the *Bed &*
Breakfast

Second Edition
1999

DIRECTORY

Published by: KGP Publishing, 54 Castlegate, Penrith, Cumbria CA11 7HY England

ACKNOWLEDGMENTS

Editor - Ken Plant
Design and Layout - Jennie Prior
Administration - Joanne Cullen & Carole Douglas
Foreword - Jacqui Kelsey
County Editorials - Karl Stedman
Illustrations on County Pages - Jonathon Robinson

Front Cover - *The White Horse, Cambridgeshire; Tower Bank Arms, Cumbria; Lamperts Cottage, Dorset; The Haven, Hay on Wye*
First Page - *Curtain Call, Stratford upon Avon; Albany Hotel, Manchester;*
Back Cover - *Cranleigh, Bath*
Page 6 - *Photograph of Kennet & Avon Canal* supplied by West Country Tourist Board
Page 30 - *Photograph of Ely Cathedral* from 'East Anglia in Colour' by John Worrall
Page 42 - *Photograph of Chalmondeley Castle* supplied by North West Tourist Board
Page 60 - *Photograph of St Michael's Mount* supplied by West Country Tourist Board
Page 90 - *Photograph of River Derwent* supplied taken by Val Corbett
Page 132 - *Photograph of Old Glossop* supplied by North West Tourist Board
Page 146 - *Photograph of Clovelly* supplied by West Country Tourist Board
Page 182 - *Photograph of Hardy's Cottage* supplied by West Country Tourist Board
Page 204 - *Photograph of Epping Forest* supplied by East of England Tourist Board Collection
Page 214 - *Photograph of Painswick* supplied by National Trust Photographic Library/David Noton
Page 233 - *Photograph of Portsmouth Harbour* taken by Peter Titmuss and supplied by Southern Tourist Board
Page 252 - *Photograph of Malvern* supplied by Heart of England Tourist Board
Page 266 - *Photograph of River Stour* supplied and taken by Claire Page
Page 282 - *Photograph of The Ribble Valley* supplied by North West Tourist Board
Page 296 - *Photograph of Robin Hood Statue* supplied by Nottingham City Council
Page 310 - *Photograph of Steep Hill* supplied by Lincolnshire County Council
Page 320 - *Photograph of Houses of Parliament* supplied and taken by Claire Page
Page 350 - *Photograph of Norfolk Broads* supplied and taken by John Worrall
Page 366 - *Photograph of Beamish Open Air Museum* supplied by Durham County Council
Page 388 - *Photograph of Hertford College Bridge* taken by Peter Titmuss and supplied by Southern Tourist Board
Page 400 - *Photograph of View from Clunbury Hill* supplied by National Trust Photographic Library/Joe Cornish
Page 412 - *Photograph of Wells Cathedral* supplied by West Country Tourist Board
Page 424 - *Photograph of Lady Street, Lavenham* from 'East Anglia in Colour' by John Worrall
Page 434 - *Photograph of Abinger Hammer clock* supplied by South East England Tourist Board
Page 442 - *Photograph of The Old Bookshop, Lewes* supplied and taken by Claire Page
Page 462 - *Photograph of Gardens at Packwood House* supplied by National Trust Photographic Library/Stephen Robson
Page 484 - *Photograph of Longleat* supplied by West Country Tourist Board
Page 496 - *Photograph of Swaledale* supplied and taken by Val Corbett
Page 554 - *Photograph of Loch Eilein* supplied and taken by Val Corbett

ISBN Number 0-9522807 6 0
Distributed worldwide by: Portfolio

KGP PUBLISHING 54 Castlegate, Penrith, Cumbria CA11 7HY England

The Bed & Breakfast
DIRECTORY

The Bed & Breakfast Directory is an invaluable companion for all who travel through England, Scotland and Wales. It is designed to give you the information you need to find the accommodation you want, where you want it. The Directory will help you find accommodation with facilities and services that are right for you, at a price to suit your budget.

"Bed and Breakfast" is a great British tradition, offered in a wide range of establishments, from private homes to guest houses and larger hotels. Unlike many accommodation guides, The Bed & Breakfast Directory does not attempt to fit properties into categories. It is, as the name suggests, a directory, listing over three thousand properties which offer bed and breakfast accommodation. Whether you are a visitor, traveller or holiday-maker, whether you are looking for an overnight stay or a longer break, whether you are travelling alone or with companions, with or without children, you will have specific requirements for your stay away from home. We feel sure you will find what you need in this volume.

The Bed & Breakfast Directory is easy to use. Areas are listed alphabetically and each is introduced with a short travel guide pointing out local attractions and the interesting features of the region. A simple map follows each introduction.

You can use The Directory in a number of ways. If you need to be in a particular place, you can start to plan your stay away by referring first to the map and then reading the entries nearest to your destination. If these are unsuitable or unavailable, the map will show you where to find the next closest property. With so many listings we feel confident that, if your first choice is unavailable, you will easily be able to find an alternative.

If your destination has not already been determined, the most important aspect of your stay may be the nature of the property and the facilities it offers. Having decided on the region, simply look through the easy to read entries. When you have found an establishment that is suitable, refer to the map to find its location.

The Bed & Breakfast Directory is also good for browsing. With such a variety of properties in such a wide range of locations, you can sit back and dream of all the places you may one day visit.

Many people from both home and abroad have discovered the pleasures and freedom of bed and breakfast accommodation. Possibly one of the reasons why the 'short break' has been so popular over the last decade is the rise in the number and the variety of places offering good accommodation and food at reasonable prices.

Whether you want to stay in the city, by the coast, or deep in the heart of our beautiful countryside, you will find something to suit your needs. The Directory lists properties within easy reach of Chelsea and Earls Court, others a stones throw from the sea or in a country village.

The range of properties offering this unique style of holiday is immense. The Directory lists cottages and grand houses, town houses and inns. There are small guests houses and large hotels. Just as diverse as the type of property is the range of facilities they offer. There are properties with swimming pools and bars, houses with libraries, and some with beautiful gardens. Some offer evening meals and a number are happy to cater for special diets. A great number have guest rooms with en suite facilities, and television is often available along with tea and coffee making facilities. Many establishments welcome children and a number allow pets.

We have resisted the temptation to use complicated codes. After a brief description of the property, you will find the tariff, details of rooms and facilities and a contact 'phone number along with the address. It couldn't be simpler!

At **KGP Publishing** we work hard to ensure all entries are accurate but changes can occur and we make no guarantees. Please let us know of any errors or omissions. We are continually trying to improve our service to the travelling public and will be pleased to have your comments on any of the properties listed - and any you feel we should attempt to include in our next edition. Our grateful thanks to the generous readers who found time to comment on last year's edition. Your help has been invaluable.

Whether you are away from home on business or for pleasure, we hope you travel safely, enjoy your break and arrive home refreshed.

Bath, Bristol & North East Somerset

Bath is Britain's best preserved and most complete Georgian city - earning it the title of the country's only World Heritage City. It is also one of the country's oldest cities, famous since Roman times for its warm mineral springs and attracting visitors for over 2,000 years.

Bath was prosperous throughout the Middle Ages, but it is most famous for its 18th century life when a handful of architects and arbiters of social taste transformed the city into a fashionable centre. Today there is still a rich cultural life in Bath, culminating every year in the Bath International Festival. There are plenty of fine Georgian streets and buildings in Bath. There is the famous circus, designed by John Wood and the Royal Crescent, the work of his son John Wood the Second. Robert Adam designed the Pultney Bridge along with the Upper Assembly Rooms, one of the city's grandest buildings. Bath is also a great place to shop with its indoor markets and narrow lanes lined with shops, cafes and restaurants.

Modern day attractions and excellent shopping facilities combine perfectly with the history of Bristol which grew up around its harbour on the River Avon, flourishing as a port since the 10th century. By the 18th and 19th centuries the dockside, which had extended outwards to Broadmead, was a bustling quay scene dominated by the masts of tall ships from all over the world.

At the Avon Gorge where the River Avon flows beneath steep limestone cliffs is Bristol's most distinctive landmark, the Clifton Suspension Bridge, two hundred and forty five feet above the water. The quiet seaside resort of Clevedon, just south of Bristol, retains much of its Victorian charm in its houses, hotels and public gardens and it has many peaceful seaside and country walks.

Weston-super-Mare offers entertainment, attractive parks, gardens and beautiful surroundings. The town has two piers, a marine lake and miniature railway as well as the Tropicana Pleasure Beach. The Burrington Combe winds its way to the top of the Mendips which gives fine views across the Bristol Channel. Near the bottom is the Rock of Ages where the Rev A Toplady, sheltering from a storm, received inspiration to write the famous hymn. The Kennet and Avon Canal which stretches between Bristol and Reading, is ideal for boating, canoeing, walking, cycling and fishing. Chew Valley Lake is a well loved beauty spot near Bristol. The man-made reservoir is a haven for fishermen, sailors, bird watchers and all who enjoy nature. Another landmark in the area is the Severn Suspension Bridge, with a centre span of 3,240ft, is a vital link on the M4 motorway to South Wales.

left, Kennet & Avon Canal

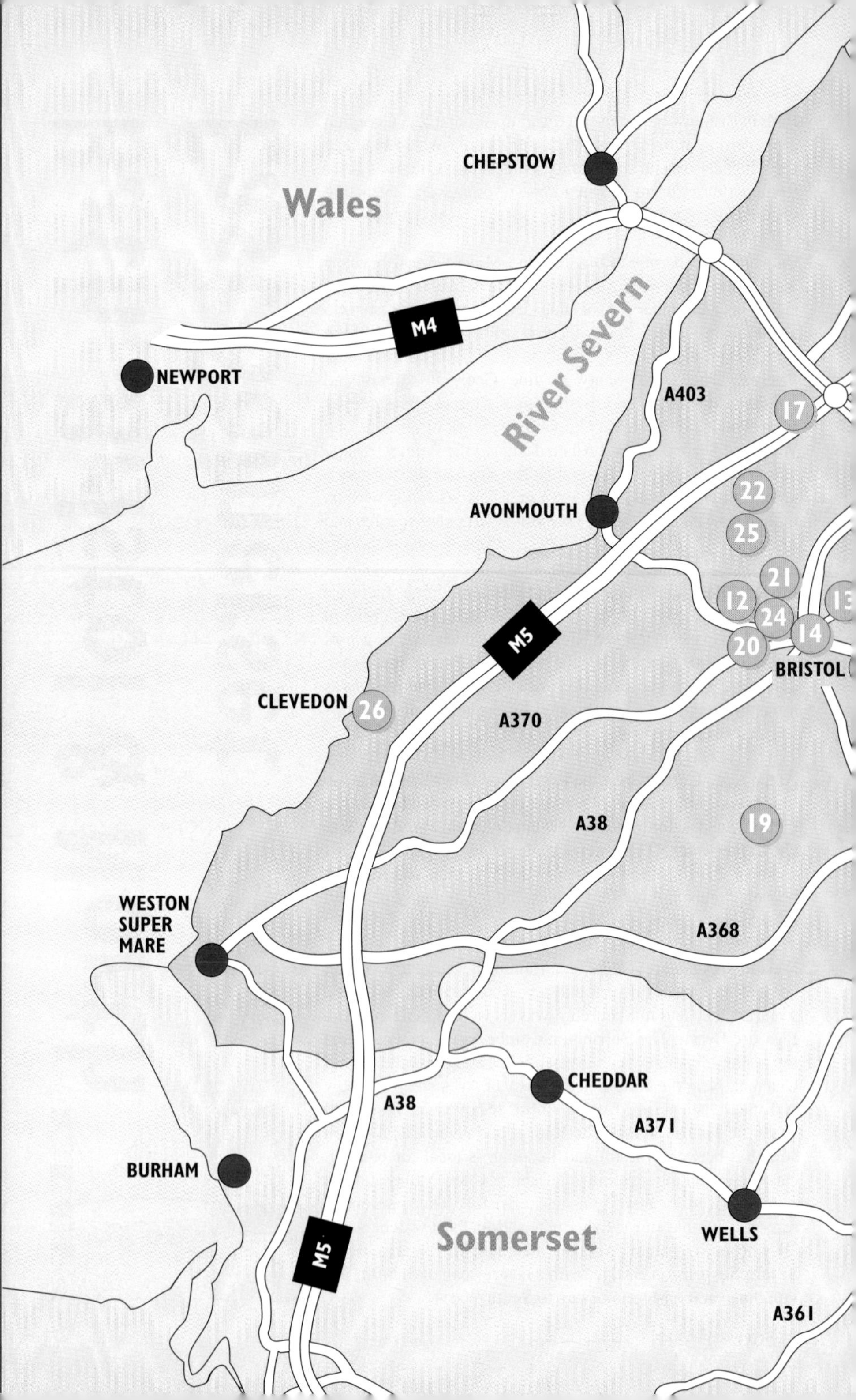

CHEPSTOW

Wales

NEWPORT

M4

River Severn

A403

17

22

25

AVONMOUTH

21

12

13

M5

24

14

20

BRISTOL

CLEVEDON 26

A370

A38

19

A368

WESTON
SUPER
MARE

A38

CHEDDAR

A371

BURHAM

M5

Somerset

WELLS

A361

9 BATHWICK HILL, a Georgian family home in desirable part of Bath. Two twin bedrooms with baths and tea/coffee facilities. Full English breakfast. TV in drawing room. Conservatory lounge. Garden. Short walk to city centre. Bus service and parking outside property. No alcohol license. No smoking. Children over 12. No credit cards.

B&B from £24pp, Rooms 2 twin, both en-suite, No smoking or pets, Children over 12, Open all year except Christmas.
Mrs Elspeth Bowman, **9 Bathwick Hill,** Bath BA2 6EW
Tel: 01225 460812   **Map Ref 1**

....

SOMERSET HOUSE HOTEL & RESTAURANT, a restaurant with rooms, this Regency house (1827) is owned and run by the Seymour family. Large garden. Good views of the city. Non-smoking house. Lunch available on Sundays in winter. Car Parking. ETB 3 Crowns Highly Commended.

B&B from £23.50 Dinner available, Rooms 1 single, 2 double, 2 twin, 5 triple, all en-suite, Children welcome, No smoking.
Somerset House Hotel & Restaurant, 35 Bathwick Hill, Bath BA2 6LD
Tel: 01225 466451 & 463471 Fax 01225 317188   **Map Ref 1**

....

HOTEL SAINT CLAIR, is a small friendly hotel just 5 minutes walk from the city, 2 minutes from Royal Crescent. Large public car park 1 minute away. One night stays welcome. ETB 2 Crowns Commended.

B&B from £25, Rooms 4 double, 2 twin, 2 triple, 1 family, most en-suite, Children from 3 years, Open all year.

Hotel Saint Clair, 1 Crescent Gardens, Upper Bristol Road, Bath BA1 2NA
Tel: 01225 425543 Fax: 01225 425543   **Map Ref 1**

....

PARADE PARK HOTEL, centrally situated, friendly bed and breakfast hotel. The Roman Baths and many of the city's finest restaurants are on the doorstep, railway and bus stations are 3 minutes' walk. All rooms have TV, tea/coffee and telephone. ETB 2 Crowns Commended.

B&B from £30, Rooms 7 single, 7 double, 2 twin, 2 family, most en-suite, Children welcome, No smoking, No pets, Open all year.
Parade Park Hotel, 10 North Parade, Bath BA2 4AL
Tel: 01225 463384 Fax: 01225 442322   **Map Ref 1**

....

WENTWORTH HOUSE, is an imposing Victorian Mansion, enjoying a peaceful location, secluded gardens, outdoor swimming pool. Rooms have TV, alarm, telephone, hair dryer and tea/coffee. Some have four poster beds, many with antiques beds. Alcohol license. Delicious breakfasts. Large free car park in hotel grounds. Quality B&B, hotel Recommended.

B&B from £25-£45pp, Rooms 3 twin, 13 double, 1 family, all en-suite, Restricted smoking, Children over 5, No pets, Open all year except Christmas & New Year.
Avril & Geoff Kitching, **Wentworth House,** 106 Bloomfield Rd, Bath BA2 2AP
Tel: 01225 339193 Fax: 01225 310460   **Map Ref 1**

....

CHESTERFIELD HOTEL, is a centrally situated Grade I listed Georgian building. Family-run hotel with individually decorated en-suite rooms and reasonable B&B rates. Limited garage parking by prior arrangement only. Car parking. ETB 2 Crowns Commended.

B&B from £35, Rooms 4 single, 12 double, 2 twin, most en-suite, Children welcome, No pets, Open all year.

Chesterfield Hotel, 11 Great Pulteney Street, Bath BA2 4BR
Tel: 01225 460953 Fax: 01225 448770   **Map Ref 1**

EDGAR HOTEL, is a Georgian town house hotel, close to city centre and Roman Baths. Privately run. All rooms with en-suite facilities.ETB 2 Crown Approved.
B&B from £30, Rooms 2 single, 9 double, 4 twin,1 triple, all en-suite, Children welcome, No smoking, Open all year.
Edgar Hotel, 64 Great Pulteney Street, Bath BA2 4DN
Tel: 01225 420619   **Map Ref 1**

....

CARFAX HOTEL, in a famous Georgian street, surrounded by the beautiful Bath hills. The rear of Carfax overlooks Henrietta Park. A well maintained, listed building.Car Parking. ETB 3 Crowns Commended.
B&B from £34, Dinner available, Rooms 13 single, 12 double, 10 twin, 3 triple, 37 en-suite, 2 public, Children welcome, No pets, Open all year. Facilities for wheelchairs and lifts to all floors.
Carfax Hotel, Great Pulteney Street, Bath BA2 4BS
Tel: 01225 462089 Fax: 01225 443257   **Map Ref 1**

....

DUKES HOTEL, is an elegantly refurbished, family run Grade I Georgian town house hotel, in the city centre. Restaurant offers finest local produce and reasonably priced wines carefully selected by a Master of Wine.

B&B from £55, Dinner available, Rooms 4 single, 11 double, 4 twin, 4 triple, 23 en-suite, Children welcome,No smoking, Open all year.
Dukes Hotel, Great Pulteney Street, Bath BA2 4DN
Tel: 01225 463512 Fax: 01225 483733   **Map Ref 1**

....

LAURA PLACE HOTEL, is an 18th Century town house, centrally located in Georgian square. 2 minutes from the Roman Baths, Pump Rooms and Abbey. Car Parking Available. ETB 2 Crowns Commended.

B&B from £62, Rooms 6 double, 1 twin, 1 family, suite available, all en-suite /private facilities, Children from 6 years old, No smoking, No pets, Open March - December.
Laura Place Hotel, 3 Laura Place, Great Pulteney Street, Bath BA2 4BH
Tel: 01225 463815 Fax: 01225 310222   **Map Ref 1**

....

KENNARD HOTEL, a Georgian town house hotel of charm and character in a quiet street. A few minutes' level walk to the Abbey and Roman Baths. ETB 2 Crowns Highly Commended.

B&B from £35, Rooms 2 single, 9 double, 1 twin, 1 family room, most en-suite, No children, pets, No smoking, Open all year.
Kennard Hotel, 11 Henrietta Street, Bath BA2 6LL
Tel: 01225 310472 Fax: 01225 460054 Email: kennard@dircon.co.uk
                                                                                                                   Map Ref 1

....

WILLIAMS GUEST HOUSE, a long established, non smoking guesthouse, run from a Victorian town house with good views to the front. Four minutes' walk to the city, British Rail and National Express stations. Private parking available. A warm welcome awaits. ETB Listed Approved.
B&B from £20, Rooms 1 single, 2 double, Children from 5 years, No smoking, No pets. Open all year.
Williams Guest House, 81 Wells Road, Bath BA2 3AN
Tel: 01225 312179   **Map Ref 1**

....

WELLSGATE, offers peaceful Victorian elegance. Breakfasts with homemade jams. Large colourful gardens and panoramic views. Only 5 minutes stroll into town. With garages and off-street parking it's ideal for business persons too. CTV, tea/coffee making, en-suite rooms and guests lounge. Non smoking. Vegetarians welcome. ETB 3 Crowns Commended.

B&B from £20pp, Dinner from £12, Rooms 3 single, 2 twin, 3 double, 1 family, Open all year.
Mrs Long, **Wellsgate,** 131 Wells Road, Bath BA2 3AN
Tel: 01225 310688 Fax: 01225 310143   **Map Ref 1**

LEIGHTON HOUSE, an elegant detached Victorian house in own large and attractive gardens. Well placed for the Cotswolds, Somerset and Wiltshire. 10 minutes walk to city centre. Parking. TV, hair dryer, tea/coffee facilities, bath and shower in every individually decorated room. ETB Highly Commended, AA QQQQQ Premier Selected, RAC Highly Acclaimed. EMail: leighton-house@which.net
B&B from £27.50pp, Rooms, 3 twin, 4 double, 1 family, all en-suite, No smoking, Children from 8, No pets, Open all year.
Colin & Marilyn Humphrey, **Leighton House,** 139 Wells Rd, Bath BA2 3AL
Tel: 01225 314769 Fax: 01225 443079 **Map Ref 1**

Away from the traffic and noise but just minutes from the heart of Bath. **CRANLEIGH** has lovely views, private parking and secluded sunny gardens. Guest bedrooms are all en-suite and exceptionally spacious. Ground floor bedrooms available. A non smoking house. AA 4Q. Recommended by Which and Good B&B. Email: cranleigh@btinternet.com

B&B from £28pp, Rooms 2 twin, 2 double, 1 family, all en-suite, No smoking or pets, Children over 5, Open all year except Christmas & New.
Christine & Arthur Webber, **Cranleigh,** 159 Newbridge Hill, Bath BA1 3PX
Tel: 01225 310197 Fax: 01225 423143 **Map Ref 1**

APSLEY HOUSE HOTEL, built for the Duke of Wellington in 1830, a small privately run hotel just over 1 mile from centre with parking. The interior includes many period features. A sumptuous breakfast is served in the delightful dining room. AA QQQQQ, ETB Highly Commended. Licensed Bar.

B&B from £32.50pp, Rooms 3 twin, 7 double, 1 family, all en-suite, Restricted smoking, Children over 5, No pets, Open all year except Christmas week.
David & Annie Lanz, **Apsley House Hotel,** Newbridge Hill, Bath BA1 3PT
Tel: 01225 336966 Fax: 01225 425462 Email: apsleyhouse@easynet.co.uk **Map Ref 1**

HAUTE COMBE HOTEL, has fully equipped non-smoking en-suite rooms in comfortable period surroundings. Easy access to city attractions. Special off season rates. Telephone for brochure. ETB 3 Crown Commended. Car parking.
B&B from £39, Dinner available, Rooms 2 single, 3 double, 2 twin, 3 triple, 2 family rooms, all en-suite/private facilities, Open all year.
Haute Combe Hotel, 174-176 Newbridge Road, Bath BA1 3LE
Tel: 01225 420061 & 339064 Fax: 01225 420061 Email: ID/101352.42@compuserve.com **Map Ref 1-**

OAKLEIGH HOUSE, a warm welcome awaits you at this quietly situated Victorian home overlooking Georgian Bath. All luxury rooms are en-suite with little extras to make your stay special. Only 10 minutes walk to city centre. Private car park. Contact David and Jenny King for brochure.

B&B from £29pp, Rooms 1 twin, 3 double, all en-suite, Restricted smoking, Open all year.
Mr & Mrs King, **Oakleigh House,** 19 Upper Oldfield Park, Bath BA2 3JX
Tel: 01225 315698 Fax: 01225 448223 **Map Ref 1**

ASHLEY VILLA HOTEL, is a comfortably furnished licensed hotel with relaxing informal atmosphere, close to the city centre. All rooms are en-suite. Swimming pool and parking for 10 cars. ETB 3 Crowns.
B&B from £49, Dinner available, Rooms 2 single, 7 double, 2 twin,3 triple, 14 en-suite, No smoking, Children welcome, No pets, Open all year.
Ashley Villa Hotel, 26 Newbridge Road, Bath BA1 3JZ
Tel: 01225 421683 & 428887 Fax: 01225 313604 **Map Ref 1**

MEADOWLAND, is set in quiet, secluded grounds and offering the highest standard in de-luxe en-suite accommodation, Meadowland is elegantly furnished and decorated. Private parking, lovely gardens. A peaceful retreat for discerning travellers. ETB 2 Crown De-Luxe.
B&B from £58, Rooms 2 double, 1 twin, all en-suite, Children welcome, No smoking, No pets, Open all year.
Meadowland, 36 Broomfield Park, Bath BA2 2BX
Tel: 01225 311079 Fax:01225 311079 **Map Ref 1**

HOLLY LODGE, an elegant Victorian house set in its own grounds, enjoying magnificent views of the city.

B&B from £37.50pp, Rooms 1 single, 2 twin, 4 double, No smoking, Children welcome, No pets, Open all year.

Mr George H. Hall, **Holly Lodge,** 8 Upper Oldfield Park, Bath BA2 3JZ
Tel: 01225 424042 Fax: 01225 481138 **Map Ref 1**

HARINGTONS HOTEL, enjoy warm hospitality, good food and wine in this charming hotel set in a picturesque cobbled street in the very heart of Bath. Just minutes from the Roman baths, theatre premier shopping and major attractions. ETB 3 Crowns Commended.
B&B from £55, Lunch & Dinner available, Rooms 10 double, 1 twin, 2 triple, all en-suite, No pets or smoking. Open all year.
Haringtons Hotel, 8-10 Queen Street, Bath BA1 1HE
Tel: 01225 461728 Fax: 01225 444804 **Map Ref 1**

With stunning panoramic views over the city, **PARADISE HOUSE** is an elegant Bath stone Georgian house just 5 minutes walk from the centre. Behind its classic and dignified exterior it conceals more than half an acre of splendid walled garden. Delightful en-suite rooms, TV, tea/coffee facilities. Parking.
B&B from £32.50pp, Rooms 3 twin, 4 double, 1 family, all en-suite, Restricted smoking, Children welcome, No pets, Open all year except Christmas week.
David & Annie Lanz, **Paradise House,** 88 Holloway, Bath BA2 4PX
Tel: 01225 317723 Fax: 01225 482005 Email: paradise@apsleyhouse.easynet.co.uk **Map Ref 1**

Built in 1850, **THE HOLLIES** is a Grade II listed family-run guesthouse within walking distance of city, Overlooking Parish Church and gardens. All rooms have en-suite/private facilities, colour TV, alarm clocks, hair dryers and hostess trays. Private off-street parking. No smoking.

B&B from £21pp, Rooms 1 twin, 2 double, all en-suite, No smoking or pets, Children over 5, Open all year except Christmas & New Year
Mr & Mrs David & Nicky Stabbins, **The Hollies,** Hatfield Road, Bath BA2 2BD
Tel: 01225 313366 Fax: 01225 313366 **Map Ref 1**

BROMPTON HOUSE HOTEL, a charming Georgian residence, (former Rectory 1777). Family owned and run. Car park and beautiful secluded gardens. Only 6 minutes level walk to Baths historic sights. Comfortable and tastefully furnished en-suite bedrooms. Delicious English, Continental or wholefood breakfasts. Email: bromptonhouse@btinternet.com

B&B from £30pp, Rooms 2 single, 7 twin, 7 double, 2 family, all en-suite, No smoking or pets, Children over 10, Open all year except Christmas & New Year.
The Selby Family, **Brompton House Hotel,** St. Johns Rd, Bath BA2 6PT
Tel: 01225 420972 Fax: 01225 420505 **Map Ref 1**

SYDNEY GARDENS HOTEL, an elegant and spacious Victorian house in a scenic parkland setting, 10 minutes' walk from the city centre. All facilities. Car Park. ETB 2 Crowns Commended.

B&B from £45, Rooms 3 double, 2 twin, 1 triple, all en-suite, Children from 4 years, No smoking, Open all year.
Sydney Gardens Hotel, Sydney Road, Bath BA2 6NT
Tel: 01225 464818   **Map Ref 1**

BATH TASBURGH HOTEL is a beautifully refurbished Victorian house set in lovely gardens with breathtaking views. 4 poster, double, twin & family rooms, all en-suite, with comfort facilities. Elegant dining room, drawing room and conservatory. Gourmet dinners and snack meals, full license and friendly service. Parking. Lovely walks and close to city.

B&B from £32.50pp, Rooms 1 single, 1 twin, 3 double, 4 poster 3 family, No smoking No pets, Children welcome, Open all year.
David & Susan Keeling, **Bath Tasburgh Hotel,** Warminster Rd, Bath BA2 6SH
Tel: 01225 425096 Fax: 01225 463842   **Map Ref 1**

GAINSBOROUGH HOTEL, a spacious and comfortable country house hotel situated on high ground with nice views. Near Botanical Gardens and centre. Colour satellite TV, beverage facilities, direct dial telephones, hair dryers etc. Large lounge. Friendly bar. Two sun terraces. Private car park. A warm welcome from friendly staff.

B&B from £27pp, Rooms 2 single, 6 twin, 6 double, 2 family, all en-suite, Restricted smoking, Children welcome, No pets, Open all year.
Mr & Mrs Warwick, **Gainsborough Hotel,** Weston Lane, Bath BA1 4AB
Tel: 01225 311380 Fax: 01225 447411   **Map Ref 1**

COMBE GROVE MANOR HOTEL & COUNTRY CLUB, a beautiful 18th century manor house and more recently built garden lodge. 2 miles from centre of Bath and with excellent sporting facilities. Car parking. ETB 5 Crowns Highly Commended.
B&B from £99, Dinner available, Rooms 27 double, 11 twin, 2 triple, 40 en-suite, suites available, Children welcome, No pets or smoking, Open all year.
Combe Grove Manor Hotel & Country Club, Brassknocker Hill, Monkton Combe, Bath BA2 7HS
Tel: 01225 834644 Fax: 01225 834961   **Map Ref 2**

ORCHARD LODGE, offers good quality accommodation. We are close to local village and city centre, well place for local attractions. All bedrooms equipped with en-suite, TV, radio, tea/coffee facilities and telephone. Warm welcome assured. Email: orchardlo@aol.com.uk

B&B from £49per room, Rooms 14 single, 5 twin, 8 double, 1 family, all en-suite, Children welcome, Pets by arrangement, Open all year except Christmas.
Monica & Melvin Curtis, **Orchard Lodge,** Warminster Road, Bathampton, Bath BA2 6XG
Tel: 01225 466115 Fax: 01225 446050   **Map Ref 3**

EAGLE HOUSE, a delightful large old Georgian house with a friendly atmosphere in 2 acres of garden, 3 miles from Bath. Home baked croissants, open fire in winter, car parking, good public transport and excellent local pubs within walking distance.

B&B from £24pp, Rooms 1 single, 2 twin, 4 double, 1 family, all en-suite, Children & pets welcome, Open all year except Christmas & New Year.
John & Rosamund Napier, **Eagle House,** Church Street, Bathford, Bath BA1 7RS
Tel: 01225 859946 Fax: 01225 859946 Email: jonap@psionworld.net   **Map Ref 4**

PICKFORD HOUSE, is an elegant house overlooking the surrounding countryside. The perfect place to relax after a day's sightseeing. Spacious rooms fully equipped and tastefully furnished are the ideal prerequisite to Angela's excellent pot-luck meal accompanied by wine from Ken's extensive list.
B&B from £16pp, Dinner from £13, Rooms 1 twin, 1 double, 2 family en-suite, Restricted smoking, Children welcome, Pets by arrangement, Open all year except Christmas.
Ken & Angela Pritchard, **Pickford House,** Bath Road, Beckington, Bath BA3 6SJ
Tel: 01373 830 329 Fax: 01373 830 329   **Map Ref 5-**

BOX HEDGE FARM, is set in 200 acres of rural countryside on the edge of the Cotswolds. Local to M4/M5, central for Bristol and Bath. We offer a warm family atmosphere with traditional farmhouse cooking. The large spacious bedrooms have colour TV and tea/coffee facilities.

B&B from £17.50-£30pp, Dinner from £7.50, Rooms 1 single, 1 twin, 2 double (1 en-suite), 1 family, Restricted smoking, Children welcome, Pets by arrangement, Open all year.
Marilyn Collins, **Box Hedge Farm,** Coalpit Heath, Bristol BS36 2UW
Tel: 01454 250786 Fax: 01454 250786   **Map Ref 15**

CROSS HANDS HOTEL, situated two miles from M4 (exit 18) towards Stroud. In 6 acres, with a garden and orchard. A la carte restaurant and large meeting rooms for up to 100 delegates with private bars.

B&B from £39.50pp, Dinner available, Rooms 9 single, 9 double 3 twin, some en-suite, Restricted smoking, Children & pets welcome, Open all year.

Cross Hands Hotel, Old Sodbury, Bristol BS17 6RJ
Tel: 01454 313000 Fax: 01454 324409   **Map Ref 16**

GREEN LANE HOUSE, is 5 miles south of Bath in conservation village on Somerset/Wiltshire border. Restored 18th century Bath stone cottages combining modern comforts with original features. Distinctively decorated guest bedrooms, homely residents lounge with log fire. Traditional English breakfast. Inns within walking distance.
B&B from £20pp, Rooms 2 twin, 2 double, 2 en-suite, No smoking, Children over 8, Pets by arrangement, Open all year.
Christopher & Juliet Davies, **Green Lane House,** Hinton Charterhouse, Bath BA3 6BL
Tel: 01225 723631 Fax: 01225 723773   **Map Ref 7**

FORRES GUEST HOUSE, an Edwardian family guest house with helpful hosts, who are ex-teachers and love Bath. River Avon and Cotswold Way close by. Traditional and vegetarian breakfasts. Colour TV and beverages in all rooms.

B&B from £20pp, Rooms 3 double, 2 triple, all en-suite, Children welcome, No pets, Open April - October.

Forres Guest House, 172 Newbridge Road, Lower Weston, Bath BA1 3LE
Tel: 01225 427698   **Map Ref 8**

CENTURION HOTEL, is an ideally situated hotel, midway between Bath & Wells. Well-appointed bedrooms, golf, squash, swimming pool, indoor & outdoor bowls. Ample car parking. ETB 5 Crowns Commended.

B&B from £55 Lunch & evening meal available, Rooms 15 double, 27 twin, 2 triple, suite available, all en-suite, Children welcome, No smoking or pets.
Centurion Hotel, Charlton Lane, Midsomer Norton, Bath BA3 4BD
Tel: 01761 417711 Fax: 01761 418357   **Map Ref 9**

THE ROOKERY, is a homely, family run guesthouse with licensed restaurant, situated between Bath and Wells. Ideal for touring the West Country. Private car parking. ETB 3 Crowns Approved.

B&B from £25, Dinner available, Rooms 3 double, 3 twin, 3 triple, all en-suite, Children welcome, No smoking, Open all year.
The Rookery, Wells Road, Radstock, Bath BA3 3RS
Tel: 01761 432626 Fax: 01761 432626 **Map Ref 10**

....

OLD MALT HOUSE HOTEL, six miles south of Bath, in beautiful unspoilt countryside. Built in 1835 as a brewery malt house, now a hotel with character and comfort. car parking available. ETB 3 Crowns Commended.

B&B from £33, Lunches and Dinner available, Rooms 1 single, 4 double, 5 twin, 2 triple, all en-suite, Children welcome, No smoking, Open all year.
Old Malt House Hotel, Radford, Timsbury, Bath BA3 1QF
Tel: 01761 470106 Fax: 01761 472726 **Map Ref 11**

....

WESTBURY PARK HOTEL, a friendly family run hotel on the Durdham Downs, close to city centre and M5, junction 17. Car parking. ETB 2 Crowns Highly Commended.

B&B from £29, Rooms 1 single, 5 double, 2 twin, all en-suite, Children welcome, Open all year.
Westbury Park Hotel, 37 Westbury Road, Bristol BS9 3AU
Tel: 0117 9620465 Fax: 0117 9628607 **Map Ref 12**

....

ALCOVE GUEST HOUSE, a clean and comfortable accommodation with personal service. Easy access from M32, M4. Private car park. ETB 1 Crown Approved.

B&B from £23, Rooms 1 single, 3 double, 3 twin, 1 triple, 1 family room, most en-suite, Children welcome. Open all year.
Alcove Guest House, 508-510 Fishponds Road, Bristol BS16 3DT
Tel: 0117 965 3886 & 965 2436 Fax: 0117 965 3886 **Map Ref 13**

....

THE TOWN & COUNTRY LODGE, recently refurbished hotel in glorious rural surroundings halfway between the City centre and Bristol airport. Restaurant with extensive menu. Function and conference rooms. Ample car parking. ETB 3 Crowns Commended.
B&B from £39, Lunch & Evening meals available, Rooms 10 single, 12 double, 10 twin, 4 triple, all en-suite, Children welcome, No smoking, Open all year.
The Town & Country Lodge, A38 Bridgwater Road, Bristol BS13 8AG
Tel: 01275 392441 Fax: 01275 393362 **Map Ref 14**

....

SWALLOW ROYAL HOTEL, enjoys a prime position in the centre of Bristol. Exceptionally well-appointed with air conditioning and award winning food and Roman theme leisure club. Short break packages available. Wheelchair access. Ample car parking. ETB 5 Crowns Highly Commended.

B&B from £125, Lunch and Evening meal available, Rooms 16 single, 104 double, 108 twin, 14 triple, all en-suite, Children welcome, No smoking , Open all year.
Swallow Royal Hotel, College Green, Bristol BS1 5TA
Tel: 0117 9255100 & 9255200 Fax: 0117 9251515 **Map Ref 14**

....

JURYS BRISTOL HOTEL, Best Western/Utell International. Modern hotel, recently refurbished. Overlooking quay and close to city centre. Special weekend rates. Restaurant lounge bar and waterfront tavern. Ample car parking. ETB 4 Crowns Commended.
B&B from £84, Lunch and Evening meal available, Rooms 20 single, 81 double, 86 twin, all en-suite, Children welcome, No smoking, Open all year.
Jurys Bristol Hotel, Prince Street, Bristol BS1 4QF
Tel: 0117 9230333 Fax: 0117 9230300 **Map Ref 14**

THE BOWL INN & RESTAURANT, a 12th century building, once a priory, nestling on the edge of the River Severn Vale. 3 minutes from the M4/M5 interchange. Car Parking. ETB 3 Crowns Commended.

B&B from £32.45-£108.35 Lunch and Evening meal available, Rooms 6 double, 4 twin, all en-suite, Children from 4 years, No smoking, No pets.

The Bowl Inn & Restaurant, 16 Church Road, Lower Almondsbury, Almondsbury, Bristol BS12 4DT
Tel: 01454 612757 Fax: 01454 619910 Email: thebowl@3wa.co.uk   **Map Ref 17**

....

A4 HOTEL, a small comfortable hotel. TV, hospitality tray, direct dial telephone, radio alarm, clock, hair dryer in our en-suite rooms. Licensed restaurant. Small bar. Private car park. A warm welcome and good food awaits you at the A4. 11/4 miles city centre. Ideal for touring Bath, Wells, Glastonbury area.

B&B from £30pp, Dinner from £12.95, Rooms 6 single, 1 twin, 3 double, all en-suite, Children & pets welcome, Open all year.
Anne Morgan, **A4 Hotel,** 511 Bath Road Brislington, Bristol BS4 3LA
Tel: 0117 9715492 Fax: 0117 9711791   **Map Ref 18**

....

ORCHARD HOUSE, comfortable accommodation in a carefully modernised Georgian house and coach house annex. Home cooking using local produce. Car parking. ETB 2 Crown Commended.

B&B from £18, Evening meals available, Rooms 1 single, 2 double, 3 twin, 1 family, most en-suite, Children welcome, No pets, Open all year.

Orchard House, Bristol Road, Chew Stoke, Bristol BS18 8UB
Tel: 01275 333143 Fax: 01275 333754   **Map Ref 19**

....

OAKFIELD HOTEL, a Georgian facade with open views at the front and rear. Well proportioned rooms. car parking available. ETB 1 Crown Approved.

B&B from £27 single, £37 for double/twin room, Rooms 10 single, 3 double, 10 twin, 4 triple, Evening meals available, Children welcome, Open all year except Christmas.

Oakfield Hotel, 52 Oakfield Road, Clifton, Bristol BS8 2BG
Tel: 0117 9735556 & 9733643   **Map Ref 20**

....

ARCHES HOTEL, is a small friendly private hotel close to central stations and 100 yards from the main A38. Option of traditional or vegetarian breakfast. ETB 1 Crown Commended.

B&B from £22.50 Rooms 3 single, 4 double, 1 twin, 2 triple, some en-suite, Children welcome, No smoking, Open all year.

Arches Hotel, 132 Cotham Brow, Cotham Brow, Bristol BS6 6AE
Tel: 0117 924 7398 Fax: 0117 924 7398   **Map Ref 21**

....

HENBURY LODGE HOTEL, one mile from junction 17 off M5, 15 minutes' drive from city centre. Local interest includes Blaise Castle and Blaise Hamlet. Various special diets catered for. Car parking. ETB 3 Crowns Commended.

B&B from £41, Lunch & evening meals available, Rooms 1 single, 12 double, 2 twin, 4 triple, all en-suite, Children welcome, No smoking, Open all year.

Henbury Lodge Hotel, Station Road, Henbury, Bristol BS10 7QQ
Tel:0117 9502615 Fax: 0117 9509532   **Map Ref 22**

GRASMERE COURT HOTEL, a well appointed hotel with high standard of decor and accommodation. Private facilities. Situated on A4 between Bath and Bristol. Car Parking. ETB 2 Crowns Commended.

B&B from £35, Evening meal available, Rooms 2 single, 9 double, 3 twin, 2 family rooms, all en-suite, Children welcome, No smoking, No pets, Open all year.
Grasmere Court Hotel, 22-24 Bath Road, Keynsham, Bristol BS18 1SN
Tel: 0117 9862662 Fax: 0117 9862762   **Map Ref 23**

OLD MANOR HOUSE, has a well deserved reputation for quality and comfort. En-suite bedrooms with TV and tea/coffee. Guest lounge with well stocked bar, comfortable seating and inglenook fireplace. The restaurant is served by 4 fully qualified chefs, English cooking with continental overtones. Car park.. 5-6 miles from Bristol & Bath. Email: oldmanorhouse@compuserve.com

B&B from £30pp, Dinner from £8, Rooms 1 single, 1 twin, 9 double, 1 family, all en-suite, Children welcome, No pets, Open all year.
Brenda Binge, **Old Manor House,** 5 Bristol Rd, Keynsham, Bristol BS31 2BA
Tel: 0117 986 3107 Fax: 0117 986 5940   **Map Ref 23**

COURTLANDS HOTEL, a comfortable, family run town house hotel, located in a quiet residential area overlooking Redland Grove. Close to all main attractions. Car parking available. ETB 3 Crowns Commended.

B&B from £44, Lunch & Evening meal available, Rooms 5 single, 10 double, 4 twin, 3 triple, 1 family room, all en-suite, Children welcome, No smoking, Open all year.
Courtlands Hotel, 1 Redland Court Road, Redland, Bristol BS6 7EE
Tel: 0117 9424432 Fax: 0117 923 2432   **Map Ref 24**

8 SOUTHOVER CLOSE,, a semi detached house in quiet cul-de-sac, 3 miles from the centre of Bristol. Situated off main Falcondale Road, just outside Westbury village. Car Parking. ETB Listed Commended.

B&B from £16, Rooms 1 single 1 double, No smoking, No pets, Open January - November.
8 Southover Close,, Westbury-on-Trym, Bristol BS9 3NG
Tel: 0117 9500754   **Map Ref 25**

MAYFAIR HOTEL, a small hotel run by owners, situated close to the downs and within easy reach of both the city and motorway. Car Parking. ETB 2 Crowns Commended.
B&B from £28, Rooms 4 single, 2 double, 2 twin, 1 triple, some en-suite, Children welcome, Open all year.
Mayfair Hotel, 5 Henleaze Road, Westbury-on-Trym, Bristol BS9 4EX
Tel: 0117 9622008 & 9493924   **Map Ref 25**

WALTON PARK HOTEL, a country house hotel overlooking the Severn Estuary. 2 miles from M5 junction 20. Ideal base for touring West Country.

B&B from £36.75pp, Dinner available, Rooms 10 single, 19 twin, 11 double, Restricted smoking, Open all year.
Walton Park Hotel, 1 Wellington Terrace, Clevedon, North Somerset BS21 7BL
Tel: 01275 874253 Fax: 01275 343577   **Map Ref 26**

LUCKNAM PARK, Utell International, Built in 1720, Lucknam Park is a magnificent Georgian country house hotel with extensive leisure facilities. Set in 500 acres of parkland north-east of bath. Half board available. Car Parking, ETB 5 Crowns Highly Commended.
B&B from £157 Dinner available, Rooms 1 single, 27 double, 14 twin, all en-suite, Children welcome, No pets, Open all year.
Lucknam Park, Colerne, Chippenham, Wiltshire SN14 8AZ
Tel: 01225 742777 Fax:01225 743536   **Map Ref 27**

The counties of Bedfordshire, Berkshire, Buckinghamshire and Hertfordshire have some of the loveliest countryside in England, yet are all just an hour's travelling distance from central London.

Bedfordshire ranges from the Greensand Ridge in the heart of the county with its wooded slopes and wildlife, to the chalk hills in the south and limestone villages along the banks of the River Great Ouse in the North. Not only is there wonderful landscape, but there are museums, galleries, stately homes, shopping centres, markets, towns and pretty villages. Ampthill is a fine historic town with picturesque narrow streets with Georgian houses and Tudor bridges. The ancient county town of Bedford dates back to before Saxon times and River Great Ouse flows through it on its journey to the Wash. The Dunstable Downs offer stunning views and are rich in wildlife.

Royal Berkshire is perhaps one of the most interesting English counties. Stretching from the outskirts of London, west to the border with Wiltshire. The River Thames flows through its beautiful countryside, providing boating and walking. To the west are the market towns of Newbury and Hungerford. Newbury is famous for its racecourse and international spring festival and Hungerford for its serene canal side setting and antiques arcade. Royal Windsor conjures up everything that is English and its historic buildings including Windsor Castle and streets make it an interesting place to visit. Nearby on the banks of the Thames are places like Maidenhead and Eton.

Buckinghamshire is rich in literary and cultural history as well as having beautiful countryside. In the north is the new city of Milton Keynes, created around several towns and villages in 1967, now boasting one of the largest indoor shopping centres in Europe. There are also some fine old towns, such as Buckingham and Olney. The Vale of Aylesbury lies in the centre of the county with the town of Aylesbury at its heart. The River Thames flows along the county's southern boundary through charming scenery, although mainly residential with pretty villages, parks, heaths and woods.

Hertfordshire has got something for everyone, rolling countryside, picturesque villages, busy market towns, stately homes and many tourist attractions. Watford is Hertfordshire's largest town with a busy centre with modern shopping. Welwyn Garden City is laid out along curved tree lined boulevards and a town centre offers excellent shopping. Hertford is a quiet country town which has many old buildings including the castle. There are numerous antique shops. Both Stevenage and Hemel Hempstead are new towns.

Bedfordshire, Berkshire, Buckinghamshire & Hertfordshire

BEDFORD OAK HOUSE, a comfortable motor hotel bed and breakfast accommodation in a large mock Tudor house, close to the railway station and town centre. En-suite facilities and large car park. ETB 2 Crowns Approved.

B&B from £30, Dinner available, Rooms 3 single, 10 double, 1 twin, most en-suite, Children welcome, No pets, Open all year.
Bedford Oak House, 33 Shakespeare Road, Bedford, Bedfordshire MK40 2DX
Tel: 01234 266972 Fax: 01234 266972 **Map Ref 1**

....

1 RAVENSDEN GRANGE, well appointed accommodation in spacious Georgian manor house overlooking lawns with great cedar trees. Cooking, comfort, hospitality all first class. Car parking. ETB 2 Crowns Commended.

B&B from £18, Lunch & evening meals available, Rooms 1 single, 1 double, 1 twin, Children over 3, No smoking, Open all year.
1 Ravensden Grange, Sunderland Hill, Ravensden, Bedford, Bedfordshire MK44 2SH
Tel: 01234 771771 **Map Ref 2**

....

OLD PALACE LODGE HOTEL, parts of the hotel are believed to date back to lodge at Norman palace of Dunstable circa 1100 AD. The hotel lies on the edge of the Chilterns, 6 miles from Luton Airport. ETB 4 Crowns Commended.

B&B from £58.75 Lunch and evening meal available, Rooms 5 single, 52 double, 11 twin, all en-suite, Children welcome, No smoking, Open all year.
Old Palace Lodge Hotel, Church Street, Dunstable, Bedfordshire LU5 4RT
Tel: 01582 662201 Fax: 01582 696422 **Map Ref 4**

....

STIRRUPS COUNTRY HOUSE HOTEL, a privately owned hotel in Berkshire, situated between Windsor, Ascot and Bracknell and only 3 miles from the Windsor Legoland park. All rooms have tea/coffee making facilities. Ample car parking. ETB 4 Crowns Highly Commended.
B&B from £60, Lunch and evening meal available, Rooms 19 double, 4 twin, 1 triple, Children welcome, Open all year.
Stirrups Country House Hotel, Maidens Green, Bracknell, Berkshire RG42 6LD
Tel: 01344 882284 Fax: 01344 882300 **Map Ref 6**

....

THE BEAR AT HUNGERFORD, a 13th century coaching inn, traditionally furnished, with timber beams and open fires. 3 miles from junction 14 of the M4, ideally situated for the Cotswolds, Berkshire Downs and Newbury races. A Jarvis hotel, refurbished in July 1997. Ample car parking. ETB 4 Crowns Commended.

B&B from £46.50 Lunch and Evening meal available, Rooms 3 single, 29 double, 9 twin, suites available, all en-suite, Children welcome, No smoking, Open all year.
The Bear at Hungerford, Charnham Street, Hungerford, Berkshire RG17 0EL
Tel: 01488 682512 Fax: 01488 684357 **Map Ref 7**

....

FISHERS FARM, an attractive farmhouse with all modern comforts on a working sheep and arable farm. Surrounded by large garden and farmland in a peaceful and secluded location yet only 1 mile from junction 14 of the M4. Heated indoor pool. Excellent cooking using home grown produce.

B&B from £25pp, Dinner from £18, Rooms 1 twin, 1 double, 1 family, all en-suite, Restricted smoking, Children welcome, Pets by arrangement, Open all year.
Mary & Henry Wilson, **Fishers Farm,** Shefford Woodlands, Hungerford, Berkshire RG17 7AB
Tel: 01488 648466 Fax: 01488 648706 **Map Ref 9**

....

ELVA LODGE HOTEL, is a family run hotel in central Maidenhead. Friendly atmosphere and personal attention. Ideal for Heathrow, Windsor, Henley and Ascot. M4 5 minutes, M40 and M25 10 minutes. ETB 2 Crowns Commended.
B&B from £36.50, Lunch and evening meal available, Rooms 10 single, 10 double, 4 twin, 2 triple, 1 family room, some en-suite, Children welcome, Open all year.
Elva Lodge Hotel, Castle Hill, Maidenhead, Berkshire SL6 4AD
Tel: 01628 22948 & 34883 Fax: 01628 38855 **Map Ref 10**

THE INN ON THE GREEN, has an extensive restaurant menu, offering freshly cooked dishes for all meals. Residents' menu available for midday until midnight. Car Parking. ETB 3 Crowns Commended.

B&B from £45, Rooms 1 single, 4 double, 3 twin, all en-suite, Children welcome, Open all year.
The Inn on the Green, The Old Cricket Common, Cookham Dean, Cookham, Maidenhead SL6 9NZ
Tel: 01628 482638 Fax: 01628 487474   **Map Ref 11**

The recently refurbished **THE QUEENS HOTEL** provides comfortable surroundings whilst maintaining the traditional features of a nineteenth century coaching inn. Each uniquely designed room is themed after a different Queen and features modern facilities including SKY TV, trouser press, hair dryer, alarm clock and tea/coffee facilities.
B&B from £60 per room, Dinner from £3.95, Rooms 9 en-suite double, Restricted smoking, Children welcome, Pets by arrangement, Open all year.
Eldridge Pope & Co. Plc, **The Queens Hotel,** Market Place, Newbury, Berkshire RG14 5BD
Tel: 01635 47447 Fax: 01635 569626   **Map Ref 12**

DONNINGTON VALLEY HOTEL & GOLF COURSE, a stylish country house hotel set in Berkshire countryside. 18-hole golf course, award winning restaurant. Excellent touring base for southern England. Ample car parking. ETB 5 Crowns Highly Commended.
B&B from £45, Lunch and evening meals available, Rooms 43 double, 15 twin, suites available, all en-suite, Children welcome, No smoking. Open all year.
Donnington Valley Hotel & Golf Course, Old Oxford Road, Donnington, Newbury, Berkshire RG14 3AG
Tel: 01635 551199 Fax: 01635 551123   **Map Ref 13**

JARVIS ELCOT PARK HOTEL, an elegant and peaceful 18th century mansion, in beautiful park and gardens laid out by the Royal Gardener, Sir William Paxton. Log fires, individually decorated bedrooms and Seb Coe Health Club. Ample car parking. ETB 4 Crowns Highly Commended.

B&B from £47.50, Lunch and evening meal available, Rooms 2 single, 64 double, 9 twin, all en-suite, Children welcome, No smoking, Open all year.
Jarvis Elcot Park Hotel, Elcot, Newbury, Berkshire RG20 8NJ
Tel: 01488 658100 Fax: 01488 658288   **Map Ref 14**

REGENCY PARK HOTEL, standing in 5 acres of Berkshire countryside, 7 minutes from junction 13 of M4. Renowned restaurant and bar. Ideal weekend breaks from £49.50 per person per night.

B&B from £40pp, Dinner available, Rooms 4 single, 14 twin, 31 double, 1 triple, all en-suite, Children welcome, Open all year.

Regency Park Hotel, Bowling Green Road, Thatcham, Newbury, Berkshire RG18 3RP
Tel: 01635 871555 Fax: 01635 871571   **Map Ref 14**

LYNDRICK GUEST HOUSE, offers quality accommodation, 25 minutes from Heathrow. Bedrooms have colour TV, tea/coffee, hair dryer and radio alarm. Breakfast served in a pleasant conservatory. London, Waterloo 45 minutes by rail convenient for Wentworth and surrounding golf courses. Easy access to motorways, close to Bracknell and Windsor.

B&B from £25pp, Rooms 1 single, 2 twin, 2 double, most en-suite,
Sue & Graham Chapman, **Lyndrick Guest House,** The Avenue, North Ascot, Berkshire SL5 7ND
Tel: 01344 883520 Fax: 01344 891243   **Map Ref 15**

THE SHIP HOTEL, town centre location, with easy access to M4, A4 and M40. A few minutes ' walk to the railway station. Private free parking. ETB 4 Crowns Commended.

B&B from £40, Lunch and evening meal available, Rooms 10 single, 17 double, 4 twin, 1 triple, Suite available, all en-suite, Children welcome, No smoking, Open all year.

The Ship Hotel, 4-8 Duke Street, Reading, Berkshire RG1 4RY
Tel: 0118 958 3455 Fax: 0118 950 4450 **Map Ref 16**

....

UPCROSS HOTEL, a privately owned country house hotel of character and warmth, featured on BBC TV. Reputed to have one of the best restaurants in Berkshire. Large garden, ample parking. Town centre/railway station 10 minutes. Easy access to M4, junction 11 and 12.

B&B from £62.50pp, Dinner available, Rooms 8 single, 7 double, 5 twin, 2 triple, 1 family, all en-suite, Restricted smoking, Children & pets welcome, Open all year.
Upcross Hotel, 68 Berkeley Avenue, Reading, Berkshire RG1 6HY
Tel: 01189 590796 Fax: 01189 576517 **Map Ref 16**

....

BIRD IN HAND, an extended 14th century coaching inn, between London and Oxford. Close to Henley, Maidenhead and Windsor. 25 minutes from Heathrow. Ample car parking. ETB 4 Crowns, Highly Commended.

B&B from £55, Lunch and Evening meal available, Rooms 1 single, 4 double, 10 twin, all en-suite, Children welcome, Open all year.

Bird in Hand, Bath Road, Knowl Hill, Reading, Berkshire RG10 9UP
Tel: 01628 822781 & 826622 Fax: 01628 826748 **Map Ref 16**

....

THE COPPER INN HOTEL & RESTAURANT, elegantly restored Georgian coaching inn with a restaurant overlooking secluded gardens. Good base for exploring the beautiful Thames Valley and all its attractions. Special weekend rates. ETB 4 Crowns Highly Commended.

B&B from £42.50, Lunch and evening meal available, Rooms 2 single, 14 double, 5 twin, 1 triple, all en-suite, Children welcome, Open all year.

The Copper Inn Hotel & Restaurant, Church Road, Pangbourne, Reading, Berkshire RG8 7AR
Tel: 0118 984 2244 Fax: 0118 984 5542 **Map Ref 17**

....

THE GREAT HOUSE AT SONNING, a riverside hotel, dating back from the 16th century, in 4 acre estate. Moorings Restaurant overlooking gardens and river. Riverside terrace during summer. Beautiful traditional bedrooms. ETB 4 Crowns Highly Commended.

B&B from £52, Lunch and evening meal available, Rooms 6 single, 25 double, 8 twin, 2 triple, all en-suite, Children welcome, Open all year.

The Great House at Sonning, Thames Street, Sonning-on-Thames, Reading, Berkshire RG4 6UT
Tel: 0118 969 2277 Fax: 0118 944 1296 **Map Ref 18**

....

CHESHAM HOUSE, is situated in a triangle formed by Reading, Maidenhead and Henley-on-Thames. Each room has an en-suite bathroom, colour TV, refrigerator and tea/coffee facilities. Three-quarters of an acre of garden. Private parking in grounds. ETB 2 Crowns Highly Commended.

B&B from £22, Rooms 1 double, 1 twin, both en-suite, Children from 6 years, No smoking, No pets, Open all year.
Chesham House, 79 Wargrave Road, Twyford, Reading, Berkshire RG40 9PE
Tel: 0118 932 0428 **Map Ref 19**

RAMBLER GUEST HOUSE, a small family run quality guest house, close to town centre, bus, train station. Ideal for Windsor, Legoland, Heathrow, M4 junctions. All rooms with colour TV. Full Fire Certificate. Main road (A4) location. Own car park. Tea making facilities. Full English breakfast. En-suite and family rooms available.

B&B from £20pp, Rooms 3 single, 5 twin, 2 double, 2 family, most en-suite, Restricted smoking, Children welcome, No pets, Open all year.

Mr & Mrs Jeer, **Rambler Guest House,** 1 Rambler Lane, London Road, Slough, Berkshire SL3 7RR

Tel/Fax: 01753 517665 **Map Ref 20**

WEXHAM PARK HALL, a converted farmhouse within a 200 acre sports complex. Elegant, en-suite rooms, friendly service and excellent restaurant. Convenient for Heathrow. Ample free parking.

B&B from £45pp, Dinner available (Monday - Friday), Rooms 1 single, 4 twin, all en-suite, Children welcome, No pets, Open all year.

Wexham Park Hall, Wexham Street, Wexham, Stoke Poges, Berkshire SL3 6NB

Tel: 01753 663254 Fax: 01753 662005 **Map Ref 21**

THE SWAN DIPLOMAT, is beautifully situated on the banks of the River Thames, within one hours drive of Oxford, Windsor, London and London Heathrow Airport. Special half board weekend rates available. ETB 4 Crowns Highly Commended.

B&B from £66.50, Lunch and evening meal available, Rooms 9 single, 27 double, 10 twin, all en-suite, Indoor swimming pool & gym, Children welcome, No smoking, Open all Year.

The Swan Diplomat, Streatley on Thames, Berkshire RG8 9HR

Tel: 01491 873737 Fax: 01491 872554 Email: sales@swan_diplomat.co.uk **Map Ref 22**

FAIRLIGHT LODGE ROYAL WINDSOR HOTEL, comfortable Victorian property, once a mayoral residence, quietly situated, but close to the River Thames, castle and town centre. Fully licensed bar and restaurant. ETB 3 Crowns Commended.

B&B from £50, Dinner available, Rooms 2 single, 5 double, 2 twin, 1 family room, all en-suite, Children welcome, No smoking, Open all year.

Fairlight Lodge Royal Windsor Hotel, 41 Frances Road, Windsor, Berkshire SL4 3AQ

Tel: 01753 861207 Fax: 01753 865963 **Map Ref 23**

ALMA LODGE, is a tastefully decorated Victorian House. it offers comfortable accommodation. All rooms are en-suite with colour TV, radio, tea/coffee facilities. There is off road parking if required. It is situated close to the town centre and is a few minutes from M4 Junction 6. Email: almalodge@aol.com

B&B from £21pp, Rooms 1 single, 2 twin, 2 double, 1 family, all en-suite, Restricted smoking, Children & pets welcome, Open all year.

Mr Shipp, **Alma Lodge,** 58 Alma Road, Windsor, Berkshire SL4 3HA

Tel: 01753 855620 Fax: 01753 855620 **Map Ref 23**

OSCAR HOTEL, situated near J6 M4 in Windsor. Walking distance to Thames River and town centre. Ten minutes drive to Legoland and 20 minutes to Heathrow. All rooms en-suite with TV, Direct Dial phone and tea/coffee facilities. Own car park and bar. 2 Crown Approved. ETB Approved.

B&B from £30pp, Rooms 4 single, 4 family, 5 double/twin, Children welcome, Open all year.

Oscar Hotel, 65 Vansittart Road, Windsor, Berkshire SL4 5DB

Tel: 01753 830613 Fax: 01753 833744 **Map Ref 23**

CLARENCE HOTEL, a comfortable hotel with licensed bar and steam room, near the town centre, castle and Eton. All rooms en-suite, have TV, hair dryer, radio and tea maker. Convenient for Heathrow Airport. ETB Listed Commended.

B&B from £35, Rooms 4 single, 4 double, 7 twin, 4 triple, 2 family, all en-suite, Children welcome, Open all year.
Clarence Hotel, 9 Clarence Road, Windsor, Berkshire SL4 5AE
Tel: 01753 864436 Fax: 01753 857060   **Map Ref 23**

....

THE CHRISTOPHER HOTEL, once a coaching inn, backing onto the playing fields at Eton College. Close to Royal Windsor and the Thames, offering a high level of comfort, hospitality and food. ETB 3 Crowns Approved.
B&B from £45, Lunch and evening meal available, Rooms 8 single, 12 double, 5 twin, 5 triple, 3 family rooms, all en suite, Children welcome, Open all year.
The Christopher Hotel, 110 High Street, Eton, Windsor, Berkshire SL4 6AN
Tel: 01753 852359 Fax: 01753 830914   **Map Ref 24**

....

CANTLEY HOUSE HOTEL, a Victorian country house hotel of great charm and character, set in quiet parkland just outside Wokingham. En-suite rooms, splendid restaurant and bistro. Only 5 minutes from M4, junction 10. ETB 4 Crowns Highly Commended.

B&B from £45, Lunch and evening meal available, Rooms 15 single, 12 double, 2 twin, suite available, all en-suite, Children welcome, No smoking, Open all year.
Cantley House Hotel, Milton Road, Wokingham, Berkshire RG41 5QG
Tel: 0118 978 9912 Fax: 0118 977 4294   **Map Ref 25**

....

VILLIERS HOTEL, individually designed bedrooms are set around an old coaching inn courtyard, incorporating English restaurant, Italian bistro and Jacobean pub. Car parking. ETB 5 Crowns Highly Commended.

B&B from £59, Lunch & evening meal available, Rooms 3 single, 18 double, 17 twin, suites available, all en-suite, Children welcome, No pets, Open all year.
Villiers Hotel, 3 Castle Street, Buckingham MK18 1BS
Tel: 01280 822444 Fax: 01280 822113   **Map Ref 26**

....

WEST LODGE HOTEL, an elegant Victorian hotel with Montgolfier French restaurant. Indoor swimming pool, sauna, hot air balloon trips. On A41 within 50 minutes of London, Heathrow and Birmingham and close to Aylesbury. Car parking, ETB 3 Crowns Commended.
B&B from £32, Dinner available, Rooms 2 single, 2 double, 2 twin, all en-suite, Children from 8 years, No smoking, No pets, Open all year.
West Lodge Hotel, 45 London Road, Aston Clinton, Aylesbury, Buckinghamshire HP22 5HL
Tel: 01296 630331 & 630362 Fax: 01296 630151   **Map Ref 27**

....

HIGHCLERE FARM, with views of the horse paddock, in a quiet location but close to M25, M40 and only half an hour by train to London (Marylebone). Car parking. ETB 2 Crowns Commended.

B&B from £35, Rooms 1 single, 6 twin, 2 family rooms, Children welcome, No smoking, No pets, Open January, March - December.
Highclere Farm, Newbarn Lane, Seer Green, Beaconsfield, Buckinghamshire HP9 2QZ
Tel: 01494 875665 & 874505 Fax: 01494 875238   **Map Ref 28**

....

CLIFTON LODGE HOTEL, is situated on the A40 approximately 1 mile from the M40 Oxford to London motorway. Ideal for touring the Thames Valley and Oxford. ETB 3 Crowns Commended.

B&B from £35, Lunch and evening meal available, Rooms 10 single, 13 double, 7 twin,2 family rooms, most en-suite, Children welcome, No smoking, No pets, Open all year.
 Clifton Lodge Hotel, 210 West Wycombe Road, High Wycombe, Buckinghamshire HP12 3AR
Tel: 01494 440095 & 529062 Fax: 01494 536322   **Map Ref 29**

THE WHITE HOUSE, a Victorian house of character, convenient for M4 and M40. Evening meals on request. ETB 2 Crowns Commended.
B&B from £30, Rooms 1 single, 2 twin, all en-suite/private facilities, No smoking, No pets, Open all year.
The White House, 194 Little Marlow Road, Marlow, Buckinghamshire SL7 1HX
Tel: 01628 485765 Fax: 01628 485765 **Map Ref 30**

....

HOLLY TREE HOUSE, a detached house set in large gardens with fine views over the valley. Quiet yet a convenient location. Outdoor heated swimming pool. ETB 2 Crowns Highly Commended.
B&B from £62.50, Rooms 1 single, 4 double, all en-suite, Children welcome, Open all year.
Holly Tree House, Burford Close, Marlow Bottom, Marlow, Buckinghamshire SL7 3NF
Tel: 01628 891110 Fax: 01628 481278 **Map Ref 30**

....

SPINNEY LODGE FARM, is an arable beef and sheep far. Lovely Victorian house with delightful en-suite bedrooms with colour TV, tea/coffee facilities. Ideal for Woburn, Althorp, Silver Stone. 12 minutes Northampton, 15 minutes Milton Keynes. 8 minutes to M1 Junction 15.
B&B from £19pp, Dinner from £10, Rooms 1 twin, 1 double, all en-suite, No smoking or pets, Children over 12, Open all year except Christmas.
Mrs Payne, **Spinney Lodge Farm,** Hanslope, Milton Keynes, Buckinghamshire MK19 7DE
Tel: 01908 510267 **Map Ref 31**

....

KINGFISHERS, a large private home set in a quarter of an acre of grounds, close to Milton Keynes city centre, bus and railway stations. Car parking. ETB Listed Commended.

B&B from £20, Dinner available, Rooms 1 single, 1 double, 1 triple, 2 en-suite, Children from 2 years, Open all year.
Kingfishers, 9 Rylstone Close, Heelands, Milton Keynes, Buckinghamshire MK13 7QT
Tel: 01908 310231 Fax: 01908 310231 **Map Ref 32**

....

SWAN REVIVED HOTEL, an independently owned famous coaching inn, where guests can enjoy every modern comfort. Convenient for thriving city of Milton Keynes, Woburn, Towcester and Silverstone. ETB 3 Crowns Highly Commended.
B&B from £42.50, Lunch and evening meal available, Rooms, 17 single, 19 double, 4 twin, 1 triple, 1 family room, suites available, all en-suite, Children welcome, Open all year.
Swan Revived Hotel, High Street, Newport Pagnall, Milton Keynes, Buckinghamshire MK16 8AR
Tel: 01908 610565 Fax: 01908 210995 **Map Ref 33**

....

ROSE COTTAGE, a restored and renovated 16th century cottage and out-buildings, within 2.5 acre garden in rural villages between Milton Keynes and Woburn. AGA cooking. All rooms en-suite, colour TV, tea/coffee facilities, full central heating, own entrance, private parking. Evening meals available at village restaurant. Email: jbassc@globalnet.co.uk
B&B from £20pp, Rooms 1 twin, 5 double, all en-suite, No smoking, children or pets, Open all year except Christmas & New Year.
Adele Brazier, **Rose Cottage,** Broughton Road, Salford, Milton Keynes, Buckinghamshire MK17 8BQ
Tel: 01908 582239 Fax: 01908 282029 **Map Ref 34**

....

THE DIFFERENT DRUMMER HOTEL, an historic oak beamed coaching inn, circa 1470, tastefully restored and modernised throughout and incorporating a high class Italian and English restaurant. ETB 3 Crowns Commended.

B&B from £45, Lunches and evening meals available, Rooms 5 single, 5 double, 1 twin, 1 triple, all en-suite, Children welcome, No smoking, No pets, Open all year.
The Different Drummer Hotel, 94 High Street, Stony Stratford, Milton Keynes, Buckinghamshire MK11 1AH
Tel: 01908 564733 Fax: 01908 260646 **Map Ref 35**

THE ROSE & CROWN INN, a family run Georgian style country inn set in the Chiltern Hills. Log fires. 1 miles from village of Saunderton, half a mile from the Ridgeway Path. Car parking. ETB 3 Crowns Commended.

B&B from £42, Lunch and evening meal available, Rooms 6 single, 10 double, 1 twin, most en-suite, Children welcome, No smoking, No pets, Open all year.
The Rose & Crown Inn, Wycombe Road, Saunderton, Princes Risborough, Buckinghamshire HP27 9NP
Tel: 01844 345299 Fax: 01844 343140   **Map Ref 36**

....

WOODLANDS LODGE, a charming, detached family home offering comfortable, pleasant and friendly accommodation. In own grounds with ample parking. Easy reach of Stansted Airport and M11, junction 8. ETB 2 Crowns Commended.

B&B from £30, Rooms 1 double, 2 twin, 1 triple, all en-suite, Children welcome, No smoking, Open all year.
Woodlands Lodge, Dunmow Road, Bishop's Stortford, Hertfordshire CM23 5QX
Tel: 01279 504784 Fax: 01279 461474   **Map Ref 37**

....

THE COTTAGE, a 17th century listed house with panelled rooms and wood stove. Conservatory dining room overlooks large, mature garden. Quiet village setting yet near the M11 junction 8 and Stansted Airport. ETB 2 Crowns Highly Commended.

B&B from £30, Rooms 3 single, 6 double, 6 twin, en-suite/private facilities, Children welcome, No smoking, No pets, Open all year except Christmas.
The Cottage, 71 Birchanger Lane, Birchanger, Bishop's Stortford, Hertfordshire CM23 5QA
Tel: 01279 812349 Fax: 01279 812349   **Map Ref 38**

....

CHESHUNT MARRIOTT HOTEL, only a minutes drive from the M25 motorway, the Cheshunt Marriott offers an ideal base for exploring London and the South East. Wheelchair access. Ample car parking. ETB 4 Crowns Commended.

B&B from £94, Lunch and evening meal available, Rooms 104 double, 38 twin, all en-suite, Children welcome, No smoking, No pets, Open all year.
Cheshunt Marriott Hotel, Halfhide Lane, Turnford, Broxbourne, Hertfordshire EN10 6NG
Tel: 01992 451245 Fax: 01992 440120   **Map Ref 39**

....

THE BELL INN & MOTEL, beautiful bungalow-styled with executive bedrooms. Full a la carte restaurant and traditional country pub serving excellent bar meals and real ales. Very close to A1M, M25 and M1. Family run and very welcoming. Ample car parking. ETB 3 Crowns Commended.

B&B from £42.50, Lunch and evening meal available, Rooms 9 double, 16 twin, all en-suite, Children welcome, No smoking, No pets, Open all year.
The Bell Inn & Motel, High Street, Codicote, Hertfordshire SG4 8XD
Tel: 01438 820278 Fax: 01438 821671   **Map Ref 40**

....

MILTON HOTEL, a family run, comfortable hotel in a residential area close to a mainline station, junctions 9/10 of M1 and convenient for M25. Large car park. ETB 1 Crown Approved.

B&B from £22, Dinner available, Rooms 3 single, 2 double, 2 twin, Children welcome, No pets, Open all year.
Milton Hotel, 25 Milton Road, Harpenden, Hertfordshire AL5 5LA
Tel: 01582 762914   **Map Ref 41**

....

COMET HOTEL, a hotel in the style of the 1930's, combining traditional comfort and service with modern design. Ideally located for London and Hertfordshire countryside. Ample car parking. ETB 4 Crowns Commended.

B&B from £35, Lunch and evening meal available, Rooms 14 single, 63 double, 24 twin, all en-suite, Children welcome, No smoking, Open all year.
Comet Hotel, 301 St Albans Road West, Hatfield, Hertfordshire AL10 9RH
Tel: 01707 265411 Fax:01707 264019   **Map Ref 42**

THE BOBSLEIGH INN, a privately owned country hotel with a reputation for good food and service. Easy access M1 and M25. 30 minutes from Luton and London Heathrow airports. Wheelchair access. ETB 4 Crowns Commended.

B&B from £40, Lunch and evening meal available, Rooms 5 single, 27 double, 5 twin, 5 triple, 1 family room, all en-suite, Children welcome, No smoking, Open all year.

The Bobsleigh Inn, Hempstead Road, Bovingdon, Hemel Hempstead, Hertfordshire HP3 0DS
Tel: 01442 833276 & 832000 Fax: 01442 832471   **Map Ref 43**

....

HALL HOUSE, a tranquil, 15th century country house, rebuilt in woodland setting on the edge of Hertford town. Car parking. ETB 3 Crowns De Luxe.

B&B from £49, Dinner available, Rooms 3 double, all en-suite/private facilities, No smoking, No pets, Open all year.

Hall House, Broad Oak End, off Bramfield Road, Hertford, Hertfordshire SG14 2JA
Tel: 01992 582807   **Map Ref 44**

....

THE LORD LISTER HOTEL, a charming Victorian house hotel with friendly and helpful staff. Individually furnished rooms some non-smoking. Restaurant, bar, car park. Close to town centre. ETB 3 Crowns Commended.

B&B from £35, Lunch and evening meal available, Rooms 4 single, 11 double, 3 twin, 1 triple, en-suite/private facilities, Children welcome, No smoking, Open all year.

The Lord Lister Hotel, 1 Park Street, Hitchin, Hertfordshire SG4 9AH
Tel: 01462 432712 & 459451 Fax: 01462 438506   **Map Ref 45**

....

REDCOATS FARMHOUSE HOTEL, a 15th century farmhouse set in open countryside offering secluded comfort and fresh food. Luton Airport is 20 minutes away. ETB 3 Crowns Commended.

B&B from £44, Lunch and evening meal available, Rooms 1 single, 10 double, 2 twin, 1 triple, Children from 4 years, No smoking, Open all year.

Redcoats Farmhouse Hotel, Redcoats Green, Hitchin, Hertfordshire SG4 7JR
Tel: 01438 729500 Fax: 01438 723322 Email: redcoatsfarmhouse@ukbusiness.com   **Map Ref 45**

....

THE APPLES HOTEL, a family run hotel in beautiful gardens within easy reach of the city centre, station and major motorways. Heated swimming pool. Facilities for disabled. Car parking. ETB 3 Crowns Commended.

B&B from £43, Lunch and evening meal available, Rooms 1 single, 5 double, 3 twin, 1 triple, all en-suite, Children welcome, No smoking, Open all year.

The Apples Hotel, 133 London Road, St Albans, Hertfordshire AL1 1TA
Tel: 01727 844111 Fax: 01727 861100   **Map Ref 46**

....

JARVIS AUBREY PARK HOTEL, is an elegant, well appointed, friendly hotel set in 6 acres of well kept gardens and woodland. Only 25 miles north of London via the M1. ETB 4 Crowns Commended.

B&B from £50, Lunch and evening meal available, Rooms 88 double, 31 twin, all en-suite, Children welcome, No smoking, Ample car parking, Open all year.

Jarvis Aubrey Park Hotel, Hemel Hempstead Road, Redbourn, St Albans, Hertfordshire AL3 7AF
Tel: 01582 792105 Fax: 01582 792001   **Map Ref 47**

Cambridgeshire & Northamptonshire

The county of Cambridgeshire has two splendid cities rich in cultural heritage - Cambridge and Peterborough.

Cambridge has a great wealth of architectural styles and many interesting features from the courtyards, the bridges and 'Backs' along the River Cam. The city has been described as the loveliest in Britain. The university had been founded by the 13th century. The oldest college is Peterhouse, founded in 1284. Others were established over the next 700 years in superb examples of architecture. King's College Chapel is the city's crowning glory and is best viewed from the 'Backs'. Today's Cambridge is a bustling city with good shopping facilities and a wide variety of bookshops. Arts and entertainment are a central part of the city's life, from impromptu classical recitals to rock concerts. The city is surrounded by lovely countryside and attractive villages which contain a wealth of historic buildings.

Peterborough is a perfect blend of past and present. The city has been dominated by its cathedral for over 750 years. The cathedral's painted ceiling is unique and the West Front is acclaimed as one of the finest in Europe. Peterborough has retained much of its heritage despite being a new city. Careful and tasteful redevelopment, such as the Queensgate and Rivergate shopping complexes, have not resulted in the destruction of the old market town buildings.

The landscape of the Fens is unique in character with vast areas of artificially reclaimed land from its original marsh state. The area was the stronghold of Hereward the Wake, the last Saxon leader to hold out against William the Conqueror. The market town of Ely is dominated by its superb cathedral, its octagonal tower is an engineering masterpiece. To the north of the county is Wisbech which retains its character of a prosperous Georgian market town.

Northampton is one of the largest market towns in England and it is noted for its fine churches. Among the finest is the Holy Sepulchre, a rare round church founded in 1110. The town is probably best known for its shoe industry. During the Civil War, it provided 1,500 pairs of shoes for Cromwell's forces. The county is indirectly linked with American independence - George Washington's ancestors lived in the small village of Sulgrave at Sulgrave Manor, build in 1560 by Lawrence Washington. The family coat of arms over the porch is thought to be the basis for the original Stars and Stripes. Towcester claims to be one of the oldest towns in the county and has been an important road junction ever since the Romans built Watling Street. The Saracen's Head Inn features in Charles Dickens' The Pickwick Papers as one of Mr Pickwick's stopping places.

left, Ely Cathedral

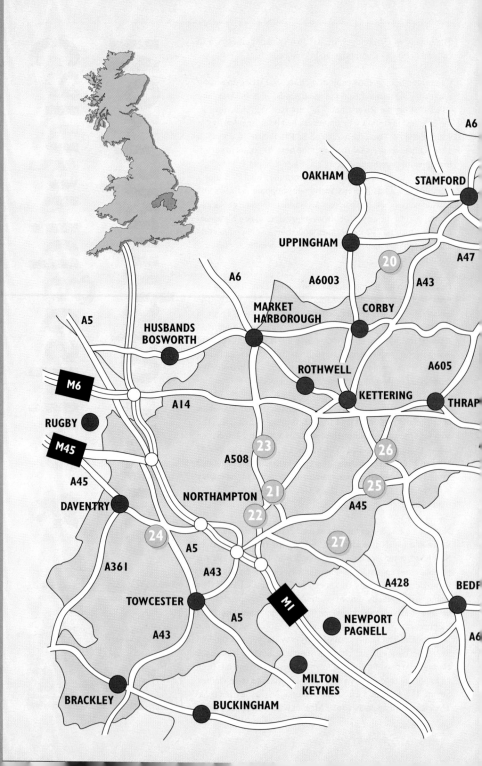

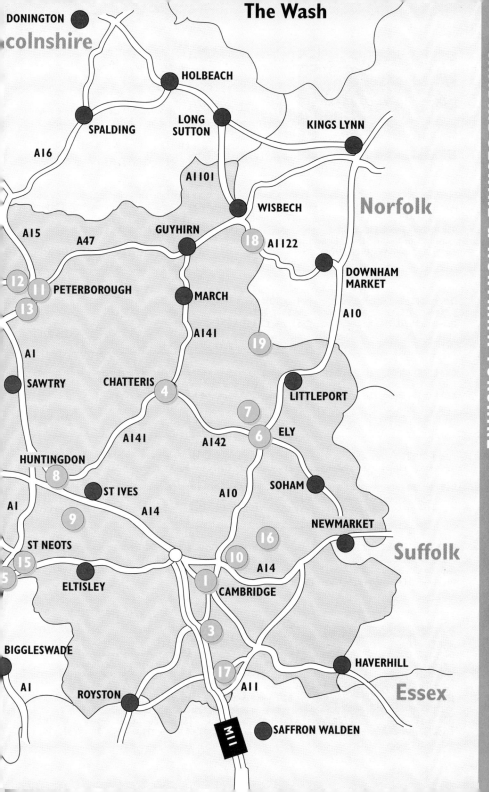

ASHTREES GUEST HOUSE, a friendly, family run guest house on main bus route to city centre and Addenbrookes Hospital. Rooms are individually decorated and have TV and tea/coffee facilities. Full English breakfast. ETB Listed Commended. RAC Listed. Car park and garden.

B&B from £18pp, Dinner from £8, Rooms 2 single, 1 twin, 3 double (1 en-suite), 1 family, No smoking or pets, Children welcome, Open 21st January - 30 December.
Mrs Irene Hill, **Ashtrees Guest House,** 128 Perne Rd, Cambridge CB1 3RR
Tel: 01223 411233   **Map Ref 1**

FAIRWAYS GUESTHOUSE, is a charming Victorian house. Family and en-suite rooms available. Direct dial telephone, clock/radio in all rooms. Close to Addenbrookes Hospital, station and golf course and 1 mile from the city centre. English/continental breakfasts, bar/lounge. ETB 2 Crowns Approved.
B&B from £20, Rooms 4 single, 4 double, 4 twin, 1 triple, 2 family rooms, Children welcome, No smoking, Open all year.
Fairways Guesthouse, 141-143 Cherry Hinton Road, Cambridge CB1 4BX
Tel: 01223 246063 Fax: 01223 212093   **Map Ref 1**

HAMILTON HOTEL, is a privately family run hotel about 1 mile from the city centre. TV's telephones, en-suite, tea and coffee making facilities. Bar, meals, car parking. ETB 3 Crowns Approved.
B&B from £22, Dinner available, Rooms 5 single, 5 twin, 3 triple, Children welcome, No pets, Open all year.
Hamilton Hotel, 156 Chesterton Road, Cambridge CB4 1DA
Tel: 01223 365664 Fax: 01223 314866   **Map Ref 1**

CAM GUESTHOUSE, is close to the River Cam, within 15 minutes' walking distance of the city centre and 5 minutes from Grafton shopping centre. En-suite jacuzzi bath. ETB Listed Commended.
B&B from £24, Rooms 3 single, 3 double, 2 triple, 1 family, Children welcome, No smoking, Open all year.
Cam Guesthouse, 17 Elizabeth Way, Cambridge CB4 1DD
Tel: 01223 354512   **Map Ref 1**

ASSISI GUESTHOUSE, warm welcoming, family-run guesthouse, ideally situated for the city, colleges and Addenbrookes Hospital. All modern facilities. Large car park. ETB 2 Crowns Approved.

B&B from £29, Rooms 4 single, 5 double, 6 twin, 1 triple, all en-suite, Children welcome, No smoking, No pets, Open all year.
Assisi Guesthouse, 193 Cherry Hinton Road, Cambridge CB1 4BX
Tel: 01223 246648 & 211466 Fax: 01223 412900   **Map Ref 1**

DRESDEN VILLA GUESTHOUSE, a family-run guesthouse offering a friendly service. All rooms en-suite with tea/coffee making facilities and satellite TV. Easy access to city, colleges and hospital. ETB 3 Crowns Approved.
B&B from £26,. Dinner available, Rooms 6 single, 3 double, 2 twin, 2 triple, all en-suite, Children welcome, No smoking, Open all year.
Dresden Villa Guesthouse, 34 Cherry Hinton Road, Cambridge CB1 4AA
Tel: 01223 247539 Fax: 01223 410640   **Map Ref 1**

CRISTINA'S GUEST HOUSE, guests are assured of a warm welcome here, quietly located in the beautiful city of Cambridge, only 15 minutes walk from the City Centre and Colleges. All rooms have colour TV and tea/coffee equipment. Some rooms have private shower and toilet. Private car park.

B&B from £35-49, Rooms 1 single, 3 twin, 1 double, 1 family, some en-suite, Restricted smoking, Children welcome, No pets, Open all year.
Cristina's Guest House, 47 St. Andrews Road, Cambridge CB4 1DH
Tel: 01223 365855 & 327700 Fax: 01223 365855   **Map Ref 1**

AYLESBRAY LODGE GUESTHOUSE, all rooms are en-suite, tastefully decorated and have complimentary extras. Four poster rooms, satellite TV. Car parking. ETB 3 Crowns Commended.

B&B from £28, Rooms 1 single, 2 double, 1 twin, 1 family room, all en-suite, Children welcome, No pets, No smoking, Open all year
Aylesbray Lodge Guesthouse, 5 Mowbray Road, Cambridge CB1 4SR
Tel: 01223 240089 Fax: 01223 240089 **Map Ref 1**

....

LENSFIELD HOTEL, a family run hotel in central location for all parts of the city's splendour - the "Bridges and Backs", Botanical Gardens, colleges, entertainment and shopping. ETB 3 Crowns.

B&B from £40, Dinner available, Rooms 7 single, 11 double, 10 twin, 2 triple, most en-suite, Children welcome, No pets, No smoking, Open all year.
Lensfield Hotel, 53 Lensfield Road, Cambridge CB2 1EN
Tel: 01223 355017 Fax: 01223 312022 **Map Ref 1**

....

SOUTHAMPTON HOUSE, is a Victorian property with friendly atmosphere, only 8 minutes' walk along the riverside to the city centre, colleges and new shopping mall. ETB Commended.

B&B from £25, Rooms 1 single, 1 double, 2 triple, 1 family room, all en-suite, Children welcome, No pets, No smoking, Open all year.

Southampton House, 7 Elizabeth Way, Cambridge CB4 1DE
Tel: 01223 357780 Fax: 01223 314297 **Map Ref 1**

....

ASHLEY HOTEL, a well appointed small hotel with modern facilities, close to city centre. Nearby Arundel House Hotel's facilities available to Ashley residents (under same ownership). ETB 3 Crowns Approved.

B&B from £29.50, Rooms 2 single, 3 double, 3 twin, 2 triple, most en-suite, Children welcome, No pets, Open all year.
Ashley Hotel, 74 Chesterton Road, Cambridge CB4 1ER
Tel: 01223 350059 **Map Ref 1**

....

ARBURY LODGE GUESTHOUSE, is a comfortable family run guesthouse, about 20 minutes walk to the city centre and colleges. Easy access from A14. Large car park and garden. Car parking. ETB Listed Commended.

B&B from £22, Rooms 1 single, 2 double, 2 twin, Children welcome, No pets, tea/coffee facilities in all rooms, Open all year.
Arbury Lodge Guesthouse, 82 Arbury Road, Cambridge CB4 2JE
Tel: 01223 364319 & 566988 Fax: 01223 566988 **Map Ref 1**

....

BROOKLANDS GUESTHOUSE, a friendly guesthouse, well decorated. All rooms en-suite and with telephone. Satellite TV, jacuzzi, sauna, four poster bed. ETB 3 Crowns Commended.

B&B from £28, Dinner available, Rooms 3 double, 2 twin, all en-suite, Children welcome, No smoking, Open all year.
Brooklands Guesthouse, 95 Cherry Hinton Road, Cambridge CB1 4BS
Tel: 01223 242035 Fax: 01223 242035 **Map Ref 1**

....

ARUNDEL HOUSE HOTEL, is an elegant, privately run 19th century terraced hotel. Beautiful location overlooking the River Cam and open parkland, near city centre and colleges. Reputation for some of the best food in the area. ETB 3 Crowns Commended.

B&B from £39.50, Lunch and evening meal available, Rooms 43 single, 33 double, 23 twin, 5 triple, 1 family, most en-suite, Children welcome, No pets, No smoking, Open all year.

Arundel House Hotel, Chesterton Road, Cambridge CB4 3AN
Tel: 01223 367701 Fax: 01223 367721 **Map Ref 1**

HOLIDAY INN (CAMBRIDGE), a centrally located, fully air conditioned hotel. Bloomsbury's Bar Restaurant with theatre-style kitchen open all day. Quinn's Irish pub - an alternative venue at the hotel for food and drink. ETB 4 Crowns Highly Commended.

B&B from £118, Lunch and evening meal available, Rooms 85 double, 112 twin, suites available, all en-suite, Children welcome, No smoking, Open all year.
Holiday Inn (Cambridge), Downing Street, Cambridge CB2 3DT
Tel: 01223 464466 Fax: 01223 464440   **Map Ref 1**

....

GONVILLE HOTEL, occupies one of the most favoured positions in Cambridge, overlooking Parkers Piece and close to most of the colleges and shopping areas. ETB 4 Crowns Commended.

B&B from £82.50 Lunch and evening meal available, Rooms 24 single, 19 double, 21 twin, 1 triple, all en-suite, Children welcome, No smoking, Open all year.
Gonville Hotel, Gonville Place, Cambridge CB1 1LY
Tel: 01223 366611 Fax: 01223 315470   **Map Ref 1**

....

3 DEAN DRIVE, is in a private road, 10 minutes walk from the station. Our rooms are tastefully furnished, have their own bathroom, and overlook the garden. They have tea and coffee making facilities, colour television, hair dryer and clock radio. There is ample safe parking.

B&B from £20pp, Rooms 1 twin, 1 double, No smoking, Children welcome, No pets, Open all year except Christmas Day & Boxing Day.

Mrs Carol Dennett, **3 Dean Drive,** Holbrook Rd, Cambridge CB1 4SW
Tel: 01223 210404   **Map Ref 1**

....

PURLINS, an attractive country house set in two acres of fields and woodland, in village four miles south of Cambridge. Ideal centre. All bedrooms en-suite with colour TV, radio, tea/coffee facilities. A conservatory serves as guests lounge. Restaurants nearby. On-drive parking.

B&B from £22pp, Rooms 1 twin, 2 double, all en-suite, No smoking or pets, Children over 8, Open February - mid December.
Olga & David Hindley, **Purlins,** 12 High Street, Little Shelford, Cambridge CB2 5ES
Tel: 01223 842643 Fax: 01223 842643   **Map Ref 3**

....

CROSS KEYS INN HOTEL, is an Elizabethan coaching inn built around 1540, Grade II listed. A la carte menu and bar meals. Friendly atmosphere, oak-beamed lounge with log fires. Ideally placed in the heart of the Fens. ETB 3 Crowns Commended.

B&B from £21, Lunch and evening meal available, Rooms 2 double, 4 twin, 1 triple, most en-suite, Children welcome, No smoking, Open all year.
Cross Keys Inn Hotel, 12-16 Market Hill, Chatteris, Cambridgeshire PE16 6BA
Tel: 01354 693036 & 692644 Fax: 01354 693036   **Map Ref 4**

....

THE GREEN WELLY MOTEL, there is a cafe open 6.00am to 10.00pm everyday serving home cooked dishes and grills. A large spacious parking area, licensed bar and colour TV's in each room. Make the stay in this purpose built budget motel affordable and pleasant.

B&B from £10.60pp, Dinner from £3, Rooms 3 single, 8 twin, 2 double, 3 family, most en-suite, Children & Pets welcome, Open all year except Christmas and Boxing Day.

Mark & Maria Hobbs, **The Green Welly Motel,** 2a Doddington Road, Chatteris, Cambridgeshire PE16 6UA
Tel: 01354 695490   **Map Ref 4**

HAMDEN GUESTHOUSE, the owner of this guesthouse guarantees you will not be disappointed with the comfortable en-suite bedrooms, most of which have a garden view. Full English breakfast. Bus service to city centre. Shops, pubs and restaurants within walking distance.

B&B from £25, Rooms 1 single, 1 double, 1 twin, 1 triple, 1 family room, private facilities, Children welcome, No pets, No smoking, Open all year.
Hamden Guesthouse, 89 High Street, Cherry Hinton, Cambridgeshire CB1 4LU
Tel: 01223 413263 Fax: 01223 245960   **Map Ref 1**

....

THE WHITE HORSE, a comfortable 13th Century Coaching Inn, with tea/coffee facilities in all rooms. Large car park. Good food, wine and ales. Convenient for all A1 destinations.

B&B from £39.50pp, Dinner from £5, Rooms 1 twin, 2 double, all en-suite, Children over 5, Pets by arrangement, Open all Year except Christmas & New Year.
The White Horse, 103 Great North Road, Eaton Socon, Cambridgeshire PE19 3EL
Tel: 01480 406650 & 474453 Fax: 01480 406650   **Map Ref 5**

....

CATHEDRAL HOUSE, Ely - capital of the Fens, situated by the cathedral and all other tourist attractions, eating places, etc. Delightful Grade II Listed house with many original features. Three well appointed en-suite rooms overlook tranquil walled garden. Parking. Easy access M11 and A14. Cambridge, Newmarket, King's Lynn, Bury St Edmunds are nearby.

B&B from £25pp, Rooms 1 twin, 1 double, 1 family, all en-suite, No smoking or pets, Children welcome, Open mid January - mid December.
Jenny & Robin Farndale, **Cathedral House,** 17 St. Mary's Street, Ely, Cambridgeshire CB7 4ER
Tel: 01353 662124 Fax: 01353 662124 Email: farndale@globalmet.co.uk   **Map Ref 6**

....

LAMB HOTEL, in the shadows of Ely Cathedral, this fully modernised former coaching inn has been used by travellers since the 14th century. ETB 4 Crowns Commended.

B&B from £62, Lunch and evening meal available, Rooms 7 single, 5 double, 13 twin, 6 triple, 1 family room, en-suite facilities, Children welcome, No smoking, Open all year.
Lamb Hotel, 2 Lynn Road, Ely, Cambridgeshire CB7 4EJ
Tel: 01353 663574 Fax: 01353 662023   **Map Ref 6**

....

NYTON HOTEL, situated in a quiet, residential area overlooking Fenland countryside and adjoining golf-course. Close to city centre and Cathedral. Car parking. ETB 3 Crowns Approved.

B&B from £38, Lunch and evening meal available, Rooms 2 single, 4 double, 2 twin, 2 family rooms, all en-suite, Children welcome, Open all year.
Nyton Hotel, 7 Barton Road, Ely, Cambridgeshire CB7 4HZ
Tel: 01353 662459 Fax: 01353 666217   **Map Ref 6**

....

HILL HOUSE FARM, a Victorian farmhouse in peaceful village 3 miles west Ely. Tastefully furnished en-suite bedrooms 1 on ground floor, colour TV, tea/coffee facilities. Guests lounge. Ely cathedral, Welney Wildfowl Trust, Newmarket, Cambridge easy access. Wicken Fen nearby. First class breakfast served in traditional dining room.

B&B from £40pp, Rooms 1 twin, 2 double, all en-suite, No smoking or pets, Children over 12, Open all year except Christmas.

Mrs Hilary Nix, **Hill House Farm,** 9 Main Street, Coveney, Ely, Cambridgeshire CB6 2DJ
Tel: 01353 778369   **Map Ref 7**

OLD BRIDGE HOTEL, a beautifully decorated Georgian town hotel by the River Ouse. Oak panelled dining room and terrace brasserie with award winning wine list, real ales and log fires. Privately owned. ETB 4 Crowns Highly Commended.

B&B from £79.50 Lunch and evening meal available, Rooms 5 single, 16 double, 4 twin, all en-suite, Children welcome, No smoking, Open all year.

Old Bridge Hotel, 1 High Street, Huntingdon, Cambridgeshire PE18 6TQ
Tel: 01480 452681 Fax: 01480 411017   **Map Ref 8**

....

PRINCE OF WALES, is a traditional village inn renowned for its traditional ales and good value food. Convenient for St Ives, Huntingdon, St Neots and Cambridge. On B1040, south east of Huntingdon. ETB 2 Crowns Commended.

B&B from £25, Lunch and evening meal available, Rooms 2 single, 1 double, 1 twin, all en-suite, Children from 5 years, Car parking, Open all year.
Prince of Wales, Potton Road, Hilton, Huntingdon, Cambridgeshire PE18 9NG
Tel: 01480 830257 Fax: 01480 830257   **Map Ref 9**

....

AMBASSADOR LODGE, a late Victorian property, family run in quiet location. 3 miles city centre. Within walking distance of River Cam and country park. Half a mile from renowned Cambridge Science Park. Easy access to A14, A1(M), M11. Usual facilities. Off road parking. Tel: 01223 860168.

B&B from £21pp, Rooms 2 single, 1 twin, 1 double, 2 family, most en-suite, Restricted smoking, Children welcome, No pets, Open all year.
Mrs V Logan, **Ambassador Lodge,** 37 High St, Milton, Cambridge CB4 6DF
Tel: 01223 860168   **Map Ref 10**

....

DALWHINNIE LODGE HOTEL, we believe we are the best hotel of our kind for location, comfort and value for money. High standards and a warm welcome guaranteed. 5 minutes from city centre, bus and train station. Ample parking. ETB 2 Crowns Approved.

B&B from £25, Dinner available, Rooms 4 single, 4 double, 2 twin, en-suite/private facilities, Children welcome, No smoking, Open all year.

Dalwhinnie Lodge Hotel, 31-33 Burghley Road, Peterborough, Cambridgeshire PE1 2QA
Tel: 01733 65968 & 565968 Fax: 01733 890838   **Map Ref 11**

....

QUEENSGATE HOTEL, is a city centre hotel 5 minutes' walk from Rivergate Centre, main shopping area Cathedral and theatre. Character building refurbished in 1996. Ample car parking. ETB 3 Crowns Commended.

B&B from £35, Dinner available, Rooms 6 single, 8 double, 3 twin, 2 triple, All en-suite, Children welcome, Open all year.
Queensgate Hotel, 5 Fletton Avenue, Peterborough, Cambridgeshire PE2 8AX
Tel: 01733 62572 & 53181 Fax: 01733 558982   **Map Ref 11**

....

HAWTHORN HOUSE HOTEL, situated in the city centre, we are a licensed hotel which offers a high standard of accommodation and service. Tastefully furnished en-suite rooms with TV and tea-making facilities. ETB 2 Crowns Commended.

B&B from £25, Dinner available, Rooms, 3 single, 3 double, 2 twin, all en-suite, Children welcome, No pets or smoking, Open all year.

Hawthorn House Hotel, 89 Thorpe Road, Peterborough, Cambridgeshire PE3 6JQ
Tel: 01733 340608 Fax: 01733 340608   **Map Ref 11**

HOTEL FORMULE 1, the benchmark in very reasonably-priced hotels (300 hotels in Europe), functional rooms (washbasin, TV, desk), one single price (£22.50) for up to 3 people. Close by, comfortable showers and toilets are equipped with a self-cleaning system. A continental breakfast costs £2.50.

£22.50 per room (up to 3 people), Breakfast £2.50, Rooms 80* (1 double bed and a bunk bed), Children welcome, Open all year.
Mr & Mrs Neary, **Hotel Formule 1,** Boongate, Peterborough PE1 5QT
Tel: 01733 894400   **Map Ref 11**

....

BUTTERFLY HOTEL, by the water's edge at Thorpe Meadows, this modern hotel maintains all the traditional values of design and comfort. Special weekend rates available. ETB 4 Crowns Commended.
B&B from £30, Lunch and evening meal available, Rooms 33 single, 18 double, 15 twin, 4 suites, all en-suite, Children welcome, No smoking, Open all year.
Butterfly Hotel, Thorpe Meadows, off Longthorpe Parkway, Peterborough, Cambridgeshire PE3 6GA
Tel: 01733 564240 Fax: 01733 565538   **Map Ref 12**

....

ORTON HALL HOTEL, a 17th century manor house set in 20 acres of mature parkland. En-suite bedrooms with four poster beds. Huntly restaurant or country pub for a choice of dining. ETB 4 Crowns Commended.

B&B from £73, Lunch and evening meal available, Rooms 9 single, 32 double, 7 twin, 2 triple, all en-suite, Children welcome, No smoking, Open all year.
Orton Hall Hotel, The Village, Orton Longueville, Peterborough, Cambridgeshire PE2 7DN
Tel: 01733 391111 Fax: 01733 231912   **Map Ref 13**

....

THE BELL INN HOTEL, is an old coaching inn, restored as a hotel including restaurant, village bar and banqueting facilities. 6 miles south of Peterborough off the A1. ETB 4 Crowns Highly Commended.
B&B from £45, Lunch and evening meal available, Rooms 2 single, 15 double, 1 twin, 1 triple, all en-suite, Children welcome, No pets, No smoking, Open all year.
The Bell Inn Hotel, Great North Road, Stilton, Peterborough, Cambridgeshire PE7 3RA
Tel: 01733 241066 Fax: 01733 245173   **Map Ref 14**

....

THOMAS COOK BLUEBELL LODGE LEISURE CENTRE, a friendly and efficient service is provided at this modern hotel. Bar, Restaurant and leisure facilities available. Ample car parking. ETB 3 Crowns Commended.
B&B from £30, Lunch and evening meal available, Rooms 2 double, 9 twin, 2 triple, all en-suite, Children welcome, No smoking, No pets, Open all year.
Thomas Cook Bluebell Lodge Leisure Centre, PO Box 36, Thorpe Wood, Peterborough, Cambridgeshire PE3 6SB
Tel: 01733 502555 & 503008 Fax: 01733 502020   **Map Ref 11**

....

ABBOTSLEY GOLF HOTEL, Charming country hotel amidst its own 2 excellent 18 hole golf courses. Golf Monthly: "The design is a revelation, the presentation superb". Non golfers just as welcome. ETB 2 Crowns Approved.
B&B from £40, Lunch and evening meal available, Rooms 2 single, 13 twin, 2 triple, all en-suite, Tea/coffee facilities in all rooms, Children welcome, Open all year.
Abbotsley Golf Hotel, Eynesbury Hardwicke, St Neots, Cambridgeshire PE19 4XN
Tel: 01480 474000 Fax: 01480 471018   **Map Ref 15**

....

BRIDGE HOTEL (MOTEL), a picturesque 17th century riverside hotel with motel rooms, between A45 and A10(B1047), 4 miles from Cambridge. Fishing, walking, boating. ETB 3 Crowns Approved.
B&B from £35, Lunch and evening meal available, Rooms 3 single, 20 double, 5 twin, suites available, all en-suite, Children from 5 years, No smoking, Open all year.
Bridge Hotel (Motel), Clayhythe, Waterbeach, Cambridgeshire CB5 9NZ
Tel: 01223 860252 Fax: 01223 440448   **Map Ref 16**

RED LION HOTEL, is a traditional 13th century English inn with modern facilities. Well situated for Cambridge with excellent road and rail connections, 1 miles from Duxford Imperial War Museum. Ample car parking. ETB 3 Crowns Approved.

B&B from £35, Lunch and evening meal available, Rooms 7 single, 6 double, 1 twin, 2 triple, 2 family, all en-suite, Children welcome, No smoking, open all year.
Red Lion Hotel, Station Road East, Whittlesford, Cambridgeshire CB2 4NL
Tel: 01223 832047 & 832115 Fax: 01223 837576   **Map Ref 17**

....

THE OLDE MILL HOTEL, a converted mill which has been tastefully extended. In a small town on the outskirts of Wisbech, Providing a good base for touring the fens. Close to Norfolk coast. ETB 3 Crowns Approved.

B&B from £31 Lunch and evening meal available, Rooms 3 double, 1 twin, 3 triple, all en-suite, tea/coffee making facilities, Children welcome, No smoking, Open all year

The Olde Mill Hotel, Town Street, Upwell, Wisbech, Cambridgeshire PE14 9AF
Tel: 01945 772614 Fax: 01945 772614   **Map Ref 18**

....

We welcome you to our former farmhouse, **STOCKYARD FARM** situated between Ely and Wisbech. Both bedrooms have washbasins and hot drinks facilities. Breakfast served in the conservatory. Guest's lounge with books and TV. Bathroom has corner bath and shower. Wildfowl & Wetlands Centre and Ouse Washes Nature Reserve nearby, making this an ideal base for bird watchers.
B&B from £16pp, Rooms 1 twin, 1 double, No smoking Minimum age 5, Pets welcome, Open all year except Christmas.
Mr & Mrs Bennett, **Stockyard Farm,** Wisbech Rd, Welney, Wisbech PE14 9RQ
Tel: 01354 610433   **Map Ref 19**

....

AARANDALE REGENT HOTEL & GUESTHOUSE, a small and cosy, family run hotel/guesthouse within easy walking distance of the town centre, bus and train stations. Car parking. Tea/coffee making facilities. ETB 1 Crown Approved.

B&B from £22, Dinner available, Rooms 4 single, 6 double, 6 twin, 4 triple, Children welcome, Open all year.

Aarandale Regent Hotel & Guesthouse, 6-8 Royal Terrace, Barrack Road (A508), Northamptonshire NN1 3RF
Tel: 01604 31096 Fax: 01604 21035   **Map Ref 22**

....

THE FALCON, a proprietor-managed country cottage hotel. Ideal touring centre for Oxford, Cambridge, Stratford, Warwick and the National Exhibition Centre. Good restaurant and bar open daily. Sky TV in all rooms. ETB 4 Crowns Commended.

B&B from £65, Lunch and evening meal available, Rooms 4 single, 10 double, 2 twin, all en-suite, Tea/coffee making facilities in all rooms. Children welcome, Open all year.
The Falcon, Castle Ashby, Northamptonshire NN7 1LF
Tel: 01604 696200 Fax: 01604 696673   **Map Ref 27**

....

WHITE SWAN, is a 15th century coaching inn offering en-suite accommodation, in a delightful village, close to many historic sites. Home cooked food and real ales. Car parking. Tea/coffee making facilities. ETB 3 Crowns Commended.

B&B from £38.50, Lunch and evening meal available, Rooms 1 single, 4 double, 1 twin, all en-suite, Children welcome, No pets, No smoking, Open all year.

White Swan, Seaton Road, Harringworth, Corby, Northamptonshire NN17 3AF
Tel: 01572 747543 Fax: 01572 747323   **Map Ref 20**

POPLARS HOTEL, personal attention is given at this small country hotel in the heart of Northamptonshire. Within easy reach of many tourist attractions. Tea/coffee making facilities. Car parking. ETB 3 Crowns Commended,

B&B from £25, Dinner available, Rooms 6 single, 4 double, 1 twin, 7 family rooms, some en-suite, Children welcome, No smoking, Open all year.
Poplars Hotel, Cross Street, Moulton, Northamptonshire NN3 7RZ
Tel: 01604 643983 Fax: 01604 790233 **Map Ref 21**

....

LIME TREES HOTEL, a delightful hotel in a conservation area. Owner managed with great care. Fine restaurant. Secure courtyard car park. Half a mile from town centre. ETB 4 Crowns Commended.

B&B from £45, Lunch and evening meal available, Rooms 7 single, 13 double, 1 twin, 2 triple, all en-suite, Children welcome, No smoking, Open all year.
Lime Trees Hotel, 8 Langham Place, Barrack Road, Northampton, Northamptonshire NN2 6AA
Tel: 01604 32188 Fax: 01604 233021 **Map Ref 22**

....

BROOMHILL COUNTRY HOUSE HOTEL & RESTAURANT, is a converted Victorian country house with some splendid views. As a welcomed guest you will be offered relaxed, old fashioned hospitality, while chef will tempt you with his interesting and varied menus. 6 miles north of Northampton, 6 miles from A14. ETB 4 Crowns Commended.
B&B from £37, Lunch and evening meal available, Rooms 2 single, 4 double, 7 twin, all en-suite, Children welcome, Tea/coffee making facilities, Open all year.
Broomhill Country House Hotel & Restaurant, Holdenby Road, Spratton, Northamptonshire NN6 8LD
Tel: 01604 845959 Fax: 01604 845834 **Map Ref 23**

....

GLOBE HOTEL, is a 19th century countryside inn. Old world atmosphere and freehouse hospitality with good English cooking, available all day. Meeting rooms. Close to the M1, Stratford and many tourist attractions. Send for information pack. ETB 4 Crown Commended.

B&B from £32, Lunch & evening meal available, Rooms 4 single, 6 double, 5 twin, 3 triple, all en-suite, Children welcome, Open all year.
Globe Hotel, High Street, Weedon, Northamptonshire NN7 4QD
Tel: 01327 340336 Fax: 01327 349058 **Map Ref 24**

....

HIGH VIEW HOTEL, a large, detached house, modernised building with pleasant gardens. In quiet tree lined area near town centre and railway station. All rooms are en-suite.Tea/coffee facilities. ETB 3 Crowns.

B&B from £28, Dinner available, Rooms 5 single 5 double, 4 twin, all en-suite, Children from 4 year, No pets or smoking, Open all year.
High View Hotel, 156 Midland Road, Wellingborough, Northamptonshire NN8 1NG
Tel: 01933 278733 **Map Ref 25**

....

OAK HOUSE PRIVATE HOTEL, is a small, homely hotel with a comfortable atmosphere, on the edge of the town centre. Double-glazed. Enclosed car park. ETB 3 Crowns Approved.

B&B from £28, Dinner available, Rooms 5 single, 5 double, 6 twin, all en-suite/private facilities, Children welcome, Tea/coffee making facilities. Open all year.
Oak House Private Hotel, 8-11 Broad Green, Wellingborough, Northamptonshire NN8 4LE
Tel: 01933 271133 Fax: 01933 271133 **Map Ref 25**

....

TUDOR GATE HOTEL, is a converted 17th century farmhouse, with 3 four-poster beds. Close to the new A1/M1 link. 30 antique businesses within walking distance and a wide range of leisure activities locally. Wheelchair access. ETB 3 Crowns Commended.

B&B from £45, Lunch and evening meal available, Rooms 4 single, 20 double, 3 twin, all en-suite, Children welcome, No smoking, Open all year.
Tudor Gate Hotel, 35 High Street, Finedon, Wellingborough, Northamptonshire NN9 5JN
Tel: 01933 680408 Fax: 01933 680745 **Map Ref 26**

Charming countryside, history and the arts meet in Cheshire and Merseyside. South Cheshire is one of the prettiest areas, famous for its beautiful black and white timbered buildings, waterways and, of course, Cheshire cheese. The Cheshire cheese trail can be followed through the farms, pubs and the countryside.

Chester is known the world over as Britain's finest shopping city outside London. Much of the city's finest architecture is now shops. Many of them are in two-tier Medieval galleries known as The Rows where they open onto balustraded walkways reached only by steps from the road. The Chester Summer Music Festival has become a celebrated major annual event and the Gateway Theatre runs an innovative programme of traditional and contemporary drama.

To the east of Chester is Tarporley, surrounded by rich farmlands and woodland. North of here is the 4,000 acre Delamere Forest and on a summit to the south is Beeston Castle on the summit of the Peckforton Hills. Knutsford is another attractive town with narrow streets and old black and white houses. Two miles north is Tatton Hall, surrounded by formal gardens and woodland, it is one of the National Trust's most visited properties. Nantwich is an old salt mining town on the River Weaver where black and white timbered houses are crowded together in narrow streets. Wallasey on the Wirral Peninsula is connected to the busy shipbuilding and industrial centre of Birkenhead by docks and wharves. Dominating the scene is the Liver Building, the offices of the Royal Liver Friendly Society. Its two main towers are topped by mythical Liver birds from which the city is said to get its name.

During the last century tons of cargo arrived daily from all over the world in the Port of Liverpool. The main trade was from America to supply the cotton merchants and mill owners of the north west during the textile boom. Liverpool's historic waterfront is today one of the country's popular tourist attractions. Converted Victorian warehouses at The Albert Dock are the home of the Merseyside Maritime Museum and next to it, the Tate Gallery houses the most important collection of contemporary art outside London. The Beatles Story, a shrine to the legendary 60's pop group and sons of Liverpool is also within the renovated dockland area. The city also has a wide range of theatres, art galleries and arts centres. Liverpool is known for its boundless artistic talent and for the many playwrights, poets, comedians, musicians and actors who began their careers there. Apart from New York, more films, plays and television series have been made in Liverpool than any other city.

Cheshire, Merseyside & Greater Manchester

left, Chalmondeley Castle

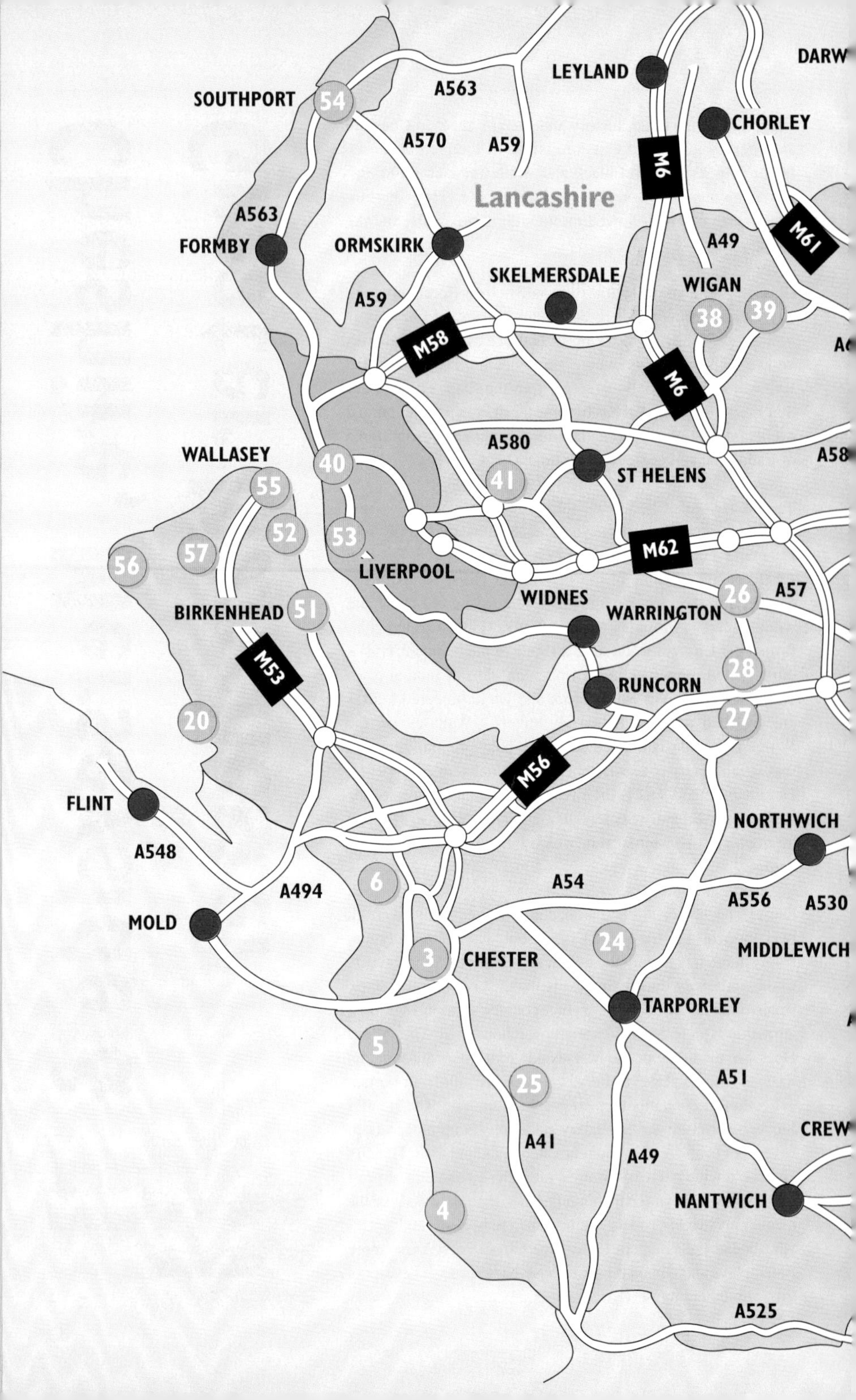

SOUTHPORT
54
A563
A570
A59
LEYLAND
DARW
CHORLEY
M6
Lancashire
A563
FORMBY
ORMSKIRK
A49
M61
SKELMERSDALE
WIGAN
38
39
A59
A(
M58
M6
WALLASEY
A580
A58
55
40
41
ST HELENS
52
53
M62
57
LIVERPOOL
56
WIDNES
26
A57
BIRKENHEAD
51
WARRINGTON
28
M53
RUNCORN
27
20
M56
FLINT
NORTHWICH
A548
A54
A556
A530
6
MOLD
A494
MIDDLEWICH
3
CHESTER
24
5
TARPORLEY
25
A51
A41
A49
CREW
4
NANTWICH
A525

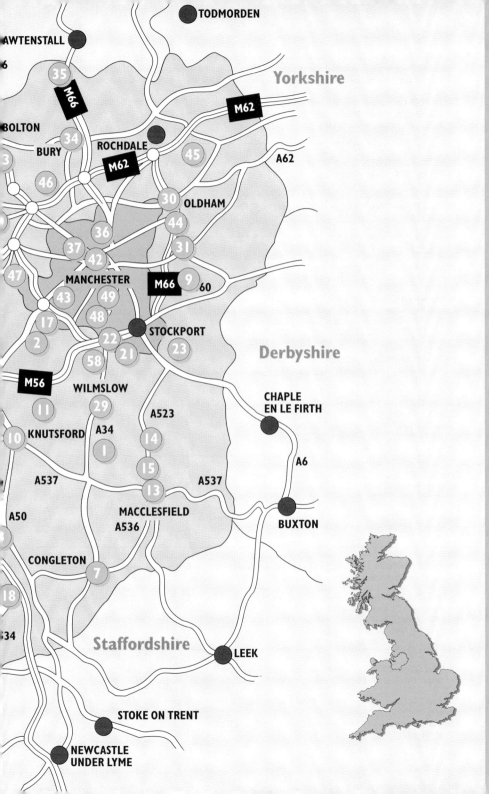

THE ALDERLEY EDGE HOTEL,, a converted country mansion built originally for one of the Manchester cotton barons. Close to the Edge beauty spot and near the village of Alderley, Jodrell Bank and Gawsorth Hall. Restaurant featuring fish and produce from the hotel bakery. Award winning head chef. ETB 4 Crowns Highly Commended.

B&B from £40, Lunch and evening meal available, Rooms 46 double, all en-suite, Children welcome, No pets, Open all year.
The Alderley Edge Hotel, Macclesfield Road, Alderley Edge, Cheshire SK9 7BJ
Tel: 01625 583033 Fax: 01625 586343 **Map Ref 1**

....

MILVERTON HOUSE HOTEL, a well appointed Victorian villa on main road with open country views. Home cooking. Car Parking. ETB 3 Crowns Approved.

B&B from £25, Dinner available, Rooms 1 single, 7 double, 4 twin, some en-suite, Children welcome, Open all year.
Milverton House Hotel, Wilmslow Road, Alderley Edge, Cheshire SK9 7QL
Tel: 01625 583615 & 585555 **Map Ref 1**

....

OASIS HOTEL, an independent family run hotel within easy reach of Manchester Airport and city centre. Convenient for public transport and shopping centre. ETB 2 Crowns Approved.

B&B from £32.50, (weekend rate from £25), Dinner available, Rooms 12 single, 7 double, 10 twin, 3 triple, all en-suite, Children welcome, No pets, Open all year.
Oasis Hotel, 46 Barrington Road, Altrincham, Cheshire WA14 1HN
Tel: 0161 928 4523 Fax: 0161 928 1055 **Map Ref 2**

....

CRESTA COURT HOTEL, a privately owned town centre hotel, opened in 1973 and designed to provide modern facilities. Easy access to M56, M6, M62, M63. 10 minutes from Manchester Airport. Tea/coffee making facilities. Car parking, ETB 4 Crowns Commended.

B&B from £72.50, Lunch and evening meal available, Rooms 114 single, 13 double, 8 twin, 3 triple, all en-suite, Children welcome, No smoking, Open all year.
Cresta Court Hotel, Church Street, Altrincham, Cheshire WA14 4DP
Tel: 0161 927 7272 Fax: 0161926 9194 **Map Ref 2**

....

LYNWOOD HOTEL, a small, comfortable, family run hotel in quiet position. Convenient for motorways, G-Mex, The Arena and National Cycling Centre. 20 minutes to Manchester Airport. ETB 2 Crowns Commended.

B&B from £20, Rooms 2 single, 2 twin, Children welcome, No pets, Tea/coffee making facilities in rooms, Open all year.
Lynwood Hotel, 3 Richmond Street, Ashton-under-Lyne, Cheshire OL6 7TX
Tel: 0161 330 5358 **Map Ref 31**

....

YORK HOUSE HOTEL, a refurbished hotel with restaurant and function room. Emphasis on good food and fine wines. Garden (Britain in Bloom" winner). Ideal base for touring north of England. ETB 4 Crowns Highly Commended.

B&B from £55, Lunch and evening meal available, Rooms 9 single, 18 double, 5 twin, 2 triple, all en-suite, Children welcome, Tea/coffee making facilities, Open all year.
York House Hotel, York Place, off Richmond Street, Ashton-under-Lyne, Cheshire OL6 7TT
Tel: 0161 330 9000 Fax: 0161 343 1613 **Map Ref 31**

....

MALVERN GUEST HOUSE, a Victorian terraced 2 storey town house, within 8 minutes' walk of the cathedral and the city centre. TV, radio and tea/coffee making facilities in all rooms. ETB 1 Crown Approved.

B&B from £13, Dinner available, Rooms 2 single, 1 double, 2 twin, 1 triple, 1 family room, Children from 2 years, No pets, Open all year.
Malvern Guest House, 21 Victoria Road, Chester, Cheshire CH2 3NJ
Tel: 01244 380865 **Map Ref 3**

EATON HOTEL, is ideally situated in the heart of Chester with the advantage of own parking. Friendly atmosphere with traditional standards of service and cuisine. Tea/coffee making facilities. ETB 3 Crowns Approved.

B&B from £32.50, Lunch and evening meal available, Rooms 3 single, 5 double, 5 twin, 2 triple, 3 family, all en-suite/private facilities, Children welcome, No smoking, Open all year.
Eaton Hotel, 29-31 City Road, Chester, Cheshire CH1 3AE
Tel: 01244 320840 Fax: 01244 320850   **Map Ref 3**

....

CURZON HOTEL, a warm welcome awaits you in this large Victorian house with beautiful gardens. Close to the racecourse, River Dee and golf course. Fine cuisine prepared by chef-proprietor Marcus Imfeld. ETB 3 Crowns Commended.

B&B from £40, Dinner available, Rooms 1 single, 7 double, 1 twin, 4 triple, 3 family rooms, all en-suite, Children welcome, No smoking, Open all year.
Curzon Hotel, 52-54 Hough Green, Chester, Cheshire CH4 8JQ
Tel: 01244 678581 Fax: 01244 680866   **Map Ref 3**

....

GREEN BOUGH HOTEL & RESTAURANT, is a comfortable, family run Victorian hotel with friendly, relaxed atmosphere. Tastefully decorated with many antique furnishings. Restaurant renowned for traditional English cooking. ETB 4 Crowns Highly Commended.

B&B from £40, Lunch and evening meal available, Rooms 2 single, 16 double, 1 twin, 3 triple, all en-suite, Children welcome, No pets, No smoking, Tea/coffee making facilities, Open all year.
Green Bough Hotel & Restaurant, 60 Hoole Road, Chester, Cheshire CH2 3NL
Tel: 01244 326241 & 0410 353370 Fax: 01244 326265   **Map Ref 3**

....

EDWARDS HOUSE HOTEL, a Victorian property with well proportioned bedrooms, all en-suite. Convenient for the city centre, Chester Zoo, M53/M56 motorways and A55 North Wales trunk road. ETB 3 crowns Commended.

B&B from £22, Dinner available, Rooms 2 single, 5 double, 3 triple, all en-suite, Children welcome, No pets, No smoking, Open all year.
Edwards House Hotel, 61-63 Hoole Road, Chester, Cheshire CH2 3NJ
Tel: 01244 318055 & 319888 Fax: 01244 319888   **Map Ref 3**

....

CHEYNEY LODGE HOTEL, is a small, friendly hotel of unusual design, featuring indoor garden and fish pond. 10 minutes' walk from city centre and on main bus route. Personally supervised with emphasis on good food. ETB 3 Crowns Commended.

B&B from £24, Lunch and evening meal available, Rooms 1 single, 4 double, 2 twin, 1 triple, all en-suite, Children welcome, No pets, Open all year.
Cheyney Lodge Hotel, 77-79 Cheyney Road, Chester, Cheshire CH1 4BS
Tel: 01244 381925   **Map Ref 3**

....

STAFFORD HOTEL, is a comfortable, family run hotel, close to the city centre and railway station. Restaurant and licensed bar. Parking available. Short breaks available all year. Brochure on request. ETB 3 Crowns Commended.

B&B from £34, Dinner available, Rooms 7 single, 10 double, 4 twin, 1 triple, all en-suite, Children welcome, No pets, No smoking, Open all year.
Stafford Hotel, City Road, Chester, Cheshire CH1 3AE
Tel: 01244 326052 Fax: 01244 311403   **Map Ref 3**

....

BELGRAVE HOTEL, is near the railway station and 5 minutes walk to the city centre. Two bars, entertainment some evenings. En-suite rooms with colour TV, Tea/coffee making facilities. ETB 2 Crowns Approved.

B&B from £20, Dinner available, Rooms 12 single, 4 double, 13 twin, 5 triple, all en-suite, Children welcome, Open all year.
Belgrave Hotel, City Road, Chester, Cheshire CH1 3AF
Tel: 01244 312138 Fax: 01244 324951   **Map Ref 3**

QUEEN HOTEL, a fully modernised hotel that still retains an elegant Victorian air. It is close to the station and all amenities. TV & radio, tea/coffee making facilities in all rooms. ETB 5 Crowns Highly Commended.

B&B from £80, Lunch and evening meal available, Rooms 9 single, 49 double, 60 twin, 10 triple, suite available, all en-suite, Children welcome, No smoking, Open all year.
Queen Hotel, City Road, Chester, Cheshire CH1 3AH
Tel: 01244 350100 Fax: 01244 318483   **Map Ref 3**

....

CITY WALLS HOTEL & RESTAURANT, is a charming Georgian hotel situated on the old city walls, overlooking Chester racecourse. Noted for accommodation food and service. ETB 3 Crowns Approved.

B&B from £40, Lunch and evening meal available, Rooms 4 single, 6 double, 2 twin,4 triple, all en-suite, Children welcome, Tea/coffee making facilities, Open all year.
City Walls Hotel & Restaurant, City Walls Road, 14 Stanley Place, Chester, Cheshire CH1 2LU
Tel: 01244 313416 Fax: 01244 313416   **Map Ref 3**

....

DENE HOTEL, set in its own grounds, adjacent to Alexandra Park and 1 mile from the city centre. A la carte restaurant, rooms for no-smokers, ample parking. ETB 4 Crown Commended.

B&B from £39.50, Lunch and evening meal available, Rooms 9 single, 23 double,12 twin, 3 triple, 2 family rooms, all en-suite, Children welcome, No smoking, Open all year.
Dene Hotel, Hoole Road, Chester, Cheshire CH2 3ND
Tel: 01244 321165 Fax: 01244 350277   **Map Ref 3**

....

THE GREYHOUND HOTEL, a family run bed and breakfast in picturesque village on River Dee. Comfortable rooms with TV and coffee/tea facilities. Good home cooking. Excellent cask conditioned beer. Cot available. Self catering holiday cottage. Great base for golfing breaks, 10 courses within 30 minutes including Carden Park.
B&B from £25, Dinner available, Rooms 1 single, 2 twin, 1 double, 1 family en-suite, Children welcome, Pets by arrangement, Open all year.
Sarah & Marco Paoloni, **The Greyhound Hotel,** High Street, Farndon, Chester, Cheshire CH3 6PU
Tel: 01829 270 244 Fax: 01829 270 244   **Map Ref 4**

....

THE MOUNT, 'somewhere special'. Victorian country house. Easy for North Wales/Cheshire. Extensive gardens, home grown vegetables. Tennis croquet. Spacious bedrooms, en-suite bathrooms, TV and tea/coffee facilities. Elegant dining room and conservatory for guests use. 5 minutes walk to village pub. Evening meals on request. Bring own wine.

B&B from £20pp, Dinner from £16, Rooms 2 twin, 1 double, all en-suite, No smoking, Children over 12, Open all year except Christmas & New Year.

Jonathan & Rachel Major, **The Mount,** Lesters Lane, Higher Kinnerton, Chester, Cheshire CH4 9BQ
Tel: 01244 660275 Fax: 01244 660275   **Map Ref 5**

....

CRABWALL MANOR HOTEL & RESTAURANT, is an exclusive country house hotel set in 11 acres of formal gardens and parkland. 2 miles north of Chester. Reputation for excellent food in the conservatory restaurant. ETB 5 Crowns Highly Commended.

B&B from £95, Lunch and evening meal available, Rooms 4 double, 44 twin, suites available, all en-suite, Children welcome, No pets, No smoking, Open all year.

Crabwall Manor Hotel & Restaurant, Parkgate Road, Mollington, Chester, Cheshire CH1 6NE
Tel: 01244 851666 & 0800 964470 Fax: 01244 851400 Email: sales@crabwall.com   **Map Ref 6**

LION & SWAN HOTEL, is a 16th century hotel with oak beamed restaurant. High standards create an ideal base for business and leisure. 6 miles from the M6. Ample car parking. ETB 4 Crowns Highly Commended.

B&B from £33, Lunch and evening meal available, Rooms 4 single, 15 double, 2 twin, all en-suite, Children welcome, No pets, No smoking, Open all year.
Lion & Swan Hotel, Swan Bank, Congleton, Cheshire CW12 1JR
Tel: 01260 273115 Fax: 01260 299270   **Map Ref 7**

....

HOLLY LODGE HOTEL, is a charming Victorian country hotel, professionally managed and family owned. Friendly and efficient service. Close to junction 18 just off the M6. A la carte restaurant, conference and meeting rooms. Four poster, jacuzzi and water bed. ETB 4 Crowns Commended.

B&B from £39, Lunch and evening meal available, Rooms 6 single, 21 double, 9 twin, 2 triple, all en-suite, Children welcome, No smoking, Open all year.
Holly Lodge Hotel, 70 London Road, Holmes Chapel, Cheshire CW4 7AS
Tel: 01477 537033 Fax: 01477 535823   **Map Ref 8**

....

NEEDHAMS FARM, a 500 year old farmhouse surrounded by scenic views, residential license. Views from all rooms. Log fires in winter. Plenty of car parking. Eve meals served 7pm to 9pm. Ideally situated for Manchester city and airport. Nearest rail station Romiley. Working farm offering a warm welcome.
B&B from £20pp single, £32pp double, Dinner from £7, Rooms 1 single, 1 twin, 4 double, 1 family, some en-suite, Children & pets welcome, Open all year.
Charlotte & Ian Walsh, **Needhams Farm,** Uplands Road, Werneth Low, Gee Cross, Hyde, Cheshire SK14 3QQ
Tel: 0161 368 4610 Fax: 0161 367 9106   **Map Ref 9**

....

LONGVIEW HOTEL & RESTAURANT, is a period Victorian hotel with many antiques and a relaxed, comfortable atmosphere, overlooking town common. High quality varied food. Close to exit 19 of M6 and airport. ETB 4 Crowns Highly Commended.

B&B from £39, Lunch and evening meal available, Rooms 6 single, 9 double, 7 twin, 1 triple, all en-suite, Children welcome, Tea/coffee making facilities, Open all year.
Longview Hotel & Restaurant, Manchester Road, Knutsford, Cheshire WA16 0LX
Tel: 01565 632119 Fax: 01565 652402   **Map Ref 10**

....

THE HINTON, a bed and breakfast for both business and private guests. Within easy reach of M6, M56, Manchester Airport and Intercity rail network. Ideal touring base, on the B5085 between Knutsford and Wilmslow. Car parking. ETB 3 Crowns Highly Commended. AA Selected QQQQ.

B&B from £38, Dinner available, Rooms 3 single, 2 double, 1 twin, all en-suite, Children welcome, No smoking, No pets, Open all year.
The Hinton, Town Lane, Mobberley, Knutsford, Cheshire WA16 7HH
Tel: 01565 873484 Fax: 01565 873484   **Map Ref 11**

....

THE OLD VICARAGE PRIVATE HOTEL, set in 2 acres of naturally wooded gardens, in the heart of rural Cheshire and yet only 3 minutes drive from M6 Junction 19 (Knutsford). In addition to traditional rural hospitality, the beautiful restored and furnished 19th century vicarage offers an impressive range of outstanding features designed for your comfort and convenience.
B&B from £27.50pp, Supper from £4.50, Rooms 2 twin, 2 double, 1 family, all en-suite, No smoking or pets, Children over 10, Open all year except Christmas & New Year.
Norma & Alfred Weston, **The Old Vicarage Private Hotel,** Moss Lane, Over Tabley, Knutsford WA16 0PL
Tel: 01565 652221 Fax: 01565 755918   **Map Ref 12**

CHADWICK HOUSE, a tastefully refurbished large town house, close to the town centre and stations. Licensed bar, restaurant, sauna solarium and gym available. Sky TV, tea/coffee making facilities in all rooms. ETB 3 Crowns Commended.

B&B from £25, Dinner available, Rooms, 6 single, 6 double, 1 twin, all en-suite, Children welcome, No smoking or pets. Open all year.
Chadwick House, 55 Beech Lane, Macclesfield, Cheshire SK10 2DS
Tel: 01625 615558 & 0858 154816 Fax: 01625 610265   **Map Ref 13**

SHRIGLEY HALL HOTEL GOLF & COUNTRY CLUB, is a country house hotel built in 1825 in 262 acre estate of Shrigley Park. Overlooks the Cheshire plain and peak District. 18 hole golf course and full leisure club. TV and tea/coffee making facilities in all rooms. ETB 5 Crowns Commended.

B&B from £99, Lunch and evening meal available, Rooms 25 single, 92 double, 34 twin, 5 triple, all en-suite, Children welcome, No smoking, Open all year.
Shrigley Hall Hotel Golf & Country Club, Shrigley Park, Pott Shrigley, Macclesfield, Cheshire SK10 5SB
Tel: 01625 575757 Fax: 01625 573323   **Map Ref 14**

MOORHAYES HOUSE HOTEL, a modern comfortable house in attractive garden, half a miles from town centre, 5 minutes from Peak District National Park, 20 minutes from Manchester Airport.

B&B from £21pp, Rooms 2 single, 1 twin, 6 double, most en-suite, Children & pets welcome, Open all year.

Moorhayes House Hotel, 27 Manchester Road, Tytherington, Macclesfield, Cheshire SK10 2JJ
Tel: 01625 433228   **Map Ref 15**

LEA FARM, a charming farmhouse set in landscaped gardens where peacocks roam on a pedigree dairy farm. Ample car parking, in beautiful rolling countryside. Spacious bedrooms, luxury lounge. Pool/snooker, fishing available. Colour TV, drinks making facilities, radio alarms. Convenient for M6 Junction 16.

B&B from £16.50pp, Dinner from £10, Rooms 1 twin, 1 double, 1 family, 2 en-suite, Restricted smoking, Children welcome, Open all year except Christmas.

Mrs Jean Callwood, **Lea Farm,** Wrinehill Road, Wyburnbury, Nantwich, Cheshire CW5 7NS
Tel: 01270 841429 Fax: 01270 841429   **Map Ref 16**

CORNERSTONES, an elegantly refurbished hotel, offering every comfort and service. Ideally situated on the A56 only minutes from city and airport. 5 minutes walk to Metro station. ETB 3 Crowns Highly Commended.

B&B from £23, Dinner available, Rooms 3 single, 3 double, 3 twin, all en-suite/private facilities, Children welcome, No pets, No smoking, Open all year.
Cornerstones, 230 Washway Road, Sale, Cheshire M33 4RA
Tel: 0161 283 6909 & 881 0901 Fax: 0161 283 6909   **Map Ref 17**

SAXON CROSS HOTEL, is conveniently situated in the heart of Cheshire at junction 17 of the M6. Just 1 mile from the quaint town of Sandbach. Wheelchair access. ETB 3 Crowns Commended.

B&B from £40, Lunch and evening meal available, Rooms 10 single, 10 double, 18 twin, 14 triple, all en-suite, Children welcome, No smoking, Open all year.

Saxon Cross Hotel, M6 Junction 17, Holmes Chapel Road, Sandbach, Cheshire CW11 1SE
Tel: 01270 763281 Fax: 01270 768723   **Map Ref 18**

GROVE HOUSE HOTEL & RESTAURANT, a restaurant with rooms in Georgian House. Family owned and run. Welcoming feel, relaxed ambience, just eight individually styled en-suite bedrooms. Excellent restaurant offering ambitious, modern cooking prepared by chef-proprietor. In quiet village on Trent and Mersey Canal, 2 miles from J17, M6.
B&B from £30pp, Dinner from £14, Rooms 1 single, 1 twin, 6 double, all en-suite, Children welcome, Pets by arrangement, Open all year except Christmas.
Richard & Katherine Shaw, Roger & Brenda Curtis, **Grove House Hotel & Restaurant,** Mill Lane, Wheelock, Sandbach, Cheshire CW11 4RD
Tel: 01270 762582 Fax: 01270 759465   **Map Ref 19**

....

SPRING COTTAGE GUEST HOUSE, a beautifully furnished Victorian house in a historic part of Cheadle Hulme. Convenient for the airport, rail station and variety of local restaurants. ETB Listed Highly Commended.

B&B from £18.50, Rooms 1 single, 1 double, 4 twin, Car parking, Children welcome, Tea/coffee making facilities, Open all year.

Spring Cottage Guest House, 60 Hulme Hall Road, Cheadle Hulme, Stockport, Cheshire SK8 6JZ
Tel: 0161 485 1037   **Map Ref 21**

....

PYMGATE LODGE HOTEL, is within 1 mile of Manchester Airport. Every bedroom overlooks garden or open fields. Decorated and furnished to a high standard. Licensed a la carte restaurant. Courtesy tray in each room. All bedrooms non smoking.

B&B from £38, Lunch and evening meal available, Rooms 5 twin, 3 triple, some en-suite, Children from 3 years. No pets, Open all year.
Pymgate Lodge Hotel, 147 Styal Road, Gatley, Stockport, Cheshire SK8 3TG
Tel: 0161 436 4103 Fax: 0161 499 9171   **Map Ref 22**

....

Real home from home accommodation at **SHIRE COTTAGE** with views over Etherow Country Park and wooded valleys. All rooms have central heating, TV, tea/coffee facilities. Situated on the edge of the Peak District yet only 10 miles from airport and 15 miles from Manchester city centre. Car parking.
B&B from £19pp, Rooms 1 single, 1 twin, 1 double, 1 family, most en-suite, Children welcome, Dogs by arrangement, Open all year except Christmas & New Year.
Mrs Monica Sidebottom, **Shire Cottage Farmhouse,** Benches Lane, Marple Bridge, Stockport, Cheshire SK6 5RY
Tel: 01457 866536   **Map Ref 23**

....

WILLINGTON HALL HOTEL, is a country house hotel set in its own park with good views over surrounding countryside. All rooms have tea/coffee making facilities. Car parking available. ETB 4 crowns Commended.

B&B from £46, Lunch and evening meal available, Rooms 2 single, 3 double, 5 twin, all en-suite, Children from 5 years, Open all year.

Willington Hall Hotel, Willington, Taporley, Cheshire CW6 0NB
Tel: 01829 752321 Fax: 01829 752596   **Map Ref 24**

....

ROUGHLOW FARM, an 18th century sandstone farmhouse in an outstanding position with wonderful views to Shropshire and Wales. Friendly family home, elegantly furnished to a very high standard. 3 comfortable en-suite bedrooms. Attractive garden with cobbled courtyard. Tennis court. Very peaceful location.

B&B from £25pp, Rooms 3 twin, No smoking or pets, Children over 6, Open all year.

Mrs Sutcliffe, **Roughlow Farm,** Willington, Tarporley, Cheshire CW6 0PG
Tel: 01829 751199 Fax: 01829 751199   **Map Ref 24**

THE PHEASANT INN, a three hundred year old inn nestling on top of Peckforton Hills. Rooms in Award Winning barn conversion with spectacular views over Cheshire Plain. Halfway along sandstone trail in wonderful walking country. Excellent food served in farmhouse kitchen.

B&B from £35pp, Dinner from £12, Rooms 2 twin, 6 double, 2 family, all en-suite, Restricted smoking, Children welcome, Pets by arrangement, Open all year.
Mr David Greenhaugh, **The Pheasant Inn,** Higher Burwardsley, Tattenhall, Cheshire CH3 9PF Email: dave1pheas@aol.com
Tel: 01829 770434 Fax: 01829 771097   **Map Ref 25**

....

ROCKFIELD HOTEL, an elegant Edwardian house, full of character and tastefully modernised. Swiss family owned. Award winning restaurant with Swiss and English cuisine. 5 minutes from M6 junction 20 , off A50. ETB 4 Crowns Highly Commended.

B&B from £30, Lunch and evening meal available, Rooms 5 single, 6 double, 1 twin, all en-suite/private facilities, Children welcome, No smoking, Open all year.
Rockfield Hotel, Alexandra Road, Grappenhall, Warrington, Cheshire WA4 2EL
Tel: 01925 262898 Fax: 01925 263343   **Map Ref 26**

....

TALL TREES LODGE, is 2.5 miles south of junction 10 of the M56. Take A49 towards Whitchurch. Little Chef and Mobil garage on site. Tea/coffee making facilities. Car parking.

B&B from £39.50, Rooms 13 double, 1 twin, 6 triple, all en-suite, Children welcome, No smoking, Open all year.
Tall Trees Lodge, Tarporley Road, Lower Whitley, Warrington, Cheshire WA4 4EZ
Tel: 01928 790824 & 715117 Fax: 01928 791330   **Map Ref 27**

....

THE PARK ROYAL INTERNATIONAL HOTEL, HEALTH & LEISURE SPA , set in the heart of the Cheshire countryside, 2 minutes from junction 10 of the M56. Special weekend rates available. Superb health and leisure spa.
B&B from £68, Lunch and evening meal available, Rooms 2 single, 91 double, 44 twin, 2 triple, 2 family rooms, suites available, all en-suite, Children welcome, No smoking, Open all year.
The Park Royal International Hotel, Health & Leisure Spa , Stretton Road, Stretton, Warrington WA4 4NS
Tel: 01925 730706 Fax: 01925 730740   **Map Ref 28**

....

HOLLOW BRIDGE GUEST HOUSE, a newly refurbished house, en-suite bedrooms, garden room, dining room, reading room. Homely atmosphere. Manchester Airport and Motorway 10 minutes away. 5 minutes from Wilmslow centre. ETB 2 Crowns Highly Commended.

B&B from £35, Rooms 2 single, 1 double, 1 twin, all en-suite, Children welcome, Open all year.
Hollow Bridge Guest House, 90 Manchester Road, Wilmslow, Cheshire SK9 2JY
Tel: 01625 537303 Fax: 01625 528718   **Map Ref 29**

....

DEAN BANK HOTEL, is a family run, countryside hotel in a peaceful setting, ideal for leisure breaks, long or short stay business accommodation and Manchester Airport. Home cooked evening meals. ETB 3 Crowns Commended.
B&B from £33, Dinner available, Rooms 1 single, 5 double, 6 twin, 5 triple, all en-suite, Children welcome, No pets, Open all year.
Dean Bank Hotel, Adlington Road, Wilmslow, Cheshire SK9 2BT
Tel: 01625 524268 Fax: 01625 549715   **Map Ref 29**

....

RYLANDS FARM GUEST HOUSE, is a family-run guesthouse with many exposed beams, colour coordinated en-suite rooms, secure parking. Free travel to airport. Only 7 minutes from Junction 6, M56. ETB 2 Crowns Commended.

B&B from £33, Dinner available, Rooms 4 double, 2 twin, all en-suite, Children welcome, No smoking, Open all year.
Rylands Farm Guest House, Altringham Road, Wilmslow, Cheshire SK9 4LT
Tel: 01625 535646 & 548041 Fax: 01625 535646   **Map Ref 29**

STANNEYLANDS HOTEL, the ideal blend of comfort and facilities makes Stanneylands a perfect setting for business meetings or entertaining in the exclusive restaurant.

B&B from £55, Lunch and evening meal available, Rooms 7 single, 11 double, 14 twin, suites available, all en-suite, Children welcome, No smoking, Open all year.
Stanneylands Hotel, Stanneylands Road, Wilmslow, Cheshire SK9 4EY
Tel: 01625 525225 Fax: 01625 537282 Email: gordonbeech@thestanneylandshotel.co.uk   **Map Ref 29**

....

FERN BANK GUEST HOUSE, a detached Victorian house, built in 1881 and standing in its own grounds. Tastefully furnished with antiques, large south facing conservatory. Manchester Airport 10 minutes by car. Long stay car parking next door.ETB 2 Crowns Commended.

B&B from £30, Rooms 2 single, 1 double, 1 twin, all en-suite, Children welcome, No smoking, Open all year.
Fern Bank Guest House, 188 Wilmslow Road, Handforth, Wilmslow, Cheshire SK9 3JX
Tel: 01625 523729 Fax: 01625 539515   **Map Ref 30**

....

LISIEUX, is a deceptively large, homely bungalow with high standard of accommodation. Extensive breakfast menu available early morning. 3 miles from Manchester Airport. ETB 3 Crowns Highly Commended.

B&B from £27, Dinner available, Rooms 1 single, 1 double, 1 twin, Children welcome, Open all year.
Lisieux, 199 Wilmslow Road, Handforth, Wilmslow, Cheshire SK9 3JX
Tel: 01625 522113 Fax: 01625 526313   **Map Ref 30**

....

BELFRY HOTEL, a modern hotel on the B5358 (old A34), noted for good food and service. Convenient for business in Manchester and Wilmslow area. 10 minutes from Manchester Airport (courtesy transport available with prior notice). ETB 5 Crowns Highly Commended.
B&B from £40, Lunch and evening meal available, Rooms 25 single, 30 double, 18 twin, 7 triple, suites available, all en-suite, Children welcome, No pets, No smoking, Open all year.
Belfry Hotel, Stanley Road, Handforth, Wilmslow, Cheshire SK9 3LD
Tel: 0161 437 0511 Fax: 0161 499 0597 Email: andrew.beech@the-belfry-hotel.co.uk   **Map Ref 30**

....

LAST DROP VILLAGE HOTEL, a collection of 18th century farm buildings transformed into a "living village", with 2 restaurants, tea shop, leisure club and hotel. Ample car parking. ETB 4 Crowns Highly Commended.

B&B from £91.50 Lunch and evening meal available, Rooms 85 double, 6 twin, 37 triple, all en-suite, Children welcome, No smoking, Open all year.
Last Drop Village Hotel, Hospital Road, Bromley Cross, Bolton, Lancashire BL7 9PZ
Tel: 01204 591131 Fax: 01204 304122   **Map Ref 32**

....

COMMERCIAL ROYAL HOTEL, is a quality hotel offering the standard of service and facilities rarely found in small hotels. Noted English/Italian restaurant. Two minutes from motorway network, 15 minutes Manchester, 5 minutes from Bolton. Car parking. ETB 3 Crowns Commended.

B&B from £24, Dinner available, 5 single, 4 double, 1 triple, some en-suite, Children welcome, No smoking, Open all year.
Commercial Royal Hotel, 13-15 Bolton Road, Moses Gate, Farnworth, Bolton, Lancashire BL4 7JN
Tel: 01204 573661 Fax: 01204 862488   **Map Ref 33**

....

NORMANDIE HOTEL, a modern, comfortable hotel noted nationally for the preparation and presentation of modern French.British cooking. Tea/coffee making facilities. Car parking. ETB 4 Crowns Highly Commended.

B&B from £49, Lunch and evening meal available, Rooms 7 single, 10 double, 6 twin, all en-suite, Children welcome, No pets, No smoking, Open all year.
Normandie Hotel, Elbut Lane, Birtle, Bury Lancashire BL9 6UT
Tel: 0161 764 3869 & 764 1170 Fax: 0161 764 4866   **Map Ref 34**

53

ROSTREVOR HOTEL & BISTRO, a small family run hotel and bistro opposite open parkland, close to the town centre, markets and steam railway. A warm welcome and friendly atmosphere. ETB 3 Crowns Commended.

B&B from £29, Lunch and evening meal available, Rooms 5 single 5 double, 4 twin, all en-suite, Children welcome, Open all year.
Rostrevor Hotel & Bistro, 148 Manchester Road, Bury, Lancashire BL9 0TL
Tel: 0161 764 3944 Fax: 0161 764 8266   **Map Ref 34**

....

THE BOLHOLT COUNTRY PARK HOTEL, is a family run hotel and conference centre, set in 50 acres of beautiful parkland, lakes and gardens. Large swimming pool and full leisure facilities. Tea/coffee making facilities in all rooms, ETB 4 Crowns Commended.

B&B from £58, Lunch and evening meal available, Rooms 14 single, 31 double, 4 twin, 4 triple, 1 family, all en-suite, Children welcome, Open all year.
The Bolholt Country Park Hotel, Walshaw Road, Bury, Lancashire BL8 1PU
Tel: 0161 764 5239 & 763 7007 Fax: 0161 763 1789   **Map Ref 34**

....

THE OLD MILL HOTEL & RESTAURANT, a converted mill with old world appearance but very modern bedrooms. Standing in its own grounds, close to the city and country life. Full leisure centre, swimming pool, sauna, whirlpool, solarium and gymnasium. ETB 5 Crowns Commended.

B&B from £35, Lunch and evening meal available, Rooms 12 single, 13 double, 12 twin, all en-suite, No pets, Open all year.
The Old Mill Hotel & Restaurant, Springwood, Ramsbottom, Bury, Lancashire BL0 9DS
Tel: 01706 822991 Fax: 01706 822291   **Map Ref 35**

....

All rooms at **MABS CROSS HOTEL** are en-suite with colour TV's and tea/coffee making facilities. Restaurant. Lady Mabels wine bar and nightly entertainment. Large car park. Free entry to one of our three town centre nightclubs right next to central park and town centre.

B&B from £15pp, Dinner £5-£12, Rooms 4 single, 5 twin, 4 double, 2 family, all en-suite, Children welcome, No pets, Open all year.
Mabs Cross Hotel, 136 Standishgate, Wigan, Lancashire WN1 1XP
Tel: 01942 248180 Fax: 01942 230340 Email: skleisure@aol.com   **Map Ref 38**

....

COACHING INN HOTEL, is approximately one mile from the town centre on good regular bus route. All rooms are en-suite with tea/coffee making facilities, TV and office desks. Secure car park. ETB 3 Crowns Approved.

B&B from £22, Lunch and evening meal available, Rooms 12 single, 2 double, 3 twin, 1 triple, all en-suite, Children welcome, No pets, Open all year.
Coaching Inn Hotel, Warrington Road, Lower Ince, Wigan, Lancashire WN3 4NJ
Tel: 01942 866330 Fax: 01942 749990   **Map Ref 39**

....

BLUNDELLSANDS HOTEL, a majestic Victorian character hotel in a quiet suburb of Crosby. Easy access to Liverpool centre and Southport. Car parking. Tea/coffee making facilities. ETB 4 Crowns Commended.

B&B from £66, Lunch and evening meal available, Rooms 12 single, 17 double, 4 twin, 4 triple, all en-suite, Children welcome, No smoking, Open all year.
Blundellsands Hotel, The Serpentine, Blundellsands, Crosby, Liverpool L23 6YB
Tel: 0151 924 6515 Fax: 0151 931 5364   **Map Ref 40**

....

ROCKLAND HOTEL, a Georgian hotel set in its own grounds in a quiet suburban location. Easy access to the motorway (1 mile) and ten miles from Liverpool city centre. ETB 3 Crowns Approved.

B&B from £25, Lunch and evening meal available, Rooms 4 single, 2 double, 3 twin, 2 triple, most en-suite, Children welcome, Open all year.
Rockland Hotel, View Road, Rainhill, Prescot, Liverpool L35 0LG
Tel: 0151 426 4603 Fax: 0151 426 0107   **Map Ref 41**

IMPERIAL HOTEL, is a well maintained hotel run by the same owner for over 10 years, offering reasonably priced accommodation. Close to university and hospitals. ETB 3 Crowns Commended.

B&B from £30, Dinner available, Rooms 13 single, 5 double, 9 twin, most en-suite, Children welcome, No pets, No smoking.
Imperial Hotel, 157 Hathersage Road, Manchester M13 0HY
Tel: 0161 225 6500 Fax: 0161 225 6500 **Map Ref 42**

THE PALACE HOTEL, is a listed building of character in the city centre, designed in a country house hotel style. TV, hair dryer and tea/coffee making facilities in all rooms. ETB 5 Crowns Highly Commended.

B&B from £94, Lunch and evening meal available, Rooms 5 single, 103 double, 53 twin, 10 family rooms, all en-suite, Children welcome, No smoking, Open all year.
The Palace Hotel, Oxford Street, Manchester M60 7HA
Tel: 0161 288 1111 Fax: 0161 288 2222 **Map Ref 42**

BENTLEY GUEST HOUSE, is a comfortable, friendly house, 10 minutes from the M62 and close to shops and bus for city centre. Private parking, garden and patio. Personal attention, freshly cooked meals, dinner optional. ETB 1 Crown Commended.

B&B from £16, Dinner available, Rooms 1 single, 2 double, Children from 8 years, No smoking, Open all year.
Bentley Guest House, 64 Mill Lane Blackley, Manchester M9 6PF
Tel: 0161 795 1115 **Map Ref 42**

Family run **LYNDHURST HOTEL** is in a quiet location, close to a variety of shops and restaurant. All rooms have TV and tea/coffee making facilities. Comfortable bar lounge and quiet lounge. Close to football and cricket grounds and motorways. 10 minutes to city centre and airport

B&B from £20pp, Rooms 5 single, 5 twin, 2 double, 3 family, some en-suite, Restricted smoking, Children welcome, No pets, Open all year.
Mr S D Bottomley, **Lyndhurst Hotel,** 22-24 Whitelow Road, Chorlton-cum-Hardy, Manchester M21 9HQ
Tel: 0161 862 9001 Fax: 0161 881 3556 **Map Ref 43**

HOTEL MONTANA, family orientated. Warm, friendly atmosphere. Licensed Bar and restaurant. Large private car park. Sky TV. Rural area. Close to North/South motorway. Airport 5 miles. City Centre 3 miles. All amenities close by. Greek, Spanish and French spoken.

B&B from £25pp, Dinner from £9, Rooms 8 single, 6 twin, 6 double, 5 family, most en-suite,
Mrs Fanos, **Hotel Montana,** 59 Palatine Road, Didsbury, Manchester M20 3LT
Tel: 0161 445 6427 Fax: 0161 448 9458 **Map Ref 48**

WILMSLOW HOTEL, is a comfortable, family run hotel with Sky TV in all rooms. Special group and long term rates available. Convenient for Manchester University, city centre, airport, railway stations and M56, M63. ETB 3 Crowns Approved.

B&B from £16.65, Dinner available, Rooms 14 single, 4 double, 6 twin, 1 triple, 3 family rooms, some en-suite, Children welcome, Open all year.

Wilmslow Hotel, 356 Wilmslow Road, Fallowfield, Manchester M14 6AB
Tel: 0161 225 3030 & 224 5815 Fax: 0161 257 2854 **Map Ref 49**

HOLIDAY INN GARDEN COURT, all rooms comfortably sleep up to 4 people. 200 meters from airport, with complimentary transfer to and from airport. Discounted long term parking on airport complex. ETB 3 Crowns Commended.

B&B from £51, Dinner Available, Rooms 85 double, 78 twin, all en-suite, Children welcome, No pets, No smoking, Open all year.
Holiday Inn Garden Court, Outward Lane, Manchester Airport, Manchester M90 4HL
Tel: 0161 498 0333 & Freephone 0800 897121 (reservations) Fax: 0161 498 0222   **Map Ref 58**

....

HOTEL SMOKIES PARK, is a beautifully appointed hotel with spacious en-suite bedrooms. Good function facilities for up to 500 people. Nightclub, trimnasium and ample free parking. ETB 4 Crowns Highly Commended.

B&B from £35, Lunch and evening meal available, Rooms 34 double, 16 twin, all en-suite, Children welcome, Open all year.
Hotel Smokies Park, Ashton Road, Bardsley, Oldham, Manchester OL8 3HX
Tel: 0161 624 3405 Fax: 0161 627 5262   **Map Ref 44**

....

LA PERGOLA HOTEL & RESTAURANT, a country hotel set in Pennine hills, only 5 minutes from M62. All bedrooms en-suite with TV, telephone, hair dryer and trouser press (non smoking available). Lounge bar with log fire, restaurant and pizzeria. ETB 4 Crowns Commended.

B&B from £40, Lunch and evening meal available, Rooms 2 single, 15 double, 7 twin, 2 triple, suite available, all en-suite, Children welcome, No smoking, Open all year.
La Pergola Hotel & Restaurant, Rochdale Road, Denshaw, Oldham, Manchester OL3 5UE
Tel: 01457 871040 Fax: 01457 873804   **Map Ref 45**

....

THE PORTLAND THISTLE HOTEL, is a traditional style hotel, combining old world charm with full modern facilities, including a leisure spa and the recently acclaimed Winstons Restaurant. Overlooks Piccadilly Gardens in the heart of the city's commercial and shopping area. ETB 5 Crowns Highly Commended.

B&B from £108, Lunch and evening meal available, Rooms 107 single, 75 double, 11 twin, 12 triple, all en-suite, Children Welcome, No smoking, Open all year.
The Portland Thistle Hotel, Portland Street, Piccadilly Gardens, Manchester M1 6DP
Tel: 0161 228 3400 Fax: 0161 228 6347   **Map Ref 42**

....

HAWTHORN HOTEL & RESTAURANT, a comfortable family hotel with restaurant, convenient for M62 junction 17, motorway network and Metrolink system. Close to Bury, Bolton and Manchester. ETB 2 Crowns Approved.

B&B from £29.50, Dinner available, Rooms 1 single, 4 double, 7 twin, 1 triple, 1 family room, all en-suite, Children welcome, No smoking, Open all year.
Hawthorn Hotel & Restaurant, 139-143 Strand Lane, Radcliffe, Manchester M26 1JR
Tel: 0161 723 2706 Fax: 0161 723 2706   **Map Ref 46**

....

WHITE LODGE PRIVATE HOTEL, a small, friendly family-run hotel close to the city centre amenities and sporting facilities. ETB 1 Crown Approved.

B&B from £20, Rooms 3 single, 3 double,3 twin, Children from 2 years, Open all year.
White Lodge Private Hotel, 87-89 Great Cheetham Street West, Broughton, Salford, Manchester M7 9JA
Tel: 0161 792 3047   **Map Ref 36**

....

HAZELDEAN HOTEL, a renovated Victorian mansion in a residential area of Salford. Two miles from exit 17 M62, 2.5 miles from city centre on M56. Fully stocked bar leading onto beautiful garden. Restaurant, TV lounge. ETB 3 Crowns Approved.

B&B from £30, Lunch and evening meal available, Rooms 10 single, 4 double, 5 twin, 2 triple, most en-suite, Children welcome, No pets, No smoking, Open all year.
Hazeldean Hotel, 467 Bury New Road, Kersal Bar, Salford, Manchester M7 3NE
Tel: 0161 792 6667 & 792 2079 Fax: 0161 792 6668   **Map Ref 37**

MANOR HEY HOTEL, a comfortable and friendly family-run hotel. Five minutes from Trafford Park, 15 minutes from Manchester Airport. TV and tea/coffee making facilities in all rooms. ETB 3 crowns Commended.

B&B from £30, Lunch and evening meal available, Rooms 1 double, 10 twin, 1 triple, all en-suite, Children welcome, Open all year.

Manor Hey Hotel, 130 Stretford Road, Urmston, Manchester M41 9LT
Tel: 0161 748 3896 Fax: 0161 746 7183   **Map Ref 47**

....

THE DROP INN HOTEL, is a 28 roomed hotel with private baths and showers. TV, radio and Tea/coffee making facilities in all rooms. Special rates for weekend breaks. ETB 3 Crowns Approved.

B&B from £35, Lunch and evening meal available, Rooms 10 single, 8 double, 10 twin, all private facilities, Children welcome, No smoking, Open all year.
The Drop Inn Hotel, 393 Wilmslow Road, Withington, Manchester M20 4WA
Tel: 0161 286 1919 Fax: 0161 286 8880   **Map Ref 49**

....

GRANADA HOTEL, a comfortable hotel close to the city centre and airport. En-suite rooms, colour TV, telephone, hair dryer. Lounge bar and restaurant. ETB 3 Crowns Approved.

B&B from £35, Dinner available, Rooms 3 single, 2 double, 3 twin, 2 triple, all private facilities, Children welcome, No pets, Open all year.

Granada Hotel, 404 Wilmslow Road, Withington, Manchester M20 9BM
Tel: 0161 286 9551 & 434 3480 Fax: 0161 286 9553   **Map Ref 49**

....

NOVOTEL MANCHESTER WEST, is a new hotel, restaurant, banqueting and conference centre. Ideal for business or pleasure. Junction 13 on M62. Restaurant open 6am-midnight. For early risers, breakfast available from 4.30am. Tea/coffee making facilities . ETB 4 Crowns Commended.

B&B from £77.50, Lunch and evening meal available, Rooms 38 single, 38 double, 38 twin, 5 triple, all en-suite, Children welcome, No smoking, Open all year.
Novotel Manchester West, Worsley Brow, Worsley, Manchester M28 2YA
Tel: 0161 799 3535 Fax: 0161 703 8207   **Map Ref 50**

....

THE ROYALS HOTEL, at the heart of Manchester's motorway network, 2 miles from Manchester Airport. Recently renovated mock Tudor building in own grounds with beautiful Conservatory Restaurant. Ample car parking. ETB 3 Crowns Approved.

B&B from £52, Lunch and evening meal available, Rooms 9 single, 9 double, 8 twin, 1 triple, 6 family rooms, All en-suite, Children welcome, No smoking, No pets, Open all year.

The Royals Hotel, Altringham Road, Wythenshawe, Manchester M22 4BJ
Tel: 0161 988 9011 Fax: 0161 998 4641   **Map Ref 58**

....

ALBANY HOTEL, est. 1967, referred to as "The Hidden Gem" of Manchester Hotels. A Victorian property built in the 1860s still retaining the charm and character of a bygone era. With all the facilities excepted of a modern hotel, and offering quality accommodation and service only found in somewhere special.
B&B from £25pp, Dinner £14.95, Rooms 3 single, 6 twin, 5 double, 4 family, all en-suite, Children welcome, Open all year except Christmas & New Year.
Margaret & Bernard Satterthwaite, **Albany Hotel,** 21 Albany Road, Chorlton-cum-Hardy, Manchester, M21 0AY
Tel: 0161 881 6774 Fax: 0161 862 9405   **Map Ref 43**

CENTRAL HOTEL, a town centre hotel opposite the railway station with direct service to Liverpool and Chester. Near the Liverpool tunnel entrance. Car Parking. ETB 3 Crowns Approved.

B&B from £29, Lunch & evening meal available, Rooms 13 single, 8 double, 9 twin, 1 triple, most en-suite, Children welcome, Open all year.
Central Hotel, Clifton Crescent, Birkenhead Merseyside L41 2QH
Tel: 0151 647 6347 Fax: 0151 647 5476   **Map Ref 51**

....

PINE LODGE, is an exclusive property with large en-suite bedrooms. The heated enclosed swimming pool is set in delightful wooded gardens adjacent to National Trust land. Car Parking. ETB 2 Crowns Commended.

B&B from £22.50, Rooms 2 single, 1 double, 1 twin, 1 triple, all en-suite, Children from 4, No pets, Open all year.
Pine Lodge, Coral Ridge, Bidston, Birkenhead Merseyside L43 7XE
Tel: 0151 652 4138   **Map Ref 52**

....

BLENHEIM GUEST HOUSE, is a large Victorian villa overlooking Sefton Park, offering first class bed and breakfast accommodation at a very reasonable price. Former family home of Beatle Stu Sutcliffe. ETB 2 Crowns Commended.

B&B from £17.50, Rooms 2 single, 2 double, 8 twin, 2 triple, 2 family rooms, some en-suite, Children welcome, No pets, Tea/coffee making facilities, Open all year.
Blenheim Guest House, 37 Aigburth Drive, Liverpool, Merseyside L17 4JE
Tel: 0151 727 7380 Fax: 0151 727 5833   **Map Ref 53**

....

GLADSTONE HOTEL, a conveniently located hotel in the heart of the city centre, adjacent to Lime Street Station. 6 miles from the airport. Meeting facilities for up to 600 people. Business services available.

B&B from £33, Lunch and evening meal available, Rooms 29 single, 52 double, 69 twin, 4 triple, suites available, all en-suite, Children welcome, No smoking, Tea/coffee making facilities, Open all year.
Gladstone Hotel, Lord Nelson Street, Liverpool, Merseyside L3 5QB
Tel: 0151 709 7050 Fax: 0151 709 2193   **Map Ref 53**

....

DUKES FOLLY HOTEL, a licensed family-run hotel noted for its high standards and friendly atmosphere. On the corner of Duke Street and Lord Street and within easy reach of all local amenities.

B&B from £38.50, Evening meal available, Rooms 5 single, 7 double, 7 twin, all en-suite, Children welcome, No smoking, Open all year.
Dukes Folly Hotel, 11 Duke Street, Southport, Merseyside PR8 1LS
Tel: 01704 533355 Fax: 01704 530065   **Map Ref 54**

....

ROSEDALE HOTEL, a well established, centrally situated private hotel with licensed bar and reading room. All bedrooms have colour TV with satellite link. Weekly rates available. Car Parking. ETB 3 Crowns Commended.

B&B from £19, Dinner available, Rooms 4 single, 2 double, 3 twin, 1 family, most en-suite, Children welcome, No pets, Open all year.
Rosedale Hotel, 11 Talbot Street, Southport, Merseyside PR8 1HP
Tel: 01704 530604 Fax: 01704 530604   **Map Ref 54**

....

AMBASSADOR PRIVATE HOTEL, a delightful small quality hotel with residential license, 200 yards from the promenade and conference facilities. All bedrooms have TV, hair dryer and tea/coffee making facilities. Pets Welcome. ETB 3 Crowns Commended.

B&B from £30, Lunch and evening meal available, Rooms 4 double, 2 twin, 2 triple, all en-suite, Children from 4 years, No smoking, Open all year.
Ambassador Private Hotel, 13 Bath Street, Southport, Merseyside PR9 0DP
Tel: 01704 530459 & 543998 Fax: 01704 536269   **Map Ref 54**

SCARISBRICK HOTEL, a prominent town centre traditional hotel, A la carte and table d'hote restaurant, several bars, function rooms and conference suites. Wheelchair access category 3.Car parking. ETB 4 Crowns Commended.

B&B from £45, Lunch and evening meal available, Rooms 7 single, 40 double, 24 twin, 6 triple, all en-suite, Children welcome, No smoking, Open all year.
Scarisbrick Hotel, 239 Lord Street, Southport, Merseyside PR8 1NZ
Tel: 01704 543000 Fax: 01704 533335   **Map Ref 54**

....

LEICESTER HOTEL, a family run hotel with personal attention, clean and comfortable, close to all amenities. Car park. Licensed Bar. TV in all rooms. ETB 2 Crowns Approved.

B&B from £17.50, Dinner available, Rooms 2 single, 3 double, 3 twin, some en-suite, Children welcome, Open all year.
Leicester Hotel, 24 Leicester Street, Southport, Merseyside PR9 0EZ
Tel: 01704 530049 Fax: 01704 530049 Email: leicester.hotel@mail.cybase.co.uk   **Map Ref 54**

....

METROPOLE HOTEL, a fully licensed, privately owned family hotel, centrally located, 50 yards from famous Lord Street shopping Boulevard. Close to Royal Birkdale Golf Course. Car parking. ETB 3 crowns Commended.

B&B from £30, Lunch and evening meal available, Rooms 13 single, 3 double, 5 twin, 3 triple, most en-suite, Children welcome, Open all year.
Metropole Hotel, 3 Portland Street, Southport, Merseyside PR8 1LL
Tel: 01704 536836 Fax: 01704 549041   **Map Ref 54**

....

STUTELEA HOTEL & LEISURE CLUB, a charming licensed hotel in pleasant gardens. Heated indoor swimming pool, sauna, jacuzzi, gymnasium, steam room, solarium and games room. Convenient from promenade, marina, golf course and shopping centre. Also self catering apartments. ETB 4 Crowns Highly Commended.

B&B from £50, Lunch & evening meal available, Rooms 8 double, 9 twin, 3 triple, all en-suite, Children welcome, No pets, Open all year.
Stutelea Hotel & Leisure Club, Alexandra Road, Southport, Merseyside PR9 0NB
Tel: 01704 544220 Fax: 01704 500232 Email: stutlea@mail.cybase.co.uk   **Map Ref 54**

....

SEA LEVEL HOTEL, is a homely, family run hotel offering a warm welcome and wholesome food. Light meals available until 11pm. TV and Tea/coffee making facilities. ETB 1 Crown Approved.

B&B from £17.50, Dinner available, Rooms 8 single, 3 double, 2 twin, 2 triple, Children welcome, Open all year.
Sea Level Hotel, 126 Victoria Road, New Brighton, Wallasey, Merseyside L45 9LD
Tel: 0151 639 3408 Fax: 0151 639 3408   **Map Ref 55**

....

KINGS GAP COURT HOTEL, an old established family run hotel, close to the sea front and many championship golf courses. Ideal for Wales, Chester and Liverpool. ETB 3 Crowns Approved.

B&B from £33, Lunch and evening meal available, Rooms 3 single, 4 double, 17 twin, 2 triple, 1 family room most en-suite, Children welcome, No smoking, Open all year.
Kings Gap Court Hotel, Valentia Road, Hoylake, Wirral, Merseyside L47 2AN
Tel: 0151 632 2073 Fax: 0151 632 0247   **Map Ref 56**

....

LEASOWE CASTLE HOTEL & CONFERENCE CENTRE, is a 16th century building converted into a hotel. All rooms with direct dial telephone, trouser press and hair dryer. 3 bars, health club, a la carte restaurant. Golf course adjacent. ETB 4 Crowns Commended.

B&B from £42.50, Lunch and evening meal available, Rooms 25 double, 25 twin, all en-suite, Children welcome, No pets, No smoking, Open all year.
Leasowe Castle Hotel & Conference Centre, Leasowe Road, Moreton, Wirral, Merseyside L46 3RF
Tel: 0151 606 9191 Fax: 0151 678 5551   **Map Ref 57**

Much of Cornwall's coastline, which is never more than twenty miles away, is designated as of Outstanding Natural Beauty. The Atlantic Ocean crashes onto the north coast's long stretches of beautiful beaches while in contrast the south has numerous fishing villages, sheltered coves and tiny unspoilt bays, as well as sub-tropical gardens and wooded rivers. Cornwall offers opportunities for anglers and water sports enthusiasts. Cornwall is a land of history and tradition. As the Britons were driven west by invading Saxon tribes, Cornwall became, with Wales, a bastion of old Celtic ways. It kept a separate Celtic language until the Middle Ages and the county remained virtually isolated from the rest of the country until modern times.

Land's End which tumbles into the sea at the end of the Penwith Peninsula, is the English mainland's furthest point West. Just 5 miles wide, the walker can take in the bracing Atlantic Northern coast and then travel to take in the milder breezes from the Channel shore. Twenty eight miles beyond Land's End, the Isles of Scilly have five inhabited islands, including Tresco, with its sub-tropical gardens. The climate is so mild that the islands are said to have only two seasons - spring and summer. The most southerly part of England, the Lizard is made up of rugged cliffs and rocks which stretch down to Lizard Point. Its hazardous waters mean that more sailors have lost their lives here than in any other part of Cornwall.

At Mousehole colour washed houses surround the small harbour and the popular Polperro maintains its distinctive flavour of a Cornish fishing village. Fowey is a network of narrow streets climbing the hills. The town's fierce seamen, nicknamed the Fowey Gallants, who raided the coast of France during the 100 Years' War, continued their raids even after Edward IV had made peace. Megavissey, one of Cornwall's most celebrated resorts, whose simple beauty has attracted a number of writers and artists.

On the south side is Penzance, facing St Michael's Mount, whose climate is so mild that palm trees and other sub-tropical plants thrive. On the north coast is St Ives, whose cluster of coloured stone cottages grew around a small chapel built by St Ia in the 6th century.

Newquay on the north coast is a popular resort and the centre of a stretch of spectacular coastal scenery and miles of golden beaches. As well as being an important shipping port, Falmouth in its spectacular setting on Falmouth Bay is a leading holiday resort. The area's sub-tropical climate and sparkling blue sea have earned its resemblance to the continental Riviera.

left, St Michael's Mount

Cornwall

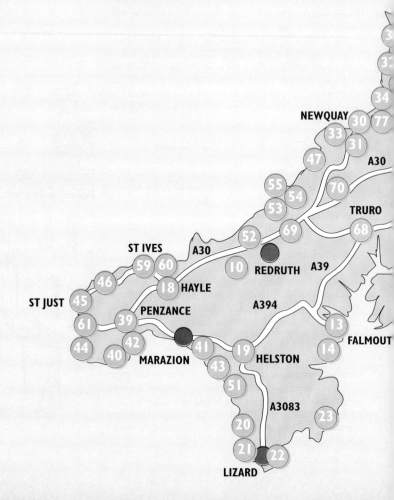

NEWQUAY

A30

TRURO

ST IVES A30

REDRUTH A39

HAYLE

ST JUST

PENZANCE A394

FALMOUT

MARAZION HELSTON

A3083

LIZARD

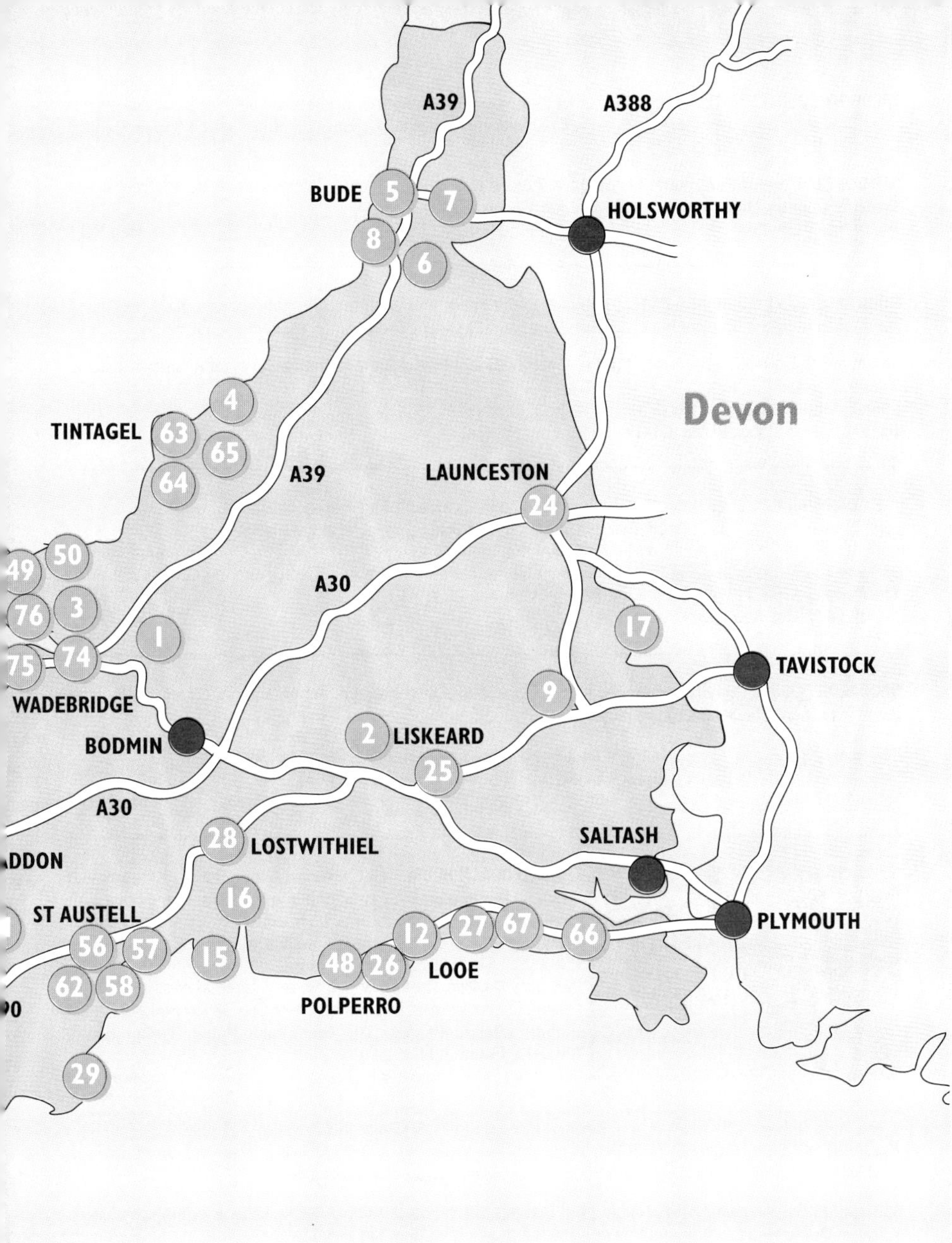

A39

A388

BUDE

5

7

HOLSWORTHY

8

6

Devon

4

TINTAGEL

63

65

64

A39

LAUNCESTON

24

49

50

A30

17

76

3

TAVISTOCK

75

74

1

9

WADEBRIDGE

2 LISKEARD

BODMIN

25

A30

28 LOSTWITHIEL

SALTASH

DDON

16

12 27 67

66 PLYMOUTH

ST AUSTELL

15

48 26 LOOE

56 57

62 58

POLPERRO

O

29

TREDETHY COUNTRY HOTEL, gracious living with spacious rooms, log fires in winter and absolute peace and quiet in beautiful surroundings. From Bodmin take the Launceston road, then the Helland turn off to Helland Bridge. Tredethy is up the hill over the bridge.

B&B from £32, Dinner available, Rooms 1 single, 3 twin, 7 double, all en-suite, No smoking, Children welcome, No pets, Open all year.
Tredethy Country Hotel, Hellandbridge, Bodmin, Cornwall PL30 4QS
Tel: 01208 841262 Fax: 01208 841707   **Map Ref 1**

MOUNT PLEASANT MOORLAND HOTEL, a charming countryside hotel with friendly, relaxing atmosphere. Residents' bar, TV, sun lounges. Delicious home cooking. Gardens, safe parking and beautiful secluded swimming pool.

B&B from £22, Dinner available, Rooms 1 single, 1 twin, 3 double, 1 triple, 1 family, all en-suite, No smoking, Children welcome, No pets, Open April - September.
Mount Pleasant Moorland Hotel, Mount, Bodmin, Cornwall PL30 4EX
Tel: 01208 821342 Fax: 01208 821417   **Map Ref 2**

THE CORNISH ARMS, a delightful 16th century coaching inn, surrounded by unspoilt countryside with views down to north Cornish coast. Noted for food. Charming, spacious bedrooms. Special breaks available.

B&B from £34.95, Dinner available, Rooms 3 twin, 4 double, most en-suite, No smoking, Children welcome, Open all year.
The Cornish Arms, Pendoggett, St Kew, Bodmin, Cornwall PL30 3HH
Tel: 01208 880263 Fax: 01208 880335   **Map Ref 3**

ORCHARD LODGE, all rooms are furnished and decorated to a high standard. Set in our own gardens with ample parking. Vegetarian breakfasts can be provided.

B&B from £20pp, Rooms 2 twin, 3 double, all en-suite, No smoking, children or pets, Open April - November.
Mrs Eileen Purslow, **Orchard Lodge,** Gunpool Lane, Boscastle, Cornwall PL35 0AT
Tel: 01840 250418   **Map Ref 4**

THE OLD COACH HOUSE, relax in former Coach House (300 years old) which is close to coast and coastal path in area of outstanding beauty. All rooms en-suite with tea/coffee facilities, colour TV, hair dryers, etc. A lounge, car parking and within easy walking distance of eating places.
EMail: Parsons@oldcoach.demon.co.uk
B&B from £34.40pp, Rooms 1 twin, 4 double, 3 family, all en-suite, Restricted smoking, Children welcome, Pets by arrangement, Open all year except Christmas.
Ruth & Michael Parsons, **The Old Coach House,** Tintagel Road, Boscastle, Cornwall PL35 0AS
Tel: 01840 250398 Fax: 01840 250346   **Map Ref 4**

TOLCARNE HOUSE HOTEL & RESTAURANT, a delightful late Victorian house in spacious grounds with lovely views to the dramatic Cornish coastline. All rooms en-suite. Restaurant and bar. Warm welcome.

B&B from £25, Dinner available, Rooms 1 single, 2 twin, 5 double, most en-suite, No smoking, Children welcome, Open March - October.
Tolcarne House Hotel & Restaurant, Tintagel Road, Boscastle, Cornwall PL35 0AS
Tel: 01840 250654 Fax: 01840 250654   **Map Ref 4**

THE FALCON HOTEL, a character hotel in lovely position overlooking the Bude Canal. Close to beaches and shops. Self catering apartments also available.

B&B from £34, Dinner available, Rooms 4 single, 5 twin, 14 double, all en-suite, No smoking, Children welcome, Open all year.
The Falcon Hotel, Breakwater Road, Bude, Cornwall EX23 8SD
Tel: 01288 352005 Fax: 01288 356359   **Map Ref 5**

CAMELOT HOTEL, a comfortable family run hotel situated close to the famous Crooklets Beach and overlooking a championship golf course.

B&B from £24, Dinner available, Rooms 2 single, 6 double, 12 twin, 1 triple, all en-suite, No smoking, Children welcome, No pets, Open February - November.
Camelot Hotel, Downs View, Bude, Cornwall EX23 8RE
Tel: 01288 352361 Fax: 01288 355470   **Map Ref 5**

....

ATLANTIC HOUSE HOTEL, a superb location overlooking beach, downs and town. Renowned for good food and fine wines. Five choice menu daily in award winning restaurant.

B&B from £22.65, Dinner available, Rooms 1 single, 2 twin, 7 double, 3 family, all en-suite, No smoking, Children welcome, Open March - November.
Atlantic House Hotel, Summerleaze Crescent, Bude, Cornwall EX23 8HJ
Tel: 01288 352451 Fax: 01288 356666   **Map Ref 5**

....

HOTEL PENARVOR, on the edge of National Trust coastline, with views across the magnificent sweep of Bude Bay,only 50 yards from the beach. Professionally prepared English and French cuisine.

B&B from £23, Dinner available, Rooms 3 single, 4 twin, 9 double, all with private or en-suite, No smoking, Children welcome, Open March - October.
Hotel Penarvor, Crooklets Beach, Bude, Cornwall EX23 8NE
Tel: 01288 352036 Fax: 01288 355027   **Map Ref 5**

....

MAER LODGE HOTEL, in own grounds in semi rural setting overlooking the seaward end of the golf course, near Crooklets surfing beach.

B&B from £22.50, Dinner from £9, Rooms 2 single, 4 twin, 9 double, 2 triple, 2 family, all en-suite and No smoking, Children welcome, Open all year.
Maer Lodge Hotel, Maer Down Road, Crooklets Beach, Bude, Cornwall EX23 8NG
Tel: 01288 353306 Fax: 01288 354005   **Map Ref 5**

....

OLD RECTORY, offering spacious, quality en-suite accommodation, 2 minutes to Atlantic Highway (A39). Spectacular unspoilt coastline. Plentiful home cooking.

B&B from £18, Dinner available, Rooms 1 twin, 2 double, all en-suite, No smoking, Children welcome, No pets, Open March - November.
Old Rectory, Marhamchurch, Bude, Cornwall EX23 0ER
Tel: 01288 361379   **Map Ref 6**

....

STRATTON GARDENS HOTEL, a charming 16th century grade II listed hotel personally run by resident proprietors. Lovely home cooked food. Quiet location in conservation area.

B&B from £20, Dinner available, Rooms 1 twin, 3 double, 1 triple, most en-suite, No smoking, Children over 5, No pets, Open all year.
Stratton Gardens Hotel, Cot Hill, Stratton, Bude, Cornwall EX23 9DN
Tel: 01288 352500 Fax: 01288 352500   **Map Ref 7**

....

MEVA-GWIN HOTEL, on Marine Drive between Bude and Widemouth Bay. Coastal and rural views from all rooms, friendly atmosphere, traditional English cooking.

B&B from £22, Dinner available, Rooms 2 single, 1 twin, 4 double, 2 triple, 3 family, most en-suite, Children welcome, No pets, Open April - September.
Meva-Gwin Hotel, Upton, Bude, Cornwall EX23 0LY
Tel: 01288 352347 Fax: 01288 352347   **Map Ref 8**

A few minutes walk from the bustling town of Callington. **DOZMARY,** is situated in a peaceful quiet cul-de-sac. Tea/coffee, colour TV, radio alarm, central heating in all rooms. A reduction of £100 per person per night for 4 nights or more consecutive stay.

B&B from £16pp, Rooms 1 twin, 1 double, 1 family, all en-suite, No smoking or pets, Children welcome, Open all year except Christmas & New Year.

Thelma & Henry Wills, **Dozmary,** Tor View Close, Tavistock Road, Callington, Cornwall PL17 7DY
Tel: 01579 383677   **Map Ref 9**

Colour TV, tea/coffee facilities and hot and cold water in every room at **THE PLOUGH INN.** Restaurant open for breakfast, lunch and dinner. Alfrescot dining in flowering courtyard. Bar open all day. Car parking. Central for north and south coast resorts and theme parks. Special rates for long stay and children.

B&B from £15pp, Dinner from £3.50, Rooms 1 twin, 1 double, 2 family, Children & pets welcome, Open January 5th - December 20th.

Steve & Eileen Robinson, **The Plough Inn,** 7 College Street, Camborne, Cornwall TR14 7JU
Tel: 01209 713014   **Map Ref 10**

COMMONWOOD MANOR HOTEL, a spacious Victorian family villa in 6 acres grounds and woodland. Spectacular views over Looe. River Valley and countryside. Only 5 minutes walk to town and harbour. Friendly Cornish hospitality. Swimming pool, car park, lounge, TV room. All rooms en-suite with Sky TV, telephone and tea making. Luxury stone cottages also available.

B&B from £31, Dinner from £13.50, Rooms 1 single, 3 twin, 6 double, 1 family, all en-suite, Restricted smoking, Children welcome, Open all year except Christmas.

Mr & Mrs T Foxall, **Commonwood Manor Hotel,** St. Martins Rd, East Looe, Cornwall PL13 1LP
Tel: 01503 262929 Fax: 01503 262632   **Map Ref 12**

THE SEAGULL HOTEL, Victorian licensed hotel close to sea front, beaches, castle and town. Comfortable en-suite rooms with TV, tea making and some sea views. Bar, lounge, office facilities. Relaxed atmosphere, friendly service. Good fresh home cooked food, full Cornish breakfasts, optional evening meals, interesting wine list, vegetarians welcome. Email: seagull@mcmail.com

B&B from £18.50pp, Dinner from £8, Rooms 2 single, 1 twin, 1 double, 3 family, most en-suite, Children over 5, No pets, Open all year.

Derek & Stephanie Penn, **The Seagull Hotel,** 10 Melvill Road, Falmouth, Cornwall TR11 4AS
Tel: 01326 314988 Fax: 01326 314988   **Map Ref 13**

WICKHAM GUEST HOUSE, a small guest house in quiet road a few minutes walk from main beaches. Most rooms with sea views, some with colour TV and some en-suite.

B&B from £17.50, Dinner available, Rooms 2 single, 1 twin, 2 double, 1 family, most en-suite, No smoking, Children welcome, No pets, Open all year.

Wickham Guest House, 21 Gyllyngvase Terrace, Falmouth, Cornwall TR11 4DL
Tel: 01326 311140   **Map Ref 13**

TRESILLIAN HOUSE HOTEL, a family run hotel in a quiet area, close to safe beaches, town and harbours. Traditional English menus.

B&B from £20, Dinner available, Rooms 2 single, 3 twin, 3 double, 4 triple, all en-suite, No smoking, Children welcome, No pets, Open March - October.

Tresillian House Hotel, 3 Stracey Road, Falmouth, Cornwall TR11 4DW
Tel: 01326 312425 & 311139   **Map Ref 13**

Are you planning a holiday or a short break? Then why not stay at **TELFORD GUEST HOUSE**? Offering en-suite rooms with colour TV's, tea/coffee facilities and central heating. Private off road parking. Convenient for town, beaches and gardens. Please mention this publication when making enquiries.
B&B from £16pp, Rooms 1 single, 1 twin, 4 double, most en-suite, Restricted smoking, Open March - November.
Ann Eschenauer, **Telford Guest House,** 47 Melvill Road, Falmouth, Cornwall TR11 4DG
Tel: 01326 314581   **Map Ref 13**

DOLVEAN HOTEL, enjoy watching the sun rise, linger over breakfast, browse through some guide books, and let us, and Cornwall, do the rest. We offer 'old fashioned' service and charm together with excellent facilities including colour televisions, private car park, credit cards accepted. AA Recommended.
B&B from £22pp, Rooms 2 single, 4 twin, 5 double, 1 family, all en-suite, No smoking or pets, Children over 5, Open all year except Christmas & New Year's Eve.
Paul & Carol Crocker, **Dolvean Hotel,** 50 Melvill Road Falmouth, Cornwall TR11 4DQ
Tel: 01326 313658 Fax: 01326 313995   **Map Ref 13**

CARTHION HOTEL, a family hotel, situated in pleasant gardens, with panoramic view of the sea from Pendennis Point to the Manacles.

B&B from £27, Dinner available, Rooms 2 single, 4 twin, 8 double, 4 triple, all en-suite, Children over 10, No pets, Open all year.
Carthion Hotel, Cliff Road, Falmouth, Cornwall TR11 4AP
Tel: 01326 313669 Fax: 01326 212828   **Map Ref 13**

ROYAL DUCHY HOTEL, Falmouth's first and foremost hotel situated overlooking the bay. High standard accommodation with extensive leisure facilities. Varied seasonal break rates available.

B&B from £53, Dinner available, Rooms 5 single, 17 twin, 17 double, 4 triple, 1 family, all en-suite, Children welcome, No pets, Open all year.

Royal Duchy Hotel, Cliff Road, Falmouth, Cornwall TR11 4NX
Tel: 01326 313042 Fax: 01326 319420   **Map Ref 13**

GROVE HOTEL, a harbour side Georgian hotel offering a warm welcome, good food and good value. Central to all local amenities. Public car and dinghy parks opposite.

B&B from £20, Dinner available, Rooms 2 single, 3 twin, 2 double, 6 triple, 2 family, most en-suite, No smoking, Children welcome, Open January - November.
Grove Hotel, Grove Place, Falmouth, Cornwall TR11 4AU
Tel: 01326 319577 Fax: 01326 319577   **Map Ref 13**

FALMOUTH BEACH RESORT HOTEL, a modern hotel, right by the beach, with lifts to most floors. No steps/stairs from sea front to public rooms. Superb sea views. Leisure complex and tennis.

B&B from £40, Dinner available, Rooms 15 single, 55 twin, 34 double, 23 family, all en-suite, No smoking, Children welcome, Open all year.

Falmouth Beach Resort Hotel, Gyllyngvase Beach, Falmouth, Cornwall TR11 4NA
Tel: 01326 318084 Fax: 01326 319147   **Map Ref 13**

ROSEMULLION HOTEL, an imposing Tudor style building offering quality accommodation in a smoke-free atmosphere. All rooms en-suite, colour televisions, heating, tea/coffee facilities. Large car park, sea views and balcony rooms with king size beds. Selected 4Q's AA. Completely refurbished, full English breakfast and excellent choice for vegetarians.
Email: gail@rosemullionhotel.demon.co.uk
B&B from £39-£48pp, Rooms 1 single, 3 twin, 10 double, all en-suite, No smoking, children or pets, Open all year except Christmas & New Year.
Gail Jones, **Rosemullion Hotel,** Gyllyngvase Hill, Falmouth TR11 4DF
Tel: 01326 314690 Fax: 01326 210098 **Map Ref 13**

BOSANNETH HOTEL, with a delightful garden and views over Falmouth Bay to the Lizard. We are a quality licensed, small hotel offering a relaxing holiday or short break. Full en-suite facilities in tastefully decorated rooms and personal service will assure your comfort. All rooms have full facilities.
B&B from £21pp, Dinner from £9, Rooms 1 single, 1 twin, 6 double, all en-suite, Restricted smoking, Children over 5, No pets, Open March - October.
Eric & Ann McGonagle, **Bosanneth Hotel,** Gyllyngvase Hill, Falmouth, Cornwall TR11 4DW
Tel: 01326 314649 Fax: 01326 314649 **Map Ref 13**

HOTEL ANACAPRI, overlooking the beach and Falmouth Bay. Pretty bedrooms, all en-suite with colour TV. English breakfast and 5 course dinner. Bar.

B&B from £27, Dinner available, Rooms 1 single, 7 twin, 76 double, 1 triple, all en-suite, Children welcome, No pets, Open all year.
Hotel Anacapri, Gyllyngvase Road, Falmouth, Cornwall TR11 4DJ
Tel: 01326 311454 Fax: 01326 311454 **Map Ref 13**

GREENBANK HOTEL, a privately owned, historic hotel with panoramic views across one of the world's finest harbours. Uninterrupted views of yachting and shipping.

B&B from £64, Dinner available, Rooms 9 single, 32 twin, 16 double, 4 triple, most en-suite, No smoking, Children welcome, Open all year.

Greenbank Hotel, Harbourside, Falmouth, Cornwall TR11 2SR
Tel: 01326 312440 Fax: 01326 211362 **Map Ref 13**

PARK GROVE HOTEL, a family run, long established hotel, centrally situated for harbour, beaches and town centre. Spacious restaurant serving excellent cuisine. Large car park.

B&B from £21, Dinner available, Rooms 3 single, 6 twin, 5 double, 5 triple, most en-suite, Children welcome, Open all year.

Park Grove Hotel, Kimberley Park Road, Falmouth, Cornwall TR11 2DD
Tel: 01326 313276 Fax: 01326 211926 **Map Ref 13**

GYLLYNGDUNE MANOR HOTEL, an old Georgian manor house situated in an acre of beautiful gardens. 10 minutes walk from town centre, 2 minutes walk from beach overlooking Falmouth Bay.

B&B from £30, Dinner available, Rooms 3 single, 10 twin, 13 double, 4 triple, all en-suite, No smoking, Children welcome, Open all year.

Gyllyngdune Manor Hotel, Melvill Road, Falmouth, Cornwall TR11 4AR
Tel: 01326 312978 Fax: 01326 211881 **Map Ref 13**

MADEIRA HOTEL, well situated with views over Falmouth Bay. Entertainment most evenings.

B&B from £25, Dinner available, Rooms 6 single, 19 twin, 16 double, 8 triple, most en-suite, No smoking, Children welcome, No pets, Open March - November & Christmas.
Madeira Hotel, Sea Front, Falmouth, Cornwall TR11 4NY
Tel: 01326 313531 Fax: 01326 319143   **Map Ref 13**

....

GREEN LAWNS HOTEL, an elegant chateau style hotel situated between the main beaches and town, with indoor leisure complex. Honeymoon and executive suites.
B&B from £49, Dinner available, Rooms 6 single, 9 twin, 16 double, 2 triple, 6 family, all en-suite, No smoking, Children welcome, Open all year.
Green Lawns Hotel, Western Terrace, Falmouth, Cornwall TR11 4QJ
Tel: 01326 312734 Fax: 01326 211427   **Map Ref 13**

....

BUDOCK VEAN GOLF & COUNTRY HOUSE HOTEL, enjoy the quiet dignity of this country house hotel. Set in 65 acres of sub tropical gardens and parkland. Own golf course, tennis courts and indoor pool.

B&B from £45, Dinner available, Rooms 6 single, 30 twin, 16 double, 2 triple, all en-suite, No smoking, Children welcome, Open February - December.
Budock Vean Golf & Country House Hotel, Mawnan Smith, Falmouth, Cornwall TR11 5LG
Tel: 01326 250288 Fax: 01326 250892   **Map Ref 14**

....

THE WHEELHOUSE, on South Cornwall Coastal Path. En-suite rooms and breakfast room/bar have fine views of sea and river. Speciality: Best of British & Belgian Bottled Beers. Five minutes walk to sandy beach, shops, restaurants and pubs. Open all year.
B&B from £18pp, Rooms 1 double, 1 family/twin, all en-suite, No smoking, Children over 5, No pets, Open all year.
Rick & Wai Chee Nisbet, **The Wheelhouse,** 60 The Esplanade, Fowey, Cornwall PL23 1JA
Tel: 01726 832452   **Map Ref 15**

....

 Situated in the historic estuary town of Fowey. **TREVANION GUEST HOUSE**, is a comfortable listed Merchants house. In the heart of Daphne Da Maurier country. An ideal base from which to walk the coastal path, visit the lost gardens of Heligan and explore the Cornish Riviera.

B&B from £20pp, Rooms 2 single, 1 twin, 1 double, 1 family, most en-suite, No smoking & pets, Children over 5, Open March - November.
Jill & Bob Bullock, **Trevanion Guest House,** 70 Lostwithiel Street, Fowey, Cornwall PL23 1BQ
Tel: 01726 832602   **Map Ref 15**

....

MARINA HOTEL, a privately run, comfortably appointed Georgian hotel of character with river views and some balcony rooms. Own moorings, waterside garden and restaurant.

B&B from £40, Dinner available, Rooms 5 twin, 5 double, all en-suite, No smoking, Children welcome, Open March - December.
Marina Hotel, Esplanade, Fowey, Cornwall PL23 1HY
Tel: 01726 833315 Fax: 01726 832779   **Map Ref 15**

....

CARNETHIC HOUSE HOTEL, a Regency house in 15. acres of mature gardens. Heated pool. Home cooking with local fish a speciality. Informal atmosphere.
B&B from £30, Dinner available, Rooms 1 single, 1 twin, 4 double, 2 triple, most en-suite, No smoking, Children welcome, Open February - November.
Carnethic House Hotel, Lambs Barn, Fowey, Cornwall PL23 1HQ
Tel: 01726 833336 Fax: 01726 833336   **Map Ref 15**

CORMORANT HOTEL, a small, attractive family run hotel with magnificent views of the Fowey estuary. Noted for hospitality and food. Indoor heated swimming pool. Special rates for short breaks all year round.

B&B from £44, Dinner available, Rooms 4 twin, 7 double, all en-suite, No smoking, Children welcome, Open all year.

Cormorant Hotel, Golant, Fowey, Cornwall PL23 1LL
Tel: 01726 833426 Fax: 01726 833426   **Map Ref 16**

THE WHITE HART INN, a quiet country inn overlooking Tamar Valley. Warm, friendly welcome, good hearty breakfast. Tea/coffee in all rooms. Car park. Close to St. Mellion Golf Club, Tavistock and Plymouth. Lots of beautiful walks, horse riding. 1 hour to Looe or Tintagel.

B&B from £15pp, Dinner from £4, Rooms 1 single, 1 twin, 1 double, 1 family, No smoking, Children welcome, Open all year.
Stella & Mike Steward, **The White Hart Inn,** Chilsworthy, Gunnislake, Cornwall PL18 9PB
Tel: 01822 832307   **Map Ref 17**

PENELLEN HOTEL, a small family beach side hotel overlooking St Ives Bay, offering sea bathing and glorious views. Ideal centre for touring. Restaurant, and safe parking.

B&B from £20, Dinner available, Rooms 6 double, 2 twin, 2 family, most en-suite, No smoking, Children welcome, Open all year.

Penellen Hotel, Riviere Towans, Hayle, Cornwall TR26 5AF
Tel: 01736 753777   **Map Ref 18**

LYNDALE GUEST HOUSE, a pretty cottage guest house on edge of the historic market town of Helston. Central for Helford River, Lizard, beaches and coastal walks. 6 well appointed rooms, most en-suite. All rooms have TV. Private parking, home cooking. Residential licence, satellite TV lounge, fax facilities. ETB 3 Crowns Commended.
B&B from £15.50pp, Dinner from £11.50, Rooms 6, 3 en-suite, Children & Pets welcome, Open all year.
Mr & Mrs Tucker, **Lyndale Guest House,** 4 Greenbank, Meneage Road, Helston, Cornwall TR13 8JA
Tel: 01326 561082 Fax: 01326 565813   **Map Ref 19**

GWEALDUES HOTEL, a licensed modern hotel with en-suite rooms. Bar meals and a la carte restaurant. Satellite TV lounge. Beer garden with fishpond and waterfall.

B&B from £30, Dinner available, Rooms 3 single, 2 twin, 9 double, 2 triple, 1 family, most en-suite, No smoking, Children welcome, Open all year.

Gwealdues Hotel, Falmouth Road, Helston, Cornwall TR13 8JX
Tel: 01326 572808 & 573331 Fax: 01326 561388   **Map Ref 19**

MULLION COVE HOTEL, a beautiful late Victorian hotel with spectacular harbour and coastal views. Outstanding food and fine wines. Guaranteed warmth and relaxation.

B&B from £25, Dinner available, Rooms 6 single, 12 twin, 13 double, 4 triple, most en-suite, Children welcome, Open all year.

Mullion Cove Hotel, Mullion, Helston, Cornwall TR12 7EP
Tel: 01326 240328 Fax: 01326 240998   **Map Ref 20**

RIDGEBACK LODGE HOTEL, set between 3 coves with views overlooking countryside and 5 minutes from beaches. 15th century Mullion offers riding, golfing, walking and shooting. Our restaurant offers traditional and exotic foods made from local produce. We have a bar, guests lounge and car park.

B&B from £16.50pp, Dinner from £9.95, Rooms 1 single, 1 twin, 3 double, 2 family, some en-suite, Children welcome, Pets by arrangement, Open all year. Peter & Jennifer Dann, **Ridgeback Lodge Hotel,** Nansmellyon Road, Mullion, Helston, Cornwall TR12 7DH
Tel: 01326 241300 Fax: 01326 241330   **Map Ref 20**

....

POLURRIAN HOTEL, APARTMENTS & LEISURE CLUB, an idyllic setting for family run hotel with own beach, surrounded by National Trust coastline. Indoor leisure club and outdoor amenities. Personal service.

B&B from £35, Dinner available, Rooms 17 twin, 18 double, 4 triple, most en-suite, No smoking, Open February - December.

Polurrian Hotel, Apartments & Leisure Club, Polurrian Cove, Mullion, Helston, Cornwall TR12 7EN
Tel: 01326 240421 Fax: 01326 240083   **Map Ref 21**

....

THE LIZARD HOTEL, friendly Victorian charm in 1.5 acres. Breathtaking views across Kynance Cove. Tea/coffee facilities. Reductions short breaks/weeks. Cosy bar. Dinner optional - good home-cooked choice. Parking. Coastal Path and the "Most Southerly Point" within yards. Serpentine rocks. Walker's paradise. ETB 2 Crowns Commended. "Which" Good Bed & Breakfast Guide Recommended.

B&B from £17.50pp, Dinner £13.50, Rooms 1 single, 1 twin, 4 double, 1 family, some en-suite, Restricted smoking. Children & pets welcome. Open all year

Tess & John Barlow, **The Lizard Hotel,** Penmenner Road, The Lizard, Helston, Cornwall TR12 7NP
Tel: 01326 290305   **Map Ref 22**

....

MELLAN HOUSE, stands in a large garden and is 5 minutes from a safe sandy beach. Bedrooms have sea views and garden views, tea/coffee facilities and there is a comfortable lounge with colour television available for guests' use.

B&B from £18pp, Rooms 1 single, 1 twin, 3 double, Restricted smoking, Children welcome, Open all year.

Muriel Fairhurst, **Mellan House,** Coverack, Heslton, Cornwall TR12 6TH
Tel: 01326 280482 Fax: 01326 280482   **Map Ref 23**

....

GLENCOE VILLA, a large 3 storey, hilltop Victorian type house with superb views across Tamar Valley. 4 minutes from town centre.

B&B from £15, Rooms 1 twin, 1 double, 1 triple, 1 family, most en-suite, No smoking, Children welcome, Open all year.

Glencoe Villa, 13 Race Hill, Launceston, Cornwall PL15 9BB
Tel: 01566 773012 & 775819   **Map Ref 24**

....

ELNOR GUEST HOUSE, home from home with friendly family atmosphere in 100 year old town house between the station and market town.

B&B from £18, Dinner available, Rooms 4 single, 1 twin, 1 double, 3 triple, most en-suite, Children welcome, No pets, Open all year.

Elnor Guest House, 1 Russell Street, Liskeard, Cornwall PL14 4BP
Tel: 01579 342472   **Map Ref 25**

THE PENCUBITT COUNTRY HOUSE HOTEL, a beautiful Victorian mansion house in 2 acres of mature gardens. Private, superb views. Award winning cuisine by chef/proprietor. Family owned and run.

B&B from £30, Dinner available, Rooms 3 single, 2 twin, 3 double, 1 family, Children welcome, Open all year.

The Pencubitt Country House Hotel, Station Road, Liskeard, Cornwall PL14 4EB
Tel: 01579 342694   **Map Ref 25**

....

THE PANORAMA HOTEL, a family run hotel, good food, friendly atmosphere. Magnificent setting overlooking harbour, beach and miles of beautiful coastline.

B&B from £23.50, Dinner available, Rooms 2 single, 1 twin, 4 double, 2 triple, 1 family, most en-suite, Children welcome, No pets, Open all year.
The Panorama Hotel, Hannafore Road, Looe, Cornwall PL13 2DE
Tel: 01503 262123 Fax: 01503 265654   **Map Ref 12**

....

FIELDHEAD HOTEL, a turn of the century house set in lovely gardens in quiet area, with panoramic views of the sea and bay. Intimate candlelit restaurant.

B&B from £38.50, Dinner available, Rooms 1 single, 3 twin, 9 double, 1 triple, all en-suite, Children over 5, Open February - December.
Fieldhead Hotel, Portuan Road, Hannafore, Looe, Cornwall PL13 2DR
Tel: 01503 262689 Fax: 01503 264114   **Map Ref 25**

....

ALLHAYS COUNTRY HOUSE, set in extensive gardens, overlooking the sea. En-suite bedrooms with Sky-TV and tea/coffee making facilities. Comfortable licensed lounge with log fire during cooler weather. Dinner freshly prepared and cooked in a AGA. Awarded A.A. Rosette. Ample parking. Close by Cornish Coastal Path and Polperro.
B&B from £28pp, Dinner from £16, Rooms 3 twin, 3 double, all en-suite, Restricted smoking, Children over 10, Pets welcome, Open all year except Christmas & New Year.
Brian & Lynda Spring, **Allhays Country House,** Talland Bay, Looe PL13 2JB
Tel: 01503 272434 Fax: 01503 272929   **Map Ref 26**

....

COOMBE FARM, experience the magic of Cornwall. Enjoy warm, friendly hospitality, delicious food, luxurious surroundings. Lovely grounds and superb views down a wooded valley to the sea. All bedrooms en-suite with satellite TV, tea/coffee facilities and direct dial telephone. ETB 3 Crowns Highly Commended.

B&B from £28pp, Dinner from £16, Rooms 3 twin, 3 double,4 family, all en-suite, No smoking, Children over 10, Dogs welcome, Open March - November.
Alexander & Sally Low, **Coombe Farm,** Widegates, Looe PL13 1QN
Tel: 01503 240223 Fax: 01503 240895   **Map Ref 27**

....

RESTORMEL LODGE HOTEL, set in the beautiful Fowey Valley. Warm, spacious well-equipped bedrooms. Imaginative menus of delicious food and friendly, efficient service.

B&B from £33, Dinner available, Rooms 2 single, 13 twin, 14 double, 3 triple, all en-suite, Children welcome, Open all year.
Restormel Lodge Hotel, 19 Castle Hill, Lostwithiel, Cornwall PL22 0DD
Tel: 01208 872223 Fax: 01208 873568   **Map Ref 28**

LOSTWITHIEL GOLF & COUNTRY CLUB, overlooking the beautiful River Fowey valley in idyllic setting. Charm, character and high levels of comfort and service. Bedrooms are converted from Cornish stone farm buildings.

B&B from £33, Dinner available, Rooms 2 single, 3 double, 13 twin, all en-suite, Children welcome, Open all year.
Lostwithiel Golf & Country Club, Lower Polscoe, Lostwithiel, Cornwall PL22 0HQ
Tel: 01208 873550 Fax: 01208 873479   **Map Ref 28**

....

SEAPOINT HOUSE HOTEL, a family run hotel with beautiful views overlooking the bay and harbour. All bedrooms with en-suite facilities, colour TV and hot drinks.
B&B from £25, Dinner available, Rooms 1 twin, 3 double, 2 triple, 3 family, most en-suite, No smoking, Children welcome, Open March - December.
Seapoint House Hotel, Battery Terrace, Mevagissey, Cornwall PL26 6QS
Tel: 01726 842684 Fax: 01726 842266   **Map Ref 29**

....

SPA HOTEL, Detached hotel with own grounds, in a traffic free position away from the bustle, yet within walking distance of the village. Weekend and midweek bookings available.

B&B from £22.50, Dinner available, Rooms 2 twin, 4 double, 3 triple, 2 family, all en-suite, No smoking, Children welcome, Open March - October.
Spa Hotel, Polkirt Hill, Mevagissey, Cornwall PL26 6UY
Tel: 01726 842244   **Map Ref 29**

....

TREMARNE HOTEL, in a quiet secluded area with views of sea and country. Within easy reach of Mevagissey harbour and Portmellon bathing beach.
B&B from £25, Dinner available, Rooms 2 single, 3 twin, 7 double, 1 triple, 1 family, all en-suite, No smoking, Children welcome, Open March - December.
Tremarne Hotel, Polkirt, Mevagissey, Cornwall PL26 6UY
Tel: 01726 842213 Fax: 01726 843420   **Map Ref 29**

....

TREVALSA COURT HOTEL, cliff top position with superb sea views and access to beach, in peaceful surroundings. Ideal for touring. Ample car parking. Accent on fresh food, vegetarian/special diets. Ground floor room ideal for semi disabled persons.

B&B from £25, Dinner available, Rooms 2 single, 4 twin, 8 double, 1 triple, all en-suite, No smoking, Children welcome, Open February - November.
Trevalsa Court Hotel, Polstreath Hill, Mevagissey, Cornwall PL26 6TH
Tel: 01726 842468   **Map Ref 29**

....

STEEP HOUSE, a comfortable house with large garden and covered (summertime) pool. Superb seaside views, licensed and free off road parking.
B&B from £20, Rooms 1 single, 1 twin, 5 double, 1 triple, most en-suite, No smoking, Children over 10, No pets, Open all year.
Steep House, Portmellon Cove, Mevagissey, Cornwall PL26 6PH
Tel: 01726 843732   **Map Ref 29**

....

SHARKSFIN HOTEL & RESTAURANT, formerly an eighteenth-century fish warehouse tastefully converted into a small hotel and waterside restaurant which dominates the waterfront. Harbour views on en-suite rooms, 2 superior double or twin rooms. TV, tea/coffee facilities. Guest lounge. Licensed bar.
B&B from £44 per room, Dinner from £8-£10, Rooms 2 single, 2 twin, 8 double, 1 family, some en-suite, Children welcome, Open February - December.
Mrs C.J. King, **Sharksfin Hotel & Restaurant,** The Quay, Mevagissey, Cornwall PL26 6QU
Tel: 01726 843241 Fax: 01726 842552   **Map Ref 29**

KERRYANNA COUNTRY HOUSE, enjoys a superb position overlooking Mevagissey. Within easy walking distance to the village. Romantic en-suite rooms. Beautiful gardens with gorgeous views and summer heated pool. Delicious suppers and hearty breakfasts. Licensed conservatory bar, games rooms and putting green. A warm and friendly welcome assured. **B&B from £20-£26pp,** Dinner from £11.50, Rooms 1 twin, 4 double, 1 family, all en-suite, Restricted smoking, Children over 5, No pets, Open March - October.
Linda Hennah, **Kerryanna Country House,** Treleaven Farm, Mevagissey, Cornwall PL26 6RZ
Tel/Fax: 01726 843558   **Map Ref 29**

TREBARWITH HOTEL, on the sea edge with 350 feet of private sea frontage, in a central position away from traffic noise. Same ownership since 1964.

B&B from £24, Dinner available, Rooms 3 single, 20 double, 12 twin, 6 family, all with private or en-suite, Children welcome, No pets, Open March - October.
Trebarwith Hotel, Newquay, Cornwall TR7 1BZ
Tel: 01637 872288 Fax: 01637 875431   **Map Ref 30**

ALOHA HOTEL, a friendly licensed hotel with en-suite rooms and home comfort. Well situated for beaches and touring Cornwall. Conservatory and garden overlooking Trencreek Valley.

B&B from £13, Dinner available, Rooms 2 single, 5 double, 3 triple, 3 family, most en-suite, No smoking, Children welcome, No pets, Open all year.
Aloha Hotel, 122/124 Henver Road, Newquay, Cornwall TR7 3EQ
Tel: 01637 878366 EMail: Aloh aNewqu@compuserve.com   **Map Ref 30**

CHICHESTER, a comfortable, licensed establishment convenient for shops, beaches and gardens. Showers in most bedrooms, many extras. Walking, mineral collecting and Discover Cornwall holidays provided in spring and autumn.

B&B from £14, Dinner available, Rooms 2 single, 2 twin, 2 double, 1 triple, most private showers, No smoking, Children over 1, No pets, Open March - November.
Chichester, 14 Bay View Terrace, Newquay, Cornwall TR7 2LR
Tel: 01637 874216   **Map Ref 30**

THE THREE TEE'S HOTEL, a first class friendly, family run hotel. Extensive refurbishment 97/98. 5 minutes walk from town centre. Ample parking. Large conservatory. Licensed bar. Close to zoo, golf course's, several beaches. Tea/coffee facilities. One child free February, March, September, October.
B&B from £13-£15pp, Dinner from £5, Rooms 1 single, 2 twin, 4 double, 5 family, all with own shower, Restricted smoking, Children welcome, Pets by arrangement, Open all year.
Mrs Tina Parton, **The Three Tee's Hotel,** 21 Carminow Way, Newquay, Cornwall TR7 3AY
Tel: 01637 872055 24hr Tel: 0585 958758   **Map Ref 30**

ELIOT - CAVENDISH HOTEL, a large family hotel situated close to beaches. Heated outdoor pool, sauna and solarium. Extensive parking.

B&B from £22, Dinner available, Rooms 6 single, 22 twin, 37 double, 11 triple, all en-suite, No smoking, Children welcome, No pets, Open January, March - December.

Eliot - Cavendish Hotel, Edgecumbe Avenue, Newquay, Cornwall TR7 2NH
Tel: 01637 878177 Fax: 01637 852053   **Map Ref 30**

FISTRAL BEACH HOTEL, overlooks Fistral - UK's most famous beach break, adjacent golf course, close to Newquay's town centre/entertainment/night life. Ideally situated for touring Cornwall. All en-suite rooms have satellite, video, tea makers, even one with four poster. Licensed bar, tea terrace, swimming pool, private car park.
B&B from £12.50pp, Dinner from £6, Rooms 3 twin, 6 double, 7 family, Children & pets welcome, Open all year.
Ken & Denise Monet, **Fistral Beach Hotel,** Esplanade Road, Newquay, Cornwall TR7 1QA
Tel: 01637 850626 & 873044 Fax: 01637 850626   **Map Ref 30**

EDGCUMBE HOTEL, a family hotel on sea front, only 5 minutes level walking to town centre. Good congenial atmosphere, friendly staff and renowned for excellent fare.

B&B from £22pp, Dinner available, Rooms 9 single, 30 double, 8 twin, 13 treble, 28 family, all en-suite, Children welcome, Open all year.
Edgcumbe Hotel, Narrowcliffe, Newquay, Cornwall TR7 2RR
Tel: 01637 872061 Fax: 01637 852524   **Map Ref 30**

TREGARN HOTEL, a family hotel with facilities for all weathers. Entertainment most nights. Few minutes walk to Fistral Beach and the River Gannel estuary.

B&B from £16, Dinner available, Rooms 4 single, 11 double, 5 twin, 9 triple, 10 family, most en-suite, Children welcome, Open March - December.
Tregarn Hotel, Pentire Crescent, Newquay, Cornwall TR7 1PX
Tel: 01637 874292 Fax: 01637 850116   **Map Ref 30**

CLIFFSIDE HOTEL, a forty bedroomed sea front hotel. One minutes to town centre. All rooms have colour TV, tea/coffee facilities and central heating. Excellent cuisine. Reasonable rates. Entertainment. Licensed bar. Business persons most welcome. Child reductions. Off street parking. Daily or weekly rates. Contact Maria for a colour brochure.
B&B from £16pp, Dinner from £6.50, Rooms 5 single, 14 twin, 12 double, 5 family, all en-suite, Restricted smoking, Children welcome, Open March - January.
Maria & Richard Machin, **Cliffside Hotel,** The Crescent, Newquay, Cornwall TR7 1DT
Tel: 01637 872897 Fax: 01637 872897   **Map Ref 30**

CRANTOCK BAY HOTEL, a long established family hotel on headland, with grounds leading directly on to beach. Wonderful walking country.

B&B from £51, Dinner available, Rooms 9 single, 15 twin, 8 double, 2 family, all en-suite, No smoking, Children welcome, Open March - November.
Crantock Bay Hotel, Crantock, Newquay, Cornwall TR8 5SE
Tel: 01637 830229 Fax: 01637 831111   **Map Ref 31**

HIGHFIELD LODGE HOTEL, is situated in the picturesque coastal village of Crantock which is a few minutes walk of one of Cornwall's finest beaches. First class accommodation with tea/coffee facilities and colour TV's in all rooms. Licensed Bar. Private car park. No smoking. No pets.

B&B from £17pp, Bar meals from £3, Rooms 1 single, 1 twin, 7 double, 2 family, most en-suite, No smoking, Children welcome, No pets, Open all year.
Rob & Jean Boston, **Highfield Lodge Hotel,** Halwyn Road, Crantock, Newquay, Cornwall TR8 5TR
Tel: 01637 830744   **Map Ref 31**

TREGENNA HOUSE, situated in the village of Crantock with sandy beach and coastal path. Ideal for touring Cornwall, fishing, riding and golf nearby. Ample parking. Heated pool. Tea/coffee facilities and TV, many rooms en-suite. A warm welcome is provided with home cooking and friendly atmosphere.
B&B from £17.50pp, Dinner from £9, Rooms 1 single, 1 twin, 1 double, 3 family, all en-suite, Restricted smoking, Children & pets welcome, Open all year.
Sue & David Wrigley, **Tregenna House,** West Pentire Road, Crantock, Newquay, Cornwall TR8 5RZ
Tel: 01637 830222 Fax: 01637 831267 **Map Ref 31**

....

TREDRAGON HOTEL, grounds lead directly to sandy cove. Magnificent coastal walks/views. Relax in our indoor pool complex. Excellent food and wine. Open all year. Ideal for short breaks.

B&B from £18.50, Dinner available, Rooms 2 single, 5 twin, 9 double, 13 family, all en-suite, Children welcome, Open all year.
Tredragon Hotel, Mawgan Porth, Newquay, Cornwall TR8 4DQ
Tel: 01637 860213 Fax: 01637 860269 **Map Ref 32**

....

PHILEMA HOTEL, furnished to a high standard with magnificent views overlooking Fistral Beach and golf course. Friendly informal hotel with good facilities, including indoor pool, leisure complex and apartments.

B&B from £20, Dinner available, Rooms 2 single, 3 twin, 8 double, 5 triple, 11 family, most en-suite, Children welcome, Open March - October.
Philema Hotel, 1 Esplanade Road, Pentire, Newquay, Cornwall TR7 1PY
Tel: 01637 872571 Fax: 01637 873188 **Map Ref 33**

....

THE ESPLANADE HOTEL, a modern hotel overlooking beautiful Fistral Bay. Good food, friendly service and excellent facilities for a happy, relaxing holiday.

B&B from £20, Dinner available, Rooms 6 single, 10 twin, 21 double, 17 triple, 20 family, most en-suite, No smoking, Children welcome, Open February - December.
The Esplanade Hotel, 9 Esplanade Road, Pentire, Newquay, Cornwall TR7 1PS
Tel: 01637 873333 Fax: 01637 851413 **Map Ref 33**

....

CORISANDE MANOR HOTEL, an unique turreted Austrian design, quietly situated, commanding an unrivalled position in 3 acre secluded grounds with private foreshore. Extensive wine cellar and chef/proprietor.

B&B from £29, Dinner available, Rooms 2 single, 2 twin, 7 double, all en-suite or private, Children welcome, Open all year.
Corisande Manor Hotel, Riverside Avenue, Pentire, Newquay, Cornwall TR7 1PL
Tel: 01637 872042 Fax: 01637 874557 **Map Ref 33**

....

WINDWARD HOTEL, a modern hotel of fine quality with large car park and situated on the coastal road to Padstow overlooking Porth Bay. 1.5 miles north of Newquay.

B&B from £25, Dinner available, Rooms 1 twin, 10 double, 1 triple, 2 family, all en-suite, Children welcome, No pets, Open March - October.
Windward Hotel, Alexandra Road, Porth, Newquay, Cornwall TR7 3NB
Tel: 01637 873185 & 852436 Fax: 01637 852436 **Map Ref 33**

....

PENDEEN HOTEL, a well established hotel, in its own grounds, 2 miles from Newquay and close to beach. Good food served with friendly and efficient service.

B&B from £21.50, Dinner available, Rooms 2 single, 2 twin, 8 double, 2 triple, 1 family, all en-suite, No smoking, Children welcome, No pets, Open January - October.
Pendeen Hotel, Alexandra Road, Porth, Newquay, Cornwall TR7 3ND
Tel: 01637 873521 Fax: 01637 873521 **Map Ref 34**

WHIPISDERRY HOTEL, set in own grounds overlooking Porth Beach and Newquay Bay. Noted for fine cuisine. Watch the badgers feed and play only a few feet away.

B&B from £18.50, Dinner available, Rooms 2 single, 12 double,1 twin, 1 triple, 4 family, most en-suite, Children welcome, Open March - October & December.
Whipisderry Hotel, Trevelgue Road, Porth, Newquay, Cornwall TR7 3LY
Tel: 01637 874777 Fax: 01637 874777   **Map Ref 34**

....

TREVALSA HOTEL, a modern, licensed hotel above beautiful Whipisderry beach. Panoramic views of Newquay's coastline. Golf, fishing, wind surfing, surfing, coastal and countryside walking.

B&B from £19, Dinner available, Rooms 4 single, 10 double, 2 twin, 5 triple, 3 family, most en-suite, No smoking, Children welcome, Open March - October.
Trevalsa Hotel, Watergate Road, Porth, Newquay, Cornwall TR7 3LX
Tel: 01637 873336 Fax: 01637 878843   **Map Ref 34**

....

TREGURRIAN HOTEL, on coast road between Newquay and Padstow, just 100 yards from golden sandy beach in an area reputed to have some of the finest beaches and coastline in Europe.

B&B from £22, Dinner available, Rooms 4 single, 11 double, 4 twin, 2 triple, 6 family, most en-suite, Children welcome, Open March - October.
Tregurrian Hotel, Watergate Bay, Newquay, Cornwall TR8 4AB
Tel: 01637 860280 Fax: 01637 860540   **Map Ref 35**

....

WOODLANDS COUNTRY HOUSE, a delightful country house in rural setting near beaches and golf courses, offering picturesque walks, modern amenities and choice of cuisine.

B&B from £26, Dinner available, Rooms 2 twin, 5 double, 2 triple, all en-suite, No smoking, Children welcome, Open March - October.
Woodlands Country House, Treator, Padstow, Cornwall PL28 8RU
Tel: 01841 532426 Fax: 01841 532426   **Map Ref 36**

....

TREVONE BAY HOTEL, you will find friendship, relaxation and good food in our spotless, family run hotel. Tranquil village position overlooking beach/coastal footpath.

B&B from £26, Dinner available, Rooms 3 single, 3 twin, 3 double, 1 triple, 3 family, all en-suite, No smoking, Children welcome, Open April - October.
Trevone Bay Hotel, Trevone Bay, Padstow, Cornwall PL28 8QS
Tel: 01841 520243 Fax: 01841 521195   **Map Ref 37**

....

GREEN WAVES HOTEL, a long established, small, family run hotel in quiet cul-de-sac. Set in garden facing south to the sea. All rooms have colour TV and tea making facilities. Half size snooker table available.

B&B from £26, Dinner available, Rooms 2 single, 6 twin, 11 double, most en-suite, Children over 4, Open April - October.
Green Waves Hotel, Trevone, Padstow, Cornwall PL28 8RD
Tel: 01841 520114   **Map Ref 37**

....

WATERBEACH HOTEL, designed to take advantage of the sunshine and views across the Atlantic. Accommodates 30 people in comfort.

B&B from £25, Dinner available, Rooms 4 single, 5 twin, 5 double, 7 triple, most en-suite, Children welcome, Open March - December.
Waterbeach Hotel, Treyarnon Bay, Padstow, Cornwall PL28 8JW
Tel: 01841 520292 Fax: 01841 521102   **Map Ref 38**

TARBERT HOTEL, a Georgian hotel, centrally located, with emphasis on quality and personal service. Restaurant featuring a la carte with fish specialities. Short breaks available.

B&B from £29, Dinner available, Rooms 2 single, 4 twin, 6 double, all en-suite, No smoking, Children over 7, No pets, Open February - December.
Tarbert Hotel, 11 Clarence Street, Penzance, Cornwall TR18 2NU
Tel: 01736 363758 Fax: 01736 331336   **Map Ref 39**

WARWICK HOUSE HOTEL, a family run hotel near the sea, station and heliport. Tastefully decorated rooms, most en-suite and with sea views. Car parking.
B&B from £17, Dinner available, Rooms 1 single, 1 twin, 3 double, 1 triple, most en-suite, No smoking,Children welcome, Open January - November.
Warwick House Hotel, 17 Regent Terrace, Penzance, Cornwall TR18 4DW
Tel: 01736 363881   **Map Ref 39**

WOODSTOCK HOUSE, is situated in central Penzance, just off the sea front. All rooms have TV, radio, tea/coffee facilities. Most rooms have en-suite bathrooms with one premier double room with 4-poster bed on the ground floor. Ideal for touring the Lands End peninsula. Email: woodstocp@aol.com
B&B from £15pp, Rooms 2 single, 2 twin, 3 double, 2 family, most en-suite, Restricted smoking, Children welcome, Pets by arrangement, Open all year.
John & Cherry Hopkins, **Woodstock House,** 29 Morrab Road, Penzance, Cornwall TR18 4EZ
Tel: 01736 369049 Fax: 01736 369049   **Map Ref 39**

A warm welcome awaits you at Victorian **LYNWOOD GUEST HOUSE**. Situated between town centre and promenade. 7 well decorated bedrooms with colour TV and tea/coffee making facilities. English & continental breakfast menu. Ideal base for visiting Lands End, Lizard, St. Michael Mount & Isles of Scilly. ETB 2 Crown, RAC.
B&B from £12pp, Rooms 1 single, 2 twin, 2 double, 2 family, some en-suite, Restricted smoking, Children welcome, Pets by arrangement, Open all year.
Roy & Teresa Stacey, **Lynwood Guest House,** 41 Morrab Rd, Penzance, Cornwall TR18 4EX
Tel: 01736 365871 Fax: 01736 365871   **Map Ref 39**

ESTORIL HOTEL, an elegant Victorian house offering comfortable, comprehensive accommodation. A warm welcome and personal service in peaceful and immaculate surroundings await you.
B&B from £24, Dinner available, Rooms 1 single, 3 twin, 4 double, 1 triple, 1 family, all en-suite, No smoking, Children welcome, No pets, Open February - November.
Estoril Hotel, 46 Morrab Road, Penzance, Cornwall TR18 4EX
Tel: 01736 362468 & 367471 Fax: 01736 367471   **Map Ref 39**

CORNERWAYS GUEST HOUSE, is a listed town house close to bus/rail stations. Ideal touring base. All rooms colour TV, tea/coffee facilities. One double en-suite. B&B from £15 per person. Evening meal £6.50, vegetarians welcome. 10% discount weeks stay.

B&B from £15pp, Dinner from £6.50, Rooms 3 single, 2 double, 1 en-suite, Restricted smoking, Children welcome, Pets by arrangement, Open all year.
John & Andrea Leggatt, **Cornerways Guest House,** 5 Leskinnick Street, Penzance, Cornwall TR18 2HA
Tel: 01736 364645   **Map Ref 39**

RIVIERA INN

RIVIERA INN, satellite colour televisions in all rooms. Tea and coffee making facilities. Fully licensed. Full catering facilities. Situated near bus and train stations. Ideal for visiting Scilly Isles. Close to all Cornwalls beaches and attractions.

B&B from £15pp, Dinner available, Rooms 5 single, 2 twin, 3 double, 1 family, Children & Pets welcome, Open all year.

Mr P Galvin & Mrs J Fiorillo, **Riviera Inn,** 52 Market Jew Street, Penzance, Cornwall TR18 2HZ
Tel: 01736 362576   **Map Ref 39**

THE SEA & HORSES HOTEL, in a quiet sea front location enjoying breathtaking views across Mount's Bay to St Michaels Mount. Former Victorian gentlemen's residence retaining original features. Excellent cuisine and wines.

B&B from £28, Dinner available, Rooms 3 single, 3 twin, 1 double, 3 triple, 1 family, all en-suite, Children welcome, Open all year.

The Sea & Horses Hotel, 6 Alexandra Terrace, Penzance, Cornwall TR18 4NX
Tel: 01736 361961 Fax: 01736 330499   **Map Ref 39**

TREVENTON GUEST HOUSE, genuine Cornish granite guest house, 200 yards walk to promenade. Homely atmosphere. Our guest book is your guarantee.

B&B from £14, Rooms 1 single, 3 double, 2 twin, 1 triple, most en-suite, Children over 5, No pets, Open all year.

Treventon Guest House, Alexandra Place, Penzance, Cornwall TR18 4NE
Tel: 01736 363521   **Map Ref 39**

KEIGWIN HOTEL, smoke free, quiet, comfortable, family run hotel, close to all amenities. Good cooking, on street parking and colour TV. Pre-booking advised.

B&B from £14, Dinner available, Rooms 2 single, 1 twin, 4 double, 1 triple, most en-suite, No smoking, Children welcome, No pets, Open all year.

Keigwin Hotel, Alexandra Road, Penzance, Cornwall TR18 4LZ
Tel: 01736 363930   **Map Ref 39**

PENMORVAH HOTEL, 350 yards from promenade in tree lined avenue. Easy reach of town centre and an ideal location for touring.

B&B from £15, Dinner available, Rooms 2 single, 1 double, 1 twin, 4 triple, all en-suite, Children welcome, Open all year.

Penmorvah Hotel, Alexandra Road, Penzance, Cornwall TR18 4LZ
Tel: 01736 363711   **Map Ref 39**

Warm welcome and excellent breakfast in lovely quiet **CAMILLA HOUSE HOTEL** overlooking Mount's Bay. Bus and rail stations and town centre nearby. Parking, sea views and en-suites available. Clean comfortable rooms have TV, tea/coffee facilities and central heating. Licensed. Ideal for Land's End Peninsular. Agents for Scillonian Sky Bus. AA QQQ, RAC Acclaimed.
B&B from £17pp, Rooms 3 single, 1 twin, 4 double, some en-suite Restricted smoking, Children over 10, Pets welcome, Open all year.
Bill & Rosemary Wooldridge, **Camilla House Hotel,** Regent Terrace, Penzance, Cornwall TR18 4DW
Tel/Fax: 01736 363771   **Map Ref 39**

SOUTHERN COMFORT, a family run guest house, magnificent sea views. All rooms en-suite, televisions, tea/coffee facilities. Private car park. Open all year. Convenient for boat or helicopter. Isles of Scilly within easy reach of Lands End.

B&B from £18-£20pp, Rooms 2 single, 3 twin, 3 double, 2 family, all en-suite, Restricted smoking, Children welcome, Pets by arrangement, Open all year. Mrs Christine Robinson, **Southern Comfort,** Seafront, 8 Alexandra Terrace, Penzance, Cornwall TR18 4NX
Tel: 01736 366333   **Map Ref 39**

THE LAMORNA COVE COUNTRY HOUSE HOTEL, a superbly situated historic country house overlooking the cove and coastal path, with many paintings and antiques contained within its granite walls. All bedrooms are en-suite and have remote control colour television, tea/coffee facilities and hair dryers. There is also a lift.
B&B £34.50pp, Dinner £15, Rooms 2 single, 3 twin, 7 double, all en-suite, No smoking, Pets by arrangement, Open March - end October, Christmas & New Year. Lisa & Malcolm Gray, **The Lamorna Cove Country House Hotel,** Lamorna, Penzance, Cornwall TR19 6XH
Tel: 01736 731411   **Map Ref 40**

CARN DU HOTEL, an elegant Victorian house in an elevated position above Mousehole. Cosy lounge, delightful cocktail bar and licensed restaurant specialising in seafood and local vegetables. Terraced gardens.
B&B from £25, Dinner available, Rooms 1 single, 3 twin, 3 double, all en-suite or private facilities, No smoking, Children welcome, No pets, Open all year.
Carn Du Hotel, Raginnis Hill, Mousehole, Penzance, Cornwall TR19 6SS
Tel: 01736 731233   **Map Ref 42**

THE KINGS ARMS, a licensed public house serving good beers and home made food. All rooms have tea/coffee facilities. Large car park. Set in beautiful village of Paul. Close to villages of Mousehole and Newlyn. Beaches nearby. Lands End 10 minutes drive.

B&B from £15pp, Dinner from £2, Rooms 1 twin, 1 double, 2 family, Restricted smoking, Children and pets welcome, Open all year except Christmas. Calvin & Anna Yould, **The Kings Arms,** Paul, Penzance, Cornwall TR19 6TZ
Tel: 01736 731224   **Map Ref 42**

EDNOVEAN HOUSE, a beautiful Victorian country house offering comfortable rooms most having en-suite facilities and panoramic sea views overlooking St Michaels Mount and Mounts Bay. Situated in one acre of gardens. Excellent home cooking. TV lounge, car park, library, informal bar, candlelit dining room. ETB 3 Crowns. AA Recommended QQQ.
B&B from £23pp, Dinner from £15, Rooms 2 single, 2 twin, 4 double, some en-suite, Restricted smoking, Children over 7, Open all year except Christmas. Clive & Jackie Whittington, **Ednovean House,** Perranuthnoe, Penzance, Cornwall TR20 9LZ
Tel: 01736 711071   **Map Ref 43**

THE LANDS END HOTEL, situated on the cliff tops at Lands End. The sea views are breathtaking!
B&B from £49, Dinner available, Rooms 4 single, 13 double, 13 twin, 3 family, all en-suite, No smoking, Children welcome, Open all year.
The Lands End Hotel, Lands End, Sennen, Penzance, Cornwall TR19 7AA
Tel: 01736 871844 Fax: 01736 871599   **Map Ref 44**

WELLINGTON HOTEL, an imposing granite building overlooking Market Square. En-suite accommodation overlooking garden.TV, tea/coffee, full license. Good value menu, fresh fish, crab, steaks, daily specials. Ideal centre for climbing, walking, bird watching, water sports, beaches, golf, fishing. Near Lands End, St. Ives, Newlyn. Ideal centre for touring **B&B from £12.50-£21pp,** Dinner from £4-£13, Rooms 6 single, 2 twin, 9 double, 3 family, most en-suite, Children & pets welcome, Open all year except Christmas.

Rod & Jennifer Gray, **Wellington Hotel,** Market Square, St Just, Penzance, Cornwall TR19 7HD
Tel: 01736 787319 Fax: 01736 787906 **Map Ref 45**

THE BLACK WELL, situated on the scenic coast road between Lands End and St. Ives. All bedrooms are en-suite and have either sea or country views. There are no parking problems. Guests enjoy walking the coastal footpath with its rugged coastline and magnificent views. Personal attention assured at all times.

B&B from £15pp, Rooms 2 twin, 1 double, 2 family, all en-suite, Restricted smoking, Children & Pets welcome, Open all year.
Reg Blackwell, **The Black Well,** Botallack, St. Just, Penzance TR19 7QH
Tel: 01736 787461 **Map Ref 46**

CHY AN KERENSA, enjoy a superb position directly overlooking miles of sea, sand and cliffs. 200 metres from beach and Perranporth centre. Our comfortable bedrooms have colour TV, CH, tea/coffee facilities. Many have panoramic sea views, as do our licensed bar/lounge and dining room

B&B from £16pp, Room only, weekly rates available, Rooms 2 single, 2 twin, 6 double, 2 family, most en-suite, Discount for children, Pets welcome, Open all year.
Will & Wendy Woodcock, **Chy An Kerensa,** Cliff Rd, Perranporth, Cornwall TR6 0DR
Tel: 01872 572470 **Map Ref 47**

PONSMERE HOTEL, a family hotel with plenty of facilities for children, situated by Perranporth's golden beach. Well placed for touring Cornwall.

B&B from £18, Dinner available, Rooms 9 single, 16 double, 6 twin, 46 family rooms, all en-suite, No smoking, Children welcome, Open April - October & Christmas.
Ponsmere Hotel, Ponsmere Road, Perranporth, Cornwall TR6 0BW
Tel: 01872 572225 Fax: 01872 572225 **Map Ref 47**

BEACH DUNES HOTEL, situated in the sand dunes and adjoining the golf course, overlooking Perranporth beach and its 3 miles of golden sands.

B&B from £26.50, Dinner available, Rooms 4 double, 2 triple, 2 family, all en-suite, No smoking, Children over 4, Open January - October.
Beach Dunes Hotel, Ramoth Way, Perranporth, Cornwall TR6 0BY
Tel: 01872 572263 Fax: 01872573824 **Map Ref 47**

CLAREMONT HOTEL, a family run hotel in the heart of fishing village. Splendid coastal walks and places of interest nearby. Award winning restaurant, sun trap patio. Off season breaks.

B&B from £18.95, Dinner available, Rooms 1 twin, 7 double, 1 triple, 1 family, all en-suite, Children welcome, Open April - December.
Claremont Hotel, The Coombes, Polperro, Cornwall PL13 2RG
Tel: 01503 272241 Fax: 01503272241 **Map Ref 48**

PENRYN HOUSE, a charming Victorian hotel offering comfortable accommodation and fine dining in candlelit restaurant. Fabulous coastal walks and National Trust properties. Murder Mystery weekends.

B&B from £28, Dinner available, Rooms 1 twin, 9 double, most en-suite, No smoking, Children welcome, Open all year.
Penryn House, The Coombes, Polperro, Cornwall PL13 2RQ
Tel: 01503 272157 Fax: 01503 273055 **Map Ref 48**

....

SEASCAPE HOTEL, renowned for food and a high degree of comfort, with magnificent sea views. Honeymoon and Christmas specials. Four poster and balcony rooms available.

B&B from £25, Dinner available, Rooms 2 twin, 13 double, all en-suite, No smoking, Children over 12, Open February - October & December.
Seascape Hotel, Polzeath, Cornwall PL27 6SX
Tel: 01208 863638 Fax: 01208 862940 **Map Ref 49**

....

PORT GAVERNE HOTEL, a 17th century hotel and restaurant in a tiny paradise on the North Cornwall coast.

B&B from £48, Dinner available, Rooms 3 single, 2 twin, 7 double, 5 triple, all en-suite or private facilities, No smoking, Children welcome, Open February - December.
Port Gaverne Hotel, Port Gaverne, Port Isaac, Cornwall PL29 3SQ
Tel: 01208 880244 & 0550 657867 Fax: 01208 880151 **Map Ref 50**

....

HARBOUR INN, a 150 year old inn on harbour edge. Restaurant open 7 days a week. Most bedrooms en-suite, many with harbour views.

B&B from £30.95, Dinner available, Rooms 1 single, 2 twin, 6 double, 1 family, most en-suite, No smoking, Children welcome, No pets, Open all year.
Harbour Inn, Commercial Road, Porthleven, Cornwall TR13 9JD
Tel: 01326 573876 **Map Ref 51**

....

AVIARY COURT HOTEL, a charming country house hotel set in over 2 acres of secluded gardens. Portreath 5 minutes by car or a 20 minute woodland walk.

B&B from £40, Dinner available, Rooms 1 twin, 4 double, 1 triple, all en-suite, Children welcome, No pets, Open all year.
Aviary Court Hotel, Marys Well, Illogan, Redruth, Cornwall TR16 4QZ
Tel: 01209 842256 Fax: 01209 843744 **Map Ref 52**

....

SUNHOLME HOTEL, a comfortable country house in extensive grounds with magnificent country and coastal views and walks. Traditional food, personal service and en-suite rooms.

B&B from £23, Dinner available, Rooms 1 single, 2 twin, 4 double, 2 triple, 1 family, most en-suite, No smoking, Children over 7, Open March - October.
Sunholme Hotel, Goonvrea Road, St Agnes, Cornwall TR5 0NW
Tel: 01872 552318 **Map Ref 53**

....

PENKERRIS, an enchanting Edwardian residence with own grounds in unspoilt Cornish village. Beautiful rooms, TV, piano, log fires in winter and superb home cooking. All facilities, dramatic cliff walks and beaches nearby. RAC, AA, 2 Crowns, Les Routiers recommended.

B&B from £15pp, Dinner from £7.50, Rooms 1 single, 3 twin, 6 double, 3 family, some en-suite, Children & pets welcome, Open all year.
Dorothy Gill-Carey, **Penkerris,** Penwinnick Road, St Agnes, Cornwall TR5 0PA
Tel: 01872 552262 Fax: 01872 552262 **Map Ref 53**

ROSE IN VALE COUNTRY HOUSE HOTEL, a secluded Georgian country house in secret wooded valley. Recently refurbished. High standards of comfort, service and cuisine. Extensive grounds. Beaches close by. Excellent touring base.

B&B from £45, Dinner available, Rooms 2 single, 8 twin, 9 double, all en-suite, No smoking, Children welcome, Open all year.
Rose in Vale Country House Hotel, Mithin, St Agnes, Cornwall TR5 0QD
Tel: 01872 552202 Fax: 01872 552700 **Map Ref 54**

....

DRIFTWOOD SPARS HOTEL, a delightful old inn with enormous beams, stone walls and log fires. Most bedrooms have wonderful sea views. Candlelit restaurant. Parking.

B&B from £30, Dinner available, Rooms 1 twin, 7 double, 1 family, all en-suite, Children welcome, Open all year.
Driftwood Spars Hotel, Trevaunance Cove, St Agnes, Cornwall TR5 0RT
Tel: 01872 552428 & 553323 Fax: 01872 552428 **Map Ref 55**

....

ALEXANDRA HOTEL, in a quiet position just 5 minutes from town centre. Within easy reach of St Austell Bay and very near bus and rail station.

B&B from £24, Dinner available, Rooms 5 single, 3 twin, 4 double, most en-suite, Children welcome, Open all year.
Alexandra Hotel, 52-54 Alexandra Road, St Austell, Cornwall PL25 4QN
Tel: 01726 66111 Fax: 01726 74242 **Map Ref 56**

....

WHITE HART HOTEL, built in the late 16th century, it became the chief coaching inn in the 17th century and is now a family run hotel.

B&B from £44, Dinner available, Rooms 2 single, 2 twin, 13 double, 1 triple, all en-suite, Children welcome, Open all year.
White Hart Hotel, Church Street, St Austell, Cornwall PL25 4AT
Tel: 01726 72100 Fax: 01726 74705 **Map Ref 56**

....

CARLYON BAY HOTEL, high standard accommodation complemented by extensive leisure facilities, including an 18 hole golf course. Seasonal break rates available.

B&B from £68, Dinner available, Rooms 13 single, 41 twin, 16 double, 2 triple, most en-suite, Children welcome, No pets, Open all year.

Carlyon Bay Hotel, Sea Road, Carlyon Bay, St Austell, Cornwall PL25 3RD
Tel: 01726 812304 Fax: 01726 814938 **Map Ref 57**

....

DUKE OF CORNWALL HOTEL, a family run public house with bed and breakfast. All rooms have shower, TV's and coffee making facilities. Car park available. Herbivore and Carnivore menu, child size meals available. We are situated in central Cornwall. All of Cornwall is within a 2 hour drive.

B&B from £15pp, Dinner from £2.50, Rooms 1 single, 2 twin, 1 double, 1 family, No smoking, Children welcome, Pets by arrangement, Open all year.
Russ & Gill Smith, **Duke of Cornwall Hotel,** 98 Victoria Road, Mount Charles, St Austell, Cornwall PL25 4QD
Tel: 01726 72031 **Map Ref 58**

....

PONDAROSA HOTEL, a private licensed hotel with en-suite rooms. Warm and friendly atmosphere. Quiet location yet convenient for town and beaches. Large private car park.

B&B from £16, Dinner available, Rooms 5 double, 2 triple, 2 family, all en-suite, No smoking, Children welcome, No pets, Open all year.
Pondarosa Hotel, 10 Porthminster Terrace, St Ives, Cornwall TR26 2DQ
Tel: 01736 795875 **Map Ref 59**

83

PRIMAVERA PRIVATE HOTEL, a small, friendly hotel overlooking Porthminster Beach, with warm, personal and efficient service. Carefully prepared food - special dietary needs catered for. Bar meals served all day.

B&B from £17, Dinner available, Rooms 2 single, 1 double, 1 triple, 1 family, some en-suite, No smoking, Children welcome, No pets, Open July - August.

Primavera Private Hotel, 14 Draycott Terrace, St Ives, Cornwall TR26 2EF
Tel: 01736 795595 **Map Ref 59**

....

CHY HARBRO, superb sea views overlooking the harbour. Reputation for good food and hospitality. Some rooms en-suite and with sea views.

B&B from £17, Dinner available, Rooms 1 single, 1 twin, 3 double, all private or en-suite, No smoking, Children over 12, Open all year.

Chy Harbro, 16 Parc Avenue, St Ives, Cornwall TR26 2DN
Tel: 01736 794617 **Map Ref 59**

....

GARRACK HOTEL & RESTAURANT, a delightful family owned hotel. Quiet location. Superb coastal views. Ample parking. Heated indoor pool and leisure centre. Fabulous bargain breaks October - March.

B&B from £65.50, Dinner available, Rooms 1 single, 5 twin, 8 double, 3 triple, most en-suite, Children welcome, Open all year.

Garrack Hotel & Restaurant, Higher Ayr, Burthallan Lane, St Ives, Cornwall TR26 3AA
Tel: 01736 796199 Fax: 01736 798955 **Map Ref 59**

....

PORTHMINSTER HOTEL, established family hotel overlooking Porthminster Beach, with magnificent views of bay from most bedrooms and public rooms.

B&B from £49.50, Dinner available, Rooms 5 single, 15 twin, 13 double, 1 triple, 13 family, all en-suite, Children welcome, Open all year.

Porthminster Hotel, The Terrace, St Ives, Cornwall TR26 2BN
Tel: 01736 795221 Fax: 01736 797043 **Map Ref 59**

....

BLUE HAYES, a country house by the sea at St. Ives. ETB 3 Crowns Highly Commended.

B&B from £28pp, Dinner from £15.50, Rooms 2 single, 1 twin, 5 double, most en-suite, Restricted smoking, Children over 5, Pets by arrangement, Open mid March - mid October.

Jan & Joan Shearn, **Blue Hayes,** Trelyon Avenue, St Ives, Cornwall TR26 2AD
Tel: 01736 797129 **Map Ref 59**

....

DEAN COURT HOTEL, a former gentlemen's residence set in own grounds. Enjoys panoramic views across St Ives Bay and overlooks Porthminster Beach and St Ives harbour. Good food and ample parking.

B&B from £30, Dinner available, Rooms 2 single, 2 twin, 8 double, all en-suite,No smoking, No pets, Open March - October.

Dean Court Hotel, Trelyon Avenue, St Ives, Cornwall TR26 2AD
Tel: 01736 796023 Fax: 01736 796233 **Map Ref 59**

NOOK HOTEL, a family hotel in secluded gardens, near cliff path, beaches and harbour. Childrens play area and car park. Traditional home cooking.

B&B from £17, Rooms 1 single, 2 twin, 7 double, 3 family, most en-suite, Children welcome, No pets, Open March - September.

Nook Hotel, Ayr, St Ives, Cornwall TR26 1EQ
Tel: 01736 795913   **Map Ref 59**

....

TREGORRAN HOTEL, a Mediterranean style villa hotel in own grounds overlooking St Ives Bay, with panoramic sea views, safe beaches and tropical garden.

B&B from £20.50, Dinner available, Rooms 2 twin, 7 double, 1 triple, 6 family, all en-suite, No smoking, Children welcome, Open Easter - October.
Tregorran Hotel, Headland Road, Carbis Bay, St Ives, Cornwall TR26 2NU
Tel: 01736 795889   **Map Ref 60**

....

WHITE HOUSE HOTEL, a relaxed and friendly family run hotel situated at the bottom of a woody valley, 150 yards to Carbis Bay beach. Cosy a la carte restaurant.

B&B from £19, Dinner available, Rooms 2 twin, 4 double, 1 triple, 1 family, all en-suite, Children welcome, No pets, Open March - October.

White House Hotel, The Valley, Carbis Bay, St Ives, Cornwall TR26 2QY
Tel: 01736 797405 Fax: 01736 797426   **Map Ref 60**

....

ROSEUDIAN, a comfortable modernised cottage in rural surroundings. Friendly, relaxing atmosphere. Good home cooking based on own produce. South facing terraced gardens. Dogs by arrangement.

B&B from £18, Dinner available, Rooms 1 twin, 2 double, all en-suite, No smoking, Children over 10, Open March - October.

Roseudian, Crippa Hill, Kelynack, St Just, Cornwall TR19 7RE
Tel: 01736 788556   **Map Ref 61**

....

THE WHEAL LODGE, situated just above the sea opposite golf course. Beautiful area, offering old fashioned personal service, every facility and comfort, excellent food, spacious safe parking. Licensed, near Heligan Gardens, and many well known beauty spots. Real Cornish welcome with peace and quiet. RAC Highly Acclaimed, AA QQQQ.
B&B from £35pp, Rooms 1 single, 2 twin/trebles, 2 double, 1 family, all en-suite, Restricted smoking, Children over 12, Open all year except Christmas & New Year.
Jeanne & Don Martin, **The Wheal Lodge,** 91 Sea Road, Carlyon Bay, St. Austell, Cornwall PL25 3SH
Tel: 01726 815543 Fax: 01726 815543   **Map Ref 57**

....

ANCHORAGE HOUSE GUEST LODGE, has delightful en-suite rooms, each furnished with every comfort including large beds, Sky TV and many special touches. Superb cooking and relaxed atmosphere. Ideally situated for visiting Cornwall's historic treasures. Private parking and flower filled garden.

B&B from £26pp, Dinner £22.50, Rooms 3 double, all en-suite, No smoking or pets, Children over 16, Open all year except Christmas.

Commander & Mrs Epperson, **Anchorage House Guest Lodge,** Nettles Corner, Tregreham, St. Austell, Cornwall PL25 3RH
Tel: 01726 814071   **Map Ref 57**

HEMBAL MANOR, a beautiful 16th century manor in six acres of grounds and gardens, tastefully decorated with period furniture. TV, tea/coffee making facilities and central heating in all bedrooms. Traditional or continental breakfasts served. Centrally situated to explore all places of interest. Especially the Lost Gardens of Heligan.

B&B from £25pp, Rooms 1 twin, 2 double, all en-suite, No smoking or pets, Children over 12, Open all year except Christmas & New Year.

Sue & Mike Higgs, **Hembal Manor,** Hembal Lane, Trewoon, St. Austell, Cornwall PL25 5TD
Tel/Fax: 01726 72144 Email: sue@hembalmanor.demon.co.uk   **Map Ref 62**

....

THE TOBY JUG, is run by a qualified chef and his wife this family guest house is in an ideal situation. Rooms overlooking harbour, the main shopping centre and many beaches. Nearby is fishing, surfing, tennis, golf, squash, bathing, boating, horse riding and trekking.

B&B from £15pp, Dinner from £7.50, Rooms 2 single, 3 twin, 2 double, 3 family, some en-suite, Children welcome, No pets, Open all year.
Bill & Margaret Stirling, **The Toby Jug,** 1 Park Avenue, St. Ives, Cornwall TR26 2DN
Tel: 01736 794250   **Map Ref 59**

....

CHY AN DOUR HOTEL, a former sea captains house with superb views over harbour, beaches and St Ives bay. All rooms en-suite with TV, tea/coffee making facilities. Ample car parking. Lift. Some ground floor rooms. Chef proprietor.
B&B from £31pp, Dinner from £15, Rooms 9 twin, 11 double, 3 family, all en-suite, Restricted smoking, Children over 5, No pets, Open all year except Christmas & New Year.
Mr & Mrs D B Watson, **Chy an Dour Hotel,** Trelyon Avenue, St. Ives, Cornwall TR26 2AD
Tel: 01736 796436 Fax: 01736 795772   **Map Ref 59**

....

POLKERR GUEST HOUSE, a period country house offering quality accommodation, central heating, TV and tea/coffee making facilities in all rooms. Ideal for touring, bathing, golf and coastal walks.

B&B from £17, Dinner available, Rooms 1 single, 1 twin, 3 double, 1 triple, 1 family, all private or en-suite, Children welcome, No pets, Open all year.

Polkerr Guest House, Tintagel, Cornwall PL34 0BY
Tel: 01840 770382   **Map Ref 63**

....

KING ARTHUR'S CASTLE HOTEL, located in one of the most spectacular parts of Cornwall, standing on a very high and rugged coastline which commands majestic views. Overlooks the ruins of Tintagel Castle, reputedly the home of King Arthur.

B&B from £25, Dinner available, Rooms 12 single, 18 twin, 14 double, 6 triple, most en-suite, No smoking, Children welcome, No pets, Open April - October.

King Arthur's Castle Hotel, Atlanta Road, Tintagel, Cornwall PL34 0DQ
Tel: 01840 770202 Fax: 01840 770978   **Map Ref 63**

BOSSINEY HOUSE HOTEL, a family run hotel set in two and a half acres of garden. Close to the castle and overlooking the beautiful north Cornwall coast.

B&B from £28, Dinner available, Rooms 9 twin, 8 double, 2 triple, 1 family, all en-suite or private facilities, Children welcome, Open March - October.

Bossiney House Hotel, Bossiney Road, Tintagel, Cornwall PL34 0AX
Tel: 01840 770240 & 370 951411 Fax: 01840 770501   **Map Ref 63**

....

THE WOOTONS COUNTRY HOTEL, located at entrance road to Tintagel Castle, reputedly home to King Arthur, and overlooking the Vale of Avalon.

B&B from £20, Dinner available, Rooms 1 single, 3 twin, 7 double, all en-suite, No smoking, Children welcome, No pets, Open all year.

The Wootons Country Hotel, Fore Street, Tintagel, Cornwall PL34 0DD
Tel: 01840 770170 Fax: 01840 770978   **Map Ref 63**

....

PORT WILLIAM INN, probably the best located inn in Cornwall, overlooking sea and beach. All rooms en-suite with TV and telephone. Extensive menu, including local seafood.

B&B from £35, Dinner available, Rooms 1 twin, 2 double, 1 triple, 2 family, all en-suite, No smoking, Children welcome, Open all year.

Port William Inn, Trebarwith Strand, Tintagel, Cornwall PL34 0HB
Tel: 01840 770230 Fax: 01840 770936   **Map Ref 64**

....

WILLAPARK MANOR HOTEL, one of the most beautifully situated hotels in England, set in 14 acres of garden and woodland, overlooking bay. Warm welcome and good cuisine ensure a memorable stay.

B&B from £26, Dinner available, Rooms 3 single, 2 twin, 7 double, 1 triple, 1 family, all en-suite, Children welcome, Open all year.

Willapark Manor Hotel, Bossiney, Tintagel, Cornwall PL34 0BA
Tel: 01840 770782   **Map Ref 65**

....

WHITSAND BAY HOTEL, a spectacularly sited elegant country mansion with sea views. Own 18 hole golf course. Indoor heated pools and leisure complex. Self catering units also available.

B&B from £21, Dinner available, Rooms 5 single, 9 twin, 9 double, 2 triple, 11 family, most en-suite, No smoking, Children welcome, Open March - December.

Whitsand Bay Hotel, Portwrinkle, Torpoint, Cornwall PL11 3BU
Tel: 01503 230276 Fax: 01503 230329   **Map Ref 66**

....

BLUE HAVEN HOTEL, is a small friendly licensed hotel in a spectacular peaceful location with panoramic sea views. Close to Looe and Polperro fishing harbours. Ideal for quiet, relaxing, touring/walking holidays. Nearby beach and village amenities. Bedrooms en-suite, tea/coffee, TV, central heating. Private parking.
B&B from £17pp, Dinner from £7.50, Rooms 1 single, 1 twin, 3 double, 1 family, all en-suite, Restricted smoking, Children welcome, Pets by arrangement,
Pat & David Rowlandson, **Blue Haven Hotel,** Looe Hill, Seaton, Torpoint, Cornwall PL11 3JQ
Tel: 01503 250310   **Map Ref 67**

87

MARCORRIE HOTEL, a family run hotel, 5 minutes walk from city centre and cathedral. Ideal for business or holiday, central for visiting the country houses and gardens of Cornwall.

B&B from £33, Dinner available, Rooms 3 single, 2 twin, 3 double, 1 triple, 3 family, most en-suite, No smoking, Children welcome, Open all year.

Marcorrie Hotel, 20 Falmouth Road, Truro, Cornwall TR1 2HX
Tel: 01872 277372 Fax: 01872 241666   **Map Ref 68**

....

CARLTON HOTEL, established, family run hotel with friendly atmosphere. Varied choice of menus. Sauna, spa bath and solarium available.

B&B from £33.50, Dinner available, Rooms Children welcome, Open all year.
Carlton Hotel, Falmouth Road, Truro, Cornwall TR1 2HL
Tel: 01872 272450 Fax: 01872 223938   **Map Ref 68**

....

ROCK COTTAGE, an 18th century beamed, cob cottage. Haven for non smokers. Bedrooms centrally heated, colour television, radio, beverage tray, hair dryer. Television/sitting room. Cosy dining room with antique Cornish range. Village location, 6 miles Truro, 3 miles ocean. Ample parking. Delightful gardens. ETB 3 Crown Highly Commended. VISA, Mastercard, Switch accepted.
B&B from £24pp, Dinner available, Rooms 1 twin, 2 double, all en-suite, No smoking, children or pets, Open all year except Christmas & New Year.
Shirley Wakeling, **Rock Cottage,** Blackwater, Truro, Cornwall TR4 8EU
Tel: 01872 560252 Fax: 01872 560252   **Map Ref 69**

....

VENTONGIMPS MILL BARN, is a converted mill barn of Cornish slate and stone. A steam runs through large gardens and lake. The cathedral city of Truro is 6 miles away. Evening meals served in our licensed bar. All rooms are en-suite and have TV. Perranporth with sandy beaches is 12 miles away.
B&B from £16pp, Dinner from £10.50, Rooms 1 single, 1 twin, 2 double, 4 family, all en-suite Restricted smoking, Children welcome, Open all year.
Mr & Mrs Gibson, **Ventongimps Mill Barn,** Ventongimps, Callestick, Truro, Cornwall TR4 9LH
Tel: 01872 573275   **Map Ref 70**

....

BISSICK OLD MILL, a 17th century water mill sympathetically converted to provide well appointed accommodation with exceptional standards of comfort, cuisine and hospitality. Central rural location makes ideal base for touring or business.

B&B from £35.25, Dinner available, Rooms 1 single, 1 twin, 2 double, all en-suite, No smoking, Children over 10, Open all year.

Bissick Old Mill, Ladock, Truro, Cornwall TR2 4PG
Tel: 01726 882557 Fax: 01726 884057   **Map Ref 71**

....

LUGGER HOTEL & RESTAURANT, a 17th century smugglers inn, at the waters edge in a quiet, picturesque cove, where fishing boats moor alongside.

B&B from £55, Dinner available, Rooms 3 single, 7 twin, 9 double, all en-suite, No smoking, Children over 12, No pets, Open March - October.
Lugger Hotel & Restaurant, Portloe, Truro, Cornwall TR2 5RD
Tel: 01872 501322 Fax: 01872 501691   **Map Ref 72**

GERRANS BAY HOTEL, set in superb countryside, near sandy beaches. Noted for food. Personal service and en-suite rooms.

B&B from £29, Dinner available, Rooms 2 single, 5 twin, 5 double, 2 family, all en-suite or private facilities, Children welcome, Open April - October.
Gerrans Bay Hotel, 12 Tregassick Road, Portscatho, Truro, Cornwall TR2 5ED
Tel: 01872 580338 Fax: 01872 580250   **Map Ref 73**

....

THE HUNDRED HOUSE HOTEL, a delightful 19th century house in a three acre garden, near St Mawes, Fal Estuary and twelve miles from Truro. Antiques, log fires and delicious dinners. Pretty en-suite bedrooms. Ideal for walking, touring, gardens and National Trust properties.

B&B from £37, Dinner available, Rooms 2 single, 4 double, 4 twin, 2 family, all en-suite, No smoking, Children welcome, Open March - October.
The Hundred House Hotel, Ruan High Lanes, Truro, Cornwall TR2 5JR
Tel: 01872 501336 Fax: 01872 501151   **Map Ref 68**

....

THE OLD MILL COUNTRY HOUSE, an 16th century mill with waterwheel. Set in own streamside gardens. Furnished with antiques and artifacts. Licensed. Guests lounge and own parking. Situated two miles from Padstow and centrally located for touring Cornwall. Personal attention from your hosts. Access at all times. Modern amenities with old world hospitality.

B&B from £26.75pp, Rooms 2 twin, 5 double, all en-suite, Restricted smoking, Children over 14, No pets, Open March - October.
Michael & Pat Walker, **The Old Mill Country House,** Little Petherick, Padstow, Wadebridge, Cornwall PL27 7QT
Tel: 01841 540388   **Map Ref 75**

....

SILVERMEAD GUEST HOUSE, a ten bedroom family run licensed guest house overlooking the Camel Estuary. Adjoining St. Enodoc Golf courses, two minutes walk to beach and water sports centre. Spacious accommodation, most en-suite. ETB Three Crown Commended.

B&B from £17.50-£23pp, Dinner from £10, Rooms 2 single, 2 twin, 2 double, 3 family, some en-suite, Restricted smoking, Children welcome, Open all year.
Barbara & Matthew Martin, **Silvermead Guest House,** Rock, Wadebridge, Cornwall PL27 6LB
Tel: 01208 862425 http://www.yell.co.uk/sites/silvermead/ **Map Ref 76**

....

HENDRA COUNTRY HOUSE, a 19th century manor house in quiet seclusion in rural tranquillity, situated three miles north east of Wadebridge. Exceptional menu using home grown produce. Warm, friendly atmosphere.

B&B from £22, Dinner available, Rooms 1 single, 2 twin, 2 double, all private facilities or en-suite, Children welcome, Open February - November & Christmas.
Hendra Country House, St Kew Highway, nr Wadebridge, Bodmin, Cornwall PL30 3EQ
Tel: 01208 841343 Fax: 01208 841343   **Map Ref 74**

....

WATERGATE BAY HOTEL, a family run hotel beside own beach on the coastal path. Wonderful indoor and outdoor leisure facilities. Dogs welcome. Spring and autumn super breaks available.

B&B from £25, Dinner available, Rooms 8 single, 4 twin, 20 double, 7 triple, 18 family, most en-suite, No smoking, Children welcome, Open March - November.

Watergate Bay Hotel, Watergate Bay, Cornwall TR8 4AA
Tel: 01637 860543 Fax: 01637 860333   **Map Ref 77**

Cumbria is a county for all seasons. Visitors are greeted by lambs and daffodils in the spring and the summer is perfect for enjoying the outdoor activities the county has to offer. Autumn's mellow hues and the snow-clad winter peaks have their own magic. The county's only city, Carlisle, still retains a fortress air with its mighty sandstone castle, city walls, cathedral and traffic free centre with a variety of shops.

Half a million acres of some of the most breathtaking landscape in the country lie in the Eden Valley. Alston, England's highest town at a thousand feet above sea level is surrounded by the North Pennines and villages which along with the town prospered with lead mining. The red sandstone town of Penrith is a popular shopping and market town. Further up the Eden Valley is the original county town of Westmorland, Appleby, famous for its horse fair in June. Beyond Brough and Kirkby Stephen in the Howgill Fells, the River Eden has its source and the landscape reflects the nearby Dales. To the west of the Lakes is St Bees Head with its priory church, extensive beaches and cliff head bird reserve. Other coastal towns include Whitehaven, Workington and Maryport with its maritime attractions.

In the north, Keswick is surrounded by superb walks with views of Derwentwater and Bassenthwaite Lake. In the Western Lakes, lanes meander inland from the coast towards peaks and valleys. Wastwater's screes lift straight from the deep water at the base of Scafell, England's highest point. Steep mountain passes such as Hardknott with a gradient of one in three climb over the mountains to the coast. Cockermouth is the birthplace of Wordsworth. South of Ullswater, over Kirkstone Pass, the highest region open to cars, is Ambleside at the head of Windermere, England's longest lake. Always crowded with walkers, Ambleside is the setting for the customary rush-bearing each July when children parade carrying rushes and flowers - a tradition from the Middle Ages when rushes carpeted churches. Boat trips can be taken from Waterhead, just south of Ambleside, along the full length of the lake.

Windermere has many easily reached vantage points with spectacular views. Kendal, the southern gateway to the Lakes grew up around the woollen trade and is known for its many fine old houses and buildings. On the western side of Lake Windermere is Far Sawrey where the children's writer Beatrix Potter lived at Hill Top Farm in the early 1900s. Donald Campbell made many attempts on the world waterspeed record at Coniston and was killed there in 1967. Grasmere is possibly most famous as the home of the poet William Wordsworth (1770-1850) who moved to Dove Cottage in 1799. Wordsworth's home from 1813 until his death was Rydal Mount, south of the village.

left, River Derwent, Borrowdale

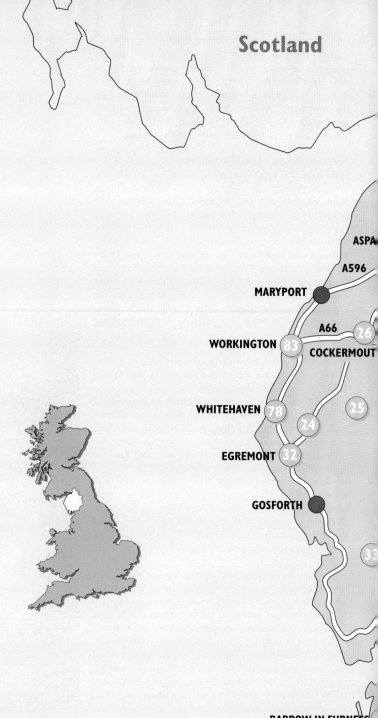

Scotland

ASPA

A596

MARYPORT

A66

WORKINGTON 83

COCKERMOUT

26

WHITEHAVEN 78

24

25

EGREMONT 32

GOSFORTH

33

BARROW IN FURNESS

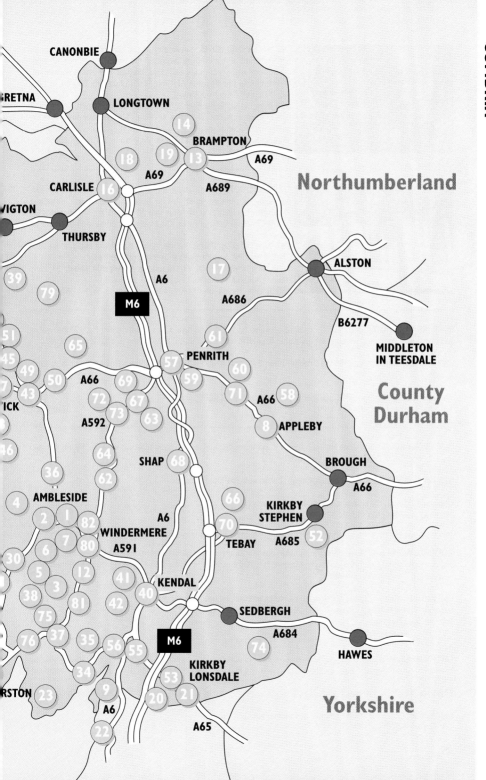

CUMBRIA

THE WATERHEAD HOTEL, situated on the shores of Lake Windermere with spectacular views from many of the rooms. A choice of three contrasting settings to relax and dine. Elegant Waterfront Restaurant. Mediterranean Bar Bistro or McGinity's Irish Fun Pub. Full use of Low Wood Leisure Club 1 mile away.
B&B from £41pp, Dinner from £8.95, Rooms 4 single, 11 twin, 11 double, 2 family, most en-suite, Restricted smoking, Children welcome, Pets by arrangement, Open all year.
Michael Kay, **The Waterhead Hotel,** Ambleside, Cumbria LA22 0ER
Tel: 015394 32566 Fax: 015394 31255 **Map Ref 1**

CHURCHILL HOTEL, main street location in the centre of Ambleside, private parking to the rear. 10 minutes from lake Windermere, shops and local amenities literally on the door step. Very popular public bar with the hearty Churchill Eatery. Tea/coffee making facilities to each room, all rooms en-suite.
B&B from £21.50pp, Rooms 2 single, 2 twin, 8 double, 2 family, all en-suite, Children welcome, No pets, Open all year except Christmas.
Mark, Michelle, Craig & Mel Routledge, **Churchill Hotel,** 33 Lane Road, Ambleside, Cumbria LA22 0BH
Tel: 015394 33192 Fax: 015394 34900 **Map Ref 1**

BORRANS PARK HOTEL, is peacefully situated between the village and lake. Enjoy candlelit dinners, 120 fine wines and four poster bedrooms with private spa baths. Tea.coffee making facilities. ETB 3 Crowns Highly Commended.

B&B from £30, Dinner available, Rooms 9 double, 1 twin, 2 triple, all en-suite, Children from 7 years, No pets, No smoking, Open all year.

Borrans Park Hotel, Borrans Road, Ambleside, Cumbria LA22 0EN
Tel: 015394 33454 Fax: 015394 33003 **Map Ref 1**

CLAREMONT HOUSE, all rooms have a colour TV and tea/coffee making facilities, most are en-suite. Family run and friendly atmosphere. ETB 2 Crowns Approved.

B&B from £14, Rooms 2 single, 3 double, 1 triple, Children welcome, Open all year.

Claremont House, Compston Road, Ambleside, Cumbria LA22 9DJ
Tel: 015394 33448 Fax: 015394 33448 **Map Ref 1**

EASEDALE GUEST HOUSE, a charming Victorian house with private car park. Overlooking Loughrigg Fell and tennis courts. Friendly and comfortable, serving generous breakfasts. Advice given for walking and sightseeing. No smoking, please. ETB 2 Crowns Commended.

B&B from £32, Rooms 7 double, some en-suite, Children welcome, No pets, Open all year.
Easedale Guest House, Compston Road, Ambleside, Cumbria LA22 9DJ
Tel: 015394 32112 **Map Ref 1**

LATTENDALES, a traditional Lakeland home in the heart of Ambleside. A central base for walking and touring, offering comfortable accommodation and local produce. Tea/coffee making facilities in all rooms. ETB 2 Crowns Commended.

B&B from £15, Dinner available, Rooms 2 single, 2 double, 2 twin, some en-suite, Children welcome, No smoking, Open all year.

Lattendales, Compston Road, Ambleside, Cumbria LA22 9DJ
Tel: 015394 32368 **Map Ref 1**

SMALLWOOD HOUSE HOTEL, a family run hotel in a central position offering a warm and friendly service, good home cooking and value-for-money quality and standards. ETB 3 Crowns Commended.

B&B from £25, Lunch and evening meal available, Rooms 6 double, 3 twin, 2 triple, 2 family rooms, most en-suite, Children welcome, No smoking, Open all year.
Smallwood House Hotel, Compston Road, Ambleside, Cumbria LA22 9DJ
Tel: 015394 32330   **Map Ref 1**

....

THORNEYFIELD GUEST HOUSE, is a cosy family run guest house in the town centre with friendly and helpful service. Close to the park, miniature golf, tennis and lake. Large family rooms available. ETB 2 Crowns Commended.

B&B from £14, Rooms 3 double, 1 triple, 2 family, all en-suite/private facilities, Children over5, No pets, No smoking, Open all year.
Thorneyfield Guest House, Compston Road, Ambleside, Cumbria LA22 9DJ
Tel: 015394 32464 Fax: 015394 32464 Email: doano@thorneyfield.demon.co.uk   **Map Ref 1**

....

KIRKSTONE FOOT COUNTRY HOUSE HOTEL, is a secluded 17th century manor house and renowned restaurant. Set in its own grounds, with adjoining self contained apartments and cottages.ETB 4 Crowns Highly Commended.

B&B from £35, Dinner available, Rooms 9 double, 3 twin, 1 triple, all en-suite, Children welcome, No pets, No smoking, Open February - December.
Kirkstone Foot Country House Hotel, Kirkstone Pass Road, Ambleside, Cumbria LA22 9EH
Tel: 015394 32232 Fax: 015394 32232   **Map Ref 1**

....

ROWANFIELD COUNTRY GUESTHOUSE, is idyllicly set with panoramic views of the lake and mountains. Laura Ashley style decor. Scrumptious food created by proprietor/chef. Superior room available at supplement. Car parking. ETB 2 Crowns Highly Commended.

B&B from £60, Dinner available, Rooms 5 double, 1 twin, 1 triple, all en-suite, Children over 8, No pets, No smoking, Open March - December.
Rowanfield Country Guesthouse, Kirkstone Road, Ambleside, Cumbria LA22 9ET
Tel: 015394 33686 Fax: 015394 31569   **Map Ref 1**

....

ELDER GROVE HOTEL, a delightful small hotel, owned and managed by the Haywood family, offering comfortable en-suite accommodation, delicious food and wines. Heating. Car parking. ETB 3 Crowns Commended.

B&B from £25, Dinner available, Rooms 2 single, 7 double, 2 twin, 1 triple, all en-suite, Children over 5, No smoking, Open February - November.
Elder Grove Hotel, Lake Road, Ambleside, Cumbria LA22 0DB
Tel: 015394 32504 Fax: 015394 32504   **Map Ref 1**

....

LAUREL VILLA, a detached Victorian house, visited by Beatrix potter. En-suite bedrooms overlooking the fells. Within easy reach of Lake Windermere and village. Private car park. ETB 3 Crowns Highly Commended.

B&B from £50, Dinner available, Rooms 7 double, 1 twin, all en-suite, No pets, No smoking, Open all year.
Laurel Villa, Lake Road, Ambleside, Cumbria LA22 0DB
Tel: 015394 33240   **Map Ref 1**

....

FISHERBECK HOTEL, noted for hospitality, service and comfort, with some refurbished superior rooms. Fine food, sheltered garden, car parking and fell views. Special breaks available. Leisure club facilities. Fishing. ETB 4 Crowns Commended.

B&B from £29, Lunch and evening meal available, Rooms 1 single, 14 double, 2 twin, 3 triple, most en-suite, Children welcome, No pets, Open all year.
Fisherbeck Hotel, Lake Road, Ambleside, Cumbria LA22 0DH
Tel: 015394 33215 Fax: 015394 33600   **Map Ref 1**

WATERHEAD HOTEL, situated on the edge of Lake Windermere, an ideal central base for touring the lovely English Lakes. Ample car parking. Tea/coffee making facilities. ETB 4 Crowns Commended.

B&B from £40, Lunch and evening meal available, Rooms 4 single, 12 double, 11 twin, 1 triple, all en-suite, Children welcome, No smoking, Open all year.
Waterhead Hotel, Lake Road, Ambleside, Cumbria LA22 0ER
Tel: 015394 32566 Fax: 015394 31255   **Map Ref 1**

....

THE SALUTATION HOTEL, a traditional hotel overlooking central Ambleside, with comfortable rooms and leisure facilities available. Warm and friendly welcome assured. Car parking. ETB 4 Crowns Highly Commended.

B&B from £34, Lunch and evening meal available, Rooms 3 single, 21 double, 8 twin, 4 triple, all en-suite, Children welcome, Open all year.
The Salutation Hotel, Lake Road, Ambleside, Cumbria LA22 9BX
Tel: 015394 32244 Fax: 015394 34157   **Map Ref 1**

....

QUEENS HOTEL, In the heart of the Lakes and convenient for walking, climbing and other leisure activities. 2 fully licensed bars, choice of restaurant or bar meals. Tea/coffee making facilities. ETB 3 Crowns Commended.

B&B from £25, Lunch and evening meal available, Rooms 4 single, 14 double, 3 twin, 2 triple, 3 family rooms, all en-suite, Children welcome, No pets, No smoking, Open all year.
Queens Hotel, Market Place, Ambleside, Cumbria LA22 9BU
Tel: 015394 32206 Fax: 015394 32721   **Map Ref 1**

....

RIVERSIDE LODGE, superbly situated in a unique riverside setting just a short walk from the centre of Ambleside and the head of Lake Windermere. The house has been refurbished to a high standard exuding great character and charm with stone-flag floors and beamed ceilings.

B&B from £23-£30pp, Rooms 1 twin, 3 double, 1 family, all en-suite, Restricted smoking, No children or pets, Open all year.
Alan & Gillian Rhone, **Riverside Lodge,** Rothay Bridge, Ambleside, Cumbria LA22 0EH
Tel: 015394 34208   **Map Ref 1**

....

ROTHAY MANOR HOTEL, an elegant Regency country house hotel with a well known restaurant. Balcony rooms overlook the garden. Suites for families and disabled guests. Free use of nearby leisure club. ETB 4 Crowns Highly Commended.

B&B from £79, Lunch and evening meal available, Rooms 2 single, 5 double, 3 twin, 5 triple, 3 family rooms, suites available, all en-suite, Children welcome, No pets, No smoking, Open February - December.
Rothay Manor Hotel, Rothay Bridge, Ambleside, Cumbria LA22 0EH
Tel: 015394 33605 Fax: 015394 33607   **Map Ref 1**

....

ROTHAY GARTH HOTEL, is a distinctive Victorian country house with elegant Loughrigg restaurant overlooking lovely garden and nearby mountains. Close to village centre and Lake Windermere. All season breaks. ETB 4 Crowns Commended.

B&B from £36, Lunch and evening meal available, Rooms 2 single, 9 double, 2 twin, 2 triple, 1 family room, most en-suite, Children welcome, No smoking, Open all year.
Rothay Garth Hotel, Rothay Road, Ambleside, Cumbria LA22 0EE
Tel: 015394 32217 Fax: 015394 34400   **Map Ref 1**

THE RYSDALE HOTEL, a family run hotel with magnificent views over park and fells. Good food, licenced bar. Friendly, personal service. Ideal walking base. Limited car parking. ETB 2 Crowns Commended.

B&B from £16, Rooms 4 single, 4 double, 1 triple, most en-suite, Children from 8 years, No smoking, Open all year.
The Rysdale Hotel, Rothay Road, Ambleside, Cumbria LA22 0EE
Tel: 015394 32140 & 33999   **Map Ref 1**

....

THE ANCHORAGE, is a modern detached guesthouse offering a good standard of accommodation and own private car park. 300 metres from the town centre and amenities. ETB 2 Crowns Commended.

B&B from £36, Rooms 4 double, 1 twin, most en suite, No smoking, No pets, Open February-November.
The Anchorage, Rydal Road, Ambleside, Cumbria LA22 9AY
Tel: 015394 32046   **Map Ref 1**

....

2 SWISS VILLAS, a small Victorian terrace house set just off the main road in the centre of Ambleside. There are three double bedrooms (one with twin beds) recently refurbished in the traditional style. Each room has central heating, tea/coffee facilities and colour TV. A full English or vegetarian breakfast available.

B&B from £18pp, Rooms 1 twin, 2 double, Open all year.
David Sowerbutts, **2 Swiss Villas,** Vicarage Road, Ambleside, Cumbria LA22 9AE
Tel: 015394 32691   **Map Ref 1**

....

THE OLD VICARAGE, a quietly situated hotel in own grounds in the heart of the village. Car park, quality en-suite accommodation, friendly service. Family run. ETB 2 Crowns Commended.

B&B from £46, Rooms 7 double, 1 twin, 1 triple, 1 family room, all en-suite, Children & pets welcome, No smoking Open all year.
The Old Vicarage, Vicarage Road, Ambleside, Cumbria LA22 9DH
Tel: 015394 33364 Fax: 015394 34734   **Map Ref 1**

....

LYNDHURST HOTEL, a small, attractive Lakeland hotel with private car park. Quietly situated for the town and lake. Pretty rooms, delicious food - a delightful experience. ETB 2 Crowns Commended.

B&B from £20, Dinner available, Rooms 5 double, 1 twin, all en-suite, No pets, Open all year.
Lyndhurst Hotel, Wansfell Road, Ambleside, Cumbria LA22 0EG
Tel: 015394 32421   **Map Ref 1**

....

Small family run hotel on quiet country lane, yet only 5 minutes walk into Ambleside. **RIVERSIDE HOTEL** is central for most walking and sightseeing trips. There are tea/coffee making facilities, hair dryers, bath robes and TV's in all rooms. Private parking.

B&B from £30pp, Rooms 4 en-suite double, Restricted smoking, Children over 10, No pets, Open March - November.
James & Jean Hainey, **Riverside Hotel,** Under Loughrigg, Ambleside, Cumbria LA22 9LJ
Tel/Fax: 015394 32395   **Map Ref 1**

....

WATEREDGE HOTEL, a delightfully situated hotel on the shores of Windermere, the family run Wateredge offers quiet relaxation, elegant comfort, excellent cuisine, beautiful lake views and, above all, personal unobtrusive service. ETB 4 Crowns Highly Commended.

B&B from £45, Lunch and evening meal available, Rooms 3 single, 11 double, 8 twin, all en-suite, Children from 7 years, Car parking, Open February - December.
Wateredge Hotel, Waterhead Bay, Ambleside, Cumbria LA22 0EP
Tel: 015394 32332 Fax: 015394 31878   **Map Ref 1**

GHYLL HEAD HOTEL, a family hotel in a good position overlooking Lake Windermere and ideal for touring the Lake District. Car Parking. ETB 3 Crowns Approved.

B&B from £24.50, Dinner available, Rooms 3 single, 3 double, 1 twin, 7 triple, 1 family room, most en-suite, Children welcome, Open all year.
Ghyll Head Hotel, Waterhead, Ambleside, Cumbria LA22 0HD
Tel: 015394 32360 & 0500 200148 (Freephone)   **Map Ref 1**

....

ELTERMERE COUNTRY HOUSE HOTEL, a friendly country house hotel in a quiet rural setting in the heart of the Langdale valley. Personally run by the owners.

B&B from £27, Dinner available, Rooms 3 single, 9 double, 6 twin, most en-suite, Children welcome, No pets, No smoking, Open all year.
Eltermere Country House Hotel, Elterwater, Ambleside, Cumbria LA22 9HY
Tel: 015394 37207   **Map Ref 2**

....

THE SAWREY HOTEL, a fully licensed 18th century inn, one mile from Windermere car ferry on B5285. 18 bedrooms with bath. Two bars. Excellent traditional English cooking, menu changed daily. Bar snacks served daily at lunchtime. Ample parking. Children and dogs welcome.

B&B from £29pp, DBB £39, Dinner from £16.50, Rooms 2 single, 8 twin, 6 double, 3 family, all en-suite, Children & pets welcome, Open all year except Christmas.

The Sawrey Hotel, Far Sawrey, Ambleside LA22 0LQ
Tel: 015394 43425   **Map Ref 3**

....

WEST VALE COUNTRY GUEST HOUSE, a warm welcome awaits you at this peaceful family run guest house, with home cooking, log fire and fine views.

B&B from £24, Evening meal available, Rooms 5 double, 1 twin, 2 triple, all en-suite/private facilities, Children from 7 years, No pets, Open March - October.
West Vale Country Guest House, Far Sawrey, Ambleside, Cumbria LA22 0LQ
Tel: 015394 42817   **Map Ref 3**

....

LANGDALE HOTEL & COUNTRY CLUB, an en-suite hotel, winner of the 1986 Civic Trust environmental award, in 35 acres of wooded grounds. Indoor country club, large pool, spa bath, sports facilities, restaurants and bars. Minimum stay 2 nights. ETB 5 Crowns Highly Commended.

B&B from £85, Lunch and evening meal available, Rooms 41 double, 24 twin, all en-suite, Children welcome, No pets, No smoking, Open all year.
Langdale Hotel & Country Club, Great Langdale, Ambleside, Cumbria LA22 9JD
Tel: 015394 37302 Fax: 015394 37694   **Map Ref 4**

....

GREENBANK HOUSE HOTEL, offers a friendly personal service, lovely views, open fire, central heating, good home cooking, tea/coffee making facilities and a cosy lounge with colour TV. Residential licensed. Ample parking. Centrally positioned for exploring the Lake District, either by car or on foot.

B&B from £21pp, Rooms 4 single, 1 twin, 6 double, 1 family, some en-suite, Restricted smoking, Children welcome, Pets by arrangement, Open all year.
Frank & Barbara Squires, **Greenbank House Hotel,** Hawkshead, Ambleside, Cumbria LA22 0NS
Tel: 015394 36497   **Map Ref 5**

BORWICK LODGE, an award winning accommodation of the highest standards. A rather special 17th century country house with magnificent panoramic views. Quietly secluded in the heart of the Lakes, close to restaurants and inns. Beautiful bedrooms all en-suite also two four poster king size rooms. Non-smoking. Residential licence.
B&B from £20pp, Rooms 1 twin,4 double, 1 family, No smoking or pets, Children over 8, Open all year.
Colin & Rosemary Haskell, **Borwick Lodge,** Outgate, Hawkshead, Ambleside, Cumbria LA22 0PU
Tel: 015394 36332 Fax: 015394 36332   **Map Ref 5**

....

BELMOUNT COUNTRY HOUSE, a fine, family-run Georgian house standing in 3 acres . Superb views. Warm welcome.

B&B from £22.50, Dinner available, Rooms 3 double, 2 twin, 3 triple, 2 family, Children welcome, No smoking, Open all year.

Belmount Country House, Outgate, Ambleside, Cumbria LA22 0NJ
Tel: 015394 36535   **Map Ref 6**

....

TOWER BANK INN, is next door to Hilltop, the home of the late Beatrix Potter Ideally situated for walking, bird watching and sailing. Rooms have colour TV, tea/coffee making facilities and full central heating. There is no separate guests lounge. Bar meals available every day, lunch and night.

B&B from £24pp, Dinner from £6, Rooms 1 twin, 2 double, all en-suite, Smokers welcome, Pets by arrangement, Open all year except Christmas.
Philip James Broadley, **Tower Bank Inn,** Sawrey, Hawkshead, Ambleside, Cumbria LA22 0LF
Tel: 015394 36334 Fax: 015394 36334   **Map Ref 3**

....

THREE SHIRES INN, a traditional Lakeland inn near the foot of Wrynose Pass in beautiful Little Langdale Valley. An ideal area for walkers and touring.

B&B from £27, Lunch & evening meal available, Rooms 5 double, 5 twin, all en-suite, Children welcome, No pets or smoking, Open February - December.

Three Shires Inn, Little Langdale, Ambleside, Cumbria LA22 9NZ
Tel: 015394 37215 Fax: 015394 37127   **Map Ref 4**

....

SAWREY HOUSE COUNTRY HOTEL, a warm friendly atmosphere. Quality bedrooms, many with lake views, good food, log fire. Hotel overlooks Esthwaite Waters, magnificent views.

B&B from £35, Dinner available, Rooms 1 single, 6 double, 2 twin, 2 triple, all en-suite, Children welcome, No smoking, Open February - December.

Sawrey House Country Hotel, Near Sawrey, Ambleside, Cumbria LA22 0LF
Tel: 015394 36387 Fax: 015394 36010   **Map Ref 3**

....

BUCKLE YEAT GUEST HOUSE, an old cottage guest house with log fires. Centrally situated for touring Lakeland, walking, bird-watching. Central heating throughout.

B&B from £22.50, Rooms 1 single, 4 double, 2 twin, all en-suite/private facilities, Children welcome, Open all year.

Buckle Yeat Guest House, Sawrey , Ambleside, Cumbria LA22 0LF
Tel: 015394 36446 & 36538 Fax: 015394 36446   **Map Ref 3**

EES WYKE COUNTRY HOUSE, a charming Georgian country house overlooking the peaceful and beautiful Esthwaite Water. Fine views of the lake, mountains and fells.

B&B from £42, Dinner available, Rooms 5 double,3 twin, all en-suite/private facilities, Children from 8 years, No smoking, Open March - December.

Ees Wyke Country House, Sawrey, Ambleside, Cumbria LA22 0JZ
Tel: 015394 36393 Fax: 015394 36393   **Map Ref 3**

....

THE DOWER HOUSE, the house overlooks Lake Windermere, 3 miles from Ambleside. Through the main gates of Wray Castle and up the drive. Tea/coffee making facilities in all rooms. ETB 2 Crowns Commended.

B&B from £22, Dinner available, Rooms 2 double, 1 twin, Children from 5 years, No pets, Open all year.
The Dower House, Wray Castle, Ambleside, Cumbria LA22 0JA
Tel: 015394 33211   **Map Ref 7**

....

BONGATE HOUSE, a family run Georgian guesthouse on the outskirts of a small market town. Large garden. Relaxed atmosphere, good home cooking. ETB 3 Crowns Commended.

B&B from £17.50, Dinner available, Rooms 1 single, 3 double, 2 twin, 1 triple, 1 family room, some en-suite, Children from 7 years, No smoking, Open all year.

Bongate House, Appleby-in-Westmorland, Cumbria CA16 6UE
Tel: 017683 51245   **Map Ref 8**

....

APPLEBY MANOR COUNTRY HOUSE HOTEL, everything you need for a perfect time: beautiful, spotlessly-clean en-suite bedrooms, log fires in luxurious lounges, imaginative meals in the award-winning restaurant and a super indoor leisure club. Explore the breathtaking beauty of the Lake District and Yorkshire Dales, play golf, ride horseback enjoy yourself. Email: appleby.manor@btinternet.com
B&B from £49pp, Dinner from £9, Rooms 8 twin, 13 double, 9 family, all en-suite, Restricted smoking, Children & pets welcome, Open all year.
Nick & Rachel Swinscoe, **Appleby Manor Country House Hotel,** Roman Road, Appleby-in-Westmorland, Cumbria CA16 6JB
Tel: 017683 51571 Fax: 017683 52888   **Map Ref 8**

....

WILLOWFIELD HOTEL, a relaxing, family-run, small private hotel for non-smokers. Quietly located with stunning estuary views towards the Lakeland hills. Separate lounge and well furnished bedrooms with colour TV etc. Good traditional English food (table license) including hearty breakfasts. Only 71/2 miles from M6 J36.

B&B from £24pp, Dinner from £12, Rooms 2 single, 3 twin, 3 double, 2 family, most en-suite, No smoking, Children welcome, Pets by arrangement, Open all year.
Ian & Janet Kerr, **Willowfield Hotel,** The Promenade, Arnside LA5 0AD
Tel: 01524 761354   **Map Ref 9**

....

CASTLEMONT, is a Victorian family residence set in 2 acres of garden with unrestricted views of the Northern Lakeland fell and Solway Firth. Built of Lazonby stone Castlemont combines the best of gracious living with all modern facilities. Full breakfast menu. Major credit cards accepted.

B&B from £18pp, Rooms 1 single, 1 twin, 1 double en-suite, 1 family, No smoking, Children welcome, Open all year.
David & Eleanor Lines, **Castlemont,** Aspatria, Cumbria CA5 2JU
Tel: 016973 20205   **Map Ref 10**

ARLINGTON HOUSE HOTEL & RESTAURANT, a relaxed hotel with elegant restaurant. In the town, yet not far away from the Lakes and sea. Tea/coffee making facilities. ETB 4 Crowns Highly Commended.

B&B from £52, Dinner available, Rooms 2 double, 6 twin, all en-suite, Children welcome, No pets, Open all year.
Arlington House Hotel & Restaurant, 200-202 Abbey Road, Barrow-in-Furness, Cumbria LA14 5LD
Tel: 01229 831976 Fax: 01229 870990 **Map Ref 11**

....

ABBEY HOUSE HOTEL, a friendly country house hotel, in idyllic location for that romantic weekend and excellent base for touring the Lake District. Car parking. ETB 4 Crowns Commended.

B&B from £44.95, Lunch and evening meal available, Rooms 3 single, 14 double, 5 twin, 6 triple, all en-suite, Children welcome, No smoking, Open all year.
Abbey House Hotel, Abbey Road, Barrow-in-Furness, Cumbria LA13 0PA
Tel: 01229 838282 Fax: 01229 820403 **Map Ref 11**

....

CRANLEIGH HOTEL, is a comfortable, clean and quiet and only 2 minutes walk to the lake and village with free use of private leisure club. Centrally heated, en-suite rooms with colour TV and tea trays. Two lounges. Bar. Dining room. Garden. Car park. Lots to do locally. Good centre for Lakes, Dales and south west Scotland.
B&B from £23pp, Dinner from £12.95, Rooms 3 twin, 8 double, 4 family, all en-suite, Restricted smoking, Children welcome, No pets, Open all year except Christmas.
Mr & Mrs A D Wigglesworth, **Cranleigh Hotel,** Kendal Road, Bowness on Windermere, Cumbria LA23 3EW
Tel: 015394 43293 **Map Ref 12**

....

VIRGINIA COTTAGE, a charming 19th century cottage, 1 minute from the lake, shops, restaurants and entertainment. Wide range of rooms, friendly atmosphere, family run.

B&B from £18, Rooms 1 single, 7 double, 3 triple, most en-suite, Children welcome, Open all year.
Virginia Cottage, 1-2 Crown Villas, Kendal Road, Bowness-on-Windermere, Cumbria LA23 3EJ
Tel: 015394 44891 **Map Ref 12**

....

LANGDALE VIEW GUEST HOUSE, a quiet guest house with home cooking. En-suite rooms, some with views. Non smoking. friendly atmosphere. Will collect from station.

B&B from £17, Dinner available, Rooms 1 single, 3 double, 1 twin, all en-suite/private facilities, Children from 5 years, No pets or smoking, Open all year.
Langdale View Guest House, 114 Craig Walk, off Helm Road, Bowness-on-Windermere, Cumbria LA23 3AX
Tel: 015394 44076 **Map Ref 12**

....

BELSFIELD HOUSE, a family run guesthouse in the heart of Bowness, 2 minutes walk from the lake front.

B&B from £21, Rooms 2 single, 3 double, 4 triple, all en-suite, Children welcome, No pets, Open all year.
Belsfield House, 4 Belsfield Terrace, Kendal Road, Bowness-on-Windermere, Cumbria LA23 3EQ
Tel: 015394 45823 **Map Ref 12**

....

THE BURN HOW GARDEN HOUSE HOTEL & MOTEL, a unique combination of Victorian houses and private chalets in secluded gardens in the heart of a picturesque village. Full facilities. Four poster beds available.

B&B from £57, Lunch and evening meal available, Rooms 2 single, 8 double, 8 twin, 8 triple, all en-suite, Children welcome, No pets, No smoking, Open February - December.
The Burn How Garden House Hotel & Motel, Back Belsfield Road, Bowness-on-Windermere, Cumbria LA23 3HH
Tel: 015394 46226 Fax: 015394 47000 **Map Ref 12**

ELIM HOUSE, family run, warm, friendly accommodation with lake and shops close by. Offers breakfast, en-suite rooms with TV and tea/coffee making facilities. Private car park.

B&B from £18, Rooms 8 double, most en-suite, Children from 10 years, No pets, Open all year.

Elim House, Biskey Howe Road, Bowness-on-Windermere, Cumbria LA23 2JP
Tel: 015394 42021   **Map Ref 12**

....

THE FAIRFIELD, is a small friendly 200 year old Lakeland hotel set in a peaceful garden environment. Close to Bowness village and Lake Windermere. The en-suite bedrooms are tastefully furnished having colour TV and welcome trays. Residents lounge with bar. Breakfasts are a speciality. Leisure facilities.
B&B from £24-£31pp, Rooms 1 single, 1 twin, 5 double, 2 family, all en-suite, No smoking or pets, Children welcome, Open February - November.
Ray & Barbara Hood, **The Fairfield,** Brantfell Road, Bowness-on-Windermere, Cumbria LA23 3AE
Tel/Fax: 015394 46565 Email: ray+barb@the-fairfield.co.uk   **Map Ref 12**

....

LINTHWAITE HOUSE HOTEL, situated in a peaceful location, in 14 acres of gardens, 1 mile south of the village and with panoramic views over the lake.

B&B from £90, Lunch and evening meal available, Rooms 1 single, 13 double, 4 twin, suite available, all en-suite, Children from 7 years, No pets, No smoking, Open all year.

Linthwaite House Hotel, Crook Road, Bowness-on-Windermere, Cumbria LA23 3JA
Tel: 015394 88600 Fax: 015394 88601 Email: admin@linhotel.u-net.com   **Map Ref 12**

....

OAKBANK HOUSE, has panoramic views of the lake , and just 1 minute from shops and restaurants. Spacious, comfortable, tastefully furnished rooms, all en-suite. Friendly family-run hotel.

B&B from £25, Rooms 3 double, 2 twin, 6 triple, all en-suite/private facilities, Children welcome, No smoking, Open all year.

Oakbank House, Helm Road, Bowness-on-Windermere, Cumbria LA23 3BU
Tel: 015394 43386   **Map Ref 12**

....

BURNSIDE HOTEL, set in extensive gardens with superb views over Lake Windermere, 300 yards from the steamboat pier and village centre. Full leisure centre. Wheelchair access.

B&B from £50, Lunch and evening meal available, Rooms 1 single, 30 double, 11 twin, 11 triple, 4 family, suites available, all en-suite, Children welcome, No pets or smoking, Open all year.

Burnside Hotel, Kendal Road, Bowness-on-Windermere, Cumbria LA23 3EP
Tel: 015394 42211 & 44530 Fax: 015394 43824   **Map Ref 12**

....

LINDETH HOWE COUNTRY HOUSE HOTEL, a 19th Century country house hotel hidden in 6 acres of beautiful, secluded gardens overlooking Lake Windermere. Cosy bar and log fires on chilly evenings. All rooms have satellite colour TV, direct dial telephone and baby listening, some have spa bath. Sauna, sunbeds. Free membership of local leisure club.

B&B from £48.50, Dinner available, Rooms 9 double, 2 twin, 3 triple, all en-suite, Children welcome, No pets or smoking, Open February - December.

Lindeth Howe Country House Hotel, Longtail Hill, Bowness-on-Windermere, Cumbria LA23 3JF
Tel: 015394 45759 Fax: 015394 46368 Email: lindeth.howe@dialin.net   **Map Ref 12**

FAYRER GARDEN HOUSE HOTEL, overlooks Lake Windermere in 5 acres grounds. Elegant lounges. Award winning air conditioned Restaurant. Some 4 posters bedrooms with whirlpool baths. Free use of local leisure centre. Peaceful yet convenient for touring. Lakeland special breaks. Colour brochure available.
B&B from £32.50pp, Dinner from £21, Rooms 1 single, 4 twin, 17 double, 3 family, all en-suite, Restricted smoking, Children welcome, Open all year.
Mr & Mrs I Garside, **Fayrer Garden House Hotel,** Lyth Valley Road, Bowness-on-Windermere, Cumbria LA23 3JP
Tel: 015394 88195 Fax: 015394 45986 **Map Ref 12**

BOWFELL COTTAGE, set in a delightful location, about 1 mile south of Bowness just off the A5074, offering traditional Lakeland hospitality.

B&B from £18, Dinner available, Rooms 1 double, 1 twin, 1 triple, Children welcome, Open all year.

Bowfell Cottage, Middle Entrance Drive, Storrs Park, Bowness-on-Windermere, Cumbria LA23 3JY
Tel:015394 44835 **Map Ref 12**

THE ROYAL HOTEL, offering hotel accommodation in the Lake District at affordable prices. For a completely unique holiday experience, try out one of the theme rooms. Two superb hotel bars with McGinty's Irish Fun Pub and Circuit Sports Bar. Full use of Low Wood Leisure Club and 50ft pool.

B&B from £29.50pp, Rooms 6 single, 3 twin, 15 double, 5 family, all en-suite, Children & pets welcome, Open all year.
Maria Walker, **The Royal Hotel,** Queen's Square, Bowness-on-Windermere, Cumbria LA23 3DB
Tel: 015394 43045 Fax: 015394 44990 **Map Ref 12**

ROYAL HOTEL, a hotel with a difference. Exciting new themed rooms, McGinty's Irish fun pub and the Circuit sports bar. Free unlimited use of superb leisure club.

B&B from £25.95, Rooms 6 single, 14 double, 3 twin, 6 triple, all en-suite, Children welcome, No smoking, Open all year.

Royal Hotel, Queens Square, Bowness-on-Windermere, Cumbria LA23 3DB
Tel: 015394 43045 Fax: 015394 44990 **Map Ref 12**

BROOKLANDS, a comfortable guesthouse in rural setting on the outskirts of Bowness village, with lake and mountain views. Close to Lake Windermere marina and shops. Golf nearby. Car parking.

B&B from £16, Rooms 1 single, 1 double, 1 twin, 3 triple, all en-suite/private facilities, Children welcome, Open all year.

Brooklands, Ferry View, Bowness-on-Windermere, Cumbria LA23 3JB
Tel: 015394 42344 **Map Ref 12**

SANDS HOUSE HOTEL, is a fully licenced 17th century coaching inn, with famous restaurant. En-suite rooms with colour TV, tea/coffee making facilities and telephone. On A69, close to Hadrians Wall and Lanercost Priory. ETB 1 Crown Commended.

B&B from £34, Lunch and evening meal available, Rooms 4 double, 4 twin, 2 triple, some en-suite, Children welcome, Open all year.

Sands House Hotel, The Sands, Brampton, Cumbria CA8 1UG
Tel: 016977 3085 Fax: 016977 3297 **Map Ref 13**

CENTURION INN, lies on Hadrians Wall and is open from 12.30 daily, lunch and dinner evening meals available. All rooms have TV and coffee facilities. Carlisle and sections of the Roman Wall are within easy reach of the inn. A car park is provided.

B&B from £16pp, Dinner from £3.50, Rooms 1 twin, 2 double, Children welcome, No pets, Open all year.
Eric & Barbara Summers, **Centurion Inn,** Walton, Brampton, Cumbria CA8 2DH
Tel: 01697 72438   **Map Ref 14**

THE GARNER GUEST HOUSE, a comfortable Victorian family house of character, with sunny walled garden. On the outskirts of this old market town. Tea/coffee making facilities. ETB 2 Crowns Commended.

B&B from £23, Rooms 1 double, 1 twin, both en-suite, Children from 5 years, Open all year.
The Garner Guest House, Church Street, Broughton-in-Furness, Cumbria LA20 6HJ
Tel: 01229 716462   **Map Ref 15**

ECCLE RIGGS MANOR HOTEL & LEISURE PARK LTD, is a Victorian mansion set in 60 acres with panoramic views of the Coniston hills. Own golf course and swimming pool. ETB 3 Crowns Commended.

B&B from £39.50, Lunch & evening meal available, Rooms 5 double, 1 twin, 3 triple, 3 family, all en-suite, Children welcome, Open all year.
Eccle Riggs Manor Hotel & Leisure Park Ltd, Foxfield Road, Broughton-in-Furness, Cumbria LA20 6BN
Tel: 01229 716398 & 716780 Fax: 01229 716958   **Map Ref 15**

CORNERWAYS GUEST HOUSE, five minutes from the bus and railway stations and city centre. M6 exit 43. Colour TV central heating in all bedrooms. Tea/coffee making facilities. Lounge, pool table, payphone.

B&B from £14, Dinner available, Rooms 3 single, 1 double, 4 twin, 1 triple, 1 family, Children welcome, No smoking, Open all year.
Cornerways Guest House, 107 Warwick Road, Carlisle, Cumbria CA1 1EA
Tel: 01228 21733   **Map Ref 16**

CALREENA GUEST HOUSE, a comfortable, friendly guesthouse. Central heating, home cooking. Colour TV and tea making facilities in all rooms. 2 minutes from city centre, railway and bus stations and from M6 Junction 43.

B&B from £15, Dinner available, Rooms 1 single, 1 double, 1 twin, 1 triple, Children welcome, Open all year.
Calreena Guest House, 123 Warwick Road, Carlisle, Cumbria CA1 1JZ
Tel: 01228 25020 & 0410 577171   **Map Ref 16**

AVONDALE, Michael & Angela Hayes welcome you to their attractive Edwardian house. Comfortable, spacious rooms. Quiet situation. Private parking. Close to city centre. ETB 2 Crowns Highly Commended.

B&B from £40, Dinner available, Rooms 1 double, 2 twin, Children welcome, No pets, Open all year.
Avondale, 2 St Aidan's Road, Carlisle, Cumbria CA1 1LT
Tel: 01228 23012   **Map Ref 16**

CARTREF, a family run guest house central to shopping, bus/rail stations and restaurants. Personal service. Colour TV and tea/coffee making facilities in all rooms.

B&B from £17, Lunch and evening meal available, Rooms 4 single, 1 double, 2 twin, 4 triple, Children welcome, No pets, No smoking, Open all year.
Cartref, 44 Victoria Place, Carlisle, Cumbria CA1 1EX
Tel: 01228 22077   **Map Ref 16**

LANGLEIGH HOUSE, a beautifully restored late Victorian house, 5 minutes from the city centre. Friendly atmosphere. All rooms en-suite. Private car park.

B&B from £25, Rooms 1 single, 1 double, 1 twin, Children welcome, No pets, No smoking, Open all year.
Langleigh House, 6 Howard Place, Carlisle, Cumbria CA1 1HR
Tel: 01228 30440   **Map Ref 16**

COUNTY HOTEL, is near to Lakes, Hadrians Wall, Gretna. By shops, cathedral, castle. Historic 84 en-suite bedroom hotel. Varied dining includes formal non smoking restaurant and informal Bistro. Some live music. Yards from station. On-site close circuit TV, car park. More info free Talking Pages 0800 600900. Special Offers! Email: cohot@enterprise.net.uk

B&B from £34pp, Dinner from £13.95, Rooms 27 single, 32 twin, 16 double, 9 family, all en-suite, Restricted smoking, Children welcome, Open all year.
Donald Whyte, **County Hotel,** 9 Botchergate, Carlisle CA1 1QP
Tel: 01228 531316 Fax: 01228 401805   **Map Ref 16**

ROYAL HOTEL, a family run hotel. All bedrooms have colour TV. Breakfast, bar lunches and evening meals served.

B&B from £21, Lunch and evening meal available, Rooms 8 single, 4 double, 8 twin, 3 triple, Children welcome, Open all year.
Royal Hotel, 9 Lowther Street, Carlisle, Cumbria CA3 8ES
Tel: 01228 22103 Fax: 01228 23904   **Map Ref 16**

VALLUM HOUSE GARDEN HOTEL, is situated in a select residential area on the west side of the city, en-route to the Solway coast. Close to Stoneyholm Golf Course and Edward 1 monument. Bar meals available lunchtime and evenings plus a la carte.

B&B from £28, Lunch and evening meal available, Rooms 6 single, 2 twin, 1 triple, some en-suite, Children welcome, No smoking, Open all year.
Vallum House Garden Hotel, Burgh Road, Carlisle, Cumbria CA2 7NB
Tel: 01228 21860   **Map Ref 16**

SWALLOW HILLTOP HOTEL, a comfortable, modern hotel with leisure facilities. Ideal touring base for the Borders, Lakes, Hadrians Wall and the Solway Coast. Special cabaret weekends. Short break packages available.

B&B from £80, Lunch and evening meal available, Rooms 2 single, 46 double, 42 twin, 2 family room, all en-suite, Children welcome, No smoking, Open all year
Swallow Hilltop Hotel, London Road, Carlisle, Cumbria CA1 2PQ
Tel: 01228 529255 Fax: 01228 25238   **Map Ref 16**

HAZELDENE GUEST HOUSE, a detached property with garden area access to swimming pool and children's play area. 2 miles west of Carlisle on bus route. Comfortable accommodation. Residential licence.

B&B from £16, Lunch and evening meal available, Rooms 2 single, 2 double, some en-suite, Children welcome, No smoking, No pets, Open all year.
Hazeldene Guest House, Orton Grange, Wigton Road, Carlisle, Cumbria CA5 6LA
Tel: 01228 711953   **Map Ref 16**

WARWICK LODGE, a well restored and appointed town house built in the 1880's. Within walking distance of the city centre and historic sites.

B&B from £23, Rooms 2 triple, both en-suite, Children welcome, No smoking, Open all year.
Warwick Lodge, Warwick Road, Carlisle, Cumbria CA1 1LF
Tel: 01228 23796   **Map Ref 16**

Croglin, home of the legendary vampire, is an isolated farming village time has forgot - no shops, buses or crowds. The 17th Century **ROBIN HOOD INN** is an old fashioned village pub, surrounded by spectacular scenery and yet central for the Lakes, Pennines, Borders and Northumbria.

B&B from £17.50pp, Dinner from £4.25, Rooms 1 twin, 1 double, both en-suite, Pets welcome, Open all year.
Gill & Clive Caygill, **Robin Hood Inn,** Croglin, Carlisle CA4 9RZ
Tel: 01768 896227   **Map Ref 17**

CROSBY LODGE COUNTRY HOUSE HOTEL, an 18th century country mansion overlooking parkland and the river. Chef/proprietor provides a renowned English and continental menu complemented by outstanding wine list.
B&B from £75, Lunch and evening meal available, Rooms 1 single, 4 double, 3 twin, 3 triple, all en-suite, Children welcome, No smoking, Open February - December.
Crosby Lodge Country House Hotel, High Crosby, Crosby-on-Eden, Carlisle, Cumbria CA6 4QZ
Tel: 01228 573618 Fax: 01228 573428   **Map Ref 18**

THE GOLDEN FLEECE

THE GOLDEN FLEECE, ideally situated six miles east of Carlisle centre. Ideal for shopping or sightseeing and within easy reach of Hadrians Wall and historic Roman Fort. All rooms en-suite with coffee/tea facilities and sky TV. Ample car parking. Bar menu available.

B&B from £28pp, Dinner available, Rooms 1 twin, 3 double, 1 family, all en-suite, No smoking or pets, Children welcome, Open all year.

The Golden Fleece, Ruleholme, Irthington, Carlisle, Cumbria CA6 4NF
Tel: 01228 573686 Fax: 01228 573271   **Map Ref 19**

CORNER HOUSE HOTEL & BAR, refurbished, friendly, family run. Open all year. All rooms en-suite, colour TV, radio, tea/coffee, phone, hair dryers, toiletries etc. Bar Sky TV. Lounge, games room. Easy access bus/trains, city centre attractions. M6 J42/43. Golf, racing, walking, horse riding, lakes, Roman Wall, 3 scenic train journeys. Bus tours to other historical cities.
B&B from £21pp, Dinner from £12, Rooms 3 single, 6 twin, 6 double, 3 family, Children & pets welcome, Open all year.
Mary Anderson, **Corner House Hotel & Bar,** 4 Grey Street, London Road, Carlisle, Cumbria CA1 2JP
Tel: 01228 533239 Fax: 01228 546628   **Map Ref 16**

KING ARMS HOTEL, is a 16th century coaching house with five letting rooms. Bar. Food. Dining room. Lounge bar. All are welcome to our village hotel.

B&B from £30 per room, Dinner from £1.75, Rooms 1 twin, 2 double, 2 family, Children & pets welcome, Open all year. Small parties catered.

Roger & Jackie Quartermain, **King Arms Hotel,** Main Street, Burton in Kendal, Carnforth, Cumbria LA6 1LR
Tel: 01524 781409   **Map Ref 20**

THE COPPER KETTLE, is part of an old manor house, built in 1610, on the border between the Yorkshire Dales and the Lakes.
B&B from £23, Lunch and evening meal available, Rooms 2 double, 1 twin, 1 triple, Children welcome, No smoking, Open all year.
The Copper Kettle, 3-5 Market Street Kirkby Lonsdale, Carnforth, Cumbria LA6 2AU
Tel: 015242 71714   **Map Ref 21**

WHOOP HALL INN, is a 17th century coaching inn offering super food and local specialities. between lakes and Dales, 6 miles from M6 junction 36. Ideal for business or pleasure.

B&B from £50, Lunch and evening meal available, Rooms 3 single, 13 double, 3 twin, 3 triple, 1 family, all en-suite, Children welcome, No smoking, Open all year.

Whoop Hall Inn, Burrow with Burrow, Kirkby Lonsdale, Carnforth, Cumbria LA6 2HP
Tel: 01524 271284 Fax: 01524 272154 **Map Ref 21**

PHEASANT INN, Old world country inn specialising in food and service, ideal for touring the Lakes, dales and coast. Situated amidst the peaceful Lunesdale Fells.

B&B from £37.50, Lunch and evening meal available, Rooms 2 single, 6 double, 2 twin, all en-suite, Children welcome, No smoking, Open all year.

Pheasant Inn, Casterton, Kirkby Lonsdale, Carnforth, Cumbria LA6 2RX
Tel: 015242 71230 Fax: 015242 71230 **Map Ref 22**

THE CAVENDISH

Originally the villages coaching inn, **THE CAVENDISH** dates from 15th Century, now fully modernised but not spoiled. Exuding ambience with brasses and log fires. 58% of our business is repeats or recommendations by friends. Cartmel is best described as a cathedral city in miniature.
Email: thecavendish@compuserve.com

B&B from £54 per room, Dinner available, Rooms 2 twin, 8 double, all en-suite, Restricted smoking, No pets, Open all year.
Howard Murray, **The Cavendish,** Cartmel, Cumbria LA11 6QA
Tel: 015395 36240 Fax: 015395 36620 **Map Ref 23**

GROVE COURT, a family run hotel with a reputation for good food. Convenient for the lake district and Solway coast. Popular meeting place for meals.

B&B from £47.50, Lunch and evening meal available, Rooms 5 double, 4 twin, 1 family, suite available, all en-suite, Children welcome, No pets, no smoking, Open all year.

Grove Court, Cleator Moor, Cumbria CA23 3DT
Tel: 01946 810503 Fax: 01946 815412 **Map Ref 24**

SHEPHERD'S ARMS HOTEL, is a small hotel with an informal and relaxed atmosphere, situated in the centre of Ennerdale Bridge. Bar and restaurant, open fires. Popular with walkers.

B&B from £26, Lunch and evening meal available, Rooms 1 single, 3 double, 4 twin, all en-suite/private facilities, Children welcome, Open all year.
Shepherd's Arms Hotel, Ennerdale Bridge, Ennerdale, Cleator, Cumbria CA23 3AR
Tel: 01946 861249 Fax: 01946 8612 49 **Map Ref 25**

TROUT HOTEL, Attractive black and white listed building, dating back from 1670, on the banks of the River Derwent adjacent to own award winning gardens. 12 miles west of Keswick off A66.

B&B from £59.95, Lunch and evening meal available, Rooms 4 single, 20 double, 8 twin, 2 triple, all en-suite, Children welcome, No smoking, Open all year.

Trout Hotel, Crown Street, Cockermouth, Cumbria CA13 0EJ
Tel: 01900 823591 Fax: 01900 827541 **Map Ref 26**

ROSE COTTAGE, in a pleasant position, this guest house is within easy reach of the Lakes and the Coast.

B&B from £22, Dinner available, Rooms, 1 single, 3 double, 1 twin, 2 triple, some en-suite, Children welcome, No smoking, Open all year.
Rose Cottage, Lorton Road, Cockermouth, Cumbria CA13 9DX
Tel: 01900 822189   **Map Ref 26**

....

THE ALLERDALE COURT HOTEL, a 17th century listed building with two smart and fashionable restaurants. A cosy cocktail bar and 22 en-suite bedrooms. All with colour TV, tea/coffee making facilities, Direct Dial telephone, radio, period furniture, oak beams. Located at the Northern gateway to the Lake District.
B&B from £30pp, Dinner from £17.95, Rooms 6 single, 6 twin, 10 double, 2 family, all en-suite, Children & Pets welcome, Open all year.
John & Kay Carlin, **The Allerdale Court Hotel,** Market Place, Cockermouth, Cumbria CA13 9NQ
Tel: 01900 823654 Fax: 01900 823033   **Map Ref 26**

....

PHEASANT INN, a peacefully situated hotel just off the A66 at the northern end of Bassenthwaite Lake. A 16th century farmhouse with all the charm and character of that age. ETB 1 Crown Highly Commended.

B&B from £68, Lunch and evening meal available, Rooms 5 single, 8 double, 7 twin, all en-suite, Children welcome, No smoking, Open all year.

Pheasant Inn, Bassenthwaite Lake, Cockermouth, Cumbria CA13 9YE
Tel: 017687 76234 Fax: 017687 76002   **Map Ref 27**

....

OUSE BRIDGE HOTEL, a small family run hotel quietly situated overlooking Bassenthwaite Lake and Skiddaw. Only 8 miles from Keswick. Home cooking. Country location. ETB 3 Crowns Commended.

B&B from £24, Evening meal available, Rooms 2 single, 4 double, 2 twin, 2 triple, most en-suite, Children from 5 years, No pets, Open February - December.
Ouse Bridge Hotel, Dubath, Bassenthwaite Lake, Cockermouth, Cumbria CA13 9YD
Tel: 017687 76322   **Map Ref 27**

....

BRIDGE HOTEL, an historic Lakeland hotel with modern comforts and facilities, in an area of outstanding natural beauty. Superb walking country. Dogs welcome.

B&B from £38, Lunch and evening meal available, Rooms 2 single, 8 double, 12 twin, all en-suite/private facilities, Children welcome, No smoking, Open all year.

Bridge Hotel, Buttermere, Cockermouth, Cumbria CA13 9UZ
Tel: 017687 70252 Fax: 017687 70252   **Map Ref 28**

....

This is the real Lake District without the crowds. With superb views from every window, **NEW HOUSE FARM** offers en-suite bedrooms, two lounges, a cosy dining room, open fires and fine traditional cooking. Simply the best place to relax and unwind!

B&B from £35pp, Dinner from £20, Rooms 2 twin, 3 double, all en-suite, No smoking, Children over 10, Pets by arrangement, Open all year except Christmas.

Hazel Hatch, **New House Farm,** Lorton, Cockermouth CA13 9UU
Tel: 01900 85404 Fax: 01900 85404   **Map Ref 29**

CROWN HOTEL, At the foot of Coniston Old Man, 10 minutes walk to the lake where Donald Campbell attempted to break the world water speed record.

B&B from £20, Lunch and evening meal available, Rooms 4 double, 1 twin, 3 triple, Children welcome, No pets, Open all year.
Crown Hotel, Coniston, Cumbria LA21 8EA
Tel: 015394 41243 Fax: 015394 41804   **Map Ref 30**

....

SUN HOTEL CONISTON, a country house hotel and 16th century inn, in spectacular mountain setting on the fringe of the village and at the foot of Coniston Old Man.
B&B from £25, Lunch and evening meal available, Rooms 1 single, 7 double, 3 twin, all en-suite/private facilities, Children welcome, No smoking, Open all year.
Sun Hotel Coniston, Coniston, Cumbria LA21 8HQ
Tel: 015394 41248   **Map Ref 30**

....

SHEPHERDS VILLA, a friendly, comfortable, family run guesthouse. Spacious accommodation in a quiet spot on the edge of the village. A warm welcome to everyone.

B&B from £17, Lunch available, Rooms 4 double, 1 twin, 3 triple, 2 family rooms, some en-suite, Children over 5, No pets or smoking, Open all year.
Shepherds Villa, Tilberthwaite Avenue, Coniston, Cumbria LA21 8EE
Tel: 015394 41337   **Map Ref 30**

....

OLD RECTORY HOTEL, a tastefully converted rectory offering delightful accommodation, set in 3 acres with pastoral views. Imaginative cooking in conservatory dining room. Superb local walks.
B&B from £19.50, Evening meal available, Rooms 1 single, 4 double, 2 twin, 1 triple, all en-suite, Children welcome, No smoking, Open all year.
Old Rectory Hotel, Torver, Coniston, Cumbria LA21 8AY
Tel: 015394 41353 Fax: 015394 41156   **Map Ref 31**

....

WILSON ARM'S, full licensed restaurant. Home cooked meals. TV's in bedrooms, tea/coffee, hair dryers, radio alarms. Car parking. Beer garden. Well stocked bar. Good central area for touring the Lakes. Excellent walking, cycling, horse riding, fishing. Nearby Coniston Lake, surrounded by beautiful Lakeland fells. Log fire.

B&B from £21.50pp, Dinner from £5.90, Rooms 1 single, 1 twin, 4 double, 2 family, all en-suite, Restricted smoking, Children welcome, Open all year except Christmas.
Frances Mayvers, **Wilson Arm's,** Torver, Coniston, Cumbria LA21 8BB
Tel: 015394 41237 Fax: 015394 41590   **Map Ref 31**

....

WHEELGATE COUNTRY HOUSE, a delightful 17th century country house with attractive bedrooms, oak beamed lounge and dining room. Complimentary leisure facilities. Perfect Lakeland retreat.

B&B from £25, Rooms 2 single, 3 double, all en-suite, Children welcome, No pets, No smoking, Open February - December.
Wheelgate Country House, Little Arrow, Torver, Coniston, Cumbria LA21 8AU
Tel: 015394 41418   **Map Ref 31**

....

WOOLPACK INN, a comfortable hotel serving real ale and home cooked food, set in beautiful scenery at the head of the Eskdale Valley.
B&B from £19.50, Lunch and evening meal available, Rooms 3 double, 4 twin, 1 family, Children welcome, No pets, No smoking, Open all year.
Woolpack Inn, Boot, Eskdale, Cumbria CA19 1TH
Tel: 01946 723230 Fax: 01946 723230   **Map Ref 33**

THORNLEIGH CHRISTIAN HOTEL, With its magnificent views across Morecambe Bay and easy access to the Lake District, Thornleigh is excellent for holidays or short breaks. Highly-acclaimed cuisine, comfortable accommodation and rich fellowship, make this hotel worthy of its splendid reputation. A warm Christian welcome awaits.
B&B from £22pp, Dinner from £7, Rooms 6 single, 13 twin, 6 double/twin/family, some en-suite, Children welcome, Open February - November and Christmas & New Year.
Susanna & David Mycock, **Thornleigh Christian Hotel,** The Esplanade, Grange over Sands, Cumbria LA11 7HH
Tel: 015395 32733 Fax: 015395 36088 **Map Ref 34**

....

NETHERWOOD HOTEL, built in 1893 and a building of high architectural and historical interest. Ample car parking.

B&B from £45, Lunch and evening meal available, Rooms 4 single, 16 double, 4 twin, 2 triple, 3 family, all en-suite, Children welcome, No smoking, Open all year.
Netherwood Hotel, Grange-over-Sands, Cumbria LA11 6ET
Tel: 015395 32553 Fax: 015395 34121 **Map Ref 34**

....

MAYFIELDS, a Victorian terraced town house, tastefully furnished and equipped to a high standard. In a pleasant position on the fringe of the town close to the promenade and open countryside. ETB 3 Crowns Commended.

B&B from £19, Lunch and evening meal available, Rooms 1 single, 1 double, 1 twin, all en-suite/private facilities, Children welcome, No pets or smoking, Open all year.
Mayfields, 3 Mayfield Terrace, Kents Bank Road, Grange-over-Sands, Cumbria LA11 7DW
Tel: 015395 34730 **Map Ref 34**

....

HAMPSFELL HOUSE HOTEL, a peaceful country setting in own grounds. Fresh and imaginatively prepared food. Extensive wine list. Ample safe parking.

B&B from £25, Lunch and evening meal available, Rooms 4 double, 4 twin, 1 triple, all en-suite, Children welcome, No smoking, Open all year.

Hampsfell House Hotel, Hampsfell Road, Grange-over-Sands, Cumbria LA11 6BG
Tel: 015395 32567 **Map Ref 34**

....

METHVEN HOTEL, a pleasantly proportioned Victorian building with half an acre of garden and superb panoramic views across Morecambe Bay. Ideal for a quiet and peaceful holiday.

B&B from £25, Lunch and evening meal available, Rooms 4 double, 4 twin, 2 triple, all en-suite, Children welcome, No pets, Smoking areas, Open all year.
Methven Hotel, Kents Bank Road, Grange-over-Sands, Cumbria LA11 7DU
Tel: 015395 32031 **Map Ref 34**

....

THE CUMBRIA GRAND HOTEL, set in 25 acres of grounds overlooking Morecambe Bay, with easy access to the M6 and the Lake District. Tennis court, trim trail, snooker room.

B&B from £42, Lunch and evening meal available, Rooms 17 single, 26 double, 80 twin, 6 triple, all en-suite/private facilities, Children welcome, No smoking, Open all year.

The Cumbria Grand Hotel, Lindale Road, Grange-over-Sands, Cumbria LA11 6EN
Tel: 015395 32331 Fax: 015395 34534 **Map Ref 34**

CLARE HOUSE, a charming hotel with well appointed bedrooms and pleasant lounges, set in grounds with magnificent bay views. Delightful meals prepared from the best ingredients.

B&B from £30, Lunch and evening meal available, Rooms 3 single, 2 double, 11 twin, 1 triple, all en-suite, Children welcome, No pets, Open April - October.
Clare House, Park Road, Grange-over-Sands, Cumbria LA11 7HQ
Tel: 015395 33026 & 34253   **Map Ref 34**

....

GRANGE HOTEL, a Victorian hotel with panoramic views over Morecambe Bay. Renowned for its service, food and leisure facilities.

B&B from £45, Lunch and evening meal available, Rooms 4 single, 15 double, 16 twin, 6 triple, all en-suite, Children from 1 year, Open all year.
Grange Hotel, Station Square, Grange-over-Sands, Cumbria LA11 6EJ
Tel: 015395 33666 Fax: 015395 35064   **Map Ref 34**

....

AYNSOME MANOR HOTEL, a lovely manor house, nestling in the vale of Cartmel. Good food, attentive service and log fire comfort. Lunches served on Sunday. No smoking in restaurant.

B&B from £46, Dinner available, Rooms 6 double, 4 twin, 2 triple, all en-suite, Children welcome, No smoking, Open February - December.
Aynsome Manor Hotel, Cartmel, Grange-over-Sands, Cumbria LA11 6HH
Tel: 015395 36653 Fax: 015395 36016   **Map Ref 23**

....

THE OLD VICARAGE COUNTRY HOUSE HOTEL, near the lakes, but far from the crowds. Enjoy award winning food and wine in a beautiful family owned historic house.

B&B from £59, Dinner available, Rooms 9 double, 4 twin, 1 triple, all en-suite, Children welcome, No smoking, Open all year.
The Old Vicarage Country House Hotel, Church Road, Witherslack, Grange-over-Sands, Cumbria LA11 6RS
Tel: 015395 52381 Fax: 015395 52373 Email: hotel@old-vic.demon.co.uk   **Map Ref 35**

....

THE SWAN, a homely hotel at the foot of Dunmail Raise on the Windermere to Keswick road. Car parking. ETB 4 Crowns Highly Commended.

B&B from £45, Lunch and evening meal available, Rooms 2 single, 20 double, 14 twin, all en-suite, Children welcome, No smoking, Open all year.
The Swan, Grasmere, Cumbria LA22 9RF
Tel: 015394 35551 Fax: 015394 35741   **Map Ref 36**

....

MOSS GROVE HOTEL, an elegant Lakeland hotel. Some four-poster bedrooms with south facing balconies. Cosy bar, conservatory, sauna and use of adjacent indoor swimming pool.

B&B from £26, Lunch and evening meal available, Rooms 2 single, 7 double, 3 twin, 1 triple, 1 family room, most en-suite, Children welcome, No pets, No smoking, Open February - November.
Moss Grove Hotel, Grasmere, Cumbria LA22 9SW
Tel: 015394 35251 Fax: 015394 35691 Email: martinw@globalnet.co.uk   **Map Ref 36**

....

OLD BANK HOTEL, a gem rarely to be found. Family run since 1981. A small hotel of superior accommodation and award winning cordon bleu cuisine.

B&B from £27.50, Dinner available, Rooms, 1 single, 9 double, 4 twin, 1 family, Children welcome, No smoking, Open February - December.
Old Bank Hotel, Broadgate, Grasmere, Cumbria LA22 9TA
Tel: 015394 35217 Fax: 015394 35685   **Map Ref 36**

LAKE VIEW COUNTRY HOUSE, in private grounds overlooking the lake and with private access. Located in the village but off the main road.

B&B from £24.50, Dinner available, Rooms 1 single, 3 double, 1 twin, some en-suite, Open February - November.

Lake View Country House, Lake View Drive, Grasmere, Cumbria LA22 9TD
Tel: 015394 35384   Map Ref 36

....

ASH COTTAGE GUEST HOUSE, a detached guest house with its own award winning garden, in the centre of Grasmere village. English home cooking our speciality.

B&B from £21, Dinner available, Rooms 1 single, 3 double, 3 twin, 1 triple, all en-suite, Children from 7 years, No pets, No smoking, Open all year.

Ash Cottage Guest House, Red Lion Square, Grasmere, Cumbria LA22 9SP
Tel: 015394 35224   Map Ref 36

....

RED LION, a 200 year old coaching inn refurbished to highest standards, including our own leisure facilities. Good food and friendly staff.

B&B from £39.80, Lunch and evening meal available, Rooms 3 single, 17 double, 12 twin, 4 family, all en-suite, Children welcome, No smoking, Restaurant open all year.

Red Lion, Red Lion Square, Grasmere, Cumbria LA22 9SS
Tel: 015394 35456 Fax: 01354 35579   Map Ref 36

....

BRIDGE HOUSE HOTEL, a comfortable hotel in 2 acres of peaceful woodland gardens beside the River Rothay in the village centre. King-sized rooms, king sized beds. Imaginative cuisine. Ample parking (yes, really!) relaxation guaranteed.

B&B from £36, Dinner available, 9 double, 9 twin, all en-suite, Children welcome, No pets, Open February - November and Christmas.

Bridge House Hotel, Stock Lane Grasmere, Cumbria LA22 9SN
Tel: 015394 35425 Fax: 015394 35523   Map Ref 36

....

RAISE VIEW GUEST HOUSE, Situated at the northern edge of Grasmere, with uninterrupted views of Easdale and easy access to many fine walks. Log fires and homely atmosphere. http://www.raisevw.demon.co.uk.

B&B from £46, Rooms 4 double, 3 twin, all en-suite, Children from 5 years, No smoking, No pets, Open February - November.

Raise View Guest House, White Bridge, Grasmere, Cumbria LA22 9RQ
Tel: 015394 35215 & 0378 146313 Fax: 015394 35126 Email: john@raisevw.demon.   Map Ref 36

....

THE GRASMERE HOTEL, a Victorian country house hotel, close to the centre of Wordsworth's Grasmere. All rooms have private facilities, colour televisions, telephones and tea/coffee facilities. Rooms are individually appointed. There is ample parking and an award winning restaurant. ETB 4 Crowns Highly Commended. Special breaks available. Telephone for brochure.

B&B from £25pp, Dinner from £12.50pp, Rooms 2 single, 2 twin, 8 double, all en-suite, Restricted smoking, Children over 6, Open February - December.

Paul & Gretchen Riley, The Grasmere Hotel, Broadgate, Grasmere LA22 9TA
Tel: 015394 35277 Fax: 015394 35277   Map Ref 36

HOW FOOT LODGE, a lovely Victorian house standing in own peaceful grounds close to Grasmere Lake and Wordsworths Dove cottage. Six spacious bedrooms en-suite; colour television; tea/coffee facilities. Substantial breakfasts. Comfortable lounge for guests and ample car parking. Ideal for walkers and conveniently situated for exploring lakeland.

B&B from £23pp, Rooms 2 twin, 4 double, all en-suite, Restricted smoking, Children over 5, Dogs by arrangement, Open February - mid December.
How Foot Lodge, Town End, Grasmere, Cumbria LA22 9SQ
Tel: 015394 35366   **Map Ref 36**

....

SILVERHOLME, set in its own grounds, overlooking Lake Windermere and with lake access, this small mansion house provides a quiet, comfortable, relaxed atmosphere. Home cooking.

B&B from £22, Lunch and evening meal available, Rooms 2 double, 1 triple, all en-suite, Children welcome, No smoking, Open all year.
Silverholme, Graythwaite, Cumbria LA12 8AZ
Tel: 015935 31332   **Map Ref 37**

....

QUEENS HEAD HOTEL, located between Lakes Windermere and Coniston. The home of Beatrix Potter, Wordsworth's grammar school and Ann Tyson's cottage. Fishing and bowling green facilities available.

B&B from £35, Lunch and evening meal available, Rooms 10 double, 1 twin, 2 triple, all en-suite/private facilities, Children welcome, No smoking, Open all year.
Queens Head Hotel, Main Street, Hawkshead, Cumbria LA22 0NS
Tel: 015394 36271 Fax: 015394 36722   **Map Ref 5**

....

RED LION INN, a 14th century coaching inn in the centre of Hawkshead, a uniquely beautiful village in England's most beautiful corner.

B&B from £29, Lunch and evening meal available, Rooms 9 double, 2 twin, 1 triple, all en-suite, Children welcome, No smoking, Open all year.

Red Lion Inn, The Square, Hawkshead, Cumbria LA22 0NS
Tel: 015394 36213 Fax: 015394 36747   **Map Ref 5**

....

GRIZEDALE LODGE HOTEL & RESTAURANT IN THE FOREST, a comfortable former shooting lodge with sun terrace and log fires. In magnificent Grizedale forest, midway between Coniston and Windermere. Close to forest walk and sculpture trails.

B&B from £28, Lunch and evening meal available, Rooms 6 double, 2 twin, 1 triple, all en-suite, Children welcome, No smoking, Open February - December.
Grizedale Lodge Hotel & Restaurant in the Forest, Grizedale, Hawkshead, Cumbria LA22 0QL
Tel: 015394 36532 Fax: 015394 36572   **Map Ref 38**

....

WOODLANDS COUNTRY HOUSE, set in a traditional Cumbrian village, 4 miles north of Bassenthwaite. Victorian former vicarage, in its own grounds, overlooking the fells. Pets, walkers and wheelchair users welcome. Warm welcome assured.

B&B from £55, Dinner available, Rooms, 3 double, 2 twin, 2 triple, all en-suite, Children welcome, No smoking, Open March - October and Christmas.

Woodlands Country House, Ireby, Cumbria CA5 1EX
Tel: 016973 71791 Fax: 016973 71482
                                                          Map Ref 39

HEAVES HOTEL, a Georgian mansion in 10 acres, 4 miles from junction 36, M6 and Kendal. Billiard room, library, family owned and run. Private car parking.

B&B from £20, Lunch and evening meal available, Rooms 4 single, 4 double, 5 twin, 1 triple, 1 family, most en-suite, Children welcome, Open all year.
Heaves Hotel, Kendal, Cumbria LA8 8EF
Tel: 015395 60269 & 60396 Fax: 015395 60269   **Map Ref 40**

....

FAIRWAYS GUEST HOUSE, on the main Kendal - Windermere road. Victorian guesthouse with en-suite facilities. TV, tea/coffee making facilities in all rooms. Four poster bedrooms. Private parking.
B&B from £17, Rooms 3 double, all en-suite, Children welcome, No pets, No smoking, Open all year.
Fairways Guest House, 102 Windermere Road, Kendal, Cumbria LA9 5EZ
Tel: 01539 725564   **Map Ref 40**

....

SAWYERS ARMS, all rooms colour TV, teamaking, hair dryers. Recently refurbished. Rooms still retain character of yesteryear. 5 minutes walk from centre of Kendal, which hosts may excellent restaurants. 8 miles from Windermere. An ideal base for the Lakes and Yorkshire Dales.

B&B from £18.50pp, Rooms 2 single, 2 twin, 3 double, 1 family, all en-suite, Children welcome, No pets, Open all year.
Geoff & Babs Wilson, **Sawyers Arms,** 137 Stricklandgate, Kendal, Cumbria LA9 4RF
Tel: 01539 729737   **Map Ref 40**

....

UNION TAVERN, a newly refurbished family hotel on main Windermere A5284 road, close to market town centre. Evening restaurant, live entertainment at weekends.

B&B from £18, Lunch and evening meal available, Rooms 2 double, 4 twin, some en-suite, Children welcome, No smoking, Open all year.
Union Tavern, 159 Stricklandgate, Kendal, Cumbria LA9 4RF
Tel: 01539 724004   **Map Ref 40**

....

NEWLANDS, a friendly Victorian guesthouse, within walking distance of the town centre, shops and museums. Ideally situated for the Lakes and Yorkshire Dales.

B&B from £16, Dinner available, Rooms 1 single, 2 double, 2 triple, Children welcome, Open all year.
Newlands, 37 Milnthorpe Road, Kendal, Cumbria LA9 5QG
Tel: 01539 725340   **Map Ref 40**

....

HILLSIDE GUEST HOUSE, a small elegant Victorian guesthouse near the shops and towns facilities, convenient for the Lakes, Yorkshire Dales and Morecambe Bay. Tourist Board, Two Crown Commended.

B&B from £17, Rooms 2 single, 3 double, 1 twin, some en-suite, Children from 3 years, No pets, Open March - November.
Mrs B Denison, **Hillside Guest House,** 4 Beast Banks, Kendal, Cumbria LA9 4JW
Tel: 01539 722836   **Map Ref 40**

....

BRANTHOLME, a family-run guesthouse in own grounds. All rooms with private facilities. Good meals from fresh local produce. Car parking.

B&B from £19, Dinner available, Rooms 3 twin, all en-suite/private facilities, Children welcome, No pets, No smoking, Open March - November.
Brantholme, 7 Sedbergh Road, Kendal, Cumbria LA9 6AD
Tel: 01539 722340   **Map Ref 40**

GARDEN HOUSE, an elegant country house offering personal service. Ideal touring base for Lakes and dales. Ample car parking. 2 day breaks available. All rooms have private facilities.
B&B from £49.50, Lunch and evening meal available, Rooms 2 single, 4 double, 3 twin, 1 triple, 1 family, all en-suite, Children welcome, No smoking, Open all year.
Garden House, Fowling Lane, Kendal, Cumbria LA9 6PH
Tel: 01539 731131 Fax: 01539 740064 **Map Ref 40**

....

WILD BOAR HOTEL, a 17th century former inn, renowned for its food. In Gilpin Valley, on B5284, 3 miles from the lake and half a mile from golf course.
B&B from £39.50, Lunch and evening meal available, Rooms 1 single, 16 double,17 twin, 2 triple, all en-suite, Children welcome, No smoking, Open all year.
Wild Boar Hotel, Crook, Kendal, Cumbria LA23 3NF
Tel: 015394 45225 Fax: 015394 42498 **Map Ref 41**

....

THE WILD BOAR HOTEL, surrounded by acres of open countryside, situated in the secluded Gilpin Valley. The Lake and Windermere Golf Course nearby. Dining is special in the unique award winning restaurant with famous house specialities and extensive cellar. Full use of sister hotel's superb pool and leisure club facilities.
B&B from £39.50pp, Dinner from £19.95, Rooms 1 single, 16 twin, 20 double, 6 family, all en-suite, Restricted smoking, Children welcome, Pets by arrangement, Open all year.
Jon Bennett, **The Wild Boar Hotel,** Crook, Windermere LA23 3NF
Tel: 015394 45225 Fax: 015394 42498 **Map Ref 41**

....

CROSTHWAITE HOUSE, a mid 18th century building with unspoilt views of the Lyth and Winster valleys, 5 miles from Bowness and Kendal. Family atmosphere and home cooking. Self catering cottages also available.
B&B from £20, Dinner available, Rooms 1 single, 3 double, 2 twin, all en-suite, Children welcome, Open March - November.
Crosthwaite House, Crosthwaite, Kendal, Cumbria LA8 8BP
Tel: 015395 68264 **Map Ref 42**

....

DAMSON DENE HOTEL, experience the unique atmosphere of this hotel, set in the tranquil Lyth Valley, near Windermere. Leisure centre open all year, roaring log fires in winter.
B&B from £30, Lunch and evening meal available, Rooms 5 single, 17 double, 10 twin, 2 family, all en-suite, Children welcome, No smoking, Open all year.
Damson Dene Hotel, Crosthwaite, Kendal, Cumbria LA8 8JE
Tel: 015395 68676 Fax: 015395 68227 **Map Ref 42**

....

SUMMERLANDS TOWER, is a fine Victorian country guesthouse offering spacious accommodation, surrounded by 3 acres of mature gardens and woodlands. 3 miles from M6 junction 36.
B&B from £27, Rooms 1 double, 1 twin, en-suite.private facilities, Children from 13 years, No pets, No smoking, Open all year.
Summerlands Tower, Endmoor, Kendal, Cumbria LA8 0ED
Tel: 015395 61081 **Map Ref 40**

....

RAVENSWORTH HOTEL, ideally situated near the town centre and all it's amenities, the lake and lower fells are just a short walk away. Tastefully furnished en-suite bedrooms have beverage tray, and colour television. Starting with our hearty breakfast you may enjoy the lakes by day and then while away the evening in the Herdwick Bar or relax in the spacious lounge. Personally run for twelve years we now rank among the top small hotels in Keswick. RAC Highly Acclaimed. AA Premier Selected. ETB Two Crowns Highly Commended.

B&B from £18pp, Rooms 1 twin, 6 double, 1 family, all en-suite, No smoking or pets, Children over 6, Open February - November.
John & Linda Lowrey, **Ravensworth Hotel,** 29 Station Road, Keswick on Derwentwater, Cumbria CA12 5HH
Tel: 017687 72476 **Map Ref 43**

CLARENCE HOUSE, high quality accommodation, all en-suite, Four-poster and ground floor rooms. 5 minutes' walk from lake, parks and shops. Non smoking.

B&B from £38, Dinner available, Rooms 1 single, 4 double, 3 twin, 1 triple, all en-suite/private facilities, Children from 4 years, No smoking, No pets, Open all year.
Clarence House, 14 Eskin Street, Keswick, Cumbria CA12 4DQ
Tel: 017687 73186   **Map Ref 43**

....

CHERRY TREES, attractive en-suite rooms, substantial home cooked meals. Non smokers only, please. 5 minutes' walk from town centre, 10 minutes to the lake.

B&B from £19, Dinner available, Rooms 1 single, 2 double, 1 twin, 1 triple, all en-suite/private facilities, Children from 8 years, No smoking, Open February - October and Christmas.
Cherry Trees, 16 Eskin Street, Keswick, Cumbria CA12 4DQ
Tel: 017687 71048   **Map Ref 43**

....

BONSHAW GUEST HOUSE, a small, friendly, comfortable guesthouse, providing good home cooking. Convenient for town centre and all amenities. En-suite rooms available. Car parking.

B&B from £15, Dinner available, Rooms 3 single, 2 double, 1 twin, 1 triple, Children from 5 years, No smoking, Open all year.
Bonshaw Guest House, 20 Eskin Street, Keswick, Cumbria CA12 4DG
Tel: 017687 73084   **Map Ref 43**

....

BRIERHOLME GUEST HOUSE, a select guesthouse in the town centre. High quality accommodation, all rooms having mountain views. tea-making facilities and colour TV. Private parking.
B&B from £36, Dinner available, Rooms 6 double, most en-suite/private facilities, Children welcome, No smoking, Open all year.
Brierholme Guest House, 21 Bank Street, Keswick, Cumbria CA12 5JZ
Tel: 017687 72938   **Map Ref 43**

....

THORNLEIGH, is a traditional lakeland building situated in Keswick town. All rooms have views of the mountains and fells, making this an idyllic base for walking or touring the northern Lakes. We offer a warm welcome and delicious full English breakfast to all our guests.

B&B from £21pp, Rooms 6 double, all en-suite, Restricted smoking, No pets or children, Open all year.
Ron & Pauline Graham, **Thornleigh,** 23 Bank Street, Keswick, Cumbria CA12 5JZ
Tel: 017687 72863   **Map Ref 43**

....

HUNTERS WAY GUEST HOUSE, a spacious, attractive guesthouse, 5 minutes walk from the town centre and beautiful countryside. Imaginative menu with home cooking - vegetarians welcome.

B&B from £18, Dinner available, Rooms 2 single, 3 double, 1 twin, most en-suite/private facilities, Children from 6 years, No pets, No smoking, Open February - November.

Hunters Way Guest House, 4 Eskin Street, Keswick, Cumbria CA12 4DH
Tel: 017687 72324 & 0374 818366   **Map Ref 43**

....

LINNETT HILL HOTEL, a charming 1812 hotel overlooking Skiddaw and Latrigg Hills. Opposite parks, gardens and river. Fresh home-cooked food, including a la carte menus with quality wines. Secure car park. Non smoking establishment.

B&B from £25, Dinner available, Rooms 1 single, 7 double, 2 twin, all en-suite, Children from 5 years, No pets, No smoking, Open all year.
Linnett Hill Hotel, 4 Penrith Road, Keswick, Cumbria CA12 4HF
Tel: 017687 73109   **Map Ref 43**

116

THE CARTWHEEL, is a family run guesthouse in a quiet area yet close to the town and park, only a short walk away from the lake.

B&B from £15, Dinner available, Rooms 1 single, 3 double, 2 twin, some en-suite, Children welcome, No pets, No smoking, Open all year.
The Cartwheel, 5 Blencathra Street, Keswick, Cumbria CA12 4HW
Tel: 017687 73182   **Map Ref 43**

....

ACORN HOUSE HOTEL, an elegant Georgian house set in colourful garden. All bedrooms tastefully furnished, some four-poster beds. Cleanliness guaranteed. Close to town centre. Good off-street parking.

B&B from £27.50, Rooms 6 double, 1 twin, 3 triple, all en-suite/private facilities, Children from 6 years, No pets, No smoking, Open February - November.
Acorn House Hotel, Ambleside Road, Keswick, Cumbria CA12 4DL
Tel: 017687 72553 Fax: 017867 75332   **Map Ref 43**

....

GREYSTONES, is situated in a tranquil location overlooking the grounds of Saint John's church. It is just a short walk to the market square and lake. There are eight delightful en-suite rooms, each with television and hot drinks tray. ETB Highly Commended. Parking, Non smoking.

B&B from £23.50pp, Rooms 1 single, 2 twin, 5 double, all en-suite, No smoking or pets, Children over 10, Open January - November.
Mr Jones, **Greystones,** Ambleside Road, Keswick, Cumbria CA12 4DP
Tel: 017687 73108   **Map Ref 43**

....

PRIORHOLME HOTEL, this Georgian hotel with charm and character has a 200 year old bar and is on a quiet road 3 minutes walk from the town, the lake and the theatre.

B&B from £18, Dinner available, Rooms 2 single, 5 double, 1 twin, most en-suite, Children welcome, No pets, Open February - December.
Priorholme Hotel, Borrowdale Road, Keswick, Cumbria CA12 5DD
Tel: 017687 72745   **Map Ref 43**

....

CHAUCER HOUSE HOTEL, a beautiful Victorian house. Quiet family run hotel overlooked by Skiddaw, Grizedale and Derwentwater. Delicious home cooked meals including bread, jams and chutney.

B&B from £29, Lunch and evening meal available, Rooms 7 single, 13 double, 11 twin, 3 triple, 1 family, most en-suite, Children welcome, No smoking, Open February - November.
Chaucer House Hotel, Derwentwater Place, Ambleside Road, Keswick, Cumbria CA12 4DR
Tel: 017687 72318 & 73223 Fax: 017687 75551   **Map Ref 43**

....

THE GRANGE COUNTRY HOUSE HOTEL, a building of charm, fully restored and refurbished, with many antiques. Quiet, overlooking Keswick with panoramic mountain views. Log fires, freshly prepared food and attractive bedrooms.

B&B from £64, Dinner available, Rooms 7 double, 3 twin, all en-suite, Children from 7 years, No smoking, Open March - November.
The Grange Country House Hotel, Manor Brow, Ambleside Road, Keswick, Cumbria CA12 4BA
Tel: 017687 72500   **Map Ref 43**

....

SKIDDAW HOTEL, a family owned town centre hotel offering true hospitality and excellent cuisine. In house saunas, free midweek golf, free use of nearby exclusive leisure club.

B&B from £36, Lunch & Dinner available, Rooms 7 single, 14 double, 11 twin, 8 triple, all en-suite, Children welcome, No smoking, Open all year.
Skiddaw Hotel, Market Square, Keswick, Cumbria CA12 5BN
Tel: 017687 72071 Fax: 017687 74850   **Map Ref 43**

LATRIGG HOUSE, a homely guesthouse offering a warm and friendly welcome and good food, in quiet area of the town with views of Skiddaw.
B&B from £14, Dinner available, Rooms 1 single, 2 double, 2 twin, 1 family, some en-suite, Children welcome, No pets or smoking, Open all year.
Latrigg House, St Herbert Street, Keswick, Cumbria CA12 4DF
Tel: 017687 73068   **Map Ref 43**

....

BERKELEY GUEST HOUSE, On a quiet road overlooking Borrowdale Valley, with splendid views from each comfortable room. Close to the town centre and lake.

B&B from £29, Rooms 1 single, 3 double, 1 triple, Children from 1 year, No pet or smoking, Open February - November.
Berkeley Guest House, The Heads, Keswick, Cumbria CA12 5ER
Tel: 017687 74222   **Map Ref 43**

....

HAZELDENE HOTEL, a beautiful and central location with open views of Skiddaw and Borrowdale and Newlands Valleys. Situated midway between town centre and Lake Derwentwater. Car parking.

B&B from £24, Dinner available, Rooms 5 single, 9 double, 4 twin, 4 triple, all en-suite/private facilities, Children welcome, Open February - November.
Hazeldene Hotel, The Heads, Keswick, Cumbria CA12 5ER
Tel: 017687 72106 Fax: 017687 75435   **Map Ref 43**

....

HIGHFIELD HOTEL, a friendly, family-run hotel quietly situated between town and lake. Superb views, cheerful, relaxed atmosphere. Large private car park.
B&B from £28, Dinner available, Rooms 2 single, 8 double, 5 twin, 2 triple, all en-suite, Children over 5, No smoking, Open all year.
Highfield Hotel, The Heads, Keswick, Cumbria CA12 5ER
Tel: 017687 72508   **Map Ref 43**

....

WEST VIEW GUEST HOUSE, comfortable centrally heated non smoking Victorian Guest House. Central position for touring and walking. Beautiful views of lakeland scenery. Three minutes walk to lake or town centre. Residents lounge with colour TV. All rooms have shaver points, tea/coffee facilities. Drying facilities available.
B&B from £17.50pp, Rooms 1 twin, 6 double, some en-suite, No smoking, children or pets, Open all year except Christmas.
John & Carole Fullagar, **West View Guest House,** The Heads, Keswick, Cumbria CA12 5ES
Tel: 017687 73638   **Map Ref 43**

....

APPLETHWAITE COUNTRY HOUSE HOTEL, a characterful Victorian Lakeland-stone residence in idyllic, peaceful setting 1.5 miles from Keswick. Superb elevated position, stunning panoramic views. Relaxed informal atmosphere. Delicious home cooking, vegetarians welcome.
B&B from £29, Dinner available, Rooms 1 single, 7 double, 2 twin, 2 triple, all en-suite, Children from 5 years, No pets, No smoking, Open February - November.
Applethwaite Country House Hotel, Applethwaite, Keswick, Cumbria CA12 4PL
Tel: 017687 72413 Fax: 017687 75706   **Map Ref 45**

....

CASTLE INN HOTEL, a hotel with extensive leisure facilities, including a large indoor swimming pool. Two good restaurants. Free children's accommodation. Friendliest welcome. Superb views.
B&B from £59, Lunch and evening meal available, Rooms 2 single, 24 double, 15 twin, 2 triple, 5 family, suite available, all en-suite, Children welcome, No smoking, Open all year.
Castle Inn Hotel, Bassenthwaite, Keswick, Cumbria CA12 4RG
Tel: 017687 76401 Fax: 017687 76604 Email: partners@castlinn.demon.co.uk   **Map Ref 27**

RAVENSTONE HOTEL, a charming dower house offering comfort and relaxation in beautiful surrounding. Elegant lounge and bar with log fires. Games room with full size snooker table. ETB 3 Crowns Highly Commended.

B&B from £30, Dinner available, Rooms 2 single, 10 double, 5 twin, 2 triple, 1 family room, all en-suite, Children welcome, Open February - October.

Ravenstone Hotel, Bassenthwaite Hotel, Bassenthwaite, Keswick, Cumbria CA12 4QG
Tel: 017687 76240 Fax: 017687 76240   **Map Ref 27**

....

MARY MOUNT, set in 4.5 acres of gardens and woodlands on the shores of Derwentwater, 2.5 miles from Keswick. Views across lake to Catbells and Maiden Moor. Families and pets welcome. ETB 3 Crowns Commended.

B&B from £25, Lunch and evening meal available, Rooms 1 single, 5 double, 5 twin, 2 triple, 1 family room, all en-suite, Car parking, Open February - December.
Mary Mount, Borrowdale, Keswick, Cumbria CA12 5UU
Tel: 017687 77223   **Map Ref 46**

....

STAKIS KESWICK LODORE HOTEL, is a largely refurbished hotel with excellent sports and family facilities. Fantastic view of lake and fells beyond. Beautiful grounds and gardens for a relaxing holiday. ETB 4 Crowns Highly Commended.

B&B from £35, Lunch and evening meal available, Rooms 10 single, 20 double, 44 twin, 1 triple, suites available, all en-suite, Children welcome, No smoking, Open all year.

Stakis Keswick Lodore Hotel, Borrowdale, Keswick, Cumbria CA12 5UX
Tel: 017687 77285 Fax: 017687 77343   **Map Ref 46**

....

GREENBANK COUNTRY HOUSE HOTEL, quiet location, superb views, 10 en-suite bedrooms. Residential license, log fires, TV lounges. Tea and coffee facilities, car parking. Excellent chef. Excellent centre for walking and exploring the Lakes.

B&B from £22pp, Dinner from £12.00, Rooms 1 single, 2 twin, 7 double, 1 family, all en-suite, Restricted smoking, Children welcome, No pets, Open February - December. Jean Wissett Wood **Greenbank Country House Hotel,** Borrowdale, Keswick, Cumbria CA12 5UY
Tel: 017687 77215   **Map Ref 46**

....

LEATHES HEAD HOTEL & RESTAURANT, an Edwardian country house with a warm welcome and magnificent views in the heart of Borrowdale. Menus change daily, with emphasis on fresh local produce. ETB 3 Crowns Highly Commended.

B&B from £39, Dinner available, Rooms 2 single, 4 double, 2 twin, 2 triple, 1 family, all en-suite, Children welcome, No pets, No smoking, Open February - December.

Leathes Head Hotel & Restaurant, Borrowdale, Keswick, Cumbria CA12 5UY
Tel: 017687 77247 Fax: 017687 77363 Email: 100755,2245@compuserve.uk   **Map Ref 46**

....

HAZEL BANK, a comfortable and well appointed country house in the beautiful, peaceful Borrowdale Valley. Ideal base for walking or touring. Non smokers only, please. Car parking. ETB 3 Crowns Highly Commended.

B&B from £46, Dinner available, Rooms 1 single, 2 double, 3 twin, all en-suite, Children from 6 years, Open April - October.
Hazel Bank, Rosthwaite, Borrowdale, Keswick, Cumbria CA12 5BX
Tel: 017687 77248 Fax: 017687 77373   **Map Ref 46**

119

ROYAL OAK HOTEL, a small, family-run traditional Lakeland Hotel, 6 miles south of Keswick. Cosy atmosphere, home cooking and friendly service.

B&B from £22, Dinner available, Rooms 2 single, 4 double, 2 twin, 3 triple, 1 family, Children welcome, Open all year.
Royal Oak Hotel, Rosthwaite, Borrowdale, Keswick, Cumbria CA12 5XB
Tel: 017687 77214   **Map Ref 46**

....

SEATOLLER HOUSE, this 300 year old house has accommodated visitors to Borrowdale for well over a century. It continues to be known for its homely, friendly and informal atmosphere, good food and fine location. ETB Listed Commended.

B&B from £29, Dinner available, Rooms 1 double, 3 twin, 5 triple, all en-suite/private facilities, Children from 5 years, No smoking, Open March - November.
Seatoller House, Seatoller, Borrowdale, Keswick, Cumbria CA12 5XN
Tel: 017687 77218 Fax: 017687 77218   **Map Ref 46**

....

MAPLE BANK, a friendly country guest house with magnificent views of Skiddaw and surrounding countryside. Delicious home cooking. Open four seasons, including Christmas and New Year.

B&B from £46, Dinner available, Rooms 6 double, 1 twin, all en-suite, Children from 12 years, No pets, No smoking, Open all year.
Maple Bank, Braithwaite, Keswick, Cumbria CA12 5RY
Tel: 017687 78229 Fax: 017687 78066 Email: maplebank@msn.com   **Map Ref 47**

....

COLEDALE INN, is a Victorian country house hotel and Georgian INN, in a peaceful hillside position away from traffic, with superb mountain views. Families and pets welcome.

B&B from £20, Lunch and evening meal available, Rooms 1 single, 6 double, 1 twin, 3 triple, 1 family, all en-suite, Children welcome, No smoking, Open all year.
Coledale Inn, Braithwaite, Keswick, Cumbria CA12 5TN
Tel: 017867 78727   **Map Ref 47**

....

DERWENT HOUSE, is a Victorian, family run guesthouse in lovely Borrowdale. Comfortable rooms enjoy beautiful views of surrounding fells. No smoking in bedrooms and dining rooms, please. ETB 3 Crowns Commended.

B&B from £25, Dinner available, Rooms 1 single, 5 double, 3 twin, 1 triple, some en-suite, Children welcome, No pets, Open February - December.
Derwent House, Grange-in-Borrowdale, Keswick, Cumbria CA12 5UY
Tel: 017687 77658 Fax: 017687 77217   **Map Ref 48**

....

LITTLETOWN FARM, a 150 acre mixed farm. in the beautiful, unspoilt Newlands Valley. En-suite, bedrooms. Comfortable residents' lounge, dining room and cosy bar. Traditional 4 course dinner 6 nights a week.

B&B from £24, Dinner available, Rooms 1 single, 4 double, 2 twin, 1 triple, 1 family, most en-suite, Children welcome, Open March - December.
Littletown Farm, Newlands, Keswick, Cumbria CA12 5TU
Tel: 017687 78353   **Map Ref 43**

....

SWINSIDE LODGE, is a quietly situated informal country hotel offering the highest standards of comfort, service and hospitality. Noted for enjoyable food which demonstrates a serious and dedicated approach to the cooking.

B&B from £47, Dinner available, Rooms 5 double, 2 twin, all en-suite, Children from 10 years, No pets, No smoking, Open February - November and Christmas.
Swinside Lodge, Newlands, Keswick, Cumbria CA12 5UE
Tel: 017687 72948 Fax: 017687 72948   **Map Ref 43**

DERWENTWATER HOTEL, Award winning with a unique and unrivalled lakeshore location in 16 acres of conservation grounds. Panoramic views from our conservatory. Deluxe and Premier rooms. Half board available for minimum 2 night stays.Email: derwentwater.hotel@dial.pipex.com

B&B from £49.50pp, Dinner available, Rooms 7 single, 23 double, 20 twin, 2 triple, all en-suite, Restricted smoking, Children & pets welcome, Disabled rooms available. Open all year.
Derwentwater Hotel, Portinscale, Keswick, Cumbria CA12 5RE
Tel: 017687 72538 Fax: 017687 71002 **Map Ref 49**

RICKERBY GRANGE, a detached country hotel in its own gardens, in a quiet village on the outskirts of Keswick. Provides imaginative cooking, a cosy bar and quiet lounge. Ground floor bedrooms available.

B&B from £27, Dinner available, Rooms 2 single, 7 double, 1 twin, 3 triple, most en-suite, Children from 5 years, No smoking, Open February - November.
Rickerby Grange, Portinscale, Keswick, Cumbria CA12 5RH
Tel: 017687 72344 **Map Ref 49**

DALEGARTH HOUSE COUNTRY HOTEL, an Edwardian house 1 mile from Keswick, with views of Skiddaw and Derwentwater. Licenced bar, 2 lounges and 6 course evening meal. Non-smokers only, please.
B&B from £27, Dinner available, Rooms 1 single, 5 double, 3 twin, 1 triple, all en-suite, Children from 5 years, No pets, No smoking, Open all year.
Dalegarth House Country Hotel, Portinscale, Keswick, Cumbria CA12 5RQ
Tel: 017687 72817 Fax: 017687 72817 **Map Ref 49**

THWAITE HOWE HOTEL, a traditional country house hotel in a tranquil position with magnificent views. Award winning food and fine wines.

B&B from £41, Dinner available, Rooms 5 double, 3 twin, all en-suite, Children from 12 years, No smoking, Open March - October.
Thwaite Howe Hotel, Thornthwaite, Keswick, Cumbria CA12 5SA
Tel: 017687 78281 Fax: 017687 78529 **Map Ref 44**

SWAN HOTEL & COUNTRY INN, is set amidst magnificent Lakeland scenery, in a quiet, elevated position overlooking Skiddaw and the Derwent Valley.
B&B from £20, Lunch and evening meal available, Rooms 5 double, 4 twin, 2 single, 1 family, all en-suite, Children welcome, No smoking, Open February - December.
Swan Hotel & Country Inn, Thornthwaite, Keswick, Cumbria CA12 5SQ
Tel: 017687 78256 **Map Ref 44**

SCALES FARM COUNTRY GUEST HOUSE, is a tastefully restored 17th century farmhouse, 10 minutes drive from Keswick. From a separate entrance our guests have access to a private lounge and dining room, and we provide colour TV and fridges in our fully en-suite bedrooms. Private car park. ETB Highly Commended.

B&B from £23pp, Rooms 2 twin, 3 double, 1 family, all en-suite, No smoking, Children welcome, Dogs welcome, Open all year except Christmas.
Chris & Caroline Briggs, **Scales Farm Country Guest House,** Scales, Threlkeld, Keswick, Cumbria CA12 4SY
Tel: 017687 79660 Fax: 017687 79660 Email: scalesfarm@scalesfarm.demon.co.uk **Map Ref 50**

LYZZICK HALL HOTEL, Peaceful country house hotel in its own grounds, with panoramic views, good food and a friendly, relaxed atmosphere. Heated indoor swimming pool, sauna and spa.
B&B from £39, Lunch and evening meal available, Rooms 3 single, 12 double, 7 twin, 3 family, all en-suite, Children welcome, No pets, No smoking, Open February - December.
Lyzzick Hall Hotel, Underskiddaw, Keswick, Cumbria CA12 4PY
Tel: 017687 72277 Fax: 017687 72278 **Map Ref 51**

THE BLACK SWAN HOTEL, a delightful family-run hotel, set amidst beautiful countryside in a picturesque village. Renowned for food, comfort and hospitality. Private fishing. 5 minutes from M6 junction 38. AA 2 Star and Rosette, RAC 2 Star, ETB 4 Crowns Commended.

B&B from £40, Lunch and evening meal available, Rooms 1 single, 9 double, 5 twin, all en-suite, Children welcome, No smoking, Open all year.
The Black Swan Hotel, Ravenstonedale, Kirkby Stephen, Cumbria CA17 4NG
Tel: 015396 23204 Fax: 015396 23604 Freephone: 0500 657860 **Map Ref 52**

....

THE PLOUGH HOTEL, a tastefully refurbished country inn renowned for the warmth of its welcome. Superb food, real ales and well appointed rooms.
B&B from £35, Lunch and evening meal available, Rooms 8 double, 2 twin, 1 triple, 2 family, suite available, all en-suite, Children welcome, Open all year.
The Plough Hotel, Cow Brow, Lupton, Cumbria LA6 1PJ
Tel: 015395 67227 Fax: 015395 67848 **Map Ref 53**

....

THE BLUE BELL AT HEVERSHAM, a country hotel in a rural haven, an ideal touring centre. Adjacent to A6 south of Kendal. Readily accessible from junction 35 or 36 of M6. Ample car parking.

B&B from £39.50, Lunch and evening meal available, Rooms 1 single, 14 double, 6 twin, 1 triple, all en-suite, Children welcome, No smoking, Open all year.
The Blue Bell at Heversham, Princes Way, Heversham, Milnthorpe, Cumbria LA7 7EE
Tel: 015395 62018 Fax: 015395 62455 **Map Ref 55**

....

KINGFISHER HOUSE & RESTAURANT, overlooking the Kent Estuary and Lakeland hills, perfect for bird watching, golf and rambling. All food home cooked using fresh produce.

B&B from £25, Lunch and evening meal available, Rooms 1 single, 1 double, 1 twin, 1 family, all en-suite, Children welcome, No smoking, Open all year.
Kingfisher House & Restaurant, Sandside, Milnthorpe, Cumbria LA7 7HW
Tel: 015395 63909 **Map Ref 56**

....

GEORGE HOTEL, an historic coaching inn with beamed ceilings and open fires. Centrally positioned. Local reputation for hospitality, food and wine. Ideal touring base for the Lakes, Pennines and Eden Valley.
B&B from £42.75, Lunch and evening meal available, Rooms 11 single, 10 double, 9 twin, all en-suite, Children welcome, Open all year.
George Hotel, Penrith, Cumbria CA11 7SU
Tel: 01768 862696 Fax: 01768 868223 **Map Ref 57**

....

BEACON BANK HOTEL, a Victorian house of character, set in peaceful landscaped gardens. Residential licence, good food and service, spacious, comfortable, high standard of accommodation. Five minutes from M6 junction 40. A no smoking hotel.

B&B from £29, Dinner available, Rooms 2 single, 5 double, 1 twin, all en-suite, Children welcome, Open all year.
Beacon Bank Hotel, Beacon Edge, Penrith, Cumbria CA11 7BD
Tel: 01768 862633 Fax: 01768 899055 **Map Ref 57**

....

NORCROFT GUEST HOUSE, a spacious Victorian house with large comfortable rooms. In a quiet residential area near town centre. Colour TV, coffee/tea facilities in all rooms. Ample private parking. We are ideally situated for exploring Eden Valley, Lakes and Pennines and only 5 minutes from M6 junction 40. Come and see!

B&B from £16pp, Dinner from £8, Rooms 1 single, 2 twin, 2 double, 2 family, some en-suite, Restricted smoking, Children welcome, No pets, Open all year.
Sylvia & Philip Jackson, **Norcroft Guest House,** Graham Street, Penrith, Cumbria CA1 9LQ
Tel/Fax: 01768 862365 **Map Ref 57**

CROWN & MITRE HOTEL

CROWN & MITRE HOTEL, enjoy peace and tranquillity in our friendly country hotel specialising in home cooking, log fires, good company. Children and pets welcome. Bar. Tea/coffee facilities, central heating. An unspoilt corner of the Lake District. Home of the Golden Eagles on route to the coast to coast.
B&B from £15pp, Dinner from £4.75, Rooms 1 single, 1 twin, 2 double, 2 family, Children & pets welcome, Open all year.
Mrs Frith, **Crown & Mitre Hotel,** Bampton Grange, Bampton, Penrith, Cumbria CA10 2QR
Tel: 0191 713 225   **Map Ref 58**

....

HORNBY HALL COUNTRY GUEST HOUSE, a 16th century recently restored farmhouse providing comfortable accommodation, set in tranquil countryside. All bedrooms face south overlooking the garden. Ideally situated for trips to Lakes, Dales, Hadrians Wall and historic Carlisle. All meals are served in the great hall using fresh local food. Fishing available.

B&B from £52pp, Dinner from £12, Rooms 1 single, 4 twin, 2 double, 1 family, some en-suite, Restricted smoking, Children welcome, Pets by arrangement, Open all year except Christmas & New Year.
Ros Sanders, **Hornby Hall Country Guest House,** Hornby Hall, Broughton, Penrith, Cumbria CA10 2AR
Tel: 01768 891114 Fax: 01768 891114   **Map Ref 59**

....

THE BLACK SWAN INN, owner run, traditional 17th century Cumbrian inn close to the River Eden and Settle Carlisle Railway. We offer quality in food, ale and en-suite accommodation with oak beams an open fire and beer garden. All our food is home cooked using only fresh produce. Three Crown Commended.

B&B from £27.50pp, Dinner from £5.95, Rooms 3 twin, 4 double, all en-suite, Restricted smoking, Children over 5, Pets by arrangement, Open all year.
Chris Pollard, **The Black Swan Inn,** Culgaith, Penrith CA10 1QW
Tel: 01768 88223 Fax: 01768 88223   **Map Ref 60**

....

EDENHALL HOTEL, in the Eden Valley. A peaceful country house hotel with good food and wines. Plenty of country walks for the energetic.

B&B from £50, Lunch and evening meal available, Rooms 6 single, 9 double, 11 twin, 2 triple, 1 family, all en-suite, Children welcome, Open all year.
Edenhall Hotel, Edenhall, Penrith, Cumbria CA11 8SX
Tel: 01768 881454 Fax: 01768 881454   **Map Ref 61**

....

MOSS CRAG, a traditional Westmorland stone built house by Glenridding Beck and Dodd. Only 5 minutes walk to Ullswater Lake where one can sail, fish canoe or windsurf.

B&B from £17.50-£25pp, Lunch and evening meal available, Rooms 5 double, 1 twin, some en-suite, Children from 5 years, No pets, No smoking, Open January - November.
Moss Crag, Glenridding, Penrith, Cumbria CA11 0PA
Tel: 017684 82500   **Map Ref 62**

....

GLENRIDDING HOTEL, an old established family hotel, adjacent to the lake and surrounded by mountains. We offer value breaks, log fires, real ales and good food. 2 restaurants, pub. Children and pets welcome.

B&B from £66, Lunch and evening meal available, Rooms 5 single, 20 double, 11 twin, 4 family, all en-suite,Open all year.
Glenridding Hotel, Glenridding, Penrith, Cumbria CA11 0PB
Tel: 017684 82228 Fax: 017684 82555   **Map Ref 62**

BECKFOOT COUNTRY HOUSE, nestling the Lakeland Fells of the Lowther Valley near Haweswater. Ideal walking base. M6 exit 39 (south) and 40 (north).

B&B from £26, Dinner available, Rooms 1 single, 2 double, 2 twin, 1 triple, all en-suite, Children welcome, No smoking, Open March - November.
Beckfoot Country House, Helton, Penrith, Cumbria CA10 2QB
Tel: 01931 713241 Fax: 01931 713391 Email: malcolmwh@aol.com   **Map Ref 63**

....

PATTERDALE HOTEL, a family run hotel, within the same family for 65 years. All rooms with private facilities, colour TV and telephone. Lift to all floors.

B&B from £30, Lunch & evening meal available, Rooms 13 single, 16 double, 24 twin, 2 family, Children welcome, Open March - December.
Patterdale Hotel, Lake Ullswater, Penrith, Cumbria CA11 0NN
Tel: 017684 82231 Fax: 017684 82440   **Map Ref 64**

....

NEAR HOWE HOTEL, a family home in 300 acres of moorland. Many bedrooms have private facilities, all have tea/coffee facilities. Home cooking with every meal freshly prepared. TV lounge. Games room. Smaller lounge with bar and on cooler evenings an log fire. Local activities include golf, fishing, pony trekking, boating and walking. Commended 3 Crowns.
B&B from £34pp, Dinner from £11, Rooms 1 twin, 3 double, 3 family, most en-suite, Restricted smoking, Children welcome, Open March - January.
Christine & Gordon Weightman, **Near Howe Hotel,** Mungrisdale, Penrith, Cumbria CA11 0SH
Tel: 017687 79678 Fax: 017687 79678   **Map Ref 65**

....

MOUNTAIN LODGE HOTEL, nestling above the Lune Gorge on the outskirts of the Lake District, with easy access from M6. Outstanding, friendly service with excellent food and large en-suite bedrooms.

B&B from £50, Lunch and evening meal available, Rooms 20 double, 24 twin, 9 family, all en-suite, Children welcome, No smoking, Open all year.

Mountain Lodge Hotel, Orton, Penrith, Cumbria CA10 3SB
Tel: 015396 24351 Fax: 015396 24354   **Map Ref 66**

....

ULLSWATER HOUSE, a centrally situated hotel in Pooley Bridge. The well appointed rooms are quiet, and each has a fridge containing alcoholic and soft drinks.

B&B from £20, Dinner available, Rooms 2 double, 1 twin, all en-suite, Children welcome, Open all year.

Ullswater House, Pooley Bridge, Penrith, Cumbria CA10 2NN
Tel: 017684 86259   **Map Ref 67**

....

GREYHOUND HOTEL, an old coaching inn, situated on the southern approach to Shap village on the A6 and approximately 1 mile from jct39 of the M6. Family run business with all en-suite rooms having colour TV and hostess tray. Good food. Licensed bar. Games rooms. Car park.

B&B from £19.50pp, Bar meals from £4.50, Rooms 2 single, 4 twin, 3 double, 1 family, all en-suite, Children welcome, Pets by arrangement, Open all year except Christmas.
Bob & Elizabeth Sneath, **Greyhound Hotel,** Main Street, Shap, Penrith, Cumbria CA10 3PW
Tel: 01931 716474   **Map Ref 68**

BRANTWOOD HOTEL, is 3 miles from Lake Ullswater in the Lake District. Small family hotel, close to M6 J40 off A66 west. Large safe car park. Full liquor license. All rooms are en-suite with TV, telephone and tea/coffee making facilities. Oak beams and log fires in winter. Open to non residents.

B&B from £28.50pp, Dinner from £15.95, Rooms 2 single, 2 twin, 9 double, 3 family, all en-suite, Restricted smoking, Children welcome, No pets, Open all year. Susan & John Harvey, **Brantwood Hotel,** Stainton, Penrith CA11 0EP
Tel: 01768 862748 Fax: 01768 890164   **Map Ref 69**

CROSS KEYS INN, Peter & Jackie Baister provide visitors with a homely and cosy atmosphere in pleasant surroundings. The bedrooms are tastefully furnished and have TV, tea/coffee facilities, hand basin and towels. Food is served in the bar of in our cosy restaurant from extensive menu.

B&B from £16.50pp, Dinner from £4.25, Rooms 1 twin, 3 double, 2 family, Restricted smoking, Children welcome, Open all year except Christmas & New Year. Jacqueline & Peter Baister, **Cross Keys Inn,** Tebay, Penrith CA10 3UY
Tel: 015396 24240 Fax: 015396 24240   **Map Ref 70**

The Lake District, **TEMPLE SOWERBY HOUSE HOTEL**, ideal touring within minutes. Two nights special breaks for less than £60 per night, including dinner, bed and breakfast. Award winning cuisine. Log fires. Welcoming owners. Christmas and New Year breaks also available. Reservations Information: 0800 146157
B&B from £45pp, Dinner a la carte from £25, Rooms 3 twin, 7 double, 2 family, all en-suite, Restricted smoking, Children & pets welcome, Open all year. Cecile & Geoffrey Temple, **Temple Sowerby House Hotel,** Temple Sowerby, Penrith, Cumbria CA10 1RZ
Tel: 017683 61578 Fax: 017683 61958   **Map Ref 71**

LANE HEAD FARM GUEST HOUSE, a charming 17th century former farmhouse in a quiet location, 4 miles from Ullswater. Good home cooking, table licence. Log fire, some en-suite and four poster rooms.
B&B from £18, Dinner available, Rooms 1 single, 5 double, 2 twin, 1 family, Children welcome, No smoking, Open April - December.
Lane Head Farm Guest House, Troutbeck, Penrith, Cumbria CA11 0SY
Tel: 017687 79220   **Map Ref 72**

LAND ENDS COUNTRY LODGE, is a charming 18th century farmhouse set in 7 acre gardens with 2 small lakes, offering peace and tranquillity in a fellside location. All rooms have tea/coffee, TV. Cosy lounge and bar. Excellent varied breakfasts. M6 only ten minutes.

B&B from £25pp, Rooms 3 single, 2 twin, 4 double, 1 family, all en-suite, Restricted smoking, Children welcome, No pets, Open all year. Barbara Holmes, **Land Ends Country Lodge,** Watermillock, Penrith, Cumbria CA11 0NB
Tel: 017684 86438 Fax: 017684 86959   **Map Ref 73**

WOODLAND HOUSE HOTEL, an elegant and spacious red sandstone house with library of books and maps for walkers, nature lovers and sightseers. Ideal base for exploring the Eden Valley, Pennines and Lakes. A non smoking hotel.
B&B from £23, Dinner available, Rooms 3 single, 2 double, 2 twin, 1 triple, all en-suite/private facilities, Children welcome, No pets or smoking, Open all year.
Woodland House Hotel, Wordsworth Street, Penrith, Cumbria CA11 7QY
Tel: 01768 864177 Fax: 01768 890152 Email: idaviesa@cix.compulink.co.uk
          Map Ref 57

GEORGE & DRAGON HOTEL, an excellent centre for exploring the Yorkshire Dales National Park. Owned by, and serves beer from Dent's own small brewery.

B&B from £25, Lunch and evening meal available, Rooms 4 double, 3 twin, 2 triple, some en-suite, Children welcome, Open all year.
George & Dragon Hotel, Main Street, Dent, Sedbergh, Cumbria LA10 5QL
Tel: 01539 625256   **Map Ref 74**

....

SWAN HOTEL, a privately owned hotel enjoying a beautiful site at the foot of Lake Windermere. We offer facilities appreciated by both holiday and business visitors.
B&B from £25, Lunch and evening meal available, Rooms 7 single, 13 double, 10 twin, 6 triple, all en-suite, Children welcome, No pets, No smoking, Open all year.
Swan Hotel, Newby Bridge, Ulverston, Cumbria LA12 8NB
Tel: 015395 31681 Fax: 015395 31917   **Map Ref 75**

....

WHITEWATER HOTEL, an old mill built of Lakeland stone, and converted into a hotel with all facilities, including a leisure centre in the grounds.

B&B from £50, Lunch and evening meal available, Rooms 4 single, 14 double, 7 twin, 10 triple, all en-suite, Children welcome, No pets, No smoking, Open all year.
Whitewater Hotel, The Lakeland Village, Newby Bridge, Ulverston, Cumbria LA12 8PX
Tel: 015395 31133 Fax: 015395 31881   **Map Ref 76**

....

TRINITY HOUSE HOTEL, a Georgian former rectory, elegant licenced restaurant with local food. En-suite bedrooms are spacious and stylishly decorated.
B&B from £45, Lunch and evening meal available, Rooms 5 double, 2 twin, all en-suite, Children welcome, Open all year.
Trinity House Hotel, Prince's Street, Ulverston, Cumbria LA12 7NB
Tel: 01229 587639 & 080222 6273 Fax: 01229 588552 Email: hotel@trinityhouse.furness.co.uk.   **Map Ref 77**

....

CORKICKLE GUEST HOUSE, a small Georgian guesthouse offering high standards of comfort. Conveniently situated for business of leisure visitors. Residential Licence.

B&B from £24.50, Dinner available, Rooms 2 single, 2 double, 2 twin, all en-suite/private facilities, Children welcome, No smoking, Open all year.
Corkickle Guest House, 1 Corkickle, Whitehaven, Cumbria CA28 8AA
Tel: 01946 692073 & 0850 172828 Fax: 01946 692073   **Map Ref 78**

....

ODDFELLOWS ARMS, an excellent B&B, self catering accommodation and a warm Cumbrian welcome awaits you in the beautiful unspoilt Lake District village of Caldbeck. All rooms are en-suite with TV and beverage facilities. Locally acclaimed. Public bar and restaurant offering quality food daily.

B&B from £22.50pp, Dinner from £4.95, Rooms 2 twin, 4 double, all en-suite, Restricted smoking, Children welcome, Pets by arrangement, Open all year.
Graham & Ruth Davis, **Oddfellows Arms,** Calbeck, Wigton CA7 8EA
Tel: 016974 78227 Fax: 016974 78134   **Map Ref 79**

....

LOW WOOD HOTEL, almost a mile of lake frontage. Boat launching, water ski tuition and superb lake and mountain views. Also leisure centre, indoor heated swimming pool, bubble beds, sauna room, health and beauty centre, gymnasium, conference centre, syndicate rooms, video and computer link-up.
B&B from £55, Lunch and evening meal available, Rooms 19 single, 17 double, 15 twin, 8 family, all en-suite, Children welcome, No smoking, Open all year.
Low Wood Hotel, Windermere, Cumbria LA23 1LP
Tel: 015394 33338 Fax: 015394 34072 Email: lowwood@elh.co.uk   **Map Ref 80**

LANGDALE CHASE HOTEL, a country house hotel in landscaped gardens on the edge of lake Windermere. Excellent views of mountains and lake. Great dining experience.

B&B from £47, Lunch and evening meal available, Rooms 1 single, 12 double, 17 twin, all en-suite, Children welcome, Open all year.
Langdale Chase Hotel, Windermere, Cumbria LA23 1LW
Tel: 015394 32201 Fax: 015394 32604 **Map Ref 80**

....

LINDETH FELL COUNTRY HOUSE HOTEL, beautifully situated in magnificent private grounds on the hills above Lake Windermere, Lindeth Fell offers brilliant views, modern English cooking and elegant surroundings. All bedrooms have full facilities, many have lake views.

B&B from £50, Lunch and evening meal available, Rooms 2 single, 5 double, 5 twin, 2 triple, all en-suite, Children from 7 years, No pets, Open all year.

Lindeth Fell Country House Hotel, Windermere, Cumbria LA23 3JP
Tel: 015394 43286/44287 Fax: 015394 47455 **Map Ref 80**

....

HOLLY PARK HOUSE, an elegant stone-built Victorian guesthouse with nicely furnished spacious rooms. Quiet area, convenient for village shops and coach/rail services.

B&B from £26, Dinner available, Rooms 2 double, 4 triple, all en-suite, Children welcome, No smoking, Open all year.
Holly Park House, 1 Park Road, Windermere, Cumbria LA23 2AW
Tel: 015394 42107 Fax: 015394 48997 **Map Ref 80**

....

ASHLEIGH GUEST HOUSE, a beautiful, comfortable, Victorian home in quiet, central location with stunning mountain views. All rooms en-suite, old pine furniture. Breakfast choice.

B&B from £15, Rooms 1 single, 3 double, 1 triple, all en-suite, No smoking, Children from 5 years, No pets, Open all year.
Ashleigh Guest House, 11 College Road, Windermere, Cumbria LA23 1BU
Tel/Fax: 015394 42292 Mobile: 0468 026634 **Map Ref 80**

....

OSBOURNE GUEST HOUSE, a traditional Lakeland house, central for all transport, tours and walks. Clean, comfortable,accommodation. Full breakfast. Developed by present owners since 1982.

B&B from £15, Rooms 2 double, 2 triple, all en-suite/private facilities, Children welcome, No pets, No smoking, Open all year.
Osbourne Guest House, 3 High Street, Windermere, Cumbria LA23 1AF
Tel: 015394 46452 **Map Ref 80**

....

BOSTON HOUSE, a charmingly peaceful Victorian listed building within 5 minutes walk of trains and town centre. Delicious food, panoramic views and/or four poster beds, private parking.

B&B from £39, Dinner available, Rooms 3 double, 1 twin, 1 family, all en-suite, Children welcome, No smoking, Open January - November.
Boston House, 4 The Terrace, Windermere, Cumbria LA23 1AJ
Tel: 015394 43654 Fax: 015394 43654 **Map Ref 80**

....

HOLLY LODGE, a traditional Lakeland stone guesthouse, built in 1854. In a quiet area off the main road, close to the village centre, buses, railway station and all amenities.

B&B from £18, Dinner available, Rooms 1 single, 5 double, 2 twin, 3 triple, Children welcome, No pets, Open all year.
Holly Lodge, 6 College Road, Windermere, Cumbria LA23 1BX
Tel: 015394 43873 Fax: 015394 43873 **Map Ref 80**

ROCKSIDE, is situated in Windermere village, 150 yards from railway station. Rooms have en-suite shower and toilet, tea/coffee making, clock, radio, telephone, hair dryer, remote TV. Menu for breakfast. Help given with planning days out. Large car park. RAC Acclaimed. Tariff £19.50 to £24.50.

B&B from £19.50pp, Rooms 2 single, 4 twin, 5 double, 4 family, most en-suite, Restricted smoking, Children over 2, No pets, Open all year except Christmas.
Mavis & Neville Fowles, **Rockside**, Ambleside Road, Windermere, Cumbria LA23 1AQ
Tel: 015394 45343 Fax: 015394 45343 **Map Ref 80**

....

MOUNTAIN ASH HOTEL, a Lakeland stone hotel refurbished to provide comfortable accommodation including four poster beds and spa baths. Cocktail bar, conservatory and locally renowned traditional cuisine.

B&B from £50, Lunch & evening meal available, Rooms 3 single, 19 double, all en-suite, Children welcome, No smoking, Open all year.
Mountain Ash Hotel, Ambleside Road, Windermere, Cumbria LA23 1AT
Tel: 015394 43715 Fax: 015394 88480 **Map Ref 80**

....

RAVENSWORTH HOTEL, close to the village centre, lake and fells. English and continental cooking. Variety of accommodation including four-poster beds.
B&B from £27.50, Dinner available, Rooms 2 single, 9 double, 2 twin, 1 triple, all en-suite, Children welcome, No smoking, Open all year.
Ravensworth Hotel, Ambleside Road, Windermere, Cumbria LA23 1BA
Tel: 015394 43747 Fax: 015394 43903 **Map Ref 80**

....

THE WILLOWSMERE HOTEL, offers a comfortable and friendly atmosphere. Run by the fifth generation of local hoteliers. Varied food using fresh local produce.

B&B from £26, Lunch and evening meal available, Rooms 2 single, 4 double, 1 twin, 6 triple, all en-suite, Children welcome, No smoking, Open February - November.
The Willowsmere Hotel, Ambleside Road, Windermere, Cumbria LA23 1ES
Tel: 015394 43575 & 44962 Fax: 015394 43575 **Map Ref 80**

....

FIRGARTH, an elegant Victorian house offering good breakfasts, friendly atmosphere, private parking and close to lake viewpoint. Ideally situated for touring all areas of Lakeland. Tours arranged. Full en-suite facilities. Colour TV and tea/coffee making facilities.
B&B from £16.50, Rooms 1 single, 4 double, 2 triple, 1 family, all en-suite, Children from 4 years, No smoking, Open all year.
Firgarth, Ambleside Road, Windermere, Cumbria LA23 1EU
Tel: 015394 46974 **Map Ref 80**

....

ROCKLEA, a charming, family-run, traditional Lakeland stone guesthouse in a quiet location. Very comfortable with warm, friendly atmosphere. Parking.

B&B from £17, Rooms 1 single, 4 double, 2 twin, most en-suite, Children from 3 years, Open all year.
Rocklea, Brookside, Lake Road, Windermere, Cumbria LA23 2BX
Tel: 015394 45326 **Map Ref 80**

....

APPLEGARTH HOTEL, an elegant Victorian mansion house with individually designed bedrooms and four poster suites. Lovely fell views from most rooms. Cosy restaurant and bar. Please pre-book dinner to avoid disappointment. Complimentary use of local country club.
B&B from £23, Dinner available, Rooms 4 single, 11 double 2 triple, 1 family, all en-suite, Children welcome, Open February - November and Christmas.
Applegarth Hotel, College Road, Windermere, Cumbria LA23 1BU
Tel: 015394 43206 **Map Ref 80**

GILPIN LODGE COUNTRY HOUSE HOTEL & RESTAURANT, an elegant and friendly hotel in rural setting. Situated 2 miles from Windermere. Sumptuous bedrooms, renowned cuisine and gardens. Country club nearby. Telephone 0800 269460 (toll free in UK).

B&B from £75, Lunch and evening meal available, Rooms 11 double, 3 twin, all en-suite, Children from 7 years, No Pets, No smoking, Open all year.
Gilpin Lodge Country House Hotel & Restaurant, Crook Road, Windermere, Cumbria LA23 3NE
Tel: 015394 88818 Fax: 015394 88058   **Map Ref 80**

SOUTH VIEW, unique in Windermere village - the only guesthouse with own heated indoor swimming pool open all year. Excellent breakfasts served. Quiet yet central location.
B&B from £19, Dinner available, Rooms 1 single, 3 double, 1 twin, 1 family, Children welcome, No pets or smoking, Open all year.
South View, Cross Street, Windermere, Cumbria LA23 1AE
Tel: 015394 42951   **Map Ref 80**

ORREST HEAD HOUSE, is a charming country house dating back to the 16th century. All bedrooms are en-suite and have TV and tea/coffee facilities. It is set in 3 acres of garden and woodland and has distant views to mountains and lake. Close to the station and village with a very homely atmosphere.
B&B from £22-£25pp, Rooms 2 twin, 3 double, all en-suite, No smoking or pets, Children over 6, Open February - December.
Brenda Butterworth, **Orrest Head House,** Kendal Road, Windermere, Cumbria LA23 1JG
Tel: 015394 44315   **Map Ref 80**

Situated midway between Windermere and Bowness villages, **FIR TREES** offers luxurious bed and breakfast in a Victorian guest house. Antiques and beautiful prints abound in the public areas, while the bedrooms, all with en-suite, are immaculately furnished and decorated. Breakfasts are simply scrumptious. ETB Highly Commended and is recommended by leading guides.

B&B from £22-£28pp, Rooms 2 twin, 4 double, 2 family, all en-suite, No smoking, Children welcome, Open all year except Christmas.
Mr & Mrs I Fishman, **Fir Trees,** Lake Road, Windermere LA23 2EQ
Tel: 015394 42272 Fax: 015394 42272   **Map Ref 80**

GLENVILLE HOTEL, standing in its own grounds, midway between Windermere and Bowness and perfectly positioned for access to all amenities. The lake is an easy 10 minute walk. Car park.
B&B from £20, Dinner available, Rooms 1 single, 4 double, 3 triple, all en-suite/private facilities, Children welcome, No pets or smoking, Open February - December.
Glenville Hotel, Lake Road, Windermere, Cumbria LA23 2EQ
Tel: 015394 43371   **Map Ref 80**

ST. JOHN'S LODGE, a fourteen bedroomed private licensed guest house situated midway between Windermere and the Lake. Convenient for all amenities. Fabulous food prepared by resident chef/proprietor. Beamed dining room, en-suite rooms with colour TV, tea/coffee facilities. Parking. Use of nearby leisure facilities. Bargain breaks available.
B&B from £18pp, Dinner from £11.50, Rooms 2 single, 1 twin, 3 double, 3 family, all en-suite, Restricted smoking, Children over 4, Pets by arrangement, Open all year except Christmas.
Barry & Sue Watts, **St. John's Lodge,** Lake Rd, Windermere LA23 2EQ
Tel: 015394 43078   **Map Ref 81**

THE POPLARS, a small family-run guesthouse on the main lake road, offering en-suite accommodation coupled with fine cuisine and homely atmosphere. Golf and fishing can be arranged.

B&B from £20, Dinner available, Rooms 1 single, 3 double, 2 twin, 1 triple, all en-suite/private facilities, Children from 3 years, Open February - December.

The Poplars, Lake Road, Windermere, Cumbria LA23 2EQ
Tel: 015394 42325 & 46690 Fax: 015394 42325   Map Ref 80

....

WESTLAKE, a family - run, private hotel between Windermere and the lake. All rooms en-suite, with colour TV and tea making facilities. Private parking.

B&B from £19, Dinner available, Rooms 1 single, 3 double, 1 twin, 2 triple, all en-suite, Children from 5 years, No pets, No smoking, Open all year.

Westlake, Lake Road, Windermere, Cumbria LA23 2EQ
Tel: 015394 43020 & 0850 779886   Map Ref 80

....

KNOLL HOTEL, situated in quiet grounds, with magnificent views overlooking Lake Windermere and the mountains. Free use of Parklands leisure club.

B&B from £25, Dinner available, Rooms 4 single, 4 double, 1 twin, 3 triple, most en-suite, Children from 3 years, No pets, Open all year.

Knoll Hotel, Lake Road, Windermere, Cumbria LA23 2JF
Tel: 015394 43756 Fax: 015394 88496 Email: knoll.hotel@ccs.prestel.co.uk   Map Ref 80

....

WHITE LODGE HOTEL, a Victorian family-owned hotel with good home cooking, only a short walk from Bowness Bay. All bedrooms have private bathroom, colour TV and tea-making facilities, some with lake views and four posters.

B&B from £24, Lunch and evening meal available, Rooms 3 single, 6 double, 2 twin, 1 triple, all en-suite, Children welcome, No pets, No smoking, Open March - November.

White Lodge Hotel, Lake Road, Windermere, Cumbria LA23 2JJ
Tel: 015394 43624 Fax: 015394 47000   Map Ref 80

....

GLENBURN HOTEL, has 16 en-suite bedrooms. All rooms have TV, radio, telephone and tea/coffee making facilities. Some four posters. Spa baths. A la carte menu. Free leisure centre nearby. Swimming pool. Gym. Sauna. Steam room. Snooker. Squash. Large private car park. Ideally located for most Lakeland attractions.
B&B from £25pp, Dinner from £16.50, Rooms 2 twin, 12 double, 2 family, all en-suite, No smoking, Children over 5, No pets, Open all year except Christmas.
David & Evelyne Limbrey, **Glenburn Hotel**, New Rd, Windermere, Cumbria LA23 2EE
Tel: 015394 42649 Fax: 015394 88998   Map Ref 80

....

WOODLANDS, a family run hotel in a quiet convenient location. Renowned for its high standard of cleanliness and comfort. Ample car parking.

B&B from £22, Dinner available, Rooms 2 single, 10 double, 1 twin, 1 family, all en-suite, Children from 5 years, No pets or smoking, Open all year.

Woodlands, New Road, Windermere, Cumbria LA23 2EE
Tel: 015394 43915 & 0468 596142 Fax: 015394 48558   Map Ref 80

OLDFIELD HOUSE, A friendly informal atmosphere within a traditionally built Lakeland stone residence. Quiet central location. Ideal for touring the Lake District. All rooms are en-suite with TV, telephone and tea/coffee facilities. We offer drying facilities. Guests have free use of Parklands swimming/leisure club. Car park. Email: oldfield.house@virgin.net

B&B from £20-£34pp, Rooms 2 single, 2 twin, 2 double, 2 family, all en-suite, No smoking, Children welcome, No pets, Open February - December.

Mr & Mrs Theobald, **Oldfield House,** Oldfield Road, Windermere, Cumbria LA23 2BY

Tel: 015394 88445 Fax: 015394 43250   **Map Ref 80**

BECKSIDE, Bed and Breakfast is perfectly situated near Windermere Lake in a superb garden setting. Near the famous "Miller How". Private parking for cars. English and vegetarian breakfast's. Maps and guides for walks and car tours provided. Tea/coffee facilities, TV. No smoking.

B&B from £17.50pp, Rooms 2 double en-suite, 1 family, No smoking, Children over 3, Pets by arrangement, Open all year.

Pauline Threlfall, **Beckside,** Rayrigg Road, Windermere LA23 1EY

Tel: 015394 43565 Mobile: 0402 111 012   **Map Ref 80**

BRAEMOUNT HOUSE, situated in a quiet location, only 5 minutes walk from Windermere and Bowness. Offering individually designed and comprehensively equipped bedrooms. Including a beautiful four poster suite. Super breakfast. Relax in pretty gardens with complimentary tea/cake for afternoon arrivals. Private car park. A warm welcome awaits.

B&B from £23pp, Rooms 1 twin, 3 double, 1 family, all en-suite, No smoking, Children welcome, Pets by arrangement, Open all year.

Duncan & Janine Hatfield, **Braemount House,** Sunny Bank Road, Windermere, Cumbria LA23 2EN

Tel: 015394 45967 Fax: 015394 45967   **Map Ref 80**

LINDISFARNE, a traditional detached Lakeland house. Situated in quiet area, close to the lake, shops and scenic walks. Varied breakfast. Friendly and flexible hosts.

B&B from £17, Dinner available, Rooms 2 double, 1 twin, 1 family, Children & pets welcome, Open all year.

Lindisfarne, Sunny Bank Road, Windermere, Cumbria LA23 2EN

Tel: 015394 46295   **Map Ref 80**

HIGH GREEN LODGE, Here all Mornings are Magical - Sun, Swans, Swallows and Amazons. Cosy en-suite/kingsize rooms in peaceful lodge with fantastic views down valley/Lake Garbon Pass. Four posters, Walkers/Motorists Paradise. Fabulous Breakfast, Gourmet food at pubs nearby.

B&B from £35pp, Rooms 2 double, 1 twin, all en-suite, No smoking, Open all year.

High Green Lodge, High Green, Troutbeck, Windermere, Cumbria LA23 1PN

Tel: 015394 33005   **Map Ref 82**

HUNDAY MANOR HOTEL, a manor house set in 4 acres of woodland and gardens overlooking the Solway and Scottish coastline.

B&B from £40, Lunch and evening meal available, Rooms 5 single, 4 double, 4 twin, all en-suite, Children welcome, No smoking, Open all year.

Hunday Manor Hotel, Hunday, Workington, Cumbria CA14 4JF

Tel: 01900 61798 Fax: 01900 601202   **Map Ref 83**

Rich upland scenery and industrial heritage offer a wide variation for the visitor to Derbyshire and Staffordshire. A focus of the area is the Peak District National Park, England's most southerly highland country with Britain's first national park more than 40 years ago at its heart. Most of the Peak District's 555 square miles are in Derbyshire, but include parts of surrounding counties, one of them being Staffordshire. Rich and varied countryside from moorland, grassy hills and dales to craggy rocks. It is not surprising that the area offers plenty of activities, whether on foot, horseback or by bicycle. The area has over four thousand miles of public paths and areas where walkers have free access for most of the year there is also climbing, caving, sailing and gliding.

Buxton is in the heart of the national park and although one of the highest towns in England, is sheltered by the surrounding hills. The spa town owes its fame to the 5th Duke of Devonshire who, at the end of the 18th century, built the town's beautiful Crescent as a rival to fashionable Bath. Just as they did in Roman times, the town's springs emerge at a constant temperature.

Not far from Buxton, at Edale is the start of the Pennine Way, which runs along the Pennine chain to the Scottish border. The River Wye flows from Bakewell where the surrounding wooded hills stretch up to high moorland. The town is perhaps most famous for its Bakewell Tarts. Known locally as Bakewell pudding, the recipe began when the cook from the Rutland Arms spread egg mixture on top of the jam in a strawberry tart instead of using it in the pastry.

At the centre of Derbyshire is the city of Derby with its parks, theatre, shopping, sporting facilities and attractions. Derby's recent history was founded on silk and the railways. Some of the city's finest houses date from the 18th century.

The area around Stoke-on-Trent is dominated by industry. The towns of the Potteries have plenty to offer the visitor with many of the pottery shops and factories open to the public. The area was a natural place for the making of pottery with its ample supplies of clay, as well as water and coal. Fragments of pottery dating back to Neolithic times and Roman and Saxon wares have also been discovered.

The county town of Stafford on the River Saw was listed as a borough in the Domesday Book in 1086. Both Leek and Uttoxeter are market towns. Uttoxeter is known for its National Hunt steeplechase course. Lichfield is dominated by its cathedral's three sandstone spires, known as "The Ladies of the Vale". Dr Samuel Johnson was born in Breadmarket Street, Lichfield in 1709.

Derbyshire & Staffordshire

left, Old Glossop, Derbyshire

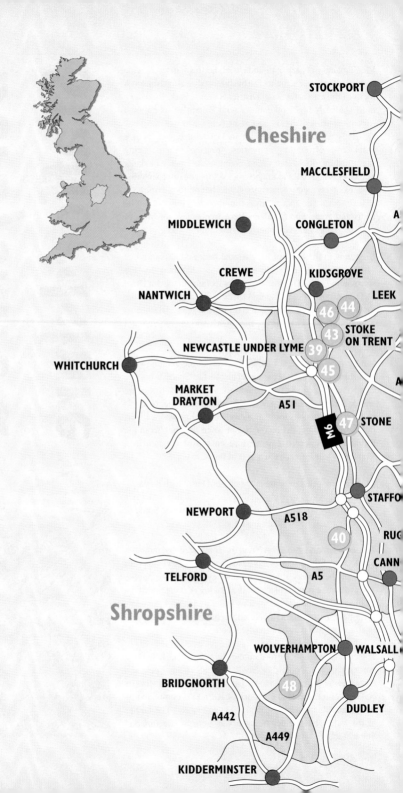

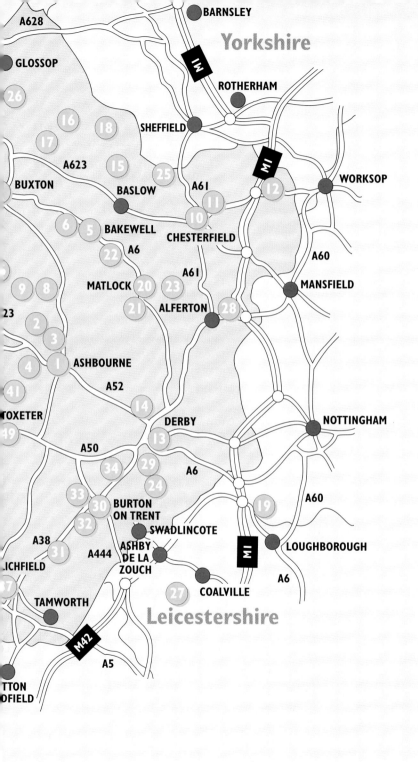

HANOVER INTERNATIONAL HOTEL & CLUB ASHBOURNE, purpose-built hotel offering en-suite cottage-style bedrooms, luxury leisure centre, two restaurants and bars. Within easy reach of Alton Towers and ideally located for exploring the Peak District, including Dovedale, Haddon Hall and Chatsworth.

B&B from £68.50, Dinner available, Rooms 2 single, 25 double, 10 twin, 8 triple, 5 family, all en-suite, Open all year.
Hanover International Hotel & Club Ashbourne, Derby Road, Ashbourne, Derbyshire DE6 1XH
Tel: 01335 346666 Fax: 01335 346549 **Map Ref 1**

Situated in the beautiful Peak District National Park, in a tranquil hamlet overlooking Dovedale. **THE OLD RECTORY** provides everything you would expect of an English country house! Dinner is by candlelight with your hosts, in a formal house party atmosphere. The property is licensed!

B&B from £39, Dinner from £22, Rooms 1 twin, 2 double, all en-suite or private, Restricted smoking, No children or pets, Open all year except Christmas.
Mr & Mrs Stuart Worthington, **The Old Rectory,** Blore, Ashbourne, Derbyshire DE6 2BS
Tel: 01335 350287 Fax: 01335 350287 **Map Ref 2**

CALLOW HALL COUNTRY HOUSE HOTEL & RESTAURANT, half a mile from the centre of Ashbourne and set in an elevated position in unspoilt countryside, surrounded by its own woodland and overlooking the valleys of Bentley Brook and River Dove.

B&B from £70, Dinner available, Rooms 10 double, 6 twin, all en-suite, Open all year.
Callow Hall Country House Hotel & Restaurant, Mappleton, Ashbourne, Derbyshire DE6 2AA
Tel: 01335 343403 Fax: 01335 343624 **Map Ref 3**

LICHFIELD GUEST HOUSE, Georgian house set in 2 acres of landscaped gardens. Magnificent views over River Dove and valleys. Convenient for Alton Towers, Chatsworth and Peaks. Non-smoking.

B&B from £21-£22, Rooms 1 double, 1 twin, 1 family, all en-suite, Open all year.
Lichfield Guest House, Bridge View, Mayfield, Ashbourne, Derbyshire DE6 2HN
Tel: 01335 344422 Fax: 01335 344422 **Map Ref 4**

CASTLE CLIFFE PRIVATE HOTEL, Victorian stone house overlooking beautiful Monsal Dale. Noted for its friendly atmosphere, good food and exceptional views.

B&B from £30, Dinner available, Rooms 1 single, 2 double, 4 twin, 2 family, most en-suite, Open all year.
Castle Cliffe Private Hotel, Monsal Head, Bakewell, Derbyshire DE45 1NL
Tel: 01629 640258 Fax: 01629 640258 **Map Ref 5**

RIVERSIDE COUNTRY HOUSE HOTEL, 17th century manor house with its own river frontage and an acre of garden which supplies home produce. Panelled bar, antiques, four-poster beds and an inglenook fireplace with log fires.

B&B from £75, Dinner available, Rooms 10 double, 5 twin, all en-suite, Open all year.
Riverside Country House Hotel, Fennel Street, Ashford in the Water, Bakewell, Derbyshire DE4 1QF
Tel: 01629 814275 Fax: 01629 812873 **Map Ref 6**

CHY-AN-DOUR, Bungalow overlooking a pretty village and offering a friendly welcome. An ideal base for visiting the nearby stately homes and Derbyshire Dales.

B&B from £30, Rooms 2 double, 1 twin, all en-suite, Open all year.

Chy-an-Dour, Vicarage Lane, Ashford in the Water, Bakewell, Derbyshire DE45 1QN
Tel: 01629 813162 **Map Ref 6**

GROSVENOR HOUSE HOTEL, privately-run Victorian residence enjoying splendid views of Pavilion Gardens/theatre. Homely and peaceful atmosphere. Bedrooms non-smoking. Home-cooked traditional food. Comfort and hospitality assured.

B&B from £25pp, Dinner available, Rooms 5 double, 1 twin, 2 triple, all en-suite, Open all year.
Grosvenor House Hotel, 1 Broad Walk, Buxton, Derbyshire SK17 6JE
Tel: 01298 72439 Fax: 01298 72439   **Map Ref 7**

....

FAIRHAVEN, within easy reach of the Opera House, Pavilion Gardens, 2 golf courses and the many and varied attractions of Derbyshire's Peak District.

B&B from £17, Dinner available, Rooms 1 single, 1 double, 1 twin, 2 triple, 1 family, Open all year.
Fairhaven, 1 Dale Terrace, Buxton, Derbyshire SK17 6LU
Tel: 01298 24481 Fax: 01298 24481   **Map Ref 7**

....

LAKENHAM GUESTHOUSE, elegant Victorian house in own grounds overlooking Pavilion gardens. Furnished in Victorian manner and offering personal service in a friendly, replaced atmosphere.

B&B from £30, Dinner available, Rooms 2 double, 2 twin, 2 family, all en-suite, Open all year.
Lakenham Guesthouse, 11 Burlington Road, Buxton, Derbyshire SK17 9AL
Tel: 01298 79209   **Map Ref 7**

....

FORD SIDE HOUSE, elegant, Edwardian house for non-smokers, in premier residential area yet close to all amenities. Stylish accommodation and delicious home cooking with flair.

B&B from £19, Dinner available, Rooms 2 double, 1 twin, all en-suite, Open all year.
Ford Side House, 125 Lightwood Road, Buxton, Derbyshire SK17 6RW
Tel: 01298 72842   **Map Ref 7**

....

PORTLAND HOTEL & PARK RESTAURANT, situated just 100 yards from Buxton's famous Opera House, the hotel and its noted restaurant make the perfect base for touring the Peak District.

B&B from £48, Dinner available, Rooms 6 single, 11 double, 7 twin, 1 triple, all en-suite, Open all year.
Portland Hotel & Park Restaurant, 32 St John's Road, Buxton, Derbyshire SK17 6XQ
Tel: 01298 71493 Fax: 01298 27464   **Map Ref 7**

....

BUXTON VIEW, guest house built from local stone, offering a friendly and relaxed atmosphere. In a quiet area with a commanding view over the town and surrounding hills, yet only a few minutes walk from the towns amenities.

B&B from £19, Dinner available, Rooms 1 single, 2 double, 1 twin, 1 triple, most en-suite, Open all year.
Buxton View, 74 Corbar Road, Buxton, Derbyshire SK17 6RJ
Tel: 01298 79222   **Map Ref 7**

....

HAWTHORN FARM GUEST HOUSE, is a listed building circa 1600 and has been in the Smith family for ten generations. There is a guests lounge with TV. Bedrooms have colour TV, tea/coffee facilities. We have parking for twelve cars. A golf course is nearby.

B&B from £22p, Rooms 4 single, 2 twin, 2 double, 4 family, some en-suite, Restricted smoking, Children & pets welcome, Open April - October.
David J.S. Smith, **Hawthorn Farm Guest House,** Fairfield Road, Buxton, Derbyshire SK17 7ED
Tel: 01298 23230   **Map Ref 7**

BIGGIN HALL, 17th century hall, Grade II listed, sympathetically modernised. Set tranquillity in the Peak District National Park. Fresh home cooking and comforts. Beautiful, uncrowded walks from the grounds.

B&B from £30, Dinner available, Rooms 7 double, 7 twin, 3 triple, 1 family, all en-suite, Open all year.
Biggin Hall, Biggin-by-Hartington, Buxton, Derbyshire SK17 0DH
Tel: 01298 84451 Fax: 01298 84681   **Map Ref 8**

CRESSBROOK HALL, accommodation with a difference. Enjoy this magnificent family home built in 1853, set in 23 acres, with spectacular views around the compass.

B&B from £62, Dinner available, Rooms 2 double, 1 twin, all en-suite, Open all year.
Cressbrook Hall, Cressbrook, Buxton, Derbyshire SK17 8SY
Tel: 01298 871289 Fax: 01298 871845   **Map Ref 7**

THE MANIFOLD INN, is a 200 year old coaching inn offering warm hospitality and good pub food at sensible prices Accommodation is in the old blacksmith's shop in secluded rear courtyard. All rooms have en-suite shower rooms, colour TV, tea/coffee facilities and telephone. Well lit car park in courtyard. ETB 3 Crown Commended.
B&B from £21-£30pp, Dinner from £5, Rooms 1 twin, 4 double, all en-suite, Children welcome, Pets in outside kennel, Open all year except Christmas Day.
Mr & Mrs F Lipp, **The Manifold Inn,** Hulme End, Hartington, Buxton, Derbyshire SK17 0EX
Tel: 01298 84537   **Map Ref 9**

ABIGAILS, relax taking breakfast in the conservatory overlooking Chesterfield and surrounding moor lands. Garden with pond and waterfall, private car park.

B&B from £21.50, Dinner available, Rooms 2 single, 3 double, 2 twin, all en-suite, Open all year.
Abigails, 62 Brockwell Lane, Chesterfield, Derbyshire S40 4EE
Tel: 01246 279391   **Map Ref 10**

ABBEYDALE HOTEL, residence proprietors. Quiet location within walking distance of town centre, close to Peak District and Chatsworth. Short breaks available.

B&B from £49.50, Dinner available, Rooms 3 single, 7 double, 1 twin, 1 triple, all en-suite, Open all year.
Abbeydale Hotel, Cross Street, Chesterfield, Derbyshire S40 4TD
Tel: 01246 277849 Fax: 01246 558223   **Map Ref 10**

RINGWOOD HALL HOTEL & CONFERENCE CENTRE, country house hotel, circa 1804, in its own grounds. A bowling green and various activities. Conferences and functions are a speciality.

B&B from £50, Dinner available, Rooms 1 single, 15 double, 8 twin, all en-suite, Open all year.
Ringwood Hall Hotel & Conference Centre, Brimington, Chesterfield, Derbyshire S43 1DQ
Tel: 01246 280077 Fax: 01246 472241 Email: ringwood@enterprise.net   **Map Ref 11**

THE VAN DYK HOTEL, elegant country house hotel in beautiful countryside, with 2 bars, a restaurant, banqueting and conference facilities. Approximately 1 mile from M1 junction 30.

B&B from £45, Dinner available, Rooms 8 single, 1 double, 5 twin, 2 triple, all en-suite, Open all year.

The Van Dyk Hotel, Worksop Road, Clowne, Chesterfield, Derbyshire S43 4TD
Tel: 01246 810219 Fax: 01246 819566   **Map Ref 12**

SANDPIPER HOTEL, in a prime location with easy access to Chesterfield, Sheffield and the Peak District. Sky TV, full restaurant, conference and banqueting facilities.

B&B from £35, Dinner available, Rooms 8 double, 16 twin, 3 triple, 1 family, all en-suite, Open all year.
Sandpiper Hotel, Sheffield Road, Sheep Bridge, Chesterfield, Derbyshire S41 9EH
Tel: 01246 450550 Fax: 01246 452805 **Map Ref 10**

....

CLARENDON GUEST HOUSE, Victorian town residence, near town centre, cricket ground, leisure facilities and Peak District National Park. Special diets catered for.

B&B from £14, Dinner available, Rooms 2 single, 1 double, 1 twin, most en-suite, Open all year.
Clarendon Guest House, 32 Clarence Road, West Bars, Chesterfield, Derbyshire S40 1LN
Tel: 01246 235004 **Map Ref 10**

....

ROSE & THISTLE, eight bedrooms, all with TV and tea/coffee facilities. Children welcome.

B&B from £18, Dinner available, Rooms 2 single, 5 double, 1 triple, Open all year.
Rose & Thistle, 21 Charnwood Street, Derby, Derbyshire DE1 2GU
Tel: 01332 344103 **Map Ref 13**

....

HOTEL RISTORANTE "LA GONDOLA", privately owned hotel with bar, restaurant and private car park. Close to the city centre and all amenities.

B&B from £48.50, Dinner available, Rooms 11 double, 2 twin, 6 triple, 1 family, all en-suite, Open all year.
Hotel Ristorante "La Gondola", 220 Osmaston Road, Derby, Derbyshire DE23 8JX
Tel: 01332 332895 Fax: 01332 384512 **Map Ref 13**

....

THE GEORGIAN HOUSE HOTEL, country style hotel in town. Beautiful Georgian architecture built circa 1765, situated city's West End. Few minutes walk from centre. Cosy cocktail bay and lively Tavern bar and restaurant. Outside courtyard dining in summer. Large car park and gardens. All bedrooms en-suite, colour TV and telephone.

B&B from £26pp, Dinner from £6.50, Rooms 4 single, 2 twin, 10 double, 4 family, all en-suite, Children & Pets welcome, Open all year.
The Georgian House Hotel, Ashbourne Road, Derby DE22 3AD
Tel: 01332 349806 Fax: 01332 349959 **Map Ref 13**

....

INTERNATIONAL HOTEL & RESTAURANT, situated close to the city centre, this privately owned hotel makes an excellent base from which to explore the Peak District Park. Good quality restaurant offers an extensive selection of fare.
B&B from £36, Dinner available, Rooms 12 single, 40 double, 6 twin, 4 triple, all en-suite, Open all year.
International Hotel & Restaurant, Burton Road, Derby, Derbyshire DE23 6AD
Tel: 01332 369321 Fax: 01332 294430 **Map Ref 13**

....

EUROPEAN INN, is a stylish modern hotel offering good quality bed and breakfast accommodation. All rooms have televisions, trouser press, drinks facilities and hair dryer. Continental restaurant on -site, full buffet style English breakfast. Near Derby railway station, 10 minutes off M1. An ideal base from which to explore Derbyshire. Email: admin@euro-derby.co.uk
B&B from £25pp, Rooms 22 twin, 66 double/family, all en-suite, Children welcome, Pets by arrangement, Open all year.
John Rowland & Richard Cooper, **European Inn,** Midland Rd, Derby DE1 2SL
Tel: 01332 292000 Fax: 01332 293940 **Map Ref 13**

THE MACKWORTH HOTEL, hotel with ample car parking in a rural setting. Recently refurbished restaurant and bedrooms. Within easy reach of city centre, Peak District and Alton Towers.
B&B from £32, Dinner available, Rooms 4 single, 5 double, 1 twin, 3 triple, 1 family, all en-suite, Open all year.
The Mackworth Hotel, Ashbourne Road, Mackworth, Derby DE22 4LY
Tel: 01332 824324 Fax: 01332 824692　　　　　　　　　　　　　**Map Ref 14**

MAYNARD ARMS HOTEL, established hotel with a relaxed, friendly atmosphere and extensive facilities. Picturesque gardens with lovely views of Hope Valley and Peak Park. Excellent walking country.
B&B from £63, Dinner available, Rooms 8 double, 2 twin, all en-suite. Open all year.
Maynard Arms Hotel, Main Road, Grindleford S32 2HE
Tel: 01433 630321 Fax: 01433 630445　　　　　　　　　　　　　**Map Ref 15**

SNAKE PASS INN, all rooms have satellite TV, plus tea/coffee facilities. There is a large car park. As it is a pub the bar is open all day. Set amidst dramatic scenery of the Peak District. Ideal for walking, cycling or relaxing. Close to the Pennine Way.

B&B From £??pp, Dinner from £5, Rooms 1 twin, 4 double, 1 family, all en-suite. Children welcome, No pets, Open all year except Christmas & New Year.
Tony & Maureen Murphy, Snake Pass Inn, Snake Road, Bamford, Hope Valley, Derbyshire S33 0BJ
Tel: 01433 651 480 Fax: 01433 651 480　　　　　　**Map Ref 16**

THE RAMBLERS REST, is a quietly situated 17th century guest house in the picturesque village of Castleton. Close to the castle and caverns. We have five double rooms, all have television and tea making facilities. A warm welcome awaits you.

B&B from £16pp, Rooms 2 single, 2 twin, 5 double, 1 family, some en-suite, Children & pets welcome, Open all year except Christmas.
Mary Gillott, The Ramblers Rest, Mill Bridge, Castleton, Hope Valley, Derbyshire S33 8WR
Tel: 01433 620125　　　　　　　　　　　　　　　　**Map Ref 17**

HIGHLOW HALL, is a 16th century manor in the heart of the Peak District with splendid views, peace and quiet. It is an ideal base for walking. All rooms are en-suite and have tea/coffee. One has a 4-poster bed.

B&B from £29pp, Rooms 2 double, 1 family/twin, No smoking or dogs, Children over 12. Open all year except Christmas & New Year.

Mr & Mrs M B Walker, Highlow Hall, Hathersage, Hope Valley, Derbyshire S32 1AX
Tel/Fax: 01433 650393　　　　　　　　　　　　　　　**Map Ref 18**

KEGWORTH HOUSE, a fine Georgian residence in superb grounds. Access to M1, M42, A50, EMA, Donington Circuit - all 5 minutes. Nottingham, Derby, Leicester, Birmingham & Derby Dales - all 30 minutes. Luxurious accommodation. Fine English cuisine with fresh vegetables from our own garden. ETB 3 Crowns Highly Commended.

B&B from £29.50pp, Dinner from £18, Rooms 3 double, all en-suite, No smoking, Pets by arrangement, Open all year except Christmas & New Year.
Tony & Diana Belcher, Kegworth House, 42 High St, Kegworth DE74 2DA
Tel: 01509 672575 Fax: 01509 670645　　　　　　**Map Ref 19**

RIBER HALL, relax in this tranquil and historic Derbyshire Country House, enjoy excellent cuisine and stroll in the old walled garden and orchard. Nominated as 'One of the most romantic hotels in Britain' and recommended by all major hotel and restaurant guides.

B&B from £83pp, Dinner available, Rooms 14 double, all en-suite, Restricted smoking, Children & pets welcome, Open all year.

Riber Hall, Matlock, Derbyshire DE4 5JU
Tel: 01629 582795 Fax: 01629 580475 **Map Ref 20**

....

WINSTAFF GUESTHOUSE, in a pleasant, quiet cul-de-sac, with a garden backing on the the River Derwent and the park, central for many tourist attractions. Private forecourt parking. Colour TV in all rooms.

B&B from £18, Rooms 5 double, 1 twin, 1 triple, some en-suite, Open all year.
Winstaff Guesthouse, Derwent Avenue, off Old English Rd, Matlock, Derbyshire DE4 3LX
Tel: 01629 582593 **Map Ref 20**

....

ROBERTSWOOD, spacious Victorian residence on the edge of Matlock, with panoramic views. Near Chatsworth. Friendly warm welcome.

B&B from £23, Dinner available, Rooms 6 double, 2 twin, all en-suite, Open all year.
Robertswood, Farley Hill, Matlock, Derbyshire DE4 3LL
Tel: 01629 55642 Fax: 01629 55642 **Map Ref 21**

....

HODGKINSONS HOTEL, Georgian hotel, beautifully restored, with original features. Open fires, antique shop and hairdressing salon. Terraced garden with lovely views.

B&B from £30, Dinner available, Rooms 1 single, 6 double, all en-suite. Open all year.
Hodgkinsons Hotel, 150 South Parade, Matlock Bath, Matlock, Derbyshire DE4 3NR
Tel: 01629 582170 Fax: 01629 584891 **Map Ref 21**

....

EAST LODGE COUNTRY HOUSE HOTEL & RESTAURANT, tastefully furnished country house hotel and restaurant, set in 10 acres of grounds close to Chatsworth, Haddon Hall and the market town of Bakewell.

B&B from £63, Dinner available, Rooms 3 single, 6 double, 6 twin, all en-suite, Open all year.

East Lodge Country House Hotel & Restaurant, Rowsley, Matlock, Derbyshire DE4 2EF
Tel: 01629 734474 Fax: 01629 733949 **Map Ref 22**

....

GROUSE AND CLARET, a delightful country inn, in the heart of the Peak District, providing a friendly, comfortable atmosphere and easy access attractions.

B&B from £20, Dinner available, Rooms 2 single, 3 double, Open all year.
Grouse and Claret, Station Road, Rowsley, Matlock, Derbyshire DE4 2EL
Tel: 01629 733233 **Map Ref 22**

....

THE TAVERN, 17th century country village inn serving real ales and with extensive lunch and dinner menus. Close to the main road, M1 and numerous places of local interest.

B&B from £25, Dinner available, Rooms 1 double, 1 twin, both en-suite, Open all year.
The Tavern, Nottingham Road, Tansley, Matlock, Derbyshire DE4 5FR
Tel: 01629 57735 & 57840 **Map Ref 23**

BOWER LODGE, a beautifully furnished Victorian house in four acres. Ideal for visiting Chatsworth, Kedleston, Calke, Alton Towers, Donnington Race Track, Melbourne, Sudbury. One hour from NEC. Superb cuisine and licensed.

B&B from £25pp, Dinner £17.50, Rooms 1 single, 4 twin, 2 double en-suite, Children welcome, Pets by arrangement, Open all year except Christmas, New Year & Easter.
Elizabeth & Peter Plant, **Bower Lodge,** Well Lane, Repton, Derbyshire DE65 6EY
Tel: 01283 702245 Fax: 01283 704361 **Map Ref 24**

....

SPRINGWOOD HOUSE, situated in 5 acres with beautiful open views of the surrounding countryside in a peaceful location with off-road parking. Both bedrooms have drinks tray, colour TV, and are comfortably furnished. IT is near Chatsworth House, Haddon Hall, Sheffield, Chesterfield. Local hostelries serve excellent food. A warm welcome awaits each guest.

B&B from £20pp, Rooms 1 twin, 1 double, both en-suite, Restricted smoking, Children welcome, Pets by arrangement, Open all year except Christmas & New Year.

Avril Turner, **Springwood House,** Cowley Lane, Holmesfield, Sheffield, Derbyshire S18 7SD
Tel: 0114 2890253 Fax: 0114 2891365 **Map Ref 25**

....

MOORGATE, distinctive country guesthouse in the heart of the Peak District. En-suite facilities available. Boot and drying room. Packed lunches. Ideal for walking and touring.

B&B from £18.50, Dinner available, Rooms 8 single, 3 double, 15 twin, some en-suite, Open all year.
Moorgate, Edale Road, Hope, Sheffield, Derbyshire S30 2RF
Tel: 01433 621219 **Map Ref 26**

....

THE ODD HOUSE INN

THE ODD HOUSE INN, a 300 year old coaching inn. 3 bars, 2 function rooms, breakfast room, restaurant seating 200, adventure playground, skittles alley, pool. Sky TV, darts, caravan and camping. Bar food, traditional beers, beer garden. All rooms have TV, tea/coffee. Ideal for weddings, conferences, disco's, party's. Situated in open countryside.
B&B from £29.50pp, Dinner from £4.95, Rooms 10 single, 5 twin, 5 double, 2 family, all en-suite, Children & pets welcome, Open all year.
Mr Richardson, **The Odd House Inn,** Bosworth Road, Snarestone, Derbyshire DE12 7DQ
Tel: 01530 270223 Fax: 01530 270938 **Map Ref 27**

....

SWALL HOTEL, modern hotel at junction 28 of M1 motorway. Ideal for Peak District, Chatsworth House, Sherwood Forest, Alton Towers (Discounted tickets available). Leisure facilities. Short break packages available.

B&B from £55, Dinner available, Rooms 54 single, 66 double, 41 twin, all en-suite, Open all year.
Swall Hotel, Carter Lane East, South Normanton, Derbyshire DE55 2EH
Tel: 01773 812000 Fax: 01773 580032 **Map Ref 28**

....

THE WILLINGTON

THE WILLINGTON, Eighteenth century property. Twelve en-suite rooms. Ideal location for Burton and Derby. A cosy country pub offering. A la carte meals and bar snacks. Traditional restaurant. Mature garden and 120 space car park. A member of the English Tourist Board. Tea/coffee facilities. Direct dial telephone, TV.

B&B from £37.50pp, Dinner from £4.50, Rooms 5 twin, 7 double, all en-suite, Children & pets welcome, Open all year.
The Willington, 28 Hall Lane, Willington, Derbyshire DE65 6DR
Tel: 01283 702104 Fax: 01283 701570 **Map Ref 29**

THE QUEENS HOTEL, a historic 3 Star hotel in centre of county town renowned for it's beers. Rebuilt in 1991, all rooms are en-suite including 4 posters and suites. With free car parking. Welcoming bar and an excellent restaurant. First class friendly hotel ideally located for Alton Towers and Peak District. Email: aardvark@bigfoot.com
B&B from £22.50pp, Dinner from £12.50, Rooms 10 single, 3 twin, 13 double, 1 family, all en-suite, Children welcome, No smoking, Open all year.
Andrea Stickland, **The Queens Hotel,** One Bridge Street, Burton upon Trent, Staffordshire DE14 1SY
Tel: 01283 564993 Fax: 01283 517556   **Map Ref 30**

CLAYMAR HOTEL, homely inn and Rafters Restaurant. Bar food also available. Sunday lunches available in Rafters.

B&B from £35, Dinner available, Rooms 2 single, 10 double, 4 twin, 3 triple, all en-suite, Open all year.
Claymar Hotel, 118a Main Street, Alrewas, Burton upon Trent, Staffordshire DE13 7AE
Tel: 01283 790202 Fax: 01283 791465   **Map Ref 31**

FAIRFIELD GUEST HOUSE, spacious, early-Victorian residence, recently carefully restored, with modern facilities but retaining many original features.

B&B from £30, Dinner available, Rooms 2 double, 1 twin, all en-suite, Open all year.
Fairfield Guest House, 55 Main Street, Barton under Needwood, Burton upon Trent, Staffordshire DE13 8AB
Tel: 01283 716396 Fax: 01827 61594   **Map Ref 32**

RIVERSIDE HOTEL, character hotel with restaurant offering a wide choice of food, in peaceful surroundings with own river frontage.

B&B from £28, Dinner available, Rooms 16 single, 6 double, all en-suite, Open all year.
Riverside Hotel, Riverside Drive, Branston, Burton upon Trent, Staffordshire DE14 3EP
Tel: 01283 511234 Fax: 01283 511441   **Map Ref 33**

THREE HORSESHOES INN & RESTAURANT, log fire, slate floor, oak and pine beams, good food and wines. Cottage-style rooms. Convenient for Peak District National Park and Alton Towers.

B&B from £45, Dinner available, Rooms 4 double, 2 twin, all en-suite, Open all year.
Three Horseshoes Inn & Restaurant, Buxton Road, Blackshaw Moor, Leek, Staffordshire ST13 8TW
Tel: 01538 300296 Fax: 01538 300320   **Map Ref 35**

THE BLACK LION INN, an 18th century atmospheric country inn situated in a picturesque village close to the beautiful Manifold Valley. Abundance of exposed beams, log fires. En-suite B&B rooms with television, tea/coffee facilities, guests' lounge, car park. Bar meals, restaurant. Fifteen minutes from Alton Towers.

B&B from £25pp, Dinner from £4.95, Rooms 2 double, 1 family, all en-suite, Children welcome, No pets, Open all year.
Tim & Lynn Lowes, **The Black Lion Inn,** Butterton, Leek ST13 7ST
Tel: 01538 304232   **Map Ref 36**

THE OLD SCHOOL TEA ROOM B&B, tastefully converted Victorian village school in beautiful Peak Park. Approx. 20 minutes' from Alton Towers. Homely ground-floor en-suite B & B.
B&B from £19.50, Rooms 1 double, 1 family, both en-suite, Open all year.
The Old School Tea Room B&B, Pot Hooks Lane, Butterton, Leek, Staffordshire ST13 7SY
Tel: 01538 304320   **Map Ref 36**

OAKLEIGH HOUSE HOTEL, country house hotel standing in its own grounds, alongside a small lake, just behind Lichfield Cathedral.

B&B from £35, Dinner available, Rooms 4 single, 2 double, 4 twin, most en-suite, Open all year.
Oakleigh House Hotel, 25 St. Chad's Road, Lichfield, Staffordshire WS13 7LZ
Tel: 01543 262688 Fax: 01543 418556 **Map Ref 37**

....

COPPER'S END, a charming detached guest house. Centrally heated. Bedrooms have vanity units, tea/coffee facilities, colour TV and radios. Residential license. Lovely conservatory dining room. Large attractive garden. 2 ground floor bedrooms, en-suite. Parking. Rural setting on A461. Easy access to NEC and motorway network.
B&B from £18.50pp, Rooms 3 double 2 en-suite, 3 twin, 1 en-suite, some en-suite, Restricted smoking, Open all year except Xmas & New Year.
Malcolm & Tricia Lumb, **Copper's End,** Walsall Road, Muckley Corner, Lichfield, Staffordshire WS14 0BG
Tel: 01543 372910 Fax: 01543 360423 **Map Ref 38**

....

THE OLDE CORNER HOUSE HOTEL, 17th century and Victorian premises furnished to a high standard. Ideal for tourists and business. Easy access to motorway network. Fully licensed.

B&B from £28, Dinner available, Rooms 4 single, 16 double, 3 twin, all en-suite, Open all year.
The Olde Corner House Hotel, Walsall Road, Muckley Corner, Lichfield, Staffordshire WS14 0BG
Tel: 01543 372182 Fax: 01543 372211 **Map Ref 38**

....

JARVIS CLAYTON LODGE HOTEL, conveniently located for M6, Potteries and Alton Towers, offering a quiet and comfortable setting overlooking the Lyme Valley. Top-rate conference and events facilities available.

B&B from £37.50, Dinner available, Rooms 11 single, 18 double, 20 twin, 1 triple, all en-suite, Open all year.
Jarvis Clayton Lodge Hotel, Clayton Road, Newcastle-under-Lyme, Staffordshire ST5 4AF
Tel: 01782 613093 Fax: 01782 711896 **Map Ref 39**

....

HATHERTON COUNTRY HOTEL & LEISURE CENTRE, listed building set in its own grounds. Leisure facilities include indoor pool, squash, sauna and gym. Walking distance to picturesque Penkridge village. Leisure breaks.

B&B from £30, Dinner available, Rooms 13 double, 22 twin, 2 triple, all en-suite, Open all year.
Hatherton Country Hotel & Leisure Centre, Pinfold Lane, Penkridge, Stafford, Staffordshire ST19 5QP
Tel: 01785 712459 Fax: 01785 715532 **Map Ref 40**

....

FERNLEA GUEST HOUSE, stone country guest house in the heart of the village. Homely, friendly atmosphere guaranteed. Families most welcome. Walking distance to pub/restaurants.

B&B from £20, Rooms 1 double, 1 triple, 1 family, all en-suite, Open all year.
Fernlea Guest House, Cedar Hill, Alton, Stoke-on-Trent, Staffordshire ST10 4BH
Tel: 01538 702327 **Map Ref 41**

....

HAYDON HOUSE HOTEL, country house in the city. Fine food and service. Executive accommodation, including suites. A land mark in Staffordshire.

B&B from £38, Dinner available, Rooms 7 single, 7 double, 7 twin, 2 triple, all en-suite, Open all year.

Haydon House Hotel, Haydon Street, Basford, Stoke-on-Trent, Staffordshire ST4 6JD
Tel: 01782 711311 Fax: 01782 717470 **Map Ref 42**

GEORGE HOTEL, attractive neo-Georgian building in Burslem's elegant Swan Square. Conveniently situated between Midlands, Liverpool and Manchester.
B&B from £50, Dinner available, Rooms 7 single, 17 double, 11 twin, 2 triple, all en-suite, Open all year.
George Hotel, Swan Square, Burslem, Stoke-on-Trent, Staffordshire ST6 2AE
Tel: 01782 577544 Fax: 01782 837496   **Map Ref 43**

....

THE HOLLIES, a delightful Victorian family house, quietly situated off the B5051, 5 miles from the city in lovely countryside. Well appointed bedrooms with TV, tea/coffee facilities. Private parking, large garden. Choice of breakfast own preserves. A warm friendly welcome. Visit the Potteries, Staffordshire moorland and Alton Towers.
B&B from £18pp, Rooms 2 twin, 2 double, 1 family, all en-suite, No smoking, Children welcome, Pets by arrangement, Open all year.
Mrs Anne Hodgson, **The Hollies,** Clay Lake, Endon, Stoke-on-Trent, Staffordshire ST9 9DD
Tel: 01782 503252   **Map Ref 44**

....

THE OLD VICARAGE, a spaciously built in 1914 with original features an modern amenities. Well back from main road with private parking. Rooms have colour TV, tea/coffee facilities, wash basins. Staffordshire Moorlands, Peak District, Alton Towers, Potteries, gardens, museums within reach. Restaurant close by. Short breaks or overnight stops.
B&B from £17.50pp, Rooms 2 twin, 1 double, No smoking or pets, Children welcome, Open all year except Christmas & New Year.
Mrs I Grey, **The Old Vicarage,** Leek Road, Endon, Stoke-on-Trent, Staffordshire ST9 9BH
Tel: 01782 503686   **Map Ref 44**

....

TRENTSIDE HOTEL, by the River Trent is just one mile from the M6 junction 15. Home to the worlds greatest pottery manufacturers. Stoke-on-Trent is an unique city made up of six separate towns, only 12 miles from Alton Towers. All rooms have tea/coffee facilities and TV.

B&B from £16pp, Rooms 1 single, 2 twin, 3 double, 1 family, some en-suite, Restricted smoking, Children & pets welcome, Open all year.
Anne & Ian Hall, **Trentside Hotel,** 260 Stone Road, Hanford, Stoke-on-Trent, Staffordshire ST4 8NJ
Tel: 01782 642443 Fax: 01782 641910   **Map Ref 45**

....

VERDON GUEST HOUSE, large, friendly guest house almost in town centre and close to bus station. Convenient for all pottery factory visits, museum and Festival Park. Alton Towers 20 minutes, M6 10 minutes. All rooms with cable TV.
B&B from £17, Rooms 2 double, 2 twin, 5 triple, 1 family, some en-suite, Open all year.
Verdon Guest House, 44 Charles Street, Hanley, Stoke-on-Trent, Staffordshire ST1 3JY
Tel: 01782 264244   **Map Ref 43**

....

SNEYD ARMS HOTEL, restaurant and public house with function suite, gym, sauna and sun beds. En-suite and budget accommodation available.
B&B from £20, Dinner available, Rooms 4 single, 3 double, 4 twin, 2 triple, all en-suite, Open all year.
Sneyd Arms Hotel, Tower Square, Tunstall, Stoke-on-Trent, Staffordshire ST6 5AA
Tel: 01782 826722 Fax: 01782 826722   **Map Ref 46**

....

STONE HOUSE HOTEL, elegant building, set in its own delightful grounds, offer extensive leisure facilities, including tennis courts and swimming pool.
B&B from £60, Dinner available, Rooms 9 single, 29 double, 8 twin, 1 triple, all en-suite, Open all year.
Stone House Hotel, Stone, Staffordshire ST15 0BQ
Tel: 01785 815531 Fax: 01785 814764   **Map Ref 47**

....

BLAKELANDS COUNTRY GUEST HOUSE & RESTAURANT, dating from 1722, with original rooms and period features. Set in 6 acres of grounds including walled gardens, orchard and carp lake.

B&B from £45, Dinner available, Rooms 6 double, 2 twin, all en-suite, Open all year.
Blakelands Country Guest House & Restaurant, Halfpenny Green, Bobbington, Stourbridge DY7 5DP
Tel: 01384 221464 Fax: 01384 221585   **Map Ref 48**

Devon provides the cream of coast and country. Inland the countryside is ideal for a relaxed holiday, with opportunities to explore on foot, horseback or by bike. Around the coast is a wealth of lovely resorts with some of the best beaches in the country.

There are several popular seaside resorts in the region. Ilfracombe is the largest seaside resort in North Devon and is built around its old harbour. There are many good shingle beaches, two of them reached by tunnels through the rocks. Coastal walks take advantage of the hilly landscape. Westward Ho! was named after Charles Kingsley's famous novel published in 1855. It has good beaches, a golf course and the famous two mile long Pebble Ridge.

Dartmoor is the largest tract of open country left in southern England and most of it lies in the Dartmoor National Park which covers 365 square miles between Okehampton and Ivybridge, Tavistock and Christow. The market town of Okehampton, the "capital of the Northern moor" is set on the River Okement. South of the town are the highest tors or peaks of Dartmoor - High Willhays at 2,039ft and Yes Tor, 2028 ft. Another important market town is Tavistock, traditionally regarded as the western capital of the moor which grew up around its Benedictine abbey, founded in the 10th century. Widdecombe in the Moor is a picturesque village in a high fold of Dartmoor. Widdecombe Fair, made famous by the Uncle Tom Cobleigh song, is held in September. To the west is Hameldown Beacon which has on its west side a well preserved group of Bronze Age barrows. Princetown, the moor's largest town and the bleakest was named after the Prince of Wales (later George IV) who gave land from the Duchy of Cornwall to build a prison to house the captives of the Napoleonic Wars.

From Brixham to Dawlish the Devon coast has colourful, luxuriant vegetation, golden sands and vivid blue sea. Visitors can enjoy a variety of activities from golf to boating and fishing and other seaside amenities. Brixham is in two parts - the old village climbing a hill and the fishing village half a mile below with early 19th century houses clustered around the harbour.

Teignmouth is one of Devon's oldest resorts with a long history of fishing and ship building. Torquay's superb setting has helped make it the largest and most famous seaside resort in the county. east Devon is a region of contrasts. The westernmost chalk headland along the Channel coast is at Beer Head and not far away are the vivid red cliffs of Budleigh Salterton. Axminster, a small town on the River Axe, is famous for its carpets and likewise Honiton is famous for its lace, produced since Elizabethan times.

left, Clovelly

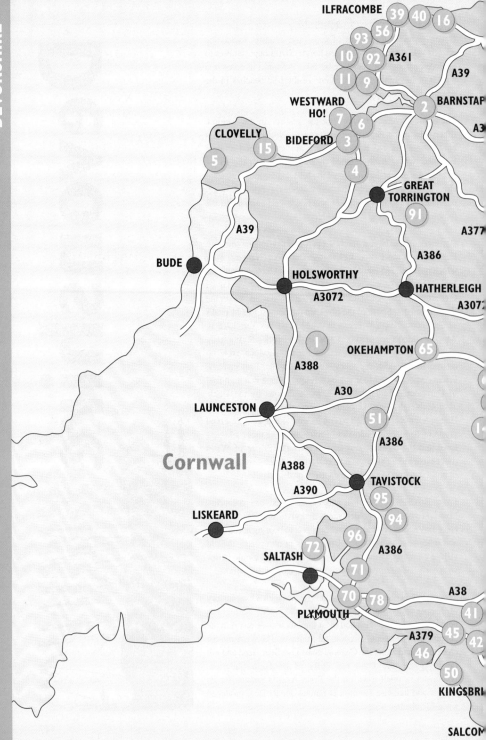

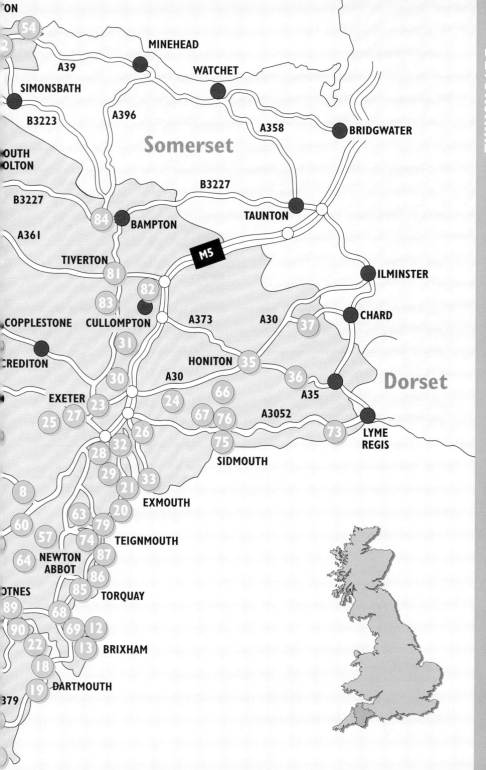

BLAGDON MANOR COUNTRY HOTEL, a 17th century manor nestling in eight acres with superb views of rolling countryside. Beautifully appointed en-suite guest rooms. Log fires during the cooler months and a profusion of fresh flowers throughout the spring and summer providing a relaxing and welcoming country house party atmosphere.

B&B from **£55pp**, Dinner from £19.50, Rooms 2 twin, 5 double, all en-suite, Restricted smoking, No children or pets, Open all year except Christmas.
Tim & Gill Casey, **Blagdon Manor Country Hotel**, Ashwater, Devon EX21 5DF
Tel: 01409 211224 Fax: 01409 211634 **Map Ref 1**

....

ROYAL & FORTESCUE HOTEL, a traditional market town hotel centrally located. Extensive refurbishment have retained the hotels coaching inn charm while adding fine modern facilities, the latest being 'The Bank', a stylish bistro.

B&B from **£44**, Dinner available, Rooms 4 single, 20 twin, 18 double, 5 triple, all en-suite, Children welcome, Open all year.
Royal & Fortescue Hotel, Boutport Street, Barnstaple, Devon EX31 1HG
Tel: 01271 42289 Fax: 01271 42289 **Map Ref 2**

....

BARNSTAPLE HOTEL, located outside the town centre, an ideal base for touring North Devon. Excellent facilities include indoor and outdoor swimming pools with sun terrace, a gymnasium, meeting rooms and two full sized snooker tables.

B&B from **£47**, Dinner available, Rooms 33 twin, 24 double, 3 triple, all en-suite, Children welcome, No pets, Open all year.
Barnstaple Hotel, Braunton Road, Barnstaple, Devon EX31 1LE
Tel: 01271 76221 Fax: 01271 24101 **Map Ref 2**

....

THE PARK HOTEL, overlooking parkland and River Taw, a short walk to town centre. Leisure facilities available at sister hotel, the Barnstaple Hotel.

B&B from **£42**, Dinner available, Rooms 7 single, 19 twin, 16 double, all en-suite, Children welcome, Open all year.
The Park Hotel, Taw Vale, Barnstaple, Devon EX32 8NJ
Tel: 01271 72166 Fax: 01271 23157 **Map Ref 3**

....

LOWER WINSFORD, come and enjoy traditional service with care at Lower Winsford. Comfortable, relaxing atmosphere in this former farmhouse. Minutes away from historic port town of Bideford. Visit RHS Rosemoor Gardens and Dartington Crystal at Torrington. Beautiful countryside abounds. Dartmoor and Exmoor. Easily accessible.

B&B from **£21pp**, Rooms 1 twin, 2 double, 2 en-suite, No smoking or pets, Children over 8, Open April - September.
Mr & Mrs J.D. Ogle, **Lower Winsford**, Abbotsham Road, Bideford, North Devon EX39 3QP
Tel: 01237 475083 Fax: 01237 425802 **Map Ref 3**

....

ROYAL HOTEL, overlooking historic Bideford Bridge and the River Torridge. Bideford's leading hotel with locally renowned restaurant and well appointed lounges.

B&B from **£42**, Dinner available, Rooms 5 single, 14 twin, 10 double, 1 triple, most en-suite, Children welcome, Open all year.
Royal Hotel, Barnstaple Street, Bideford, Devon EX39 4AE
Tel: 01237 472005 Fax: 01237 478957 **Map Ref 3**

....

SUNSET HOTEL, a small, quality country hotel in peaceful, picturesque location, specialising in home cooking. Delightful en-suite bedrooms with beverage and colour TV. Book with confidence.

B&B from **£25**, Dinner available, Rooms 1 twin, 1 double, 1 triple, 1 family, all en-suite, No smoking, Children welcome, Open March - October.

Sunset Hotel, Landcross, Bideford, Devon EX39 5JA
Tel: 01237 472962 **Map Ref 4**

RIVERSFORD HOTEL, peace and tranquillity, overlooking the River Torridge. Delightful restaurant offering home cooked foods (fresh fish a speciality). Individual en-suite bedrooms with character and river views, four poster bedrooms. Take A386 from Bideford to Northam then turn right into Limers Lane.

B&B from £40, Dinner available, Rooms 7 twin, 6 double, 1 family, all en-suite, Children welcome, Open all year.
Riversford Hotel, Limers Lane, Bideford, Devon EX39 2RG
Tel: 01237 474239 Fax: 01237 421661   **Map Ref 3**

....

THE MOUNT HOTEL, a small, family run hotel over 200 years old, with character and charm. Home cooking. Peaceful garden. Short walk to town centre and quay. Ideal base for touring North Devon and 'Tarka' country.

B&B from £21, Dinner available, Rooms 2 single, 2 twin, 3 double, 1 triple, all en-suite, No smoking, Children welcome, No pets, Open all year.
The Mount Hotel, Northdown Road, Bideford, Devon EX39 3LP
Tel: 01237 473748   **Map Ref 3**

....

HARTLAND QUAY HOTEL, family hotel offering home cooking, en-suite rooms with TV, tea/coffee, guest lounge, dining room. Bar food. Fully licensed. Car park. Important geology area overlooking Devons rugged Atlantic coastline. Coastal walks. Beaches. Clovelly nearby.

B&B from £40pp, Dinner from £9, Rooms 2 single, 5 twin, 5 double, 2 family, some en-suite, Children & pets welcome, Open Easter - November.
Nancy Johns, **Hartland Quay Hotel,** Hartland, Bideford, North Devon EX39 6DU
Tel: 01237 441218 Fax: 01237 441371   **Map Ref 5**

....

YEOLDON COUNTRY HOUSE HOTEL & RESTAURANT, a Victorian country house overlooking river. Quality English and continental cuisine and an interesting wine list. Hospitable owners, friendly and efficient staff. Individually decorated rooms.

B&B from £45, Dinner available, Rooms 3 twin, 7 double, all en-suite, No smoking, Children welcome, Open all year.
Yeoldon Country House Hotel & Restaurant, Durrant Lane, Northam, Bideford, Devon EX39 2RL
Tel: 01237 474400 Fax: 01237 476618   **Map Ref 6**

....

BUCKLEIGH LODGE, a fine late Victorian house in own grounds, with magnificent views over the bay and close to a large safe beach. Ideal touring centre.

B&B from £20, Dinner available, Rooms 1 single, 2 twin, 3 double, all en-suite, Children welcome, No pets, Open all year.
Buckleigh Lodge, 135 Bay View Road, Westward Ho! Bideford, Devon EX39 1BJ
Tel: 01237 475988   **Map Ref 7**

....

CULLODEN HOUSE HOTEL, a carefully converted Victorian house with fabulous sea views. Family run, good food and an ideal base for golfing, walking and family holidays.

B&B from £22.50, Dinner available, Rooms 7 twin, 2 family, most en-suite, Children welcome, Open February - December.
Culloden House Hotel, Fosketh Hill, Westward Ho! Bideford, Devon EX39 1JA
Tel: 01237 479421   **Map Ref 7**

....

EDGEMOOR HOTEL, a country house hotel in peaceful wooded setting on the edge of Dartmoor National Park. Good food. Elegance without pretension.

B&B from £46.50, Dinner available, Rooms 3 single, 3 twin, 9 double, 1 triple, 1 family, all en-suite, No smoking, Children welcome, Open all year.
Edgemoor Hotel, Haytor Road, Lowerdown Cross, Bovey Tracey, Devon TQ13 9LE
Tel: 01626 832466 Fax: 01626 834760   **Map Ref 8**

NEILDON, close to local beach. Both rooms have TV with tea/coffee facilities. One twin/double en-suite, one double with private bathroom. Guest lounge with log fire, TV. Off road parking. Bed and breakfast from £15.

B&B from £15pp, Room 1 twin, 2 double, all en-suite/private facilities, No smoking, children or pets, Open all year except Christmas & New Year.
Shirley & John Houle, **Neildon,** Exeter Road, Braunton, North Devon EX33 2JL
Tel: 01271 815874   **Map Ref 9**

....

CROYDE BAY HOUSE HOTEL, a small, friendly hotel beside beach, where comfort, good food and personal care are still found. Beautifully positioned sun deck and sun lounge.

B&B from £34, Dinner available, Rooms 2 twin, 3 double, 2 triple, all en-suite, Children welcome, Open March - November.
Croyde Bay House Hotel, Moor Lane, Croyde, Braunton, Devon EX33 1PA
Tel: 01271 890270   **Map Ref 10**

....

SAUNTON SANDS HOTEL, directly overlooking 5 miles of golden sands and surrounded by unspoilt countryside, offering a wealth of sports and leisure facilities. Seasonal break rates available.

B&B from £65, Dinner available, Rooms 17 single, 28 twin, 15 double, 32 family, most en-suite, Children welcome, No pets, Open all year.
Saunton Sands Hotel, Saunton, Braunton, Devon EX33 1LQ
Tel: 01271 890212 Fax: 01271 890145   **Map Ref 11**

....

THE BERRY HEAD HOTEL, steeped in history, nestling on water's edge in 6 acres of grounds and in an area of outstanding natural beauty.

B&B from £35, Dinner available, Rooms 1 single, 6 twin, 6 double, 3 family, all en-suite, No smoking, Children welcome, Open all year.
The Berry Head Hotel, Berry Head Road, Brixham, Devon TQ5 9AJ
Tel: 01803 853225 Fax: 01803 882084   **Map Ref 12**

....

RICHMOND HOUSE HOTEL, a detached Victorian house with well appointed accommodation, sun trap garden and adjacent car park. Convenient for shops and harbour, yet quiet location.

B&B from £16, Rooms 1 single, 4 double, 1 triple, most en-suite, No smoking, Children welcome, Open all year.
Richmond House Hotel, Higher Manor Road, Brixham, Devon TQ5 8HA
Tel: 01803 882391 Fax: 01803 882391   **Map Ref 13**

....

THORNWORTHY HOUSE, a family house high on the moor with magnificent views. Stroll straight onto the moor and reservoir. Ideal for walkers, artists, fishermen or just relaxing in the gardens. Lounge with log fire. TV and tea making in all rooms. Licensed car parking. Tennis, Croquet, riding, Rosemoor & interesting places nearby. ETB 2 Crown Recommended. AA 4Q Selected.
B&B from £30.50pp, Dinner from £17, Rooms 1 single, 1 twin, 1 double, some en-suite, Restricted smoking, Children & pets welcome, Open February - December.
Hugh & Sheila Rogers, **Thornworthy House,** Chagford TR13 8EY
Tel: 01647 433297 Fax: 01647 433297   **Map Ref 14**

....

THE NEW INN, a 17th century inn hidden deep within the cobbled streets of this historic village. Newly restored. Lovely bedrooms. Rare views. Wonderful atmosphere.

B&B from £30, Dinner available, Rooms 1 single, 7 double, all en-suite, No smoking, Children welcome, No pets, Open all year.
The New Inn, High Street, Clovelly, Devon EX39 5TQ
Tel: 01237 431303 Fax: 01237 431636   **Map Ref 15**

RED LION HOTEL, a newly refurbished ancient inn. Dramatic quayside setting in unique heritage village. Splendid bedrooms. Stunning sea views. Seafood a speciality.

B&B from £37, Dinner available, Rooms 2 twin, 7 double, 2 triple, all en-suite, No smoking, Children welcome, No pets, Open all year.

Red Lion Hotel, The Quay, Clovelly, Devon EX39 5TF
Tel: 01237 431237 Fax: 01237 431044   **Map Ref 15**

....

BLAIR LODGE HOTEL, is a small licensed hotel overlooking Combe Martin Bay. Rooms have en-suites, tea/coffee facilities and televisions. choice of menu. RAC Acclaimed. Exmoor National Park and coastal walks nearby. No smoking or pets, Special breaks, weekly rates.

B&B from £22pp, Dinner from £10.50, Rooms 2 single, 2 twin, 6 double, all en-suite, Children over 12, Open March - end October.

Mr & Mrs K Smith, **Blair Lodge Hotel,** Moory Meadow, Combe Martin, Devon EX34 0DG
Tel: 01271 882294   **Map Ref 16**

....

COOMBE HOUSE COUNTRY HOTEL, a Georgian manor house in 5 acres. Rural heart of Devon between Dartmoor and Exmoor, equidistant north and south coasts and 15 minutes from Exeter. Croquet, swimming and tennis.

B&B from £36.50, Dinner available, Rooms 6 twin, 9 double, all en-suite, Children welcome, Open all year.

Coombe House Country Hotel, Coleford, Crediton, Devon EX17 5BY
Tel: 01363 84487 Fax: 01363 84722   **Map Ref 17**

....

VICTORIA HOTEL, a small, elegant hotel in town centre with en-suite rooms. Candlelit restaurant serving finest local produce, prepared with flair. 2 bars. Friendly and efficient staff.

B&B from £30, Dinner available, Rooms 3 twin, 7 double, all en-suite, No smoking, Open all year.

Victoria Hotel, 27-29 Victoria Road, Dartmouth Devon TQ6 9RT
Tel: 01803 832572 & 832573 Fax: 01803 835815   **Map Ref 18**

....

FORD HOUSE, king size beds. Parking, Walk to centre. Breakfast 8.30 to 12 noon. Beverage tray, fridges, telephone, colour TV's. AA 5Q's, RAC Highly Acclaimed, ETB 3 Crowns Highly Commended.

B&B from £27.50pp, Dinner from £25, Rooms 2 twin, 2 double, all en-suite, Children & pets welcome, Open March - October.

Richard Turner, **Ford House,** 44 Victoria Road, Dartmouth, Devon TQ6 9DX
Tel: 01803 834047 Fax: 01803 834047   **Map Ref 18**

....

BROOME COURT, overlooks 3 copses and is surrounded by south Devon countryside rich in wildlife. The old farm building surround a courtyard with flowers, shrubs and goldfish pond. Breakfast is served in the old farmhouse kitchen.

B&B from £30pp, Dinner from £17.50, Rooms 1 twin, 2 double, 1 family unit, all en-suite, Restricted smoking, Children over 12, Pets by arrangement, Open all year.

Jan Bird & Tom Boughton, **Broome Court,** Broomhill, Dartmouth, Devon TQ6 0LD
Tel: 01803 834275 Fax: 01803 833260   **Map Ref 18**

STOKE LODGE HOTEL, a country house hotel with sea and village views. Heated indoor and outdoor swimming pools and leisure facilities, including all weather tennis court.

B&B from £45, Dinner available, Rooms 2 single, 8 twin, 8 double, 7 triple, all en-suite, No smoking, Children welcome, Open all year.
Stoke Lodge Hotel, Stoke Fleming, Dartmouth, Devon TQ6 0RA
Tel: 01803 770523 Fax: 01803 770851   **Map Ref 19**

....

WEST HATCH HOTEL, a delightful, tastefully coordinated licensed hotel overlooking sea in restful resort. Well equipped bedrooms, all en-suite, some on ground floor. Many extra touches. Luxurious four poster. Recognised for quality, high standards, relaxation, comfort and excellent breakfast menu. ETB 2 Crowns Highly Commended, RAC Highly Acclaimed, AA QQQQ.
B&B from £23pp, Rooms 1 twin, 7 double, 2 family, all en-suite, Restricted smoking, Children welcome, No pets, Open all year except Christmas & New Year.
Pat & Dave Badcock, **West Hatch Hotel,** 34 West Cliff, Dawlish, South Devon EX7 9DN
Tel: 01626 864211 & 862948 Fax: 01626 864211   **Map Ref 20**

....

LANGSTONE CLIFF HOTEL, situated in 20 acre grounds overlooking the sea. 500 metres from the beach, golf course and bird sanctuary. Indoor and outdoor swimming pools, hard tennis court and play area. Toddler rooms, snooker, table tennis, weekend entertainment and cabaret weekends. All rooms with TV, telephone, tea/coffee facilities, hair dryer and trouser press.

B&B from £25pp, Dinner from £14.50, Rooms 4 single, 22 double, 41 family, all en-suite, Smoking, children & pets welcome, Open all year.
Geoff Rogers, **Langstone Cliff Hotel,** Dawlish Warren, Dawlish EX7 0NA
Tel: 01626 865155 Fax: 01626 867166   **Map Ref 21**

....

THE WHITE HOUSE, a traditional 18th century stone built house in picturesque village setting, overlooking the beautiful River Dart, close to the coast. 2 good pubs within walking distance. Guest sitting room. Sun terrace. Parking. Usual TV and refreshment facilities. Friendly atmosphere. Ideal for walkers, peace and quiet.

B&B from £25pp, Rooms 1 twin, 2 double, all en-suite/private, No smoking or pets, Children welcome, Open all year except Christmas.
Hugh Treseder, **The White House,** Manor Street, Dittisham, Devon TQ6 0EX
Tel: 01803 722355 Fax: 01803 722355   **Map Ref 22**

....

ST ANDREWS HOTEL, a warm welcome awaits you at this long established family run hotel. Whilst retaining the features of a large Victorian house it provides all the facilities of a modern hotel. Brochure and tariff on request. Weekend breaks available all year.
B&B from £41, Dinner available, Rooms 4 single, 3 twin, 8 double, 2 triple, all en-suite, Children welcome, Open all year except Christmas.
St Andrews Hotel, 28 Aplhington Road, Exeter, Devon EX2 8HN
Tel: 01392 276784 Fax: 01392 250249   **Map Ref 23**

....

HOTEL GLEDHILLS, an attractive red brick Victorian hotel, situated conveniently close to shops, leisure centre and Exeter famous Quay. All modern comfortably furnished bedrooms with full facilities, beverage trays and colour TV. Sunny guests lounge, licensed bar and large rear car park.

B&B from £22.50pp, Rooms 5 single, 2 twin, 3 double, 2 family, most en-suite, No smoking dining room, Children welcome, No pets, Open all year except Christmas.
David & Suzanne Greening, **Hotel Gledhills,** 32 Alphington Rd, Exeter, Devon EX2 8HN
Tel: 01392 430469 & 271439 Fax: 01392 430469   **Map Ref 23**

PARK VIEW HOTEL, a charming family run hotel, noted for peace and quiet and high standards, near city centre and stations. Tea/coffee, colour TV and telephone in all rooms.

B&B from £20, Rooms 3 single, 3 twin, 7 double, 2 triple, most en-suite, No smoking, Children welcome, Open all year.
Park View Hotel, 8 Howell Road, Exeter, Devon EX4 4LG
Tel: 01392 271772 Fax: 01392 253047   **Map Ref 23**

....

THE SOUTH GATE HOTEL, part of the Forte Heritage Collection, the Southgate is an elegant hotel offering first class facilities including a health club with indoor pool.

B&B from £59, Dinner available, Rooms 48 twin, 56 double, 6 triple, all en-suite, No smoking, Children welcome, Open all year.
The South gate Hotel, Southernhay East, Exeter, Devon EX1 1QF
Tel: 01392 412812 & 413549 Fax: 01392 413549   **Map Ref 23**

....

HOLBROOK FARM, enjoy the warm welcome, spectacular views and peaceful surrounding of our diary farm. Spacious en-suite rooms furnished to a high standard. All with colour TV and hot drinks facilities, off road parking. Excellent local eating. The cathedral city of Exeter is only a short drive away as are coast and moors making this an ideal base for any holiday.

B&B from £19pp, Rooms 1 twin, 1 double, 1 family, all en-suite, No smoking or pets, Children welcome, Open all year.
Heather Glanvill, **Holbrook Farm,** Clyst Honiton, Exeter, Devon EX5 2HR
Tel: 01392 367000   **Map Ref 24**

....

THE LORD HALDON HOTEL, a family run, historic former mansion within own grounds, offering panoramic views. 5 miles south west of Exeter and well placed for Dartmoor and coast.

B&B from £42.50, Dinner available, Rooms 5 twin, 10 double, 3 triple, 1 family, most en-suite, No smoking, Children welcome, Open all year.
The Lord Haldon Hotel, Dunchideock, Exeter, Devon EX6 7YF
Tel: 01392 832483 Fax: 01392 833765   **Map Ref 25**

....

EBFORD HOUSE HOTEL, a beautiful Georgian country house surrounded by lovely gardens and fine views. Noted restaurant. Relax in our leisure area. Convenient for 8 golf courses, sea, sand and moors.

B&B from £61, Dinner available, Rooms 3 single, 2 twin, 11 double, all en-suite, No smoking, Children welcome, Open all year.
Ebford House Hotel, Exmouth Road, Ebford, Exeter, Devon EX3 0QH
Tel: 01392 877658 Fax: 01392 874424   **Map Ref 26**

....

DRAKES FARM HOUSE, a 15th century farmhouse, large garden, quiet village. Two public houses, two restaurants. Two miles M5/Exeter centre. Convenient coast/Moors. Guests lounge. Laundry facilities. Tea/coffee/TV in all rooms. Ample private parking.

B&B from £16-£18.50pp, Rooms 1 single, 1 twin, 1 double, 1 family, 2 en-suite, No smoking or pets, Children welcome, Open all year.
Nova Easterbrook, **Drakes Farm House,** Ide, Exeter, Devon EX2 9RQ
Tel: 01392 256814 & 495564 Fax: 01392 256814   **Map Ref 27**

....

FAIRWINDS HOTEL, a friendly little 'no smoking' hotel, offering real value for money in beautiful rural surroundings. Comfortable, well equipped en-suite bedrooms. Excellent choice of home made food. Perfect touring base.

B&B from £35, Dinner available, Rooms 1 single, 2 twin, 3 double, 1 triple, all en-suite, No smoking, Children welcome, No pets, Open January - November.
Fairwinds Hotel, Kennford, Exeter, Devon EX6 7UD
Tel: 01392 832911 Fax: 01392 832911   **Map Ref 28**

DEVON ARMS, situated on A379, 5 miles from Dawlish Warren, 8 miles from Cathedral city of Exeter, adjacent to Powderham Castle. All rooms have colour TV, tea/coffee making facilities. We have lunchtime and evening menus. Large car park. Booking advisable. Discounts for multi night stays.

B&B from £20pp, Rooms 1 twin, 1 double, 4 family, all en-suite, Children welcome, No pets, Open all year except Christmas.

George & Thelma Vickery, **Devon Arms,** Fore St, Kenton, Exeter EX6 8LD
Tel: 01626 890213   **Map Ref 29**

DEVON HOTEL, set in beautiful countryside, yet offering easy accessibility to the M5 and the centre of Exeter. Recent refurbishment has seen the addition of a further banqueting suite and 'Carriages', a stylish bistro.

B&B from £44, Dinner available, Rooms 7 single, 17 twin, 15 double, 2 family, all en-suite, No smoking, Children welcome, Open all year.

Devon Hotel, Exeter By Pass, Matford, Exeter, Devon EX2 8XU
Tel: 01392 259268 Fax: 01392 413142   **Map Ref 23**

GIPSY HILL HOTEL & RESTAURANT, a peaceful country house hotel with magnificent views. 1 mile form M5, junction 30 and 2 miles from Exeter, just off the A30. Adjacent M5 junction 29.

B&B from £37.50, Dinner available, Rooms 9 single, 10 twin, 16 double, 2 triple, 1 family, all en-suite, No smoking, Children welcome, Open all year.

Gipsy Hill Hotel & Restaurant, Gipsy Hill Lane, Pinhoe, Exeter, Devon EX1 3RN
Tel: 01392 465252 Fax: 01392 464302   **Map Ref 30**

THE GREAT WESTERN HOTEL, with easy access to railway station. Bar, restaurant, lounge, conference room and car park.

B&B from £32, Dinner available, Rooms 23 single, 9 twin, 7 double, 1 triple, most en-suite, No smoking, Children welcome, Open all year.

The Great Western Hotel, Station Approach, St David's, Exeter, Devon EX4 4NU
Tel: 01392 274039 Fax: 01392 425529   **Map Ref 23**

BARTON CROSS HOTEL, a harmonious blend of 17th century charm and 20th century comfort. International standard accommodation with superb cuisine in glorious Devon country side, just 4 miles north of Exeter.

B&B from £63.50, Dinner available, Rooms 1 single, 2 twin, 3 double, all en-suite, No smoking, Children welcome, Open all year.

Barton Cross Hotel, Huxham, Stoke Canon, Exeter, Devon EX5 4EJ
Tel: 01392 841245 Fax: 01392 841942   **Map Ref 31**

THE GLOBE HOTEL, we are a traditional English Inn situated in the beautiful and historic estuary town of Topsham. (Exeter city centre 4 miles). 17 en-suite bedrooms (some four posters). Oak panelled bars serving traditional ales and fine wines. Elizabethan Restaurant (closed Sundays). Bar snacks also available.

B&B from £26.50pp, Dinner from £14.50, Rooms 1 single, 7 twin, 6 double, 3 family, all en-suite, Children welcome, Pets by arrangement, Open all year except Christmas.

Mrs Hodges, **The Globe Hotel,** Fore Street, Topsham, Exeter EX3 0HR
Tel: 01392 873471 Fax: 01392 873879   **Map Ref 32**

THE DEVONCOURT HOTEL, the ideal family resort, spectacular sea views over golden sandy beaches. Set in 4 acres of sub tropical gardens, with full leisure complex, 2 pools, tennis, putting, croquet and much more. Sky TV, baby listening. 8 miles from Exeter and M5.

B&B from £50, Dinner available, Rooms 6 single, 6 twin, 11 double, 17 triple, 11 family, all en-suite, No smoking, Children welcome, Open all year.

The Devoncourt Hotel, Douglas Avenue, Exmouth, Devon EX8 2EX
Tel: 01395 272277 Fax: 01395 269315   **Map Ref 33**

....

HONITON HOTEL, a comfortable, friendly licensed motel. Ideal touring base or for a one night stay. Midway stop between Cornwall and north.

B&B from £32, Dinner available, Rooms 1 single, 8 twin, 4 double, 2 triple, all en-suite, Children welcome, Open all year.

Honiton Hotel, Turks Head Corner, Exeter Road, Honiton, Devon EX14 8BL
Tel: 01404 43440 & 45400 Fax: 01404 47767   **Map Ref 35**

....

HOME FARM HOTEL & RESTAURANT, a thatched 16th century farmhouse hotel in lovely countryside. Restaurant uses local produce to serve food of high standard. Bar with light meals. Log fires. 6 miles from sea.

B&B from £32, Dinner available, Rooms 3 single, 2 twin, 4 double, 4 triple, most en-suite,No smoking Children welcome,Open all year.
Home Farm Hotel & Restaurant, Wilmington, Honiton, Devon EX14 9JR
Tel: 01404 831278 & 831246 Fax: 01404 831411   **Map Ref 36**

....

THE BELFRY COUNTRY HOTEL, tastefully converted Victorian village school in picturesque valley with lovely views. Relaxed and friendly atmosphere, all rooms en-suite, scrumptious award winning home cooking. Log fire.

B&B from £34, Dinner available, Rooms 2 twin, 3 double, 1 triple, all en-suite, No smoking, Children over 12, Open all year.

The Belfry Country Hotel, Yarcombe, Honiton, Devon EX14 9BD
Tel: 01404 861234 Fax: 01404 861579   **Map Ref 37**

....

Delightful Victorian hotel with the emphasis on quality, good food, wine and relaxation. **STRATHMORE HOTEL** has a central location for discovering North Devon's many attractions and beautiful Exmoor. The hotel offers en-suite accommodation, a choice of excellent menu, licensed bar and parking.
B&B from £18pp, Dinner from £9.50, Rooms 1 single, 1 twin, 4 double, 3 family, all en-suite, Children & pets welcome, Open all year.
Rosemary Pilch, **Strathmore Hotel,** 57 St. Brannock's Road, Iffracombe, North Devon EX34 8EQ
Tel: 01271 862248   **Map Ref 39**

....

THE DARNLEY HOTEL

THE DARNLEY HOTEL, is a friendly family run hotel. Centrally heated en-suite rooms with colour TV's, tea/coffee facilities. Licensed bar and restaurant, varied menu. Excellent wine list. Pets welcome. Ideal for golfing, walking holidays. Ample parking. Special breaks available throughout the year. Email: darnley.hotel@btinternet.com
B&B from £20-£25pp, Dinner from £9, Rooms 1 twin, 8 double, 3 family, all en-suite, Children & pets welcome, Open all year.
Nicol, Sue & Michael, **The Darnley Hotel,** 3 Belmont Road, Ilfracombe, North Devon EX34 8DR
Tel: 01271 863955 Fax: 01271 864076   **Map Ref 39**

LYNCOTT, Devon's romantic Atlantic coast. 'Lyncott' combines elegance, moderate terms and old fashioned hospitality. Delightful en-suite bedrooms. Scrumptious fare!

B&B from £13.50, Dinner available, Rooms 1 twin, 4 double, 2 triple, most en-suite, No smoking, Children welcome, Open all year.

Lyncott, 56 St Brannock's Road, Ilfracombe, Devon EX34 8EQ
Tel: 01271 862425   **Map Ref 39**

....

Paul and Karen welcome you to **GRAYSTOKE HOTEL,** bed and breakfast from £15, dinner £10. Rooms with TV and tea/coffee facilities. Children and pets welcome. Parking. Ideal base for beaches and Exmoor. Open all year.

B&B from £15pp, Dinner £10, Rooms 1 twin, 3 double, 4 family, some en-suite, Restricted smoking, Children & Pets welcome,
Paul & Karen Dudley, **Graystoke Hotel,** 58 St. Brannocks Road, Ilfracombe, Devon EX34 8EQ
Tel: 01271 862328   **Map Ref 39**

....

THE ILFRACOMBE CARLTON HOTEL, a premier resort in central location adjacent to beach and sea front. Comfortable rooms with good facilities. Buttery, dancing and 1 non smoking lounge.

B&B from £27.50, Dinner available, Rooms 10 single, 14 twin, 18 double, 6 triple, most en-suite, No smoking, Children welcome, No pets, Open March - December.

The Ilfracombe Carlton Hotel, Runnacleave Road, Ilfracombe, Devon EX34 8AR
Tel: 01271 862446 & 863711 Fax: 01271 865379   **Map Ref 39**

....

CAPSTONE HOTEL & RESTAURANT, a family run hotel with restaurant on ground floor. Close to harbour and all amenities. Local seafood a speciality.

B&B from £14, Dinner available, Rooms 1 single, 1 twin, 7 double, 3 family, all en-suite, Children welcome, Open April - October.

Capstone Hotel & Restaurant, St James Place, Ilfracombe, Devon EX34 9BJ
Tel: 01271 863540 Fax: 01271 862277   **Map Ref 39**

....

MERLIN COURT HOTEL, a listed detached hotel, peacefully situated in own lovely terraced gardens and ideally located for exploring beautiful North Devon. Four poster bed available. Car park.

B&B from £19.99, Dinner available, Rooms 7 double, 2 triple, 4 family, most en-suite, Children welcome, Open all year.

Merlin Court Hotel, Torrs Park, Ilfracombe, Devon EX34 8AY
Tel: 01271 862697   **Map Ref 39**

....

SHERBORNE LODGE HOTEL, is a friendly, family run hotel with parking in beautiful Torrs Park. Short walk to sea front, harbour, theatre and all amenities. Explore the many facets of Devon from coastline to moor. Golfing, fishing and shooting days arranged. Storage for sports equipment and drying rooms available. Email: 113121.222@compuserve.com
B&B from £15.50pp, Dinner from £8, Rooms 3 twin, 7 double, 1 family, most en-suite, Restricted smoking, Children welcome, Pets by arrangement, Open all year.
Kirsten & Warren Millington, **Sherborne Lodge Hotel,** Torrs Park, Ilfracombe, North Devon EX34 8AY
Tel: 01271 862297 Fax: 01271 865520   **Map Ref 39**

THE TORRS HOTEL, a Victorian mansion with fine views. Quiet location beside the National Trust Torrs Coastal Walk. Close to seafront and town centre.

B&B from £20, Dinner available, Rooms 3 twin, 6 double, 5 triple, all en-suite, Children welcome, Open February - November.
The Torrs Hotel, Torrs Park, Ilfracombe, Devon EX34 8AY
Tel: 01271 862334   **Map Ref 39**

....

BEECHWOOD HOTEL, a small Victorian mansion peacefully situated in own garden and woodlands bordering National Trust coastline. Splendid views over town and sea.

B&B from £20, Dinner available, Rooms 1 single, 2 twin, 6 double, most en-suite, No smoking, Children welcome, No pets, Open all year.

Beechwood Hotel, Torrs Park, Ilfracombe, Devon EX34 8AZ
Tel: 01271 863800 Fax: 01271 893800   **Map Ref 39**

....

ELMFIELD HOTEL, stands in 1 acre of gardens, with car parking. Heated indoor swimming pool, jacuzzi, sauna and solarium. Two bedrooms have four posters.

B&B from £32, Dinner available, Rooms 2 single, 4 twin, 8 double, all en-suite, No smoking, Children welcome, No pets, Open April - October & Christmas.
Elmfield Hotel, Torrs Park, Ilfracombe, Devon EX34 8AZ
Tel: 01271 863377 Fax: 01271 866828   **Map Ref 39**

....

EPCHRIS HOTEL, an old stone house with a country feel, near centre of Ilfracombe and Torrs Walks. Bar, lovely terraced gardens and swimming pool.

B&B from £19, Dinner available, Rooms 1 single, 1 double, 2 triple, 5 family, most en-suite, No smoking, Children welcome, No pets Open January - October, December.

Epchris Hotel, Torrs Park, Ilfracombe, Devon EX34 8AZ
Tel: 01271 862751   **Map Ref 39**

....

THE EXCELSIOR HOTEL, a comfortable hotel with friendly atmosphere. Lovely position, providing wonderful views. Well stocked for serving cocktails and usual drinks. En-suite rooms, colour TV's and beverage making. Car park. 5 minutes walk, tunnels, beaches and town. Woolacombe 10 minutes drive. Central for variety attractions. Excellent walks.
B&B from £19pp, Dinner from £8, Rooms 4 single, 3 twin, 8 double, 4 family, most en-suite, Restricted smoking, Children & pets welcome, Open all year.
Bernard Mills & Caroline Brennan, **The Excelsior Hotel,** Torrs Park, Ilfracombe, North Devon EX34 8AZ
Tel: 01271 862919 Fax: 01271 862919   **Map Ref 39**

....

WESTWELL HALL HOTEL, the elegant Victorian licensed hotel is set in its own grounds in an elevated position, enjoying views of sea and countryside. All rooms are en-suite with colour TV and tea/coffee facilities. Ample parking. AA Recommended. RAC Acclaimed. ETB Three Crowns Commended.
B&B from £21pp, Dinner from £10, Rooms 1 single, 2 twin, 7 double, all en-suite, Restricted smoking, Children & pets welcome, Open all year.
Colin & Rosemary Lomas, **Westwell Hall Hotel,** Torrs Park, Ilfracombe, Devon EX34 8AZ
Tel: 01271 862792 Fax: 01271 862792   **Map Ref 39**

WOODLANDS HOTEL, nestles in peaceful, lightly wooded grounds in a scenic location. Stroll to beaches, the bustling harbour and all entertainments. Coast and moorland walks, golf and fishing nearby. Home cooked meals, friendly relaxed atmosphere. Colour TV and tea/coffee in en-suite rooms, licensed bar. Parking.
B&B from £21pp, Dinner from £11, Rooms 2 twin, 5 double, 3 family, most en-suite, Restricted smoking, Children over 5, Open March - December.
Doreen & Alan Wilkinson, **Woodlands Hotel,** Torrs Park, Ilfracombe, North Devon EX34 8AZ
Tel: 01271 863098 Fax: 01271 863098   **Map Ref 39**

IMPERIAL HOTEL, on the seafront close to all amenities and a few minutes' walk from beautiful harbour. Entertainment 5 nights a week.

B&B from £19, Dinner available, Rooms 16 single, 39 twin, 41 double, 8 triple, all en-suite, No smoking, Children welcome, No pets, Open March - October, December.
Imperial Hotel, Wilder Road, Ilfracombe, Devon EX34 9AL
Tel: 01271 862536 Fax: 01271 862571   **Map Ref 39**

SANDY COVE HOTEL, in many acres of own grounds incorporating garden, cliffs, own beach and woods. Overlooks Combe Martin Bay, the beaches, sea and Exmoor. Outdoor/indoor pools, sauna, sunbed, gym equipment and whirlpool.

B&B from £25, Dinner available, Rooms 2 single, 5 twin, 16 double, 10 triple, all en-suite, Children welcome, Open all year.
Sandy Cove Hotel, Old Coast Road, Berrynarbor, Ilfracombe, Devon EX34 9SR
Tel: 01271 882243 & 882888 Fax: 01271 883830   **Map Ref 40**

SAFFRON HOUSE HOTEL, a 17th century hotel set in own grounds close to beaches and Exmoor. Well appointed en-suite rooms. Heated pool. Ideal touring base.

B&B from £19, Dinner available, Rooms 1 twin, 4 double, 2 triple, 2 family, most en-suite, No smoking, Children & pets welcome, Open January - November.
Saffron House Hotel, King Street, Combe Martin, Ilfracombe, Devon EX34 0BX
Tel: 01271 883521   **Map Ref 16**

ERMEWOOD HOUSE HOTEL, a Georgian country hotel with glorious river views. Unspoilt South Hams coastline 4 miles south, Dartmoor National Park 4 miles North. 10 bedrooms en-suite with colour TV, tea/coffee facilities. Ermewood is noted for its position, comfort, hospitality, good food and wines.
B&B from £31.50pp, Dinner from £16.50, Rooms 3 single, 2 twin, 4 double, 1 family, all en-suite, Restricted smoking, Children over 11, Pets by arrangement, Open all year except Christmas Day.
Mike & Claire Loseby, **Ermewood House Hotel,** Totnes Road, Ermington, Ivybridge, South Devon PL21 9NS
Tel: 01538 830741 Fax: 01548 830741   **Map Ref 41**

MODBURY INN, a 17th century coaching inn, with a cosy lounge bar plus family room and a well established restaurant. All rooms have wash basins, tea/coffee facilities and colour TV. Close to beaches, children's activity centres and Dartmoor for walkers.

B&B from £15pp, Dinner from £5.25, Rooms 2 single, 2 family (1 en-suite), Children & pets welcome, Open all year.
Mrs M.B. Paine, **Modbury Inn,** Brownston Street, Modbury, Ivybridge, Devon PL21 0RQ
Tel: 01548 830275   **Map Ref 42**

COURT BARTON FARMHOUSE, a delightful 16th century farmhouse in peaceful setting and within easy walking distance of village. Choice of seven bedrooms with en-suite facilities and colour TV's. Lots of car parking. Start your day with our scrumptious breakfast and relax in our comfortable lounge or extensive gardens. Email: jill@courtbarton.avel.co.uk

B&B from £20pp, Rooms 1 single, 2 twin, 2 double, 2 family, most en-suite, Restricted smoking, Children welcome, No pets, Open all year except Christmas. John & Jill Balkwill, **Court Barton Farmhouse,** Aveton Gifford, Kingsbridge, Devon TQ7 4LE
Tel: 01548 550312 Fax: 01548 550312   **Map Ref 44**

HELLIERS FARM, is a small working sheep farm on a hillside, set in the heart of Devons unspoilt countryside, within easy reach of beaches, moors, golf courses, National Trust houses and walks. The charming bedrooms all have tea/coffee trays, family, double and twin are en-suite and 1 single bedroom. No smoking. ETB 2 Crown Highly Commended.

B&B from £19pp, Rooms 1 single, 1 twin, 1 double, 1 family, most en-suite, No smoking, Children welcome, Open all year except Christmas.
Helliers Farm, Ashford, Aveton Gifford, Kingsbridge, South Devon TQ7 4ND
Tel: 01548 550689 Fax: 01548 550689   **Map Ref 45**

THE HENLEY HOTEL, a small, comfortable hotel on the edge of the sea. Spectacular views with private steps through garden down to lovely beach.

B&B from £27, Dinner available, Rooms 2 single, 2 twin, 4 double, all en-suite, No smoking, Children welcome, Open April - October.
The Henley Hotel, Folly Hill, Bigbury-on-Sea, Kingsbridge, Devon TQ7 4AR
Tel: 01548 810240 Fax: 01548 810020   **Map Ref 46**

ODDICOMBE HOUSE HOTEL, a country house standing in three acres of delightful grounds with lovely views to the hills beyond. All en-suite rooms with tea/coffee facilities. TV only in lounge. Private parking. Licensed. Situated 4 miles east of Kingsbridge. Ideal for Dartmouth, Kingsbridge and Salcombe.

B&B from £23pp, Dinner from £15, Rooms 2 single, 2 twin, 2 double, 1 family, all en-suite, Restricted smoking, Pets welcome, Open Easter - October.
Bob & Monica Yapp, **Oddicombe House Hotel,** Chillington, Kingsbridge, Devon TQ7 2JD
Tel: 01548 531234   **Map Ref 47**

HYGH DOWNE HOUSE, an acclaimed country house with picturesque views to the sea. Superbly appointed interior, en-suite spa bath, emperor bed, all facilities to make an extremely comfortable stay.
B&B from £25, Dinner available, Rooms 4 double, en-suite, No smoking, Open all year.
Hygh Downe House, East Prawle, Kingsbridge, Devon TQ7 2NL
Tel: 01548 511210 Fax: 01548 511210   **Map Ref 48**

OLD WALLS, is a beautiful 17th century traditional cob and thatch cottage set in private gardens with a stream. We have 3 cosy and comfortably furnished en-suite rooms, they have TV, hot drink trays and other touches to make your stay as enjoyable as possible. Breakfast features local produce, fresh baked bread and homemade preserves. Dinner is served in the candlelit dining room.

B&B from £25-£37.50pp, Dinner from £15.50, Rooms 3 en-suite double, No smoking, Open Easter - end October.
Barbara & Malcolm Wesley, **Old Walls,** Combe, Salcombe, Kingsbridge, Devon TQ7 3DN
Tel: 01548 842241   **Map Ref 49**

THURLESTONE HOTEL, a peaceful setting in old world village with thatched cottages. International cuisine and outstanding indoor sporting amenities.

B&B from £40, Dinner available, Rooms 5 single, 26 twin, 18 double, 13 triple, 3 family, all en-suite,No smoking, Children welcome, Open all year.

Thurlestone Hotel, Thurlestone, Kingsbridge, Devon TQ7 3NN
Tel: 01548 560382 Fax: 01548 561069   **Map Ref 50**

LYDFORD HOUSE HOTEL, a delightful country house in secluded garden setting on edge of Dartmoor. Charming bedrooms with every facility. Comfortable lounges and cosy bar. Recommended restaurant serving traditional English fare. Interesting wine list. Friendly personal service. Parking. Own BHS approved riding stables in the grounds. Email: Lydfordhousehotel@compuserve.com
B&B from £36pp, Dinner from £15.50, Rooms 2 single, 4 twin, 3 double, 3 family, all en-suite, Restricted smoking, Children over 5, Pets by arrangement, Open all year except Christmas & New Year.
The Boulter Family, **Lydford House Hotel,** Lydford, Devon EX20 4AU
Tel: 01822 820347 Fax: 01822 820442   **Map Ref 51**

MOOR VIEW HOUSE, a family run country house hotel on the edge of Dartmoor, peacefully set in 2 acres of gardens. Fine food, sound wine and log fires. Walking, fishing, riding, shooting and golf. Excellent touring base.

B&B from £40, Dinner available, Rooms 3 double, 1 twin, all en-suite, No smoking, Children over 12, Open all year.

Moor View House, Vale Down, Lydford, Devon EX20 4BB
Tel: 01822 820220   **Map Ref 51**

BATH HOTEL, a friendly, family run hotel by picturesque Lynmouth harbour. Ideal centre for exploring Exmoor National Park.

B&B from £29, Dinner available, Rooms 1 single, 8 twin, 12 double, 3 triple, all en-suite, Children welcome, Open February - December.

Bath Hotel, Lynmouth, Devon EX35 6EL
Tel: 01598 752238 Fax: 01598 752544   **Map Ref 52**

TREGONWELL RIVERSIDE GUESTHOUSE, an elegant, Victorian former sea captains house on riverside, alongside waterfalls, cascades, dramatic scenery and enchanting harbour in romantic old world smugglers village. Nature lovers and walkers paradise.

B&B from £19.50, Dinner available, Rooms 1 twin, 5 double, 1 triple, most en-suite, No smoking, Children welcome, Open all year.

Tregonwell Riverside Guesthouse, 1 Tors Road, Lynmouth, Devon EX35 6ET
Tel: 01598 753369   **Map Ref 52**

INGLESIDE HOTEL, a family run hotel with high standards in elevated position overlooking village. Ideal centre for exploring Exmoor.

B&B from £24, Dinner available, Rooms 1 twin, 4 double, 2 triple, all en-suite, No smoking, Children welcome, No pets, Open March - October.

Ingleside Hotel, Lynton, Devon EX35 6HW
Tel: 01598 752223   **Map Ref 53**

ALFORD HOUSE HOTEL, an elegant Georgian hotel with spectacular views over Lynton and Exmoor coastline. Delightful en-suite rooms, some four poster beds. Relaxing and peaceful, warm hospitality, outstanding food and fine wine.

B&B from £23, Dinner available, Rooms 1 single, 2 twin, 5 double, most en-suite, No smoking,No pets, Open February - November & Christmas.
Alford House Hotel, Alford Terrace, Lynton, Devon EX35 6AT
Tel: 01598 752359   **Map Ref 53**

....

SANDROCK HOTEL, a relaxing Edwardian hotel with modern comforts, in delightful sunny position close to Exmoor's superb coastal scenery and beauty spots.

B&B from £19.50, Dinner available, Rooms 2 single, 3 twin, 4 double, most en-suite,Children welcome, Open all year.
Sandrock Hotel, Longmead, Lynton, Devon EX35 6DH
Tel: 01598 753307 Fax: 01598 752665   **Map Ref 53**

....

KINGFORD HOUSE, a private hotel close to Valley of Rocks. Attractive, comfortable rooms, good home cooked meals with choice of menu. Individual attention assured.

B&B from £18, Dinner available, Rooms 2 single, 1 twin, 3 double, all en-suite, No smoking, Children welcome, No pets, Open February - December.
Kingford House, Longmead, Lynton, Devon EX35 6DQ
Tel: 01598 752361   **Map Ref 53**

....

LONGMEAD HOUSE HOTEL, a delightful old house set in a large garden, quietly situated towards the Valley of Rocks. Comfortable, pretty en-suite bedrooms, No smoking. Home cooking a speciality.

B&B from £17, Dinner available, Rooms 1 single, 1 twin, 4 double, 1 triple, most en-suite, No smoking, Children welcome, Open March - October.
Longmead House Hotel, Longmead, Lynton, Devon EX35 6DQ
Tel: 01598 752523   **Map Ref 53**

....

SEAWOOD HOTEL, a family run country house hotel nestling on wooded cliffs overlooking Lynmouth Bay and headland. Varied menu and friendly service.

B&B from £27, Dinner available, Rooms 1 single, 2 twin, 9 double, most en-suite, No smoking, Children welcome, Open April - October.
Seawood Hotel, North Walk Drive, Lynton, Devon EX35 6HJ
Tel: 01598 752272   **Map Ref 53**

....

CHOUGH'S NEST HOTEL, a detached cliffside retreat with 2 acre grounds and magnificent sea views. Good food. Value for money. Within walking distance of shops.

B&B from £29, Dinner available, Rooms 2 single, 1 twin, 7 double, 2 triple, all en-suite, No smoking, Children welcome, No pets, Open March - October.
Chough's Nest Hotel, North Walk, Lynton, Devon EX35 6HJ
Tel: 01598 753315   **Map Ref 53**

....

THE EXMOOR SANDPIPER INN, a beamed character inn/hotel, part 13th century, amidst thousands of acres of rolling Exmoor hills. A few hundred yards from Countisbury sea cliffs and 1 mile from Lynmouth harbour.

B&B from £25, Dinner available, Rooms 1 twin, 9 double, 4 triple, 2 family, all en-suite, Children welcome, Open all year.
The Exmoor Sandpiper Inn, Countisbury, Lynton, Devon EX35 6NE
Tel: 01598 741263 Fax: 01598 741358   **Map Ref 54**

PINE LODGE, where Exmoor meets the sea, overlooking the wooded West Lyn valley. Comfortable bedrooms most en-suite with TV, tea/coffee facilities. Large garden and private car park. Pedestranised easy walk into Lynton village. Dinner optional. Non smoking B&B from £18.00 per night.

B&B from £18pp, Dinner available, Rooms 4 double, 2 twin, most en-suite, No smoking, Open all year.
Mrs Davies, **Pine Lodge,** Lynway, Lynton, Devon EX35 6AX
Tel: 01598 753230 **Map Ref 53**

WOOSTON FARM, where a friendly welcome awaits you, where all rooms are tastefully furnished, two en-suite, one four-poster bed. The farm is situated high above the Teign valley where there are numerous walks. Peaceful, relaxing. AA Listed 4Q's, ETB 2 Crown Highly Commended.

B&B from £19pp, Rooms 1 twin, 2 double, all en-suite/private, No smoking or pets, Children over 8, Open all year.
Mrs Cuming, **Wooston Farm,** Moretonhampstead, Devon TQ13 8QA
Tel: 01647 440367 Fax: 01647 440367 **Map Ref 55**

GREAT SLONCOMBE FARM, share the magic of Dartmoor whilst staying in our lovely 13th century farmhouse. Set amongst meadows and woodland full of flowers and wildlife. A welcoming place to relax and explore our beautiful area. Comfortable en-suite rooms with every facility. Delicious farmhouse food.

B&B from £21-£22pp, Dinner from £11-£12, Rooms 1 twin, 2 double, all en-suite, No smoking, Children over 8, Pets by arrangement, Open all year.
Trudie Merchant, **Great Sloncombe Farm,** Moretonhampstead, Devon TQ13 8QF
Tel: 01647 440595 Fax: 01647 440595 **Map Ref 55**

MANOR HOUSE HOTEL & GOLF COURSE, this beautiful Jacobean manor is set in 270 acres of estate and is home to a par-69 championship golf course.

B&B from £75, Dinner available, Rooms 23 single, 36 twin, 28 double, 3 triple, most en-suite, Children welcome, Open all year.
Manor House Hotel & Golf Course, Moretonhampstead, Devon TQ13 8RE
Tel: 01647 440355 Fax: 01647 440961 **Map Ref 55**

WHITE HART HOTEL, is a 17th century former Coaching Inn on edge of Dartmoor. All rooms have colour TV, radio, direct dial telephone, hair dryer, trouser press, iron and ironing board, tea/coffee facilities. Cosy bar and lounges. Excellent Award Winning restaurant serving fresh local produce. Warmest welcome guaranteed.

B&B from £30pp, Dinner from £7.50, Rooms 1 single, 6 twin, 11 double, 2 family, all en-suite, Restricted smoking, Children & pets welcome, Open all year.
Alan Pope, **White Hart Hotel,** The Square, Moretonhampstead TQ13 8NF
Tel: 01647 440406 Fax: 01647 440565 **Map Ref 55**

GATE HOUSE, in Dartmoor National Park is 15th century thatched home in mediaeval village amidst breathtaking scenery. Rooms charmingly furnished offering classical country elegance with modern facilities. Beamed ceilings and massive fireplace with bread oven in sitting room. Secluded garden with swimming pool.

B&B from £25pp, Dinner from £14, Rooms 1 twin 2 double, all en-suite, No smoking, Pets welcome, Open all year.

John & Sheila Williams **Gate House,** North Bovey, Moretonhampstead, Devon TQ13 8RB
Tel: 01647 440479 Fax: 01647 440479 **Map Ref 38**

LUNDY HOUSE HOTEL, magnificently situated on coastal path with spectacular sea views. Traditional home cooking, licensed bar/lounge. Bargain breaks.

B&B from £17.50, Dinner available, Rooms 1 single, 4 double, 3 triple, 1 family, most en-suite, No smoking, Children welcome, Open all year.
Lundy House Hotel, Chapel Hill, Mortehoe, Devon EX34 7DZ
Tel: 01271 870372 & 870469 Fax: 01271 871001   **Map Ref 56**

....

HAZELWOOD HOTEL, an attractive, turn-of-the-century building in quiet residential location, 5 minutes walk from town centre, rail and coach stations. Licensed restaurant, residents lounge, garden and car park.

B&B from £30, Dinner available, Rooms 1 single, 3 twin, 4 double, most en-suite, Children welcome, Open all year.
Hazelwood Hotel, 33a Torquay Road, Newton Abbot, Devon TQ12 2LW
Tel: 01626 66130 Fax: 01626065021   **Map Ref 57**

....

MILL END, family owned, situated in the Dartmoor National Park on the banks of the River Teign. 3 miles from A30, Whiddon Down on A382.

B&B from £47, Dinner available, Rooms 2 single, 8 twin, 5 double, 2 triple, all with private or en-suite, Children welcome, Open all year.
Mill End, Sandy Park, Dartmoor National Park, Newton Abbot, Devon TQ13 8JN
Tel: 01647 432282 Fax: 01647 433106   **Map Ref 61**

....

GAGES MILL, a 14th century former millhouse set in beautiful countryside on the edge of Dartmoor. Comfortable accommodation, quality home cooking, large well kept gardens.
B&B from £20, Dinner available, Rooms 1 single, 1 twin, 6 double, all en-suite, Limited smoking, Children over 10, No pets, Open March - November.
Gages Mill, Buckfastleigh Road, Ashburton, Newton Abbot, Devon TQ13 7JW
Tel: 01364 652391   **Map Ref 58**

....

WELLPRITTON FARM, Dartmoor farmhouse 3 miles from A38 expressway half an hour Exeter, Plymouth, Torbay. Most rooms en-suite, all with tea/coffee facilities. Central heating, lounge with wood burner. Outdoor swimming pool, garden, pet goats, lambs, horse and chickens. Most country pursuits nearby. ETB 2 Crown Highly Recommended. AA QQQQ Selected.

B&B from £19pp, Dinner from £9, Rooms 1 twin, 1 double, 2 family, Restricted smoking, Children welcome, Open all year.
Colin & Susan Gifford, **Wellpritton Farm,** Holne, Ashburton, Newton Abbot, South Devon TQ13 7RX
Tel: 01364 631273   **Map Ref 59**

....

HOLNE CHASE HOTEL & RESTAURANT, a stunning estate setting inside Dartmoor National Park. River Dart for fishing. Excellent cuisine, comfortable, friendly hospitality, peaceful and relaxing. Lovely gardens and walks.
B&B from £60, Dinner available, Rooms 1 single, 8 twin, 9 double, all en-suite, Children welcome, Open all year.
Holne Chase Hotel & Restaurant, Tavistock Road, Ashburton, Newton Abbot, Devon TQ13 7NS
Tel: 01364 631471 Fax: 01364 631453   **Map Ref 58**

....

In the Dartmoor National Park with secluded beautiful woodland gardens, hard tennis court and glorious panoramic views, **PENPARK** is an elegant country house, designed by Clough Williams Ellis of Portmeirion fame. All rooms have private bathroom or shower, washbasins, tea and coffee making facilities and colour TV. Brochure with colour photograph sent by return.

B&B from £22pp, Dinner from £16 by arrangement, Reductions for children, Rooms 1 single, 1 twin/double, 1 double, all private facilities, No smoking, Open all year.
Madeleine Gregson, **Penpark,** Bickington, Newton Abbot TQ12 6LH
Tel: 01626 821314 Fax: 01626 821101   **Map Ref 60**

165

GLENDARAH HOUSE, a comfortable Victorian house with beautiful views in peaceful location, a short walk from village centre. Friendly service, en-suite rooms with all facilities.

B&B from £25, Rooms 3 twin, 3 double, all en-suite, No smoking, Children welcome, No pets, Open all year.
Glendarah House, Chagford, Newton Abbot, Devon TQ13 8BZ
Tel: 01647 433270 Fax: 01647 433483   **Map Ref 61**

....

GIDLEIGH PARK, a luxurious hotel and restaurant on the banks of the River Teign. Regarded by many as having the finest restaurant between Bath & Land's End.

B&B from £167.50, Dinner available, Rooms 13 twin, 1 double, all en-suite, No smoking, Children welcome, Open all year.
Gidleigh Park, Chagford, Newton Abbot, Devon TQ13 8HH
Tel: 01647 432367 &432225 Fax: 01647 432574 Email: gidleighpark@gidleigh.co.uk   **Map Ref 61**

....

EASTON COURT HOTEL, a thatched 15th century hotel of great charm and character on the edge of Dartmoor, offering peace, comfort and good food.

B&B from £45, Dinner available, Rooms 2 twin, 6 double, all en-suite, No smoking, Children welcome, Open February - December.
Easton Court Hotel, Easton Cross, Chagford, Newton Abbot, Devon TQ13 8JL
Tel: 01647 433469 Fax: 01647 433654   **Map Ref 62**

....

THE THATCHED COTTAGE RESTAURANT, a grade II listed 16th century Devon longhouse of great character. Licensed restaurant featuring large open fireplace serving home cooked food of the finest standard. Rooms have colour TV, tea/coffee facilities. Private car park and easy access to Dartmoor and to beaches and coastline.
B&B from £20pp, Dinner from £12.95, Rooms 1 single, 1 twin, 2 double, 1 family, all en-suite, No smoking, Children welcome, Open all year.
Klaus & Janice Wiemeyer, **The Thatched Cottage Restaurant,** 9 Crossley Moor Road, Kingsteignton, Newton Abbot, Devon TQ12 3LE
Tel: 01626 365650   **Map Ref 63**

....

OLD CHURCH HOUSE INN, a 13 th century coaching house of immense character and old world charm with inglenook fireplaces, stone walls and oak beamed ceilings. Situated in a beautiful valley between Dartmoor and Torquay.

B&B from £ 40, Dinner available, Rooms 5 double, 5 triple, all en-suite, No smoking, Children welcome, No pets, Open all year.
Old Church House Inn, Torbryan, Newton Abbot, Devon TQ12 5UR
Tel: 01803 812372 & 812180 Fax: 01812180   **Map Ref 64**

....

WHITE HART HOTEL, a town centre 17th century coaching inn. Fully licensed freehouse with bars, restaurant, function suites and car parking.

B&B from £35, Dinner available, Rooms 2 single, 11 double, 6 twin, 1 triple, all en-suite, Children welcome, No pets, Open all year.
White Hart Hotel, Fore Street, Okehampton, Devon EX20 1HD
Tel: 01837 52730 & 54514 Fax: 01837 53979   **Map Ref 65**

....

HEATHFIELD HOUSE, a friendly country guest house specialising in the personal touch. Noted for cuisine. The ideal stopover for business or pleasure. Comfort assured. Heated pool.

B&B from £20, Dinner available, Rooms 1 single, 21 twin, 1 double, 1 family, all en-suite, No smoking, Children welcome, Open January - November.
Heathfield House, Klondyke Road, Okehampton, Devon EX20 1EW
Tel: 01837 54211 & 850 881547 Fax: 01837 54211   **Map Ref 65**

FLUXTON FARM HOTEL, a former farmhouse in beautiful country setting. Comfortable en-suite bedrooms, 2 sitting rooms and large gardens. Home cooked food served in candlelit dining room. Log fires in season. Cat loves paradise.

B&B from £23, Dinner available, Rooms 3 single, 4 twin, 3 double, 2 triple, most en-suite, No smoking, Children welcome, Open all year.

Fluxton Farm Hotel, Ottery St Mary, Devon EX11 1RJ
Tel: 01404 812818   **Map Ref 66**

....

SALSTON MANOR HOTEL, a welcoming country house hotel in the heart of East Devon, with amenities for all the family. Indoor pool, squash, sauna and solarium. Ideal for business or pleasure.

B&B from £37.50, Dinner available, Rooms 3 single, 4 twin, 7 double, 1 family, 12 triple, all en-suite, No smoking, Children welcome, Open all year.

Salston Manor Hotel, Ottery St Mary, Devon EX11 1RQ
Tel: 01404 815581 Fax: 01404 815581   **Map Ref 66**

....

VENN OTTERY BARTON HOTEL, a 16th century country hotel. Great food, jolly atmosphere, special interest holidays, short breaks etc. Lovely gardens, ample parking. Ground floor rooms available.

B&B from £32, Dinner available, Rooms 2 single, 7 twin, 5 double, 3 triple, most en-suite, No smoking, Children welcome, Open all year.

Venn Ottery Barton Hotel, Venn Ottery, Ottery St Mary, Devon EX11 1RZ
Tel: 01404 812733 Fax: 01404 814713   **Map Ref 67**

....

SOUTH SANDS HOTEL, family run, wonderful fresh food. Superb, peaceful location overlooking sea, beach, park and close to harbour. Large car park.

B&B from £20, Dinner available, Rooms 2 single, 1 twin, 3 double, 5 triple, 8 family, most en-suite, No smoking, Children welcome, Open April - October & Christmas.

South Sands Hotel, 12 Alta Vista Road, Paignton, Devon TQ4 6BZ
Tel: 01803 557231 & 0500 432153 Fax: 01803 529947   **Map Ref 68**

....

LYNCOURT HOTEL, situated in a quiet tree lined road on a level location a short distance from shops, beaches and leisure facilities.

B&B from £14, Dinner available, Rooms 3 single, 3 twin, 3 double, 1 triple, 1 family, most en-suite, No smoking, Children welcome, No pets, Open all year.

Lyncourt Hotel, 14 Elmsleigh Park, Paignton, Devon TQ4 5AT
Tel: 01803 557124 & 0410 209291   **Map Ref 68**

....

THE SANDPIPER VEGETARIAN HOTEL, 100% vegetarian. Vegans also catered for. Colour TV's, tea and coffee in rooms. Licensed dining room. 2 minutes picturesque harbour, coves and beaches. Coastal walks. Take the steam train to Dartmouth. Cruise down the River Dart to historical Totnes. Take a ramble on Dartmoor.

B&B from £18pp, Dinner from £6.50, Rooms 4 twin, 11 double, 5 family, most en-suite, Restricted smoking, Children welcome, Open all year.

Angela & Marion, **The Sandpiper Vegetarian Hotel,** 14 Roundham Road, Paignton, Devon TQ4 6DN
Tel: 01803 551397 Fax: 01803 551397   **Map Ref 68**

ROSSLYN HOTEL, a cosy and friendly licensed hotel, close to all amenities and 100 yards to beach. En-suite rooms with satellite TV and tea/coffee making facilities. Old worlde bar. Central heating. Parking. A warm welcome assured from your hosts.

B&B from £16pp, Dinner from £7.50, Rooms 1 single, 2 twin, 6 double, 3 family, most en-suite, Children welcome, No pets, Open all year except Christmas.

Val & Bob Adams, **Rosslyn Hotel,** 16 Colin Rd, Paignton, Devon TQ3 2NR
Tel: 01803 525578   **Map Ref 68**

HARTLEY BRIAR, we have colour TVs in rooms. Guest lounge. Dining room. 2 minutes walk beach. 5 minutes walk family resort of Paignton with Theatre, Leisure Centre, Zoo, cinema and stream train. Usual seaside attractions. Within a few miles drive beautiful Dartmoor and countryside.

B&B from £13pp, Dinner from £3.50, Rooms 1 single, 3 double, 3 family, all with vanity units, Restricted smoking, Children welcome, No pets, Open February - November.
Helen Roberts, **Hartley Briar,** 18 Leighon Road, Paignton, Devon TQ3 2BQ
Tel: 01803 556819 Fax: 01803 556819   **Map Ref 68**

WYNNCROFT HOTEL, centrally situated hotel, with traditional cuisine from an a la carte menu, in the comfort of a refurbished Victorian home. ETB 3 Crowns Highly Commended.

B&B from £18, Dinner available, Rooms 3 twin, 6 double, 2 triple, most en-suite, Children welcome, No pets, Open January - November.
Wynncroft Hotel, 2 Elmsleigh Park, Paignton, Devon TQ4 5AT
Tel: 01803 525728   **Map Ref 68**

REDCLIFFE HOTEL, choice location in 3 acres of grounds directly adjoining the beach. Heated outdoor swimming pool and new indoor leisure complex.

B&B from £40, Dinner available, Rooms 12 single, 22 twin, 23 double, 2 triple, most en-suite, No smoking, Children welcome, No pets, Open all year.

Redcliffe Hotel, Marine Drive, Paignton, Devon TQ3 2NL
Tel: 01803 526397 Fax: 01803 528030 EMail: Redclfe@aol.com   **Map Ref 68**

TORBAY COURT HOTEL, situated in a quiet, secluded position. A few yards level walk to the seafront. Close to park and amenities.

B&B from £13, Dinner available, Rooms 11 single, 27 twin, 16 double, 3 triple, 1 family, most en-suite, Children welcome, No pets, Open March - December.
Torbay Court Hotel, Steartfield Road, Paignton, Devon TQ3 2BG
Tel: 01803 663332 Fax: 01803 522680   **Map Ref 68**

TORBAY HOLIDAY MOTEL, on the A385 in peaceful countryside, close to all amenities of Torbay. Ideal base for touring Devon.

B&B from £30, Dinner available, Rooms 2 single, 5 twin, 7 double, 2 triple, all en-suite, Children welcome, Open all year.

Torbay Holiday Motel, Totnes Road, Paignton, Devon TQ4 7PP
Tel: 01803 558226 Fax: 01803 663375   **Map Ref 68**

HARWIN HOTEL, is a family run hotel specialising in friendly, personal service. Safe bathing from hotel in picturesque Bay. Direct access to open park land. Near sports complex, water theme park and harbour. Radio/baby listener, colour TV's/video channel in all rooms. Reductions for children in family rooms. Mini-break specials.
B&B from £20pp, Dinner from £10.50, Rooms 4 single, 5 twin, 4 double, 13 family, most en-suite, Restricted smoking, Children welcome, Open May - September.
Ruth & Stephen Gorman, **Harwin Hotel**, Alta Vista Road Goodrington Sands, Paignton, South Devon TQ4 6DA
Tel: 01803 558771 Fax: 01803 558771   **Map Ref 69**

SUMMERHILL HOTEL, comfortable hotel with spacious, secluded, suntrap gardens, adjacent to sandy beaches and park. Close to harbour, leisure centre and water theme park.

B&B from £20, Dinner available, Rooms 2 single, 5 twin, 10 double, 9 triple, all en-suite, Children welcome, Open March - November.
Summerhill Hotel, Braeside Road, Goodrington, Paignton, Devon TQ4 6BX
Tel: 01803 558101 Fax: 01803 588101   **Map Ref 69**

LAMPLIGHTER HOTEL, a small friendly hotel on Plymouth Hoe, 5 minutes walk from the city centre and seafront.

B&B from £18, Dinner available, Rooms 2 twin, 5 double, 1 triple, 1 family, most en-suite, Children welcome, Open all year.

Lamplighter Hotel, 103 Citadel Road, The Hoe, Plymouth, Devon PL1 2RN
Tel: 01752 663855 Fax: 01752 228139   **Map Ref 70**

INVICTA HOTEL, an elegant Victorian hotel opposite Sir Francis Drake bowling green and famous Plymouth Hoe. Very close to the city centre and historic Barbican.

B&B from £40, Dinner available, Rooms 4 single, 7 twin, 6 double, 3 triple, 3 family, most en-suite, Children welcome, Open all year.
Invicta Hotel, 11-12 Osborne Place, The Hoe, Plymouth, Devon PL1 2PU
Tel: 01752 664997 Fax: 01752 664994   **Map Ref 70**

GROSVENOR PARK HOTEL, a popular, comfortable, recently refurbished hotel offering good food and drink and great value. Nearest hotel to the station an d all city centre amenities. Look no further! Golf, bowls and diving package breaks a speciality.

B&B from £20, Dinner available, Rooms 5 single, 5 twin, 5 double, 1 family, most en-suite, No smoking, Children welcome, No pets, Open all year.

Grosvenor Park Hotel, 114-116 North Road East, Plymouth, Devon PL4 6AH
Tel: 01752 229312 Fax: 01752 252777   **Map Ref 70**

AVALON GUEST HOUSE, is a family run establishment situated on Plymouth Hoe, adjacent to Drakes Bowling Green. Two minutes to sea front. Barbican Theatre, Royal Pavilions and Brittany Ferries. Colour TV and tea/coffee facilities in all rooms. Full central heating. Own keys, no restrictions.

B&B from £15pp, Rooms 2 single, 1 twin/double en-suite, 2 double with shower, 1 family, Restricted smoking, Children welcome, No pets, Open all year except Christmas.
Bob & Cindy Wright, **Avalon Guest House**, 167 Citadel Road, The Hoe, Plymouth, Devon PL1 2HU
Tel: 01752 668127   **Map Ref 70**

169

ST. MALO GUEST HOUSE, close to sea front and Brittany ferries, coach and railway stations. All rooms colour TV, tea/coffee facilities. Snacks available. Central heating and very comfortable. S.A.E for details.

B&B from £13-£14pp, Rooms 2 single, 4 twin, 3 double, 3 family, Restricted smoking, Children & pets welcome,

Delphine & Bernard James, **St. Malo Guest House,** 19 Garden Court, West Hoe, Plymouth, Devon PL1 3DA
Tel: 01752 262961   **Map Ref 70**

THE TEVIOT GUEST HOUSE, an early Victorian town house situated close to university, rail, bus and ferry terminals. Within a short walking distance of Plymouth Hoe and Barbican.

B&B from £18, Rooms 1 single, 2 double, 2 twin, 1 triple, most en-suite, No smoking, Children welcome, No pets, Open all year.

The Teviot Guest House, 20 North Road East, Plymouth, Devon PL4 6AS
Tel: 01752 262656 Fax: 01752 251660   **Map Ref 70**

WATER'S EDGE HOTEL, is a character building dating from 1855. Facilities include, TV, hair dryers, tea/coffee facilities, central heating, beautiful terrace overlooking the Sound. Early breakfast available for ferry travellers. Fully licensed bar. Scenic views. Situated close to the historic Plymouth Hoe. Within easy reach of the Plymouth's city centre. **B&B from £18pp,** Rooms 2 single, 1 twin, 2 double, 4 family, all en-suite, Children & pets welcome, Open all year except Christmas & New Year. Roy & Maureen Bullard, **Water's Edge Hotel,** 29 Grand Parade, West Hoe, Plymouth, Devon PL1 3DQ
Tel: 01752 266449   **Map Ref 70**

ATHENAEUM LODGE, an elegant Georgian grade II listed guest house, furnished to high standard. In a central position for the Hoe, historic Barbican and ferry port. Reputation for comfort and hospitality. Free private parking.

B&B from £16, Rooms 3 twin, 4 double, 3 triple, most en-suite, No smoking, Children over 5, No pets, Open all year.

Athenaeum Lodge, 4 Athenaeum Street, The Hoe, Plymouth, Devon PL1 2RH
Tel: 01752 665005   **Map Ref 70**

BERKELEYS OF ST JAMES, a non smoking charming Victorian house in secluded square on Plymouth Hoe. Quality stay assured. Awarded healthy option/eats award 1997/8. En-suite accommodation.

B&B from £21, Rooms 1 single, 3 double, 1 triple, all en-suite, No smoking, Children welcome, Open all year.

Berkeleys of St James, 4 St James Place East, The Hoe, Plymouth, Devon PL1 3AS
Tel: 01752 221654   **Map Ref 70**

SQUIRES GUEST HOUSE, an elegant Victorian establishment in a quiet secluded square on Plymouth Hoe. Converted to a high standard. Within easy walking distance of all amenities. Winner of Chairman's Cup for Excellence, awarded by Plymouth's Marketing Bureau.

B&B from £18, Rooms 2 single, 4 double, 2 triple, most en-suite, No smoking, Children welcome, No pets, Open all year.

Squires Guest House, 7 St James Place East, The Hoe, Plymouth, Devon PL1 3AS
Tel: 01752 261459 Fax: 01752 261459   **Map Ref 70**

THE GRAND HOTEL, a Victorian hotel on Plymouth Hoe. Magnificent sea views, close to city centre and historic Barbican. Leisure breaks available all year round. Live entertainment every Saturday. Balcony rooms and suites.

B&B from £40, Dinner available, Rooms 34 twin, 38 double, 3 triple, 2 family, all en-suite, No smoking, Children welcome, Open all year.
The Grand Hotel, Elliot Street, The Hoe, Plymouth, Devon PL1 2PT
Tel: 01752 661195 Fax: 01752 600653   **Map Ref 70**

....

NEW CONTINENTAL HOTEL, a beautifully refurbished grade II listed Victorian building in city centre. Within easy walking distance of the shops,Barbican and Hoe. Adjacent to Pavillions conference centre. Superb indoor leisure complex. Leisure breaks available.

B&B from £42, Dinner available, Rooms 22 single, 14 twin, 37 double, 2 triple, 24 family, all en-suite, No smoking, Children welcome, Open all year.
New Continental Hotel, Millbay Road, Plymouth, Devon PL1 3LD
Tel: 01752 220782 Fax: 01752 227013   **Map Ref 70**

....

THE VILLA, is a small family run guest house close to rail station and to city centre and all tourist attractions. All rooms have colour televisions, tea/coffee facilities. A guest lounge is available with television and video. Anne and Derek look forward to welcoming you.

B&B from £16pp, Rooms 3 single, 1 twin, 2 family, most en-suite, Children & pets welcome, Open all year.
Anne & Derek Albano **The Villa,** 1 Glen Park Avenue, Mutley, Plymouth, Devon PL4 6BA
Tel: 01752 223158 Fax: 01752 223158   **Map Ref 70**

....

ROSALAND HOTEL, a quiet Victorian hotel recommended by 'Which' in is 'Best Bed & Breakfast Guide'. Close to city centre and railway station. We have a comfortable TV lounge and licensed bar. Car parking. Satellite TV, tea/coffee facilities, hair dryers and telephones in all bedrooms.

B&B from £15pp, Dinner by arrangement £10, Rooms 4 single, 1 twin, 2 double, 2 family, some en-suite, Restricted smoking, Children welcome, No pets, Open all year.
Heather & Peter Shaw, **Rosaland Hotel,** 32 Houndiscombe Road, Mutley, Plymouth, Devon PL4 6HQ
Tel: 01752 664749 Fax: 01752 256984   **Map Ref 70**

....

MILLSTONES COUNTRY HOTEL, an elegant country hotel set in an acre of delightful lawned gardens with private parking. Located 4 miles north of the centre of Plymouth on main A386 road.

B&B from £47, Dinner available, Rooms 2 single, 2 twin, 5 double, most en-suite, Children welcome, No pets, Open all year.
Millstones Country Hotel, 436-438 Tavistock Road, Roborough, Plymouth, Devon PL6 7HQ
Tel: 01752 773734 Fax: 01752 769435   **Map Ref 71**

....

MOUNTBATTEN HOTEL, is a Victorian residence situated in a conservation area. It is a small hotel located in a quiet cul-de-sac, overlooking parkland with River views. Garage/free street parking. Well appointed bedrooms with telephone, tea/coffee, colour TV. Licensed bar. 3 Crown Commended.

B&B from £21.50pp, Dinner from £8.50, Rooms 4 single, 1 twin, 3 double, 3 family, mainly en-suite, Children & pets welcome, Open all year.
Mike Hendy, **Mountbatten Hotel,** 52 Exmouth Road, Stoke, Plymouth, Devon PL1 4QH
Tel: 01752 563843 Fax: 01752 606014   **Map Ref 70**

TORRE VIEW HOTEL, a detached Victorian residence with every modern comfort, commanding extensive views of the estuary and surrounding countryside. Congenial atmosphere.

B&B from £25, Dinner available, Rooms 2 twin, 6 double, all en-suite, No smoking, Children over 4, No pets, Open March - October.
Torre View Hotel, Devon Road, Salcombe, Devon TQ8 8HJ
Tel: 01548 842633 Fax: 01548 842633 **Map Ref 49**

....

HERON HOUSE HOTEL, an idyllic sea edge location, surrounded by National Trust countryside and adjacent to bird reserve. Beautifully appointed. Noted for food.

B&B from £30, Dinner available, Rooms 1 single, 2 twin, 13 double, 1 triple, 1 family, all en-suite, No smoking, Children welcome, Open all year.
Heron House Hotel, Thurlestone Sands, Salcombe, Devon TQ7 3JY
Tel: 01548 561308 & 561600 Fax: 01548 560180 **Map Ref 50**

....

ST MELLION HOTEL, GOLF & COUNTRY CLUB, the compass pivot of Devon and Cornwall. The visitor's perfect choice with world class golf, new leisure facilities, award winning food and lodge/hotel accommodation.

B&B from £50, Dinner available, Rooms 16 twin, 8 double, all en-suite, No smoking, Children welcome, No pets, Open all year.
St Mellion Hotel, Golf & Country Club, St Mellion, Saltash, Devon PL12 6SD
Tel: 01579 351351 Fax: 01579 350537 **Map Ref 72**

....

BEACH END GUEST HOUSE, enjoy unrivalled views of Seaton Bay. We offer fine food, friendly and attentive service in our lovely Edwardian guest house.

B&B from £43, Dinner available, Rooms 1 twin, 4 double, all en-suite, No pets, Open February - October.
Beach End Guest House, 8 Trevelyan Road, Seaton, Devon EX12 2NL
Tel: 01297 23388 **Map Ref 73**

....

BEAUMONT, an attractive and spacious guest house in select seafront position, offering en-suite comfort, personal attention and traditional home cooking.

B&B from £19, Dinner available, Rooms 2 double, 2 triple, 1 family, all en-suite, Children welcome, Open January - October & December.
Beaumont, Castle Hill, Seaton, Devon EX12 2QW
Tel: 01297 20832 **Map Ref 73**

....

GLENSIDE HOTEL, an 18th century cottage hotel in conservation village over looking river and an easy stroll to the Beach. All meals prepared and cooked by resident proprietors. Sunny gardens. Car park. 3 Crown Commended. Bargain Breaks Brochure.

B&B from £19pp, Dinner form £13, Rooms 1 single, 3 twin, 5 double, 1 family, all en-suite, Restricted smoking, Children over 4, Pets by arrangement, Open all year.

Mr & Mrs Underwood, **Glenside Hotel,** Shaldon, South Devon TQ14 0EP
Tel: 01626 872448 **Map Ref 74**

....

VIRGINIA COTTAGE, a grade II listed 17th century house set in one acre garden. Bedrooms with private facilities and tea/coffee makers. Large inglenook fireplace. Car parking in grounds.

B&B from £24pp, Rooms 2 twin, 1 double, No smoking or pets, Children over 12, Open March - December.
Jennifer & Michael Britton, **Virginia Cottage,** Brook Lane, Shaldon, Teignmouth, Devon TQ14 0HZ
Tel: 01626 872634 Fax: 01626 872634 **Map Ref 74**

RYTON GUEST HOUSE, is a friendly, well established guest house. Quietly situated within walking distance of town and sea front. All rooms have televisions, tastefully decorated, clean and comfortable. We are proud of our reputation for serving plenty of varied home prepared meals. Patio garden. Full licence. Free private parking.
B&B from £18pp, Dinner from £9, Rooms 2 single, 3 twin, 3 double, 2 family, most en-suite, Restricted smoking, Children welcome, Open March - October.
Mary & Vic Williams, **Ryton Guest House,** 52-54 Winslade Road, Sidmouth, Devon EX10 9EX
Tel: 01395 513981   Map Ref 75

WOODLANDS HOTEL, a family owned Regency country house, set in award winning seaside gardens, offering complete relaxation. Near sea and shops. Traditionally high standards.

B&B from £18.50, Dinner available, Rooms 5 single, 15 twin, 6 double, most en-suite, No smoking, Children over 3, Open all year.
Woodlands Hotel, Cotman Cross, Sidmouth, Devon EX10 8HG
Tel: 01395 513120 & 513166 Fax: 01395 513292   Map Ref 75

WILLOW BRIDGE HOTEL, E.T.B Highly Commended. AA Selected 4Q's. Delightful riverside position. Short level walk to sea and town. En-suite rooms with tea/coffee making facilities, colour TV's, radios, hair dryers, shaver points. Guests car park. Licensed. Non smoking. Many local attractions. Beautiful natural countryside.
B&B from £21pp, Dinner from £10, Rooms 2 twin, 4 double, en-suite facilities, No smoking, Children & Pets welcome, Open March - November.
David & Brenda Smith **Willow Bridge Hotel,** Millford Road, Sidmouth, Devon EX10 8DR
Tel: 01395 513599 Fax: 01395 513599   Map Ref 75

LITTLECOURT HOTEL, a Regency country house built for the Duke of St Albans. Tastefully modernised yet retaining its charm and elegance. Set in award winning gardens. Excellent cuisine, mainly Devon/Dorset regional dishes. Short walk to sea and shops.

B&B from £28.50, Dinner available, Rooms 4 single, 8 twin, 5 double, 3 triple, most en-suite, No smoking, Children welcome, Open March - October & Christmas.
Littlecourt Hotel, Seafield Road, Sidmouth, Devon EX10 8HF
Tel: 01395 515279   Map Ref 75

HOTEL ELIZABETH, superbly positioned Victorian seafront hotel on the level esplanade. Refurbished and now totally non smoking. Comfortable rooms, excellent food and friendly staff.

B&B from £27, Dinner available, Rooms 1 single, 7 double, 20 twin, most en-suite, No smoking, Children welcome, No pets, Open February - November.
Hotel Elizabeth, The Esplanade, Sidmouth, Devon EX10 8AT
Tel: 01395 513503   Map Ref 75

DEVORAN HOTEL, a family run hotel overlooking beach, very close to town centre and amenities. relaxed, happy atmosphere with traditional home cooked food using local produce.

B&B from £27, Dinner available, Rooms 5 single, 7 twin, 7 double, 4 triple, most en-suite, No smoking, Children welcome, Open March - November.

Devoran Hotel, The Esplanade, Sidmouth, Devon EX10 8AU
Tel: 01395 513151 & 0800 317171 Fax: 01395 579929   Map Ref 75

KINGSWOOD HOTEL, delightful central location on Sidmouth's Regency seafront. Emphasis on good food. Comfortable relaxed atmosphere in former Victorian spa baths. 45 years of same ownership.

B&B from £30, Dinner available, Rooms 8 single, 2 double, 9 twin, 7 triple, all with en-suite or private bathroom, No smoking, Children welcome, Open March - November.

Kingswood Hotel, The Esplanade, Sidmouth, Devon EX10 8AX
Tel: 01395 516367 Fax: 01395 513185   **Map Ref 75**

....

HOTEL RIVIERA, a majestic Regency hotel on the Esplanade, with panoramic sea views and a splendid terrace overlooking Lyme Bay.

B&B from £66, Dinner available, Rooms 7 single, 14 twin, 6 double, most en-suite, No smoking, Children welcome, Open February - December.

Hotel Riviera, The Esplanade, Sidmouth, Devon EX10 8AY
Tel: 01395 515201 Fax: 01395 577775 EMail: enquiries@hotelriviera.co.uk   **Map Ref 75**

....

ROYAL YORK & FAULKNER HOTEL, a charming Regency hotel on centre of Sidmouth's delightful Esplanade. Long established, family run hotel offering all amenities and excellent leisure facilities.

B&B from £25.75, Dinner available, Rooms 22 single, 29 twin, 9 double, 8 triple, most en-suite, No smoking, Children welcome, Open February - December
Royal York & Faulkner Hotel, The Esplanade, Sidmouth, Devon EX10 8AZ
Tel: 01395 513043 & 513184 Fax: 01395 577472   **Map Ref 75**

....

THE BELMONT HOTEL, traditionally one of Sidmouth's finest seafront hotels. Leisure facilities are available at adjacent hotel, the Victoria. Seasonal break breaks available.

B&B from £57, Dinner available, Rooms 9 single, 11 double, 28 twin, 3 family, all en-suite, No smoking, Children welcome, Open all year.

The Belmont Hotel, The Esplanade, Sidmouth, Devon EX10 8RX
Tel: 01395 512555 Fax: 01395 579101   **Map Ref 75**

....

THE VICTORIA HOTEL, one of England's finest hotels on Sidmouth's famous Esplanade. Guests are assured of high standards of service, comfort and cuisine. Seasonal break rates available.

B&B from £65, Dinner available, Rooms 14 single, 20 twin, 18 double, 9 triple, all en-suite, No smoking, Children welcome, No pets, Open all year.

The Victoria Hotel, The Esplanade, Sidmouth, Devon EX10 8RY
Tel: 01395 512651 Fax: 01395 579154   **Map Ref 75**

....

CHERITON GUEST HOUSE, is a large town house which backs on to the River Sid, with the 'Byes' parkland beyond.Private parking. Comfortable lounge with TV. Beautiful secluded garden. Rooms have central heating, TV and tea/coffee facilities and all rooms are en-suite. Individual winners of Sidmouth in Bloom.
B&B from £20, Dinner from £9, Rooms 3 single, 5 double/twin, 2 family, all en-suite, No smoking, Pets by arrangement, Open all year.
Diana & John Lee, **Cheriton Guest House,** Vicarage Road, Sidmouth, Devon EX10 8UQ
Tel: 01395 513810   **Map Ref 75**

SID VALLEY COUNTRY HOUSE HOTEL, outdoor heated pool set in five acres. Horses. Walking. Offering peace in a tranquil setting near Saxon village of Sidbury. All rooms have tea/coffee and TV. Restaurant resident license. A warm welcome awaits you and also self catering available. 4 Crowns Highly Commended.
B&B from £20pp, Dinner from £10, Rooms 2 single, 7 twin, 5 double, 1 family, all en-suite, Restricted smoking, Children & Pets welcome, Open all year.
Stephen & Sarah Hills-Ingyon, **Sid Valley Country House Hotel,** Sidbury, Sidmouth, Devon EX10 0QJ
Tel: 01395 597274   **Map Ref 76**

THE GEORGE HOTEL, a 17th century grade II listed building, formerly the town's main coaching inn and known as the George Inn and Theatre.

B&B from £25, Dinner available, Rooms 1 single, 3 twin, 4 double, 2 triple, most en-suite, No smoking, Children welcome, No pets, Open all year.
The George Hotel, 1 Broad Street, South Molton, Devon EX36 3AB
Tel: 01769 572514 & 574816 Fax: 01769 572514   **Map Ref 77**

WELBECK MANOR HOTEL, is a licensed hotel, built by Isambard Kingdom Brunel , set in 60 acres of park land, golf course, near Dartmoor and historic Plymouth. Victorian style bedrooms, tea/coffee facilities, colour TV's, en-suite bathrooms. Special weekend and weekly rates available. Ask about our Murder Mystery Weekends. Email: welbeckm@aol.com

B&B from £25pp, Dinner from £6.50, Rooms 2 twin, 3 double, 1 family, all en-suite, Children welcome, Pets by arrangement, Open all year.
Peter Barraud, **Welbeck Manor Hotel,** Blacklands, Sparkwell PL7 5DF
Tel: 01752 837374 Fax: 01752 837219   **Map Ref 78**

LONDON HOTEL, situated in town centre with easy access to beaches and moors. Families catered for. Leisure facilities include indoor swimming pool.

B&B from £22, Dinner available, Rooms 1 single, 2 twin, 17 double, 6 triple, 6 family, all en-suite, Children welcome, Open all year.

London Hotel, Bank Street, Teignmouth, Devon TQ14 8AW
Tel: 01626 776336 Fax: 01626 778457   **Map Ref 79**

BELVEDERE HOTEL, a comfortable detached family run Victorian villa with its own garden and car park. Close to beach and town centre. Many rooms with sea views.

B&B from £20, Dinner available, Rooms 1 single, 2 twin, 7 double, 2 family, 1 triple, all en-suite, Children welcome, No pets, Open all year.

Belvedere Hotel, Barnpark Road, Teignmouth, Devon TQ14 8PJ
Tel: 01626 774561 Fax: 01626 770009   **Map Ref 79**

THE COOMBE BANK HOTEL, a spacious, detached Victorian house, quietly situated above town centre, 10 minute's walk from shops and beach. Well appointed bedrooms with private facilities. Private parking.

B&B from £25, Dinner available, Rooms 6 twin, 3 double, 1 triple, all with private or en-suite facilities, Children welcome, No pets, Open all year.

The Coombe Bank Hotel, Landscore Road, Teignmouth, Devon TQ14 9JL
Tel: 01626 772369 Fax: 01626 774159   **Map Ref 79**

BRIDGE GUEST HOUSE, an attractive Victorian town house on a bank of the River Exe, with pretty riverside tea garden. Ideal for touring the heart of Devon.

B&B from £18.50, Dinner available, Rooms 4 single, 1 twin, 2 double,2 triple, most en-suite,children welcome, Open all year.
Bridge Guest House, 23 Angel Hill, Tiverton, Devon EX16 6PE
Tel: 01884 252804 Fax: 01884 253949   **Map Ref 81**

....

POOLE FARM, an attractive farmhouse recently renovated. En-suite bedrooms with colour TV and tea/coffee facilities. Quiet hamlet but only 15 minutes from M5 and Tiverton Parkway railway station. Ideal touring centre for Dartmoor, Exmoor and coast. Lovely houses, gardens and places of interest nearby.

B&B £24pp, Dinner by prior arrangement, Rooms 1 twin, 1 double, both en-suite, No smoking, Children welcome, Pets by arrangement, Open all year except Christmas & New Year.
Jenny Shaw, **Poole Farm,** Ash Thomas, Tiverton, Devon EX16 4NS
Tel: 01884 820201   **Map Ref 82**

....

Situated by the River Exe near Bickleigh Bridge. **BICKLEIGH COTTAGE HOTEL,** has been owned by the Cochrane family since 1933. The original cottage was built circa 1640. All bedrooms are en-suite with tea/coffee facilities. A perfect centre for touring Devon, Exeter and Tiverton Castle.

B&B from £23.50pp, Dinner from £11.40, Rooms 2 single, 3 twin, 4 double, all en-suite, Restricted smoking, Children over 14, Open April - October.
R S H & P M Cochrane, **Bickleigh Cottage Hotel,** Bickleigh, Tiverton, Devon EX16 8RJ
Tel: 01884 855230   **Map Ref 83**

....

LITTLE HOLWELL, we offer a warm welcome in our 13th century home. A refreshing cup of tea, evening meal optional. The house is centrally heated, log fires in winter. Tea/coffee facilities, clock/radios and hair dryers. Ideal overnight stop or good base for touring.

B&B from £16pp, Dinner from £9, Rooms 2 double, 1 family, 2 en-suite, No smoking or pets, Children welcome, Open all year except Christmas.
Mrs Hill-King **Little Holwell,** Collipriest, Tiverton, Devon EX16 4PT
Tel/Fax: 01884 257590   **Map Ref 81**

....

THE OLD RECTORY, a beautiful house, in its own vineyard, in the tranquil Domesday village of Oakford. Lovely views, walks, and fishing in the Exe. Deer watching on Exmoor. Central heating. Car parking. Tea/coffee. TV. Full English breakfast, diets by request. German, Spanish and French spoken.

B&B from £15pp, Dinner from £9, rooms 1 twin, 1 double en-suite, No smoking, Children over 16, No pets, Open all year except Christmas & New Year.
Mrs Rostron, **The Old Rectory,** Oakford, Tiverton, Devon EX16 9EW
Tel: 01398 351486 Fax: 01398 351486   **Map Ref 84**

....

BAHAMAS HOTEL, a family hotel with emphasis on food and service. 5 minutes from the sea and English Riviera Centre. All en-suite rooms with TV, radio and central heating.

B&B from £19, Dinner available, Rooms 1 single, 4 twin, 3 double, 1 triple, 2 family, all en-suite, No smoking, Children welcome, Open all year.
Bahamas Hotel, 17 Avenue Road, Torquay, Devon TQ2 5LB
Tel: 01803 296005 & 0500 526022   **Map Ref 85**

HOTEL FIESTA, is family run, catering for weekend or longer breaks in a relaxed friendly atmosphere. This listed building set in its own grounds is a short walk from the town and a 5 minutes drive to the beach. Ideal centre for touring South Devon.

B&B from £15pp, Dinner from £8, Rooms 1 single, 2 twin, 3 double, 1 family, most en-suite, Children & pets welcome, Open all year except Christmas & New Year. Keith & Catriona Pearson, **Hotel Fiesta,** 50 St. Marychurch Road, Torquay, Devon TQ1 3JE
Tel: 01803 292388 Fax: 01803 292388   **Map Ref 85**

....

CRANBORNE HOTEL, a family run hotel, close to town centre, seafront and conference centre. We take pride in our service, home cooking and friendly atmosphere.

B&B from £15, Dinner available, Rooms 2 single, 1 twin, 4 double, 4 triple, 2 family, most en-suite, Children welcome, No pets, Open all year.
Cranborne Hotel, 58 Belgrave Road, Torquay, Devon TQ2 5HY
Tel: 01803 298046 Fax: 01803 298046   **Map Ref 85**

....

TORBAY STAR GUEST HOUSE, a friendly guest house in level position. Free car park, own keys, tea/coffee making facilities and TV. En-suite or private facilities.

B&B from £26, Rooms 2 double, 1 triple, 2 family, all en-suite, No smoking, Children welcome, No pets, Open all year.
Torbay Star Guest House, 73 Avenue Road, Torquay, Devon TQ2 5LL
Tel: 01803 293998   **Map Ref 85**

....

WILSBROOK GUEST HOUSE, an attractive Victorian house, a level walk to seafront, Torre Abbey Gardens and Riviera Centre. En-suite non smoking bedrooms with tea making and TV. Guest lounge and car park.

B&B from £13, Dinner available, Rooms 1 single, 3 double, 1 family, most en-suite, No smoking, Children welcome, No pets, Open all year.
Wilsbrook Guest House, 77 Avenue Road, Torquay, Devon TQ2 5LL
Tel: 01803 298413   **Map Ref 85**

....

CRANMORE GUEST HOUSE, a friendly, family run, small hotel offering home cooking. No restrictions, close to all amenities. Level walk to seafront.

B&B from £14, Dinner available, Rooms 2 twin, 4 double, 2 family, all en-suite, Children welcome, No pets, Open all year.
Cranmore Guest House, 89 Avenue Road, Torquay, Devon TQ2 5LH
Tel: 01803 298488   **Map Ref 85**

....

PALACE HOTEL, a gracious former Bishop's Palace situated in 25 acres of beautiful gardens and woodland. Extensive and unrivalled leisure facilities.

B&B from £65, Dinner available, Rooms 45 single, 36 twin, 40 double, 6 triple, 14 family, all en-suite, Children welcome, No pets, Open all year.
Palace Hotel, Babbacombe Road, Torquay, Devon TQ1 3TG
Tel: 01803 200200 Fax: 01803 299899   **Map Ref 85**

....

BUTE COURT HOTEL, a family run hotel overlooking Torbay and adjoining English Riviera Centre, Large lounges and bar. 5 course choice menu.

B&B from £20, Dinner available, Rooms 10 single, 11 twin, 14 double, 8 triple, 2 family, most en-suite, Children welcome, Open all year.
Bute Court Hotel, Belgrave Road, Torquay, Devon TQ2 5HQ
Tel: 01803 213055 Fax: 01803 213429   **Map Ref 85**

GROSVENOR HOUSE HOTEL, a comfortable, licensed hotel in quiet, central area, run by Christian family. Sea 400 metres. Excellent home cooked food with choice of menu.

B&B from £18, Dinner available, Rooms 1 single, 1 twin, 5 double, 2 triple, 1 family, all en-suite, Children welcome, No pets, Open all year.
Grosvenor House Hotel, Falkland Road, Torquay, Devon TQ2 5JP
Tel: 01803 294110   **Map Ref 85**

PALM COURT HOTEL, on seafront opposite sandy beach, sunny level position - short walk to harbour and shops. Four bars, restaurant and self catering units available.

B&B from £21, Dinner available, Rooms 7 single, 14 double, 8 twin, 6 triple, 1 family, all en-suite,No smoking, Children welcome, Open March - December.
Palm Court Hotel, Sea Front, Torquay, Devon TQ2 5HD
Tel: 01803 294881 & 0468 738070 Fax: 01803 211199   **Map Ref 85**

ELLINGTON COURT HOTEL, affordable elegance in an informal, non smoking, atmosphere. Situated in South facing gardens within a few minutes walk to beach and town centre. All rooms en-suite, TV and hair dryers, some sea views Sauna Solarium, Snooker and Gym for residents use.
Email: raysan@compuserve.com
B&B from £15pp, Dinner from £8, Rooms 2 single, 3 twin, 7 double, 4 family, Open all year.
Ray & Rita Peters **Ellington Court Hotel,** St Lukes Road South, Torquay, Devon TQ2 5NZ
Tel: 01803 294957 Fax: 01803 201383   **Map Ref 85**

HOTEL REGINA, a pleasant hotel adjacent to Torquay harbour, in level position and within walking distance of many of the resort's amenities.

B&B from £23, Dinner available, Rooms 9 single, 21 double, 34 twin, 5 triple, all en-suite, Children welcome, No pets, Open March - November & Christmas.

Hotel Regina, Victoria Parade, Torquay, Devon TQ1 2BE
Tel: 01803 292904 Fax: 01803 290270   **Map Ref 85**

NORCLIFFE HOTEL, a traditional family hotel in a seafront corner position, close to beaches, shops and golf course. Swimming pool,sauna and keep fit facilities.

B&B from £20, Dinner available, Rooms 4 single, 6 twin, 7 double, 4 triple, all en-suite,No smoking, Children welcome, Open all year.
Norcliffe Hotel, Sea Front, Babbacombe Downs, Torquay, Devon TQ1 3LF
Tel: 01803 328456   **Map Ref 86**

COOMBE COURT HOTEL, situated in picturesque Babbacombe 50 yards from Babbacombe Downs which command spectacular views. Close to Model Village, shops etc. All rooms en-suite, TV, radio and tea/coffee facilities. Licensed. Large sun lounge. Large car park. Traditional family run hotel. Balcony rooms available.
B&B from £20pp, Dinner from £10, Rooms 1 single, 4 twin/family, 10 double, all en-suite, No smoking, Children welcome, No pets, Open all year.
Phil & Jackie Lyons, **Coombe Court Hotel,** 67 Babbacombe Downs Road, Babbacombe, Torquay, Devon TQ1 3LP
Tel: 01803 327097 Fax: 01803 327097   **Map Ref 86**

FAIRMOUNT HOUSE HOTEL, an award winning hotel, peacefully situated in lovely gardens near Cockington village. Excellent home cooking, comfortable, spotless accommodation and great hospitality.

B&B from £28, Dinner available, Rooms 2 single, 4 double, 2 triple, all en-suite, Children welcome, Open March - October.
Fairmount House Hotel, Herbert Road, Chelston, Torquay, Devon TQ2 6RW
Tel: 01803 605446 Fax: 01803 605446 **Map Ref 85**

....

MILLBROOK HOUSE HOTEL, a small, elegant hotel noted for comfort and food. Level walk to seafront and Abbey Gardens. Cellar bar, games room and satellite TV.

B&B from £18, Dinner available, Rooms 3 twin, 6 double, 2 family, all en-suite, No smoking, Children welcome, No pets, Open all year.

Millbrook House Hotel, Old Mill Road, Chelston, Torquay, Devon TQ9 6AP
Tel: 01803 297394 Fax: 01803 297394 **Map Ref 85**

....

ELMDENE HOTEL, a rural setting close to seafront and amenities. Warm, friendly and welcoming. Licensed,open all year. Car park.

B&B from £17, Dinner available, Rooms 2 single, 5 double, 2 triple, 2 family, most en-suite, Children welcome, Open all year.
Elmdene Hotel, Rathmore Road, Chelston, Torquay, Devon TQ2 6NZ
Tel: 01803 294940 Fax: 01803 294940 **Map Ref 85**

....

BARN HAYES COUNTRY HOTEL, a warm, friendly and comfortable country house hotel in an area of outstanding natural beauty overlooking countryside and sea. Relaxation is guaranteed in these lovely surroundings by personal service, good food and fine wines.

B&B from £25, Dinner available, Rooms 2 single, 2 twin, 4 double, 2 triple, 2 family, all en-suite, No smoking, Children welcome, Open February - December.

Barn Hayes Country Hotel, Brim Hill, Maidencombe Torquay, Devon TQ1 4TR
Tel: 01803 327980 Fax: 01803 327980 **Map Ref 87**

....

THE OLD FORGE AT TOTNES, is a delightfully converted 600 year old historic stone building with cobbled drive, coach arch and walled garden. Cosy cottage style bedrooms - luxuriously appointed. Golf breaks (15 courses). Leisure (Conservatory) lounge, whirlpool spa. Ground floor rooms, suitable for families/disabled. Licensed. Extensive breakfast menu including vegetarian. Working forge. As featured on BBC TV's holiday programme.
B&B from £26pp, Rooms 1 single, 2 twin, 3 double, 4 family, all en-suite, No smoking, Children welcome, Dogs in cars only, Open all year.
Jeannie Allnutt, **The Old Forge at Totnes,** Seymour Place, Totnes TQ9 5AY
Tel: 01803 862174 Fax: 01803 865385 **Map Ref 89**

....

ROYAL SEVEN STARS, charming town centre 1660 Coaching Inn near River Dart. Torbay and Dartmoor 6-8 miles drive. Ideal touring location. Fully licensed. Restaurant. Bar meals. All rooms colour TV, radio, beverage tray. and central heating. Individually decorated to a good standard. Colour brochures available. Weekly terms from £245 half board.

B&B from £27-£31, Dinner from £14, Rooms 1 single, 2 twin, 8 double, 3 family, most en-suite, Restricted smoking, Children & Pets welcome, Open all year.
Mr K Stone, **Royal Seven Stars,** The Plains, Totnes, Devon TQ9 5DD
Tel: 01803 862125 Fax: 01803 867925 **Map Ref 89**

THE MALTSTERS' ARMS, is an old stone pub on Bow Creek.Several cosy rooms, one with a log fire, and the restaurant overlooks the quayside, the creek and the woods beyond, as do the 3 main bedrooms. 3-4 hours drive from South West London. Glorious walks all around and many lovely places within a short drive.
B&B from £27.50pp, Dinner from £15, rooms 4 double, all en-suite, Children & Pets welcome, Open all year.
Quentin & Denise Thwaites, **The Maltsters' Arms,** Bow Creek, Tuckenhay, Totnes, Devon TQ9 7EQ
Tel: 01803 732350 Fax: 01803 732823 **Map Ref 90**

BEAFORD HOUSE HOTEL, a beautiful country hotel overlooking the River Torridge and 5 miles south east of Torrington, near Tarka Trail. Excellent cuisine, friendly atmosphere. Ideal for a peaceful break. Heated pool, tennis, golf and riding. Near Rosemoor Gardens.
B&B from £29, Dinner available, Rooms 1 single, 1 twin, 1 double, 2 triple, 4 family, most en-suite, Children welcome, Open January, March - December.
Beaford House Hotel, Beaford, Winkford, Devon EX19 8AB
Tel: 01805 603305 & 603330 **Map Ref 91**

Carlos and Teresa welcome you to the **HOLMESDALE HOTEL & ST GEMA RESTAURANT**, where comfort and superb cuisine are the chefs order of the day. English and continental delicacies served daily. Honeymoon suite. Licensed bar with friendly atmosphere. Overlooking the sea, short walk to the beach.
B&B from £20pp, Dinner from £10, Rooms 2 single, 2 twin, 3 double, 8 family, all en-suite, Restricted smoking, Children & pets welcome, Open March - December.
Carlos & Teresa Oyarzabal, **Holmesdale Hotel & St Gema Restaurant,** Bay View Road, Woolacombe, Devon
Tel: 01271 870335 Fax: 01271 870088 **Map Ref 92**

NARRACOTT GRAND HOTEL, a superbly situated seafront hotel with extensive leisure facilities, ideal for family holidays, breaks and large parties.
B&B from £16, Dinner available, Rooms 11 single, 24 double, 6 twin, 41 triple, 18 family, most en-suite, Children welcome, No pets, Open February - December.
Narracott Grand Hotel, Beach Road, Woolacombe, Devon EX34 7BS
Tel: 01271 870418 Fax: 01271 870600 **Map Ref 92**

SANDUNES, offers clean comfortable, centrally heated accommodation. All rooms with en-suite, tea/coffee trays and television. Although not licensed for alcohol we are happy to chill and serve your own when having dinner. Ample car parking facilities are available. Ideal base for relaxing/touring.

B&B from £18pp, Dinner £10, Rooms 1 single, 1 twin, 5 double, all en-suite, No smoking, children or pets, Open March - October.
Jean & Charles Boorman, **Sandunes,** Beach Rd, Woolacombe EX34 7BT
Tel: 01271 870661 **Map Ref 92**

Our small family run licensed hotel for non-smokers offers a friendly and informal atmosphere, enabling you to enjoy the tranquillity and magnificent views over coast and countryside. Varied cuisine, inexpensive bar and wine prices and home-from-home comforts, **SUNNYSIDE HOTEL** makes the perfect base for your break.
B&B from £22.50pp, Dinner from £7.50, Rooms 1 twin, 2 double, 2 family, all en-suite, No smoking or pets, Children welcome, Open March - October.
Jan & Clive Webber, **Sunnyside Hotel,** Sunnyside Road, Woolacombe, North Devon EX34 7DG
Tel: 01271 870267 **Map Ref 92**

CROSSWAYS HOTEL, a friendly, family run hotel in quiet seafront position overlooking Combesgate beach and Lundy.

B&B from £20, Dinner available, Rooms 1 single, 2 twin, 3 double, 3 family, most en-suite, No smoking, Children & pets welcome, Open March - October.
Crossways Hotel, The Esplanade, Woolacombe, Devon EX34 7DJ
Tel: 01271 870395 Fax: 01271 870395   **Map Ref 92**

....

PEBBLES HOTEL & RESTAURANT, a family run hotel with restaurant standard cuisine. Adjoining National Trust land, with spectacular views of sea and coast and direct access to beach. Short breaks available.

B&B from £23, Dinner available, Rooms 1 single, 1 twin, 6 double, 3 family, all with private or en-suite, Children welcome, Open February - December.
Pebbles Hotel & Restaurant, Combesgate Beach, Mortoehoe, Woolacombe, Devon EX34 7EA
Tel: 01271 870426   **Map Ref 93**

....

THE OLD ORCHARD, a quietly elegant house on the edge of the Dartmoor National Park. 6 miles from Princetown. Providing a warm, friendly home from home. Guest lounge with colour TV. Tea/coffee facilities in bedrooms. Parking. Cot available.

B&B from £19.50pp, Rooms 1 twin, 1 en-suite double, Restricted smoking, Children & pets welcome, Open all year except Christmas & New Year.
Barbara Greig, **The Old Orchard,** Harrowbeer Lane, Yelverton, Devon PL20 6DZ
Tel: 01822 854310 Fax: 01822 854310   **Map Ref 94**

....

OVERCOMBE HOTEL, situated in west Dartmoor, between Plymouth and Tavistock. Ideal for walking and touring. Friendly, comfortable hotel offering personal service.

B&B from £23, Dinner available, Rooms 1 single, 3 twin, 5 double, 2 triple, all en-suite, Children welcome, Open all year.
Overcombe Hotel, Horrabridge, Yelverton, Devon PL20 7RA
Tel: 01822 853501 & 853602 Fax: 01822 853501   **Map Ref 95**

....

BLOWISCOMBE BARTON, a modernised farmhouse surrounded by rolling farmland. Beautiful garden and heated swimming pool. Close to village pub and Dartmoor National Park. Plymouth and Tavistock 8 miles.

B&B from £22, Dinner available, Rooms 1 twin, 2 double, all en-suite,Children welcome, No pets, Open all year.
Blowiscombe Barton, Milton Combe, Yelverton, Devon PL20 6HR
Tel: 01822 854853 Fax: 01822 854853   **Map Ref 96**

....

PRINCE HALL HOTEL, a small, friendly country house hotel set in the heart of Dartmoor. Owner/chef. Good wine list. Ideal for walking, riding and fishing.

B&B from £52.50, Dinner available, Rooms 1 single, 3 twin, 3 double, 1 triple, all en-suite, No smoking, Children over 8, Open February - December.
Prince Hall Hotel, Two Bridges, Yelverton, Devon PL20 6SA
Tel: 01822 890403 Fax: 01822 890676   **Map Ref 94**

....

TWO BRIDGES HOTEL, an 18th century riverside inn, old world atmosphere, log fires, good food, wine and own real ales. Ideal for walking, riding, fishing and golf. Heart of Dartmoor. Addictive.

B&B from £38, Dinner available, Rooms 1 single, 16 double, 6 twin, 2 triple, all en-suite, No smoking, Children welcome, Open all year.
Two Bridges Hotel, Two Bridges, Yelverton, Devon PL20 6SW
Tel: 01822 890581 Fax: 01822 890575   **Map Ref 94**

So beautiful is the county of Dorset that it has been almost entirely designated as an area of Outstanding Natural Beauty. It has a wealth of rolling chalk hills and fertile green valleys. Its villages of thatch and golden sandstone contrast with the large lively resorts.

In the heart of mid Dorset is Dorchester, a bustling county town and shopping centre. The lines of its main road were laid by the Romans and there is plenty of other evidence of Roman life in the town.

At Milton Abbas thatched cottages line the street of this 18th century model village while Wool, a mellow village on the River Frome, has one of the most beautiful 17th century bridges in the county. Along the coast are unspoilt chalk cliffs and the notable beauty spot of Lulworth Cove. Here the cliffs suddenly end and Portland and Purbeck stone almost encircle a lake of water. The climb and walk westwards leads to Man O'War Bay and the huge limestone arch, Durdle Door, jutting out into the sea.

Rolling chalk hills stretch to the sea in west Dorset. from south of Sherborne to Lyme Regis. Sherborne is an ideal place from which to explore the area. Close by are the remains of ancient tracks and earthworks cut from the chalk, including the Cerne Abbas Giant, cut out of the turf about 1,500 years ago. Sherborne abounds in old inns and 16th and 17th century houses built in the same golden stone as the town's imposing abbey which has one of the most graceful fan-vaulted roofs in England. Sherborne Old Castle, where Sir Walter Raleigh lived for 5 years, is now a ruin while Sherborne New Castle is rich in art treasures.

Lyme Regis, once a medieval port, became a seaside resort in the 18th century, earning its royal title when Edward I used its harbour during the war against the French. The resort was a favourite of the novelist Jane Austen, who set part of Persuasion in the town. Lyme Regis and neighbouring Charmouth are a paradise for fossil collectors.

The undulating country of North East Dorset reflects rural tranquillity. Shaftesbury, built on the edge of a seven hundred foot plateau, has fine views over the Blackmoor Vale and figures under its old name, Shaston, in Hardy's novels. Grey-green sandstone houses line the steep, cobbled gold Hill. There are numerous other little farming villages.

Poole, Dorset's largest town has a harbour with an 18th century atmosphere. Swanage is a busy holiday resort. Once a Saxon port, it is referred to in the Domesday Book as Swanic.

left, Thomas Hardy's Cottage

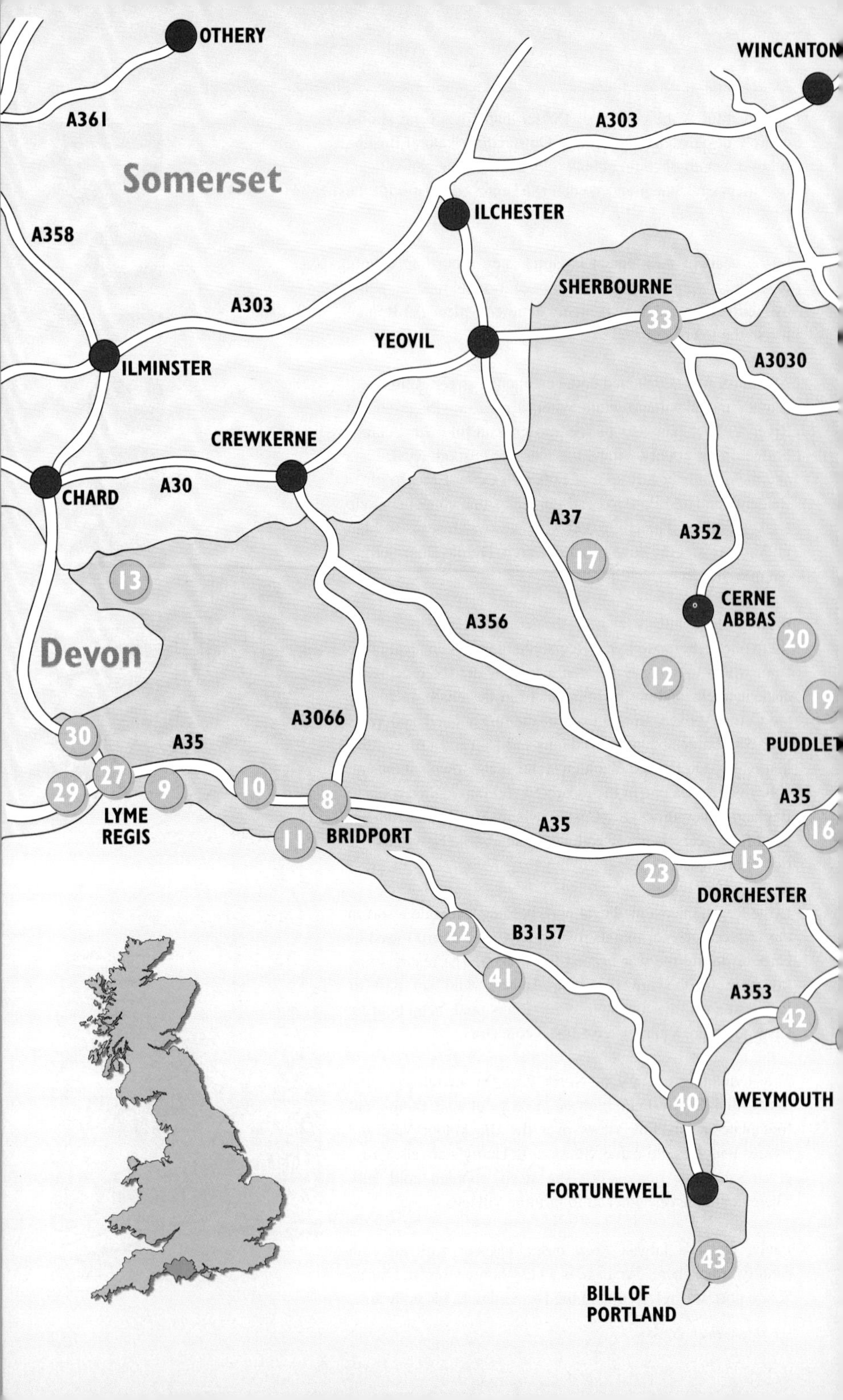

OTHERY

WINCANTON

A361

A303

Somerset

A358

A303

ILCHESTER

SHERBOURNE

33

YEOVIL

A3030

ILMINSTER

CREWKERNE

A37

A352

CHARD

A30

17

CERNE
ABBAS

13

A356

20

Devon

12

19

A3066

PUDDLET

30

A35

27

9

10

8

A35

16

29

LYME
REGIS

11

BRIDPORT

15

23

DORCHESTER

22

B3157

41

A353

42

40

WEYMOUTH

FORTUNEWELL

43

BILL OF
PORTLAND

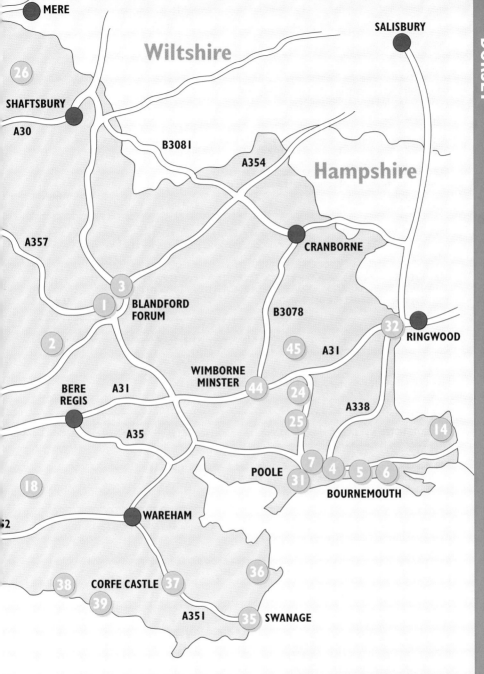

CROWN HOTEL, an original Georgian coaching hotel built in 1756, overlooking water meadows on the southern edge of town.

B&B from £50, Dinner available, Rooms 12 single, 7 double, 11 twin, 2 family rooms, all en-suite, open all year.
Crown Hotel, 1 West Street, Blandford Forum, Dorset DT1 7AJ
Tel: 01258 456626 Fax: 01258 451084   **Map Ref 1**

....

DUNBURY HEIGHTS, always a friendly welcome at this brick and flint cottage. Outstanding views to Poole and Isle of Wight. 6 miles from Blandford Forum. Rural countryside, ideal for walking and touring.

B&B from £17.50, Rooms 1 double, 1 twin, 1 en-suite, Open all year.
Dunbury Heights, Milton Abbas, Blandford Forum, Dorset DT11 0DH
Tel: 01258 880445   **Map Ref 2**

....

ANVIL HOTEL & RESTAURANT, a picturesque 16th century thatched, fully licensed hotel. Separate beamed a la carte restaurant with log fire. Mouth-watering menu with delicious desserts. Comprehensive tasty bar meals. Clay pigeon tuition.

B&B from £45, Dinner & lunch available, Rooms 1 single, 7 double, 2 twin, 1 triple, all en-suite, Open all year.
Anvil Hotel & Restaurant, Salisbury Road, Pimperne, Blandford Forum, Dorset DT11 8UQ
Tel: 01258 453431 & 480182 Fax: 01258 480182   **Map Ref 3**

....

DENE COURT HOTEL, a family run hotel 5 minutes from sandy beach. Good home cooking served in relaxed surroundings. Come as a guest, leave as a friend.

B&B from £12.50, Dinner available, Rooms 1 single, 6 double, 5 twin, 8 triple, most en-suite, Open all year.
Dene Court Hotel, 19 Boscombe Spa Road, Bournemouth, Dorset BH5 1AR
Tel: 01202 394874   **Map Ref 4**

....

WYCHCOTE HOTEL, a small, well-appointed Victorian house hotel standing in its own tree-lined grounds. Quiet but near all facilities. Home Cooking.

B&B from £20, Dinner available, Rooms 2 single, 5 double, 3 twin, 1 triple, most en-suite, Open February - November.
Wychcote Hotel, 2 Somerville Road, Bournemouth, Dorset BH2 5LH
Tel: 01202 557898   **Map Ref 4**

....

WESTLEIGH HOTEL, central location close to shops and beaches. All rooms with colour TV, tea/coffee facilities, hair dryer. Sauna, spa bath, solarium, indoor pool, lift, car park.

B&B from £40, Dinner available, Rooms 3 single, 13 double, 9 twin, 1 triple, 4 family, most en-suite, Open all year.
Westleigh Hotel, 26 West Hill Road, Bournemouth, Dorset BH2 5PG
Tel: 01202 296989 Fax: 01202 296989   **Map Ref 4**

....

GERVIS COURT HOTEL, a Victorian detached house. Centrally located for all of Bournemouth's wonderful facilities. Few minutes walk to beach, shops, conference centre, clubs and theatres. Ample parking. All rooms en-suite and have TV and kettles. Excellent location for visiting Bournemouth, New Forest and Purbecks. http://www.gerviscourthotel.co.uk
B&B from £18-£25, Rooms 1 single, 3 twin, 7 double, 2 family, all en-suite, No smoking or pets, Children welcome, Open all year.
Alan & Jackie Edwards, **Gervis Court Hotel,** 38 Gervis Road, Bournemouth, Dorset BH1 3DH
Tel: 01202 556871 Fax: 01202 556871   **Map Ref 4**

CARISBROOKE HOTEL, a modernised traditional family-owned hotel in excellent location close to the sea and International Centre. High standards of home cooking. Special diets. Ground floor rooms. Golf holidays arranged.

B&B from £19, Dinner available, Rooms 3 single, 6 double, 6 twin, 7 triple, most en-suite, Open all year.
Carisbrooke Hotel, 42 Tregonwell Road, Bournemouth, Dorset BH2 5NT
Tel: 01202 290432 Fax: 01202 310499 **Map Ref 4**

....

MAYFIELD PRIVATE HOTEL, overlooking public gardens with tennis, bowling greens, crazy-golf. Central for sea, shops and main rail/coach stations. Some rooms have shower or toilet/shower. Licensed.

B&B from £15, Dinner available, Rooms 1 single, 4 double, 2 twin, 1 family, some en-suite, Open all year.
Mayfield Private Hotel, 46 Frances Road, Bournemouth, Dorset BH1 3SA
Tel: 01202 551839 **Map Ref 4**

....

EAST CLIFF COTTAGE HOTEL, a high standard old world hotel in central position. Some sea views. Large family rooms, good food, garden, car park. Long or short stays.

B&B from £19.50, Dinner available, Rooms 1 single, 3 double, 1 twin, 5 triple, some en-suite, Open all year.
East Cliff Cottage Hotel, 57 Grove Road, Bournemouth, Dorset BH1 3AT
Tel: 01202 552788 Fax: 01202 556400 **Map Ref 4**

....

SYDNEY HOUSE HOTEL, 150 yards from sea front on West Cliff and a few minutes from entertainments and shops. Tea room serving cream teas. Parking. Special interest Dorset holidays available.

B&B from £15, Rooms 2 single, 7 double, 2 twin, 2 triple, 2 family, most en-suite, Open all year.
Sydney House Hotel, 6 Westcliff Road, Bournemouth, Dorset BH2 5EY
Tel: 01202 555536 **Map Ref 4**

....

SEACREST LODGE HOTEL, is situated at the head of beautiful Alum Chine, leading on to miles of golden sands. Close to restaurants, shops and Bournemouth's entertainment. Short drive into New Forest and Poole harbour. Colour TV and tea/coffee in all rooms. Superb breakfast, large garden and ample parking.
B&B from £17.50pp, Rooms 1 twin, 4 double, 2 family, Restricted smoking, Children welcome, Pets by arrangement, Open all year except Christmas & New Year.
Jane & Bob Clarke, **Seacrest Lodge Hotel,** 63 Alum Chine Road Bournemouth, Dorset BH4 8DU
Tel: 01202 767438 **Map Ref 4**

....

BELVEDERE HOTEL, centrally located with a large car park. Superb food and friendly service. Ideal for both business and holidays, offering high standards all round. Group rates available on request.

B&B from £35, Dinner available, Rooms 11 single, 25 double, 13 twin, 11 triple, 1 family, all en-suite, Open all year.
Belvedere Hotel, Bath Road, Bournemouth, Dorset BH1 2EU
Tel: 01202 297556 Fax: 01202 294699 Email: 101452.2567 @ compuserve.com **Map Ref 4**

....

CUMBERLAND HOTEL, a family hotel on East Cliff overlooking the bay and offering a high standard of service and cuisine for all ages. Complimentary use of nearby indoor leisure facility.

B&B from £39.50, Dinner available, Rooms 12 single, 34 double, 44 twin, 12 triple, suites available, all en-suite. Open all year.

Cumberland Hotel, East Overcliff Drive, Bournemouth, Dorset BH1 3AF
Tel: 01202 290722 Fax: 01202 311394 **Map Ref 4**

187

SUNCLIFF HOTEL, a cliff top location overlooking bay. Short walk to sandy beach and town centre. Extensive indoor leisure facilities including pool and evening entertainment.

B&B from £25, Rooms 12 single, 29 double, 24 twin, 18 triple, 11 family rooms, all en-suite, Open all year.

Suncliff Hotel, East Overcliff Drive, Bournemouth, Dorset BH1 3AG
Tel: 01202 291711 Fax: 01202 293788   **Map Ref 4**

....

CLIFFESIDE HOTEL, on East Cliff with views to the Isle of Wight and the Purbeck Hills. Within easy reach of the town centre.

B&B from £35, Dinner available, Rooms 7 single, 27 double, 23 twin, 1 triple, 3 family, all en-suite, Open all year.
Cliffeside Hotel, East Overcliff Drive, Bournemouth, Dorset BH1 3AQ
Tel: 01202 555724 Fax: 01202 314534   **Map Ref 4**

....

ARLINGTON HOTEL, a family run hotel overlooking Bournemouth pine gardens. 100 metres traffic-free, level walk to square, beach, shops and Bournemouth International Centre.

B&B from £28, Dinner available, Rooms 4 single, 11 double, 9 twin, 4 triple, most en-suite, Open all year.

Arlington Hotel, Exeter Park Road, Lower Gardens, Bournemouth, Dorset BH2 5BD
Tel: 01202 552879 & 553012 Fax: 01202 298317   **Map Ref 4**

....

QUEEN'S HOTEL, a modern, family run hotel near the beach, ideal for family holidays and with leisure facilities for business conventions. Leisure club.

B&B from £39.50, Dinner available, Rooms 12 single, 43 double, 46 twin, 8 triple, all en-suite, Open all year.
Queen's Hotel, Meyrick Road, Bournemouth, Dorset BH1 3DL
Tel: 01202 554415 Fax: 01202 294810   **Map Ref 4**

....

FIRCROFT HOTEL, a long-established family hotel, close to sea and comprehensive shopping. Free entry to hotel-owned sports and leisure club (indoor pool,gym, sauna, squash) 9am-6pm. Licensed, entertainment in season. Large car park.

B&B from £18, Dinner available, Rooms 6 single, 16 double, 12 twin, 16 triple, all en-suite, Open all year.

Fircroft Hotel, Owls Road, Bournemouth, Dorset BH5 1AE
Tel: 01202 309771 Fax: 01202 395644   **Map Ref 4**

....

TROUVILLE HOTEL, centrally located close to all amenities, the Trouville boasts a leisure centre and has a fine reputation for friendly service and superb food.

B&B from £45, Dinner available, Rooms 9 single, 28 double, 29 twin, 13 triple, all en-suite, Open all year.

Trouville Hotel, Priory Road, Bournemouth, Dorset BH2 5DH
Tel: 01202 552262 Fax: 01202 293324   **Map Ref 4**

....

WINTERBOURNE HOTEL, enjoying a prime position with magnificent sea views, the hotel is within 400 metres of shops, theatres, pier and beaches. Free golf tickets.

B&B from £25, Dinner available, Rooms 6 single, 13 double, 10 twin, 8 triple, 4 family, all en-suite, Open all year.

Winterbourne Hotel, Priory Road, Bournemouth, Dorset BH2 5DJ
Tel: 01202 296366 Fax: 01202 780073   **Map Ref 4**

MARSHAM COURT HOTEL, overlooking bay in quiet central situation with sun terraces, outdoor swimming pool. Edwardian bar and summer entertainment. Free accommodation for children. Snooker. Parking.http://www.marshamcourt.co.uk

B&B from £37-46, Dinner available, Rooms 8 single, 23 double, 44 twin, 11 triple, suites available, all en-suite, Open all year.
Marsham Court Hotel, Russell-Cotes Road, Bournemouth, Dorset BH1 3AB
Tel: 01202 552111 Fax: 01202 294744 Email: reservations@marshamcourt.co.uk **Map Ref 4**

ROSEDENE COTTAGE HOTEL, a town centre location. Old world cottage hotel, quiet. A short stroll to pier, shops, gardens, Bournemouth International Centre, theatres and beaches. 20 minutes from airport.

B&B from £18, Rooms 3 single, 5 double, 1 twin, 1 triple, some en-suite, Open all year.
Rosedene Cottage Hotel, St. Peter's Road, Bournemouth, Dorset BH1 2LA
Tel: 01202 554102 Fax: 01202 246995 **Map Ref 4**

SHADY NOOK GUEST HOUSE, is a centrally located, charming Victorian residence close to shops, gardens, beaches, entertainment and conference centre. Tea/coffee facilities. Sky TV and full central heating. Special diets. Parking by arrangement. Bright, comfortable room, most en-suite. Cheerful atmosphere. Special rates for children.
B&B from £15pp, Dinner from £6.50, Rooms 2 twin, 3 double, 2 family, most en-suite, Children & pets welcome, Open all year except Christmas & New Year.
Paul & Avril Holdaway, **Shady Nook Guest House,** Upper Terrace Road, Bournemouth, Dorset BH2 5NW
Tel: 01202 551557 **Map Ref 4**

HOTEL RIVIERA, on the West Cliff of Bournemouth overlooking the sea, with an award-winning garden which has direct access to the cliff top.

B&B from £24, Dinner available, Rooms 8 single, 14 double, 8 twin, 4 triple, all en-suite, Open April - October & Christmas.
Hotel Riviera, Westcliff Gardens, Bournemouth, Dorset BH2 5HL
Tel: 01202 552845 **Map Ref 4**

ULLSWATER HOTEL, on the West Cliff, a few minutes from the town centre and shops, 150 yards from the cliff top and path to beach.

B&B from £25, Dinner available, Rooms 9 single, 13 double, 13 twin, 7 triple, all en-suite, Open all year.
Ullswater Hotel, Westcliff Gardens, Bournemouth, Dorset BH2 5HW
Tel: 01202 555181 Fax: 01202 317896 **Map Ref 4**

NEW DURLEY DEAN HOTEL, this elegant Victorian hotel, situated on the West Cliff in close proximity to both beaches and town, offers the latest in modern amenities, whilst maintaining the charm of a bygone era.

B&B from £49.50, Dinner available, Rooms 25 single, 32 double, 25 twin, 28 triple, 3 family, all en-suite, Open all year.
New Durley Dean Hotel, Westcliff Road, Bournemouth, Dorset BH2 5HE
Tel: 01202 557711 Fax: 01202 292815 **Map Ref 4**

WEST DENE HOTEL, quiet, select cliff top position overlooking Bournemouth Bay, 150 yards from sandy beach and woodland glade of Alum Chine.

B&B from £24.50, Dinner available, Rooms 1 single, 7 double, 4 twin, 3 triple, 2 family, some en-suite, Open March - October.
West Dene Hotel, 117 Alumhurst Road, Alum Chine, Bournemouth, Dorset BH4 8HS
Tel: 01202 764843 **Map Ref 4**

RIVIERA HOTEL, a family hotel in Alum Chine. Views of the Isle of Wight. Short walk to sandy beach. Extensive leisure facilities including indoor/outdoor pools.

B&B from £45, Dinner available, Rooms 6 single, 22 double, 20 twin, 17 triple, 12 family, all en-suite, Open February - December.

Riviera Hotel, 12-16 Burnaby Road, Alum Chine, Bournemouth, Dorset BH4 8JF
Tel: 01202 763653 Fax: 01202 768422   **Map Ref 4**

....

HIGHCLERE HOTEL, this pretty "Victorian" hotel is close to the sea. Rooms are well furnished with en-suites, colour TV, tea/coffee facilities, direct dial telephone, and clock radio alarm. A home cooked meal is available in the spacious dining room. AA. RAC and ETB Awards.
B&B from £19-£23.69pp, Dinner from £6.50, Rooms 1 twin, 4 double, 4 family, all en-suite, Restricted smoking, Children over 3, Pets by arrangement, Open April - October.
David & Averil Baldwin, **Highclere Hotel,** 15 Burnaby Road, Alum Chine, Bournemouth, Dorset BH4 8JF
Tel: 01202 761350 Fax: 01202 767110   **Map Ref 4**

....

MOUNT LODGE HOTEL, close to Bournemouth, Poole, New Forest. Few minutes walk through the Chine to sandy blue flag beaches. Comfortable en-suite rooms with TV, tea/coffee facilities. Residents bar, parking and own keys. Close to golfing, bowling, windsurfing, shops, restaurants. Good home cooked food.
B&B from £15-£21pp, Dinner from £6.50, Rooms 2 single, 2 twin, 6 double, 1 family, most en-suite, Children over 2, No pets, Open all year except Christmas & New Year.
Allan & Gill Gillham, **Mount Lodge Hotel,** 19 Beaulieu Road, Alum Chine, Bournemouth, Dorset BH4 8HY
Tel: 01202 761173   **Map Ref 7**

....

LANGDALE HOTEL, quietly located in pine-clad Alum Chine, close to sea front. All rooms en-suite (bath or shower) with TV and radio alarm. Trouble free parking.

B&B from £20, Dinner available, Rooms 2 single, 5 double, 2 twin, 1 triple, all en-suite, Open all year.

Langdale Hotel, 6 Earle Road, Alum Chine, Bournemouth, Dorset BH4 8JQ
Tel: 01202 761174 Fax: 01202 761174   **Map Ref 4**

....

THE GOLDEN SOVEREIGNS HOTEL, an attractive decorated Victorian hotel. Quiet, convenient location, beach 4 minutes walk. Comfortable rooms, traditional home-cooking. Early booking special discounts.

B&B from £15.50, Dinner available, Rooms 2 single, 2 double, 1 twin, 2 triple, 2 family, some en-suite, Open all year.

The Golden Sovereigns Hotel, 97 Alumhurst Road, Alum Chine, Bournemouth, Dorset BH4 8HR
Tel: 01202 762088   **Map Ref 4**

....

HOLMCROFT HOTEL, a subtly elegant family run hotel, quietly situated. Enjoy a choice of menu, all fresh vegetables, within a relaxed, friendly atmosphere. No smoking.

B&B from £16, Dinner available, Rooms 2 single, 12 double, 3 twin, 2 triple, most en-suite, Open all year.

Holmcroft Hotel, Earle Road, Alum Chine, Bournemouth, Dorset BH4 8JQ
Tel: 01202 761289 Fax: 01202 761289   **Map Ref 4**

CHASE LODGE, a charming Edwardian family run hotel. Tea/coffee and colour televisions in all rooms. Quiet, comfy residents' lounge with daily paper. Short walk to sandy beach, or shops and restaurant in Westbourne. Car park. Delicious breakfast and mouth-watering picnics in cool bags. Masses of tourist information.
B&B from £16.50pp, Rooms 1 twin, 3 double, 2 family, all en-suite or private, No smoking or pets, Children welcome, Open all year except New Year.
Mr & Mrs W Webb, **Chase Lodge,** Herbert Road, Alum Chine, Bournemouth, Dorset BH4 8HD
Tel: 01202 768515 Fax: 01202 757847 **Map Ref 7**

WRENWOOD HOTEL, a licensed, family hotel, 5 minutes' walk to pier, shopping centre and entertainments. Convenient for tennis, bowling, golf and New Forest area.

B&B from £15.50, Dinner available, Rooms 5 double, 3 triple, 2 family, all en-suite, Open all year.

Wrenwood Hotel, 11 Florence Road, Boscombe, Bournemouth, Dorset BH5 1HH
Tel: 01202 395086 Fax: 01202 396511 **Map Ref 5**

CARLTON HOUSE

CARLTON HOUSE, a warm and friendly atmosphere. All rooms colour TV, tea/coffee facilities, shower/toilet bathroom/toilet. Ample parking. Close to golden sandy beaches, main shops, cafe's, restaurants. Minutes from coach terminals and reliable local transport. Golf courses, lovely walks and gardens, parks, sea angling.
B&B from £14.50-£17pp, Rooms 3 twin, 2 double, 3 family, some en-suite, Restricted smoking, Children welcome, Pets by arrangement, Open all year.
Jay & June Shortland, **Carlton House,** 12 Westby Road, Boscombe, Bournemouth, Dorset BH5 1HD
Tel: 01202 303650 **Map Ref 6**

CROSBIE HALL HOTEL, a delightful character hotel offering comfort, cleanliness, fine food, friendly atmosphere and good value. Near beach, gardens, shops and transport.

B&B from £15, Dinner available, Rooms 3 single, 8 double, 2 twin, 4 triple, some en-suite, Open all year.

Crosbie Hall Hotel, 21 Florence Road, Boscombe, Bournemouth, Dorset BH5 1HJ
Tel: 01202 394714 Fax: 01202 394714 **Map Ref 5**

AUDMORE HOTEL, a friendly, family run licensed hotel only a few minutes from the beach, shops and theatre.

B&B from £15, Dinner available, Rooms 2 single, 3 double, 1 twin, 2 triple, 2 family, some en-suite, Open March to November.
Audmore Hotel, 3 Cecil Road, Boscombe, Bournemouth, Dorset BH5 1DU
Tel: 01202 395166 **Map Ref 5**

SANDELHEATH HOTEL, excellent position, convenient for beach and town centre. Full English breakfast. Tea making facilities, colour TV, most rooms en-suite. Car parking. 5 minutes rail and coach station. Own key access.

B&B from £15.50pp, Rooms 3 single, 4 twin, 7 double, 3 family, most en-suite, Children over 3, No pets, Open all year except Christmas & New Year.
Caroline & Derek Buick, **Sandelheath Hotel,** 1 Knyveton Road, East Cliff, Bournemouth, Dorset BH1 3QF
Tel: 01202 555428 **Map Ref 4**

191

THE COTTAGE HOTEL, a small select, family run, licensed private hotel in peaceful surroundings. Noted for fresh home prepared cooking, cleanliness and tastefully furnished accommodation. Ground floor/en-suite rooms with TV, tea/coffee facilities, radio-alarm clocks and hair dryers. Ample parking. Les Routiers. ETB 3 Crown Highly Commended. **B&B from £18.50pp,** Dinner from £8, Rooms 1 single, 2 twin, 2 double, 2 family, most en-suite, No smoking, Children over 8, Open mid February - mid October. Ronald & Valarie Halliwell, **The Cottage Hotel,** 12 Southern Road, Southbourne, Bournemouth, Dorset BH6 3SR
Tel: 01202 422764   **Map Ref 6**

ACORNS HOTEL, a family run hotel, all rooms en-suite with TV. Good food. Only 5 minutes from the sea.

B&B from £15, Dinner available, Rooms 1 single, 2 double, 1 twin, 2 triple, all en-suite, Open March - October.
Acorns Hotel, 14 Southwood Avenue, Southbourne, Bournemouth, Dorset BH6 3QA
Tel: 01202 422438   **Map Ref 6**

FIELDEN COURT HOTEL, a relaxing, family run hotel. All rooms en-suite, with tea/coffee and TV. 3 minutes' walk to cliff top/lift/shops. Licensed.

B&B from £15 Dinner available, Rooms 1 single, 3 double, 2 twin, 1 triple, 1 family, all en-suite, Open all year.

Fielden Court Hotel, 20 Southern Road, Southbourne, Bournemouth, Dorset BH6 3SR
Tel: 01202 427459 Fax: 01202 427459   **Map Ref 6**

PENNINGTON HOTEL, a small detached hotel, approximately 100 yards from the cliff top. Easy access to Bournemouth, Christchurch and New Forest. All bedrooms have electric fires, colour TVs and tea/coffee making facilities. Dining room with separate tables, lounge with TV. Car parking available. Good food assured.
B&B from £16.50pp, Dinner from £22.50, Rooms 1 single, 1 twin, 3 double, 2 family, most en-suite, Restricted smoking, Children welcome, Open February - November.
Valerie & Ron Anderton, **Pennington Hotel,** 26 Southern Road, Southbourne, Bournemouth, Dorset BH6 3SS
Tel: 01202 428653   **Map Ref 6**

SHERWOOD HOTEL, situated in a quiet position opposite the cliff-top at Southbourne. All rooms have TV, tea/coffee facilities and are en-suite. A guests' lounge with a license. Shops, Theatres, Museums nearby. Friendly, family run hotel with a warm welcome.

B&B from £15pp, Dinner from £6.50, Rooms 1 single, 2 twin, 2 double, 5 family, Children & Pets welcome, Open all year except Christmas & New Year.
Jackie Manning, **Sherwood Hotel,** 44 Pinecliffe Avenue, Southbourne, Bournemouth, Dorset BH6 3PZ
Tel: 01202 427693   **Map Ref 6**

SHORELINE HOTEL, a small, licensed hotel providing comfortable accommodation and home cooking. Close to beach and local shops, in quiet area.

B&B from £14, Dinner available, Rooms 2 single, 6 double, 2 triple, some en-suite, Open all year.

Shoreline Hotel, 7 Pinecliff Avenue, Southbourne, Bournemouth, Dorset BH6 3PY
Tel: 01202 429654   **Map Ref 6**

WINTERDENE HOTEL, is a Victorian villa offering comfortable surroundings for your holiday. All rooms en-suite, colour TV and tea/coffee facilities. Family run. Just 5 minutes walk from the beach and Bournemouth centre. Car park. Excellent home cooking. Residential license.
B&B from £23pp, Dinner from £9, Rooms 3 single, 4 twin, 4 double, 3 family, all en-suite, Children welcome - reduced rates, Small dogs by arrangement, Open all year except February.
Renzo & Heather Dei Cas, **Winterdene Hotel,** 11 Durley Road South, West Cliff, Bournemouth, Dorset BH2 5JH
Tel: 01202 554150 Fax: 01202 555426　　　　　**Map Ref 4**

....

BABBACOMBE COURT HOTEL, a family run hotel, with good home cooking. Close to shops, beach and Bournemouth International Centre. Ample parking.

B&B from £16, Dinner available, Rooms 4 single, 6 double, 2 twin, 2 triple, 1 family room, all en-suite, Open all year.
Babbacombe Court Hotel, 28 Westhill Road, West Cliff, Bournemouth, Dorset BH2 5PG
Tel: 01202 552823 & 551746 Fax: 01202 789030　　　　　**Map Ref 4**

....

SOUTHERNHAY HOTEL, a welcoming hotel, a short walk to beach and Westbourne shops and restaurants. Large car park. Full English breakfast.

B&B from £15, Rooms 1 single, 4 double, 1 twin, 1 triple, most en-suite, Open all year.
Southernhay Hotel, 42 Alum Chine Road, Westbourne, Bournemouth, Dorset BH4 8DX
Tel: 01202 761251 Fax: 01202 761251　　　　　**Map Ref 7**

....

WESTBROOK PRIVATE HOTEL, an immaculate hotel providing fresh, clean, smoke free surroundings. Extra touches include a courtesy car between rail and coach stations. The beach, village shops and restaurants are nearby. Bournemouth centre and New Forest are just minutes away. Sorry no children or pets.
B&B from £18pp, Rooms 1 twin, 4 double, all en-suite, No smoking, children or pets, Open all year.
Kenny & Denise Connolly, **Westbrook Private Hotel,** 64 Alum Chine Road, Westbourne, Bournemouth, Dorset BH4 8DZ
Tel: 01202 761081　　　　　**Map Ref 7**

....

CLEVELAND HOTEL, all rooms with colour TV and tea/coffee facilities. Bright and sunny guests lounge. Resident License. Hot bar food. Car parking. Frequent buses to Bournemouth. Situated between Bournemouth and Poole near head of Alum Chine. Westbourne Village 3 minutes level walk many shops, pubs and restaurants.
B&B from £15pp, Rooms 3 twin, 3 double, 4 family, some en-suite, Restricted smoking, Children over 5, No pets, Open all year.
John & Margaret Jolly, **Cleveland Hotel,** 90 West Cliff Road, Westbourne, Bournemouth, Dorset BH4 8BG
Tel: 01202 760993 Fax: 01202 760733　　　　　**Map Ref 7**

....

BULL HOTEL, 16th century historic town centre Coaching Inn. ETB 3 Crowns. A la Carte restaurant/bar food. Perfect touring centre. Spectacular coastal countryside. Many local attractions and National Trust Properties. Conferences. Receptions. Car park.

B&B from £19.50pp, Dinner from £5, Rooms 7 single, 2 twin, 9 double, 4 family, some en-suite, Children & pets welcome, Open all year.
Mr & Mrs Buzza, **Bull Hotel,** 34 East Street, Bridport, Dorset DT6 3LF
Tel/Fax: 01308 422878　　　　　**Map Ref 8**

DORSET

ROUNDHAM HOUSE HOTEL, an attractive stone built house in an elevated position, within its own one acre gardens, giving superb country and sea views. Noted for its excellent food (using home grown and local produce) and hospitality.

B&B from £33, Dinner available, Rooms 1 single, 2 twin, 3 double, 2 family, all en-suite, No smoking, Children welcome, Open March - December.

Roundham House Hotel, Roundham Gardens, West Bay Road, Bridport, Dorset DT6 4BD
Tel: 01308 422753 Fax: 01308 421500 **Map Ref 8**

....

HENSLEIGH HOTEL, a family-run hotel with a reputation for friendly service, comfort, hospitality and delicious food. All bedrooms are en-suite with central-heating, colour television and hospitality trays. The hotel is situated between the village and the beach and has a large private car park.
B&B from £25pp, Dinner from £14.50, Rooms 2 single, 4 twin, 4 double, 1 family, all en-suite, Restricted smoking, Children welcome, Pets by arrangement, Open March - October.
Mary MacNair, **Hensleigh Hotel,** Lower Sea Lane, Charmouth, Bridport, Dorset DT6 6LW
Tel: 01297 560830 Fax: 01297 560830 **Map Ref 9**

....

WARREN HOUSE, a 17th century listed thatched house in area of designated outstanding natural beauty. Family run business with warm and friendly atmosphere. Tea/coffee facilities, TV and central heating in all rooms. Private car parking. Varied breakfast menu close to beach and south coastal path, ramblers paradise.

B&B from £20pp, Rooms, 1 twin, 2 double, 1 family, all en-suite, No smoking or pets, Children welcome, Open all year except Christmas.
Eric & Denny Tweddle, **Warren House,** Chideock, Bridport DT6 6JW
Tel: 01297 489704 Fax: 01297 489704 **Map Ref 10**

....

CHIDEOCK HOUSE HOTEL, a warm, friendly, family-run 15th century thatched hotel. ETB 3 Crowns Commended. AA 2 Star. AA Rosette. Oak beamed restaurant/bar General Fairfaxs Headquarter. Car park. 7 miles to Lyme Regis. Minutes walk to a sea town, stunning Dorset village. Coastal walks a must. Fossil searching in Charmouth. Golf, swimming, horse riding all nearby.
B&B from £27.50-£35pp, Dinner from £18, Rooms 1 twin, 8 double, all en-suite, Children & pets welcome, Open February - December.
Anna & George Dunn, **Chideock House Hotel,** Main Street, Chideock, Bridport, Dorset DT6 6JN
Tel: 01297 489242 Fax: 01297 489184 **Map Ref 10**

....

At **BRITMEAD HOUSE**, we put 'your comfort first' and offer you hospitality and delicious meals. Twixt Briport, West Bay Harbour, Chesil Beach and Dorset Coastal Path. Our bedrooms have many thoughtful extras you'll appreciate. Spacious lounge and dining room overlooking the garden. Licensed. Parking. ETB 3 Crown Highly Commended.
B&B from £21-£30pp, Dinner £14, Rooms 2 twin (1 of 2 twins on ground floor), 4 double, 1 family, all en-suite, Restricted smoking, Children over 5, Pets by arrangement, Open all year.
Ann & Dan Walker, **Britmead House,** West Bay Road, Bridport DT6 4EG
Tel: 01308 422941 Fax: 01308 42216 **Map Ref 11**

HADDON HOUSE HOTEL, a country house hotel, renowned for cuisine, situated 500 yards from picturesque harbour, coast and golf course. Well situated for touring Dorset, Devon and Somerset.

B&B from £40, Dinner available, Rooms 2 single, 3 twin, 6 double, 2 triple, all en-suite, Children welcome, Open all year.
Haddon House Hotel, West Bay, Bridport, Dorset DT6 4EL
Tel: 01308 423626 & 425323 Fax: 01308 427348   **Map Ref 11**

....

WESTPOINT TAVERN, on the seafront and promenade. All rooms en-suite with TV, tea/coffee facilities and sea or harbour views. Fishing, golf, cliff walks in Thomas Hardy country. Daily half board prices apply to 2 day breaks.

B&B from £23, Dinner available, Rooms 3 twin, 2 double, all en-suite, Children welcome, No pets, Open all year.
Westpoint Tavern, The Esplanade, West Bay, Bridport, Dorset DT6 4HG
Tel: 01308 423636   **Map Ref 11**

....

LAMPERTS COTTAGE, a 16th century thatched listed cottage with stream running in front. Bedrooms are prettily decorated. Breakfast is served in the dining room with inglenook fireplace, bread oven and beams. Central heating and tea/coffee makers. Excellent countryside for walking with footpaths over chalk hills and hidden valleys. Guidebooks and maps available to borrow. Credit cards accepted.
B&B from £19pp, Rooms 1 twin, 1 double, 1 family, Restricted smoking, Children over 8, Pets by arrangement, Open all year.
Nicky Willis, **Lamperts Cottage,** Syding St. Nicholas, Cerne Abbas DT2 9NU
Tel: 01300 341659 Fax: 01300 341699   **Map Ref 12**

....

ROSE COTTAGE, a former Sadborow Estate dwelling, recently enlarged in flintstone and brick with pretty garden. The Synderford valley is near Forde Abbey and Lyme Regis, with excellent walking. The bedrooms are comfortably furnished with fine views and TV, tea/coffee.
B&B from £18pp, Dinner from £8, Rooms 1 twin, 1 double, both en-suite, Restricted smoking, Children over 5, Pets by arrangement, Open all year except Christmas & New Year.
Mr & Mrs Fortescue-Thomas, **Rose Cottage,** Holway, Thorncombe, Chard, Somerset TA20 4PZ
Tel/Fax: 01460 30578   **Map Ref 13**

....

THE WHITE HOUSE HOTEL, a listed Regency house with many original period features including Regency windows and bow doors. Warmly furnished for peace and relaxation.

B&B from £38, Dinner available, Rooms 1 single, 2 twin, 7 double, all with private or en-suite, No smoking, Children welcome, Open February - October & December.
The White House Hotel, 2 Hillside, The Street, Charmouth, Dorset DT6 6PJ
Tel: 01297 560411 Fax: 01297 560702   **Map Ref 9**

....

Welcome to **THE CLOCK HOUSE**, a 16th century thatched freehouse family run pub in the beautiful village of Chideock in Dorset near the coast. The pub offers a good restaurant and weekend entertainment. All accommodation is en-suite and has tea/coffee facilities and colour TV's.

B&B from £17.50pp, Dinner from £4.50, Rooms 1 twin, 1 double, 1 family, all en-suite, Restricted smoking, Children welcome, Pets by prior arrangement, Open all year.
Mr William Black, **The Clock House,** Main Street, Chideock, Dorset DT6 6JW
Tel: 01297 489423   **Map Ref 10**

This delightful **OLD VICARAGE HOTEL** is set in ten acres of gardens comprising woods, lawns, flower beds and the hotel boasts its own cricket pitch. All rooms have coffee facilities and the restaurant has won awards for its cuisine. A relaxing retreat.

B&B from £17pp, Dinner from £10, Rooms 6 twin, all en-suite, Children welcome, No pets, Open all year except Boxing Day & New Years Day.
Linda Harrison, **The Old Vicarage Hotel,** Lyndhurst Road, Hinton, Christchurch, Dorset BH23 7DR
Tel: 01425 277006 Fax: 01425 273599 **Map Ref 14**

THE OLD POST OFFICE, is a stone and slate Georgian cottage use as a post office until 1950. Part of a row of listed buildings. Good rural base. The bedrooms have wash basins, tea making facilities. Near to Dorchester, Maiden Castle, Abbotsbury and Weymouth.

B&B from £16.20pp, Dinner from £10-£12.50, Rooms 2 twin, 1 double, Children & pets welcome, Open all year.

Jane Rootham, **The Old Post Office,** Dorchester, Dorset DT2 9LF
Tel: 01305 889 254 **Map Ref 15**

WESSEX ROYAL HOTEL, a Georgian town centre hotel, recently refurbished to a high standard, with extensive restaurant, bar and function facilities.

B&B from £25, Dinner available, Rooms 3 single, 2 twin, 17 double, 2 triple, most en-suite, Children welcome, Open all year.
Wessex Royal Hotel, 32 High West Street, Dorchester, Dorset DT1 1UP
Tel: 01305 262660 Fax: 01305 251941 **Map Ref 15**

YALBURY COTTAGE HOTEL & RESTAURANT, a 17th century thatched hotel in beautiful countryside 2 miles east of Dorchester, near Hardy's Cottage. Comfortable, oak beamed lounge and excellent restaurant with friendly, attentive service. Well equipped en-suite bedrooms.

B&B from £36, Dinner available, Rooms 6 double, 1 twin, 1 family, all en-suite, Children welcome, Open February - December.
Yalbury Cottage Hotel & Restaurant, Lower Bockhampton, Dorchester, Dorset DT2 8PZ
Tel: 01305 262382 Fax: 01305 266412 **Map Ref 16**

BRAMBLES, a beautifully appointed thatched cottage set in lovely countryside. Offering every comfort. Log fire on winter mornings and evenings. Close to Sherborne, Yeovil, Dorchester, Beaminster. Wide choice of breakfast. Relaxed friendly atmosphere. Colour TV, coffee/tea facilities in rooms. En-suites available. Parking in grounds.

B&B from £20pp, Dinner from £14, Rooms 2 single, 1 twin, 1 double, some en-suite, No smoking or pets, Children welcome, Open all year except Christmas & New Year.
Anita & Andre Millorit, **Brambles,** Woolcombe, Melbury Bubb, Dorchester, Dorset DT2 0NJ
Tel: 01935 83672 Fax: 01935 83003 **Map Ref 17**

VARTREES HOUSE, a peaceful secluded country house, in Thomas Hardy countryside, set in 3 acres of picturesque woodland gardens. Spacious and comfortable accommodation throughout. Tea/coffee facilities, TV. Near coast and places of interest. Moreton Railway Station a quarter a mile. Excellent local pubs. Ideal base for a relaxing holiday.

B&B from £18pp, Rooms 1 twin, 2 double, 2 en-suite, Restricted smoking, Children over 10, Pets by arrangement, Open January - November.
Mrs D.M Haggett, **Vartrees House,** Moreton, Dorchester, Dorset DT2 8BE
Tel: 01305 852704 **Map Ref 18**

MUSTON MANOR, a 17th century manor house built by Churchill family. Set in five acres surrounded by farmland in peaceful Piddle Valley. Large comfortable, well furnished rooms with tea/coffee making facilities, TV and central heating. Outdoor heated swimming pool in season.
B&B from £19pp, Rooms 2 double, 1 en-suite, No smoking, Children over 10, Pets by arrangement, Open March - October.
Barry & Paddy Paine, **Muston Manor,** Piddlehinton, Dorchester, Dorset DT2 7SY
Tel: 01305 848242 Fax: 01305 848242　　　　　　　　　　　　　　　　　　**Map Ref 19**

....

THE POACHERS INN, an inn situated in lovely Piddle Valley on B3143. En-suite rooms with colour TV, telephone, tea/coffee. Restaurant. Stay 2 nights half board October - March, get third night free.
B&B from £33, Dinner available, Rooms 1 twin, 9 double, 2 family, all en-suite, Children welcome, Open all year.
The Poachers Inn, Piddletrenthide, Dorchester, Dorset DT2 7QX
Tel: 01300 348358　　　　　　　　　　　　　　　　　　　　　　　　　**Map Ref 20**

....

THE CREEK, on the heritage coastal path, garden leads directly to sea. 2 rooms available, both look North over National Trust farmland, dining and sitting rooms look across garden to sea, Portland in distance. Ideal for walking, touring. Weymouth and Dorchester each 7 miles away. Fabulous views.
B&B from £18.50pp, Dinner from £12.50, Rooms 2 double, both en-suite, No smoking or pets, Children over 10, Open all year.
Freda Fisher, **The Creek,** Ringstead, Dorchester, Dorset DT2 8NG
Tel: 01305 852251　　　　　　　　　　　　　　　　　　　　　　　　　**Map Ref 21**

....

16th century **THE MANOR HOTEL,** 500 yards to Chesil Beach. Jacobean panelling and flagstone floors. Panoramic views of Dorset coast from most bedrooms, all have en-suite facilities, tea/coffee and TV. Two residents lounges. No smoking conservatory. Excellent reputation for cuisine and service. Character cellar bar. Three real ales. Log fires.
B&B from £44pp, Dinner £18.95, Rooms 1 single, 3 twin, 8 double, 1 family, all en-suite, Smoking & children welcome, No pets, Open all year except Christmas.
Richard & Jayne Childs, **The Manor Hotel,** West Bexington, Dorchester, Dorset DT2 9DF
Tel: 01308 897616 Fax: 0130 897035　　　　　　　　　　　　　**Map Ref 22**

....

THE OLD RECTORY, built in 1850 on 1 acre of land in a quiet hamlet with beautiful surroundings. Close to Weymouth, beaches, Dorchester and their restaurants. We specialise in a good nights sleep and a copious breakfast with many homemade produces. French spoken. No credit card facilities. Private dining on request.
http://homepage.eurobell.co.uk/trees/Welcome.html Email:trees@eurobell.co.uk
B&B from £20pp, Dinner for minimum of 6, Rooms 4 twin/double, all en-suite/private bathroom, No smoking or pets, Open all year except Christmas & New Year.
Capt & Mrs Tree, **The Old Rectory,** Winterbourne Steepleton, Dorchester, Dorset DT2 9LG
Tel: 01305 889468 Fax: 01305 889737　　　　　　　　　　　　**Map Ref 23**

....

COACH HOUSE INN, set in beautiful wooded surroundings, close to the New Forest and 6 miles from Bournemouth with its golden beaches.
B&B from £40, Dinner available, Rooms 16 double, 20 twin, 3 triple, 4 family, all en-suite. Open all year.
Coach House Inn, 579 Winbourne Road East, Ferndown, Dorset BH22 9NW
Tel: 01202 861222 Fax: 01202 894130　　　　　　　　　　　　　　　**Map Ref 24**

....

BRIDGE HOUSE HOTEL, located between Poole and Bournemouth, on the banks of the beautiful River Stour. A la carte restaurant, carvery bar. Four poster bed available.
B&B from £30, Dinner available, Rooms 4 single, 21 double, 11 twin, 1 triple, all en-suite, Open all year.
Bridge House Hotel, 2 Ringwood Road, Longham, Ferndown, Dorset BH22 9AN
Tel: 01202 578828 Fax: 01202 572620　　　　　　　　　　　　　　　**Map Ref 25**

STOCK HILL COUNTRY HOTEL, a deluxe country house - a haven of peace, offering a personal hospitality, service and food at its best.

B&B from £120, Dinner available, Rooms 2 single, 3 double, 3 twin, 1 triple, all en-suite, suite available, Open all year.

Stock Hill Country Hotel, Stock Hill, Gillingham, Dorset SP8 5NR
Tel: 01747 823626 Fax: 01747 825628   **Map Ref 26**

....

SHAMIEN HOUSE, a centrally situated Georgian House with full central heating. Close to shops and the sea. Friendly atmosphere. Good breakfast with wide choice. Small car park at rear. Colour TV and hospitality tray in all rooms. Great centre for walkers, fishing, sailing or fossil hunting.

B&B from £15.60-£21pp, Rooms 1 single, 2 twin, 2 double, 1 family, most en-suite, No smoking, Children welcome, Dogs welcome, Open February - January.
Diane Drummond, **Shamien House,** 8 Pound Street, Lyme Regis, Dorset DT7 3HZ
Tel: 01297 442339 Fax: 01297 444898   **Map Ref 27**

....

KERSBROOK HOTEL & RESTAURANT, a thatched 18th century listed hotel and restaurant in its own picturesque gardens, set high above Lyme Bay. For those who prefer peace and tranquillity.

B&B from £50, Dinner available, Rooms 2 single, 2 twin, 6 double, all en-suite, No smoking, Children welcome, Open February - December.
Kersbrook Hotel & Restaurant, Pound Road, Lyme Regis, Dorset DT7 3HX
Tel: 01297 442596 & 442576 Fax: 01297 442596   **Map Ref 27**

....

HOTEL BUENA VISTA, a Regency house with a country house atmosphere in an unrivalled position overlooking the bay. Close to the town and beaches.

B&B from £37, Dinner available, Rooms 4 single, 9 double, 4 twin, 1 family, all en-suite, No smoking, Children welcome, Open February - November.

Hotel Buena Vista, Pound Street, Lyme Regis, Dorset DT7 3HZ
Tel: 01297 4424/94   **Map Ref 27**

....

THATCH, a picturesque thatched octagonal house located on the outskirts of Lyme Regis. Views of country and sea. Tea/coffee facilities, TV in all rooms. Ironing, trouser press and hair drying facilities. Ample safe parking. Central heating. Sumptuous English breakfast. Attractive rates for longer stays. Concessionary rates for golfers. Discount: £4 per round per person.

B&B from £18.50-£25pp, Rooms 1 single, 1 twin/en-suite, 1 double/private bathroom, Children welcome, Pets by arrangement, Open all year.
Rhoda Elwick, **Thatch,** Uplyme Road, Lyme Regis, Dorset DT7 3LP
Tel: 01297 442212 Fax: 01297 443485   **Map Ref 27**

....

ROTHERFIELD, an exceptionally spacious, comfortable accommodation with own car park, home cooking, licensed, panoramic sea and countryside views. Warm welcome assured. Completely refurbished.

B&B from £17.50, Dinner available, Rooms 2 single, 2 double, 2 twin, 1 family, most en-suite,

Rotherfield, View Road, Lyme Regis, Dorset DT7 3AA
Tel: 01297 445585   **Map Ref 27**

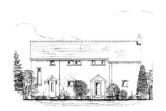

WILLOW COTTAGE, enjoys tranquillity and unrivalled views over National Trust pastureland and coastline. Close to the renowned undercliff nature trail and the Cobb, Lyme's harbour. The en-suite double bedded studio has colour TV and tea/coffee. For a third member of a party there is an adjoining single room. The main room opens on to a sun balcony which commands sea views.
B&B from £23pp, Rooms 1 single, 1 double, both en-suite, Children over 8, Pets by arrangement, Open March - November.
Geoffrey & Elizabeth Griffin, **Willow Cottage,** Ware Lane, Lyme Regis, Dorset DT7 3EL
Tel: 01297 443199   **Map Ref 27**

THATCH LODGE HOTEL, a picture postcard 14th century thatched hotel offering tranquillity, discerning quality, superb chef inspired cuisine. World famous fossil beach 3 minutes walk away. Non smoking throughout.
B&B from £39.50, Dinner available, Rooms 1 twin, 6 double, all with bathroom, No smoking, No pets, Open January, March - December.
Thatch Lodge Hotel, The Street, Charmouth, Lyme Regis, Dorset DT6 6PQ
Tel: 01297 560407 Fax: 01297 560407   **Map Ref 9**

THE DOWER HOUSE HOTEL, originally a dower house, now a country house hotel in its own idyllic grounds. Open fires. Emphasis on good food and comfort.
B&B from £38, Dinner available, Rooms 1 single, 2 twin, 3 double, 3 triple, all en-suite, Children welcome, Open all year.
The Dower House Hotel, Rousdon, Lyme Regis, Dorset DT7 3RB
Tel: 01297 21047 Fax: 01297 24748   **Map Ref 29**

ORCHARD COUNTRY HOTEL, offers good food, comfortable accommodation, gentle relaxing atmosphere and a friendly welcome are assured. Ideal base for motorists and walkers.
B&B from £30, Dinner available, Rooms 2 single, 5 twin, 5 double, all with private or en-suite facilities, Children welcome, Open March - December.
Orchard Country Hotel, Rousdon, Lyme Regis, Dorset DT7 3XW
Tel: 01297 442972   **Map Ref 29**

LYDWELL HOUSE, is ideal for Dorset and Devon countryside, Lyme Regis town and beaches are nearby. Large gardens, ponds, ample parking, easy to find from the main road. Rooms have television, direct dial phone, tea making facilities. Good home cooked food, alcoholic drinks and quiet guests' lounge available.
B&B from £21pp, Dinner from £12, Rooms 1 single, 1 twin, 1 double, 2 family, most en-suite, No smoking or pets, Children welcome, Open all year.
Mr P Brittain, **Lydwell House,** Lyme Road, Uplyme, Lyme Regis, Dorset DT7 3TJ
Tel: 01297 443522   **Map Ref 30**

VIEWPOINT GUEST HOUSE, just over a mile from Poole, 3 miles Bournemouth. The magnificent bedrooms are en-suite with the four poster featuring a corner 'spa' bath. Rooms have colour cable TV, clock radio, tea/coffee facilities, direct dial telephones, full length dress mirrors and hair dryers. Bus and taxi opposite.
B&B from £20pp, Dinner from £5.50, Rooms 2 double or 1 twin, 1 family, all en-suite, No smoking or pets, Children welcome, Open all year except Christmas.
Steve & Heather **Viewpoint Guest House,** 11 Constitution Hill, Parkstone, Poole, Dorset BH14 0QB
Tel: 01202 733 586 Fax: 01202 733 586   **Map Ref 31**

HARMONY HOTEL, a friendly service in peaceful, residential area close to all amenities. Ideally placed as a touring centre.

B&B from £16, Dinner available, Rooms 5 double, 4 twin, 2 triple, most en-suite, Open all year.
Harmony Hotel, 19 St. Peter's Road, Parkstone, Poole, Dorset BH14 0NZ
Tel: 01202 747510 Fax: 01202 747510 **Map Ref 31**

THE ST LEONARDS HOTEL, a rural hotel set in attractive grounds, convenient for the New Forest and Bournemouth. Local attractions include Beaulieu, Corfe Castle and Poole Harbour.

B&B from £37.50, Dinner available, Rooms 20 double, 8 twin, 6 family, suites available, all en-suite, Open all year.
The St Leonards Hotel, 185 Ringwood Road, St Leonards, Ringwood, Dorset BH24 2NP
Tel: 01425 471220 Fax: 01425 480274 **Map Ref 32**

EASTBURY HOTEL, a gracious Georgian town house hotel with attractive walled garden, near town centre. Private car park.
B&B from £45, Dinner available, Rooms 6 single, 4 twin, 5 double, all en-suite, Children welcome, No pets, Open all year.
Eastbury Hotel, Long Street, Sherbourne, Dorset DT9 3BY
Tel: 01935 813131 Fax: 01935 817296 **Map Ref 33**

BRITANNIA INN, originally the Lord Digby School for Girls, built in 1743, now a listed building.

B&B from £18.50, Dinner available,Rooms 1 single, 1 double, 3 twin, 2 triple, Children welcome, Open all year.
Britannia Inn, Westbury, Sherbourne, Dorset DT9 3EH
Tel: 01935 813300 **Map Ref 33**

PLUMBER MANOR, run as a restaurant with bedrooms and supervised by the family. Set in the middle of Hardy's Dorset and surrounded by the home farm. Email: plumber@btinternet.com

B&B from £47.50pp, Dinner available, Rooms 10 double, 6 twin, all en-suite, Open January, March - December.

Plumber Manor, Sturminster Newton, Dorset DT10 2AF
Tel: 01258 472507 Fax: 01258 473370 **Map Ref 34**

300 year old **STOURCASTLE LODGE** with en-suite rooms all with TV, telephone and tea/coffee facilities. Log fires in lounge. Excellent hospitality and cuisine. NG's garden many country and riverside walks and National Trust properties locally.

B&B from £27.50pp, Dinner from £17, Rooms 1 twin, 3 double, 1 family, Restricted smoking, Children welcome, No pets, Open all year.
Jill & Ken Hookham-Bassett, **Stourcastle Lodge,** Gough's Close, Sturminster Newton, Dorset DT10 1BU
Tel: 01258 472320 Fax: 01258 473381 **Map Ref 34**

HAVENHURST HOTEL, a charming detached, licensed hotel, quietly situated on level. Short walk to beach and shops. Special attention given.

B&B from £18, Dinner available, Rooms 3 single, 6 double, 4 twin, 2 triple, 2 family, all en-suite, Open all year.
Havenhurst Hotel, 3 Cranborne Road, Swanage, Dorset BH19 1EA
Tel: 01929 424224 Fax: 01929 422173 **Map Ref 35**

GLENLEE HOTEL, a delightful position overlooking beach gardens, bowling green and tennis courts. 150 yards to beach. All rooms en-suite, with colour TV and hot drinks facilities.

B&B from £40, Dinner available, Rooms 4 double, 2 twin, 1 triple, all en-suite, Open March - October.
Glenlee Hotel, 6 Cauldon Avenue, Swanage, Dorset BH19 1PQ
Tel: 01929 425794 **Map Ref 35**

SEASHELLS VEGETARIAN HOTEL, we are a nonsmoking vegetarian hotel situated on a quiet sunny road, opposite a safe sandy beach - 5 minutes from coastal path. All our rooms are en-suite, and have TV, drinks facilities, some with balconies and sea views. We have a generous car park, license, and welcome families! We happily cater for special diets etc.
B&B from £20pp, Dinner from £12, Rooms 2 single, 1 twin, 3 double, 3 family, all en-suite, No smoking or pets, Children welcome, Open all year.
Annie Campbell & Mary Lloyd, **Seashells Vegetarian Hotel,** 7 Burlington Road, Swanage, Dorset BH19 1LR
Tel: 01929 422794 **Map Ref 35**

THE PINES HOTEL, a family run hotel set amid the Purbeck countryside at quiet end of Swanage Bay. Own access to beach. Wheelchair access category 3.

B&B from £35, Dinner available, Rooms 4 single, 10 double, 11 twin, 24 triple, most en-suite, Open all year.
The Pines Hotel, Burlington Road, Swanage, Dorset BH19 1LT
Tel: 01929 425211 Fax: 01929 422075 **Map Ref 35**

KNOLL HOUSE HOTEL, an independent country hotel in National Trust reserve. Access to 3-mile beach from 100-acre grounds. Many facilities.

B&B from £64, Dinner available, Rooms 29 single, 20 twin, 30 family suites, Open April - October.

Knoll House Hotel, Studland, Swanage, Dorset BH19 3AH
Tel: 01929 450450 Fax: 01929 450423 **Map Ref 36**

The romantic 18th century **MANOR HOUSE HOTEL**, set in 20 acres of secluded grounds overlooking the sea. Residential and restaurant license. All rooms en-suite with central heating, TV, telephone, radio, hair dryer, tea/coffee facilities and some 4 poster beds. Menus feature fresh local seafood. Oak panelled bar and dining room with conservatory. 2 tennis court, riding and golf nearby.
B&B from £35pp, Dinner from £15, Rooms 6 twin, 6 double, 6 family, all en-suite, Restricted smoking, Children over 5, Pets welcome, Open February - mid December.
Manor House Hotel, Studland, Swanage, Dorset BH19 3AU
Tel: 01929 450288 Fax: 01929 450288 **Map Ref 36**

MAGISTON FARM, is a 16th century farmhouse with inglenook fireplaces and antiques furniture. Tea/coffee facilities and arm chairs in bedrooms. Evening meals on request. Ideal touring spot in the centre of Hardy Country. Very peaceful.

B&B from £17.50-£18.50pp, Dinner from £9.50, Rooms 1 single, 2 twin (1 en-suite), 1 double, Restricted smoking, Children over 10, Pets by arrangement, Open all year except Christmas.
Mrs T Barraclough, **Magiston Farm,** Sydling St. Nicholas, Dorset DT2 9NR
Tel: 01300 320 295 **Map Ref 12**

MORTONS HOUSE HOTEL, an attractive Elizabethan manor house with castle views. Walled gardens, coastal and country pursuits. Suites and four-poster bed. Licensed gourmet restaurant.
B&B from £45, Dinner available, Rooms 13 double, 3 twin, 1 family, all en-suite, Open all year.
Mortons House Hotel, East Street, Corfe Castle, Wareham, Dorset BH20 5EE
Tel: 01929 480988 Fax: 01929 480820   **Map Ref 37**

....

SHIRLEY HOTEL, in the country by the sea. Small, friendly hotel close to Lulworth Cove. Good food and relaxed atmosphere. Indoor heated pool and jacuzzi.
B&B from £32, Dinner available, Rooms 3 single, 8 double, 4 twin, 1 triple, 2 family, all en-suite, Open February - November.
Shirley Hotel, West Lulworth, Wareham, Dorset BH20 5RL
Tel: 01929 400358 Fax: 01929 400167   **Map Ref 38**

....

CROMWELL HOUSE HOTEL, a family hotel on the Dorset Heritage Coast footpath. Outstanding sea views over Lulworth Cove. Secluded garden. Good walking country. Swimming pool.
B&B from £23, Dinner available, Rooms 1 single, 7 double, 5 twin, 1 triple, all en-suite, Open all year.
Cromwell House Hotel, Lulworth Cove, West Lulworth, Wareham, Dorset BH20 5RJ
Tel: 01929 400253 Fax: 01929 400566   **Map Ref 39**

....

LULWORTH COVE HOTEL, one hundred yards from the cove on the Dorset Coastal Path. Some sea-view balcony rooms. Wide variety of restaurants.

B&B from £21, Dinner available, Rooms 1 single, 12 double, 1 triple, 1 family, some en-suite, Open all year.
Lulworth Cove Hotel, Main Road, West Lulworth, Wareham, Dorset BH20 5RQ
Tel: 01929 400333 Fax: 01929 400534 Email: lulworthcove@saqnet.co.uk   **Map Ref 38**

....

REMBRANDT HOTEL, a premier hotel in Weymouth, walking distance from the seafront and town centre. Hotel has leisure club with sauna, whirlpool bath, sun beds, toning beds and large heated swimming pool.
B&B from £40, Dinner available, Rooms 6 single, 12 twin, 27 double, 35 triple, 8 family, most en-suite,No smoking, Children welcome, Open all year.
Rembrandt Hotel, 12-16 Dorchester Road, Weymouth, Dorset DT4 7JU
Tel: 01305 764000 Fax: 01305 764022   **Map Ref 40**

....

OAKDALE GUEST HOUSE, a family run guest house in a quiet avenue, few minutes walk to beach and town centre. Eight rooms, seven are en-suite, all centrally heated with colour televisions, tea/coffee facilities. Ground floor en-suite room. Own key access. Car parking on premises.

B&B from £15pp, Dinner from £6, Rooms 1 single, 1 twin, 6 double, 5 family, most en-suite, No smoking or pets, Children welcome, Open all year except Christmas.
Sue Robinson, Oakdale Guest House, 14 Kirtleton Avenue, Weymouth, Dorset DT4 7PT
Tel: 01305 774179   **Map Ref 40**

....

THE PEBBLES GUEST HOUSE, comfortable, friendly, family run guest house. Private parking. Tea/coffee facilities, TV and radio in all rooms. Central heating. Few minutes from sea front. Close to Nature Reserve and Sea Life Centre. Ground floor en-suite room. Optional home cooked evening meal and full English Breakfast.
B&B from £95pp, Dinner from £7, Rooms 2 single, 4 twin, 2 double, 4 family, most en-suite, Children welcome, Pets by arrangement, Open all year except Christmas.
Gail & Stephen Blackshaw, The Pebbles Guest House, 18 Kirtleton Avenue, Weymouth, Dorset DT4 7PT
Tel: 01305 784331 Fax: 01305 784695   **Map Ref 40**

SUNNINGDALE HOTEL, a family hotel with a relaxed and comfortable atmosphere, set in attractive gardens with an out door swimming pool. 2 miles to the town centre.

B&B from £22, Dinner available, Rooms 1 single, 3 twin, 7 double, 3 triple, 4 family, most en-suite, Children welcome, Open April - October.
Sunningdale Hotel, 52 Preston Road, Weymouth, Dorset DT3 6QD
Tel: 01305 832179 Fax: 01305 832179   **Map Ref 40**

....

SWAN LODGE, situated on the B3157 coastal road between Weymouth and Bridport. Swan inn public house opposite, where food is served all day, is under same ownership.

B&B from £22, Dinner available, Rooms 2 twin, 2 double, 1 en-suite, most en-suite, Children welcome, Open all year.
Swan Lodge, Rodden Row, Abbotsbury, Weymouth, Dorset DT3 4JL
Tel: 01305 871249 Fax: 01305 871249   **Map Ref 41**

....

Osmington is a quiet, picturesque village in an area of outstanding natural beauty, a mile from the coast. **THE BEEHIVE**, which is thatched, has comfortable well-equipped rooms and a sitting room with TV. It is an ideal place for a peaceful relaxing holiday or break.

B&B from £17pp, Rooms 1 single, 1 twin, 1 double en-suite, No smoking, Children over 6, Pets by arrangement, Open February - December.
Mary Kempe, **The Beehive,** Church Lane, Osmington, Weymouth, Dorset DT3 6EL
Tel: 01305 834095   **Map Ref 42**

....

ALESSANDRIA HOTEL & RESTAURANT, an 18th century, portland stone building. Quiet location. Beautiful scenery. Excellent food cooked by chef/proprietor 30 years first class experience. All rooms have colour TV's, tea/coffee, new comfortable beds, guest toiletries. Well stocked bar, restaurant and lounge. Car park. Call Giovanni or Rose for reservations and brochure.
B&B from £22.50pp, Dinner from £12, Rooms 3 single, 3 twin, 6 double, 3 family, most en-suite, Restricted smoking, Children welcome, Pets by arrangement, Open all year.
Rose Cliffe & Giovanni Bisogno, **Alessandria Hotel & Restaurant,** 71 Wakeham Easton, Portland, Weymouth, Dorset DT5 1HW
Tel: 01305 822 270 & 820 108 Fax: 01305 820 561   **Map Ref 43**

....

ALBION HOTEL, a 17th century coaching house in the centre of Wimborne. TV, tea/coffee making facilities available. Large car park and beer garden. Places to visit - Wimborne Minster and three day market - Friday, Saturday and Sunday.
B&B from £19.50pp, Rooms 1 single, 3 twin, 3 double, 1 family, some en-suite, Children & pets welcome, Open all year.
Colin Ray, **Albion Hotel,** 19 High Street, Wimborne, Dorset BH21 1HR
Tel: 01202 882492   **Map Ref 44**

....

GORDON HOUSE, town centre location, 250 year old property. Tea/coffee making facilities. Car parking off road. Many places of interest, National Trust Kingston Lacey House and grounds, 11th Century Wimborne Minster, New Forest, Athelhampton Beauleiu House, Longleat House, Safari Park and beaches at Bournemouth and Poole.

B&B from £ 15pp, Rooms 1 single, 2 twin, 1 double, 1 family, 2 en-suite, Children & Pets welcome, Open all year except Christmas.
Peter & Conchita Abineri, **Gordon House,** 42 Westborough, Wimborne, Dorset BH21 1NQ
Tel: 01202 885547   **Map Ref 44**

....

THORNHILL, a large thatched family home with a separate lounge and TV. The house is set well away from the road but is within walking distance of the local pub. Excellently situated for visiting Poole, Bournemouth and other coastal areas. Also Salisbury and the New Forest.
B&B from £20pp, Rooms 1 single, 1 twin, 1 double en-suite, No smoking, children or pets, Open all year.
John & Sara Turnbull, **Thornhill,** Holt, Wimborne, Dorset BH21 7DJ
Tel: 01202 889434   **Map Ref 45**

Essex is a county of many parts. On the fringe of Greater London is Epping Forest. Epping, a busy little market town, dates from the thirteenth century and was once an important coaching centre and some of the old coaching inns still survive along the attractive main street. Epping's long High Street follows the line of one of the 'purlieu banks' that marked the edge of Epping Forest. In contrast to the rough heaths and trees of the forest is the built-up area along the Thames from Purfleet to Shoeburyness, including Southend with its pier and illuminations. Sweeping north from Shoeburyness to the Blackwater estuary, and peculiar to the area, is the coastal belt of marsh reclaimed from the sea by the Dutch in the seventeenth century. Behind the sea wall the miles of mudflats, saltings and remote islands are a haven for wildlife.

Essex has many seaside resorts. Southend-on-Sea has seven miles of beach-lined promenades, with pretty parks, elegant esplanades and lively amusements. It has the longest pleasure pier in the world with unique pier trains. The resort was winner of the Tidy Britain Group Seaside award for cleanliness of beach and water at East Beach, Shoeburyness and Three Shells Beach. Clacton-on-Sea's seven mile long sandy beach forms the sunshine holiday coast of Essex. The strikingly clean town has tree lined streets and colourful gardens. Nearby Holland-on-Sea has sandy beaches which are usually quieter than Clacton. Frinton-on-Sea is for the more energetic. It has a golf course plus excellent cricket, tennis and squash facilities. Burnham-on-Crouch is the largest town in the area known as the Dengie Hundred, a peninsula stretching into the North Sea, bounded by the River Blackwater in the north and the River Crouch in the south.

Colchester, one of the greatest Roman fortress cities in England after London. The town is a marvellous mix of the old and new with centuries old streets blending in with modern shopping centres. Colchester's famed history is everywhere from parts of the original Roman wall to the Norman castle keep, the largest in Britain. Braintree and Coggeshall were wool centres. Braintree now depends on the manufacture of silk and other textiles. Coggeshall is on the route of the old Roman Stane Street and among its many fine old houses is Paycocke's, a well known wool merchant's house of 1500.

The ancient town of Saffron Walden has revolved around its market for many generations. The medieval market rows are well preserved and there are many timber-framed buildings, many decorated by the traditional pargetting. The Saffron Crocus can be seen flowering outside the town's museum in the autumn. To the south are the Rodings, a group of farming villages along the valley of the River Roding, rich in half timbered houses, moated manor farms and ancient churches.

Essex

left, Epping Forest

STOWMARKET

Suffolk

IPSWICH

A12

18

17

15

FELIXSTOWE

HARWICH

A120

7

COLCHESTER

WALTON ON THE NASE

11

A133

B1015

6

REE

10

ST OSYTH

CLACTON ON SEA

WEST MERSEA

BRADWELL ON SEA

B1021

1010

BURNHAM ON CROUCH

ERNESS

ESSEX

COTTAGES GUEST HOUSE, situated in a quiet rural area. Cosy, modern facilities. Specialising in commercial trade. Long term available. Licensed bar. Large car park. Satellite TV. 15 minutes from Southend, Basildon or Chelmsford. One mile from Battlesbridge Station and extensive antiques market. Mini bus available to hire.

B&B from £17.50pp, Dinner from £3.50, Rooms 1 single, 4 twin, 2 double, 1 family, some en-suite, Restricted smoking, Children & pets welcome, Open all year except Christmas week.
Miss Carr, **Cottages Guest House,** Beeches Road, Battlesbridge, Essex SS11 8TJ
Tel: 01702 232105   **Map Ref 1**

....

WHITE HART HOTEL, a warm and cosily furnished, town centre hotel, created around an original 16th century coaching inn. Excellent base for visiting East Anglia.

B&B from £36, Dinner available, Rooms 3 single, 14 double, 6 twin, 8 triple, all en-suite, No smoking, Children welcome, Open all year.

White Hart Hotel, Bocking End, Braintree, Essex CM7 9AB
Tel: 01376 321401 Fax: 01376 552628   **Map Ref 2**

....

BRENTWOOD GUESTHOUSE, a Victorian detached guest house, recently refurbished. Close to Brentwood centre and local parks. 2 minutes walk from rail station (London 25 minutes), 1 mile to M25. TV in all rooms, en-suite rooms available.

B&B from £25, Rooms 2 single, 2 twin, 4 double, 2 triple, most en-suite, No smoking, Children welcome, No pets, Open all year.
Brentwood Guesthouse, 75-77 Rose Valley, Brentwood, Essex CM14 4HJ
Tel: 01277 262713 & 0410 523757 Fax: 01277 211146   **Map Ref 3**

....

MARYGREEN MANOR HOTEL, an original Tudor building dating back to 1512. Hunting lodge visited by Catherine of Aragon. Old world garden.

B&B from £108.50, Dinner available, Rooms 16 double, 17 twin, all en-suite, No smoking, Children welcome, Open all year.
Marygreen Manor Hotel, London Road, Brentwood, Essex CM14 4NR
Tel: 01277 225252 Fax: 01277 262809   **Map Ref 3**

....

BOSWELL HOUSE HOTEL, a Victorian town house in central location, offering high standard accommodation in friendly and informal surroundings. Family atmosphere with home cooking.

B&B from £45, Dinner available, Rooms 5 single, 6 double, 2 triple, all en-suite, No smoking, Children welcome, No pets, Open all year.
Boswell House Hotel, 118 Springfield Road, Chelmsford, Essex CM2 6LF
Tel: 01245 287587 Fax: 01245 287587   **Map Ref 4**

....

THE CHELMER HOTEL, a friendly and homely atmosphere. Close to all amenities and priding itself as the most economic hotel in Chelmsford.

B&B from £19, Rooms 2 single, 1 double, 2 twin, 2 triple, Children welcome, No pets, Open all year.

The Chelmer Hotel, 2-4 Hamlet Road, Chelmsford, Essex CM2 0EU
Tel: 01245 353360 & 609055 Fax: 0181 574 3912   **Map Ref 4**

....

BEECHCROFT PRIVATE HOTEL, central hotel offering clean and comfortable accommodation with friendly service. Under family ownership and management. Within walking distance of town centre.

B&B from £31, Rooms 12 single, 3 double, 3 twin, 1 triple, 1 family, most en-suite, Children welcome, Open all year.
Beechcroft Private Hotel, 211 New London Road, Chelmsford, Essex CM2 0AJ
Tel: 01245 352462 & 250861 Fax: 01245 347833   **Map Ref 4**

COUNTY HOTEL, a privately owned hotel, 10 minutes walk from town centre. Families welcome - free cots, extra beds. Popular restaurant offering £18 - £20 3 course meals.

B&B from £28, Dinner available, Rooms 18 single, 7 double, 10 twin, all en-suite, No smoking, Children welcome, Open all year.
County Hotel, Rainsford Road, Chelmsford, Essex CM1 2QA
Tel: 01245 491911 Fax: 01245 492762   **Map Ref 4**

THE WINDMILL MOTOR INN, is situated 300 metres off the A131 in the hamlet of Chatham Green, Essex. The accommodation is in chalet style rooms adjoining the old village pub - 4 in the windmill roundhouse, 3 in the rebuilt stable block. All have en-suite bathrooms. Two have disabled facilities.
B&B single £40 per night, double £55 per night, Dinner £7.95, Rooms ???single,???double, ???twin, ???family, Open all year.
Mr Hooper, **The Windmill Motor Inn,** Chatham Green, Little Waltham, Chelmsford, Essex CM3 3LE
Tel: 01245 361188   **Map Ref 5**

SANDROCK HOTEL, a private hotel in central position, just off sea front and close to town. Comfortable bedrooms with coordinated soft furnishings. Excellent, freshly cooked food. Licensed. Car park.

B&B from £22, Dinner available, Rooms 5 double, 2 twin, 1 triple, all en-suite, No smoking, Children welcome, Open all year.
Sandrock Hotel, 1 Penfold Road, Marine Parade West, Clacton on Sea, Essex CO15 1JN
Tel: 01255 428215 Fax: 01255 428215   **Map Ref 6**

THE GRAND HOTEL, is situated on the seafront at Clacton. Panoramic views of the North Sea. All rooms fully en-suite with colour satellite TV, video, electric blankets and courtesy trays. Food of the finest quality. Fully licensed. Two lounge bars. Near to shops and theatres and opposite pier. Borders on the beautiful Constable country. Braile menu. Toilets for the disabled.
B&B from £25pp, Dinner from £7.50, Rooms 9 single, 8 twin, 10 double, 3 family, all en-suite, Children & pets welcome, Open all year except Christmas.
Mrs Chapman Webb, **The Grand Hotel,** Marine Parade East, Clacton on Sea, Essex CO15 1PS
Tel: 01255 222020 Fax: 01255 220698   **Map Ref 6**

HAMELIN HOTEL, a friendly family atmosphere in this Christian run retreat and small conference hotel. Full central heating, coloured TV, tea/coffee facilities in all rooms. Guest lounge, small bar, limited parking. Situated close to beach and shops.

B&B from £16pp, Dinner from £6, Rooms 1 single, 2 twin, 2 double, 3 family, some en-suite, Restricted smoking, Children welcome, Pets by arrangement, Open all year except Christmas.
Mrs F.C. Baker, **Hamelin Hotel,** 20 Penfold Road, Clacton-on-Sea Essex CO15 1JN
Tel: 01255 474456 Fax: 01255 428053 Email: linkministries@enterprise.net   **Map Ref 6**

ST. JOHNS GUEST HOUSE, well situated, attractive house with access to country park. Luxury en-suite. Leisure centre and restaurants close by. Short drive to town centre. Convenient A12 and A120 to Harwich. Parking within own grounds. Colour TV, tea/coffee in all rooms.

B&B from £18pp, Rooms 2 single, 2 twin, 2 double, 2 family, some en-suite, No smoking, Children welcome, Pets by arrangement, Open all year.

Colin Knight, **St. Johns Guest House,** 330 Ipswich Road, Colchester Essex CO4 4ET
Tel: 01206 852288   **Map Ref 7**

THE SALISBURY, a family run hotel near town centre. Fully licensed restaurant/bar, private meeting facilities, pool and darts. Specialises in small, informal dinner parties.

B&B from £30, Dinner available, Rooms 3 single, 2 double, 2 twin, 1 triple, all en-suite, No smoking, Children welcome, No pets, Open all year.
The Salisbury, 112 Butt Road, Colchester, Essex CO3 3DL
Tel: 01206 572338 & 508508 Fax: 01206 797265   **Map Ref 7**

....

SCHEREGATE HOTEL, interesting 15th century building, centrally situated, providing accommodation at moderate prices.

B&B from £18, Rooms 12 single, 6 double, 8 twin, 1 triple, 1 family, most en-suite, Children welcome, No pets, Open all year.
Scheregate Hotel, 36 Osborne Street, via St John's Street, Colchester, Essex CO2 7DB
Tel: 01206 573034   **Map Ref 7**

....

PEVERIL HOTEL, a friendly, family run hotel with fine restaurant and bar. All rooms have colour TV and all facilities. Some en-suite available.

B&B from £25, Dinner available, Rooms 5 single, 7 double, 4 twin, 1 triple, some en-suite, Children welcome, Open all year.
Peveril Hotel, 51 North Hill, Colchester, Essex CO1 1PY
Tel: 01206 574001 Fax: 01206 574001   **Map Ref 7**

....

BUTTERFLY HOTEL, a purpose built hotel in traditional style. Modern coaching inn by the waters edge on the outskirts of Colchester at the junction of A12 and A120.

B&B from £51.95, Dinner available, Rooms 22 single, 12 double, 12 twin, 4 family, all en-suite, No smoking, Children welcome, Open all year.
Butterfly Hotel, A12-A120 Ardliegh Junction, Old Ipswich Road, Colchester, Essex CO7 7QY
Tel: 01206 230900 Fax: 01206 231095   **Map Ref 7**

....

COLCHESTER MILL HOTEL, converted flour mill set alongside the River Calne, just a few minutes from the ancient town centre of Colchester. The quayside restaurant overlooks the river and has a reputation locally for good food and service.

B&B from £45, Dinner available, Rooms 6 single, 34 double, 15 twin, 2 triple, 4 family, all en-suite, No smoking, Children welcome, Open all year.
Colchester Mill Hotel, East Street, Colchester, Essex CO1 2TS
Tel: 01206 865022 Fax: 01206 860851   **Map Ref 7**

....

ROSE & CROWN, the oldest inn in the oldest recorded town in England. Early 15th century inn with charming en-suite bedrooms, log fire, bar and noted restaurant. On Ipswich road 2 miles off A12 and half a mile from town centre.

B&B from £62, Dinner available, Rooms 1 single, 23 double, 2 twin, 4 triple, all en-suite, No smoking, Children welcome, No pets, Open all year.
Rose & Crown, East Street, Colchester, Essex CO1 2TZ
Tel: 01206 866677 Fax: 01206 866616   **Map Ref 7**

....

THE WHITE HART HOTEL, a Tudor inn dating from 1432, built on a Roman road and signed off the A120 and A12, 7 miles west of Colchester.

B&B from £49.20, Dinner available, Rooms 2 single, 14 double, 2 twin, all en-suite, Children welcome, No pets, Open all year.
The White Hart Hotel, Market End, Coggeshall, Colchester, Essex CO6 1NH
Tel: 01376 561654 Fax: 01376 561789   **Map Ref 8**

THE LODGE, a modern hotel at The Essex Golf and Country Club. West of Colchester in some of the most beautiful countryside in the country.

B&B from £45, Dinner available, Rooms 12 double, 30 twin, all en-suite, No smoking, Children welcome, No pets, Open all year.
The Lodge, The Essex Golf & Country Club, Earls Colne, Colchester, Essex CO6 2NS
Tel: 01787 224466 Fax: 01787 224410   **Map Ref 9**

THE BLACKWATER HOTEL & RESTAURANT, a family run hotel a short walk from beach. Private gardens and parking. Restaurant Le Champagne, which offers French Cuisine, and specialises in fresh fish. The Mussel Pan, offers a speciality mussels cooked in various ways, and again local fish.Tea/Coffee, Lunch and light snacks from 11am - 4pm. Email: blackwaterhotel@dial.pipex.com
B&B from £14pp, DB&B from £40, Rooms 6 single/double, 2 twin, 2 family, all en-suite or with private bathroom.
Saskia Niessen, **The Blackwater Hotel & Restaurant,** 20-22 Church Road, West Mersea, Colchester, Essex CO5 8QH
Tel: 01206 383338 Fax: 01206 383038   **Map Ref 10**

WIVENHOE HOUSE HOTEL & CONFERENCE CENTRE, a Georgian mansion in 200 acres of parkland on the outskirts of Colchester.

B&B from £54.80, Dinner available, Rooms 7 single, 10 double, 30 twin, all en-suite, Children welcome, Open all year.
Wivenhoe House Hotel & Conference Centre, Wivenhoe Park, Colchester, Essex CO4 3SQ
Tel: 01206 863666 Fax: 01206 868532   **Map Ref 11**

MILL HOUSE, is an 18th century listed town house with a delightful garden sloping down to the River Colne. Adjoining the house, straddling the River is Townsford Mill antiques centre. Rooms are decorated in period style, teas making, TV's. Pubs, restaurants close by. Tourist Board Highly Commended.

B&B from £48pp, Rooms 1 twin, 2 double, all en-suite, No smoking or pets, Children over 12, Open all year except Christmas & New Year.
Geraldine Stuckey, **Mill House,** The Causeway, Halstead, Essex CO9 1ET
Tel: 01787 474451   **Map Ref 12**

HARLOW MOAT HOUSE, a modern 120 bedroomed hotel with comprehensive conference facilities. Ideally located for business people and tourists.

B&B from £85, Dinner available, Rooms 30 double, 90 twin, all en-suite, No smoking, Children welcome, Open all year.
Harlow Moat House, Southern Way, Harlow, Essex CM18 7BA
Tel: 01279 829988 Fax: 01279 635094   **Map Ref 13**

CHURCHGATE MANOR HOTEL, a spacious hotel in secluded grounds with large indoor leisure complex and swimming pool. Close to M11, M25 and Stansted Airport. 16th century restaurant and bars. Extensive conference facilities for up to 200 persons. Special value weekend breaks.

B&B from £62, Dinner available, Rooms 22 single, 24 double, 24 twin, 15 triple, all en-suite, No smoking, Children welcome, Open all year.
Churchgate Manor Hotel, Churchgate Street Village, Old Harlow, Essex CM17 0JT
Tel: 01279 420246 Fax: 01279 437720   **Map Ref 14**

THE PIER AT HARWICH, two restaurant both with excellent views of twin estuaries of Stour and Orwell rivers, serving the freshest fish available from the quay opposite. En-suite accommodation.

B&B from £52.50, Dinner available, Rooms 4 double, 2 twin, all en-suite, Children welcome, No pets, Open all year.
The Pier at Harwich, The Quay, Harwich, Essex CO12 3HH
Tel: 01255 241212 Fax: 01255 551922   **Map Ref 15**

IVY HILL HOTEL, a converted mansion house in the countryside near A12. Complex includes conference centre, banquetting, bar and elegant restaurant.

B&B from £75, Dinner available, Rooms 24 double, 10 twin, all en-suite, Children welcome, No pets, Open all year.
Ivy Hill Hotel, Writtle Road, Margaretting, Ingatestone, Essex CM4 0EH
Tel: 01277 353040 Fax: 01277 355038   **Map Ref 16**

THORN HOTEL, situated close to the picturesque River Stour, the hotel has recently been refurbished. All rooms en-suite.

B&B from £30, Dinner available, Rooms 2 single, 2 double, all private facilities, Children welcome, No smoking, No pets, Open all year.
Thorn Hotel, High Street, Mistley, Manningtree, Essex CO11 1HE
Tel: 01206 392821 Fax: 01206 392133   **Map Ref 17**

NEW FARM HOUSE, a modern comfortable farmhouse in large garden, 10 minutes drive to Harwich and convenient for Constable country. From Wix village crossroads, take Bradfield Road, turn right at top of hill, first house on left.

B&B from £22, Dinner available, Rooms 3 single, 1 double, 3 twin, 5 family, most en-suite, No smoking, Children welcome, Open all year.

New Farm House, Spinnell's Lane, Wix, Manningtree, Essex CO11 2UJ
Tel: 01255 870365 Fax: 01255 870837   **Map Ref 18**

GIDEA PARK HOTEL

GIDEA PARK HOTEL, we are a small family run business offering excellent accommodation. Our rooms offer tea/coffee facilities, 39 channel cable television in all rooms and Direct Dial telephones. We are Licensed and offer a good variety of food. All our rooms offer en-suite facilities.

B&B from £27.91pp, Dinner from £10, Rooms 6 single, 4 twin, 4 double, 2 family, all rooms en-suite, Children welcome, No pets, Open all year.
Donald & Michelle Camilleri, **Gidea Park Hotel,** 115 Main Road, Gidea Park, Romford, Essex RM2 5EL
Tel: 01708 746676 Fax: 01708 764044   **Map Ref 19**

SAFFRON HOTEL, a 16th century hotel in market town. South of Cambridge, close to Duxford Air Museum and Stansted Airport. Noted restaurant.

B&B from £42.50, Dinner available, Rooms 3 single, 10 double, 3 twin, 1 triple, all with en-suite or private facilities, No smoking, Children welcome, Open all year.

Saffron Hotel, 10-18 High Street, Saffron Walden, Essex CB10 1AY
Tel: 01799 522676 Fax: 01799 513979   **Map Ref 20**

ARCHWAY GUEST HOUSE, unusual property, decorated with wall to wall original paintings, rock and pop memorabilia and old toys. Situated right in the centre of town. Rooms have tea and coffee. Cambridge 15 miles. Stanstead Airport 10 miles. M11 2 miles. Audley End House 5 minutes.

B&B from £22.50, Rooms 1 single, 2 twin, 3 double, 2 family, some en-suite, Children & Pets welcome, Open all year.
Flora Miles, **Archway Guest House,** Church Street, Saffron Walden, Essex CB10 1JW
Tel: 01799 501500 Fax: 01799 501500   **Map Ref 20**

THE CRICKETERS, a 16th century freehouse with beamed and attractively decorated interior. Well established restaurant and bar meals. Accommodation adjacent.

B&B from £60, Dinner available, Rooms 2 double, 4 twin, all en-suite, No smoking,Children welcome, No pets, Open all year.
The Cricketers, Clavering, Saffron Walden, Essex CB11 4QT
Tel: 01799 550442 Fax: 01799 550882 **Map Ref 21**

....

QUEENS HEAD INN, a family run freehouse and hotel close to Audley End. All rooms en-suite. Good Pub Guide 'Best Pub in Essex' 1995. Interesting and unusual menu.

B&B from £32.95, Dinner available, Rooms 2 single, 1 twin, 2 double, 1 family, all en-suite, No smoking, Children welcome, No pets, Open all year.
Queens Head Inn, Littlebury, Saffron Walden, Essex CB11 4TD
Tel: 01799 522251 Fax: 01799 513522 **Map Ref 22**

....

TOWER HOTEL & RESTAURANT, a restored Victorian hotel in conservation area, 10 minutes walk from Cliff Gardens, the sea, Cliffs Pavilion Theatre, High Street and British Rail.

B&B from £36, Dinner available, Rooms 12 single, 14 double, 2 twin, 2 triple, 1 family, most en-suite, Children welcome, Open all year.
Tower Hotel & Restaurant, 146 Alexandra Road, Southend on Sea, Essex SS1 1HE
Tel: 01702 348635 Fax: 01702 433044 **Map Ref 23**

....

BALMORAL HOTEL, a highly appealing hotel, designer furnished in 1995. En-suite rooms, excellent bar and restaurant. 24 hour service. Near station, buses, shops and sea. Secure parking.

B&B from £39, Dinner available, Rooms 10 single, 13 double, 6 twin, all en-suite, Children welcome, Open all year.

Balmoral Hotel, 32-36 Valkyrie Road, Southend on Sea, Essex SS0 8BU
Tel: 01702 342947 Fax: 01702 337828 **Map Ref 23**

....

HAVEN HOUSE HOTEL, central location, modern building and car park.

B&B from £19, Rooms 2 single, 2 double, 4 twin, 1 triple, Children welcome, Open all year.
Haven House Hotel, 47 Heygate Avenue, Southend on Sea, Essex SS1 2AN
Tel: 01702 619246 **Map Ref 23**

....

ROSLIN HOTEL, overlooking the Thames Estuary in residential Thorpe Bay. Within easy reach of Southend and 45 minutes from London.

B&B from £30pp, Dinner available, Rooms 16 single, 8 double, 10 twin, 4 triple, all en-suite, No smoking, Children welcome, Open all year.

Roslin Hotel, Thorpe Esplanade, Thorpe Bay, Southend on Sea, Essex SS1 3BG
Tel: 01702 586375 Fax: 01702 586663 **Map Ref 24**

....

THE CHICHESTER HOTEL, a picturesque family run hotel with restaurant, dinner dance restaurant and functions complex. Surrounded by farmland in the Basildon, Chelmsford, Southend triangle.

B&B from £47.50, Dinner available, Rooms 17 single, 10 double, 8 twin, all en-suite, No pets, Open all year.

The Chichester Hotel, Old London Road, Wickford, Essex SS11 8UE
Tel: 01268 560555 Fax: 01268 560580 **Map Ref 25**

213

Mention the county of Gloucestershire and the immediate image is of mellow Cotswold villages surrounded by countryside. As well as many picturesque towns and villages, a focus of the county is the Regency spa town of Cheltenham, along with nearby Gloucester, with its magnificent cathedral. The Forest of Dean stretches between the rivers Severn and Wye in the west of the county.

Stow-on-the-Wold was once a bustling centre of the wool industry, its importance growing in the Middle Ages as it stood at the junction of several main roads. As well as the wealth of the wool trade and its heritage of superb buildings, the area is also characterised by its soft, natural limestone used in its buildings and dry stone walls.

There are world famous larger villages such as Bourton-on-the-Water, Broadway, Chipping Campden and Bibury, but plenty of smaller "undiscovered" villages like Stanton, Snowshill and Bisley offer local character. With a number of long distance footpaths, the area is a walker's paradise.

The source of the Thames is three miles south west of the Roman town of Cirencester, an excellent centre for walking or touring. Three Roman roads - Akeman Street, the Foss Way and one of the two Ermine Streets radiate from Cirencester, whose many Roman finds can be seen in the Corinium Museum. Cheltenham is a centre of music, art and sport. It is one of the most famous spa towns in England. The only alkaline springs in England run underground and are available at the Pittville Pump Room, the town's most beautiful building. Also with Roman origins is Gloucester, for centuries the guardian to the routes to Wales which converged at the lowest crossing point of the River Severn. The city's industrial heritage can be seen at Gloucester Docks, a collection of Victorian warehouses, restored with shops, restaurants and cafe bars. It has superb shopping facilities, pubs and plenty of night life. To the west of the River Severn is the beautiful Wye Valley, dominated by the splendour of Symonds Yat and the ruined Tintern Abbey and the Forest of Dean.

The Forest of Dean has an estimated 20 million trees, mainly oak and beech but with birch, ash, conifers and massive holly trees. Decreed a Royal hunting ground in 1016, the forest offers facilities for outdoor activities. Traditional industries include charcoal making and mining. Foresters, the people who live and work in the forest, have traditional privileges granted to them centuries ago. Miners have the right to dig coal free and the quarrymen can cut stone. Half the forest is fenced and the other half is grazed by Foresters' sheep. A natural phenomenon is the Severn Bore, when the river meets the incoming tide and forms a great wave.

Gloucestershire

left, Painswick from Scottsquar Hill

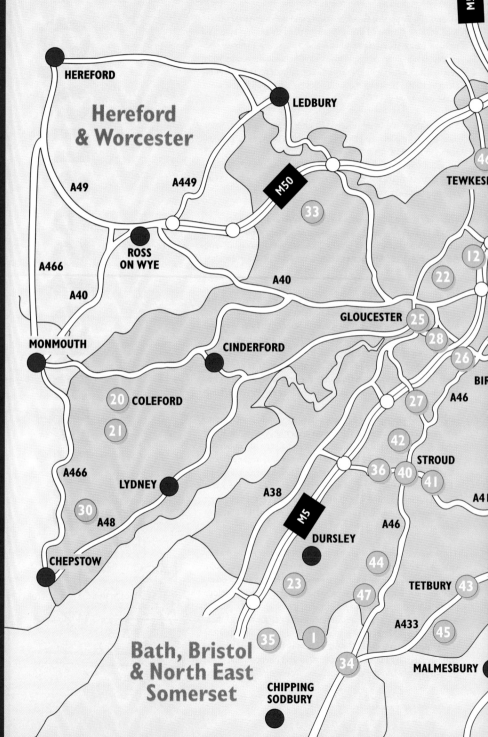

GLOUCESTERSHIRE

BODKIN HOUSE HOTEL, ideal for Bath and Cotswolds. Beautifully restored 17th century Cotswold coaching inn, providing large, well appointed en-suite bedrooms. Renowned for good food.

B&B from £49.95, Dinner available, Rooms 2 twin, 7 double, 2 triple, all en-suite, Children welcome, Open all year.
Bodkin House Hotel, A46, Bath to Stroud Road, Badminton, Gloucestershire GL9 1AF
Tel: 01454 238310 Fax: 01454 238422   **Map Ref 1**

....

PETTY FRANCE HOTEL, an informal country house atmosphere on the edge of the Cotswolds. Good walking, many sights to visit, convenient for Bath and Bristol.
B&B from £59, Dinner available, Rooms 2 single,12 double, 5 twin, 1 triple, all en-suite, No smoking, Children welcome, Open all year.
Petty France Hotel, A46, Dunkirk, Badminton, Gloucestershire GL9 1AF
Tel: 01454 238768   **Map Ref 1**

....

COOMBE HOUSE, a Cotswold home providing accommodation for guests who enjoy the highest levels of cleanliness and comfort in gentle elegance. ETB Highly Commended. AA QQQQ Selected. 7 rooms with en-suite colour TV and refreshment tray. VISA/MC/AMEX. Liquor license. Pretty plantsmans garden. Private parking.
B&B from £31pp, Rooms 2 twin, 5 double, all en-suite, No smoking or pets, Children by arrangement, Open all year except Christmas Eve/Day & New Year's Eve.
Graham & Diana Ellis, **Coombe House,** Rissington Road, Bourton-on-the-Water, Gloucestershire GL54 2DT
Tel: 01451 821966 Fax: 01451 810477   **Map Ref 2**

....

OLD MANSE HOTEL, listed 18th century village centre hotel fronting the River Windrush. A la carte, table d'hote and vegetarian menus, real ales, four-poster with whirlpool spa, log fire.

B&B from £39.50, Dinner available, Rooms 9 double, 3 twin, all en-suite, Open all year.
Old Manse Hotel, Victorian Street, Bourton-On-The-Water, Cheltenham, Gloucestershire GL54 2BX
Tel: 01451 820082 Fax: 01451 810381   **Map Ref 2**

....

OLD NEW INN, this local Inn with its pictures and log fires retain the character and ambience which has been built up over the last 200 years.

B&B from £30, Dinner available, Rooms 3 single, 9 double, 4 twin, 1 triple, most en-suite, Open all year.
Old New Inn, Bourton-on-the-Water, Cheltenham, Gloucestershire GL54 2AF
Tel: 01451 820467 Fax: 01451 810236   **Map Ref 2**

....

DIAL HOUSE, 17th Century hotel in 1.5 acres of beautiful walled garden, peacefully situated in village centre. Log fires, four-posters, noted a la carte restaurant.

B&B from £30, Dinner available, Rooms 1 single, 6 double, 3 twin, most en-suite, Open all year.
Dial House, The Chestnuts, High Street, Bourton-on-the-Water, Cheltenham, Gloucestershire GL54 2AN
Tel: 01451 822244 Fax: 01451 810126   **Map Ref 2**

....

BOURTON LODGE HOTEL, family-run hotel with friendly atmosphere and traditional home cooking. Panoramic views of surrounding countryside from most bedrooms. Bourton-on-the-Water close by. Within easy driving distance of Cirencester, Cheltenham and Stratford.

B&B from £43.50, Dinner available, Rooms 7 double, 1 twin, 1 triple, 1 family, all en-suite, Open all year.

Bourton Lodge Hotel, Whieshoots Hill, Bourton-on-the-Water, Cheltenham, Gloucestershire GL54 2LE
Tel: 01451 820387 Fax: 01451 821635   **Map Ref 2**

BUCKLAND MANOR, 13th century Cotswold manor in 10 acres, in idyllic secluded valley. Log fires, central heating. Tennis, riding and complete tranquillity.

B&B from £175, Dinner available, Rooms 8 double, 5 twin, all en-suite. Open all year.

Buckland Manor, Buckland, Broadway, Worcestershire WR12 7LY
Tel: 01386 852626 Fax: 01386 853557   **Map Ref 3**

The Cotswold stone 17th century **THE OLD RECTORY** is tucked away opposite the Church. Superb breakfasts in dining room, log fires in winter. Many places for eating close by. Specialist paint finishes in the en-suite bedrooms. 4 poster beds, TV and all facilities. Crabtree and Evelyn toiletries. Special Winter rates. Parking. Good base for walking and touring. Email: beauvoisin@btinternet.com
B&B from £32.50pp, Rooms 1 twin, 5 double, 2 family, 6 en-suite, 2 private, No smoking or pets, Children over 8, Open all year except Christmas.
Mrs E Beauvoisin, **The Old Rectory,** Church Street, Willersey, Broadway, Gloucestershire WR12 7PN
Tel: 01386 853729 Fax: 01386 858061   **Map Ref 4**

4 PITTVILLE CRESCENT, lovely Regency house with airy rooms, beautifully situated overlooking charming parkland. 5 minutes from town centre.

B&B from £17.50, Rooms 1 single, 2 twin, Open all year.

4 Pittville Crescent, Cheltenham, Gloucestershire GL52 2QZ
Tel: 01242 575567 Email: sparrey@tr250.demon.co.uk   **Map Ref 5**

MOOREND PARK HOTEL, an elegant Victorian house, recently renovated and refurbished. Ample private parking. Fine swiss orientated cuisine. Close to town centre and M5 (junction 11A).

B&B from £35, Dinner available, Rooms 1 single, 2 double, 3 twin, 2 triple, 1 family, all en-suite, Open all year.

Moorend Park Hotel, 11 Moorend Park Road, Cheltenham, Gloucestershire GL53 0LA
Tel: 01242 224441 Fax: 01242 572413   **Map Ref 5**

HOLLINGTON HOUSE HOTEL, easy to find, 700 yards from London road/A40. Plenty of free on-site parking. Victorian house, a la carte menus, licensed bar. Standards maintained by resident proprietors. Special interest tours by arrangement in our own mini-bus. Nous parlons francais. Chakap bahasa sidikit. Wir sprechan Deutsch.

B&B from £30, Dinner available, Rooms 2 single, 2 double, 1 twin, 1 triple, 3 family, all en-suite, Open all year.

Hollington House Hotel, 115 Hales Road, Cheltenham, Gloucestershire GL52 6ST
Tel: 01242 256652 Fax: 01242 570280   **Map Ref 5**

BATTLEDOWN HOTEL, a family run Grade II listed Victorian house in French colonial style within walking distance of town centre and race course. All rooms complete with beverage facilities and colour TV. Off street parking for guests at the rear of the building.

B&B from £25pp, Dinner from £11, Rooms single, 2 twin, 3 double, 1 family, most en-suite, Restricted smoking, Children welcome, No pets, Open all year.
Peter & Gay Smurthwaite, **Battledown Hotel,** 125 Hales Road, Cheltenham, Gloucestershire GL52 6ST
Tel: 01242 233881 Fax: 01242 524198   **Map Ref 5**

BEECHWORTH LAWN HOTEL, carefully modernised and well-appointed, detached Victorian hotel, set in conifer and shrub gardens. Convenient for shopping centre and all amenities.

B&B from £25, Dinner available, Rooms 2 double, 4 twin, 2 triple, most en-suite, Open all year.
Beechworth Lawn Hotel, 133 Hales Road, Cheltenham, Gloucestershire GL52 6ST
Tel: 01242 522583 Fax: 01242 522583   **Map Ref 5**

IVY DENE HOUSE HOTEL, ideal base for exploring the Cotswolds. A charming corner house in its own grounds, situated in a residential area within walking distance of the town.

B&B from £20, Rooms 3 single, 1 twin, 4 triple, 1 family, most en-suite, Open all year.
Ivy Dene House Hotel, 145 Hewlett Road, Cheltenham, Gloucestershire GL52 6TS
Tel: 01242 521726   **Map Ref 5**

ST. MICHAELS, an elegant Edwardian guesthouse offering delightful non-smoking accommodation with parking, five minutes' walk from town centre. Excellent breakfast menu and a warm welcome.

B&B from £25, Rooms 2 double, 1 twin, 2 triple, some en-suite, Open all year.
St. Michaels, 4 Montpellier Drive, Cheltenham, Gloucestershire GL50 1TX
Tel: 01242 513587 Fax: 01242 513587   **Map Ref 5**

CRESSY GUEST HOUSE, a fine friendly Edwardian home, family atmosphere. Close to town centre, restaurants and colleges and private schools. Special diets catered for. Choice of Breakfast, cooked freshly (no microwave). Non smoking bedrooms and dining room. TV lounge (smokers). M5 junction 11.
B&B from £20pp, Rooms 2 twin, 1 double, Restricted smoking, Children over 10, Pets by arrangement, Open all year.
Mrs Diane Cresswell, **Cressy Guest House,** 44 St. Stephens Road, Cheltenham, Gloucestershire GL51 5AD
Tel: 01242 525012   **Map Ref 5**

HANOVER HOUSE, well-appointed and spacious accommodation in elegant, listed Victorian Cotswold-stone house. Close to theatre, town hall, gardens and shopping facilities.

B&B from £23, Dinner available, Rooms 1 single, 3 double, 1 twin, 1 triple, some en-suite, Open all year.
Hanover House, 65 St. Georges Road, Cheltenham, Gloucestershire GL50 3DU
Tel: 01242 529867 Fax: 01242 222779   **Map Ref 5**

CENTRAL HOTEL, family-run hotel, close to town centre, shops, coach station, racecourse, cinema and theatre. Fully-licensed bar and restaurant.

B&B from £25, Dinner available, Rooms 2 single, 4 double, 6 twin, 2 triple, some en-suite, Open all year.
Central Hotel, 7-9 Portland Street, Cheltenham, Gloucestershire GL52 2NZ
Tel: 01242 582172   **Map Ref 5**

SAVOY HOTEL, located in a quiet tree-lined avenue in the prestigious Montpellier area of this Regency spa town. Excellent English restaurant. Parking.

B&B from £52, Dinner available, Rooms 16 single, 17 double, 8 twin, all en-suite. Open all year.

Savoy Hotel, Bayshill Road, Cheltenham, Gloucestershire GL50 3AS
Tel: 01242 527788 Fax: 01242 226412   **Map Ref 5**

CLARENCE COURT HOTEL

CLARENCE COURT HOTEL, once the townhouse of the Duke of Wellington this beautiful Regency hotel, overlooks gardens in a tree-lined square and is only a short stroll from the town centre. We provide free parking, a bar, TV's and hospitality trays in all our individually decorated rooms.

B&B from £27.50-£33.50pp, Dinner from £10, Rooms 6 single, 9 twin, 4 double, 2 family, all en-suite, Children welcome, Pets by arrangement, Open all year.
Brian & Susan Howe, **Clarence Court Hotel,** Clarence Square, Cheltenham, Gloucestershire GL50 4JR
Tel: 01242 580411 Fax: 01242 229609   **Map Ref 5**

....

LONSDALE HOUSE, Regency house situated 5 minutes' walk from the town hall, Promenade, shopping centre, parks and theatre. Easy access to main routes.

B&B from £19, Rooms 4 single, 2 double, 1 twin, 2 triple, 1 family, some en-suite, Open all year.
Lonsdale House, Montpellier Drive, Cheltenham, Gloucestershire GL50 1TX
Tel: 01242 232379 Fax: 01242 232379   **Map Ref 5**

....

CARLTON HOTEL, in quiet, first class position, 250 yards from famous Promenade and award-winning parks. Emphasis on traditional friendly service. Tasteful bedrooms offer today's guest all modern comforts. Excellent restaurant and bar facilities.

B&B from £40, Dinner available, Rooms 16 single, 16 double, 43 twin, all en-suite, Open all year.
Carlton Hotel, Parabola Road, Cheltenham, Gloucestershire GL50 3AQ
Tel: 01242 514453 Fax: 01242 226487   **Map Ref 5**

....

STRETTON LODGE HOTEL, nestling in the heart of Cheltenham, a family-managed Victorian hotel with parking. Home-cooked dinners and personal service ensure a relaxing stay.

B&B from £30, Dinner available, Rooms 1 single, 2 double, 1 twin, 1 triple, all en-suite, Open all year.
Stretton Lodge Hotel, Western Road, Cheltenham, Gloucestershire GL50 3RN
Tel: 01242 570771 Fax: 01242 528724   **Map Ref 5**

....

MILTON HOUSE, beautiful Regency listed building with individually styled spacious bedrooms, set among tree-lined avenues, only 4 minutes stroll from promenade.

B&B from £38.50, Dinner available, Rooms 2 single, 3 double, 1 twin, 2 triple, all en-suite, Open all year.
Milton House, 12 Royal Parade, Bayshill Road, Cheltenham, Gloucestershire GL50 3AY
Tel: 01242 582601 Fax: 01242 222326   **Map Ref 5**

....

THE FROGMILL, a magnificent building set in 5 acres by the River Coln. Turning ornamental waterwheel in the garden. 4 miles from Cheltenham, 9 miles from Gloucester.

B&B from £39, Dinner available, Rooms 6 double, 6 twin, 4 family, all en-suite, Open all year.
The Frogmill, Shipton Oliffe, Andoversford, Cheltenham, Gloucestershire GL54 4HT
Tel: 01242 820547 Fax: 01242 820237   **Map Ref 6**

....

BARN END, large, spacious and comfortable detached house. Convenient for Cheltenham (4 miles) and its racecourse (2 miles), also Tewkesbury, Stratford and Cotswolds. Horse Riding, walking and golf on Cleeve Common (1 mile)

B&B from £38, Rooms 1 double, 2 twin, 1 en-suite, Open all year.
Barn End, 23 Cheltenham Road, Bishops Cleeve, Cheltenham, Gloucestershire GL52 4LU
Tel: 01242 672404   **Map Ref 7**

THE CHELTENHAM PARK HOTEL, stylish Regency hotel in own colourful gardens in the heart of the Cotswolds. On the edge of Cheltenham, the hotel enjoys splendid views over the adjoining golf course and Cotswold Hills. Leisure club with pool, spa bath, steam room, sauna and gyms.

B&B from £90, Dinner available, Rooms 17 single, 58 double, 68 twin, 2 family, all en-suite, Open all year.
The Cheltenham Park Hotel, Cirencester Road, Charlton Kings, Cheltenham, Gloucestershire GL53 8EA
Tel: 01242 222021 Fax: 01242 254880 **Map Ref 8**

....

CHARLTON KINGS HOTEL, 2.5 miles from town centre in an area of outstanding beauty. Friendly staff, interesting menus and quality accommodation.

B&B from £35.50, Dinner available, Rooms 2 single, 8 double, 2 twin, 1 triple, 1 family, all en-suite, Open all year.
Charlton Kings Hotel, London Road, Charlton Kings, Cheltenham, Gloucestershire GL52 6UU
Tel: 01242 231061 Fax: 01242 241900 **Map Ref 8**

....

RISING SUN HOTEL, spectacular hilltop location with panoramic Cotswold views, close to race course and golf course. Ideal for exploring the Cotswolds.

B&B from £36.50, Dinner available, Rooms 3 single, 15 double, 6 twin, all en-suite, Open all year.
Rising Sun Hotel, Cleeve Hill, Cheltenham, Gloucestershire GL52 3PX
Tel: 01242 676281 Fax: 01242 673069 **Map Ref 9**

....

NORTHFIELD BED & BREAKFAST, detached family house in the country with large gardens and home-grown produce. Excellent centre for visiting the Cotswolds and close to local services.

B&B from £26, Dinner available, Rooms 1 double, 2 family, all en-suite, Open all year.
Northfield Bed & Breakfast, Cirencester Road, Northleach, Cheltenham, Gloucestershire GL54 3JL
Tel: 01451 860427 Email: nrth-fieldo@aol.com **Map Ref 10**

....

COTTESWOLD HOUSE, relax in our 400 year old Cotswold stone wealthy wool merchants home. Luxury private suite or en-suite double rooms - all spacious, elegant and well-equipped. Ideal touring base. AA 4Q's selected. ETB 3 Crown Commended. No smoking.

B&B from £22.50-£35pp, Rooms 1 twin, 2 double, all en-suite, No smoking, children or pets, Open all year except Christmas & New Year.
Graham & Elaine Whent, **Cotteswold House,** Market Place, Northleach, Cheltenham, Gloucestershire GL54 3EG
Tel: 01451 860493 Fax: 01451 860493 **Map Ref 10**

....

MARKET HOUSE, a 400 year old house of 'old worlde' charm and characterised by exposed beams and inglenook fireplace, yet with modern facilities, washbasins, central heating, tea/coffee facilities and touring guides. Located in an unspoilt tiny town, amidst a selection of inns and restaurants, surrounded by beautiful countryside.

B&B from £19pp, Rooms 2 single, 1 twin, 1 double en-suite, No smoking Children over 12, Open February - November.
Mike & Theresa Eastman, **Market House,** The Square, Northleach, Cheltenham, Gloucestershire GL54 3EJ
Tel: 01451 860557 **Map Ref 10**

....

REGENCY HOUSE HOTEL, restored Regency house in a quiet Georgian square. Near Pittville Park, but only minutes' walk from all town centre amenities.

B&B from £34, Dinner available, Rooms 5 double,3 triple, all en-suite, Open all year.

Regency House Hotel, 50 Clarence Square, Pittville, Cheltenham, Gloucestershire GL50 4JR
Tel: 01242 582718 Fax: 01242 262697 Email: regency1.demon.co.uk **Map Ref 5**

THE PRESTBURY HOUSE HOTEL & RESTAURANT, 300-year-old Georgian country manor house set in 4 acres of secluded grounds beneath Cleeve Hill. Only 1 mile from Cheltenham centre.

B&B from £70, Dinner available, Rooms 1 single, 10 double, 6 twin, all en-suite, Open all year.
The Prestbury House Hotel & Restaurant, The Burgage, Prestbury, Cheltenham, Gloucestershire GL52 3DN
Tel: 01242 529533 Fax: 01242 227076 **Map Ref 11**

....

WHITE HOUSE HOTEL, peacefully located hotel, just a few minutes' drive from Cheltenham or Gloucester city centre. Ideal base for Cotswolds.

B&B from £40, Dinner available, Rooms 1 single, 6 double, 37 twin, 3 triple, 2 family, all en-suite, Open all year.
White House Hotel, Gloucester Road, Staverton, Cheltenham, Gloucestershire GL51 0ST
Tel: 01452 713226 Fax: 01452 857590 **Map Ref 12**

....

MALT HOUSE, listed 16th Century Cotswold home set in 7.5 acres of secluded gardens. Bedrooms individually decorated, four-poster room available. Public rooms furnished with English antiques and with log fires. Noted restaurant serving table d'hote evening menu.

B&B from £49.50, Dinner available, Rooms 4 double, 3 twin, 1 triple, all en-suite. Open all year.

Malt House, Broad Campden, Chipping Campden, Gloucestershire GL55 6UU
Tel: 01386 840295 Fax: 01386 841334 **Map Ref 13**

....

THREE WAYS HOUSE, Cotswold village hotel close to Chipping Campden, Broadway and Stratford-upon-Avon. Comfortable bedrooms, cosy bar, good food and friendly service. Known a "Home of the pudding club" for many years.

B&B from £60, Dinner available, Rooms 3 single, 14 double, 19 twin, 3 triple, 2 family, all en-suite, Open all year.
Three Ways House, Chapel Lane, Mickleton, Chipping Campden, Gloucestershire GL55 6SB
Tel: 01386 438429 Fax: 01386 438118 **Map Ref 14**

....

WARWICK COTTAGE GUEST HOUSE, an attractive Victorian town house, 5 minutes from the town centre. Good base for touring the Cotswolds. Bargain breaks available.

B&B from £32, Dinners available, Rooms 2 double, 2 triple, most en-suite, Open all year.

Warwick Cottage Guest House, 75 Victoria Road, Cirencester Gloucestershire GL7 1ES
Tel: 01285 656279 **Map Ref 15**

....

KING'S HEAD HOTEL, a comfortable town centre hotel (historic coaching inn) with old world charm, secret passage. English cuisine, Lift and night porter.

B&B from £75, Dinner available, Rooms 15 single, 20 double, 26 twin, 2 triple, 3 family, all en-suite, Open all year.
King's Head Hotel, Market Place, Cirencester, Gloucestershire GL7 2NR
Tel: 01285 653322 Fax: 01285 655103 **Map Ref 15**

....

CROWN OF CRUCIS, privately owned traditional Cotswold hotel with elegant bedrooms. Quiet riverside location, 2 miles east of Cirencester on A417. Excellent local reputation for quality food and service.

B&B from £39, Dinner available, Rooms 9 double, 16 twin, all en-suite, Open all year.

Crown of Crucis, Ampney Crucis, Cirencester, Gloucestershire GL7 5RS
Tel: 01285 851806 Fax: 01285 851735 **Map Ref 16**

THE SWAN HOTEL, deluxe family-run hotel, with riverside gardens, cosy parlours, noted restaurant, sumptuous bedrooms all with extravagant bathrooms (3 with four-posters and jacuzzi). Centrally located for touring the Cotswolds, Stratford, Oxford and Bath.

B&B from £97, Dinner available, Rooms 13 double, 4 twin, 1 family, all en-suite, Open all year.
The Swan Hotel, Bibury, Cirencester, Gloucestershire GL7 5NW
Tel: 01285 740695 Fax: 01285 740473   **Map Ref 17**

THE ELIOT ARMS HOTEL, we have retained the character of a traditional coaching inn and added modern hotel facilities to all rooms, add to this meals of the finest quality fine kept beers, wines and over 100 malt whiskeys. Riverside gardens and patio. Log fires in winter. A word wide reputation for hospitality. Two and a half mile from Cirencester.
B&B from £26.25pp, Dinner from £5.95, Rooms 1 single, 4 twin, 5 double, 2 suites, all en-suite, Children welcome, Pets by arrangement, Open all year.
Linda & Duncan Hickling, **The Eliot Arms Hotel,** Clarks Hay, South Cerney, Cirencester, Gloucestershire GL7 5UA
Tel: 01285 860215 Fax: 01285 861121   **Map Ref 18**

GOLDEN FARM INN, situated in the heart of the Cotswolds. 17th Century former farmhouse with large gardens, car park, patio and function room. Skittles, darts, pool. 10 minutes walk from Cirencester. Surrounded by activities of all types. Rooms all have TV and tea/coffee. http://www.s-h-systems.co.uk/hotels/goldenfr.html Email:RFealmarti@aol.com
B&B from £18pp, Dinner from £2.50, Rooms 1 single, 2 twin, 2 double/family, Children & Pets welcome, Open all year except Christmas Day & Boxing Day.
Bob & Barbara Feal-Martinez, **Golden Farm Inn,** Upper Churnside, Cirencester, Gloucestershire GL7 1AR
Tel: 01285 652927 Fax: 01285 657011   **Map Ref 19**

FOREST HOUSE HOTEL, 18th century listed former home of industrial steel pioneers. Spacious, comfortable rooms, imaginative cuisine. Close to town centre. Ideal touring/outdoor pursuits base.

B&B from £17, Dinner available, Rooms 2 single, 3 double, 2 twin, some en-suite, Open all year.

Forest House Hotel, Cinder Hill, Coleford, Gloucestershire GL16 8HQ
Tel: 01594 832424   **Map Ref 20**

WYNDHAM ARMS, stay free on Sundays in this historic hotel. Under the competent management of the Stanford family since 1973.

B&B from £52.50, Dinner available, Rooms 2 single, 4 double, 9 twin, 2 triple, all en-suite, Open all year.

Wyndham Arms, Clearwell, Coleford, Gloucestershire GL16 8JT
Tel: 01594 433666 Fax: 01594 836450   **Map Ref 21**

FROGFURLONG COTTAGE, built in 1812 is situated in the Gloucestershire green belt surrounded by fields. The accommodation is totally self-contained and comprises a double room with luxury en-suite bathroom and jacuzzi. Facilities include TV, tea/coffee tray and heated indoor swimming pool. Ample parking.

B&B from £18pp, Dinner from £10.50, Rooms 1 double en-suite, No smoking, children or pets, Open all year except Christmas.

Clive & Anna Rooke, **Frogfurlong Cottage,** Frogfurlong Lane, Down Hatherley, Gloucestershire GL2 9QE
Tel: 01452 730430   **Map Ref 22**

BURROWS COURT, 18th century country house in idyllic setting. Peaceful, quiet and relaxing. Exposed beams, acre of gardens. Ideal for Cotswolds and Bath.

B&B from £29, Dinner available, Rooms 3 double, 1 twin, 2 triple, all en-suite, Open all year.
Burrows Court, Nibley Green, North Nibley, Dursley, Gloucestershire GL11 6AZ
Tel: 01453 546230   **Map Ref 23**

BULL HOTEL, a 15th century family-run Cotswold hotel with a la carte restaurant. Rooms with private facilities, TV, teasmaid, telephone. Private fishing.

B&B from £29.50, Dinner available, Rooms 3 single, 13 double, 5 twin, 1 family, most en-suite, Open all year.
Bull Hotel, Market Place, Fairford, Gloucestershire GL7 4AA
Tel: 01285 712535 Fax: 01285 713782   **Map Ref 24**

DENMARK HOTEL, small family hotel close to city centre.

B&B from £21, Dinner available, Rooms 7 single, 2 double, 1 triple, some en-suite, Open all year.
Denmark Hotel, 36 Denmark Road, Gloucester, Gloucestershire GL1 3JQ
Tel: 01452 303808   **Map Ref 25**

ROTHERFIELD HOUSE HOTEL, an elegant Victorian detached property in quiet side road location, 1 mile from city centre and minutes from M5. Family business. Choice of freshly cooked dishes.

B&B from £22, Dinner available, Rooms 8 single, 2 double, 1 twin, 2 triple, some en-suite, Open all year.
Rotherfield House Hotel, 5 Horton Road, Gloucester, Gloucestershire GL1 3PX
Tel: 01452 410500 Fax: 01452 381922   **Map Ref 25**

THE BLACK SWAN, is 250m from the historic docks in the city centre, close to Blackfriars and the beautiful cathedral. It has private car parking and is C.A.M.R.A. Recommended. All rooms are en-suite with televisions. ETB Three Crowns facilities.

B&B Single - £35pp, Twin/Double - £50pp, Dinner from £4, Rooms 13 twin, 4 double, 2 family, all en-suite, Children welcome, No pets, Open all year.
Bob Keech, **The Black Swan,** 68-70 Southgate Street, Gloucester, Gloucestershire, GL1 2DR
Tel: 01452 523642 Fax: 01452 308840   **Map Ref 25**

HETHERLEY MANOR HOTEL, a beautiful hotel in 37 acre with notable restaurant. Mini-breaks available. Ideal base for visiting Cotswolds and Cheltenham.

B&B from £35, Dinner available, Rooms 8 single, 43 double, 5 twin, all en-suite, Open all year.

Hetherley Manor Hotel, Down Hatheley Lane, Gloucester, Gloucestershire GL2 9QA
Tel: 01452 730217 Fax: 01452 731032   **Map Ref 25**

CHELTENHAM/GLOUCESTER MOAT HOUSE, recently built hotel with leisure facilities, set in extensive landscaped grounds. Directly accessible from M5, junction 11a.

B&B from £48, Dinner available, Rooms 55 double, 41 twin, all en-suite, Open all year.

Cheltenham/Gloucester Moat House, Shurdington Road, Brockworth, Gloucester, Gloucestershire GL3 4PB
Tel: 01452 519988 Fax: 01452 519977   **Map Ref 26**

BROOKTHORPE LODGE, this handsome three storey Georgian licensed guest house is three miles from Gloucester at the foot of the Cotswold Scarp on A4173. Excellent accommodation, TV and tea/coffee facilities in all rooms. Most with en-suite. Guest lounge, private parking, all diets catered for. Smoking restricted to conservatory please.
B&B from £20pp, Dinner from £9.50, Rooms 3 single, 3 twin, 2 double, 2 family, 1 4-poster, most en-suite, Restricted smoking, Children welcome, Open all year.
Judith Cockroft, **Brookthorpe Lodge,** Stroud Road, Brookthorpe, Gloucester GL4 0UQ
Tel: 01452 812645 Fax: 01452 812645   **Map Ref 27**

....

JARVIS GLOUCESTER HOTEL & COUNTRY CLUB, hotel and country club specialising in golf, skiing and leisure facilities, within the boundaries of the Roman city of Gloucester. Convenient for touring the Cotswolds and the Wye Valley.

B&B from £45, Dinner available, Rooms 9 single, 34 double, 57 twin, 7 triple, all en-suite, Open all year.
Jarvis Gloucester Hotel & Country Club, Matson Lane, Robinswood Hill, Gloucester GL4 6EA
Tel: 01452 525653 Fax: 01452 307212   **Map Ref 25**

....

TUDOR ARMS LODGE, recently-built lodge adjoining a 18th century freehouse, alongside Gloucester and Sharpness Canal. Renowned Slimbridge wildfowl and Wetlands Trust Centre only 800 yards away.

B&B from £34, Dinner available, Rooms 4 double, 5 twin, 2 triple, 1 family, all en-suite, Open all year.
Tudor Arms Lodge, Shepherds Patch, Slimbridge, Gloucester GL2 7BP
Tel: 01453 890306 Fax: 01453 890103   **Map Ref 25**

....

PEMBURY GUEST HOUSE, licensed family-run detached house, close to ski-slope and golfing facilities. Ideal base for Cotswolds, Gloucester Docks and cathedral.

B&B from £18, Dinner available, Rooms 1 single, 4 double, 3 twin, 2 triple, some en-suite, Open all year.
Pembury Guest House, 9 Pembury Road, St. Barnabas, Gloucester GL4 9UE
Tel: 01452 521856 Fax: 01452 303418   **Map Ref 25**

....

NOTLEY HOUSE, a family owned beamed property offering comfortable accommodation at realistic prices. ETB 3 Crown Commended. Ideal for Gloucester, Regency Cheltenham and the Cotswolds. Tea/coffee facilities, colour TV, clock radios and car parking. Self-contained 2 level Coach House with four-poster bedroom, bathroom, separate lounge and fitted kitchen.
B&B from £20pp, Dinner from £11.50, Rooms 1 single, 2 twin, 3 double, 1 family, all en-suite, No smoking, Children welcome, Pets by arrangement, Open all year.
Sara & Simon Wright, **Notley House,** 93 Hucclecote Road, Hucclecote, Gloucestershire GL3 3TR
Tel: 01452 611584 Fax: 01452 371229   **Map Ref 28**

....

Attractive village on the River Thames. Family run **CAMBRAI LODGE** is close to River, garden. Ample off road parking. Burford A361, 5 miles Swindon, A361 12 miles. Ideal base for touring the Cotswolds. Nearby is Kemscott Manor with its William Morris furnishing and the 18th century Buscot House
B&B from £19pp, Rooms 2 single, 1 twin, 1 double, 1 family, some en-suite, Restricted smoking, Children welcome, Pets by arrangement, Open all year.
Mr Titchener, **Cambrai Lodge,** Oak Street, Lechlade, Gloucestershire GL7 3AY
Tel: 01367 253173 Mobile: 0860 150467   **Map Ref 29**

INN HOTEL, situated in a tranquil riverside setting, offering a comfortable blend of traditional hospitality and all modern advantages. Private parking.

B&B from £40, Dinner available, Rooms 2 single, 16 double, 1 2 twin, all en-suite, Open all year.

New Inn Hotel, Market Square, Lechlade-on-Thames, Lechlade, Gloucestershire GL7 3AB

Tel: 01367 252296 Fax: 01367 252315 **Map Ref 29**

THE FLORENCE COUNTRY HOTEL, overlooking the River Wye at Bigsweir, in 5 acres of woodland. Area of outstanding beauty. Adjacent to Offa's Dyke path.

B&B from £30, Dinner available, Rooms 1 single, 2 double, 1 twin, 1 triple, all en-suite, Open all year.

The Florence Country Hotel, Bigsweir, St. Briavels, Lower Wye Valley, Gloucestershire GL15 6QQ

Tel: 01594 530830 **Map Ref 30**

MORETON HOUSE, family-run w providing full English breakfast and optional evening meal. Tea shop, open 6 days a week, lounge bar with restaurant. Ideal for touring the Cotswolds. Children and dogs welcome.

B&B from £22, Dinner available, Rooms 2 single, 7 double, 2 twin, most en-suite, Open all year.

Moreton House, Moreton-in-Marsh, Gloucestershire GL56 0LQ

Tel: 01608 650747 Fax: 01608 652747 **Map Ref 31**

TOWNEND COTTAGE & COACH HOUSE, A warm welcome is guaranteed in our 17th century cottage and coach house. Rooms are beamed with distinct character. Heart of Cotswolds. Rooms have TV, tea/coffee facilities. Large gardens. Car parking. Licensed plus tea rooms. Easy access to Stratford, Stow, Broadway. Families are welcome.

B&B from £19pp, Rooms 1 twin, 2 double, 1 family, all en-suite/private bathroom, Restricted smoking, Children welcome, No pets, Open all year.

Chris & Jenny Gant, **Townend Cottage & Coach House,** High Street, Moreton-in-Marsh, Gloucestershire GL56 0AD

Tel: 01608 650846 **Map Ref 31**

BLUE CEDAR HOUSE, an attractive detached residence set in half-acre garden in the Cotswolds, with pleasantly decorated, well-equipped accommodation and garden room. Complementary tea/coffee. Close to village centre.

B&B from £19, Dinner available, Rooms 1 single, 1 double, 1 twin, 1 family, some en-suite, Open all year.

Blue Cedar House, Stow Road, Moreton-in-Marsh, Gloucestershire GL56 0DW

Tel: 01608 650299 **Map Ref 31**

HORSE & GROOM INN, 16th century old world character inn off A436. In quiet village yet only 2 miles from Stow-on-the-Wold and close to the motorway and trunk roads. En-suite rooms, lunchtime and evening meals. Families welcome.

B&B from £40, Dinner available, Rooms 5 double, 2 twin, all en-suite, Open all year,

Horse & Groom Inn, Upper Oddington, Moreton-in-Marsh, Gloucestershire GL56 0XH

Tel: 01451 830584 Fax: 01451 870494 **Map Ref 32**

OLD COURT HOTEL, magnificent Manor House set in delightful one acre walled gardens. Elegant public rooms retain many period features. All bedrooms en-suite with tea/coffee, telephone, colour TV, radio, etc. The four-poster room is perfect for special occasions. Georgian Restaurant offers superb cuisine. Nearby Wine tasting, Falconry. Walking. ETB 3 Crown.

B&B from £22.50pp, Dinner from £13.75, Rooms 1 twin, 3 double, 1 family, all en-suite, Children welcome, Pets by arrangement. Open all year except Christmas & New Year.

Ron & Sue Wood, **Old Court Hotel,** 26 Church Street, Newent, Gloucestershire GL18 1AB

Tel: 01531 820522 **Map Ref 33**

GEORGE HOTEL, family-run 17th century coaching house in Newent town centre, offering bed and breakfast and extensive bar and restaurant menus. In Good Beer Guide.

B&B from £18, Dinner available, Rooms 2 double, 5 twin, 2 triple, some en-suite, Open all year.
George Hotel, Church Street Newent, Gloucestershire GL18 1PU
Tel: 01531 820203 Fax: 01531 822899 **Map Ref 33**

....

CROSS HANDS HOTEL, two miles from M4 (exit 18) towards Stroud. In 6 acres, with garden and orchard. A la carte restaurant and large meeting rooms with private bar for over 100 delegates.

B&B from £35, Dinner available, Rooms 9 single, 6 twin, 9 double, most en-suite, No smoking, Children welcome, Open all year.
Cross Hands Hotel, Old Sodbury, Gloucestershire BS17 6RJ
Tel: 01454 313000 Fax: 01454 324409 **Map Ref 34**

....

CROSS HANDS HOTEL, two miles from M4 (exit 18) towards Stroud. In 6 acres, with garden and orchard. A la carte restaurant and large meeting rooms with private bar for over 100 delegates.

B&B from £35, Dinner available, Rooms 9 single, 6 twin, 9 double, most en-suite, No smoking, Children welcome, Open all year.
Cross Hands Hotel, Old Sodbury, Gloucestershire BS17 6RJ
Tel: 01454 313000 Fax: 01454 324409 **Map Ref 34**

....

A warm welcome awaits at **SODBURY HOUSE HOTEL** where service and quality are important. Set in attractive grounds on the Cotswolds edge. 12 miles from Bristol and Bath, an ideal base to explore the area. The well appointed rooms include colour TV, radio, welcome tray, hair dryer and trouser press. Residential license.
B&B from £29.50pp sharing double room, Rooms 6 single, 2 twin, 3 double, 2 family, all en-suite, Restricted smoking, Open all year except Xmas & New Year.
David & Margaret Warren, **Sodbury House Hotel,** Badminton Road, Old Sodbury, Gloucestershire BS17 6LU
Tel: 01454 312847 Fax: 01454 273105 **Map Ref 34**

....

RANGEWORTHY COURT HOTEL, a 17th century country manor house with relaxing, peaceful atmosphere and popular restaurant. Less than 20 minutes from M4, M5 and Bristol.

B&B from £42, Dinner available, Rooms 3 single, 2 twin, 7 double, 2 triple, all en-suite, Children welcome, Open all year.

Rangeworthy Court Hotel, Church Lane, Wotton Road, Rangeworthy, Gloucestershire BS37 7ND
Tel: 01454 228347 Fax: 01454 228945 **Map Ref 35**

....

ROSE & CROWN INN, a300 year old inn, in quiet Cotswold village, close to Cotswold Way. Easy access to M4 and M5.

B&B from £30, Rooms 1 double, 3 triple, most en-suite, Open all year.
Rose & Crown Inn, Nympsfield, Stonehouse, Gloucestershire GL10 3TU
Tel: 01453 860240 Fax: 01453 860240 Email: roseandcrowninn@btinternet **Map Ref 36**

....

FOSSE MANOR HOTEL, rurally located Cotswold manor house in beautiful gardens. Tastefully decorated throughout. Elegant restaurant serving traditional and continental cuisine. Central to all Cotswold attractions.

B&B from £57, Dinner available, Rooms 3 single, 8 double, 3 twin, 3 triple, all en-suite, Open all year.

Fosse Manor Hotel, Stow-on-the-Wold, Gloucestershire GL54 1JX
Tel: 01451 830354 Fax: 01451 832486 **Map Ref 37**

CORSHAM FIELD FARMHOUSE, 100-acre mixed farm. Homely farmhouse with breathtaking views. Ideally situated for exploring the Cotswolds. En-suite and standard rooms. TV's , guest lounge, tea/coffee facilities. Good food pub 5 minutes' walk away.

B&B from £15, Rooms 2 double, 2 twin, 3 family, most en-suite, Open all year.

Corsham Field Farmhouse, Bledington Road, Stow-on-the-Wold, Gloucestershire GL54 1JH
Tel: 01451 831750   **Map Ref 37**

....

THE LIMES, is a large Victorian house with lovely scenery all around. All our rooms are very comfortable with tea/coffee facilities, hair dryers, Sky TV, and lovely breakfast room and guests' lounge. Where 4 minutes to town centre and very central of place to visit in the Cotswold's.

B&B from £17.50pp, Rooms 2 twin, 4 double, 1 family, all en-suite, Children & pets welcome, Open all year except Christmas & New Year.

Helen & Graham Keyte, **The Limes,** Evesham Road, Stow-on-the-Wold, Gloucestershire GL54 1EJ
Tel: 01451 830034   **Map Ref 37**

....

FARMERS LODGE HOTEL & RESTAURANT, new, privately owned and operated budget lodge in Central Cotswold location. Adjoining bar and restaurant.

B&B from £45, Dinner available, Rooms 9 double, 4 twin, 5 family, all en-suite, Open all year.

Farmers Lodge Hotel & Restaurant, Fosse Way, Stow-on-the-Wold, Gloucestershire GL54 1JX
Tel: 01451 870539 Fax: 01451 870639   **Map Ref 37**

....

OLD FARMHOUSE HOTEL, sympathetically converted 16th Century Cotswold-stone farmhouse in a quiet hamlet, 1 mile west of Stow-on-the-Wold. Warm and unpretentious hospitality.

B&B from £20, Dinner available, Rooms 7 double, 4 twin, 2 family, most en-suite, Open all year.

Old Farmhouse Hotel, Lower Swell, Stow-on-the-Wold, Gloucestershire GL54 1LF
Tel: 01451 830232 Fax: 01451 870962 Email: oldfarm@globalnet.co.uk   **Map Ref 38**

....

GRAPEVINE HOTEL, exceptional small hotel in antique centre of Cotswolds. Accent on food and hospitality. Lovely furnishings complement the romantic, vine-clad conservatory restaurant.

B&B from £80, Dinner available, Rooms 3 single, 7 double, 10 twin, 2 triple, all en-suite, Open all year.

Grapevine Hotel, Sheep Street, Stow-on-the-Wold, Gloucestershire GL54 1AU
Tel: 01451 830344 Fax: 01451 832278   **Map Ref 37**

....

UNICORN HOTEL, 17th century coaching inn, well placed for touring the Cotswolds. Its hospitality is second to none, with an award-winning restaurant. The inn is full of old world charm.

B&B from £54, Dinners available, Rooms 2 single, 14 double, 4 twin, all en-suite, Open all year.

Unicorn Hotel, Sheep Street, Stow-on-the-Wold, Gloucestershire GL54 1HQ
Tel: 01451 830257 Fax: 01451 831090   **Map Ref 37**

STOW LODGE HOTEL, family-run, Grade II listed manor house in pretty gardens overlooking market square. Open fires in bar and lounge, en-suite comfortably furnished bedrooms, candlelit restaurant with interesting wine list, private car park.

B&B from £45, Dinner available, Rooms 1 single, 9 double, 9 twin, 2 triple, all en-suite, Open all year.

Stow Lodge Hotel, The Square, Stow-on-the-Wold, Gloucestershire GL54 1AB
Tel: 01451 830485 Fax: 01451 831671   **Map Ref 37**

....

AULD STOCKS HOTEL, 17th century Grade II listed hotel facing quiet village green on which the original penal stocks still stands. Refurbished to combine modern comforts and original charm and character. Friendly and caring staff make this an ideal base for exploring the Cotswolds.

B&B from £37, Dinner available, Rooms 1 single, 14 double, 2 twin, 1 triple, all en-suite, Open all year.

Auld Stocks Hotel, The Square, Stow-on-the-Wold, Gloucestershire GL54 1AF
Tel: 01451 830666 Fax: 01451 870014   **Map Ref 37**

....

WOODLANDS, a luxurious small guest house set in a quarter acre of gardens. In quaint Cotswold village with breathtaking views over lake and hills. All bedrooms are en-suite with colour TV and tea/coffee making facilities. There is a lounge for guests where light snacks are served. Ample car parking is available.

B&B from £26pp, Rooms 1 single, 1 twin, 3 double, all en-suite, Children & Pets welcome, Open all year.

Brian & Kathryn Sykes, **Woodlands,** Upper Swell, Stow-on-the-Wold, Gloucestershire GL54 1EW
Tel: 01451 832346   **Map Ref 39**

....

DOWNFIELD HOTEL, imposing hotel in quiet location. Home cooking. 1 mile from the town centre, 5 miles from M5 motorway, junction 13, on main A419 road.

B&B from £20, Dinner available, Rooms 4 single, 9 double, 7 twin, 1 triple, some en-suite, Open all year.

Downfield Hotel, 134 Cainscross Road, Stroud, Gloucestershire GL5 4HN
Tel: 01453 764496 Fax: 01453 753150   **Map Ref 40**

....

ASHLEIGH HOUSE, an ideal Cotswold touring centre in a peaceful setting, offering good food, cleanliness and comfort.

B&B from £21, Dinner available, Rooms 3 double, 3 twin, 3 triple, all en-suite, Open all year.

Ashleigh House, Bussage, Stroud, Gloucestershire GL6 8AZ
Tel: 01453 883944 Fax: 01453 886931   **Map Ref 41**

....

THE FALCON HOTEL, a famous old coaching inn and posting house dating from 1554, situated in the heart of the village of Painswick. Recently refurbished to very high standards, with antique furniture and many original oil paintings. Renowned restaurant.

B&B from £35, Dinner available, Rooms 2 double, 4 twin, 2 triple, most en-suite, Open all year.

The Falcon Hotel, New Street, Painswick, Stroud, Gloucestershire GL6 6UN
Tel: 01452 814222 Fax: 01452 813377   **Map Ref 42**

BELL HOTEL

BELL HOTEL, situated on the banks of the Stroudwater Canal, the hotel offers a warm, friendly welcome to all. All rooms en-suite, tea/coffee, colour TV. Full A La Carte restaurant and a wide range of bar snacks. Special offer on minimum two day breaks.

B&B from £21pp, Dinner from £6, Rooms 1 single, 4 twin, 5 double, 2 family, all en-suite, Children welcome, Pets by arrangement, Open all year.

Mr M. R. Williams, **Bell Hotel,** Wallbridge, Stroud, Gloucestershire GL5 3JS
Tel: 01453 763556 Fax: 01453 758611 **Map Ref 40**

Idyllic Tetbury, famous for antiques. Ideal base for touring the Cotswolds. **ORMONDS HEAD COACHING INN** offers twenty en-suite bedrooms, tea/coffee makers, TV's. All day bar. Grill Room. Bar food. Sunday roast. Privately owned. Lively town centre inn. Excellent value. Warm welcome. Access. VISA
B&B from £31pp, Dinner from £4.95, Rooms 2 single, 1 twin, 11 double, 4 family, all en-suite, Children welcome, Guide dogs welcome, Open all year except Christmas Day.
Lyndon & Judy Booth **Ormonds Head Coaching Inn,** Long Street, Tetbury, Gloucestershire GL8 8AA
Tel: 01666 505690 Fax: 01666 505956 **Map Ref 43**

HUNTERS HALL INN, a 16th century coaching inn with open fireplaces and beamed ceilings. The old stable block has been converted into bedrooms. Situated on the A4135 between Tetbury and Dursley.
B&B from £45, Dinner available, Rooms 6 double, 5 twin, 1 triple, all en-suite, Open all year.
Hunters Hall Inn, Kingscote, Tetbury, Gloucestershire GL8 8XZ
Tel: 01453 860393 Fax: 01453 860707 **Map Ref 44**

TAVERN HOUSE, a delightfully situated 17th century former Cotswold coaching inn. 1 mile from Westonbirt Arboretum. All rooms en-suite, direct-dial phone, TV, tea maker, hair dryer, trouser press. Guests lounge. Charming secluded walled garden. Parking. Convenient for visiting Bath, Bourton-on-the-Water, Stow, Bristol, Cheltenham. ETB Silver Award winner 1993.
B&B from £29.50pp, Rooms 1 twin, 3 double, all en-suite, Restricted smoking, Children over 10, No pets, Open all year.
Janet & Tim Tremellen, **Tavern House,** Willesley, Tetbury, Gloucestershire GL8 8QU
Tel: 01666 880444 Fax: 01666 880254 **Map Ref 45**

JESSOP HOUSE HOTEL, a Georgian house facing the abbey and mediaeval cottages, peacefully overlooking Tewkesbury's "Ham".
B&B from £55, Dinner available, Rooms 3 double, 4 twin, 1 triple, all en-suite, Open all year.
Jessop House Hotel, 65 Church Street, Tewkesbury, Gloucestershire GL20 5RZ
Tel: 01684 292017 Fax: 01684 273076 **Map Ref 46**

WOTTON GUEST HOUSE, a 17th century house nestling in a walled garden offers, TV, tea/coffee, parking, lounge, central heating. Coffee shop adjoining, lunches, coffees/tea all homemade. Towns equidistant Gloucester, Bristol and Bath. Nearby Arboretum, Slimbridge, Berkeley Castle. Views from most rooms.
B&B from £22.50pp, Rooms 2 single, 2 twin, 2 double, 1 family, all en-suite, Restricted smoking, Children & Pets welcome, Open all year.
Sandra Nixon, **Wotton Guest House,** 31a Long Street, Wotton Under Edge, Gloucestershire GL12 7BX
Tel: 01453 843158 Fax: 01453 842410 **Map Ref 47**

Hampshire & Isle of Wight

Hampshire's vital role in England's defence from sea invasion spans many centuries. In the many busy ports such as Portsmouth, Southampton and Gosport, this maritime past is depicted in museums and heritage sites. Inland, high, rolling downs dip to small villages, complete with Norman churches and thatched cottages.

In Portsmouth, historic ships, castles, forts and museums combine with the city's resort of Southsea to create an excellent holiday centre from which to explore the area. For much of England's history Portsmouth has been the traditional home of the Royal Navy and was the strongest fortress in medieval England. At its heart is Nelson's flagship, HMS Victory, and nearby the remains of the Mary Rose, Henry VIII's favourite warship, are being conserved.

Years of traditional seaside holidays have developed the city's own resort of Southsea into the grandstand of the Solent, with four miles of seafront. The New Forest occupies the south western corner of Hampshire on its border with Dorset. For centuries it was the haunt of English kings. Nova Foresta, as it was named by William the Conqueror, is still subject to the special laws which he created to protect his sport of the forest's red deer. Over nine hundred years later visitors can explore the mosaic of ancient forest and heathland that is a unique survivor of England's royal hunting forests.

On the western edge of the New Forest is the seaside town of Christchurch, the annual regatta is held in mid-August with rowing on the River Stour, displays on the quay and culminating in a spectacular fireworks display.

To the East of the town and at the entrance to Christchurch Harbour is Mudeford, a popular holiday area with sandy beaches and good watersports facilities. Basingstoke is a thriving commercial centre set in unspoilt rural North Hampshire. A large part of the borough has been designated as part of the North Wessex Downs Area of Outstanding Natural Beauty. Less than an hour away from both London and the South coast makes it a popular tourist area. To the North of Basingstoke, is Watership Down, immortalised in Richard Adams' novel of the same name.

Winchester, founded by the Romans, was King Alfred's capital and it first acquired a church in 648, and its cathedral was built nine centuries ago. The famous Arthurian Round Table, weighing well over a ton, is housed in the Great Hall, the only remaining part of Winchester's castle where the first English Parliament met. Winchester College was founded as far back as 1382.

left, Portsmouth Harbour

233

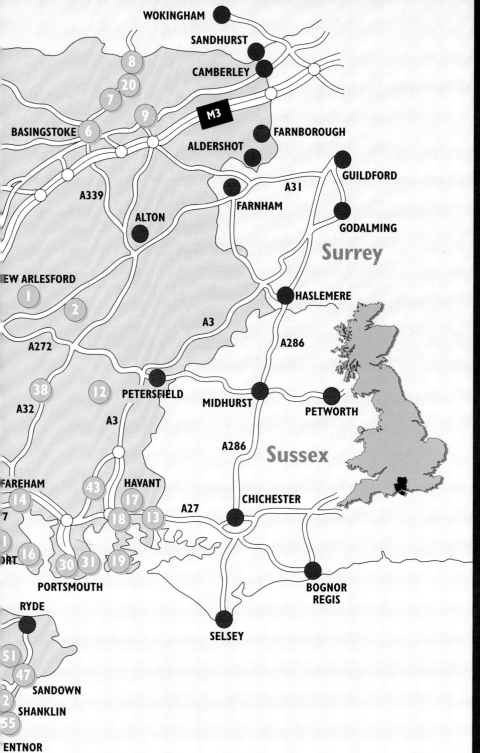

WOKINGHAM

SANDHURST

CAMBERLEY

8

20

7

9

M3

FARNBOROUGH

ALDERSHOT

BASINGSTOKE 6

A339

A31

GUILDFORD

FARNHAM

ALTON

GODALMING

EW ARLESFORD

Surrey

1

2

A272

A3

A286

HASLEMERE

A32

38

12

PETERSFIELD

MIDHURST

PETWORTH

A3

A286

Sussex

FAREHAM

HAVANT

14

43

17

CHICHESTER

18

13

A27

16

30 31 19

PORTSMOUTH

BOGNOR
REGIS

RYDE

51

47

SANDOWN

SHANKLIN

55

ENTNOR

SELSEY

THE SWAN HOTEL, warm and friendly, 18th century coaching inn.

B&B from £35, Dinner available, Rooms 1 single, 14 double, 5 twin, 3 family, all en-suite. Open all year.
The Swan Hotel, 11 West Street, Alresford, Hampshire SO24 9AD
Tel: 01962 732302 & 734427 Fax: 01962 735274   **Map Ref 1**

....

THICKETS, a spacious house in large garden with fine views. Two comfortable twin bedded rooms. Tea/coffee facilities available. Guests's sitting room with TV. Full English breakfast. Local attractions Jane Austen's House ten minutes by car. Winchester, Salisbury, Portsmouth within easy reach. Heathrow Airport one hour.

B&B from £20pp, Rooms 2 twin, both private facilities, Restricted smoking, Children over 10, No pets, Open all year except Christmas & New Year.
David & Sue Lloyd-Evans, **Thickets,** Swelling Hill, Ropley, Alresford, Hampshire SO24 0DA
Tel: 01962 772467   **Map Ref 2**

....

AMBERLEY HOTEL, a small, comfortable furnished hotel, with attractive restaurant open to non-residents. Private meetings, luncheons and wedding receptions can be booked.

B&B from £29, Dinner available, Rooms 6 single, 4 double, 5 twin, 1 triple, 1 family, some en-suite. Open all year.
Amberley Hotel, 70 Weyhill Road, Andover, Hampshire SO24 9AD
Tel: 01962 352224 Fax: 01264 392555   **Map Ref 3**

....

ASHLEY COURT HOTEL, half a mile from town centre, quietly set in nearly 3 acres of grounds. Friendly atmosphere, good restaurant, conference and air conditioned banqueting facilities.

B&B from £39.50 Dinner available, Rooms 7 single, 16 double, 12 twin, all en-suite, Open all year.

Ashley Court Hotel, Micheldever Road, Andover, Hampshire SP11 6LA
Tel: 01264 374344 Fax: 01264 356755   **Map Ref 3**

....

AMPORT INN, friendly inn in attractive Hampshire village with racecourses, riding and fishing nearby. Business people welcome weekdays. Breakaway weekends available. Sauna and indoor pool.

B&B from £27.50 Dinner available, Rooms 3 double, 4 twin, 2 triple, all en-suite, Open all year.

Amport Inn, Amport, Andover, Hampshire SP11 8AE
Tel: 01264 710371 Fax: 01264 710112   **Map Ref 5**

....

FERNBANK HOTEL, extremely well-appointed family-run hotel, full of character. In residential area within a short walk of town's facilities. Charming conservatory/lounge. First class breakfast.

B&B from £47, Rooms 8 single, 6 double, 2 twin, all en-suite, Open all year.

Fernbank Hotel, 4 Fairfields Road, Basingstoke, Hampshire RG21 3DR
Tel: 01256 321191 Fax: 01256 321191   **Map Ref 6**

....

THE CENTRE COURT HOTEL, hotel is complemented by a superb purpose-built tennis centre, including 5 indoor and 5 outdoor tennis courts, indoor heated pool, spa bath, steam room, sauna and gym.

B&B from £60, Dinner available, Rooms 24 double, 26 twin, all en-suite. Open all year.

The Centre Court Hotel, Centre Drive, Chineham, Basingstoke, Hampshire RG24 8FY
Tel: 01256 816664 Fax: 01256 816727   **Map Ref 7**

THE NEW INN, 15th Century inn set in the picturesque country side of North Hampshire, recently extended but retaining its unique character. Conference facilities and restaurant.

B&B from £42.50, Dinner available, 9 double rooms, 7 twin, all en-suite.
The New Inn, Heckfield, Basingstoke, Hampshire RG27 OLE
Tel: 0118 932 6374 Fax: 0118 932 6550   **Map Ref 8**

....

CEDAR COURT, comfortable ground floor accommodation with delightful gardens. On B3349 between the M3 and M4, 6 miles east of Basingstoke, 1 hour from London and coast.
B&B from £22, Rooms 2 single, 3 double, 1 twin, most en-suite, Open all year.
Cedar Court, Reading Road, Hook, Basingstoke, Hampshire RG27 9DB
Tel: 01256 762178 Fax: 01256 762178   **Map Ref 9**

....

RAVEN HOTEL, in Hook village, convenient for Basingstoke and Hampshire countryside. Local attractions include Birdworld and Stratfield Saye House. Weekly jazz.

B&B from £36.50, Dinner available, Rooms 2 single, 21 double, 15 twin, all en-suite. Open all year.
Raven Hotel, Station Road, Hook, Basingstoke, Hampshire RG27 9HS
Tel: 01256 762541 Fax: 01256 7686077   **Map Ref 9**

....

NEW PARK MANOR HOTEL, prestigious and romantic country house hotel, dating from 16th Century former royal hunting lodge of Charles II, set amidst New Forest parklands. Log fire ambience. Stag Head Restaurant, individually designed rooms. Horse riding, seasonal heated swimming pool, tennis court.

B&B from £75, Dinner available, Rooms 16 double, 5 twin, all en-suite. Open all year.
New Park Manor Hotel, Lyndhurst Road, Brockenhurst, Hampshire SO42 7QH
Tel: 01590 623467 Fax: 0101590 622268   **Map Ref 10**

....

THE COTTAGE HOTEL, a delightfully converted cosy oak-beamed forester's cottage, noted for comfort and service. Two minutes' walk from forest and village centre. Email: 100604.22@compuserve.com

B&B from £49, Rooms 1 single, 5 double, 1 twin, all en-suite. Open all year.

The Cottage Hotel, Sway Road, Brockenhurst, Hampshire SO42 7SH
Tel: 01590 622296 Fax: 01590 623014   **Map Ref 10**

....

DRAYTON COTTAGE, is a 200 year old flint and chalk building surrounded by fields. Antiques and oak beams, and a conservatory overlooking the garden, provide a luxurious yet cosy atmosphere. Bedrooms have TV, tea/coffee facilities and excellent beds. Views are superb and parking easy.

B&B from £20pp, Rooms 1 double/twin en-suite,1 double private facilities, Restricted smoking, No pets, Open all year except Christmas.
Joan Rockett, **Drayton Cottage,** East Meon, Hampshire GU32 1PW
Tel: 01730 823 472   **Map Ref 12**

....

JINGLES HOTEL, fully modernised and comfortably furnished Victorian house located between the South Downs and Chichester harbour.

B&B from £24, Dinner available, rooms 5 single, 5 double, 3 twin, some en-suite.
Jingles Hotel, 77 Horndean Road, Emsworth, Hampshire PO10 7PU
Tel: 01243 373755 Fax: 01243 373755   **Map Ref 13**

THE BROOKFIELD HOTEL, privately owned and run country house hotel, near the old fishing village of Emsworth and close to Chichester and its festival theatre. Bargain break rates at weekends.

B&B from £54.00 Dinner available, Rooms 5 single, 23 double, 12 twin, all en-suite. Open all year.

The Brookfield Hotel, Havant Road, Emsworth, Hampshire PO10 7LF
Tel: 01243 373363 Fax: 01243 376342 **Map Ref 13**

....

AVENUE HOUSE HOTEL, comfortable, small hotel, with charm and character, set in mature gardens. 5 minutes' walk to town centre, railway station and restaurants.

B&B from £41.50 Rooms 3 single, 8 double, 3 twin, 3 triple, all en-suite. Open all year.
Avenue House Hotel, 22 The Avenue, Fareham, Hampshire PO14 1NS
Tel: 01329 232175 Fax: 01329 232196 **Map Ref 14**

....

THE RED LION HOTEL, restored coaching inn, a Grade II listed building, in the heart of Fareham and convenient for Portsmouth and Southampton.

B&B from £24, Dinner available, Rooms, 15 Single, 18 double, 7 twin, 2 family rooms, all en-suite. Open all year.

The Red Lion Hotel, East Street, Fareham, Hampshire PO16 OBP
Tel: 01329 822640 Fax: 01329 823579 **Map Ref 14**

....

HENDLEY HOUSE, a beautiful south facing 16th century house in picturesque village with good pub to walk to. So much to visit in Hampshire, Wiltshire and Dorset. Walking and cycling in New Forest, surrounding countryside and south coast. Attractive en-suite twin and double bedroom with private bathroom.

B&B from £25pp, Rooms 1 twin, 1 double, both en-suite/private, Children over 10, No pets, Open February - November.
Mrs Pat Ratcliffe, Hendley House, Rockbourne, Fordingbridge, Hampshire SP6 3NA
Tel: 01725 518303 Fax: 01725 518546 **Map Ref 15**

....

THE MANOR HOTEL, very popular private hotel and public house. Close to Portsmouth's naval history. Midway between Fareham & Gosport.

B&B from £35, Rooms 1 single, 6 double, 1 twin, 4 triple, 2 family, most en-suite. Open all year.
The Manor Hotel, Brewers Lane, Gosport, Hampshire PO13 0JY
Tel: 01329 232946 Fax: 01329 220392 **Map Ref 16**

....

BEAR HOTEL, a hotel in a town centre location, close to shops, A27/M27, bus and rail station, Chichester and Portsmouth. Half board prices shown apply at weekends.

B&B from £33.50, Dinner available, Rooms 10 single, 25 double, 7 twin, all en-suite, Open all year.

Bear Hotel, East Street, Havant, Hampshire PO9 1AA
Tel: 01705 486501 Fax: 01705 470551 **Map Ref 17**

....

THE OLD MILL GUEST HOUSE, Georgian house in large grounds by a lake abundant in wildlife. Modernised, comfortable retreat. John Keates rested here.

B&B from £24, Rooms 1 double, 4 triple, all en-suite, Open all year.

The Old Mill Guest House, Mill Lane, Bedhampton, Havant, Hampshire PO9 3JH
Tel: 01705 454948 Fax: 01705 499677 **Map Ref 18**

NEWTOWN HOUSE HOTEL, 18th Century converted farmhouse, set in own grounds a quarter of a mile from seafront. Indoor leisure complex with heated pool, gym, steam room, jacuzzi and sauna. Tennis.

B&B from £30, Dinner available, Rooms 9 single, 9 double, 4 twin, 3 triple, all en-suite. Open all year.
Newtown House Hotel, Manor Road, Hayling Island, Hampshire PO11 0QR
Tel: 01705 466131 Fax: 01705 461366   **Map Ref 19**

....

HAYLING BAY HOTEL, seafront location with panoramic views of the Solent. All rooms have TV's, radio alarms, clocks and tea/coffee facilities. There is a guests' lounge. Licensed bar and private parking. There are various sporting facilities nearby, also the South Downs, Portsmouth historic ships and Goodwood.

B&B from £18pp, Rooms 1 single, 3 twin, 3 double, 4 family, some en-suite, Restricted smoking, Children & pets welcome, Open all year.
Mike Brassington, **Hayling Bay Hotel,** Seafront, Hayling Island, Hampshire PO11 9JE
Tel: 01705 462507 Fax: 01705 462507   **Map Ref 19**

....

THE WHITE HART HOTEL, all rooms are en-suite and have tea/coffee facilities, trouser presses, hair dryers, televisions and direct dial telephones. Home cooked meals and up to 8 real ales are served daily in the olde worlde lounge bar. Ample car parking facilities are available.

B&B from £39.50 per room, Dinner from £4.95, Rooms 2 four-poster, 6 twin, 11 double, 2 family, all en-suite, Children welcome, Pets by arrangement, Open all year.
Mr & Mrs E.A. Henderson **The White Hart Hotel,** London Road, Hook, Hampshire RG27 9DZ
Tel: 01256 762462 Fax: 01256 768351   **Map Ref 9**

....

THE WELLINGTON ARMS, a traditional coaching inn on the Duke of Wellington's estate. Situated midway between Basingstoke and Reading on the main A33. Motorway access is from junction 6 of M3 junction 11 of M4.
B&B from £50, Dinner available, Rooms 7 single, 19 double, 5 twin, 2 family, all en-suite. Open all year.
The Wellington Arms, Stratfield Turgis, Hook, Hampshire RG27 0AS
Tel: 01256 882214 Fax: 01256 882934   **Map Ref 20**

....

BELLE VUE HOTEL, modern hotel on the seafront with uninterrupted views across the Solent. Lounge Bar, fine restaurant and banqueting facilities, entertainment.

B&B from £49.50 Dinner available, Rooms 3 single, 20 double, 4 twin, all en-suite. Open all year.
Belle Vue Hotel, 39 Parade East, Lee on the Solent Hampshire PO13 9BW
Tel: 01705 550258 Fax: 01705 552624   **Map Ref 21**

....

JEVINGTON, a comfortable family home, situated in a quiet lane midway between High street/Marina. Ideal base for New Forest, solent walks, 10 minutes drive to Isle of Wight ferry. Tea/coffee facilities, TV. Off street parking. Children welcome, No smoking. Convenient for Bournemouth, Southampton, Winchester. Bike hire, sailing, walks can all be arranged.

B&B from £18pp, Rooms 1 twin, 1 double, 1 family, all en-suite, No smoking, Children & pets welcome, Open all year.
Ian & June Carruthers, **Jevington,** 47 Waterford Lane, Lymington, Hampshire SO41 3PT
Tel: 01590 672148   **Map Ref 22**

....

SOUTH LAWN HOTEL, an attractive country hotel in peaceful surroundings, where chef/proprietor ensures that food, comfort and personal service predominate.
B&B from £49, Rooms 6 double, 18 twin, all en-suite. Open all year.
South Lawn Hotel, Lymington Road, Milford-on- sea, Lymington, Hampshire SO41 ORF
Tel: 01590 643911 Fax: 01590 644820   **Map Ref 23**

COMPTON HOTEL, small, private hotel with en-suite rooms and TV. Outdoor heated swimming pool. English and vegetarian cooking. Licensed.

B&B from £26, Dinner available, Rooms 2 single, 3 double, 1 twin, 1 family room, most en-suite. Open all year.
Compton Hotel, 59 Keyhaven Road, Milford-on-Sea, Lymington, Hampshire SO41 0QX
Tel: 01590 643117   **Map Ref 23**

....

WESTOVER HALL HOTEL, a Grade II listed Victorian mansion with stunning views of Christchurch Bay and the Needles. Stylish and individual with excellent service and award winning Italian cuisine.
B&B from £55, Dinner available, Rooms 1 single, 5 double, 6 twin, all en-suite. Open all year.
Westover Hall Hotel, Park Lane, Milford-on-Sea, Lymington, Hampshire SO41 0PT
Tel: 01590 643044 Fax: 01644490   **Map Ref 23**

....

OUR BENCH, all en-suite bedrooms with TV. Indoor heated pool, jacuzzi and sauna. Non-smokers only, please. Sorry, no children. Large quiet garden. Close to forest. England for Excellence. Silver Award Winner.

B&B from £20, Dinner available, Rooms 2 double, 1 twin, all en-suite. Open all year.
Our Bench, 9 Lodge Road, Pennington, Lymington, Hampshire SO41 8HH
Tel: 01590 673141 Fax: 01590 673141 Email: ourbench@newforest.demon.co.uk   **Map Ref 24**

....

STRING OF HORSES, a unique, secluded hotel set in 4 acres in the New Forest. Individually designed bedrooms with fantasy bathrooms. Intimate candlelit restaurant.
B&B from £52.50, Dinner available, Rooms 7 en-suite double. Open all year.
String of Horses, Mead End Road, Sway, Lymington, Hampshire SO41 6EH
Tel: 01590 682631 Fax: 01590 682631   **Map Ref 25**

....

THE FOREST LODGE HOTEL

THE FOREST LODGE HOTEL, a Georgian Country House set on the outskirts of Lyndhurst village. Country style decor and attentive but friendly service makes the hotel a fine example of English hospitality. Indoor pool, delicious food, direct forest access. Breaks include tickets to local attraction. AA 2, RAC 3 Star.
B&B from £42pp, Dinner from £20.50, Rooms 7 twin, 13 double, 8 family, all en-suite, Children & pets welcome, Open all year.
Mr M Johnson, **The Forest Lodge Hotel,** Pikes Hill, Romsey Road, Lyndhurst, Hampshire SO43 7AS
Tel: 01703 283677 Fax: 01703 282940   **Map Ref 26**

....

BURWOOD LODGE, a lovely house in half-acre garden, near the village centre. All rooms with en-suite shower, WC and washbasin. Parking in grounds.
B&B from £22, Rooms 1 single, 3 double, 1 triple, 1 family, all en-suite, Open all year.
Burwood Lodge, Romsey Road, Lyndhurst, Hampshire SO43 7AA
Tel: 01703 282445 Fax: 01703 282445   **Map Ref 26**

....

THE PENNY FARTHING HOTEL, welcome to our cheerful hotel, ideally situated in Lyndhurst village centre. Hotel rooms all have en-suite facilities, colour TV, tea/coffee tray and telephones. A further four rooms available in our new "Laura Ashley" cottage Annex. Also bar, bike store and large private car park. AA, RAC, ETB.
B&B from £25-£35pp, Rooms 1 single, 1 twin, 11 double, 2 family, most en-suite, Restricted smoking, Children & pets welcome, Open all year except Christmas week.
Pauline or Mike, **The Penny Farthing Hotel,** Romsey Road, Lyndhurst, Hampshire SO43 7AA
Tel: 01703 284422 Fax: 01703 284488   **Map Ref 26**

KNIGHTWOOD LODGE, on the edge of Lyndhurst overlooking the New Forest. Facilities include an indoor health centre with spa, sauna, swimming pool and steam room. Cosy bar. Parking.

B&B from £30, Dinner available, Rooms 2 single, 9 double, 1 twin, 2 triple, all en-suite. Open all year.
Knightwood Lodge, Southampton Road, Lyndhurst, Hampshire SO43 7AA
Tel: 01703 282502 Fax: 01703 283730   **Map Ref 26**

....

FOREST GATE LODGE, a charming, large country house in the New Forest, direct access New Forest, country pubs. Restaurants. Golf courses, horse riding, theme park, wild life etc. Beverages. Satellite TV in rooms. Central for all New Forest attractions. Some en-suites. Car parking. 5 minutes walk train station.

B&B from £17pp, Rooms ??single, ??double, ??twin, ?? family, Open January - November.
Forest Gate Lodge, 161 Lyndhurst Road, Ashurst, New Forest, Hampshire SO40 7AW
Tel: 01703 293026   **Map Ref 27**

....

CHEWTON FLEN HOTEL, HEALTH & COUNTRY CLUB, a house of Georgian origin with unobtrusive additions and high standard of interior decoration. Set in 70 acres of parkland.

B&B from £210, Dinner available, Rooms 52 double suites, all en-suite. Open all year.
Chewton Flen Hotel, Health & Country Club, Christchurch Road, New Milton, Hampshire BH25 6QS
Tel: 01425 275341 Fax: 01425 272310   **Map Ref 28**

....

THE OLD COASTGUARD HOTEL, peaceful cliff top hotel close to the New Forest, with excellent cuisine and personal service in a friendly atmosphere. Some ground floor rooms.

B&B from £22, Dinner available, Rooms 1 single, 3 double, 3 twin, all en-suite. Open all year.
The Old Coastguard Hotel, 53 Marine Drive East, Barton on Sea, New Milton, Hampshire BH25 7DX
Tel: 01425 612987 Fax: 01425 612987   **Map Ref 29**

....

FORTITUDE COTTAGE, a charming quayside cottage at entrance to Portsmouth harbour. All bedrooms immaculately maintained, and attractively furnished, each with en-suite/private bathrooms, TV, tea/coffee facilities. Breakfast room overlooking fishing quay. Waterbus 100 yards away, takes 5 minutes to HMS Victory Mary Rose and HMS Warrior. Car park opposite £2 per day. Restaurants nearby.

B&B from £23pp, Rooms 2 twin, 1 double, all en-suite, No smoking or pets, Children over 8, Open all year except Christmas.

Mrs C A. Harbeck, **Fortitude Cottage,** 51 Broad Street, Old Portsmouth, Hampshire PO1 2JD
Tel: 01705 823748 Fax: 01705 823748   **Map Ref 30**

....

LANGRISH HOUSE, delightful old English manor house with panoramic views set in 13 acres of beautiful countryside. Idyllic country walks and 7 golf-courses nearby.

B&B from £35, Dinner available, Rooms 6 single, 6 double, 6 twin, all en-suite. Open all year.
Langrish House, Langrish, Petersfield, Hampshire GU32 1RN
Tel: 01730 266941 Fax: 01730 260543   **Map Ref 31**

....

SALLY PORT INN, a 16th Century timber-framed inn, with a charming atmosphere of bygone days. Situated opposite the cathedral in the heart of the "old" city. Nearby are museums, promenades and historic ships.

B&B from £32, Dinner available, Rooms 4 single, 3 double, 2 twin, 1 triple, most en-suite. Open all year.

Sally Port Inn, 57-58 High Street, Portsmouth, Hampshire PO1 2LU
Tel: 01705 821860 Fax: 01705 821293   **Map Ref 30**

UNIVERSITY OF PORTSMOUTH, set in the heart of Maritime England, is superbly located for the naval attractions as well as en-route stopovers to the Continent and Isle of Wight. B&B from £22.95, en-suite rooms, tea/coffee facilities. Lunches and dinner by arrangement. Available mid June to mid September. Email: reservations@port.ac.uk
B&B from £20pppn, Rooms 200 single, 25 twin, all en-suite, Restricted smoking, Children welcome, No pets, Open mid June - mid September.
University of Portsmouth, Accommodation & Hospitality Services, Nuffield Centre, BBD, St. Michaels Road, Portsmouth PO1 2ED
Tel: 01705 843178 Fax: 01705 843423   **Map Ref 30**

FORTE POSTHOUSE PORTSMOUTH, completely refurbished to include full leisure facilities. In a central position overlooking the seafront at Southsea. Business services available. Half board prices based on a minimum 2-night stay.
B&B from £68.95, Dinner available, Rooms 79 double, 75 twin, 9 family, all en-suite. Open all year.
Forte Posthouse Portsmouth, Pembroke Road, Portsmouth, Hampshire PO1 2TA
Tel: 01705 827651 Fax: 01705 756715   **Map Ref 30**

KEPPEL'S HEAD HOTEL, a hotel with historic naval connections, close to HMS Victory and the Continental ferries.

B&B from £49, Dinner available, Rooms 9 single, 10 double, 5 twin, 3 triple, all en-suite. Open all year.
Keppel's Head Hotel, The Hard, Portsmouth, Hampshire PO1 3DT
Tel: 01705 833231 Fax: 01705 838688   **Map Ref 30**

BEMBELL COURT HOTEL, a friendly, family-run, licensed hotel, ideally situated in Southsea's prime holiday area, with an excellent selection of shops, pubs and restaurants nearby.

B&B from £25, Dinner available, Rooms 2 single, 4 double, 4 twin, 3 triple, 1 family, most en-suite. Open all year.
Bembell Court Hotel, 69 Festing Road, Southsea, Portsmouth, Hampshire PO4 0NQ
Tel: 01705 735915 Fax: 01705 756497   **Map Ref 31**

BEAUFORT HOTEL, with en-suite bedrooms, standing in its own grounds. 1 minutes walk from seafront. Car Park.

B&B from £40, Dinner available, Rooms 3 single, 11 double, 2 twin, 2 triple, 1 family, all en-suite. Open all year.
Beaufort Hotel, 71 Festing Road, Southsea, Portsmouth, Hampshire PO4 0NQ
Tel: 01705 823707 Fax: 01705 870270   **Map Ref 31**

MOORHILL HOUSE HOTEL, quiet country house hotel in secluded two and a half acres, half a mile from picturesque village of Burley. Will appeal to those who love beauty, quiet surroundings and complete freedom of the New Forest. Daily half board price based on minimum 2-night stay.
B&B from £55, Dinner available, Rooms 2 single, 13 double, 2 twin, 7 triple, all en-suite. Open all year.
Moorhill House Hotel, Burley, Ringwood, Hampshire BH24 4AG
Tel: 01425 403285 Fax: 01425 403715   **Map Ref 32**

ABBEY HOTEL, is a Victorian pub/hotel in the ancient market town of Romsey. Good old fashioned service offering home-made English food, excellent real ales and social chatter our only music. An ideal base for visiting the many local interests.
B&B from £25pp, Dinner available, Rooms 2 single, 2 twin, 2 double,1 family, all en-suite, Children welcome, Pets by arrangement, Open all year except Christmas & New Year.
John & Diane Hilsley, **Abbey Hotel,** 11 Church Street, Romsey, Hampshire SO51 8BT
Tel: 01794 513360 Fax: 01794 524318   **Map Ref 33**

HIGHFIELD HOUSE, in unspoilt village, overlooking golf-course. Delightful setting and charming gardens. Home cooking a speciality. Close to Mottisfont Abbey National Trust and Hillier Arboretum.

B&B from £45, Dinner available, Rooms 1 double, 2 twin, all en-suite. Open all year.

Highfield House, Newtown Road, Awbridge, Romsey, Hampshire SO51 0GG
Tel: 01794 340727 Fax: 01794 341450   **Map Ref 34**

....

COUNTRY ACCOMMODATION, character rooms in ground floor independent annexe. Quiet village, 3 miles from Romsey.. from Romsey. All en-suite, tea/coffee, TV Good local pubs and restaurants.

B&B from £28, Rooms 2 double, 1 single, all en-suite. Open all year.
Country Accommodation, The Old Post Office, New Road, Michelmersh, Romsey, Hampshire SO51 0NL
Tel: 01794 368739   **Map Ref 35**

....

PARKHOUSE MOTEL, 17th Century former coaching inn built of brick and flint with slate roof. 5 miles east of Stonehenge, 10 miles north of Salisbury and 7 miles west of Andover.

B&B from £24, Dinner available, Rooms 6 single, 18 double, 6 twin, 3 triple, suites available, some en-suite.

Parkhouse Motel, Cholderton, Salisbury, Hampshire SP4 0EG
Tel: 01980 629256 Fax: 01980 629256   **Map Ref 36**

....

EATON COURT HOTEL, a comfortable, small, owner-run hotel for business or leisure stays. Bedrooms have all amenities and the breakfasts are generous.

B&B from £23, Dinner available, Rooms 8 single, 3 double, 3 twin, most en-suite. Open all year.
Eaton Court Hotel, 32 Hill Lane, Southampton, Hampshire SO15 5AY
Tel: 01703 223081 Fax: 01703 322006   **Map Ref 37**

....

BANISTER HOUSE HOTEL, a friendly welcome in this family-run hotel which is central and in a residential area. Off A33 (The Avenue) into Southampton.

B&B from £22.50, Dinner available, 13 single, 4 double, 3 twin, 2 triple, 1 family, some en-suite, Open all year.

Banister House Hotel, Banister Road, Southampton, Hampshire SO15 2JJ
Tel: 01703 221279 Fax: 01703 221279   **Map Ref 37**

....

DE VERE GRAND HARBOUR, a magnificent granite and glass building offering luxurious yet comfortable accommodation. Conveniently situated overlooking the waterfront, adjacent to the mediaeval city walls.

B&B from £75pp, Dinner available, Rooms 98 double, 34 twin, 20 triple, 20 family, suites available, all en-suite. Open all year.

De Vere Grand Harbour, West Quay Road, Southampton, Hampshire SO15 1AG
Tel: 01703 633033 Fax: 01703 633066   **Map Ref 37**

....

UPLAND PARK HOTEL, family-run hotel in picturesque country surroundings, well situated for touring Southern England. Good reputation for cuisine.

B&B from £35.00 Dinner available, Rooms 3 single, 9 double, 3 twin, 2 family, all en-suite. Open all year.

Upland Park Hotel, Garrison Hill, Droxford, Southampton, Hampshire SO32 3QL
Tel: 01489 878507 Fax: 01489 877853   **Map Ref 38**

243

LA CASA BLANCA, small, pleasantly situated licensed hotel. Friendly welcome, well-equipped en-suite bedrooms and home cooking.

B&B from £26, Dinner available, Rooms 4 single, 1 double, 1 twin, 2 triple, 1 family, all en-suite. Open all year.

La Casa Blanca, 48 Victoria Road, Nestley Abbey, Southampton, Hampshire SO31 5DQ
Tel: 01703 453718 Fax: 01703 453718   **Map Ref 39**

....

HUNTERS LODGE HOTEL, you will receive a warm welcome at this personally-run hotel. Convenient for city centre, ferry ports and motorways. Attractive en-suite rooms with telephone and satellite TV. Cosy lounge with well-stocked bar.

B&B from £29.38, Dinner available, Rooms 5 single, 7 double, 4 twin, 1 triple, all en-suite. Open all year.
Hunters Lodge Hotel, 25 Landguard Road, Shirley, Southampton, Hampshire SO15 5DL
Tel: 01703 227919 Fax: 01703 230913   **Map Ref 40**

....

ADDENRO HOUSE HOTEL, a family-run small hotel, offering friendly, reliable service at a reasonable cost.

B&B from £15, Rooms 7 single, 2 double, 4 twin, 5 triple, some en-suite. Open all year.

Addenro House Hotel, 40-42 Howard Street, Shirley, Southampton, Hampshire SO15 5BD
Tel: 01703 227144   **Map Ref 40**

....

THE LODGE, a friendly owner-managed hotel in quiet surroundings, close to city centre and university and convenient for airport.

B&B from £21.50, Dinner available, Rooms 9 single, 2 double, 2 twin, 1 triple, some en-suite. Open all year.
The Lodge, 1 Winn Road, The Avenue, Southampton, Hampshire SO12 1EH
Tel: 01703 557537   **Map Ref 37**

....

BUSKETTS LAWN HOTEL, a delightful family-run country house hotel in quiet forest surroundings, 8 miles west of Southampton. Heated swimming pool. Every amenity.

B&B from £37.50, Dinner available, Rooms 4 single, 5 double, 3 twin, 2 triple, all en-suite. Open all year.

Busketts Lawn Hotel, 174 Woodlands Road, Woodlands, Southampton, Hampshire SO40 7GL
Tel: 01703 292272 & 292077 Fax: 01703 272487   **Map Ref 41**

....

THE DOLPHINS HOTEL, on the seafront, overlooking the common. Attractive bar and restaurant. Near Mary Rose , HMS Victory, HMS Warrior, ferry terminals, shopping centres

B&B from £24, Dinner available, Rooms 10 single, 6 double, 13 twin, 4 triple, most en-suite. Open all year.

The Dolphins Hotel, 10-11 Western Parade, Southsea, Hampshire PO5 3JF
Tel: 01705 823823 Fax: 01705 820833   **Map Ref 31**

....

NEWLEAZE GUEST HOUSE, small friendly establishment with home cooking, giving good value for money. Within easy reach of ferry port.

B&B from £16.00 Dinner available, Rooms 1 single, 1 double, 3 twin, 1 family room. Open all year.

Newleaze Guest House, 11 St. Edward's Road, Southsea, Hampshire PO5 3DH
Tel: 01705 832735   **Map Ref 31**

OAKLEIGH GUEST HOUSE, a family-run guesthouse, 5 minutes from the seafront and ferries. All modern amenities, colour TV and tea/coffee making facilities.

B&B from £14, Dinner available, Rooms 2 single, 2 double, 1 twin, 2 family, some en-suite. Open all year.
Oakleigh Guest House, 48 Festive Grove, Southsea, Hampshire PO4 9QD
Tel: 01705 812276   **Map Ref 31**

....

GLENCOE GUEST HOUSE, a Victorian family run guest house only 2 minutes from sea front and a short drive to the continental ferry port. Well situated for all amenities and places of historic interest. Glencoe offers high standards of comfort with attractive en-suite bedrooms.

B&B from £18.50pp, Rooms 2 single, 2 twin, 2 double, 1 family, all en-suite, Restricted smoking, Children welcome, No pets, Open all year.
June Gwilliam, **Glencoe Guest House,** 64 Whitwell Road, Southsea, Hampshire PO4 0QS
Tel: 01705 737413 Fax: 01705 737413   **Map Ref 31**

....

WESTFIELD HALL HOTEL, a small, exclusive hotel in own grounds, with large car park, 3 minutes from Southsea's seafront, promenade and canoe lake.

B&B from £38.00 Dinner available, Rooms 2 single, 7 double, 4 twin, 4 triple, 3 family, all en-suite. Open all year.
Westfield Hall Hotel, 65 Festing Road, Southsea, Hampshire PO4 0NQ
Tel: 01705 826971 Fax: 01705 870200   **Map Ref 31**

....

OAKDALE GUEST HOUSE, an elegant, comfortable Edwardian house, 5 minutes from flower-filled seafront and handy for historic ships, shops and restaurants.

B&B from £23, Dinner available, Rooms 2 single, 2 double, 2 twin, all en-suite. Open all year.
Oakdale Guest House, 71 St Ronans Road, Southsea, Hampshire PO4 0PP
Tel: 01705 737358 Fax: 01705 737358   **Map Ref 31**

....

OCEAN HOTEL & APARTMENTS, an imposing building in foremost seafront position between South Parade Pier and Canoe Lake with magnificent sea views. Choice of hotel rooms, suites, or self-contained apartments. Lift to all floors. Car park.
B&B from £20, Dinner available, 1 single, 4 double, 4 triple, 7 family rooms, most en-suite. Open all year.
Ocean Hotel & Apartments, 8-10 St. Helens Parade, Southsea, Hampshire PO4 0RW
Tel: 01705 73423 Fax: 01705 297046   **Map Ref 31**

....

RYDEVIEW HOTEL, a very friendly family hotel with character. Two minutes' walk from sea and other attractions. Recently refurbished. Private car park.

B&B from £19, Dinner available, Rooms 6 single, 5 double, 3 twin, 4 triple, suites available, some en-suite. Open all year.
Rydeview Hotel, 9 Western Parade, Southsea, Hampshire PO5 3JF
Tel: 01705 820865 Fax: 01705 863664   **Map Ref 31**

....

THE SANDRINGHAM HOTEL, a seafront hotel with sea views from most bedrooms. Recently refurbished to the highest standards. 100-seat restaurant, function/conference room, large ballroom. Free car park opposite. Two minutes' walk to Southsea shopping centre.

B&B from £25, Dinner available, Rooms 8 single, 19 double, 9 twin, 4 triple, 4 family, all en-suite. Open all year.
The Sandringham Hotel, Osborne Road, Clarence Parade, Southsea, Hampshire PO5 3LR
Tel: 01705 826969 Fax: 01705 822330   **Map Ref 31**

CARBERRY GUEST HOUSE, a fine old Georgian house in an acre of landscaped gardens and lawns, overlooking the River Test. Games and swimming facilities, riding and fishing can be arranged. Ideal for touring the South Coast and the New Forest.

B&B from £25, Dinner available, Rooms 4 single, 3 double, 2 twin, 1 triple, 1 family, most en-suite. Open all year.
Carberry Guest House, Salisbury Hill, Stockbridge, Hampshire SO20 6EZ
Tel: 01264 810771 Fax: 01264 811022 **Map Ref 42**

....

FOREST GATE, a Georgian house on the outskirts of the village overlooking farm land. Two twin en-suite bedrooms with tea/coffee making facilities and TV. Large garden with tennis court. Off road car parking. Within easy reach of maritime Portsmouth and continental ferries.

B&B from £18pp, Dinner from £10, Rooms 2 twin, both en-suite, No smoking or pets, Children over 10, Open all year except Christmas & New Year.
Torfrida & David Cox, **Forest Gate,** Hambledon Road, Denmead, Waterlooville, Hampshire PO7 6EX
Tel: 01705 255901 **Map Ref 43**

....

PORTLAND HOUSE HOTEL, a family run elegant Georgian townhouse situated in a quiet mews. Close to city centre and minutes from the station. All rooms en-suite with cable TV and tea/coffee facilities. Traditional English or continental breakfast.

B&B from £24pp, Rooms 2 twin, 2 double, 1 family, all en-suite, Smoking & children welcome, No pets, Open all year except Christmas & New Year.
Kristina Wehr, **Portland House Hotel,** 63 Tower Street, Winchester, Hampshire SO23 8TA
Tel: 01962 865195 Fax: 01962 865195 **Map Ref 44**

....

CATHEDRAL VIEW, a guesthouse with views across historic city and cathedral. 5 minutes' walk from city centre. En-suite facilities, TV, Parking.

B&B from £33, Rooms 4 double, 1 twin, 1 family, some en-suite. Open all year.
Cathedral View, 9A Magdalen Hill, Winchester, Hampshire SO23 OHJ
Tel: 01962 863802 **Map Ref 44**

....

HARESTOCK LODGE HOTEL, a privately-run country house hotel set in secluded gardens on the edge of historic Winchester. Offering a warm welcome and good food with menus to suit all tastes.
B&B from £46, Dinner available, Rooms 4 single, 8 double, 4 twin, 2 triple, all en-suite. Open all year.
Harestock Lodge Hotel, Harestock Road, Winchester, Hampshire SO22 6NX
Tel: 01962 881870 & 880038 Fax: 01962 886959 **Map Ref 44**

....

LAINSTON HOUSE, a magnificent, Georgian, listed 17th Century country house set in 63 acres of parkland. Recently refurbished. Noted for food and service.

B&B from £95, Dinner available, Rooms 7 single, 16 double, 14 twin, 1 triple, most en-suite. Open all year.
Lainston House, Sparsholt, Winchester, Hampshire SO21 2LT
Tel: 01962 863588 Fax: 01962 776672 **Map Ref 45**

....

STRATTON HOUSE, a lovely old Victorian house with an acre of grounds, in an elevated position on St. Giles Hill.

B&B from £33, Dinner available, Rooms 1 single, 3 double, 2 twin, 1 triple, most en-suite. Open all year.
Stratton House, Stratton Road, St. Giles Hill, Winchester, Hampshire SO23 0JQ
Tel: 01962 863919 & 864529 Fax: 01962 842095 **Map Ref 44**

BOTLEY PARK HOTEL, GOLF & COUNTRY CLUB, a purpose-designed to cater for the leisure and business demands of the 1990's. Few minutes drive from M27, 60 minutes from London, 50 minutes to Heathrow. Golf, sauna, solarium, gymnasium, jacuzzi, indoor heated pool, tennis and squash courts.

B&B from £70, Dinner available, Rooms 44 double, 56 twin, all en-suite. Open all year.
Botley Park Hotel, Golf & Country Club, Winchester Road, Boorley Green, Botley, Southampton SO3 2UA
Tel: 01489 780888 Fax: 01489 789242 **Map Ref 46**

....

WILLOW DENE GUEST HOUSE, a small friendly guesthouse, offering home cooking and a homely atmosphere. Near station and a few minutes from shops, beach and buses to all parts of the Island. Pets welcome.

B&B from £12, Dinner available, Rooms 1 single, 1 double, 2 triple, 1 family, Open January - November.
WIllow Dene Guest House, 110 Station Avenue, Sandown, Isle of WIght PO36 8HD
Tel: 01983 403100 **Map Ref 47**

....

CLARENDON HOTEL & WIGHT MOUSE INN, a 17th Century coaching hotel overlooking Freshwater Bay and the Needles. Children most welcome. 6 real ales, 365 whiskies and live entertainment nightly, all year round. Well appointed bedrooms, good food, service and hospitality.

B&B from £25, Dinner available, Rooms 1 single, 3 double, 9 family, suites available, all en-suite. Open all year.
Clarendon Hotel & Wight Mouse Inn, Blackgang, Chale, Isle of Wight PO38 2HA
Tel: 01983 730431 Fax: 01983 730431 **Map Ref 56**

....

ROYAL STANDARD HOTEL, is a family-run eleven-bedroomed Hotel and Free House which offers a warm and friendly welcome. Situated in the centre of Freshwater at the western end of the Island, it is in ideal area for walking, fishing and golf.
B&B from £20pp, Dinner available, Rooms 4 single, 3 twin, 3 double, 1 family, all en-suite, Children & Pets welcome, Open all year.
Raymond, Mary & Graham Garlick, **Royal Standard Hotel,** 15 School Green Rd, Freshwater, Isle of Wight PO40 9AJ
Tel: 01983 753227 **Map Ref 48**

....

FARRINGFORD HOTEL, set in 33-acre grounds, offering traditional hotel service and also self-catering suites, the best of both worlds. 9 hole golf -course, swimming and tennis.

B&B from £26.00 Dinner available, Rooms 3 single, 2 double, 7 twin, 7 triple, all en-suite. Open all year.
Farringford Hotel, Bedbury Lane, Freshwater, Isle of Wight PO40 9PE
Tel: 01983 752500 Fax: 01983 756515 **Map Ref 48**

....

BROOKSIDE FORGE HOTEL, located in picturesque west Wight, close to all bays and downs. All bedrooms en-suite with colour TV and tea/coffee facilities. Large gardens and car park. Good quality home cooked food. Special diets catered for. Licensed bar. Reductions for groups and out of season discount.
B&B from £19.50pp, Dinner from £8.95, Rooms 2 single, 3 twin, 5 double, 1 family, all en-suite, Children & pets welcome, Open all year.
Mr & Mrs Chettle, **Brookside Forge Hotel,** Brookside Road, Freshwater, Isle of Wight PO40 9ER
Tel: 01983 754644 **Map Ref 48**

....

ONTARIO PRIVATE HOTEL, four minutes from seaside award beach, offering accommodation of a high standard with licensed bar, choice of menu. Children and pets welcome.
B&B from £20, Dinner available, Rooms 1 single, 2 double, 2 triple, 1 family, some en-suite. Open March - December.
Ontario Private Hotel, Colwell Common Road, Colwell Bay, Freshwater, Isle of Wight PO39 0DD
Tel: 01983 75237 **Map Ref 49**

THE FERNSIDE PRIVATE HOTEL, a friendly and relaxing stay at our licensed hotel is guaranteed. All rooms have tea/coffee facilities and colour TV's in a tree lined avenue and close to all amenities. Any day to any day bookings. Ground floor rooms available.
B&B from £22pp, Dinner from £6, Rooms 2 single, 2 twin, 6 double, 4 family, some en-suite, Restricted smoking, Children welcome, Pets by arrangement, Open all year.
Sarah Brown, **The Fernside Private Hotel,** 30 Station Avenue, Sandown, Isle of Wight PO36 9BW
Tel: 01983 402356 Fax: 01983 402356   **Map Ref 47**

CULVER LODGE HOTEL, a warm, comfortable hotel offering traditional English hospitality. Overlooking sun terrace, swimming pool and garden. Close to town, beach and leisure facilities.

B&B from £19, Dinner available, Rooms 4 single, 7 double, 4 twin, 4 triple, 1 family, all en-suite, Open March - October.
Culver Lodge Hotel, Albert Road, Sandown, Isle of Wight PO36 8AW
Tel: 01983 403819 Fax: 01983 403819   **Map Ref 47**

REGINA HOTEL, a small seafront hotel with all rooms en-suite, specialising in personal service, food, comfort and the desire to give value for money.

B&B from £18, Dinner available, Rooms 7 double, 2 twin, 4 triple, all en-suite, Open January - October & Christmas.
Regina Hotel, Esplanade, Sandown, Isle of Wight PO36 8AE
Tel: 01983 403219   **Map Ref 47**

THE GRANGE, is in the centre of the hamlet of Alverstone with Nature trail reserve as part of the village. Set in peaceful gardens with ample car parking. A comfortable lounge with log fire and bright airy rooms. Well situated for all aspects of the Island.

B&B from £19pp, Rooms 1 single, 2 twin, 4 double, 1 family, all en-suite, No smoking, Children welcome, No pets, Open February - November.
David & Geraldine Watling, **The Grange,** Alverstone, Sandown, Isle of Wight PO36 0EZ
Tel: 01983 403729   **Map Ref 51**

HAZELWOOD HOTEL, is a detached hotel in a quiet tree-lined road, close to sea, shops and town. All rooms are en-suite, have TV and tea making, parking available. We offer all home cooking with choice for breakfast and dinner A warm welcome awaits for all.
B&B from £18pp, Dinner from £7, Rooms 1 single, 2 twin, 2 double, 3 family, all en-suite, Children welcome, Pets by arrangement, Open all year except Christmas & New Year.
Pete & Barbara Tubbs, **Hazelwood Hotel,** 14 Clarence Road, Shanklin, Isle of Wight PO37 7BH
Tel: 01983 862824 Fax: 01983 862824   **Map Ref 52**

ALVERSTONE MANOR HOTEL, a charming country house hotel overlooking Sandown/Shanklin Bay. Within easy reach of Old Village, town and beach. 2 acres of gardens with heated swimming pool, lawn tennis court and putting green.

B&B from £25, Dinner available, Rooms 1 single, 3 double, 1 twin, 6 triple, all en-suite. Open March - October.

Alverstone Manor Hotel, 32 Luccombe Road, Shanklin, Isle of Wight PO37 6RR
Tel: 01983 862586 Fax: 01983 865127   **Map Ref 52**

ST GEORGE'S HOUSE HOTEL, car park. Close to sea front, old village and Shanklin town centre. Children and pets welcomed. Friendly family run hotel. We are here to give you a holiday to remember. Bar and dining room, dry lounge. TV and coffee facilities in rooms.

B&B from £16.50pp, Dinner from £6, Rooms 2 single, 1 twin, 5 double, 2 family, some en-suite, Restricted smoking, Children & pets welcome, Open April - October.
Colin & June Withers, **St George's House Hotel,** St George's Road, Shanklin, Isle of Wight PO37 6BA
Tel: 01983 863691 Fax: 01983 863091 **Map Ref 52**

COUNTRY GARDEN HOTEL, a country house hotel set in lovely gardens overlooking the sea. In the words of one hotel reviewer: "Relish the superb cuisine, fantastic walks, wonderful views".

B&B from £38, Dinner available, Rooms 2 single, 9 double, 5 twin, suites available, all en-suite. Open March - October.

Country Garden Hotel, Church Hill, Totland Bay, Isle of Wight PO39 1QE
Tel: 01983 754521 Fax: 01983 754521 **Map Ref 53**

HIGHDOWN INN, a country pub close to scenic National Trust downland and interesting landmarks. Ideal base for walkers, strollers and cyclists. Car park. Attractive gardens. Real ales. Wide range of home cooked food including seasonal variety of fresh local game, fish and vegetables available in our well appointed restaurant.
B&B from £18pp, Dinner from £4.95, Rooms 2 twin, 2 double, 1 en-suite, Restricted smoking, Children & pets welcome, Open all year.
Susan White, **Highdown Inn,** Highdown Lane, Totland Bay, Isle of Wight PO39 0HY
Tel: 01983 752450 **Map Ref 53**

SENTRY MEAD HOTEL, a tranquil location. Ideal base for walking. Two minutes' walk to beach. Comfortable and tastefully furnished. Delicious 5-course dinner menus.

B&B from £22, Dinner available, Rooms 2 single, 5 double, 3 twin, 3 triple, 1 family, all en-suite. Open all year.
Sentry Mead Hotel, Madeira Road, Totland Bay, Isle of Wight PO39 0BJ
Tel: 01983 753212 Fax: 01983 753212 **Map Ref 53**

BURLINGTON HOTEL, a friendly family-run hotel with heated swimming pool, commanding wonderful sea views. Central, yet affords peace and quiet.

B&B from £28, Dinner available, Rooms 4 single, 5 double, 9 twin, 5 triple, all en-suite. Open March - October.
Burlington Hotel, Bellevue Road, Ventnor, Isle of Wight PO38 1DB
Tel: 01983 852113 Fax: 01983 852113 **Map Ref 54**

LECONFIELD HOTEL, family run country house non-smoking hotel. All rooms en-suite with tea/coffee facilities and colour TV. Comfortable residents lounge with log fire. Large private car park. Fully licensed Bar. Outdoor heated swimming pool (may-sept). One of the finest Channel views on the Isle of Wight.
B&B from £22pp, Dinner from £8.50, Rooms 1 single, 3 twin, 6 double, 4 family, all en-suite, No smoking, Children over 5, No pets, Open March - November.
Mike & Jean Barker **Leconfield Hotel,** 85 Leeson Road, Upper Bonchurch, Ventnor, Isle of Wight PO38 1PU
Tel: 01983 852196 Fax: 01983 856525 **Map Ref 55**

249

Hereford and Worcester is steeped in history and its two principal cities reflect this. Worcester is famed as a Royalist city: Charles I passed through on his way west and fought his last battle south of Worcester and then fled, hiding in the famous Royal Oak. Worcester Cathedral is in a beautiful situation on the River Severn and away from the town centre. The county cricket ground is an archetypal feature of an English summer and there is an all year racing at Worcester Racecourse.

It was thanks to the richness of the surrounding agricultural land that Hereford grew up on the banks of the River Wye. Hereford Cathedral, built overlooking the river and associated with the church since the 7th century, is famous as the home of the Mappa Mundi, a unique map of the world drawn at the end of the 13th century.

In south Herefordshire the River Wye dissects some of the finest farming country in Britain - yet the area is also secluded, wild in places and an area of outstanding natural beauty. A horse shoe gorge has been carved through sandstone by the river at Symonds Yat forming spectacular cliffs above the water.

Ross-on-Wye, south Herefordshire's largest town, stands on a stone outcrop overlooking the river. The area is popular for a variety of outdoor activities from angling and watersports to climbing and rambling. Offa's Dyke Footpath, the long distance trail, runs along the entire length of the border between England and Wales. It passes the unique town of Hay-on-Wye which has the world's largest second hand and antiquarian book centre. Leominster is a beautiful old wool town on the River Lugg, with a number of black and white half-timbered houses. Ledbury, to the east of Hereford, also has a number of half timbered houses. It makes a good centre from which to explore the Malvern Hills. The hills have a number of walks and trails and it is said that fourteen counties can be seen from the ridge on a fine day. Much of the building of Great Malvern was carried out by the Victorians who came to take the waters. Malvern is the site of the Three Counties Showground which hosts the Three Counties Agricultural Show in June and the Spring Gardening Show in May.

The area around Evesham and Pershore has the greatest concentration of market gardening and fruit orchards and in the spring motorists can follow the lanes for the Blossom trail. Towards Droitwich and Ombersley the land is more rolling and Bromsgrove is set in undulating farm land. Redditch grew up in the Industrial Revolution becoming, among other things, the needle capital of the world. Today it is a prime example of a new town, over half is made up of countryside, parks and woodlands.

left, Malvern, Worcestershire

Herefordshire & Worcestershire

Shropshire

CRAVEN ARMS

A49

LUDLOW

KNIGHTON

A488

TENBURY WELLS

A49

A4112

LEOMINSTER

KINGTON

A44

10

BROMY

7

A4112

18

17

417

19

A41

3

A438

5

NEWTOWN

9

4

6

A4103

1

HAY ON WYE

20

HEREFORD

A438

21

A465

A49

16

2

A466

11

15

14

12

ROSS ON WYE

A40

13

Wales

MONMOUTH

NEWNHA

A466

A48

LYDNEY

THE OLD RECTORY. Our home is very welcoming. Visitors have own sitting room with logfire and colour TV. Blue bedroom - double four poster. Pink bedroom - twin beds. Both have hand basin, TV and tea/coffee facility. Shared bathroom also shower room. Peaceful gardens, beautiful views to Brecon Beacons and Black mountains. Dinner by arrangement.

B&B from £20pp, Dinner from £16, Rooms 1 twin, 1 double, No smoking or pets, Children over 8, Open all year except Christmas & New Year.

Caroline Ailesbury, **The Old Rectory,** Garway, Herefordshire HR2 8RH
Tel: 01600 750363 Fax: 01600 750364   **Map Ref 2**

....

THE HAVEN, enjoy the spacious rooms, log fires, books and deep peace of this early Victorian vicarage, visited by Kilvert. Imaginative food. Licensed. Tea/coffee facilities, TV. Self catering flat for 2. Ground floor bedroom suitable for wheelchair user. Large garden. Car park. Near Hay and Black Mountains.
B&B from £23pp, Dinner from £14, Rooms 1 single, 2 twin, 2 double, 1 family, all en-suite, Restricted smoking, Children welcome, Pets by arrangement, Open March - November.
Mark & Janet Robinson, **The Haven,** Hardwicke, Hay-on-Wye HR3 5TA
Tel/Fax: 01497 831254   **Map Ref 3**

....

THE SOMERVILLE, quiet guesthouse with views, convenient for city centre and station. Well-appointed bedrooms. No lunches. Children welcome. Ample parking.

B&B from £20, Dinner available, Rooms 4 single, 3 double, 2 twin, 1 triple, all en-suite, Open all year.

The Somerville, 12 Bodenham Road, Hereford, Herefordshire HR1 2TS
Tel: 01432 273991   **Map Ref 1**

....

COLLINS HOUSE, fully restored early Georgian town house, c 1722, combining comfort, character and convenience in historic town centre. Private parking. No smoking, please.

B&B from £30, Dinner available, Rooms 1 double, 2 twin, all en-suite, Open all year.

Collins House, 19 St, Owen Street, Hereford, Herefordshire HR1 2JB
Tel: 01432 272416 Fax: 01432 357717   **Map Ref 1**

....

AYLESTONE COURT HOTEL, three-story Georgian building, listed Grade II, tastefully renovated throughout,. Spacious, comfortable public rooms and en-suite bedrooms. Lawns and gardens. 4 minutes' walk to city centre.

B&B from £30, Dinner available, Rooms 7 double, 3 twin, 1 triple, all en-suite, Open all year.

Aylestone Court Hotel, Aylestone Hill, Hereford, Herefordshire HR1 1HS
Tel: 01432 341891 Fax: 01432 267691   **Map Ref 1**

....

THREE COUNTIES HOTEL, excellently appointed hotel set in 3.5 acres. Emphasis on traditional, friendly service. Tasteful bedrooms, restaurant and bar offer today's guest all modern comforts. Ideal base for touring Wye Valley. Town centre 1 mile.

B&B from £25, Dinner available, Rooms 17 double, 43 twin, all en-suite, Open all year.

Three Counties Hotel, Belmont Road, Hereford, Herefordshire HR2 7BP
Tel: 01432 299955 Fax: 01432 275114   **Map Ref 1**

CASTLE POOL HOTEL, the hotel garden is part of the old castle moat. Located minutes from the Cathedral, river and sports facilities.

B&B from £38, Dinner available, Rooms 8 single, 8 double, 8 twin, 2 triple, all en-suite, Open all year.
Castle Pool Hotel, Castle Street, Hereford, Herefordshire HR1 2NW
Tel: 01432 356321 Fax: 01432 356321   **Map Ref 1**

....

MERTON HOTEL, Georgian origin , this charming town house hotel has been modernised to provide comfortable, well-appointed accommodation with elegant "Governor's" restaurant.

B&B from £45, Dinner available, Rooms 8 single, 5 double, 3 twin, a triple, all en-suite, Open all year.
Merton Hotel, Commercial Road, Hereford, Herefordshire HR1 2BD
Tel: 01432 265925 Fax: 01432 354983 Email: 106317.2760@compuserve.com   **Map Ref 1**

....

HEDLEY LODGE, guesthouse set within the historic estate of Belmont Abbey, a Benedictine monastery on the A465 Hereford to Abergavenny road.

B&B from £18.50, Dinner available, Rooms 8 twin, all en-suite, Open all year.
Hedley Lodge, Belmont Abbey, Hereford, Herefordshire HR2 9RZ
Tel: 01432 277475 Fax: 01432 277597   **Map Ref 1**

....

BELMONT LODGE & GOLF COURSE, comfortable hotel situated off the A465, 2 miles south of Hereford city centre. Overlooking the River Wye and Herefordshire countryside, offering beautiful views.

B&B from £29.50, Dinner available, Rooms 26 twin, 4 triple, all en-suite, Open all year.
Belmont Lodge & Golf Course, Belmont, Hereford, Herefordshire HR2 9SA
Tel: 01432 352666 Fax: 01432 358090   **Map Ref 20**

....

THE HARP INN, a Welsh village pub, nearby River Wye, 4 miles Hay-on-Wye town of books. Ideal touring Black Mountains, Brecon Beacons. All rooms central heating, TV, tea/coffee facilities. Car parking. Canoeing, pony trekking, golf, walking available locally, also popular area artists, bird watchers. Home cooked food including Vegetarian. Children meals. Real Ale.
B&B from £17.50pp, Dinner from £8, Rooms 2 twin, 2 double, all en-suite, Restricted smoking, Children welcome, No pets, Open all year.
David & Lynda White, **The Harp Inn,** Hay Road, Glasbury-on-Wye, Hereford, Herefordshire HR3 5NR
Tel: 01497 847 373   **Map Ref 4**

....

THE NEW PRIORY HOTEL, really friendly family hotel set in pleasant peaceful surroundings, 2 miles from the centre of Hereford. Good home-cooked food, lots of historical interest. En-suite four-poster rooms.

B&B from £25, Dinner available, Rooms 2 single, 5 double, 1 twin, most en-suite, Open all year.
The New Priory Hotel, Stretton Sugwas, Hereford, Herefordshire HR4 7AR
Tel: 01432 760264 Fax: 01432 761809   **Map Ref 5**

....

CEDAR GUEST HOUSE, situated on touring route, approx. 1 mile from Hereford, this Georgian family guesthouse has private parking.

B&B from £19, Rooms 2 double, 1 twin, 2 triple, 1 family, Open all year.

Cedar Guest House, 123 Whitecross Road, Whitecross, Hereford, Herefordshire HR4 0LS
Tel: 01432 267235   **Map Ref 6**

BURTON HOTEL, attractively modernised, authentic coaching inn, in centre of small market town near Welsh border and Offa's Dyke footpath.

B&B from £42, Dinner available, Rooms 1 single, 5 double, 3 twin, 6 triple, all en-suite, Open all year.
Burton Hotel, Mill Street, Kington, Herefordshire HR5 3BQ
Tel: 01544 230323 Fax: 01544 230323   **Map Ref 7**

....

FEATHERS HOTEL, traditional Elizabethan coaching inn, situated in the centre of Ledbury. Ideal for touring Malverns and the Marches.

B&B from £65, Dinner available, Rooms 4 double, 4 twin, 3 triple, all en-suite, Open all year.
Feathers Hotel, High Street, Ledbury, Herefordshire HR8 1DS
Tel: 01531 635266 Fax: 01531 632001   **Map Ref 8**

....

HIGHFIELD, Two Crowns Commended. Comfortable, spacious Edwardian house with garden surrounded by fields and views of distance hills. Friendly relaxed atmosphere. Good food tailored to tastes and needs, wine list available. Drink making facilities in bedrooms. TV lounge with open fire. Definitely a pleasant happy stay.
B&B from £18.50pp, Dinner from £12.50, Rooms 2 twin,1 double, all en-suite/private bathroom, Restricted smoking, No pets, Open March - October.
Catherine & Marguerite Fothergill, **Highfield,** Newtown, Ivington Road, Leominster, Herefordshire HR6 8QD
Tel: 01568 613216   **Map Ref 9**

....

ROYAL OAK HOTEL, Grade II listed Georgian coaching house dating from 1723, with log fires in winter, real ales and an emphasis on good food and wines at reasonable prices.

B&B from £31.50, Dinner available, Rooms 2 single, 9 double, 5 twin, 2 triple, all en-suite, Open all year.
Royal Oak Hotel, South Street, Leominster, Herefordshire HR6 8JA
Tel: 01568 612610 Fax: 01568 612710   **Map Ref 10**

....

COPPER HALL, comfortable 17th century house with spacious garden. Good English cooking and homely atmosphere. Convenient touring centre for Wales, Wye Valley and the Malverns.

B&B from £20, Dinner available, Rooms 1 double, 2 twin, 1 triple, Open all year.
Copper Hall, South Street, Leominster, Herefordshire HR6 8JN
Tel: 01568 611622   **Map Ref 10**

....

TALBOT HOTEL, 15th century coaching inn with oak beams and log fire, now offering 20th century facilities. Ideal location for touring Mid-Wales, Shropshire and Herefordshire.

B&B from £42, Dinner available, Rooms 2 single, 8 double, 7 twin, 2 triple, 1 family, all en-suite, Open all year.
Talbot Hotel, West Street, Leominster, Herefordshire HR6 8EP
Tel: 01568 616347 Fax: 01568 614880   **Map Ref 10**

....

PENGETHLEY MANOR, elegant Georgian country house in superb gardens with magnificent views over Herefordshire countryside. extensive wine list. Restaurant specialises in fresh local produce.

B&B from £60, Dinner available, Rooms 2 single, 11 double, 10 twin, 1 triple, all en-suite, Children welcome, Open all year.

Pengethley Manor, Ross on Wye, Herefordshire HR9 6LL
Tel: 01989 730211 Fax: 01989 730238   **Map Ref 11**

RUDHALL FARM, an elegant early Georgian farmhouse perfect to explore Wye Valley and beyond. In attractive valley with lake and mill stream. All rooms with vanity units, beverage trays etc. Friendly welcoming hospitality. AGA cooked breakfasts, diets catered for. Terraced mature English garden much loved by the owner. Fourth generations at the farm.

B&B from £20pp, Rooms 2 double, No smoking or pets, Open all year except Christmas.
Mrs Gammond, **Rudhall Farm,** Ross on Wye, Herefordshire HR9 7TL
Tel: 01989 780240 **Map Ref 11**

....

THE CHASE HOTEL, a Georgian country house set in 11 acres of lovely grounds. Short walk to town centre. Enthusiastic staff provide a professional service in a friendly and relaxed atmosphere. Ideal touring centre.

B&B from £70, Dinner available, Rooms 17 double, 21 twin, 1 triple, all en-suite, No smoking, Children welcome, Open all year.

The Chase Hotel, Gloucester Road, Ross on Wye, Herefordshire HR9 5LH
Tel: 01989 763161 Fax: 01989 768330 **Map Ref 11**

....

SUNNYMOUNT HOTEL, a warm, comfortable hotel in quiet location on edge of town,offering French and English cooking with home grown and local produce freshly cooked for each meal.

B&B from £25, Dinner available, Rooms 3 single, 3 double, 3 twin, most en-suite, No smoking, Children welcome, No pets, Open all year.

Sunnymount Hotel, Ryefield Road, Ross on Wye, Herefordshire HR9 5LU
Tel: 01989 563880 **Map Ref 11**

....

THE ARCHES HOTEL, a small, family run hotel, set in half an acre of lawned gardens, 10 minutes walk from town centre. Warm, friendly atmosphere. All rooms furnished to a high standard and with views of the garden. Victorian style conservatory in which to relax.

B&B from £20, Dinner available, Rooms 1 single, 4 double, 1 twin, 1 triple, most en-suite, No smoking, Children welcome, No pets, Open all year.

The Arches Hotel, Walford Road, Ross on Wye, Herefordshire HR9 5PT
Tel: 01989 563348 **Map Ref 11**

....

PENCRAIG COURT HOTEL, a Georgian country house hotel, privately owned, providing both English and French cooking. Elegant restaurant and extensive wine cellars. Large attractive garden with glorious views overlooking River Wye. Email: mike@pencraig.court.co.uk

B&B from £32.25pp, Dinner available, Rooms 1 single, 4 double, 4 twin, 2 triple, all en-suite, Children welcome, Open all year.

Pencraig Court Hotel, Pencraig, Ross on Wye, Herefordshire HR9 6HR
Tel: 01989 770306 Fax: 01989 770040 **Map Ref 12**

....

ROYAL HOTEL, a quiet country house in Alpine type setting, next to the River Wye,. Ideal touring location. Only 6 miles from Ross on Wye, and Monmouth.

B&B from £30, Dinner available, Rooms 1 single, 15 double, 4 twin, all en-suite, Children over 12, Open all year.

Royal Hotel, Symonds Yat East, Ross on Wye, Herefordshire HR9 6JL
Tel: 01600 890238 Fax: 01600 890238 **Map Ref 13**

257

RIVERSDALE LODGE HOTEL, a high standard of accommodation, set in 2 acres on the banks of the River Wye,. Spectacular views of the rapids and gorge. Traditional food.

B&B from £25, Dinner available, Rooms 3 double, 1 twin, 1 family, most en-suite, No smoking,Children welcome, Open all year.
Riversdale Lodge Hotel, Symonds Yat West, Ross on Wye, Herefordshire HR9 6BL
Tel: 01600 890445 Fax: 01600 890445 **Map Ref 13**

....

WOODLEA HOTEL, a family run Victorian country house hotel set in a secluded woodland valley close to River Wye,. Only one and half miles from A40, between Ross and Monmouth. Excellent food and wines, friendly welcome.

B&B from £25, Dinner available, Rooms 1 single, 4 double, 1 twin, 1 triple, 1 family, most en-suite, Children welcome, Open all year.
Woodlea Hotel, Symonds Yat West, Ross on Wye, Herefordshire HR9 6BL
Tel: 01600 890206 Fax: 01600 890206 **Map Ref 13**

....

BRIDGE HOUSE HOTEL, a riverside hotel with panoramic views from the gardens and pride in its comfort and cuisine. All rooms en-suite.

B&B from £33.50, Dinner available, Rooms 4 double, 3 twin, 1 triple, most en-suite, Children over 10, Open all year.
Bridge House Hotel, Wilton, Ross on Wye, Herefordshire HR9 6AA
Tel: 01989 562655 Fax: 01989 567652 **Map Ref 14**

....

MILL BARN, a converted barn in tranquil Lakeside setting with large gardens. 4 miles from Ross-on-Wye with many local walks. Rooms have TV, tea/coffee facilities. Ample car parking.

B&B from £25pp, Rooms 1 double en-suite, 1 double with private bathroom, No smoking or children, Pets by arrangement, Open all year except Christmas week.

Penny & Mike Smith, **Mill Barn,** Bromsash, Ross-on-Wye, Herefordshire HR9 7SB
Tel: 01989 780300 Fax: 01989 780324 **Map Ref 15**

....

YE OLDE FERRIE INNE, is situated on the banks of the River Wye in an area of designated natural beauty, midway between Ross and Monmouth. Ideally located as a base when visiting the surrounding area. Local activities include walking, fishing, boating, cycling, golf, pony trekking.

B&B from £24.50pp, Dinner from £5, Rooms 2 single, 2 twin, 4 double, some en-suite, Children welcome, Pets by arrangement, Open all year except Christmas.
Liz & Brian Cheney, **Ye Olde Ferrie Inne,** Symonds Yat West, Ross-on-Wye, Herefordshire HR9 6BL
Tel: 01600 890232 **Map Ref 13**

....

THE NEW INN, a delightful 16th century coaching inn offering a wealth of warm character, oak beams and open fireplaces with two en-suite 4-poster letting rooms. An extensive menu of home-made dishes available in the bar or restaurant, together with an excellent choice of well kept real ales.

B&B from £35pp, Dinner from £7-£15, Rooms 2 double, both en-suite, Children & pets welcome, Open all year except Christmas.
Jane & Nigel Donovan, **The New Inn,** St Owens Cross, Herefordshire HR2 8LQ
Tel: 01989 730274 **Map Ref 16**

THE STEPPES, a 17th century listed building with oak beams, log fires and inglenook fireplaces. Cordon Bleu cuisine. Intimate atmosphere. En-suite accommodation in restored barns.

B&B from £45, Dinner available, Rooms 4 double, 2 twin, all en-suite, No smoking, Children over 12, Open all year.

The Steppes, Ullingswick, Herefordshire HR1 3JG
Tel: 01432 820424 Fax: 01432 820042   **Map Ref 17**

....

YE OLDE SALUTATION INN, a traditional black and white country inn overlooking the main Broad Street. Quality home cooked bar meals and a la carte menu. Inglenook fireplace. Homely atmosphere.

B&B from £37, Dinner available, Rooms 2 single, 1 double, 1 twin, 1 family, most en-suite, No smoking, Children over 14, Open all year.

Ye Olde Salutation Inn, Market Pitch, Weobley, Herefordshire HR4 8SJ
Tel: 01544 318443 Fax: 01544 318216   **Map Ref 18**

....

HURSTWOOD COTTAGE, a country cottage set in two thirds of an acre of grounds, surrounded by 200 acre fields with panoramic views across the Black Mountains.

B&B from £15pp, Dinner available, Rooms 1 double, 1 triple, en-suite, Restricted smoking, Open all year.

Hurstwood Cottage, Winforton, Herefordshire HR3 6EB
Tel: 01544 327328   **Map Ref 19**

....

PILGRIM HOTEL, country house hotel combining modern facilities with old world charm. Popular with country lovers and golfers. Set in 4 acres of grounds, south of Hereford.

B&B from £39.50, Dinner available, Rooms 1 single, 9 double, 8 twin, 2 triple, all en-suite, Open all year.

Pilgrim Hotel, Ross Road, Much Birch, Hereford, Herefordshire HR2 8HJ
Tel: 01981 540742 Fax: 01981 540620   **Map Ref 21**

....

WYCHE KEEP, is a unique arts and crafts castle style house, perched high on the Malvern Hills, built by the family of Sir Stanley Baldwin, Prime Minster to enjoy the spectacular 60 mile views. Guests can savour memorable four course candle-lit dinners. Fully licensed. Parking.

B&B from £25-£30pp, Dinner from £18, Rooms 2 twin, 1 double, all en-suite, No smoking or pets, Children over 13, Open all year.
Mr & Mrs Williams, **Wyche Keep,** 22 Wyche Road, Malvern, Worcestershire WR14 4EG
Tel: 01684 567018 Fax: 01684 892304   **Map Ref 22**

....

THE MANOR ARMS HOTEL, a fully licensed 300 year old inn, with old oak beams and lots of character. Within easy reach of Worcester, Birmingham and National Exhibition Centre. A la carte restaurant and bar food always available.

B&B from £35, Dinner available, Rooms 4 single, 3 double, 1 family, all en-suite, No smoking, Children welcome, Open all year.

The Manor Arms Hotel, Abberley Village, Worcestershire WR6 6BN
Tel: 01299 896507 Fax: 01299 896723   **Map Ref 23**

TARN, an attractive country family home with library, set in 17 acres of gardens and fields with views excellent breakfasts, home baking. Conveniently situated for Worcestershire way walk (guests collected). Safari park, Severn Valley Steam Railway, gardens, stately homes, golf. Ample parking.

B&B from £18pp, Rooms 2 single, 2 twin, No smoking or pets, Children welcome, Open February - November.
Topsy Beves, **Tarn,** Long Bank, Bewdley, Worcestershire DY12 2QT
Tel: 01299 402243   **Map Ref 24**

Built 1913, **ROSA LODGE** has three beautifully furnished bedrooms with en-suite facilities. All luxuriously appointed with television, trouser press, tea/coffee facilities. Parking. Excellent food served in Edwardian dining room. M42/M5 motorway complex one and a quarter miles, NEC 25 minutes, Birmingham ICC and NIA 20 minutes.
B&B from £25pp, Dinner from £11.50, Rooms 1 single, 1 twin, 1 double, all en-suite, Restricted smoking, Children over 12, Pets by arrangement, Open all year.
Sandra Shakespeare, **Rosa Lodge,** 38 Station Road, Blackwell, Worcestershire B60 1PZ
Tel: 0121 445 5440 Fax: 0121 445 5440   **Map Ref 25**

BANK HOUSE HOTEL, GOLF & COUNTRY CLUB, sympathetically y converted country house hotel and golf course set in 123 acres of countryside, 3 miles from Worcester. On A4103 Worcester to Hereford road, close to many local attractions.

B&B from £67.50, Dinner available, Rooms 11 single, 32 double, 23 twin, all en-suite, No smoking, Children welcome, Open all year.
Bank House Hotel, Golf & Country Club, Hereford Road, Bransford, Worcestershire WR6 5JD
Tel: 01886 833551 Fax: 01886 832461   **Map Ref 26**

THE LYGON ARMS, 16th century coaching inn set in the heart of the Cotswolds, with all comforts of the 20th century. Well situated for touring the Cotswolds and Shakespeare country.

B&B from £185, Dinner available, Rooms 2 single, 48 double, 9 twin, 6 triple, all en-suite, Open all year.

The Lygon Arms, Broadway, Worcestershire WR12 7DU
Tel: 01386 852255 Fax: 01386 858611 Email: info@the-lygon-arms.co.uk   **Map Ref 27**

OLIVE BRANCH GUEST HOUSE, 16th century house with modern amenities close to centre of village. Traditional English breakfast served. Reduced rates for 3 or more nights.

B&B from £19, Rooms 2 single, 3 double, 2 twin, 1 triple, most en-suite, Open all year.

Olive Branch Guest House, 78 High Street, Broadway, Worcestershire WR12 7AJ
Tel: 01386 853440 Fax: 01386 853440 Email: mark@olivebr.u-net.com   **Map Ref 27**

PATHLOW HOUSE, a comfortable period house, situated centrally for all amenities.

B&B from £42, Rooms 4 double, 1 twin, 1 family, most en-suite. Open all year.

Pathlow House, 82 High Street, Broadway, Worcestershire WR12 7AJ
Tel: 01386 853444   **Map Ref 27**

COLLIN HOUSE HOTEL & RESTAURANT, 16th century secluded Cotswold hotel, with traditional atmosphere and charm. Four-poster bedrooms, inglenook fireplaces. Fine views, extensive gardens. Noted for food.

B&B from £46, Dinner available, Rooms 1 single, 3 double, 3 twin, most en-suite, Open all year.
Collin House Hotel & Restaurant, Collin Lane, Broadway, Worcestershire WR12 7PB
Tel: 01386 858354   **Map Ref 27**

....

EASTBANK, quiet location, half a mile from village. All rooms fully en-suite (bath/shower), with colour TV and beverage facilities. Homely atmosphere. Free brochure.

B&B from £20, Rooms 2 double, 2 twin, 2 triple, all en-suite, Open all year.
Eastbank, Station Drive, Broadway, Worcestershire WR12 7DF
Tel: 01386 852659   **Map Ref 27**

....

SOUTHWOLD GUEST HOUSE, warm welcome, friendly service, good cooking at this large Edwardian house, only 4 minutes' walk from village centre.

B&B from £20, Rooms 1 single, 4 double, 2 twin, 1 family, suites available, most en-suite, Open all year.
Southwold Guest House, Station Road, Broadway, Worcestershire WR12 7DE
Tel: 01386 853681 Fax: 01386 854610   **Map Ref 27**

....

WHITE ACRES GUESTHOUSE, spacious Victorian house with en-suite bedrooms, 3 with four-poster beds. Off-road parking. 4 minutes' walk from the village centre. Reductions for 3 or more nights. Bargain winter breaks.

B&B from £40, Rooms 5 double, 1 twin, all en-suite, Open March - October.

White Acres Guesthouse, Station Road, Broadway, Worcestershire WR12 7DE
Tel: 01386 852320   **Map Ref 27**

....

WINDRUSH HOUSE, a spacious Edwardian house offering traditional English breakfast. All rooms en-suite with welcome trays, colour TV and hair dryers. Private parking within 2 minutes walk to village. Reductions in tariff after 2 nights. Bargain winter breaks. Open all year.

B&B from £20pp, Rooms 1 twin, 3 double, all en-suite, Restricted smoking, Pets by arrangement, Open all year except Christmas.
Joan Nadin, **Windrush House,** Station Road, Broadway, Worcestershire WR12 7DE
Tel: 01386 853577   **Map Ref 27**

....

BROADWAY HOTEL, Grade II listed 16th century hotel in the heart of picturesque village. Combines old world charm with the comforts and amenities of a modern hotel, recently refurbished.

B&B from £47.50, Dinner available, Rooms 2 single, 10 double, 6 twin, all en-suite, Open all year.
Broadway Hotel, The Green, Broadway, Worcestershire WR12 7AA
Tel: 01386 852041 Fax: 01386 853879   **Map Ref 27**

....

LEASOW HOUSE, 17th century Cotswold-stone farmhouse tranquilly set in open countryside close to Broadway village.

B&B from £53, Rooms 3 double, 2 twin, 2 triple, all en-suite, Open all year.

Leasow House, Laverton Meadow, Broadway, Worcestershire WR12 7NA
Tel: 01386 584526 Fax: 01386 584596 Email: bmeeking@compuserve.com   **Map Ref 28**

PINE LODGE HOTEL, with convenient access to the motorway network, in beautiful countryside. This Spanish design hotel has 2 restaurants, lounge bar, 12 conference and banqueting suites and leisure club. Close to NEC, Birmingham, Cadbury World and Warwick Castle.
B&B from £35, Dinner available, Rooms 15 single, 70 double, 12 twin, 17 triple, all en-suite. Open all year.
Pine Lodge Hotel, Kidderminster Road, Bromsgrove, Worcestershire B61 9AB
Tel: 01527 576600 Fax: 01527 878981 **Map Ref 30**

....

BROMSGROVE COUNTRY HOTEL, a quiet, elegant Victorian residence with modern amenities, suitable for business or pleasure. Close to the M6/M42/M5 junctions and historic countryside. A pleasant stay ensured under the personal supervision of the proprietors.
B&B from £40, Dinner available, Rooms 4 double, 2 twin, 3 triple, most en-suite, Open all year.
Bromsgrove Country Hotel, 249 Worcester Road, Stoke Heath, Bromsgrove, Worcestershire B61 7JA
Tel: 01527 835522 Fax: 01527 871257 **Map Ref 31**

....

THE CEDARS GUEST HOUSE, in own grounds on edge of Cotswolds (Broadway 7 miles). Private parking. Pretty Riverside village. Ideal for touring/business. In the heart of England, Cotswold, Cheltenham and Stratford on Avon. Good walks. All rooms tea/coffee, colour TV. Guest Lounge and bar. Dogs and children welcome.
B&B from £15pp, Rooms 1 single, 2 twin, 1 double, 2 family, some en-suite, Restricted smoking, Pets by arrangement, Open all year except Christmas & New Year.
Mrs Joan & Mr Douglas Faulkner, **The Cedars Guest House,** Evesham Road, Cropthorne, Worcestershire WR10 3JU
Tel: 01386 860219 **Map Ref 32**

....

THE WATERSIDE HOTEL, family-run hotel offering comfortable accommodation in a friendly atmosphere. Riverside situation, close to town centre. Ideal base for touring the Cotswolds and Shakespeare country.
B&B from £20.50, Rooms 10 single, 4 double, 10 twin, 1 triple, 1 family, most en-suite, Open all year.
The Waterside Hotel, 56 Waterside, Evesham, Worcestershire WR11 6BS
Tel: 01386 442639 Email: mike.spires@btinternet.com **Map Ref 33**

....

EVESHAM HOTEL, family-run Tudor mansion in 2.5 acre garden, offering unusual food and wine and all modern facilities. Ideal touring centre. Indoor pool designed for fun.
B&B from £58, Dinner available, Rooms 6 single, 22 double, 11 twin, 1 family, all en-suite, Open all year.
Evesham Hotel, Cooper's Lane, off Waterside, Evesham, Worcestershire WR11 6DA
Tel: 01386 765566 Fax: 01386 765443 **Map Ref 33**

....

THE MILL AT HARVINGTON, peaceful, owner-run riverside hotel tastefully converted from beautiful house and mill. In acres of gardens, quarter of a mile from Evesham to Stratford road.
B&B from £58, Dinner available, Rooms 12 double, 3 twin, all en-suite, Open all year.
The Mill at Harvington, Anchor Lane, Harvington, Evesham, Worcestershire WR11 5NR
Tel: 01386 870688 Fax: 01386 870688 **Map Ref 34**

....

THE BULLS HEAD INN, boasts real log fires in inglenook fireplaces, original 14th century flagstone floors and a wealth of old oak beams. A family owned and run business situated opposite the village green and offering delightful accommodation, extensive well-cooked food and local ales.

B&B from £35pp, Dinner from £10, Rooms 1 twin, 3 double, 1 family, all en-suite, Children & pets welcome, Open all year.
Garry Cant, **The Bulls Head Inn,** The Village Green, Inkberrow, Worcestershire WR7 4DY
Tel: 01386 792233 Fax: 01386 793090 **Map Ref 35**

GAINSBOROUGH HOUSE HOTEL, traditional hotel close to River Severn. The Severn Valley Railway, West Midlands safari Park and Worcestershire countryside are all close at hand.

B&B from £35, Dinner available, Rooms 1 single, 12 double, 24 twin, 5 triple, all en-suite, Open all year.

Gainsborough House Hotel, Bewdley Hill, Kidderminster, Worcestershire DY11 6BS
Tel: 01562 820041 Fax: 01562 66179   **Map Ref 36**

....

CEDARS HOTEL, charming conversion of a Georgian building close to the River Severn, Severn Valley Railway and Worcestershire countryside, 15 minutes from M5.

B&B from £33.25, Dinner available, Rooms 2 single, 8 double, 6 twin, 4 triple, 2 family, all en-suite, Open all year.

Cedars Hotel, Mason Road, Kidderminster, Worcestershire DY11 6AG
Tel: 01562 515595 Fax: 01562 751103   **Map Ref 36**

....

THE GRANARY HOTEL & RESTAURANT, family-owned restaurant and hotel renowned for food and good service. Close to Severn Valley Railway and safari park. Rural location.

B&B from £45, Dinner available, Rooms 5 double, 13 twin, all en-suite, Open all year.
The Granary Hotel & Restaurant, Shenstone, Kidderminster, Worcestershire DY10 4BS
Tel: 01562 777535 Fax: 01562 777722   **Map Ref 37**

....

BREDON HOUSE HOTEL, quiet, relaxed and friendly family-run hotel with spectacular views. 100 yards from town centre, Winter gardens and theatre. Wonderful walks. Car park, pets welcome.

B&B from £35, Rooms 2 single, 2 double, 2 twin, 2 triple, 1 family, all en-suite, Open all year.

Bredon House Hotel, 34 Worcester Road, Malvern, Worcestershire WR14 4AA
Tel: 01684 566990 Fax: 01684 575323   **Map Ref 22**

....

MOUNT PLEASANT HOTEL, Georgian building with Orangery, in 1.5 acres of garden with beautiful views. Close to theatre and shops and the direct access to Malvern Hills.

B&B from £42.50, Dinner available, Rooms 3 single, 7 double, 5 twin, most en-suite, Open all year.
Mount Pleasant Hotel, Belle Vue Terrace, Malvern, Worcestershire WR14 4PZ
Tel: 01684 561837 Fax: 01684 569968   **Map Ref 22**

....

GREAT MALVERN HOTEL, in Malvern's central conservation area, close to the Priory and Winter Gardens, this early Victorian hotel was refurbished in 1997. Run by the proprietors.

B&B from £40, Dinner available, Rooms 1 single, 8 double, 2 twin, 3 triple, most en-suite, Open all year.

Great Malvern Hotel, Graham Road, Malvern, Worcestershire WR14 2HN
Tel: 01684 563411 Fax: 01684 560514   **Map Ref 22**

....

COTFORD HOTEL, peaceful situation near town centre and hills. Ample car parking, good food, good service and value for money.

B&B from £40, Dinner available, Rooms 8 single, 3 double, 1 twin, 4 triple, all en-suite, Open all year.

Cotford Hotel, Graham Road, Malvern, Worcestershire WR14 2HU
Tel: 01684 572427 Fax: 01684 572952   **Map Ref 22**

COLWALL PARK HOTEL, charming country house hotel set on the western side of the Malvern Hills. Well-appointed bedrooms. Good views of hills and mature hotel garden. Enjoy award-winning cuisine in relaxing and comfortable surroundings.
B&B from £59.50, Dinner available, Rooms 3 single, 9 double, 7 twin, 2 triple, 2 family, all en-suite, Open all year.
Colwall Park Hotel, Walwyn Road, Colwall, Malvern, Worcestershire WR13 6QG
Tel: 01684 540206 Fax: 01684 540847 **Map Ref 38**

HOLDFAST COTTAGE HOTEL, small oak-beamed country house set in 2 acres of gardens at the foot of the Malvern Hills. Pretty bedrooms, log fires, wonderful views. Award-winning restaurant.

B&B from £42, Dinner available, Rooms 1 single, 5 double, 2 twin, all en-suite, Open all year.
Holdfast Cottage Hotel, Marlbank Road, Little Malvern, Malvern, Worcestershire WR13 6NA
Tel: 01684 310288 Fax: 01684 311117 **Map Ref 39**

THE COTTAGE IN THE WOOD HOTEL, set high on the Malvern Hills with 30-mile views to the Cotswolds. Family-owned and run. Exceptional food. Breaks available all week, all year.
B&B from £70, Dinner available, Rooms 16 double, 4 twin, all en-suite, Open all year.
The Cottage in the Wood Hotel, Holywell Road, Malvern Wells, Malvern, Worcestershire WR14 4LG
Tel: 01684 575859 Fax: 01684 560662 **Map Ref 40**

HARCOURT COTTAGE, nestling on the west side of the Malvern Hills, well placed for walking holidays or as a base for touring. English and French cuisine.

B&B from £38, Dinner available, Rooms 2 double, 1 twin, all en-suite, Open all year.
Harcourt Cottage, 252 West Malvern Road, West Malvern, Malvern, Worcestershire WR14 4DQ
Tel: 01684 574561 **Map Ref 41**

MALVERN HILLS HOTEL, enchanting hotel sitting atop the Malvern Hills. Magnificent views, prettily decorated en-suite rooms, oak panelled lounge, friendly and efficient staff.
B&B from £32-£50pp, Dinner available, Rooms 2 single, 6 double, 7 twin, 2 triple, all en-suite, Open all year.
Malvern Hills Hotel, British Camp, Wynd's Point, Malvern, Worcestershire WR13 6DW
Tel: 01684 540690 Fax: 01684 540327 **Map Ref 42**

HOTEL MONTVILLE & GRANNY'S RESTAURANT, perfect location for NEC, Birmingham station and airport, Stratford, Cotswolds, M5, M6, M42 and M40. Privately owned and managed. Free car parking.
B&B from £30, Dinner available, 10 single, 3 double, 1 twin, 2 triple, most en-suite, Open all year.
Hotel Montville & Granny's Restaurant, 101 Mount Pleasant, Southcrest, Redditch, Worcestershire B97 4JE
Tel: 01527 544411 Fax: 01527 544341 **Map Ref 43**

THE MAXIMILLIAN HOTEL, a warm and friendly, 6 minutes walk from city centre, 2 minutes from Shrub Hill station. 2 miles from M5, junction 6 or 7. Ample car parking.
B&B from £38.50, Dinner available, Rooms 4 single, 5 double, 4 twin, all en-suite, No smoking, Children welcome, No pets, Open all year.
The Maximillian Hotel, Shrub Hill Road, Shrub Hill, Worcestershire WR4 9EF
Tel: 01905 23867 & 21694 Fax: 01905 724935 **Map Ref 44**

ST. ELIZABETH'S COTTAGE, a beautiful country cottage in tranquil setting. Heated outdoor swimming pool. Lovely country walks. TV in all rooms plus tea/coffee facilities. Ample parking space. Plenty of pubs and restaurants nearby. Destinations within easy reach. Symphony Hall, Convention centre, Birmingham, Black country museum, Dudley.

B&B from £24pp, Rooms 1 twin, 2 double, all en-suite, No smoking, Children & pets welcome, Open all year.
Sheila Blankstone, **St. Elizabeth's Cottage,** Woodman Lane, Clent, Stourbridge, Worcestershire DY9 9PX
Tel: 01562 883883 **Map Ref 45**

THE WHITE LION HOTEL, the Inn of Henry Fieldings Tom Jones as seen on BBC TV, with historical connections during the Civil War. Ideal centre for visiting the Malvern Hill, Cotswolds, Cheltenham, Worcester, Ledbury etc. Excellent food, lunch time, cafe, evenings, Brasserie. Individually decorated rooms, all en-suite. Phone for brochure and info. **B&B from 72.50,** Dinner from £14, Rooms 1 single, 4 twin, 6 double, all en-suite, Children welcome, Pets by arrangement, Open all year.

Jon Lear **The White Lion Hotel,** 21 High Street Upton Upon Severn, Worcestershire WR8 9HJ
Tel: 01684 592551 Fax: 01684 592551 **Map Ref 46**

....

TILTRIDGE FARM & VINEYARD, a 9 acre vineyard and farm. Fully renovated period farmhouse close to Upton and Malvern showground. Warm welcome, bumper breakfast and wine from our own vineyard.

B&B from £23, Rooms 2 double, 1 twin, all en-suite, No smoking, Children welcome, Open all year.
Tiltridge Farm & Vineyard, Upper Hook Road, Upton upon Severn, Worcestershire WR8 0SA
Tel: 01684 592906 Fax: 01684 594142 **Map Ref 46**

....

BRIDGE HOUSE, originally a cottage, benefits from extensive and tasteful renovation, with each room enjoying lovely views. ETB 2 Crowns Highly Commended.

B&B from £20, Rooms 2 double, 1 twin, all en-suite, No smoking, Children over 5, Open all year.
Bridge House, Welland Stone, Upton upon Severn, Worcestershire WR8 0RW
Tel: 01684 593046 Fax: 01684 593046 **Map Ref 46**

....

LOCH RYAN HOTEL, a historic hotel, once home of Bishop Gore, close to cathedral, Royal Worcester porcelain factory and Commandery. Attractive terraced garden. Imaginative food. Holders of Heartbeat and Worcester City clean food awards.

B&B from £42, Dinner available, Rooms 1 single, 4 double, 4 twin, 1 family, all en-suite, No smoking, Children welcome, No pets, Open all year.
Loch Ryan Hotel, 119 Sidbury, Worcester, Worcestershire WR5 2DH
Tel: 01905 351143 Fax: 01905 351143 **Map Ref 44**

....

BURGAGE HOUSE, an elegant Georgian Mews House, is right next to the Cathedral in a small cobbled street. Comfortable colour coordinated rooms all have TV and tea/coffee. Cricket grounds, shops, restaurants and most amenities are nearby. Guests inglenook lounge. English breakfast with free range eggs.
B&B from £20pp, Rooms 1 single, 1 twin, 1 double,1 family, most en-suite, Restricted smoking, Children welcome, No pets, Open all year except Christmas.
Mrs J. A. Ratcliffe, **Burgage House,** 4 College Precincts, Worcester, Worcestershire WR1 2LG
Tel: 01905 25396 Fax: 01905 25396 **Map Ref 44**

....

OLD PARSONAGE FARM, is an 18th century country residence, enjoying views of the Malvern Hills and countryside. The house is beautifully decorated thanks to Ann Addison's natural flair for interior design. Besides this she is an accomplished cook producing imaginative dishes of a high standard. To complement this, husband Tony, is a wine expert with over 100 wines in stock.

B&B from £20.50pp, Dinner from £15.40, Rooms 3 double, all en-suite, Restricted smoking, Children over 12, Pets by arrangement, Open mid January - mid December.

Mrs Ann Addison, **Old Parsonage Farm,** Hanley Castle, Worcester, Worcestershire WR8 0BU
Tel: 01684 310124 **Map Ref 44**

Kent is a county for all seasons with its orchards and gardens but is also a county steeped in history. Its great passenger port, Dover, is the gateway to Britain, whose harbours are thronged with cross-Channel ferries, cargo boats and yachts, all overlooked by the grey walls of Dover Castle. Known since the height of the Cinque Ports - powerful, prosperous ports whose men and ships guarded their king and country - as the Key to England, Dover is one of the most strategic strongholds in Europe. Inland there are also dramatic castles. The thirteenth century splendour of Leeds Castle has been enlarged and enriched over the century by Kings of England. Both Leeds and Lullingstone were loved by Henry VIII and Anne Boleyn, whose childhood home was Hever Castle.

Kent has hundreds of well preserved historical buildings and many eminent people have been associated with the county, leaving houses as reminders of their lives and times. One of the county's most famous landmarks is Canterbury Cathedral. Canterbury is the cradle of Christianity in Saxon England, standing on a site that had been occupied for three hundred and fifty years when the Romans arrived in AD 43.

Maidstone, the county town of Kent, is a thriving commercial and business centre with excellent shopping and leisure facilities - but there are many reminders of the town's historical past from the old gatehouse to the Archbishop's Palace. Sevenoaks is still a typical market town, despite its closeness to London. In the town centre there are many old buildings including the Market House and the Red House, the home of Jane Austen's uncle whom she often visited.

Royal Tunbridge Wells was a fashionable spa in the seventeenth to nineteenth centuries and in Georgian times the aristocracy flocked here to indulge in high society life.

Kent's holiday coast in the north thrives on its good sands, safe bathing and record for long hours of sunshine and low rainfall. The towns mix the grace and charm of Regency houses with Victorian Gothic, yet there is plenty of modern entertainment. Off the coast are two islands. Thanet is an island in name only although in Roman and Saxon times it was separated from the mainland by the Rivers Stour and Wantsum. Sheppey (Isle of Sheep) is cut off from the mainland by the narrow Swale Channel and crossed only by the Kingsferry Bridge. Margate and Ramsgate are popular resorts and both have miles of safe sands and plenty of entertainment, although Ramsgate is more of a sea-going and olde worlde town. Broadstairs is another popular seaside town and there are reminders of the Flemish weavers in Sandwich, an ancient Cinque Port now two miles from the sea.

left, The River Stour, Canterbury

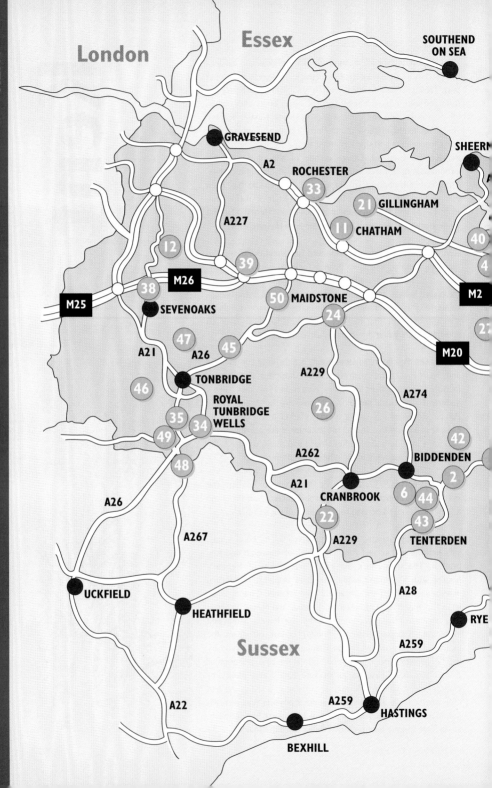

MARGATE

HERNE BAY

WHITSTABLE

28 29

BROADSTAIRS

7

51

A253

*ERSHAM

A299

32

RAMSGATE

A28

A2

8

10

36

SANDWICH

CANTERBURY

37 16

A2

A256

13

DEAL

9

15

3

14

ASHFORD

5

17

4

DOVER

070

20

23

FOLKESTONE

18

30

NEW ROMNEY

THE COACH HOUSE, is one mile from Bethersden village, well served with country pubs for evening meals. TV's, tea/coffee facilities. Breakfast of your choice from local produce. Dutch spoken. Guests warmly welcomed with an informal atmosphere. easy reach Euro Tunnel, Leeds castle and Canterbury.
B&B from £17.50pp, Rooms 1 twin, 1 double, 1 family, all en-suite or private, Restricted smoking, Children welcome, No pets, Open March - October.
Bernard & Else Broad, **The Coach House,** Oakmead Farm, Bethersden, Ashford, Kent TN26 3DU
Tel: 01233 820583 **Map Ref 1**

LION HOUSE, is a listed Queen Anne farmhouse set in a large mature garden. Comfortable centrally heated accommodation with en-suite bath and shower, TV, tea/coffee facilities and trouser press etc. Private dining room and patio garden.
B&B from £20pp, Dinner from £5, Rooms 1 single, 1 twin, 1 family, all en-suite, Restricted smoking, Children welcome, No pets, Open all year except Christmas.
Gerald & Caroline Mullins, **Lion House,** Church Hill, High Malden, Ashford, Kent TN26 3LS
Tel: 01233 850 446 Fax: 01233 850 446 **Map Ref 2**

CROFT HOTEL, a country house in 2 acres of gardens. Channel Tunnel 10 miles, Canterbury 12 miles, Dover 22 miles. Ideal for business people and tourists alike.

B&B from £40, Dinner available, Rooms 6 single, 8 double, 9 twin, 4 triple, 1 family all en-suite, Open all year.

Croft Hotel, Canterbury Road, Kennington, Ashford, Kent TN25 4DU
Tel: 01233 622140 Fax: 01233 635271 **Map Ref 3**

BULLTOWN FARMHOUSE, is a 15th century timber framed farmhouse in countryside of outstanding natural beauty on the southwestern side of the North Downs, but still close enough to Ports, Channel Tunnel and Canterbury. Tea/coffee facilities in rooms. Excellent country pubs, close by for dining out.
B&B from £20pp, Rooms 1 twin, 1 double, 1 family, all en-suite, No smoking or pets, Children welcome, Open all year.
Mrs L Wilton, **Bulltown Farmhouse,** Bulltown Lane, West Brabourne, Ashford, Kent TN25 5NB
Tel: 01233 813505 **Map Ref 4**

WARREN COTTAGE HOTEL, a 17th century hotel and restaurant, set in 2.5 acres, where a cosy atmosphere awaits. All rooms en-suite with colour TV, large car park. M20 junction 10 and minutes from Ashford International Station, Channel Tunnel, Dover and Folkestone.
B&B from £34.90, Dinner available, Rooms 2 single, 2 double, 1 twin, 1 triple, 1 family, all en-suite, Open all year.
Warren Cottage Hotel, 136 The Street, Willesborough, Ashford, Kent TN24 0NB
Tel: 01233 621905 Fax: 01233 623400 **Map Ref 5**

BISHOPSDALE OAST, a relaxing Oast house secluded in the heart of Kent, away from all traffic. Near to various garden, castles and places of historical interest. Bedrooms are large with super king sized beds, colour TV, tea/coffee facilities. Breakfast or dinner on the terrace or dining room.

B&B from £25pp, Dinner from £17, 3 rooms can be single/twin/double/family, all en-suite, Restricted smoking, Children over 12, No pets, Open all year.
Iain & Jane Drysdale, **Bishopsdale Oast,** Biddenden, Kent TN27 8DR
Tel: 01580 291027 & 292065 Fax: 01580 292321 **Map Ref 6**

CASTLEMERE HOTEL, is a 37 bedroom family run hotel. It is a 19th century Victorian building set on it's own grounds and overlooks the English Channel. Most rooms are en-suite with tea/coffee facilities, television, telephone. Broadstairs makes a perfect location to relax by the sea.

B&B from £25pp, Dinner from £12, Rooms 10 single, 14 twin, 10 double, 2 family, all en-suite, Children & pets welcome, Open all year.
Mr Ian Baverstock & Miss Fiona Munro, **Castlemere Hotel,** 15 Western Esplanade, Broadstairs, Kent CT10 1TD
Tel: 01843 861566 Fax: 01843 866379 **Map Ref 7**

....

MAYNARD COTTAGE, dates to 1695. Oak timber framed with Kent-peg tiled roof. Period furniture throughout. Bedrooms comfortably equipped with televisions, radio-alarms, tea/coffee and goodie tray. Breakfast generous enough to satisfy the heartiest appetite. All diets catered for. 5-6 minutes walk city centre. Canterbury east/rail 2 minutes on Ashford A28 road.

B&B from £19pp, Dinner from £14.50, Rooms 1 twin/double, 1 family, Restricted smoking, Children welcome, No pets, Open all year.
Fiona Ely, **Maynard Cottage,** 106 Wincheap, Canterbury, Kent CT1 3RS
Tel: 01227 454991 Mobile: 0468 074177 **Map Ref 8**

....

ZAN STEL LODGE, a gracious Edwardian house offering value for money accommodation, and individually styled bedrooms with little niceties that usually meet with guests approval. The elegant dining room overlooks a pretty cottage garden including fishponds. Enjoy your stay in a very homely atmosphere. ETB 2 Crown Highly Commended.
B&B from £22pp, Rooms 1 twin, 2 double, 1 family, 2 en-suite, No smoking or pets, Open all year except Christmas.
Zandra & Ron Stedman, **Zan Stel Lodge,** 140 Old Dover Road, Canterbury, Kent CT1 3NX
Tel: 01227 453654 **Map Ref 8**

....

ORIEL LODGE, situated in a tree-lined residential avenue, very near the city centre and restaurants, is an attractive Edwardian house with six well-furnished bedrooms and clean, up-to-date facilities. Afternoon tea served in the garden or lounge with log fire. ETB 2 Crowns, Highly Commended. AA, RAC and Which? Recommended. Private parking.
B&B from £20pp, Rooms 1 single, 1 twin, 3 double, 1 family, some en-suite, Restricted smoking, Children over 6, No pets, Open all year.
Keith & Anthea Rishworth, **Oriel Lodge,** 3 Queens Avenue, Canterbury, Kent CT2 8AY
Tel: 01227 462845 Fax: 01227 462845 **Map Ref 8**

....

CATHEDRAL GATE HOTEL, a mediaeval family run hotel next to Canterbury Cathedral. Beams, sloping floors, winding corridors and warm welcome. TV, tea/coffee facilities and direct dial telephone in all rooms. Residents licence, bar and lounge. Continental breakfast included, full English breakfast extra from March onwards.

B&B from £20pp, Dinner from £10, Rooms 5 single, 7 twin, 7 double, 5 family, some en-suite, Children welcome, Pets by arrangement, Open all year.
Mrs C Jubber, **Cathedral Gate Hotel,** 36 Burgate, Canterbury CT1 2HA
Tel: 01227 464381 Fax: 01227 462800 **Map Ref 8**

....

MAGNOLIA HOUSE, a quiet Georgian house in attractive city street. Close to university, gardens, river and city centre. Pretty walled garden in which to relax. Winner 1995 "Welcome to Kent Hospitality Award".
B&B from £36, Dinner available, Rooms 1 single, 4 double, 2 twin, all en-suite, Open all year.
Magnolia House, 36 St. Dunstan's Terrace, Canterbury, Kent CT2 8AX
Tel: 01227 765121 Fax: 01227 765121 **Map Ref 8**

CHAUCER LODGE, Maria and Alistair Wilson extend a warm, friendly welcome to this comfortable family guest house. City 10 minutes' walk, county cricket grounds 5 minutes'. High standard of cleanliness and furnishings.

B&B from £22, Dinner available, Rooms 2 double, 2 twin, 1 triple, 1 family, all en-suite, Open all year.
Chaucer Lodge, 62 New Dover Road, Canterbury, Kent CT1 3DT
Tel: 01227 459141 Fax: 01227 459141 **Map Ref 8**

....

CANTERBURY HOTEL, an elegant Victorian hotel 10 minutes from city centre, providing high standards of personal service and comfort. Famed for its "La Bonne Cuisine" French restaurant. Some executive rooms, one four poster-suite.

B&B from £45, Dinner available, Rooms 5 single, 5 double, 13 twin, 1 triple, 2 family, all en-suite, Open all year.
Canterbury Hotel, 71 New Dover Road, Canterbury, Kent CT1 3DZ
Tel: 01227 450551 Fax: 01227 780145 **Map Ref 8**

....

CLARE ELLEN GUEST HOUSE, 2 Crown Highly Commended. A warm welcome and B&B in style. Large elegant en-suite rooms, all with colour TV, clock radio, hair dryer and tea/coffee making facilities. Six minutes walk to town centre and bus station, five minutes to Canterbury East train station. Private car park and garage available. Email: loraine.williams@virgin.net
B&B from £22.50pp, Rooms 1 single, 3 double, 2 twin, (2 family), all en-suite, Children welcome, No pets, Open all year.
Mrs Loraine Williams, **Clare Ellen Guest House,** 9 Victoria Road, Canterbury, Kent CT1 3SG
Tel: 01227 760205 Fax: 01227 784482 **Map Ref 8**

....

COUNTY HOTEL, situated in the heart of the city, close to the cathedral, with gourmet restaurant and coffee shop.

B&B from £88.95, Dinner available, Rooms 15 single, 27 double, 30 twin, 1 family, all en-suite, Open all year,
County Hotel, High Street, Canterbury, Kent CT1 2RX
Tel: 01227 766266 Fax: 01227 451512 **Map Ref 8**

....

IFFIN FARMHOUSE, a warm welcome awaits you in this old 18th century farmhouse, renovated to a high standard in the mid 50's. Offering luxury en-suite bedrooms with TV and tea/coffee trays and set in 10 acres of gardens, orchards and paddocks in a quiet rural setting only 6 minutes drive to the centre of historic Canterbury.

B&B from £22.50pp, Rooms 1 twin, 2 double, 2 family, all en-suite, No smoking or pets, Children over 5, Open all year except Christmas & New Year.
Colin & Rosemary Stevens, **Iffin Farmhouse,** Iffin Lane, Canterbury, Kent CT4 7BE
Tel: 01227 462776 Fax: 01227 462776 **Map Ref 8**

....

EBURY HOTEL, a family run Victorian hotel just outside the city centre. Licensed restaurant, large public rooms and bedrooms. Heated indoor pool and spa.
B&B from £45, Dinner available, Rooms 2 single, 7 double, 4 twin, 1 triple, 1 family, all en-suite, Open all year.
Ebury Hotel, New Dover Road, Canterbury, Kent CT1 3DX
Tel: 01227 768433 Fax: 01227 459187 **Map Ref 8**

....

THE OLD COACH HOUSE, originally a coaching inn (c1815), the hotel is run along the lines of a French auberge by chef/patron. Licensed restaurant specialising in local fish and game. Large car park. Ideally placed for Dover and Canterbury.
B&B from £47, Dinner available, Rooms 2 double, 2 twin, 1 family, all en-suite.
The Old Coach House, Dover Road, Barham, Canterbury, Kent CT4 6SA
Tel: 01227 831218 Fax: 01227 831932 **Map Ref 9**

CROCKSHARD FARMHOUSE, an exceptionally attractive period farmhouse in beautiful gardens and countryside. Breakfast with home produced bread, jam and eggs. Tea/coffee facilities available in the comfortable bedrooms. Drawing room with TV. Swimming pool. 3 family bedrooms. Ideal for Canterbury, channel ports and for visiting the whole of Kent. Golf, horse riding and many places to eat nearby.
B&B from £17.50pp, (Children sharing parents room £12), Rooms 1 twin, 3 family, Children welcome, Restricted smoking, Pets by arrangement, Open all year.
Mrs Nicola Ellen **Crockshard Farmhouse,** Wingham, Canterbury CT3 1NY
Tel: 01227 720464 Fax: 07070 604027 **Map Ref 10**

HOLMWOOD HOTEL, takes great pleasure in introducing you, your clients or personnel to a pleasantly run family hotel. All rooms are centrally heated with vanity basins colour TV, tea/coffee facilities and radio alarm. Spacious drawing room and sun lounge. Residential license. ETB 2 Crown Listed.
B&B from £19.50pp, Dinner from £2.50, Rooms 7 single, 3 twin, 1 double, 1 family, most en-suite, Smoking & Children welcome, Pets by arrangement, Open all year except January.
Maurice Walters, **Holmwood Hotel,** 158 Maidstone Rd, Chatham ME4 6EN
Tel: 01634 842849 Fax: 01634 832905 **Map Ref 11**

THE BRANDS HATCH THISTLE, set at the entrance to the world-famous motor racing circuit, the hotel offers elegance and varied cuisine. Easy access, near M20, M25 and M26.

B&B from £60, Dinner available, Rooms 65 double, 51 twin, 4 triple, all en-suite, Open all year.
The Brands Hatch Thistle, Brands Hatch, Dartford, Kent DA3 8PE
Tel:01474 854900 Fax: 01474 853220 **Map Ref 12**

ROYAL HOTEL, a Georgian town hotel, famous for hosting Lord Nelson and Lady Hamilton. Delightful rooms with sea views. Excellent restaurant specialising in fish.

B&B from £40, Dinner available, Rooms 1 single, 5 double, 4 twin, 2 family, all en-suite, Open all year.
Royal Hotel, Beach Street, Deal, Kent CT14 6JD
Tel: 01304 375555 Fax: 01304 375555 **Map Ref 13**

KINGSDOWN COUNTRY HOTEL & CAPTAINS TABLE, a family run village hotel with full en-suite bedrooms, bar, comfortable dining room, secluded rear car park and gardens with a gate to the beach.

B&B from £22, Dinner available, Rooms 1 single, 2 double, 1 twin, all en-suite, Open all year.

Kingsdown Country Hotel & Captains Table, Cliffe Road, Kingsdown, Deal, Kent CT14 8AJ
Tel: 01304 373755 Fax: 01304 373755 **Map Ref 14**

HILLSIDE GUEST HOUSE, a regency house, terrace and garden. Off street parking. Hospitality trays and colour TV in rooms. Early breakfast available. 10 minutes to Port of Dover. 20 minutes Channel Tunnel. Convenient for golf, fishing and historic sites.

B&B from £18pp, Rooms 1 twin, 1 double, 1 family, all en-suite, Children welcome, No pets, Open all year except Christmas.
Mr & Mrs Cavell, **Hillside Guest House,** 214 Dover Road, Walmer, Deal, Kent CT14 7NB
Tel: 01304 372652 **Map Ref 15**

ILEX COTTAGE, a renovated 1736 house with lovely conservatory and country views. Secluded yet convenient village location north of Deal. Sandwich 5 minutes, Canterbury, Dover and Ramsgate 25 minutes.

B&B from £20, Dinner available, Rooms 1 double, 2 twin, all en-suite. Open all year.
Ilex Cottage, Temple Way, Worth, Deal, Kent CT14 0DA
Tel: 01304 617026   **Map Ref 16**

CASTLE HOUSE, looking for comfortable accommodation, good food and genuine hospitality then come to our Grade II listed guest house. All rooms non-smoking. En-suite rooms with colour televisions and hospitality trays. Ideally situated below Dover castle, close to ferries, cruise liners. 10 minutes Channel Tunnel.
B&B from £18pp, Dinner from £8.50, Rooms 1 single, 1 twin, 3 double, 1 family, all en-suite, No smoking, Children welcome, Pets by arrangement, Open all year.
Rodney & Elizabeth Dimech, **Castle House,** 10 Castle Hill Road, Dover, Kent CT16 1QW
Tel: 01304 201656 Fax: 01304 210197   **Map Ref 17**

CONIFERS GUEST HOUSE, a family guest house, 5 minutes' from rail station, town centre, sea front and Channel Tunnel terminus. Early breakfast available.

B&B from £16, Rooms 1 single, 2 double, 1 twin, 2 family, most en-suite, Open all year.
Conifers Guest House, 241 Folkestone Road, Dover, Kent CT17 9LL
Tel: 01304 205609   **Map Ref 17**

WHITMORE GUEST HOUSE, a warm welcome awaits you at this lovely Victorian Guest House. All rooms are clean, comfortable with en-suite facilities, colour TV, tea/coffee facilities, alarm clocks, hair dryers, shaver plugs. central heating, double glazed. Convenient for ferries, Hoverport, station, Channel Tunnel. Car parking.
B&B from £14pp, Rooms 1 single, 1 twin, 1 double, 2 family, all en-suite, Restricted smoking, Children welcome, Open all year except Christmas.
Mike & Margi Brunt, **Whitmore Guest House,** 261 Folkestone Road, Dover, Kent CT17 9LL
Tel: 01304 203080 Fax: 01304 240110   **Map Ref 17**

BLAKES OF DOVER, a family run bistro, wine bar and restaurant, having en-suite guest suites (bed, lounge and bath). Special tourist and early bird menus, real ales.

B&B from £37.50, Dinner available, Rooms 3 double, 2 twin, 1 triple, all en-suite, Open all year.

Blakes of Dover, 52 Castle Street, Dover, Kent CT16 1PJ
Tel: 01304 202194 Fax: 01304 202194   **Map Ref 17**

ST ALBANS BED & BREAKFAST, opposite Dover Priory Railway Station (courtesy bus ports). Friendly, homely atmosphere welcomes you to this comfortable family run guest house. Ideal stop over en-route to continent, 3 minutes ports, 10 minutes Tunnel. All rooms colour TV, tea/coffee. Cooked breakfasts from 0645hrs. Cards: Switch, Delta, Visa, Mastercard, Solo, Eletron, Amex.
B&B from £13-£25pp, Evening meals by arrangement from £6, includes wine/beer, Rooms 3 twin, 3 double, 1 family, 3 en-suite, non smoking rooms available, Children welcome, No pets, Open all year.
Mr Martin **St Albans Bed & Breakfast,** 71 Folkestone Rd, Dover CT17 9RZ
Tel: 01304 206308   **Map Ref 17**

THE CHURCHILL, under the white cliffs, between East and West docks and only 10 minutes away from the Channel Tunnel. Rooms have satellite TV.

B&B from £63, Dinner available, Rooms 6 single, 37 double, 20 twin, 5 family, all en-suite. Open all year.
The Churchill, Dover Waterfront, Dover, Kent CT17 9BP
Tel: 01304 203633 Fax: 01304 216320 **Map Ref 17**

WATERSIDE GUEST HOUSE, overlooking Romney Marsh which boasts numerous historical churches. Channel Tunnel 20 minutes. Port Lympne Wild Animal Park, Romney, Hythe and Dymchurch Railway close by. Ideal for touring Kent and Sussex. Private car park. Licensed lounge with satellite TV. Bedrooms have colour TV's and tea/coffee facilities. Good food.
B&B from £15pp, Dinner from £5, Rooms 1 single, 2 twin, 2 double, 1 family, some en-suite, Children welcome, No pets, Open all year.
Mrs Tinklin, **Waterside Guest House,** 15 Hythe Road, Dymchurch, Kent TN29 0LN
Tel/Fax: 01303 872253 **Map Ref 18**

FRITH FARM HOUSE, an elegant Georgian house, high on the North Downs. Beautiful gardens and its own cherry orchard. All rooms en-suite with TV and tea tray. Dinner by prior arrangement. A wonderful quiet situation.

B&B from £26pp, Rooms 1 twin, 2 double, No smoking or pets, Children over 10, Open all year except Christmas.
Markham & Susan Chesterfield, **Frith Farm House,** Otterden, Faversham, Kent ME13 0DD
Tel: 01795 890701 Fax: 01795 890009 **Map Ref 19**

HARBOURSIDE BED & BREAKFAST HOTEL, a Victorian house, superior en-suite rooms. The service, hospitality and views are truly unique. Licensed. No smoking.
B&B from £35, Rooms 4 double, 2 twin, most en-suite, Open all year.
Harbourside Bed & Breakfast Hotel, 14 Wear Bay Road, Folkestone, Kent CT19 6AT
Tel: 01303 256528 Fax: 01303 241299 EMail: r.j.pye@dial.pipex.com **Map Ref 20**

NORMANDIE GUEST HOUSE, central, near all local amenities, with parking nearby. Early breakfast served. Convenient for the harbour and trips to the continent.
B&B from £16, Rooms 2 single, 2 double, 2 twin, 2 family, Open all year.
Normandie Guest House, 39 Cheriton Road, Folkestone, Kent CT20 1DD
Tel: 01303 256233 **Map Ref 20**

WARDS HOTEL & RESTAURANT, a family run hotel, AA 3 Star, with ten beautifully designed double en-suite rooms with tea making facilities, Sky TV and direct dial telephone. Superb Bistro offering dishes from around the world, prices start for £5.95 for main courses. Voted 'Best Kept Hotel' for two years on the south east coast. Car park.
B&B from £50per room, Dinner from £5.95, Rooms 3 twin, 5 double, 2 family, all en-suite, Restricted smoking, Children welcome, No pets, Open all year.
Mr & Mrs J Ward, **Wards Hotel & Restaurant,** 39 Earls Avenue, Folkestone, Kent CT20 2HB
Tel: 01303 245166 Fax: 01303 254480 **Map Ref 20**

AUGUSTA HOTEL, a small, licensed hotel in central position, close to sea and Leas and with easy access to ferries and Eurotunnel. Spacious patio with access to private gardens. An elegant Victorian building with style. No lift.
B&B from £15, Dinner available, Rooms 3 single, 8 double, 1 twin, all en-suite, Open all year.
Augusta Hotel, 4 Augusta Gardens, Folkestone, Kent CT20 2RR
Tel: 01303 850952 Fax: 01303 240282 **Map Ref 20**

BANQUE HOTEL, hotel near sea front and shops. All rooms en-suite with colour TV, telephone, radio, tea/coffee facilities. Exercise room with sauna and solarium. Car park.

B&B from £20, Rooms 3 single, 5 double, 4 twin, all en-suite, Open all year.
Banque Hotel, 4 Castle Hill Avenue, Folkestone, Kent CT20 2QT
Tel: 01303 253797 Fax: 01303 253797   **Map Ref 20**

SUNNY LODGE GUEST HOUSE, the place to stay, a Victorian house with lovely garden and noted for high standards. Choice of breakfast. Central heating. Colour TV. Hospitality trays. Minutes to channel tunnel, town centre, stations and M20 Jn12. Private car park. ETB 2 Crown. Look forward to meeting you.
B&B from £16pp, Rooms 2 single, 2 twin, 2 double, 2 family, Children over 3 welcome, Open all year except Christmas & New Year.
Mrs J Young, **Sunny Lodge Guest House,** 85 Cheriton Rd, Folkestone, Kent CT20 2QL
Tel: 01303 251498   **Map Ref 20**

CLIFTON HOTEL, a Regency-style house in centre of the Leas, minutes from town centre, ferry and Channel Tunnel and with views of the English Channel. Good base for Canterbury. Weald of Kent and France.

B&B from £56, Dinner available, Rooms 20 single, 25 double, 29 twin, 5 triple, all en-suite, Open all year.
Clifton Hotel, The Leas, Clifton Gardens, Folkestone, Kent CT20 2EB
Tel: 01303 851231 Fax: 01303 851231   **Map Ref 20**

KING CHARLES HOTEL, a friendly, modern hotel run by family, catering for all requirements at very reasonable rates in comfortable accommodation.

B&B from £25, Dinner available, Rooms 1 single, 30 double, 21 twin, 21, triple, 5 family, all en-suite, Open all year.
King Charles Hotel, Brompton Road, Gillingham, Kent ME7 5QT
Tel: 01634 830303 Fax: 01634 829430   **Map Ref 21**

WOODHAM HALL HOTEL, a country house on the edge of the village, in interesting historic surroundings. Personal, friendly service. Tennis, snooker and horse-riding available. Ideal for holidays or business.

B&B from £35, Rooms 3 double, 2 family, all en-suite, Open all year.
Woodham Hall Hotel, Rye Road, Hawkhurst, Kent TN18 5DA
Tel: 01580 753428 Fax: 01580 753428   **Map Ref 22**

STADE COURT HOTEL, a sea front hotel, with well appointed family suites, indoor pool, golf, squash, sauna, solarium and so much more, 600 metres away at our sister hotel.

B&B from £67.50, Dinner available, Rooms 10 single, 11 double, 16 twin, 5 triple, all en-suite. Open all year.
Stade Court Hotel, West Parade, Hythe, Kent CT21 6DT
Tel: 01303 268263 Fax: 01303 261803   **Map Ref 23**

RUSSELL HOTEL, a converted convent school a few minutes from Maidstone and 1.5 miles from the M20. Set in secluded grounds with ample parking.

B&B from £45, Dinner available, Rooms 14 single, 16 double, 7 twin, 2 triple, 2 family, all en-suite, Open all year.

Russell Hotel, 136 Boxley Road, Maidstone, Kent ME14 2AH
Tel: 01622 692221 Fax: 01622 762084   **Map Ref 24**

GRANGEMOOR HOTEL, one hour from London and the Kent coast, in a quiet position on the edge of town. The hotel has rear gardens, restaurant and bar.

B&B from £35, Dinner available, Rooms 10 single, 15 double, 15 twin, 15 triple, 2 family, most en-suite, Open all year.
Grangemoor Hotel, St. Michael's Road, Maidstone, Kent ME16 8BS
Tel: 01622 677623 Fax: 01622 678246 **Map Ref 24**

WILLINGTON COURT, a charming Grade II listed building. Antiques, four-poster bed. All rooms have television, hospitality tray, hair dryer, trouser press plus extras for that touch of luxury. Adjacent to Mote Park and near Leeds Castle. ETB 2 Crown Highly Commended. AA Selected QQQQ.

B&B form £21pp, Rooms 2 double, 1 twin, all private facilities, Restricted smoking, No pets, Open all year.

Willington Court, Willington Street, Maidstone, Kent ME15 8JW
Tel: 01622 738885 Fax: 01622 631790 **Map Ref 24**

MERZIE MEADOWS, provides peaceful accommodation in a beautiful countryside setting, central to Leeds, Sissinghurst and many historic houses. Convenient for London . The guests accommodation is private, spacious and overlooking landscaped gardens with swimming pool. Near good eating places for evening meals. Spacious parking for cars.

B&B from £22-£22.50pp, Rooms 2 double, all en-suite, No smoking or pets, Children over 12, Open mid January - mid December
Rodney & Pamela Mumford, **Merzie Meadows,** Hunton Road, Harden, Maidstone, Kent TN12 9SL
Tel: 01622 820500 **Map Ref 26**

THE RINGLESTONE INN & FARMHOUSE HOTEL, a Kentish character farmhouse, furnished in rustic oak, one bedroom with canopied 4 poster bed. Surrounded by tranquil, landscaped gardens and farmland. Adjoining famous 16th century inn recommended by major guide books for Kentish fare, English fruit wines and real ales. Situated 10 minutes from J8 M20.Email: michelle@ringlestone.com
B&B from £47.50pp, Dinner from £6, Rooms 2 twin, 1 double, all en-suite, Restricted smoking, Children welcome, No pets, Open all year except Christmas & New Year.
Michael Millington-Buck, Stanley, **The Ringlestone Inn & Farmhouse Hotel,** Ringlestone Hamlet, Harrietsham, Maidstone, Kent ME17 1NX
Tel: 01622 859900 Fax: 01622 859966 **Map Ref 27**

THE NAYLAND ROCK HOTEL, we are a large, comfortable, family run, licensed hotel with gardens leading directly onto the promenade. All rooms with welcome tray, hair dryer, telephone and satellite TV, and are furnished to a high standard. Our restaurant overlooks the harbour and sands as so many of our rooms. Email: reception@nayland.co.uk
http://www.nayland.co.uk
B&B from £49.50pp, Dinner from £10.95, Rooms 6 single, 19 twin, 29 double, 10 family, all en-suite, Smoking & children welcome, No pets, Open all year.
The Nayland Rock Hotel, 1-5 Royal Crescent, Canterbury Rd, Margate CT9 2AJ
Tel: 01843 299992 Fax: 01843 292666 **Map Ref 28**

LONSDALE COURT HOTEL, a family run hotel near sea and shops. En-suite bedrooms with TV, telephone and tea making. Entertainment, bars, coffee shop. Sports hall for badminton, indoor bowls, sauna, solarium and heated pool.

B&B from £29, Dinner available, Rooms 11 single, 17 double, 15 suites, 18 triple, 2 family, most en-suite, Open all year.
Lonsdale Court Hotel, 51-61 Norfolk Road, Cliftonville, Margate, Kent CT9 2HX
Tel: 01843 221053 Fax: 01843 299993 **Map Ref 29**

MALVERN HOTEL, is a small private hotel overlooking the sea and lawns. Close to shops, amenities, restaurants, etc., with Canterbury (cathedral), cross-channel Ferryports and Channel Tunnel within easy reach. En-suite rooms have shower and toilet; All have TV, tea/coffee facilities. Non-smoking dining room.

B&B from £18-£21pp, Rooms 1 single, 2 twin, 5 double, 2 family, most en-suite, No pets, Open all year.
Malvern Hotel, Eastern Esplanade, Cliftonville, Margate, Kent CT9 2HL
Tel/Fax: 01843 290192   **Map Ref 29**

....

CLINTONS, set in illuminated garden square, this elegant hotel offers comfortable en-suite bedrooms, spacious lounge, licensed restaurant, saunas, jacuzzi, gym and solarium.

B&B from £28, Dinner available, Rooms 5 double, 5 twin, 3 triple, all en-suite, Open all year.
Clintons, 9 Dalby Square, Cliftonville, Margate, Kent CT9 2ER
Tel: 01843 290598   **Map Ref 29**

....

BROADACRE HOTEL, a small 16th century family run hotel offering a warm, friendly welcome and personal attention. Intimate restaurants, lounge, bar, garden.

B&B from £35, Dinner available, Rooms 3 single, 4 double, 2 twin, 1 family, all en-suite, Open all year.
Broadacre Hotel, North Street, New Romney, Kent TN28 8DR
Tel: 01797 362381 Fax: 01797 362381   **Map Ref 30**

....

ABBEYGAIL GUEST HOUSE, gives a friendly welcome at our family run guest house, near to Sandy beach, Chalk Cliffs and town. All rooms have colour TV, tea/coffee facilities. Some ground floor bedrooms. There is a guest lounge. Weekly half board rates available.
B&B from £13pp, Dinner from £6, Rooms 2 single, 1 twin, 2 double, 3 family, some en-suite, Restricted smoking, Children welcome, No pets, Open all year except Christmas.
Hazel & John Nash, **Abbeygail Guest House,** 17 Penshurst Road, Ramsgate, Kent CT11 8EG
Tel: 01843 594154   **Map Ref 32**

....

GOODWIN VIEW HOTEL, a sea front licensed hotel in Grade II listed historic building overlooking harbour and beach. Terminal and town within walking distance. Ideal base for touring Kent. Ferry travellers welcome.

B&B from £19, Rooms 4 single, 3 double, 2 twin, 2 triple, 2 family, some en-suite, Open all year.
Goodwin View Hotel, 19 Wellington Crescent, Ramsgate, Kent CT11 8DT
Tel: 01843 592345   **Map Ref 32**

....

EASTWOOD GUEST HOUSE, a pretty Victorian villa, close to ferry port and amenities. Comfortable rooms, mostly en-suite. Lock-up garages available. Breakfast served from 6.45 am.

B&B from £20, Dinner available, Rooms 1 single, 4 double, 4 twin, 6 family, some en-suite, Open all year.
Eastwood Guest House, 28 Augusta Road, Ramsgate, Kent CT11 8JS
Tel: 01843 591505 Fax: 01843 591505   **Map Ref 32**

....

ROYALE GUEST HOUSE, our homely, comfortable and friendly guest house welcomes you to bed and full English breakfast. Very close to the port and harbour and all amenities. Reductions for children. Mid week and one night bookings welcome. Colour TV and tea/coffee making facilities in all rooms.

B&B from £15pp, Rooms 4 single, 2 twin, 2 double, 1 family, 1 en-suite, Children over 2, Pets by arrangement, Open all year.
Sylvia & Anthony Barry, **Royale Guest House,** 7 Royal Road, Ramsgate, Kent CT11 9LE
Tel: 01843 594712   **Map Ref 32**

SHIRLEY'S HOTEL, overlooking Ramsgate harbour and Sally Line ferry terminal. 2 minutes from town centre. All rooms have colour TV and tea -making facilities.
B&B from £15, Rooms 2 single, 2 double, 2 twin, 3 triple, 2 family, some en-suite, Open all year.
Shirley's Hotel, 8 Nelson Crescent, Ramsgate, Kent CT11 9JF
Tel: 01843 584198 Fax: 01843 586759   **Map Ref 32**

....

SAN CLU HOTEL, a Grade II listed Victorian cliff top hotel, recently refurbished. Overlooking sea and sands and near cross-Channel ferry terminals and harbour. Quiet location out of town centre, but within easy reach of ample parking.

B&B from £45, Dinner available, Rooms 7 single, 18 double, 5 twin, 12 triple, 2 family, all en-suite, Open all year.
San Clu Hotel, Victoria Parade, East Cliff, Ramsgate, Kent CT11 8DT
Tel: 01843 592345 Fax: 01843 580157   **Map Ref 32**

....

BRIDGEWOOD MANOR HOTEL, a modern manor built around a classical courtyard. Superb leisure facilities make it an ideal choice for exploring Kent's many attractions.
B&B from £73.50, Rooms 57 double, 43 twin, all en-suite. Open all year.
Bridgewood Manor Hotel, Bridgewood Roundabout, Maidstone Road, Rochester, Kent ME5 9AX
Tel: 01634 201333 Fax: 01634 201330   **Map Ref 33**

....

RUSSELL HOTEL, a large Victorian house facing common, only minutes from town centre. Totally refurbished to highest modern standards.

B&B from £40, Dinner available, Rooms 11 double, 10 twin, 3 triple, all en-suite, Open all year.
Russell Hotel, 80 London Road, Royal Tunbridge Wells, Kent TN1 1DZ
Tel: 01892 544833 Fax: 01892 515846   **Map Ref 34**

....

THE SPA HOTEL, an elegant mansion overlooking the historic town of Royal Tunbridge Wells, Extensive leisure facilities and fine dining. Ideal for weekend breaks.
B&B from £88, Dinner available, Rooms 16 single, 32 double, 22 twin, 4 triple, all en-suite.
The Spa Hotel, Mount Ephraim, Royal Tunbridge Wells, Kent TN4 8XJ
Tel: 01892 520331 Fax: 01892 510575   **Map Ref 35**

....

BELL HOTEL, a 17th century riverside inn extended during Victorian times, recently refurbished in traditional manner to provide individual and comfortable accommodation with quality restaurant and cellar. Own golf club.

B&B from £70, Dinner available, Rooms 7 single, 6 double, 19 twin, 1 family, all en-suite, Open all year.
Bell Hotel, The Quay, Sandwich, Kent CT13 9EF
Tel: 01304 613388 Fax: 01304 615308   **Map Ref 36**

....

THE BLAZING DONKEY COUNTRY HOTEL & INN, one of East Kent's most atmospheric country inns. Situated in the heart of the countryside, between the coastal towns of Sandwich and Deal.
B&B from £35, Dinner available, Rooms 7 double, 6 twin, 6 triple, all en-suite, Open all year.
The Blazing Donkey Country Hotel & Inn, Hay Hill, Ham, Sandwich, Kent CT13 0HU
Tel: 01304 617362 Fax: 01304 615264   **Map Ref 37**

....

DONNINGTON MANOR HOTEL, hotel with full leisure facilities, in delightful countryside of Kent. Close to M25 and M26. Good base for many places of interest.

B&B from £55, Dinner available, Rooms 34 double, 27 twin, 2 family, all en-suite, Open all year.
Donnington Manor Hotel, London Road, Dunton Green, Sevenoaks, Kent TN13 2TD
Tel: 01732 46281 Fax: 01732 458116   **Map Ref 38**

THE BULL HOTEL, a privately run 14th century coaching inn, in secluded historic village 15 minutes from Sevenoaks. Just off M20 and M25/26, 30 minutes from Gatwick and London, 1 hour from Dover. Oak beams and inglenook fireplaces. Ideal for places of interest.
B&B from £37, Dinner available, Rooms 1 single, 3 double, 6 twin, some en-suite, Open all year.
The Bull Hotel, Wrotham, Sevenoaks, Kent TN15 7RF
Tel: 01732 885522 Fax: 01732 886288   **Map Ref 39**

....

THE BEAUMONT, clean, comfortable, quality accommodation with good food and friendly service. Most rooms en-suite, including 4-poster. Television, tea/coffee and telephone in every room. Superb prize - winning breakfast menu. Private car park. Conveniently located for historic Canterbury and Rochester. M2/M20 within 5-10 minutes. ETB Highly Commended.

B&B from £20pp, Dinner by arrangement from £8, Rooms 3 single, 2 twin, 4 double, 1 family, some en-suite, Restricted smoking, Children welcome, Pets by arrangement, Open all year.
Duncan Wetherall, **The Beaumont,** 74 London Road, Sittingbourne, Kent ME10 1NS
Tel: 01795 472536 Fax: 01795 426921 Email: beaumont74@aol.com   **Map Ref 40**

....

HEMPSTEAD HOUSE, an exclusive private Victorian country house on main A2 between Canterbury and Sittingbourne, offering quality accommodation, fine cuisine and friendly hospitality.
B&B from £62, Dinner available, Rooms 11 double, 2 twin, all en-suite. Open all year.
Hempstead House, London Road, Bapchild, Sittingbourne, Kent ME9 9PP
Tel: 01795 428020 Fax: 01795 428020   **Map Ref 41**

....

THE CHEQUERS INN 14th century country inn in Kent's Best Kept Village. All rooms have colour TV and tea/coffee facilities. has been owned and run by the Stevens family for thirty years. Renowned for good fresh food and is close to several stately homes, gardens and golf courses.

B&B from £22.50pp, Dinner from £4.95, Rooms 1 single, 2 twin, 2 double, 1 family, some en-suite, Smoking, children & pets welcome, Open all year except Christmas Day.
Frank & Frances Stevens, **The Chequers Inn,** Smarden, Kent TN27 8QA
Tel: 01233 770217 Fax: 01233 770623   **Map Ref 42**

....

COLLINA HOUSE HOTEL, an Edwardian house overlooking orchards and garden, within walking distance of picturesque town. Swiss-trained proprietors offering both English and Continental cooking.
B&B from £28, Dinner available, Rooms 1 single, 5 double, 1 twin, 4 triple, 3 family, all rooms en-suite. Open all year.
Collina House Hotel, East Hill, Tenterden, Kent TN30 6RL
Tel: 01580 764852 Fax: 01580 762224   **Map Ref 43**

....

LITTLE SILVER COUNTRY HOTEL, quality accommodation in Tudor-style country house hotel. Four-poster, brass bedded, family room and disabled facilities . A la carte menu. Personal service in a truly delightful and unique atmosphere. Landscaped gardens.
B&B from £60, Dinner available, Rooms 5 double, 3 twin, 1 triple, 1 family, all en-suite.
Little Silver Country Hotel, Ashford Road, St. Michaels, Tenterden, Kent TN30 6SP
Tel: 01233 850321 Fax: 01233 850647   **Map Ref 44**

....

A warm welcome awaits you at **LEAVERS OAST**. All rooms are spacious and comfortably furnished with TV and tea/coffee facilities. An excellent base for touring the many historic buildings and gardens including Hever and Leeds Castles, Chartwell, Sissinghurst, Knole and Penshurst place.
B&B from £27pp, Dinner from £20, Rooms 1 twin, 2 en-suite double, No smoking or pets, Children over 12, Open all year.
Anne Turner, **Leavers Oast,** Stanford Lane, Hadlow, Tonbridge, Kent TN11 0JN
Tel: 01732 850924 Fax: 01732 850924   **Map Ref 45**

SWALE COTTAGE, listed Grade II, is a large converted Kentish barn. In a unique and tranquil setting, it overlooks a mediaeval manor house, gardens and glorious countryside. Three spacious en-suite rooms with TV and tea/coffee trays. 1 romantic 4 poster. Parking. Near Penshurst Place, Hever, Chartwell and Tunbridge Wells. ETB Listed Highly Commended. AA Premier Selected.

B&B from £28pp, Rooms 1 twin, 2 double, all en-suite, No smoking or pets, Children over 10, Open all year.
Cynthia Dakin, **Swale Cottage,** Poundsbridge Lane, Penshurst, Tonbridge, Kent TN11 8AH
Tel: 01892 870 738 Fax: 01892 870 738   **Map Ref 46**

....

THE CHASER INN, a recently refurbished village inn next to Shipbourne Church and set around an attractive courtyard. Imaginative bar and restaurant food serves. All rooms with private facilities.

B&B from £40, Dinner available, Rooms 5 single, 6 double, 4 twin, all rooms en-suite.
The Chaser Inn, Stumble Hill, Shipbourne, Tonbridge, Kent TN11 9PE
Tel: 01732 810360 Fax: 01732 810941   **Map Ref 47**

....

THE OLD PARSONAGE, a magnificent Georgian house in quiet, pretty village providing superior accommodation: luxurious en-suite bedrooms with all modern comforts, antique - furnished reception rooms and sunny conservatory - lounge for afternoon tea and evening drinks. Short walk to village pubs and excellent restaurant. England for Excellence Award - Winner.

B&B from £32pp, Rooms 1 twin, 3 double, all en-suite, Restricted smoking, Children welcome, Pets by arrangement, Open all year.
Mary Dakin, **The Old Parsonage,** Church Lane, Frant, Tunbridge Wells, Kent TN3 9DX
Tel: 01892 750773 Fax: 01892 750773   **Map Ref 48**

....

DANEHURST HOUSE, is a charming gabled house in a village setting in the heart of Kent. Our tastefully furnished bedrooms afford you excellent accommodation. Breakfast is served in our Victorian conservatory. Guests can enjoy a relaxing drink in our drawing room. We would be delighted to welcome you to our home once you are in our care you can relax. Private parking.
B&B from £25pp, Rooms 3 twin, 2 double, most en-suite, No smoking or pets, Children over 8, Open all year except Christmas.
Angela & Michael Godbold, **Danehurst House,** 41 Lower Green Road, Rusthall, Tunbridge Wells, Kent TN4 8TW
Tel: 01892 527739 Fax: 01892 514804   **Map Ref 49**

....

SCOTT HOUSE, is a Grade II Listed Georgian town house. A family home from which we run an antique and interior design business as well as offering B&B. All bedrooms are en-suite with all facilities and furnished to a very high standard. M20 junction 4. A228.

B&B from £49pp, Rooms 1 twin, 2 double, all en-suite, No smoking, children or pets, Open all year except Christmas.

Ernest Smith, **Scott House,** 37 High Street, West Malling ME19 6QH
Tel: 01732 841380 Fax: 01732 870025   **Map Ref 50**

....

MARINE, a hotel of original character recently refurbished with every modern facility. Good food, Kentish beers, comfortable en-suite accommodation and sea-facing bedrooms.

B&B from £35, Dinner available, Rooms 4 double, 6 twin, 1 triple, all en-suite, Open all year.

Marine, Marine Parade, Tankerton, Whitstable, Kent CT5 2BE
Tel: 01227 272672 Fax: 01227 264721   **Map Ref 51**

Natural beauty, industrial heritage and seaside resorts are just some of the reasons for visiting Lancashire. East Lancashire is wild moorland, interspersed with wooded dales and river valleys. The coastal "lung" has been the north's most popular resort area since the mid 18th century. Lancashire's industrial centres are in an arc north of Manchester, in the south of the county and include the cotton spinning towns of Bolton, Blackburn, Rochdale and Oldham. The towns are wedged between ridges running from north to south, including the Forest of Rossendale and Pendle Hill.

The Weaver's Shuttle walk around Pendle, land of the famous Pendle Witches, takes ramblers around the splendour of Lancashire's hill country with views of the mills and towns. Bolton was the birthplace of Samuel Crompton, inventor of the spinning mule which revolutionised the textile industry and Blackburn's history of cotton weaving goes back to the fourteenth century when it became the home of the Flemish weavers. Cotton weaving was the main industry of Burnley and Chorley. Rochdale was the birthplace of the Co-operative Movement. The depression of the early 19th century prompted a group of men to set up their own co-operative shop in 1844, dividing the surplus for the benefit of all. Wigan, one of the oldest boroughs in Lancashire, the town's leading tourist attraction, Wigan Pier, takes a step back in time to the year 1900.

Lancashire boasts some world famous seaside resorts. Blackpool attracts over seventeen million visitors a year. While much of the resort's original charm remains, these days hi-tech funfair rides blend with tea dances in the Tower Ballroom. One of the country's most famous traditions is the Blackpool Illuminations. Lytham St Annes is famous for its golf courses, delightful parks, gardens and floral displays, sandy beaches and gentler pace of life. Morecambe and Heysham have combined to form a lively resort. At low tide you can walk across Morecambe Bay from Hest Bank to Grange-over-Sands.

Lancaster, an important university city these days, has a seafaring history still in evidence today with its Georgian Quay and Maritime Museum. The home of wealthy cotton, rum and sugar merchants, the city's history goes back much further. Its skyline is dominated by Lancaster Castle which tells eight hundred years of history and goes back to Henry IV's father. It is probably best known for its imprisonment of the Lancashire Witches.

Preston, lying at the crossroads of the region's motorway network, makes an ideal touring centre. To the west is beautiful moorland country. From the M6 motorway at Forton Services the road goes through ancient forest to Abbeystead. From here a road goes by Marshaw to Dunsop Bridge through the Trough of Bowland.

Lancashire

left, The Ribble Valley

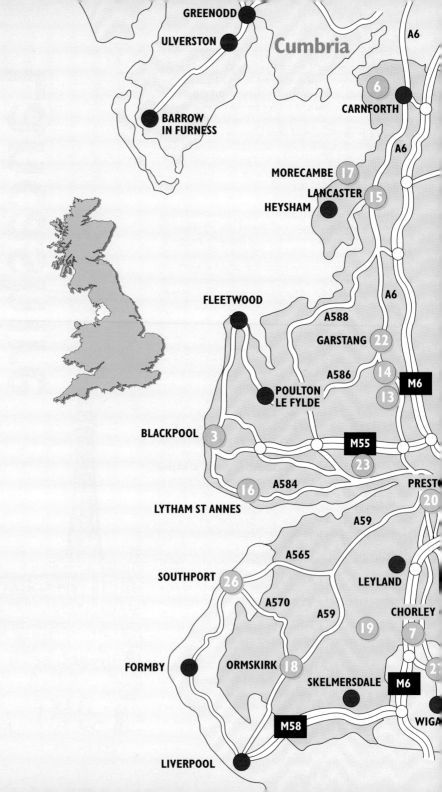

KIRKBY LONSDALE

INGLETON

CLAPHAM

A65

Yorkshire

SETTLE

LONG PRESTON

A65

A59

SKIPTON

SLAIDBURN

B6478

GISBURN

9

A59

BARNOLDSWICK

A6068

12

CLITHEROE

8

11

COLNE

10

WHALLEY

M65

25

A671

59

24

2

5

1

4

BURNLEY

BLACKBURN

ACCRINGTON

RWEN

RAWTENSTALL

TODMORDEN

BACUP

RAMSBOTTOM

A58

M66

A666

ROCHDALE

M61

BOLTON

BURY

A6

Greater Manchester

SPARTH HOUSE HOTEL, privately owned by the Coleman family. Built in1740, and set in its own peaceful grounds, the hotel offers the perfect location for short stays, conferences and functions alike.

B&B from £38, Lunch & evening meal available, Rooms 2 single, 11 double, 2 twin, 1 triple, all en-suite, Children welcome, No smoking, Open all year.
Sparth House Hotel, Whalley Road, Clayton-le-Moors, Accrington, Lancashire BB5 5RP
Tel: 01254 872263 Fax: 01254 872263   **Map Ref 1**

....

NORTHCOTE MANOR HOTEL, Privately-owned refurbished manor house with an outstanding restaurant, offering the best in hospitality. Ideal location 9 miles from M6 junction 31, off A59. One night dinner bed and breakfast gourmet breaks: £165 for two.

B&B from £80, Lunch & evening meal available, Rooms 10 double, 4 twin, all en-suite, Children welcome, No pets, Open all year.
Northcote Manor Hotel, Northcote Road, Old Langho, Blackburn, Lancashire BB6 8BE
Tel: 01254 240555 Fax: 01254 246568   **Map Ref 2**

....

MYTTON FOLD HOTEL & GOLF COMPLEX, a family owned, award winning hotel, 10 miles from exit 31 of M6. Peacefully secluded, yet only 300 yards from the A59. Own private 18 hole golf course.

B&B from £39, Lunch & evening meal available, Rooms 13 double, 14 twin, all en-suite, Children welcome, No pets, No smoking, Open all year.
Mytton Fold Hotel & Golf Complex, Whalley Road, Old Langho, Blackburn, Lancashire BB6 8AB
Tel: 01254 240662 Fax: 01254 248119   **Map Ref 2**

....

MAY-DENE LICENCE HOTEL, in a sun trap area close to South Promenade, Sandcastle, Pleasure Beach, markets and pier. Clean, friendly and good food.

B&B from £19, Dinner available, Rooms 5 double, 1 triple, 4 family, most en-suite, Children welcome, No pets, Open all year.
May-Dene Licence Hotel, 10 Dean Street, Blackpool, Lancashire FY4 1AU
Tel: 01253 343464   **Map Ref 3**

....

GLENROY PRIVATE HOTEL, a small licensed hotel, 50 yards from the beach. En-suite facilities available. No hidden extras.

B&B from £16, Dinner available, Rooms 6 double, 1 triple, 3 family, all en-suite, Children welcome, Open all year.
Glenroy Private Hotel, 10 Trafalgar Road, Blackpool, Lancashire FY1 6AW
Tel: 01253 344607   **Map Ref 3**

....

PEMBROKE PRIVATE HOTEL, a warm welcome assured to all at this small, beautifully decorated hotel, which offers a quiet, relaxed atmosphere.

B&B from £17.50, Dinner available, Rooms 4 single, 4 double, 2 twin, 1 triple, most en-suite, Children welcome, Open March - October.
Pembroke Private Hotel, 11 King Edward Avenue, Blackpool, Lancashire FY2 9TD
Tel: 01253 351306 Fax: 01253 351306   **Map Ref 3**

....

GLENAYRE, 12 cheerfully decorated bedrooms all with hot and cold, ample wardrobe space, colour TV's, tea/coffee facilities, heating to all rooms. Bathroom plus 4 shower. Every effort is made to ensure the comfort and happiness of our guests during their stay.

B&B from £12pp, Dinner from £4, Rooms 2 single, 2 twin, 4 double, 4 family, Restricted smoking, Children welcome, Open Easter - October.
Barbara & Peter Biggs, **Glenayre,** 111 Reads Avenue, Blackpool, Lancashire FY1 4JH
Tel: 01253 621770   **Map Ref 3**

CLIFTON COURT HOTEL, comfortable value for money accommodation, very close to sea and Pleasure Beach. In a select location, refurbished rooms with TV, tea/coffee facilities, licensed bar, car park. Midweek special offers always available. For friendliness, cleanliness and affordability telephone Clifton Court Blackpool 01253 342385.

B&B from £28 double/twin, Dinner from £5, Rooms 1 single, 2 twin, 5 double, 2 family, Restricted smoking, Children welcome, Pets by arrangement, Open March - November.

Mr Muller, **Clifton Court Hotel,** 12 Clifton Drive, Blackpool FY4 1NX
Tel/Fax: 01253 342385   **Map Ref 3**

ASH LODGE HOTEL, within easy reach of Blackpool Tower, Winter Gardens, Golden Mile, Central pier, main shopping centre. The hotel offers quiet, clean, comfortable accommodation. Most bedrooms are en-suite, all offer tea/coffee facilities. TV lounge, well stocked bar. Own car park.

B&B from £15pp, Dinner from £5.50, Rooms 2 twin, 7 double, 3 family, some en-suite, Children welcome, No pets, Open all year except Christmas & New Year.
Margaret & Mary Harrison, **Ash Lodge Hotel,** 131 Hornby Road, Blackpool, Lancashire FY1 4JG
Tel: 01253 627637   **Map Ref 3**

ALANDENE PRIVATE HOTEL, is a private detached hotel, private parking, licensed bar, lounge. Ground floor en-suite rooms and annex rooms available. All rooms have colour TV's, tea/coffee facilities. Situated behind Blackpool Tower and close to the Pleasure Beach. Children and pets welcome, Illuminations September and October. Email: alandene@aol.com

B&B from £12pp, Dinner from £4.50, Rooms 1 twin, 6 double, 3 family, some en-suite, Restricted smoking, Children welcome, Pets by arrangement, Open all year.
Keith Sagar, **Alandene Private Hotel,** 131 Park Rd, Blackpool FY1 4ET
Tel: 01253 623356 Fax: 01253 623356   **Map Ref 3**

THE OAKWOOD, is a Blackpool family run Hotel. All rooms en-suite, TV's, tea makers, central heating. Good home cooking. Well Stocked bar. Very clean and friendly. Ideally situated for all Blackpool's varied entertainment clubs, pubs, bingo, Pleasure beach, Tower, Sea Life Centre, all the piers shows etc.

B&B from £14pp, Dinner from £4, Rooms 1 single, 2 twin, 6 double, 1 family, all en-suite, Restricted smoking, Children welcome, Pets by arrangement, Open all year.
Mr & Mrs Molyneux, **The Oakwood,** 18 Shaw Rd, Blackpool FY1 6HB
Tel: 01253 341340   **Map Ref 3**

REGENT HOTEL, clean, comfy hotel. Good food and service. Near North Station, Winter Gardens, Theatres. All amenities hair dryers, en-suite rooms, tea/coffee facilities. Licensed. Open all year. Children and pets welcome. Special diets catered for. OAP's reductions, illumination special rates. Near Promenade, Trams and town centre.
B&B from £12-£15pp, Dinner from £4, Rooms 2 single, 4 twin, 4 double, 1 family, most en-suite, Children & pets welcome, Open all year.
Mrs E Woods, **Regent Hotel,** 18 Springfield Road, Blackpool, Lancashire FY1 1QL
Tel: 01253 620299   **Map Ref 3**

THE ROYAL SEABANK HOTEL, this recently refurbished hotel enjoys one of the finest positions on the Central Promenade, with unobstructed views of the Irish Sea. Only 700 yards from the Tower.
B&B from £17.50, Dinner available, Rooms 5 single, 18 double, 14 twin, 17 triple, 3 family rooms, all en-suite, Children welcome, No smoking, Open all year.
The Royal Seabank Hotel, 219-221 Central Promenade, Blackpool, Lancashire FY1 5DL
Tel: 01253 22717 & 22173 Fax: 01253 295148   **Map Ref 3**

CAMELOT HOUSE, is family run providing highly maintained comfortable accommodation and good home cooking choice of menu. All bedrooms have central heating and tea/coffee facilities, personal keys, comfortable lounge with satellite TV, en-suite available. Adjoining promenade midway between central and south piers. Convenient for all amenities. Small parties welcome. **B&B from £10pp,** Dinner from £14, Rooms 5 double, 5 family, some en-suite, Smoking & children welcome, Open Easter - November.
Noreen Westhead, **Camelot House,** 24 Crystal Road, South Shore, Blackpool, Lancashire FY1 6BS
Tel: 01253 345636   **Map Ref 3**

SUNNYSIDE & HOLMSDALE, is conveniently situated a few yards from North Railway Station close to Promenade, Theatre, shops and most of Blackpool's famous amenities. Comfortable lounge with colour TV. Senior citizens reductions May - June. Special diets catered for. Morning tea available. Excellent food assured. Fire certificate granted. **B&B from £18pp,** Dinner from £7, Rooms 2 single, 4 twin, 4 double, 3 family, No smoking or Pets, Children welcome, Open March - February.
Ron & Elsie Platt, **Sunnyside & Holmsdale,** 25-27 High Street, Blackpool, Lancashire FY1 2BN
Tel: 01253 623781   **Map Ref 3**

THE HOTEL BAMBI, a friendly, family-run guesthouse with good facilities. Ideally situated for Pleasure Beach, Promenade and South Shore shopping area.
B&B from £18, Rooms 2 double, 1 twin, 1 triple, 1 family, all en-suite, Children welcome, No pets, Car parking, Open February - November.
The Hotel Bambi, 27 Bright Street, Blackpool, Lancashire FY4 1BS
Tel: 01253 343756   **Map Ref 3**

Located minutes from Blackpool North Station. **CARLTON HOTEL** has ample car parking. All rooms are pleasantly furnished with en-suite facilities, tea/coffee, colour TV and direct dial telephones. Conference facilities available. Sea view restaurant. Fully licensed bars, all complimented by cheerful, efficient staff.
B&B from £20pp, Dinner from £10, Rooms 18 single, 8 twin, 23 double, 9 family, all en-suite, Children welcome, No pets, Open all year.
Shilpa Patel, **Carlton Hotel,** 282-286 North Promenade, Blackpool, Lancashire FY1 2EZ
Tel: 01253 628966 Fax: 01253 752587   **Map Ref 3**

BEDFORD HOTEL, a well managed family-run hotel on the seafront, with indoor swimming pool, sauna, spa and large, comfortable bedrooms. Choice of menu at all meals. Large free car park.
B&B from £20, Lunch & evening meal available, Rooms 20 double, 5 twin, 12 triple, 5 family rooms, suites available, all en-suite, Children welcome, Open all year.
Bedford Hotel, 298-300 North Promenade, Blackpool, Lancashire FY1 2EY
Tel: 01253 23475 & 290163 Fax: 01253 21878   **Map Ref 3**

BOBINS GUEST HOUSE, a small cosy guest house. 2 minutes walk from the pleasant North Shore. All heated bedrooms include complimentary tea/coffee, biscuits, TV's and hair dryers. En-suite rooms available. The south facing lounge and separate dining room with variable meal times, are for exclusive guest use.
B&B from £13pp, Dinner from £5, Rooms 1 single, 2 double, 1 family, some en-suite, Restricted smoking, Children welcome, No pets, Open all year.
Jo, Jack & Nigel Lock, **Bobins Guest House,** 30 Empress Drive, North Shore, Blackpool, Lancashire FY2 9SD
Tel: 01253 356907 Fax: 01253 595101   **Map Ref 3**

PARK HOUSE HOTEL, a beautifully situated hotel on the promenade within easy reach of Winter Gardens, piers, golf-courses, town centre and Stanley Park.

B&B from £23.75, Lunch & evening meal available, Rooms 13 single, 34 double, 35 twin, 14 triple, 8 family, all en-suite, Children welcome, No pets, Open all year.
Park House Hotel, 308 North Promenade, Blackpool, Lancashire FY1 2HA
Tel: 01253 20081 Fax: 01253 290181 **Map Ref 3**

....

ST CHADS HOTEL, a splendid promenade location offering live entertainment in season. Choice of menu. Home from home.

B&B from £20, Lunch & evening meal available, Rooms 7 single, 21 double, 22 twin, 2 triple, 6 family, all en-suite, Children welcome, No smoking, Open all year.
St Chads Hotel, 317-321 Promenade, Blackpool, Lancashire FY1 6BN
Tel: 01253 346348 Fax: 01253 348240 **Map Ref 3**

....

RAYNERS HOTEL, is family run, situated between central and south Piers. About 20 metres from sea front. Central position for shops, Pleasure Beach, Sandcastle Tower, nightclubs, amusements and entertainments. All rooms have tea/coffee facilities with colour TV and full central heating.

B&B from £13pp, Dinner from £5, Rooms 6 double, 1 twin, 4 family, 1 treble, Children welcome, No pets, Open all year.
Mrs Sturgess, **Rayners Hotel,** 4 Woodfield Road, South Shore, Blackpool, Lancashire FY1 6AX
Tel: 01253 346036 **Map Ref 3**

....

ASHCROFT HOTEL, a small friendly hotel off Queens Promenade, 2 minutes from the sea and Gynn Gardens. Offering personal service. Cleanliness assured.

B&B from £16, Dinner available, Rooms 3 single, 3 double, 1 twin, 2 triple, 1 family, some en-suite, Children from 2 years, No pets, Open all year.
Ashcroft Hotel, 42 King Edward Avenue, Blackpool, Lancashire FY2 9TA
Tel: 01253 351538 **Map Ref 3**

....

SUNRAY, modern semi in quiet residential part of north Blackpool. Friendly personal service and care. 1.75 miles north of Tower along the promenade. Turn right at Uncle Tom's Cabin. Sunray is about 300 yards on left.

B&B from £26, Dinner available, Rooms 3 single, 2 double, 2 twin, 2 triple, all en-suite, Children welcome, Open all year.
Sunray, 42 Knowle Avenue, Blackpool, Lancashire FY2 9TQ
Tel: 01253 351937 Fax: 01253 593307 **Map Ref 3**

....

THE ASHBEIAN GUEST HOUSE, has 5 bedrooms, all en-suite. Good public parking. Splendid menus. Terrific value, just off seafront. A very easy walk to everywhere in the town.

B&B from £16, Dinner available, Rooms 1 single, 2 double, 1 triple, 1 family, all en-suite, Children from 5 years, No smoking, Open all year.
The Ashbeian Guest House, 49 High Street, Blackpool, Lancashire FY1 2BN
Tel: 01253 26301 changing to 01253 626301 **Map Ref 3**

....

THE OLD COACH HOUSE, a large detached house set in beautiful grounds, near the promenade and South Pier.

B&B from £24, Dinner available, Rooms 3 double, 2 twin, 1 triple, 1 family, all en-suite, Children welcome, No pets, No smoking, Open all year.
The Old Coach House, 50 Dean Street, Blackpool, Lancashire FY4 1BP
Tel: 01253 349195 Fax: 01253 344330 **Map Ref 3**

WINDSOR HOTEL, clean comfortable en-suite rooms. Four posters available. Good home cooking. Guests' individual needs catered for. Close to promenade and entertainments.

B&B from £16, Dinner available, Rooms 2 single, 5 double,3 twin, 2 triple, Children welcome, No smoking, No pets, Open all year.

Windsor Hotel, 53 Dean Street, Blackpool, Lancashire FY4 1BP
Tel: 01253 400232 & 346886 Fax: 01253 346886 **Map Ref 3**

WESTDEAN HOTEL, ETB 2 Crown Commended, AA "QQQ" and RAC Acclaimed. Family run licensed and sure to please. Choice menu and separate dining tables. Ideally located adjacent to Promenade by South Pier. The perfect hotel for your next holiday. Credit and Debit cards accepted.

B&B from £19pp, Dinner from £8, Rooms 2 single, 1 twin, 5 double, 3 family, all en-suite, No smoking in Dining room, Children welcome, No pets, Open all year. Michael & Carole Ball, **Westdean Hotel,** 59 Dean Street, Blackpool, Lancashire FY4 1BP
Tel: 01253 342904 Fax: 01253 342904 **Map Ref 3**

THE HEADLANDS, a superior seafront hotel, with all rooms en-suite. Lift, parking and entertainment. Weekend breaks and midweek specials available. Excellent service, cuisine and quality. Open Christmas and New Year.

B&B from £29.50, Lunch & evening meal available, Rooms 10 single, 8 double, 14 twin, 10 triple, 1 family, all en-suite, Children welcome, No smoking, Open all year.

The Headlands, 611-613 South Promenade, Blackpool, Lancashire FY4 1NJ
Tel: 01253 341179 Fax: 01253 342047 **Map Ref 3**

THE KNOWLSLEY PRIVATE HOTEL, a friendly, family-run hotel in quiet area of South Shore. Close to the beach, shops, Pleasure Beach. Easy access to M55 and Airport.

B&B from £20, Dinner available, Rooms 2 single, 4 double, 2 twin, 2 triple, 2 family, some en-suite, Children welcome, No pets, Open all year.

The Knowlsley Private Hotel, 68 Dean Street, Blackpool, Lancashire FY4 1BP
Tel: 01253 343414 **Map Ref 3**

RAFFLES HOTEL, Excellent location for theatres, promenade, shops, restaurants, tourist spots and conference venues. Family-run private hotel with character. The proprietor is also the chef.

B&B from £18, Dinner available, Rooms 11 double, 3 twin, 2 family, most en-suite, Children welcome, No pets, Open all year.

Raffles Hotel, 73-75 Hornby Road, Blackpool, Lancashire FY1 4QJ
Tel: 01253 294713 Fax: 01253 294713 **Map Ref 3**

COLLINGWOOD HOTEL, in a select area just off Queens promenade and Gynn Gardens. Good reputation for service, home cooking, cleanliness and value for money. All rooms are en-suite. Excellence is our standard.

B&B from £18, Lunch & evening meal available, Rooms 2 single, 9 double, 2 twin, 2 triple, 2 family, all en-suite, Children welcome, No pets, Open all year.

Collingwood Hotel, 8-10 Holmfield Road, Blackpool, Lancashire FY2 9SL
Tel: 01253 352929 Fax: 01253 352929 **Map Ref 3**

NORDELPH HOTEL, a small luxury hotel. Situated near to Promenade and with easy access to town centre. Relaxed, comfortable atmosphere. Excellent food. Tea/coffee facilities and TV's in rooms. Most rooms en-suite. Free car parking for all guests.

B&B from £17pp, Dinner from £4, Rooms 2 single, 5 double, 1 family, most en-suite, Restricted smoking, Children welcome, No pets, Open March - November.
Paul & Andrea Jones, **Nordelph Hotel,** 9 Empress Drive, North Shore, Blackpool, Lancashire FY2 9SE
Tel: 01253 351925   **Map Ref 3**

....

SURREY HOUSE HOTEL, a friendly, family-run hotel close to the promenade, Gynn Gardens and with easy access to the town's entertainments. Central heating and en-suite facilities.

B&B from £19, Dinner available, Rooms 1 single,6 double, 2 twin, 2 triple, all en-suite/private facilities, Children welcome, Open all year.
Surrey House Hotel, 9 Northumberland Avenue, Blackpool, Lancashire FY2 9SB
Tel: 01253 351743   **Map Ref 3**

....

WAVERLEY HOTEL, small, licensed hotel close to Tower, Winter Gardens, shopping precinct and promenade. For those special occasions, book our four-poster or canopied rooms. Comfort and quality assured, at prices you can afford.

B&B from £15, Dinner available, Rooms 1 single, 10 double, 1 triple, 1 family, most en-suite, Children welcome, Open all year.
Waverley Hotel, 95 Reads Avenue, Blackpool, Lancashire FY1 4DG
Tel: 01253 21633   **Map Ref 3**

....

IMPERIAL HOTEL- FORTE, imposing 19th century Victorian hotel set back from the North Promenade, with its own health and fitness club comprising of indoor swimming pool, sauna, solarium, gymnasium, steam room, massage and jacuzzi.

B&B from £59, Lunch & evening meal available, Rooms 26 single, 93 double, 62 twin, 2 family, suites available, all en-suite, Children welcome, No smoking, Open all year.
Imperial Hotel- Forte, North Promenade, Blackpool, Lancashire FY1 2HB
Tel: 01253 623971 Fax: 01253 751784   **Map Ref 3**

....

BERWYN HOTEL, and elegant licensed hotel overlooking Gynn Gardens and Queens Promenade. Our standards of cuisine, service and cleanliness are high and our aim is to please.
B&B from £28, Dinner available, Rooms 1 single, 14 double, 3 twin, 2 triple, all en-suite, Children welcome, No pets, Open all year.
Berwyn Hotel, 1 Finchley Road, Gynn Square, Blackpool, Lancashire FY1 2LP
Tel: 01253 352896 Fax: 01253 594391   **Map Ref 3**

....

THE WINDSOR HOTEL, has quality furnishings in all bedrooms. Fine public rooms displaying antiques and watercolours. Exquisite dining room serving traditional English cuisine.
B&B from £19.50, Dinner available, Rooms 3 single, 4 double, 1 twin, 1 triple, all en-suite, Children from 6 years, No pets or smoking, Open April - October and Christmas.
The Windsor Hotel, 21 King Edward Avenue, North Shore, Blackpool, Lancashire FY2 9TA
Tel: 01253 353735   **Map Ref 3**

....

ORMEROD HOTEL, small bed and breakfast hotel in a quiet and pleasant area facing local parks. Recently refurbished, all en-suite facilities, 5 minutes from the town centre.

B&B from £20, Rooms 4 single, 2 double, 2 twin, 2 triple, Children welcome, Open all year.
Ormerod Hotel, 121-123 Ormerod Road, Burnley, Lancashire BB11 3QW
Tel: 01282 423255   **Map Ref 4**

ALEXANDER HOTEL, family run hotel with accent on personal service. Near the town centre, in quiet residential area close to Towneley Hall.

B&B from £25, Lunch & evening meal available, Rooms 8 single, 5 double, 2 twin, 1 triple, most en-suite, Children welcome, Open all year.

Alexander Hotel, 2 Tarleton Avenue, Todmoreden Road, Burnley, Lancashire BB11 3ET
Tel: 01282 422684 Fax: 01282 424094　　　　　　　　　　　　　　　　　**Map Ref 4**

....

EAVES BARN FARM, is a working farm, set in 30 acres. Elegant guest lounge, has a welcoming open log fire. Individually designed rooms offering luxurious facilities TV, welcome trays. Breakfast is served in the Victorian style conservatory. Best B&B in Lancashire 1992. Situated within easy reach of the coast - Lake District, Yorkshire Dales, Lancashire hills and Manchester Airport can be reached using the motorway network.
B&B from £21pp, Dinner from £12, Rooms 1 single, 1 twin, 1 double, all en-suite, Restricted smoking, Children over 10, Open all year except Christmas & New Year.
Mrs Butler, **Eaves Barn Farm,** Hapton, Burnley, Lancashire BB12 7LP
Tel: 01282 771591 Fax: 01282 771591　　　　　　　　　**Map Ref 5**

....

THE LIMES VILLAGE GUEST HOUSE, charming Victorian house set in beautiful landscaped gardens, has been tastefully refurbished. The spacious bedrooms, decorated with flair, have private bathrooms, TV, easy chairs and tea/coffee tray. the owners serve delicious food, with an incredibly wide breakfast choice and an optional five course candlelit dinner.
B&B from £17.50pp, Dinner from £12.50, Rooms 1 twin, 1 double, 1 family, all private bathrooms, No smoking or pets, Open all year.
Noel & Andree Livesey **The Limes Village Guest House,** 23 Stankelt Road, Silverdale, Carnforth LA5 0TF
Tel/Fax: 01524 701454　　　　　　　　　　　　　　　　　　**Map Ref 6**

....

PARK HALL HOTEL, LEISURE & CONFERENCE CENTRE, hotel, village and conference centre set in 130 acres of beautiful ground, close to both M6 and M61 motorways. Conference and superb leisure facilities.
B&B from £79.98, Lunch & evening meal available, Rooms 41 double, 42 twin, 53 family, suites available, all en-suite, Children welcome, No smoking, Open all year.
Park Hall Hotel, Leisure & Conference Centre, Park Hall Road, Charnock Richard, Chorley, Lancashire PR7 5LP
Tel: 01257 452090 Fax: 01257 451838　　　　　　　　　　　　**Map Ref 7**

....

BROOKLYN, a small, family-run licensed guesthouse close to the town centre, where the proprietors assure you of a warm welcome.
B&B from £23, Dinner available, Rooms 1 single, 1 double, 2 twin, all en-suite, Children welcome, No pets or smoking, Open all year.
Brooklyn, 32 Pimlico Road, Clitheroe, Lancashire BB7 2AH
Tel: 01200 428268/423861　　　　　　　　　　　　　　　　**Map Ref 8**

....

MIDDLE FLASS LODGE GUESTHOUSE & RESTAURANT, a tasteful barn conversion in beautiful countryside of the Forest of Bowland. Chef-prepared cuisine in restaurant open to non residents. Licensed, ample parking.
B&B from £20, Evening meal available, Rooms 2 double, 2 twin, 4 family all en-suite, Children over 1, No pets or smoking, Open all year.
Middle Flass Lodge Guesthouse & Restaurant, Settle Road, Bolton-by-Bowland, Clitheroe, Lancashire BB7 4NY
Tel: 01200 447259 Fax: 01200 447300　　　　　　　　　　　　**Map Ref 9**

....

SHIREBURN ARMS HOTEL, a 16th century family-run hotel, with unrivalled views, renowned for food and comfort, log fires, real ale, bar food. Within easy reach of the motorway network.

B&B from £40, Lunch & evening meal available, Rooms 9 double, 3 twin, 1 triple, 1 family, all en-suite, Children welcome, No smoking, Open all year.
Shireburn Arms Hotel, Whalley Road, Hurst Green, Clitheroe, Lancashire BB7 9QJ
Tel: 01254 826518 Fax: 01254 826208　　　　　　　　　　　　**Map Ref 10**

MITTON HALL LODGINGS, a 16th century listed hall in the Ribble Valley. Restaurant, pizzeria, tavern, lodgings. Two miles Whalley Abbey, 3 miles Clitheroe Castle, close to Trough of Bowland. Eleven miles junction 31 of M6, 7 miles M65.

B&B from £41.50, Lunch & evening meal available, Rooms 2 single, 6 double, 5 twin, 1 triple, all en-suite, Children welcome, Open all year.

Mitton Hall Lodgings, Mitton Road, Mitton, Clitheroe, Lancashire BB7 9PQ
Tel: 01254 826544 Fax: 01254 826386   **Map Ref 11**

....

THE MOORCOCK INN, 3 Crown Commended. A friendly, family-run hostelry overlooking the Ribble Valley with all modern amenities and home cooked food. All major credit cards accepted.

B&B from £38pp, Dinner from £8, 11 en-suite rooms, Children welcome, Pets by arrangement, Open all year.

Peter & Susan Fillary, **The Moorcock Inn,** Waddington, Clitheroe, Lancashire BB7 3AA
Tel: 01200 422333 Fax: 01200 429184   **Map Ref 12**

....

GUYS THATCHED HAMLET, a friendly, family run thatched canal side tavern, restaurant, pizzeria, lodgings, craft shops, cricket ground with thatched pavilion and crown green bowling. Conference centre. Off junction 32 of M6, then 3 miles north on A6 to Garstang.

B&B from £41.50, Lunch & evening meal available, Rooms 28 double, 20 twin, 5 family, all en-suite, Children welcome, No smoking, Open all year.

Guys Thatched Hamlet, Canalside, St Michael's Road, Bilsborrow, Garstang, Lancashire PR3 0RS
Tel: 01995 640849/640010 Fax: 01995 640141   **Map Ref 13**

....

GARSTANG COUNTRY HOTEL & GOLF CLUB, The ideal location for business or pleasure, this new family-owned hotel and 18 hole golf course has every amenity for an enjoyable stay. Golf breaks a speciality.

B&B from £40, Lunch & evening meal available, Rooms 4 double, 28 twin, all en-suite, Children welcome, No pets or smoking, Open all year.

Garstang Country Hotel & Golf Club, Garstang Road, Bowgreave, Garstang, Lancashire PR3 1YE
Tel: 01995 600100 Fax: 01995 600950   **Map Ref 14**

....

LANCASTER HOUSE HOTEL, an elegant country house with extensive leisure facilities, perfectly located for exploring the nearby Lake District, Yorkshire Dales and historic Lancaster.

B&B from £77.45, Lunch & evening meal available, Rooms 38 double, 42 twin, all en-suite, Children welcome, No smoking, Open all year.

Lancaster House Hotel, Green Lane, Lancaster, Lancashire LA1 4GJ
Tel: 01524 844822 Fax: 01524 844766 Email: Head Office @lancasterhousehotel.telme.com   **Map Ref 15**

....

CHADWICK HOTEL, a modern family-run hotel and leisure complex with reputation for food, comfort, personal service and value for money.

B&B from £38, Lunch & evening meal available, Rooms 10 single, 11 double, 29 twin, 14 triple, 8 family, all en-suite, Children welcome, No pets, No smoking, Open all year.

Chadwick Hotel, South Promenade, Lytham St Annes, Lancashire FY8 1NP
Tel: 01253 720061 Fax: 01253 714455   **Map Ref 16**

THE MARINA HOTEL, is a small family run hotel with good quality English cooking, bar, TV, lounge, patio, some en-suite rooms. All with shaver points, tea/coffee facilities, heating and colour TV's. Close to all amenities trains, buses, town centre. Sea front location. Ideal base for Lakes and Yorkshire Dales.

B&B from £16.50-£20pp, Dinner from £6, Rooms 2 single, 3 double/twin, 6 double, some en-suite, Restricted smoking, Children welcome, No pets, Open all year.

Ann & Allan Norton, **The Marina Hotel,** 324 Marine Road Central, Morecambe, Lancashire LA4 5AA
Tel: 01524 423979   **Map Ref 17**

THORN TREE FARM, is set in eight acres of rural farmland you are certain of a warm welcome together with comfortable beds, TV and coffee facilities in all rooms. Golf courses near by also bird watching - pub within walking distance.

B&B from £40pp, Rooms 1 single, 2 twin, 1 en-suite, 1 family, No smoking, Children welcome, Pets by arrangement, Open all year.

Winifred & Richard Pemberton, **Thorn Tree Farm,** Prescot Road, Aughton, Ormskirk, Lancashire L39 6RS
Tel: 01695 422109   **Map Ref 18**

MAWDESLEYS EATING HOUSE & HOTEL, set in the picturesque village of Mawdesley, which has been voted "best kept village". Its peaceful setting will be appreciated by business people and pleasure travellers alike.

B&B from £43.50, Lunch & evening meal available, Rooms 39 double, 6 twin, all en-suite, Children welcome, Open all year.

Mawdesleys Eating House & Hotel, Hall Lane, Mawdesley, Ormskirk, Lancashire L40 2QZ
Tel: 01704 822552/821874 Fax: 01704 822096   **Map Ref 19**

TULKETH HOTEL, a hotel of fine quality and with personal service, in a quiet residential area. A la carte menu. 5 minutes from the town centre, 10 minutes from M6 motorway.

B&B from £35, Dinner available, Rooms 5 single, 2 double, 5 twin, all en-suite/private facilities, Children welcome, No pets, Open all year.

Tulketh Hotel, 209 Tulketh Road, Ashton, Preston, Lancashire PR2 1ES
Tel: 01772 728096/726250 Fax: 01772 723743   **Map Ref 20**

GIBBON BRIDGE HOTEL, a privately owned country house hotel in the heart of some of Lancashire's finest countryside, yet only 20 minutes from M6, exit 32. Award winning hotel. Excellent dining facilities and executive accommodation, leisure facilities and beauty studio.

B&B from £70, Lunch & evening meal available, Rooms 3 single, 8 double, 15 twin, 4 triple, suites available, all en-suite, Children welcome, Open all year.

Gibbon Bridge Hotel, Forest of Bowland, Chipping, Preston, Lancashire PR3 2TQ
Tel: 01995 61456 Fax: 01995 61277   **Map Ref 21**

CROFTERS HOTEL, a family owned and managed hotel with all modern facilities, situated midway between Preston and Lancaster.

B&B from £50, Lunch & evening meal available, Rooms 1 single, 5 double, 10 twin, 3 triple, all en-suite, Children welcome, No smoking, Open all year.

Crofters Hotel, A6, Cabus, Garstang, Preston, Lancashire PR3 1PH
Tel: 01995 604128 Fax: 01995 601646   **Map Ref 22**

THE SADDLE INN. Comfortable family accommodation in recently refurbished quiet country Inn. Tea/coffee facilities. Accent on high quality meals and real ales. Large grassed play area with swings, slides etc. Ample parking. 20 minutes Blackpool, 1 hour Lakes, yet only 10 minutes Preston town centre.
B&B from £20pp, Dinner from £8, Rooms 1 double, 1 family, Children welcome, Cot available, Open all year except Christmas & New Year.
Mr J.G. Smith, **The Saddle Inn,** Sidgreaves Lane, Lea Town, Preston, Lancashire PR4 0RS
Tel: 01772 726982   **Map Ref 23**

ROSE COTTAGE, is a picturesque 200 year old cottage on A59, 5 miles from M6 and M65. Comfortable, well appointed rooms with private facilities, beverages, satellite TV, heated towel rail, radio, alarms, smoke detectors, guest fridge, hair dryers, fans. Excellent overnight stop for Scotland. Hearty English breakfast awaits. Pubs and restaurants nearby.
B&B from £18pp, Rooms 2 twin, 1 double, all en-suite, Restricted smoking, Children welcome, Pets by arrangement, Open all year.
Marj Adderley, **Rose Cottage,** Longsight Road, Clayton-le-Dale Ribble Valley, Lancashire BB1 9EX
Tel: 01254 813223 Fax: 01254 813831   **Map Ref 25**

NORLAND HOTEL, offers tea/coffee facilities in all rooms, colour TV with text. Lounge bar. Eating places within walking distance, close to fair ground. Car parking on Hotel forecourt. Close to motorway network, M6/M57, Liverpool, Manchester, Albert Dock, Preston.

B&B from £16.50pp, Rooms 2 single, 1 twin, 5 double/family, Children welcome, pets by arrangement, Open all year except Christmas & New Year.
Maureen Chan, **Norland Hotel,** 11 Bath Street, Southport, Lancashire PR9 0DP
Tel: 01704 530 890   **Map Ref 26**

EDENDALE HOTEL, has comfortable rooms, colour TV, tea/coffee facilities, radio alarms, hair dryers, individually heated. Licensed. Car park. Delicious 3/4 course evening meals. Extensive breakfast menu. Quietly situated. Short stroll to Lord Street Boulevard, the Promenade, Marina Lake, Floral Hall Theatre Complex, Pleasureland, two golf courses.
B&B from £19.50pp, Dinner from £7, Rooms 1 single, 2 twin, 3 double, 2 family, all en-suite, No smoking or pets, Children welcome, Open all year except New Year.
Shirley & Michael Whiting, **Edendale Hotel,** 83 Avondale Road North, Southport, Lancashire PR9 0NE
Tel: 01704 530718 Fax: 01704 547299   **Map Ref 26**

BAY HORSE PREMIER LODGE

Originally built in 1824, the **BAY HORSE PREMIER LODGE** is the ideal location for exploring the areas delights, including Gullivers World, Haydock Park, Wigan Pier and many more. We have a license for alcohol. All rooms with en-suite facilities and tea/coffee facilities. Car park.

B&B from £54.14pp, Rooms 28 double, all en-suite, Restricted smoking, Children welcome, Pets by arrangement, Open all year.
Mr & Mrs Bonnister, **Bay Horse Premier Lodge,** 52 Warrington Road, Ashton in Makerfield, Wigan, Lancashire NN4 9PJ
Tel: 01942 725032 Fax: 01942 719302   **Map Ref 27**

Leicestershire, Nottinghamshire & Rutland

There's plenty of opportunities to delve into the past in Leicestershire and Nottinghamshire. Throughout history the area has been at the heart of events which are still evident in the number of museums, castles, historic houses and heritage centres.

Leicester's Castle Park turns back the clock. The history of Leicester can be traced from the Jewry Wall, the grand entrance to the town's public baths in Roman times, to the Saxon church of St Nicholas. Fascinating narrow streets wind back to St Martin's Square with its Victorian lights and specialist shops, through one of the largest permanent open air markets to the modern department stores of the Shires Centre and the theatres. A warm and friendly welcome awaits in Leicestershire's market towns. Ashby-de-la-Zouch has a five-aisled church and a ruined castle. The former Saxon settlement of Lutterworth has ancient inns and Melton Mowbray is famed for its pork pies and Stilton cheese.

Nottingham is known throughout the world for its lace. The city has many museums, including the Brewhouse Yard Museum, five seventeenth century cottages at the foot of Nottingham Castle, which houses displays on the city's social history.

At Rutland Water there is a twenty seven mile cycle track around the shoreline and there are numerous waterside paths which encircle one of the largest man-made lakes in western Europe. Red and fallow deer roam in Bradgate Park among the natural parkland with its rocky hills, woods, heath and bracken. From the summit of Beacon Hill Country Park there are superb views and there are nature reserves at Watermead and Melton Country Parks. Nottinghamshire provides a variety of landscapes. Rolling arable farmland and ancient oak woodlands blend harmoniously with grand ducal estates and picturesque villages. Clumber Park is a notable example of eighteenth century landscape design. It is famed for its Dukes Drive, a double avenue of lime trees over two miles long.

There are more woodland walks at Rufford Country Park, with its lake and gardens. Close by is the most famous parkland of all, the Sherwood Forest Country Park at Edwinstowe. In the days of the Norman kings when Sherwood was a royal hunting forest, it covered one hundred thousand acres, although it is much smaller today. It is preserved much as it it would have been in Robin Hood's time with its thousand ancient oak trees. Waymarked paths lead to the Mighty Major Oak and an interpretative exhibition "Robin Hode and Mery Scherwode". The legends really come to life in the Robin Hood Festival, a week long feast of medieval entertainment held every summer, with jousting, story-telling and hunt the outlaw games.

left, Robin Hood Statue

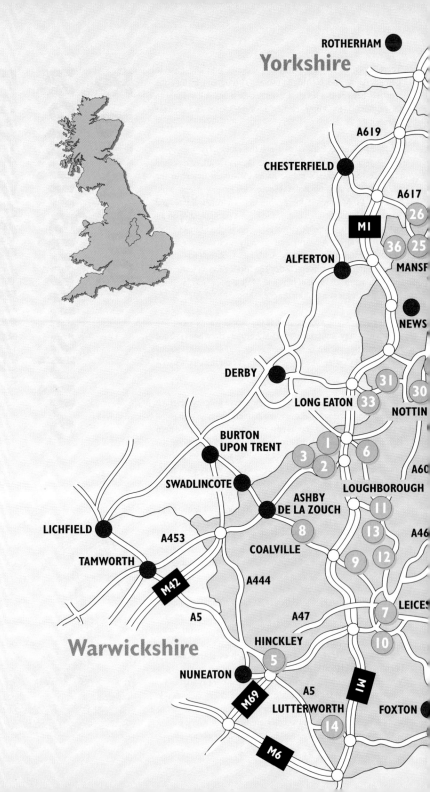

DELVEN HOTEL, a small, family run hotel, 1 mile from Donington race track and 2 miles from East Midlands Airport.

B&B from £18, Rooms 2 double, 4 twin, 1 triple, some en-suite, Open all year.
Delven Hotel, 12 Delven Lane, Castle Donington, Leicestershire DE7 2LJ
Tel: 01332 810153   **Map Ref 1**

....

FOUR-POSTER GUESTHOUSE, some four-poster beds are available in this old world accommodation in a quiet location opposite the church.

B&B from £15, Rooms 3 single, 3 double, 2 twin, 3 family, some en-suite, Open all year.
Four-poster Guesthouse, 73 Clapgun Street, Castle Donington, Leicestershire DE27 2LF
Tel: 01332 810335 Fax: 01332 812418   **Map Ref 1**

....

MORTON HOUSE HOTEL, a family run private hotel with friendly atmosphere and lounge bar, only 1.5 miles from M1, junction 24, and East Midlands International Airport. 1 mile from Donington Park race circuit.

B&B from £21, Dinner available, Rooms 2 single, 3 double, 1 twin, 1 triple, some en-suite, Open all year.
Morton House Hotel, 78 Bondgate, Castle Donington, Leicestershire DE7 2NR
Tel: 01332 812415 Fax: 01332 812415   **Map Ref 1**

....

DONINGTON MANOR HOTEL, this 18th Century coaching inn with modern bedroom extensions has French and English menus, is 2 miles from junction 24 of the M1 and is close to the Donington Park motor circuit and East Midlands Airport.

B&B from £65, Dinner available, Rooms 2 single, 12 double, 11 twin, 1 family, all en-suite, Open all year.
Donington Manor Hotel, High Street, Castle Donington, Leicestershire DE74 2PP
Tel: 01332 810253   **Map Ref 1**

....

LITTLE CHIMNEYS GUESTHOUSE, a modern building in the pleasant village of Diseworth, close to the M1, East Midlands International Airport and Donington race track.

B&B from £24.50, Rooms 4 twin, 1 triple, all en-suite, Open all year.
Little Chimneys Guesthouse, 19 The Green, Diseworth, Castle Donington, Leicestershire DE7 2QN
Tel: 01332 812458   **Map Ref 2**

....

DONINGTON PARK FARMHOUSE HOTEL, a half-timbered 17th century farmhouse, in its own grounds. Spacious rooms, farmhouse suppers. Located at competitors' entrance to Donington Park.

B&B from £49, Dinner available, Rooms 2 single, 3 double, 3 twin, 2 triple, 1 family, most en-suite, Open all year.

Donington Park Farmhouse Hotel, Melbourne Road, Isley Walton, Castle Donington, Leicestershire DE74 2RN
Tel: 01332 862409 Fax: 01332 862364 EMail: park.farmhouse@dial.pipex.com   **Map Ref 3**

....

THE RED HOUSE INN, situated in the beautiful vale of Belvoir within sight of Belvoir Castle. 18th century listed hunting lodge stands in own attractive gardens. Experience excellent food, good beer and fine wines in our conservatory restaurant. All rooms have TV and tea facilities. Extensive car parking.
B&B from £26pp, Dinner from £6, Rooms 2 single, 3 twin, 3 double, most en-suite, Children welcome, Pets by arrangement, Open all year.
David & Janet Cotterell, **The Red House Inn,** 6 Croxton Road, Knipton, near Grantham, Leicestershire NG32 1RH
Tel: 01476 870352 Fax: 01476 870429   **Map Ref 4**

SKETCHLEY GRANGE HOTEL, a country house hotel set in green fields, yet only 2 minutes from the M69. Friendly and efficient service assured. Located on the border of Leicestershire/Warwickshire.

B&B from £60, Dinner available, Rooms 7 single, 23 double, 23 twin, 5 triple, 4 suites, all en-suite, Open all year.
Sketchley Grange Hotel, Sketchley Lane, Burbage, Hinckley, Leicestershire LE10 3HU
Tel: 01455 251133 Fax: 01455 631384 **Map Ref 5**

....

HOLIDAY INN LEICESTER, a city centre hotel with extensive leisure facilities. Ideal for sporting and cultural attractions. Three miles from M1 junction 21, with free resident parking. Major refurbishment completed in 1996.
B&B from £59, Dinner available, Rooms 89 double, 99 twin, all en-suite, Open all year.
Holiday Inn Leicester, 129 St Nicholas Circle, Leicester LE1 5LX
Tel: 0116 253 1161 Fax: 0116 251 3169 **Map Ref 7**

....

THE GRAND HOTEL, a recently refurbished city centre hotel, close to railway station, theatres, cinemas, shops and sporting venues.
B&B from £80, Dinner available, Rooms 25 single, 42 double, 25 twin, all en-suite, Open all year.
The Grand Hotel, Granby Street, Leicester LE1 6ES
Tel: 0116 255 5599 Fax: 0116 254 4736 **Map Ref 7**

....

CRAIGLEIGH HOTEL, a small friendly run hotel 1 mile from the city centre, with easy access to the M1 and M69. Close to sporting venues.

B&B from £20pp, Rooms 3 single, 3 double, 4 twin, some en-suite, Children & pets welcome, Open all year.

Craigleigh Hotel, 17-19 Westleigh Road, Leicester LE3 0HH
Tel: 0116 2546875 Fax: 0116 2546875 **Map Ref 7**

....

BEAUMARIS, a friendly, family run guesthouse, away from the heavy traffic, yet on a bus route to town and within 15 minutes walking distance of it.
B&B from £17, Rooms 2 single, 1 double, 2 twin, 1 triple, Open all year.
Beaumaris, 18 Westcotes Drive, Leicester LE3 0QR
Tel: 0116 254 0261 **Map Ref 7**

....

REGENCY HOTEL, an exquisitely restored Victorian town house hotel formerly a convent with many interesting historical features. Is the ideal venue for all your hospitality needs. Two restaurants/Langtry's Brasserie/The Town House Restaurant/separate banqueting facilities. Ample free car parking.

B&B from £26pp, Dinner from £13.95, Rooms 15 single, 1 twin, 14 double, 2 family, all en-suite, Children welcome, Pets by arrangement, Open all year.
Hazel Goodwin, **Regency Hotel,** 360 London Road, Leicester LE2 2PL
Tel: 0116 270 9634 Fax: 0116 270 1375 **Map Ref 7**

....

GLENFIELD LODGE HOTEL, a small, friendly hotel with an interesting ornamental courtyard, home-cooked food and cosy, relaxed surroundings. Close to city centre.

B&B from £15.50, Dinner available, Rooms 6 single, 3 double, 4 twin, 2 triple, Open all year.
Glenfield Lodge Hotel, 4 Glenfield Road, Leicester LE3 6AP
Tel: 0116 262 7554 **Map Ref 7**

WALTHAM HOUSE, a Victorian detached house. Close to M1/M69 junction and approx. 2 miles from city centre. Very large rooms. Warm, friendly welcome assured.

B&B from £19, Rooms 1 single, 1 double, 1 triple, 1 en-suite, Open all year,

Waltham House, 500 Narborough Road, Leicester LE3 2FU
Tel: 0116 289 1129   **Map Ref 7**

....

HERMITAGE PARK HOTEL, a modern hotel, located in the heart of the National Forest, offering a comfortable atrium bar and restaurant, leisure suite and friendly professional service.

B&B from £35, Dinner available, Rooms 21 double, 4 twin, all en-suite, Open all year.
Hermitage Park Hotel, Whitwick Road, Coalville, Leicester LE67 3FA
Tel: 01530 814814 Fax: 01530 814202   **Map Ref 8**

....

FIELD HEAD HOTEL, located on the A50, 1 mile from junction 22 of the M1. Originally an old farmhouse, the hotel has been built in local stone.

B&B from £33.50, Dinner available, Rooms 11 double, 16 twin, 1 triple, all en-suite, Open all year.
Field Head Hotel, Markfield Lane, Markfield, Leicester LE67 9PS
Tel: 01530 245454 Fax: 01530 243740   **Map Ref 9**

....

BURLINGTON HOTEL, a friendly welcome awaits you at this family run hotel. Situated in a quiet residential area close to the town centre.

B&B from £30, Dinner available, Rooms 9 single, 4 double, 2 twin, 1 triple, some en-suite, Open all year.

Burlington Hotel, Elmfield Avenue, Stoneygate, Leicester LE2 1RB
Tel: 0116 270 5112 Fax: 0116 270 4207   **Map Ref 7**

....

LEICESTER STAGE HOTEL, on the A50, 3 miles south of the city centre and the M1/M69, this friendly, privately-owned hotel has en-suite bedrooms, a health and leisure club, indoor heated pool, excellent bar and restaurant.

B&B from £40, Dinner available, Rooms 37 double, 39 twin, all en-suite, Open all year.

Leicester Stage Hotel, Leicester Road, Wigston, Leicester LE18 1JW
Tel: 0116 288 6164 Fax: 0116 281 1874   **Map Ref 10**

....

GARENDON LODGE GUEST HOUSE, a spacious Victorian guesthouse, completely refurbished. In quiet surroundings but with in 5 minutes of town centre and nearby Charnwood Forest.

B&B from £25, Dinner available, Rooms 2 single, 3 double, all en-suite, Open all year.
Garendon Lodge Guest House, 136 Leicester Road, Loughborough, Leicestershire LE11 2AQ
Tel: 01509 211120   **Map Ref 11**

....

THE HIGHBURY GUESTHOUSE, a guesthouse on the A6 road from Loughborough to Leicester. Within 5 minutes' walking distance of the town centre. Convenient for steam railway, junction 23 of M1, university, airport and Donington Park.

B&B from £19, Dinner available, Rooms 4 single, 4 double, 3 triple, most en-suite, Open all year.

The Highbury Guesthouse, 146 Leicester Road, Loughborough, Leicestershire LE11 0BJ
Tel: 01509 230545 Fax: 01509 233086   **Map Ref 11**

PEACHNOOK GUEST HOUSE, a family run guest house, all nations welcome. Built around 1880, Victorian villa near to all amenities town centre, motorway, airport, train station and post office. Full English breakfast or continental. Cater for vegans and vegetarians. Packed lunches on request.
B&B from £15-£19pp, Rooms 1 single, 1 double/family en-suite, Restricted smoking, No pets, Open all year.
Valerie Wood, **Peachnook Guest House,** 154 Ashby Rd, Loughborough, Leicestershire LE11 3AG
Tel: 01509 264390   **Map Ref 11**

FOREST RISE HOTEL, friendly personal service. Excellent order throughout. Easy access to M1 motorway, university and town centre. Car park at rear.

B&B from £32, Dinner available, Rooms 8 single, 10 double, 1 twin, 3 triple, most en-suite, Open all year.

Forest Rise Hotel, 55 Forest Road, Loughborough, Leicestershire LE11 3NW
Tel: 01509 215928 Fax: 01509 210506   **Map Ref 11**

DEMONTFORT HOTEL, one of Loughborough's oldest hotels. family run, warm, friendly service, rooms tastefully decorated, restaurant, bar lounge. Close to town centre, university and Steam Trust.

B&B from £23, Dinner available, Rooms 1 single, 3 double, 2 twin, 3 triple, some en-suite, Open all year.

Demontfort Hotel, 88 Leicester Road, Loughborough, Leicestershire LE11 2AQ
Tel: 01509 216061 Fax: 01509 233667   **Map Ref 11**

The **GARDENDON PARK HOTEL** has well furnished en-suite bedrooms, all with radio, colour satellite TV and tea/coffee making facilities. Restaurant with an a la carte selection. We are licensed to serve drinks. The hotel is located 5 minutes from town centre. Local attractions are Great Central Railway and Bell Foundry.
B&B from £17.50pp, Dinner from £5.50, Rooms 3 single, 5 twin, 6 double, 4 family, most en-suite, Restricted smoking, Children welcome, Pets by arrangement, Open all year.
Trisha & Andrew Hassall, **Gardendon Park Hotel,** 92 Leicester Road, Loughborough, Leicestershire LE11 2AQ
Tel: 01509 236557 Fax: 01509 265559   **Map Ref 11**

GREAT CENTRAL HOTEL & MASTER CUTLER RESTAURANT, a friendly, family-owned pub/hotel offering excellent value food/accommodation functions.

B&B from £25, Dinner available, Rooms 3 single, 9 double, 5 twin, 1 triple, 2 family, all en-suite, Open all year.

Great Central Hotel & Master Cutler Restaurant, Great Central Road, Loughborough, Leicestershire LE11 1RW
Tel: 01509 263405 Fax: 01509 264130   **Map Ref 11**

JARVIS KINGS HEAD HOTEL, a Georgian style hotel located midway between Leeds and London, only 3 miles off M1. Many interesting places to visit in the nearby shires.

B&B from £37.50, Dinner available, Rooms 18 single, 34 double, 26 twin, all en-suite, Open all year.

Jarvis Kings Head Hotel, High Street, Loughborough, Leicestershire LE11 2QL
Tel: 01509 233222 Fax: 01509 262911   **Map Ref 11**

BARLEYLOFT GUEST HOUSE, spacious bungalow close to the A6 between Leicester and Loughborough. Quiet, rural location with outstanding riverside walks. Comfortable base for working away from home or exploring local historical attractions. TV and tea/coffee in all rooms, guest's fridge, microwave, toaster. Extensive parking. Suitable disabled.
B&B from £16pp, Rooms 1 single, 1 twin, 2 double, 2 family, Children & Pets welcome, Long term reduced rates, Open all year.
Mrs M.A. Pegg, **Barleyloft Guest House**, 33a Hawcliffe Road, Mountsorrel, Loughborough, Leicestershire LE12 7AQ
Tel: 01509 413514   **Map Ref 12**

QUORN GRANGE HOTEL & RESTAURANT, an old country house on the edge of Bradgate park, set in its own gardens.

B&B from £50, Rooms 10 double, 5 twin, suites available, all en-suite, Open all year.
Quorn Grange Hotel & Restaurant, 88 Wood Lane, Quorn, Loughborough, Leicestershire LE12 8DB
Tel: 01509 412167 Fax: 01509 415621   **Map Ref 13**

THE DENBIGH ARMS HOTEL, is an attractive Georgian coaching inn in the heart of Lutterworth. Characteristic restaurant and Players bar provide the ideal setting in which to relax or enjoy the company of friends and colleagues.

B&B from £58pp, Dinner from £12.95, Rooms 5 single, 10 twin, 14 double, 3 family, all en-suite, Children welcome, Pets by arrangement, Open all year.
Angela Psaras, **The Denbigh Arms Hotel**, High Street, Lutterworth, Leicestershire LE17 4AD
Tel: 01455 553537 Fax: 01455 556627   **Map Ref 14**

HOTHORPE HALL, a family run hotel/conference centre in Georgian country house in a delightful, quiet rural setting. 12 acres of gardens and grounds. Car parking. 5 miles from Market Harborough.

B&B from £18.75, Dinner available, Rooms 2 single, 4 double, 28 twin, 3 triple, 17 family, some en-suite, Open all year.
Hothorpe Hall, Theddingworth, Lutterworth, Leicestershire LE17 6QX
Tel: 01858 880257 Fax: 01858 880979   **Map Ref 15**

HOMESTEAD HOUSE, in an elevated position overlooking the Welland Valley on the outskirts of Medbourne, a picturesque village dating back to Roman times.
B&B from £24, Dinner available, Rooms 3 twin, all en-suite, Open all year.
Homestead House, 5 Ashley Road, Medbourne, Market Harborough, Leicestershire LE16 8DL
Tel: 01858 565724 Fax: 01858 565324   **Map Ref 16**

QUORN LODGE HOTEL, originally a hunting lodge. Short walk from busy market town. Family owned and run. Restaurant overlooking garden serving a la carte and table d'hote meals. Large car park.

B&B from £39.50, Dinner available, Rooms 6 single, 6 double, 3 twin, 1 triple, 2 four-poster, all en-suite, Open all year.
Quorn Lodge Hotel, 46 Asfordby Road, Melton Mowbray Leicestershire LE13 0HR
Tel: 01664 66660 Fax: 01664 480660   **Map Ref 17**

SYSONBY KNOLL HOTEL, a friendly, family run hotel set in its own grounds with river frontage. Tastefully extended, offering comfortable accommodation and good food, both lunchtime and evening.
B&B from £38, Dinner available, Rooms 6 single, 10 double, 6 twin, 2 triple, all en-suite, Open all year.
Sysonby Knoll Hotel, Asfordby Road, Melton Mowbray, Leicestershire LE13 0HP
Tel: 01664 563563 Fax: 01664 410364   **Map Ref 17**

HILLSIDE HOUSE, a charmingly converted old farm-building overlooking rolling countryside. Comfortable accommodation offered in 3 bedrooms with en-suite/private bathrooms. Rooms have TV, hospitality trays, central heating, radio/alarm, hair dryers. Close to Melton Mowbray, Rutland and centrally located for many interesting places. Guests welcome to use garden.
B&B from £17.00pp, Rooms 2 twin, 1 double, all en-suite, Restricted smoking, Children over 10, No pets, Open all year except Christmas & New Year.
Sue Goodwin, **Hillside House,** 27 Melton Road, Burton Lazars, Melton Mowbray, Leicestershire LE14 2UR
Tel: 01664 566312 Fax: 01664 501819   **Map Ref 18**

....

THE GRANGE, this beautiful country house surrounds you with elegance comfort and friendly care, outstanding views and a lovely formal garden of two and a half acres. Each bedroom is en-suite with telephone, TV and tea/coffee facilities. The drawing room is furnished with antiques and has open log fire. One and a half miles Melton Mowbray. 7 miles Oakham.

B&B from £22.25pp, Rooms 1 single, 1 twin, 2 double, 1 family, all en-suite, Restricted smoking, Children welcome, No pets, Open all year.
Pam Holden, **The Grange,** New Road, Burton Lazars, Melton Mowbray, Leicestershire LE14 2UU
Tel: 01664 560775 Fax: 01664 560775   **Map Ref 18**

....

BOULTONS COUNTRY HOUSE HOTEL, in the county of Rutland. Unspoilt surroundings with many attractions including Rutland Water. Country house ambience, pub circa 1604 and intimate restaurant.

B&B from £60, Dinner available, Rooms 7 single, 12 double, 6 twin, all en-suite, Open all year.
Boultons Country House Hotel, 4 Catmosd Street, Oakham, Leicestershire LE15 6HW
Tel: 01572 722844 Fax: 01572 724473   **Map Ref 19**

....

BARNSDALE COUNTRY CLUB & HOTEL, set in 60 acres overlooking Rutland Water, offering extensive leisure and sporting facilities and a gourmet restaurant.
B&B from £46.75, Dinner available, Rooms 3 single, 40 double, 6 twin, all en-suite, Open all year.
Barnsdale Country Club & Hotel, Barnsdale, Exton, Oakham, Leicestershire LE15 8AB
Tel: 01572 757901 Fax: 01572 756235   **Map Ref 20**

....

BARNSDALE LODGE HOTEL, a country farmhouse hotel furnished in Edwardian style. On the side of Rutland Water, 2 miles from Oakham.

B&B from £58, Dinner available, Rooms 8 single, 12 double, 7 twin, 2 triple, all en-suite, Open all year.
Barnsdale Lodge Hotel, The Avenue, Exton, Oakham, Leicestershire LE15 8AH
Tel: 01572 724678 Fax: 01572 724961   **Map Ref 20**

....

LAKE ISLE HOTEL, this 18th century hotel absorbs more than a little of Uppingham's charm. The personal touch will make your stay extra special with weekly changing menus and a list of over 300 wines.

B&B from £45, Dinner available, Rooms 1 single, 9 double, 2 twin, all en-suite, Open all year.
Lake Isle Hotel, 16 High Street East, Uppingham, Oakham, Leicestershire LE15 9PZ
Tel: 01572 822591 Fax: 01572 822951   **Map Ref 21**

....

RUTLAND HOUSE, a family run B & B. Close to Rutland Water. Full English breakfast. Well-placed for exploring Rutland's villages and countryside.

B&B from £30, Rooms 2 double, 2 twin, 1 triple, all en-suite, Open all year.
Rutland House, 61 High Street East, Uppingham, Leicestershire LE15 9PY
Tel: 01572 822497 Fax: 01572 822497   **Map Ref 21**

GARDEN HOTEL, offers en-suite rooms with colour TV, telephone, radio, and tea/coffee facilities. Comfortable lounge bar. Walled garden. Traditional British home cooking. Good wine list. French Bistro also available. Historic hotel with friendly reputation and homely service. Same day laundry. Near to Rutland Water, sailing, fishing and walking. The best kept secret in Rutland. Private car park.
B&B from £35pp, Dinner from £20, Rooms 4 single, 1 twin, 4 double, 1 family, all en-suite, No smoking, Children & pets welcome, Open all year.
Garden Hotel, High Street West, Uppingham, Leicestershire LE15 9QD
Tel: 01572 822352 Fax: 01572 821156 **Map Ref 21**

SPINDLE LODGE HOTEL, a Victorian house with friendly atmosphere, within easy walking distance of city centre, university, station, civic and entertainment centres.
B&B from £29.50, Dinner available, Rooms 5 single, 3 double, 3 twin, 2 triple, some en-suite, Open all year.
Spindle Lodge Hotel, 2 West Walk, Leicester, Leicestershire, LE1 7NA
Tel: 0116 233 8801 Fax: 0116 233 8804 **Map Ref 7**

HOLLY LODGE, an attractive 19th century former Hunting Lodge, delightfully situated in peaceful country surroundings. Approximately 10 miles north of Nottingham. The Victorian outbuildings have been converted to provide comfortable en-suite accommodation. Rooms have colour TV, tea/coffee, central heating throughout. Parking. Tennis, golf, riding, walks nearby.
B&B from £23pp, Rooms 2 single, 1 twin, 2 double, all en-suite, No smoking or pets, Children welcome, Open all year.
Ann Shipside, **Holly Lodge,** Ricket Lane, Blidworth, Nottinghamshire NG21 0NQ
Tel: 01623 793853 Fax: 01623 490977 **Map Ref 22**

OAKMONT HOUSE GUEST HOUSE, a delightful Victorian house, ten minutes from city centre offering en-suite rooms, centrally heated, tea/coffee facilities, television, guests lounge. Satellite TV. Private parking. Full English breakfast, home cooked natural produce. All with very warm welcome. Strictly non smoking.
B&B from £25pp, Rooms 1 twin, 3 double, all en-suite, Non smoking, Open all year except Christmas.
Jean Plaskitt, **Oakmont House Guest House,** 51 Shearing Hill, Gedling, Nottinghamshire NG4 3GY
Tel: 0115 9616534 **Map Ref 23**

PINE LODGE HOTEL, friendly and informal. Good food, good value, excellent service.
B&B from £35, Dinner available, Rooms 5 single, 5 double, 7 twin, 2 triple, all en-suite, Open all year.
Pine Lodge Hotel, 281-283 Nottingham Road, Mansfield, Nottinghamshire NG18 3HS
Tel: 01623 622308 Fax: 01623 656819 **Map Ref 25**

TITCHFIELD GUEST HOUSE, a family run guest house with adjoining garage for parking facilities. TV lounge. TV in all bedrooms. Kitchen available for making hot drinks etc. Garden for guests. Sherwood Forest and Peak District easy accessible and forward travel. A warm and friendly welcome is assured here.
B&B from £17pp, Rooms 4 single, 2 twin, 1 double, 1 family, Restricted smoking, Children welcome, Pets by arrangement, Open all year.
Bette Hinchley, **Titchfield Guest House,** 300-302 Chesterfield Road, Mansfield, Nottinghamshire NG19 7QU
Tel: 01623 810356 & 810921 Fax: 01623 810356 **Map Ref 26**

THE FRINGE HOTEL & LEISURE COMPLEX, a modern, well-equipped hotel with extensive leisure facilities including squash, tennis, gymnasium and sunbeds. Comfortable, pleasant interior and friendly service.

B&B from £25, Dinner available, Rooms 6 single, 3 double, 6 twin, all en-suite, Open all year.
The Fringe Hotel & Leisure Complex, Briar Lane, Mansfield, Nottinghamshire NG18 3HS
Tel: 01623 641337 Fax: 01623 27521   **Map Ref 25**

....

SOUTH PARADE HOTEL, a family run Georgian listed hotel in quiet location, 5 minutes' walk from market place. Good home-cooked food. All rooms, restaurant and bar recently renovated, refurbished and redecorated.

B&B from £39.50, Dinner available, Rooms 5 single, 5 double, 1 twin, 2 triple, 1 family, most en-suite, Open all year.
South Parade Hotel, 117 Balderton Gate, Newark, Nottinghamshire NG24 1RY
Tel: 01636 703008 Fax: 01636 605593   **Map Ref 27**

....

THE GRANGE HOTEL, a family run hotel with en-suite rooms, candlelit restaurant and excellent food. Spacious restaurant and excellent food. Spacious restaurant and bar with good selection of wines and malt whiskies.

B&B from £45, Dinner available, Rooms 2 single, 9 double, 3 twin, 1 triple, all en-suite, Open all year.
The Grange Hotel, 73 London Road, Newark, Nottinghamshire NG24 1RZ
Tel: 01636 703399 Fax: 01636 702328   **Map Ref 27**

....

WILLOW TREE INN, a 17th century village inn, conveniently placed for historic Lincoln, Grantham, Newark and Sherwood. Known locally for good food and ales. Off the A17 and A1.

B&B from £35, Dinner available, Rooms 3 single, 1 double, some en-suite, Open all year.
Willow Tree Inn, Front Street, Barnby-in-the-Willows, Newark, Nottinghamshire NG24 2SA
Tel: 01636 626613 Fax: 01636 626060   **Map Ref 28**

....

RACECOURSE FARM, charming two hundred year old cottage. Beamed ceilings. Large attractive bedrooms, TV, tea/coffee facilities in rooms. Peaceful surroundings. Facing the church in a small village. Safe parking. Three miles Minster Town. Southwell five miles, Newark/Trent, A1. Racecourse, Golf Course 1/2 mile. Sherwood Forest ten miles.

B&B from £18.20pp, Rooms 1 twin, 1 double, 1 family, 1 en-suite, No smoking, Children over 14, No pets, Open all year.
Ann Lee, **Racecourse Farm,** Station Road, Rolleston, Newark, Nottinghamshire NG23 5SE
Tel: 01636 812176   **Map Ref 29**

....

THE NOTTINGHAM GATEWAY HOTEL, a comfortable hotel with modern facilities and friendly staff, is well located for guests wishing to explore Robin Hood country, Newtstead Abbey - Lord Byron's birth place, Nottingham Lace Hall and the many more historical and literary places of interest.

B&B from £32.50pp, Dinner from £12.95-£15.50, Rooms 31 twin, 50 double, 25 family, all en-suite, Restricted smoking, Children welcome, No pets, Open all year.
Mandy Goldsmith, **The Nottingham Gateway Hotel,** Nuthall Road, Nottingham NG8 6AZ
Tel: 0115 979 4949 Fax: 0115 979 4744   **Map Ref 30**

....

FORTE POSTHOUSE NOTTINGHAM CITY, a modern city centre hotel, with variety of dining/bar experiences, ideally placed for theatres, shopping and such major attractions as Nottingham Castle.

B&B from £78, Dinner available, Rooms 93 single, 13 double, 24 twin, all en-suite, Open all year.
Forte Posthouse Nottingham City, St James Street, Nottingham NG1 6BN
Tel: 0115 947 0130 Fax: 0115 948 4366   **Map Ref 30**

GREENWOOD LODGE, one mile from Nottingham city centre, in quiet location. Sheila and Michael welcome you to this fine Victorian house. All rooms en-suite with hospitality tray, trouser press, TV, hair dryer and fine four poster. Magnificent conservatory dining room in elegant gardens. Ample off-street car parking provided. ETB 3 Crowns Highly Commended.
B&B from £24pp, Dinner from £9.50, Rooms 1 single, 1 twin, 4 double, all en-suite, Restricted smoking, Children welcome, Pets by arrangement, Open all year.
Michael & Sheila Spratt, **Greenwood Lodge,** Third Avenue, Sherwood Rise, Nottingham NG7 6JH
Tel: 0115 9621206 Fax: 0115 9621206   **Map Ref 30**

....

FAIRHAVEN PRIVATE HOTEL, a family run private hotel close to the university and rail station, midway between the M1 and Nottingham city centre.

B&B from £21, Dinner available, Rooms 5 single, 4 double, 2 twin, 1 triple, some en-suite, Open all year.

Fairhaven Private Hotel, 19 Meadow Road, Beaston Rylands, Nottingham, Nottinghamshire NG9 1JP
Tel: 0115 922 7509 Email: fairhavenb@aol.com   **Map Ref 31**

....

LANGAR HALL, a charming small hotel in peaceful rural setting, 12 miles south-east of Nottingham, Central for touring or as a stop-off for travellers between north and south.

B&B from £75, Dinner available, Rooms 9 double, 1 twin, all en-suite. Open all year.

Langar Hall, Langar, Nottingham, Nottinghamshire NG13 9HG
Tel: 01949 860559 Fax: 01949 861045   **Map Ref 32**

....

CLIFTON HOTEL, a friendly, family run hotel, close to M1, exit 25. 10 minutes from Donington Racecourse, East Midlands Airport, Derby and Nottingham.

B&B from £19, Dinner available, Rooms 5 single, 2 double, 1 twin, 2 triple, some en-suite, Open all year.

Clifton Hotel, 126 Nottingham Road, Long Eaton, Nottingham, Nottinghamshire NG10 2BZ
Tel: 0115 973 4277   **Map Ref 33**

....

SWANS HOTEL & RESTAURANT, ideally placed for all Nottingham's major sporting facilities. Good value, excellent service, wonderful food.

B&B from £35, Dinner available, Rooms 5 single, 19 double, 3 twin, 2 triple, 1 family, all en-suite, Open all year.

Swans Hotel & Restaurant, 84 - 90 Radcliffe Road, West Bridgford, Nottingham, Nottinghamshire NG2 5HH
Tel: 0115 981 4042 Fax: 0115 945 5745   **Map Ref 34**

....

THE OLD FORGE, once a working forge, now a pretty house. Antique furnishings, quietly but centrally situated within short walk of beautiful Minster, restaurants, pubs and shops. Also within short drive of many historic places. Friendly and informal. Pretty garden. Private parking.

B&B from £25pp, Rooms 2 twin, 2 double, 1 family, all en-suite, No smoking, Children & pets welcome, Open all year.

Hilary Marston, **The Old Forge,** 2 Burgage Lane, Southwell, Nottinghamshire NG25 0ER
Tel: 01636 812809 Fax: 01636 816302   **Map Ref 35**

DALESTORTH HOUSE, 18th century Georgian ancestral house modernised, to hotel standard. Clean, comfortable, family run with colour TVs and tea/coffee facilities. Ideal for visiting relations, friends, business people to Mansfield/Sutton area. Car parking. 5 miles from junction 28,M1.

B&B from £15pp, Rooms 5 single, 3 twin, 3 double, 2 family, Children welcome, No pets, Open all year.

Mr & Mrs Jordan, **Dalestorth House,** Skegby Lane, Skegby, Sutton-in-Ashfield, Nottinghamshire NG17 3DH
Tel: 01623 551110 Fax: 01623 442241   **Map Ref 36**

....

CROFT HOTEL, this charming Victorian private bed and breakfast hotel is family run. Situated in a quiet suburb of Nottingham, close to all amenities, 1.5 miles from city centre. All rooms have washbasins, tea/coffee and colour TV. Variety of breakfasts.

B&B from £17pp, Rooms 7 single, 2 twin, 3 double, 3 family, Restricted smoking, Children & pets welcome, Open all year except Christmas & New Year.

Mr & Mrs Kennedy, **Croft Hotel,** 6-8 North Road, West Bridgford, Nottinghamshire NG2 7NH
Tel: 0115 9812744   **Map Ref 34**

....

DUKERIES GUEST HOUSE, all rooms have colour TV, tea/coffee facilities. Close to all local amenities, restaurants and pubs. Many places of historical interest nearby including Sherwood Forest and Clumber Park which is part of the National Trust. Car park. Major refurbishment planned Autumn 1998 offering extended facilities.

B&B from £22.50pp, Dinner by arrangement from £6.50, Rooms 2 single, 1 twin, 2 double,1 family, some en-suite, Restricted smoking, Children welcome, No pets, Open all year except Christmas.

Janice & Allen Crookes, **Dukeries Guest House,** 29 Park Street, Worksop, Nottinghamshire S80 1HW
Tel: 01909 476674   **Map Ref 37**

....

SHERWOOD GUESTHOUSE, in Robin Hood country, near M1 and A1 and close to station and town centre. Comfortable rooms with TV and tea/coffee facilities.

B&B from £19, Rooms 1 single, 4 twin, 2 triple, some en-suite, Open all year.

Sherwood Guesthouse, 57 Carlton Road, Worksop, Nottinghamshire S80 1PP
Tel: 01909 474209   **Map Ref 37**

....

GRANTHAM HOTEL, a family run licensed hotel offering modern accommodation in a comfortable atmosphere. Convenient for the centre of Nottingham, Trent Bridge and the National Water Sports Centre.

B&B from £21, Dinner available, Rooms 13 single, 2 double, 4 twin, 2 triple, 1 family, some en-suite, Open all year.
Grantham Hotel, 24-26 Radcliff Road, West Bridgfrod, Nottingham, Nottinghamshire, NG2 5FW
Tel: 0115 981 1373 Fax: 0115 981 8567   **Map Ref 34**

....

THE OLD RECTORY, a Victorian country house and guest annexe in charming conservation village overlooking the Eyebrook valley. Small farm environment and excellent farmhouse breakfast. Lots to see and do; cycling, riding, walking - Rutland Water, castles, stately homes, country parks, forestry and Barnstable TV gardens. 2 Crown Commended. Email: bb@stablemate.demon.co.uk
B&B from £22pp, Rooms 1 single, 3 twin, 1 double, 1 family, most en-suite, No smoking, Children welcome, Pets by arrangement, Open all year.
Richard & Vanessa Peach, **The Old Rectory,** Belton in Rutland, Oakham, Rutland LE15 9LE
Tel: 01572 717279 Fax: 01572 717 343   **Map Ref 38**

If you think of the county of Lincolnshire as being flat and dull, take a look for yourself. The gentle rolling landscape of the peaceful Wolds, ancient woods, winding roads and pretty villages along with the mysterious beauty of the Fens will all come as a surprise. The Wolds are a forty mile stretch of chalk upland containing rolling hills and deep valleys, rising to five hundred and fifty two feet near Normanby le Wold. The area is one of England's most prosperous for growing wheat and peas.

There are three thousand miles of public rights of way and another thousand miles of Green Lanes so there is plenty of opportunity to explore Lincolnshire's unspoilt countryside. There are plenty of quiet roads with places of interest to discover. From Woodhall Spa, set amid splendid pine woods, there are numerous picturesque walks. From the top of Tattershall Castle's brick tower, both Lincoln Cathedral and the Boston "Stump", the octagonal church tower of St Botolph's Church, can be seen on a clear day.

The bulb-growing region of the Lincolnshire Fens is a riot of colour in the spring time when daffodils and tulips come into flower around Holbeach and Spalding. Here the highlight of the year is the Spalding Flower Parade in early May, with its floats covered in brilliant coloured flower heads. One of the country's premier show gardens, Springfields, has over a million spring bulbs and Summer bedding plants.

Lincolnshire's coast stretches from Gibraltar Point to the mouth of the River Humber. Here the North Sea often retreats so far it almost disappears. Cleethorpes is at the mouth of the river and neighbouring Grimsby, until the mid 1970s was one of the world's greatest fishing ports.

Skegness has always been described as "bracing" because of its East winds. It is not surprising that windmills are a feature of the Lincolnshire landscape - the five sailed tower mill at Alford was built in 1837.

As well as beautiful countryside, Lincolnshire has many places of historic interest. The poet Alfred Lord Tennyson was born in the village of Somersby where his father was rector. The gardens of Gunby Hall were Tennyson's "haunts of ancient peace" and exhibitions commemorating his work can be seen at Stockwith Mill and in Lincoln's Usher Gallery.

Lincolnshire's busy market towns offer a wealth of attractions for visitors. Horncastle was a walled settlement in Roman times and is now noted for its many antique shops. Stamford with its honey-coloured stone buildings was England's first conservation area.

left, Steep Hill

SPURN HEAD

MSBY

CLEETHORPES

THAM

A1031

LOUTH

MABLETHORPE

A16

A52

16

PARTNEY

15 SKEGNESS

A52

6

BOSTON

6

7

HUNSTANTON

Norfolk

7

LONG SUTTON

OLBEACH

A17

KING'S LYNN

WISBECH

COMFORT FRIENDLY INN, conveniently located at the junction of the A17/A52. Well equipped bedrooms, all day restaurant, meeting and conference facilities and ample free car parking.

B&B from £25, Dinner available, Rooms 20 double, 35 twin, all en-suite, No smoking, Children welcome, Open all year.
Comfort Friendly Inn, Junction A17/A52, Donington Road, Boston, Lincolnshire PE20 3AN
Tel: 01205 820118 Fax: 01205 820228   **Map Ref 1**

....

YE OLDE MAGNET TAVERN, a traditional 17th century English pub with cask ales, serving home cooked food in a friendly atmosphere. Opposite the historic Guildhall Museum and within easy reach of all local amenities.

B&B from £31.75, Dinner available, Rooms 1 single, 2 double, 1 twin, all en-suite, Children welcome, Open all year.
Ye Olde Magnet Tavern, South Square, Boston, Lincolnshire PE21 6HX
Tel: 01205 369186   **Map Ref 1**

....

BLACK HORSE INN, a coaching inn since 1717, nestling in the shadow of Grimsthorpe Castle. A hostelry of individually from its furnishings to its food. All guests treated personally.

B&B from £40, Dinner available, Rooms 4 double, 2 twin, most en-suite, No smoking, Children over 10, No pets, Open all year.
Black Horse Inn, Grimsthorpe, Bourne, Lincolnshire PE10 0LY
Tel: 01778 591247 Fax: 01778 591373   **Map Ref 2**

....

WHITE HART HOTEL, a family run, town centre coaching inn. Set within pedestrianised area of this bustling market town. The hotel is fully modernised with full central heating. All rooms en-suite with colour TV, tea/coffee facilities. Olde World restaurant, good menu. Lively weekends. Parking for 15+cars.
B&B from £45pp, Dinner from £7, Rooms 3 single, 7 twin, 2 double, 2 family, all en-suite, Children welcome, Pets by arrangement, Open all year.
Mr & Mrs Davies, **White Hart Hotel,** 49 Lord Street, Gainsborough, Lincolnshire DN21 2DD
Tel: 01427 612018 Fax: 01427 811756   **Map Ref 4**

....

KINGS HOTEL, a privately owned hotel serving Grantham and the East Midlands, with a tradition of good hospitality and great value since 1974.
B&B from £35, Dinner available, Rooms 10 double, 10 twin, 1 family, all en-suite, No smoking, Children welcome, Open all year.
Kings Hotel, North Parade, Grantham, Lincolnshire NG31 8AU
Tel: 01476 590800 Fax: 01476 590800   **Map Ref 5**

....

KEELBY GUEST HOUSE, a rural village setting, close to Immingham, Sallingborough and Humberside Airport. Colour TV, tea/coffee facilities in all rooms. Private car park. Two excellent local pubs. Golf breaks from £74 for 2 nights, no supplement for single occupancy.
B&B from £14pp, Dinner from £3.50, Rooms 1 single, 5 twin, Restricted smoking, Children welcome, No pets, Open all year except Christmas & New Year.
Mr S Parker, **Keelby Guest House,** 3 Victoria Road, Keelby, Grimsby, North East Lincolnshire DN41 8EH
Tel: 01469 561399   **Map Ref 6**

....

CACKLE HILL HOUSE, a warm welcome awaits you at our comfortable home set in a rural position. All rooms have en-suite private facilities and hospitality trays. Guests lounge with colour TV. Situated near the borders of Norfolk and Cambridgeshire. ETB 2 Crowns Highly Commended.
B&B from £20pp, Rooms 2 twin, 1 double, all en-suite, No smoking, Children over 10, Pets by arrangement, Open all year except Christmas & New Year.
Maureen Biggadike, **Cackle Hill House,** Cackle Hill Lane, Holbeach, Lincolnshire PE12 8BS
Tel: 01406 426721 Fax: 01406 424659   **Map Ref 7**

ADMIRAL RODNEY HOTEL, located in pleasant market town just off main Lincoln to Skegness road - ideal touring base. Large car park, en-suite bedrooms and fine restaurant.

B&B from £33.50, Dinner available, Rooms 19 double, 9 twin, 1 triple, 2 family, all en-suite, Children welcome, No smoking, Open all year.
Admiral Rodney Hotel, North Street, Horncastle, Lincolnshire LN9 5DX
Tel: 01507 523131 Fax: 01507 523104 **Map Ref 8**

GEORGE HOTEL, a 17th century coaching inn where the owners take pride in the international menu and their collection of over 500 whiskies from all over the world.

B&B from £20, Dinner available, Rooms 2 single, 2 double, 3 twin, most en-suite, Children welcome, Open all year.
George Hotel, High Street, Leadenham, Lincolnshire LN5 0PN
Tel: 01400 272251 Fax: 01400 272091 **Map Ref 9**

CARLINE GUEST HOUSE, is a charming double fronted Edwardian House. A short stroll from the Cathedral area. Each room is fully equipped with TV, radio, trouser press, hospitality tray, en-suite. For your comfort and safety we are a non smoking establishment. Private garaging and parking available.

B&B from £20pp, Rooms 2 twin, 8 double, 2 family, all en-suite, No smoking or pets, Children welcome, Open all year except Christmas & New Year.
Gillian & John Pritchard, **Carline Guest House,** 1-3 Carline Road, Lincoln, Lincolnshire LN1 1HL
Tel: 01522 530422 Fax: 01522 530422 **Map Ref 10**

HILLCREST HOTEL, a Victorian rectory overlooking gardens and park. Peaceful location, 5 minutes walk to cathedral and city. Short breaks available.

B&B from £37, Dinner available, Rooms 6 single, 6 double, 1 twin, 4 triple, all en-suite, No smoking, Children welcome, Open all year.
Hillcrest Hotel, 15 Lindum Terrace, Lincoln, Lincolnshire LN2 5RT
Tel: 01522 510182 Fax: 01522 510182 **Map Ref 10**

HOLLIES HOTEL, a privately owned Victorian residence of considerable charm and character. A short and picturesque walk to the town, tourist areas and Brayford Marina.
B&B from £35, Dinner available, Rooms 2 single, 4 double, 2 twin, 1 triple, 1 family, most en-suite, No smoking, Children over 6, Open all year.
Hollies Hotel, 65 Carholme Road, Lincoln, Lincolnshire LN1 1RT
Tel: 01522 522419 Fax: 01522 522419 **Map Ref 10**

TENNYSON HOTEL, a comfortable atmosphere, overlooking the South Park, 1 mile from the city centre. Personally supervised. Leisure breaks available.

B&B from £29, Rooms 2 single, 3 double, 1 twin, 2 triple, all en-suite, Children welcome, No pets, Open all year.
Tennyson Hotel, 7 South Park Avenue, Lincoln, Lincolnshire LN5 8EN
Tel: 01522 521624 Fax: 01522 521624 **Map Ref 10**

DAMON'S MOTEL, a purpose built, 2 storey motel on the Lincoln ring road. Adjacent restaurant, indoor pool, gym and solarium. Satellite TV.
B&B from £42, Dinner available, Rooms 24 double, 18 twin, 5 triple, all en-suite, No smoking, Children welcome, No pets, Open all year.
Damon's Motel, 997 Doddington Road, Lincoln, Lincolnshire LN6 3SE
Tel: 01522 887733 Fax: 01522 887734 **Map Ref 10**

GRAND HOTEL, a family owned hotel, in the centre of beautiful historic city. Getaway breaks available throughout the year.

B&B from £43.50, Dinner available, Rooms 19 single, 14 double, 13 twin, 2 triple, all en-suite, No smoking, Children welcome, Open all year.
Grand Hotel, St Marys Street, Lincoln, Lincolnshire LN5 7EP
Tel: 01522 524211 Fax: 01522 537661 **Map Ref 10**

CASTLE HOTEL, privately owned traditional English hotel offering hospitality at its best. Listed building in Lincoln's historic heart. Impressive castle and cathedral views. Ample free parking. A unique welcome, and one we're confident you'll wish to experience again.
B&B from £42.50, Dinner available, Rooms 4 single, 9 double, 5 twin, 1 triple, all en-suite, No smoking, Children welcome, Open all year.
Castle Hotel, Westgate, Lincoln, Lincolnshire LN1 3AS
Tel: 01522 538801 Fax: 01522 575457 **Map Ref 10**

BRANSTON HALL HOTEL, situated three miles from historic Lincoln city. We offer full A'la Carte and Table D'Hote dining. Fully licensed bar, ample car parking. Eighty eight acres of parkland and beautiful lake make Branston Hall Hotel ideal for a relaxing break in a country house in a traditional style.

B&B from £49 per room, Dinner from £15.95, Rooms 4 single, 4 double, 30 double, 2 family, all en -suite, Restricted smoking, Children welcome, Open all year.
Mr N Pratt, **Branston Hall Hotel,** Lincoln Rd, Branston, Lincoln LN4 1PD
Tel: 01522 793305 Fax: 01522 790549 **Map Ref 11**

THE WAVENEY GUEST HOUSE, is highly recommended for comfort, cleanliness and home cooked food. All rooms en-suite with CTV and tea making facilities. Guests lounge and dining room. Private car park. Within easy reach of biggest antiques centre in the country, the Lincolnshire Wolds and the coast. Pets welcome.
B&B from £16pp, Dinner £7.50, Rooms 2 twin, 1 family, all en-suite, No smoking, Children & pets welcome, Open all year.
Mrs M E Dawson-Margrave, **The Waveney Guest House,** Willingham Road, Market Rasen, Lincolnshire LN8 3DN
Tel: 01673 843236 **Map Ref 12**

ABBEY HOUSE & COACH HOUSE, a grade II listed former rectory, dating in part from 1190 AD, located in quiet, predominantly stone, village east of Stamford. Attractive gardens. Ideal for touring the Eastern Shires.
B&B from £23, Rooms 1 single, 4 double, 3 twin, 1 triple, 1 family, most en-suite, No smoking, Children over 6, No pets, Open all year.
Abbey House & Coach House, West End Road, Maxey, Lincolnshire PE6 9EJ
Tel: 01778 344642 **Map Ref 13**

IVY LODGE HOTEL, is situated in a picturesque village, an ideal stopover or base. The en-suite rooms have tea/coffee and TV. Residents licensed restaurant provides delicious home cooked food. Comfortable lounge, drinks service, spacious garden. Car park. ETB 3 Crowns Commended. Credit Cards accepted.
B&B from £22pp, Dinner from £5.95, Rooms 2 single, 1 twin, 1 double, 1 family, all en-suite, Restricted smoking, Children welcome, Pets by arrangement, Open all year except Christmas & New Year.
Mrs Pat Mewis, **Ivy Lodge Hotel,** Messingham Road (A159), Scotter, Lincolnshire DN21 3UQ
Tel: 01724 763723 Fax: 01724 763770 **Map Ref 14**

SAXBY HOTEL, a family run hotel on a corner in a quiet residential area of Skegness. 300 yards from seafront and close to all amenities.

B&B from £25, Dinner available, Rooms 1 single, 10 double, 2 twin, 2 triple, most en-suite, Children welcome, Open all year.

Saxby Hotel, 12 Saxby Avenue, Skegness, Lincolnshire PE25 3LG
Tel: 01754 763905 Fax: 01754 763905   **Map Ref 15**

CRAIGSIDE HOTEL, is close to town and sea front attractions. All rooms have private facilities, tea/coffee making. Guest lounge, games/entertainment room, dining room and bar are all wheelchair accessible. Car park to rear. We offer a choice of menu, all diets catered for.
B&B from £20pp, Dinner from £6, Rooms 3 single, 3 twin, 5 double, 5 family, most en-suite, Restricted smoking, Children welcome, No pets, Open March - September.
Ken & Deborah Milner, **Craigside Hotel,** 26 Scarborough Avenue, Skegness, Lincolnshire PE25 2SY
Tel: 01754 763307 Fax: 01754 763307   **Map Ref 15**

CROWN HOTEL, a family run hotel in a quiet part of Skegness, near Gibraltar Point and Seacroft Golf Club.

B&B from £40.50, Dinner available, Rooms 1 single, 4 double, 13 twin, 8 triple, 1 family, all private or en-suite, Children welcome, No pets, Open all year.

Crown Hotel, Drummond Road, Skegness, Lincolnshire PE25 3AB
Tel: 01754 610760 Fax: 01754 610847   **Map Ref 15**

GROSVENOR HOUSE HOTEL, midway along the seafront near the bathing pool, bowling greens, Sun Castle and the Embassy Conference Centre.

B&B from £23.60, Dinner available, Rooms 9 single, 9 double, 3 twin, 11 triple, 1 family, most en-suite, Children welcome, No pets, Open April - October.

Grosvenor House Hotel, North Parade, Skegness, Lincolnshire PE25 2TE
Tel: 01754 763376 Fax: 01754 764650   **Map Ref 15**

THE VINE, attractive, detached brick built property in this popular seaside resort.

B&B from £45, Dinner available, Rooms 3 single, 10 double, 3 twin, 4 triple, 1 family, all private or en-suite, Children welcome, Open all year.

The Vine, Vine Road, Skegness, Lincolnshire PE25 3DB
Tel: 01754 610611 & 763018 Fax: 01754 769845   **Map Ref 15**

SEAYR HOTEL, a small family run hotel with very high standards. In pleasant seaside village between Skegness and Mablethorpe. TV lounge and bar. Car park. Tea/coffee facilities and TV in all bedrooms. Full English breakfast.

B&B from £14pp, Rooms 1 twin, 4 double, 2 family, some en-suite, Smoking & Children welcome, Open all year except December.
Mr & Mrs Hanes, **Seayr Hotel,** 25 South Road, Chapel St Leonards, Skegness, Lincolnshire PE24 5TL
Tel: 01754 872810   **Map Ref 16**

THE LINCOLNSHIRE OAK HOTEL, situated on the edge of a market town, this comfortable hotel offers an ideal central base for exploring Lincolnshire. Excellent food and wines.

B&B from £39, Dinner available, Rooms 5 single, 7 double, 2 twin, all en-suite, No smoking, Children welcome, No pets.
The Lincolnshire Oak Hotel, East Road, Sleaford, Lincolnshire NG34 7EH
Tel: 01529 413807 Fax: 01529 413710 **Map Ref 17**

....

THE TALLY HO INN, a traditional, friendly 17th century listed country inn. En-suite rooms carefully converted stables, a la carte restaurant and bar meals. Plenty of welcoming atmosphere and character.

B&B from £30, Dinner available, Rooms 2 double, 4 twin, all en-suite, Children welcome, Open all year.
The Tally Ho Inn, Aswarby, Sleaford, Lincolnshire NG34 8SA
Tel: 01529 455205 **Map Ref 18**

....

CLEY HALL HOTEL, a Georgian manor house by the River Welland, 500 metres from town centre, with unique candlelit cellar restaurant. Own car park.

B&B from £30, Dinner available, Rooms 4 single, 5 double, 3 twin, all en-suite, No smoking, Children welcome, Open all year.
Cley Hall Hotel, 22 High Street, Spalding, Lincolnshire PE11 1TX
Tel: 01775 725157 Fax: 01775 710785 **Map Ref 19**

....

TRAVEL STOP, converted from farm buildings, the motel complements the 17th century farmhouse. Three quarters of a mile from centre of Spalding on the Travelstop round about and B1173, A1073 Peterborough road. Most units are on ground floor with own porches and all are equipped with fridge and colour TV.

B&B from £30, Rooms 3 single, 5 double, 2 twin, all en-suite, No smoking, Children welcome, Open all year.
Travel Stop, Locks Mill Farm, 50 Cowbit Road, Spalding, Lincolnshire PE11 2RJ
Tel: 01775 767290 Fax: 01775 767716 **Map Ref 19**

....

PIPWELL MANOR, bed and breakfast in a Georgian Manor House in a small Fenland village just off the A17. Bedrooms are attractive and well furnished with all facilities. Parking is available and guests are welcomed with home made cakes and tea. A lovely place to stay. AA QQQQ Selected. Two Crowns Highly Commended.

B&B from £20pp, Rooms 1 twin, 2 double, all en-suite, No smoking or pets, Children welcome, Open all year except Christmas & New Year.
Mrs Lesley Honnor, **Pipwell Manor,** Washway Road, Sarcens Head, Holbeach, Spalding, Lincolnshire PE12 8AL
Tel: 01406 423119 **Map Ref 20**

....

DOLPHIN GUEST HOUSE, offer luxury en-suite accommodation next to the Dolphin Inn, renowned for its Cast Ales and food. All rooms with satellite TV and hospitality tray's. Off road parking and only 100 yards from Stamford town centre, listed by Les Routiers, the Good Beer Guide and ETB Three Crowns. Also Room at the Inn by CAMRA.
B&B from £20pp, Dinner £4, Rooms 3 twin, 3 double, 2 family, all en-suite, Smoking & Children welcome, Pets by arrangement, Open all year.
Mike & Tina Maksimovic, **Dolphin Guest House,** 12 East Street, Stamford, Lincolnshire PE9 1QD
Tel: 01780 757515 Fax: 01780 757515 **Map Ref 21**

....

THE PRIORY, a listed 16th century country house in peaceful setting. Award winning bed and breakfast. En-suite rooms with every comfort overlook splendid gardens. Resident chef. Choice of menus. Brochure available.

B&B from £54, Dinner available, Rooms 2 double, 1 twin, all en-suite, No smoking, Children welcome, No pets, Open all year.
The Priory, Church Road, Ketton, Stamford, Lincolnshire PE9 3RD
Tel: 01780 720215 Fax: 01780 721881 **Map Ref 22**

GARDEN HOUSE HOTEL, a charming 18th century town house converted to a hotel, where guests are treated as such by their hosts. Features a conservatory, full or floral extravaganza and a meandering garden of 1 acre.

B&B from £30pp, Dinner available, Rooms 2 single, 9 double, 8 twin, 1 triple, all en-suite, Children & pets welcome, Open all year.

Garden House Hotel, St. Martins, Stamford, Lincolnshire PE9 2LP
Tel: 01780 763359 Fax: 01780 763339   **Map Ref 21**

GILLINGHAM REST, a quiet, extremely comfortable high class guest house, situated four miles from Humberside International Airport and close to Humber Bank Industries. Private parking. Television, tea/coffee facilities in all rooms. Guest lounge. A friendly welcome always assured.
http://www.yell.co.uk/sites/gillinghamrest/
B&B from £20pp, Dinner from £6, Rooms 2 single, 2 twin, all private facilities, Children welcome, Open all year except Christmas.
Susan Connole, **Gillingham Rest,** Spruce Lane, Ulceby, North Lincolnshire DN39 6UL
Tel: 01469 588427   **Map Ref 24**

GILLINGHAM REST

WASHINGBOROUGH HALL COUNTRY HOUSE HOTEL, a stone built, former manor house in grounds of 3 acres, in a pleasant village 2.5 miles from the historic cathedral city of Lincoln.
B&B from £56.50, Dinner available, Rooms 6 double, 6 twin, most en-suite, No smoking, Children welcome, Open all year.
Washingborough Hall Country House Hotel, Church Hill, Washingborough, Lincolnshire LN4 1BE
Tel: 01522 790340 Fax: 01522 792936   **Map Ref 23**

B&B in the **CLAREMONT GUEST HOUSE**, a homely traditional unspoilt Victorian house, in Lincolnshire's unique resort. TV and tea/coffee facilities in all rooms. Off-street parking and peaceful garden available for guests and good food nearby. Ideal for exploring Lincolnshire or enjoying Woodhall Spa's many attractions.
B&B from £15pp, Rooms 2 single, 1 twin, 3 double, 3 family, some en-suite, Restricted smoking, Children & pets welcome, Open all year.
Claire Brennan, **Claremont Guest House,** 9-11 Witham Road, Woodhall Spa, Lincolnshire LN10 6RW
Tel: 01526 352000   **Map Ref 25**

DOWER HOUSE HOTEL, is surrounded by three acres of well tended gardens, with own private car park. Overlooking the internationally famous Woodhall Spa golf course. The hotel has an excellent restaurant and fully licensed bar. Television, tea/coffee facilities in all rooms. Three Crowns Commended.
B&B from £34-44pp, Dinner from £14.95, Rooms 6 twin, 1 double/family, most en-suite, Children welcome, Pets by arrangement, Open all year.
Mr H & Mrs C Plumb, **Dower House Hotel,** Manor Estate, Woodhall Spa, Lincolnshire LN10 6PY
Tel/Fax: 01526 352588   **Map Ref 25**

EAGLE LODGE HOTEL, a mock Tudor country house hotel, close to many good golf courses and a short drive from Lincoln, Boston and the East Coast. Good food, real ales and a good atmosphere.
B&B from £25, Dinner available, Rooms 5 single, 7 double, 9 twin, 1 triple, 1 family, all en-suite or private facilities, Children welcome, Open all year.
Eagle Lodge Hotel, The Broadway, Woodhall Spa, Lincolnshire LN10 6ST
Tel: 01526 353231 Fax: 01526 352797   **Map Ref 25**

London & Middlesex

There need never be a dull moment in England's capital city, London. It offers such a bewildering choice of things to do and places to visit that the difficulty is in deciding exactly what to do and see in a short break there.

The Queen has opened her 300 year old London home, Buckingham Palace to the public. Eighteen major rooms are included in the tour from the Throne Room, State Dining Room, the Green, Blue and White Drawing Rooms and the Music Room. London Zoo undergone a £1 million major refurbishment project to update and extend the Children's Zoo and at the Science Museum a £1.2 million gallery explores the rapid development in 20th century medicine with plenty of hands-on exhibits. The Tower of London has a new Jewel House, now three times larger than the previous one, allowing 20,000 visitors a day to pass through and view the treasures.

London was the first capital city in the world to experience the industrial revolution, and its attractions and river still pay tribute to those days. Many of these attractions are best reached by river boat such as the National Maritime Museum, the Old Royal Observatory and the London Docklands.

The docklands rising in the east alongside the Thames is almost a mini-Manhattan. New and imaginative buildings have replaced areas where the world's shipping used to load and unload cargo and redundant warehouses have been converted into fashionable apartments and a shopping village.

Getting around the capital city is easy whether you take the bus or the underground train. There are also numerous bus companies offering sightseeing tours and if you want to get onto the streets, walking tours are also given.

London is the place where you can really 'shop till you drop' but the difficulty could be knowing where to start as you may well 'drop' before you've visited half of the shops. There are the large department stores from Selfridges in Oxford Street, to Harrods in Knightsbridge and Liberty in Regent Street while at the other extreme are the wide selection of small specialist shops selling everything from cheese to china.

It is the evening when London comes to life. Theatre in London centres mainly around Shaftesbury Avenue, but there is also the Barbican Centre, home to the Royal Shakespeare Company and the Royal National Theatre on the South Bank. As well as classical music, opera there is an array of restaurants unrivalled by other major cities, a range of night-clubs, wine bars and cinemas.

left, Houses of Parliament along the Thames

Beautiful B&B in London

Anita Harrison and Rosemary Richardson specialise in arranging good quality Bed and Breakfast accommodation in London homes. All have their individual style and offer exceptional value for money - a very affordable alternative to hotels.

Most of the accommodation is located in the leafy west London areas of Chiswick, Hammersmith, Ealing and Parsons Green, convenient to shops and restaurants and public transport for the central sights. *London Home-to-Home* also represents a select number of homes in more central areas where prices are higher.

The accommodation has been chosen with great care with hosts who take pleasure in welcoming guests to their homes. The guest rooms are comfortable and attractively decorated, with the emphasis on cleanliness and warmth. Tea and coffee making facilities are provided and a generous breakfast is included in the tariff. Parking is available at most of the addresses.

Typical Cost: £30 per person per night including breakfast

Telephone Anita or Rosemary to discuss options:

LONDON HOME-TO-HOME
19 Mount Park Crescent, London W5 2RN
Tel and Fax: +44 181 566 7976
Email: londonhh@btinternet.com

WANT TO COME TO LONDON?

We can find you lovely accommodation from our wide selection of delightful homes in many areas of London. Our homes are in attractive, interesting neighbourhoods with shops and restaurants nearby, convenient to public transport and the central sightseeing areas. You will be offered a generous continental breakfast by our friendly and helpful families who enjoy welcoming visitors from all over the world. A cooked breakfast can sometimes be arranged with the family for a small supplement.

the
LONDON
BED & BREAKFAST
agency limited

DON'T KNOW WHERE TO STAY?

CATEGORY A *Top quality homes* in or very near the centre, many with private facilities: **£30-£40**

CATEGORY B+ *Lovely homes* offering private facilities, for two people minimum, approximately 15-20 minutes to the centre, **£25**

CATEGORY B *Delightful homes* with easy access to the centre, **£21**

CATEGORY C *Attractive homes* generally a little further to the centre or the underground, **£18** (Prices quoted are per person per night)

Accommodation with private facilities for the single visitor is from £35 per night. This accommodation is generally within 10-20 minutes of the centre. We have a few special homes in the centre @ **£50-£55** per night for the single visitor.

For an efficient and professional service contact

THE LONDON BED & BREAKFAST AGENCY LIMITED
Telephone +44 171 586 2768 Fax +44 171 586 6567
EMail londonbb@dircon.co.uk
Or book via our website http://www.dircon.co.uk/londonbb/
71 FELLOWS ROAD LONDON NW3 3JY

HOW DO I BOOK?

Simply fax, e-mail, post (remember to enclose a cheque) or telephone your booking request. Give us your name, the exact dates of your stay, the number of people in your group, and the maximum price you wish to pay. We also ask for your credit card details (Visa/Mastercard/Switch). We then make the reservation, debit your card and send you full confirmation details within 24 hours. There is a **£5 booking charge** for all reservations. **Please note** there is a minimum stay requirement of 3 consecutive nights; 2 night stays can only be booked a few days in advance. **We regret we are unable to arrange stays of one night only.**

A listing of homes and locations will be sent on request.

All prices are correct
at the time of going to print

WEST LODGE PARK, a white painted William IV country house set in 35 acres of grounds in rolling countryside. Fine restaurant and very comfortable bedrooms with lots of cossetting extras. Leisure club nearby.
B&B from £84.50, Lunch & evening meal available, Rooms 13 single, 23 double, 7 twin, all en-suite, Children welcome, No pets, No smoking, Open all year.
West Lodge Park, Cockfosters Road, Hadley Wood, Barnet, Hertfordshire EN4 0PY
Tel: 0181 440 8311 Fax: 0181 449 3698

SWALLOW HOTEL, easy access to London and just minutes from junction 2 of the M25. Spacious, double size bedrooms with marble finish bathrooms, leisure club with extensive facilities including fitness room with the latest computerised equipment. Short break packages available.

B&B from £70, Lunch & evening meal available, Rooms 54 single, 35 double, 35 twin, 10 triple, 8 family, suites available, all en-suite, Children welcome, No smoking, Open all year.
Swallow Hotel, 1 Broadway, Bexley Heath, Kent DA6 7JZ
Tel: 0181 298 1000 Fax: 0181 298 1234 Email: info@swallowhotel.com

---

BUXTED LODGE, a Victorian lodge retaining many original features. 30 minutes to central London by British Rail.
B&B from £25, Dinner available, Rooms 2 single, 3 double, 2 twin, 2 triple, some en-suite, Children from 14 years, No smoking, Open all year.
Buxted Lodge, 40 Parkhurst Road, Bexley, Kent DA5 1AS
Tel: 01322 554010 & 0831 794031

GLENDEVON HOUSE HOTEL, a small hotel with private car park. Convenient for central London. Caters for tourists and business people.

B&B from £26.50, Rooms 5 single, 3 double, 1 twin, 1 triple, Children welcome, Open all year.
Glendevon House Hotel, 80 Southborough Road, Bickley, Bromley, Kent BR1 2EN
Tel: 0181 467 2183

THE MARY ROSE HOTEL, a 16th century listed inn. Land traversed by the River Cray. 30 minutes from Hever and Leeds Castles, Chartwell, Greenwich. 25 minutes from central London, convenient for M25 and British Rail.
B&B from £22.50, Lunch & evening meal available, Rooms 4 single, 12 double, 6 twin, 5 triple, 7 family, most en-suite/private facilities, Children welcome, Open all year.
The Mary Rose Hotel, 40-50 High Street, St Mary Cray, Orpington, Kent BR5 3NJ
Tel: 01689 871917 & 875369 Fax: 01689 839445

ANCHOR HOTEL, charming small hotel offering a friendly atmosphere and comfort. Well appointed accommodation. Bedrooms do vary in size, tastefully decorated with modern furniture and have colour TV, tea/coffee facilities and direct dial telephone. Danish style buffet breakfast. Car park facilities.
B&B from £23pp, Rooms 2 single, 4 twin, 5 double, 1 family, some en-suite, Restricted smoking, Children welcome, No pets, Open all year.
Anchor Hotel, (Nova Management), 10 West Heath Drive, London NW11 7QH
Tel: 0181 458 8764 Fax: 0181 455 3204

RILUX HOUSE, high standards, all private facilities, kitchenette and garden. Quiet. Close to underground, buses, M1, 20 minutes West End. Convenient for Wembley, easy route to Heathrow, direct trains to Gatwick and Luton airports. Close to Middlesex University.
B&B from £30, Rooms 1 twin, en-suite, Children welcome, No pets, No smoking, Open all year.
Rilux House, 1 Lodge Road, London NW4 4DD
Tel: 0181 203 0933 Fax: 0181 203 6446

ROSE COURT HOTEL, Privately run Victorian town house in a quiet garden square. Close to Paddington and the West End.

B&B from £40, Lunch & evening meal available, Rooms 7 single, 11 double, 16 twin, 5 triple, 3 family, all en-suite, Children welcome, No smoking, No pets, Open all year.
Rose Court Hotel, 1-3 Talbot Square, London W2 1TR
Tel: 0171 723 5128 & 723 8671 Fax: 0171 723 1855

....

ABCONE HOTEL, close to Gloucester Road underground and convenient for High Street Kensington, Knightsbridge, Olympia, Earls Court, museums and Hyde Park.

B&B from £40, Dinner available, Rooms 17 single, 15 double, 3 twin, Children from 1 year, No pets, Open all year.
Abcone Hotel, 10 Ashburn Gardens, London SW7 4DG
Tel: 0171 460 3400 Fax: 0171 460 3444 Email: aliuk@compuserve.com.

....

THE BERNERS HOTEL, an Edwardian building restored to its original beauty and elegance, a few minutes walk from Oxford Circus and Soho.

B&B from £175, Lunch & evening meal available, Rooms 37 single, 135 double, 45 twin, suites available, all en-suite, Children welcome, No smoking, Open all year.
The Berners Hotel, 10 Berners Street, London W1A 3BE
Tel: 0171 666 2000 Fax: 0171 666 2001 Email: berners@berners.co.uk

....

SASS HOUSE HOTEL, budget accommodation, convenient for central London, Hyde Park and West End. Paddington and Lancaster Gate underground stations nearby. Easy access to tourist attractions.
B&B from £26, Rooms 8 double, 7 twin, 8 triple, all en-suite, Children welcome, No pets, Open all year.
Sass House Hotel, 10-11 Craven Terrace, London W2 3QD
Tel: 0171 262 2325 Fax: 0171 262 0889

....

EBURY HOUSE HOTEL, a small clean Bed & Breakfast in the heart of Belgravia, very near Victoria tube and coach stations. All rooms have colour TV's and hair dryers, some with private shower, toilets. All prices include full English breakfast and VAT.

B&B from £30-£38pp, Rooms 3 single, 4 twin, 4 double, 2 family, some en-suite, Children welcome, No pets, Open all year.
Tony & Kay Ahmed, **Ebury House Hotel,** 102 Ebury Street, London SW1W 9QD
Tel: 0171 730 1350 Fax: 0171 259 0400

....

VEGAS HOTEL, close to Victoria coach and underground stations and 15 minutes from Buckingham Palace. Satellite colour TV, telephone, radio, alarm clock in all rooms.

B&B from £40, Rooms 1 single, 3 double, 9 twin, most en-suite, Children welcome, No pets, No smoking, Open all year.
Vegas Hotel, 104 Warwick Way, London SW1V 1SD
Tel: 0171 834 0082 Fax: 0171 834 5623

....

NOVOTEL LONDON WATERLOO, 3 minutes from Waterloo Station by car. Conveniently located opposite the Houses of Parliament and Big Ben. Good transport links. Air conditioned rooms with mini bar, hair dryers.
B&B from £121, Lunch & evening meal available, Rooms 187 double, suites available, all en-suite, Children welcome, No smoking, Open all year.
Novotel London Waterloo, 113 Lambeth Road, London SE1 7LS
Tel: 0171 793 1010 Fax: 0171 793 0202

PARKLAND WALK GUEST HOUSE, a friendly Victorian family house in a residential area, Highgate/Crouch End. Near many restaurants and convenient for central London. Non smokers only.

B&B from £26, Rooms 3 single, 1 double, 1 twin, 1 family Most en-suite, Children welcome, No pets or smoking, Open all year.
Parkland Walk Guest House, 12 Hornsey Rise Gardens, London N19 3PR
Tel: 0171 263 3228 & 0973 382982 Fax: 0171 263 3965 Email: parklandwalk@monomark.demon.co.uk

....

WINDSOR HOUSE, a budget priced b& B establishment in Earl's Court. Easily reached from airports and motorway. The West End is minutes away by underground.NCP parking.

B&B from £26, Rooms 2 single, 4 double, 4 twin, 1 triple, 7 family, some en-suite, Children welcome, Open all year.
Windsor House, 12 Penywern Road, London SW5 9ST
Tel: 0171 373 9087 Fax: 0171 385 2417

....

BARCLAY COURT PRIVATE HOTEL, a family run establishment on main A3. Direct rail connection to Gatwick Airport and Victoria station from nearby Clapham Junction.

B&B from £30, Rooms 6 single, 3 double, 3 twin, 2 triple, Children welcome, No pets, No smoking, Open all year.

Barclay Court Private Hotel, 12-14 Hafer Road, London SW11 1HF
Tel: 0171 228 5272 Fax: 0171 924 5431

....

NAYLAND HOTEL, centrally located, close to many amenities and within walking distance of Hyde Park and Oxford Street. Quality you can afford.

B&B from £46, Dinner available, Rooms 11 single, 8 double, 17 twin, 5 triple, all en-suite, Children welcome, No pets, Open all year.
Nayland Hotel, 132-134 Sussex Gardens, London W2 1UB
Tel: 0171 723 4615 Fax: 0171 402 3292

....

LONDON LODGE HOTEL, an attractive hotel ideally situated in a quiet residential street in the heart of Kensington. Perfectly placed for business, shopping and seeing London. Special weekday/weekend packages available.

B&B from £75, Lunch & evening meal available, Rooms 7 single, 8 double, 12 twin, 1 triple, all en-suite, Children welcome, No pets, Open all year.

London Lodge Hotel, 136 Lexham Gardens, London W8 6JE
Tel: 0171 244 8444 Fax: 0171 373 6661

....

BEVERLEY HOUSE HOTEL, refurbished bed and breakfast hotel, serving traditional English breakfast and offering high standards at low prices. Close to Paddington station, Hyde Park and museums.

B&B from £40, Dinner available, Rooms 6 single, 5 double, 6 twin, 6 triple, all en-suite, Children welcome, Open all year.
Beverley House Hotel, 142 Sussex Gardens, London W2 1UB
Tel: 0171 723 3380 Fax: 0171 262 0324

....

ASHLEY COURT, Very popular town house hotel in quiet garden square. Quality rooms with private showers and toilets, TV, tea-making facilities. Owned and managed by the same Welsh family for 30 years.

B&B from £31, Rooms 18 single, 16 double, 6 twin, 8 triple, 5 family, Children welcome, No pets, Open all year.

Ashley Court, 15 Norfolk Square, London W2 1RU
Tel: 0171 723 3375 Fax: 0171 723 0173

THE LEONARD, four 18th Century town houses, elegantly restored. Accommodation is mainly suites, all with air conditioning and hifi systems. 24 hour room service and friendly staff.

B&B from £205, Lunch available, Rooms 22 double, 1 triple, 3 family, suites available, all en-suite, Children welcome, No pets, No smoking, Open all year.
The Leonard, 15 Seymour Street, London W1H 5AA
Tel: 0171 935 2010 Fax: 0171 935 6700

....

WESTLAND HOTEL, small friendly hotel, well located for West End shopping, touring or relaxing in a beautiful park. Your home-from-home.

B&B from £80, Lunch & evening meal available, Rooms 2 single, 6 double, 19 twin, 3 triple, 1 family, all en-suite, Children welcome, Open all year.
Westland Hotel, 154 Bayswater Road London W2 4HP
Tel: 0171 229 9191 Fax: 0171 727 1054

....

SPRINGFIELD HOTEL, small hotel close to Hyde Park and Marble Arch.
B&B from £40, Rooms 2 single, 6 double, 6 twin, 6 triple, all en-suite, Children welcome, Open all year.
Springfield Hotel, 154 Sussex Gardens, London W2 1UD
Tel: 0171 723 9898 Fax: 0171 723 0874

....

ALBRO HOUSE HOTEL, ideally located in pleasant area near public transport. Nice rooms, all en-suite. English breakfast. Languages spoken. Friendly and safe. Some parking available.

B&B from £38, Rooms 2 single, 6 double, 5 twin, 4 triple, 3 family, most en-suite, Children welcome, No pets, Open all year.
Albro House Hotel, 155 Sussex Gardens, London W2 2RY
Tel: 0171 724 2931 & 706 8153 Fax: 0171 262 2278

....

KNIGHTSBRIDGE GREEN HOTEL, a small family-owned and run hotel close to Harrods, offering spacious accommodation at competitive rates.

B&B from £109.50, Rooms 7 single, 3 double, 5 twin, 12 triple, suites available, all en-suite, Children welcome, No pets, Open all year.
Knightsbridge Green Hotel, 159 Knightsbridge, London SW1X 7PD
Tel: 0171 584 6274 Fax: 0171 225 1635 Email: theKGHotel@aol.com

....

VIENNA GROUP OF HOTELS, offer a range of accommodation in London and Oxford. Along with over 150 apartments and 4 Three Star hotels, Vienna Budget Hotels are perfect for those wishing to travel to London and pay sensible prices for clean, comfortable, basic accommodation.
B&B from £52 per room, 245 rooms many with en-suite, Children welcome, Pets by arrangement, Open all year.
Peter M Lowy, **Vienna Group of Hotels,** 16 Leinster Square, London W2 4PR
Tel: 0171 221 1400 Fax: 0171 229 3917 Email: hotels@vienna-group.co.uk

....

CECIL COURT HOTEL, is a clean family run house conveniently located ten minutes from the Marble Arch, central London. It is an ideal choice for joyful visitors on a budget. Home cooked breakfast each morning. Free parking (limited). 3 minutes from Edgware Road Underground.

B&B from £25pp, Rooms 2 single, 4 twin, 4 double, 3 family, some en-suite, Children welcome, No pets, Open all year.

Alvaro Silvares, **Cecil Court Hotel,** 16 Sussex Gardens, London W2 1UL
Tel: 0171 262 3881 Fax: 0171 262 3881

RUDDIMANS HOTEL, comfortable hotel close to the West End and London's attractions, offering generous English breakfast and good service at reasonable prices. Car park.

B&B from £26, Rooms 8 single, 13 double, 6 twin, 11 triple, 3 family, Children Welcome, No pets, Open all year.
Ruddimans Hotel, 160-162 Sussex Gardens, London W2 1UD
Tel: 0171 723 1026 & 723 6715 Fax: 0171 262 2983

....

HOTEL LA PLACE, small, friendly and safe (especially for single women) townhouse hotel with a bar (open 24 hrs) and restaurant. ETB 3 Crowns Commended.

B&B from £79, Lunch & evening meal available, Rooms 7 single, 6 double, 3 twin, 2 triple, 3 family, suites available, Children welcome, No pets, Open all year.

Hotel La Place, 17 Nottingham Place, London W1M 3FF
Tel: 0171 486 2323 Fax: 0171 486 4335

....

ACADEMY HOTEL, "one of London's top 10 most stylish hotels"- LA Times '96. Georgian hotel if immense charm and character. Restaurant/bar/library and patio garden.

B&B from £103, Lunch & evening meal available, Rooms 8 single, 24 double, 4 twin, suites available, all en-suite, Children welcome, No pets, Open all year.
Academy Hotel, 17-25 Gower Street, London WC1E 6HG
Tel: 0171 631 4115 Fax: 0171 636 3442

....

WESTPOINT HOTEL, inexpensive accommodation in central London. Close to Paddington and Lancaster gate underground stations. Easy access to tourist attractions, shopping and Hyde park.

B&B from £28, Rooms 12 single, 15 double, 16 twin, 14 triple, 6 family, some en-suite, Children welcome, No pets, Open all year.
Westpoint Hotel, 170-172 Sussex Gardens, London W2 1TP
Tel: 0171 402 0281 Fax: 0171 224 9114

....

SWISS HOUSE HOTEL, High quality budget priced hotel, conveniently situated near London museums, shopping/exhibition centres. Gloucester Road underground station is with easy walking distance.

B&B from £42, Rooms 5 single, 5 double, 2 twin, 4 triple, most en-suite, Children welcome, No smoking, Open all year.
Swiss House Hotel, 171 Old Brompton Road, London SW5 0AN
Tel: 0171 373 2769 & 373 9383 Fax: 0171 373 4983 Email: recep@swiss-hh.demon.co.uk

....

ABBEY COURT HOTEL, a central London hotel, reasonable prices. Within walking distance of Lancaster Gate, Paddington station and Hyde park. Easy access to tourist attractions and shopping. Car parking at modest charge.

B&B from £29, Rooms 14 single, 24 double, 7 triple, 10 triple, 2 family, all en-suite, Children welcome, No pets, Open all year.
Abbey Court Hotel, 174 Sussex Gardens, London W2 1TP
Tel: 0171 402 0704 Fax: 0171 262 2055

....

LONDON KENSINGTON HILTON, a modern hotel with easy access to shops, exhibition centres and Heathrow Airport by Airbus A2 service.
B&B from £140, Lunch & evening meal available, Rooms 193 single, 136 double, 247 twin, Suite available, all en-suite, Children welcome, No smoking, Open all year.
London Kensington Hilton, 179-199 Holland Park Avenue, London W11 4UL
Tel: 0171 603 3355 Fax: 0171 602 9397

HOTEL ATLAS-APOLLO, a friendly, log established hotel, situated close to Earls Court and Olympia. Shopping areas of Knightsbridge and Kensington High Street nearby.

B&B from £60, Rooms 26 single, 7 double, 44 twin, 14 triple, all en-suite, Children welcome, No pets, Open all year.

Hotel Atlas-Apollo, 18-30 Lexham Gardens, London W8 5JE
Tel: 0171 835 1155 Fax: 0171 370 4853

....

REGENCY HOTEL

REGENCY HOTEL, this recently refurbished hotel offers en-suite, well-appointed bedrooms equipped to a high standard with hair-dryer, coffee-making, satellite TV/radio, trouser press, ironing board and fridge. Located in the heart of Londons west-end within walking distance of Oxford Street, Madame Tussaud's, Theatreland and Regents Park. AA Selected hotel.

B&B from £39.50pp, Rooms 6 single, 3 twin, 9 double, 2 family, all en-suite, Restricted smoking, Children welcome, Pets by arrangement, Open all year.
Mrs Naela Bhanji, **Regency Hotel,** 19 Nottingham Lane, London W1M 3FF
Tel: 0171 486 5347 Fax: 0171 224 6057

....

MERLYN COURT HOTEL, a well established, family-run, good value hotel in quiet An edwardian square, close to Earls Court and Olympia. Direct underground link to Heathrow, the West End and rail stations. car park nearby.

B&B from £28, Rooms 4 single, 4 double, 4 twin, 2 triple, 3 family rooms, some en-suite, Children welcome, No smoking, Open all year.

Merlyn Court Hotel, 2 Barkston Gardens, London SW5 0EN
Tel: 0171 370 1640 Fax: 0171 370 4986

....

ST ATHAN'S HOTEL, Simple, small but clean family run hotel offering bed and breakfast.

B&B from £30, Rooms 16 single, 15 double, 15 twin, 4 triple, 5 family, some en-suite, Children welcome, Open all year.

St Athan's Hotel, 20 Tavistock Place, Russell Square, London WC1H 9RE
Tel: 0171 837 9140 & 837 9627 Fax: 0171 822 8352

....

ROYAL ADELPHI HOTEL, a centrally located hotel ideal for theatreland, near embankment and Charing Cross underground. All rooms with colour TV, hair dryer, tea/coffee making facilities. Most rooms have private bathrooms.

B&B from £45, Lunch & evening meal available, Rooms 20 single, 12 double, 13 twin, 2 triple, Children welcome, Open all year.

Royal Adelphi Hotel, 21 Villiers Street, London WC2N 6ND
Tel: 0171 930 8764 Fax: 0171 930 8735

....

CHARLOTTE GUEST HOUSE, with central heating, TV and tea/coffee facilities. Licensed restaurant. Free London travel card for 7 nights stay or longer. 12 minutes to Piccadilly. Good access to airports. Local shopping area. Close to Hampstead Heath.

B&B from £17.50pp, Dinner from £10, Rooms 12 single, 12 twin, 12 double, 2 family, some en-suite, Smoking, children & pets welcome, Open all year.

Mr L Koch, **Charlotte Guest House,** 221 West End Lane, London NW6 1XJ
Tel: 0171 7946476 Fax: 0171 4313584

RUSKIN HOTEL, a family run hotel opposite British Museum. Easy access to Oxford Street and West End, close to public transport. Hair dryers, tea/coffee facilities in room. Lift to all main floors. TV lounge.

B&B from £30pp, Rooms 11 single, 3 twin, 12 double, 6 double/single, some en-suite, Children welcome, No pets, Open all year.
Mr A Sedeno, **Ruskin Hotel,** 23-24 Montaque Street, Russell Square, London WC1B 5BH
Tel: 0171 636 7388 Fax: 0171 323 1662

....

LORD JIM HOTEL, a budget priced, well serviced bed and breakfast, ideally situated for Earls Court and Olympia. Convenient for museums, city and Heathrow and Gatwick airports.

B&B from £20, Rooms 8 single, 6 double, 5 twin, 9 triple, 7 family, Children welcome, No pets, Open all year.
Lord Jim Hotel, 23-25 Penywern Road, London SW5 9TT
Tel: 0171 370 6071 & 0956 238277 Fax: 0171 373 8919

....

CAVENDISH GUEST HOUSE, in a quiet residential street, 5 minutes walk from Kilburn underground station, 15 minutes travelling time to the West End. Easy access to Wembley Stadium, Heathrow, Gatwick. 10 mins from M1.

B&B from £26, Rooms 4 single, 1 double, 1 twin, 2 triple, Children welcome, No pets, Open all year.
Cavendish Guest House, 24 Cavendish Road, London NW6 7XP
Tel: 0181 451 3249

....

WELLMEADOW LODGE HOTEL, charming establishment combining the highest hotel standards with the atmosphere of a private home. EN-suite facilities, delicious breakfasts second to none with home made items.

B&B from £65, Evening meal available, Rooms 3 single, 4 double, 3 twin, all en-suite, Children welcome, NO pets, No smoking, Open all year.
Wellmeadow Lodge Hotel, 24 Wellmeadow Road, London W7 2AL
Tel: 0181 567 7294 Fax: 0181 566 3468

....

CASWELL HOTEL, a pleasant family-run hotel, near Victoria coach and rail stations, yet in a quiet location.

B&B from £30, Rooms 1 single, 6 double, 6 twin, 3 triple, 2 family rooms, Children from 5 years, No pets, Open all year.
Caswell Hotel, 25 Gloucester Street, London SW1V 2DB
Tel: 0171 834 6345

....

INTER ATTICA HOTEL

INTER ATTICA HOTEL, offers clean budget accommodation with most rooms with en-suite facilities. Located in the heart of London's west-end. The hotel is within walking distance of Oxford Street, Marble-Arch and Theatreland. Central heating, all rooms with TV and direct dial telephone. Excellent value in central London.

B&B from £25pp, Rooms 10 single, 6 twin, 8 double, 2 family, most en-suite, Restricted smoking, Children welcome, Pets by arrangement, Open all year.
Mr S Bhanji, **Inter Attica Hotel,** 25 Nottingham Lane, London W1M 3PF
Tel: 0171 935 8344 Fax: 0171 487 4330

....

YORK HOUSE HOTEL, a conveniently located hotel hotel close to Earls Court, Olympia and the West End. Underground direct to Heathrow Airport.

B&B from £29, Rooms 16 single, 3 double, 3 twin, 2 triple, 2 family, Children welcome, No pets, Open all year.

York House Hotel, 27-28 Philbeach Gardens, London SW5 9EA
Tel: 0171 373 7519 & 373 7579 Fax: 0171 370 4641

GARDEN COURT HOTEL, a friendly, family run town house hotel established in 1954, in a quiet Victorian garden square in central London. Convenient for all transport. All rooms have TV, telephone and hair dryers.
B&B from £34, Rooms 13 single, 7 double, 6 twin, 6 triple, 2 family, some en-suite, Children welcome, No smoking, Open all year.
Garden Court Hotel, 30-31 Kensington Gardens Square, London W2 4BG
Tel: 0171 229 2553 Fax: 0171 727 2749

JUBILEE B&B HOTEL, in a quiet position this private hotel is conveniently situated within walking distance Victoria coach, rail and underground station, Buckingham Palace, Westminster Abbey, Houses of Parliament, Trafalgar Square. Every room has TV, telephone, tea/coffee facilities. Car parking near by at special rates to Jubilee Hotel.

B&B from £30, Rooms 5 single, 2 twin, 7 double, 7 triple, 3 family, some en-suite, Children welcome, No pets, Open all year.
Jubilee B&B Hotel, 31 Eccleston Square, London SW1V 1NZ
Tel: 0171 834 8045 & 834 0873 Fax: 0171 976 6332

LINCOLN HOUSE HOTEL, a Georgian hotel of distinctive character and ambience. Close to Oxford Street, fashionable shops, theatre land and major attractions. En-suite rooms with modern comforts including satellite TV, direct dial telephone, hair dryer, trouser press and beverages. Commended by consumer associations, European motoring organisations and world famous guide books. Email: reservations@lincoln-house-hotel.co.uk
B&B from £39pp, Rooms 5 single, 4 twin, 9 double, 4 family, most en-suite, Children welcome, No pets, Open all year.
Joesph Shariff, **Lincoln House Hotel,** 33 Gloucester Place, London W1H 3PD
Tel: 0171 486 7630 Fax: 0171 486 0166

BLAIR HOUSE HOTEL, a homely hotel in a quiet, elegant street, close to Harrods and museums.

B&B from £70, Rooms 1 single, 4 double, 6 twin, all en-suite, Children welcome, No pets, Open all year.
Blair House Hotel, 34 Draycott Place, London SW3 2SA
Tel: 0171 581 2323 & 225 0771 Fax: 0171 823 7752

DUKE OF LEINSTER , centrally located near Hyde Park, 10 minutes walk from Queensway underground. Former residence of the Duke of Leinster.

B&B from £49, Rooms 4 single, 21 double, 9 twin, 8 triple, all en-suite, Children welcome, Open all year.
Duke of Leinster , 34 Queen's Gardens, London W2 3AA
Tel: 0171 258 0079 Fax: 0171 262 0741

ALBANY HOTEL, a small friendly hotel in the centre of London.

B&B from £34, Lunch & evening meal available, Rooms 3 single, 3 double, 4 twin, 1 triple, Children welcome, Open all year.
Albany Hotel, 34 Tavistock Place, London WC1H 9RE
Tel: 0171 837 9139 & 833 0459 Fax: 0171 833 0459

MELITA HOUSE HOTEL, a family-run, budget B&B (full English breakfast), close to Victoria station. Warm, friendly and with extensive facilities.

B&B from £30, Rooms 6 single, 5 double, 5 twin, 1 triple, 2 family, some en-suite, Children welcome, No pets, No smoking, Open all year.
Melita House Hotel, 35 Charlwood Street, London SW1V 2DU
Tel: 0171 828 0471 & 834 1387 Fax: 0171 932 0988 Email: reserve@melita.co.uk

GRESHAM HOTEL

GRESHAM HOTEL, a privately-owned hotel in central London, close to theatreland, Covent Garden and the British Museum, the Gresham prides itself on the number of guests who return year after year. Economic and convenient, friendly and clean. Colour TV and telephone in all of them.

Single from £35 per room, Twin/double from £55 per room, family from £75 per room, Open all year.

Mr Parsons, **Gresham Hotel,** 36 Bloomsbury Street, London WC1B 3QJ
Tel: 0171 580 4232 Fax: 0171 436 6341

....

LONDON GUARDS HOTEL, an air conditioned and completely refurbished hotel, opened in May 1997, in a quiet residential area of Lancaster Gate. Bar and coffee shop facilities.

B&B from £95, Lunch & evening meal available, Rooms 2 single, 13 double, 11 twin, 9 triple, 4 family, all en-suite, Children welcome, No smoking, Open all year.
London Guards Hotel, 36-37 Lancaster Gate, London W2 3NA
Tel: 0171 402 1101 Fax: 0171 262 2551

....

PARKWOOD HOTEL, smart town house only 1 minute's walk from Oxford Street and Speakers' Corner, Hyde Park.

B&B from £45, Rooms 5 single, 2 double, 7 twin, 4 triple, some en-suite, Children welcome, No smoking, Open all year.
Parkwood Hotel, 4 Stanhope Place, London W2 2HB
Tel: 0171 402 2241 Fax: 0171 402 1574

....

SPRING PARK HOTEL, overlooking Finsbury Park, next to Manor House underground station for Piccadilly line direct to West End and Heathrow Airport.

B&B from £29, Lunch & evening meal available, Rooms 10 single, 19 double, 20 twin, 1 triple, some en-suite, Children welcome, No smoking, Open all year.
Spring Park Hotel, 400 Seven Sisters Road, London N4 2LX
Tel: 0181 800 6030 Fax: 0181 802 5652

....

KENT HALL HOTEL, close to Manor House underground, 10 minutes from central London. Ideal for groups and school parties.

B&B from £25, Rooms 3 single, 11 twin, 11 triple, all en-suite/private facilities, Children welcome, No pets, Open all year.
Kent Hall Hotel, 414 Seven Sisters Road, London N4 2LX
Tel: 0181 802 0800 & 802 5100 Fax: 0181 802 9070

....

PRINCE WILLIAM HOTEL, central location in Paddington, close to Hyde Park and Oxford Street. Clean, comfortable accommodation, residents' lounge, restaurant and bar. Secretarial and fax services.

B&B from £39, Dinner available, Rooms 23 single, 7 double, 11 twin, 2 triple, most en-suite, Children welcome, Open all year.
Prince William Hotel, 42-44 Gloucester Terrace, London W2 3DA
Tel: 0171 724 7414 Fax: 0171 706 2411

....

DOVER HOTEL, a small friendly bed and breakfast hotel with easy access to all major attractions and 3 minutes from Victoria rail and coach stations.

B&B from £40, Rooms 4 single, 9 double, 7 twin, 9 triple, 4 family, Children welcome, No pets, Open all year.
Dover Hotel, 44 Belgrave Road, London SW1V 1RG
Tel: 0171 821 9085 Fax: 0171 834 6425

LUNA-SIMONE HOTEL, a friendly, good value, bed and breakfast hotel. Within easy walking distance of Victoria rail, underground and coach stations. Opposite bus stop.
B&B from £25, Rooms 3 single, 11 double, 11 twin, 10 triple, children welcome, No pets, No smoking, Open all year.
Luna-Simone Hotel, 47 Belgrave Road, London SW1V 2BB
Tel: 0171 834 5897 Fax: 0171 828 2472

....

CRESCENT HOTEL, recently refurbished, comfortable, family-run hotel in a quiet Georgian crescent, with private gardens and tennis courts. All rooms have a colour TV and tea/coffee making facilities.

B&B from £38, Rooms 9 single, 2 double, 2 twin, 9 triple, 2 family, some en-suite, Children welcome, No pets, Open all year.
Crescent Hotel, 49-50 Cartwright Gardens, London WC1H 9EL
Tel: 0171 387 1515 Fax: 0171 383 2054

....

The **ROYAL PARK HOTEL** is well placed for central London and Hyde Park. All rooms have TV, radio and tea/coffee facilities. There is a bar, Thai restaurant and car park. All rates include full English breakfast. We are close to Kensington Palace and Portobello Road Antiques.

B&B from £60pp, Dinner from £10.20, Rooms 6 single, 30 twin, 13 double, 11 family, all en-suite, Smoking, children & pets are welcome, Open all year.

David Cartwright, **Royal Park Hotel,** 5 Westbourne Terrace, London W2 3UL
Tel: 0171 4026187 Fax: 0171 2249426

....

GOWER HOUSE HOTEL, a friendly bed and breakfast hotel, close to Goodge Street underground station and within easy walking distance of the British Museum, shops, theatres and restaurants.
B&B from £35, Rooms 4 single, 2 double, 6 twin, 3 triple, 1 family, Children welcome, NO pets, No smoking, Open all year.
Gower House Hotel, 57 Gower Street, London WC1E 6HJ
Tel: 0171 636 4685 Fax: 0171 636 4685

....

BEAVER HOTEL, situated in a quiet, tree lined crescent of late Victorian terraced houses, close to Earls Court Exhibition Centre and 10 minutes from the West End.
B&B from £30, Rooms 17 single, 6 double, 10 twin, 4 triple, some en-suite, Children welcome, No smoking, Open all year.
Beaver Hotel, 57-59 Philbeach Gardens, London SW5 9ED
Tel: 0171 373 4553 Fax: 0171 373 4555

....

GEORGE HOTEL, a central London hotel in a quiet square. Comfortable, bright rooms with satellite TV, direct dial telephone, tea/coffee. Gardens and tennis court available for guests use.
B&B from £39.50, Rooms 15 single, 4 double, 4 twin, 10 triple, 7 family, some en-suite, Children welcome, No pets, No smoking, Open all year.
George Hotel, 58-60 Cartwright Gardens, London WC1H 9EL
Tel: 0171 387 8777 Fax: 0171 387 8666

....

BUCKLAND HOTEL, all rooms have tea/coffee making facilities, TV with some satellite stations, direct dial telephones. Only four minutes from local shops, restaurants, pubs and underground. Local bus passes door. Near Hampstead Heath. Near library, swimming pool. Ten minutes by tube to centre of town.

B&B from £28pp, Rooms 3 single, 2 twin, 9 double/triple, 2 family, most en-suite, Restricted smoking, Children welcome, No pets Open all year.
Miss Charters, **Buckland Hotel,** 6 Buckland Crescent, London NW3 5DX
Tel: 0171 722 5574 Fax: 0171 722 5594

PALACE COURT HOTEL, all rooms TV, continental breakfast included in price. En-suite rooms have extra tea/coffee making facilities. Telephones in all rooms. Friendly receptionist. All our rooms are newly refurbished and every thing is new. Special weekday discounts.

B&B from £60per night, Rooms 4 single, 8 twin, 18 double, 8 family, most en-suite, Children welcome, No pets, Open all year.

Mr Jaffer, **Palace Court Hotel,** 64-65 Princes Square London W2 4PX
Tel: 0171 7274412 Fax: 0171 7276626

....

KANDARA GUEST HOUSE, a small family-run guest house near the Angel, Islington. Free street parking and good public transport to West End and city.

B&B from £33, Rooms 4 single, 2 double, 2 twin, 2 triple, Children welcome, No pets, Open all year.
Kandara Guest House, 68 Ockendon Road, London N1 3NW
Tel: 0171 226 5721 Fax/Ans: 0171 226 3379

....

GARTH HOTEL, centrally situated family run bed and breakfast accommodation, convenient for shops, theatres and travel. TV in rooms. Tea/coffee making facilities.

B&B from £32, Rooms 3 single, 4 double, 5 twin, 3 triple, 2 family, some en-suite, Children welcome, Open all year.
Garth Hotel, 69 Gower Street, London WC1E 6HJ
Tel: 0171 636 5761 Fax: 0171 637 4854

....

AMSTERDAM HOTEL, a comfortable, attractively furnished hotel, rooms all with private bathroom, colour TV and direct dial telephone.
B&B from £65, Rooms 6 single, 6 double, 4 twin, 2 triple, 2 family rooms, all en-suite, Children welcome, No pets, No smoking, Open all year.
Amsterdam Hotel, 7 Trebovir Road, London SW5 9LS
Tel: 0171 370 5048 Fax: 0171 244 7608

....

DAWSON HOUSE HOTEL, a truly charming Victorian house, lovingly restored and tastefully decorated, set within its own gardens. The hotel typifies the great Victorian town houses of the past, yet offers every modern amenity, ensuring that guests enjoy a relaxing and memorable stay.

B&B from £35, Rooms 6 single, 5 double, 1 twin, 2 triple, 1 family, all en-suite, Children from 5 years, No pets, No smoking, Open all year.
Dawson House Hotel, 72 Canfield Gardens, London NW6 3ED
Tel: 0171 624 0079 & 624 6525 Fax: 0171 372 3469

....

CHISWICK HOTEL, a large tastefully converted Victorian hotel. Self contained apartment available. Relaxed atmosphere. Close to Heathrow Airport and central London.

B&B from £70, Dinner available, Rooms 28 single, 11 double, 7 twin, 4 triple, 3 family, all en-suite, Children welcome, Open all year.
Chiswick Hotel, 73 High Road, London W4 2LS
Tel: 0181 994 1712 Fax: 0181 742 2585

....

ARRAN HOUSE HOTEL, a small comfortable, family-run bed and breakfast hotel in central London, convenient for theatres, shopping and public transport.

B&B from £35, Rooms 6 single, 6 double, 4 twin, 10 triple, 2 family, some en-suite, Children welcome, No smoking,Open all year.
Arran House Hotel, 77 Gower Street, London WC1E 6HJ
Tel: 0171 636 2186 & 637 1140 Fax: 0171 436 5328

BLAIR VICTORIA, close to Victoria Station, behind a period facade, the hotel offers comfort, service and interior-decorated accommodation.

B&B from £54, Rooms 9 single, 10 double, 9 twin, 4 triple, 1 family room, all en-suite, Children welcome, No pets, No smoking, Open all year.

Blair Victoria, 78-82 Warwick Way, London SW1V 1RZ
Tel: 0171 828 8603 & 0468 660098 Fax: 0171 976 6536

....

MELBOURNE HOUSE, a family run bed and breakfast. All rooms en-suite with tea/coffee facilities, colour TV, hair dryers. Good value. Book early.

B&B from £40, Rooms 2 single, 5 double, 5 twin, 1 triple, 1 family, suites available, all en-suite, Children welcome, No pets, No smoking, Open all year.

Melbourne House, 79 Belgrave Road, London SW1V 2 BG
Tel: 0171 828 3516 Fax: 0171 828 7120

....

THANET HOTEL, a comfortable, family-run hotel, with colour TV, tea/coffee making facilities and direct dial telephone. All en-suite rooms, Next to the British Museum, close to London's famous Theatreland, Full English breakfast.

B&B from £54, Rooms 4 single, 5 double, 4 twin, 3 family, Children welcome, No pets, Open all year.

Thanet Hotel, 8 Bedford Place, London WC1B 5JA
Tel: 0171 580 3377 & 636 2869 Fax: 0171 323 6676

....

BLANDFORD HOTEL, is a small quality hotel situated in the heart of London in Baker Street. The hotel has recently been refurbished and offers comfortable bedrooms with en-suite facilities. A warm, friendly atmosphere awaits the business traveller and visitors to London.

B&B from £60pp, Rooms 5 single, 9 twin, 9 double, 10 family, all en-suite, Children welcome, No pets, Open all year.
Mr H Bhayani, **Blandford Hotel,** 80 Chiltern Street, Baker Street, London W1M 1PS
Tel: 0171 486 3103 Fax: 0171 487 2786

....

KENSINGTON GARDENS HOTEL, beautifully refurbished Victorian building, centrally situated close to Bayswater and Queensway underground stations. Easy access to airports and British Rail stations.

B&B from £45, Lunch & evening meal available, Rooms 8 single, 5 double, 2 twin, 2 triple, some en-suite, Children welcome, No pets, No smoking, Open all year.

Kensington Gardens Hotel, 9 Kensington Gardens Square, London W2 4BH
Tel: 0171 221 7790 Fax: 0171 792 8612

....

THE BONNINGTON IN BLOOMSBURY, situated between the City and the West End. Close to mainline stations and on the underground to Heathrow Airport. Wheelchair access.

B&B from £68, Lunch & evening meal available, Rooms 109 single, 44 double, 45 twin, 17 triple, all en-suite, Children welcome No smoking, Open all year.

The Bonnington in Bloomsbury, 92 Southampton Row, London WC1B 4BH
Tel: 0171 242 2828 Fax: 0171 831 9170

BROWN'S HOTELS, situated in Mayfair, close to Bond Street, Royal Academy, Sotherby's, Brown's offers the perfect location to enjoy the best of British hospitality.

B&B from £249, Lunch & evening meal available, Rooms 21 single, 51 double, 30 twin, 12 triple, 3 family, suites available, all en-suite.

Brown's Hotels, Albemarle Street and Dover Street, London W1X 4BP
Tel: 0171 493 6020 Fax: 0171 493 9381 Email: brownshotel@UKbusiness.com

....

SWALLOW INTERNATIONAL HOTEL, a bright modern hotel offering an exclusive leisure club. Near Earl's Court and Olympia Exhibition Halls, fashionable Knightsbridge and Kensington's parks and museum. Short break packages available.

B&B from £138, Lunch & evening meal available, Rooms 28 single, 131 double, 226 twin, 36 triple, suites available, all en-suite, Children welcome, No smoking, Open all year.

Swallow International Hotel, Cromwell Road, London SW5 0TH
Tel: 0171 973 1000 Fax: 0171 244 8194

....

DOLPHIN SQUARE HOTEL, an all-suite hotel/apartment complex, with private gardens, in central London. Exclusive leisure facilities include own sports and health club with swimming pool, gym and squash.

B&B from £100, Lunch & evening meal available, Rooms 19 single, 95 double, 35 twin, 2 triple, all en-suite, Children welcome, No smoking, Open all year.

Dolphin Square Hotel, Dolphin Square, London SW1V 3LX
Tel: 0171 834 3800 Fax: 0171 798 8735 Email: dolphin-square-hotel@Compuserve.com

....

ACTON PARK HOTEL, a small, friendly, family-run hotel, just off the North Circular Road. Between Heathrow and the West End, overlooking parkland. Ample parking.

B&B from £47, Lunch & evening meal available, Rooms 7 single, 4 double, 8 twin, 2 triple, all en-suite, Children welcome, Open all year.

Acton Park Hotel, 116 The Vale, Acton, London W3 7JT
Tel: 0181 743 9417 Fax: 0181 743 9417

....

PEACE HAVEN, lovely Edwardian house in half acre of gardens. Close to London with easy access to Heathrow Airport. Traditional English cooking offered. Individual needs catered for. Off road parking, TV lounge, library, games room, tea/coffee and vending drinks machine. Suitable for group bookings.
B&B from £14pp, Dinner from £6, Rooms 1 single, 14 twin, 1 double, 5 family, 6 en-suite, Restricted smoking, Children welcome, Pets by arrangement, Open all year.
Pam Matthews & Kate Gilbert, **Peace Haven,** 3 Creswick Road, Acton, London W3 9HE
Tel: 0181 7520055 Fax: 0181 7520066

....

ACTON GRANGE GUEST HOUSE, a family-run, small friendly establishment. Ten minutes from Heathrow Airport; excellent transport facilities (central London 25 minutes).

B&B from £22, Rooms 1 single, 3 double, 1 twin, 1 triple, Children from 4 years, No pets, No smoking, Open all year.

Acton Grange Guest House, 317 Uxbridge Road, Acton, London W3 9QU
Tel: 0181 992 0586

THE BYRON HOTEL, a superb Victorian conversion to bring modern standards of comfort in traditional surroundings. All rooms fully en-suite with trouser press, hair dryers and tea making facilities. The hotel is also fully air conditioned. Excellent location to all shopping and tourist attractions.

B&B from £40pp, Rooms 4 single, 16 twin, 19 double, 4 family, all en-suite, Children welcome, No pets, Open all year.
The Byron Hotel, 36-38 Queensborough Terrace, Bayswater, London W2 3SH
Tel: 0171 243 0987 Fax: 0171 792 1957

HESPER LEWIS HOTEL, a friendly very central guest house. Former home of Noel Coward continues the article tradition with regular theatre specials. Five minutes walk to Victoria tube and rail. Facilities include TV, English breakfast, mini-bars, fax, laundry-service, theatre-bookings. We except all major credit cards. Open all year.
B&B from £60pp, Dinner from £7, Rooms 3 twin, 3 double, 2 family, all en-suite, Restricted smoking, Children welcome, Pets by arrangement, Open all year.
Mark, Anthony, Steven Dos Santos, **Hesper Lewis Hotel**, 111 Ebury Street, Belgravia, London SW1W 9 QU
Tel: 0171 7302094 Fax: 0171 7308697

BARDON LODGE HOTEL, within walking distance of Greenwich Park, the Observatory and Blackheath village. One minute's drive from the A2 and three quarters of a mile from the Millennium site.
B&B from £60, Dinner available, Rooms 13 triple, 11 double, 3 twin, 1 triple, 3 family, most en-suite, Children welcome, Open all year.
Bardon Lodge Hotel, 15-17 Stratheden Road, Blackheath, London SE3 7TH
Tel: 0181 853 4051 Fax: 0181 858 7357

CLARENDON HOTEL, facing the heath and 22 minutes by train to central London. 10 minutes' walk from Greenwich, 5 minutes' walk from Greenwich Royal Park.

B&B from £56.50, Lunch & evening meal available, Rooms 44 single, 54 double, 69, 24 triple, 2 family rooms, suites available, most en-suite, Children welcome, No smoking, Open all year.
Clarendon Hotel, 8-16 Montpelier Row, Blackheath, London SE3 0RW
Tel: 0181 318 4321 Fax: 0181 318 4378

HOLIDAY INN GARDEN COURT, located just of the north circular road at the foot of the M1. Hotel ideal for those travelling to London by car. Free parking. Linked by tube (northern line). All rooms en-suite, satellite TV and tea/coffee facilities. Bar and restaurant in hotel. Close to RAF Museum, Campden Market, Wembley and Hamsptead. Central London 7 miles. Opposite Brent Cross shopping centre. Disabled rooms available.
B&B from £49.50pp, Dinner from £15, Rooms 89 double, 64 family, all en-suite, Children welcome, Pets by arrangement, Open all year.
Holiday Inn Garden Court, Tilling Road, Brent Cross, London NW2 1LP
Tel: 0181 201 8686 Fax: 0181 967 6372

KINGS ARMS HOTEL

Traditional public house, the **KINGS ARMS HOTEL** has 7 exceptional en-suite rooms, all with TV, tea/coffee making facilities etc. Ideal for central London and Heathrow, 1 minute walk Brentford British Rail and 10 minute walk Boston Manor Tube. "Claiming highest hotel standards" with family run business.
B&B from £45pp, Dinner from £5, Rooms 3 single, 2 twin, 2 double, all en-suite, Smoking & Children welcome, No pets, Open all year.
Joanne Antick, **Kings Arms Hotel**, 19 Boston Manor, Brentford, London TW8 8EA
Tel: 0181 560 5860 Fax: 0181 876 5512

WINDMILL ON THE COMMON, has well appointed bedrooms overlooking Clapham Common. A la carte/table d'hote restaurant and traditional busy Young pub serving good bar food. Easy access into central London.

B&B from £70, Lunch & evening meal available, Rooms 20 double, 9 twin, all en-suite, Children welcome, No smoking, Open all year.

Windmill on the Common, Southside, Clapham Common, London SW4 9DE
Tel: 0181 673 4578 Fax: 0181 675 1486

SEVEN DIALS HOTEL, is situated in the heart of Covent Garden where Leicester Square, Piccadilly Circus and Oxford Street are three minutes walking distance. Rooms have en-suite shower/bath and all rooms are equipped with: remote control colour TV, tea/coffee facilities, direct dial telephone.

B&B from £32.50pp, Rooms 6 single, 3 twin, 6 double, 3 family/twin/double, all en-suite, Children welcome, No pets, Open all year.

Mr Dipopolo, **Seven Dials Hotel,** 7 Monmouth Street, Convent Garden, London WC2H 9DA
Tel: 0171 2400823 & 6810791 Fax: 0171 6810792

THE EALING PARK HOTEL

THE EALING PARK HOTEL, is a friendly, comfortable, affordable B&B in Ealing Common. Ideal for weekend breaks, shopping, theatre, business trips. Colour TV's tea/coffee tray in all rooms. Full English breakfast. Weekend/Weekly rates. Credit cards welcome. Ealing Common/Broadway Tubes - ten minutes' walk. Easy access to M4, M40, A406.

B&B from £29pp, Rooms, 12 single, 4 twin, 8 double, 5 family, most en-suite, Restricted smoking, Children over 8, Open all year except Christmas & New Year.

Nayna Kumari, **The Ealing Park Hotel,** 40-41 Grange Park, Ealing Common, London W5 3PR
Tel: 0181 567 1373 Fax: 0181 840 0165

CREFFIELD LODGE, a Victorian property on 3 floors, located in residential road, adjacent to and with use of all the facilities of the 150 bedroom Jarvis Carnarvon Hotel.

B&B from £32, Lunch & evening meal available, Rooms 12 single, 7 double, 4 twin, 1 triple, some en-suite, Children welcome, No pets, Open all year.

Creffield Lodge, 2-4 Creffield Road, Ealing, London W5 3HN
Tel: 0181 993 2284 Fax: 0181 992 7082

GRANGE LODGE HOTEL, a quiet, comfortable hotel within a few hundred yards of the underground station. Midway between central London and Heathrow.

B&B from £35, Rooms 8 single, 2 double, 2 twin, 2 triple, some en-suite, Children welcome, Open all year.

Grange Lodge Hotel, 48-50 Grange Road, Ealing, London W5 5BX
Tel: 0181 567 1049 Fax: 0181 579 5350

ABBEY LODGE HOTEL, all rooms are en-suite and with remote control colour TV. Complimentary hot drinks 24 hours a day. very close to 3 underground lines.

B&B from £35, Rooms 10 single, 2 double, 1 twin, 2 triple, 1 family, all en-suite, Children welcome, Open all year.

Abbey Lodge Hotel, 51 Grange park, Ealing, London W5 3PR
Tel: 0181 567 7914 Fax: 0181 579 5350

RASOOL COURT HOTEL, is situated close to Earl's Court exhibition and underground station. Within easy reach of West End, Marble Arch, Piccadilly and Knightsbridge. All rooms with colour TV's with Sky Channels and Direct Dial phones. Lift and residential lounge open 24 hours. Email: younis@rasool.demon.co.uk

B&B from £22pp, Rooms 27 single, 7 twin, 16 double, 7 family, some en-suite, Children welcome, No Pets, Open all year.
Mr Younis, **Rasool Court Hotel,** 19-21 Penywern Road, Earl's Court, London SW5 9TT
Tel: 0171 373 8900 Fax: 0171 244 6835

RAMSEES HOTEL, family run hotel located in fashionable Kensington, close to the heart of city within one minute walk from Earl's Court station. All rooms with colour TV's, sky channel and Direct Dial phones. Tourist attractions of Buckingham Palace, Tower of London and Oxford Street are very close. Email: younis@rasool.demon.co.uk

B&B from £22pp, Rooms 13 single, 19 twin, 18 double, 8 family, some en-suite, Children welcome, No pets, Open all year.
Ramsees Hotel, 32-36 Hogarth Road, Earl's Court, London SW5 0PU
Tel: 0171 370 1445 Fax: 0171 244 6835

MOWBRAY COURT HOTEL, a tourist class hotel near Earls Court Exhibition Centre.
B&B from £40, Rooms 30 single, 15 double, 20 twin, 8 family, most en-suite, Children welcome, No smoking, Open all year.
Mowbray Court Hotel, 28-32 Penywern Road, Earls Court, London SW5 9SU
Tel: 0171 370 2316 & 370 3690 Fax: 0171 370 5693

BEDKNOBS, a carefully restored Victorian family-run house, offering many home comforts excellent service and a warm welcome.
B&B from £25, Rooms 1 double, 2 twin, Children welcome, No pets, No smoking, Open all year.
Bedknobs, 58 Glengarry Road, East Dulwich, London SE22 8QD
Tel: 0181 299 2004 Fax: 0181 693 5611

WESTON HOUSE, a recently refurbished, friendly comfortable hotel in Greenwich conservation area close to the National Maritime Museum. 20 minutes from central London, convenient for A2, M20 and A205.
B&B from £30, Rooms 3 single, 2 double, 3 twin, 1 triple, 1 family room, Children welcome, No pets, Open all year.
Weston House, 8 Eltham Green, Eltham, London SE9 5LB
Tel: 0181 850 5191 Fax: 0181 850 0030

NEW PEMBURY HOTEL, a recently renovated, welcoming hotel. Modern rooms, all en-suite, with tea/coffee making facilities, direct dial telephone and Sky TV. Friendly bar/cafe. Easy access to West End and central London. Competitive prices.
B&B from £40, Lunch & evening meal available, Rooms 22 single, 15 double, 16 twin, 5 triple, 1 family, all en-suite, Children welcome, No pets, No smoking, Open all year.
New Pembury Hotel, 328 Seven Sisters Road, Finsbury Park, London N4 2AP
Tel: 0181 800 5310 Fax: 0181 809 6362

COSTELLO PALACE HOTEL, a fully refurbished, family run, attractive hotel. Conveniently situated for all amenities. All rooms are en-suite with Sky TV, telephone. Full English breakfast. Free car park.

B&B from £45, Rooms 3 single, 17 double, 20 twin, 4 triple, all en-suite, Children welcome, No pets, Open all year
Costello Palace Hotel, 374 Seven Sisters Road, Finsbury Park, London N4 2PG
Tel: 0181 802 6551 Fax: 0181 802 9461

GRANGEWOOD LODGE HOTEL, comfortable budget accommodation in a quiet road. Pleasant garden. Easy access to central London, Docklands and M11. 12 minutes to Liverpool Street station.

B&B from £18, Rooms 10 single, 1 double, 5 twin, 2 triple, Children welcome, No pets, Open all year.
Grangewood Lodge Hotel, 104 Clova Road, Forest Gate, London E7 9AF
Tel: 0181 534 0637 & 503 0941 Fax: 0181 217 0392

FOREST VIEW HOTEL, catering for business and tourist clientele, this hotel has en-suite rooms with tea/coffee making facilities, direct dial telephone and TV. Full English breakfast. Warm and friendly atmosphere, competitive rates.

B&B from £38, Dinner available, Rooms 8 single, 5 double, 2 twin, 2 triple, 3 family, Children over 2, No smoking, Open all year.
Forest View Hotel, 227 Romford Road, Forest Gate, London E7 9HL
Tel: 0181 534 4844 Fax: 0181 534 8959

DALMACIA HOTEL, a family-run bed and breakfast within easy reach of the West End. All rooms en-suite with satellite TV, hair dryer, tea/coffee making facilities and direct dial telephone.

B&B from £32, Dinner available, Rooms 3 single, 6 double, 4 twin, 3 triple, all en-suite, Children from 5 years, No smoking, No pets, Open all year.
Dalmacia Hotel, 71 Shepherds Bush Road, Hammersmith, London W6 7LS
Tel: 0171 603 2887 & 602 5701 Fax: 0171 602 9226

LA GAFFE, is in quaint Hampstead village. Twelve minutes by tube from the centre of London, close to Hampstead Heath and Hampstead Tube. La Gaffe offers eighteen en-suite rooms, all with television, telephone, hair dryers as well as tea/coffee facilities.

B&B from £40pp, Dinner from £5, Rooms 4 single, 4 twin, 9 double, 1 family, all en-suite, No smoking or pets, Children welcome, Open all year.
Giuseppe Graziani, Bernardo & Lorenzo Stella, **La Gaffe,** 107-111 Heath Street, Hampstead, London NW3 6SS
Tel: 0171 435 8965 Fax: 0171 794 7592 Email: lagaffe@msn.com

THE LANGORF, 3 minutes walk from Finchley Road underground, this elegant Edwardian residence in Hampstead boasts attractive bedrooms with full facilities.

B&B from £73, Lunch & evening meal available, Rooms 1 single, 18 double, 8 twin, 4 triple, all en-suite, Children welcome, No pets, Open all year.
The Langorf, 20 Frognal, Hampstead, London NW3 6AG
Tel: 0171 794 4483 Fax: 0171 435 9055

DILLONS HOTEL, a small private guest house, close to central London, with excellent transport facilities nearby.

B&B from £26, Rooms 3 single, 2 double, 5 twin, 1 triple, 2 family, some en-suite, Children welcome, No pets, Open all year.
Dillons Hotel, 21 Belsize Park, Hampstead, London NW3 4DU
Tel: 0171 794 3360 Fax: 0171 431 7900

WHITE LODGE HOTEL, a small, friendly family guest hotel offering personal service. Easy access to all transport, for sightseeing and business trips.

B&B from £26, Dinner available, Rooms 7 single, 3 double, 3 twin, 3 family, some en-suite, Children welcome, No pets, Open all year.
White Lodge Hotel, 1 Church Lane, Hornsey, London N8 7BU
Tel: 0181 340 7851 Fax: 0181 340 7851

HYDE PARK ROOMS HOTEL, small centrally located private hotel with personal service. Clean, comfortable and friendly. Within walking distance of Hyde Park and Kensington Gardens. Car Parking available.

B&B from £26, Rooms 5 single, 6 double, 2 twin, 1 triple, Children welcome, No pets, Open all year.

Hyde Park Rooms Hotel, 137 Sussex Gardens, Hyde Park, London W2 2RX
Tel: 0171 723 0225 & 723 0965

....

ST DAVID'S & NORFOLK COURT HOTEL, a small friendly hotel in front of a quiet garden square. central location, economical prices. Reckons to serve the "best English breakfast" in London.

B&B from £30, Rooms 14 single, 18 double, 14 twin, 12 triple, Children welcome, No pets, Open all year.
St David's & Norfolk Court Hotel, 16 Norfolk Square, Hyde Park, London W2 1RS
Tel: 0171 723 3856 & 723 4963 Fax: 0171 402 9061

....

VICARAGE PRIVATE HOTEL, this splendid Victorian house which retains many original features is situated in a quiet residential garden square in a particularly pleasant part of the Royal Borough of Kensington, yet only a stroll away from the exciting shopping in High Street Kensington, Knightsbridge and Portobello Market. Email: reception@londonvicaragehotel.com
B&B from £32pp, Rooms 7 single, 2 twin, 6 double, 3 family, Restricted smoking, Children welcome, No pets, Open all year.
Martin & Eileen Diviney, **Vicarage Private Hotel,** 10 Vicarage Gate, Kensington, London W8 4AG
Tel: 0171 229 4030 Fax: 0171 792 5989

....

HOGARTH HOTEL, a modern hotel near Earls court within walking distance of Olympia and Earl's Court Exhibition Centres. All en-suite designer bedrooms are well equipped and have benefited from recent refurbishment.

B&B from £93.50, Lunch & evening meal available, Rooms 7 single, 27 double, 50 twin, 1 triple, all en-suite, Children welcome, No smoking, Open all year.

Hogarth Hotel, 33 Hogarth Road, Kensington, London SW5 0QQ
Tel: 0171 370 6831 Fax: 0171 373 6179

....

COTTESPAR HOTEL, a very friendly, clean, family run B&B. Full English breakfast, tea/coffee facilities on request, no charge. Very central near to three main railway stations, St Pancras, Kings Cross, Thames Link under ground, Victoria, Piccadilly, Northern Circle Metropolitan. Colour TV, central heating in all rooms.

B&B from £25-£40pp, Rooms 9 single, 3 twin, 4 double, 2 family, all en-suite, Children welcome, No pets, Open all year.

Mr A Joseph, **Cottespar Hotel,** 11 Wicklow Street, Camden, King Cross, London WC1X 9JX
Tel: 0171 837 8738 & 278 0585 Fax: 0171 837 9762

....

CLIFTON HOTEL, a small, friendly, family run B&B hotel. 5 minutes walk from King's Cross St, Pancras Stations, 10 minutes' walk from Euston Station, 15 minutes by underground to Oxford Street, West End, and city. All rooms with colour TV.

B&B from £15pp, Rooms 4 single, 2 twin, 2 double 1 en-suite, 1 family, Children welcome, No pets, Open all year.
Ann Lawrence & Enzo Danelon, **Clifton Hotel,** 7 St. Chad's Street, King's Cross, London WC1H 8BD
Tel: 0171 8374452

DYLAN HOTEL, a small hotel in central location, 4 minutes from Paddington and Lancaster Gate underground stations. Marble Arch, Hyde park and Oxford Street close by. No t just a hotel, a home from home.

B&B from £30, Rooms 4 single, 4 double, 7 twin, 3 triple, Children welcome, No pets, Open all year.
Dylan Hotel, 14 Devonshire Terrace, Lancaster Gate, London W2 3DW
Tel: 0171 723 3280 Fax: 0171 402 2443

....

ALLANDALE HOTEL, a small select family hotel will impress you with its careful service. Full English breakfast. All bedrooms have private shower and toilet, colour TV and central heating. Close to Hyde park, West End, Lancaster Gate/Paddington Stations.

B&B from £38, Rooms 2 single, 8 double, 5 twin, 2 triple, 3 family, Children welcome, Open all year.
Allandale Hotel, 3 Devonshire Terrace, Lancaster Gate, London W2 3DN
Tel: 0171 723 8311 & 723 7807 Fax: 0181 905 4891

....

SLEEPING BEAUTY MOTEL, all rooms en-suite with bath and shower, satellite TV, direct dial telephone, hair dryer, hospitality tray, trouser press, mini fridge, safe. Ironing facilities, 24 hour reception, lift, free car park, bar.

B&B from £40, Rooms 16 double, 61 twin, 4 triple, all en-suite, Children from 3 years, No pets, Open all year.
Sleeping Beauty Motel, 543 Lea Bridge Road, Leyton, London E10 7EB
Tel: 0181 556 8080 Fax: 0181 556 8080

....

BOSTON COURT HOTEL, is a small comfortable and friendly B&B in central London. Only two minutes walk from Marble Arch, Oxford St shops and Hyde Park. Continental breakfast included. Modern private bath, shower and toilet, direct dial telephone, satellite colour TV, refrigerator, fans, tea/coffee making facilities and hair dryer available in all rooms. Access at all times.
Price range, single from £49(sh)- £55(sh+wc), Double from £55(sh)- £73(sh+wc), Open all year.
Boston Court Hotel, 26 Upper Berkley Street, Marble Arch, London W1H 7PF
Tel: 0171 723 1445 Fax: 0171 262 8823

....

THE EDWARD LEAR HOTEL, a family-run Georgian town residence, once the home of Edward Lear, famous poet and painter, with informal but efficient atmosphere. In a central location, 1 minute from Oxford Street and Marble Arch.

B&B from £39.50, Rooms 13 single, 4 double, 10 twin, 2 triple, 2 family, Children welcome, No pets, Open all year.
The Edward Lear Hotel, 30 Seymour Street, Marble Arch, London W1H 5WD
Tel: 0171 402 5401 Fax: 0171 706 3766

....

MARBLE ARCH INN, a friendly hotel at Marble Arch, within minutes from Hyde Park and Oxford Street and within easy reach of other major attractions.

B&B from £40, Rooms 2 single, 8 double, 9 twin, 6 triple, 4 family, most en-suite, Children welcome, No pets, No smoking, Open all year.
Marble Arch Inn, 49-50 Upper Berkley Street, Marble Arch, London W1H 7PN
Tel: 0171 723 7888 Fax: 0171 723 6060

....

RAGLAN HALL HOTEL, located in a quiet treelined avenue of north London. Lovely secluded garden and patio. Modern English food. Friendly relaxed atmosphere.

B&B from £96.95, Dinner available, Rooms 8 single, 20 double, 10 twin, 8 triple, all en-suite, Children welcome,No smoking, Open all year.
Raglan Hall Hotel, 8-12 Queens Avenue, Muswell Hill, London N10 3NR
Tel: 0181 883 9836 Fax: 0181 883 5002 Email: raglanhall@aol.com

MEADOW CROFT LODGE, between A2 and A20, near New Eltham station with easy access to London. Warm and friendly atmosphere. TV in rooms.

B&B from £20, Rooms 4 single, 3 double, 9 twin, 1 family, Children welcome, No pets, No smoking, Open all year.
Meadow Croft Lodge, 96-98 Southwood Road, New Eltham, London SE9 3QS
Tel: 0181 859 1488 Fax: 0181 850 8054

....

OXFORD HOTEL, refurbished budget hotel, all rooms with en-suite shower/toilet. Close to bus routes and underground. Family rooms available. All have microwave and fridge.

B&B from £60, Rooms 1 double, 8 twin, 9 family, Children from 12 years, No smoking, Open all year.
Oxford Hotel, 13-14 Craven Terrace, Paddington, London W2 3QD
Tel: 0171 402 6860 & 0800 318798 Fax: 0171 706 4318

....

THE PARK LANE HOTEL, on Piccadilly overlooking Green Park towards Buckingham Palace, offering good service and modern facilities.

B&B from £222.63, Lunch & evening meal available, Rooms 50 single, 100 double, 100 twin, 20 triple, 40 family rooms, suites available, all en-suite, Children welcome, No smoking, Open all year.

The Park Lane Hotel, Piccadilly, London W1Y 8BX
Tel: 0171 499 6321 Fax: 0171 499 1965

....

THE WHITE HOUSE, near Regent's Park, the zoo and Madame Tussaud's. A few minutes from Euston Station and about 10 minutes walk from Oxford Circus. There are 3 underground stations within walking distance.

B&B from £155, Lunch & evening meal available, Rooms 53 single, 216 double, 239 twin, 53 triple, all en-suite, Children welcome, No pets, No smoking, Open all year.
The White House, Albany Street, Regent's Park, London NW1 3UP
Tel: 0171 287 1200 Fax: 0171 388 0091

....

HOTEL NUMBER SIXTEEN, with atmosphere of a comfortable town house in very attractive street. Secluded award-winning gardens.

B&B from £85, Rooms 9 single, 23 double, 4 triple, all en-suite, Children welcome, NO pets, Open all year.

Hotel Number Sixteen, 16 Sumner Place, South Kensington, London SW7 3EG
Tel: 0171 589 5232 Fax: 0171 584 8615

....

FIVE SUMNER PLACE HOTEL, situated in South Kensington, the most fashionable area. This family owned and run hotel offers first-class service and personal attention.

B&B from £81, Rooms 3 single, 5 double, 5 twin, all en-suite, Children from 6 years, No pets, No smoking, Open all year.
Five Sumner Place Hotel, 5 Sumner Place, South Kensington, London SW7 3EE
Tel: 0171 584 7586 Fax: 0171 823 9962 Email: no.5@dial.pipex.com

....

FIVE KINGS GUEST HOUSE, a privately run guesthouse in a quiet residential area. 15 minutes to central London. Unrestricted parking in road.

B&B from £20, Rooms 6 single, 3 double, 3 twin, 2 triple, 2 family, some en-suite, Children from 3 years, No pets, Open all year.

Five Kings Guest House, 59 Anson Road, Tufnell Park, London N7 0AR
Tel: 0171 607 3996 & 607 6466

WINDERMERE HOTEL, a small friendly hotel with well equipped bedrooms and a cosy lounge. English breakfast and dinner are served in the elegant licenced restaurant.

B&B from £49, Dinner available, Rooms 3 single, 11 double, 5 twin, 1 triple, 3 family, Children welcome, No pets, No smoking, Open all year.

Windermere Hotel, 142-144 Warwick Way, Victoria, London SW1V 4JE
Tel: 0171 834 5163 & 834 5480 Fax: 0171 630 8831 Email: 100773.1171@compuserve.com

....

HOLLY HOUSE HOTEL

HOLLY HOUSE HOTEL, Bed & Breakfast in the heart of London. Comfort and convenience at a budget price. Hot and cold water in all rooms with central heating. All rooms with central heating. All rooms with colour TV, tea/coffee facilities. Two minutes from Victoria Station. All major credit cards accepted.
B&B from £17.50pp, Rooms ??single, ??twin, ??double, ?? family, Restricted smoking, Children welcome, No pets, Open all year.
Manager A. Jessa, **Holly House Hotel,** 20 Hugh Street, Victoria, London SW1V 1RP
Tel: 0171 834 5671 Fax: 0171 233 5154

....

AIRWAYS HOTEL, NATION LODGE LTD, within walking distance of Buckingham Palace and Westminster Abbey. Convenient for Harrods and theatreland. friendly personal service. Full English breakfast.

B&B from £40, Rooms 8 single, 9 double, 11 twin, 5 triple, 5 family, all en-suite, Children welcome, No smoking, Open all year.

Airways Hotel, Nation Lodge Ltd, 29-31 St George's Drive, Victoria, London SW1V 4DG
Tel: 0171 834 0205 Fax: 0171 932 0007

....

ELIZABETH HOTEL, a friendly, quiet hotel overlooking magnificent gardens of stately residential square (circa 1835), close to Belgravia yet within 5 minutes' walk of Victoria. Free colour brochure.

B&B from £40, Rooms 6 single, 5 double, 4 twin, 16 triple,7 family, Children welcome, No smoking, No pets, Open all year.

Elizabeth Hotel, 37 Eccleston Square, Victoria, London SW1V 1PB
Tel: 0171 828 6812

....

CARLTON HOTEL, a small, friendly bed and breakfast near Victoria station and within walking distance of famous landmarks such as Buckingham Palace, Trafalgar Square and Piccadilly Circus.

B&B from £39, Rooms 4 single, 5 double, 2 twin, 6 triple, most en-suite, Children welcome, No pets, Open all year.

Carlton Hotel, 90 Belgrave Road, Victoria, London SW1V 2BJ
Tel: 0171 976 6634 & 932 0913 Fax: 0171 821 8020

....

COLLIERS HOTEL, a clean reasonably priced hotel, centrally situated in Victoria a few minutes walk from railway, coach and underground stations. Central heating throughout. All rooms with TV and telephone. London Tourist Board Listed.

B&B from £18pp, Rooms 4 single, 4 twin, 8 double, 3 family, 2 en-suite, Children welcome, No pets, Open all year.
Mr I. A. Akhtar, **Colliers Hotel,** 97 Warwick Way, Victoria, London SW1V 1QL
Tel: 0171 834 6931 Fax: 0171 834 8439

DIANA HOTEL, a pleasant, comfortable, converted Victorian house near Dulwich Village. Ten minutes by train from Victoria in central London. TV, tea/coffee facilities, guests' lounge/breakfast room, bar, some off street parking. Near Dulwich Picture Gallery, Dulwich College, Horniman Museum/Gardens and Crystal Palace National Sports Centre. **B&B from £22.50pp,** Rooms 2 single, 5 twin, 5 double, 1 family, some en-suite, Children welcome, No pets, Open all year.
Mr & Mrs Chong, **Diana Hotel,** 88 Thurlow Park Road, West Dulwich, London SE21 8HY
Tel: 0181 670 3250 Fax: 0181 761 8300

....

THE WHITE HOUSE, a listed Georgian house with forecourt parking, on main road. Buses and trains to the city and 15 minutes by train to Wimbledon. Close to Crystal Palace National Sports Centre.

B&B from £16, Rooms 2 single, 1 family, all en-suite, Children welcome, No pets, Open all year.
The White House, 242 Norwood Road, West Norwood, London SE27 9AW
Tel: 0181 670 36607 & 761 8892 Fax: 0181 670 6440

....

POLANKA, all rooms have colour TV, tea/coffee making facilities, a guest lounge. Car parking facilities, free nearby. 24 hour check-in. Free storage of your luggage. Walking distance to Portobello Market, Little Venice Queensway. Nearest underground station Westbourne Park. Free Courtesy car service from any mine line station.
B&B from £19pp, Rooms 4 twin, 2 double, 2 family, Children welcome, No pets, Open all year.
Michael Banaszkiewicz, **Polanka,** 406 Harrow Road, Westbourne Park, London W9 2HU
Tel: 0171 223 6364 Fax: 0171 289 5747

....

J & T GUEST HOUSE, a small guest house in north west London close to the underground. Easy access to Wembley Stadium complex. 5 mins from M1.

B&B from £30, Rooms 1 single, 1 double, 3 twin, 1 triple, all en-suite, Children welcome, No pets, Open all year.
J & T Guest House, 98 Park Avenue North, Willesden Green, London NW10 1 JY
Tel: 0181 452 4085 Fax: 0181 450 2503

....

COMPTON GUEST HOUSE

COMPTON GUEST HOUSE, a family run guesthouse in pleasant, peaceful area, 5 minutes from Wimbledon station. Easy access to the West End, central London, M1, M2, M3, M4, and M25. Quality rooms, with excellent service. 12 minutes walk from Wimbledon tennis courts.

B&B from £35, Rooms 2 single, 1 double, 2 twin, 1 triple, 2 family rooms, Children from 5 years, No pets, No smoking, Open all year.

Compton Guest House, 65 Compton Rd, Wimbledon, London SW19 7QA
Tel: 0181 947 4488 & 879 3245 Fax: 0181 947 4488

....

ROYAL CHACE HOTEL, pleasant hotel of character, set in Green Belt, with access to London and M25. Ideal for business and tourists. Special weekend rates available.

B&B from £50, Lunch & evening meal available, Rooms 70 double, 19 twin, 3 family, all en-suite, Children welcome, No pets, Open all year.
Royal Chace Hotel, 162 The Ridgeway, Enfield, Middlesex EN2 8AR
Tel: 0181 366 6500 Fax: 0181 367 7191 Email: royal.chace@dial.pipex.com

....

THE QUALITY HARROW HOTEL, a friendly, family-run hotel near Wembley and convenient for central London. New air-conditioned restaurant and function suite. Non-smoking conservatory. Easy access to motorways and Heathrow. Free parking.
B&B from £74, Lunch & evening meal available, Rooms 17 single, 19 double, 14 twin, 2 family, all en-suite, Children welcome, No smoking, Open all year.
The Quality Harrow Hotel, 12-22 Pinner Road, Harrow, Middlesex HA1 4HZ
Tel: 0181 427 3435 Fax: 0181 861 1370

LINDAL HOTEL, in the busy town centre. Easy reach motorways, central London, Wembley complex and Heathrow. 8 minutes' walk to the tube stations.

B&B from £45, Lunch & evening meal available, Rooms 7 single, 4 double, 5 twin, 2 triple, 1 family, all en-suite, Children welcome, No smoking, Open all year.

Lindal Hotel, 2 Hindes Road, Harrow, Middlesex HA1 1SJ
Tel: 0181 863 3164 Fax: 0181 427 5435

....

CRESCENT HOTEL, a modern, friendly hotel with full facilities in the heart of Harrow. Five minutes to underground, easy access to Wembley, West End, Heathrow and major motorways. Website: http://www.crsnthtl.demon.co.uk.

B&B from £40-£65, Rooms 9 single, 3 double, 6 twin, 2 family, some en-suite, Children welcome, Open all year.

Crescent Hotel, 58-62 Welldon Crescent, Harrow, Middlesex HA1 1QR
Tel: 0181 863 5491 & 863 5163 Fax: 0181 427 5965 Email: jivraj@crsnthtl.demon.co.uk.

....

HINDES HOTEL, a homely owner-run bed and breakfast hotel near the M1. West End 15 minutes by underground. Convenient for Wembley Stadium complex.

B&B from £31, Rooms 4 single, 4 double, 6 twin, some en-suite, Children welcome, Open all year.

Hindes Hotel, 8 Hindes Road, Harrow, Middlesex HA1 1SJ
Tel: 0181 427 7468 Fax: 0181 424 0673

....

SHEPISTON LODGE, a homely guest house, ten minutes from Heathrow. Easy access A4/M4, A/M40, M25. All rooms with colour TV, tea/coffee facility. Licensed bar, Evening meals. Parking for holiday period. AA Q, RAC Listed, Approved Tourist Board Crown.

B&B from £40pp, Dinner from £5, Rooms 3 single, 6 twin, 1 double, 3 family, Children welcome, No pets, Open all year.
Rana Dhawan, **Shepiston Lodge,** 31 Shepiston Lane, Hayes, Middlesex UB3 1LJ
Tel: 0181 573 0266 Fax: 0181 569 2536

....

SKYLARK BED & BREAKFAST, is three miles from Heathrow second underground station from Heathrow. All rooms have TV's, tea/coffee facilities and en-suite. Car park. Central London is only 30 minutes away. Shopping centre, restaurants nearby. Single £40, Double £55, Twin £55, Family £24 per person, all rates includes full English breakfast.
B&B from £27.50pp, Rooms single, twin, double, family, all en-suite, Restricted smoking, Children welcome, No pets, Open all year.
Mr Parmar, **Skylark Bed & Breakfast,** 297 Bath Road, Hounslow West, Middlesex TW3 3DB
Tel: 0181 577 8455 Fax: 0181 577 8741

....

ASHDOWNE HOUSE, a very comfortable Victorian house with elegant rooms, all en-suite and non smoking. Conveniently situated for travel to Heathrow and central London.

B&B from £49.50, Rooms 2 single, 3 double, 2 twin, all en-suite, Children welcome, No smoking, No pets, Open all year.

Ashdowne House, 9 Pownall Gardens, Hounslow, Middlesex TW3 1YW
Tel: 0181 572 0008 Fax: 0181 570 1939

BARN HOTEL, a 17th century hotel set in two acres of landscaped rose gardens and lawns. Just minutes from central London and Heathrow. Adjacent to underground station. Own free car park.

B&B from £55, Lunch & evening meal available, Rooms 25 single, 21 double, 11 twin, all en-suite, Children welcome, No smoking, Open all year.

Barn Hotel, Sherley's Farm, West End Road, Ruislip, Middlesex HA4 6JB
Tel: 01895 636 057 Fax: 01895 638 379

....

ELM HOTEL, ten minutes walk from Wembley Stadium and Conference centre. 150 yards from Wembley Central underground and mainline station.

B&B from £35, Rooms 5 single, 8 double, 8 twin, 3 triple, 2 family, suites available, all en-suite, Children welcome, Open all year.

Elm Hotel, 1-7 Elm Road, Wembley, Middlesex HA9 7JA
Tel: 0181 902 1764 Fax: 0181 903 8365

....

THE BROOKSIDE HOTEL, 20 minutes from central London, a stone's throw from Wembley Stadium and Conference Centre. Overlooks Wembley Park station.

B&B from £28, Rooms 3 single, 3 double, 1 twin, 2 triple, 2 family, most en-suite, Children welcome, No pets, Open all year.

The Brookside Hotel, 32 Brook Avenue, Wembley, Middlesex HA9 8PH
Tel: 0181 904 333 & 908 5725 Fax: 0181 908 3333

....

ADELPHI HOTEL, close to Wembley Stadium and Wembley Park underground, 15 minutes from the West End. Attractive decor. TV lounge, tea/coffee in rooms.

B&B from £30, Dinner available, Rooms 4 single, 4 double, 3 twin, some en-suite, Children welcome, No pets, Open all year.

Adelphi Hotel, 4 Forty Lane, Wembley, Middlesex HA9 9EB
Tel: 0181 904 5629 Fax: 0181 908 5314

....

ARENA HOTEL, spacious en-suite accommodation with TV and satellite link in every room. Recent refurbishment, only 1800 yards from Wembley Stadium complex. Easy access by all transport routes. Parking.

B&B from £35, Dinner available, Rooms 2 single, 2 double, 3 twin, 3 triple, 3 family rooms, all en-suite, Children welcome, Open all year.

Arena Hotel, 6 Forty Lane, Wembley, Middlesex HA9 9EB
Tel: 0181 908 0670 & 908 2850 Fax: 0181 908 2007

....

KIRKDALE HOTEL, a characterful Victorian house decorated to a high standard. Close to Croydon's shopping and business areas, theatre, restaurants and station. Easy travel to London, Gatwick and Brighton.

B&B from £30, Rooms 8 single, 9 double, 2 twin, all en-suite, Children from 3 years, No pets, No smoking, Open all year.

Kirkdale Hotel, 22 St Peter's Road, Croydon, Surrey CR0 1HD
Tel: 0181 688 5898 Fax: 0181 680 6001

CROYDON HOTEL, close to central Croydon (route A222) and 10 minutes' walk from East Croydon Station. Opposite shops and restaurants. Frequent direct trains to Victoria and Gatwick Airport.

B&B from £24, Rooms 1 single, 2 double, 3 twin, 2 triple, most en-suite, Children welcome, No pets, Open all year.

Croydon Hotel, 112 Lower Addiscombe Road, Croydon, Surrey CR0 6AD
Tel: 0181 656 7233 Fax: 0181 655 0211

....

HAYESTHORPE HOTEL, a quiet, family style hotel located in South Croydon, just off the London Brighton Road.

B&B from £40, Dinner available, Rooms 10 single, 5 double, 7 twin, 3 triple, all en-suite, Children welcome, No pets, No smoking, Open all year.

Hayesthorpe Hotel, 48-52 Augustine's Avenue, Croydon, Surrey CR2 6JJ
Tel: 0181 688 8120 Fax: 0181 680 1099

....

MITRE HOTEL, an historic 17th century building overlooking Hampton Court Palace and the River Thames. Elegantly decorated, with spacious en-suite rooms, including a four poster bed.

B&B from £75, Lunch & evening meal available, Rooms 15 double, 20 twin, 1 triple, suite available, all en-suite, Children welcome, No smoking, Open all year.

Mitre Hotel, Hampton Court Road, Hampton Court, East Mosesey, Surrey KT8 9BN
Tel: 0181 979 9988 Fax: 0181 979 9777

....

HOTEL ANTOINETTE OF KINGSTON, a tourist hotel located 20 minutes by train from London. An ideal base for visiting Hampton Court, Kew, Windsor, Chessington World of Adventures and Thorpe Park.

B&B from £44, Dinner available, Rooms 24 single, 8 double, 34 twin, 24 triple, 9 family rooms, all en-suite, Children welcome, No smoking, Open all year.

Hotel Antoinette of Kingston, Beaufort Road, Kingston-upon Thames, Surrey KT1 2TQ
Tel: 0181 546 1044 Fax: 0181 547 2595

....

CHASE LODGE HOTEL, a small hotel in quiet conservation area. Close to Hampton Court, River Thames and 23 minutes to the centre of London. Excellent restaurant open to non-residents.

B&B from £48, Lunch & evening meal available, Rooms 2 single, 7 double, 3 twin, all en-suite, Children welcome, No smoking, Open all year.

Chase Lodge Hotel, 10 Park Road, Hampton Wick, Kingston-upon-Thames, Surrey KT14AS
Tel: 0181 943 1862 Fax: 0181 943 9363

....

RIVERSIDE HOTEL, an elegant Victorian house overlooking the Thames, close to Richmond Bridge. En-suite rooms, colour TV and tea/coffee making facilities.

B&B from £36, Rooms 4 single, 5 double, 3 twin, 1 triple, all en-suite/private facilities, Children welcome, Open all year.

Riverside Hotel, 23 Petersham Road, Richmond, Surrey TW10 6UH
Tel: 0181 940 1339

RICHMOND PARK HOTEL, a privately owned hotel in the heart of Richmond. All rooms are en-suite with direct-dial telephone, colour TV, radio and tea/coffee making facilities.

B&B from £55, Rooms 6 single, 14 double, 2 twin, Children welcome, No smoking, Open all year.

Richmond Park Hotel, 3 Petersham Road, Richmond, Surrey TW10 6UH
Tel: 0181 948 4666 Fax: 0181 940 7376

....

QUINNS HOTEL, ideally located for business or pleasure, within easy reach of central London, airports and local places of interest.

B&B from £35, Rooms 8 single, 16 double, 10 twin, 3 triple, 1 family, some en-suite, Children welcome, Open all year.

Quinns Hotel, 48 Sheen Road, Richmond, Surrey TW9 1AW
Tel: 0181 940 5444 Fax: 0181 940 1828

....

MARKINGTON HOTEL, a friendly, comfortable private hotel with fully equipped rooms, all en-suite. Free car parking. Bar and restaurant. Close to public transport.

B&B from £35, Dinner available, Rooms 10 single, 6 double, 2 twin, 2 triple, all en-suite, Children welcome, No pets, No smoking, Open all year.

Markington Hotel, 9 Haling Park, South Croydon, Surrey CR2 6NG
Tel: 0181 681 6494 Fax: 0181 688 6530

....

SELSDON PARK, a country house hotel, 10 minutes from the M25, 30 minutes from London and Gatwick, set in 200 acres of Parkland. Special weekend Rates.

B&B from £107, Lunch & evening meal available, Rooms 40 single, 50 double, 80 twin, suite available, all en-suite, Children welcome, No smoking, Open all year.

Selsdon Park, Sanderstead, South Croydon, Surrey CR2 8YA
Tel: 0181 657 8811 Fax: 0181 651 6171

....

ASHLING TARA HOTEL, situated opposite open parkland. Short walk to Sutton town centre. All rooms are en-suite, lounge/bar and restaurant. On-site parking. Convenient for M25, Heathrow and Gatwick Airports.

B&B from £60, Dinner available, Rooms 5 single, 4 double, 4 twin, 2 family, most en-suite, Children welcome, No smoking, No pets, Open all year.

Ashling Tara Hotel, 50 Rosehill, Sutton, Surrey SM1 3EU
Tel: 0181 641 6142 Fax: 0181 644 7872

....

ALPHA GUEST HOUSE, a modern, family run residence in ideal location near to Croydon (20 minutes from Victoria Station). Tea/coffee making facilities, satellite TV, free parking and varied breakfasts.

B&B from £22, Rooms 5 single, 1 double, 4 twin, 1 triple, some en-suite, Children welcome, No pets, No smoking, Open all year.

Alpha Guest House, 99 Brigstock Road, Thornton Heath, Surrey CR7 7JL
Tel: 0181 684 4811 & 665 0032 Fax: 0181 405 0302

Norfolk is probably best known for the Broads and the seaside resorts of Great Yarmouth, Cromer and Hunstanton - but the county has much more to offer. Peaceful and unspoilt, Norfolk is easy to reach with good road and rail links to the rest of the country.

Norfolk's gentle terrain is ideal walking and cycling country. For the energetic there is the Around Norfolk Walk which joins the Peddars Way from Thetford to the Coastal Path, running from Holme to Cromer, and then along the Weavers Way to Great Yarmouth.

The landscape of the Fens with its patchwork of fields has its own dramatic beauty. The marshland was drained by Dutch engineers in the seventeenth century and the remains of the wind pumps are still visible - without them the water contained within the high banks of the rivers and dykes would still cover this fertile, black farmland.

The coastline stretches from the flat tidal marshes of the Wash, past Hunstanton, and along the salt marshes and lonely beaches and dunes passing a number of picturesque villages. The cliffs re-emerge at Weybourne Hope and climb steadily past Cromer to Mundesley. Here the coast curves southwards and dunes replace the cliffs, which between Sea Palling and Winterton are all that prevent the sea from flooding into the Broads at Horsey Mere. Within the triangle from Norwich, Lowestoft and Sea Palling lie more than 30 Broads, networks of rivers and lakes, formed by flooded medieval peat digging, which today form lock free waterways. The real character of the Broads is best appreciated from a boat and many boatyards offer craft to hire for the day. For the fisherman the waters are a delight.

Norfolk's county town, Norwich, has one of England's best preserved historic centres with its medieval street pattern contained by the remains of the city walls. The city has exceptionally good shopping and also hosts a regular arts festival, with events held in various venues around the centre.

Great Yarmouth is a combination of a large bustling seaside resort and an historic port. The seafront has its traditional visitor attractions while the river quay has been home of the herring and merchant fleet for centuries, but is now more familiar to cargo ships. Cromer became a seaside resort in Victorian times with the coming of the railway and has remained popular ever since.

King's Lynn has two market places and two medieval guildhalls, one of which is now the town hall. Thetford is an ancient town and a thousand years ago was the capital of East Anglia. Its continuing importance during the middle ages left a legacy of historic sites.

left, Norfolk Broads

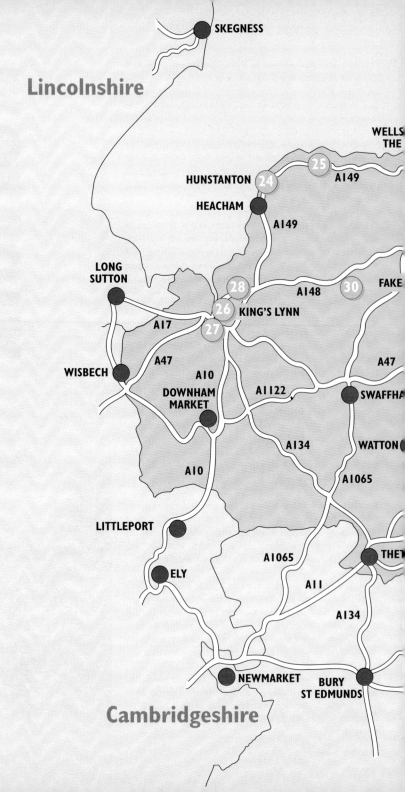

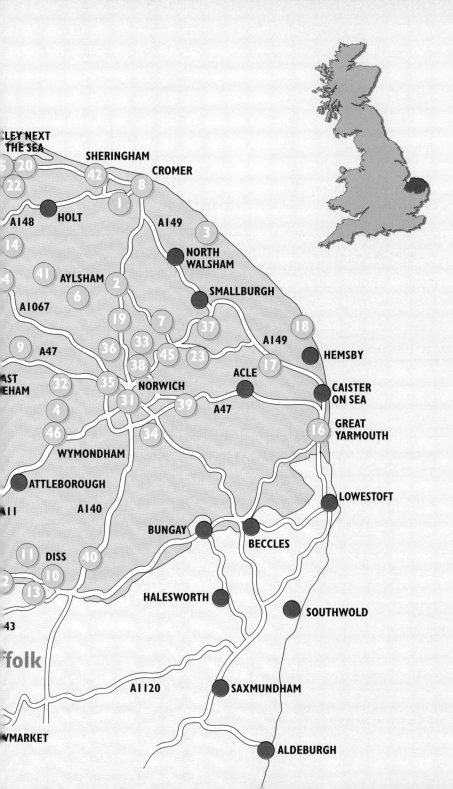

LEY NEXT
THE SEA

SHERINGHAM

CROMER

HOLT

A148

A149

NORTH
WALSHAM

AYLSHAM

SMALLBURGH

A1067

A149

HEMSBY

A47

ACLE

NORWICH

CAISTER
ON SEA

AST
EHAM

A47

GREAT
YARMOUTH

WYMONDHAM

ATTLEBOROUGH

LOWESTOFT

A140

BUNGAY

BECCLES

DISS

HALESWORTH

SOUTHWOLD

43

folk

A1120

SAXMUNDHAM

MARKET

ALDEBURGH

FELBRIGG LODGE, hidden in 4 acres of spectacular gardens and woods. Large, comfortable bedrooms, well appointed with every facility and all en-suite. Delicious dinners. 10 minutes from Holt.

B&B from £38, Rooms 2 twin, 1 double, all en-suite, No smoking, Children over 8, Open all year.
Felbrigg Lodge, Aylmerton, Norfolk NR11 8RA
Tel: 01263 837588 Fax: 01263 838012   **Map Ref 1**

....

THE OLD PUMP HOUSE, creature comforts, steps everywhere and home cooking. Rambling 1750's house beside the thatched pump, a minute from church and marketplace. Pine shuttered breakfast room overlooks peaceful garden. Non smoking.

B&B from £18, Dinner available, Rooms 2 twin, 3 double, most en-suite, Children welcome, No smoking, Open all year.
The Old Pump House, Holman Road, Aylsham, Norfolk NR11 6BY
Tel: 01263 733789   **Map Ref 2**

....

THE AYLSHAM MOTEL, a family run motel. Relaxed and friendly atmosphere in peaceful surroundings. All rooms en-suite. Close to North Norfolk and Broads. Bar and a la carte meals available.

B&B from £29, Dinner available, Rooms 10 twin, 3 double, 2 triple, all en-suite, No smoking, Children welcome, Open all year.
The Aylsham Motel, Norwich Road, Aylsham, Norfolk NR11 6JH
Tel: 01263 734851 Fax: 01263 734851   **Map Ref 2**

....

SEACROFT PRIVATE HOTEL, a large Victorian house close to shops and beach. Home cooking and personal supervision. Off B1159, via Seacroft caravan park.

B&B from £19.50, Dinner available, Rooms 2 single, 2 twin, 3 double, 1 triple, 1 family, most en-suite, Children welcome, No pets, Open February - December.
Seacroft Private Hotel, Beach Road, Bacton on Sea, Norfolk NR12 0HS
Tel: 01692 650302   **Map Ref 3**

....

BARNHAM BROOM HOTEL, GOLF, CONFERENCE & LEISURE CENTRE, in 250 acres of beautiful countryside, with a relaxed and friendly atmosphere. Excellent sports facilities, 2 18 hole golf courses. Large conference complex, indoor heated pool.

B&B from £68, Dinner available, Rooms 1 single, 36 twin, 8 double, 1 triple, 7 family, all en-suite, No smoking, Children welcome, No pets, Open all year.
Barnham Broom Hotel, Golf, Conference & Leisure Centre, Honingham Rd, Barnham Broom, Norfolk NR9 4DD
Tel: 01603 759393 Fax: 01603 758224   **Map Ref 4**

....

WHITE HORSE HOTEL, an old Norfolk inn near picturesque harbour, offering traditional food and real beer. Restaurant closed Sunday and Monday evenings. Bar food 7 days a week. Local fish and game used.

B&B from £30, Dinner available, Rooms 2 single, 1 twin, 4 double, 2 triple, all en-suite, No smoking, Children welcome, No pets, Open all year.
White Horse Hotel, 4 High Street, Blakeney, Norfolk NR25 7AL
Tel: 01263 740574 Fax: 01263 741303   **Map Ref 5**

....

GREY GABLES COUNTRY HOUSE HOTEL & RESTAURANT, a former rectory in pleasant, rural setting, 10 miles from Norwich, coast and Broads. Wine cellar, emphasis on food. Comfortably furnished with many antiques.

B&B from £21, Dinner available, Rooms 2 single, 5 double, 1 twin, most en-suite, No smoking, Children welcome, Open all year.
Grey Gables Country House Hotel & Restaurant, Norwich Road, Cawston, Norfolk NR10 4EY
Tel: 01603 871259   **Map Ref 6**

THE NORFOLK MEAD HOTEL, a beautiful Georgian country house set in 12 secluded acres of parkland and gardens with river frontage. Boating, birdlife, fishing, outdoor swimming pool and restaurant.

B&B from £49, Dinner available, Rooms 3 twin, 6 double, 2 family, all en-suite, No smoking, Children welcome, Open all year.

The Norfolk Mead Hotel, The Mead, Coltishall, Norfolk NR12 7DN
Tel: 01603 737531 Fax: 01603 737521   **Map Ref 7**

KNOLL GUEST HOUSE, warm, friendly, family run Victorian guest house. TV in guest lounge, bar, tea/coffee facilities. Close to sea front, town centre, bus/rail station.

B&B from £16pp, Dinner from £7.50, Rooms 1 single, 1 twin, 1 double, 1 family, Restricted smoking, Children & pets welcome, Open all year except Christmas.

Mr Arnold, **Knoll Guest House**, 23 Alfred Rd, Cromer, Norfolk NR27 9AN
Tel: 01263 512753   **Map Ref 8**

THE GROVE GUESTHOUSE, a Georgian holiday home set in three acres, with beautiful walks through fields and woods to the cliffs and beach. We also have self catering cottages in a range of converted barns which are very popular.

B&B from £23, Dinner available, Rooms 1 single, 2 twin, 4 double, 2 family, all en-suite, Children welcome, No pets, Open April - September.

The Grove Guesthouse, 95 Overstrand Road, Cromer, Norfolk NR27 0DJ
Tel: 01263 512412 Fax: 01263 513416   **Map Ref 8**

HOTEL DE PARIS, a large hotel of historic and architectural interest, overlooking the pier and close to shops.

B&B from £22, Dinner available, Rooms 10 single, 27 twin, 14 double, 5 triple, most en-suite, No smoking, Children welcome, No pets, Open March - December.

Hotel De Paris, High Street, Cromer, Norfolk NR27 9HG
Tel: 01263 513141 Fax: 01263 515217   **Map Ref 8**

CLIFTONVILLE HOTEL, a beautifully restored Edwardian hotel on the seafront. En-suite bedrooms all with sea view. All day coffee shop/bar, Boltons Seafood Bistro and fine a la carte restaurant.

B&B from £25, Dinner available, Rooms 8 single, 9 twin, 10 double, 2 triple, 1 family, most en-suite, No smoking, Children welcome, Open all year.

Cliftonville Hotel, Runton Road, Cromer, Norfolk NR27 9AS
Tel: 01263 512543 Fax: 01263 515700   **Map Ref 8**

BARTLES LODGE, a river location, set in twelve acres of landscaped meadows with its own fishing lakes. All rooms are en-suite and tastefully decorated in country style with colour TV and tea/coffee making facilities. Village inn within 100 metres for evening meals.

B&B from £22.50pp, Rooms 3 twin, 3 double, 1 family, all en-suite, Children over 10, Pets by arrangement, Open all year.

David & Annie Bartlett, **Bartles Lodge**, Church Street, Elsing, Dereham, Norfolk NR20 3EA
Tel: 01362 637177   **Map Ref 9**

THE PARK HOTEL, a beautifully restored East Anglian house located near to the town centre. Fine restaurant and bar. All rooms en-suite with colour TV, direct dial telephone and hospitality tray. Ideal for touring Norfolk and for conferences up to 200. Ample parking. All set in our own grounds. We pride ourselves on offering high standards of comfort and friendly service.
B&B from £23.50pp, Dinner from £12, Rooms 1 single, 5 twin, 8 double, 2 family, all en-suite, Restricted smoking, Children welcome, Pets by arrangement, Open all year.
Robin Twigge, **The Park Hotel,** 29 Denmark St, Diss, Norfolk IP22 3LE
Tel: 01379 642244 Fax: 01379 644218   **Map Ref 10**

STRENNETH, a family run country Bed and Breakfast. Renovated period property, rural location close to Bressingham gardens. Log fires, central heating, four-poster and executive. All rooms individually styled, en-suite, colour TV's, hospitality trays, most on ground floor. Parking. Extensive breakfast menu. Local walks. Kennels if required. Colour brochure. Email: ken@mainline.co.uk
B&B from £22.50pp, Rooms 1 single, 2 twin, 4 double, all en-suite, Restricted smoking, Children & pets welcome, Open all year.
Ken & Brenda Webb, **Strenneth,** Airfield Road, Fersfield, Diss IP22 2BP
Tel: 01379 688182 Fax: 01379 688260   **Map Ref 11**

INGLENEUK LODGE, a modern single level home, family run. South facing patio, riverside walk. Very friendly atmosphere. On B1111, 1 mile south of village.

B&B from £33, Rooms 1 single, 1 double, 2 twin, all en-suite, No smoking, Children welcome, Open all year.

Ingleneuk Lodge, Hopton Road, Garboldisham, Diss, Norfolk IP22 2RQ
Tel: 01953 681541 Fax: 01953 681633   **Map Ref 12**

MALT HOUSE, a 17th century malt house, beautifully renovated and with all modern amenities. Candlelit dinners in elegant dining room, after dinner coffee in beamed lounge. 1 acre of landscaped garden with walled kitchen garden. 10 minutes walk, 2 miles Bressingham Gardens.

B&B from £35, Dinner available, Rooms 1 twin, 2 double, all en-suite, No smoking, Children over 2, No pets, Open all year.

Malt House, Denmark Hill, Palgrave, Diss, Norfolk IP22 1AE
Tel: 01379 642107 Fax: 01379 640315   **Map Ref 13**

MANOR FARM HOUSE, is set in 500 acres of arable farmland. All bedrooms have tea/coffee making facilities and colour TV. Credit cards accepted. Many stately homes are within a half an hour drive. The coast is 20 minutes drive away. Parking available.

B&B from £20pp, Dinner from £13.50, Rooms 1 twin, 2 double, No smoking, Children over 7, Open all year.
Anne Savage, **Manor Farm House,** Stibbard Road, Fulmodeston, Fakeham, Norfolk NR21 0LX
Tel: 01328 829353 Fax: 01328 829741   **Map Ref 14**

WENSUM LODGE HOTEL, a riverside location. Private gardens, freshly prepared a la carte menu. All bedrooms en-suite with colour TV.

B&B from £45, Dinner available, Rooms 2 single, 8 twin, 7 double, all en-suite, Children welcome, Open all year.

Wensum Lodge Hotel, Bridge Street, Fakenham, Norfolk NR21 9AY
Tel: 01328 862100 Fax: 01328 863365   **Map Ref 15**

TROTWOOD PRIVATE HOTEL, opposite bowling greens on seafront, giving unrivalled sea views. Close to Britannia Pier and all amenities. En-suite bedrooms, licensed bar and own car park.
B&B from £24, Rooms 1 twin, 8 double, most en-suite, No smoking, Children welcome, Open all year.
Trotwood Private Hotel, 2 North Drive, Great Yarmouth, Norfolk NR30 1ED
Tel: 01493 843971   **Map Ref 16**

....

SPINDRIFT PRIVATE HOTEL, attractively situated small private hotel, close to all amenities and with Beach Coach Station and car park at rear. Front bedrooms overlook gardens and sea.

B&B from £20, Rooms 2 single, 1 twin, 2 double, 1 triple, 1 family, most en-suite, Children over 3, No pets, Open all year.
Spindrift Private Hotel, 36 Wellesley Road, Great Yarmouth, Norfolk NR30 1EU
Tel: 01493 858674 Fax: 01493 858674   **Map Ref 16**

....

SOUTHERN HOTEL, a comfortable and friendly hotel within easy walking distance of seafront and attractions.
B&B from £16, Dinner available, Rooms 3 single, 1 twin, 11 double, 6 triple, most en-suite, Children welcome, No pets, Open March - October.
Southern Hotel, 46 Queens Road, Great Yarmouth, Norfolk NR30 3JR
Tel: 01493 843313 Fax: 01493 853047   **Map Ref 16**

....

REGENCY DOLPHIN HOTEL, a friendly, relaxing hotel with many amenities. Suites, presidential suite, jacuzzis, heated swimming pool in summer. Short breaks available.
B&B from £38.50, Dinner available, Rooms 6 single, 6 twin, 32 double, 4 triple, all en-suite, Children welcome, Open all year.
Regency Dolphin Hotel, Albert Square, Great Yarmouth, Norfolk NR30 3JH
Tel: 01493 855070 Fax: 01493 853798   **Map Ref 16**

....

THE CORNER HOUSE HOTEL, a bay fronted Victorian house adjacent to seafront, enjoying a high reputation for good cooking and personal, courteous service.
B&B from £19, Dinner available, Rooms 2 twin, 5 double, 1 triple, most en-suite, Children welcome, No pets, Open March - September.
The Corner House Hotel, Albert Square, Great Yarmouth, Norfolk NR30 3JH
Tel: 01493 842773   **Map Ref 16**

....

BURLINGTON PALM COURT HOTEL, sea views, heated indoor pool, sauna, solarium, lift and car park, in a resort with sandy beaches and crammed with history.

B&B from £40, Dinner available, Rooms 9 single, 29 twin, 17 double, 9 triple, 8 family, most en-suite, Children welcome, No pets, Open February - December.
Burlington Palm Court Hotel, North Drive, Great Yarmouth, Norfolk NR30 1EG
Tel: 01493 844568 Fax: 01493 331848   **Map Ref 16**

....

IMPERIAL HOTEL, modern, comfortable accommodation is offered in this family run seafront hotel, locally renowned for fine food, wine and service.
B&B from £41, Dinner available, Rooms No smoking, Children welcome, Open all year.
Imperial Hotel, North Drive, Great Yarmouth, Norfolk NR30 1EQ
Tel: 01493 851113 Fax: 01493 852229   **Map Ref 16**

....

HORSE & GROOM MOTEL, recently built motel on A149 in Norfolk Broads area. All rooms en-suite with satellite TV and tea/coffee facilities.

B&B from £39, Dinner available, Rooms 3 twin, 13 double, 4 family, all en-suite, Children welcome, Open all year.
Horse & Groom Motel, Rollesby, Great Yarmouth, Norfolk NR29 5ER
Tel: 01493 740624 Fax: 01493 740022   **Map Ref 17**

THE OLD COURT HOUSE, an 18th century workhouse set in 4 acres in a peaceful, rural location near the Broads. Family run with private bar and home cooking. Large games area. Bicycles for hire. Tennis, fishing and riding nearby.

B&B from £20, Dinner available, Rooms 1 twin, 2 double, 1 triple, 3 family, most en-suite, Children welcome, Open February - October.
The Old Court House, Court Road, Rollesby, Great Yarmouth, Norfolk NR29 5HG
Tel: 01493 369665   **Map Ref 17**

....

TOWER COTTAGE,, a charming cottage in a pretty village, with a sandy beach and pub, a short stroll away. Attractive bedrooms with TV, tea/coffee facilities (one is en-suite, with sitting room in a converted bar). Norfolk Broads 2 miles, Norwich 19 miles, Great Yarmouth 8 miles. "Which" entry.

B&B from £18pp, Rooms 1 twin, 2 double, 1 en-suite, Restricted smoking, Children over 8, Pets by arrangement, Open all year except Christmas & New Year.

Alan & Muriel Webster, **Tower Cottage,,** Black Street, Winterton-on-Sea, Great Yarmouth, Norfolk NR29 4AP
Tel: 01493 394053   **Map Ref 18**

....

MARSHAM ARMS INN, set in peaceful Norfolk countryside within reach of Norfolk, the Broads and the coast. Comfortable and spacious accommodation, good food and a fine selection of ales.

B&B from £38, Dinner available, Rooms 5 twin, 3 double, all en-suite, No smoking, Children welcome, Open all year.
Marsham Arms Inn, Holt Road, Hevingham, Norfolk NR10 5NP
Tel: 01603 754268 Fax: 01603 754839   **Map Ref 19**

....

CLEY MILL, nestles on the edge of Cley village in a position of great peace, commanding stunning views of Blakeney Harbour, the Salt Marshes and Cley Bird Sanctuary. Dinner is served 'En Famille' in the 18th Century dining room. Self catering apartments in converted boathouses available.

B&B from £25pp, Dinner from £15, Rooms 2 twin, 4 double, most en-suite, Restricted smoking, Children welcome, No pets, Open all year.
Jeremy Bolam, **Cley Mill,** Cley-next-the-Sea, Holt, Norfolk NR25 7RP
Tel: 01263 740 209 Fax: 01263 740 209   **Map Ref 20**

....

MORSTON HALL, a 17th century country house hotel with delightful gardens, 2 miles from Blakeney. Fine restaurant, fully licensed. Attractive bedrooms. Peaceful.

B&B from £80, Dinner available, Rooms 1 twin, 5 double, all en-suite, No smoking, Children welcome, Open February - December.

Morston Hall, Morston, Holt, Norfolk NR25 7AA
Tel: 01263 741041 Fax: 01263 740419   **Map Ref 21**

....

FLINTSTONES GUEST HOUSE, is one mile from Blakeney and Cley situated near village green and pub. All rooms have TV, hospitality trays, central heating. Ample parking. Ideal for bird watching. Several National Trust properties nearby. Coastal path and several walks. AA, RAC, ETB.
B&B from £17.50-£19.50pp, Rooms 1 single, 1 double, 3 family, all en-suite, No smoking, Children welcome, Pets by arrangement, Open all year except Christmas & New Year.
Pat & Malcolm Ormerod, **Flintstones Guest House,** Blakeney Road, Wiveton, Holt, Norfolk NR25 7TL
Tel: 01263 740337   **Map Ref 22**

PETERSFIELD HOUSE HOTEL, set slightly back from the banks of the River Bure, the hotel occupies one of the choicest positions on the Broads. Weekend breaks available.

B&B from £37.50, Dinner available, Rooms 3 single, 5 twin, 9 double, 1 family, all en-suite, Children welcome, Open all year.

Petersfield House Hotel, Lower Street, Horning, Norfolk NR12 8PF
Tel: 01692 630741 Fax: 01692 630745 **Map Ref 23**

....

ORIEL LODGE, Victorian charm with elegant accommodation. Rooms have TV, radio, beverage facilities, toilet requisites, hair dryers and luxurious bath robes. Sumptuous breakfast served in our oak panelled dining-room. Log fire compliments large lounge. Licensed Bar, sea views and ample parking. Golf, Coast, Nature Reserves, Walsingham and Sandringham close by. Email: info@orielodge.demon.co.uk
B&B from £23pp, Rooms 3 double, 2 family, some en-suite,
Inga Osborne, **Oriel Lodge,** 24 Homefields Road, Hunstanton, Norfolk PE36 5HJ
Tel: 01485 532368 Fax: 01485 535737 **Map Ref 24**

....

THE LINKSWAY COUNTRY HOUSE HOTEL, in a quiet location overlooking Hunstanton Golf Course, Close to beach and RSPB bird sancutries.

B&B from £22, Dinner available, Rooms 2 single, 8 twin, 2 double, 2 family, most en-suite, No smoking, Children over 3, No pets, Open March - December.

The Linksway Country House Hotel, Golf Course Road, Old Hunstanton, Norfolk PE36 6JE
Tel: 01485 532209 & 0860 330178 Fax: 01485 532209 **Map Ref 24**

....

BRIARFIELDS, a traditional, privately owned hotel, overlooking Titchwell RSPB Reserve, salt marshes and beaches. Renowned for comfort and excellent menus. Ideally situated for bird watching, beach walking, golf or visiting places of local interest. Special breaks all year round.

B&B from £35.50, Dinner available, Rooms 5 twin, 10 double, 2 family, all en-suite, No smoking, Children welcome, No pets, Open all year.

Briarfields, Main Street, Titchwell, King's Lynn Norfolk PE31 8BB
Tel: 01485 210742 Fax: 01485 210933 **Map Ref 25**

....

MARANATHA GUESTHOUSE, a large carrstone and brick residence with gardens front and rear, 10 minutes walk from town centre. Lynnsport and Queen Elizabeth Hospital.

B&B from £17, Dinner available, Rooms 2 single, 2 twin, 2 double, 1 triple, some en-suite, Children welcome, Open all year.
Maranatha Guesthouse, 115 Gaywood Road, King's Lynn, Norfolk PE30 2PU
Tel: 01553 774596 **Map Ref 26**

....

HAVANA GUEST HOUSE, Barry and Rosemary welcome you to their comfortable Victorian guest house. All bedrooms are colour coordinated with hospitality tray and colour TV. Most rooms en-suite including two on ground floor overlooking garden. Ample off-street parking. Easy walking distance to town centre. ETB 2 Crown Commended.

B&B from £16pp, Rooms 1 single, 3 twin, 2 double, 1 family, some en-suite, Restricted smoking, Children welcome, No pets, Open all year except Christmas & New Year.

Barry & Rosemary Breed, **Havana Guest House,** 117 Gaywood Road, King's Lynn, Norfolk PE30 2PU
Tel: 01553 772331 **Map Ref 26**

RUSSET HOUSE HOTEL, a lovely old house with pretty en-suite rooms. Four poster available. Bar, dining room, gardens and ample parking. Good food.

B&B from £30, Dinner available, Rooms 3 single, 2 twin, 5 double, 2 triple, all en-suite, No smoking, Children welcome, Open all year.
Russet House Hotel, 53 Goodwins Road, Vancouver Avenue, King's Lynn, Norfolk PE30 5PE
Tel: 01553 773098 Fax: 01553 773098 **Map Ref 26**

....

BUTTERFLY HOTEL, a modern building with rustic style and decor, set around an open central courtyard. Special weekend rates available.

B&B from £51.95, Dinner available, Rooms 23 single, 15 double, 12 twin, all en-suite, No smoking, Children welcome, Open all year.
Butterfly Hotel, A10-A47 Roundabout, Hardwick Narrows, King's Lynn, Norfolk PE30 4NB
Tel: 01553 771707 Fax: 01553 768027 **Map Ref 27**

....

THE TUDOR ROSE HOTEL, built around 1500 by a local merchant and extended in 1640, the hotel offers comfortable accommodation, traditional British cooking and a choice of 4 real ales in 2 bars.

B&B from £30, Dinner available, Rooms 5 single, 3 twin, 5 double, most en-suite, No smoking, Children welcome, Open all year.
The Tudor Rose Hotel, St Nicholas Street, off Tuesday Market Place, King's Lynn, Norfolk PE30 1LR
Tel: 01553 762824 Fax: 01553 764894 **Map Ref 26**

....

THE DUKE'S HEAD, one of the finest classical buildings in the town. Overlooking the delightful market square, it holds a prime position from which to enjoy this interesting town.

B&B from £39, Dinner available, Rooms 18 single, 37 double, 14 twin, 2 triple, all en-suite, No smoking, Children welcome, Open all year.
The Duke's Head, Tuesday Market Place, King's Lynn, Norfolk PE30 1JS
Tel: 01553 774996 Fax: 01553 763556 **Map Ref 26**

....

THE BEECHES GUESTHOUSE, a detached Victorian house, all rooms with TV, tea/coffee facilities and telephone. Most rooms en-suite. Full English breakfast and 3 course evening meal with coffee.

B&B from £20, Dinner available, Rooms 3 twin, 2 double, 2 triple, most en-suite, Children welcome, Open all year.
The Beeches Guesthouse, 2 Guanock Terrace, Kings Lynn, Norfolk PE30 5QT
Tel: 01553 766577 Fax: 01553 776664 **Map Ref 26**

....

THE STUART HOUSE HOTEL, a quiet, centrally located hotel situated within it's own grounds next to the town park. Superb accommodation, licensed bar, restaurant, and gardens. Off street parking. Close to Royal Sandringham, countryside and beach. Email: stuarthousehotel@btinternet.com

B&B from £32.50pp, Dinner from £15, Rooms 2 single, 6 twin, 8 double, 2 family, all en-suite, Restricted smoking, Children welcome, Open all year.
David Armes, **The Stuart House Hotel,** 35 Goodwins Road, Kings Lynn, Norfolk PE30 5QX
Tel: 01553 772169 Fax: 774788 **Map Ref 26**

....

KNIGHTS HILL HOTEL, sympathetically restored farm complex offering a choice of accommodation styles, 2 restaurants, a country pub and an extensive health club. Special breaks available.

B&B from £43pp, Dinner available, Rooms 5 single, 13 twin, 37 double, all en-suite, No smoking, Children welcome, Open all year.

Knights Hill Hotel, Knights Hill Village, South Wootton, King's Lynn, Norfolk PE30 3HQ
Tel: 01553 675566 Fax: 01553 675568 **Map Ref 28**

LOWER FARM, is set in delightful countryside, off the beaten track. It is south east of Sandringham and 20 minutes from the coast. There is an excellent pub in the village. Stabling available for horses. Lovely garden and trees. Comfortable bedrooms with TV, tea/coffee facilities and fridge. Parking.

B&B from £18pp, Rooms 1 twin, 2 double, all en-suite/private facilities, Restricted smoking, Children over 12, Pets by arrangement, Open all year except Christmas week.

Mrs Amanda Case, **Lower Farm,** Harpley, Kings Lynn PE31 6TU
Tel: 01485 520240 **Map Ref 30**

ABERDALE LODGE, a friendly, family run guest house close to city centre, University, Norfolk Broads. Good English breakfast, special diets by arrangement. TV's, tea/coffee in all rooms. Personal keys.

B&B from £15.50pp, Rooms 3 single, 1 twin, 1 double, 1 family, Restricted smoking, Children over 3, No pets, Open all year except Christmas.

Margaret Gilbert, **Aberdale Lodge,** 211 Earlham Road, Norwich Norfolk NR2 3RQ
Tel: 01603 502100 **Map Ref 31**

HOTEL NORWICH, a modern hotel conveniently located on the ring road, with easy access to the city centre, countryside, coastlines and Norfolk Broads. Leisure centre with indoor Pool.

B&B from £49.50, Dinner available, Rooms 18 single, 38 twin, 42 double, 8 triple, all en-suite, No smoking, Children welcome, No pets, Open all year.

Hotel Norwich, 121-131 Boundary Road, Norwich, Norfolk NR3 2BA
Tel: 01603 787260 Fax: 01603 400466 **Map Ref 31**

FUCHSIAS GUESTHOUSE, a friendly, family run guesthouse, convenient for city centre, university and surrounding countryside. Special diets available. Own keys.

B&B from £20, Rooms 1 single, 2 twin, 2 double, 1 triple, 1 en-suite, No smoking, Children welcome, No pets, Open all year.

Fuchsias Guesthouse, 139 Earlham Road, Norwich, Norfolk NR2 3RG
Tel: 01603 451410 Fax: 01603 259696 **Map Ref 31**

Comfortable, friendly family run Victorian **ROSEDALE GUEST HOUSE,** situated on B1108. Easy access to country, coast and city centre. Local shops and restaurants so park and relax. TV, tea/coffee and hot/cold in all rooms. Full English breakfast or vegetarian if required.

B&B from £16pp, Rooms 3 single, 2 twin, 2 double, 1 family, Restricted smoking, Children over 4, No pets, Open all year except Christmas.
Diane & Brian Curtis, **Rosedale Guest House,** 145 Earlham Road, Norwich, Norfolk NR3 2RG
Tel: 01603 453743 Fax: 01603 408473 **Map Ref 31**

CONIFERS HOTEL, a friendly hotel, close to city centre, university, sports village and showground. All rooms have colour TV, tea/coffee and hair dryers.

B&B from £19, Rooms 4 single, 3 twin, 1 double, 1 en-suite, Children welcome, Open all year.

Conifers Hotel, 162 Dereham Road, Norwich, Norfolk NR2 3AH
Tel: 01603 628737 **Map Ref 31**

CROFTERS HOTEL, tastefully restored Victorian house set in beautiful landscaped gardens. Comfortable accommodation at affordable rates in central Norwich.

B&B from £42, Dinner available, Rooms 5 twin, 6 double, 1 triple, all en-suite, Open all year.
Crofters Hotel, 2 Earlham Road, Norwich, Norfolk NR2 3DA
Tel: 01603 613287 Fax: 01603 766864 **Map Ref 31**

....

MARLBOROUGH HOUSE HOTEL, a long established family hotel, close to city centre, Castle Mall, museum, cathedral and Elm Hill. 3 minutes from railway station. Full central heating. All double, twin and family rooms are en-suite. Tea/coffee making facilities, licensed bar and car park.

B&B from £20, Dinner available, Rooms 5 single, 2 twin, 3 double, 1 triple, most en-suite, No smoking, Children welcome, Open all year.
Marlborough House Hotel, 22 Stracey Road, Norwich, Norfolk NR1 1EZ
Tel: 01603 628005 Fax: 01603 628005 **Map Ref 31**

....

THE GEORGIAN HOUSE HOTEL, comfortable we may be, expensive we are not. Two tastefully furnished linked Victorian houses, set in beautiful gardens, form the heart of this popular hotel. Ample parking, intimate bar and relaxed restaurant.

B&B from £40, Dinner available, Rooms 10 single, 5 twin, 10 double, 2 triple, all en-suite, No smoking, Children welcome, Open all year.
The Georgian House Hotel, 32-34 Unthank Road, Norwich, Norfolk NR2 2RB
Tel: 01603 615655 Fax: 01603 765689 **Map Ref 31**

....

BEECHES HOTEL & VICTORIAN GARDENS, a welcoming hotel, with unique and tranquil English Heritage wooded gardens. Tastefully restored and refurbished to offer high standards of comfort in a relaxed, informal atmosphere. An oasis in the heart of historic Norwich.

B&B from £44.50, Dinner available, Rooms 8 single, 3 twin, 14 double, all en-suite, No smoking, Children welcome, No pets, Open all year.
Beeches Hotel & Victorian Gardens, 4-6 Earlham Road, Norwich, Norfolk NR2 3DB
Tel: 01603 621167 Fax: 01603 620151 **Map Ref 31**

....

WEDGEWOOD HOUSE, a family run hotel, close to coach station and within walking distance of shops and places of interest. Parking.

B&B from £20, Rooms 2 single, 2 twin, 5 double, 3 triple, 1 family, most en-suite, No smoking, No pets, Open all year.
Wedgewood House, 42 St Stephens Road, Norwich, Norfolk NR1 3RE
Tel: 01603 625730 Fax: 01603 615035 **Map Ref 31**

....

THE GABLES GUESTHOUSE, high standard of accommodation with a friendly and relaxed atmosphere, snooker table and car park. Close to city and UEA.

B&B from £35, Rooms 4 twin, 5 double, 1 triple, all en-suite, No smoking, Children welcome, No pets, Open all year except Christmas & New Year.
The Gables Guesthouse, 527 Earlham Road, Norwich, Norfolk NR4 7HN
Tel: 01603 456666 Fax: 01603 250320 **Map Ref 31**

....

ANNESLEY HOUSE HOTEL, three listed Georgian buildings, restored and refurbished to a high standard. Set in landscaped grounds in a conservation area, yet a stroll to the city centre.

B&B from £50, Dinner available, Rooms 8 single, 2 twin, 16 double, all en-suite, Children welcome, No pets, Open all year.

Annesley House Hotel, 6 Newmarket Road, Norwich, Norfolk NR2 2LA
Tel: 01603 624553 Fax: 01603 621577 **Map Ref 31**

THE CORNER HOUSE, a large Victorian house with friendly atmosphere, 10 minutes from city centre. TV and tea/coffee facilities in all bedrooms, residents lounge area. Car parking.
B&B from £20, Rooms 2 double, 1 triple, all private or en-suite, No smoking, Children welcome, Open all year.
The Corner House, 62 Earlham Road, Norwich, Norfolk NR2 3DF
Tel: 01603 627928   **Map Ref 31**

EDMAR LODGE, a warm welcome awaits you. Most rooms en-suite with cable TV, tea/coffee facilities, hair dryer etc. Close to city centre and UEA, with 2 car parks. Excellent breakfasts.
B&B from £18, Rooms 1 single, 1 twin, 1 double, 1 triple, most en-suite, No smoking, Children welcome, No pets, Open all year.
Edmar Lodge, 64 Earlham Road, Norwich, Norfolk NR2 3DF
Tel: 01603 615599 Fax: 01603 632977   **Map Ref 31**

HOTEL NELSON, a modern, purpose built hotel on the riverside close to railway station and city centre. Easy access to the Broads and coast. Leisure club with indoor swimming pool.
D,B&B from £55pp, (2 nights or more), Rooms 27 single, 38 twin, 67 double, all en-suite, Children welcome, No pets, Open all year.
Hotel Nelson, Prince of Wales Road, Norwich, Norfolk NR1 1DX
Tel: 01603 760260 Fax: 01603 620008   **Map Ref 31**

Standing in three acres of grounds with Lakes, **THE UGLY BUG INN** offers a stay in the peaceful countryside of Norfolk. Friendly, informal restaurant and bar selling a selection of real ales. En-suite or private bathroom. Television, tea/coffee facilities.
B&B from £27pp, Dinner from £9.95, Rooms 1 single, 1 twin, 1 family, 2 en-suite, Restricted smoking, Children & pets welcome, Open all year except Christmas & New Year.
Sheila & Peter Crowland, **The Ugly Bug Inn,** High House Farm Lane, Colton, Norwich, Norfolk NR9 5DG
Tel: 01603 880794 Fax: 01603 880909   **Map Ref 32**

OLD RECTORY, an old Victorian rectory with bedroom extension, set amidst 3.5 acres of mature trees. Well placed for the Broads and 5 miles from Norwich. Homely accommodation.

B&B from £36, Dinner available, Rooms 6 twin, 5 double, 2 family, all en-suite, No smoking, Children welcome, Open all year.
Old Rectory, North Walsham Road, Crostwick, Norwich, Norfolk NR12 7BG
Tel: 01603 738513 Fax: 01603 738712   **Map Ref 33**

THE OLD RECTORY, a beautifully renovated and extended 17th century house set in 2 acres of garden adjacent to Saxon church of St. Andrews. Convenient for Broads and Norfolk/Suffolk coasts. Situated in beautiful countryside 4.5 miles south of the historic city of Norwich. Visitor's lounge with wood burner and a wealth of beams. Ample parking.

B&B from £20pp, Rooms 1 double/family, 1 twin, No smoking, Children welcome, no pets, Open all year.
The Old Rectory, Hall Road, Framingham Earl, Norwich NR14 7SB
Tel: 01508 493590   **Map Ref 34**

NORWICH SPORT VILLAGE HOTEL, situated on outer Norwich ring road on the A1067. Providing sports facilities, including tennis, squash, badminton, snooker, health centre, sauna and £4.5m Aquapark. Three bars and three restaurants. Many facilities free to residents.
B&B from £45, Dinner available, Rooms 42 twin, 11 double, 2 family, all en-suite, No smoking, Children welcome, Open all year.
Norwich Sport Village Hotel, Drayton High Road, Hellesdon, Norwich, Norfolk NR6 5DU
Tel: 01603 789469 Fax: 01603 406845   **Map Ref 35**

BECKLANDS, quietly located modern house overlooking open countryside. 5 miles north of Norwich. Central for the Broads and coastal areas.
B&B from £18, Rooms 4 single, 2 twin, 3 double, most en-suite, Children welcome, No pets, Open all year.
Becklands, 105 Holt Road, Horsford, Norwich, Norfolk NR10 3AB
Tel: 01603 898582 & 898020 Fax: 01603 891649   **Map Ref 36**

REGENCY GUEST HOUSE, 17th century property in picturesque Broads village. Generous English breakfast. Laura Ashley decorated rooms with TV and tea/coffee. Oak panelled breakfast room. Ideal for rambles, cycling, bird watching and boating. 6 miles coast, 10 miles Norwich. Self catering cottage available.
B&B from £19pp, Dinner from £5, Rooms 2 twin, 2 double, 1 family, some en-suite, Restricted smoking, Children & pets welcome, Open all year.
Sue & Alan Wrigley, **Regency Guest House,** The Street, Neatishead, Norwich, Norfolk NR12 8AD
Tel: 01692 630233   **Map Ref 37**

ELM FARM COUNTRY HOUSE. recently refurbished chalet accommodation in attractive village of Horsham St. Faith. En-suite rooms with colour television, radio alarms, hair dryers, tea/coffee facilities. Ample parking. Guests lounge. English breakfasts, coffee, lunches, afternoon tea. Residents license. Dining room in the 17th century farm house.
B&B from £28pp, Rooms 3 single, 6 twin, 6 double, 1 family, all en-suite, Restricted smoking, Children welcome, No pets, Open all year.
Maurice & Pam Parkerbrown, **Elm Farm Country House,** 55 Norwich Road, St. Faith, Norwich, Norfolk NR10 3HH
Tel: 01603 898366 Fax: 01603 897129   **Map Ref 38**

THE OLD RECTORY, a delightful Georgian house in an acre of gardens overlooking the Yare valley. Personally run by the owners who offer traditional hospitality in a friendly atmosphere.
B&B from £55, Dinner available, Rooms 1 twin, 7 double, all en-suite, No smoking, Open all year.
The Old Rectory, 103 Yarmouth Road, Thorpe St Andrew, Norwich, Norfolk NR7 0HF
Tel: 01603 700772   **Map Ref 39**

THE OLD RAM COACHING INN, a 17th century coaching inn (15 miles south of Norwich) with oak beams and log fires. En-suite accommodation and extensive menu.
B&B from £49, Dinner available, Rooms 8 double, 2 family, all en-suite, No smoking, Children welcome, No pets, Open all year.
The Old Ram Coaching Inn, Ipswich Road, Tivetshall St Mary, Norwich, Norfolk NR15 2DE
Tel: 01379 676794 Fax: 01379 608399   **Map Ref 40**

WESTWOOD BARN, outstanding accommodation, all on ground floor level. All rooms en-suite with TV, tea/coffee facilities. Beautiful four poster bedded room. Building of historical interest. ETB Highly Commended. Two miles from the picturesque village of Heydon, Norwich, coast, Broads, National Trust properties within 12 miles radius.
B&B from £22pp, Dinner from £16, Rooms 1 twin, 2 double, all en-suite, Restricted smoking, Children welcome, No pets, Open all year.
Geoffrey & Sylvia Westwood, **Westwood Barn,** Crabgate Lane South, Wood Dalling, Norwich, Norfolk NR11 6SW
Tel: 01263 584108   **Map Ref 41**

THE BAY LEAF GUEST HOUSE, a charming Victorian guesthouse with licensed bar, open all year. Conveniently situated in the town. Near golf course and woodlands, adjacent to steam railway and 5 minutes from sea.

B&B from £17, Dinner available, Rooms 2 twin, 2 double, 2 triple, all en-suite, Children over 8, Open all year.
The Bay Leaf Guest House, 10 St Peters Road, Sheringham, Norfolk NR26 8QY
Tel: 01263 823779   **Map Ref 42**

BEAUMARIS HOTEL, a family run hotel established in 1947. Reputation for personal service and English cuisine. Quietly located close to beach, shops and golf club.

B&B from £30, Dinner available, Rooms 5 single, 7 twin, 10 double, all en-suite, Children welcome, Open March - December.

Beaumaris Hotel, 15 South Street, Sheringham, Norfolk NR26 8LL
Tel: 01263 822370 Fax: 01263 821421   **Map Ref 42**

....

OLIVEDALE GUESTHOUSE, a charming family home, close to town centre, sea and amenities. Ideal base for exploring this beautiful area. All rooms have colour TV, radio alarm and tea/coffee facilities.

B&B from £20, Rooms 1 single, 1 twin, 3 double, some en-suite, No smoking, Children over 10, No pets, Open all year.
Olivedale Guesthouse, 20 Augusta Street, Sheringham, Norfolk NR26 8LA
Tel: 01263 825871   **Map Ref 42**

....

THE NORMANS, listed Georgian house 100 yards from the quay. All rooms en-suite with colour TV and tea/coffee. Some rooms have views over salt marshes to the sea.

B&B from £30, Rooms 1 twin, 5 double, 1 triple, most en-suite, No smoking, Children over 10, Open all year.
The Normans, Invaders Court, Standard Road, Wells next the Sea, Norfolk NR23 1JW
Tel: 01328 710657 Fax: 01328 710468   **Map Ref 43**

....

THE OLD RECTORY, this fascinating house dating from 17th century set in beautiful grounds of 5 acres. Large bedrooms, double with huge canopied brass bedstead, twin room/private bathroom, very attractive. Both have colour TV, tea/coffee facilities. All with a friendly family atmosphere.

B&B from £20pp, Dinner from £12.50, Rooms 1 twin, 1 double, all en-suite, Restricted smoking, Children welcome, Pets by arrangement, Open all year except Christmas & New Year.
Jo & Giles Winter, The Old Rectory, Wood Norton, Norfolk NR20 5AZ
Tel: 01362 683785   **Map Ref 44**

....

THE BROADS HOTEL, a family hotel in the heart of Broadland, 2 minutes from shops, boat hire and fishing. Ideal touring base for the coast and the city of Norwich.

B&B from £35, Dinner available, Rooms 7 single, 17 double, 3 twin, 1 family, all private facilities, No smoking, Children welcome, Open all year.

The Broads Hotel, Station Road, Wroxham, Norfolk NR12 8UR
Tel: 01603 782869 Fax: 01603 784066   **Map Ref 45**

....

ABBEY HOTEL, a quiet location opposite 12th century abbey. Character Victorian town house with friendly, relaxed atmosphere. Proprietor run with high rate of repeat business.

B&B from £60.45, Dinner available, Rooms 3 single, 10 double, 9 twin, 1 triple, all en-suite, Children welcome, Open all year.
Abbey Hotel, 10 Church Street, Wymondham, Norfolk NR18 0PH
Tel: 01953 602148 Fax: 01953 606247   **Map Ref 46**

....

WYMONDHAM CONSORT HOTEL, totally refurbished. Restaurant award. Walled gardens and secure private car parking.

B&B from £34, Dinner available, Rooms 5 single, 9 double, 5 twin, 1 triple, all en-suite, No smoking, Children welcome, Open all year.

Wymondham Consort Hotel, 28 Market Street, Wymondham, Norfolk NR18 0BB
Tel: 01953 606721 Fax: 01953 601361   **Map Ref 46**

Northumbria & County Durham

The former ancient kingdom on Northumbria now encompasses 4 counties - Northumberland, Tyne and Wear, Durham and Cleveland - and each has its own unique identity. Excellent motorways and trunk roads link the region with the rest of Britain. The area has wild National Parks and a spectacular coastline with high cliffs, castles and golden beaches. Northumbria's miles of unspoilt beaches are guarded by a string of fortresses built hundreds of years ago that bear witness to the area's violent past. England's most Northerly town, Berwick-upon-Tweed boasts a compelling history. The town changed hands fourteen times as the English and Scots fought to control the border.

Lindisfarne Castle on Holy Island was built in the mid 1500's and was given to the National Trust in 1944. Holy Island is set apart from the mainland and is accessible at low tides by a causeway. The village of Bamburgh is dominated by its castle, which dates from the twelfth century when it was the capital of the region ruled by the Saxon Kings. The nearby town of Seahouses is the embarkation point for the Farne Islands, a collection of twenty eight islands, some only visible at low tide. Inner Farne became a retreat for St Aidan and St Cuthbert and chapel remains can still be seen there. The eerie ruin of Dunstanburgh Castle can be seen from the fishing village of Craster. There are popular resorts at Tynemouth and Whitley Bay, which both have stretches of golden sands and leisure facilities. The ancient market town of Alnwick grew up around its castle, erected in the tenth century as a defence against the Scots. It is not surprising that the area is peppered with battle sites. Otterburn was the site of one of the most desperate border battles immortalised in the Ballad of Chevy Chase in 1388. History goes back even further the Roman times with Hadrian's Wall. Large sections of the wall built nearly two thousand years ago remain with the surrounding moors and valleys forming a stunning backdrop.

The Cheviot Hills form the backbone of Northumberland and make up the Northumberland National Park, popular with ornithologists, ramblers and archaeologists. South of the River Tyne, one of the area's main rivers, is the rural district of Weardale, once governed by the wealthy and all powerful Prince Bishops, who assumed the role when William the Conqueror declared Durham a palatinate. The River Tees rises at Cross Fell and courses down to Middleton-in-Teesdale. Teesdale's scenery has been recognised by its inclusion in the North Pennines Area of Outstanding Natural Beauty. High Force, in upper Teesdale, drops seventy feet over the Great Whin Sill. Barnard Castle is the gateway to Teesdale and has associations with the present royal family. Darlington is known as the birthplace of the railway and George Stephenson's steam engine Locomotion 1 can be seen at the Railway Museum in North Road.

left, Part of the town at Beamish Open Air Museum

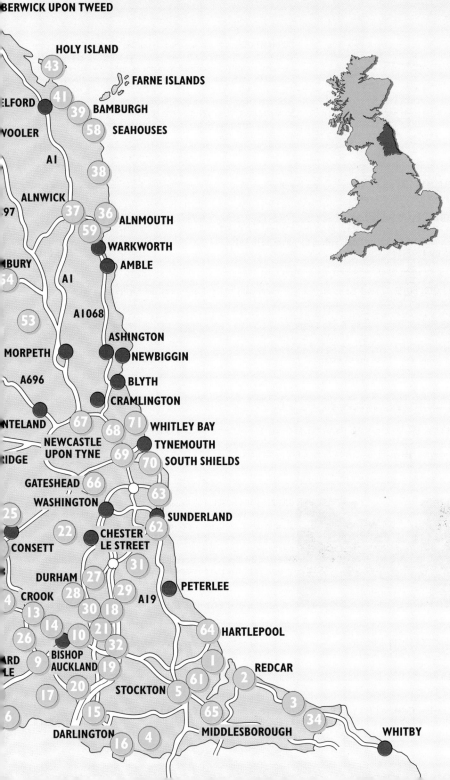

BERWICK UPON TWEED

HOLY ISLAND

43

FARNE ISLANDS

41

ELFORD

39 BAMBURGH

WOOLER

58 SEAHOUSES

A1

38

ALNWICK

97

37 36 ALNMOUTH

59

WARKWORTH

BURY

AMBLE

54

A1

A1068

53

ASHINGTON

MORPETH

NEWBIGGIN

A696

BLYTH

CRAMLINGTON

NTELAND

67 68 71 WHITLEY BAY

NEWCASTLE UPON TYNE

69 TYNEMOUTH

RIDGE

70 SOUTH SHIELDS

GATESHEAD 66

WASHINGTON

63

25

SUNDERLAND

22

62

CONSETT

CHESTER LE STREET

DURHAM 27

31

CROOK 28

29 PETERLEE

4

A19

13

30 18

14

26

10

64 HARTLEPOOL

ARD

21

LE

9

32

BISHOP AUCKLAND

19

1

20

REDCAR

17

61 2

15

5

65

3

6

34

DARLINGTON

MIDDLESBOROUGH

WHITBY

16 4

DURHAM HOTEL, a family run hotel on seafront location. Noted for good food and friendly service. All rooms have central heating and colour TV. En-suites available. Tea/coffee available in guest TV lounge. Ideally situated for many leisure activities including Hartlepool's Historic Quay, Marina golfing and fishing.

B&B from £15pp, Dinner from £4.50, Rooms 5 single, 4 twin, 5 double, 2 family, some en-suite, Children welcome, Open all year except Christmas & New Year. Mrs N Bell, **Durham Hotel,** 38/39 The Front, Seaton Carew, Hartlepool, Cleveland TS25 1DA
Tel: 01429 236502   **Map Ref 1**

FALCON HOTEL, a licenced hotel in the centre of town with new extension of en-suite twins and singles. Within easy reach of the Cleveland Hills.

B&B from £16, Dinner available, Rooms 8 single, 7 twin, 1 triple, 3 family, some en-suite, Children welcome, Open all year.

Falcon Hotel, 13 Station Road, Redcar, Cleveland TS10 1AH
Tel: 01642 484300   **Map Ref 2**

CLAXTON HOTEL, a hotel facing the sea with traditionally-styled dining room and bar featuring huge inglenook fireplace.

B&B from £20, Dinner available, Rooms 3 single, 3 double, 18 twin, 1 family, most en-suite, Children welcome, Open all year.

Claxton Hotel, 196 High Street, Redcar, Cleveland TS10 3AW
Tel: 01642 486745 Fax: 01642 486522   **Map Ref 2**

WATERSIDE HOUSE, large terraced property overlooking the sea, close to town centre and leisure centre. Warm, friendly atmosphere with true Yorkshire hospitality.

B&B from £14, Dinner available, Rooms 2 single, 3 triple, 1 family, Children welcome, Open all year.

Waterside House, 35 Newcomen Terrace, Redcar, Cleveland TS10 1DB
Tel: 01642 481062   **Map Ref 2**

GRINKLE PARK HOTEL, a 19th century country house hotel set in 35 acres of parkland. The hotel comprises of 20 individually decorated bedrooms all with private facilities. Welcoming hall area with open fire. Recently refurbished bedrooms. Bar area. Full size snooker table. Outdoor tennis court. Open to non residents.

B&B from £45.50pp, Dinner from £19.50, Rooms 5 single, 6 twin, 9 double, all en-suite, Children welcome, Pets by arrangement, Open all year. Mrs Jane Norton, **Grinkle Park Hotel,** Easington, Saltburn-by-the-Sea, Cleveland TS13 5UB
Tel: 01287 640515 Fax: 01287 641278   **Map Ref 3**

SUNNYSIDE HOTEL, a friendly, family hotel, ideal for touring Cleveland and North Yorkshire, with easy access to main roads, the station and Teeside Airport.

B&B from £25, Lunch & evening meal available, Rooms 7 single, 11 double, 3 twin, 2 triple, all en-suite, Children welcome, Open all year.

Sunnyside Hotel, 580-582 Yarm Road, Eaglescliffe, Stockton-on-Tees, Cleveland TS16 0DF
Tel: 01642 780075 Fax: 01642 783789   **Map Ref 4**

PARKMORE HOTEL & LEISURE CLUB, a warm, friendly hotel with leisure club, opposite golf course near Yarm. Ideal for visiting North York Moors, the dales, Durham and York.

B&B from £50, Lunch & evening meal available, Rooms 18 single, 18 double, 16 twin, 3 triple, all en-suite, Children welcome, No smoking Restaurant, Open all year.
Parkmore Hotel & Leisure Club, 636 Yarm Road, Eaglescliffe, Stockton-on-Tees, Cleveland TS16 0DH
Tel: 01642 786815 Fax: 01642 790485 **Map Ref 4**

HOTEL FORMULE 1, the benchmark in very reasonably-priced hotels (300 hotels in Europe), functional rooms (washbasin, TV,desk), one single price (£22.50) for up to 3 people. Close by, comfortable showers and toilets are equipped with a self-cleaning system. A continental breakfast costs £2.50.
£22.50 per room (up to 3 people), Breakfast £2.50, Rooms 64* (1 double bed and a bunk bed), Children welcome, Open all year.
Mr & Mrs Vieira, **Hotel Formule 1,** Teesway, North Tees. Ind. Estate, Stockton-on-Tees, Cleveland TS18 2RT
Tel: 01642 606 560 **Map Ref 5**

TREVELYAN COLLEGE

TREVELYAN COLLEGE, set in parkland within easy walking distance of Durham City. Comfortable Cloister Bar, TV lounges, ample car parking, Standard and en-suite rooms available. Email: trev.coll@dur.ac.uk

B&B from £18.50, Lunch & evening meal available, Rooms 261 single, 27 twin, some en-suite, Children welcome, No pets, Open January, March-April, June - September, December.

Trevelyan College, Elvet Hill Road, County Durham DH1 3LN
Tel: 0191 374 3765 & 374 3768 Fax: 0191 374 3789 **Map Ref 27**

THE MORRITT ARMS HOTEL, a hidden gem, twixt Yorkshire and Durham Dales. Charming 17th century inn. Private gardens, good food, log fires, cosy lounges real. Excellent walking.

B&B from £49.50, Lunch & evening meal available, Rooms 3 single, 11 double, 4 twin, Children welcome, No smoking, Open all year.

The Morritt Arms Hotel, Greta Bridge, Rokeby, Barnard Castle County Durham DL12 9SE
Tel: 01833 627232 Fax: 01833 627392 **Map Ref 6**

MONTALBO HOTEL, a small, family-run hotel offering attractive and comfortable bedrooms at reasonable prices. Excellent choice of food served every evening.

B&B from £25, Lunch & evening meal available, Rooms 2 single, 2 double, 2 twin, 1 triple, all en-suite, Children welcome, No smoking, open all year.
Montalbo Hotel, Montalbo Road, Barnard Castle, County Durham DL12 8BP
Tel: 01833 637342 Fax: 01833 637342 **Map Ref 7**

TEESDALE HOTEL, a tastefully modernised, family-run 18th century coaching inn serving home cooking and fine wines. All rooms with telephone, radio and TV. Also 4 comfortable holiday cottages in hotel courtyard. Dogs welcome free of charge.

B&B from £38.50, Lunch & evening meal available, Rooms 2 single, 5 double, 3 twin, all en-suite, Children welcome, Open all year.

Teesdale Hotel, Middleton-in-Teesdale, Barnard Castle, County Durham DL12 0QG
Tel: 01833 640264 & 640537 Fax: 01833 640651 **Map Ref 8**

WHEATSIDE HOTEL, a popular, friendly, family-run hotel in beautiful countryside on the main scenic route to Scotland. A warm welcome awaits you.

B&B from £32, Lunch & evening meal available, Rooms 6 single, 4 double, 2 twin, all en-suite, Children welcome, No pets, Open all year.
Wheatside Hotel, Bildershaw Bank, West Auckland, Bishop Auckland, County Durham DL14 9PL
Tel: 01388 832725 & 832485   **Map Ref 9**

....

PARK HEAD HOTEL, an attractive family run hotel with en-suite bedrooms, half a mile north of Bishop Auckland and 6 miles south of Durham. Food served in restaurant, carvery and bar.

B&B from £48, Lunch & evening meal available, Rooms 8 single, 8 double, 13 twin, 4 triple, suites available, all en-suite, Children welcome, No smoking, Open all year.
Park Head Hotel, New Coundon, Bishop Aukland, County Durham DL14 8QB
Tel: 01388 661727   **Map Ref 10**

....

BEE COTTAGE FARM, a 46 acre livestock farm. 1.5 miles west of the A68, between Castleside and Tow Law. Unspoilt views. Ideally located for Beamish Museum and Durham. No smoking. Tea-room open 1-6pm.

B&B from £25, Lunch & evening meal available, Rooms 1 single, 3 double, 2 twin, 1 triple, 2 family, suites available, Children welcome, No smoking, Open all year.
 Bee Cottage Farm, Castleside, Consett, County Durham DH8 9HW
Tel: 01207 508224   **Map Ref 11**

....

LORD CREWE ARMS HOTEL, Originally Blanchland Abbey (built in the 13th century), now a hotel, reputedly with a delightful ghost. Set in the Derwent Valley and surrounded by Northumberland moors.

B&B from £80, Dinner available, Rooms 12 double, 6 twin, 2 triple, all en-suite, Children welcome, Open all year.
Lord Crewe Arms Hotel, Blanchland, Consett, County Durham DH8 9SP
Tel: 01434 675251 Fax: 01434 675337   **Map Ref 12**

....

HELME PARK HALL HOTEL, a comfortable, fully refurbished hotel with open fires and warm, welcoming atmosphere. In 5 acres of grounds, with spectacular views over the dales. A haven of peace and tranquillity.

B&B from £40, Lunch & evening meal available, Rooms 2 single, 7 double, 4 twin, all en-suite, Children welcome, No pets, Open all year.
Helme Park Hall Hotel, Fir Tree, Crook, County Durham DL13 4NW
Tel: 01388 730970 Fax: 01388 730970   **Map Ref 13**

....

KENSINGTON HALL HOTEL, a comfortable family-run hotel with lounge bar, restaurant and function suite. Excellent meals daily. South west of Durham on A690 to Crook.

B&B from £24, Lunch & evening meal available, Rooms 3 double, 4 twin, 2 triple, 1 family, all en-suite, Children welcome, No smoking, Open all year.
Kensington Hall Hotel, Kensington Terrace, Willington, Crook, County Durham DL15 0PJ
Tel: 01388 745071 Fax: 01388 745800   **Map Ref 14**

....

ALBERLADY GUEST HOUSE, a large Victorian house near the town centre. Short walking distance to Railway Museum. Within easy reach of 4 golf courses and leisure centre.

B&B from £13.50, Rooms 2 single, 3 twin, 1 triple, 1 family, Children welcome, Open all year.
Alberlady Guest House, 51 Corporation Road, Darlington, County Durham DL3 6AD
Tel: 01325 461449   **Map Ref 15**

THE CRICKETERS HOTEL, a small, family-run hotel close to the town centre. En suite rooms, friendly bar/lounge and restaurant for 50 people.

B&B from £30, Lunch & evening meal available, Rooms 4 single, 7 double, 4 twin, 1 triple, all en-suite, Children welcome No smoking, Open all year.
The Cricketers Hotel, 55 Parkgate, Darlington, County Durham DL1 1RR
Tel: 01325 384444   **Map Ref 15**

....

BALMORAL HOUSE, is a Victorian town house built in 1876. Tastefully decorated bedrooms with all amenities.

B&B from £20, Rooms 3 single, 1 double, 2 twin, 3 triple, Children welcome, No smoking, open all year.
Balmoral House, 63 Woodland Road, Darlington, County Durham DL3 7BQ
Tel: 01325 461908   **Map Ref 15**

....

GRANGE HOTEL, an imposing stately mansion built in 1804, once the home of Joseph Pease, first Quaker MP and promoter of early railways. Was also a convent from 1905 to 1975. Here we offer you the comfort and contentment of gracious living.

B&B from £25, Dinner available, Rooms 2 single, 2 double, 5 twin, 1 triple, all en-suite, Children welcome, No smoking, open all year.
Grange Hotel, South End, Coniscliffe Road, Darlington, County Durham DL3 7HZ
Tel: 01325 464555 Fax: 01325 464555   **Map Ref 15**

....

THE COACHMAN HOTEL, a comfortable family-run hotel close to the town centre, railway station and all leisure facilities. Easy access to the A1(M).

B&B from £29.50, Lunch & evening meal available, Rooms 7 single, 3 double, 8 twin, 1 triple,1 family, all en-suite, Children welcome, Open all year.
The Coachman Hotel, Victoria Road, Darlington, County Durham DL1 5JJ
Tel: 01325 286116 Fax: 01325 382796   **Map Ref 15**

....

NEWBUS ARMS HOTEL & RESTAURANT, a country house hotel of immense beauty, dating from 1610. Set in its own grounds, 3.5 miles from Darlington, between Hurworth and Neasham.

B&B from £49.50, Lunch & evening meal available, Rooms 3 single, 9 double, 4 twin, some en-suite, Children welcome, Open all year.
Newbus Arms Hotel & Restaurant, Newbus Arms, Neasham, Darlington, County Durham DL2 1PE
Tel: 01325 721071 Fax: 01325 721770   **Map Ref 16**

....

WALWORTH CASTLE HOTEL, a 12 century castle in 18 acres of lawns and woods, privately owned, offering comfort and food at modest prices. 3 miles west of Darlington off the A68.
B&B from £35, Lunch & evening meal available, Rooms 4 single, 23 double, 5 twin, 4 triple, all en-suite, Children welcome, open all year.
Walworth Castle Hotel, Walworth, Darlington, County Durham DL2 2LY
Tel: 01325 485470 Fax: 01325 462257   **Map Ref 17**

....

ASH HOUSE, a charming Victorian house situated on a quiet conservation village green. The elegant rooms furnished to a high standard, having lovely open views. Adjacent A1M motorway, junction 61, 8 minutes Durham city. Ideally placed between York and Edinburgh. Private parking. A warm welcome assured. Excellent value.

B&B from £18pp, Rooms 1 twin, 1 double, 1 family, Restricted smoking, Children welcome, Pets by arrangement, Open all year except Christmas & New Year.
Delia Slack, **Ash House,** 24 The Green, Cornforth, Durham DL17 9JH
Tel: 01740 654654   **Map Ref 18**

THE BURY GUEST HOUSE, tea/coffee and colour TV in all rooms. Close to pubs, clubs and town. Only a short distance from Trading Estate. Good home cooking and a friendly atmosphere. Large garden for sunbathing available. When possible we have BBQ's, all are welcome to join us.

B&B from £15pp, Dinner from £5, Rooms 4 single, 5 twin, Children over 6, No pets, Open all year.

Brenda & Harry Craggs, **The Bury Guest House,** 8-10 Bury Road, Newton Aycliffe, County Durham DL5 5DL
Tel: 01325 300203   **Map Ref 19**

....

REDWOTH HALL, a beautiful 17th century country house hotel, providing, excellent leisure and conference facilities. An ideal venue for business or pleasure.

B&B from £105, Lunch & evening meal available, Rooms 3 single, 35 double, 42 twin, 7 triple, 13 family, all en-suite, Children welcome, Non smoking bedrooms available, Open all year.
Redwoth Hall, Redworth, Newton Aycliffe, County Durham DL5 6NL
Tel: 01388 772442 Fax: 01388 775112   **Map Ref 20**

....

THE GABLES, Victorian House. Quite area. Off road parking. TV, tea/coffee in all rooms. Ground floor rooms. Near Durham City. Within easy reach Beamish Museum, Hadrians Wall, Metro Centre, Bowe's Museum, Weardale and Teesdale.

B&B from £15pp, Dinner from £10, Rooms 4 twin, 2 double, some en-suite, Restricted smoking, Children & Pets welcome, Open all year.
Terry & Norma Shortman, **The Gables,** 10 South View, Middlestone Moor, Spennymoor, County Durham DL16 7DF
Tel: 01388 817544   **Map Ref 21**

....

HARPERLEY HOTEL, a converted granary on the outskirts of Stanley, in the country park area close to the old water mill. Fishing and shooting can be arranged.

B&B from £30, Lunch & evening meal available, Rooms 2 single, 3 double, all en-suite, Children welcome, Open all year.

Harperley Hotel, Harperley, Stanley, County Durham DH9 9TY
Tel: 01207 234011   **Map Ref 22**

....

There is something special about **GREENWELLS FARM.** A friendly welcome for visitors to this 18th century Bann and Gingan. Beautifully furnished with antique oak and pine. En-suite rooms. Quality breakfasts, farm conservation. Central for Beamish, Durham, Barnard Castle and Dales. Good for cycling and walking. Email: greenwell@aol.com
B&B from £40pp, Dinner from £8.50, Rooms 1 single, 2 twin, 2 double, 1 family, all en-suite, Restricted smoking, Open all year except Christmas & New Year.
Mike & Linda Vickers, **Greenwells Farm,** Wolsingham, Tow Law, County Durham DL13 4PH
Tel: 01388 527248 Fax: 01388 526735   **Map Ref 24**

....

THE MANOR HOUSE INN, a small family-run inn, offering warm, comfortable,accommodation. Delicious food, ales and wines. Overlooking an Area of Outstanding Natural Beauty and Derwent reservoir.

B&B from £24, Lunch & evening meal available, Rooms 2 double, 1 twin, 1 family, Children welcome, No smoking, Open all year.

The Manor House Inn, Carterway Heads, Shotley Bridge, Consett, County Durham, DH8 9LX
Tel: 01207 255268   **Map Ref 25**

GREENHEAD COUNTRY HOUSE HOTEL, perfectly situated at the foot of Weardale, north-west of Bishop Auckland. Surrounded by open fields and woodland yet only 15 minutes from Durham City. Its tranquillity is enhanced as only private resident guests are catered for - no public bars or discos.

B&B from £40, Dinner available, Rooms 1 single, 3 double, 2 twin, all en-suite, Children from 13 years, No pets, Open all year.

Greenhead Country House Hotel, Fir Tree, Crook, County Durham, DL15 8BL
Tel: 01388 763143 Fax: 01388 763143   **Map Ref 26**

....

DRUMFORKE, near the city centre and providing a useful base for touring the beautiful dales of Weardale and Teesdale.

B&B from £20, Rooms 2 twin, 1 triple, Children from 1 year, Open all year.
Drumforke, 25 Crossgate Peth, Durham DH1 4PZ
Tel: 0191 384 2966   **Map Ref 27**

....

CASTLE VIEW GUEST HOUSE, a 250 year old listed building in the heart of the old city, with woodland and riverside walks and a magnificent view of the cathedral and castle.

B&B from £38, Rooms 1 single, 3 double, 2 twin, all en-suite, Children welcome, No pets, No smoking, Open all year.
Castle View Guest House, 4 Crossgate, Durham DH1 4PS
Tel: 0191 386 8852 Fax: 0191 386 8852   **Map Ref 27**

....

BEES COTTAGE GUEST HOUSE, Durham's oldest cottage, in the city centre and convenient for shops, rail and bus. Hospitality tray, English or vegetarian breakfast, early morning call. All rooms en-suite with TV. No smoking, please. private parking.

B&B from £36, Rooms 1 double, 2 twin, 1 triple, all en-suite, Children welcome, No pets, No smoking, Open all year.

Bees Cottage Guest House, Bridge Street, Durham DH1 4RT
Tel: 0191 348 5775   **Map Ref 27**

....

QUEENS HEAD HOTEL, is under a mile away from the city centre in a main road position. bar with pool and darts, beer garden.

B&B from £18, Lunch available, Rooms 1 single, 3 double, 3 twin, 1 triple, 1 family, Children welcome, No pets, Open all year.
Queens Head Hotel, Gilesgate, Durham DH1 2JR
Tel: 0191 386 5649   **Map Ref 27**

....

THREE TUNS HOTEL, was originally a coaching inn, the hotel has been tastefully modernised to provide first-class facilities. Within easy walking distance of the magnificent Norman Cathedral. Short break packages available.

B&B from £39, Lunch & evening meal available, Rooms 15 single, 12 double, 18 twin, 1 triple, Suite available, all en-suite, Children welcome, No smoking, Open all year.
Three Tuns Hotel, New Elvet, Durham DH1 3AQ
Tel: 0191 386 4326 Fax: 0191 386 1406   **Map Ref 27**

....

ROYAL COUNTY HOTEL, situated in the heart of this cathedral city. Steeped in history the hotel is very well appointed. Choice of restaurants and superbly equipped leisure club.

B&B from £95, Lunch & evening meal available, Rooms 35 single, 56 double, 55 twin, 4 family, suite available, all en-suite, Children welcome, No smoking, Open all year.
Royal County Hotel, Old Elvet, Durham DH1 3JN
Tel: 0191 386 6821 Fax: 0191 386 0704   **Map Ref 27**

BAY HORSE INN, ten stone chalets 3 miles from Durham city centre. All have shower, toilet, TV, tea/coffee making facilities and telephone. Ample car parking.

B&B from £31, Lunch & evening meal available, Rooms 3 double, 6 twin, 1 family, all en-suite, Children welcome, No smoking, Open all year.
Bay Horse Inn, Brandon Village, Durham DH7 8ST
Tel: 0191 378 0498   **Map Ref 28**

....

BOWBURN HALL HOTEL, a large country house set in 5 acres of private grounds, 3 miles from Durham City.

B&B from £50, Lunch & evening meal available, Rooms 4 single, 11 double, 4 twin, all en-suite, Children welcome, Open all year.

Bowburn Hall Hotel, Bowburn, Durham DH6 5NH
Tel: 0191 377 0311 Fax: 0191 377 3459   **Map Ref 29**

....

HILL RISE GUEST HOUSE, conveniently placed 200 yards from A1(M). Family, twin and double rooms with en-suite facilities. Quality home cooked evening meals available.

B&B from £18, Dinner available, Rooms 2 single, 1 twin, 2 triple, 1 family, some en-suite, Children welcome, No pets, Open all year.
Hill Rise Guest House, 13 Durham Road West, Bowburn, Durham DH6 5AU
Tel: 0191 377 0302 Fax: 0191 377 0302   **Map Ref 29**

....

REDHILLS HOTEL, a small, friendly hotel with well-appointed bedrooms and personal service, only 2 minutes from Durham city centre.

B&B from £20, Lunch & evening meal available, Rooms 5 single, 1 double, Children welcome, Open all year.
Redhills Hotel, Redhills Lane, Crossgate Moor, Durham DH1 4AW
Tel: 0191 386 4331 Fax: 0191 386 9612   **Map Ref 27**

....

CROXDALE INN, a recently refurbished family-run hotel, 3 miles south of the city. Spacious bedrooms, all with private facilities, satellite TV, telephone and hair dryer. Four poster suite with sauna and jacuzzi. Restaurant serving home cooked food.

B&B from £28, Lunch & evening meal available, Rooms 4 single, 4 double, 3 twin, 1 triple, all en-suite, Children welcome,Open all year.

Croxdale Inn, Croxdale, Durham DH6 5HX
Tel: 01388 815727 & 420294 Fax: 01388 815368   **Map Ref 30**

....

HALLGARTH MANOR HOTEL, is a country house hotel in 4 acres of grounds. Restaurant, lounge, cocktail bar. Attractively furnished.

B&B from £48, Lunch & evening meal available, Rooms 4 single, 13 double, 6 twin, all en-suite, Children welcome, Open all year.
Hallgarth Manor Hotel, Pittington, Durham DH6 1AB
Tel: 0191 372 1188 Fax: 0191 372 1249   **Map Ref 31**

....

EDEN ARMS SWALLOW HOTEL, a 17th century coaching inn with leisure club, 10 miles south of Durham city. Ideal base for visiting Durham and the Tees Valley. Short break packages available.

B&B from £80, Lunch & evening meal available, Rooms 13 single, 20 double, 8 twin, 4 triple,all en-suite, Children welcome, No smoking, Open all year.

Eden Arms Swallow Hotel, Rushyford, Durham DL17 0LL
Tel: 01388 720541 Fax: 01388 721871   **Map Ref 32**

376

HADRIAN LODGE, a conversion of a single storey hunting/fishing lodge. In 18 acres with trout lake, near Housesteads Roman Fort and Hadrians Wall. Cosy residents' bar, tea-room/lounge, Brochure available.

B&B from £15, Dinner available, Rooms 1 single, 1 double, 1 twin, 1 triple, 1 family, Children welcome, No pets, Open all year.
Hadrian Lodge, Hindshield Moss, North Road, Haydon Bridge, Hexham NE47 6NF
Tel: 01434 688688 Fax: 01434 684867   **Map Ref 33**

....

ANCHOR HOTEL, a riverside inn, set in a village close to the Roman Wall. Ideal centre for touring the North Pennines and Northumberland National park.

B&B from £36, Lunch & evening meal available, Rooms 5 double, 3 twin, 2 triple, all en-suite, Children welcome, No smoking, Open all year.
Anchor Hotel, John Martin Street, Haydon Bridge, Hexham, Northumberland NE47 6AB
Tel: 01434 684227 Fax: 01434 684586   **Map Ref 33**

....

HUNLEY HALL GOLF CLUB & HOTEL, situated on the Captain Cook trail between Middlesborough and Whitby, with unrivalled coastal views.

B&B from £25, Lunch & evening meal available, Rooms 2 double, 5 twin, 1 triple, all en-suite, Children welcome, No pets, No smoking, Open all year.
Hunley Hall Golf Club & Hotel, Brotton, Saltburn-by-the-Sea, North Yorkshire TS12 2QQ
Tel: 01287 676216 Fax: 01287 678250   **Map Ref 34**

....

THORNLEY HOUSE, a beautiful country house in spacious grounds, 1 mile out of Allendale near Hadrian's wall. 3 bedrooms with facilities, tea/coffee makers. Home baking. Wonderful walks, maps provided. Vegetarian meals and packed lunches available. Bring your own wine.

B&B from £18.50pp, Dinner from £11, Rooms 1 twin, 2 double, all en-suite, No smoking, Children over 8, Pets by arrangement, Open all year.
Mrs Finn, **Thornley House,** Allendale, Northumberland NE47 9NH
Tel: 01434 683255   **Map Ref 35**

....

SADDLE HOTEL, personally supervised by the owners and offering a high standard of accommodation. Fourteen awards for food in seven years.

B&B from £30, Lunch & evening meal available, Rooms 4 double, 4 twin, 1 triple, all en-suite, Children welcome, Open all year.
Saddle Hotel, 24-25 Northumberland Street, Alnmouth, Alnwick, Northumberland NE66 2RA
Tel: 01665 830476   **Map Ref 36**

....

21 BOULMER VILLAGE, Traditional fishermans cottage overlooking the North sea in a working fishing village. Easy access.

B&B from £20, Rooms 1 double, 1 twin, both en-suite, Children welcome, No pets, No smoking, Open all year.
21 Boulmer Village, Alnwick, Northumberland NE66 3BS
Tel: 01665 577262   **Map Ref 37**

....

BONDGATE HOUSE HOTEL, a small family-run hotel near the medieval town gateway and interesting local shops. Well placed for touring. Most rooms and en-suite.

B&B from £24, Dinner available, Rooms 1 single, 2 double, 2 twin, 2 triple, 1 family, some en-suite, Children welcome, No pets, Open all year.
Bondgate House Hotel, 20 Bondgate Without, Alnwick, Northumberland NE66 1PN
Tel: 01665 602025   **Map Ref 37**

WHITE SWAN HOTEL, a former coaching inn, partly traditional with log fire in the cosy reception are/lounge. Groups welcome.

B&B from £65, Lunch & evening meal available, Rooms 4 single, 14 double, 36 twin, 1 triple, 3 family, all en-suite, Children welcome, No smoking, Open all year.
White Swan Hotel, Bondgate Within, Alnwick, Northumberland NE66 1TD
Tel: 01665 602109 Fax: 01665 510400   **Map Ref 37**

HOTSPUR HOTEL, originally a coaching inn, centrally located, offering a warm welcome and friendly hospitality. Tastefully furnished bedrooms, all en-suite. High standard of food, fine ales.

B&B from £30, Lunch & evening meal available, Rooms 2 single, 9 double, 11 twin, 1 family, most en-suite, Children welcome, No pets, Open all year.
Hotspur Hotel, Bondgate Without, Alnwick, Northumberland NE66 1PR
Tel: 01665 510101 Fax: 01665 605033   **Map Ref 37**

THE SPORTSMAN, a family run hotel, recently refurbished. Includes dormitory facilities for golfing parties, etc. Bar meals available.

B&B from £20, Lunch & evening meal available, Rooms 2 single, 1 double, 2 twin, 1 triple, 3 family, some en-suite, Children from 2 years, No pets, Open all year.
The Sportsman, Embleton, Alnwick, Northumberland NE66 3XF
Tel: 01665 576588 Fax: 01665 576524   **Map Ref 38**

EAST FARM HOUSE, a grade II listed building in this tranquil coastal village whose beach and golf course are outstanding. Quality B&B and devotion to their guests' comfort have generated a loyal clientele - now better served by the conversion of a stable block to a private licensed dining room.
B&B from £15.50pp, Dinner from £17.50, Rooms 2 twin, 1 double, No smoking, Children over 11, No pets, Open March - October.
Sara & Keith East Farm House, Embleton, Alnwick, Northumberland NE66 3XU
Tel: 01665 576653 Fax: 01665 576727   **Map Ref 38**

THE GREENHOUSE- Seven bedroomed Guest House on main street in the quiet coastal village of Bamburgh. All rooms en-suite with complimentary hot drinks tray, some rooms with colour TV. Full Northumbrian breakfast included in price. A la Carte restaurant and licensed bar on premises, run by the owner/chef. Booking essential Peak season.
B&B from £19.95pp, Dinner from £14, Rooms 1 twin, 4 double, 2 king size, all en-suite, No smoking or children, Pets by arrangement, Open March - December.
Jan Chattaway The Greenhouse, 5-6 Front Street, Bamburgh, Northumberland NE69 7BW
Tel: 01668 214513   **Map Ref 39**

MIZEN HEAD HOTEL, a privately-owned, fully licenced hotel in own ground, with accent on good food and service. Convenient for beaches, castle and golf. 2 minutes' walk from the village centre.

B&B from £22.50, Lunch & evening meal available, Rooms 2 single, 5 double, 4 twin, 4 family, most en-suite, Children welcome, Open all year.

Mizen Head Hotel, Lucker Road, Bamburgh, Northumberland NE 69 7BS
Tel: 01668 214254   **Map Ref 39**

VALLUM LODGE HOTEL, a comfortable cottage style hotel in quiet countryside by Hadrian's Wall. Renowned for choice of excellent food and good home cooking. Lounge with TV. Residents bar. Lovely rooms with tea/coffee facilities and clock/radio. Garden. Large car park. Central for touring or walking.

B&B from £21pp, Dinner from £15, Rooms 1 single, 3 twin, 3 double, 4 en-suite, Restricted smoking, Pets by arrangement, Open March - October.

Jack & Christine Wright, **Vallum Lodge Hotel,** Military Road, Twice Brewed, Bardon Mill, Northumberland NE47 7AN
Tel: 01434 344248 Fax: 01434 344488 **Map Ref 40**

....

WAREN HOUSE HOTEL, a traditional, beautifully restored, award winning country house in 6 acres overlooking Holy Island. Quality accommodation and food, 250+ bin win list. Adults only.

B&B from £55, Dinner available, Rooms 6 double, 3 twin, suites available, No children, No smoking, Open all year.

Waren House Hotel, Waren Mill, Belford Northumberland NE70 7EE
Tel: 01668 214581 Fax: 01668 214484 **Map Ref 41**

....

RIVERDALE HALL HOTEL, a spacious country hall in large grounds. Indoor swimming pool, sauna, fishing, cricket field and golf opposite. Award winning hotel restaurant. The Cocker family's 20th year.

B&B from £40, Lunch & evening meal available, Rooms 3 single, 4 double, 9 twin, 4 triple, all en-suite, Children welcome, Open all year.

Riverdale Hall Hotel, Bellingham, Northumberland NE48 2JT
Tel: 01434 220254 Fax: 01434 220457 **Map Ref 47**

....

QUEENS HEAD HOTEL, near the town centre, opposite the swimming baths and adjacent to the historic town walls.

B&B from £30, Lunch & evening meal available, Rooms 1 single, 1 double, 2 twin, 2 triple, all en-suite, Children welcome, No smoking, open all year.

Queens Head Hotel, Sandgate, Berwick-upon-Tweed, Northumberland TD15 1EP
Tel: 01289 307852 Fax: 01289 307852 **Map Ref 42**

....

LINDISFARNE HOTEL, a small, comfortable, family-run hotel providing coffees, lunches and evening meals. An ideal place for ornithologists and within walking distance of Lindisfarne Castle and priory.

B&B from £16.50 Lunch & evening meal available, Rooms 2 single, 1 double, 1 twin, 3 triple, some en-suite, Children welcome, No pets, No smoking, Open all year.

Lindisfarne Hotel, Holy Island, Berwick-upon-Tweed, Northumberland TD15 2SQ
Tel: 01289 389273 Fax: 01289 389284 **Map Ref 43**

....

NORTH VIEW, a 400 year old listed building on historic and beautiful island. Ideally situated for visiting many or Northumberland's tourist attractions.

B&B from £25, Evening meal available, Rooms 2 double, 1 twin, all en-suite, No smoking, Open all year.

North View, Marygate, Holy Island, Berwick-upon-Tweed, Northumberland TD15 2SD
Tel: 01289 389222 **Map Ref 43**

Built in 1840 as the village school, **CLIVE HOUSE** offers lovely en-suite bedrooms one with 4-poster. All facilities including telephone. Only minutes walk from charming village centre. Near Hadrians Wall and an ideal break between York and Edinburgh. ETB 2 Crowns Highly Commended. No smoking house.
B&B from £24pp, Rooms 1 single, 2 double, all en-suite, No smoking, children or pets, Open March - November.
Ann Hodgson, **Clive House,** Appletree Lane, Corbridge, Northumberland NE45 5DN
Tel: 01434 632617   **Map Ref 44**

LION OF CORBRIDGE HOTEL, a family-run hotel on the bank of the River Tyne with emphasis on comfort and good food. Room on ground floor especially equipped for disabled.
B&B from £45, Lunch & evening meal available, Rooms 8 double, 6 twin, all en-suite, Children welcome, No pets, No smoking, Open all year.
Lion of Corbridge Hotel, Bridge End, Corbridge, Northumberland NE45 5AX
Tel: 01434 632504 Fax: 01434 632571   **Map Ref 44**

HAYES GUEST HOUSE, a spacious guest house with single, double and family rooms, tea/coffee facilities, stair lift. Guests television lounge. Large garden. Car parking. Pay-phone. 1 Crown approved. Also self catering accommodation. Hadrians Wall country, Kielder Water, Metro Centre within easy reach.
B&B from £16.50pp, Rooms 2 single, 2 twin, 1 double/family, Restricted smoking, Children welcome, Pets by arrangement, Open January - mid December.
Miss G Matthews, **Hayes Guest House,** Newcastle Road, Corbridge, Northumberland NE45 5LP
Tel: 01434 632010   **Map Ref 44**

FOX & HOUNDS HOTEL, a 400 year old coaching inn with a 70 seat conservatory restaurant. Owners operate and live on premises.

B&B from £30, Lunch & evening meal available, Rooms 1 single, 3 double, 3 twin, 1 triple, all en-suite, Children welcome, No pets, Open all year.
Fox & Hounds Hotel, Stagshaw Bank, Corbridge, Northumberland NE45 5QW
Tel: 01434 633024 Fax: 01434 633024   **Map Ref 44**

THE SPOTTED COW INN, a traditional pub-restaurant with beamed ceilings, dating from 18th century, serving real ales and fresh food cooked to order. En-suite bedrooms with colour TV, tea/coffee facilities. Children welcome.
B&B from £20, Lunch & evening meal available, Rooms 2 double, 1 twin, all en-suite, Children welcome, No smoking, Open all year.
The Spotted Cow Inn, Castle Hill, Haltwhistle, Northumberland NE49 0EN
Tel: 01434 320327   **Map Ref 45**

MANOR HOUSE HOTEL, centrally situated in small town, very near the Roman Wall. Hotel over 400 years old. Recently refurbished.
B&B from £15, Lunch & evening meal available, Rooms 1 double, 4 twin, 1 family, some en-suite, Children welcome, No pets, Open all year.
Manor House Hotel, Main Street, Haltwhistle, Northumberland NE49 0BS
Tel: 01434 322588 & 320975   **Map Ref 45**

BARRASFORD ARMS, a small country hotel in this lovely hamlet, only 8 miles from Hexham and 4 miles to the Roman Wall. An ideal centre for touring Northumberland.

B&B from £20, Dinner available, Rooms 1 double, 3 twin, 1 triple, most en-suite, Children welcome, Open all year.
Barrasford Arms, Barrasford, Hexham, Northumberland NE48 4AA
Tel: 01434 681237   **Map Ref 46**

ETB 3 Crowns Highly Commended, RAC Acclaimed. **LYNDALE GUEST HOUSE** our pretty bungalow, between Hadrian's Wall and Kielder Lake with pleasant walled garden and sun lounge with panoramic views. Quality ground floor en-suite. Good food, good walking and quiet roads. National Park area. Cycle lock-up and private parking. http://www.smoothHound.co.uk/Hotels/Lyndale.html
B&B from £25pp, Dinner from £12.50, Rooms 1 double, 1 twin, 1 family, all en-suite, No smoking, Open all year.
Lyndale Guest House, Off The Square, Bellingham, Hexham, Northumberland NE48 2AW
Tel: 01434 220361   **Map Ref 47**

....

THE PHEASANT INN (BY KIELDER WATER), an historic inn with beamed ceilings and open fires. Home cooking. Fishing, riding and all water sports nearby. Close to Kielder Water, Hadrian's Wall and the Scottish border.

B&B from £22, Lunch & evening meal available, Rooms 4 double, 3 twin, 1 family, all en-suite, Children welcome, No smoking, Open all year.
The Pheasant Inn (by Kielder Water), Stannersburn, Falstone, Hexham, Northumberland NE48 1DD
Tel: 01434 240382   **Map Ref 48**

....

LANGLEY CASTLE, a 14th century castle restored to a magnificent and comfortable hotel. 2 miles south west of Haydon bridge, 30 minutes from Newcastle and 40 minutes from Newcastle Airport. A69-A686 junction.

B&B from £74.50, Lunch & evening meal available, Rooms 14 double, 2 twin, all en-suite, Children welcome, No smoking, Open all year.
Langley Castle, Langley-on-Tyne, Hexham, Northumberland NE47 5LU
Tel: 01434 688888 Fax: 01434 684019 Email: langleycastle@dial.pipex.com   **Map Ref 49**

....

RYE HILL FARM, offers you the freedom to enjoy the pleasures of Northumberland. En-suite bedrooms with large bath towels. A full English breakfast and optional 3 course dinner are served in the dining room with open log fire and a table licence. Telephone and tourist information in the reception lounge. Guests are invited to use the games room and look around the farm. Email: enquiries@courage.u-net.co
B&B from £20pp, Dinner from £12, Rooms 1 twin, 3 double, 2 family, all en-suite, Restricted smoking, Children & pets welcome, Open all year.
Elizabeth Courage, **Rye Hill Farm,** Slaley, Hexham, Northumberland NE47 0AH
Tel: 01434 673259 Fax: 01434 673608 m   **Map Ref 50**

....

STOTSFORD HALL, a beautiful house surrounded by 15 acres of gardens and woodland with streams and flowers. 6 miles south of Hexham.

B&B from £19.50, Rooms 2 single, 1 double, 1 twin, Children welcome, No pets, open all year.

Stotsford Hall, Steel, Hexham, Northumberland NE47 0HP
Tel: 01434 673270   **Map Ref 51**

....

BATTLESTEADS HOTEL, an 18th century inn, formerly a farmhouse, in the heart of rural Northumberland, close to the Roman Wall and Kielder Water. An ideal centre for exploring Border country and for relaxing.

B&B from £30, Lunch & evening meal available, Rooms 1 single, 3 double, 5 twin, 1 family, all en-suite, Children welcome, Open all year.

Battlesteads Hotel, Wark, Hexham, Northumberland NE48 3LS
Tel: 01434 230209 Fax: 01434 230730 Email: thebattlesteads@btinternet.com   **Map Ref 52**

LINDEN HALL HOTEL, a Georgian country house hotel, north of Morpeth, set in a 450 acre estate with extensive leisure facilities including an 18 hole golf course.
B&B from £97.50, Lunch & evening meal available, Rooms 2 single, 28 double, 20 twin, suites available, all en-suite, Children welcome, No smoking, Open all year.
Linden Hall Hotel, Longhorsley, Morpeth, Northumberland NE65 8XF
Tel: 01670 516611 Fax: 01670 788544   **Map Ref 53**

....

ORCHARD GUEST HOUSE, a charming guesthouse in the middle of a lovely village, an ideal centre for visiting all Northumbria's attractions. Comfortable surroundings.
B&B from £21, Rooms 2 double, 4 twin, some en-suite, Children welcome, No pets, Open March - October.
Orchard Guest House, High Street, Rothbury, Morpeth, Northumberland NE65 7TL
Tel: 01669 620684   **Map Ref 54**

....

SHEILDHALL, a charmingly restored 18th century farmhouse, centres around an attractive courtyard onto which each beautifully furnished guest suite and lounge open. Rooms are en-suite with TV's, coffee etc. The secret licensed bar opens before dinner, when local, seasonal produce is complimented by excellent English cooking.

B&B from £21pp, Dinner from £15, Rooms 1 single, 1 twin, 2 double, 1 family, Restricted smoking, Children over 10, Pets by arrangement, Open February - December.
Stephen & Celia Gay, **Sheildhall**, Wallington, Morpeth, Northumberland NE61 4AQ
Tel: 01830 540387   **Map Ref 55**

....

THE BUTTERCHURN GUEST HOUSE, in the village centre, on the River Rede. Central for Roman Wall and Kielder Water. Within easy reach of Northumberland coast. All rooms en-suite.
B&B from £22, Rooms 2 double, 2 twin, 3 triple, Children welcome, Open all year.
The Butterchurn Guest House, Main Street, Otterburn, Northumberland NE19 1NP
Tel: 01830 520585   **Map Ref 56**

....

REDESDALE ARMS HOTEL, a family-run old coaching inn, central for Hadrian' Wall and Kielder Forest. All rooms en-suite. Super home cooked food.
B&B from £36, Lunch & evening meal available, Rooms 3 double, 5 twin, 2 triple, all en-suite, Children welcome, No smoking, Open all year.
Redesdale Arms Hotel, Rochester, Otterburn, Northumberland NE19 1TA
Tel: 01830 520668 Fax: 01830 520063   **Map Ref 57**

....

OLDE SHIP INN, with a long established reputation for food and drink in comfortably relaxing old fashioned surroundings.
B&B from £30, Lunch & evening meal available, Rooms 1 single, 9 double, 5 twin, 1 triple, suites available, all en-suite, Children from 10 years, No pets, No smoking, Open February - November.
Olde Ship Inn, Seahouses, Northumberland NE68 7RD
Tel: 01665 720200 Fax: 01665 721383   **Map Ref 58**

....

BEACH HOUSE HOTEL, is situated on the Sea Front of this small fishing village, overlooking the Farne Islands. All rooms are en-suite and are equipped with tea/coffee makers and complimentary toiletries. Home cooking and baking from locally grown produce. Guests lounge. Lounge Bar. Car parking facilities. Colour TV in all rooms.
B&B from £25-£35pp, Dinner from £14.75, Rooms 2 single, 8 twin, 9 double, 6 family, all en-suite, No smoking or pets, Children welcome, Open February - December.
Malcolm & Hazel Brown, **Beach House Hotel,** Sea Front, 12A St. Aidans, Seahouses, Northumberland NE68 7SR
Tel: 01665 720337 Fax: 01665 720921   **Map Ref 58**

Dating back to the 17th century, **NORTH COTTAGE** offers substantial full breakfasts. Afternoon tea is served free on arrival. Bedrooms are on the ground floor and have tea/coffee facilities, electric blanket, clock radio and colour TV. The double and twin rooms are en-suite and the single room has a wash basin.

B&B from £20pp, Rooms 1 single, 1 twin, 2 double, most en-suite, No smoking, Children or pets, Open all year except Christmas & New Year.

John & Edith Howliston, **North Cottage,** Birling, Warkworth, Northumberland NE65 0EX

Tel: 01665 711263 **Map Ref 59**

LORETO GUEST HOUSE, a family-run early Georgian house in spacious grounds, in lovely Cheviot village. Central for touring and walking and close to coastline. All home cooking, all rooms en-suite.

B&B from £18, Dinner available, Rooms 1 single, 3 double, 1 twin, 1 family, all en-suite, Children welcome, Open all year.

Loreto Guest House, 1 Ryecroft Way, Wooler, Northumberland NE71 6BW

Tel: 01668 281350 **Map Ref 60**

TANKERVILLE ARMS HOTEL, a charming 17th century family owned coaching inn. All facilities, fine cuisine. Central for beautiful coast, National Trust properties and Scottish borders.

B&B from £45.50, Lunch & evening meal available, Rooms 2 single, 6 double, 6 twin, 1 triple, 1 family, all en-suite, Children welcome, Open all year.

Tankerville Arms Hotel, 22 Cottage Road, Wooler, Northumberland NE71 6AD

Tel: 01668 281581 Fax: 01668 281387 **Map Ref 60**

SWALLOW HOTEL, a smart, modern hotel in Stockton town centre, with Swallow Leisure Club, bar, restaurant and Brasserie. An ideal base for visiting the north east for business or pleasure. Short break packages available.

B&B from £95, Dinner available, Rooms 76 double, 49 twin, all en-suite, No smoking, Children welcome, Open all year.

Swallow Hotel, John Walker Square, High Street, Stockton on Tees, Cleveland, Northumbria TS18 1AQ

Tel: 01642 679721 Fax: 01642 601714 **Map Ref 61**

ANTHONY LODGE, a licensed family run guest house with easy access to town, buses and trains. Parking area to rear.

B&B from £16, Rooms 5 single, 1 double, 2 twin, No smoking, Children welcome, No pets, Open all year.

Anthony Lodge, 5 Brookside Terrace, Ashbrook, Sunderland, Northumbria SR2 7RN

Tel: 0191 567 7108 **Map Ref 62**

FELICITATIONS, refurbished, all rooms spacious with own hot and cold water. Family and single have own adjacent shower rooms, double has private bathroom with additional WCs. Large comfortable TV lounge/bar.

B&B from £18, Dinner available, Rooms 1 single, 1 double, 1 family, No smoking, Children over 5, No pets, Open all year.

Felicitations, 94 Ewesley Road, High Barnes, Sunderland, Northumbria SR4 7RJ

Tel: 0191 522 0960 & 551 8915 **Map Ref 62**

SWALLOW HOTEL, a highly commended hotel with leisure facilities and spectacular seaside location. Good base for seeing Northumbria's coastline and castles.

B&B from £90, Dinner available, Rooms 3 single, 36 double, 23 twin, 3 family, all en-suite, No smoking, Children welcome, Open all year.

Swallow Hotel, Queens Parade, Seaburn, Sunderland, Northumbria SR6 8DB

Tel: 0191 529 2041 Fax: 0191 529 4227 **Map Ref 62**

THE PULLMAN LODGE HOTEL, on the coast. Restaurant is in genuine Pullman carriages with sea view. Railway theme throughout. Large children's play area, family room.

B&B from £35, Dinner available, Rooms 8 twin, 8 family, all en-suite, Children welcome, Open all year.

The Pullman Lodge Hotel, Whitburn Road, Seaburn, Sunderland, Northumbria SR6 8AA
Tel: 0191 529 2020 Fax: 0191 529 2077   **Map Ref 62**

....

BRENDON HOUSE, all rooms have television, tea/coffee making and washing facilities. Private enclosed parking. Local attractions Gateshead Metro Centre and Arena, Beamish Museum, Durham Cathedral, Washington Old Hall, ancestral home of George Washington, Washington Wildfowl Park, National Glass Centre and Sunderland Stadium of Light.

B&B from £14pp, Dinner by arrangement, Rooms 1 single, 1 twin, 2 double, 3 family, Children & Pets welcome, Open all year.

Eileen Hughes, **Brendon House,** 49 Roker Park Road, Roker, Sunderland SR6 9PL
Tel: 0191 5489303   **Map Ref 63**

....

GRAND HOTEL, a traditional 19th century city centre hotel close to modern enclosed shopping centre. Extensively refurbished and on excellent base for visiting the Metro Centre, Beamish and Durham.

B&B from £49.50, Lunch & evening meal available, Rooms 14 single, 18 double, 13 twin, suites available, all en-suite, Children welcome, No smoking, Open all year.

Grand Hotel, Swainson Street, Hartlepool, Cleveland, Tees Valley TS24 8AA
Tel: 01429 266345 Fax: 01429 265217   **Map Ref 64**

....

BALTIMORE HOTEL, close to the heart of both commercial and residential Middlesbrough and 1 mile from the central station. Teesdale Airport 18 miles.

B&B from £36.75, Lunch & evening meal available, Rooms 18 single, 5 double, 7 twin, 1 triple, suite available, all en-suite Children welcome, open all year.

Baltimore Hotel, 250 Marton Road, Middlesbrough, Cleveland, Tees Valley TS4 2EZ
Tel: 01642 224111 Fax: 01642 226156   **Map Ref 65**

....

SHAFTESBURY HOUSE HOTEL, a charming, Victorian, family hotel. central for Metro centre, Newcastle City and Arena, Gateshead Stadium, Beamish and local transport. opposite Gateshead Leisure Centre. A1 to Gateshead (south), then A167.

B&B from £22, Dinner available, Rooms 2 double, 6 twin, 2 triple, Children welcome, No smoking, Open all year.

Shaftesbury House Hotel, 245 Prince Consort Road, Gateshead, Tyne & Wear NE8 4DT
Tel: 0191 478 2544 Fax: 0191 478 2544   **Map Ref 66**

....

SWALLOW HOTEL, a friendly hotel , 1 mile from Newcastle city centre just south of the River Tyne. Leisure complex incorporating pool, sauna, solarium and cardiovascular gym. Well placed for visiting the Metro Centre. Short break packages available.

B&B from £85, Lunch & evening meal available, Rooms 37 single, 29 double, 33 twin, 4 family, all en-suite, Children welcome, No smoking, Open all year.

Swallow Hotel, High West Street, Gateshead, Tyne & Wear NE8 1PE
Tel: 0191 477 1105 Fax: 0191 478 7214   **Map Ref 66**

SURTEES HOTEL, a city centre hotel within walking distance of Eldon Square, the quayside and station, with a 24 hour multi storey car park adjacent. Cocktail and public bar, restaurant and nightclub. All bedrooms are en-suite with satellite TV and tea-making facilities.

B&B from £57.50, Lunch & evening meal available, Rooms 12 single, 9 double, 6 twin, all en-suite, Children welcome, No pets, Open all year.

Surtees Hotel, 12-16 Dean Street, Newcastle-upon Tyne, Tyne & Wear NE1 1PG
Tel: 0191 261 7771 Fax: 0191 230 1322   **Map Ref 67**

....

SWALLOW GOSFORTH PARK HOTEL, a beautifully appointed hotel set in 12 acres of woodland, 5 miles north of city centre. Facilities include restaurants, bars, leisure complex and conference facilities. Short break packages available.

B&B from £70, Lunch & evening meal available, Rooms 110 double, 63 twin, 5 triple, Suites available, all en-suite, Children welcome, No smoking, Open all year.

Swallow Gosforth Park Hotel, High Gosforth Park, Newcastle-upon Tyne, Tyne & Wear NE3 5HN
Tel: 0191 236 4111 Fax: 0191 236 8192   **Map Ref 67**

....

IMPERIAL SWALLOW HOTEL, elegantly furnished, following recent major refurbishment. Traditionally styled bedrooms, cocktail bar and lounge, a fully equipped leisure club. Free car park. One mile from Newcastle city centre, 200 yards from Jesmond Metro Station. Short break packages available.

B&B from £75, Lunch & evening meal available, Rooms 53 single, 45 double, 18 twin, 3 triple, 3 family, all en-suite, Children welcome, No smoking, Open all year.

Imperial Swallow Hotel, Jesmond Road, Newcastle-upon Tyne, Tyne & Wear NE2 1PR
Tel: 0191 281 5511 Fax: 0191 281 8472   **Map Ref 67**

....

ROYAL STATION HOTEL, was opened by Queen Victoria in 1858, the hotel combines elegant Victorian architecture with up to date facilities. Fully refurbished, family-run. We take pride in offering a friendly and courteous service to all our clients.

B&B from £60, Lunch & evening meal available, Rooms 43 single, 42 double, 28 twin, 7 triple, 6 family, all en-suite, Children welcome, Open all year.

Royal Station Hotel, Neville Street, Newcastle-upon Tyne, Tyne & Wear NE1 5DH
Tel: 0191 232 0781 Fax: 0191 222 0786   **Map Ref 67**

....

THE COPTHORNE NEWCASTLE, set amidst the historic quayside, all bedrooms, restaurant, bars and leisure club pool overlook the river. Free on-site car parking.

B&B from £89, Lunch & evening meal available, Rooms 132 double, 24 twin, all en-suite, Children welcome, No smoking, Open all year.

The Copthorne Newcastle, The Close, Quayside, Newcastle-upon Tyne, Tyne & Wear NE1 3RT
Tel: 0191 222 0333 Fax: 0191 230 1111   **Map Ref 67**

....

WESTLAND HOTEL, is a well established hotel in a quiet residential area, convenient for city centre, coast, countryside and Gateshead Metro Centre.

B&B from £20, Rooms 11 single, 2 double, 2 triple, some en-suite, Children welcome, Open all year.

Westland Hotel, 27 Osbourne Avenue, Jesmond, Newcastle-upon Tyne, Tyne & Wear NE2 1JR
Tel: 0191 281 0412 Fax: 0191 281 5005   **Map Ref 68**

DENE HOTEL, set in a quiet residential area close to beautiful Jesmond Dene with its small children's zoo. Within easy reach of the city centre. Passenger lift.

B&B from £25.50, Lunch & evening meal available, Rooms 13 single, 5 double, 5 twin, some en-suite, Children welcome, No smoking, Open all year.

Dene Hotel, 38-42 Grosvenor Road, Jesmond, Newcastle-upon Tyne, Tyne & Wear NE2 2RP
Tel: 0191 281 1502 Fax: 0191 281 8110 **Map Ref 68**

....

JESMOND PARK HOTEL, a clean and friendly hotel offering good English breakfast, in a quiet area close to the city centre.

B&B from £24, Rooms 8 single, 2 double, 3 twin, 1 triple, 2 family, some en-suite, Children welcome, Open all year.

Jesmond Park Hotel, 74-76 Queens Road, Jesmond, Newcastle-upon Tyne, Tyne & Wear NE2 2PR
Tel: 0191 281 2821 & 281 1913 Fax: 0191 281 0515 **Map Ref 68**

....

GROSVENOR HOTEL, a friendly hotel in quiet residential suburb, offering a wide range of facilities. Close to city centre.

B&B from £25, Lunch & evening meal available, Rooms 17 single, 8 double, 9 twin, 7 triple, most en-suite, Children welcome, Open all year.

Grosvenor Hotel, Grosvenor Road, Jesmond, Newcastle-upon Tyne, Tyne & Wear NE2 2RR
Tel: 0191 281 0543 Fax: 0191 281 9217 **Map Ref 68**

....

HOSPITALITY INN, set in a quiet residential area of Newcastle, just 1 mile from the city centre and close to the city's universities and Jesmond Dene.

B&B from £30, Lunch & evening meal available, Rooms 10 single, 17 double, 52 twin, 6 triple, Suite available, all en-suite, Children welcome, No smoking, Open all year.

Hospitality Inn, Osbourne Road, Jesmond, Newcastle-upon Tyne, Tyne & Wear NE2 2AT
Tel: 0191 281 7881 Fax: 0191 281 6241 **Map Ref 68**

....

THE OSBORNE HOTEL, is a licensed, 22 bedroom hotel situated one and a half miles from city centre. All bedrooms are en-suite with tea/coffee facilities, TV, radio and telephone. Also dine in our 60 seater Apollo Restaurant.

B&B from £35, Rooms 14 single, 3 twin, 4 double, 1 family, all en-suite, Restricted smoking, Children welcome, Pets by arrangement, Open all year.
Kiran Venayak, **The Osborne Hotel,** 13-15 Osborne Road, Jesmond, Newcastle-upon-Tyne, Tyne & Wear NE7 7QX
Tel: 0191 2813385 Fax: 0191 2817717 **Map Ref 68**

....

GRAND HOTEL, high on the cliffs overlooking beautiful Long Sands beach, this imposing Victorian building was the seaside home of the Duchess of Northumberland. Building is now completely modernised to offer every comfort.

B&B from £45, Lunch & evening meal available, Rooms 29 double, 7 twin, 8 triple, 2 family, all en-suite, Children welcome, No pets, Open all year.

Grand Hotel, Grand Parade, Tynemouth, North Shields, Tyne & Wear NE30 4ER
Tel: 0191 293 6666 Fax: 0191 293 6665 **Map Ref 69**

RIVER'S END GUEST HOUSE, is situated in 'Catherine Cookson Country' the 'River's End' looks out across parkland to the Tyne harbour and piers. There are miles of coastal walks and the Roman Fort is just around the corner. Most rooms are en-suite, have TV, plus the usual facilities.

B&B from £19pp, Rooms 2 single, 1 twin, 1 double, 2 family, most en-suite, Restricted smoking, Children welcome, Pets by arrangement, Open all year.
Brian Pearson, **River's End Guest House,** 41 Lawe Road, South Shields, Tyne & Wear NE33 2EU
Tel: 0191 4564229 Fax: 0191 4564229 **Map Ref 70**

....

SEA HOTEL, on the seafront in the heart of Catherine Cookson country. Popular restaurant offering French and English cooking. Secure car park.

B&B from £60, Lunch & evening meal available, Rooms 20 single, 6 double, 5 twin, 2 triple, all en-suite, Children welcome, Open all year.
Sea Hotel, Sea Road, South Shields, Tyne & Wear NE33 2LD
Tel: 0191 427 0999 Fax: 0191 454 0500 Email: seahot@aol.com **Map Ref 70**

....

MARLBOROUGH HOTEL, a traditional seaside hotel with fine sea views. Comfortable, modern accommodation with friendly service.

B&B from £20, 4 single, 5 double, 4 twin, 1 triple, 1 family, most en-suite, Children from 2 years, No pets, No smoking, Open all year.
Marlborough Hotel, 20-21 East Parade, The Promenade, Whitley Bay, Tyne & Wear NE26 1AP
Tel: 0191 251 3628 Fax: 0191 251 3628 **Map Ref 71**

....

SHAN-GRI-LA, a small family-run guesthouse. Close to all amenities, near seafront and shopping area.

B&B from £17, Dinner available, Rooms 4 single, 3 twin, 3 triple, Children welcome, Open all year.
Shan-Gri-La, 29 Esplanade, Whitley Bay, Tyne & Wear NE26 2AL
Tel: 0191 253 0230 **Map Ref 71**

....

YORK HOUSE HOTEL, ideally located for exploring historic Northumbria or visiting the excellent shopping facilities at Newcastle and Metro Centre. High standard en-suite accommodation and imaginative menu choice. No charge charge for children when sharing. Secure car parking.

B&B from £25, Lunch & evening meal available, Rooms 4 single, 8 double, 2 twin, all en-suite/private facilities, Children welcome, No smoking, Open all year.
York House Hotel, 30 Park Parade, Whitley Bay, Tyne & Wear NE26 1DX
Tel: 0191 252 8313 Fax: 0191 251 3953 **Map Ref 71**

....

WINDSOR HOTEL, a private hotel close to the seafront and town centre. An excellent base in the north east for business or pleasure.

B&B from £50, Lunch & evening meal available, Rooms 4 single, 16 double, 43 twin, all en-suite, Children welcome, Open all year.
Windsor Hotel, South Parade, Whitley Bay, Tyne & Wear NE26 2RF
Tel: 0191 251 8888 Fax: 0191 297 0272 **Map Ref 71**

....

HIGH POINT HOTEL, a prominent, refurbished hotel with panoramic sea views, only 5 minutes' walk from Whitley Bay. Restaurant.

B&B from £52, Lunch & evening meal available, Rooms 3 single, 4 double, 5 twin, 1 triple, 2 family, all en-suite, Children welcome, No pets, Open all year.
High Point Hotel, The Promenade, Whitley Bay, Tyne & Wear NE26 2NJ
Tel: 0191 251 7782 Fax: 0191 251 6318 **Map Ref 71**

Mention Oxfordshire and the city of Oxford immediately springs to mind. A city like no other, Oxford is a seat of learning and a centre for the arts. The city, in only one square mile, has more than six hundred buildings of architectural and historical interest. The medieval origins of Oxford University have produced a blend of architectural styles. It consists of forty two different colleges and halls sited in various parts of the city.

Sir Christopher Wren was Professor of Astronomy when he designed one of the university's best known buildings, the Sheldonian Theatre. The students have created their own vibrant culture from restaurants, pubs, markets and artistic events. As well as a wide variety of entertainment for the visitor from concerts to art exhibitions and museums, there are many walks through gardens - and there is always the famous pastime, punting!

To the south west of Oxford is the famous Vale of the White Horse. From Uffington, there are good views of the horse cut into the chalk of White Horse Hill. There is still dispute over when the figure was cut into the hillside. One theory is that it was cut in Saxon times to commemorate a ninth century victory by King Alfred, other theories say its style means it could date back to as early as 350 BC and be the art of the Iron Age Celts. North Oxfordshire's Cotswold country is very much the English heartland with sleepy villages of olden ironstone or grey limestone.

What remains of the great royal hunting forest of Wychwood overlooks the valley of the River Evenlode. Here Tudor monarchs, including Henry VIII, hunted. Now there is a nature reserve in the one thousand five hundred acres which survive. Burford, on the River Windrush, is a mixture of Tudor houses and Georgian facades. A feature of the High Street is the Tolsey, an upper storey supported on pillars which was where the market was held and tolls collected.

Chipping Norton, at seven hundred feet, is the highest town in the county. Mentioned in the Domesday Book as Norton, the "chipping" or "cheapening" meaning market was added to the name in the thirteenth century. Banbury is famous for its cakes, made from flaky or puff pastry filled with dried spiced fruit.

Much of the eastern side of Oxfordshire is off the tourist map, with its vast cornfields and wide open tracts of land. Ot Moor, a bleak expanse is surrounded by a string of attractive villages. There are also attractive villages in the south of the area along the River Thame and the River Cherwell in the north. By the Cherwell near Bicester is Rousham House, one of the finest Jacobean mansions in the country.

left, Hertford College Bridge, Oxford

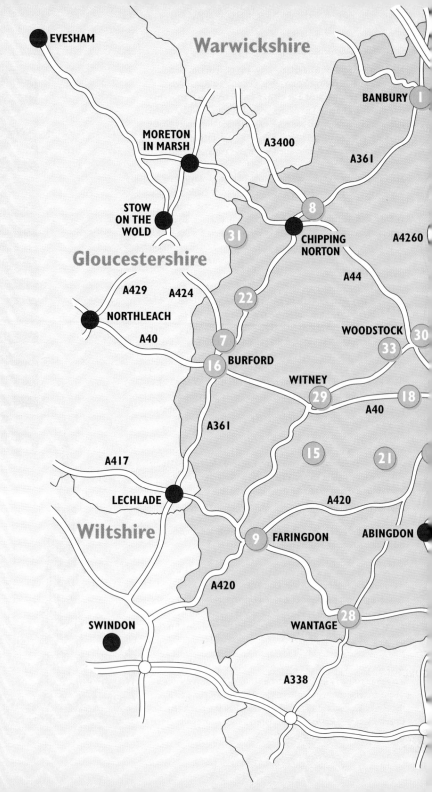

BANBURY CROSS B&B, is a small family run business within 400 yards of the famous Banbury Cross, with the Town Centre only minutes away. We are a NON-SMOKING establishment offering ample off street parking. Quality accommodation with full English breakfast, vegetarians and special diets catered for.
B&B from £22.50pp, Rooms 2 single, 1 twin, 4 double, 1 family, most en-suite, Children welcome, Open all year.
Anne & Ron Carroll, **Banbury Cross B&B,** 1 Broughton Road, Banbury, Oxon OX16 9QB
Tel: 01295 266048   **Map Ref 1**

....

PROSPECT HOUSE GUEST HOUSE, a detached house with lovely grounds, in the most convenient area of town.

B&B from £30.00 Rooms 1 single, 6 double, 2 twin, 1 triple, all en-suite, Open all year.
Prospect House Guest House, 70 Oxford Road, Banbury, Oxfordshire OX16 9AN
Tel: 01295 268749 & Mobile 0468 525538 Fax: 01295 268749   **Map Ref 1**

....

BANBURY HOUSE HOTEL, an elegant Georgian building with all modern facilities. Ideal for touring the Cotswolds, Stratford upon Avon and Oxford.

B&B from £35.00 Dinner available, Rooms 16 single, 28 double, 15 twin, 4 triple. Suite available, all en-suite, Open all year
Banbury House Hotel, Oxford Road, Banbury, Oxfordshire OX16 9AH
Tel: 01295 259361 Fax: 01295 270954   **Map Ref 1**

....

RED LION INN, a 16th century coaching inn with superb rooms, restaurant and conference facility. A4260 Banbury Oxford road. Junction 11, M40, Banbury.

B&B from £49.50, Dinner available, Rooms 2 single, 9 double, 3 twin, most en-suite, Open all year.
Red Lion Inn, The Green, Oxford Road, Adderbury, Banbury, Oxfordshire OX17 3LU
Tel: 01295 810269 Fax: 01295 811906   **Map Ref 2**

....

THE DEDDINGTON ARMS, a 16th century coaching inn, tasteful refurbished to provide air conditioned restaurant and en-suite bedrooms whilst retaining the village in atmosphere. Ideal base for Banbury, Oxford, Stratford, Warwick, Blenheim Palace and the Cotswolds.

B&B from £49.50, Dinner available, Rooms 18 double, 3 twin, 1 triple, 1 family room, suites available, most en-suite.
The Deddington Arms, Horsefair, Deddington, Banbury, Oxfordshire OX15 OSH
Tel: 01869 338364 Fax: 01869 337010   **Map Ref 3**

....

HOLCOMBE HOTEL & RESTAURANT, a delightful 17th century award winning family run hotel in lovely village on A4260 Banbury to Oxford road, M40 exit 10. Ideal forvisiting the Cotswolds, Stratford, Warwick, Woodstock and Blenheim.

B&B from £59.50, Dinner available, Rooms 2 single, 8 double, 6 twin, 1 triple, all rooms en-suite, Open all year.
Holcombe Hotel & Restaurant, High Street, Deddington, Banbury, Oxfordshire OX15 0SL
Tel: 01869 338274 Fax: 01869 337167   **Map Ref 3**

....

LITTLEBURY HOTEL, a family owned and run town centre hotel in quiet location with plenty of parking, offering fine food and hospitality.

B&B from £51.50 Dinner available, Rooms 5 single, 5 double, 16 twin, 2 triple, 7 family rooms, all en-suite, Open all year.
Littlebury Hotel, Kings End, Bicester, Oxfordshire OX6 7DR
Tel: 01869 252595 Fax: 01869 253225   **Map Ref 4**

BIGNELL PARK HOTEL, a Cotswold period house circa 1740, set in 2.5 acres with mature gardens in rural Oxfordshire.

B&B from £60, Dinner available, Rooms 1 single, 11 double, 2 twin, 2 en-suite
Bignell Park Hotel, Chesterton, Bicester, Oxfordshire OX6 8UE
Tel: 01869 241444 & 241192 Fax: 01869 241444   **Map Ref 5**

The **KINGS HEAD INN,** a quintessential Cotswold Inn, located on village green with brook and attendant ducks. Retains olde world charm, fireplaces, pews, settles. Delightful en-suite bedrooms complement thoughtful extras. Award winning restaurant offering bar fare, table d'hote, a la Carte. A hot buttered Cotswold experience. Ideally located for main tourist attractions Warwick, Stratford etc.
B&B from £60 per room, Dinner from £10.95, Rooms 2 single, 2 twin, 12 double, 2 family, all en-suite, Restricted smoking, Children welcome, Open all year except Christmas.
Annette & Michael Royce, **Kings Head Inn,** The Green, Bledington, Oxon OX7 6XQ
Tel: 01608 658365 Fax: 01608 658902   **Map Ref 31**

TILBURY LODGE PRIVATE HOTEL, is situated in a quiet country lane just 2 minutes west of city centre, 1 mile to the railway and 2 miles to Farmoor Reservoir. En-suite rooms with telephone, hair dryer, TV, radio and tea/coffee. Ground floor bedrooms. Lounge, jacuzzi, 4 poster and parking. Ideal for the Cotswolds, Blenheim and Stratford. AA Selected, RAC Highly Acclaimed.
B&B from £30pp, Rooms 2 single, 2 twin, 3 double, 2 family, all en-suite, No smoking or pets, Children welcome, Open all year.
Eileen & Eddie Trafford, **Tilbury Lodge Private Hotel,** 5 Tilbury Lane, Eynsham Road, Eynsham Road, Botley, Oxfordshire OX2 9NB
Tel: 01865 862138 Fax: 01865 863700   **Map Ref 6**

ELM HOUSE HOTEL, a Cotswold stone manor style house with attractive walled gardens. Homely, welcoming atmosphere, fine home cooked food served in comfortable surroundings. Centrally located for exploring Cotswolds and Oxfordshire.
B&B from £41.00 Dinner available, Rooms 4 double, 3 twin, most en-suite, Open all year.
Elm House Hotel, Meadow Lane, Fulbrook, Burford, Oxfordshire OX18 4BW
Tel: 01993 823611 Fax: 01993 82397   **Map Ref 7**

SOUTHCOMBE LODGE GUEST HOUSE, a well decorated pebbledash guest house set in 3.5 acres, at the junction of the A44/A3400, close to Chipping Norton.

B&B from £22, Dinner available, Rooms 2 double, 3 twin, 1 triple, 2 en-suite.
Southcombe Lodge Guest House, Southcombe, Chipping Norton, Oxfordshire OX7 5QH
Tel: 01608 643068   **Map Ref 8**

SUDBURY HOUSE HOTEL, peacefully situated midway between Oxford & Swindon, within an easy drive of the Cotswolds, Blenheim Palace and Warwick Castle. Special weekend rates.
B&B from £45, Dinner available,Rooms 39 double, 10 twin, all en-suite. Open all year.
Sudbury House Hotel, 56 London Street, Faringdon, Oxfordshire SN7 8AA
Tel: 01367 241272 Fax: 01367 242346   **Map Ref 9**

FARINGDON HOTEL, all en-suite rooms equipped with remote control colour TV, direct dial telephone, tea/coffee making facilities, hair dryer. Open fire, lounge bar and restaurant.
B&B from £45, Dinner available, Rooms 3 single, 13 double, 1 twin, 3 triple, all rooms en-suite. Open all year.
Faringdon Hotel, Market Place, Faringdon, Oxfordshire SN7 7HL
Tel: 01367 240536 Fax: 01367 243250   **Map Ref 9**

PORTWELL HOUSE HOTEL, in the centre of the market place of this country market town. Within easy reach of the Cotswolds.

B&B from £32, Dinner available, Rooms 1 single, 2 double, 2 twin, 3 triple, all en-suite. Open all year.

Portwell House Hotel, Market Place, Faringdon, Oxfordshire SN7 7HU
Tel: 01367 240197 Fax: 01367 244330   **Map Ref 9**

....

THE WHITE HART HOTEL, a historic coaching inn, combining traditional architecture with modern facilities. Convenient for Henley and Oxford.

B&B from £49.50, Dinner available, Rooms 3 double, 3 twin, all en-suite. Open all year.

The White Hart Hotel, High Street, Nettlebed, Henley On Thames, Oxfordshire RG9 5DD
Tel: 01491 641245 Fax: 01491 641423   **Map Ref 10**

....

Comfortable and welcoming, **SHEPHERDS** is a part 18th century house set in gardens. All rooms have en-suite or private facilities, clock radio and tea/coffee facilities, some have TV. Guests drawing room with antiques and open fire. Conveniently situated for Windsor, Oxford, the Chilterns and Heathrow.

B&B from £21pp, Rooms 2 twin, 2 double, all en-suite, Restricted smoking, Children over 12, No pets, Open all year except Christmas.

Susan Fulford-Dobson, **Shepherds,** Shepherds Green, Rotherfield Greys, Henley on Thames, Oxfordshire RG9 4QL
Tel: 01491 628413   **Map Ref 11**

....

WYNFORD HOUSE, a warm welcome awaits you in our comfortable home. Colour TV and tea/coffee facilities in all rooms. Good local pubs within walking distance. Conveniently situated for Oxford, Woodstock and Cotswolds. Many good walks in local countryside.

B&B from £19pp, Rooms 1 twin, 1 double, 1 family en-suite, No smoking, Children welcome, Pets by arrangement, Open all year except Christmas & New Year.
Carol Ellis, **Wynford House,** 79 Main Road, Long Hanborough, Oxon OX8 8JX
Tel: 01993 881402 Fax: 01993 883661   **Map Ref 33**

....

HENLEY HOUSE, an elegant spacious property, set in a Victorian walled garden in an area of outstanding natural beauty. All modern comforts, with a relaxed, friendly atmosphere. Very convenient for M4 and access to London, Oxford & Windsor.
B&B from £45, Rooms 4 double, all en-suite. Open all year
Henley House, School Lane, Medmenham, Marlow, Oxfordshire SL7 2HJ
Tel: 01491 576100 Fax: 01491 571764   **Map Ref 12**

....

THE OLD BAKERY, a 18th century large country cottage, conservation village. Inglenook fireplace, oak beams well furnished, good breakfast, tea/coffee facilities. 5 miles Oxford centre. Plentiful parking. Pleasant walks. TV in rooms. Pleasant host, hostess. Believed to be oldest planted village in England next to beautiful Arboretum. Easy access reach M40.
B&B from £25pp, Rooms 1 single, 1 twin, 1 double, 1 family, most en-suite, No smoking, Children welcome, Open all year.
Maggie Howard, **The Old Bakery,** Nuneham Courtenay, Oxfordshire OX44 9NX
Tel: 01865 343585 Fax: 01865 343585   **Map Ref 13**

THE OLD PARSONAGE HOTEL, an independently owned hotel in the centre of the city. 17th century building with an informal restaurant, open from 7 am until late.

B&B from £120, Dinner available, 1 single, 19 double, 6 twin, 4 triple, all rooms en-suite. Open all year.
The Old Parsonage Hotel, 1 Banbury Road, Oxford, Oxfordshire OX2 6NN
Tel: 01865 310210 Fax: 01865 311262 EMail: oldparsonage@dial.pipex.com   **Map Ref 14**

....

THE OLD BLACK HORSE HOTEL, a former coaching inn with private car park, close to Magdalen Bridge, colleges, riverside walks and city centre. Easy access M40 north and south.

B&B from £50, Dinner available, Rooms 1 single, 4 double, 3 twin, 2 triple, all rooms en-suite. Open all year.
The Old Black Horse Hotel, 102 St. Clements, Oxford, Oxfordshire OX4 1AR
Tel: 01865 244691 Fax: 01865 242771   **Map Ref 14**

....

COMBERMERE HOUSE, a family run Victorian house in quiet tree lined road in residential north Oxford, 1 mile from city centre and colleges.

B&B from £23.00 Rooms 4 single, 1 double, 3 triple, 1 family room, all rooms en-suite. Open all year.
Combermere House, 11 Polstead Road, Oxford, Oxfordshire OX2 6TW
Tel: 01865 556971 Fax: 01865 556971   **Map Ref 14**

....

HIGHFIELD WEST, ETB 2 Crowns Highly Commended. Situated west Oxford. No smoking. Vegetarian very welcome. Excellent village pubs with meals nearby. Our comfortable home is centrally heated. Guest lounge. Most rooms are en-suite and all have colour TV and refreshment trays. Large outdoor pool, heated in season. Fire certificate. Car parking. Cotswolds, London easily reached. Email: highfieldwest@email.msn.com
B&B from £20pp, Rooms 2 single, 1 twin, 1 double, 1 family, most en-suite, Children over 3, Pets by arrangement, Open all year except Christmas & New Year.
Diana & Richard Mitchell, **Highfield West,** 188 Cumnor Hill, Oxford OX2 9PJ
Tel: 01865 863007   **Map Ref 14**

....

BRAVALLA GUEST HOUSE, a small family run guest house, mostly en-suite, within half a mile of Magdalen College with its famous deer park. 1 mile from city centre.

B&B from £25, Rooms 2 double, 2 twin, 1 triple, 1 family , some rooms en-suite. Open all year.
Bravalla Guest House, 242 Iffley Road, Oxford OX4 1SE
Tel: 01865 241326 & 250511 Fax: 01865 250511   **Map Ref 14**

....

ACORN GUEST HOUSE, a Victorian house situated midway between the city centre and the ring road. Convenient for all local amenities and more distant attractions.

B&B from £22, Dinner available, Rooms 4 single, 2 twin, 7 triple, some en-suite. Open all year.
Acorn Guest House, 260 Iffley Road, Oxford OX4 1SE
Tel: 01865 247998   **Map Ref 14**

....

PINE CASTLE HOTEL, a characterful Edwardian guest house close to the city centre and picturesque River Thames. A warm welcome awaits you from the resident proprietor.

B&B from £55, Dinner available, Rooms 5 double, 2 twin, 1 family, all rooms en-suite. Open all year.

Pine Castle Hotel, 290 Iffley Road, Oxford OX4 4AE
Tel: 01865 241497 Fax: 01865 727230 EMail: pinebeds.oxfhotel@pop3.hiway.co.uk   **Map Ref 14**

THE BALKAN LODGE HOTEL, a delightful small hotel, recently refurbished. En suite bedrooms with Sky, TV, hair dryer, trouser press, direct dial telephone, tea/coffee facilities. Car park at rear.

B&B from £50, Dinner available, Rooms 3 single, 9 double, 1 twin, all en-suite. Open all year.
The Balkan Lodge Hotel, 315 Iffley Road, Oxford OX4 4AG
Tel: 01865 244524 **Map Ref 14**

MARLBOROUGH HOUSE HOTEL, one and a half miles from Oxford city centre. All rooms en-suite with telephone, TV, fridge, desk, armchair, tea/coffee facilities. Continental breakfast. Parking.

B&B from £59.5 Rooms 2 single, 8 double, 4 twin, 2 triple, all rooms en-suite. Open all year.
Marlborough House Hotel, 321 Woodstock Road, Oxford OX2 7NY
Tel: 01865 311321 Fax: 01865 515329 **Map Ref 14**

EARLMONT GUEST HOUSE, is a non-smoking house with most rooms en-suite, each equipped with television, radio/alarm clock, hair dryers and tea/coffee making facilities for your comfort. Close to a good selection of restaurants; ample car parking frequent bus service, 10 minute walk to first Colleges and Botanic Gardens.
B&B from £25pp, Rooms 1 single, 1 twin, 5 double, 1 family, No smoking, Children over 5 , No pets, Open all year except Christmas & New Year.
Peter & Georgette Facer, **Earlmont Guest House,** 322-324 Cowley Road, Oxford OX4 2AF
Tel: 01865 240236 Fax: 01865 434903 **Map Ref 14**

COTSWOLD HOUSE, a well situated elegant property offering a high standard of furnishings and facilities in each of its rooms.

B&B from £41 single, £62 double, Rooms 2 single, 2 double, 1 twin, 2 triple, all rooms en-suite. Open all year.
Cotswold House, 363 Banbury Road, Oxford OX2 7PL
Tel: 01865 310558 Fax: 01865 310558 **Map Ref 14**

MILKA'S GUEST HOUSE, a pleasant semi detached house on a main road, 1 mile from city centre.

B&B from £25, Rooms 2 double, 1 twin, 1 en-suite room. Open all year.

Milka's Guest House, 379 Iffley Road, Oxford OX4 4DP
Tel: 01865 778485 Fax: 01865 776477 **Map Ref 14**

ISIS GUEST HOUSE, a modernised, Victorian, city centre guest house within walking distance of colleges and shops. Easy access to ring road.

B&B from £22, Rooms 12 single, 6 double, 17 twin, 2 triple, some rooms en-suite. Open July, August & September.
Isis Guest House, 45-53 Iffley Road, Oxford OX4 1ED
Tel: 01865 248894 Fax: 01865 243492 **Map Ref 14**

FALCON PRIVATE HOTEL, a Victorian building with modern facilities, overlooking Queens College playing fields. 10 minutes' walk to colleges and city centre.

B&B from £29, Rooms 2 single, 5 double, 2 twin, 1 triple, 2 family rooms, all rooms en-suite. Open all year.

Falcon Private Hotel, 88 90 Abingdon Road, Oxford OX1 4PX
Tel: 01865 722995 Fax: 01865 246642 **Map Ref 14**

THE RANDOLPH, Oxford's most famous hotel, with magnificent public rooms and bedrooms in a traditional style. Situated in the heart of the city.

B&B from £59, Dinner available, Rooms 41 single, 41 double, 20 twin, 7 family rooms, suites available, all rooms en-suite. Open all year.
The Randolph, Beaumont Street, Oxford OX1 2LN
Tel: 01865 247481 Fax: 01865 791678   **Map Ref 14**

....

ROMANY INN, a 19th century listed Georgian building, recently refurbished, at nearby Bampton. Lounge bar , separate restaurant, chef/proprietor. Noted in pub and beer guides. Brochure available.

B&B from £19.50, Dinner available, Rooms 4 double, 2 twin, 3 triple, all rooms en-suite, Open all year.
Romany Inn, Bridge Street, Bampton, Oxford OX18 2HA
Tel: 01993 850237   **Map Ref 15**

....

THE HIGHWAY HOTEL, a beamed mediaeval Cotswold guest house, rooms with TV. Ideal touring base for Cotswolds. Incorporates acclaimed needlecraft centre.

B&B from £30, Rooms 9 double, 2 triple, most rooms en-suite.
The Highway Hotel, 117 High Street, Burford, Oxford OX18 4RG
Tel: 01993 8221136 Fax: 01993 822136   **Map Ref 16**

....

GOLDEN PHEASANT HOTEL, a beautifully restored 15th century inn with informal and friendly atmosphere. Large open fireplaces, antique furniture and individually styled rooms.

B&B from £50, Dinner available, Rooms 8 double, 4 twin, most en-suite, Open all year.

Golden Pheasant Hotel, High Street, Burford, Oxford OX18 4QA
Tel: 01993 823223 Fax: 01993 822621   **Map Ref 16**

....

THE BAT & BALL INN, an old coaching inn with scenic views and interesting collection of cricket memorabilia. Cuddesdon is an attractive small village, well placed for Oxford and the M40.

B&B from £30, Dinner available, rooms 2 single, 3 double, 1 twin, 1 triple, all en-suite, Open all year.

The Bat & Ball Inn, 28 High Street, Cuddesdon, Oxford OX44 9HJ
Tel: 01865 874379 Fax: 01865 873363   **Map Ref 17**

....

ALL VIEWS, a 7 acre nursery, 1991 built Cotswold stone chalet bungalow, adjacent A40 between Oxford & Witney. Designed with guests' comfort in mind. All rooms have full facilities.

B&B from £39.95, Rooms 1 single, 2 double, 1 twin, all rooms en-suite. Open all year.

All Views, 67 Old Witney Road,On main A40, Eynsham, Oxford OX8 1PU
Tel: 01865 880891   **Map Ref 18**

....

ALL SEASONS GUEST HOUSE, a Victorian house with lots of of character, spacious rooms, car parking, patio, 2 miles from city centre. Frequent bus service. Convenient for Cotswolds and close to M40 motorway.

B&B from £25.00 Rooms 1 single, 3 double, 2 twin, some rooms en-suite. Open all year.

All Seasons Guest House, 63 Windmill Road, Headington, Oxford OX3 7BP
Tel: 01865 742215   **Map Ref 19**

MOUNT PLEASANT, a small, no smoking, family run hotel offering full facilities. On the A40 and convenient for Oxford shopping, hospitals, colleges, visiting the Chilterns and the Cotswolds.
B&B from £37.50, Dinner available, Rooms 2 double, 5 twin, 1 triple, all rooms en-suite. Open all year.
Mount Pleasant, 76 London Road, Headington, Oxford OX3 9AJ
Tel: 01865 62749 Fax: 01865 62749   **Map Ref 19**

....

STUDLEY PRIOR HOTEL, a converted Elizabethan manor house in a rural setting north east of Oxford, with a restaurant that specialises in English cooking.

B&B from £100, Dinner available, Rooms 6 single, 8 double, 5 twin suites, all rooms en-suite. Open all year.
Studley Prior Hotel, Horton cum Studley, Oxford OX33 1AZ
Tel: 01865 351203 Fax: 01865 351613   **Map Ref 20**

....

KINGS ARMS HOTEL, a charming Cotswold stone country hotel in village location with golf course nearby. Ideal base for visiting Oxford, Blenheim Palace and the Cotswolds.
B&B from £30, Dinner available, Rooms 2 single, 5 double, 2 twin, 1 triple, all rooms en-suite. Open all year.
Kings Arms Hotel, The Old Green, Horton cum Studley, Oxford OX33 1AY
Tel: 01865 351235 Fax: 01865 351721   **Map Ref 20**

....

THE FERRYMAN INN, a riverside inn on site of ancient ferry crossing. Recently renovated to give two bars, restaurant and en-suite bedrooms.

B&B from £35, Dinner available, Rooms 3 double, 1 twin, 2 triple, all en-suite. Open all year.
The Ferryman Inn, Bablock Hythe, Northmoor, Oxford OX8 1BL
Tel: 01865 880028 Fax: 01865 88028   **Map Ref 21**

....

THE SHAVEN CROWN HOTEL, an Abbey hospice built around a courtyard garden, delightfully located in the Cotswolds. Midway between Oxford and Stratford upon Avon. Baronial Hall, beautiful Tudor archway.
B&B from £35, Dinner available, Rooms 1 single, 4 double, 3 twin, 1 family, most en-suite. Open all year.
The Shaven Crown Hotel, High Street, Shipton under Wychwood, Oxford OX7 6BA
Tel: 01993 830330 Fax: 01993 830330   **Map Ref 22**

....

HOPCROFTS HOLT HOTEL, a 15th century hotel with en-suite bedrooms, restaurant and extensive banqueting facilities. Located 11 miles north of Oxford.

B&B from £65, Dinner available, Rooms 17 Single, 44 double, 25 twin, 2 triple, most rooms en-suite. Open all year.
 Hopcrofts Holt Hotel, Banbury Road, Steeple Aston, Oxford OX6 3QQ
Tel: 01869 340529 Fax: 01869 340865   **Map Ref 23**

....

CASA VILLA GUEST HOUSE, a detached guest house in north Oxford, one and three quarter miles from city centre. Friendly and pleasant service provided. Close to all amenities and easy access to M40.
B&B from £29, Dinner available, Rooms 2 single, 5 double, 1 twin, 1 family room, some rooms en-suite. Open all year.
Casa Villa Guest House, 388 Banbury Road, Summertown, Oxford OX2 7PW
Tel: 01865 512642 Fax: 01865 512642   **Map Ref 24**

....

MILLER OF MANSFIELD, an ivy covered inn with Tudor style exterior. Interior has original beams, open fires and comfortable bedrooms.

B&B from £30, Dinner available, Rooms 2 single, 5 double, 3 twin, most en-suite. Open all year.
Miller of Mansfield, High Street, Goring, Reading, Oxfordshire RG8 9AW
Tel: 01491 872829 Fax: 01491 874200   **Map Ref 25**

THE SPREAD EAGLE HOTEL, a converted 17th century coaching inn, in centre of small country market town. Fothergills Restaurant features a choice of menus. Banqueting and conference facilities. Good base for touring the Thames Valley.
B&B from £92.90 Dinner available, Rooms 5 single, 22 double, 5 twin, 1 triple, suites available, most rooms en-suite. Open all year.
The Spread Eagle Hotel, Cornmarket, Thame, Oxfordshire OX9 2BW
Tel: 01844 213661 Fax: 01844 261380 **Map Ref 26**

OXFORD BELFRY HOTEL, a Tudor style country hotel, privately owned. Well placed for touring. Indoor leisure complex with swimming pool, sauna, solarium, mini gym. Half board daily prices based on a min. 2 night stay.
B&B from £98.50, Dinner available, Rooms 11 Single, 54 double, 32 twin, all rooms en-suite. Open all year,
Oxford Belfry Hotel, Milton Common, Thame, Oxfordshire OX9 2JW
Tel: 01844 279381 Fax: 01844 279624 **Map Ref 27**

THE BEAR HOTEL, a historic coaching inn with renowned cuisine and traditional ales. Friendly staff and comfortable accommodation. Ideal for visiting Oxford and excellent location for relaxing with the family.
B&B from £59 Dinner available, Rooms 9 single, 14 double, 10 twin, 3 triple, all rooms en-suite. Open all year.
The Bear Hotel, Market Place, Wantage, Oxfordshire OX12 8AB
Tel: 01235 766366 Fax: 01235 768826 **Map Ref 28**

FOX & HOUNDS, 17th century inn, CAMRA recommended. Serving traditional and international cuisine 7 days per week. Tea/coffee facilities and TV's in rooms. Half a mile from the Ridgeway. Ornithologists heaven: red kites in abundance. Situated in the town centre surrounded by amenities. Just 3 miles from J6 M40.Email:foxandhounds.watlington@dial.pipex.com
B&B from £22.50pp, Dinner from £5.50, Rooms 2 twin, No smoking, Children & Pets welcome, Open all year except Christmas Day.
Ian & Julia Kingsford, **Fox & Hounds**, 13 Shirburn Street, Watlington, Oxon OX9 5BU
Tel: 01491 612142 Fax: 01491 614571 **Map Ref 34**

GREYSTONES LODGE HOTEL, q quiet comfortable private hotel set in three quarters of an acre of pleasant garden. Conveniently located for visiting Oxford and the Cotswolds.
B&B from £27.00 Dinner available, Rooms 4 single, 4 double, 2 twin, 1 triple, most rooms en-suite. Open all year.
Greystones Lodge Hotel, 34 Tower Hill, Witney, Oxfordshire OX8 5ES
Tel: 01993 771898 Fax: 01993 771898 **Map Ref 29**

FIELD VIEW, an attractive Cotswold stone house set in 2 acres, situated on picturesque Wood green, Witney, midway between Oxford University and the Cotswolds. Ideal centre for touring. Three comfortable en-suite rooms, with colour TV, tea/coffee facilities. ETB 2 Crowns Highly Commended.

B&B from £21pp, Rooms 2 twin, 1 double, all en-suite, No smoking or pets, Children over 13, Open all year except Christmas.
Liz & John Simpson, **Field View,** Wood Green, Witney, Oxfordshire OX8 6DE
Tel: 01993 705485 Email: Jsimpson@netcomuk.co.uk **Map Ref 29**

A traditional English pub with oak beams and open fireplaces. **THE STAR INN** has been welcoming both travellers and locals for over three hundred years. Our four well appointed bedroom, which include one four poster, provide the modern day comforts expected by the discerning guest.

B&B from £65, Dinner from £6.95, Room s 1 twin, 3 double, all en-suite, Children & pets welcome, Open all year except Christmas & Boxing Day.
Mel & Sarah Phipps, **The Star Inn,** 22 Market Place, Woodstock, Oxfordshire OX20 1TA
Tel: 01993 811373 Fax: 01993 812007 **Map Ref 30**

Upland and lowland Britain meet in Shropshire; wild, high moorland encounters soft, lush lowland farms. Shropshire's contrasts give it its distinctive quality - its Roman city and 20th century new town; ruined castles and elegant country houses; the birthplace of industry and rich farmland. Shropshire is also Cadfael Country - the dark, close setting of the Medieval marches that inspired the Brother Cadfael Chronicles. Local author Ellis Peters created her best selling medieval who-dunits around the Benedictine monk at Shrewsbury Abbey.

Shropshire has many small, but interesting towns, most of which have half-timbered houses. One of the most beautiful Tudor towns in England is Shropshire's county town, Shrewsbury. Lying on a peninsula of the River Severn, which is spanned by twin bridges, the town's narrow streets and half timbered houses give it a unique character. The town is ornamented by its castle, originally Norman and renovated by Thomas Telford, the engineer and architect, whom the new town of Telford was named after. He was Surveyor Of Public Works for Shropshire and the aqueduct he designed to carry the Shropshire Union Canal at Longdon upon Tern is the oldest cast iron aqueduct in the world, dating from 1794.

The market town of Shifnal, with its fine half-timbered and Georgian houses, was described by Charles Dickens in The Old Curiosity Shop. Wem is famous for its strong ales. It was the infamous Judge Jeffreys who became Baron of Wem in 1685. Bridgnorth is built on a red sandstone ridge. The Low Town is connected to the High Town by a two-car funicular railway and flights of steep steps.

North of the town the River Severn flows through the Ironbridge Gorge, one of the major centres in Britain's Industrial Revolution. The bridge spans the gorge and was built in 1779 marking the first use of iron in industrial architecture. The town of Ludlow has its own history, if not tumultuous with its Welsh border raids, and its own mellow beauty. Its ruined castle stands above the River Teme.

South of the River Severn the landscape is studded by country houses in rich parkland. Shropshire is ideal walking country, from the lake lands in the north at Ellesmere, to the rolling hills in the south and the rugged Welsh border country. There are many trails and walks in the county. At Knighton the long distance trail, Offa's Dyke Path enters Shropshire from Wales. A 10 mile ridge called the Long Mynd to the west of Church Stretton also provides excellent walking country on its heath and moorland owned by the National Trust. A track of unknown age, The Port Way runs the entire length of the ridge.

left, View from Clunbury Hill

Shropshire

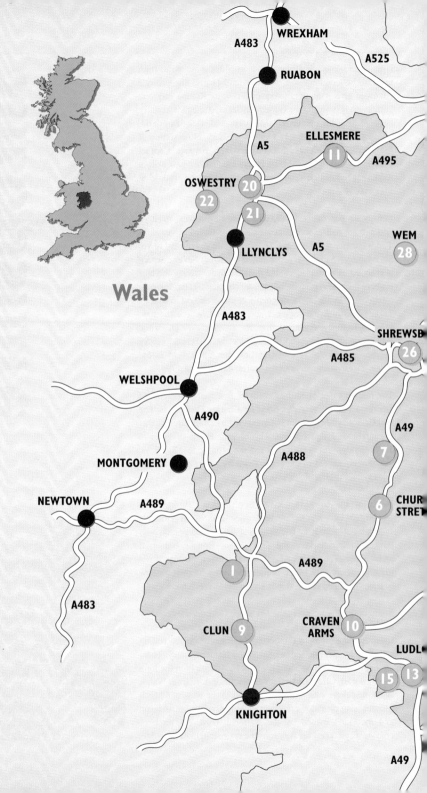

eshire

A51

A530

A425

ITCHURCH

MARKET
DRAYTON

A51

STONE

16

Staffordshire

HODNET

A41

M6

A53

A518

A442

NEWPORT   19

STAFFORD

A518

35   34

25

A5

33   TELFORD

32

CANNOCK

IRONBRIDGE

23

30

31

M54

5   12

24

17   18

A442

4

WOLVERHAMPTON

BRIDGNORTH

2

DUDLEY

4368

3

14

A442

8

KIDDERMINSTER

A456

TENBURY WELLS

A449

Iereford & Worcester

THE BOARS HEAD HOTEL, an old world inn, with en-suite accommodation in original stables. Comfortable dining area serves wide choice of bar meals. A la carte restaurant also available.

B&B from £33, Dinner available, Rooms 1 double, 2 twin, 1 family, all en-suite, Open all year.
The Boars Head Hotel, Church Street, Bishop's Castle, Shropshire SY9 5AE
Tel: 01588 638521 & 0468 882248 Fax: 01588 630126 EMail: GreatBoars@aol.com   **Map Ref 1**

....

THE CROFT HOTEL, a listed building with a wealth of oak beams, in an old street. Family-run and an ideal centre for exploring the delightful Shropshire countryside.

B&B from £23.50, Dinner available, Rooms 3 single, 4 double, 1 twin, 4 triple, most en-suite, Open all year.
The Croft Hotel, St. Mary's Street, Bridgnorth, Shropshire WV16 4DW
Tel: 01746 762416 & 767155   **Map Ref 2**

....

MILL HOTEL, a beautiful hotel in a delightful, tranquil setting. Bedrooms overlooking the mill pool and landscaped gardens. Superb waterside restaurant.

B&B from £58, Dinner available, Rooms 2 single, 13 double, 6 twin, all en-suite, Open all year.
Mill Hotel, Alveley, Bridgnorth, Shropshire WV15 6HL
Tel: 01746 780437 Fax: 01746 780850   **Map Ref 3**

....

PARLORS HALL HOTEL, a 15th century residence of the Parlor family, built in 1419, with fine carved wood fireplaces and 18th century panelled lounge.

B&B from £39, Dinner available, Rooms 2 single, 8 double, 1 twin, 2 triple, all en-suite, Open all year.
Parlors Hall Hotel, Mill Street, Low Town, Bridgnorth, Shropshire WV15 5AL
Tel: 01746 761931 Fax: 01746 767058   **Map Ref 2**

....

OLD VICARAGE HOTEL, a peaceful location, ideal for business or pleasure, close to Ironbridge Gorge and Severn Valley Railway.

B&B from £70, Dinner available, Rooms 8 double, 5 twin, 1 triple, all en-suite, Open all year.
Old Vicarage Hotel, Worfield, Bridgnorth, Shropshire WV15 5JZ
Tel: 01746 716497 Fax: 01746 716552   **Map Ref 4**

....

BROSELEY GUEST HOUSE, a well-appointed spacious accommodation in the centre of Broseley, 1 mile from Ironbridge and convenient for Telford business centres.

B&B from £26, Rooms 2 single, 2 double, 1 twin, 1 triple, all en-suite, Open all year.

Broseley Guest House, The Square, Broseley, Shropshire TF12 5EW
Tel: 01952 882043   **Map Ref 5**

....

BELVEDERE GUEST HOUSE, is set in superb walking country just 100 yards from 6000 acres of National Trust hills. Very convenient for Church Stretton town centre and an ideal base for exploring Ludlow, Shrewsbury or Ironbridge. There are two lounges for guests use. ETB 3 Crown Commended. AA 4Q's Selected. Licensed.
B&B from £23pp, Dinner from £10, Rooms 3 single, 3 twin, 4 double, 2 family, some en-suite, Restricted smoking, Children & pets welcome, Open all year except Christmas.
Don & Rita Rogers, **Belvedere Guest House,** Burway Road, Church Stretton, Shropshire SY6 6DP
Tel: 01694 722232 Fax: 01694 722232   **Map Ref 6**

LONGMYND HOTEL, a family run country hotel commanding panoramic views of the south Shropshire highlands. Situated in an Area of Outstanding Natural Beauty. Self-catering lodges available.

B&B from £50, Dinner available, Rooms 22 double, 6 single, 13 twin, 6 triple, 3 family, all en-suite, Open all year.
Longmynd Hotel, Cunnery Road, Church Stretton, Shropshire SY6 6AG
Tel: 01694 722244 Fax: 01694 722718 EMail: neil@neilski.demon.co.uk   **Map Ref 6**

DENEHURST HOTEL & LEISURE CENTRE, in the heart of beautiful Shropshire, with a comfortable, friendly family atmosphere. En-suite rooms. Suitable for all the family. Leisure for all the family. Leisure facilities, including indoor pool.

B&B from £35, Dinner available, Rooms 1 single, 7 double, 6 twin, 2 triple, all en-suite, Open all year.
Denehurst Hotel & Leisure Centre, Shrewsbury Road, Church Stretton, Shropshire SY6 6EU
Tel: 01694 722699 Fax: 01694 724110   **Map Ref 6**

WILLOWFIELD GUEST HOUSE, beautiful panoramic views of Shropshire hills, rural countryside and gardens. Delightful en-suite bedrooms - lounge area, TV, beverages and telephone. Quiet lounge - open fire. Elizabethan dining room, candlelit dinners, delicious traditional home cooking. Licensed. Parking. ETB 3 Crowns Highly Commended. Warm and friendly welcome. Brochure.
B&B from £24pp, Dinner from £17, Rooms 3 twin, 3 double, all en-suite, No smoking, Open March - October.
Philip & Jane Secrett, **Willowfield Guest House,** Lower Wood, Church Stretton, Shropshire SY6 6LF
Tel/Fax: 01694 751471   **Map Ref 7**

THE REDFERN HOTEL, a family run 2 Star AA/RAC hotel, AA Rosette for good food. All in room facilities. Attractive conservatory for breakfast, which are served all morning. Car park. Close to Ludlow, Ironbridge, Industrial Museum, Severn Valley, Steam Railway, National Trust and English Heritage properties. A warm welcome awaits.
B&B from £37pp, Dinner from £15, Rooms 5 twin, 5 double, 1 family, all en-suite, Restricted smoking, Children & pets welcome, Open all year.
Jon & Liz Redfern, **The Redfern Hotel,** Cleobury Mortimer, Shropshire DY14 8AA
Tel: 01299 270395 Fax: 01299 271011   **Map Ref 8**

NEW HOUSE FARM, isolated 18th century farmhouse set in Clun hills near Welsh borders. Hill farm includes iron age hill fort. Walks from doorstep. Accommodation spacious with scenic views. Tea/coffee facilities, TV and furnished to high standard. Books to browse. Large country garden.

B&B from £45pp, Rooms 1 twin, 1 family, all en-suite, No smoking, Children over 5, Pets by arrangement, Open Easter - October.

Miriam Ellison, **New House Farm,** Clun, Shropshire SY7 8NJ
Tel: 01588 638314   **Map Ref 9**

THE ANCHOR INN, a 14th century Drovers Inn. Horses welcome, can be stabled. Excellent riding and walking country. Offa's Dyke and Kerry Ridgway close proximity. Imaginative menu using fresh local produce. Tea/coffee in all rooms. Fully licensed. Golf, shooting, fishing available nearby. Ludlow, Shrewsbury 25 miles. Car parking. Informal atmosphere.
B&B from £25pp, Dinner from £7.50, Rooms 1 single, 2 twin, 5 double, some en-suite, Children over 12 & pets by arrangement, Open all year except Christmas.
Michael Steedman & Alexandra Melville, **The Anchor Inn,** Anchor, nr Craven Arms, Shropshire SY7 8PR
Tel: 01686 670900 Fax: 01686 670900   **Map Ref 10**

SHROPSHIRE

THE ELLESMERE HOTEL, a 17th century coaching inn in the centre of an attractive market town. Restaurant, lounge and bar serving wholesome, hearty food. Quality wines, spirits and cask conditioned ales.

B&B from £27, Dinner available, Rooms 3 single, 7 double, 2 twin, all en-suite, Open all year.
The Ellesmere Hotel, High Street, Ellesmere, Shropshire SY12 0ES
Tel: 01691 622055 Fax: 01691 622055   **Map Ref 11**

....

VALLEY HOTEL, a Georgian listed building situated in World Heritage Site of Ironbridge. Riverside location with large car park. All Ironbridge Gorge Museum attractions are within walking distance of the hotel.
B&B from £55, Dinner available, Rooms 9 single, 24 double, 2 twin, all en-suite, Open all year.
Valley Hotel, Ironbridge, Telford, Shropshire TF8 7DW
Tel: 01952 432247 Fax: 01952 432308   **Map Ref 12**

....

THE LIBRARY HOUSE, a fascinating 18th century house, 60 metres from the Ironbridge, where you are assured of a friendly, personal welcome, comfortable rooms and home cooking. Free car park passes available.

B&B from £38, Rooms 1 double, 2 triple, some en-suite, Open all year.
The Library House, 11 Severn Bank, Ironbridge, Telford, Shropshire TF8 7AN
Tel: 01952 680068 Fax: 01952 684275   **Map Ref 12**

....

SEVERN LODGE, a Georgian house set in a lovely garden and situated a few yards from the famous iron bridge and River Severn.
B&B from £40, Rooms 2 double, 1 twin, 2 en-suite, Open all year.
Severn Lodge, New Road, Ironbridge, Telford, Shropshire TF8 7AS
Tel: 01952 432148 Fax: 01952 432148   **Map Ref 12**

....

TONTINE HOTEL, a family hotel with personal service and attention built 200 years ago by the makers of the first iron bridge.
B&B from £20, Dinner available, Rooms 2 single, 4 double, 2 twin, 2 triple, 2 family, some en-suite, Open all year.
Tontine Hotel, The Square, Ironbridge, Telford, Shropshire TF8 7AL
Tel: 01952 432127 Fax: 01952 432094   **Map Ref 12**

....

For centuries, travellers have enjoyed the hospitality of **THE SEVERN TROW**, a former ale house, lodgings and brothel, catering for boatmen of the river. Today, guests can enjoy 4-poster beds. Some rooms have TV, all have tea/coffee facilities. English breakfast served, vegetarian or special diets on request. Guests of limited mobility welcome. TV lounge. Residential licence. Parking.
B&B from £20pp, Rooms 1 twin, 2 double, all en-suite, No smoking or pets, Open all year except Christmas & New Year.
Jim & Pauline Hannigan, **The Severn Trow,** Church Road, Jackfield, Ironbridge, Shropshire TF8 7ND
Tel: 01952 883551   **Map Ref 12**

....

THE FEATHERS AT LUDLOW, a historic inn with Jacobean interior, sited within the mediaeval walls of Ludlow, historic capital of the English/Welsh Marches.
B&B from £64.25, Dinner available, Rooms 11 single, 15 double, 11 twin, 2 triple, all en-suite, Open all year.
The Feathers at Ludlow, Bull Ring, Ludlow, Shropshire SY8 1AA
Tel: 01584 875261 Fax: 01584 876030   **Map Ref 13**

....

OVERTON GRANGE HOTEL, a country house hotel in its own grounds, with commanding views over the Shropshire countryside. Noted for comfort and cuisine.

B&B from £40, Dinner available, Rooms 1 single, 10 double, 4 twin, 1 triple, most en-suite, Open all year.
Overton Grange Hotel, Old Hereford Road, Ludlow, Shropshire SY8 4AD
Tel: 01584 873500 Fax: 01584 873254   **Map Ref 13**

CECIL GUEST HOUSE, one mile form centre of historic market town of Ludlow. Bedrooms have colour televisions, tea/coffee. Guests lounge, no smoking except in separate licensed bar. Central heating. Quiet secluded garden. Off road parking. Nearby attractions include Offas Dyke, Ironbridge, Severn Valley Railway, Mortimer Forest, Castle.
B&B from £19pp, Dinner £12, Rooms 2 single, 4 twin, 2 double, 1 family, some en-suite, Restricted smoking, Children welcome, No pets, Open all year except Christmas & New Year.
Sue & Ron Green, **Cecil Guest House,** Sheet Rd, Ludlow, Shropshire SY8 1LR
Tel: 01584 872442 Fax: 01584 872442   **Map Ref 13**

THE MOOR HALL, built in 1789 circa and set in 5 acres of mature grounds with pools, amid unspoilt countryside and yet close to Ludlow. Relaxed, informal atmosphere. Fishing.

B&B from £22, Dinner available, Rooms 2 double, 1 twin, all en-suite, Open all year.
The Moor Hall, Cleedownton, Ludlow, Shropshire SY8 3EG
Tel: 01584 823209 Fax: 01584 823387   **Map Ref 14**

DINHAM WEIR HOTEL & RESTAURANT, beautifully situated on the banks of the River Teme. All bedrooms with riverside views. Intimate candlelit restaurant.
B&B from £30, Dinner available, Rooms 4 double, 2 twin, all en-suite, Open all year.
Dinham Weir Hotel & Restaurant, Dinham Bridge, Ludlow, Shropshire SY8 1EH
Tel: 01584 874431   **Map Ref 15**

DINHAM HALL HOTEL & RESTAURANT, a splendid Georgian residence opposite Ludlow Castle and with open views of the countryside from all rooms. Restaurant noted for cuisine.

B&B from £65, Dinner available, Rooms 2 single, 6 double, 4 twin, all en-suite, Open all year.
Dinham Hall Hotel & Restaurant, Dinham By The Castle, Ludlow, Shropshire SY8 1EJ
Tel: 01584 876464 Fax: 01584 876019   **Map Ref 15**

CLIFFE HOTEL, a hotel in its own garden conveniently placed on the edge of town, near the castle, river and forest.

B&B from £30, Dinner available, Rooms 1 single, 4 double, 4 twin, all en-suite.
Cliffe Hotel, Dinham, Ludlow, Shropshire SY8 2JE
Tel: 01584 872063 Fax: 01584 873991   **Map Ref 15**

THE BEAR HOTEL, a privately owned 16th century inn, with the character of bygone age but 20th century comforts and a warm and friendly atmosphere.
B&B from £30, Dinner available, Rooms 1 single, 3 double, 2 twin, all en-suite, Open all year.
The Bear Hotel, Hodnet, Market Drayton, Shropshire TF9 3NH
Tel: 01630 685214 Fax: 01630 685787   **Map Ref 16**

THE TALBOT HOTEL, a 15th century Coaching Inn in the heart of Shropshire. Facilities include Bed & Breakfast, tea/coffee facilities, colour TV, hair dryer. Licensed. The market town of Ludlow and Bewdley are only a short distance away.

B&B from £40, Rooms 1 single, 2 twin, 5 double, most en-suite, Children welcome, No pets, Open all year except Christmas Eve.
Stuart Hunt, **The Talbot Hotel,** 29 High Street, Cleobury, Mortimer, Shropshire DY14 8DQ
Tel: 01299 270036 Fax: 01299 270205   **Map Ref 8**

GASKELL ARMS HOTEL, a 17th century coaching inn built of stone and brick, with beamed ceilings, log fires. Family-run freehouse. Situated on the outskirts of small mediaeval town and Wenlock Edge, close to Ironbridge.

B&B from £29, Dinner available, Rooms 7 double, 3 twin, 1 family, some en-suite, Open all year.

Gaskell Arms Hotel, Much Wenlock, Shropshire TF13 6HF
Tel: 01952 727212 Fax: 01952 727736   **Map Ref 17**

RAVEN HOTEL & RESTAURANT, a fine coaching inn which has provided hospitality since 1700. Beautifully appointed accommodation, making this an ideal base for discovering this an ideal base for discovering Shropshire. Close to Ironbridge Gorge.

B&B from £48, Dinner available, Rooms 1 single, 11 double, 3 twin, all en-suite. Open all year.

Raven Hotel & Restaurant, Barrow Street, Much Wenlock, Shropshire TF13 6EN
Tel: 01952 727251 Fax: 01952 728416   **Map Ref 17**

THE WENLOCK EDGE INN, a family run freehouse of Wenlock limestone, built about 1700. Peaceful location, fine views. Four miles from Wenlock on B4371.

B&B from £40, Dinner available, Rooms 2 double, 1 twin, all en-suite. Open all year.

The Wenlock Edge Inn, Hilltop, Wenlock Edge, Much Wenlock, Shropshire TF13 6DJ
Tel: 01746 785678 Fax: 01746 785285   **Map Ref 18**

ADAMS HOUSE HOTEL, eight bedrooms offering both en-suite and budget family accommodation. Restaurant, 40 seats, specialises in English/French cuisine. Newport is an ideally situated market town "Stopping-Off" point. Surrounding area includes Ironbridge, Weston Park and Shugborough Hall Stately Homes, RAF Cosford Air Museum.
B&B from £50pp, Dinner from £10.95, Rooms 1 single, 1 twin, 3 en-suite double, 3 family, Restricted smoking, Children welcome, No pets, Open all year.
Pat & Mike Hill, **Adams House Hotel,** 5-7 High Street, Newport, Shropshire TF10 7AR
Tel/Fax: 01952 820085   **Map Ref 19**

NORWOOD HOUSE HOTEL & RESTAURANT, a hotel of character just off the A41 Whitchurch to ~Wolverhampton road, close to Lilleshall National Sports Centre.

B&B from £25, Dinner available, Rooms 1 single, 2 double, 2 twin, 1 triple, all en-suite, Open all year.

Norwood House Hotel & Restaurant, Pave Lane, Newport, Shropshire TF10 9LQ
Tel: 01952 825896   **Map Ref 19**

FOEL, relaxed family atmosphere. Short pleasant walk to town centre. Colour TV and beverage facilities in bedrooms. Private parking. Ideal base for business, golf, fishing or exploring the beautiful countryside. Convenient for North Wales, Chester, Shrewsbury and Shropshire Lakes. Many Trust properties and castles nearby.

B&B from £15pp, Rooms 1 single, 1 twin, 1 double, Children welcome, Pets by arrangement, Open all year except Christmas.
Beryl Willetts, **Foel,** 18 Hampton Road, Oswestry, Shropshire SY11 1SJ
Tel: 01691 652184   **Map Ref 20**

SEBASTIANS HOTEL & RESTAURANT, a 16th century small hotel with beautifully decorated and furnished en-suite bedrooms. Award-winning restaurant with table d'hote and a la carte menus, featuring the finest French cuisine. Original oak beams and panelling. Chef/patron Mark Sebastian Fisher.

B&B from £36.95, Dinner available, Rooms 2 double, 1 twin, all en-suite, Open all year.
Sebastians Hotel & Restaurant, 45 Willow Street, Oswestry, Shropshire SY11 1AQ
Tel: 01691 655444 Fax: 01691 653452   **Map Ref 20**

....

SWEENEY HALL HOTEL, a haven for gracious living, offering top class hospitality in an ocean of tranquillity overlooking a panorama of unspoilt countryside.
B&B from £30, Dinner available, Rooms 1 single, 4 double, 4 twin, some en-suite, Open all year.
Sweeney Hall Hotel, Morda, Oswestry, Shropshire SY10 9EU
Tel: 01691 652450 Fax: 01691 652805   **Map Ref 21**

....

PEN-Y-DYFFRYN COUNTRY HOTEL, a peaceful, stone-built Georgian former rectory in 5 acres of grounds in Shropshire/Welsh border hills. Fully licensed, extensive a la carte menu. Quiet and relaxed atmosphere. Shrewsbury and Chester 30 minutes.

B&B from £30, Dinner available, Rooms 1 single, 3 double, 3 twin, 1 triple, all en-suite, Open all year.
Pen-y-Dyffryn Country Hotel, Rhyd-y-Croesau, Oswestry, Shropshire SY10 7DT
Tel: 01691 653700 Fax: 01691 653700   **Map Ref 22**

....

HAUGHTON HALL, is an eighteenth century country house set in 35 acres near Telford. Accommodation comprises 28 rooms all en-suite, each having TV and tea/coffee facilities. Ideally located for visitors to this beautiful county with easy access to Ironbridge, Shrewsbury and other places of interest. Email: val@hostcomp.demon.co.uk

B&B from £25pp, Dinner from £12.50, rooms 6 single, 22 double, 3 family, all en-suite, Children welcome, Pets by arrangement, Open all year.
Mr Alan K Taylor, **Haughton Hall,** Haughton Lane, Shifnal TF11 8HW
Tel: 01952 468300 Fax: 01952 468313   **Map Ref 23**

....

ODFELLOWS WINE BAR, is one of the areas must popular wine bars. Self contained luxurious rooms with TV, fridge, etc. Our rates includes Continental breakfast in the room. We are near Shifnal Railway station close to M54. Ideally located for business visitors and tourists to the area.
B&B from £40-£50pp, Dinner from £5.20, Rooms 4 double, 1 family, all en-suite, Children welcome, No pets, Open all year except Christmas, Boxing & New Years Day.
Ross Ireland, **Odfellows Wine Bar,** Market Place, Shifnal, Shropshire TF11 9AU
Tel: 01952 461517 Fax: 01952 463855   **Map Ref 23**

....

PARK HOUSE HOTEL, a magnificent character hotel converted from 2 17th century country houses. Located just a few minutes' drive from exit 4 of M54. 40 minutes from Birmingham. Leisure facilities.
B&B from £55, Dinner available, Rooms 5 single, 30 double, 19 twin, all en-suite, Open all year.
Park House Hotel, Park Street, Shifnal, Shropshire TF11 9BA
Tel: 01952 460128 Fax: 01952 461658   **Map Ref 23**

....

HUNDRED HOUSE HOTEL, RESTAURANT & COUNTRY INN, a homely, family run hotel, with atmospheric historic bars, interesting bar food and intimate restaurant. Antique patchwork themed bedrooms with all facilities. Beautiful, relaxing cottage gardens.

B&B from £65, Dinner available, Rooms 2 single, 2 double, 1 twin, 5 triple, all en-suite, Open all year.
Hundred House Hotel, Restaurant & Country Inn, Bridgnorth Road, Norton, Shifnal, Shropshire TF11 9EE
Tel: 01952 730353 Fax: 01952 730355   **Map Ref 24**

VILLAGE FARM LODGE, tastefully converted farm buildings in Sheriffhales village, situated on the B4379 off the A5. Minutes from Telford and Ironbridge Gorge.
B&B from £28.50, Rooms 1 single, 2 double, 3 twin, 1 triple, 1 family, all en-suite, Open all year.
Village Farm Lodge, Sheriffhales, Shifnal, Shropshire TF11 8RD
Tel: 01952 862763 Fax: 01952 201310 **Map Ref 25**

....

CROMWELLS HOTEL & WINE BAR, a 15th century coaching inn in Shrewsbury town centre, offering comfortable, well-maintained character bedrooms. Cosy restaurant, with excellent local reputation, and lively wine bar.
B&B from £23, Dinner available, Rooms 2 single, 2 double, 1 twin, 2 triple, Open all year.
Cromwells Hotel & Wine Bar, 11 Dogpole, Shrewsbury, Shropshire SY1 1EN
Tel: 01743 361440 Fax: 01743 361440 **Map Ref 26**

....

ABBEY COURT HOUSE, is five minutes walk from Shrewsbury Quest Centre with easy access to all major roads. En-suite bedrooms (including ground floor) are provided in an adjacent annexe. All have TV, telephone and tea/coffee making facilities. Guest's lounge and private parking. Discount for 3 nights or more.
B&B from £17pp, Rooms 2 single, 3 twin, 4 double, 4 family, some en-suite, Restricted smoking, Children welcome, No pets, Open all year except Christmas.
Cherry Turnock, **Abbey Court House,** 134 Abbey Forgate, Shrewsbury, Shropshire SY2 6AU
Tel: 01743 364416 **Map Ref 26**

....

ABBOT'S MEAD HOTEL, a Georgian town house between town centre and the River Severn. All bedrooms have private facilities, colour TV, tea/coffee makers, direct dial telephone. Car parking.
B&B from £34, Dinner available, Rooms 10 double, 4 twin, all en-suite, Open all year.
Abbot's Mead Hotel, 9-10 St. Julian Friars, Shrewsbury, Shropshire SY1 1XL
Tel: 01743 235281 Fax: 01743 369133 EMail: abbotsmead@studi.erta.net **Map Ref 26**

....

ALBRIGHT HUSSEY HOTEL & RESTAURANT, a historic 16th century moated manor house, only 2 miles from Shrewsbury town centre. Renowned for fine food, fine wines and impeccable and friendly service. In the heart of Shropshire countryside yet only 5 minutes from M54 motorway link.
B&B from £73 single, £95 double, Dinner available, Rooms 10 double, 4 twin, all en-suite. Open all year.
Albright Hussey Hotel & Restaurant, Ellesmere Road, Shrewsbury, Shropshire SY4 3AF
Tel: 01939 290571 Fax: 01939 291143 **Map Ref 26**

....

THE MERMAID HOTEL, a Grade II listed manor house on the banks of the River Severn. Two miles from Shrewsbury and 7 miles from Telford.
B&B from £35, Dinner available, Rooms 2 single, 11 double, 4 twin, 1 family, all en-suite, Open all year.
The Mermaid Hotel, Atcham, Shrewsbury, Shropshire SY5 6QG
Tel: 01743 761220 Fax: 01743 761292 **Map Ref 27**

....

SOULTON HALL, super home cooking and en-suite rooms at this Tudor manor house ensure a relaxing holiday. Moated Domesday site in grounds, private riverside and woodland walks.
B&B from £33.50, Dinner available, Rooms 1 single, 3 double, 1 twin, 1 triple, most en-suite, Open all year.
Soulton Hall, Wem, Shrewsbury, Shropshire SY4 5RS
Tel: 01939 232786 Fax: 01939 234097 **Map Ref 28**

....

WINDMILL COTTAGE GUESTHOUSE, a Grade II listed 17th century black and white property with original exposed beams externally and internally. Nearby are Hawkstone Hall, Park and Follies and Hodnet Hall Garden. Ideal for golfers, walkers and countryside lovers.
B&B from £24.99, Rooms 3 twin, both en-suite.
Windmill Cottage Guesthouse, Weston-under-Redcastle, Shrewsbury, Shropshire SY4 5UX
Tel: 01939 200219 **Map Ref 29**

410

BRIDGE HOUSE, is a 17th century period residence, situated in the beautiful Ironbridge Gorge. Ideal for exploring the wonders that Shropshire has to offer. Rooms are beautifully decorated with TV, tea/coffee facilities. Residents lounge. Car park. Interesting garden for visitors to enjoy. In a relaxing and comfortable place to stay.

B&B from £48pp, Rooms 1 twin, 2 double, 1 family, all en-suite, Children welcome, No pets, Open all year except Christmas & New Year.
Janet Hedges, **Bridge House,** Buildwas, Telford, Shropshire TF8 7BN
Tel: 01952 432105 **Map Ref 30**

MADELEY COURT HOTEL, a country house style hotel converted from 16th century manor house in the heart of Ironbridge Gorge. Telford and motorway network 5 minutes' drive.

B&B from £60, Dinner available, Rooms 7 single, 31 double, 8 twin, 1 triple, all en-suite, Open all year.

Madeley Court Hotel, Castlefields Way, Madeley, Telford, Shropshire TF7 5DW
Tel: 01952 680068 Fax: 01952 684275 **Map Ref 31**

A warm welcome awaits you at **STONE HOUSE GUEST HOUSE**. Situated in a convenient and pleasant location near to many tourist attractions. Accommodation with all rooms offering en-suite facilities, colour TV and tea/coffee making facilities. On site parking is available for guests.

B&B from £20pp, Dinner from £10, Rooms 3 twin, 2 double, all en-suite, No smoking, Children welcome, No pets, Open all year.
Pauline Silcock, **Stone House Guest House,** Shifnal Road, Priorslee, Telford, Shropshire TF2 9NN
Tel: 01952 290119 Fax: 01952 290119 **Map Ref 32**

THE OAKS HOTEL & RESTAURANT, a family-owned hotel, 2.5 miles from Telford town centre. Restaurant, public bar. En-suite bedrooms with telephone, colour TV, tea/coffee facilities.

B&B from £42, Dinner available, Rooms 6 single, 3 double, 3 twin, all en-suite, Open all year.
The Oaks Hotel & Restaurant, Redhill St. Georges, Telford, Shropshire TF2 9NZ
Tel: 01952 620126 Fax: 01952 620257 **Map Ref 33**

FALCON HOTEL, a small, family run 18th century coaching hotel, 10 miles from Shrewsbury, 4 miles from Shrewsbury, 4 miles from Ironbridge, 18 miles from M6 at the end of M54 (exit 7).

B&B from £27, Dinner available, Rooms 2 single, 4 double, 4 twin, 1 family, most en-suite, Open all year.
Falcon Hotel, Holyhead Road, Wellington, Telford, Shropshire TF1 2DD
Tel: 01952 255011 **Map Ref 34**

CHURCH FARM, down a lime tree avenue in a peaceful village between Shrewsbury and Telford, lies a superbly situated beamed Georgian Farmhouse. Mature gardens with mediaeval stonework, old roses and many unusual plants. Attractive bedrooms with TV's, tea/coffee, some en-suite, with ground floor available. 1 mile M54(J7) and A5. AA QQQQ Selected.
B&B from £20pp, Rooms 2 twin, 3 double, some en-suite, Children over 10, Pets by arrangement, Open all year.
Mrs Jo Savage, **Church Farm,** Wrockwardine, Wellington, Telford, Shropshire TF6 5DG
Tel: 01952 244917 Fax: 01952 244917 **Map Ref 35**

Somerset is famed the world over for its cheddar cheese and cider. It is also known for its varied scenery from the unspoilt countryside and towns bordering with Dorset and Wiltshire to the wild expanse of Exmoor where it meets Devon in the west.

The Exmoor National Park covers two hundred and sixty five square miles from Raleigh's Cross in Somerset to Combe Martin in Devon and includes coast, pastoral moorland and heath. It is home for the red deer and the native Exmoor ponies. Exmoor has many attractive villages including Dunster, perhaps the area's most beautiful with a wide main street of old houses and the seventeenth century Yarn Market. Brendon has thatched and whitewashed cottages with a medieval packhorse bridge across the East Lyn River.

The National Park coastline meets the sea at the Bristol Channel and provides some outstanding walks along cliff-top routes. Attractive towns and villages include Lynton, a Victorian creation perched on a cliff. Lynmouth's picturesque small harbour is lined by thatched houses.

Somerset's county town and commercial centre, Taunton has much of interest for the tourist from its Norman castle, the grandest of the town's buildings, to its churches. Nearby Wellington has some fine Georgian houses and it is noted for its ancient wool industry.

Glastonbury is famous for its abbey which is in ruins. Arthurian legend links Glastonbury with Avalon, the place to which Arthur was taken after his death. The low lying marshy region of Sedgemoor stretches from the Mendips to Taunton and Ilminster and its willows are used for the local industry of basket making.

The Mendip Hills cover a broad band of Somerset from Weston-super-Mare to Frome. Composed of limestone covering old red sandstone, the area has a number of famous caves and swallow holes. Cheddar is at the foot of the famous Cheddar Gorge and there are more than four hundred holes or caverns in the area. Cheddar cheese originated here more than three hundred years ago. To the south west is Wookey, two miles away from the famous group of caves known as Wookey Hole. The River Axe flows through the caves before widening into a lake.

The town of Shepton Mallet was an important wool market in the middle ages. Wells is famous for its cathedral, which has one of the finest west fronts in Britain, originally embellished with statues of angels, saints and prophets. Yeovil is the only sizeable industrial town in south Somerset. Cadbury Castle sits on top of a steep hill. According to legend it is from here that King Arthur set out to find his sword Excalibur.

Somerset

left, Wells Cathedral

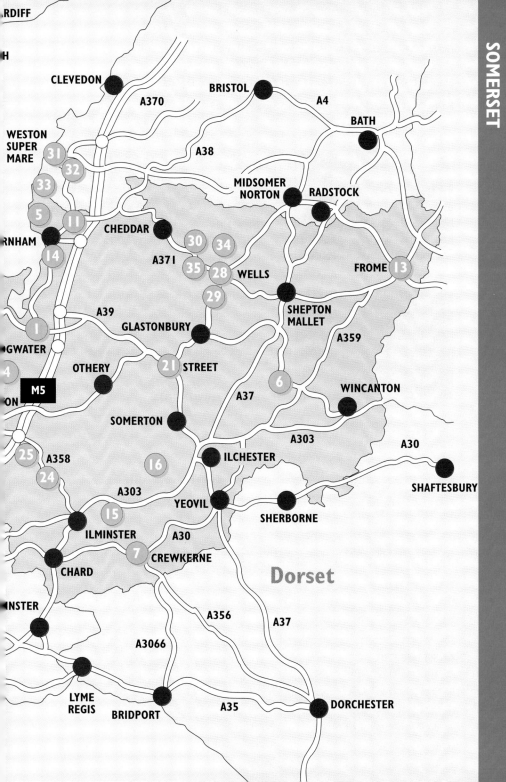

RDIFF

H

CLEVEDON

BRISTOL

A370

A4

BATH

WESTON
SUPER
MARE

31

32

A38

MIDSOMER
NORTON

RADSTOCK

33

5

11

CHEDDAR

30

34

FROME

13

RNHAM

14

A371

35

28

WELLS

A39

29

SHEPTON
MALLET

A359

1

GLASTONBURY

GWATER

4

OTHERY

21

STREET

6

WINCANTON

M5

A37

ON

SOMERTON

A303

A30

25

A358

ILCHESTER

SHAFTESBURY

24

16

A303

YEOVIL

SHERBORNE

15

ILMINSTER

A30

7

CREWKERNE

Dorset

CHARD

NSTER

A356

A37

A3066

LYME
REGIS

BRIDPORT

A35

DORCHESTER

FRIARN COURT HOTEL, a comfortable friendly hotel with restaurant and cosy bar, ideal base for business or pleasure. Double price is for special weekend breaks. Colour brochure.

B&B from £39.90, Dinner available, Rooms 2 single, 6 twin, 7 double, 1 triple, all en-suite, No smoking, Children welcome, Open all year.
Friarn Court Hotel, 37 St Mary Street, Bridgwater, Somerset TA6 3LX
Tel: 01278 452859 Fax: 01278 452988   **Map Ref 1**

....

THE OLD VICARAGE HOTEL, one of three mediaeval buildings in Bridgwater. The oak room bears carved mantel dated 1734. Opposite St. Marys Church. It now has 15 well appointed en-suite bedrooms. Licensed Bar. Car park. Lovely gardens. Relaxed, friendly atmosphere. Only 1.5 miles junction 24 M5.
B&B from £28.75pp, Dinner available from £5.20, Rooms 2 single, 3 twin, 9 double, 1 family, all en-suite, Children welcome, Pets by arrangement, Open all year except Boxing Day.
Philip & Pamela Jacobs, **The Old Vicarage Hotel,** 45-51 St. Mary Street, Bridgwater, Somerset TA6 3EQ
Tel: 01278 458891 Fax: 01287 445297   **Map Ref 1**

....

COMBE HOUSE HOTEL, a 17th century hotel in beautiful Butterfly Combe in the heart of the Quantock Hills. Traditional hospitality in rural peace and quiet.

B&B from £28pp, Dinner available, Rooms 4 single, 5 double, 7 twin, all en-suite, Restricted smoking, Children & pets welcome, Open all year.

Combe House Hotel, Holford, Bridgwater, Somerset TA5 1RZ
Tel: 01278 741382 Fax: 01278 741322   **Map Ref 2**

....

STOWEY TEA ROOMS, situated in this historic village at the foot of the Quantocks, we offer comfortable en-suite accommodation with TV, tea/coffee facilities. The village has three pubs, a farm shop, Coleridge Museum and Quantock visitor centre. Ideal base for exploring the Quantocks and Exmoor.

B&B from £15pp, Rooms 2 double, 1 family, all en-suite, No smoking, Children welcome, Pets by arrangement, Open all year except Christmas & New Year.
Mrs Morse, **Stowey Tea Rooms,** 18 Castle Street, Nether Stowey, Bridgwater, Somerset TA5 1LN
Tel: 01278 733686 Fax: 01278 733022   **Map Ref 3**

....

APPLE TREE INN & RESTAURANT, a small family hotel easily located on he main A39, surrounded by rolling Quantock Hills. Large car park and gardens. Well known restaurant. Near Nether Stowey, some 6 miles west of Bridgwater.

B&B from £36.75, Dinner available, Rooms 2 single, 3 twin, 3 double, 3 triple, most en-suite, No smoking, Children welcome, No pets, Open all year.
Apple Tree Inn & Restaurant, Keenthorne, Nether Stowey, Bridgwater, Somerset TA5 1HZ
Tel: 01278 733238 Fax: 01278 732693   **Map Ref 3**

....

WALNUT TREE HOTEL, set in the heart of Somerset. An 18th century coaching inn on A38, 1 mile from M5 exit 24. A welcome stopover for businessmen and tourists.

B&B from £37, Dinner available, Rooms 2 single, 8 twin, 23 double, all en-suite, Children welcome, Open all year.

Walnut Tree Hotel, North Petherton, Bridgwater, Somerset TA6 6QA
Tel: 01278 662255 Fax: 01278 663946   **Map Ref 4**

QUANTOCK VIEW HOUSE, a comfortable, family run guest house in central Somerset. En-suite facilities available. Close to hills and coast, yet only minutes from M5, junction 24.

B&B from £16, Dinner available, Rooms 1 twin, 1 double, 1 triple, 1 family, most en-suite, Children welcome, Open all year.

Quantock View House, Bridgwater Road, North Petherton, Bridgwater, Somerset TA6 6PR
Tel: 01278 663309   **Map Ref 4**

Part 17th Century, newly refurbished. **YEW TREE HOUSE** offers comfortable spacious rooms with tea/coffee and colour TV. Guest lounge has beamed ceilings, inglenook fireplace and colour TV. Nearby 7 miles of sandy beaches. Private car park. 5 miles J22 M5. Easy reach of Wales, Exmoor & West Country.
B&B from £22pp, Rooms 1 twin, 1 double, 1 family, all en-suite, No smoking, Children welcome, Pets by arrangement, Open January -November
Gill & Nigel Crewdson, **Yew Tree House,** Hurn Lane, Berrow, Burnham-on-Sea, Somerset TA8 2QT
Tel: 01278 751382 Fax: 01278 751382   **Map Ref 5**

GEORGE HOTEL, a 15th century thatched coaching inn with en-suite rooms, 2 bars and noted restaurant. Centrally located for many National Trust house and gardens, Cheddar, Wells, Glastonbury and Bath.

B&B from £40, Dinner available, Rooms 4 single, 3 twin, 7 double, 1 family, all en-suite, No smoking, Children welcome, Open all year.

George Hotel, Market Place, Castle Cary, Somerset BA7 7AH
Tel: 01963 350761 Fax: 01963 350035
                                                                                        Map Ref 6

THE HORSE POND INN & MOTEL, a 17th century coaching inn with its old stables converted to spacious motel units, within a few steps of the main building.

B&B from £30, Dinner available, Rooms 2 twin, 1 double, 3 triple, some en-suite, No smoking, Children welcome, Open all year.

The Horse Pond Inn & Motel, The Triangle, Castle Cary, Somerset BA7 7BD
Tel: 01963 350318 & 351762/4   **Map Ref 6**

THE GEORGE HOTEL & RESTAURANT, a recently refurbished 17th century grade II listed coaching inn in the market square. Ideally located for touring. Fine food, real ales, warm welcome!

B&B from £24, Dinner available, Rooms 3 single, 2 twin, 6 double, 1 family, 1 triple, most en-suite, Children welcome, Open all year.

The George Hotel & Restaurant, Market Square, Crewkerne, Somerset TA18 7LP
Tel: 01460 73650 Fax: 01460 72974   **Map Ref 7**

BROADVIEW GARDENS, an unusual Colonial bungalow, a winner of awards for quality, friendliness and traditional English cooking. En-suite rooms overlooking acre of beautiful secluded gardens. Dorset border, perfect   touring   base.   EMail: broadgdn@eurobell.co.uk
http://www.broadgdn.eurobell.co.uk

B&B from £25-£28, Dinner available, Rooms 2 twin, 1 double, all with en-suite or private facilities, No smoking, Children welcome, Open all year.
Broadview Gardens, East Crewkerne, Crewkerne, Somerset TA18 7AG
Tel: 01460 73424 Fax: 01460 73424   **Map Ref 7**

417

DASSELS COUNTRY HOUSE, a Georgian style country guest house, magnificently situated on the Devon and Somerset border with panoramic views.
B&B from £30, Dinner available, Rooms 1 single, 3 twin, 3 double, 3 triple, all en-suite, No smoking, Children welcome, Open all year.
Dassels Country House, Dassels, Dulverton, Somerset TA22 9RZ
Tel: 01398 341561 Fax: 01398 341203   **Map Ref 8**

THE ANCHOR INN & HOTEL,, a charming residential country inn and hotel on the banks of the River Exe, with its own fishing. Stable restaurant overlooking river. Ideal base for exploring Exmoor.

B&B from £37, Dinner available, Rooms 1 single, 2 twin, 3 doubler,all en-suite, Children welcome, Open all year.
The Anchor Inn & Hotel,, Exebridge, Dulverton, Somerset TA22 9AZ
Tel: 01398 323433 Fax: 01398 323808   **Map Ref 9**

EXTON HOUSE HOTEL, a former rectory in a delightful rural setting on side of the Exe Valley. Turn off A396 at Bridgetown and we are half a mile on the right.
B&B from £27, Dinner available, Rooms 1 single, 3 twin, 5 double, all with private or en-suite, No smoking, Children welcome, Open all year.
Exton House Hotel, Exton, Dulverton, Somerset TA22 9JT
Tel: 01643 851365 Fax: 01643 851213   **Map Ref 10**

KNOLL LODGE, comfortable accommodation and quality food in friendly and peaceful rural surroundings. Each room attractively decorated with antique pine furniture and hand made American patchwork quilts, tea/coffee facilities and colour TV. 2 and a half miles from M5, Junction 22. Guest lounge. Ample parking.
B&B from £21pp, Dinner from £11, Rooms 1 twin, 2 double, all en-suite/private bathroom, No smoking or pets, Children over 12, Open all year except Christmas.
Jaqui Collins, **Knoll Lodge,** Church Road, East Brent, Somerset TA9 4HZ
Tel: 01278 760294   **Map Ref 11**

FOURWINDS GUEST HOUSE, a comfortable and friendly guest house with all the amenities of a small hotel. Half a mile north of town centre.
B&B from £25, Dinner available, Rooms 1 single, 2 twin, 2 double, 1 family, most en-suite, No smoking, Children welcome, No pets, Open all year.
Fourwinds Guest House, 19 Bath Road, Frome, Somerset BA11 2HJ
Tel: 01373 462618 Fax: 01373 453029   **Map Ref 13**

MENDIP LODGE HOTEL, set in 3.5 acres, overlooking Mendip Hills, near Bath, Wells and Longleat. Restaurant and terrace for dining al fresco.
B&B from £42.50, Dinner available, Rooms 6 single, 14 twin, 10 double, 6 family, 4 triple, all en-suite, Children welcome, Open all year.
Mendip Lodge Hotel, Bath Road, Frome, Somerset BA11 2HP
Tel: 01373 463223 Fax: 01373 463990   **Map Ref 13**

LABURNHAM HOUSE, set in a rural location near beaches. Indoor swimming pool, clay pigeon shooting, tennis court and water skiing. Restaurant. Situated in quiet location on edge of nature reserve. 3 miles from Burnham-on-Sea.
B&B from £27, Dinner available, Rooms 11 twin, 7 double, 7 triple, all en-suite, Children welcome, Open all year.
Laburnham House, Sloway Lane, West Huntspill, Highbridge, Somerset TA9 3RJ
Tel: 01278 781830 Fax: 01278 781612   **Map Ref 14**

THE PHEASANT, a beautiful 17th century farmhouse converted into a sumptuously furnished old world style hotel and restaurant. Renowned for comfort, atmosphere and food. Just off A303.
B&B from £70, Dinner available, Rooms 2 twin, 6 double, all en-suite, Children welcome, No pets, Open all year.
The Pheasant, Seavington St Mary, Ilminster, Somerset TA19 0QH
Tel: 01460 240502 Fax: 01460 242388   **Map Ref 15**

THE DEVONSHIRE ARMS HOTEL, built as a hunting lodge by the Duke of Devonshire in 1787.

B&B from £40, Dinner available, Rooms 5 double, 3 twin, 1 triple, all en-suite, Children welcome, No pets, Open all year.
The Devonshire Arms Hotel, Long Sutton, Langport, Somerset TA10 9LP
Tel: 01458 241271 & 0385 348800 Fax: 01458 241037   **Map Ref 16**

....

MAYFAIR HOTEL, a Victorian house hotel with lovely decor and furnishings. All rooms en-suite and with refrigerator.
Family run and home cooking. 3 minutes from sea and shops.
B&B from £25, Dinner available, Rooms 2 single, 2 twin, 4 double, 5 triple, all en-suite or with private facilities, No smoking,
Children welcome, No pets, Open March - October.
Mayfair Hotel, 25 The Avenue, Minehead, Somerset TA24 5AY
Tel: 01643 702719   **Map Ref 17**

....

KILDARE LODGE, a family run, Edwin Lutyens designed, grade II listed building. Elegant a la carte licensed bar, bar
meals, well appointed en-suite accommodation, including family rooms.

B&B from £19, Dinner available, Rooms 1 single, 2 twin, 4 double, 2 family, most en-suite, Children welcome, Open all year.
Kildare Lodge, Townsend Road, Minehead, Somerset TA24 5RQ
Tel: 01643 702009 Fax: 01643 706516   **Map Ref 17**

....

FERN COTTAGE, a large 16th century traditional Exmoor cottage in National Trust wooded vale. Dramatic scenery and
wildlife. Fine classic cooking and comprehensive wine list. Special breaks available.
B&B from £26.50, Dinner available, Rooms 3 double, 1 triple, all with private or en-suite, No smoking, Open all year.
Fern Cottage, Allerford, Minehead, Somerset TA24 8HN
Tel: 01643 862215 Fax: 01643 862215   **Map Ref 18**

....

EXMOOR WHITE HORSE HOTEL, an old world inn standing on the green beside the River Exe in beautiful Exmoor
village. Local blacksmith at working village, with the rolling moors just up the road.

B&B from £25, Dinner available, Rooms 3 twin, 12 double, 3 triple, all en-suite, No smoking, Children welcome, Open all year.
Exmoor White Horse Hotel, Exford, Minehead, Somerset TA24 7PY
Tel: 01643 831229 Fax: 01643 831246   **Map Ref 19**

....

CHANNEL HOUSE HOTEL, a hotel specialising in first class food and service. Beautiful gardens in peaceful location.
The bedrooms will suit those who appreciate quality. Perfect for exploring Exmoor.
B&B from £60, Dinner available, Rooms 5 twin, 2 double, 1 triple, all en-suite, Children welcome, No pets, Open March - November
& Christmas.
Channel House Hotel, Church Path, off Northfield Road, Minehead, Somerset TA24 5QG
Tel: 01643 703229 Fax: 01643 708925 Email: channel.house@virgin.net   **Map Ref 17**

....

ANCHOR & SHIP HOTEL, an attractive, quiet, comfortable hotel on waters edge. Picturesque harbour amid Exmoors
magnificent scenery and coastline. Wildlife everywhere, ancient villages, mediaeval castle and smugglers coves.
B&B from £49, Dinner available, Rooms 2 single, 2 twin, 13 double, 2 triple, all en-suite, Children welcome, Open February - December.
Anchor & Ship Hotel, Porlock Harbour, Porlock, Minehead, Somerset TA24 8PB
Tel: 01643 862753 Fax: 01643 862843   **Map Ref 20**

....

PORLOCK VALE HOUSE, formerly a hunting lodge, now a small friendly hotel. Magnificent location, with 25 acres of
grounds sweeping down to the sea and with wonderful views across Porlock Bay.
B&B from £50, Dinner available, Rooms 5 twin, 10 double, most en-suite, No smoking, Open all year.
Porlock Vale House, Porlock Weir, Porlock, Minehead, Somerset TA24 8NY
Tel: 01643 862338 Fax: 01643 862338   **Map Ref 20**

THE LORNA DOONE HOTEL, a 15 room licensed hotel in village centre. All rooms en-suite with tea/coffee facilities and colour TV. Extensive home cooked a la carte menu with many vegetarian dishes. Residents lounge and bar. Ideal base for walking on Exmoor and the south west coastal path. ETB 3 Crowns. Non smoking restaurant.
B&B from £20pp, Dinner from £12, Rooms 2 single, 6 twin, 5 double, 2 family, all en-suite, Children & pets welcome, Open all year except Christmas.
Dick & Toni Thornton, **The Lorna Doone Hotel,** High Street, Porlock, Somerset TA24 8PS
Tel: 01643 862404 **Map Ref 20**

WESSEX HOTEL, with modern en-suite bedrooms, situated in the heart of Somerset, legendary country of King Arthur and the Knights of the Round Table. Nearby attractions include Bath, Glastonbury Abbey, Cheddar Gorge, Wookey Hole Caves and Wells Cathedral.

B&B from £40, Dinner available, Rooms 43 twin, 7 double, all en-suite, No smoking, Children welcome, Open all year.
Wessex Hotel, High Street, Street, Somerset BA16 0EF
Tel: 01458 443383 Fax: 01458 446589 **Map Ref 21**

FORDE HOUSE, in a peaceful location in the centre of town, close to all amenities, including public park and golf course. Warm welcome guaranteed.

B&B from £26, Rooms 1 single, 2 twin, 2 double, all en-suite, Children welcome, No pets, Open all year.
Forde House, 9 Upper High Street, Taunton, Somerset TA1 3PX
Tel: 01823 279042 Fax: 01823 279042 **Map Ref 22**

THE HEATHERTON GRANGE HOTEL, an old-fashioned family run Hotel, situated close to the Devon/Somerset border affording access to Dartmoor/Exmoor and all popular West Country tourist routes. Comfortable en-suite bedrooms, tea/coffee facilities and TV. Non-smoking restaurant offers a la carte. Bar meals are taken in the Grange Bar.
B&B from £27.50pp, Dinner from £5, Rooms 5 twin, 9 double, 1 family, all en-suite, Restricted smoking, Children welcome, No pets, Open all year.
Carol & John Northam, **The Heatherton Grange Hotel,** Bradford on Tone, Taunton, Somerset TA4 1ET
Tel: 01823 461777 Fax: 01823 461490 **Map Ref 23**

FARTHINGS HOTEL & RESTAURANT, an elegant Georgian house in lovely gardens, tastefully decorated and furnished. Friendly personal service in a comfortable and relaxed atmosphere. Only 5 minutes from junction 25 of M5 at Taunton.

B&B from £47.50, Dinner available, Rooms 4 twin, 4 double, all en-suite, No smoking, Children welcome, Open all year.
Farthings Hotel & Restaurant, Hatch Beauchamp, Taunton, Somerset TA3 6SG
Tel: 01823 480664 Fax: 01823 481118 **Map Ref 24**

HATCH INN, is situated in a quiet village a few minutes drive from the M5 (junction 25) and the county town of Taunton. All bedrooms have colour televisions and tea/coffee making facilities. Good home cooked food and real ales are served in our comfortable well stocked bar.

B&B from £16.50pp, Dinner from £5, Rooms 2 twin, 3 double, 1 family, Children welcome, Pets by arrangement, Open all year except Christmas.
Mr & Mrs Beck, **Hatch Inn,** Village Rd, Hatch Beauchamp, Taunton, Somerset TA3 6SG
Tel: 01823 480245 **Map Ref 24**

FALCON HOTEL, a family owned country house hotel in own grounds, only 1 mile east of M5 junction 25. Informal atmosphere, comfortable and well equipped.

B&B from £45, Dinner available, Rooms 5 twin, 3 double, 2 family, all en-suite, No smoking, Children welcome, Open all year.
Falcon Hotel, Henlade, Taunton, Somerset TA3 5DH
Tel: 01823 442502 Fax: 01823 442670   **Map Ref 25**

....

ORCHARD HOUSE, an elegant Georgian house within 5 minutes walk of town centre and all amenities. Fine selection of pubs and restaurants nearby. Easy access from M5.

B&B from £35 single, £50 double/twin, Dinner available, Rooms 5 twin, 1 double, all en-suite, No smoking or pets, Open all year.
Orchard House, Fons George, Middleway, Taunton, Somerset TA1 3JS
Tel: 01823 351783 Fax: 01823 351785   **Map Ref 22**

....

HIGHER DIPFORD FARM, a 120 acre dairy farm. 14th century listed Somerset longhouse with magnificent walks and views. Antique furniture, log fires and spacious en-suite rooms. Renowned for high class cuisine using fresh dairy produce.

B&B from £30, Dinner available, Rooms 2 twin, 1 double, all en-suite, No smoking, Children welcome, No pets, Open all year.
Higher Dipford Farm, Trull, Taunton, Somerset TA3 7NU
Tel: 01823 275770 & 257916   **Map Ref 26**

....

DOWNFIELD HOUSE, an attractive Victorian country house, set in secluded grounds with views over harbour and town. Comfortable lounge and chandeliered dining room. Situated close to the Quantocks and Exmoor.

B&B from £23, Dinner available, Rooms 2 twin, 6 double, all en-suite, No smoking, Children welcome, Open February - December.

Downfield House, 16 St Decuman's Rd, Watchet, Somerset TA23 0HR
Tel: 01984 631267 Fax: 01984 634369   **Map Ref 27**

....

TOR HOUSE, a historic, sympathetically restored 17th century building in delightful grounds overlooking the cathedral and Bishops Palace. Attractive, comfortable and tastefully furnished throughout. 3 minutes walk to town centre. Ample parking.

B&B from £22, Dinner available, Rooms 1 single, 1 twin, 3 double, 3 family, most en-suite, No smoking, Children welcome, No pets, Open all year.
Tor House, 20 Tor Street, Wells, Somerset BA5 2US
Tel: 01749 672322 & 672084 Fax: 01749 672322   **Map Ref 28**

....

SWAN HOTEL, a privately owned 15th century hotel with views of the cathedrals west front. Restaurant, saddle bar, log fires and four poster beds available.
B&B from £45, Dinner available, Rooms 9 single, 10 twin, 19 double, all en-suite, Children welcome, Open all year.
Swan Hotel, Sadler Street, Wells, Somerset BA5 2RX
Tel: 01749 678877 Fax: 01749 677647   **Map Ref 28**

....

BURCOTT MILL, a restored water mill with attached house and craft workshops. Friendly country atmosphere. Birds and animals. Home cooking. Opposite a good country pub. Accommodation available for wheelchair use.

B&B from £19, Rooms 1 single, 1 double, 3 triple, 1 family, all en-suite, Children welcome, Open all year.
Burcott Mill, Burcott, Wells, Somerset BA5 1BJ
Tel: 01749 673118 Fax: 01749 673118   **Map Ref 28**

LITTLEWELL FARM, is an 18th Century farmhouse nestling in a pretty garden enjoying extensive views over beautiful countryside. Cosy individually presented bedrooms with lovely antique pieces, offer comfort and high standards. Only one mile from the centre of Wells. A candlelight dinner if required is prepared with skill and imagination.

B&B from £18.50-£23pp, Dinner from £18, Rooms 1 single, 2 twin, 2 double, all en-suite, No smoking or pets, Children over 10, Open all year.
Gerry & Di Gnoyke, **Littlewell Farm,** Coxley, Wells, Somerset BA5 1QP
Tel: 01749 677914   **Map Ref 29**

BOX TREE HOUSE, a warm welcome is assured at this delightful converted 17th century farmhouse, situated next to an excellent village inn. Three comfortable en-suite rooms and charming TV lounge. Generous breakfast with local preserves, croissants and home made muffins. Workshop for stained glass with many unique items for sale.

B&B form £20pp, Rooms 1 single, 1 double, 1 family, all en-suite, Restricted smoking, Children welcome, Pets by arrangement, Open all year.
Carolyn White, **Box Tree House,** Westbury-sub-Mendip, Wells, Somerset BA5 1HA
Tel: 01749 870777 Email: doug@willowsys.demon.co.uk   **Map Ref 30**

STONELEIGH HOUSE, an 18th century farmhouse with wonderful views across open countryside. Excellent accommodation, rooms with TV and tea/coffee making facilities. A guests' lounge for your relaxation. A generous breakfast is served with homemade preserves and free range eggs. A large car park. Good pub nearby. Ideal position for walking or touring holiday.

B&B from £20pp, Rooms 1 twin, 2 double, all en-suite/private facilities, No smoking or pets, Children over 10, Open all year except Christmas.
Mrs Wendy Thompson, **Stoneleigh House,** Westbury-sub-Mendip, Wells, Somerset BA5 1HF
Tel: 01749 870668 Fax: 01749 870668   **Map Ref 30**

BRAESIDE HOTEL. All rooms en-suite, colour TV, coffee/tea making. Some rooms with sea views. Unrestricted on street parking. Directions: with sea on left take first right after Winter Gardens, then first left into Lower Church Road. Victoria Park is on the right after the left hand bend.
B&B £24pp, Dinner £12, Rooms 2 single, 1 twin, 5 double, 1 family, all en-suite, Restricted smoking, Children & pets welcome, Open all year except Christmas & New Year.
Hugh & Bronwyn Wallington, **Braeside Hotel,** 2 Victoria Park, Weston-Super-Mare, Somerset BS23 2HZ
Tel: 01934 626642 Fax: 01934 626642   **Map Ref 31**

SAXONIA, a friendly and family run guest house near beach, 15 minutes from Tropicana Leisure Centre and Sea Life Centre. All rooms are en-suite with shower, hair dryer and colour TV. Air conditioned dining room.

B&B from £20, Dinner available, Rooms 2 single, 3 twin, 2 double, 1 triple, 1 family, all with private/en-suite, Children welcome, Open all year.
Saxonia, 95 Locking Road, Weston-super-Mare, Somerset BS23 3EW
Tel: 01934 633856 Fax: 01934 623141   **Map Ref 31**

ROYAL PIER HOTEL, situated on the water's edge overlooking Weston Bay. Refurbished throughout to high standards, complementing food and service. Free parking.

B&B from £38, Dinner available, Rooms 7 single, 21 twin, 8 double, 4 triple, most en-suite, No smoking, Children welcome, No pets, Open all year.
Royal Pier Hotel, Birnbeck Road, Weston-super-Mare, Somerset BS23 2EJ
Tel: 01934 626644 Fax: 01934 624169   **Map Ref 31**

TRALEE HOTEL, a detached, licensed sea front hotel with views across Weston Bay. Lift. Entertainment. Easy level walk to all main amenities.
B&B from £17.50, Dinner available, Rooms 6 single, 9 twin, 7 double, 9 triple, most en-suite, Children welcome, No pets, Open April - October.
Tralee Hotel, Sea Front, Weston-super-Mare, Somerset BS23 2BX
Tel: 01934 626707 **Map Ref 31**

QUEENSWOOD HOTEL, a friendly family hotel set off the sea front with panoramic views. Emphasis on comfort, food, wine and service.
B&B from £30, Dinner available, Rooms 3 single, 11 double, 2 triple, 1 family, all en-suite, No smoking, Children welcome, Open all year.
Queenswood Hotel, Victoria Park, Weston-super-Mare, Somerset BS23 2HZ
Tel: 01934 416141 Fax: 01934 621759 **Map Ref 31**

MOORLANDS, a family run 18th century house in mature landscaped grounds. Beach 10 minutes drive. Good centre for many places of beauty and interest. Log fires.
B&B from £18.50, Rooms 1 single, 2 twin, 2 double, 1 triple, 1 family, most en-suite, Children welcome, Open all year.
Moorlands, Hutton, Weston-super-Mare, Somerset BS24 9QH
Tel: 01934 812283 **Map Ref 32**

COMMODORE HOTEL, with traditional hotel facilities and popular restaurant, lounge bar and buffet services. Situated in unspoilt bay, close to major resort amenities.
B&B from £42.50, Dinner available, Rooms 2 single, 3 twin, 10 double, 3 family, all en-suite, No smoking, Children welcome, No pets, Open all year.
Commodore Hotel, Sand Bay, Kewstoke, Weston-super-Mare, Somerset BS22 9UZ
Tel: 01934 415778 Fax: 01934 636483 **Map Ref 33**

UPHILL MANOR, a Manor House style but in town. 19 acres of grounds. 5 luxury double rooms plus library, smoke room, drawing room, panelled dining room. Gothic architecture in pugin style by Grace. Close to town, golf course, beach and all amenities, but very private tranquil and relaxing.

B&B from £37.50pp, Rooms 5 double, all en-suite, Restricted smoking, Children welcome, No pets, Open all year except Christmas.
Craig & Tina Kennedy, **Uphill Manor,** 3 Uphill Road South, Uphill Weston-super-Mare, Somerset BS23 4SD
Tel: 01934 644654 Fax: 01934 624603 **Map Ref 33**

GLENCOT HOUSE, an elegant country house in idyllic setting with river frontage. Small indoor pool, sauna, snooker and table tennis.

Double rooms from £84-£98, Dinner available, Rooms 3 single, 2 twin, 8 double, all en-suite, No smoking, Children welcome, Open all year.

Glencot House, Glencot Lane, Wookey Hole, Somerset BA5 1BH
Tel: 01749 677160 Fax: 01749 670210 **Map Ref 34**

WORTH HOUSE HOTEL, a small country hotel, dating from the 16th century, 2 miles from Wells on the B3139. Exposed beams and log fires.
B&B from £20, Dinner available, Rooms 1 single, 2 twin, 3 double, 1 family, all en-suite, No smoking, Children welcome, No pets, Open all year.
Worth House Hotel, Worth, Wookey, Somerset BA5 1LW
Tel: 01749 672041 Fax: 01749 672041 **Map Ref 35**

Suffolk

Constable's description of Suffolk two hundred years ago is just as fitting today. It is a county of peaceful countryside, ancient market towns and villages and unspoilt coast and estuaries. Britain's easternmost county stretches from the heaths of Newmarket in the west to the North Sea in the east, in the south to the Forest of Breckland and to the north, The Broads. There is plenty to do and see in Suffolk with places to visit from stately homes and castles to abbeys, windmills, vineyards and nature reserves. John Constable grew up in the county and immortalised the Stour valley in paintings. Thomas Gainsborough, painter of kings and courtiers in the eighteenth century, grew up in Sudbury.

The Suffolk coast's estuaries and creeks provide great sailing. The River Waveney in the North of Suffolk is part of the great network of Broadland waterways.

Lowestoft is Britain's most easterly point and has clean, sandy beaches. Nearby Southwold boasts a Blue Flag for its beach. Broadland comes right into the town at Oulton Broad and it makes a good centre for visiting the Broads. Felixstowe grew up as a Victorian resort but is now better known as a port. Boat trips on the estuary can be enjoyed - or even a day trip to Belgium.

Ipswich is the county town of Suffolk and its origins go back to Saxon times when it was among the principal towns of England. The sixteenth century Christchurch Mansion is set in one of the town's many parks and has a fine collection of paintings, including the best display of Gainsborough and Constable outside London. The Ancient House, now a bookshop, is a fine example of pargetting, an external plasterwork decoration peculiar to the area.

Inland, the towns of Sudbury and Hadleigh, grew up around wool and the cloth industry. Lavenham is a beautifully kept example of a Suffolk wool town with superb ancient buildings. The 16th century Guildhall is one of the countries finest Tudor half-timbered buildings. The tower of Dedham's church is in many of Constable's paintings and a footpath leads along the river to Flatford Mill and Willy Lott's cottage, the scene of his famous Hay Wain.

Ever since Charles II went to Newmarket to ride, the town has been associated with horses. One of the world centres of racing, horses are bred, trained and raced here.

Bury St Edmunds has an important place in English history. It was the capital of the Saxon Kingdom of England and here in 1215 the Barons of England swore to make King John sign the Magna Carta. The plan of streets in the town centre has not changed for nine hundred years.

left, Lavenham

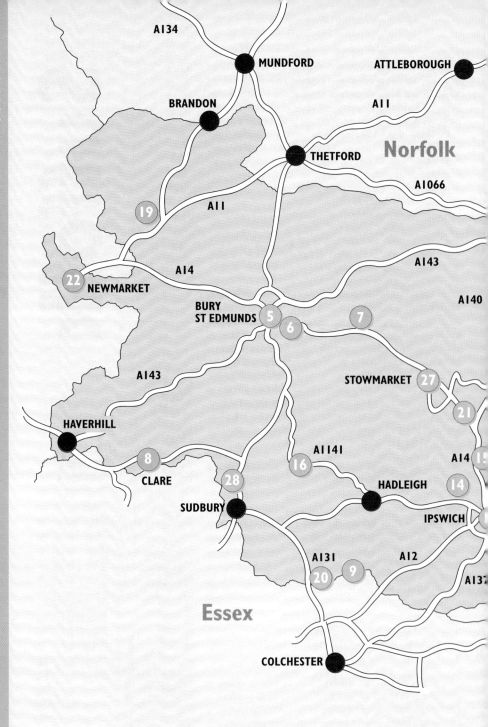

GREAT
YARMOUTH

A143

A146

A140

24

18   LOWESTOFT

23

A143

4

BUNGAY

BECCLES

3

KESSINGLAND

SCOLE

A144

A145

11

HALESWORTH

2

26   SOUTHWOLD

30

31

SAXMUNDHAM

25

A1120

17   LEISTON

A12

1   ALDEBURGH

29

WOODBRIDGE

12   FELIXSTOWE

HARWICH

WHITE LION HOTEL, an imposing hotel standing directly on the seafront of totally unspoilt fishing town of great charm, famous for classical music concerts.

B&B from £54, Dinner available, Rooms 2 single, 21 double, 14 twin, 1 triple, all en-suite, No smoking, Children welcome, Open all year.
White Lion Hotel, Market Cross Place, Aldeburgh, Suffolk IP15 5BJ
Tel: 01728 452720 Fax: 01728 452986 **Map Ref 1**

....

UPLANDS HOTEL, a comfortable family run hotel with en-suite rooms. Restaurant using local produce overlooks award winning gardens.
B&B from £35, Dinner available, Rooms 4 single, 9 twin, 5 double, 2 triple, most en-suite, No smoking, No pets, Open all year.
Uplands Hotel, Victoria Road, Aldeburgh, Suffolk IP15 5DX
Tel: 01728 452420 Fax: 01728 454872 **Map Ref 1**

....

THE ANGEL INN, a 16th century, grade II listed village inn, carefully renovated in 1995, with log fires and en-suite rooms.

B&B from £25, Dinner available, Rooms 4 double, 1 family, all en-suite, No smoking, Children welcome, Open all year.
The Angel Inn, 39 High Street, Wangford, Beccles, Suffolk NR34 8RL
Tel: 01502 578636 Fax: 01502 578535 **Map Ref 2**

....

COLVILLE ARMS MOTEL, a quiet village location, all rooms en-suite, bar, restaurant and large car park. Half hour to Norwich, Lowestoft, Yarmouth, Broads and Blue Flag beaches.
B&B from £22.50, Dinner available, Rooms 2 twin, 2 double, 1 triple, all en-suite, Children welcome, Open all year.
Colville Arms Motel, Lowestoft Road, Worlingham, Beccles, Suffolk NR34 7EF
Tel: 01502 712571 Fax: 01502 712571 **Map Ref 3**

....

THE KINGS HEAD HOTEL, a 17th century coaching inn, centre of delightful Waveney Valley market town. Central for Norwich, the Broads, Suffolk coast and countryside. Bar, restaurant and ballroom.

B&B from £25, Dinner available, Rooms 6 single, 5 twin, 2 double, 1 family, most en-suite, Children welcome, Open all year.
The Kings Head Hotel, Market Place, Bungay, Suffolk NR35 1AF
Tel: 01986 893583 Fax: 01986 893583 **Map Ref 4**

....

DUNSTON GUESTHOUSE, an attractive Victorian guest house/hotel providing high standard accommodation, quietly situated half a mile from town centre. Licensed, sun lounge, garden and car park. Groups welcome.
B&B from £20, Rooms 6 single, 3 twin, 3 double, 3 triple, most en-suite, Children welcome, No smoking, No pets, Open all year.
Dunston Guesthouse, 8 Springfield Road, Bury St Edmunds, Suffolk IP33 3AN
Tel: 01284 767981 **Map Ref 5**

....

ANGEL HOTEL, an attractive Georgian hotel with individually decorated bedrooms. Four posters and suites available. Ball room and conference rooms. Bar food and noted restaurant.

B&B from £38, Dinner available, Rooms 11 single, 12 twin, 19 double, all en-suite, Children welcome, Open all year.
Angel Hotel, Angel Hill, Bury St Edmunds, Suffolk IP33 1LT
Tel: 01284 753926 Fax: 01284 750092 **Map Ref 5**

....

BUTTERFLY HOTEL, a modern building with rustic style and decor, around open courtyard. Special weekend rates available.

B&B from £51.95, Dinner available, Rooms 32 single, 14 twin, 19 double, all en-suite, No smoking, Children welcome, Open all year.
Butterfly Hotel, A14 Bury East Exit, Moreton Hall, Bury St Edmunds, Suffolk IP32 7BW
Tel: 01284 760884 Fax: 01284 755476 **Map Ref 6**

THE GRANGE HOTEL, a family owned country house hotel with chef/proprietor, 4 miles from Bury St Edmunds.
B&B from £40, Dinner available, Rooms 2 single, 2 twin, 8 double, 1 triple, all en-suite, Children welcome, Open all year.
The Grange Hotel, Barton Road, Thurston, Bury St Edmunds, Suffolk IP31 3PQ
Tel: 01359 231260 Fax: 01359 231260   **Map Ref 7**

ETB 3 Crown Commended. **SHIP STORES** adjoins the village store and tea room in picturesque small town of Clare. All rooms en-suite with colour TV and tea/coffee facilities. Deluxe rooms in converted annexe with queen size beds and settee. Close to many historic villages.

B&B from £19.50pp, Dinner from £8.50, Rooms 1 twin, 3 double, 1 family, all en-suite, Restricted smoking, Children welcome, No pets, Open all year.
Debra & Colin Bowels, **Ship Stores,** 22 Callis Street, Clare, Suffolk CO10 3PX
Tel: 01787 277834   **Map Ref 8**

A beautifully restored 16th century village inn, situated in the heart of Constable country. **THE ANGEL INN** has an International reputation for quality food. Because of its local popularity it is recommended that table reservation are made when booking rooms.

B&B from £29.75pp, Dinner from £8.75-£25, Rooms 6 single, 1 twin, 5 double, all en-suite, Children over 10, No pets, Open all year except Christmas & New Year.
Peter Smith & Richard Wright, **The Angel Inn,** Polstead Street, Stoke-by-Nayland, Colchester, Suffolk CO6 4SA
Tel: 01206 263245 Fax: 01206 263373   **Map Ref 9**

THE CORNWALLIS ARMS, a family run country house hotel with mediaeval origins set in beautiful spacious grounds with water garden. Well appointed bedrooms with four poster beds. Characterful bar and elegant restaurant.
B&B from £60, Dinner available, Rooms 1 twin, 10 double, all en-suite, Children welcome,Open all year.
The Cornwallis Arms, Brome, Eye, Suffolk IP23 8AJ
Tel: 01379 870326 Fax: 01379 870051   **Map Ref 10**

A warm welcome awaits guests to 16th century **PRIORY HOUSE**, set in secluded lawns and gardens. Bedrooms have tea/coffee facilities. 2 have private bathroom. Wealth of beams and furnished with antiques. Guests lounge. Ideal for touring Norwich, Bury St Edmunds, the Broads, coasts and gardens. Excellent food available in the village. Colour brochure on request.
B&B from £22pp, Rooms 1 twin, 1 double, private bathroom, Restricted smoking, Children over 10, Pets by arrangement, Open all year except Christmas & New Year.
Rosemary Willis, **Priory House,** Fressingfield, Eye, Suffolk IP21 5PH
Tel: 01379 586254   **Map Ref 11**

CHIPPENHALL HALL, a listed Tudor manor, film location, heavily beamed and with inglenook fireplaces, in 7 secluded acres, Fine food and wines. 1 mile south of Fressingfield on B1116.
B&B from £31pp, Dinner available, Rooms 5 double, all en-suite, No pets, Open all year.
Chippenhall Hall, Fressingfield, Eye, Suffolk IP21 5TD
Tel: 01379 588180 & 586733 Fax: 01379 586272   **Map Ref 11**

DOLPHIN HOTEL, a private hotel, situated just five minutes from beach and ten minutes from the town centre.
B&B from £16, Dinner available, Rooms 3 single, 2 twin, 3 double, 1 triple, some en-suite, Children welcome, Open all year.
Dolphin Hotel, 41 Beach Station Road, Felixstowe, Suffolk IP11 8EY
Tel: 01394 282261   **Map Ref 12**

BROOK HOTEL, a well appointed hotel, close to town centre and seaside, offering freshly prepared snacks, mouth watering carvery, cask ales and fine wines.

B&B from £45, Dinner available, Rooms 2 single, 5 twin, 17 double, 1 family, all private or en-suite, No smoking,Children welcome,Open all year.
Brook Hotel, Orwell Road, Felixstowe, Suffolk IP11 7PF
Tel: 01394 278441 Fax: 01394 670422   **Map Ref 12**

....

WAVERLEY HOTEL, a beautifully refurbished cliff top hotel with spectacular views of the sea and promenade.

B&B from £40, Dinner available, Rooms 5 single, 8 double, 6 twin, 1 triple, all en-suite, No smoking, Children welcome, Open all year.
Waverley Hotel, Wolsey Gardens, Felixstowe, Suffolk IP11 7DF
Tel: 01394 282811 Fax: 01394 670185   **Map Ref 12**

....

THE MARLBOROUGH AT IPSWICH, a quietly situated hotel opposite Christchurch Park and Mansion. Victorian restaurant overlooking floodlit gardens. All rooms, including a suite and several with balconies, are individually decorated.
B&B from £56.50, Dinner available, Rooms 4 single, 13 double, 5 twin, all en-suite, No smoking, Children welcome, Open all year.
The Marlborough at Ipswich, Henley Road, Ipswich, Suffolk IP1 3SP
Tel: 01473 257677 Fax: 01473 226927   **Map Ref 13**

....

MULBERRY HALL, lovely old farmhouse previously owned by Cardinal Wolsey during 16th century. Log fires. Good home cooking. Prettily situated in small village 5 miles west of Ipswich. Comfortable rooms, attractively furnished with lovely garden and tennis court. Ideal venue for sightseeing.

B&B from £19pp, Dinner from £15, Rooms 1 single, 1 twin, 1 double, No smoking or pets, Children welcome, Open all year except Christmas & New Year.
Penny Debenham, **Mulberry Hall,** Burstall, Ipswich, Suffolk IP8 3DP
Tel: 01473 652348 Fax: 01473 652110   **Map Ref 14**

....

CLAYDON COUNTRY HOUSE HOTEL & RESTAURANT, a hotel with all en-suite bedrooms and table d' hote menus, excellent wines, beers and cocktail bar. Set in small village of Claydon just outside Ipswich on A45.
B&B from £48, Dinner available, Rooms 1 single, 3 twin, 10 double, all en-suite, Children welcome, No pets, Open all year.
Claydon Country House Hotel & Restaurant, Ipswich Road, Claydon, Ipswich, Suffolk IP6 0AR
Tel: 01473 830382 Fax: 01473 832476   **Map Ref 15**

....

ANGEL HOTEL, a family run 15th century inn overlooking famous Guildhall. Freshly cooked local food, menu changing daily. Saturday night stays must include dinner.

B&B from £39.50, Dinner available, Rooms 1 twin, 6 double, 1 triple, all en-suite, No smoking, Children welcome, Open all year.
Angel Hotel, Market Place, Lavenham, Suffolk CO10 9QZ
Tel: 01787 247388 Fax: 01787 248344   **Map Ref 16**

....

THE GREAT HOUSE RESTAURANT & HOTEL, renowned 16th century house with award winning restaurant offering beautifully decorated individual bedrooms with en-suite bathrooms on magnificent Lavenham Market Square. Patio and garden.

B&B from £25pp, Dinner available, Rooms 4 double, 2 twin, 1 triple, 1 family, all en-suite, Children & pets welcome, Open all year.
The Great House Restaurant & Hotel, Market Place, Lavenham, Suffolk CO10 9QZ
Tel: 01787 247431 Fax: 01747 248007   **Map Ref 16**

430

WHITE HORSE HOTEL, an 18th century Georgian hotel with a relaxed and informal atmosphere, only 2 miles from the sea, in the heart of bird watching country.
B&B from £25, Dinner available, Rooms 3 single, 4 twin, 6 double, most en-suite, No smoking, Children welcome, Open all year.
White Horse Hotel, Station Road, Leiston, Suffolk IP16 4HD
Tel: 01728 830694 Fax: 01728 833105   **Map Ref 17**

....

THE JAY'S GUEST HOUSE, a bed awaits you at sensible rates with licence bar, pool table, sea views. En-suite rooms, four poster bed, all rooms have TV, tea/coffee facilities, central heating. Open all year. Access at all times. Full English breakfast. Evening dinner. Car park. Sky TV.
B&B from £14pp, Dinner from £4.50, Rooms 2 single, 2 twin, 2 double (1 en-suite), 1 family, Children welcome, No pets, Open all year.
Brian Smith, **The Jay's Guest House,** 14 Kirkley Cliff, Lowestoft, Suffolk NR33 0BY
Tel: 01502 561124   **Map Ref 18**

....

ROYAL COURT HOTEL, is situated on the A12 in the centre of Lowestoft, close to the award winning beaches, entertainments and main shopping area. All rooms have central heating, tea/coffee, TV. Licensed bar, pool table and Sky TV. Lounge available for guests enjoyment.

B&B from £17.50pp, Dinner from £7.50, Rooms 3 single, 9 twin, 2 double, 4 family, all en-suite, Children & pets welcome, Open all year.
Terry Loman, **Royal Court Hotel,** 146 London Road South, Lowestoft, Suffolk NR33 0AZ
Tel: 01502 568901 Fax: 01502 568901   **Map Ref 18**

....

AARLAND HOUSE, for a quiet retreat, England's most easterly guest house. Hospitality trays in rooms. En-suite available. Caroline and Tony Barley welcome you.
B&B from £18, Dinner available, Rooms 1 single, 2 twin, 4 double, 1 triple, most en-suite, No smoking, Children welcome, Open all year.
Caroline & Tony Barley **Aarland House,** 36 Lyndhurst Road, Lowestoft, Suffolk NR32 4PD
Tel/Fax: 01502 585148   **Map Ref 18**

....

ALBANY HOTEL, a small, family run private hotel. 3 minutes from sandy beach and Kensington Gardens and a short distance from main shopping precinct.

B&B from £17.50, Dinner available, Rooms 2 single, 1 twin, 1 double, 1 triple, 2 family, most en-suite, Children welcome, No pets, Open all year.
Albany Hotel, 400 London Road South, Lowestoft, Suffolk NR33 0BQ
Tel: 01502 574394   **Map Ref 18**

....

THE WILLOWS GUEST HOUSE, a comfortable family run guest house, facing the Award Wining South Beach, with some en-suite facilities. Well known for our delicious meals, two course dinners by arrangement every night except Fridays and Saturdays. All rooms have colour TV's, hospitality tray, vanity units and central heating.

B&B from £14pp, Dinner from £6, Rooms 2 single, 2 twin, 1 double, 1 family en-suite, Children welcome, No pets, Open all year except Christmas.
Brenda & Ian Scott, **The Willows Guest House,** 49 Marine Parade, Lowestoft, Suffolk NR33 0QN
Tel: 01502 512561   **Map Ref 18**

....

RIVERSIDE HOTEL, a grade II Regency style manor house in picturesque riverside setting. Recently refurbished to a high standard. Easter, Christmas and New Year breaks.

B&B from £53, Dinner available, Rooms 3 single, 6 twin, 8 double, 3 triple, all en-suite, No smoking, Children welcome, Open all year.
Riverside Hotel, Mill Street Mildenhall, Suffolk IP28 7DP
Tel: 01638 717274   **Map Ref 19**

HILL HOUSE, a comfortable 16th century 'hall-house' set on edge of constable village in quiet location. Secluded garden with views over the valley. Good base for touring. Excellent restaurants and good pub food locally. Easy access A12, Colchester 6 miles. Colour TV, tea/coffee facilities. Golf course 1 miles. Good walking country.

B&B from £20pp, Rooms 1 single, 1 twin, 1 double, 1 family, all en-suite, No smoking or pets, Children over 10, Open all year except Christmas.
Mrs Heigham, **Hill House,** Gravel Hill, Nayland, Suffolk CO6 4JB
Tel: 01206 262782   **Map Ref 20**

....

THE ANNEX, close to all local amenities and recreational facilities. Family suites available if required. Payphone for guests use. Private car park.

B&B from £20, Rooms 1 single, 1 twin, 1 double, No smoking, Children over 5, Open all year.
The Annex, 17 High Street, Needham Market, Suffolk IP6 8AL
Tel: 01449 720687 Fax: 01449 722230   **Map Ref 21**

....

BEDFORD LODGE HOTEL, a former hunting lodge and one of Suffolk's most attractive country hotels. A striking combination of the classic and the new, offering every modern convenience, including fitness centre, indoor swimming pool, sauna, steam room and beauty salon. Close to town and racecourse.

B&B from £59.50, Dinner available, Rooms 13 twin, 43 double, all en-suite, Children welcome, Open all year.
Bedford Lodge Hotel, Bury Road, Newmarket, Suffolk CB8 7BX
Tel: 01638 663175 Fax: 01638 667391   **Map Ref 22**

....

BROADLANDS HOTEL, a modern hotel near Oulton Broad, gateway to Norfolk and Suffolk Broads. Own indoor swimming pool and leisure facilities. Traditional English fare served in beautiful restaurant. Mini breaks available.
B&B from £34, Dinner available, Rooms 2 single, 19 twin, 29 double, all en-suite, No smoking, Children welcome, Open all year.
Broadlands Hotel, Bridge Road, Oulton Broad, Suffolk NR32 3LN
Tel: 01502 516031 & 572157 Fax: 01502 501454   **Map Ref 23**

....

PARKHILL HOTEL, peaceful wooded grounds with gardens and lawns. The hotel offers a friendly and homely atmosphere.

B&B from £30, Dinner available, Rooms 7 single, 3 twin, 8 double, all en-suite, No smoking, Children over 1, Open all year.
Parkhill Hotel, Parkhill, Oulton, Suffolk NR32 5DQ
Tel: 01502 730322 Fax: 01502 731695 Email: parkhill.hotel@zetnet.co.uk   **Map Ref 24**

....

THE BELL HOTEL, a recently refurbished 18th century coaching inn. The principal building in Saxmundham, a tranquil hamlet town, just off the main A12.
B&B from £25, Dinner available, Rooms 3 single, 6 twin, 3 double, 1 triple, 1 family, most en-suite, Children welcome, Open all year.
The Bell Hotel, High Street, Saxmundham, Suffolk IP17 1AF
Tel: 01728 602331 Fax: 01728 833105   **Map Ref 25**

....

The 600 year old **THE BELL INN** is situated in the heart of Walberswick, near to the village green and a stone's throw from the beach. To the north across the River Blyth by foot or Ferry Southwold and to the South Dunwick, Minsmere and Blythburgh.

B&B from £30pp, Rooms 1 twin, 4 double, all en-suite, Children & pets welcome, Open all year except Christmas.
Sue Ireland Cutting, **The Bell Inn,** Ferry Road, Walerswick, Southwold, Suffolk IP18 ETN
Tel: 01502 723109   **Map Ref 26**

CEDARS HOTEL, originally a 16th century farmhouse, now a family run hotel, ideal for those wishing to tour Suffolk. Good food available in comfortable, informal atmosphere. Ample parking.

B&B from £42, Dinner available, Rooms 5 single, 4 twin, 13 double, 1 family, all en-suite, Children welcome, Open all year.

Cedars Hotel, Needham Road, Stowmarket, Suffolk IP14 2AJ
Tel: 01449 612668 Fax: 01449 674704   **Map Ref 27**

....

THE GEORGE & DRAGON, an English country inn offering traditional service and hospitalit and the best in both beer and food.

B&B from £35, Dinner available, Rooms 3 twin, 2 double, 1 triple, all en-suite, No smoking, Children welcome, Open all year.

The George & Dragon, Long Melford, Sudbury, Suffolk CO10 9JB
Tel: 01787 371285 Fax: 01787 312428   **Map Ref 28**

....

PERSEVERANCE HOTEL, a public house with converted outbuildings providing additional chalet style accommodation.

B&B from £17.50, Dinner available, Rooms 1 single, 3 twin, 1 double, 1 triple, most en-suite, Children welcome, Open all year.

Perseverance Hotel, Station Road, Long Melford, Sudbury, Suffolk CO10 9HN
Tel: 01787 375862   **Map Ref 28**

....

SECKFORD HALL HOTEL, an Elizabethan country house hotel with four poster beds, spa baths, indoor heated swimming pool and 18 hole golf course. Excellent cuisine in 2 restaurants.

B&B from £79, Dinner available, Rooms 3 single, 10 twin, 14 double, 1 triple, 4 family, all en-suite, Children welcome, Open all year.

Seckford Hall Hotel, Woodbridge, Suffolk IP13 6NU
Tel: 01394 385678 Fax: 01394 380610   **Map Ref 29**

....

GRANGE FARM, a warm welcome awaits you at our exceptional moated farmhouse dating from 13th century. Set in extensive grounds including all weather tennis court. Bedrooms have tea/coffee facilities. Lounges have TV and log fires. Snape maltings and coast nearby. Bread and marmalade are home made.

B&B from £20pp, Dinner from £10, Rooms 3 single, 2 twin, 1 double, 1 family, No smoking or pets, Children over 10, Open January 10th - December 10th.
Mrs Hickson, **Grange Farm,** Dennington, Woodbridge, Suffolk IP13 8BT
Tel: 01986 798 388   **Map Ref 30**

....

SAXTEAD NR. FRAMLINGHAM, private en-suite apartments, separate from house, each with its own lounge/dining room, TV and drink making facility. Picturesque Saxtead lies 3 miles from the historic castle town of Framlingham. From the Windmill on the village green we are three quarter miles along the Tannington Road.

B&B from £19.50pp, Dinner from £10, Rooms 1 twin, 2 double, 1 family, all en-suite, No smoking or pets, Children welcome, Open all year.
Cheryl Jones, **Bantry,** Chapel Rd, Saxtead, Woodbridge, Suffolk IP13 9RB
Tel: 01728 685578 Email: cheryl.jones@saqnet.co.uk   **Map Ref 31**

433

A hundred years ago Surrey's pine and heather country was as wild as parts of Scotland. Today the county is known as the commuter and stockbroker belt, but there are still thousands of acres of commons and heaths open to the walker and picnicker giving spectacular views.

In the north of Surrey, towns like Bagshot, Esher, Camberley and Woking have become urbanised and yet are surrounded by woodlands, commons and heaths. There are also still many attractive villages like Friday Street, Abinger, Holmbury St Mary and Peaslake. Bagshot Heath was once renowned for highwaymen and it extends south to Bisley Common, famous for modern day marksmen. Three miles south west is the Royal Military Academy, Sandhurst, built in 1807. Runnymede is where King John sealed the first draft of the Magna Carta in 1215. The broad meadow alongside the River Thames belongs to the National Trust. Virginia Water is the large artificial lake at the south eastern corner of Windsor Great Park, laid out in George III's time by landscape gardeners Paul and Thomas Sandby. The lake is alive with wildfowl and coarse fish. Guildford is believed to take its name from a "ford of golden flowers" the point where the Harrow Way, an ancient track along the North Downs, crossed the River Wey. The old county town is full of well preserved houses. Nearby Godalming is an old wool town. Its narrow streets, half timbered houses and inns date back to Tudor and Stuart days. Farnham is Surrey's most westerly town and one of the least spoilt. Here the Pilgrims' Way enters the county from Winchester. Still traceable in part along the part of the downs known as the Hog's Back, the route was used by Bronze Age traders long before medieval pilgrims. South of Farnham, at Frensham the Great Pond is one of the largest lakes in southern England. Views from nearby hills the Devil's Jumps are among the best in Surrey.

Within 20 miles of the heart of London is excellent riding country - and the race course which hosts the world's most famous flat race, the Derby. The Derby has been run since 1780 on the downs south east of Epsom and horses can be seen at exercise early in the morning.

Dorking, where the river Mole has cut a gap through the North Downs, makes an ideal touring centre. The town's High Street follows the route of the Roman Stane Street. Just to the north of Dorking is Box Hill, a popular picnic spot as long ago as the reign of Charles II and one of the most popular viewpoints in southern England. It derives its name from the ancient box trees on its slopes. More than eight hundred acres of wood and chalk downland belong to the National Trust here. To the west of Epsom, Esher is surrounded by good open spaces. Sandown Park Racecourse is just north of the town.

left, Abinger Hammer clock

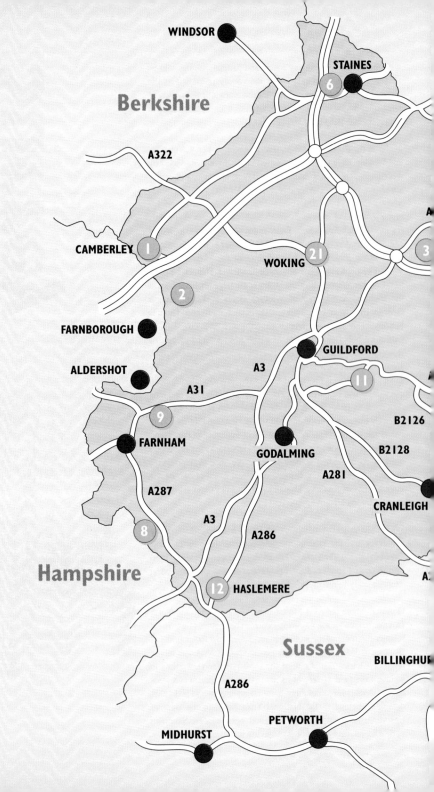

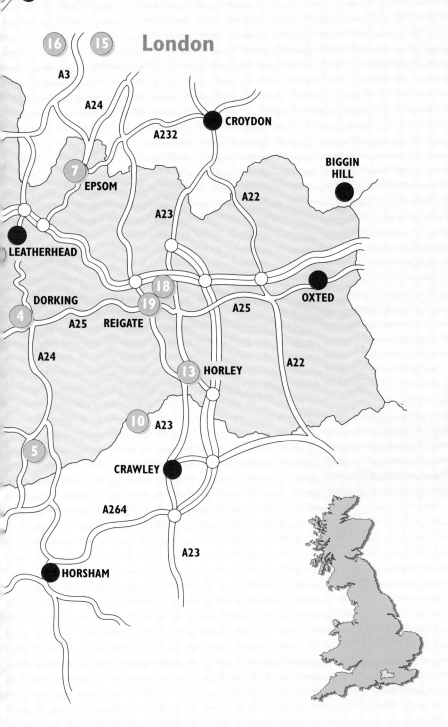

BURWOOD HOUSE HOTEL, a friendly, family run hotel where Richard and Jenny Cave enjoy looking after you. Approximately 2 miles from junction 3 and 4 of M3.

B&B from £35, Dinner available, Rooms 8 single, 7 double, 2 twin, 2 triple, all en-suite, Open all year.
Burwood House Hotel, 15 London Road, Camberley, Surrey GU15 3UQ
Tel: 01276 685686 Fax: 01276 62220   **Map Ref 1**

....

LAKESIDE INTERNATIONAL HOTEL, with fine restaurant, seminar and conference facilities. Just 5 minutes from M3 junction 4. Easy access for rail and air.

B&B from £95, Dinner available, Rooms 55 double, 43 twin, all en-suite, Open all year.
Lakeside International Hotel, Wharf Road, Frimley Green, Camberley, Surrey GU16 6JR
Tel: 01252 838000 Fax: 01252 837857   **Map Ref 2**

....

CEDAR HOUSE HOTEL & RESTAURANT, a 15th century house with later additions, popular timbered main restaurant and garden overlooking River Mole. Close to village. Excellent access to M25 and London.

B&B from £80, Dinner available, Rooms 4 double, 2 twin, all en-suite, Open all year.
Cedar House Hotel & Restaurant, Mill Road, Cobham, Surrey KT11 3AL
Tel: 01932 863424 Fax: 01932 862023   **Map Ref 3**

....

FAIRDENE GUEST HOUSE, a late-Victorian house in convenient location, close to town centre and Gatwick Airport. Friendly and homely atmosphere. Off-street parking.

B&B from £25, Rooms 2 double, 2 twin, 1 triple, Open all year.
Fairdene Guest House, Moores Road, Dorking, Surrey RH4 2BG
Tel: 01306 888337   **Map Ref 4**

....

GATTON MANOR HOTEL GOLF & COUNTRY CLUB, an 18th century manor house on 200-acre estate. Championship length golf-course, hotel, a la carte restaurant, conference suites, bowls, fishing, tennis, gym and health suite. Village is 6 miles south of Dorking.
Email: gattonmanor@enterprise.net

B&B from £40pp, Dinner available, Rooms 2 double, 14 twin, all en-suite, Restricted smoking, Children welcome, Open all year.
Gatton Manor Hotel Golf & Country Club, Ockley, Dorking RH5 5PQ
Tel: 01306 627555 Fax: 01306 627713   **Map Ref 5**

....

RUNNYMEDE HOTEL & SPA, delightfully situated overlooking the Thames at Bell-Weir lock, a privately owned modern hotel standing in 12 acres of landscaped gardens. On A308, off the M25 junction 13.

B&B from £62.95, Dinner available, Rooms 23 single, 107 double, 35 twin, 15 triple, all en-suite, Open all year.
Runnymede Hotel & Spa, Windsor Road, Egham, Surrey TW20 0AG
Tel: 01784 436171 Fax: 01784 436340 http://www.runnymedehotel.co.uk   **Map Ref 6**

....

GREAT FOSTERS, a 16th century hunting lodge, now a comfortable hotel, retaining decor and atmosphere of former times. Set in 17 acres of formal grounds.

B&B from £93, Dinner available, Rooms 25 single, 11 double, 9 twin, most en-suite, Open all year.

Great Fosters, Stroude Road, Egham, Surrey TW20 9UR
Tel: 01784 433822 Fax: 01784 472455   **Map Ref 6**

ANGLESIDE GUEST HOUSE, an owner-run establishment midway between Gatwick and Heathrow Airports, close to the High Street, downs and racecourse.

B&B from £20, Rooms 1 single, 3 twin, 3 triple, 1 family, Open all year.

Angleside Guest House, 27 Ashley Road, Epsom, Surrey KT18 5BD
Tel: 01372 724303   **Map Ref 7**

WHITE HOUSE HOTEL, a charming, spacious traditional mansion converted into a modern hotel. Epsom town and station only minutes away with regular train services to London.

B&B from £42.50, Dinner available, Rooms 7 single, 2 double, 3 twin, 1 family, most en-suite, Open all year.
White House Hotel, Downs Hill Road, Epsom, Surrey KT18 5HW
Tel: 01372 722472 Fax: 01372 744447   **Map Ref 7**

THE MARINERS HOTEL, on A287 between Farnham and Hindhead, a traditional country inn with spacious function room for conferences, receptions, etc. Comfortable bedrooms a friendly atmosphere, real ales and a reasonably-priced menu.

B&B from £49.50, Dinner available, Rooms 6 single, 4 double, 8 twin, 3 triple, some en-suite, Open all year.

The Mariners Hotel, Millbridge, Frensham, Farnham, Surrey GU10 3DJ
Tel: 01252 792050 Fax: 01252 792649   **Map Ref 8**

JARVIS HOGS BACK HOTEL, an extensively refurbished country house style hotel offering modern facilities. Magnificent views over Surrey countryside.

B&B from £42.50, Dinner available, Rooms 6 single, 41 double, 26 twin, 6 triple, all en-suite, Open all year.
Jarvis Hogs Back Hotel, Hog's Back, Seale, Farnham, Surrey GU10 1EX
Tel: 01252 782345 Fax: 01252 783113   **Map Ref 9**

GAINSBOROUGH LODGE, an extended Edwardian house set in attractive garden. Five minutes' walk from Horley Station and town centre. Five minutes' drive from Gatwick Airport.

B&B from £34, Rooms 5 single, 4 double, 6 twin, 1 triple, 2 family, most en-suite, Open all year.

Gainsborough Lodge, 39 Massetts Road, Gatwick, Surrey RH6 7DT
Tel: 01293 783982 Fax: 01293 785365   **Map Ref 10**

STREAM COTTAGE, a picturesque village location in beautiful countryside. Charming period beamed cottage with lounge, dining room, spa bath and sauna. Pub food locally. Courtesy transport to and from Gatwick/Heathrow.

B&B from £25, Rooms 1 double, 2 twin, some en-suite, Open February to December.

Stream Cottage, The Street, Albury, Guildford, Surrey GU5 9AG
Tel: 01483 202228 Fax: 01483 202793   **Map Ref 11**

LYTHE HILL HOTEL, forms a hamlet of beautifully restored historic buildings in 14 acres of parkland in the Surrey hills. French and English restaurant, Tennis, croquet. One hour from London.

B&B from £103, Dinner available, Rooms 4 single, 20 double, 8 twin, 8 family, all en-suite, Open all year.

Lythe Hill Hotel, Petworth Road, Haslemere, Surrey GU27 3BQ
Tel: 01428 651251 Fax: 01428 644131 Email: lythe@lythehill.co.uk   **Map Ref 12**

VICTORIA LODGE, Gatwick Airport 5 minutes away. Our family run guest house has many original features and spacious rooms. Cable TV, tea/coffee, hair dryers in rooms. Well located for town centre, rail station, pubs and restaurants. Central London is 35 minutes by train. Holiday parking available. Email: prnrjr@globalnet.co.uk
B&B from £17.50pp, Rooms 1 single, 4 twin, 2 double, 2 family, some en-suite, No smoking or pets, Children welcome, Open all year.
Nikki & Paul Robson, **Victoria Lodge,** 161 Victoria Road, Horley, Surrey RH6 7AS
Tel: 01293 432040 Fax: 01293 432042   **Map Ref 13**

THE LAWN GUEST HOUSE, an attractive Victorian house set in pretty gardens. 2 minutes from town centre, restaurants, shops and railway station to London and south coast. All rooms en-suite with tea/coffee/chocolate tray, colour TV, hair dryer, direct dial phone. Full English breakfast or healthy alternative. Holiday parking. Gatwick 5 minutes. Courtesy transport by arrangement.
B&B from £22.50pp, Rooms 2 twin, 1 double, 4 family, all en-suite, No smoking, Children welcome, Pets by arrangement, Open all year.
Carole & Adrian Grinsted, **The Lawn Guest House,** 30 Massetts Road, Horley, Surrey RH6 7DE
Tel: 01293 775751 Fax: 01293 821803   **Map Ref 13**

WOODLANDS GUEST HOUSE, 1 mile from Gatwick airport, all rooms en-suite with colour TV, tea/coffee facilities. Residents Lounge. Car Park. Courtesy car by arrangement. Non-smoking.

B&B from £28, Rooms 1 single, 2 double, 1 twin, 1 triple, Open all year.
Woodlands Guest House, 42 Massetts Road, Horley, Surrey RH6 7DS
Tel: 01293 782994 Fax: 01293 776358   **Map Ref 13**

MASSLINK HOUSE, a comfortable, well-maintained Victorian house with full range of rooms, including downstairs en-suite. TV and tea/coffee facilities. Near Gatwick Airport.

B&B from £20, Rooms 2 single, 2 double, 2 twin, 1 family, Open all year.
Masslink House, 70 Massetts Road, Horley, Surrey RH6 7DS
Tel: 01293 785798   **Map Ref 13**

FELCOURT GUEST HOUSE, a friendly Victorian house, close to pubs, restaurants, shopping centre and railway station. One mile from motorway and Gatwick Airport. Long term parking available at £10 per week.

B&B from £20, Dinner available, Rooms 2 single, 3 triple, some en-suite, Open all year.

Felcourt Guest House, 79 Massetts Road, Horley, Surrey RH6 7EB
Tel: 01293 782651 Fax: 01293 782651   **Map Ref 13**

HOTEL ANTOINETTE, all rooms with television, hospitality tray and telephone. Pleasant bar and lounge with cable television. Restaurant offering excellent food at affordable prices. Garden. Large free car park. 12 miles from London. Close to Kew, Windsor, Wimbledon, Twickenham, Hampton Court and Chessington World of Adventures.Email: hotelantoinette@btinternet.com
B&B from £28pp, Dinner available, Rooms 24 single, 34 twin, 8 double, 33 family, all en-suite, Children welcome, Small dogs by prior arrangement, Open all year.
Miss Alison Webb, **Hotel Antoinette,** Beaufort Road, Kingston upon Thames, Surrey KT1 2TQ
Tel: 0181 546 1044 Fax: 0181 547 2595   **Map Ref 15**

CHASE LODGE HOTEL, situated in a quiet conservation area. 20 minutes from the centre of London. 5 minutes Hampton Court Palace, River Thames, 10 minutes Kew Garden's. Fully licensed. Small award winning restaurant and hotel. A delight to stay in.

B&B from £42.50pp, Dinner from £14, Rooms 2 single, 3 twin, 8 double 2 family, all en-suite, Children & pets welcome, Open all year.
Mr & Mrs Stafford 'Haworth, **Chase Lodge Hotel,** 10 Park Road, Hampton Wick, Kingston upon Thames, Surrey KT1 4AS
Tel: 0181 943 1862 Fax: 0181 943 9363 **Map Ref 16**

BOOKHAM GRANGE HOTEL, a country house hotel in ideal location for M25, A3, Gatwick, Heathrow and central London. Good food and friendly service.

B&B from £59, Dinner available, Rooms 3 single, 8 double, 5 twin, 2 triple, all en-suite, Open all year.

Bookham Grange Hotel, Little Bookham Common, Bookham, Leatherhead, Surrey KT23 3HS
Tel: 01372 452742 Fax: 01372 450080 **Map Ref 17**

ASHLEIGH HOUSE HOTEL, a friendly, family run early Edwardian house with most rooms en-suite. Situated 500 yards from railway station, London 30 minutes and Gatwick Airport 15 minutes'.

B&B from £30, Rooms 1 single, 2 double, 3 twin, 1 triple, 1 family, most en-suite, Open all year.

Ashleigh House Hotel, 39 Redstone Hill, Redhill, Surrey RH1 4BG
Tel: 01737 764763 Fax: 01737 780308 **Map Ref 18**

CRANLEIGH HOTEL, is situated close to town centre and railway station, on the main road to the south west, within a short distance of Gatwick Airport and easy reach of the centre of London. 1 mile from M25.

B&B from £40pp, Dinner from £3-£20, Rooms 2 single, 2 twin, 3 double, 2 family, most en-suite, Children welcome, No pets, Open all year except Christmas & New Year.

Carol & Pino **Cranleigh Hotel,** 41 West Street, Reigate, Surrey RH2 9BL
Tel: 01737 223417 Fax: 01737 223734 **Map Ref 19**

BRIDGE HOUSE HOTEL & RESTAURANT, most rooms have own balcony with views over South Downs. 2 minutes from junction 8 of M25, 15 minutes from Gatwick and 35 minutes from Heathrow.

B&B from £55, Dinner available, Rooms 8 single, 20 double, 8 twin, 3 family, all en-suite, Open all year.

Bridge House Hotel & Restaurant, Reigate Hill, Reigate, Surrey RH2 9RP
Tel: 01737 246801 Fax: 01737 223756 **Map Ref 19**

THE DUTCH, a small, peaceful, private hotel, ideally situated for touring Surrey and for business visits to Woking. Located 27 minutes from London.

B&B from £52, Dinner available, Rooms 2 double, 2 twin, all en-suite, Open all year.

The Dutch, Woodham Road, Woking, Surrey GU21 4EQ
Tel: 01483 724255 Fax: 01483 724255 **Map Ref 21**

441

The Sussex coast is backed by the South Downs, the land of skylarks and sheep. Valleys cut through the chalk where Stone Age man grazed his sheep some five thousand years ago - the Arun, Adur, Cuckmere and Ouse. The South Downs face the steep escarpment of the North Downs across the Weald, once covered by deep forests and now peppered with attractive villages, mansions, farms, orchards and hop gardens.

The West Sussex Downs are rich in history. Heavily wooded to within just a few miles of Chichester, there are many ancient churches hidden there. The area is crossed by numerous ancient trackways. The South Downs Way runs along the Downs north of Chichester and eighty miles east across four river valleys to Beachy Head.

When the Romans arrived in AD 43 Chichester was already an important settlement for the Regni tribe. Chichester harbour has twenty seven square miles of navigable water, with yachting centres on numerous inlets. North of the city, Goodwood House has its own racecourse high on the downs above it famous for the Glorious Goodwood meeting starting on the last Tuesday in July and among the main events in the racing calendar.

Just west of Chichester, Fishbourne is one of Britain's major roman relics, an important palace occupied during the second and third centuries AD during the peak of the Roman occupation.

The Normans built Arundel Castle to defend the River Arun against raiders. The valley was one of six administrative divisions in Norman times. Today the valley is a place of natural beauty, complemented by the bright, friendly seaside resorts such as Bognor Regis. Bognor is a family holiday centre with five miles of sandy beaches. The medieval fishing village developed as a seaside watering place from 1790, acquiring the Regis after King George V convalesced at nearby Aldwick in 1928.

Littlehampton is also a popular family resort - nine hundred years ago it was used by travellers to and from Normandy. Many village and farm names end with fold, meaning a clearing in a forest, referring to the Wealden forest which once covered most of the area. One of the loveliest is Chiddingfold. Cowdray Park, with the imposing ruins of Cowdray House, built in 1530 and burnt down in 1793, is famous for its summer polo.

Some of the last remaining tracts of the Wealden forest stretches along north Sussex. From East Grinstead, minor roads run south through Ashdown Forest, the largest remaining area of heath and woods covering twenty square miles.

left, The Old Bookshop, Lewes

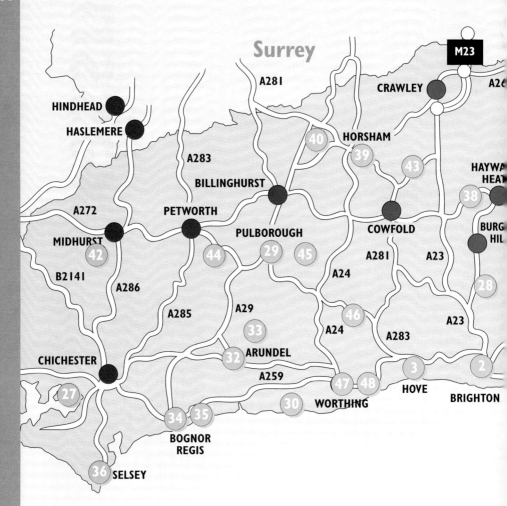

Surrey

M23

A281

CRAWLEY

A2€

HINDHEAD

HASLEMERE

40 HORSHAM

A283

39

BILLINGHURST

43

HAYWA
HEAT

A272

PETWORTH

PULBOROUGH

COWFOLD

38

MIDHURST

42

44

29

45

BURG
HIL

B2141

A286

A281

A23

28

A285

A29

A24

A23

33

46

CHICHESTER

32 ARUNDEL

A24

A283

3

2

A259

27

47 48

HOVE

BRIGHTON

34 35

30 WORTHING

36 SELSEY

BOGNOR
REGIS

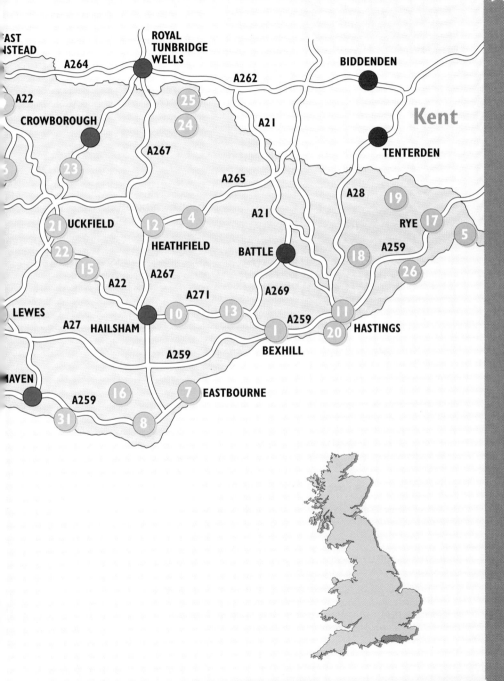

AST
NSTEAD

A264

ROYAL
TUNBRIDGE
WELLS

A262

BIDDENDEN

A22

Kent

CROWBOROUGH

25

24

A21

TENTERDEN

A267

23

A265

A28

19

21 UCKFIELD

12

4

A21

RYE

17

HEATHFIELD

BATTLE

18

A259

5

22

15

A22

A267

A269

26

LEWES

A271

10

13

11

A27

HAILSHAM

A259

20

HASTINGS

A259

1

BEXHILL

IAVEN

A259

16

7

EASTBOURNE

31

8

THE GEORGE INN & HOTEL, 14th Century Inn, oak beamed, 8 rooms, Irish linen sheets, colour television, tea/coffee facilities. Award winning candlelit restaurant. Clergy House of historic town of Lewes close by. Parking facilities in village. Tennis, horse riding, leisure complex close by. 4 poster beds.
B&B from £25-£40pp, Lunch & Dinner available, Rooms 2 single, 1 twin, 4 double, 1 family, most en-suite, Restricted smoking, Children over 10, Pets by arrangement, Open all year.
Mr Nye, **The George Inn & Hotel,** High St, Alfriston BN26 5SY
Tel: 01323 870319 Fax: 01323 871384 **Map Ref 16**

....

BRIDGE HOUSE, a family run guest house, in the centre of town, with views of the castle, river and Downs. An ideal centre for exploring beautiful Sussex, ancestral homes, Roman ruins and for visiting Fontwell and Goodwood racecourses.

B&B from £20, Dinner available, Rooms 2 single, 8 double, 2 twin, 4 triple, 3 family, some en-suite, Open all year.

Bridge House, 18 Queen Street, Arundel, West Sussex BN18 9JG
Tel: 01903 882779 Fax: 01903 883600 **Map Ref 32**

....

In the heart of Historic Arundel. The **SWAN HOTEL** has been restored to its former Victorian splendour, award-winning restaurant with traditional bar serving real ales, hot/cold food. Close to castle, river, parks, antique shops etc. All rooms en-suite bathrooms, colour TV, tea/coffee, telephone, hair dryers.
B&B from £30pp, Dinner available, Rooms 2 single, 3 twin, 10 double, all en-suite, Restricted smoking, Children welcome, No pets, Open all year.
David, Vincent & Julie Sinclair, Ryan, **Swan Hotel,** 27-29 High Street, Arundel, West Sussex BN18 9AG
Tel: 01903 882314 Fax: 01903 883759 **Map Ref 32**

....

BURPHAM COUNTRY HOUSE HOTEL, in one of the most peaceful unspoilt villages in West Sussex, with superb downland views. Ideal for walking holidays. Perfect for a stress remedy break. Award winning restaurant.

B&B from £37, Dinner available, Rooms 1 single, 6 double, 3 twin, all en-suite, Open all year,

Burpham Country House Hotel, Burpham, Arundel, West Sussex BN18 9RJ
Tel: 01903 882160 Fax: 01903 884627 **Map Ref 33**

....

THE NORTHERN HOTEL, warm and friendly hotel comprising terrace of 6 large Edwardian town houses in quiet seaside resort. Family-managed for over 40 years. Ideal touring country for 1066 country.

B&B from £30, Dinner available, Rooms 12 single, 4 double, 4 twin, all en-suite, Open all year.

The Northern Hotel, 72-82 Sea Road, Bexhill-on-Sea, East Sussex TN40 1JL
Tel: 01424 212836 Fax: 01424 213036 **Map Ref 1**

....

BEDFORD LODGE HOTEL, comfortable, family run, Victorian building in quiet residential area close to promenade and town. Appetising home cooking. Easy parking.

B&B from £21, Dinner available, Rooms 2 single, 2 double, 2 twin, some en-suite, Open all year.

Bedford Lodge Hotel, Cantelupe Road, Bexhill-on-Sea, East Sussex TN40 1PR
Tel: 01424 730097 Fax: 01424 217552 **Map Ref 1**

SEA CREST PRIVATE HOTEL, small, comfortable, private hotel near the sea with particularly attractive and modern en-suite rooms available at reasonable prices.

B&B from £19, Dinner available, Rooms 1 single, 3 double, 1 twin, 2 triple, most en-suite, Open all year.

Sea Crest Private Hotel, 19 Nyewood Lane, Bognor Regis, West Sussex PO21 2QB
Tel: 01243 821438   **Map Ref 34**

....

JUBILEE GUEST HOUSE, family run business, 75 yards from seafront and beach. Ideally situated for visiting "South Coast World", Chichester, Goodwood, Fontwell, Arundel and the South Downs.

B&B from £18, Rooms 2 single, 1 double, 1 triple, 1 family, Open February to December.
Jubilee Guest House, 5 Gloucester Road, Bognor Regis, West Sussex PO21 1NU
Tel: 01243 863016 Fax: 01243 868016   **Map Ref 34**

....

CAMELOT HOTEL & RESTAURANT, whilst away from home do what King Arthur did: think of Camelot. Situated on A259 Littlehampton-Bognor main road in the village of Felpham, West Sussex.

B&B from £32.50, Dinner available, Rooms 1 single, 7 double, 1 twin, all en-suite, Open all year.

Camelot Hotel & Restaurant, 3 Flansham Lane, Felpham, Bognor Regis, West Sussex PO22 6AA
Tel: 01243 585875 Fax: 01243 587500   **Map Ref 35**

....

BEACHCROFT HOTEL, family run hotel in south-facing beachside village location. Garden, indoor heated pool, car park. All rooms en-suite with TV, telephone, tea and coffee. Comprehensive restaurant and bar facilities.

B&B from £26, Dinner available, Rooms 9 single, 6 double, 16 twin, 2 triple, 4 family, all en-suite, Open all year.
Beachcroft Hotel, Clyde Road, Felpham, Bognor Regis, West Sussex PO22 7AH
Tel: 01243 827142 Fax: 01243 827142   **Map Ref 35**

....

KIMBERLEY HOTEL, family run hotel, 2 minutes from seafront and central amusements, shopping, marina and conference centre. Licensed residents' bar.

B&B from £20, Rooms 3 single, 3 double, 5 twin, 2 triple, 2 family, some en-suite, Open all year.

Kimberley Hotel, 17 Atlingworth Street, Brighton, East Sussex BN2 1PL
Tel: 01273 603504 Fax: 01273 603504   **Map Ref 2**

....

NEW MADEIRA HOTEL, Regency hotel overlooking the sea, directly opposite the famous dolphinarium and aquarium and next to Palace Pier.

B&B from £25, Rooms 10 single, 10 double, 13 twin, 4 triple, all en-suite, Open all year.

New Madeira Hotel, 19-23 Marine Parade, Brighton, East Sussex BN2 1TL
Tel: 01273 698331 Fax: 01273 606193   **Map Ref 2**

....

ARLANDA HOTEL, enjoy good food and company in a licensed, family run hotel. Our warm rooms have full en-suite facilities. The hotel is in a quiet 200-year-old Regency square, yet close to Brighton's attractions.

B&B from £20, Rooms 4 single, 4 double, 1 twin, 3 triple, all en-suite, Open all year.

Arlanda Hotel, 20 New Steine, Brighton, East Sussex BN2 1PD
Tel: 01273 699300 Fax: 01273 600930   **Map Ref 2**

BRIGHTON TWENTY ONE HOTEL, exquisite rooms, including the Green Room, the executive Victorian Room or the Suite.

B&B from £25, Dinner available, Rooms 4 double, 2 twin, suites available, all en-suite, Open all year.
Brighton Twenty One Hotel, 21 Charlotte Street, Brighton, East Sussex BN2 1AG
Tel: 01273 686450 Fax: 01273 695560 EMail: the21@pavilion.co.uk   **Map Ref 2**

....

ASCOTT HOUSE HOTEL, well established, popular hotel with sea views, close to all amenities. Reputation for comfort, cleanliness and delicious breakfasts.

B&B from £20, Rooms 4 single, 6 triple, 2 family, most en-suite, Open all year.

Ascott House Hotel, 21 New Steine, Brighton, East Sussex BN2 1PD
Tel: 01273 688085 Fax: 01273 623733   **Map Ref 2**

....

AMBASSADOR HOTEL, family run, licensed hotel overlooking sea, near conference centres. Colour TV, telephone, radio, tea/coffee facilities.

B&B from £25, Rooms 6 single, 8 double, 6 triple, 1 family , all en-suite, Open all year.

Ambassador Hotel, 22 New Steine, Brighton, East Sussex BN2 1PD
Tel: 01273 676869 Fax: 01689 988   **Map Ref 2**

....

FYFIELD HOUSE, established over 25 years. Excellent home-from-home hotel, close to all attractions in and out of town. Peter and Anna ensure a nice stay.

B&B from £16, Dinner available, Rooms 4 single, 5 double, some en-suite, Open all year.

Fyfield House, 26 New Steine, Brighton, East Sussex BN2 1PD
Tel: 01273 602770 Fax: 01273 602770   **Map Ref 2**

....

AINSLEY HOUSE HOTEL, elegant listed Regency house overlooking a garden square and the sea. 10 minutes from conference centre, shops and theatres.

B&B from £24, Rooms 3 single, 3 double, 1 twin, 3 double, most en-suite, Open all year.
Ainsley House Hotel, 28 New Steine, Brighton, East Sussex BN2 1PD
Tel: 01273 605310 Fax: 01273 688604   **Map Ref 2**

....

ALLENDALE HOTEL, Regency hotel, offering every facility for a comfortable, enjoyable and stress-free stay. Privately run, overlooking garden square and sea.

B&B from £25, Dinner available, 5 single, 3 double, 1 twin, 2 triple, 1 family, most en-suite, Open all year.

Allendale Hotel, 3 New Steine, Brighton, East Sussex BN2 1PD
Tel: 01273 675436 Fax: 01273 602603   **Map Ref 2**

....

COSMOPOLITAN HOTEL, in a seafront garden square with views of the beach and Palace Pier. Central for shopping, entertainments and conference centres.

B&B from £22, Dinner available, Rooms 12 single, 11 double, 3 twin, 10 triple, 2 family, most en-suite, Open all year.

Cosmopolitan Hotel, 31 New Steine, Brighton, East Sussex BN2 1PD
Tel: 01273 682461 Fax: 01273 622311   **Map Ref 2**

KEMPTON HOUSE HOTEL, seafront hotel overlooking beach and Palace Pier. Central to all amenities. En-suite sea view rooms. Licensed bar and sea-facing patio garden.

B&B from £32, Dinner available, Rooms 7 double, 2 twin, 3 triple, all en-suite, Open all year.
Kempton House Hotel, 33-34 Marine Parade, Brighton, East Sussex BN2 1TR
Tel: 01273 570248 Fax: 01273 570248   **Map Ref 2**

....

CAVALAIRE HOUSE, Victorian townhouse, close to sea and town centre. Resident proprietors offer comfortable furnished rooms with or without private facilities. Book 7 nights, get 1 night free.

B&B from £18, Rooms 1 single, 3 double, 3 twin, 2 triple, some en-suite, Open all year.
Cavalaire House, 34 Upper Rock Gardens, Brighton, East Sussex BN2 1QF
Tel: 01273 696899 Fax: 01273 600504   **Map Ref 2**

....

MELFORD HALL HOTEL, listed building, well positioned on seafront and within easy walking distance of all the entertainment that Brighton has to offer. Many rooms with sea view.

B&B from £30, Rooms 4 single, 16 double, 4 twin, 1 triple, most en-suite, Open all year.
Melford Hall Hotel, 41 Marine Parade, Brighton, East Sussex BN2 1PE
Tel: 01273 681435 Fax: 01273 624186   **Map Ref 2**

....

ADELAIDE HOTEL, an elegant Regency town house hotel, modernised but retaining the charm of yesteryear. Centrally situated in Brighton's premier seafront square with NCP parking beneath. Twelve peaceful bedrooms, individually designed, coordinating decor, phone , colour TV etc. 4 poster bedroom. Discounts for 2 nights or more. Email: adelaide@pavilion.co.uk
B&B from £32.50pp, Rooms 3 single, 1 twin, 7 double, 1 family, all en-suite, Restricted smoking, Children welcome, No pets, Open all year except Christmas.
Clive Buxton, **Adelaide Hotel,** 51 Regency Square, Brighton, East Sussex BN1 2FF
Tel: 01273 205286 Fax: 01273 220904   **Map Ref 2**

....

LEONA HOUSE, privately run guest house close to sea, conference centre and all amenities.

B&B from £18, Rooms 2 single, 3 double, 2 twin, 1 triple, some en-suite, Open all year.
Leona House, 74 Middle Street, Brighton, East Sussex BN1 1AL
Tel: 01273 327309   **Map Ref 2**

....

BRIGHTON MARINA HOUSE HOTEL, cosy, elegantly furnished, well-equipped, clean, comfortable, caring, family run. Near sea, central for Palace Pier, Royal Pavilion, conference and exhibition halls, the famous Lanes, tourist attractions. Flexible breakfast, check in/out times. Offering all facilities. Free street parking. Best in price range.

B&B from £17.50, Rooms 3 single, 3 double, 1 twin, 3 triple, some en-suite, Open all year.
Brighton Marina House Hotel, 8 Charlotte Street, Brighton, East Sussex BN2 1AG
Tel: 01273 605349 Fax: 01273 679484   **Map Ref 2**

....

OLD SHIP HOTEL, refurbished old world character hotel on Brighton's seafront. Noted restaurant. Sea views and executive rooms available.

B&B from £60, Dinner available, Rooms 11 single, 88 double, 53 twin, all en-suite, Open all year.

Old Ship Hotel, King's Road, Brighton, East Sussex BN1 1NR
Tel: 01273 329001 Fax: 01273 820718   **Map Ref 2**

449

BRIGHTON OAK HOTEL, elegant city centre hotel, designed in 1930's art deco style. Close to the seafront and adjacent to conference centre and the famous Lanes.

B&B from £56, Dinner available, Rooms 2 single, 56 double, 80 twin, all en-suite, Open all year.
Brighton Oak Hotel, West Street, Brighton, East Sussex BN1 2RQ
Tel: 01273 220033 Fax: 01273 778000   **Map Ref 2**

ST CATHERINES LODGE HOTEL, well-established seafront hotel. Restaurant specialises in traditional English dishes. Four-poster honeymoon rooms. Attractive cocktail bar, games rooms, garden and easy parking.
B&B from £36, Dinner available, Rooms 8 single, 17 double, 11 twin, 1 triple, 3 family, All rooms en-suite, Open all year.
St Catherines Lodge Hotel, Kingsway, Hove, Brighton, East Sussex BN3 2TP
Tel: 01273 735912 Fax: 01273 323525   **Map Ref 3**

THE DUDLEY HOTEL, a fine resort hotel, situated in the elegance of Regency Hove close to the seafront and all Brighton's attractions.
B&B from £35, Dinner available, Rooms 15 single, 22 double, 31 twin, 3 triple, all en-suite, Open all year.
The Dudley Hotel, Lansdowne Place, Hove, Brighton, East Sussex BN3 1HQ
Tel: 01273 736266 Fax: 01273 729802   **Map Ref 3**

HOTEL SEAFIELD, family run hotel with home-cooked food, close to the seafront and main shopping centre. Free street parking in addition to private parking.
B&B from £25, Dinner available, Rooms 2 single, 5 double, 1 twin, 2 triple, 3 family rooms, most en-suite, Open all year.
Hotel Seafield, 23 Seafield Road, Hove, Brighton, East Sussex BN3 2TP
Tel: 01273 735912 Fax: 01273 323525   **Map Ref 3**

GLYDWISH PLACE, a mock Tudor home set on a lovely wooded site with infinite peace and far reaching views. Four attractively furnished rooms, colour TV's, tea/coffee facilities for your comfort. 2 rooms have 7ft sq beds. Also available, beautiful wing (sleeps four), B&B or self catering. Sauna.
B&B from £30pp, Rooms 1 single, 4 double, 1 family, some en-suite, Restricted smoking, Children over 12, No pets, Open all year.
Dolores Collins, **Glydwish Place,** Fontridge Lane, Burwash, East Sussex TN19 7DG
Tel: 01435 882869 Fax: 01435 882749   **Map Ref 4**

GLENROSE, is situated close to the historic town of Rye on the coast road to Folkestone and Dover ferries. In sight of sea and golden sand's of Camber. We are friendly and homely with tea/coffee making facilities and television. Car parking.

B&B from £40per room, Rooms 1 twin, 2 double, all en-suite, No smoking, Children or pets, Open all year except Christmas & New Year.

Doreen & Steve, **Glenrose,** 127 Lydd Rd, Camber, East Sussex TN31 7RS
Tel: 01797 224417   **Map Ref 5**

CRITCHFIELD HOUSE, is a period house in the middle of this picturesque sailing village. The harbour is within walking distance. Bedrooms with private bathroom, TV and tea/coffee facilities. Ample parking. Excellent breakfast. Chichester, Goodwood and the South Downs nearby. ETB Listed Highly Commended.
B&B from £25pp, Rooms 1 twin, 2 double, all with private bathroom or en-suite, No smoking, Children over 8, Open March - October.
Mrs Janetta Field, **Critchfield House,** Bosham Lane, Bosham, Chichester, Sussex PO18 8HE
Tel: 01243 572370 Fax: 01243 572370   **Map Ref 27**

ST ANDREWS LODGE, family run friendly, relaxed atmosphere, licensed. Cosy lounge, log fire peaceful sun trap garden. Close to natural beaches and countryside, south of Chichester.

B&B from £25, Dinner available, Rooms 1 single, 3 double, 3 twin, 2 family. All en-suite, Open all year.
St Andrews Lodge, Chichester Road, Selsey, Chichester, West Sussex PO20 0LX
Tel: 01243 606899 Fax: 01243 607826 **Map Ref 36**

SLIDERS FARM, is a listed 16th century farmhouse situated down a quiet country lane. Rooms have colour TV and tea/coffee facilities. A guests' dining room and lounge with inglenooks and snooker table. Sheffield Park Gardens and the Bluebell Railway close by. Tennis, swimming and fishing available.
B&B from £22-£28pp, Rooms 1 twin, 2 double, all en-suite, Restricted smoking, Children welcome, No pets, Open all year except Christmas.
Jean & David Salmon, **Sliders Farm,** Furners Green, Danehill, East Sussex TN22 3RT
Tel/Fax: 01825 790258 **Map Ref 6**

CRANSTON HOUSE, situated in a quiet residential road, 10 minutes walk from railway station.15 minutes drive from Gatwick Airport. Parking. Tea making, television in all rooms.

B&B from £16pp, Rooms 1 single, 1 twin, 1 double, 1 family, en-suite available, No smoking, Children over 6, Pets by arrangement, Open all year.

Brian & Aileen Linacre, **Cranston House,** Cranston Road, East Grinstead, West Sussex RH19 3HW
Tel: 01342 323609 **Map Ref 37**

CARLTON COURT HOTEL, well-established family-owned hotel overlooking beautiful lawned square. Close to seafront, Devonshire Park and theatres.

B&B from £19.50, Dinner available, Rooms 4 single, 6 double, 14 twin, 3 triple, all en-suite, Open February to December.

Carlton Court Hotel, 10 Wilmington Square, Eastbourne, Sussex BN21 4EA
Tel: 01323 430668 Fax: 01323 732787 EMail: carlton@fastnet.co.uk **Map Ref 7**

EDELWEISS PRIVATE HOTEL, small family run hotel 50 yards from the pier. Comfortable bedrooms with TV and tea-making. En-suite rooms available. Guests' lounge and bar.

B&B from £14, Dinner available, Rooms 2 single, 6 double, 5 twin, 1 family, some en-suite, Open all year.
Edelweiss Private Hotel, 10-12 Elms Avenue, Eastbourne, Sussex BN21 3DN
Tel: 01323 732071 Fax: 01323 732071 **Map Ref 7**

MARWOOD GUEST HOUSE, on sea front. All bedrooms have shaver points, TV, tea making. Ground floor bedroom available. Dining room and comfortable lounge on ground floor. Central heating. Fire certificate. Unrestricted road parking, access at all times. English breakfast, 4 course dinner, served at separate tables. Open all year. Non smoking.
B&B from £16pp, Dinner available, Rooms 2 single, 5 twin/4 double, some en-suite, No smoking, Children over 7, Open all year except Christmas & New Year.
Mr & Mrs G Emmett, **Marwood Guest House,** 122-123 Royal Parade, Eastbourne, Sussex BN22 7JY
Tel: 01323 730791 **Map Ref 7**

ST OMER HOTEL, fine seafront, licensed, family run hotel. Sun lounge and terrace. Colour TV and tea-making facilities in all rooms. Home-cooked meals.

B&B from £19, Dinner available, Rooms 1 single, 2 double, 6 twin, 1 triple, most en-suite, Open April to September.
St Omer Hotel, 13 Royal Parade, Eastbourne, Sussex BN22 7AR
Tel: 01323 722152 Fax: 01323 726756   **Map Ref 7**

BRAYSCROFT: quiet, peaceful, elegant, small hotel. En-suite rooms with colour TV's and tea/coffee facilities. Meals prepared from fresh produce. Residents' licence. Minutes from seafront. Short walk to bandstand, western lawns, carpet gardens, theatres and Devonshire Park. Ideal for South Downs and Sussex. ETB Highly Commended. Email: Brayscroft@compuserve.com
B&B from £23pp, Dinner from £9, Rooms 1 single, 2 twin, 2 double, all en-suite, No smoking, Children over 14, Pets by arrangement, Open all year.
Gerry Crawshaw, **Brayscroft,** 13 South Cliff Avenue, Eastbourne, East Sussex BN20 7AH
Tel: 01323 647 005 Fax: 01323 720 705   **Map Ref 7**

YORK HOUSE HOTEL, exceptional seaviews and bar lunches on the terrace of the Verandah Bar. 5-course dinner, followed by dancing in the Lancaster Room. An early dip in the heated indoor pool.

B&B from £38, Dinner available, Rooms 24 single, 26 double, 40 twin, 6 triple, 1 family, all rooms en-suite. Open all year.
York House Hotel, 14-22 Royal Parade, Eastbourne, Sussex BN22 7AP
Tel: 01323 412918 Fax: 01323 646238   **Map Ref 7**

CHERRY TREE HOTEL, small hotel and restaurant. All bedrooms en-suite with colour TV, telephone, tea/coffee making. A la carte and table d'hote restaurant.

B&B from £23, Dinner available, Rooms 2 single, 3 double, 3 twin, 2 triple, all en-suite, Open all year.

Cherry Tree Hotel, 15 Silverdale Road, Eastbourne, Sussex BN20 7AJ
Tel: 01323 722406 Fax: 01323 648838   **Map Ref 7**

SAINVIA LICENSED GUEST HOUSE, situated one minute from the coach station. Close to the pier and shops. All bedrooms have tea making facilities, wash hand basins, colour TV. The dining room has separate tables and is a no smoking area. Full English breakfast. There is a comfortable lounge.
B&B from £16pp, Rooms 2 single, 2 twin, 3 double, 2 family, Children welcome, No pets, Open all year.
John Frost, **Sainvia Licensed Guest House,** 19 Ceylon Place, Eastbourne, East Sussex BN21 3JE
Tel: 01323 725943 Fax: 01323 725943   **Map Ref 7**

AMBLESIDE PRIVATE HOTEL, is a small hotel. Central to all main attractions and services in attractive Victorian Avenue. Close to seafront, shops and theatres. Pets welcome, long or short stays. Comfortable rooms, colour TV, central heating, own keys. Full compliance with fire and environmental authority standards, no restrictions.
B&B £17pp, Dinner from £6.50, Rooms 2 single, 3 twin, 3 double, Restricted smoking, Pets by arrangement, Open all year.
John Pattenden, **Ambleside Private Hotel,** 24 Elms Avenue, Eastbourne, East Sussex BN21 3DN
Tel: 01323 724991   **Map Ref 7**

ADRIAN HOUSE, small, family run private hotel in quiet area. Diets catered for. Children welcome. Ample parking.

B&B from £18, Dinner available, Rooms 2 single, 3 double, 1 twin, 2 triple, most en-suite, Open all year.
Adrian House, 24 Selwyn Road, Eastbourne, Sussex BN21 2LR
Tel: 01323 720372   **Map Ref 7**

CONGRESS HOTEL, family run hotel in peaceful location. Close to theatres and seafront. Suitable for wheelchair users.

B&B from £29, Dinner available, Rooms 14 single, 11 double, 32 twin, 5 triple, some en-suite. Open March to November.
Congress Hotel, 31-41 Carlisle Road, Eastbourne, Sussex BN21 4JS
Tel: 01323 732118 Fax: 01323 720016   **Map Ref 7**

JENRIC GUEST HOUSE, safe, comfortable, clean rooms with showers, tea/coffee-making facilities, at reasonable rates. Good breakfast. Central location, excellent connections for Ashford (Channel Tunnel), Hastings and Rye.

B&B from £13, Dinner available, Rooms 1 single, 1 double, 2 twin, all en-suite, Open all year.
Jenric Guest House, 36 Ceylon Place, Eastbourne, Sussex BN21 3JF
Tel: 01323 728857   **Map Ref 7**

DOWNLAND HOTEL, charming small hotel in quiet yet convenient location. Warm welcome, relaxed atmosphere, personal service, Award-winning restaurant, private car park.

B&B from £35, Dinner available, Rooms 1 single, 8 double, 5 twin, all en-suite, Open all year.
Downland Hotel, 37 Lewes Road, Eastbourne, Sussex BN21 2BU
Tel: 01323 732689 Fax: 01323 720321   **Map Ref 7**

TUDOR HOUSE, Eastbourne, 100 yards seafront. Close to Pier, shops, services. Town centre 10 minutes. Licensed. Separate tables. Central heating, pay phone, TV lounge, most rooms en-suite. Special rates for longer stays.

B&B from £16pp. Dinner £6.50. Half Board £22.50pp, Rooms 2 single, 2 twin, 2 double, 1 family, Restricted smoking, Children welcome, No pets, Open all year except Christmas.
Sylvia & Brian Hickman, **Tudor House,** 5 Marine Road, Eastbourne, Sussex BN22 7AU
Tel: 01323 721796   **Map Ref 7**

STIRLING HOUSE HOTEL, is two minutes from sea and is central for all theatres, gardens and restaurants. Residential licence. TV and tea/coffee facilities in all rooms with a non smoking TV lounge. This is our home as well as our business and whilst here you are one of the family. For half board weekly, ask for tariff.
B&B from £20pp, Dinner from £6.50, Rooms 5 single, 5 twin, 9 double, 11 are en-suite, Children over 10, Pets by arrangement, Open April - November.
Eric & Elisa, **Stirling House Hotel,** 5-7 Cavendish Parade, Eastbourne, Sussex BN21 1EJ
Tel: 01323 732263   **Map Ref 7**

STRATFORD HOTEL & RESTAURANT, ideally situated near promenade, coaches and shopping centre. Licensed, centrally heated throughout. Ground floor and family rooms available. Tea-making facilities and colour TV in all rooms.

B&B from £18, Dinner available, Rooms 2 single, 5 double, 4 twin, 2 triple, most en-suite, Open all year.
Stratford Hotel & Restaurant, 59 Cavendish Place, Eastbourne, Sussex BN21 3RL
Tel: 01323 724051 & 726391   **Map Ref 7**

BAY LODGE HOTEL, small seafront hotel opposite pavilion gardens and marina. Large sun-lounge. ALL double/twin bedrooms have en-suite or private facilities. Non-smokers' lounge.
B&B from £20, Dinner available, Rooms 3 single, 5 double, 3 twin, some en-suite, Open March to October and Christmas.
Bay Lodge Hotel, 61-62 Royal Parade, Eastbourne, Sussex BN22 7AQ
Tel: 01323 732515 Fax: 01323 735009   **Map Ref 7**

....

CUMBERLAND HOTEL, beautiful hotel right on the seafront, opposite bandstand. Spacious comfortable lounge and elegant dining room, both sea-facing. Friendly, professional service. Close to shops and theatres.

B&B from £28, Dinner available, Rooms 17 single, 9 double, 46 twin, all en-suite. Open all year.
Cumberland Hotel, Grand Parade, Eastbourne, Sussex BN21 3YT
Tel: 01323 730342 Fax: 01323 646314   **Map Ref 7**

....

CHATSWORTH HOTEL, elegant Victorian detached hotel in a prominent position on seafront, very close to shops and theatres.
B&B from £38, Dinner available, 10 single, 13 double, 22 twin, 2 family, all en-suite, Open March to November.
Chatsworth Hotel, Grande Parade, Eastbourne, Sussex BN21 3YR
Tel: 01323 411016 Fax: 01323 643270   **Map Ref 7**

....

LANSDOWNE HOTEL, privately owned and run hotel in premier seafront position, with bar, spacious lounges, and elegant public areas. Theatres, shops and sporting facilities nearby.

B&B from £50, Dinner available, Rooms 42 single, 18 double, 57 twin, 4 triple, all en-suite, Open all year.
Lansdowne Hotel, King Edward's Parade, Eastbourne, Sussex BN21 4BL
Tel: 01323 725174 Fax: 01323 739721   **Map Ref 7**

....

THE WISH TOWER HOTEL, elegant seaside hotel within easy reach of all attractions. Most rooms sea views. Refurbished public rooms invite total relaxation.
B&B from £27, Dinner available, Rooms 25 single, 11 double, 29 twin, all en-suite, Open all year.
The Wish Tower Hotel, King Edward's Parade, Eastbourne, Sussex BN21 4EB
Tel: 01323 722676 Fax: 01323 721474   **Map Ref 7**

....

PRINCES HOTEL, friendly family hotel, ideal centre for exploring the many historic monuments and beauty spots of Sussex.

B&B from £27.50, Dinner available, Rooms 13 single, 13 double, 16 twin, 2 triple, all en-suite, Open all year.
Princes Hotel, Lascelles Terrace, Eastbourne, Sussex BN21 4BL
Tel: 01323 722056 Fax: 01323 727469   **Map Ref 7**

....

FARRAR'S HOTEL, family run hotel in quiet square, 200 yards from the seafront, opposite Devonshire Park and Congress Theatre. Send for brochure giving details of mini-breaks.
B&B from £20, Dinner available, Rooms 13 single, 7 double, 23 twin, 2 triple, all en-suite, Open February to December.
Farrar's Hotel, Wilmington Gardens, Eastbourne, Sussex BN21 4JN
Tel: 01232 723737 Fax: 01323 732902   **Map Ref 7**

....

BIRLING GAP HOTEL, Magnificent Seven Sisters clifftop position, with views of country, sea, beach walks. Old world "Thatched Bar" and "Oak Room Restaurant". Coffee shop and games room, function and conference suite. Off A259 coast road at East Dean, 1.5 miles west of Beachy Head.
B&B from £20, Dinner available, Rooms 1 single, 2 double, 3 twin, 3 triple, all en-suite, Open all year.
Birling Gap Hotel, Birling Gap, Severn Sisters Cliffs, East Dean, Eastbourne, East Sussex BN20 0AB
Tel: 01323 423197 Fax: 01323 423197   **Map Ref 8**

ASHDOWN PARK HOTEL, built in the 1860's, sympathetically restored for luxury in the 1970's. Relaxation is guaranteed, with 187 acres of landscaped grounds. A superb restaurant and wine cellar, large elegant rooms and suites and impressive leisure facilities. Just of the A22.

B&B from £105, Dinner available, Rooms 6 single, 42 double, 47 twin, all rooms en-suite. Open all year.
Ashdown Park Hotel, Wych Cross, Forest Row, East Sussex RH18 5JR
Tel: 01342 824988 Fax: 01342 826206 **Map Ref 9**

....

OLDE FORGE HOTEL & RESTAURANT, pretty, beamed 16th century building on A271. Comfortable bedrooms, log fires and candlelit dining room. Traditional and reasonable priced menu.

B&B from £39.50, Dinner available, Rooms 2 single, 4 double, 2 twin, some en-suite. Open all year.
Olde Forge Hotel & Restaurant, Magham Down, Hailsham, East Sussex BN22 1PN
Tel: 01323 842893 Fax: 01323 842893 **Map Ref 10**

....

DOWER COTTAGE, is a large country house with beautiful views over Sussex Weald. Ideal for walking, riding, cycling on South Downs Way. Colour TV in all bedrooms. Library for guests. Off road car parking. Close to Brighton and only 35 minutes from Gatwick, Newhaven and Hassocks Station for London 10 minutes away.
B&B From £20-£25pp, Rooms 1 single, 1 twin, 2 double, 2 family en-suite, No smoking, Children welcome, Open all year except Christmas & Boxing Day.
Chris & Andy Bailey, **Dower Cottage,** Under Hill Lane, Clayton, Hassocks, Sussex BN6 9PL
Tel: 01273 843363 & 846503 Fax: 01273 846503 **Map Ref 28**

....

LIONSDOWN HOUSE, mediaeval 15th Century hall house. Historic character with exposed timbers. Tudor fireplaces and en-suite rooms with antique furnishings. In picturesque old town, 5 minuets from beach.

B&B from £20, Rooms 2 double, 1 twin, some en-suite, Open all year.
Lionsdown House, 116 High Street, Hastings, East Sussex TN34 3ET
Tel: 01424 420802 Fax: 01424 420802 **Map Ref 11**

....

WALDORF HOTEL, is premier position on the sea front close to all amenities. Friendly family run hotel where all rooms provide TV, tea/coffee facilities. Most rooms are en-suite. Guest lounge, TV rooms and licensed bar. Special family rate also. Short break packages and special discount for long stay available.

B&B from £15-£22.50pp, Dinner from £8, Rooms 3 single, 8 twin, 1 double, 8 family, most en-suite, Children welcome, No pets, Open all except Christmas.
Mr G Ozal, **Waldorf Hotel,** 4 Carlisle Parade, Hasting TN3 4NG
Tel/Fax: 01424 422185 **Map Ref 11**

....

GAINSBOROUGH HOTEL, is situated on the sea front close to the town and amenities ten minutes walk from the historic "old town" and within easy reach of parks, gardens and cliffs. Most bedrooms have sea views and en-suite bathrooms, central heating, TV, radio and tea/coffee facilities.

B&B from £17pp, Dinner from £7.50, Rooms 4 single, 2 twin, 4 double, 2 family, some en-suite, No smoking, Children & pets welcome, Open March - November.
Barbara Moules, **Gainsborough Hotel,** 5 Carlisle Parade, Hastings, East Sussex TN34 1JG
Tel: 01424 434010 **Map Ref 11**

BEECHWOOD HOTEL, late Victorian building with panoramic views of sea, castle and park, in quiet residential area. 1 mile from station and beach.

B&B from £15, Dinner available, Rooms 4 double, 2 twin, 1 triple, 2 family, some en-suite, Open all year.
Beechwood Hotel, 59 Baldslow Road, Hastings, East Sussex TN34 2EY
Tel: 01424 420078 **Map Ref 11**

....

GRAND HOTEL, seafront licensed hotel, half mile from Hastings Pier, 10 minutes Warrior Square station. Unrestricted and disabled space in front of hotel. English Tourist Board National accessible member. Radio, baby listening all rooms. Child and senior reductions packages in low season. Ici on parle Francais.
B&B from £14pp, Dinner from £8, Rooms 14 single, 8 twin, 13 double, 5 family, some en-suite, Restricted smoking, Children welcome, No pets, Open all year.
Peter Mann, **Grand Hotel,** Grand Parade, St. Leonards, Hastings, East Sussex TN38 0DD
Tel: 01424 428510 Fax: 01424 428510 **Map Ref 20**

....

HILTON PARK HOTEL, Victorian house in 3 acres of gardens, with magnificent views of South Downs from conservatory bar and bedrooms.

B&B from £55, Dinner available, Rooms 5 double, 1 twin, 3 triple, all en-suite, Open all year.
Hilton Park Hotel, Cuckfield, Haywards Heath, West Sussex RH17 5EG
Tel: 01444 454555 Fax: 01444 457222 **Map Ref 38**

....

GREAT CROUCH'S, a Grade II country house furnished with oak beams, original doors, and antiques, set in 15 acres of garden and pasture with an indoor heated swimming pool. Lots of houses and gardens to visit and local pubs serve good food. Come and enjoy life's pleasures.
B&B from £27.50pp, Rooms 1 twin, 1 double, both en-suite, No smoking, children or pets, Open all year except Christmas.
Richard & Ruth Thomas, **Great Crouch's,** Rushlake Green, Heathfield East Sussex TN21 9QD
Tel: 01435 830145 **Map Ref 12**

....

WHITE FRIARS HOTEL, 16th Century country house, with cheerful and friendly atmosphere. Log fire, some rooms with four-poster beds, excellent food. Two acres of beautiful gardens. On the A271.

B&B from £55, Dinner available, Rooms 2 single, 10 double, 5 twin, 3 triple, all en-suite, Open all year.
White Friars Hotel, Boreham Street Village, Herstmonceux, East Sussex BN27 4SE
Tel: 01323 832355 Fax: 01323 833882 **Map Ref 13**

....

THE LARCHES, a friendly, family home close to town and stations. All rooms TV, fridge, tea/coffee facilities, central heating. Car parking. Lovely countryside surrounding area offers walks and drives to public "homes and gardens". Easy reach by train to London sights and south coast.
B&B from £17.50pp, Dinner from £5, Rooms 1 single, 1 twin, 1 en-suite family, Children welcome, No pets, Open all year.
Mrs Jane Lane, **The Larches,** 28 Rusper Road, Horsham, West Sussex RH12 4BD
Tel: 01403 263392 **Map Ref 39**

....

MAGPIES, a delightful 18th century Sussex barn. Peaceful views over open countryside. Local pubs. Golf course. Public footpaths within walking distance. Guest lounge. Artist gallery. All bedrooms en-suite, TV, tea/coffee facilities. Gatwick 35 minutes. Coast 45 minutes. Good car park.

B&B from £21pp, Single occupancy £35pp, Rooms 2 twin, 1 double, all en-suite, No smoking or pets, Children over 12, Open all year except Christmas & New Year.
Daphne Davies, **Magpies,** Stane Street, Slinfold, Horsham RH13 7QX
Tel: 01403 790 764 **Map Ref 40**

THE KINGSWAY HOTEL, small friendly hotel, 15 bedrooms many with sea views and en-suite facilities. Guest rooms furnished to a high standard. All rooms have TV's, tea/coffee making facilities and trouser presses. Free street parking available. Restaurants and shopping area close by. Leisure Centre opposite with swimming pool. Email: admin@kingswayent.demon.co.uk
B&B from £25pp, Single, double, twin and family rooms available, most en-suite, Children welcome, Open all year except Christmas.
Mr Graham White, **The Kingsway Hotel,** 2 St Aubyns, Hove, East Sussex BN3 2TB
Tel: 01273 722068 Fax: 01273 778409   **Map Ref 3**

SHELLEYS HOTEL, 16th century house in 1 acre of garden. Convenient for the South Downs and Glendebourne.

B&B from £53, Dinner available, Rooms 1 single, 9 double, 9 twin, suites available, all en-suite, Open all year.
Shelleys Hotel, High Street, Lewes, East Sussex BN7 1XS
Tel: 01273 472361 Fax: 01273 486152   **Map Ref 14**

HALLAND FORGE HOTEL, a charming, fully licensed hotel in the heart of Sussex, adjacent to unspoilt woodland. The Forge Restaurant is renowned for excellent food, with a comprehensive wine list and friendly service. All rooms have TV, radio, tea/coffee facilities, telephone, trouser press and hair dryer. Ample parking.
B&B from £38.50pp, Dinner from £14, Rooms 7 twin, 11 double, 2 family, all en-suite, Restricted smoking, Children over 5, Open all year.
Jean & Max Howell, **Halland Forge Hotel,** Halland, nr Lewes, East Sussex BN8 6PW
Tel: 01825 840456 Fax: 01825 840773   **Map Ref 15**

PARK HOUSE HOTEL, beautifully situated country house Hotel, equipped to give maximum comfort, with the atmosphere and amenities of an English country home. Outdoor pool, pitch and putt course, tennis courts, conference facilities.

B&B from £49, Dinner available, Rooms 2 single, 5 double, 6 twin, 1 triple, all en-suite, open all year.

Park House Hotel, Bepton, Midhurst, West Sussex GU29 0JB
Tel: 01730 812880 Fax: 01730 815643   **Map Ref 42**

THE VILLAGE PANTRY, a comfortable house offering attractive rooms with TV and courtesy trays, some en-suite. Lovely garden. 4 miles Horsham, 5 miles Crawley, 15 minutes Gatwick, London 1 hour, coast 30 minutes. Ideal for Nymans, Leonardslee, Hickstead and Ardingly. A very warm welcome.

B&B from £17.50pp, Rooms 1 single, 1 twin, 1 double, 1 triple, 3 en-suite, No smoking, Children & pets welcome, Open all year except Christmas.

Pam Jays, **The Village Pantry,** Handcross Road, Plummers Plain, West Sussex RH13 6NU
Tel: 01403 891 319   **Map Ref 43**

WHITE LODGE COUNTRY HOUSE HOTEL, set in 5 acres of gardens overlooking scenic Sussex downland. Tasteful and elegant furnishings, excellent cooking, large comfortable bedrooms, experienced personal attention.

B&B from £50, Dinner available, Rooms 3 single, 7 double, 6 twin, 1 triple, suites available, most en-suite, Open all year.

White Lodge Country House Hotel, Sloe Lane, Alfriston, Polegate, East Sussex BN26 5UR
Tel: 01323 870265 Fax: 01323 870284   **Map Ref 16**

CHEQUERS HOTEL, country hotel, dating from 1548, in picturesque village, overlooking the South Downs. Licensed restaurant, coffee shop. Some rooms on ground food and some with four-posters. Lovely walks in private 9-acre meadow.

B&B from £49.50, Dinner available, Rooms 1 single, 5 double, 2 twin, 3 triple, most en-suite, Open all year.
Chequers Hotel, Church Place, Pulborough, Sussex RH20 1AD
Tel: 01798 872486 Fax: 01798 872715   **Map Ref 29**

....

THE SWAN INN, all rooms have a television, tea/coffee facilities, trouser presses, hair dryers. Undercover parking. Full on license public lounge, bar, restaurant. Large garden. Log fires in winter. Four posters available. Close to Arundel, Chichester, Fontwell and Goodwood Racecourse. Arun Golf courses.
B&B from £20pp, Dinner from £6.96, Rooms 3 single, 1 twin, 7 double, all en-suite, Children welcome, No pets, Open all year except Christmas.
Robert Carey, **The Swan Inn,** Lower Street, Fittleworth, Pulborough, West Sussex RH20 1GL
Tel: 01798 865429 Fax: 01798 865721   **Map Ref 44**

....

ROUNDABOUT HOTEL, Tudor-style hotel in countryside. Nowhere near a roundabout - in fact, a haven of tranquillity. Plenty of historic castles to see in the immediate area.

B&B from £65.95, Dinner available, Rooms 3 single, 7 double, 9 twin, 4 triple, all en-suite, Open all year.
Roundabout Hotel, Monkmead Lane, West Chiltington, Pulborough, West Sussex RH20 2PF
Tel: 01798 813838 Fax: 01798 812962   **Map Ref 45**

....

KENMORE, secluded Edwardian house in the heart of village close to sea. Ideal for historic towns, castles, cathedrals and stately homes.

B&B from £22.50, Rooms 1 single, 1 double, 1 twin, 3 triple, 1 family, all en-suite, Open all year.
Kenmore, Claigmar Road, Rustington, Sussex BN16 2NL
Tel: 01903 784634 Fax: 01903 784634   **Map Ref 30**

....

LITTLE SALTCOTE. Located just a few minutes walk from the centre of the picturesque town of Rye, Little Saltcote offers a warm welcome, free parking and a choice of breakfast, and has five comfortable rooms, all with central heating, colour television and complimentary beverage tray.

B&B from £18.50pp, Rooms 2 double, 3 family, 2 en-suite, Restricted smoking, Children welcome, Pets by arrangement, Open all year except Christmas.
Denys & Barbara Martin, **Little Saltcote,** 22 Military Road, Rye, East Sussex TN31 7NY
Tel/Fax: 01797 223210   **Map Ref 17**

....

WHITE VINE HOUSE, a tudor house at the heart of unspoilt Ancient Rye with its cobbled streets and rich history. Very comfortable bedrooms and excellent, generous breakfast. Oak beams, stone fireplaces, books and paintings make this beautiful home your choice for restful days. Non-smoking haven for grown-ups.
B&B from £32pp, Rooms 5 double, all en-suite, No smoking or Children, Pets welcome, Open all year.
Robert & Geraldine Bromley, **White Vine House,** High Street, Rye, East Sussex TN31 7JF
Tel: 01797 224748 Fax: 01797 223599   **Map Ref 17**

RYE LODGE HOTEL, stunning estuary views. Close to town centre. Elegant rooms. Candlelit dinners, delicious food and wine. Room service (breakfast in bed!). Attentive service. Car park.
B&B from £47.50, Dinner available, Rooms 2 single, 11 double, 7 twin, all en-suite, Open all year.
Rye Lodge Hotel, Hilders Cliff, Rye, East Sussex TN31 7LD
Tel: 01797 223838 Fax: 01797 223585 **Map Ref 17**

....

JEAKE'S HOUSE, recapture the past in this historic house, in a cobble stoned street at the heart of the old town. Honeymoon suites available.
B&B from £24.50, Rooms 1 single, 7 double, 1 twin, 2 triple, 1 family, most en-suite, Open all year.
Jeake's House, Mermaid Street, Rye, East Sussex TN31 7ET
Tel: 01797 222828 Fax: 01797 222623 EMail: jeakeshouse@btinternet.com **Map Ref 17**

....

OLD BOROUGH ARMS, a 300 year old former sailors Inn now a family run licensed hotel situated adjacent to the cobbled streets and riverside walks of Rye. A flower decked patio overlooks the bustling Strand full of interesting antique centres. Breakfasts are served in our beamed dining room. Log fire in winter months. 40 minutes from the Channel Tunnel and ferry ports of Dover and Folkestone. 11/2 hours central London.
B&B from £45pp, Dinner from £8, Rooms 2 single, 1 twin, 5 double, 1 family, all en-suite, Children over 8, No pets, Open all year except Christmas week.
Mrs Jane Cox, **Old Borough Arms,** The Strand, Rye, East Sussex TN31 7DB
Tel: 01797 222128 Fax: 01797 222128 **Map Ref 17**

....

LITTLE ORCHARD HOUSE, an informal country house atmosphere in elegant Georgian town house. Quiet central location, antique furnishings throughout. All rooms en-suite with TV and hospitality tray. Generous breakfast feature local/organic produce. Large traditional walled garden for guests use. Wide selection of good pubs/ restaurants nearby. Off-street parking available.

B&B from £30pp, Rooms 1 twin, 2 double, all en-suite, Restricted smoking, Children over 12, No pets, Open all year.
Ms S.L. Brinkhurst, **Little Orchard House,** West Street, Rye, East Sussex TN31 7ES
Tel: 01797 223831 Fax: 01797 223831 **Map Ref 17**

....

ARNDALE COTTAGE, period style country cottage set in 1.5 acres, ideally situated as a base for exploring Kent and East Sussex.

B&B from £25, Rooms 2 double, 1 twin, all en-suite, Open all year.
Arndale Cottage, Northiam Road, Broad Oak, Brede, Rye, East Sussex TN31 6EP
Tel: 01424 882813 Fax: 01424 882813 **Map Ref 18**

....

FLACKLEY ASH HOTEL & RESTAURANT, Georgian country house hotel in 5 acres. Swimming pool and leisure centre. Fresh fish and well-stocked cellar.
B&B from £69, Dinner available, Rooms 21 double, 9 twin, 1 triple, 1 family, all rooms en-suite, Open all year.
Flackley Ash Hotel & Restaurant, London Road, Peasmarsh, Rye, East Sussex TN31 6YH
Tel: 01797 230651 Fax: 01797 230510 **Map Ref 19**

....

THE SILVERDALE, is a friendly, comfortable, licensed establishment which boasts a warm welcome and generous hospitality. Very varied menu including a wide range of vegetarian items. AA 3Q Recommended, ETB 3 Crown Commended. Specialists in malt whiskies and English wines. Everything that you would expect of an establishment of our standard.
B&B from £16pp, Dinner from £8, Rooms 2 single, 6 twin, 6 double, 5 family, most en-suite, Restricted smoking, Children welcome, Pets by arrangement, Open all year.
Ted & Gilly Cowdrey, **The Silverdale,** 21 Sutton Park Rd, Seaford BN25 1RH
Tel: 01323 491849 Fax: 01323 891131 **Map Ref 31**

FILSHAM FARM HOUSE, a 17th century listed Sussex farmhouse within easy reach of town centre and surrounding countryside. Furnished with antiques, providing a high standard of accommodation. All rooms have colour TV, tea/coffee facilities and there is ample private parking space available.
B&B from £17.50pp, Rooms 1 twin, 2 double, 2 family, most en-suite, Restricted smoking, Children over 5, Pets by arrangement, Open all year except Christmas & New Year.
Barbara Yorke, **Filsham Farm House,** 111 Harley Shute Road, St Leonards on Sea, East Sussex TN38 8BY
Tel: 01424 433109 Fax: 01424 461061 **Map Ref 20**

....

ROYAL VICTORIA HOTEL, elegant Victorian building on the seafront, within walking distance of Hastings. Tastefully furnished, individually styled bedrooms. Renowned sea terrace restaurant, piano bar and 6 conference rooms. The perfect location for every occasion: business or pleasure.

B&B from £65, Dinner available, Rooms 34 double, 11 twin, 5 triple, all en-suite, Open all year.
Royal Victoria Hotel, Marina, St. Leonards-on-Sea, East Sussex TN38 0BD
Tel: 01424 445544 Fax: 01424 721995 **Map Ref 20**

....

THE OLD TOLLGATE RESTAURANT & HOTEL, beautifully appointed hotel at the foot of South Downs, Opposite Bramber Castle ruins. Stunning award-winning carvery.

B&B from £67.95, Dinner available, Rooms 21 double, 10 twin, suites available, all en-suite, Open all year.
The Old Tollgate Restaurant & Hotel, The Street, Bramber, Steyning, West Sussex BN44 3WE
Tel: 01903 879494 Fax: 01903 813399 **Map Ref 46**

....

BUXTED PARK COUNTRY HOUSE HOTEL, beautiful Georgian mansion set in 312 acres of gardens, lakes and parklands, near Ashdown Forest. Excellent cuisine, well-equipped health club and impeccable service.

B&B from £85, Dinner available, Rooms 3 single, 34 double, 7 twin, all en-suite, Open all year.
Buxted Park Country House Hotel, Uckfield, East Sussex TN22 4AY
Tel: 01825 732711 Fax: 01825 732770 **Map Ref 21**

....

HORSTED PLACE SPORTING ESTATE & HOTEL, Victorian mansion off A26 south of Uckfield, set in 22 aces of Sussex countryside. Part of 1,100-acre estate of East Sussex National Golf Club. Heated indoor pool, tennis and croquet. All rooms individually decorated.
B&B from £120, Dinner available, Rooms 9 double, 8 twin, suites available, All en-suite, Open all year.
Horsted Place Sporting Estate & Hotel, Little Horsted, Uckfield, East Sussex TN22 5TS
Tel: 01825 750581 Fax: 01825 750459 **Map Ref 22**

....

THE COTTAGE, is a 160 year old stone cottage in quiet lane with beautiful views, pretty cottage garden in unspoilt countryside with many walks on Ashdown Forest. Close to many National Trust Gardens, Houses and Castles. Historic Tunbridge Wells, Eastbourne and coast ,rolling Downs within easy reach, so much to see and do.
B&B from £18-£20pp, Rooms 1 single, 1 twin, 1 family en-suite, No smoking or pets, Children welcome, Open all year.
Fiona Brown, **The Cottage,** Chillies Lane, High Hurstwood, Uckfield, East Sussex TN22 4AA
Tel: 01825 732804 Fax: 01825 732804 **Map Ref 23**

....

TICEHURST,, set in over 300 acres, high on the Kentish Weald, a quality hotel with 2 golf-courses and swimming pool.

B&B from £58, Dinner available, Rooms 6 double, 20 twin, all en-suite. Open all year.
Ticehurst,, Wadhurst, East Sussex TN5 7DQ
Tel: 01580 200112 Fax: 01580 201249 **Map Ref 24**

CHEVIOTS, a comfortable modern guest house in beautiful Weald countryside. Off-road parking and extensive garden. Non-smoking establishment. Good home cooking. Guests lounge. All rooms colour TV and tea/coffee facilities. Close to Hever and Leeds castles. London one hour by train, Gatwick one hour by car. ETB 3 Crown Commended. Email: cheviots.guesthouse@dial.pipex.com

B&B from £22pp, Dinner from £15, Rooms 2 twin, 1 double, 2 en-suite, No smoking or pets, Children welcome, Open March - October.

Solvita Field, **Cheviots,** Cousley Wood, Wadhurst, East Sussex TN5 6HD

Tel: 01892 782952 Fax: 01892 782952 **Map Ref 25**

STRAND HOUSE, the old-world charm of one of Winchelsea's oldest houses, dating from the 15th Century, with oak beams and inglenooks. Overlooking the National Trust pastureland. Four-poster bedroom. Residents' licence. Non smoking. Log fires in winter. Lovely gardens.

B&B from £23, Dinner available, Rooms 8 double, 1 twin, 1 triple, most en-suite, Open all year.

Strand House, Winchelsea, East Sussex TN36 4JT

Tel: 01797 226276 Fax: 01797 224806 **Map Ref 26**

DELMAR HOTEL, family run licensed hotel, extensively refurbished, overlooking sea and gardens. Convenient for all local amenities and town.

B&B from £28.50, Dinner available, Rooms 5 single, 2 double, 1 twin, 4 triple, all en-suite, Open all year.

Delmar Hotel, 1-2 New Parade, Worthing, West Sussex BN11 2BQ

Tel: 01903 211834 Fax: 01903 219052 **Map Ref 47**

CAVANDISH HOTEL, fully-licensed seafront hotel with en-suite rooms. A la carte and extensive menu. Open to non-residents.

B&B from £42.50, Dinner available, Rooms 4 single, 4 double, 3 twin, 4 triple, all en-suite, Open all year.

Cavandish Hotel, 115-116 Marine Parade, Worthing, West Sussex BN11 3QG

Tel: 01903 236767 Fax: 01903 823840 **Map Ref 47**

WOODLANDS GUEST HOUSE, family run guest house providing home-cooked food and friendly service. All bedrooms are well-appointed and comfortably furnished.

B&B from £18, Dinner available, Rooms 3 single, 3 double, 3 twin, 2 triple, some en-suite, Open all year.

Woodlands Guest House, 20-22 Warwick Gardens, Worthing, West Sussex BN11 1PF

Tel: 01903 233557 Fax: 01903 233557 **Map Ref 47**

UPTON FARM HOUSE

UPTON FARM HOUSE, a lovely 15th century farmhouse situated close to the South Downs, short distance to Arundel an Brighton. All rooms have tea/coffee facilities, colour televisions, either en-suite or basin and shaverpoint. Guest lounge, car park facilities.

B&B from £18.50pp, Rooms 1 twin, 1 double, 1 family, No smoking, Children & pets welcome, Open all year.

Mrs Hall, **Upton Farm House,** Upper Brighton Road, Sompting Village, Worthing, West Sussex BN14 9JU

Tel: 01903 233706 **Map Ref 48**

The visitor to Warwickshire and the West Midlands can take a step back in the country's literary and industrial heritage. Yet the area's main cities, Coventry and Birmingham are excellent modern centres. No visit to Warwickshire can be complete without taking in Stratford-upon-Avon where the world's most famous dramatist, William Shakespeare was born. His mother Mary Arden was the daughter of a prosperous local farmer and his father was a glover and wool dealer who rose to become the town bailiff or mayor. Visitors can see the house in Henley Street where Shakespeare was born. Running from the Bancroft Basin in the heart of Stratford is the two hundred year old Stratford-upon-Avon Canal. The city of Coventry bears little evidence of its industrial heritage - after the Second World War it was largely reduced to rubble. Now, modern shops, restaurants and cinemas are set amid flower gardens and the only evidence of the war is the shell of the former cathedral, levelled along with most of the centre by one air raid.

The county town of Warwick, in contrast with Coventry, is a blend of Georgian and Tudor architecture . Warwick Castle, overlooking the River Avon is the most visited stately home in Britain and the finest medieval castle in England. The castle's 60 acres of grounds were landscaped by Capability Brown and until 1978 it was continuously inhabited by successive Earls of Warwick. Another famous castle, Kenilworth, is now in ruins on a gentle grassy slope, a short distance from the modern town centre. It is the setting for much of the action in Sir Walter Scott's "Kenilworth".

Queen Victoria granted the prefix Royal to Leamington Spa in 1838. The mineral waters first recorded in 1586 can still be taken at the Royal Pump room in the town centre Rugby is noted for its important railway junction - called Mugby Junction by Charles Dickens in a special edition of the magazine "All Year Round" - and its public school, founded in 1567. The village of Stoneleigh is probably best known as the home of the National Agricultural Centre and the Royal Agricultural Show. Birmingham and its suburbs dominate the West Midlands. In Shakespeare's day it was a market town in the heart of the English countryside - but even then it was an important industrial centre. Birmingham was noted for its smiths who used coal from the North Warwickshire mines. Birmingham became one of the world's greatest industrial cities. In recent years, massive rebuilding has transformed the city. In Shakespeare's day the Forest of Arden covered two hundred square miles to the North and West of the Avon and the names of some villages still serve as a reminder of the forest, such as Henley -in-Arden and Tamworth in Arden. Henley-in-Arden, a small market town is a fine walking centre. Edgbaston is one of Birmingham's prettiest suburbs which includes Warwickshire county cricket ground, the university and botanical gardens.

left, Gardens at Packwood House

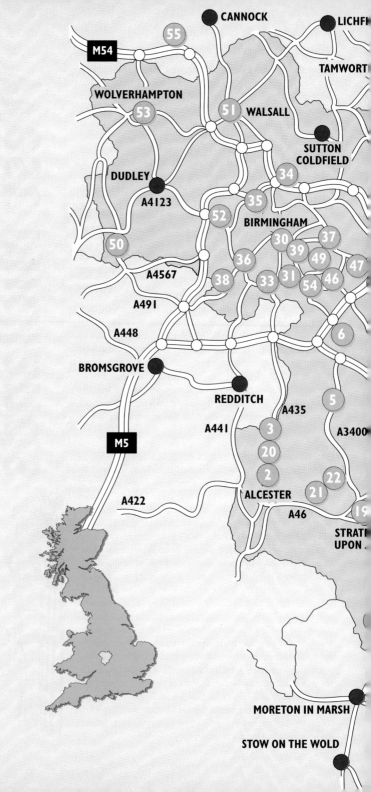

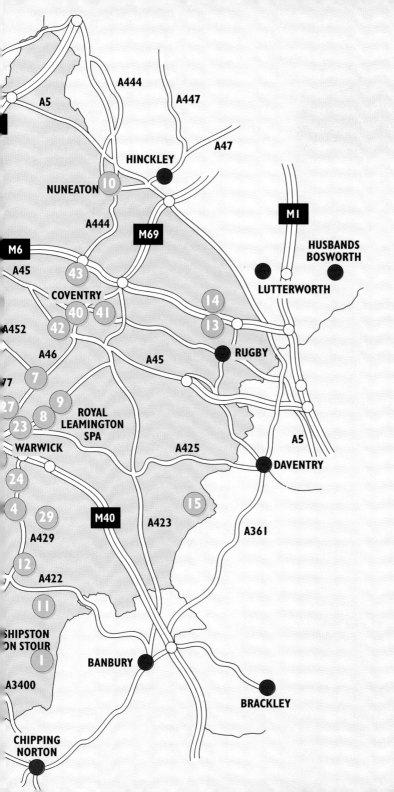

WARWICKSHIRE & WEST MIDLANDS

AGDON FARM, a Cotswold farmhouse on a working farm, set in designated area of outstanding natural beauty. Pleasant rooms with tea/coffee facilities. Guest bathroom. TV sitting room. ETB Listed. Good local pubs. Ideal for visiting Oxford, Cotswolds, Warwick, Hidcote and Upton House.

B&B from £17.50pp, Dinner from £7.50, Rooms 1 single, 1 twin, 1 double, 1 family, Restricted smoking, Children welcome, No pets, Open all year.
Margaret Cripps, **Agdon Farm,** Brailes, Banbury, Oxfordshire OX15 5JJ
Tel: 01608 685226 Fax: 01608 685226 **Map Ref 1**

....

ICKNIELD HOUSE, comfortable, well-furnished Victorian house of character, on the Birmingham road, a few hundred yards off A435. Close to Warwick and the Cotswolds and 10 minutes from Stratford-upon-Avon. Excellent touring centre.

B&B from £18, Dinner available, Rooms 2 single, 2 double, 1 twin, 1 triple, some en-suite, Open all year.
Icknield House, 54 Birmingham Road, Alcester Warwickshire B49 5EG
Tel: 01789 763287 Fax: 01789 763287 **Map Ref 2**

....

THROCKMORTON ARMS HOTEL, small family-owned and managed country hotel of quality. Friendly atmosphere, log fires, air conditioning. bar meals and restaurant. On A435 between Studley and Alcester. Exit junction 3, M42.

B&B from £27.50, Dinner available, Rooms 5 double, 5 twin, all en-suite.
Throckmorton Arms Hotel, Coughton, Alcester, Warwickshire B49 5HX
Tel: 01789 762879 Fax: 01789 762654 **Map Ref 3**

....

CHARLECOTE PHEASANT COUNTRY HOTEL, a 19th century farmhouse converted into a comfortable hotel, opposite Charlecote Park. Set in beautiful Warwickshire countryside, 4 miles from Stratford-upon-Avon and Warwick.

B&B from £60, Dinner available, Rooms 5 single, 16 double, 6 twin, 40 triple, all en-suite, Open all year.
Charlecote Pheasant Country Hotel, Charlecote, Warwickshire CV35 9EW
Tel: 01789 279954 Fax: 01789 470222 **Map Ref 4**

....

HENLEY HOTEL, although a modern building, the hotel is full of character, enhanced by its delightful situation beside the River Alne. Explore Shakespeare country or visit the NEC, both only 15 minutes away.

B&B from £33.50, Dinner available, Rooms 5 single, 22 double, 4 twin, 2 triple, all en-suite, Open all year.
Henley Hotel, Tanworth Lane, Henley-in-Arden, Warwickshire B95 5RA
Tel: 01564 794551 Fax: 01564 795044 **Map Ref 5**

....

NUTHURST GRANGE COUNTRY HOUSE HOTEL & RESTAURANT, located close to motorway network in rural setting of 7.5 acres. Relaxed country house atmosphere with acclaimed restaurant. Bedrooms en-suite with whirlpool baths.

B&B from £120, Dinner available, Rooms 10 double, 5 twin, all en-suite, Open all year.
Nuthurst Grange Country House Hotel & Restaurant, Nuthurst Grange Lane, Hockley Heath, Warwickshire B94 5NL
Tel: 01564 783972 Fax: 01564 783919 **Map Ref 6**

....

VICTORIA LODGE HOTEL, prestigious small hotel with a warming ambience. Beautiful bedrooms, with individual appeal and character, are complemented with traditional hospitality.

B&B from £37.50, Dinner available by prior arrangement, Rooms 1 single, 5 double, 1 twin, all en-suite, Open all year.
Victoria Lodge Hotel, 180 Warwick Road, Kenilworth, Warwickshire CV8 1HU
Tel: 01926 512020 Fax: 01926 858703 **Map Ref 7**

ENDERLEY GUEST HOUSE, family run guesthouse, quietly situated near town centre and convenient for Warwick, Stratford-upon-Avon, Warwick University and NEC.
B&B from £26, Rooms 2 double, 1 twin, 1 triple, all en-suite, Open all year.
Enderley Guest House, 20 Queens Road, Kenilworth, Warwickshire CV8 1JQ
Tel: 01926 855388 Fax: 01926 850450   **Map Ref 7**

....

THE COTTAGE INN, traditional English pub located centrally for Warwick, Leamington, Stratford-Upon-Avon, Coventry, Birmingham Airport, the NEC and the Royal Agricultural Showground at Stoneleigh. Home- made bar meals and snacks.

B&B from £20, Dinner available, Rooms 1 single, 3 double, 2 twin, all en-suite, Open all year.
The Cottage Inn, 36 Stoneleigh Road, Kenilworth, Warwickshire CV8 2GD
Tel: 01926 853900   **Map Ref 7**

....

FERNDALE GUEST HOUSE, delightfully modernised Victorian house. Attractive en-suite bedrooms with colour TV, tea/coffee facilities. Ideal for NEC, NAC and Warwick University. Private Parking.
B&B from £21, Rooms 1 single, 1 double, 3 twin, 2 triple, all en-suite, Open all year.
Ferndale Guest House, 45 Priory Road, Kenilworth, Warwickshire CV8 1LL
Tel: 01926 853214 Fax: 01926 858336   **Map Ref 7**

....

ABBEY GUEST HOUSE, cosy Victorian house, 10 minutes from the National Agricultural Centre, 15 minutes from NEC. Ideally placed for Warwick, Stratford-upon-Avon, Coventry and the Cotswolds.

B&B from £25, Rooms 2 single, 3 double, 2 twin, all en-suite, Open all year.
 Abbey Guest House, 41 Station Road, Kenilworth, Warwickshire, CV8 1JD
Tel: 01926 512707 Fax: 01926 859148   **Map Ref 7**

....

HOLLYHURST GUEST HOUSE, high standard family run guesthouse in quiet location close to two centre. easy access to NEC, Royal Showground and tourist areas of Stratford-upon-Avon, Warwick and Coventry.

B&B from £21, Rooms 1 single, 1 double, 3 twin, 2 triple, some en-suite, Open all year.
Hollyhurst Guest House, 47 Priory Road, Kenilworth, Warwickshire CV8 1LL
Tel: 01926 853882   **Map Ref 7**

....

MILVERTON HOUSE HOTEL, graceful, modernised, 145 year old building, licensed and centrally heated, within walking distance of the two centre. Home-cooked food.
B&B from £20, Dinner available, Rooms 2 single, 3 double, 4 twin, 1 triple, most en-suite, Open all year.
Milverton House Hotel, 1 Milverton Terrace, Leamington Spa, Warwickshire CV32 5BE
Tel: 01926 428335   **Map Ref 8**

....

EATON COURT HOTEL, privately owned and run hotel with spacious en-suite rooms and comfortable facilities including function rooms and licensed restaurant.

B&B from £40, Dinner available, Rooms 10 single, 12 double, 10 twin, 2 triple, 2 family, all en-suite, Open all year.
Eaton Court Hotel, 1-7 St Marks Road, Leamington Spa, Warwickshire CV32 6DL
Tel: 01926 885848 Fax: 01926 885848   **Map Ref 8**

....

VICTORIA PARK HOTEL, Victorian house close to bus and railway stations and town centre. Park, Plump Room, garden, bowls, tennis and river all three minutes walk away.
B&B from £30, Dinner available, Rooms 11 single, 3 double, 1 twin, 12 triple, most en-suite, Open all year.
Victoria Park Hotel, 12 Adelaide Road, Leamington Spa, Warwickshire CV31 3PW
Tel: 01926 424195 Fax: 01926 421521   **Map Ref 8**

FALSTAFF HOTEL, elegant Regency hotel offering every modern convenience to the business traveller. Ideally located in the heart of England.

B&B from £30, Dinner available, Rooms 274 single, 18 double, 21 twin, all en-suite, Open all year.
Falstaff Hotel, 16-20 Warwick New Road, Leamington Spa, Warwickshire CV32 5JQ
Tel: 01926 312044 Fax: 01926 450574   **Map Ref 8**

BEECH LODGE HOTEL, elegant Regency building with spacious lounge, dining room and residents' bar. All bedrooms with colour TV, radio, telephone and tea/coffee making facilities.

B&B from £30, Dinner available, Rooms 7 single, 6 double, 1 twin, most en-suite, Open all year.

Beech Lodge Hotel, 28 Warwick New Road, Leamington Spa, Warwickshire CV32 5JJ
Tel: 01926 422227   **Map Ref 8**

CHARNWOOD GUEST HOUSE, attractive Victorian house near railway station and two centre. All rooms have colour TV and tea/coffee.

B&B from £17, Dinner available, Rooms 1 single, 2 double, 2 twin, 1 triple, some en-suite, Open all year.
Charnwood Guest House, 47 Avenue Road, Leamington Spa, Warwickshire CV31 3PF
Tel: 01926 831074   **Map Ref 8**

THE LEAMINGTON HOTEL & BISTRO, has been completely refurbished restoring the former character and splendour into this fine example of Victorian architecture, creating a stylishly appointed town house hotel. All our bedrooms have full en-suite bathrooms with power units and luxury beds. AA 3 Star, RAC 3 Star. Parking. Bistro Restaurant, Award winning, Red Rosette.
B&B from £55pp, Dinner available, Rooms 6 double, 16 twin, all en-suite, Restricted smoking, Children welcome, No pets, Open all year.
The Leamington Hotel & Bistro, 64 Upper Holly Walk, Leamington Spa, Warwickshire CV32 4JL
Tel: 01926 883777 Fax: 01926 330467   **Map Ref 8**

COVERDALE HOTEL, a large attractive detached house situated in the centre of Leamington Spa. High quality accommodation at inexpensive rates. Car parking. Full English breakfast. All rooms have colour TV, private bath or shower, hospitality tray and direct dial telephone.

B&B from £24pp, Rooms 3 twin, 2 double, 2 family, all en-suite, Smoking, Children & pets welcome, Open all year.
David & Jean Selby, **Coverdale Hotel,** 8 Portland Street, Leamington Spa, Warwickshire CV32 5HE
Tel: 01926 330400 Fax: 01926 833388   **Map Ref 8**

STONEHOUSE FARM, a delightful Queen Anne farmhouse enjoying extensive views from all its comfortable rooms. Very close to Leamington Spa, Warwick, Stratford upon Avon. Bedrooms have tea/coffee facilities, TV and heating. A guests' snug with television and meals are taken in the traditional dining room.
B&B from £18.50pp, Rooms 3 twin, 1 en-suite, Restricted smoking, Children over 2, No pets, Open all year except Christmas & New Year.
Kate Liggins, **Stonehouse Farm,** Cubbington Heath, Leamington Spa, Warwickshire CV32 6QZ
Tel: 01926 336370   **Map Ref 9**

LA TAVOLA CALDA, a family run Italian restaurant and hotel.
B&B from £18, Dinner available, Rooms 1 single, 5 twin, 2 triple, all en-suite, Open all year.
La Tavola Calda, 70 Midland Road, Abbey Green, Nuneaton, Warwickshire CV11 5DY
Tel: 01203 383195 Fax: 01203 381816   **Map Ref 10**

NOLANDS FARM, in tranquil valley. Annexed rooms, mostly ground floor. Four posters/doubles/twin/single. All facilities. Clay Pigeon shooting, Bicycle hire, fishing, riding stables nearby. Dinner in licensed restaurant by arrangement. Very peaceful and quiet, everything for the country lover. Stratford 8 miles. M40 6 miles. Email: nolandsfm@compuserve.com

B&B from £18pp, Dinner from £16.95, Rooms 1 single, 1 twin, 5 double, 1 family, all en-suite, Restricted smoking, Children over 7, Open mid January - mid December.
Sue Hutsby, **Nolands Farm,** Oxhill, Warwickshire CV35 0RJ
Tel: 01926 640309 Fax: 01926 641662   **Map Ref 11**

DOCKERS BARN FARM, is an idyllically situated barn conversion in its own land. Handy for Warwick, Stratford, NEC, NAC, Cotswolds. M40 J12 6 miles. The beamed en-suite bedrooms and 4-poster suite have hospitality tray and colour TV. We keep sheep, horses, hens. Lovely walks. Friendly and attentive service.
B&B from £19pp, Room 2 double, 1 family, all en-suite, No smoking, Children over 8, Pets by arrangement, Open all year except Christmas.
John & Carolyn Howard, **Dockers Barn Farm,** Oxhill Bridle Road, Pillerton Hersey, Warwickshire CV35 0QB
Tel: 01926 640475 Fax: 01926 641747   **Map Ref 12**

THE GOLDEN LION INN OF EASENHALL, individually styled bedrooms, in a traditional 16th century building in beautiful village surroundings. bar and restaurant, wholesome food, secure parking.
B&B from £40, Dinner available, Rooms 2 single, 1 double, 1 twin, all en-suite, Open all year.
The Golden Lion Inn of Easenhall, Easenhall, Rugby, Warwickshire CV23 0JA
Tel: 01788 832265 Fax: 01788 832878   **Map Ref 13**

WHITE LION INN, 17th century coaching inn, recently refurbished but retaining all old world features. Close to Rugby, Coventry and Stratford. Within 2 miles of motorways.
B&B from £19.50, Dinner available, Rooms 9 twin, 5 en-suite. Open all year.
White Lion Inn, Coventry Road, Pailton, Rugby, Warwickshire CV23 0QD
Tel: 01788 832359 Fax: 01788 832 359   **Map Ref 14**

MARSTON HOUSE, is a turn of the century family home furnished with antiques. Ideal for Warwick, Stratford, Blenheim, the Cotswolds, Silverstone and Gaydon Motor Museum. TV in drawing room. Tea/coffee facilities on request. Car park. Tennis court and croquet lawn. Good pubs in the village. Our address is misleading, we are between Banbury and Leamington Spa.
B&B from £22pp, Dinner from £17, Rooms 1 twin, 1 double, both en-suite with private bathroom, No smoking, Children & pets welcome, Open all year.
Kim Mahon, **Marston House,** Priors Marston, Rugby, Warwickshire CV23 8RD
Tel: 01327 260297 Fax: 01327 262846   **Map Ref 15**

THE OLD RECTORY, a charming 17th century hotel with antiques, beams, inglenook etc. Lovely garden, secluded parking. En-suites, spa bath, antique beds available. Phones and trouser press in rooms. A la Carte restaurant. Bar. Ideal for Warwick, Stratford, NEC, also close to M40 jn 15. AA Selected, ETB, Which magazine, Major guides.
B&B from £26pp, Dinner available, Rooms 2 single, 5 twin, 5 double, 2 family, all en-suite, Children welcome, Pets by arrangement, Open all year.
Ian & Dawn Kitchen, **The Old Rectory,** Vicarage Lane, Sherbourne, Warwickshire CV35 8AB
Tel: 01926 624562 Fax: 01926 624995   **Map Ref 16**

THE OLD MILL HOTEL, situated nine miles from Stratford-upon-Avon. Foundations of original building, noted in the Domesday Book remain. All rooms with en-suite facilities.

B&B from £30pp, Dinner available, Rooms 2 single, 4 double, 1 triple, all en-suite, Restricted smoking, Children welcome, No pets, Open all year.

The Old Mill Hotel, Mill St, Shipston-on-Stour, Warwickshire CV36 4AW
Tel: 01608 661830   **Map Ref 17**

BLACKWELL GRANGE, is a Grade II listed farmhouse, part of which dates from 1603. Situated on the edge of a peaceful village with an attractive garden and views of the Ilmigton Hills. All rooms have tea/coffee (one ground floor bedroom suitable for disabled). Stone flagged dining room with inglenook fireplace, drawing room with a log fire in winter, a very relaxing place to stay.
B&B from £28pp, Dinner from £12.50-£17.50, Rooms 1 single, 1 twin, 2 double, all en-suite, No smoking, Children over 12, Open mid February - mid December.
Mrs L Vernon Miller, **Blackwell Grange,** Blackwell, Shipston-on-Stour, Warwickshire CV36 4PF
Tel: 01608 682357 Fax: 01608 682357   **Map Ref 18**

CURTAIN CALL, for a special stay away with four poster beds and en-suite rooms with hair dryer, radio and welcome tray waiting for you. Single rooms are also available. Car parking.

B&B from £17pp, Rooms 2 single, 1 twin, 3 double (four poster), 1 family, most en-suite, Restricted smoking, Children welcome, Open all year.

J & J Purlan, **Curtain Call,** 142 Alcester Road, Stratford upon Avon Warwickshire CV37 9DR
Tel: 017689 267734   **Map Ref 19**

NANDOS, a Victorian town house where Pat and Peter Short extend a warm welcome to all their guests. We pride ourselves on our quality of food and high standard of hygiene. Only minutes away from the Royal Shakespeare Theatre. 21 rooms, 7 with en-suite facilities and all with colour TV and tea/coffee facilities. TV lounge. The perfect base for visiting the surrounding area.

B&B from £15pp, Dinner from £8, Rooms 6 single, 4 twin, 6 double, 4 family, most en-suite, Restricted smoking, Children welcome, Pets by arrangement, Open all year.

Peter & Pat Short, **Nandos,** 18-20 Evesham Road, Stratford-upon-Avon Warwickshire CV37 6HT
Tel: 01789 204907 Fax: 01789 204907   **Map Ref 19**

LINHILL GUEST HOUSE, a large Victorian town house, central to town centre and local attractions. A family run guest house where a warm and friendly awaits you. Excellent home cooked food. Evening meals available. Special diets catered for and babysitting available. TV and tea/coffee facilities in all rooms.
B&B from £15pp, Dinner from £6.50, Rooms 1 single, 3 twin, 1 double, 3 family, some en-suite, Children welcome, No pets, Open all year.
Diana Tallis, **Linhill Guest House,** 35 Evesham Place, Stratford-upon-Avon Warwickshire CV37 6HT
Tel: 01789 292879 Fax: 01789 292879   **Map Ref 19**

TWELFTH NIGHT, somewhere special. Once owned by the Royal Shakespeare Company, this beautifully restored Victorian villa provides nostalgia and superior accommodation for the discerning. Non-smokers please.

B&B from £45, Rooms 6 double, all en-suite, Open all year.
Twelfth Night, Evesham Place, Stratford-upon-Avon Warwickshire CV37 6HT
Tel: 01789 414595   **Map Ref 19**

KINGS COURT HOTEL, delightful bedrooms set around main part of the hotel, which is a listed Tudor farmhouse. Excellent home-cooked bar and restaurant meals. Close to Stratford-upon-Avon and the Cotswolds.

B&B from £31, Dinner available, Rooms 6 single, 18 double, 17 twin, 1 triple, most en-suite, Open all year.
Kings Court Hotel, Kings Coughton, Stratford-upon-Avon Warwickshire B49 5QQ
Tel: 01789 763111 Fax: 01789 400242   **Map Ref 20**

HARDWICK HOUSE, a family run Victorian guesthouse in a quiet area, a short walk to town, theatre, Shakespeare properties. Non-smoking bedrooms. Large car park.

B&B from £28, Rooms 2 single, 7 double, 2 twin, 2 triple, 1 family, most en-suite, Open all year.
Hardwick House, 1 Avenue Road, Stratford-upon-Avon, Warwickshire CV37 6UY
Tel: 01789 204307 Fax: 01789 296760   **Map Ref 19**

COURTLAND HOTEL, personal attention in elegant Georgian house. Town centre situation at rear of Shakespeare's birthplace and 3-4 minutes from theatre. Home-made preserves, antique furniture.

B&B from £22, Rooms 2 single, 2 double, 1 twin, 2 family, some en-suite, Open all year.
Courtland Hotel, 12 Guild Street, Stratford-upon-Avon, Warwickshire CV37 6RE
Tel: 01789 292401 Fax: 01789 292401   **Map Ref 19**

MOONLIGHT BED & BREAKFAST, a small family guesthouse near town centre, offering comfortable accommodation at reasonable prices. Tea/coffee-making facilities and colour TV.

B&B from £15, Rooms 1 single, 1 double, 1 twin, 1 triple, some en-suite. Open all year.
Moonlight Bed & Breakfast, 144 Alcester Road, Stratford-upon-Avon, Warwickshire CV37 9DR
Tel: 01789 298213   **Map Ref 19**

THE COACH HOUSE HOTEL, a family run hotel within 6 minutes walk of town centre. Adjacent to sports centre and golf courses. Vaulted Cellar Restaurant.

B&B from £39, Dinner available, Rooms 2 single, 12 double, 4 twin, 2 triple, 1 family, most en-suite, Open all year.
The Coach House Hotel, 16-17 Warwick Road, Stratford-upon-Avon, Warwickshire CV37 6YW
Tel: 01789 204109 Fax: 01789 415916 EMail: kiwiavon@aol.com.uk   **Map Ref 19**

EAST BANK HOUSE, a fine Victorian house set in well-tended grounds just 3 minutes' walk from town centre. Friendly, good food and good value.

B&B from £32, Rooms 6 double, 3 twin, 1 triple, most en-suite, Open all year.

East Bank House, 19 Warwick Road, Stratford-upon-Avon, Warwickshire CV37 6YW
Tel: 01789 292758 Fax: 01789 292758   **Map Ref 19**

RAVENHURST, all rooms en-suite, equipped with colour TV, tea/coffee facilities. Limited off street parking available. Quietly situated yet only a few minutes walk from Shakespeare Theatre and places of historical interest. Excellent local knowledge. Substantial English breakfast. All major credit cards accepted.
B&B from £20pp, Rooms 1 twin, 3 double, 1 family, all en-suite, No smoking or pets, Children over 10, Open all year.
Mr Richard Workman, **Ravenhurst**, 2 Broad Walk, Stratford-upon-Avon, Warwickshire CV37 6HS
Tel: 01789 292515 Fax: 01789 292515 **Map Ref 19**

STRATFORD COURT HOTEL, a quietly situated Edwardian house, furnished with antiques and set in beautiful gardens with car park. Enjoy the relaxed atmosphere yet only 10 minutes' walk from the town and theatres.

B&B from £45, Dinner available, Rooms 4 single, 5 double, 2 twin, 2 triple, all en-suite, Open all year.

Stratford Court Hotel, 20 Avenue Road, Stratford-upon-Avon, Warwickshire CV37 6UX
Tel: 01789 297799 Fax: 01789 262449 **Map Ref 19**

CARLTON GUEST HOUSE, an elegantly furnished house combining Victorian origins with all modern facilities. 5 minutes walk to the theatre and town centre. Private parking.

B&B from £21, Rooms 2 single, 2 double,1 twin, 1 triple, some en-suite, Open all year.

Carlton Guest House, 22 Evesham Place, Stratford-upon-Avon, Warwickshire CV37 6HT
Tel: 01789 293548 **Map Ref 19**

ABERFOYLE GUEST HOUSE, a charming bijou Edwardian residence with spacious bedrooms, near town centre. English breakfast. Garage. Non-smokers please.

B&B from £22.00 Rooms 1 double, 2 triple,both en-suite, Open all year.

Aberfoyle Guest House, 3 Evesham Place, Stratford-upon-Avon, Warwickshire CV37 6HT
Tel: 01789 295703 Fax: 01789 295703 **Map Ref 19**

AMELIA LINHILL GUESTHOUSE, a comfortable guest house offering warm welcome and good food. 5 minutes' walk from town centre and theatres and convenient for Cotswolds. Baby sitting service.

B&B from £14, Dinner available, Rooms 1 single, 1 double, 3 twin, 2 triple, 1 family, some en-suite, Open all year.

Amelia Linhill Guesthouse, 32 Evesham Place, Stratford-upon-Avon, Warwickshire CV37 6HT
Tel: 01789 292879 Fax: 01789 414478 **Map Ref 19**

PENSHURST GUEST HOUSE, a prettily refurbished Victorian townhouse, 5 minutes walk from centre. Totally non-smoking! Perhaps you would like a lie-in while on holiday? no problem! Delicious English or continental breakfast are served from 7.00am right up until 10.30am. Excellent value for money. ETB Listed Commended.
B&B from £15pp, Dinner from £7.50, Rooms 2 single, 2 twin, 2 double, 2 family, 2 en-suite, No smoking or pets, Children welcome, Open all year.
Karen Cauvin, **Penshurst Guest House,** 34 Evesham Place, Stratford-upon-Avon, Warwickshire CV37 6HT
Tel: 01789 205259 Fax: 01789 295322 **Map Ref 19**

MELITIA PRIVATE HOTEL, appointed to a high and comfortable standard, managed by caring proprietors offering a war, friendly atmosphere. Close to town centre and an ideal base for Cotswolds and NEC. Lounge bar and beautiful award-winning garden.

B&B from £32, Rooms 3 single, 4 double, 3 twin, 1 triple, 1 family , most en-suite, Open all year.
Melitia Private Hotel, 37 Shipston Road, Stratford-upon-Avon, Warwickshire CV37 7LN
Tel: 01789 292432 Fax: 01789 204867   **Map Ref 19**

....

HAMPTON LODGE GUEST HOUSE, a comfortable guesthouse. All en-suite rooms with usual facilities. 5 minutes' walk town centre and RSC Theatre. Friendly atmosphere. Private parking.

B&B from £28, Dinner available, Rooms 1 single, 2 double, 1 twin, 2 triple, all en-suite, Open all year.
Hampton Lodge Guest House, 38 Shipston Road, Stratford-upon-Avon, Warwickshire CV37 7LP
Tel: 01789 299374 Fax: 01789 299374   **Map Ref 19**

....

AMBLESIDE GUEST HOUSE, a picturesque guesthouse, offering a warm welcome to all. Overlooking Firs Park and close to town centre. Delightfully furnished rooms. Private parking.

B&B from £23, Rooms 1 single, 2 double, 1 twin, 2 triple, some en-suite, some en-suite, Open all year.
Ambleside Guest House, 41 Grove Road, Stratford-upon-Avon, Warwickshire CV37 6PB
Tel: 01789 297239 Fax: 01789 295670   **Map Ref 19**

....

PAYTON HOTEL, a listed Georgian house in centre of Stratford, in quiet location. Theatre 3 minutes' walk. Four-poster or Victorian antique beds.

B&B from £30, Rooms 3 double, 2 twin, en-suite, Open all year.

Payton Hotel, 6 John Street, Stratford-upon-Avon, Warwickshire CV37 6UB
Tel: 01789 266442 Fax: 01789 266442   **Map Ref 19**

....

THE MYRTLES BED & BREAKFAST, a Victorian 3 storey building in town centre. En-suite bedrooms, breakfast room and patio garden.

B&B from £30, Rooms 2 double, 1 twin, all en-suite.

The Myrtles Bed & Breakfast, 6 Rother Street, Stratford-upon-Avon, Warwickshire CV37 6LU
Tel: 01789 295511   **Map Ref 19**

....

MOSS COTTAGE, Pauline and Jim Rush welcome you to their charming detached cottage. Walking distance theatre/town. Spacious accommodation. Hospitality tray, TV, Parking.

B&B from £20pp, Rooms 2 double, both en-suite. Open all year.

Pauline & Jim Rush **Moss Cottage,** 61 Evesham Road, Stratford-upon-Avon, Warwickshire CV37 9BA
Tel: 01789 294770 Fax: 01789 294770   **Map Ref 19**

....

NEWLANDS, Sue Boston's home is a short walk to the Royal Shakespeare Theatre, town centre and Shakespeare properties, and has some forecourt parking.

B&B from £19, Rooms 1 single, 1 double, 2 triple, most en-suite. Open all year.

Newlands, 7 Broad Walk, Stratford-upon-Avon, Warwickshire CV37 6HS
Tel: 01789 298449 Fax: 01789 298449   **Map Ref 19**

THE STAG AT REDHILL, a 16th century coaching inn in 4 acres of landscaped gardens, 2 miles from Stratford-upon-Avon. En-suite bedrooms with all amenities. Smoking and non-smoking restaurant renowned for splendid food.

B&B from £40, Dinner available, Rooms 4 single, 5 double, 3 twin, all en-suite. Open all year.

The Stag at Redhill, Alcester Road, Stratford-upon-Avon, Warwickshire B49 6NQ
Tel: 01789 764634 Fax: 01789 764431   **Map Ref 19**

....

STRATFORD VICTORIA, a newly-constructed, Victorian-style hotel close to the centre of Stratford-upon-Avon, Brasserie restaurant, bar,gym, whirlpool spa and conference facilities.

B&B from £75, Dinner available, Rooms 10 single, 37 double, 2 twin, 9 triple, 42 family, all en-suite. Open all year.
Stratford Victoria, Arden Street, Stratford-upon-Avon, Warwickshire CV37 6QQ
Tel: 01789 271000 Fax: 01789 271001   **Map Ref 19**

....

FALCON HOTEL, a magnificently preserved 16th century timbered inn, with a a skilfully blended modern extension, large enclosed garden and ample parking, situated in the heart of Stratford.

B&B from £60, Dinner available, Rooms 5 single, 23 double, 31 twin, 13 triple, 1 family, all en-suite, Open all year.

Falcon Hotel, Chapel Street, Stratford-upon-Avon, Warwickshire CV37 6HA
Tel: 01789 279953 Fax: 01789 414260   **Map Ref 19**

....

DUKES HOTEL, a listed Georgian town house, furnished with antiques, in town centre location. Own garden and car park. Privately owned and operated. French and German spoken.

B&B from £50, Dinner available, Rooms 4 single, 10 double, 8 twin, all en-suite, Open all year.
Dukes Hotel, Payton Street, Stratford-upon-Avon, Warwickshire CV37 6UA
Tel: 01789 269300 Fax: 01789 414700   **Map Ref 19**

....

EASTNOR HOUSE, a comfortable Victorian private hotel, oak panelled and tastefully furnished. Spacious bedrooms. Centrally located by River Avon, theatre 350 metres.

B&B from £20, Rooms 3 double, 2 twin, 2 triple, 2 family, all en-suite, Open all year.

Eastnor House, Shipston Road, Stratford-upon-Avon, Warwickshire CV37 7LN
Tel: 01789 268115 Fax: 01789 266516   **Map Ref 19**

....

STRATFORD MANOR HOTEL, a warm welcome awaits you. Superb leisure facilities. Ideal base for exploring Cotswolds and Stratford-upon-Avon.

B&B from £99.50, Dinner available, Rooms 38 double, 66 twin, all en-suite.

Stratford Manor Hotel, Warwick Road, Stratford-upon-Avon, Warwickshire CV37 0PY
Tel: 01789 731173 Fax: 01789 731131   **Map Ref 19**

....

GROSVENOR HOTEL, an independently-owned Georgian hotel, 5 minutes' walk from town centre, theatres, Shakespeare's birthplace and River Avon. Unique restaurant decor, private car park.

B&B from £78.50, Dinner available, Rooms 7 single, 35 double, 17 twin, 7 triple, 1 family, all en-suite, Open all year.

Grosvenor Hotel, Warwick Road, Stratford-upon-Avon, Warwickshire CV37 6YT
Tel: 01789 269213 Fax: 01789 266087   **Map Ref 19**

BILLESLEY MANOR HOTEL, an Elizabethan manor set in 11 acres of gardens, 4 miles from Stratford-upon-Avon on the A46. Fine oak-panelled restaurant.

B&B from £80, Dinner available, Rooms 1 single, 23 double, 17 twin, all en-suite, Open all year.

Billesley Manor Hotel, Billesley, Alcester, Stratford-upon-Avon, Warwickshire B49 6NF
Tel: 01789 279955 Fax: 01789 764145   **Map Ref 21**

....

VICTORIA SPA LODGE, open 1837, now Grade II listed building overlooking the Stratford canal. Seven beautifully appointed bedrooms, en-suite, including TV, hair dryer, radio-alarm, hostess tray. Breakfast served in large elegant dining room. Completely non smoking. Ample parking. Walks along tow-path to Stratford and other villages. http://www.scoot.co.uk/victoriaspa/
B&B from £25-£30pp, Rooms 1 twin, 3 double, 3 family, all en-suite, No smoking or pets, Children welcome, Open all year.
Paul & D'reen Tozer, **Victoria Spa Lodge,** Bishopton Lane, Bishopton, Stratford-upon-Avon, Warwickshire CV37 9QY
Tel: 01789 267985 Fax: 01789 204728   **Map Ref 19**

....

PEARTREE COTTAGE, an Elizabethan house, furnished with antiques, set in beautiful garden overlooking Mary Arden's house. Pub and restaurant within walking distance.

B&B from £30, Rooms 4 double, 2 twin, 1 triple, all en-suite, Open all year.

Peartree Cottage, 7 Church Road, Wilmcote, Stratford-upon-Avon, Warwickshire CV37 9UX
Tel: 01789 205889 Fax: 01789 262862   **Map Ref 22**

....

LORD LEYCESTER HOTEL, a historic Georgian hotel in Warwick centre. Renowned cuisine in elegant and comfortable surroundings. Easy drive to NEC, walking distance to castle.

B&B from £30, Dinner available, Rooms 13 single, 25 double, 7 twin, 2 triple, 4 family, all en-suite, Open all year.

Lord Leycester Hotel, 17 Jury Street, Warwick CV34 4EJ
Tel: 01926 491481 Fax: 01926 491561   **Map Ref 23**

....

THE OLD FOURPENNY SHOP HOTEL, recently refurbished, offering real ale, real food and friendly hospitality. Situated in a quiet side street, close to two centre.

B&B from £35, Dinner available, Rooms 2 single, 5 double, 3 twin, 1 triple, all en-suite, Open all year.

The Old Fourpenny Shop Hotel, 27-29 Crompton Street, Warwick CV34 6HJ
Tel: 01926 491360 Fax: 01926 411892   **Map Ref 23**

....

THE TUDOR HOUSE INN, is scheduled as an ancient monument. Built in 1472 it still has a wealth of old timbers. All rooms are equipped with colour TV, telephone and tea/coffee making facilities. The hotel is located opposite the car park entrance to Warwick Castle.

B&B from £32.50pp, Dinner from £6.95, Rooms 3 single, 2 twin, 5 double, 1 family, most en-suite, Children welcome, No pets, Open all year.
Erik & Rienne Blanksma, **The Tudor House Inn,** 90-92 West Street, Warwick CV34 6AW
Tel: 01926 495447 Fax: 01926 492948   **Map Ref 23**

We extend a warm welcome to our guests. At **AUSTIN HOUSE**, we have smoking and non smoking rooms and ground floor accommodation. We are only 15 minutes walk from Warwick town centre and Castle. Stratford upon Avon, Kenilworth, Coventry, Birmingham, NAC, NEC are all within easy reach.

B&B from £17pp, Rooms 1 single, 1 twin, 1 double, 4 family/double/twin, some en-suite, Restricted smoking, Children welcome, No pets, Open all year except Christmas.

Mike & Mary Winter, **Austin House,** 96 Emscote Road, Warwick CV34 5QJ
Tel: 01926 493583 Fax: 01926 493583   **Map Ref 23**

....

THE GLEBE AT BARFORD, in a country village location, 1 mile junction 15 of M40, 7 miles Stratford-upon-Avon. Four-poster beds, traditional cuisine, fine wines, leisure club.

B&B from £90, Dinner available, Rooms 4 single, 12 double, 10 twin, 9 triple, all en-suite, Open all year.

The Glebe at Barford, Church Street, Barford, Warwick CV35 8BS
Tel: 01926 624218 Fax: 01926 62465   **Map Ref 24**

....

WOODSIDE COUNTRY HOUSE, set in beautiful garden and woodland, furnished in cottage style with Victorian and antique furniture. Full central heating. Guest lounge with open fire, TV and video. Bedroom TV, tea/coffee. Five bedrooms, 3 bathrooms, one en-suite. Doreen and her bernese mountain dog offer a warm welcome.

B&B from £20pp, Dinner from £12.50, Rooms 1 single, 2 twin, 1 double en-suite, 1 family, No smoking, Children & pets welcome, Open all year except Christmas.

Doreen Bromilow, **Woodside Country House,** Langley Road, Claverdon, Warwick CV35 8PJ
Tel: 01926 842446   **Map Ref 25**

....

ARDENCOTE MANOR HOTEL & COUNTRY CLUB, historic former gentleman's residence, sympathetically refurbished, set in 40 acres of gardens and grounds. Extensive leisure and sports facilities. Easy access to M40, M42 and Shakespeare country.

B&B from £87.50, Dinner available, Rooms 6 single, 8 double, 4 twin, all en-suite, Open all year.

Ardencote Manor Hotel & Country Club, Lye Green Road, Claverdon, Warwick CV35 8LS
Tel: 01926 843111 Fax: 01926 842646   **Map Ref 25**

....

THE CROFT, friendly family atmosphere in picturesque rural setting. In Haseley Knob Village off the A4177 between Balsall Common and Warwick, convenient for NEC, National Agriculture Centre, Stratford and Coventry. 15 minutes from Birmingham Airport.

B&B from £21, Dinner available, Rooms 1 single, 1 double, 1 twin, 2 triple, all en-suite, Open all year.

The Croft, Haseley Knob, Warwick CV35 7NL
Tel: 01926 484447 Fax: 01926 484447   **Map Ref 26**

....

NORTHLEIGH HOUSE, a comfortable, peaceful country house where the elegant rooms are individually designed and have en-suite bathroom, fringe, kettle and remote-control TV.

B&B from £33, Rooms 1 single, 5 double, 1 twin, all en-suite, Open February to November.

Northleigh House, Five Ways Road, Hatton, Warwick CV35 7HZ
Tel: 01926 484203 Fax: 01926 484006   **Map Ref 27**

SHREWLEY HOUSE, a listed 17th century farmhouse and home set amidst beautiful 1.5 acre gardens. King-sized four-poster bedrooms, all en-suite, with many top extras. Four miles from Warwick.

B&B from £37, Dinner available, Rooms 3 double, 3 en-suite, Open all year.

Shrewley House, Hockley Road, Shrewley, Warwick CV35 7AT
Tel: 01926 842549 Fax: 01926 842216 **Map Ref 28**

....

WALTON HALL MEMBERS, a Victorian country mansion only 7 miles from Stratford-upon-Avon.

B&B from £80, Dinner available, Rooms 88 triple, all en-suite, Open all year.

Walton Hall Members, Walton, Wellesbourne, Warwick CV35 9HU
Tel: 01789 842424 Fax: 01789 470418 **Map Ref 29**

....

CHAMBERLAIN HOTEL, restored and refurbished Grade II listed Victorian building of character, 1 mile from city centre. Extensive conference and banqueting facilities.

B&B from £35, Dinner available, Rooms 69 single, 118 double, 63 twin, all en-suite, open all year.

Chamberlain Hotel, Alcester Street, Birmingham, West Midlands B12 0PJ
Tel: 0121 606 9000 Fax: 0121 606 9001 **Map Ref 30**

....

IBIS BIRMINGHAM, in the heart of the city, close to the main line railway station and within easy access of motorway and international airport links. Adjacent to the Chinese quarter, theatre district, shopping and restaurants.

B&B from £53.25, Dinner available, Rooms 94 double, 60 twin, 5 family, all en-suite, Open all year.
Ibis Birmingham, Ladywell Walk, Birmingham, West Midlands B5 4ST
Tel: 0121 622 6010 Fax: 0121 622 6020 **Map Ref 30**

....

ATHOLL LODGE, friendly guesthouse in a quiet location on the south side of Birmingham. The N E C , airport and two centre are all within easy reach.

B&B from £20.000, Dinner available, Rooms 4 single, 1 double, 4 twin, 1 triple, some en-suite, Open all year.

Atholl Lodge, 16 Elmdon Road, Acocks Green, Birmingham, West Midlands B27 6LH
Tel: 0121 707 4417 Fax: 0121 707 4417 **Map Ref 31**

....

ASHDALE HOUSE HOTEL, furnished to enhance its Victorian character, this quiet, friendly hotel is in an attractive location overlooking a park. Delicious organic English breakfasts and alternatives are our speciality. If needed a courtesy car is usually available to welcome you.

B&B from £20, Rooms 7 single, 2 triple, some en-suite, Open all year.
Ashdale House Hotel, 39 Broad Road, Acocks Green, Birmingham, West Midlands B27 7UX
Tel: 01212 706 3598 Fax: 0121 706 3598 EMail: Ashdale@waverider **Map Ref 31**

....

BRIDGE HOUSE HOTEL, comfortable well appointed private hotel with a range of facilities including pleasant dining room with a la carte menu, 2 licensed residential bars. TV lounge, patio and garden. Large secure car park. Executive rooms available.

B&B from £37.60, Dinner available, Rooms 15 single, 14 double, 14 twin, all en-suite, Open all year.
Bridge House Hotel, 49 Sherbourne Road, Acocks Green, Birmingham, West Midlands B27 6DX
Tel: 0121 706 5900 Fax: 0121 624 5900 **Map Ref 31**

THE WESTLEY HOTEL, close to the NEC and ICC. Two restaurants, theme bar and banqueting. Convenient for Stratford-upon-Avon and Warwick. 3 miles junction 5 of M42.

B&B from £39.50, Dinner available, Rooms 8 single, 7 double, 20 twin, 1 triple, suites available, all en-suite, Open all year.
The Westley Hotel, Westley Road, Acocks Green, Birmingham, West Midlands B27 7UJ
Tel: 0121 706 4312 Fax: 0121 706 2824   **Map Ref 31**

....

COLESHILL HOTEL, in traditional coaching inn style restaurant, lounge bar and function/conference facilities. 5 minuets drive from the NEC.

B&B from £33.50, Dinner available, Rooms 2 single, 11 double, 10 twin, all en-suite, Open all year.
Coleshill Hotel, 152 High Street, Coleshill, Birmingham, West Midlands B46 3BG
Tel: 01675 465527 Fax: 01675 464013   **Map Ref 32**

....

ASQUITH HOUSE HOTEL & RESTAURANT, listed building (1854) of architectural interest, converted into an exclusive licensed hotel and restaurant. Well suited for mini-conferences and business meetings. Weddings a speciality.

B&B from £60.50, Dinner available, Rooms 2 single, 2 double, 5 twin, 1 triple, all en-suite, Open all year.
Asquith House Hotel & Restaurant, 19 Portland Road, Edgbaston, Birmingham, West Midlands B16 9HN
Tel: 0121 454 5282 Fax: 0121 456 4668   **Map Ref 33**

....

WESTBOURNE LODGE HOTEL, family run hotel, all rooms en-suite. Good food. Ideal for city, NEC, International Convention Centre, National Indoor Arena and airport. Free parking.

B&B from £38, Dinner available, Rooms 9 single, 3 double, 2 twin, 3 triple, all en-suite, Open all year.
Westbourne Lodge Hotel, 27-29 Fountain Road, Edgbaston, Birmingham, West Midlands B17 8NJ
Tel: 0121 429 1003 Fax: 0121 429 7436   **Map Ref 33**

....

WOODVILLE HOUSE, high standard accommodation, 1 mile from city centre. Full English breakfast. All rooms have colour TV and tea/coffee making facilities.

B&B from £16, Rooms 4 single, 2 double, 2 twin, 1 triple, some en-suite, Open all year.
Woodville House, 39 Portland Road, Edgbaston, Birmingham, West Midlands B16 9HN
Tel: 0121 454 0274 Fax: 0121 421 4340   **Map Ref 33**

....

GROVE HOTEL, a Victorian style hotel, built in 1899. Tastefully furnished and offers comfortable surroundings. The majority of rooms are en-suite and all have colour TV and direct dial telephones. The hotel offers a fully licensed bar and restaurant.

B&B from £20pp, Dinner available, Rooms 15 single, 20 double, 10 twin, many en-suite, Children welcome, Pets by arrangement, Open all year.

Grove Hotel, 409 Hagley Road, Edgbaston, Birmingham B17 8BL
Tel: 0121 429 2502 Fax: 0121 420 1207   **Map Ref 33**

....

HAGLEY COURT HOTEL, a private hotel and restaurant, all rooms en-suite with TV, telephone. English breakfast. 1.5 miles from city centre.

B&B from £32, Dinner available, Rooms 8 single, 16 double, 3 twin, all en-suite, Open all year.

Hagley Court Hotel, 229 Hagley Road, Egbaston, Birmingham, West Midlands B16 9RP
Tel: 0121 454 6514 Fax: 0121 456 2722   **Map Ref 33**

FOUNTAIN COURT HOTEL, small family run hotel with friendly service and easy access to city centre.

B&B from £39, Dinner available, Rooms 11 single, 6 double, 2 twin, 4 triple, all en-suite, Open all year.

Fountain Court Hotel, 339-343 Hagley Road, Egbaston, Birmingham, West Midlands B17 8NH
Tel: 0121 429 1754 Fax: 0121 429 1209   **Map Ref 33**

....

ROLLANSON WOOD HOTEL, friendly family run hotel, 1 mile from M6, exit 6. Convenient for city centre. A la carte restaurant and bar.

B&B from £17.85, Dinner available, Rooms 19 single, 3 double, 8 twin, 5 triple, some en-suite, Open all year.

Rollanson Wood Hotel, 130 Wood End Road, Erdington, Birmingham, West Midlands B24 8BJ
Tel: 0121 373 1230 Fax: 0121 382 2578   **Map Ref 34**

....

LYNDHURST HOTEL, within half a mile of M6 (junction 6) and within easy reach of the city and NEC. Comfortable bedrooms, spacious restaurant. Personal service in a quiet friendly atmosphere.

B&B from £28, Dinner available, Rooms 10 single, 10 double, 2 twin, some en-suite, Open all year.

Lyndhurst Hotel, 135 Kingsbury Road, Erdington, Birmingham, West Midlands B24 8QT
Tel: 0121 373 5695 Fax: 0121 373 5695   **Map Ref 34**

....

SHERIDAN HOUSE HOTEL, private hotel, 3.5 miles from city centre, ICC and National Indoor Arena. 20 minutes from NEC, 5 minutes from M5 and M6. Car park.

B&B from £28, Dinner available, Rooms 2 single, 3 double, 5 twin, 1 triple, most en-suite, Open all year.

heridan House Hotel, 82 Handsworth Wood Road, Handsworth Wood, Birmingham, West Midlands B20 2PL
Tel: 0121 523 5960 Fax: 0121 551 4761   **Map Ref 35**

....

WENTWORTH HOTEL, family run hotel, all bedrooms en-suite with tea and coffee facilities. Victorian building with bar and restaurant in Victorian style. Sky TV.

B&B from £30, Dinner available, Rooms 6 single, 2 double, 4 twin, all en-suite, Open all year.

Wentworth Hotel, 103 Wentworth Road, Harborne, Birmingham, West Midlands B17 9SU
Tel: 0121 427 2839 Fax: 0121 427 2839   **Map Ref 36**

....

HEATH LODGE HOTEL, licensed family run hotel quietly situated and less than 2 mile's from the NEC and Birmingham Airport.

B&B from £30, Dinner available, Rooms 9 single, 3 double, 6 twin, most en-suite, Open all year.

Heath Lodge Hotel, Coleshill Road, Marston Green, Birmingham, West Midlands B37 7HT
Tel: 0121 779 2218 Fax: 0121 779 2218   **Map Ref 37**

....

KENSINGTON GUEST HOUSE HOTEL, family atmosphere. Full central heating, evening meals, ground floor rooms. Four-poster bed in bridal suite. Close to all amenities.

B&B from £30, Dinner available, Rooms 5 single, 7 double, 8 twin, 5 triple, 4 family, some en-suite, Open all year.
Kensington Guest House Hotel, 785 Pershore Road, Selly Park, Birmingham, West Midlands B29 7LR
Tel: 0121 472 7086 Fax: 0121 472 5520   **Map Ref 38**

CENTRAL GUEST HOUSE, aside the A45 dual carriageway into the city. This friendly, well equipped semi detached guest house caters well for the business traveller. Pay phone. The dining room overlooks the garden where breakfast is served. Directions - off M42 at NEC, jct, A45 continue past MacDonalds, Harry Ramsden, pull in after set of houses on left.
B&B from £17.50pp, Rooms 1 single, 3 twin, 2 double, 1 family, all en-suite, Children & Pets welcome, Open all year except Christmas & Boxing Day.
Marlene Mousley, **Central Guest House**, 1637 Coventry Road, South Yardley, Birmingham, West Midlands B26 1DD
Tel/Fax: 0121 706 7757   **Map Ref 39**

FALCON HOTEL, situated close to the Coventry railway station, ideal for the businessman. Ten minutes from the NEC, M6 motorway and Birmingham Airport. Large free car park. Shops, social and cultural activities readily at hand.

B&B from £45, Dinner available, Rooms 6 single, 2 double, 3 twin, 3 triple, 1 family, all en-suite, Open all year.

Falcon Hotel, 13-19 Manor Road, Coventry, West Midlands CV1 2LH
Tel: 01203 258615 Fax: 01203 520680   **Map Ref 40**

ASHLEIGH HOUSE, recently renovated guesthouse only 100 yards from the railway station. All city amenities within 5 minutes walk.

B&B from £18, Dinner available, Rooms 3 single, 3 double, 2 twin, 2 triple, most en-suite. Open all year.

Ashleigh House, 17 Park Road, Coventry, West Midlands CV1 2LH
Tel: 01203 223804   **Map Ref 40**

CHESTER HOUSE, a large white stone house with double bays, the first house off the main Holyhead road.

B&B from £14, Dinner available, Rooms 1 single, 3 triple, 1 family, 1 en-suite, Open all year.

Chester House, 3 Chester Street, Coventry, West Midlands CV1 4DH
Tel: 01203 223857   **Map Ref 40**

NORTHANGER HOUSE, a friendly home 5 minutes from the city centre. Close to the railway and bus stations, and convenient for NEC and NAC.

B&B from £15, Dinner available, Rooms 4 single, 1 twin, 2 triple, 2 family, Open all year.

Northanger House, 35 Westminster Road, Coventry, West Midlands CV1 3GB
Tel: 01203 226780   **Map Ref 40**

MERRICK LODGE HOTEL, a former manor house, just five minutes walk from the city centre. Table d'hote and a la carte restaurant. 3 bars. Comfortable, well-equipped en-suite bedrooms. Superb base for visiting the area. Private functions and conferences also catered for.

B&B from £35, Dinner available, Rooms 4 single, 8 double, 9 twin, 4 triple, 1 family, most en-suite, Open all year.

Merrick Lodge Hotel, 80-82 St Nicholas Street, Coventry, West Midlands CV1 4BP
Tel: 01203 553940 Fax: 01203 550112   **Map Ref 40**

COOMBE ABBEY, historic country house hotel, dating back to the 11th century. Quality bedrooms, atmospheric public areas. Set in 500 acres of parkland.

B&B from £115, Dinner available, Rooms 49 double, 14 twin, suites available, all en-suite, Open all year.

Coombe Abbey, Brinklow Road, Binley, Coventry, West Midlands CV3 2AB
Tel: 01203 450450 Fax: 01203 635101   **Map Ref 41**

....

KINGSTON GUEST HOUSE, is situated within an easy ten minutes walk from Railway Station and city centre where the famous Cathedrals and many other places of interest can be found. All rooms have colour TV's, tea facilities and ample on street parking. Good friendly service is speciality.

B&B from £14pp, Rooms 5 single, 3 twin, Children welcome, No pets, Open all year except Christmas & New Year.
Irena Johnson, **Kingston Guest House,** 3 Regent Street, Earlsdon, Coventry, West Midlands CV1 3EP
Tel: 01203 224932   **Map Ref 42**

....

NOVOTEL COVENTRY, Coventry and the Novotel, a venue for business, holiday weekends or as a relaxing stop-over between journeys.

B&B from £50, Dinner available, Rooms 98 triple, all en-suite. Open all year.

Novotel Coventry, Wilsons Lane, Longford, Coventry, West Midlands CV6 6HL
Tel: 01203 365000 Fax: 01203 362422   **Map Ref 43**

....

MERIDEN HOTEL, a family run hotel situated near NEC and Birmingham Airport. Convenient for Coventry, Birmingham, Solihull and surrounding districts.

B&B from £34, Dinner available, Rooms 6 single, 4 double, 5 twin, most en-suite, Open all year.

Meriden Hotel, Main Road, Meriden, Coventry, West Midlands CV7 7NH
Tel: 01676 522005 Fax: 01676 523744   **Map Ref 44**

....

NAILCOTE HALL & RESTAURANT, a historic country house hotel and restaurant. Ideally located for the Heart of England visitors. Situated on the B4101 Knowles to Coventry road.

B&B from £120, Dinner available, Rooms 25 double, 13 twin, all en-suite, Open all year.

Nailcote Hall & Restaurant, Nailcote Lane, Berkswell, Coventry, West Midlands CV7 7DE
Tel: 01203 466174 Fax: 01203 470720   **Map Ref 45**

....

CEDARWOOD HOUSE, a private guesthouse, all bedrooms elegantly furnished and with en-suite facilities. Within 2 miles of the NEC, airport, station and Solihull town centre.

B&B from £27.50, Rooms 4 single, 1 twin, all en-suite, Open all year.

Cedarwood House, 347 Lyndon Road, Solihull, West Midlands B92 7QT
Tel/Fax: 0121 743 5844   **Map Ref 46**

ST. JOHN'S SWALLOW HOTEL, a newly refurbished hotel with leisure facilities, close to Solihull town centre. A good touring base for Stratford, Warwick and Coventry.

B&B from £50, Rooms 14 single, 58 double, 100 twin, 5 family, all en-suite, Open all year.
St. John's Swallow Hotel, 651 Warwick Road, Solihull, West Midlands B91 1AT
Tel: 0121 711 3000 Fax: 0121 705 6629   **Map Ref 46**

....

ARDEN HOTEL & LEISURE CLUB, perfect location next to NEC, railway, airport and motorway network. Privately owned and managed. Leisure complex includes swimming pool, sauna and jacuzzi. Free car parking.

B&B from £73, Dinner available, Rooms 28 single, 14 double, 98 twin, 6 triple, all en-suite, Open all year.
Arden Hotel & Leisure Club, Coventry Road, Bickenhill, Solihull, West Midlands B92 0EH
Tel: 01675 443221 Fax: 01675 443221   **Map Ref 47**

....

THE HOLLIES, excellent accommodation just 2.5 miles from NEC and Birmingham International Airport. Sky TV, ample parking.

B&B from £20, Rooms 1 single, 4 double, 2 twin, 1 triple, some en-suite, Open all year.
The Hollies, Kenilworth Road, Hampton in Arden, Solihull, West Midlands B92 0LW
Tel: 01675 442941 Fax: 01675 442941   **Map Ref 48**

....

THE EDWARDIAN GUEST HOUSE, an Edwardian guesthouse of character. A warm welcome, good food. Excellent accommodation and delightful garden. 1.25 miles Solihull, 10 minutes from NEC, airport and railway, 5 minutes junction 5 of M42. No smoking please.

B&B from £30, Rooms 2 twin, both en-suite, Open all year.
The Edwardian Guest House, 7 St. Bernards Road, Olton, Solihull, West Midlands B92 7AU
Tel: 0121 706 2138   **Map Ref 49**

....

THE WATERLOO, TV in all rooms. Busy pub, restaurant, very friendly. Tea/coffee facilities. Clean and bright rooms. Car park. Easy access to good shopping.

B&B from £20pp, Dinner from £4.50, Rooms 1 single, 2 twin, Children welcome, Pets by arrangement, Open all year.
Martin & Steve Hore, **The Waterloo,** 58 Bridgnorth Road, Wollaston, Stourbridge, West Midlands DY8 3QG
Tel: 01384 394330   **Map Ref 50**

....

BEVERLEY HOTEL, situated close to the motorway network, with special facilities and rates for group bookings. Convenient for the NEC.

B&B from £40, Dinner available, Rooms 7 single, 10 double, 14 twin, 2 triple, all en-suite, Open all year.
Beverley Hotel, 58 Lichfield Road, Walsall, West Midlands WS4 2DJ
Tel: 01922 22999 Fax: 01922 724187   **Map Ref 51**

....

HOTEL DINARA, a small friendly hotel offering bed & breakfast. Modern, comfortable bedrooms most with en-suite facilities, all have colour TV, radio, telephone and central heating. Licensed bar. Car park. Function room for hear seats up to 200. Close to Birmingham city centre and the National Indoor Arena.
B&B from £17.50pp, Rooms 7 single, 4 twin, 3 double, most en-suite, Smoking & children welcome, No pets, Open all year.
John & Maria Marcetic, **Hotel Dinara,** 344 Bearwood Road, Smethwick, Warley, West Midlands B66 4ES
Tel: 0121 4292299   **Map Ref 52**

THE FOX HOTEL INTERNATIONAL, all bedrooms are decorated to the highest standard with all of the facilities you require, colour TV, telephone, tea/coffee. Ideally placed in the Black Country and the beautiful countryside of Shropshire and the Welsh borders. Car park is available. Near to Wolves Ground, University, Dunstall Race course and town centre. Email: foxhotel@aol.com
B&B from £46.98pp, Dinner from £6.50, Rooms 24 single, 2 twin, 6 double, 1 family, all en-suite, Children welcome, Pets by arrangement, Open all year.
Mr P S Kalirai, **The Fox Hotel International,** 118 School Street, Wolverhampton, West Midlands WV3 0NR
Tel: 01902 421680 Fax: 01902 711654   **Map Ref 53**

ELY HOUSE, a fine imposing Georgian building, fully restored, in a good central position adjacent to motorway network. Ideal base for touring the West Midlands.

B&B from £46, Dinner available, Rooms 6 single, 6 double, 7 twin, all en-suite, Open all year.

Ely House, 53 Tettenhall Road, Wolverhampton, West Midlands WV3 9NB
Tel: 01902 311311 Fax: 01902 21098   **Map Ref 53**

HOLIDAY INN GARDEN COURT, every room contains en-suite, tea/coffee facilities, TV and hair dryer. Licensed bar. Harry's Bistro serves a range of delicious meals. Wolverhampton Racecourse is on site with racing throughout the year, including flood-lit Saturday evening racing. Free parking. Disabled facilities. Birmingham Airport and NEC 20 miles.
B&B from £79pp, Dinner from £7, Rooms 8 twin, 33 double, 11 family, all en-suite, Restricted smoking, Children welcome, No pets, Open all year.
Holiday Inn Garden Court, Dunstall Park, Wolverhampton, West Midlands WV6 0PE
Tel: 01902 713313 Fax: 01902 714364   **Map Ref 53**

GREENWAY HOUSE HOTEL, small comfortable, private-run friendly hotel, close to the city centre, motorways, airport and National Exhibition Centre. Special weekend tariffs from £16.

B&B from £18, Dinner available, Rooms 8 single, 3 double, 2 twin, 1 triple, some en-suite, Open all year.

Greenway House Hotel, 978 Warwick Road, Acocks Green, Birmingham, West Midlands, B27 6QG
Tel: 0121 706 1361 Fax: 0121 706 1361   **Map Ref 31**

ELMDON GUEST HOUSE, family run guesthouse with en-suite facilities. TV in all rooms, including Sky. On main A45 close to the National Exhibition Centre, airport, railway and city centre.

B&B from £20, Dinner available, Rooms 2 single, 4 twin, 1 triple, most en-suite, Open all year.

Elmdon Guest House, 2369 Coventry Road, Sheldon, Birmingham, West Midlands, B26 3PN
Tel: 0121 742 1626 Fax: 0121 688 1720   **Map Ref 54**

FEATHERSTONE FARM, a 17th century farmhouse with listed barn/stables completely refurbished. Open fires. Near M6, M54 and close to Weston Hall. Restaurant offering Indian Cuisine.

B&B from £35, Dinner available, Rooms 2 single, 3 double, 3 twin, 1 triple, all en-suite, Open all year.

Featherstone Farm, New Road, Featherstone, Wolverhampton, West Midlands, WV10 7NW
Tel: 01902 725371 Fax: 01902 731741   **Map Ref 55**

In less than an hour from London the visitor can be in the heart of rural England - Wiltshire. The county stretches from the lush countryside in the north of the county where the Cotswolds spill over from Gloucestershire to the wide open spaces of Salisbury Plain to the south. There are also many famous prehistoric monuments and sites, the most noted of which are Stonehenge, and Avebury's circle of standing stones.

The Kennet and Avon Canal is fully navigable from the east to the west of Wiltshire. From Bradford-on-Avon, the canal makes its way through an impressive flight of twenty nine locks at Caen Hill, to just south of Savernake Forest at the eastern edge of the county.

Bradford-on-Avon is a town unlike any other in Wiltshire with almost every route on steep incline. The bridge across the river has two original medieval arches and a domed structure on one side, which was once a chapel. Castle Combe is one of the most photographed villages in the country - the descent to the village is dramatic. Once a wealthy weaving centre, mellowed cottages circle the stone canopied market cross. At the north and south extremities of Wiltshire are two important towns - Swindon and Salisbury. Swindon is an excellent modern shopping centre and home to the Great Western Railway Museum. Salisbury, or New Sarum, was built at the meeting point of four rivers and is one of the most beautiful cathedral cities in Britain. Founded in 1220 when Bishop Richard Poore abandoned the Norman cathedral built at Old Sarum and built another, called New Sarum.

The inn at Alderbury, The Green Dragon, was featured in Charles Dickens' Martin Chuzzlewit. Other interesting and attractive villages include Chilmark, with a wealth of seventeenth century houses, Britford, which has views to Salisbury Cathedral, Dinton and Great Wishford. Steeple Langford in the Wylye Valley has thatched brick cottages contrasting with the even older chequered flint houses. Wylye is another village with typical chequered stonework. Stonehenge, west of Amesbury, and completed around 1250 BC, retains a powerful atmosphere. The world famous Bronze Age site on Salisbury Plain probably dates back to 2150 BC.

Notable towns include Amesbury, set in a bend of the River Avon which is crossed by a five arched Palladian style bridge; Devizes a pleasant old market town with fine Georgian houses; and Trowbridge, once a major settlement for Flemish weavers who had brought with them great prosperity. Marlborough is a town noted for having one of the widest main streets in the country, with its splendid Georgian buildings and colonnaded shops.

left, Longleat

Wiltshire

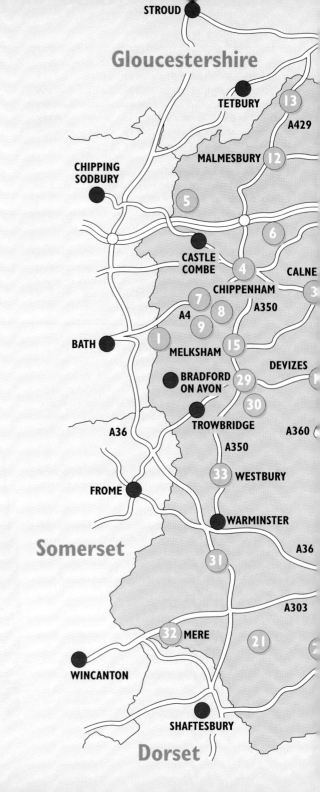

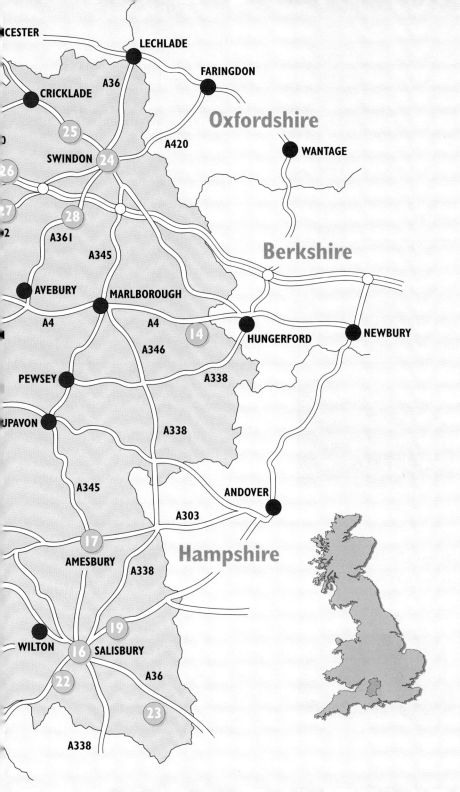

CESTER

LECHLADE

FARINGDON

A36

CRICKLADE

Oxfordshire

25

WANTAGE

26

SWINDON

24

A420

27

28

Berkshire

2

A361

A345

AVEBURY

MARLBOROUGH

A4

A4

14

HUNGERFORD

NEWBURY

A346

PEWSEY

A338

UPAVON

A338

A345

ANDOVER

A303

17

Hampshire

AMESBURY

A338

19

WILTON

16

SALISBURY

22

A36

23

A338

FERN COTTAGE, a delightful stone cottage dating from 1680 in quiet conservation village. Oak beams, open fire, antiques and family heirlooms. Three beautifully appointed bedrooms with private bath/shower, colour TV, tea/coffee facilities. Traditional English breakfast is served at a large attractively arranged table. Guests may relax in garden and conservatory. No smoking. Ample parking. Local Inn 100 yards.

B&B from £27.50pp, Rooms 3 double, all en-suite, No smoking, Children welcome, Pets by arrangement, Open all year.
Christopher & Jenny Valentine, **Fern Cottage,** Monkton Farleigh, Bradford-on-Avon, Wiltshire BA15 2QJ
Tel: 01225 859412 Fax: 01225 859018   **Map Ref 1**

LANSDOWNE STRAND HOTEL & RESTAURANT, a 16th century coaching inn noted for cuisine and high standard of accommodation. Retains all original features. Ideal touring centre for Cotswolds and Wiltshire.

B&B from £42, Dinner available, Rooms 2 single, 9 twin, 12 double, 3 family rooms, all en-suite, No smoking, Children welcome, Open all year.

Lansdowne Strand Hotel & Restaurant, The Strand, Calne, Wiltshire SN11 0EH
Tel: 01249 812488 Fax: 01249 815323   **Map Ref 3**

THE BRAMLEYS, a large Victorian listed building, close to town centre. Family run with relaxed friendly atmosphere. All home cooking.

B&B from £15, Dinner available, Rooms 1 single, 3 twin, 1 triple, No smoking, Children welcome, No pets, Open all year.
The Bramleys, 73 Marshfield Road, Chippenham, Wiltshire SN15 1JR
Tel: 01249 653770   **Map Ref 4**

MANOR FARM, is a beautiful 17th century working farm nestling in Alderton. Warm hospitality and spacious en-suite bedrooms embraces all who stay. A super selection of pubs are available within a few minutes drive. In close proximity to Bath, Bristol and M4.

B&B from £28-£30pp, Rooms 1 twin, 2 double, all en-suite, Restricted smoking, Children over 12, Pets by arrangement, Open all year except Christmas & New Year.
Mrs Victoria Lippiatt, **Manor Farm,** Alderton, Chippenham, Wiltshire SW14 6NL
Tel: 01666 840271 Fax: 01666 840271   **Map Ref 5**

BELL HOUSE HOTEL, a pretty country hotel set in a small quiet village. Suitable for a quiet weekend away, yet near M4 and town.

B&B from £45, Dinner available, Rooms 3 single, 6 twin, 5 double, all en-suite, No smoking, Children welcome, Open all year.

Bell House Hotel, High Street, Sutton Benger, Chippenham, Wiltshire SN15 4RH
Tel: 01249 720401 Fax: 01249 720401   **Map Ref 6**

PICKWICK LODGE FARM, enjoy a stay in lovely farmhouse take a short stroll or longer walk, relax in the peaceful garden. 15 minutes drive to Bath. Close to Lacock, Castle Combe, Avebury, Stonehenge, National Trust properties. Close to village pubs. 2 well appointed bedrooms. Colour TV, central heating, log fires, refreshment trays. home made biscuits. Delicious breakfast.
B&B from £20pp, Rooms 1 twin, 2 double, all en-suite, No smoking or pets, Children welcome, Open all year except Christmas & New Year.
Mrs Stafford, **Pickwick Lodge Farm,** Corsham, Wiltshire SN13 0PS
Tel: 01249 712207 Fax: 01249 701904   **Map Ref 7**

HEATHERLY COTTAGE, a 17th century cottage in a quiet country lane with ample parking, overlooking countryside. Tastefully furnished bedrooms with colour TV and tea/coffee facilities. Ideal for Avebury, Stonehenge, Lacock Abbey, Castle Combe, Corsham and other historic places of interest. Excellent pubs nearby.
B&B from £19pp, Rooms 1 twin, 2 double, all en-suite, No smoking or pets, Children over 8, Open February - December.
Peter & Jenny Daniel, **Heatherly Cottage,** Ladbrook Lane, Gastard, Corsham, Wiltshire SN13 9PE
Tel: 01249 701402 Fax: 01249 701412   **Map Ref 8**

NESTON COUNTRY INN, television, tea/coffee making facilities. Car parking. Animals, duck pond, patio and garden pond with waterfall. Gypsy caravan for children plus other things to play on for the very young. Full license. Tudor style bar with thatching. Collection of balloons and dolls hang in the bar. Close to Box 5 miles, Bath 8 miles, Laycock 5 miles, Corsham one and a half miles.
B&B from £45per room, Meals from £4.50, Rooms 1 twin, 3 double, 1 family, all en-suite, Restricted smoking, Children & pets welcome, Open all year except Boxing Day.
Janet & Ian Tucker, **Neston Country Inn,** Neston, Corsham SN13 9SN
Tel: 01225 811694 Mobile: 0498 713413   **Map Ref 9**

BLACK SWAN HOTEL, a welcoming family run hotel in picturesque market town, central for many of Wiltshire's historic sights. Excellent food, well appointed en-suite rooms, friendly service.

B&B from £40, Dinner available, Rooms 1 single, 4 twin, 5 double, all en-suite, Children welcome, No pets, Open all year.

Black Swan Hotel, Market Place, Devizes, Wiltshire SN10 1JQ
Tel: 01380 723259 Fax: 01380 729966   **Map Ref 10**

THE CASTLE HOTEL, well appointed accommodation in a busy market town. A la carte restaurant and popular bar. All rooms en-suite.

B&B from £40, Dinner available, Rooms 5 single, 7 twin, 5 double, 1 family, all en-suite, No smoking, Children welcome, Open all year.

The Castle Hotel, New Park Street, Devizes, Wiltshire SN10 1DS
Tel: 01380 729300 Fax: 01380 729155   **Map Ref 10**

SPOUT COTTAGE, a delightfully situated thatched cottage in secluded valley. Idyllic peaceful retreat. Well appointed centrally heated rooms, inglenook fireplace, beamed ceilings. Delicious, imaginative food.

B&B from £18.50, Dinner available, Rooms 1 single, 1 twin, No smoking, No pets, Open all year.

Spout Cottage, Stert, Devizes, Wiltshire SN10 3JD
Tel: 01380 724336   **Map Ref 11**

KNOLL HOUSE HOTEL, ideally located with easy access to M4, Bath, Cheltenham and Cotswolds. Country house with fine restaurant and outdoor heated pool.

B&B from £60, Dinner available, Rooms 9 single, 3 twin, 10 double, all en-suite, No smoking, Children welcome, Open all year.

Knoll House Hotel, Swindon Road, Malmesbury, Wiltshire SN16 9LU
Tel: 01666 823114 Fax: 01666 823897   **Map Ref 12**

MAYFIELD HOUSE HOTEL, a delightful country hotel with two acres of walled garden. Award wining restaurant, with warm and friendly service. Close to the M4 and ideal for touring the Cotswolds and Bath.

B&B from £29, Dinner available, Rooms 4 single, 7 twin, 8 double, 1 triple, all en-suite, Children welcome, Open all year.

Mayfield House Hotel, Crudwell, Malmesbury, Wiltshire SN16 9EW
Tel: 01666 577409 & 577198 Fax: 01666 577977 **Map Ref 13**

....

THE HARROW INN, is a small family run village pub nestling in the beautiful Wiltshire countryside, very close to the banks of the Kennet and Avon Canal. We offer good food and wine and a warm welcome. We look forward to seeing you.

B&B from £25pp, Dinner from £4.50, Rooms 1 twin, 1 double, both en-suite, No smoking Children welcome, Pets by arrangement, Open all year.

Kim & Susie Sharman, **The Harrow Inn,** Little Bedwyn, Marlborough, Wiltshire SN8 3JP
Tel: 01672 870871 Fax: 01672 811231 **Map Ref 14**

....

LONGHOPE GUEST HOUSE, situated in its own grounds on the A350 Melksham - Chippenham road. Half a mile from Melksham town centre, 10 miles from M4 junction 17.

B&B from £25, Rooms 1 single, 2 twin, 1 double, 2 triple, all en-suite, Children welcome, No pets, Open all year.

Longhope Guest House, 9 Beanacre Road, Melksham, Wiltshire SN12 8AG
Tel: 01225 706737 Fax: 01225 706737 **Map Ref 15**

....

THE KINGS ARMS HOTEL, combines old world atmosphere with modern amenities and is an ideal centre for touring historic Wiltshire.

B&B from £32, Dinner available, Rooms 6 single, 2 twin, 5 double, most en-suite, Children welcome, Open all year.

The Kings Arms Hotel, Market Place, Melksham, Wiltshire SN12 6EX
Tel: 01225 707272 Fax: 01225 702085 **Map Ref 15**

....

CONIGRE FARM HOTEL & RESTAURANT, a charming 17th century farmhouse and stable block tastefully converted to provide individually decorated en-suite accommodation and a popular restaurant. Situated 400 yards from the town centre.

B&B from £35, Dinner available, Rooms 3 single, 1 twin, 5 double, most en-suite, Children welcome, Open all year.

Conigre Farm Hotel & Restaurant, Semington Road, Melksham, Wiltshire SN12 6BZ
Tel: 01225 702229 Fax: 01225 707392 **Map Ref 15**

....

TALBOT HOTEL, a 16th century coaching inn with interesting features. Ideal for visits to Stourhead, Longleat, Stonehenge, Salisbury, Bath, Sherborne and Cheddar. Two night breaks available.

B&B from £25, Dinner available, Rooms 1 single, 1 twin, 2 double, 3 triple, all en-suite, No smoking, Children welcome, Open all year.

Talbot Hotel, The Square, Mere, Wiltshire BA12 6DR
Tel: 01747 860427 **Map Ref 32**

THE MILFORD HALL HOTEL & RESTAURANT, this fine Georgian city centre mansion has been sympathetically restored to create a magnificent hotel and restaurant that is becoming a landmark in this historic cathedral city.

B&B from £55, Dinner available, Rooms 15 twin, 20 double, all en-suite, No smoking, Children welcome, Open all year.

The Milford Hall Hotel & Restaurant, 206 Castle Street, Salisbury, Wiltshire SP1 3TE
Tel: 01722 417411 Fax: 01772 419444 **Map Ref 16**

....

THE ROKEBY GUEST HOUSE, a beautiful, nostalgic Edwardian house. Quietly situated ten minutes stroll from the city centre and cathedral. Large landscaped gardens, summerhouse, fishpond, two storey conservatory and satellite television.

B&B from £30, Dinner available, Rooms 3 twin, 1 double, 1 triple, 2 family, most en-suite, No smoking, Children welcome, No pets, Open all year.

The Rokeby Guest House, 3 Wain-a-Long Road, Salisbury, Wiltshire SP1 1LJ
Tel: 01722 329800 Fax: 01722 329800 **Map Ref 16**

....

BYWAYS HOUSE, an attractive family run Victorian house situated close to the cathedral in quiet area of the city centre. Car park. Bedrooms with private bathrooms and colour satellite television. Traditional English and vegetarian breakfasts served.

B&B from £24, Rooms 4 single, 3 twin, 7 double, 2 triple, 7 family, most en-suite, No smoking, Children welcome, Open all year.

Byways House, 31 Fowlers Road, Salisbury, Wiltshire SP1 2QP
Tel: 01722 328364 Fax: 01722 322146 **Map Ref 16**

....

STRATFORD LODGE, a charming Victorian house in quiet lane overlooking Victoria Park. Eight en-suite bedrooms. Licensed restaurant offering varied menu. Breakfast in lovely conservatory. Wonderful garden. Large car-park. Residents lounge. Comfortable rooms with tea-making facilities, TV, telephone. Credit cards. Close to Old Sarum and City. **B&B from £28pp,** Dinner from £17, Rooms 8 double, 2 family, all en-suite, No smoking or pets, Children over 5, Open all year except Christmas.
Ian & Jacqueline Lawrence, **Stratford Lodge,** 4 Park Lane, Salisbury, Wiltshire SP1 3NP
Tel: 01722 325177 Fax: 01722 325177 **Map Ref 16**

....

CRANSTON GUEST HOUSE, a large detached town house covered in Virginia creeper. 10 minutes walk from town centre and cathedral.

B&B from £17, Rooms 2 single, 1 double, 2 family, most en-suite, No smoking, Children welcome, Open all year.

Cranston Guest House, 5 Wain-a-Long Road, Salisbury, Wiltshire SP1 1LJ
Tel: 01722 336776 **Map Ref 16**

....

THE EDWARDIAN LODGE, an Edwardian house, home cooked evening meals, good parking off main road, short walk to city centre, cathedral and Old Sarum. Beautiful valley drive to Stonehenge.

B&B from £25, Dinner available, Rooms 1 single, 2 twin, 3 double, 1 family, all en-suite, No smoking, Children welcome, Open all year.

The Edwardian Lodge, 59 Castle Road, Salisbury, Wiltshire SP1 3RH
Tel: 01722 413329 & 410500 Fax: 01722 503105 **Map Ref 16**

VICTORIA LODGE GUEST HOUSE, a Victorian lodge, a short walk from city centre, cathedral and Old Sarum. Home cooked evening meals, good parking. Stonehenge 8 miles.

B&B from £25, Dinner available, Rooms 4 single, 2 twin, 2 double, 4 triple, 3 family, all en-suite, No smoking, Children welcome, Open all year.

Victoria Lodge Guest House, 61 Castle Road, Salisbury, Wiltshire SP1 3RH
Tel: 01722 320586 Fax: 01722 414507   **Map Ref 16**

....

GRASMERE HOUSE, a 19th century family residence delightfully converted into a private hotel within a setting of rural tranquillity with views of Rivers Avon, Nadder and Salisbury Cathedral. Access off A3094.

B&B from £65, Dinner available, Rooms 2 single, 10 twin, 7 double, 1 family, all en-suite,No smoking, Children welcome, Open all year.
Grasmere House, 70 Harnham Road, Salisbury, Wiltshire SP2 8JN
Tel: 01722 338388 Fax: 01772 333710   **Map Ref 16**

....

HAYBURN WYKE GUEST HOUSE, a friendly, family run guest house situated by Victoria Park, half a mile Riverside walk from city centre and cathedral. Interesting places nearby include old Sarum, Wilton House and Stonehenge. Rooms have TV's, tea/coffee facilities. Wonderful breakfasts. Car parking. Credit cards accepted. AA QQQ, ETB Commended.
B&B from £18.50pp, Rooms 2 twin, 3 double, 2 family, some en-suite, Children welcome, Pets by arrangement, Open all year.
Dawn & Alan Curnow, **Hayburn Wyke Guest House,** 72 Castle Road, Salisbury, Wiltshire SP1 3RL
Tel: 01722 412627 Fax: 01722 412627   **Map Ref 16**

....

FARTHINGS, is very quiet but central with easy parking. The rooms are comfortable with tea/coffee facilities. The guests' lounge has a TV and a collection of family photos. The garden is delightful. An ideal base for visiting Salisbury, Stonehenge and many other interesting places.

B&B from £18pp, Rooms 2 single, 1 twin, 1 double, some en-suite, No smoking or pets, Open all year.

Mrs Gill Rodwell **Farthings,** 9 Swaynes Close, Salisbury, Wiltshire SP1 3AE
Tel: 01722 330749 Fax: 01722 330749   **Map Ref 16**

....

RED LION HOTEL, originally a coaching inn, now a city centre hotel with all modern facilities. Ideal for business or pleasure.

B&B from £85, Dinner available, Rooms 11 single, 19 twin, 22 double, 2 family, all en-suite,No smoking, Children welcome, No pets, Open all year.

Red Lion Hotel, Milford Street, Salisbury, Wiltshire SP1 2AN
Tel: 01722 323334 Fax: 01722 325756   **Map Ref 16**

....

ANTROBUS ARMS HOTEL, a traditional hotel with highly acclaimed 'Fountain Restaurant'. Walled Victorian garden. Near Stonehenge, A303 half a mile, Salisbury 5 miles. Well situated for visiting countryside steeped in history and rich in culture.

B&B from £35, Dinner available, Rooms 7 single, 5 twin, 7 double, 1 family, most en-suite, Children welcome, Open all year.

Antrobus Arms Hotel, 15 Church Street, Amesbury, Salisbury, Wiltshire SP4 7EU
Tel: 01980 623163 Fax: 01980 622112   **Map Ref 17**

MORRIS FARMHOUSE, a 100 year old farmhouse with attractive garden set in open countryside. Good parking. tea/coffee facilities in each room. Excellent local pub 2 minutes walk. Ideal for Wilton House, Wilton Carpet Factory, Salisbury, Old Sarum, Stonehenge, Stowhead and Longleat.

B&B from £18pp, Rooms 1 twin, double/twin, No smoking, Children & pets welcome, Open all year except Christmas & New Year.

Martin & Judith Marriott, **Morris Farmhouse,** Baverstock, Dinton, Salisbury, Wiltshire SP3 5EL
Tel/Fax: 01722 716874 Email: marriott@dircon.co.uk   **Map Ref 18**

....

1 RIVERSIDE CLOSE, charming, well appointed home, in quiet area not far from Salisbury Cathedral. Tastefully furnished rooms with en-suite bath or shower room, TV and drinks facilities. Salisbury is the centre of an are stepped in antiquity with many places of historical interest. Your hosts are happy to plan itineraries for them.

B&B from £22.50pp, Dinner from £12, Rooms 1 double, 1 family, all en-suite, No smoking or pets, Children welcome, Open all year.
Mary Tucker, **1 Riverside Close,** Laverstock, Salisbury, Wiltshire SP1 1QW
Tel: 01722 320287 Fax: 01722 320287   **Map Ref 19**

....

HOWARDS HOUSE HOTEL, a 17th century dower house in idyllic rural setting with high quality accommodation, award winning restaurant and an atmosphere of tranquillity and friendliness.

B&B from £65, Dinner available, Rooms 1 twin, 8 double, all en-suite, No smoking, Children welcome, Open all year.

Howards House Hotel, Teffont Evias, Salisbury, Wiltshire SP3 5RJ
Tel: 01722 716392 & 716821 Fax: 01722 716820   **Map Ref 20**

....

BECKFORD ARMS, a tastefully refurbished, stylish and comfortable 18th century inn, between Tisbury and Hindon in area of outstanding beauty. 2 miles A303. Convenient for Salisbury and Shaftesbury.

B&B from £34.50, Dinner available, Rooms 3 single, 1 twin, 4 double, all with en-suite or private facilities, Children welcome, Open all year.

Beckford Arms, Fonthill Gifford, Tisbury, Salisbury, Wiltshire SP3 6PX
Tel: 01747 870385 Fax: 01747 851496   **Map Ref 21**

....

THE OLD MILL HOTEL, is a former 14th century Mill, peacefully located on River Nadder surrounded by water meadows, close to Salisbury Cathedral. Beautiful rooms and views. 2 Star. Our restaurant specialises in traditional Fayre and fresh seafood. Our pub offers real ale and real food. Riverside Beer Gardens. 10 minutes stroll city centre.
B&B from £35pp, Dinner from £15, Rooms 2 single, 4 twin, 5 double, all en-suite, Children welcome, No pets, Open all year.
Roy & Lois Thwaites, **The Old Mill Hotel,** Town Path, West Harmham, Salisbury, Wiltshire SP2 8EU
Tel: 01722 327517 Fax: 01722 333367   **Map Ref 22**

....

Salisbury 5 minutes. Lionel welcomes you to the **THREE CROWNS INN** just off the main A36. The Inn is full of character with plenty of beams and a open log fire. It is also within easy distance to Stone Henge and Wilton House, Salisbury cathedral.

B&B from £18pp, Dinner from £5.50, Rooms 1 twin, 1 double, 1 family, all en-suite, Restricted smoking, Children welcome, No pets, Open all year.

Lionel Sutton, **Three Crowns Inn,** Whaddon, Salisbury, Wiltshire SP5 3HB
Tel: 01722 710211   **Map Ref 23**

THE ROYSTON HOTEL, is an ivy-clad Victorian town house close to the town centre. All rooms have been recently refurbished and provide free cable television, direct dial telephone and refreshments. Licensed restaurant. Private parking. Special weekend breaks available. Close to Cotswolds, Oxford, Bath and Salisbury.
B&B from £30pp, Dinner from £7.50, Rooms 6 single, 6 twin, 5 double, 7 family, some en-suite, Children & pets welcome, Open all year except Christmas & New Year.
Anna-Marie Dutton, **The Royston Hotel,** 34 Victoria Road, Swindon, Wiltshire SN1 3AS
Tel: 01793 522990 Fax: 01793 522991   **Map Ref 24**

....

GODDARD ARMS HOTEL, an old world hotel built in 1790 and named after famous local family in the old town. Short distance from M4 motorway, Cotswolds, Avebury and Wiltshire Downs.

B&B from £40, Dinner available, Rooms 12 single, 237 twin, 16 double, all private bathrooms, No smoking, Children welcome, Open all year.

Goddard Arms Hotel, High Street, Swindon, Wiltshire SN1 3EG
Tel: 01793 692313 Fax: 01793 512984   **Map Ref 24**

....

BLUNSDON HOUSE HOTEL & LEISURE CLUB, peacefully set on the edge of the Cotswolds. Facilities include a leisure club and 9 hole par 3 golf course. Special breaks available.

B&B from £68, Dinner available, Rooms 9 single, 18 twin, 50 double, 10 triple, all en-suite, No smoking, Children welcome, No pets, Open all year.

Blunsdon House Hotel & Leisure Club, Blunsdon, Swindon, Wiltshire SN2 4AD
Tel: 01793 721701 Fax: 01793 721056   **Map Ref 25**

....

THE SCHOOL HOUSE HOTEL & RESTAURANT, a charming country house hotel in a converted 1860 school house. Combining modern facilities and Victorian decor. Situated in a rural hamlet but close to M4, Swindon and the Cotswolds.

B&B from £59, Dinner available, Rooms 1 twin, 9 double, all en-suite, No smoking, Children welcome, No pets Open all year.

The School House Hotel & Restaurant, Hook Street, Hook, Swindon, Wiltshire SN4 8EF
Tel: 01793 851198 Fax: 01793 851025   **Map Ref 26**

....

FAIRVIEW GUEST HOUSE, a detached guest house, situated west of Swindon, close to M4 junction 19. Ground floor rooms available.

B&B from £19.50, Rooms 5 single, 2 twin, 3 double, 2 triple, most en-suite,No smoking, Children welcome, Open all year.

Fairview Guest House, 52 Swindon Road, Wootton Bassett, Swindon, Wiltshire SN4 8EU
Tel: 01793 852283 Fax: 01793 848076   **Map Ref 27**

....

VILLIERS INN, a warm hearted, full service hotel with personality! An 18th century farmhouse with first class en-suite bedrooms and two popular restaurants.

B&B from £50, Dinner available, Rooms 9 single, 15 twin, 10 double, all en-suite, No smoking, Children welcome, No pets, Open all year.

Villiers Inn, Moorhead Road, Wroughton, Swindon, Wiltshire SN4 9BY
Tel: 01793 814744 Fax: 01793 814119   **Map Ref 28**

BROOK HOUSE, a spacious house in large grounds with swimming pool. Convenient for Bath, Avebury, Castle Combe and Lacock. Good walking along canal. Recommended pub in village Excellent breakfast and comfortable bedrooms.

B&B from £20pp, Rooms 2 twin, 1 double, 1 family, all en-suite/private facilities, Restricted smoking, Children & pets welcome, Open January - November.

Mr & Mrs Bruges, **Brook House,** Semington, Trowbridge, Wiltshire BA14 6SR
Tel: 01380 870232 Fax: 01380 871431　　　　　　　　　**Map Ref 29**

SPIERS PIECE FARM, a homely and spacious Georgian farmhouse in the heart of the Wiltshire countryside. Easy access Bath, Longleat etc. Large comfortable bedrooms, with washbasins and hospitality trays. Luxury guests bathroom, guests lounge, colour TV. TV's in two double rooms also.

B&B from £16pp, Rooms 1 twin, 2 double, Restricted smoking, Children welcome, Pets by arrangement, Open February - November.

Jill Awdry, **Spiers Piece Farm,** Steeple Ashton, Trowbridge, Wiltshire BA14 6HG
Tel: 01380 870266 Fax: 01380 870266　　　　　　　　　**Map Ref 30**

Situated in the beautiful Wylye Valley, on the edge of the famous Longleat Estate, **SPRINGFIELD HOUSE** is a charming village home dating from the 17th century with beams, open fires and fresh flowers. Private or en-suite rooms overlook the garden and grass tennis court. Ideal for touring, walking or relaxing. Bath, Salisbury, Wells, Glastonbury, Stonehenge and Stourhead Gardens easily reached.

B&B from £24pp, Dinner from £15, Rooms 1 twin, 2 double, all en-suite, No smoking or pets, Children welcome, Open all year except Christmas & New Year.

Rachel & Colin Singer, **Springfield House,** Crockerton, Warminster, Wiltshire BA12 8AU
Tel: 01985 213696　　　　　　　　　**Map Ref 31**

CHETCOMBE HOUSE HOTEL, a country house hotel set in one acre of mature gardens, close to Stourhead House and Gardens. An ideal touring centre. Home cooked local produce a speciality.

B&B from £29, Dinner available, Rooms 1 single, 2 twin, 2 double, all en-suite, No smoking, Children welcome, Open all year.
Chetcombe House Hotel, Chetcombe Road, Mere, Warminster, Wiltshire BA12 6AZ
Tel: 01747 860219 Fax: 01747 860111　　　　　　　　　**Map Ref 32**

MELTONE HOUSE, a comfortable house with beautiful views. Large car park and garden. Situated about one mile from Mere on the Shaftesbury road.

B&B from £17.50, Dinner available, Rooms 1 single, 2 double, Children welcome, No pets, Open all year.

Meltone House, The Causeway, Shaftesbury Road, Mere, Warminster, Wiltshire BA12 6BW
Tel: 01747 861383　　　　　　　　　**Map Ref 32**

THE CEDAR HOTEL, an 18th century country house with a friendly and relaxed atmosphere. Offering comfortable, well appointed accommodation and good cuisine.

B&B from £40, Dinner available, Rooms 1 single, 3 twin, 12 double, all en-suite, No smoking, Children welcome, Open all year.
The Cedar Hotel, Warminster Road, Westbury, Wiltshire BA13 3PR
Tel: 01373 822753 Fax: 01373 858423　　　　　　　　　**Map Ref 33**

Yorkshire is a county of unspoilt beauty and a wealth of heritage. The county has some spectacular scenery from the Dales to the predominantly cliff lined coast. The region's historical capital, York, dates back to the Romans nearly two thousand years ago and one of the city's quaint streets, the Shambles, is the best preserved medieval thoroughfare in Europe. Perhaps Yorkshire's most breathtaking scenery is the natural limestone landscape of upper Airedale, around Malham. The village of Malham itself is set in an amphitheatre of hills, with the giant overhang of Malham Cove a mile to the north.

Grassington is Upper Wharfedale's principal village where a medieval bridge spans the River Wharfe. To the north of the village, lead mining on Grassington Moor brought a boom in the late eighteenth and nineteenth centuries. While the Dales look purely pastoral today, moors like Grassington and gill-sides bear the scars of lead mining which declined in the 1880s because of foreign imports. Kettlewell must be one of upper Wharfedale's most attractive villages, dominated by great Whernside while three miles to the south is Kilnsey Crag which attracts serious rock climbers. In the Yorkshire Dales National Park upland moors sweep to a score of summits.

The view from the top of Richmond's eleventh century castle keep is one of England's finest. More unspoilt countryside can be found in the firsts, hills and vales of the North Yorkshire Moors, where heather covered moorland stretches from the Vale of York to the sea. Helmsley is the main town beneath the rim of the moors and a fine centre for walking. Two miles north is Rievaulx Abbey, founded in 1131, the first Cistercian house in the north of England and one of the country's most magnificent monastic ruins.

Whitby, a fishing port is dominated by its abbey, high above the town. Its first abbey was founded in AD 657 by St Hilda. Robin Hood's Bay is another seaside village well worth a visit.

The spa town of Harrogate is an attractive town with its banks of flowers and well planned open spaces. It is also well known as a conference centre. At nearby Knaresborough, Georgian houses line the narrow streets and steep steps and alleys lead down to the River Nidd. Opposite the ruined castle is the Dropping Well, where water dropping on to an overhang forms a limestone deposit, petrifying a curious assortment of objects.

Among the many Yorkshire market towns to visit are Bedale, with its wide cobbled verges, and Boroughbridge, where three stone monoliths dating from 2000 to 1500 BC stand at up to thirty feet high, and are known as the Devils Arrows.

left, Swaledale

497

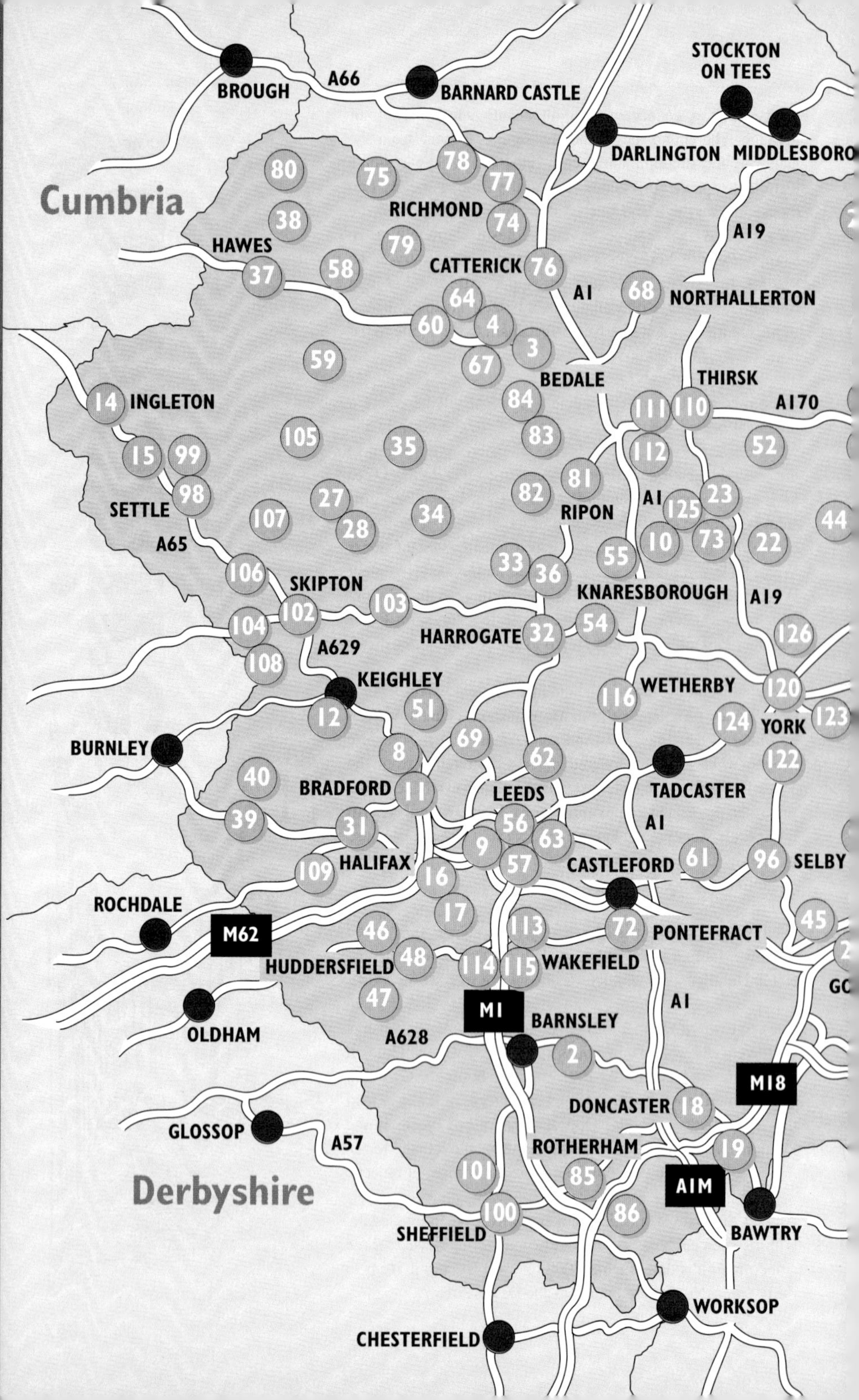
BROUGH
A66
BARNARD CASTLE
STOCKTON ON TEES
DARLINGTON
MIDDLESBORO
Cumbria
80
75
78
77
RICHMOND
38
74
HAWES
79
A19
37
58
CATTERICK
76
A1
68
NORTHALLERTON
64
60
4
3
59
67
BEDALE
THIRSK
14
INGLETON
84
111
110
A170
105
35
83
112
52
15
99
81
98
27
82
A1
125
23
SETTLE
107
34
RIPON
44
28
10
73
22
A65
33
36
55
106
SKIPTON
KNARESBOROUGH
A19
102
103
104
HARROGATE
32
54
126
A629
108
KEIGHLEY
116
WETHERBY
120
51
12
124
YORK
123
BURNLEY
69
8
62
122
40
BRADFORD
11
LEEDS
TADCASTER
56
39
31
63
A1
9
HALIFAX
109
57
CASTLEFORD
61
96
SELBY
16
ROCHDALE
17
45
M62
46
113
72
PONTEFRACT
HUDDERSFIELD
48
114
115
WAKEFIELD
47
A1
M1
BARNSLEY
OLDHAM
A628
2
M18
DONCASTER
18
GLOSSOP
A57
ROTHERHAM
19
101
85
A1M
Derbyshire
100
86
SHEFFIELD
BAWTRY
WORKSOP
CHESTERFIELD

CAR

87

117 WHITBY

118

119

93

1

90

70

89

RING

88 SCARBOROUGH

92 91

55

66

A64

24 FILEY

A165

25

21

13 BRIDLINGTON

A166

DRIFFIELD

A165

20

BEVERLEY

43 HORNSEA

7

5

6

3

A63

HULL

49

50

A1033

WITHERNSEA

A15

THORPE

94

IMMINGHAM

SPURN POINT

95

A15

30 GRIMSBY

A46

BOROUGH

Lincolnshire

APPLETON HALL COUNTRY HOUSE HOTEL, a Victorian country house set in 2 acres of mature lawns and award winning gardens. A hideaway place offering elegance, comfort and tranquillity.

B&B from £40, Dinner available, Rooms 2 single, 5 double, 2 twin, all en-suite, No smoking, Children welcome, Open all year.

Appleton Hall Country House Hotel, Appleton-le-Moors, Yorkshire YO6 6TF
Tel: 01751 417227 & 417452 Fax: 01751 417540   **Map Ref 1**

....

ARDSLEY HOUSE HOTEL, an 18th century manor house, tastefully converted to a private hotel. Extensive conference and banqueting facilities. French and English cooking.

B&B from £35, Dinner available, Rooms 17 single, 22 double, 23 twin, 11 triple, all en-suite, No smoking, Children welcome, Open all year.
Ardsley House Hotel, Doncaster Road, Ardsley, Barnsley, Yorkshire S71 5EH
Tel: 01226 309955 Fax: 01226 205374   **Map Ref 2**

....

HYPERION HOUSE, set in the market town of Bedale, gateway to the Dales. An ideal base for also touring the Yorkshire Moors National Park, Teesdale and the historic cities of York, Ripon and Harrogate. Let us spoil you in our lovely home. ETB 2 Crowns Highly Commended.

B&B from £18-£22pp, Rooms 1 twin, 2 en-suite double, No smoking or pets, Children over 8, Open all year except Christmas, New Year & February.

Sheila & Ron Dean, **Hyperion House,** 88 South End, Bedale, North Yorkshire DL8 2DS
Tel: 01677 422334 Fax: 01677 422334   **Map Ref 3**

....

ELMFIELD HOUSE, a country house in own grounds with special emphasis on standards and home cooking. All rooms en-suite. Bar, games room and solarium. Ample secure parking.

B&B from £29.50, Dinner available, Rooms 4 double, 3 twin, 2 triple, all en-suite, No smoking, Children welcome, No pets, Open all year.

Elmfield House, Arranthorne, Bedale, Yorkshire DL8 1NE
Tel: 01677 450558 Fax: 01677 450557   **Map Ref 4**

....

EASTGATE GUEST HOUSE, situated in the centre of Beverley, two minutes walk from Railway Station. Two crown commended classification with ETB, RAC Listed, AA Recommended. All rooms colour TV, central heating, Bedside lights, washing basins etc. tea/coffee making facilities available.
B&B from £17pp, Rooms 5 single, 2 twin, 5 double, 4 family, some en-suite, Restricted smoking, Children & Pets welcome, Open all year.
Julie Anderson, **Eastgate Guest House,** 7 Eastgate, Beverley, East Yorkshire HU17 0DR
Tel: 01482 868464 Fax: 01482 871899   **Map Ref 5**

....

MANOR HOUSE, a country house hotel, surrounded by trees in an idyllic setting among meadows and farms. Between Walkington and Bishop Burton, 5 minutes from Beverley. RAC Small hotel of the North 1995

B&B from £70pp, Dinner available, Rooms 6 double, 1 family, all en-suite, Children & pets welcome, Open all year.

Manor House, Newbald Road, Northlands, Walkington, Beverley, Yorkshire HU17 8RT
Tel: 01482 881645 Fax: 01482 866501   **Map Ref 6**

TICKTON GRANGE HOTEL & RESTAURANT, a family run Georgian country house set in rose gardens, 2 miles from historic Beverley. Country house cooking.

B&B from £50, Dinner available, Rooms 3 single, 10 double, 3 twin, 1 triple, all en-suite, Children welcome, Open all year.
Tickton Grange Hotel & Restaurant, Tickton, Beverley, Yorkshire HU17 9SH
Tel: 01964 543666 Fax: 01964 542556 **Map Ref 7**

FIVE RISE LOCKS HOTEL, a delightful Victorian mill owner's hose set in its own grounds, with excellent views and terraced gardens. Relaxed atmosphere complemented by interesting menus and wine list.

B&B from £32.50, Dinner available, Rooms 7 double, 2 twin, all en-suite, No smoking, Children welcome, Open all year.
Five Rise Locks Hotel, Beck Lane, Bingley, Yorkshire BD16 4DD
Tel: 01274 565296 Fax: 01274 568828 **Map Ref 8**

OAKWOOD HALL HOTEL, an impressive listed building in quiet woodland. Individually designed bedrooms, some with four poster beds. 4 ground floor bedrooms. Relaxed place to visit, serving fine food.

B&B from £55, Dinner available, Rooms 1 single, 15 double, 4 twin, all en-suite, Children welcome, Open all year.
Oakwood Hall Hotel, Lady Lane, Bingley, Yorkshire BD16 4AW
Tel: 01274 564123 & 563569 Fax: 01274 561477 **Map Ref 8**

OAKWELL MOTEL, rooms include TV, tea/coffee facilities. Car park and bar area. Lounge. Nearby there are plenty of restaurants along side the showcase Cinema. The motel also has squash and gym facilities to guests or go walking in the country park of Oakwell Hall.

B&B from £20pp, Rooms 6 single, 5 twin, all en-suite, Children welcome, Pets by arrangement, Open all year.
David, Pam & Lynn Ward, **Oakwell Motel,** Low Lane, Birstall, West Yorkshire WF17 9HD
Tel: 01924 441514 **Map Ref 9**

CROWN HOTEL, a fully modernised 12th century coaching inn, 1 mile from A1. Ideal base for Yorkshire Dales, Herriot country, York and Harrogate. Good restaurant.

B&B from £52.50, Dinner available, Rooms 5 single, 14 double, 22 twin, 1 triple, all en-suite, Children welcome, Open all year.
Crown Hotel, Horsefair, Boroughbridge, Yorkshire YO5 9LB
Tel: 01423 322328 Fax: 01423 324512 **Map Ref 10**

NEW BEEHIVE INN, an Edwardian gaslit oak panelled inn, full of character, close to centre of Bradford. Antique furniture and individually furnished bedrooms.

B&B from £27, Dinner available, Rooms 1 single, 4 double, 2 twin, 1 triple, most en-suite, Children welcome, No pets, Open all year.
New Beehive Inn, 171 Westgate, Bradford, Yorkshire BD1 3AA
Tel: 01274 721784 **Map Ref 11**

IVY GUEST HOUSE, a large detached listed house built of Yorkshire stone. Car park and gardens. Close to city centre, National Museum of Photography, Film and Television and Alhambra Theatre.

B&B from £18, Dinner available, Rooms 3 single, 2 double, 4 twin, 1 triple, Children welcome, No pets, Open all year.

Ivy Guest House, 3 Melbourne Place, Bradford, Yorkshire BD5 0HZ
Tel: 01274 727060 & 0421 509207 Fax: 01274 306347 **Map Ref 11**

PENNINGTON MIDLAND HOTEL, totally refurbished owner managed Victorian city centre hotel. Free secure parking, adjacent Intercity station and direct motorway link. Spacious rooms, ornate plaster work, glittering chandeliers and two of the finest ballrooms in Yorkshire make the venue way ahead of the rest.

B&B from £35, Dinner available, Rooms 20 single, 56 double, 15 twin, all en-suite, No smoking, Children welcome, Open all year.
Pennington Midland Hotel, Forster Square, Bradford, Yorkshire BD1 4HU
Tel: 01274 735735 & 0836 261557 Fax: 01274 720003   **Map Ref 11**

....

P.L.S. HOTEL, this attractive hotel, located in the heart of Bradford, provides the perfect base for the businessman and visitor to the University. Located within five minutes walking distance from the University and town centre and only a short drive away from Leeds and Bradford Airport. All rooms are comfortably and elegantly furnished to a high standard.

B&B from £25-£45pp, Rooms 2 single, 3 twin, 13 double, 1 family, all en-suite, Children welcome, Pets by arrangement, Open all year except Christmas & New Year.
P.L.S. Hotel, Great Horton Road, Bradford, West Yorkshire BD7 1QG
Tel: 01274 306775 Fax: 01274 724296   **Map Ref 11**

....

CEDAR COURT HOTEL BRADFORD, the first purpose built hotel in Bradford for 20 years. Situated at the top of the M606. The ideal location.

B&B from £35, Dinner available, Rooms 86 double, 33 twin, 7 triple, all en-suite, No smoking, Children welcome, Open all year.
Cedar Court Hotel Bradford, Mayo Avenue, off Rooley Lane, Bradford, Yorkshire BD5 8HZ
Tel: 01274 406606 Fax: 01274 406600   **Map Ref 11**

....

NOVOTEL BRADFORD, 10 minutes drive from Bradford city and 2 minutes from the M62, with easy access to Leeds/Bradford Airport.

B&B from £55, Dinner available, Rooms 58 double, 58 twin, 11 triple, all en-suite, No smoking, Children welcome, Open all year.
Novotel Bradford, Merrydale Road, Bradford, Yorkshire BD4 6SA
Tel: 01274 683683 Fax: 01274 651342   **Map Ref 11**

....

PARK GROVE HOTEL & RESTAURANT, a Victorian establishment in a secluded preserved area of Bradford. 1.5 miles form the city centre. Gateway to the dales.
B&B from £35, Dinner available, Rooms 6 single, 7 double, 1 twin, 2 triple, all en-suite, Children over 4, No pets, Open all year.
Park Grove Hotel & Restaurant, Park Grove, Frizinghall, Bradford, Yorkshire BD9 4JY
Tel: 01274 543444 Fax: 01274 495619 http://www.parkgrovehotel.co.uk   **Map Ref 11**

....

THE SIDINGS, colour television, tea/coffee making facilities. Car park to side of house. Within easy reach of Bradford, Keighley, Halifax, Bingley and Ilkley. Haworth home of the Brontes 5 minutes away. Public Houses for eating or drinking within short car drive distance. Quiet location.

B&B from £18pp, Dinner by arrangement from £7.50, Rooms 1 single, 1 twin, 1 double, No smoking, Children welcome, Pets by arrangement, Open all year except Christmas.
Joyce Bunton, **The Sidings,** Station Road, Harecroft, Wilsden, Bradford, West Yorkshire BD15 0BS
Tel: 01535 274943 Fax: 01535 274943   **Map Ref 12**

....

PARK DRIVE HOTEL, 'its like staying in the country!' This elegant Victorian residence in delightful woodland setting is just 1.5 miles from the city centre and has parking inside the grounds.

B&B from £30, Dinner available, Rooms 5 single, 3 double, 2 twin, 1 triple, all en-suite, No smoking, Children welcome, Open all year.
Park Drive Hotel, 12 Park Drive, Heaton, Bradford, Yorkshire BD9 4DR
Tel: 01274 480194 Fax: 01274 484869   **Map Ref 11**

BAY RIDGE HOTEL,, a friendly, comfortable and caring family run hotel near the South Beach and Spa Complex. Good value for money, all mod cons.

B&B from £19.50, Dinner available, Rooms 2 single, 6 double, 2 twin, 4 triple, most n-suite, No smoking, Children welcome, Open all year.
Bay Ridge Hotel,, 11 Summerfield Road, Bridlington, Yorkshire YO15 3LF
Tel: 01262 673425   **Map Ref 13**

THE TENNYSON HOTEL, fine cuisine in attractive surroundings, close to sea and Leisure World. Complimentary newspaper and toiletries.

B&B from £20, Dinner available, Rooms 3 double, 3 twin, most en-suite, No smoking, Children over 9, Open all year.
The Tennyson Hotel, 19 Tennyson Avenue, Bridlington, Yorkshire YO15 2EU
Tel: 01262 604382 Fax: 01262 604382   **Map Ref 13**

BAY COURT HOTEL, a small, high quality licensed hotel, 50 yards from beach, offering tasteful accommodation and a friendly welcome. Lounge with open fires, south facing sun patio that provides a haven in which to relax and enjoy sea views. Convenient for cliff walks, moors, Wolds villages, stately homes and beaches/coves.

B&B from £19, Dinner available, Rooms 2 single, 3 double, 2 twin, most en-suite, No smoking, Children welcome, No pets, Open all year.
Bay Court Hotel, 35a Sands Lane, Bridlington, Yorkshire YO15 2JG
Tel: 01262 676288   **Map Ref 13**

EXPANSE HOTEL, in a unique position overlooking the beach and sea, with panoramic views of the bay and Heritage coast.
B&B from £29.50, Dinner available, Rooms 13 single, 11 double, 20 twin, 4 triple, all en-suite, Children welcome, No pets, Open all year.
Expanse Hotel, North Marine Drive, Bridlington, Yorkshire YO15 2LS
Tel: 01262 675347 Fax: 01262 604928   **Map Ref 13**

RAGS RESTAURANT & DYL'S HOTEL, en-suite rooms with corner baths, 3 rooms with harbour views and bistro bar.

B&B from £25, Dinner available, Rooms 3 double, 3 twin, all en-suite, Children welcome, No pets, Open all year.
Rags Restaurant & Dyl's Hotel, South Pier, Southcliff Road, Bridlington, Yorkshire YO15 3AN
Tel: 01262 400355 & 674791   **Map Ref 13**

INGLENOOK GUEST HOUSE, Phil and Carolyn welcome you to their recently refurbished Victorian built guest house. The tastefully coordinated bedrooms have colour TV, tea/coffee facilities and superb views. Four poster available. Guest lounge. Picturesque village, ideal base for touring the Dales and Lake District. AA 3Q Recommended. **B&B from £18pp,** Dinner from £10, Rooms 2 twin, 3 double, most en-suite, No smoking, Children over 2, Pets by arrangement, Open all year except Christmas. Phil & Carolyn Smith, **Inglenook Guest House,** 20 Main Street, Ingleton, Carnforth, North Yorkshire LA6 3HJ
Tel: 015242 41270 Email: phillsmith@msn.com   **Map Ref 14**

FERNCLIFFE GUEST HOUSE, a lovely detached Victorian house in quiet location, with growing reputation for good food and high standard of accommodation. All rooms en-suite.
B&B from £30, Dinner available, Rooms 1 double, 4 twin, all en-suite, Children over 12, Open February - October.
Ferncliffe Guest House, 55 Main Street, Ingleton, Carnforth, Yorkshire LA6 3HJ
Tel: 015242 42405   **Map Ref 14**

INGLEBOROUGH VIEW, an attractive stone built house overlooking river. Renowned for food, comfort and hospitality. Ideally situated for local walks and touring dales and Lake District.

B&B from £20, Rooms 3 double, 1 twin, all en-suite or private facilities, Children welcome, No pets, Open all year.
Ingleborough View, Main Street, Ingleton, Carnforth, Yorkshire LA6 3HH
Tel: 015242 41523   **Map Ref 14**

....

SPRINGFIELD PRIVATE HOTEL, a detached Victorian villa in own grounds with car park. Colour TV and tea/coffee facilities in all rooms. Guests lounge. Licensed. Fishing available. Garden patios. Central for Dales, Lakes, N. Lancashire and Forest of Bowland. Local features in Ingleton include waterfalls, caves & walks.
B&B from £22pp, Dinner from £10.50, Rooms 1 single, 1 twin, 3 double, 1 family, all en-suite, Restricted smoking, Children & pets welcome, Open all year except Christmas.
Jack Thornton, **Springfield Private Hotel,** Main Street, Ingleton, Carnforth, Yorkshire LA6 3HJ
Tel: 015242 41280 Fax: 015242 41280   **Map Ref 14**

....

BRIDGE END GUEST HOUSE, a Georgian house pleasantly situated adjacent to the entrance to the waterfalls walk. It features a cantilevered patio over the River Doe and retains an elegant staircase. All rooms en-suite. Vegetarians welcome.

B&B from £19, Dinner available, Rooms 1 single, 1 double, 1 triple, all en-suite, No smoking, Children welcome, No pets, Open all year.
Bridge End Guest House, Mill Lane, Ingleton, Carnforth, Yorkshire LA6 3EP
Tel: 015242 41413   **Map Ref 14**

....

LANGBER COUNTRY GUEST HOUSE, a detached country house in hilltop position with panoramic views. Good touring centre for dales, lakes and coast. Comfortable accommodation. Friendly service - everyone welcome.
B&B from £16.50, Dinner available, Rooms 1 single, 2 double, 1 twin, 2 triple, 1 family, most en-suite, Children welcome, No smoking, Open all year.
Langber Country Guest House, Tatterthorne Road, Ingleton, Carnforth, Yorkshire LA6 3DT
Tel: 015242 41587   **Map Ref 14**

....

NEW INN HOTEL, an 18th century coaching inn in a picturesque Yorkshire Dales village 6 miles north of Settle, in dramatic river, waterfall and fell country.

B&B from £45, Dinner available, Rooms No smoking, Children welcome, Open all year.
New Inn Hotel, Clapham, Yorkshire LA2 8HH
Tel: 015242 51203 Fax: 015242 51496   **Map Ref 15**

....

PROSPECT HALL HOTEL, a hall, converted to provide a well appointed hotel, close to the M62, Bronte country, the dales and Peak District.

B&B from £40, Dinner available, Rooms 7 single, 30 double, 3 twin, all en-suite, No smoking, Children welcome, Open all year.
Prospect Hall Hotel, Prospect Road, Cleckheaton, Yorkshire BD19 3HD
Tel: 01274 873022 Fax: 01274 870376   **Map Ref 16**

....

HEATH COTTAGE HOTEL & RESTAURANT, an impressive Victorian house in well kept gardens. On the A683, 2.5 miles from M1 junction 40. Conference/banquet facilities. Large car park.
B&B from £27, Dinner available, Rooms 10 single, 13 double, 1 twin, 3 triple, all en-suite, No smoking, Children welcome, No pets, Open all year.
Heath Cottage Hotel & Restaurant, Wakefield Road, Dewsbury, Yorkshire WF12 8ET
Tel: 01924 465399 Fax: 01924 459405   **Map Ref 17**

ALMEL HOTEL, a licensed hotel in the town centre, close to racecourse and leisure park. Coach parties welcome.

B&B from £21, Dinner available, Rooms 12 single, 1 double, 15 twin, 1 triple, 1 family, most en-suite, Children welcome, Open all year.
Almel Hotel, 20 Christchurch Road, Doncaster, Yorkshire DN1 2QL
Tel: 01302 365230 Fax: 01302 341434   **Map Ref 18**

REGENT HOTEL, a family run hotel overlooking Regents Park. Two public bars, cocktail bar and a good restaurant. All rooms en-suite.

B&B from £40, Dinner available, Rooms 20 single, 9 double, 15 twin, 5 triple, all en-suite, Children welcome, Open all year.

Regent Hotel, Regent Square, Doncaster, Yorkshire DN1 2DS
Tel: 01302 364180 & 364336 Fax: 01302 322331   **Map Ref 18**

HOTEL FORMULE 1, the benchmark in very reasonably-priced hotels (300 hotels in Europe), functional rooms (washbasin, TV,desk), one single price (£22.50) for up to 3 people. Close by, comfortable showers and toilets are equipped with a self-cleaning system. A continental breakfast costs £2.50.

£22.50 per room (up to 3 people), Breakfast £2.50, Rooms 64* (1 double bed and a bunk bed), Children welcome, Open all year.
Mr Huet & Ms D'orangeville, Thierry, **Hotel Formule 1**, Ten Pound Walk, Doncaster, South Yorkshire DN4 5HX
Tel: 01302 761050   **Map Ref 18**

THE ROYAL HOTEL, recent total refurbishment, restaurant, public bars, games room, lounge, licensed, childrens play area. Car park. Places of interest Chatsworth, Doncaster Races, Earth Centre, Dome Leisure Centre. Arranged activities, fishing, jet skiing, horse riding. Courtesy transport. Coach, railway station. Doncaster, Bawtry 10 minutes drive.
B&B from £28 per night, Dinner from £3, Rooms 10 single, 4 twin, 10 double, 4 family, Restricted smoking, Children welcome, Pets by arrangement, Open all year.
Maria Clark & Stuart George, **The Royal Hotel**, Queen Mary's Road Rossington, Doncaster, South Yorkshire DN11 0SN
Tel: 01302 863390 Fax: 01302 863878   **Map Ref 19**

BURTON LODGE HOTEL, a charming country hotel set in 2 acres of grounds and gardens adjoining an 18 hole golf course (reduced green fee for guests). All bedrooms have en-suite, Sky TV, telephone and tea/coffee tray. Comfortable lounge/bar. Ample car parking. Situated on the A165. Beverly 7 miles. Hornsea 6 miles.
B&B from £23pp, Dinner from £12.50, Rooms 2 single, 4 twin, 2 double, 2 family, all en-suite, Restricted smoking, Children welcome, Open all year except Christmas.
Peter & Rosemary Atkin, **Burton Lodge Hotel**, Brandesburton, Driffield, East Yorkshire YO25 8RU
Tel: 01964 542847 Fax: 01964 542847   **Map Ref 20**

THE OLD RECTORY, a Victorian rectory set in the traditional riding of East Yorkshire. We offer classic good food, log fires and elegant en-suite rooms. In the heart of unspoilt countryside.

B&B from £47.50, Dinner available, Rooms 1 double, 2 twin, all private or en-suite, No smoking, Open all year.

The Old Rectory, Cowlam, Driffield, Yorkshire YO25 0AD
Tel: 01377 267617 Fax: 01377 267403   **Map Ref 21**

THE TRITON INN, an 18th century coaching inn nestling in the shadows of historic Sledmere house. All bedrooms have colour TV, tea/coffee facilities. Rustic bar with open log fires, games room. Separate dining room. Ideal base for walking and touring Yorkshire coast and Wolds.
B&B from £18pp, Dinner from £4.95, Rooms 1 single, 1 twin, 2 double, 1 family, some en-suite, Restricted smoking, Children welcome, Pets by arrangement, Open all year.
Peter & Irene Sellers, **The Triton Inn,** Sledmere, Driffield, East Yorkshire YO25 3XQ
Tel: 01377 236644   **Map Ref 21**

....

THE GEORGE, an 18th century coaching inn overlooking cobbled square in delightful Georgian market town. 15 minutes York, dales and moors. Good food. Cask beers.

B&B from £50, Dinner available, Rooms 8 double, 5 twin, 1 triple, 1 family, all en-suite, No smoking, Children welcome, No pets, Open all year.
The George, Market Place, Easingwold, Yorkshire YO61 3AD
Tel: 01347 821698 Fax: 01347 823448   **Map Ref 22**

....

THE OLD RECTORY, set in large country garden was built in 1737 and retains many original features and is furnished with antiques. Spacious bedrooms with tea/coffee facilities, one with 4-poster bed. Lounge with colour TV and open fire. Situated in James Herriot country. Ideal for the Dales, Moors, York and the many historic abbeys and houses.
B&B from £16pp, Rooms 1 twin, 1 en-suite double, 1 en-suite family, Restricted smoking, Children & pets welcome, Open all year except Christmas.
Mrs Rachel Ritchie, **The Old Rectory,** Thormanby, Easingwold, Yorkshire YO6 3NN
Tel: 01845 501417   **Map Ref 23**

....

SEAFIELD HOTEL, a small, friendly and comfortable hotel in the centre of Filey, close to the beach and all amenities. Car park. Family rooms.

B&B from £19, Dinner available, Rooms 4 double, 4 triple, 5 family, most en-suite, No smoking, Children welcome, No pets, Open all year.

Seafield Hotel, 9-11 Rutland Street, Filey Yorkshire YO14 9JA
Tel: 01723 513715   **Map Ref 24**

....

SEA BRINK HOTEL, sea front hotel overlooking the beach. Magnificent views, delightful en-suite rooms with all facilities. Licensed restaurant/coffee shop. German spoken.

B&B from £27, Dinner available, Rooms 5 double, 4 family, most en-suite, No smoking, Children welcome, Open all year.
Sea Brink Hotel, 3 The Beach, Filey, Yorkshire YO14 9LA
Tel: 01723 513257 Fax: 01723 514139   **Map Ref 24**

....

THE DOWNCLIFFE HOUSE HOTEL, a recently refurbished seafront hotel with magnificent views over Filey Bay. All rooms en-suite with telephone, satellite TV and tea making facilities.

B&B from £30, Dinner available, Rooms 1 single, 6 double, 1 twin, 1 triple, 1 family, all en-suite, No smoking, Children over 5, No pets, Open February - December.

The Downcliffe House Hotel, The Beach, Filey, Yorkshire YO14 9LA
Tel: 01723 513310 Fax: 01723 516141   **Map Ref 24**

FLANEBURG HOTEL, taking its name from ancient Flamborough, the hotel offers comfort, good food and a flavour of the region.Under the personal supervision of the proprietors. Ideal for bird watching, walking, rambling or golf. Good base for touring East Coast and moors.

B&B from £24, Dinner available, Rooms 1 single, 6 double, 2 twin, 3 triple, 1 family, most en-suite, Children welcome, No pets, Open all year.
Flaneburg Hotel, North Marine Road, Flamborough, Yorkshire YO15 1LF
Tel: 01262 850284 Fax: 01262 850284   **Map Ref 25**

....

CLIFTON HOTEL, a small, comfortable and friendly family run hotel convenient for Humberside, York, East Yorkshire and Lincolnshire. One mile from M62 motorway.

B&B from £28, Dinner available, Rooms 4 single, 3 double, 1 twin, 1 family, all private or en-suite, Children welcome, Open all year.
Clifton Hotel, Boothferry Road, Goole, Yorkshire DN14 6AL
Tel: 01405 761336 Fax: 01405 762350   **Map Ref 26**

....

TOWNHEAD GUEST HOUSE, all rooms have colour TV's, tea/coffee making facilities and are en-suite. Parking available.

B&B from £22pp, Rooms 1 twin, 3 double, all en-suite, No smoking or pets, Open all year except Christmas.
Marian Lister, **Townhead Guest House,** 1 Low Lane, Grassington, North Yorkshire BD23 5AU
Tel: 01756 752811   **Map Ref 27**

....

GRASSINGTON HOUSE HOTEL, a friendly, family run Georgian hotel in the Yorkshire Dales. Renowned for comfort and food. Pets welcome. Ideal touring and walking base.

B&B from £26, Dinner available, Rooms 1 single, 6 double, 2 twin, 1 triple, all en-suite, No smoking, Children welcome, Open all year.
Grassington House Hotel, 5 The Square, Grassington, Yorkshire BD23 5AQ
Tel: 01756 752406 Fax: 01756 752135   **Map Ref 27**

....

ASHFIELD HOUSE HOTEL, a quiet and secluded 17th century private hotel near the village square. Open fires and creative home cooking using only fresh produce.

B&B from £30, Dinner available, Rooms 4 double, 3 twin, all en-suite or private facilities, No smoking, Children over 5, No pets, Open February - December.
Ashfield House Hotel, Summers Fold, Grassington, Yorkshire BD23 5AE
Tel: 01756 752584 Fax: 01756 752584   **Map Ref 27**

....

CLAREDON HOTEL, a Yorkshire Dales village inn serving good food and ales. Personal supervision at all times. Steaks and fish dishes are specialities.

B&B from £30, Dinner available, Rooms 2 double, 1 twin, all en-suite, Children over 12, No pets, Open all year.
Claredon Hotel, Hebden, Grassington, Yorkshire BD23 5DE
Tel: 01756 752446   **Map Ref 28**

....

MANOR HOUSE FARM, a charming old farm house in idyllic surroundings of North Yorkshire Moors National Park. Licensed. Fine evening dinners. Guests have own entrance, lounge (with TV) and dining room. Tea/coffee machines in bedrooms. Two Crown Highly Commended by ETB. 4Q's Selected by AA. Brochure. Cards accepted.

Dinner, Bed & Breakfast from £41pp, Rooms 2 twin, 1 double, all en-suite, No smoking, Children over 12, Pets by arrangement, Open January - November.
Margaret & Martin Bloom, **Manor House Farm,** Ingleby Greenhow, Great Ayton, North Yorkshire TS9 6RB
Tel: 01642 722384 Email: mbloom@globalnet.co.uk   **Map Ref 29**

507

MILLFIELDS, exclusive yet competitively priced hotel with a wide range of leisure facilities, situated close to the commercial and retail centre of Grimsby.

B&B from £37.50, Dinner available, Rooms 13 double, 9 twin, all en-suite, No smoking, Children welcome, Open all year.
Millfields, 53 Bargate, Grimsby, North East Lincolnshire DN34 5AD
Tel: 01472 356068 Fax: 01472 250286 **Map Ref 30**

....

MOZART GUEST HOUSE, bed and breakfast near to Halifax town centre. Also easy reach to Motorways for Manchester and Leeds. Halifax is surrounded by countryside and also has the childrens Eureka Museum. All rooms en-suite with TV and tea/coffee facilities.

B&B from single £25pp, double £36, twin £36, Rooms 8 twin, all en-suite, Children welcome, No pets, Open all year except Christmas & New Year.
Anne Wilby, **Mozart Guest House,** 34 Prescott Street, Halifax, West Yorkshire HX1 2QW
Tel: 01422 340319 Fax: 01422 251025 **Map Ref 31**

....

ROCK INN HOTEL & CHURCHILLS RESTAURANT, a privately owned hostelry offering all the attractions of a wayside inn plus the sophistication of a first class hotel and conference centre. Rural setting yet only 1.5 miles from junction 24 of M62.

B&B from £45, Dinner available, Rooms No smoking, Children welcome, Open all year.
Rock Inn Hotel & Churchills Restaurant, Holywell Green, Halifax, Yorkshire HX4 9BS
Tel: 01422 379721 Fax: 01422 379110 **Map Ref 31**

....

KIMBERLEY HOTEL, a free standing Victorian terraced house, 100 yards from Harrogate Conference Centre. Within 5 minutes walk of town centre and railway station.

B&B from £32, Rooms 5 single, 24 double, 16 twin, 3 triple, all en-suite, No smoking, Children welcome, Open all year.
Kimberley Hotel, 11-19 Kings Road, Harrogate, Yorkshire HG1 5JY
Tel: 01423 505613 Fax: 01423 530276 **Map Ref 32**

....

GARDEN HOUSE HOTEL, a small, family run Victorian hotel overlooking Valley Gardens, in a quiet location with unrestricted parking. Home cooking using fresh produce.

B&B from £22, Dinner available, Rooms 3 single, 2 double, 2 twin, most en-suite, Children over 2, No pets, Open all year.

Garden House Hotel, 14 Harlow Moor Drive, Harrogate, Yorkshire HG2 0JX
Tel: 01423 503059 **Map Ref 32**

....

ASHBROOKE HOUSE HOTEL, an elegant Edwardian town house hotel, close to town, conference centre and countryside, offering quality accommodation. Children and pets most welcome.

B&B from £23, Rooms 3 single, 1 double, 2 twin,1 triple, most en-suite, No smoking, Children welcome, Open all year.
Ashbrooke House Hotel, 140 Valley Drive, Harrogate, Yorkshire HG2 0JS
Tel: 01423 564478 **Map Ref 32**

....

ABBATT & YOUNGS HOTEL, a Victorian property in a quiet conservation area. Attractive gardens, private car park. Within walking distance of town centre and Valley Gardens.

B&B from £38, Dinner available, Rooms 4 single, 2 double, 2 twin, 1 family, all en-suite, Children welcome, Open all year.

Abbatt & Youngs Hotel, 15 York Road, off Swan Road, Harrogate, Yorkshire HG1 2QL
Tel: 01423 567336 & 521231 Fax: 01423 500042 **Map Ref 32**

BRITANNIA LODGE HOTEL, a beautiful 19th century town house with delightful gardens and private parking in select Harrogate area. elegant, cosy lounge and bar with open fire, pretty bedrooms, all en-suite. Only 5 minutes walk to town centre and Valley Gardens.

B&B from £38, Dinner available, Rooms 4 single, 3 twin, 5 triple, all en-suite, No smoking, Children welcome, No pets, Open all year.
Britannia Lodge Hotel, 16 Swan Road, Harrogate, Yorkshire HG1 2SA
Tel: 01423 508482 Fax: 01423 526840 **Map Ref 32**

....

DELAINE HOTEL, a family run hotel set in beautiful award winning gardens. Very attractive en-suite rooms. Delicious home cooked fare. An ideal choice for your holiday.

B&B from £37, Dinner available, Rooms 1 single, 5 double, 2 twin, 2 triple, all en-suite, No smoking, Children welcome, No pets, Open all year.
Delaine Hotel, 17 Ripon Road, Harrogate, Yorkshire HG1 2JL
Tel: 01423 567974 Fax: 01423 561723 **Map Ref 32**

....

ACACIA LODGE, "Highly Commended", warm, lovingly restored family run Victorian hotel retaining original character with fine furnishings, antiques/paintings. All bedrooms luxuriously en-suite with every comfort and facility. Private floodlit parking for all. Entirely no smoking. Somewhere special AA QQQQ Selected. Brochure on request.

B&B from £27pp, Rooms 2 twin, 2 double, 2 family, all en-suite, No smoking or pets, Children over 10, Open all year except Christmas & New Year.
Peter & Dee Bateson, **Acacia Lodge,** 21 Ripon Road, Harrogate, North Yorkshire HG1 2JL
Tel: 01423 560752 Fax: 01423 503725 **Map Ref 32**

....

SPRING LODGE, an attractive Edwardian town house situated in a quiet cul-de-sac close to all amenities. Five minutes walk from Conference and Exhibition centre. Ideal for the business or tourist visitor, with the beautiful Yorkshire Dales nearby. TV, tea/coffee facilities, licensed, dinner on request.

B&B from £17pp, Dinner from £8.50, Rooms 1 single, 4 double, 1 family, some en-suite, No smoking or pets, Children welcome, Open all year except Christmas.
Carol & Derek Vinter, **Spring Lodge,** 22 Spring Mount, Harrogate HG1 2HX
Tel: 01423 506036 **Map Ref 32**

....

ALBANY HOTEL, a comfortable, small hotel with friendly relaxing atmosphere, overlooking the beautiful Valley Gardens. All rooms have en-suite facilities.

B&B from £25, Rooms 4 single, 3 double, 4 twin, 3 triple, most en-suite, Children welcome, No pets, Open all year.
Albany Hotel, 22-23 Harlow Moor Drive, Harrogate, Yorkshire HG2 0JY
Tel: 01423 565890 Fax: 01423 565890 **Map Ref 32**

....

ETON HOUSE, standing on the edge of open parkland close to town centre. We are a large Victorian house and have been welcoming guests for the past 20 years. Our rooms have television and tea/coffee facilities. Large car park at rear. ETB 2 Crowns Commended.
B&B from £20pp, Rooms 1 single, 1 twin, 2 double, 3 family, most en-suite, Restricted smoking, Children welcome, Pets by arrangement, Open all year except Christmas & New Year.
Janet, Keith & Daniel Wyatt, **Eton House,** 3 Eton Terrace, Harrogate, North Yorkshire HG2 7SU
Tel: 01423 886850 Fax: 01423 886850 **Map Ref 32**

CAVENDISH HOTEL, overlooking the beautiful Valley Gardens in a quiet location yet close to conference centre and extensive shopping area. Ideal for business or pleasure.

B&B from £28, Dinner available, Rooms 3 single, 4 double, 2 twin, all en-suite, No smoking, Children welcome, Open all year.

Cavendish Hotel, 3 Valley Drive, Harrogate, Yorkshire HG2 0JJ
Tel: 01423 509637   **Map Ref 32**

LYNTON HOUSE, in a central, quiet tree lined avenue, 100 yards from exhibition halls and close to Valley Gardens. Personal supervision.

B&B from £18, Rooms 2 single, 2 double, 1 twin, No smoking, Children over 9, No pets, Open March - November.

Lynton House, 42 Studley Road, Harrogate, Yorkshire HG1 5JU
Tel: 01423 504715   **Map Ref 32**

ASCOT HOUSE HOTEL, a delightful, refurbished hotel near town centre assuring you of a friendly welcome and an enjoyable stay. Quality cuisine. Parking. Ring for colour brochure.

B&B from £46, Dinner available, Rooms 3 single, 7 double, 7 twin, 1 triple, all en-suite, Children welcome, Open all year.

Ascot House Hotel, 53 Kings Road, Harrogate, Yorkshire HG1 5HJ
Tel: 01423 531005 Fax: 01423 503523   **Map Ref 32**

SHANNON COURT HOTEL, a charming Victorian house. Eight delightful en-suite bedrooms with every modern comfort including radio/alarm, colour TV and tea/coffee facilities. Licensed. For residents and their guests enjoy a home cooked evening meal. Close to town centre, we have our own car park. An excellent touring base. Licensed for residents and their guests.
B&B from £22.50pp, Dinner from £15, Rooms 2 single, 1 twin, 3 double, 2 family, all en-suite, No smoking or pets, Children welcome, Open all year except Christmas & New Year.
Carol & Jim Dodds, **Shannon Court Hotel,** 65 Dragon Avenue, Harrogate, Yorkshire HG1 5DS
Tel: 01423 509858 Fax: 01423 530606   **Map Ref 32**

ARDEN HOUSE HOTEL, a family run hotel with a warm, friendly atmosphere and real home cooking. Close to the town centre. Trouser press and hair dryer in all rooms.

B&B from £30, Dinner available, Rooms 4 single, 5 double, 4 twin, 1 triple, all en-suite, No smoking, Children welcome, Open all year.

Arden House Hotel, 69-71 Franklin Rd, Harrogate, Yorkshire HG1 5EH
Tel: 01423 509224 Fax: 01423 561170   **Map Ref 32**

ALVERA COURT HOTEL, an extensively refurbished Victorian residence placing special emphasis on comfort and personal service. Directly opposite the conference centre.

B&B from £29, Dinner available, Rooms 5 single, 1 double, 2 twin, 4 triple, all en-suite, Children welcome, No pets, Open all year.

Alvera Court Hotel, 76 Kings Road, Harrogate, Yorkshire HG1 5JX
Tel: 01423 505735 Fax: 01423 505996   **Map Ref 32**

THE ALEXANDER, a friendly, family run elegant Victorian guest house with some en-suite facilities. Ideal for conference centre and Harrogate town. Good touring centre for dales.

B&B from £22, Rooms 2 single, 1 double, 2 triple, most en-suite, No smoking, Children welcome, No pets, Open all year.
The Alexander, 88 Franklin Road, Harrogate, Yorkshire HG1 5EN
Tel: 01423 503348 Fax: 01423 540230   **Map Ref 32**

....

ALAMAH, comfortable rooms, personal attention, friendly atmosphere and full English breakfast. 300 metres from town centre. Garages/parking.

B&B from £24, Dinner available, Rooms 2 single, 2 double, 2 twin, 1 family, all en-suite or private, Children over 3, Open all year.
Alamah, 88 Kings Road, Harrogate, Yorkshire HG1 5JX
Tel: 01423 502187 Fax: 01423 566175   **Map Ref 32**

....

THE COPPICE, a warm and friendly welcome awaits. Quiet location, excellent food and service. Five minutes walk to elegant town centre, 2 minutes to conference centre and a short drive to dales.

B&B from £23, Dinner available, Rooms 1 single, 2 double, 1 twin, 1 triple, all en-suite, No smoking, Children over 5, No pets, Open all year.

The Coppice, 9 Studley Road, Harrogate, Yorkshire HG1 5JU
Tel: 01423 569626 Fax: 01423 569005   **Map Ref 32**

....

ANRO, in a central position, 2 minutes from the conference centre and near Valley Gardens, town, bus and rail stations. Ideal for touring the dales. Home cooking.

B&B from £22, Dinner available, Rooms 3 single, 1 double, 2 twin, 1 family, most en-suite, Children over 7, No pets, Open all year.
Anro, 90 Kings Road, Harrogate, Yorkshire HG1 5JX
Tel: 01423 503087   **Map Ref 32**

....

VALLEY HOTEL, overlooking Valley Gardens offering a warm welcome both to tourists and business people.Licensed restaurant.

B&B from £30, Dinner available, Rooms 4 single, 3 double, 5 twin, 2 triple, 2 family, all en-suite, No smoking, Children welcome, Open all year.

Valley Hotel, 93-95 Valley Drive, Harrogate, Yorkshire HG2 0JP
Tel: 01423 504868 Fax: 01423 531940   **Map Ref 32**

....

WHITE HART HOTEL, grade II listed building in the centre of Harrogate, overlooking West Park Stray. Recently upgraded and refurbished. Large car park.

B&B from £51.50, Dinner available, Rooms 37 single, 4 double, 13 twin, all en-suite, No smoking, No pets, Open all year.
White Hart Hotel, Cold Bath Road, Harrogate, Yorkshire HG2 0NF
Tel: 01423 505681 Fax: 01423 568354   **Map Ref 32**

....

BALMORAL HOTEL, exclusive town house with beautifully furnished rooms and a relaxed, tranquil ambience. Nine four poster rooms. Award winning restaurant with modern English menu.

B&B from £40, Dinner available, Rooms 5 single, 12 double, 4 twin, all en-suite, No smoking, Children welcome, Open all year.

Balmoral Hotel, Franklin Mount, Harrogate, Yorkshire HG1 5EJ
Tel: 01423 508208 Fax: 01423 530652   **Map Ref 32**

IMPERIAL HOTEL, recently refurbished and situated in the heart of this historic spa town, this hotel was once the home of Lord Caernarvon.

B&B from £43, Dinner available, Rooms 12 single, 22 double, 51 twin, all en-suite, No smoking, Children welcome, Open all year.
Imperial Hotel, Prospect Place, Harrogate, Yorkshire HG1 1LA
Tel: 01423 565071 Fax: 01423 500082   **Map Ref 32**

....

ST GEORGE SWALLOW HOTEL, a traditional hotel, tastefully restored, with leisure complex including pool, sauna, solarium, spa bath and exercise gym. Close to Valley Gardens and other historic attractions.

B&B from £90, Dinner available, Rooms 35 single, 28 double, 13 twin, 8 triple, 6 family, all en-suite, No smoking, Children welcome, Open all year.
St George Swallow Hotel, Ripon Road, Harrogate, Yorkshire HG1 2SY
Tel: 01423 561431 Fax: 01423 530037   **Map Ref 32**

....

STUDLEY HOTEL & LE BRETON RESTAURANT, a small, friendly hotel, ideally situated near Valley Gardens, shops and conference/exhibition centre. Le Breton French Restaurant has genuine charcoal grill. Excellent value table d'hote dinner and a la carte menu with extensive wine list.

B&B from £55, Dinner available, Rooms 15 single, 10 double, 11 twin, all en-suite, Children welcome, Open all year.
Studley Hotel & Le Breton Restaurant, Swan Road, Harrogate, Yorkshire HG1 2SE
Tel: 01423 561431 Fax: 01423 530037   **Map Ref 32**

....

BAY HORSE INN, renowned 18th century inn with oak beams, open log fires and restaurant serving traditional English fare. In Nidderdale between Ripley and Pateley Bridge. Ideal base for racing in Yorkshire, golf courses and shooting parties.

B&B from £40, Dinner available, Rooms 4 double, 6 twin, 2 triple, all en-suite, No smoking, Children welcome, Open all year.

Bay Horse Inn, Burnt Yates, Harrogate, Yorkshire HG3 3EJ
Tel: 01423 770230   **Map Ref 33**

....

HIGH WINSLEY COTTAGE, a traditional Yorkshire Dales cottage. Situated well off the road in peaceful countryside, good food and comfortable accommodation are assured. All bedrooms are en-suite with tea/coffee trays and lovely views of surroundings countryside. Two guests sitting rooms, TV in one, books, local guides, map etc.
B&B from £19-£24pp, Dinner from £12.50, Rooms 2 twin, 2 double, all en-suite, Restricted smoking, Children over 11, No pets, Open March - December.
Clive & Gill King, **High Winsley Cottage,** Burnt Yates, Harrogate, North Yorkshire HG3 3EP
Tel: 01423 770662   **Map Ref 33**

....

GRASSFIELDS COUNTRY HOUSE HOTEL, is a Georgian residence set in its own grounds. All rooms have tea/coffee making facilities, direct dial telephones and colour TV. Our chefs prepare only the freshest food from local sources served in our elegant conservatory, which compliments the private bar and fine wine cellar.
B&B from £25pp, Dinner from £13.95, Rooms 1 single, 4 twin, 3 double, 1 family, all en-suite, Children & pets welcome, Open all year.
Adrian Whitehead, **Grassfields Country House Hotel,** Low Wath Road, Pateley Bridge, Harrogate, North Yorkshire HG3 5HL
Tel: 01423 711412 Fax: 01423 712844   **Map Ref 34**

YORKE ARMS HOTEL, an 18th century hostelry on village green. In the heart of unspoilt Nidderdale at the head of Gouthwaite Reservior Nature Reserve. All bedrooms en-suite.

B&B from £50, Dinner available, Rooms 3 single, 3 double, 5 twin, 2 triple, all en-suite, Children welcome, No pets, Open all year.

Yorke Arms Hotel, Ramsgill, Harrogate, Yorkshire HG3 5RL
Tel: 01423 755243 Fax: 01423 755330   **Map Ref 35**

....

THE BOAR'S HEAD HOTEL, at the heart of this historic Ripley Castle estate, overlooking the cobbled market square. Renowned restaurant and fine village pub. One of the great inns of England.

B&B from £67.50, Dinner available, Rooms 5 double, 20 twin, all en-suite, Children welcome, Open all year.

The Boar's Head Hotel, Ripley Castle Estate, Ripley, Harrogate, Yorkshire HG3 3AY
Tel: 01423 771888 Fax: 01423 771509   **Map Ref 36**

....

WHITE HART INN, a 17th century coaching inn with a friendly a friendly welcome, offering traditional fare. Open fires, Yorkshire ales. Central for exploring the dales.

B&B from £18.50, Dinner available, Rooms 1 single, 4 double, 2 twin, Children welcome, Open all year.

White Hart Inn, Main Street, Hawes, Yorkshire DL8 3QL
Tel: 01969 667259   **Map Ref 37**

....

HERRIOTS HOTEL, an eighteenth century building situated on a cobbled street in the centre of Hawes. Accommodation comprises of seven beautifully decorated en-suite bedrooms. Our elegant restaurant with comfortable bar specialises in fresh international cuisine offering Table d'hote and A La Carte menus. ETB 3 Crowns Commended.
B&B from £25pp, Dinner from £12.95, Rooms 1 single, 2 twin, 4 double, 1 family, all en-suite, Restricted smoking, Children welcome, Pets by arrangement, Open February - 5th January.
Joanne Wright, **Herriots Hotel,** Main St, Hawes, Yorkshire DL8 3QU
Tel: 01969 667536 Fax: 01969 667536   **Map Ref 37**

....

STEPPE HAUGH GUEST HOUSE, licensed 17th century house, beamed ceilings, pine panelling, cosy rooms with colour TV, tea/coffee facilities, two bathrooms, some rooms en-suite facilities. South facing TV lounge looks out onto gardens, patio and car park. All within walking distance of Hawes many attractions, restaurants and pubs.
B&B from £18pp, Rooms 1 single, 1 twin, 2 double, 2 en-suite double, Restricted smoking, Children over 7, Pets by arrangement, Open all year.
Margaret Grattan, **Steppe Haugh Guest House,** Town Head, Hawes, North Yorkshire DL8 3RH
Tel: 01969 667645   **Map Ref 37**

....

STONE HOUSE HOTEL, a fine Edwardian country house hotel in a beautiful old English garden with panoramic views of Upper Wensleydale.

B&B from £29, Dinner available, Rooms 1 single, 10 double, 7 twin, 1 triple, most en-suite, No smoking, Children welcome, Open February - December.

Stone House Hotel, Sedbusk, Hawes, Yorkshire DL8 3PT
Tel: 01969 667571 Fax: 01969 667720   **Map Ref 38**

513

TARNEY FORS COUNTRY GUEST HOUSE, a grade II listed building. Former dales farmhouse situated in open countryside, yet with easy access. In heart of Dales National Park. Lunches and cream teas available.

B&B from £44, Dinner available, Rooms 2 double, 1 twin, all with en-suite or private facilities, No smoking, Children over 7, No pets, Open March - November.

Tarney Fors Country Guest House, Tarney Fors, Hawes, Yorkshire DL8 3LS
Tel: 01969 667475   **Map Ref 37**

....

CARLTON HOTEL, a Victorian emporium converted and lovingly restored to provide comfort and tranquillity from the town set below. Varied and interesting shops to hand and excellent walking nearby.

B&B from £54, Dinner available, Rooms 3 single, 9 double, 4 twin, all en-suite, No smoking, Children welcome, Open all year.

Carlton Hotel, Albert Street, Hebden Bridge, Yorkshire HX7 8ES
Tel: 01422 844400 Fax: 01422 843117   **Map Ref 39**

....

WHITE LION HOTEL, a family run inn, dating back to 1657, well known for a wide range of cask ales and good home cooked food.

B&B from £35, Dinner available, Rooms 5 double, 2 twin, 1 triple, 2 family, all en-suite, No smoking, Children welcome, No pets, Open all year.

White Lion Hotel, Bridge Gate, Hebden Bridge, Yorkshire HX7 8EX
Tel: 01422 842197 Fax: 01422 846619   **Map Ref 39**

....

NUTCLOUGH HOUSE HOTEL, a family run hotel offering an extensive menu with large vegetarian selection. 800 yards from town centre. Large car park.

B&B from £20, Dinner available, Rooms 3 double, 1 twin, 1 family, all en-suite, No pets, Open all year.
Nutclough House Hotel, Keighley Road, Hebden Bridge, Yorkshire HX7 8EZ
Tel: 01422 844361   **Map Ref 39**

....

REDACRE MILL, a converted canal side mill, antique furniture, central for south Pennine Hill country, Bronte parsonage, Ted Hughes centre, Holmfirth, (Last of the Summer Wine), Bradford, Leeds, Manchester, Skipton, the Dales, York and Harrogate. All rooms en-suite, TV, coffee facilities. Car park. Guests' lounge. Licensed.
B&B from £27.50pp, Dinner from £14.50, Rooms 2 twin, 2 double, all en-suite, No smoking or pets, Children welcome, Open all year.
Tony & Judith Peters, **Redacre Mill,** Mytholmroyd, Hebden Bridge, West Yorkshire HX7 5DQ
Tel: 01422 885563 Fax: 01422 885563   **Map Ref 39**

....

HARE & HOUNDS, a traditional inn enjoying panoramic views across to Heptonstall and Hebden-Bridge. Perfect for walking or just relaxing. Brand new en-suite rooms and home cooked food. Timothy Taylor's traditional ales featured in the Which Guide to Country Pubs and Good Beer Guide. Car park.
B&B from £22.50pp, Dinner from £5, Rooms 4 double, all en-suite, No smoking or pets, Children welcome, Open all year.
Mr & Mrs Greenwood, **Hare & Hounds,** Wadsworth, Hebden Bridge, West Yorkshire HX7 8TN
Tel: 01422 842671   **Map Ref 40**

CARLTON LODGE, within the North York Moors National Park, convivial resident directors offer good food in a superb walking and touring area.

B&B from £35, Dinner available, Rooms 2 single, 7 double, 3 twin, most en-suite, Children welcome, Open all year.
Carlton Lodge, Bondgate, Helmsley, Yorkshire YO62 5EY
Tel: 01439 770557 Fax: 01439 770623   **Map Ref 41**

....

FEATHERS HOTEL, fronting on to Helmsley market place, the hotel could not be more centrally or pleasantly situated.

B&B from £35, Dinner available, Rooms 9 double, 6 twin, all en-suite,Children welcome, Open all year.
Feathers Hotel, Market Place, Helmsley, Yorkshire YO6 5BH
Tel: 01439 770275 Fax: 01439 771101   **Map Ref 41**

....

THE CROWN HOTEL, a 16th century inn with Jacobean dining room offering traditional country cooking. Special breaks available. Run by the same family for 36 years.

B&B from £28, Dinner available, Rooms 5 single, 4 double, 4 twin, 1 triple, most en-suite, No smoking, Children welcome, Open all year.
The Crown Hotel, Market Place, Helmsley, Yorkshire YO6 5BJ
Tel: 01439 770297 Fax: 01439 771595   **Map Ref 41**

....

PHEASANT HOTEL, in a quiet rural village, with a terrace and gardens overlooking the village pond. Oak beamed bar in former blacksmith's shop. English food and log fires. Indoor heated swimming pool.

B&B from £55, Dinner available, Rooms 1 single, 5 double, 6 twin, all en-suite, No smoking, Children over 12, Open March - December.
Pheasant Hotel, Harome, Helmsley, Yorkshire YO6 5JG
Tel: 01439 771241 Fax: 01439 771744   **Map Ref 42**

....

 **LASKILL FARM**, a charming warm country farmhouse, lovely and tastefully furnished and decorated giving cosy elegance of a country home. All rooms with chocolate/tea/coffee trays, colour TV. Guests lounge. Natural spring water. Peace and tranquillity, stately homes, Abbey's Museums. A walkers paradise excellent eating places nearby. Lovely villages. York 40 minutes.
B&B from £24pp, Dinner from £11, Rooms 3 twin, 3 double, all en-suite, Restricted smoking, Children welcome, Pets by arrangement, Open all year except Christmas.
Sue Smith, **Laskill Farm,** Hawnby, Hemsley Yorkshire YO62 5NB
Tel: 01439 798 268   **Map Ref 41**

....

MERLSTEAD PRIVATE HOTEL, a large, well built family run property offering comfortable, spacious accommodation with a warm and friendly atmosphere, close to the sea.

B&B from £30, Dinner available, Rooms 1 double, 3 twin, 1 triple, all en-suite, Children welcome, Open all year.
Merlstead Private Hotel, 59 Eastgate, Hornsea, Yorkshire HU18 1NB
Tel: 01964 533068 Fax: 01964 536975   **Map Ref 43**

....

WORSLEY ARMS HOTEL, a Georgian coaching inn set in village birthplace of the Duchess of Kent. Sitting rooms with beautiful decor and open log fires. Food is a highlight, with local produce and game in abundance.

B&B from £55, Dinner available, Rooms 4 single, 6 double, 9 twin, all en-suite, No smoking, Children welcome, Open all year.
Worsley Arms Hotel, Hovingham, Yorkshire YO6 4LA
Tel: 01653 628234 Fax: 01653 628130   **Map Ref 44**

WELLINGTON HOTEL, a 16th century coaching inn with modern facilities in historic market town. Popular restaurant, bars and beer garden. Ideal for business or pleasure.

B&B from £25, Dinner available, Rooms 3 single, 3 double, 4 twin, most en-suite, Children welcome, Open all year.
Wellington Hotel, 31 Bridgegate, Howden, Yorkshire DN14 7JG
Tel: 01430 430258 Fax: 01430 432139 **Map Ref 45**

....

HUDDERSFIELD HOTEL & ROSEMARY LANE BISTRO, past winner of Yorkshire in Bloom. Free secure car park. Continental style brasserie, traditional pub and nightclub within the complex.

B&B from £25, Dinner available, Rooms 20 single, 13 double, 10 twin, 1 triple, 1 family, all en-suite, Children welcome, Open all year.
Huddersfield Hotel & Rosemary Lane Bistro, 33-47 Kirkgate, Huddersfield, Yorkshire HD1 1QT
Tel: 01484 512111 Fax: 01484 435262 **Map Ref 46**

....

ASHFIELD HOTEL, a family run licensed hotel with emphasis on home cooked food and friendly service. Half a mile from town centre and within 2 miles of M62.

B&B from £20, Dinner available, Rooms 8 single, 5 double, 2 twin, 5 triple, most en-suite, Children welcome, Open all year.
Ashfield Hotel, 93 New North Road, Huddersfield, Yorkshire HD1 5ND
Tel: 01484 425916 Fax: 01484 425916 **Map Ref 46**

....

BRIAR COURT HOTEL, a Yorkshire stone hotel renowned for friendly and efficient service and high standards. Tow restaurants, one being the famous Da Sandro Ristorante, very popular with local and regional guests.

B&B from £45, Dinner available, Rooms 2 single, 40 double, 2 twin, 1 triple, 2 family, all en-suite, No smoking, Children welcome, Open all year.
Briar Court Hotel, Halifax Road, Birchencliffe, Huddersfield, Yorkshire HD3 3NY
Tel: 01484 519902 Fax: 01484 431812 **Map Ref 46**

....

OLD BRIDGE HOTEL, small friendly family run hotel set in the heart of Summer Wine country. Rooms have en-suite facilities, TV and tea/coffee making equipment. Car parking at front of Hotel. We serve food all day from 7am to 9.30pm. Good food and real ales our pride.

B&B from £25pp, Dinner from £15.75, Rooms 7 single, 2 twin, 11 double, all en-suite, Children & Pets welcome, Open all year.
Mr Armitage, **Old Bridge Hotel,** Holmfirth, Huddersfield, West Yorkshire HD7 1DA
Tel: 01484 681212 Fax: 01484 687978 **Map Ref 47**

....

FLYING HORSE COUNTRY HOTEL, a country hotel within walking distance of moors, 2 miles from M62, exit 23.

B&B from £30, Dinner available, Rooms 1 single, 17 double, 15 twin, all en-suite, No smoking, Children welcome, Open all year.
Flying Horse Country Hotel, Nettleton Hill Road, Scapegoat Hill, Huddersfield, Yorkshire HD7 4NY
Tel: 01484 642368 Fax: 01484 642866 **Map Ref 46**

....

THREE ACRES INN & RESTAURANT, an attractive country inn, convenient for all Yorkshire's major conurbations and motorway network. Restaurant and traditional beers.

B&B from £30, Dinner available, Rooms 6 single, 9 double, 2 twin, 2 triple, all en-suite, Children welcome, No pets, Open all year.

Three Acres Inn & Restaurant, Roydhouse, Shelley, Huddersfield, Yorkshire HD8 8LR
Tel: 01484 602606 Fax: 01484 608411 **Map Ref 48**

THE MALLOWS GUEST HOUSE , is an impeccably maintained, elegant listed building with spacious, tastefully furnished rooms throughout. Some bedrooms with en-suite facilities, all with TV and hospitality tray. Floodlit car park and just five minutes walk from town centre. 2 miles from Junction 24 on M62.
B&B from £15pp, Rooms 1 single, 4 twin, 1 double, Restricted smoking, No pets, Open all year except Christmas & New Year.
Mrs Chantry, **The Mallows Guest House ,** 55 Spring Street, Springwood, Huddersfield, West Yorkshire HD1 4AZ
Tel: 01484 544684   **Map Ref 46**

THE EARLSMERE HOTEL, a small family run hotel in a quiet area overlooking the private grounds of Hymers College. Local buses 50 metres from door, city centre 1 mile.
B&B from £17.50, Rooms 2 single, 4 double, 3 triple, most en-suite, Children welcome, Open all year.
The Earlsmere Hotel, 76-78 Sunnybank, off Spring Bank West, Hull, Yorkshire HU3 1LQ
Tel: 01482 341977 Fax: 01482 473714   **Map Ref 49**

CONWAY-ROSEBERRY HOTEL, a homely guest house set in tree lined avenue of Victorian houses in quiet conservation area. Emphasis on food, cleanliness and comfort. High standard of service in friendly atmosphere.
B&B from £17, Dinner available, Rooms 1 single, 2 double, 1 twin, most en-suite, Children welcome, No pets, Open all year.
Conway-Roseberry Hotel, 86 Marlborough Avenue, Hull, Yorkshire HU5 3JT
Tel: 01482 445256 Fax: 01482 445256   **Map Ref 49**

QUALITY ROYAL HOTEL, a large Victorian city centre hotel with direct access to coach and railway stations, refurbished to a high standard and with an indoor leisure centre. Rooms feature en-suite bathroom, colour TV, radio alarm, tea/coffee tray.
B&B from £46.75, Dinner available, Rooms 46 single, 46 double, 63 twin, all en-suite, No smoking, Children welcome, Open all year.
Quality Royal Hotel, Ferensway, Hull, Yorkshire HU1 3UF
Tel: 01482 325087 Fax: 01482 323172   **Map Ref 49**

KINGSTOWN HOTEL, stylish, select and very friendly. Ideally placed for visiting Hull and Holderness. Large kiddies indoor/outdoor play areas. Extensive dining facilities.
B&B from £45, Dinner available, Rooms 10 single, 19 double, 5 twin, all en-suite, No smoking, Children welcome, No pets, Open all year.
Kingstown Hotel, Hull Road, Hedon, Hull, Yorkshire HU12 8DJ
Tel: 01482 890461 Fax: 01482 890713   **Map Ref 50**

ADMIRAL WYNDHAM HOTEL, a Victorian town house situated in a quiet tree lined avenue, 5 minutes city centre. All rooms individually decorated, tea/coffee, TV. SKY TV guest lounge. Car parking. Relaxing courtyard garden. Easy access Ferry, University, historic Beverley, York, east coast resorts, Lincolnshire via Humber Bridge. Warm welcome assured.
B&B from £15pp, Dinner from £3, Rooms 7 single, 3 twin, 3 double, 2 family, some en-suite, Open all year.
Valerie Chalkley, **Admiral Wyndham Hotel,** 52-54 Sunny Bank, Spring Bank West, Hull, East Yorkshire HU3 1LQ
Tel: 01482 443168 Fax: 01482 341889   **Map Ref 49**

COW & CALF HOTEL, a famous Yorkshire Inn on Ilkley Moor with superb views of Wharfedale. Restaurant, bar, lounges and award winning gardens. All rooms are fully en-suite. AA/RAC 3 Stars. Convenient for Leeds, Bradford, Harrogate and the Yorkshire Dales.

B&B from £30pp, Dinner from £13.75, Rooms 2 single, 6 twin, 8 double, 1 family, all en-suite, Children welcome, Pets by arrangement, Open all year except Christmas.
The Norfolk family, **Cow & Calf Hotel,** Moor Top, Ilkley, West Yorkshire LS29 8BT
Tel: 01943 607335 Fax: 01943 816022   **Map Ref 51**

GROVE HOTEL, a small, friendly, private hotel offering well appointed accommodation. Convenient for Ilkley town centre, shops and gardens. Short breaks available all year.

B&B from £30, Dinner available, Rooms 4 double, 2 triple, all en-suite, Children welcome, Open all year.

Grove Hotel, 66 The Grove, Ilkley, Yorkshire LS29 9PA
Tel: 01943 600298 Fax: 01943 817426   **Map Ref 51**

....

CRESCENT HOTEL, a fully modernised hotel with family rooms and self catering suites. In a central position in town. Convenient for the Dales. Meals can also be provided for residents at The Box Tree, an award winning restaurant.

B&B from £46, Dinner available, Rooms 1 single, 4 double, 15 twin, all en-suite, No smoking, Children welcome, No pets, Open all year.

Crescent Hotel, Brook Street, Ilkley, Yorkshire LS29 8DG
Tel: 01943 600012 & 600062 Fax: 01943 607186   **Map Ref 51**

....

ROMBALDS HOTEL & RESTAURANT, an elegant Georgian restoration on the edge of Ilkley Moor, 600 yards from the town centre. Award winning restaurant.

B&B from £50.45, Dinner available, Rooms 3 single, 9 double, 2 twin, 1 triple, all en-suite, No smoking, Children welcome, Open all year.
Rombalds Hotel & Restaurant, West View, Wells Road, Ilkley, Yorkshire LS29 9JG
Tel: 01943 603201 Fax: 01943 816586   **Map Ref 51**

....

OLD WHITE LION HOTEL, a family run, centuries old coaching inn. Candlelit restaurant using local fresh produce, cooked to order. Old world bars serving homemade bar meals and traditional ales.

B&B from £60, Dinner available, Rooms 3 single, 8 double, 1 twin, 2 triple, all en-suite, No smoking, Children welcome, No pets, Open all year.

Old White Lion Hotel, Haworth, Keighley, Yorkshire BD22 8DU
Tel: 01535 642313 Fax: 01535 646222   **Map Ref 12**

....

THE APOTHECARY GUEST HOUSE & TEA ROOMS, at the top of Haworth Main Street opposite the famous Bronte church, 1 minute from the Parsonage and moors.

B&B from £18, Rooms 1 single, 4 double, 1 twin, 1 triple, all en-suite or private facilities, No smoking, Children welcome, Open all year.
The Apothecary Guest House & Tea Rooms, 86 Main Street, Haworth, Keighley, Yorkshire BD22 8DA
Tel: 01535 643642 Fax: 01535 643642   **Map Ref 12**

....

FERNCLIFFE, well appointed, private hotel with panoramic views overlooking Haworth and the Worth Valley Steam Railway. Personal attention and good food.

B&B from £19.50, Dinner available, Rooms 2 single, 2 double, 1 twin, 1 triple, all en-suite, No smoking, Children welcome, Open all year.

Ferncliffe, Hebden Road, Haworth, Keighley, Yorkshire BD22 8RS
Tel: 01535 643405   **Map Ref 12**

....

BRONTE HOTEL, on the edge of the moors, 5 minutes walk from the station and 15 minutes walk to the Parsonage, the former home of the Brontes.

B&B from £20, Dinner available, Rooms 3 single, 3 double, 2 twin, 3 triple, most en-suite, Children welcome, No pets, Open all year.
Bronte Hotel, Lees Lane, Haworth, Keighley, Yorkshire BD22 8RA
Tel: 01535 644112 Fax: 01535 646725   **Map Ref 12**

518

THE OLD WHITE LION HOTEL, situated on the old cobbled main street, a stones throw from the Bronte Parsonage Church and moors. ETB 4 Crown Commended. Two old world bars, candle-lit restaurant, featured in major food guides. Ideal base for exploring Dales. Weekend breaks available. Brochure on request.
B&B from £29pp, Dinner from £4.70, Rooms 3 single, 1 twin, 8 double, 2 family, all en-suite, Smoking & children welcome, Guide dogs only, Open all year.
Chris Bradford, **The Old White Lion Hotel,** Main Street, Haworth, Keighley, West Yorkshire BD22 8DU
Tel: 01535 642313 Fax: 01535 646222   **Map Ref 12**

THE FORRESTERS ARMS HOTEL, set in the North York Moors National Park in Herriot country. 12 th century inn next door to the famous 'Mousey' Thompson.

B&B from £38, Dinner available, Rooms 7 double, 3 twin, all en-suite, Children welcome, Open all year.
The Forresters Arms Hotel, Kilburn, Yorkshire YO6 4AH
Tel: 01347 868550 & 868386 Fax: 01347 868386   **Map Ref 52**

GEORGE & DRAGON HOTEL, an inn of character adjacent to the North York Moors. Extensively modernised bedrooms, all with colour TV, en-suite bathrooms. Ideal touring location.

B&B from £45, Dinner available, Rooms 1 single, 12 double, 3 twin, 2 triple, 1 family, all en-suite, No smoking, Children welcome, Open all year.
George & Dragon Hotel, Market Place, Kirkbymoorside, Yorkshire YO6 6AA
Tel: 01751 433334 Fax: 01751 433334   **Map Ref 53**

EBOR MOUNT, a charming 18th century townhouse with private car park, providing bed and breakfast accommodation in recently refurbished rooms. Ideal touring centre.

B&B from £19, Rooms 1 single, 4 double, 1 twin, 2 triple, most en-suite, No smoking, Children welcome, No pets, Open all year.
Ebor Mount, 18 York Place, Knaresborough, Yorkshire HG5 0AA
Tel: 01423 863315 Fax: 01423 863315   **Map Ref 54**

ABBEYFIELD HOUSE, just 2 miles from the town centre, a large older type house, built in 1901, which has been modernised to a good standard.

B&B from £30, Rooms 2 double, both en-suite, No smoking, Children welcome, NO pets, Open all year.
Abbeyfield House, 25 Park Grove, Knaresborough, Yorkshire HG5 9ET
Tel: 01423 866867   **Map Ref 54**

NEWTON HOUSE HOTEL, a charming, family run 17th century former coaching inn, situated 2 minutes walk from the market square, castle and river. 10 minutes Harrogate, 20 minutes York, 30 minutes the dales.

B&B from £25, Dinner available, Rooms 1 single, 6 double, 3 twin, 2 triple, all en-suite, Children welcome, Open all year.
Newton House Hotel, 5-7 York Place, Knaresborough, Yorkshire HG5 0AD
Tel: 01423 863539 Fax: 01423 869748   **Map Ref 54**

YORKSHIRE LASS,, a detached inn on main Harrogate/York road, with attractive bedrooms overlooking River Nidd. Real ales, wines, large selection of whiskies. Specialising in traditional Yorkshire dishes.

B&B from £30, Dinner available, Rooms 1 single, 2 double, 2 twin, 1 triple, all en-suite, Children welcome, No pets, Open all year.
Yorkshire Lass,, High Bridge, Harrogate Road, Knaresborough, Yorkshire HG5 8DA
Tel: 01423 862962 Fax: 01423 869091   **Map Ref 54**

GENERAL TARLETON INN, all rooms elegantly furnished. Freehouse, traditional ales and a warm family welcome.

B&B from £55, Dinner available, Rooms 3 double, 12 twin, all en-suite, No smoking, Children welcome, Open all year.
General Tarleton Inn, Boroughbridge Road, Ferrensby, Knaresborough, Yorkshire HG5 0QB
Tel: 01423 340284 Fax: 01423 340288 **Map Ref 55**

....

FAIRBAIRN HOUSE, a Victorian mansion, dating from 1850, with modern bedroom extension. Within easy reach of Leeds city centre.
B&B from £20, Dinner available, Rooms 22 single, 8 double, most en-suite, No smoking, Open all year.
Fairbairn House, 71-75 Clarendon Road, Leeds, Yorkshire LS2 9PL
Tel: 0113 233 6633 Fax: 0113 246 0899 **Map Ref 56**

....

PINEWOOD HOTEL, an extremely attractively decorated and very well furnished, with many extra touches enhancing guests comfort. A most comfortable welcome in a small hotel of distinction.

B&B from £20, Dinner available, Rooms 5 single, 3 double, 2 twin, all en-suite, No smoking, Children welcome, Open all year.
Pinewood Hotel, 78 Potternewton Lane, Leeds, Yorkshire LS7 3LW
Tel: 0113 262 2561 & 262 8485 **Map Ref 56**

....

EAGLE TAVERN, a nice friendly atmosphere. It is a public house. Car park at rear. Tea/coffee available, TV's in all rooms. Samuel Smiths Ales. 10 minutes from town and national express station. 15 minutes from train station.
B&B from £20pp, Dinner from £4, Rooms 2 single, 5 twin, 2 family, Children welcome, No pets, Open all year.
Eric Carol Vaughan, **Eagle Tavern,** North Street, Leeds, West Yorkshire LS7 1AF
Tel: 0113 2457146 **Map Ref 56**

....

PARK HOUSE, is situated on Dewsbury Road (A653) opposite the Broadway Public House, 6 minutes from city centre. All rooms have tea/coffee facilities, colour TV's, centrally heated, double glazed and are of a very high standard.Off street parking. 1 year old everything still as new.

B&B from £18pp, Various rooms, all en-suite, Restricted smoking, Children welcome, Pets by arrangement, Open all year.
Park House, 348 Dewsbury Road, Beeston, Leeds, Yorkshire LS11 7BD
Tel: 07071 880223 Mobile: 0370 616173 Fax: 0113 225697 **Map Ref 57**

....

WOODVILLE LODGE HOTEL, is situated two to three miles from Leeds city centre. There is SKY TV in all bedrooms, tea/coffee. Free parking. Also places of interest Royal Armouries Museum, Thackray Medical Museum, Tetleys Brewery, Wharf, Yorkshire Dales, Bronte Country. Small family run hotel. Very friendly.
B&B from £17pp, Dinner from £5, Rooms 2 single, 4 twin, 1 family, Children & Pets welcome, Open all year.
Ann Haugh, **Woodville Lodge Hotel,** 7 East Grange Drive, Belle Isle, Leeds, Yorkshire LS10 3EH
Tel: 0113 2776114 **Map Ref 57**

....

HAREWOOD ARMS HOTEL, a stone built hotel and restaurant of character with a rural aspect, 8 miles from Harrogate and Leeds. Opposite Harewood House and close to all amenities, including golf and racing.

B&B from £45, Dinner available, Rooms 2 single, 10 double, 10 twin, 2 triple, all en-suite, Children welcome, Open all year.
Harewood Arms Hotel, Harrogate Road, Harewood, Leeds, Yorkshire LS17 9LH
Tel: 0113 288 6566 Fax: 0113 288 6064 **Map Ref 56**

BROOMHURST HOTEL, a small comfortable hotel in a quiet pleasantly wooded conservation area, 1.5 miles from the city centre. Convenient for Yorkshire County Cricket Ground and university. Warm welcome form friendly staff.

B&B from £25, Dinner available, Rooms 8 single, 4 double, 2 twin, 2 triple, 2 family, most en-suite, No smoking, Children welcome, Open all year.
Broomhurst Hotel, 12 Chapel Lane, Headingley, Leeds, Yorkshire LS6 3BW
Tel: 0113 278 6836 & 278 5764 Fax: 0113 230 7099   **Map Ref 56**

ASCOT GRANGE HOTEL, newly refurbished throughout to a high standard. All rooms en-suite. Two miles form city centre, close to Beckets Park and Yorkshire County Cricket Ground. Warm welcome from friendly staff.

B&B from £37, Rooms 5 single, 9 double, 6 family, all en-suite, Children welcome, No pets, Open all year.
Ascot Grange Hotel, 126-130 Otley Road, Headingley, Leeds, Yorkshire LS16 5JX
Tel: 0113 293 4444 Fax: 0113 293 5555   **Map Ref 56**

CARDIGAN PRIVATE HOTEL, a family run hotel, next to Headingley Cricket/Rugby League Ground. Near public transport and shopping facilities, 1.5 miles from city centre. Evening meals available Monday to Thursday.

B&B from £25, Dinner available, Rooms 5 singe, 1 double, 2 twin, 1 triple, 1 family, most en-suite, No smoking, Children welcome, No pets, Open all year.
Cardigan Private Hotel, 36 Cardigan Road, Headingley, Leeds, Yorkshire LS6 3AG
Tel: 0113 278 4301 Fax: 0113 230 7792   **Map Ref 56**

AINTREE HOTEL, a small, comfortable licensed family hotel in tree lined road, overlooking Headingley Cricket Ground. Close to university, public transport and shopping centre, 1.5 miles from city centre.

B&B from £24, Dinner available, Rooms 6 single, 1 double, 2 twin, most en-suite, No smoking, Children welcome, No pets, Open all year.
Aintree Hotel, 38 Cardigan Road, Headingley, Leeds, Yorkshire LS6 3AG
Tel: 0113 275 8290   **Map Ref 56**

ST MICHAEL'S TOWER HOTEL, a comfortable licensed hotel, 1.5 miles from city centre and close to Headingley Cricket Ground and university. Easy access to Yorkshire countryside. Warm welcome from friendly staff.

B&B from £24, Dinner available, Rooms 7 single, 7 double, 7 twin, 1 triple, 1 family, most en-suite, Children welcome, No pets, Open all year.
St Michael's Tower Hotel, 5 St Michael's Villas, Cardigan Road, Headingley, Leeds, Yorkshire LS6 3AF
Tel: 0113 275 5557 & 275 6039 Fax: 0113 230 7491   **Map Ref 56**

CLIFF LAWN HOTEL, a large Victorian mansion set in well kept grounds. In a quiet location, approximately 1 mile from Leeds city centre.

B&B from £31.75, Dinner available, Rooms 10 single, 7 double, 5 twin, 1 triple, most en-suite, Children welcome, Open all year.
Cliff Lawn Hotel, Cliff Road, Headingley, Leeds, Yorkshire LS6 2ET
Tel: 0113 278 5442 & 275 6192 Fax: 0113 278 5442   **Map Ref 56**

ARAGON HOTEL, a converted, late Victorian house in quiet, wooded surroundings, 2 miles from the city centre. TV, telephone and tea making facilities in all bedrooms. Free car parking.

B&B from £29.90, Dinner available, Rooms 3 single, 7 double, 3 twin, all en-suite, No smoking, Children welcome, Open all year.

Aragon Hotel, 250 Stainbeck Lane, Meanwood, Leeds, Yorkshire LS7 2PS
Tel: 0113 275 9306 Fax: 0113 275 7166   **Map Ref 56**

MONK FRYSTON HALL HOTEL, an old manor house with peaceful, comfortable accommodation on the A63 just off the A1. Friendly atmosphere and English cooking.

B&B from £72, Dinner available, Rooms 5 single, 15 double, 6 twin, 2 triple, all en-suite, No smoking, Children welcome, Open all year.
Monk Fryston Hall Hotel, Monk Fryston, Leeds, Yorkshire LS25 5DU
Tel: 01977 682369 Fax: 01977 683544   **Map Ref 61**

....

OLD VICARAGE GUEST HOUSE, within minutes of motorways, providing a Yorkshire welcome with home comforts in an authentic Victorian setting.

B&B from £27, Dinner available, Rooms 11 single, 4 double, 2 twin, all en-suite, No smoking, Children welcome, No pets, Open all year.

Old Vicarage Guest House, Bruntcliffe Road, Morley, Leeds, Yorkshire LS27 0JZ
Tel: 0113 253 2174 Fax: 0113 253 3549   **Map Ref 57**

....

STAKIS LEEDS, ideal for both business and holiday makers. On the main Leeds to York road with easy access to the airport and motorways.

B&B from £27, Dinner available, Rooms 22 single, 26 double, 50 twin, 2 family, all en-suite, No smoking, Children welcome, Open all year.
Stakis Leeds, Ring Road, Mill Green View, Seacroft, Leeds, Yorkshire LS14 5QF
Tel: 0113 273 2323 Fax: 0113 232 3018   **Map Ref 62**

....

DE VERE OULTON HALL, a fully renovated hall in the heart of Yorkshire, south east of Leeds. Adjacent to a golf course. Full leisure club.

B&B from £125, Dinner available, Rooms 88 double, 64 twin, all en-suite, Children welcome, Open all year.

De Vere Oulton Hall, Rothwell Lane, Oulton, Woodlesford, Leeds, Yorkshire LS26 8HN
Tel: 0113 282 1000 Fax: 0113 282 8066   **Map Ref 63**

....

SECRET GARDEN HOUSE, a Georgian house with secluded walled garden and conservatory, in market town, the heart of James Herriot country. Free off street parking.

B&B from £19.50, Dinner available, Rooms 3 double, 1 twin, all en-suite, No smoking, Children over 12, Open all year.

Secret Garden House, Grove Square, Leyburn, Yorkshire DL8 5AE
Tel: 01969 623589   **Map Ref 64**

....

GOLDEN LION HOTEL & LICENSED RESTAURANT, a small family run hotel in the market place of a busy dales town. A good base for touring the surrounding countryside.

B&B from £21, Dinner available, Rooms 3 single, 4 double, 3 twin, 4 triple, most en-suite, Children welcome, Open all year.

Golden Lion Hotel & Licensed Restaurant, Market Place, Leyburn, Yorkshire DL8 5AS
Tel: 01969 622161 Fax: 01969 623836   **Map Ref 64**

....

KINGS ARMS HOTEL & CLUBROOM RESTAURANT, Yorkshire Life 'Hotel of the Year' and Herriot pub. Famous for comfort, atmosphere, good food, fine wine and real ales. Central for dales, moors and Lakes.

B&B from £50, Dinner available, Rooms 10 double, 1 twin, all en-suite, No smoking, Children welcome, Open all year.

Kings Arms Hotel & Clubroom Restaurant, Askrigg, Leyburn, Yorkshire DL8 3HQ
Tel: 01969 650258 Fax: 01969 650635   **Map Ref 58**

WINVILLE HOTEL & RESTAURANT, a 19th century Georgian residence in the centre of Herriot village. Some rooms have vies of the dales. Conservatory and private gardens.

B&B from £32, Dinner available, Rooms 4 double, 2 twin, 4 triple, all en-suite, Children welcome, Open all year.
Winville Hotel & Restaurant, Main Street, Askrigg, Leyburn, Yorkshire DL8 3HG
Tel: 01969 650515 Fax: 01969 650594　　　　　　　　　　　　　　　　　　　**Map Ref 58**

....

RIVERDALE HOUSE COUNTRY HOTEL, tastefully appointed, comfortable house, with special emphasis on food. In the centre of a lovely village in Upper Wensleydale, the area used for the filming of the James Herriot stories.

B&B from £52, Dinner available, Rooms 6 double, 4 twin, 2 triple, all en-suite, No smoking, Children welcome, No pets, Open March - October.
Riverdale House Country Hotel, Bainbridge, Leyburn, Yorkshire DL8 3EW
Tel: 01969 650311 & 663381　　　　　　　　　　　　　　　　　　　　　　**Map Ref 58**

....

Situated in unspoilt Bishopdale, **EAST LANE HOUSE** is a 17th century refurbished farmhouse. Centrally heated bedrooms with en-suite and tea/coffee facilities. Traditional breakfast and 4 course evening meals if required. Guests' lounge, open fires and off road parking. Excellent centre for walking and touring.
B&B from £19.50pp, Dinner from £12, Rooms 1 twin, 1 double, all en-suite, Restricted smoking, Children & pets welcome, Open all year except Christmas & New Year.
Colin & Judith, Smith, **East Lane House,** Newbiggin in Bishopdale, Leyburn, North Yorkshire DL8 3TF
Tel: 01969 663234　　　　　　　　　　　　　　　　　　　　　　　　**Map Ref 59**

....

WENSLEYDALE HEIFER, a 17th century inn situated in Yorkshire Dales National Park. Seafood restaurant and bistro. Four poster bedrooms. Special breaks. Dogs welcome. Rustic country cooking.

B&B from £54, Dinner available, Rooms 8 double, 5 twin, 1 triple, 1 family, all en-suite, Children welcome, Open all year.
Wensleydale Heifer, West Witton, Leyburn, Yorkshire DL8 4LS
Tel: 01969 622322 Fax: 01969 624183　　　　　　　　　　　　　　　　　**Map Ref 60**

....

IVY DENE COUNTRY GUESTHOUSE, a 17th century country guest house, beautifully situated in Yorkshire Dales National Park. Quality en-suite accommodation in a friendly, informal atmosphere. Super home cooked meals prepared from fresh produce. Short break discounts.

B&B from £25, Dinner available, Rooms 3 double, 1 twin, 1 triple, most en-suite, No smoking, Children over 5, No pets, Open all year.
Ivy Dene Country Guesthouse, Main Street, West Witton, Leyburn, Yorkshire DL8 4LP
Tel: 01969 622785　　　　　　　　　　　　　　　　　　　　　　　　**Map Ref 60**

....

HEALDS HALL HOTEL, a family run hotel with award winning restaurant. Large gardens. On A62, near M1 and M62. Ideal for dales. Special weekend breaks available.

B&B from £30, Dinner available, Rooms 5 single, 11 double, 5 twin, 4 triple, all en-suite, No smoking, Children welcome, Open all year.
Healds Hall Hotel, Leeds Road, Liversedge, Yorkshire WF15 6JA
Tel: 01924 409112 Fax: 01924 401895　　　　　　　　　　　　　　　　　**Map Ref 16**

....

THE GEORGE HOTEL, a family run hotel, dating from the 16th century, now totally refurbished. In town centre location with own car park. Families welcome. Special diets.

B&B from £42, Dinner available, Rooms 1 double, 1 twin, 1 triple, 1 family, all en-suite, Children welcome, No pets, Open all year.
The George Hotel, 19 Yorkersgate, Malton, Yorkshire YO17 0AA
Tel: 01653 692884 & 468 344337　　　　　　　　　　　　　　　　　　**Map Ref 65**

THE SNOOTY FOX (A64), has motel accommodation set in 4 and a half acres overlooking the beautiful vale of Pickering. TV and tea/coffee making facilities in all rooms. Pub with log fire, serving a selection of home made meals. Ideally situated for Scarborough, Malton and North Yorkshire Moors.
B&B from £19pp, Dinner available, Rooms 1 twin, 2 double, 2 family, all en-suite, Smoking, Children & pets welcome, Open all year.
Judie Bland, **The Snooty Fox (A64),** East Heslerton, Malton, North Yorkshire YO17 8EN
Tel: 01944 710554   **Map Ref 66**

WENTWORTH ARMS HOTEL, a former coaching inn, built early 1700s and run by the same family for 100 years. 20 miles from York. An excellent base for touring the Yorkshire Dales, North York Moors and the East Coast.

B&B from £22, Dinner available, Rooms 3 double, 2 twin, most en-suite, No pets, Open all year.
Wentworth Arms Hotel, Town Street, Malton, Yorkshire YO17 0HD
Tel: 01653 692618   **Map Ref 65**

NEWSTEAD GRANGE, an elegant Georgian country house in 2.5 acres, 1.5 miles from Malton on the Beverley road. Antique furniture. Non smoking establishment.

B&B from £37, Dinner available, Rooms 4 double, 4 twin, all en-suite, No smoking, Children over 10, No pets, Open February - November.
Newstead Grange, Norton, Malton, Yorkshire YO17 9PJ
Tel: 01653 692502 Fax: 01653 696951   **Map Ref 65**

MILLERS HOUSE HOTEL, Yorkshire's Hotel of the Year runner up 96/97. Elegant Georgian country house in the heart of the dales. Privately owned and run, offering a warm welcome, quality and comfort. Noted restaurant. 20 minutes from A1.
B&B from £30, Dinner available, Rooms 1 single, 3 double, 3 twin, all en-suite, No smoking, Children over 10, No pets, Open February - December.
Millers House Hotel, Middleham, Yorkshire DL8 4NR
Tel: 01969 622630 Fax: 01969 623570   **Map Ref 67**

BLACK SWAN HOTEL, an unspoilt 17th century inn, with open fires and beamed ceilings, allied to 20th century comforts. Emphasis on food.

B&B from £27, Dinner available, Rooms 1 single, 4 double, 1 twin, 1 triple, all en-suite, Children welcome, Open all year.
Black Swan Hotel, Market Place, Middleham, Yorkshire DL8 4NP
Tel: 01969 622221 Fax: 01969 622221   **Map Ref 67**

ALVERTON GUEST HOUSE, a family run guest house convenient for county town facilities and ideal for touring the dales,moors and coastal areas.
B&B from £17, Dinner available, Rooms 2 single, 1 double, 1 twin, 1 triple, most en-suite, Children welcome, Open all year.
Alverton Guest House, 26 South Parade, Northallerton, Yorkshire DL7 8SG
Tel: 01609 776207   **Map Ref 68**

WHITE ROSE HOTEL, a family run private hotel and restaurant ideally situated in village half a mile from A1 motorway. Central for Yorkshire Dales, Heartbeat country and coastal resorts. Pets welcome.

B&B from £17.50, Dinner available, Rooms 9 single, 1 double, 6 twin, 2 triple, all en-suite, Children welcome, Open all year.
White Rose Hotel, Leeming Bar, Northallerton, Yorkshire DL7 9AY
Tel: 01677 422707 & 424941 Fax: 01677 425123   **Map Ref 68**

SOLBERGE HALL, a Victorian country house in the heart of Herriot country, convenient for the moors and dales.

B&B from £60, Dinner available, Rooms 4 single, 16 double, 5 twin, all en-suite, No smoking, Children welcome, Open all year.

Solberge Hall, Newby Wiske, Northallerton, Yorkshire DL7 9ER
Tel: 01609 779191 Fax: 01609 780472 **Map Ref 68**

....

MONKMAN'S BISTRO WITH BEDROOMS, a fine Georgian mansion 9 miles from Harrogate, Leeds and Bradford. Exceptionally warm welcome and renowned modern bistro cuisine.

B&B from £63, Dinner available, Rooms 1 single, 3 double, 2 twin, all en-suite, No smoking, Children welcome, No pets, Open all year.
Monkman's Bistro with Bedrooms, Pool Bank, Pool in Wharfdale, Otley, Yorkshire LS21 1EH
Tel: 0113 284 1105 Fax: 0113 284 3115 **Map Ref 69**

....

HEATHCOTE HOUSE, an early Victorian house 5 minutes from town centre. Ideal for walking and touring. All bedrooms have en-suite. Optional dinners. Relaxed, friendly atmosphere. Secluded parking.

B&B from £25, Dinner available, Rooms 3 double, 2 twin, most en-suite, No smoking, No pets, Open February - December.

Heathcote House, 100 Eastgate, Pickering, Yorkshire YO18 7DW
Tel: 01751 476991 Fax: 01751 476991 **Map Ref 70**

....

BRAMWOOD GUEST HOUSE, a charming 18th century house. All rooms tastefully furnished en-suite. Individual dining tables, guest lounge. Friendly and relaxed atmosphere.

B&B from £25, Dinner available, Rooms 4 double, 1 twin, all en-suite, No smoking, Children over 5, No pets, Open all year.
Bramwood Guest House, 19 Hallgarth, Pickering, Yorkshire YO18 7AW
Tel: 01751 474066 **Map Ref 70**

....

FOREST & VALE HOTEL, an old manor house with comfortable accommodation, good food and pleasant staff. Central for Yorkshire Moors, East Coast and York.

B&B from £40, Dinner available, Rooms 2 single, 9 double, 3 twin, 3 triple, all en-suite, Children welcome, Open all year.

Forest & Vale Hotel, Malton Road, Pickering, Yorkshire YO18 7DL
Tel: 01751 472722 Fax: 01751 472972 **Map Ref 70**

....

OLD MANSE GUEST HOUSE, an Edwardian house set in large garden with orchard and private car park. All rooms en-suite. 4 minutes walk to steam railway and town centre.

B&B from £18, Dinner available, Rooms 5 double, 3 twin, all en-suite, Children over 10, No pets, Open all year.

Old Manse Guest House, Middleton Road, Pickering, Yorkshire YO18 8AL
Tel: 01751 476484 Fax: 01751 477124 **Map Ref 70**

....

SUNNYSIDE, a large, south facing chalet bungalow with private parking and a garden, in an open country aspect. Some ground floor rooms.

B&B from £24, Dinner available, Rooms 1 double, 1 twin, 1 triple, all en-suite, No smoking, Children welcome, Open March - October.

Sunnyside, Carr Lane, Middleton, Pickering, Yorkshire YO18 8PD
Tel: 01751 476104 Fax: 01751 476104 **Map Ref 71**

MILBURN ARMS HOTEL, a historic inn, in a picturesque conservation area village, central to the national park and 15 miles from the Yorkshire Heritage Coast. Restaurant noted for enjoyable, well prepared food.

B&B from £32pp, Dinner available, Rooms 9 double, 2 twin, all en-suite, Children welcome, No pets, Open all year.

Milburn Arms Hotel, Rosedale Abbey, Pickering, Yorkshire YO18 8RA
Tel: 01751 417312 Fax: 01751 417312   **Map Ref 70**

FOX & HOUNDS COUNTRY INN, once an old coaching inn. Open fires and period furniture. In tranquil rural setting west of Pickering. Fishing, riding, golf and riverside walks close by.

B&B from £38, Dinner available, Rooms 1 single, 6 double, 2 twin, 1 family, all en-suite, No smoking, Children welcome, Open all year.
Fox & Hounds Country Inn, Sinnington, Pickering, Yorkshire YO6 6SQ
Tel: 01751 431577 Fax: 01751 431577   **Map Ref 71**

ROGERTHORPE MANOR COUNTRY HOUSE HOTEL, impressive grade II listed country ,manor in its own grounds. Tastefully restored and ideally located near Pontefract, the A1 and M62.

B&B from £35, Dinner available, Rooms 4 single, 4 double, 5 twin, 1 triple, No smoking, Children welcome, Open all year.

Rogerthorpe Manor Country House Hotel, Thorpe Lane, Badsworth, Pontefract, Yorkshire WF9 1AB
Tel: 01977 643839 Fax: 01977 641571   **Map Ref 72**

OLD FARMHOUSE COUNTRY HOTEL & RESTAURANT, a former farmhouse converted to a comfortable country hotel, offering home cooking, open fires and a warm, friendly welcome. In Herriot country, 3 miles from Easingwold and 15 miles from York.

B&B from £32, Dinner available, Rooms 1 single, 7 double, 1 twin, 1 triple, all en-suite, No smoking, Children welcome, No pets, Open all year.

Old Farmhouse Country Hotel & Restaurant, Raskelf, Yorkshire YO6 3LF
Tel: 01347 821971   **Map Ref 73**

MILLGATE HOUSE, a Georgian town house, award winning garden, central but secluded. Super views of River, garden and waterfalls. Ideal touring location. A very special house with enchanting character and atmosphere. Quiet exceptional, an amazing find. All rooms colour TV, tea/coffee, full facilities. mail: oztim@millgatehouse.demon.co.uk
B&B from £27.50pp, Rooms 1 twin, 1 double, both en-suite, Children over 10, Pets by arrangement, Open all year.
Austin Lynch & Tim Culkin, **Millgate House,** Richmond, North Yorkshire DL10 4JN
Tel: 01748 823571 Fax: 01748 850701 E   **Map Ref 74**

Nestling on the green, close to the river Swale with marvellous views of Richmond Castle. **THE OLD BREWERY GUEST HOUSE** was once an old inn. It has en-suite rooms, a 4 poster bed, TV and tea/coffee facilities. Home cooked meals. Lounge and patio garden.

B&B from £20pp, Dinner from £13, Rooms 1 twin, 4 double, all en-suite, Restricted smoking, Children over 8, No pets, Open February - December.
Mrs Mears, **The Old Brewery Guest House,** 29 The Green, Richmond, North Yorkshire DL10 4RG
Tel: 01748 822460 Fax: 01748 825561   **Map Ref 74**

THE RESTAURANT ON THE GREEN, a grade II listed William and Mary property with Georgian sundials at foot of Castle bluff. Near town centre, River Swale and countryside. Family run,. Bedrooms with colour TV, beverage tray, en-suite or private bathroom. Good food, fine wines.

B&B from £18.50, Dinner available, Rooms 1 double private bathroom, 1 twin en-suite, No smoking, Children over 10, No pets, Open all year.
The Restaurant on the Green, 5-7 Bridge Street, Richmond, Yorkshire DL10 4RW
Tel: 01748 826229   **Map Ref 74**

....

KING'S HEAD HOTEL, a beautiful Georgian hotel in historic market town. Ideal for touring Herriot country/Yorkshire Dales. High standard of accommodation and service. Freshly prepared cooking and extensive wine list.

B&B from £41pp, Dinner available, Rooms 7 single, 15 double, 7 twin, 1 triple, all en-suite, Restricted smoking, Children & pets welcome, Open all year.

King's Head Hotel, Market Place, Richmond, Yorkshire DL10 4HS
Tel: 01748 850220 Fax: 01748 850635   **Map Ref 74**

....

CHARLES BATHURST INN, situated in the heart of Yorkshire Dales with growing reputation for outstanding fresh food. We offer 9 en-suite rooms all with colour TV, tea/coffee making facilities. Residents lounge and off street parking. Special breaks available.

B&B from £25pp, Dinner from £12.50, Rooms 1 single, 3 twin, 5 double, all en-suite, No smoking, Children welcome, Pets by arrangement, Open all year.
Charles & Stacy Cody, **Charles Bathurst Inn,** Arkengarthdale, Richmond, North Yorkshire DL11 6EN
Tel: 01748 884567 Fax: 01748 884599 Email: cb-inn-msn.com
                                                                                                               Map Ref 75

....

THE WHITE HOUSE, a family run guest house with panoramic views of this secluded dale. Close to Richmond and Barnard Castle and 3 miles from Reeth in Swaledale. An ideal touring and walking centre.

B&B from £18.50, Dinner available, Rooms 2 double, 1 twin, most en-suite, No smoking, Children over 10, No pets, Open March - November.
The White House, Arkle Town, Arkengarthdale, Richmond, Yorkshire DL11 6RB
Tel: 01748 884203 Fax: 01748 884088   **Map Ref 75**

....

BRIDGE HOUSE HOTEL, a riverside coaching hotel dating back to the 15th century. Easily accessible from the A1. Situated midway between the dales and the North York Moors.

B&B from £40, Dinner available, Rooms 2 single, 6 double, 6 twin, 2 triple, most en-suite, Children welcome, Open all year.
Bridge House Hotel, Catterick Bridge, Richmond, Yorkshire DL10 7PE
Tel: 01748 818331 Fax: 01748 818331   **Map Ref 74**

....

ROSE COTTAGE GUEST HOUSE, a small, friendly stone built guest house. En-suite facilities, guest lounge, private parking and convenient for Richmond and Yorkshire Dales.

B&B from £20.50, Dinner available, Rooms 1 single, 2 twin, 1 triple, some en-suite, No smoking, Children welcome, Open all year.

Rose Cottage Guest House, 26 High Street, Catterick, Richmond, Yorkshire DL10 7LJ
Tel: 01748 811164   **Map Ref 76**

THE SHOULDER OF MUTTON INN, an ivy fronted country inn in an elevated position on the edge of Kirby Hall village, giving a magnificent view of the Yorkshire Dales. Rooms are en-suite with central heating, colour TV and tea/coffee facilities. Send for brochure.

B&B from £28pp, Dinner from £10, Rooms 4 double, 1 family, all en-suite, Children welcome, Pets by arrangement, Open all year except Christmas Day.
Mick & Anne Burns, **The Shoulder of Mutton Inn,** Kirkby Hill, Richmond, North Yorkshire DL11 7JH
Tel: 01748 822748   **Map Ref 77**

THE BAY HORSE INN, warm, friendly atmosphere. Old world charm overlooking beautiful village green. Home made food in bar and restaurant. Beer garden. Middle of Yorkshire Dales. Excellent walking country. 4 miles from Scotch Corner, 10 minutes Richmond, 10 minutes Barnard Castle. Twin room with en-suite TV, tea/coffee facilities in room
B&B from £18pp, Dinner from £4-£10, Rooms 1 en-suite twin, Children & Pets welcome, Open all year.
Mr Charles Hird & Miss Sue Wass, **The Bay Horse Inn,** Ravensworth, Richmond, North Yorkshire DL11 7ET
Tel: 01325 718328   **Map Ref 78**

KINGS ARMS HOTEL, a traditional Yorkshire inn dating from 1730 with spectacular views of Swaledale from the inglenook bar or residents bedrooms overlooking the village green.

B&B from £20, Dinner available, Rooms 2 double, 1 twin, 1 family, all with private showers, No smoking, Children welcome, Open all year.
Kings Arms Hotel, High Row, Reeth, Richmond, Yorkshire DL11 6SY
Tel: 01748 884259   **Map Ref 79**

KEARTON GUEST HOUSE, in the charming village of Thwaite in Swaledale, within easy reach of York, the Lake District, Herriot country and the Yorkshire Dales.

B&B from £21, Dinner available, Rooms 1 single, 4 double, 1 twin, 6 triple, 1 family, most en-suite, Children welcome, No pets, Open March - December.
Kearton Guest House, Thwaite, Richmond, Yorkshire DL11 6DR
Tel: 01748 886277 Fax: 01748 886590   **Map Ref 80**

BISHOPTON GROVE HOUSE, a restored Georgian house in a lovely rural corner of Ripon, near the River Laver and Fountains Abbey.

B&B from £20, Dinner available, Rooms 2 double, 1 twin, 1 en-suite, Children welcome, Open all year.
Bishopton Grove House, Bishopton, Ripon, Yorkshire HG4 2QL
Tel: 01765 600888   **Map Ref 81**

ST. GEORGES COURT, is set in 20 acres of secluded farmland. Our comfortable en-suite rooms all have colour TV and tea/coffee making facilities, all on ground floor. The farmhouse is a listed building with plenty of parking and new conservatory sitting room. Let the beauty, peace and tranquillity of St George's Court work its charm on you too.
B&B from £20pp, Rooms 1 twin, 3 double, 1 family, all en-suite, Restricted smoking, Children over 2, Pets by arrangement, Open all year except Christmas.
Mrs Gordon, **St. Georges Court,** Old Home Farm, Grantley, Ripon, North Yorkshire HG4 3EU
Tel: 01765 620618   **Map Ref 82**

Yorkshire Dales, 200 year old **LIME TREE FARM** set in secluded woodland. Oak panelling, beams, exposed stonework and open fires. Furnished with antiques. Private facilities, colour TV, tea/coffee facilities in all rooms. Traditional home cooked food. Ideal for touring or walking. Phone for colour brochure.

B&B from £18.50pp, Dinner from £12.50, Rooms 1 twin, 2 double, all en-suite, Smoking & children welcome, Pets by arrangement, Open all year.

Peter & Irene **Lime Tree Farm,** Hutts Lane, Grewelthorpe, Ripon, North Yorkshire HG4 3DA

Tel: 01765 658450 **Map Ref 83**

THE BUCK INN, a friendly village inn overlooking the delightful cricket green in a small village, 3 miles from Bedale on the Masham road, and close to the A1. Ideal centre for exploring both the dales and North York Moors.

B&B from £34, Dinner available, Rooms 1 single, 3 double, 2 twin, 1 triple, most en-suite, Children welcome, Open all year.
The Buck Inn, Thornton Watlass, Ripon, Yorkshire HG4 4AH
Tel: 01677 422461 Fax: 01677 422447 **Map Ref 84**

CARLTON PARK HOTEL, a modern hotel with conference facilities, extensive leisure facilities, a restaurant and a public bar. In a residential area, close to M1 and M18 motorway.

B&B from £35, Dinner available, Rooms 38 single, 11 double, 21 twin, 6 triple, all en-suite, No smoking, Children welcome, Open all year.
Carlton Park Hotel, 102-104 Moorgate Road, Rotherham, Yorkshire S60 2BG
Tel: 01709 849955 Fax: 01709 368960 **Map Ref 85**

SWALLOW HOTEL, a modern, 4 storey building with extensive conference and banqueting facilities and leisure complex. Easy access from junction 33 of M1.

B&B from £75, Dinner available, Rooms 71 double, 27 twin, 2 family, all en-suite, No smoking, Children welcome, Open all year.
Swallow Hotel, West Bawtry Road, Rotherham, Yorkshire S60 4NA
Tel: 01709 830630 Fax: 01709 830549 **Map Ref 85**

BEST WESTERN ELTON HOTEL, a 200 year old, stone built Yorkshire house with a modern extension and a restaurant. Half a mile from junction 1 of M18, 2 miles from M1.

B&B from £48.50, Dinner available, Rooms 9 single, 12 double, 4 twin, 4 triple, all en-suite, No smoking, Children welcome, Open all year.
Best Western Elton Hotel, Main Street, Bramley, Rotherham, Yorkshire S66 0SF
Tel: 01709 545681 Fax: 01709 549100 **Map Ref 85**

CONSORT HOTEL, BANQUETING & CONFERENCE SUITE, at the junction of M1 and M18 (access exits 31 and 33 of M1 and exit 1 of M18).

B&B from £30, Dinner available, Rooms 10 double, 7 twin, 1 family, all en-suite, No smoking, Children welcome, No pets, Open all year.
Consort Hotel, Banqueting & Conference Suite, Brampton Road, Thurcroft, Rotherham, Yorkshire S66 9JA
Tel: 01709 530022 Fax: 01709 531529 **Map Ref 86**

ELLERBY HOTEL, a residential country inn within the North York Moors National Park, 9 miles north of Whitby, 1 mile inland from Runswick Bay.

B&B from £35, Dinner available, Rooms 5 double, 4 triple, all en-suite, No smoking, Children welcome, Open all year.

Ellerby Hotel, Ellerby, Saltburn by the Sea, Yorkshire TS13 5LP
Tel: 01947 840342 Fax: 01947 841221 **Map Ref 87**

THE FIRS, in a coastal village, 8 miles north of Whitby. All rooms en-suite, with colour TV, tea/coffee facilities. Evening meals by arrangement.
B&B from £26, Dinner available, Rooms 1 double, 1 twin, 2 triple, 1 family, all en-suite, Children over 3, Open all year.
The Firs, 26 Hinderwell Lane, Runswick, Saltburn by the Sea, Yorkshire TS13 5HR
Tel: 01947 840433   **Map Ref 87**

....

CLIFFEMOUNT HOTEL, a relaxing hotel on the cliff top with panoramic views of Runswick Bay. 9 miles north of Whitby. Noted for cuisine.
B&B from £25, Dinner available, Rooms 1 single, 8 double, 2 triple, all en-suite or private facilities, Children welcome, Open all year.
Cliffemount Hotel, Runswick Bay, Runswick, Saltburn by the Sea, Yorkshire TS13 5HU
Tel: 01947 840103 Fax: 01947 841025   **Map Ref 87**

....

EXCELSIOR PRIVATE HOTEL, North Bay sea front corner, superb views. Traditionally cooked fresh produce and homemade bread by hosts Irene and Raymond Brown.
B&B from £20, Dinner available, Rooms 2 single, 4 double, 1 triple, 1 family, most en-suite, No smoking, Children over 4, No pets, Open April - October.
Irene & Raymond Brown **Excelsior Private Hotel,** 1 Marlborough Street, Scarborough, Yorkshire YO12 7HG
Tel: 01723 360716   **Map Ref 88**

....

SUNNINGDALE PRIVATE HOTEL, a modern, detached hotel facing Peasholm Park and close to all north side attractions. Short, level walk to North Beach.
B&B from £24, Dinner available, Rooms 2 single, 5 double, 5 triple, all en-suite, Children welcome, No pets, Open all year.
Sunningdale Private Hotel, 105 Peasholm Drive, Scarborough, Yorkshire YO12 7NB
Tel: 01723 372041 & 0850 784347 Fax: 01723 354691   **Map Ref 88**

....

NORTHCOTE NON SMOKING HOTEL, a modern, semi detached private hotel with bedrooms on 2 floors only. Special offers available for senior citizens. All rooms en-suite and with colour TV.
B&B from £16.50, Dinner available, Rooms 1 single, 4 double, 2 twin, 1 triple, 1 family, most en-suite, No smoking, Children over 5, Open March - November.
Northcote Non Smoking Hotel, 114 Columbus Ravine, Scarborough, Yorkshire YO12 8QZ
Tel: 01723 367758   **Map Ref 88**

....

HOTEL COLUMBUS, is 100% non smoking. Ideal location for all North Bay amenities and 15 minutes from town private facilities. Television, complimentary tray, hair dryer and double glazing in all bedrooms. Choice menu. Open all year. Midweek and weekend breaks available. Private brochure on request.
B&B from £20pp, Dinner from £10, Rooms 1 single, 1 twin, 7 double, 2 family, all en-suite, No smoking or pets, Children welcome, Open all year Christmas.
Mrs Purchon, **Hotel Columbus,** 124 Columbus Ravine, Scarborough, North Yorkshire YO12 7QZ
Tel: 01723 374634 Fax: 01723 374634   **Map Ref 88**

....

RICHMOND PRIVATE HOTEL, resident proprietors guarantee a warm welcome, comfortable accommodation. Colour TV and tea/coffee in all rooms. Separate guest lounge. Licensed bar and good home cooking. Convenient for town centre. Cricket ground, indoor bowls complex, North Bays sandy beaches, swimming pools and many more attractions nearby.
B&B from £13.50pp, Dinner from £5, Rooms 1 single, 3 twin, 3 double, 1 family, Restricted smoking, Children welcome, Pets by arrangement, Open all year.
Brian & Janet Shaw, **Richmond Private Hotel,** 135 Columbus Ravine, Scarborough, North Yorkshire YO12 7QZ
Tel: 01723 362934   **Map Ref 88**

THE ALBEMARLE HOTEL, offers comfortable, spacious accommodation, close to town amenities, station, theatre, bingo and chemist. Seven minutes to sea, via lift. All rooms have Sky TV and tea/coffee facilities. Bar and quiet lounge with pool table. Specialising in school and coach parties.
B&B from £14pp, Dinner from £5, Rooms 3 single, 4 twin, 5 double, 6 family, 5 en-suite, Smoking & children welcome, Pets by arrangement, Open March - October.
Mr Nick Polihronos, **The Albemarle Hotel,** 22 Albemarle Crescent, Scarborough, Yorkshire YO11 1XX
Tel: 01723 501019 **Map Ref 88**

....

LYSANDER HOTEL, in a peaceful setting between Peasholm Gardens. Close tot he beach, swimming pools, boating lakes, golf and theatres.

B&B from £20, Dinner available, Rooms 4 single, 7 double, 5 twin, 2 triple, most en-suite, Children welcome, No pets, Open April - October & Christmas.

Lysander Hotel, 22 Weydale Avenue, Scarborough, Yorkshire YO12 6AX
Tel: 01723 373369 **Map Ref 88**

....

WHARNCLIFFE HOTEL, panoramic sea views - cleanliness assured - friendly atmosphere. All rooms en-suite with colour TV, radio alarm and tea/coffee making facilities. Close to town centre and amenities.

B&B from £21, Dinner available, Rooms 7 double, 1 twin, 2 triple, 2 family, all en-suite, Children welcome, No pets, Open March - September.
Wharncliffe Hotel, 26 Blenheim Terrace, Scarborough, Yorkshire YO12 7HD
Tel: 01723 374635 **Map Ref 88**

....

RYNDLE COURT PRIVATE HOTEL, pleasantly situated overlooking Peasholm Park and near the sea. All rooms en-suite with TV and tea making facilities. residents bar and car park.

B&B from £27, Dinner available, Rooms 1 single, 6 double, 2 twin, 3 triple, 2 family, all en-suite, No smoking, Children welcome, No pets, Open all year.

Ryndle Court Private Hotel, 47 Northstead Manor Drive, Scarborough, Yorkshire YO12 6AF
Tel: 01723 375188 & 0860711517 Fax: 01723 375188 **Map Ref 88**

....

HIGHBANK HOTEL, a modern non-smoking small hotel in quiet location, close to North Bay. Well equipped en-suite rooms, high standards, experienced service in relaxing ambience, giving best value for discerning guests. Secure car parking, special requests welcome, diets catered for. Aromatherapy available from qualified practioner.

B&B from £18pp, Dinner from £7, Rooms 1 single, 1 twin, 4 double, 1 family, all en-suite, No smoking, Children welcome, Pets by arrangement, Open all year.
Harry & Chris Smith, **Highbank Hotel,** 5 Givendale Road, Scarborough, North Yorkshire YO12 6LE
Tel: 01723 365265 **Map Ref 88**

....

AVONCROFT HOTEL, a listed Georgian terrace overlooking Crown Gardens. Close to spa and sports facilities. Convenient for town centre and all entertainments.

B&B from £20.50, Dinner available, Rooms 7 single, 10 double, 5 twin, 12 triple, most en-suite, Children welcome, Open February - December.

Avoncroft Hotel, 5-7 Crown Terrace, Scarborough, Yorkshire YO11 2BL
Tel: 01723 372737 Fax: 01723 372737 **Map Ref 88**

531

MANOR HEATH HOTEL, a detached hotel with pleasant gardens and a private car park, overlooking Peasholm Park and the sea. Close to all North Bay attractions.

B&B from £20, Dinner available, Rooms 1 single, 6 double, 2 triple, 5 family, most en-suite, Children welcome, No pets, Open all year.

Manor Heath Hotel, 67 Northstead Manor Drive, Scarborough, Yorkshire YO12 6AF
Tel: 01723 365720   **Map Ref 88**

HOLMELEA GUEST HOUSE, all rooms with central heating, divans, duvets, tea/coffee making, colour TV with satellite/video link, radio alarm and hair dryer. Now facilities for deaf and hard of hearing, including Minicom.

B&B from £14, Rooms 2 single, 1 double, 2 twin, 1 family, Children welcome, Open all year.

Holmelea Guest House, 8 Belle Vue Parade, Scarborough, Yorkshire YO11 1SU
Tel: 01723 360139 Fax: 01723 360139 Minicom: 01723 363077   **Map Ref 88**

BEVERLEY HOUSE PRIVATE HOTEL, is a family run licensed hotel offering an informal atmosphere, flexible mealtimes and menus. Bedrooms have TV and hot drink facilities. Situated close to the south bay and spa complex within easy reach of Historic town centre and attractions.
B&B from £18pp, Dinner from £3.50, Rooms 3 single, 1 twin, 2 double, 3 family, en-suite available, Restricted smoking, Children welcome, No pets, Open all year except Christmas & New Year.
Ann & Terry Stafford, **Beverley House Private Hotel,** 8 Crown Crescent, South Cliff, Scarborough, North Yorkshire YO11 2BJ
Tel/Fax: 01723 364687   **Map Ref 88**

ESPLANADE HOTEL, a welcoming period style hotel in good position on Scarborough's South Cliff. Close to beach, spa and town centre. Landau restaurant, parlour bar and roof terrace.

B&B from £44, Dinner available, Rooms 18 single, 19 double, 26 twin, 8 triple, 2 family, most en-suite, No smoking, Children welcome, Open March - December.

Esplanade Hotel, Belmont Road, Scarborough, Yorkshire YO11 2AA
Tel: 01723 360382 Fax: 01723 376137   **Map Ref 88**

RED LEA HOTEL, a traditional hotel with sea views, close to the Spa Centre. Restaurant, bar, lounges, lift and colour TV. Solarium and indoor heated swimming pool.

B&B from £33, Dinner available, Rooms 19 single, 11 double, 27 twin, 7 triple, 4 family, all en-suite, No smoking, Children welcome, No pets, Open all year.

Red Lea Hotel, Prince of Wales Terrace, Scarborough, Yorkshire YO11 2AJ
Tel: 01723 362431 Fax: 01723 371230   **Map Ref 88**

AMBASSADOR HOTEL, a Victorian hotel offering en-suite bedrooms, sea views, indoor heated swimming pool, spa, solarium, entertainment, lift and free parking.

B&B from £27, Dinner available, Rooms 9 single, 17 double, 29 twin, 3 triple, 1 family, all en-suite, No smoking, Children welcome, Open all year.

Ambassador Hotel, The Esplanade, Scarborough, Yorkshire YO11 2AY
Tel: 01723 362841 Fax: 01723 362841   **Map Ref 88**

HARMONY COUNTRY LODGE, is a comfortable peaceful retreat. Unusual octagonal design with superb views overlooking sea and National Park. TV and tea/coffee in all rooms. Guests lounge, conservatory and massage available. Licensed. Parking. Ideal for walking or motoring. 4 miles Scarborough. Personal service and warm welcome guaranteed.
B&B from £18.50pp, Dinner from £10, Rooms 1 single, 1 twin, 5 double, all en-suite, No smoking, Children over 7, Pets by arrangement, Open all year.
Sue & Tony Hewitt, **Harmony Country Lodge,** Limestone Road, Burniston, Scarborough, North Yorkshire YO13 0DG
Tel: 01723 870276　　　　　　　　　　　　　**Map Ref 89**

STATION HOUSE, a recently converted country railway station in large garden, retaining many features of times past. En-suite ground floor rooms with own entrances. TV and tea/coffee facilities. 1 mile from the sea and Moors. Idyllic walking area. Bicycle hire available. Tea room open until 6pm.
B&B from £20pp, Rooms 1 double/twin, 1 family, both en-suite, No smoking or pets, Children welcome, Open all year except Christmas & New Year.
Steve & Barbara Hargreaves, **Station House,** Station Lane, Cloughton, Scarborough, North Yorkshire YO13 0AD
Tel: 01723 870896　　　　　　　　　　　　　**Map Ref 90**

EAST AYTON LODGE COUNTRY HOTEL & RESTAURANT, a country hotel and restaurant in a beautiful 3 acre setting by the River Derwent, in the North York Moors National Park, only 3 miles from Scarborough.

B&B from £49, Dinner available, Rooms 17 double, 11 twin, 2 triple, 1 family, all en-suite, Children welcome, Open February - December.
East Ayton Lodge Country Hotel & Restaurant, Moor Lane, East Ayton, Scarborough, Yorkshire YO13 9EW
Tel: 01723 864227 Fax: 01723 862680　　　　　　　**Map Ref 91**

THE FOXHOLM, a peaceful, licensed, personally run country inn in quiet picturesque village. Ground floor en-suite rooms overlooking large private garden. Lounge with French doors. All bedrooms have tea/coffee facilities, radio alarms and colour TV. Ideal for moors, coast, dales and York. Car park.
B&B from £23.50pp, Dinner from £3.95, Rooms 2 twin, 2 double, all en-suite, Smoking, Children and pets welcome, Open all year.
Kay Clyde, **The Foxholm,** Ebberston, Scarborough, North Yorkshire YO13 9NJ
Tel: 01723 859550　　　　　　　　　　　　　**Map Ref 92**

THE GRESHAM HOTEL, a beautifully appointed, detached, licensed hotel in imposing position next to Peasholm Park. Ideal for North Cliff golf course. A warm welcome awaits.

B&B from £17, Dinner available, Rooms 6 single, 6 double, 1 twin, most en-suite, No smoking, Children over 1, Open March - October.
The Gresham Hotel, 18 Lowdale Avenue, Northstead, Scarborough, Yorkshire YO12 6JW
Tel: 01723 372117　　　　　　　　　　　　　**Map Ref 88**

BIDE-A-WHILE, a small guest house offering clean, comfortable accommodation in a homely atmosphere. Home cooking with fresh produce. Sea views from all rooms. On the edge of North York Moors and ideal for exploring the Dales.
B&B from £16.50, Dinner available, Rooms 1 double, 2 family, Children welcome, No pets, Open all year.
Bide-a-While, 3 Loring Road, Ravenscar, Scarborough, Yorkshire YO13 0LY
Tel: 01723 870643　　　　　　　　　　　　　**Map Ref 93**

CRAG HILL, magnificent coastal views. Golf and pony trekking available locally. TV in all rooms. Ideal for walking and touring.

B&B from £26, Dinner available, Rooms 3 double, 2 twin, 2 family, most en-suite, No smoking, Children welcome, No pets, Open all year.
Crag Hill, Ravenhall Road, Ravenscar, Scarborough, Yorkshire YO13 0NA
Tel: 01723 870925 **Map Ref 93**

OX PASTURE HALL, a grade II listed hotel set in 30 acres. Panoramic views. Ground floor spacious quality accommodation. Good food and resident proprietors.

B&B from £31.50, Dinner available, Rooms 1 single, 8 double, 5 twin, 2 triple, 1 family, all en-suite, No smoking, Children welcome, Open all year.
Ox Pasture Hall, Lady Ediths Drive, Throxenby, Scarborough, Yorkshire YO15 5TD
Tel: 01723 365295 Fax: 01723 355156 **Map Ref 93**

BEVERLEY HOTEL, in the pleasant, quiet residential district of Old Brumby off the A18, close to Scunthorpe town centre.

B&B from £38.50, Dinner available, Rooms 5 single, 3 double, 5 twin, 2 triple, all en-suite, No smoking, Children welcome, Open all year.
Beverley Hotel, 55 Old Brumby Street, Scunthorpe, Yorkshire DN16 2AJ
Tel: 01724 282212 Fax: 01724 270422 **Map Ref 94**

WORTLEY HOUSE HOTEL, a friendly, modern hotel, close to the town centre, but with easy access to M18, M1 and Humber Bridge. Ideal base for touring Humberside and Lincolnshire.

B&B from £47.50, Dinner available, Rooms 16 single, 17 double, 3 twin, 2 triple, all en-suite, No smoking, Children welcome, Open all year.
Wortley House Hotel, Rowland Road, Scunthorpe, Yorkshire DN16 1SU
Tel: 01724 842223 Fax: 01724 280646 **Map Ref 94**

BRIGGATE LODGE INN, close to junction 4 of the M180, within easy reach of Lincoln, Hull and York, a beautifully appointed hotel set in mature woodland, with 27 hole championship golf complex and floodlit driving range.

B&B from £56, Dinner available, Rooms 38 double, 48 twin, all en-suite, No smoking, Children welcome, Open all year.
Briggate Lodge Inn, Ermine Street, Broughton, Brigg, Scunthorpe, North Lincolnshire DN20 0AQ
Tel: 01652 650770 Fax: 01652 650495 **Map Ref 95**

HAZELDENE GUEST HOUSE, a large Victorian detached house on A19, convenient for York, Leeds and Hull. En-suite or standard rooms, recently refurbished.

B&B from £18, Rooms 3 single, 2 double, 3 twin, 1 family, most en-suite, No smoking, Children over 2, No pets, Open all year.
Hazeldene Guest House, 34 Brook Street, Selby, Yorkshire YO8 0AR
Tel: 01757 704809 Fax: 01757 709300 **Map Ref 96**

LOFTSOME BRIDGE COACHING HOUSE, nestling alongside the tranquil River Derwent, just 5 minutes from the M62 and a leisurely 20 minute drive from York. Dating back to 1782, this family run country house hotel boasts a hand carved Chippendale four poster bed.

B&B from £35, Dinner available, Rooms 10 double, 4 twin, 1 family, all en-suite, Children welcome, No pets, Open all year.
Loftsome Bridge Coaching House, Loftsome Bridge, Wressle, Selby, Yorkshire YO8 7EN
Tel: 01757 630070 Fax: 01757 630070 **Map Ref 97**

WHITEFRIARS COUNTRY GUEST HOUSE, a historic family run guest house, set in spacious gardens, in the heart of Settle. Ideal for exploring the Dales, Settle-Carlisle Railway.

B&B from £17.50, Dinner available, Rooms 1 single, 3 double, 3 twin, 1 triple, 1 family, most en-suite, No smoking, Children welcome, No pets, Open all year.
Whitefriars Country Guest House, Church Street, Settle, Yorkshire BD24 9JD
Tel: 01729 823753   **Map Ref 98**

....

FALCON MANOR HOTEL, a privately owned country house hotel, grade II listed, in the dales market town of Settle. Ideal for walking, motoring and the Settle to Carlisle Railway.

B&B from £52, Dinner available, Rooms 11 double, 5 twin, 3 triple, all en-suite, No smoking, Children welcome, Open all year.
Falcon Manor Hotel, Skipton Road, Settle, Yorkshire BD24 9BD
Tel: 01729 823814 Fax: 01729 822087   **Map Ref 98**

....

THE TRADDOCK, a well known Yorkshire gem. This Georgian country house hotel is situated in the walkers paradise of the Yorkshire Dales. Emphasis on comfort, good food and wines.

B&B from £40, Dinner available, Rooms 1 single, 4 double, 3 twin, 2 triple, 1 family, most en-suite, No smoking, Open all year.
The Traddock, Austwick, Settle, Yorkshire LA2 8BY
Tel: 015242 51224 Fax: 015242 51224   **Map Ref 99**

....

WOODVIEW GUEST HOUSE, one of the oldest farmhouses in Austwick, an elegant grade II listed building on The Green. All rooms en-suite. Packed lunch available.

B&B from £22.50, Dinner available, Rooms 2 double, 1 twin, 3 triple, all en-suite, No smoking, Children welcome, Open all year.

Woodview Guest House, The Green, Austwick, Settle, Yorkshire LA2 8BB
Tel: 015242 51268   **Map Ref 99**

....

ST PELLEGRINO, comfortable, family run hotel near university and city centre, yet you can still enjoy the spacious beauty of peaceful surroundings.

B&B from £20, Rooms 3 single, 2 double, 3 twin, 3 triple, all private or en-suite, No smoking, Children welcome, No pets, Open all year.

St Pellegrino, 2 Oak Park, off Manchester Road, Sheffield, Yorkshire S10 5DE
Tel: 0114 268 1953 & 266 0151   **Map Ref 100**

....

LINDRICK HOTEL, a family run hotel with parking at the front and rear, only minutes from the city centre.

B&B from £21, Dinner available, Rooms 16 single, 3 double, 2 twin, 2 triple, most en-suite, No smoking, Children welcome, Open all year.
Lindrick Hotel, 226-230 Chippinghouse Road, Sheffield, Yorkshire S7 1DR
Tel: 0114 258 5041 Fax: 0114 255 4758   **Map Ref 100**

....

IVORY HOUSE HOTEL, within easy reach of both the city centre and countryside. Personal service from the family management. TV and tea/coffee facilities in all rooms.

B&B from £18, Rooms 5 single, 1 twin, 1 triple, 1 family, some en-suite, Children welcome, No pets, Open all year.

Ivory House Hotel, 34 Wostenholm Road, Sheffield, Yorkshire S7 1LJ
Tel: 0114 255 1853 Fax: 0114 255 1578   **Map Ref 100**

PEACE GUEST HOUSE, established for 15 years. Close to Encliffe Park, university, hospitals and Peak District Route.

B&B from £15, Dinner available, Rooms 3 single, 1 double, 2 twin, 1 triple, some en-suite, No smoking, Children welcome, No pets, Open all year.
Peace Guest House, 92 Brocco Bank, Sheffield, Yorkshire S11 8RS
Tel: 0114 268 5110 & 267 0760   **Map Ref 100**

....

SWALLOW HOTEL, set in extensive landscaped grounds with its own leisure club, this hotel is ideal for the Peaks, Meadowhall and Chatsworth. Short break packages available.

B&B from £105, Dinner available, Rooms 25 single, 58 double, 35 twin, all en-suite, No smoking, Children welcome, Open all year.
Swallow Hotel, Kenwood Road, Sheffield, Yorkshire S7 1NQ
Tel: 0114 258 3811 Fax: 0114 255 4744   **Map Ref 100**

....

ETURIA HOUSE HOTEL, a family run hotel in elegant Victorian house, close to all amenities and city centre. Ideal base for Peak District.

B&B from £26, Rooms 5 single, 3 double, 2 twin, 1 triple, most en-suite, Children welcome, Open all year.
Eturia House Hotel, 91 Crookes Road, Broomhill, Sheffield, Yorkshire S10 5BD
Tel: 0114 266 2241 & 267 0853 Fax: 0114 267 0853   **Map Ref 100**

....

WHITLEY HALL HOTEL, an Elizabethan mansion with 30 acres of gardens, lakes and woodlands, only a few miles from the centres of Sheffield, Rotherham and Barnsley. Food a speciality with full a la carte and daily menus.Open to nonresidents.

B&B from £63, Dinner available, Rooms 2 single, 8 double, 7 twin, 1 family, all en-suite, Children welcome, Open all year.

Whitley Hall Hotel, Elliott Lane, Grenoside, Sheffield, Yorkshire S35 8NR
Tel: 0114 245 4444 Fax: 0114 245 5414   **Map Ref 101**

....

UNICORN HOTEL, centrally situated, with double glazing to ensure peace and tranquillity. Ideal base for touring Bronte country and the Yorkshire Dales. Recently refurbished to a high standard.

B&B from £32, Dinner available, Rooms 6 double, 2 twin, 1 family, all en-suite, Children welcome, No pets, Open all year.
Unicorn Hotel, Devonshire Place, Keighley Road, Skipton, Yorkshire BD23 2LP
Tel: 01756 794146 & 793376   **Map Ref 102**

....

HANOVER INTERNATIONAL HOTEL & CLUB SKIPTON, situated at the gateway to the dales. Individually designed rooms and suite, Waterside restaurant, conference facilities for up to 400 people. Leisure centre with indoor pool and squash courts.

B&B from £55, Dinner available, Rooms 26 double, 29 twin, 20 triple, all en-suite, No smoking, Children welcome, Open all year.
Hanover International Hotel & Club Skipton, Keighley Road, Skipton, Yorkshire BD23 2TA
Tel: 01756 700100 Fax: 01756 700107   **Map Ref 102**

....

DEVONSHIRE HOTEL, a family run, country market town hotel with an attractive garden and childrens play area. All bedrooms have TV. Resident proprietors. Real ale. An ideal base for touring the dales and Yorkshire countryside.

B&B from £20, Dinner available, Rooms 1 single, 7 double, 4 twin, 1 triple, 2 family, most en-suite, Children welcome, Open all year.

Devonshire Hotel, Newmarket Street, Skipton, Yorkshire BD23 2HR
Tel: 01756 793078 & 01756 426640 Fax: 01756 793078   **Map Ref 102**

DEVONSHIRE ARMS COUNTRY HOUSE HOTEL, a traditional country house hotel in Yorkshire Dales. Open fires, lounges furnished with antiques from Chatsworth. Leisure, health and beauty therapy club.

B&B from £115, Dinner available, Rooms 22 double, 19 twin, all en-suite, No smoking, Children welcome, Open all year.
Devonshire Arms Country House Hotel, Bolton Abbey, Skipton, Yorkshire BD23 6AJ
Tel: 01756 710441 Fax: 01756 710564   **Map Ref 103**

....

FELL HOTEL, stands in well tended gardens overlooking the River Wharfe with views of the surrounding fells and the village of Burnsall.

B&B from £33.50, Dinner available, Rooms 9 double, 1 twin, 3 triple, all en-suite, No smoking, Children welcome, Open all year.
Fell Hotel, Burnsall, Skipton, Yorkshire BD23 6BT
Tel: 01756 720209 Fax: 01756 720605   **Map Ref 28**

....

TEMPEST ARMS HOTEL & RESTAURANT, an 18th century stone built inn on A56 between Earby and Skipton. Surrounded by green fields and edged with a stream, giving character to this traditional Yorkshire pub.

B&B from £49.50, Dinner available, Rooms 6 double, 2 twin, 2 triple, all en-suite, Children welcome, No pets, Open all year.
Tempest Arms Hotel & Restaurant, Eslack, Skipton, Yorkshire BD23 3AY
Tel: 01282 842450 Fax: 01282 843331   **Map Ref 104**

....

TENANT ARM HOTEL, a 17th century coaching inn, family owned and run. 10 en-suite rooms with colour TV and tea/coffee making facilities. Pine panelled restaurant. Bar meals served every lunch and evening in the heart of Yorkshire Dales. Ideal for fishing and walking. ETB 3 Crown Commended.
B&B from £23.50pp, Dinner from £6.75, Rooms 3 twin, 5 double, 2 family, all en-suite, Smoking & children welcome, Pets by arrangement, Open all year except Christmas.
Norrie & Dilly Dean, **Tenant Arm Hotel,** Kilnsey, Skipton, North Yorkshire BD23 5DS
Tel: 01756 752301   **Map Ref 105**

....

MAYPOLE INN, a 17th century inn, with open fires, on the village green. Easy access to many attractive walks in the surrounding dales. 4 miles from Settle.

B&B from £26, Dinner available, Rooms 1 single, 2 double, 1 twin, 1 triple, 1 family, all en-suite, No smoking, Children welcome, No pets, Open all year.
Maypole Inn, Maypole Green, Main Street, Long Preston, Skipton, Yorkshire BD23 4PH
Tel: 01729 840219   **Map Ref 106**

....

BECK HALL GUEST HOUSE, a family run guest house set in a spacious riverside garden. Homely atmosphere, four poster beds, log fires and large car park.

B&B from £17, Dinner available, Rooms 11 double, 3 twin, most en-suite, Children welcome, Open all year.
Beck Hall Guest House, Malham, Skipton, Yorkshire BD23 4DJ
Tel: 01729 830332   **Map Ref 107**

....

PLOUGH INN, once an inn and working farm which was part of a large country estate, now converted to provide high standard accommodation in a rural setting.

B&B from £34, Dinner available, Rooms 7 double, 4 twin, 1 triple, all en-suite, No smoking, Children welcome, No pets, Open all year.
Plough Inn, Wigglesworth, Skipton, Yorkshire BD23 4RJ
Tel: 01729 840243 & 840638 Fax: 01729 840243   **Map Ref 108**

THE HOBBIT, a country hotel with panoramic views. Restaurant and bistro have reputation for good food at affordable prices. Friendly inn-type atmosphere.

B&B from £32, Dinner available, Rooms 2 single, 7 double, 9 twin, 3 triple, all en-suite, No smoking, Children welcome, No pets, Open all year.
The Hobbit, Hob Lane, Norland, Sowerby Bridge, Yorkshire HX6 3QL
Tel: 01422 832202 Fax: 01422 835381 **Map Ref 109**

....

GOLDEN FLEECE, situated in the market place within easy reach of the Yorkshire Dales and Moors, this old coaching inn has a friendly atmosphere and serves traditional ales and fine fare.

B&B from £47.50, Dinner available, Rooms 1 single, 14 double, 2 twin, 1 triple, all en-suite, Children welcome, Open all year.
Golden Fleece, Market Place, Thirsk, Yorkshire YO7 1LL
Tel: 01845 523108 Fax: 01845 523996 **Map Ref 110**

....

FURWAYS GUEST HOUSE, close to the town centre, 2 minutes walk from the surgery of famous vet and author, the late James Herriot. Centrally located for touring the North York Moors and Yorkshire Dales.

B&B from £16, Dinner available, Rooms 3 single, 3 double, 3 twin, 1 triple, most en-suite, No smoking, Children welcome, Open all year.

Furways Guest House, Town End, Thirsk, Yorkshire YO7 1PY
Tel: 01845 522601 **Map Ref 110**

....

OLD RED HOUSE, a two storey Georgian building, with a bar lounge and open fire.

B&B from £20, Dinner available, Rooms 1 single, 3 double, 1 twin, 1 triple, 4 family, all en-suite, Children welcome, Open all year.
Old Red House, Station Road, Carlton Miniott, Thirsk, Yorkshire YO7 4LT
Tel: 01845 524383 **Map Ref 111**

....

ANGEL INN, a well appointed, attractive village inn, renowned for good food and traditional ales. Ideal centre for touring York and Herriot country.

B&B from £39, Dinner available, Rooms 2 single, 8 double, 4 twin, 1 family, all en-suite, Children welcome, No pets, Open all year.

Angel Inn, Long Street, Topcliffe, Thirsk, Yorkshire YO7 3RW
Tel: 01845 577237 Fax: 01845 578000 **Map Ref 112**

....

PARKLANDS HOTEL, an elegant Victorian former vicarage overlooking 680 acres of beautiful parkland. Family run for over 28 years, providing a high standard of service and cuisine and well appointed en-suite bedrooms.

B&B from £32.50, Dinner available, Rooms 9 single, 2 double, 2 twin, most en-suite, No smoking, Children welcome, Open all year.
Parklands Hotel, 143 Horbury Road, Wakefield, Yorkshire WF2 8TY
Tel: 01924 377407 Fax: 01924 290348 **Map Ref 113**

....

CEDAR COURT HOTEL, international hotel, designed for ultimate customer satisfaction. Close to the M1 and M62 motorways, halfway between London and Scotland. Suitable for business people, conferences, private functions and holidaymakers.

B&B from £50, Dinner available, Rooms 126 double, 23 twin, 1 triple, all en-suite, No smoking, Children welcome, Open all year.

Cedar Court Hotel, Denby Dale Road, Calder Grove, Wakefield, Yorkshire WF4 3QZ
Tel: 01924 276310 & 261459 Fax: 01924 280221 **Map Ref 113**

MIDGLEY LODGE MOTEL, is a luxury purpose built motel. All rooms with en-suite satellite TV, tea/coffee facilities, clock radio, telephone and panoramic countryside view. Private car parking. English continental breakfast. Whitbread Brewers Fayre in same grounds. M1 junction 38 & junction 39 minutes away.
B&B from £38pp, Rooms 4 twin, 11 double, 10 family, all en-suite, Smoking & Children welcome, Pets by arrangement, Open all year.
Mr Emmingham, **Midgley Lodge Motel,** Barr Lane Midgley, Wakefield, West Yorkshire WF4 4JJ
Tel: 01924 830069 Fax: 01924 830087   **Map Ref 113**

DIMPLE WELL LODGE HOTEL, a family run, Georgian house hotel in own picturesque gardens, offering charm and character. Close to M1 and M62.

B&B from £43, Dinner available, Rooms 5 single, 5 double, 1 twin, all en-suite, No smoking, Children over 10, No pets, Open all year.

Dimple Well Lodge Hotel, The Green, Ossett, Wakefield, Yorkshire WF5 8JX
Tel: 01924 264352 Fax: 01924 274024   **Map Ref 114**

WATERTON PARK HOTEL, a Georgian mansion, situated on an island and surrounded by a 26 acre lake. Well equipped bedrooms, restaurant, swimming pool, steam room, sauna, solarium, fly fishing, fitness room, coffee shop and 18 hole golf.

B&B from £60, Dinner available, Rooms 3 single, 31 double, 8 twin, all en-suite, No smoking, Children welcome, No pets, Open all year.

Waterton Park Hotel, Walton Hall, Walton, Wakefield, Yorkshire WF2 6PW
Tel: 01924 257911 Fax: 01924 240082   **Map Ref 115**

PROSPECT HOUSE, established 35 years. En-suite rooms available. Near York, Harrogate, Dales and Herriot country. Midway London to Edinburgh. Restaurant s nearby. Pets welcome.

B&B from £ Rooms 1 single 3 double, 2 twin, most en-suite, Children welcome, Open all year.

Prospect House, 8 Caxton Street, Wetherby, Yorkshire LS22 6RU
Tel: 01937 582428   **Map Ref 116**

JARVIS WETHERBY HOTEL, an oasis amid the Yorkshire Dales. Just off A1 hub for York, Leeds and Harrogate. Modern hotel, run with Jarvis flair and Italian charm.

B&B from £ 39, Dinner available, Rooms 17 double, 53 twin, 2 triple, all en-suite, No smoking, Children welcome, Open all year.

Jarvis Wetherby Hotel, Leeds Road, Wetherby, Yorkshire LS22 5HE
Tel: 01937 583881 Fax: 01937 580062   **Map Ref 116**

ROSSLYN HOUSE, is a spacious Victorian built home, still retaining many original features. Situated on the West Cliff of Whitby, close to all amenities. Clean and recently decorated bedrooms. Furnished to modern standards including colour TV's and hospitality trays. All meals are generous and freshly cooked.
B&B from £14.95pp, Dinner £8, Rooms 1 single, 1 twin, 4 double, 2 family, some en-suite, Children welcome, Pets by arrangement, Open all year except Christmas.
Alan & Julie Briers, **Rosslyn House,** 11 Abbey Terrace, Whitby, North Yorkshire YO21 3HQ
Tel: 01947 604086   **Map Ref 117**

SEACLIFFE HOTEL, a family hotel overlooking sea. All rooms en-suite with colour TV and tea/coffee facilities. Licensed a la Carte restaurant specialising in fresh seafood steaks and vegetarian dishes with excellent wine list. Residents lounge, and parking for 8 cars. Visit North York Moors, National Park, Whitby Abbey and local golf course's.
B&B from £59pp, Dinner from £16, Rooms 1 single, 2 twin, 15 double, 2 family, all en-suite, Restricted smoking, Children welcome, Pets by arrangement, Open all year.
Julie Wilson, **Seacliffe Hotel,** 12 North Prom, West Cliff, Whitby, Yorkshire YO21 3JX
Tel: 01947 603139 Fax: 01947 603139 Freephone 0500 202229   **Map Ref 117**

....

GLENDALE GUEST HOUSE, a family run Victorian guest house. Clean and comfortable with a pleasant atmosphere. Emphasis on food.

B&B from £17, Dinner available, Rooms 1 single, 5 double, most en-suite, Children welcome, Open March - November.

Glendale Guest House, 16 Crescent Avenue, Whitby, Yorkshire YO21 3ED
Tel: 01947 604242   **Map Ref 117**

....

SAXONVILLE HOTEL, a family owned hotel, in operation since 1946, proud of its cuisine and friendly atmosphere.

B&B from £35, Dinner available, Rooms 3 single, 10 double, 9 twin, 2 triple, all en-suite, Children welcome, No pets, Open April - October.
Saxonville Hotel, Ladysmith Avenue, Whitby, Yorkshire YO21 3HX
Tel: 01947 602631 Fax: 01947 820523 Freephone: 0500 334454 Email: saxonville@onyxnet.co.uk   **Map Ref 117**

....

LARPOOL HALL COUNTRY HOTEL & RESTAURANT, a Georgian mansion set in 14 acres overlooking Esk Valley, offering peace and tranquillity. One mile form town centre.

B&B from £45, Dinner available, Rooms 3 single, 10 double, 3 twin, 1 triple, all en-suite, No smoking, Children welcome, No pets, Open all year.

Larpool Hall Country Hotel & Restaurant, Larpool Lane, Whitby, Yorkshire YO22 4ND
Tel: 01947 602737 Fax: 01947 820204   **Map Ref 117**

....

MOORLANDS HOTEL, a family run hotel/freehouse offering home cooking and a well stocked bar. In the national park with magnificent views of the Esk Valley and the North York Moors. Ideal for walking and touring.

B&B from £23, Dinner available, Rooms 2 single, 2 double, 3 twin, 1 triple, most en-suite, No smoking, Children welcome, Open all year.

Moorlands Hotel, Castleton, Whitby, Yorkshire YO21 2DB
Tel: 01287 660206 Fax: 01287 660317   **Map Ref 117**

....

FLASK INN, has six en-suite rooms, all with colour TV, tea/coffee making facilities and central heating. Meals are available seven days a week, lunch and evening meals can be enjoyed in the main bar. Ideal for Whitby, Robin Hood's Bay and Scarborough.

B&B from £??pp, Dinner available, Rooms ?twin, ?double, ?family, Restricted smoking, Children welcome, Open all year.

Flask Inn, Robin Hood's Bay, Fylingdales, Whitby, Yorkshire YO22 4QH
Tel: 01947 880305 Fax: 01947 880592   **Map Ref 118**

WHITFIELD HOUSE HOTEL, a 17th century farmhouse proving modern comforts amidst old world charm. Peaceful location. Cottage style en-suite bedrooms with every amenity.

B&B from £26, Dinner available, Rooms 1 single, 6 double, 2 triple, all en-suite, No smoking, Children over 5, Open all year.

Whitfield House Hotel, Darnholm, Goathland, Whitby, Yorkshire YO22 5LA
Tel: 01947 896215 & 896214   **Map Ref 119**

FAIRHAVEN COUNTRY HOTEL, a comfortable hotel with old fashioned comforts, welcoming log fires and good dining facilities. An ideal centre for walking the North York Moors. Heartbeat country.

B&B from £50, Dinner available, Rooms 4 single, 12 double, 7 twin, all en-suite or private facilities, No smoking, Children welcome, Open all year.

Fairhaven Country Hotel, The Common, Goathland, Whitby, Yorkshire YO22 5AN
Tel: 01947 896486 & 896206 Fax: 01947 896327   **Map Ref 119**

STAKESBY MANOR, a Georgian house dating back to 1710,in its own grounds, on the outskirts of Whitby in the North York Moors National Park. Facing south with views of the moors.

B&B from £38, Dinner available, Rooms 8 double, 2 twin, all en-suite, No smoking, Children welcome, No pets,Open all year.

Stakesby Manor, Manor Close, High Stakesby, Whitby, Yorkshire YO21 1HL
Tel: 01947 602773 & 602140 Fax: 01947 602773   **Map Ref 117**

BARBICAN HOTEL, a charming 19th century house. Less than ten minutes walk to centre. Vegetarian or traditional English breakfast in dining room with superb Victorian range. All bedrooms en-suite/private with TV, tea/coffee, hair dryer, telephone etc. Comfy guest lounge. Private floodlit car park. Email: barbican@thenet.co.uk
B&B from £24pp, Rooms 1 single, 1 twin, 3 double, 1 family, all en-suite or private, No smoking or pets, Children welcome, Open all year.

Elsie & Len Osterman, **Barbican Hotel,** 20 Barbican Rd, York YO1 5AA
Tel: 01904 627617 Fax: 01904 647140   **Map Ref 120**

EASTONS, is centrally situated 300 yards from city wall. William Morris style, rich decor, with period furniture and original paintings. Fully equipped en-suite bedrooms. Victorian sideboard breakfast menu, including vegetarian. Yorkshire Tourist Board B&B of the Year Winner 1996. Private car park. ETB Highly Commended. RAC Highly Acclaimed.
B&B from £22pp, Rooms 2 twin, 7 double, 2 family, all en-suite, No smoking, Children over 5, No pets, Open all year.
L M Keir, **Eastons,** 90 Bishopthorpe Road, York YO23 1JS
Tel: 01904 626646   **Map Ref 120**

COTTAGE HOTEL, enchanting family run hotel within 10 minutes waking distance of the city centre, overlooking the beautiful Clifton Green.

B&B from £29.50, Dinner available, Rooms 2 single, 9 double, 5 twin, 3 triple, all en-suite, Children welcome, Open all year.

Cottage Hotel, 1 Clifton Green, York YO3 6LH
Tel: 01904 643711 Fax: 01904 611230   **Map Ref 120**

BEDFORD HOTEL, a family run hotel, a short walk along historic Bootham to the famous York Minster and city centre. Evening meals available.

B&B from £23pp, Dinner available, Rooms 4 single, 6 double, 2 twin, 3 triple, 1 family, all en-suite, Children welcome, No pets, Open all year.
Bedford Hotel, 108-110 Bootham, York YO3 07DG
Tel: 01904 624412 Fax: 01904 632851 **Map Ref 120**

TYBURN HOUSE, a family owned and run guest house overlooking the racecourse. In a quiet and beautiful area, close to city centre and railway station.

B&B from £25, Rooms 2 single, 3 double, 3 twin, 3 triple, 2 family, most en-suite, Children welcome, Open February - October.
Tyburn House, 11 Albemarle Road, York YO2 1EN
Tel: 01904 655069 **Map Ref 120**

CORNMILL LODGE, a well appointed guesthouse only 12 minutes walk from York Minster. Most rooms en-suite. No smoking indoors. Car park. Friendly welcome.

B&B from £17, Dinner available, Rooms 1 single, 2 double, 2 twin, most en-suite, No smoking, Children over 4, No pets, Open February - November.
Cornmill Lodge, 120 Haxby Road, York YO3 7JP
Tel: 01904 620566 **Map Ref 120**

ST PAUL'S HOTEL, close to York's many attractions, this small, family run hotel has a warm atmosphere and serves a hearty breakfast. Come as a guest and leave as a friend.

B&B from £25, Dinner available, Rooms 1 single, 1 double, 1 twin, 1 triple, 2 family, all en-suite, No smoking, Children welcome, Open all year.
St Paul's Hotel, 120 Holgate Road, York YO2 4BB
Tel: 01904 611514 **Map Ref 120**

AMBASSADOR, a listed building in 2 acres of garden on York's main approach road from the south and west. Only 5 minutes from the railway station, city centre and racecourse. Lift to most bedrooms.

B&B from £102, Dinner available, Rooms 17 double, 8 twin, all en-suite, No smoking, Children welcome, Open all year.
Ambassador, 123-125 The Mount, York YO2 2DA
Tel: 01904 641316 Fax: 01904 40259 **Map Ref 120**

GREENSIDE,, owner run guesthouse, fronting Clifton Green, ideally situated for all York's attractions. Offers many facilities and a homely atmosphere.

B&B from £16, Dinner available, Rooms 1 single, 3 double, 2 twin, 2 triple, most en-suite, No smoking, Children welcome, Open all year.
Greenside,, 124 Clifton, York YO3 6BQ
Tel: 01904 623631 **Map Ref 120**

PRIORY HOTEL, a family hotel in a residential area with adjacent riverside walk to the city centre.

B&B from £32.50, Dinner available, Rooms 1 single, 9 double, 3 twin, 2 triple, 3 family, all en-suite, Children welcome, Open all year.

Priory Hotel, 126-128 Fulford Road, York YO1 4BE
Tel: 01904 625280 Fax: 01904 625280 **Map Ref 120**

BLOOMSBURY HOTEL, an elegantly appointed large Victorian town house, centrally situated, with large private car park. Recently totally refurbished. Completely non smoking.

B&B from £35, Rooms 2 single, 3 double, 3 twin, 2 triple, all en-suite, No smoking, Children welcome, No pets, Open all year.
Bloomsbury Hotel, 127 Clifton, York YO3 6BL
Tel: 01904 634031   **Map Ref 120**

KILIMA HOTEL, a lovingly refurbished 19th century rectory with a fine restaurant serving a la carte and table d' hote. Walking distance to city centre. Private car park.

B&B from £50, Dinner available, Rooms 4 single, 7 double, 3 twin, 1 family, all en-suite, No smoking, Children welcome, Open all year.
Kilima Hotel, 129 Holgate Road, York YO2 4DE
Tel: 01904 625787 Fax: 01904 612083   **Map Ref 120**

CARLTON HOUSE HOTEL, a Georgian terraced home, family run for 50 years. Just outside city walls, close to all attractions and amenities.

B&B from £27, Rooms 1 single, 6 double, 1 twin, 4 triple, 1 family, most en-suite, Children welcome, No pets, Open all year.
Carlton House Hotel, 134 The Mount, York YO2 2AS
Tel: 01904 622265 Fax: 01904 637157   **Map Ref 120**

KEYS HOUSE, a comfortable Edwardian house providing spacious bedrooms with showers and WCs. Own key provided.

B&B from £24, Dinner available, Rooms 2 double, 3 triple, all en-suite, Children welcome, Open all year.
Keys House, 137 Fulford Road, York YO1 4HG
Tel: 01904 658488   **Map Ref 120**

ASHBOURNE HOUSE, a comfortable Victorian family owned and run licensed private hotel. Car parking provided on main route into York from the south and within walking distance of the city centre. All rooms en-suite excepting family room which has private facilities, tea/coffee facilities, telephone in rooms. Email: ashbourne@aol.com
B&B from £20-£30pp, Dinner from £17.50, Rooms 2 twin, 3 double, 1 family, all en-suite/private bathroom, No smoking or pets, Children welcome, Open all year except Christmas & New Year.
Aileen & David Minns, **Ashbourne House,** 139 Fulford Rd, York YO1 4HG
Tel: 01904 639912 Fax: 01904 631332   **Map Ref 120**

HOLLIES, a comfortable family run guest house, close to university and golf course and with easy access to city centre. Tea/coffee facilities, colour TV in all rooms, some en-suite. Car parking.

B&B from £16, Dinner available, Rooms 2 double, 2 triple, 1 family, some en-suite, No smoking, Children over 3, Open all year.
Hollies, 141 Fulford Road, York YO1 4HG
Tel: 01904 634279   **Map Ref 120**

MIDWAY HOUSE HOTEL, a non smoking family run hotel. Spacious en-suite bedrooms with four poster and ground floor rooms available. Close to city centre and university. Private parking.

B&B from £27, Dinner available, Rooms 8 double, 2 twin, 2 triple, most en-suite, No smoking, Children welcome, Open all year.
Midway House Hotel, 145 Fulford Road, York YO1 4HG
Tel: 01904 659272 Fax: 01904 659272   **Map Ref 120**

NEWINGTON HOTEL, in a fine Georgian terrace, next to York's famous racecourse and within walking distance of city centre. Car park, indoor swimming pool and sauna.

B&B from £30, Dinner available, Rooms 4 single, 21 double, 11 twin, 7 triple, all en-suite, No smoking, Children welcome, Open all year.

Newington Hotel, 147-157 Mount Vale, York YO2 2DJ
Tel: 01904 6625173 & 623090 Fax: 01904 679937   **Map Ref 120**

....

TOWER GUEST HOUSE, a comfortable and spacious 19th century guest house with friendly and informative hosts.Strolling distance from York Minster and city centre attractions.

B&B from £18, Dinner available, Rooms 1 single, 3 double, 1 twin, 1 triple, all en-suite, No smoking, Children welcome, No pets, Open all year.
Tower Guest House, 2 Feversham Crescent, York YO3 7HQ
Tel: 01904 655571 & 635924   **Map Ref 120**

....

ROMLEY GUEST HOUSE, a comfortable, friendly, family run guest house offering a licensed bar and a variety of other facilities. 10 minutes from city centre.

B&B from £14, Rooms 3 single, 1 double, 1 twin, 1 triple, 1 family, Children welcome, No pets, Open all year.

Romley Guest House, 2 Millfield Road, York YO2 1NQ
Tel: 01904 652822   **Map Ref 120**

....

HOLLY LODGE, beautifully appointed Georgian Grade II Listed building. Quiet en-suite room's overlooking garden or terrace. On site parking. A pleasant 10 minutes Riverside stroll to the city. Conveniently situated for all York's attractions. An ideal venue for a stay where you are assured of a warm welcome. Booking recommended. AA QQQ. ETB Commended. RAC Acclaimed.
B&B from £24pp, Rooms 1 twin, 3 double, 1 family, all en-suite, Restricted smoking, Children welcome, No pets, Open all year.
Mr & Mrs Gallagher, **Holly Lodge,** 204-206 Fulford Rd, York YO1 4DD
Tel: 01904 646005   **Map Ref 120**

....

CROSSWAYS GUEST HOUSE, ten minutes walk from city centre. En-suite rooms with colour TV. Garden. Warm welcome and hearty breakfast.

B&B from £20, Dinner available, Rooms 4 double, 1 twin, all en-suite, Children welcome, No pets, Open all year.

Crossways Guest House, 23 Wigginton Road, York YO3 7HJ
Tel: 01904 637250   **Map Ref 120**

....

Situated in the Centre of York, only 400 yards from York Minster in an extremely quiet location, with private car park and comfortable en-suite bedrooms, **THE HAZELWOOD** offers excellent value for money. Quality breakfasts, catering for all tastes including vegetarian. Non smoking. ETB 2 Crowns Commended.
B&B from £24pp, Rooms 1 single, 4 twin, 6 double, 2 family, all en-suite, No smoking or pets, Children over 6, Open all year.
Ian & Carolyn McNabb, **The Hazelwood,** 24-25 Portland Street, York YO3 7EH
Tel: 01904 626548 Fax: 01904 628032   **Map Ref 120**

GLENEAGLES LODGE GUEST HOUSE, in a cul-de-sac close to the station, city centre and museums. Within easy walking distance of the racecourse.

B&B from £25, Rooms 2 double, 1 twin, 2 family, most en-suite, No smoking, Children welcome, Open all year.
Gleneagles Lodge Guest House, 27 Nunthorpe Avenue, York YO2 1PF
Tel: 01904 637000 Fax: 01904 637000   **Map Ref 120**

....

ASHCROFT HOTEL, a Victorian former mansion in 2 acres of wooded grounds overlooking the River Ouse, only 1 mile from the city centre. All bedrooms are en-suite and have colour TV, radio, telephone, tea/coffee making facilities, hair dryer and trouser press.

B&B from £40, Dinner available, Rooms 1 single, 7 double, 4 twin, 1 triple, 2 family, all en-suite, Children over 5, Open all year.
Ashcroft Hotel, 294 Bishopthorpe Road, York YO2 1LH
Tel: 01904 659286 & 629543 Fax: 01904 640107   **Map Ref 120**

....

HEDLEY HOUSE, a family run hotel close to the city centre. 1 ground floor bedroom. All rooms en-suite. Home cooking, special diets catered for.

B&B from £20, Dinner available, Rooms 2 single, 5 double, 5 twin, 2 triple, 1 family, all en-suite, Children welcome, No pets, Open all year.
Hedley House, 3-4 Bootham Terrace, York YO3 7DH
Tel: 01904 637404   **Map Ref 120**

....

WARRENS GUEST HOUSE, centrally situated guest house. All rooms en-suite with colour TV and tea/coffee making facilities. Full English breakfast. Four poster beds available, also some ground floor bedrooms. Private car park with CCTV.

B&B from £20, Rooms 1 single, 1 double, 2 twin, 1 triple, 1 family, all private or en-suite, No smoking, Children welcome, No pets, Open March - November.
Warrens Guest House, 30 Scarcroft Road, York YO2 1NF
Tel: 01904 643139   **Map Ref 120**

....

KNAVESMIRE MANOR HOTEL, once a Rowntree family home, overlooking York Racecourse whilst close to the city centre.Award winning Brasserie restaurant. Walled gardens and car park. Private tropical pool and spa.

B&B from £34.50, Dinner available, Rooms 3 single, 9 double, 5 twin, 3 triple, 1 family, all en-suite, Children welcome, Open all year.
Knavesmire Manor Hotel, 302 Tadcaster Road, York YO2 2HE
Tel: 01904 702941 Fax: 01904 709274   **Map Ref 120**

....

CAVALIER PRIVATE HOTEL, a small family run hotel close tot he city centre, only yards from the ancient Bar Walls and many of York's famous historic landmarks.

B&B from £23, Rooms 2 single, 4 double, 2 triple, 2 family, most en-suite, Children welcome, No pets, Open all year.
Cavalier Private Hotel, 39 Monkgate, York YO3 7PB
Tel: 01904 636615 Fax: 01904 636615   **Map Ref 120**

....

BOWEN HOUSE, within a short walk of York Minster and city centre, this late Victorian, family run guest house combines high quality facilities with old style charm. Private car park. Traditional or vegetarian breakfasts.

B&B from £20, Rooms 1 single, 2 double, 1 twin, 1 family, most en-suite, No smoking, Children welcome, Open all year.
Bowen House, 4 Gladstone Street, Huntington Road, York YO3 7RF
Tel: 01904 636881 Fax: 01904 636881   **Map Ref 120**

BOOTHAM BAR HOTEL, hotel garden is bordered by the city walls, 150 yards from York Minster. Excellent full English breakfasts. Luggage lift. Parking available on request.

B&B from £20, Rooms 3 single, 7 double, 1 twin, 2 triple, 1 family, most en-suite, No smoking, Children over 2, No pets, Open all year.
Bootham Bar Hotel, 4 High Petergate, York YO1 2EH
Tel: 01904 658516   **Map Ref 120**

....

WINSTON HOUSE, close to racecourse and 10 minutes walk to city centre and railway station. Character en-suite room with all facilities. Private car park.

B&B from £30, Rooms 1 double en-suite, Children welcome, No pets, Open all year.
Winston House, 4 Nunthorpe Drive, York YO2 1DY
Tel: 01904 653171   **Map Ref 120**

....

GRANBY LODGE HOTEL, a Victorian family hotel offering all modern comforts and a mezzanine bar lounge.Most room en-suite. Car park.

B&B from £18, Dinner available, Rooms 8 single, 20 double, 23 twin, 3 family, most en-suite, Children welcome, Open all year.
Granby Lodge Hotel, 41-43 Scarcroft Road, York YO2 1DA
Tel: 01904 653291 Fax: 01904 653291   **Map Ref 120**

....

PAPILLON HOTEL, a small, friendly city centre guest house with personal attention at all times. 300 yards from York Minster. En-suite available. Car parking.

B&B from £20, Rooms 2 single, 1 double, 2 twin, 3 triple, most en-suite, No smoking, Children welcome, Open all year.
Papillon Hotel, 43 Gillygate, York YO3 7EA
Tel: 01904 636505   **Map Ref 120**

....

GRANGE LODGE, we are a family run Guest House close to city centre. All room have colour TV, tea/coffee making facilities. Special low off season rates. Easy parking.

B&B from £17-£22pp, Dinner from £9, Rooms, 1 single, 1 twin, 3 double, 2 family, some en-suite, Restricted smoking, Children welcome, Pets by arrangement, Open all year.

Jenny Robinson, **Grange Lodge,** 52 Bootham Road, York YO3 7AH
Tel: 01904 621137   **Map Ref 120**

....

GALTRES LODGE HOTEL, a Georgian brick building of character, with views of the rose window of York Minster from some rooms.

B&B from £20, Dinner available, Rooms 3 single, 5 double, 3 twin, 1 triple, most en-suite, No smoking, Children welcome, Open all year.
Galtres Lodge Hotel, 54 Low Petergate, York YO1 2HZ
Tel: 01904 622478 Fax: 01904 627804   **Map Ref 120**

....

BOOTHAM GUEST HOUSE, a family run guest house in a quiet crescent off the main thoroughfare. Only a few minutes walk from the city centre and Minster.

B&B from £18, Rooms 2 single, 3 double, 1 twin, 1 triple, most en-suite, Children welcome, No pets, Open all year.
Bootham Guest House, 56 Bootham Crescent, York YO3 7AH
Tel: 01904 672123   **Map Ref 120**

LINDEN LODGE, a Victorian town house in a quiet cul-de-sac, 10 minutes walk from racecourse, rail station and city centre. easy access A64.

B&B from £20, Rooms 2 single, 7 double, 2 twin, 2 family, most en-suite, No smoking, Children welcome, No pets, Open all year.
Linden Lodge, 6 Nunthorpe Avenue, York YO2 1PF
Tel: 01904 620107 Fax: 01904 620985   **Map Ref 120**

....

ST. GEORGES HOTEL, is a family run Victorian house in a select area of York. Close to Racecourse. Private enclosed parking. Ten minutes walk to City Walls. Tastefully furnished en-suite rooms with colour TV, tea/coffee tray. Easily reached from A64, A59 and convenient for visits to Scarborough, Bridlington and North York Moors.

B&B from £22.50pp, Dinner from £6.50, Rooms 5 double, 5 family, all en-suite, Children & Pets welcome, Open all year.
Mr Livingstone, **St. Georges Hotel,** 6 St Georges Place, York YO2 2DR
Tel: 01904 625056 Fax: 01904 625009   **Map Ref 120**

....

AVONDALE, a small, friendly guest house, close to city centre. All rooms en-suite with TV and tea/coffee facilities. Non smoking.

B&B from £30, Rooms 3 double, 1 twin, 1 triple, all en-suite, No smoking, Children welcome, No pets, Open all year.
Avondale, 61 Bishopthorpe Road, York YO2 1NX
Tel: 01904 633989   **Map Ref 120**

....

HAZELMERE GUEST HOUSE, Georgian cottages, tastefully linked to retain their original character. Very close to York Minster and to several restaurants. Established for over 30 years. All rooms on first floor level. Private parking.

B&B from £14, Rooms 2 single, 2 double, 2 twin, 2 triple, some en-suite, No smoking, Children welcome, No pets, Open all year.
Hazelmere Guest House, 65 Monkgate, York YO3 7PA
Tel: 01904 655947 Fax: 01904 626142   **Map Ref 120**

....

CITY GUEST HOUSE, a small, friendly, family run B&B in attractive Victorian town house. Ideally situated 5 minutes walk to York Minster and close to attractions. Private parking. Cosy en-suite rooms.

B&B from £16, Rooms 1 single, 4 double, 1 twin, 1 family, most en-suite, No smoking, Children welcome, No pets, Open all year.
City Guest House, 68 Monkgate, York YO3 7PF
Tel: 01904 622483   **Map Ref 120**

....

FOURPOSTER LODGE HOTEL, a Victorian villa, lovingly restored and furnished for your comfort. Just 10 minutes walk from historic York with all its fascinations.

B&B from £20, Dinner available, Rooms 8 double, 1 twin, 1 triple, most en-suite, No smoking, Children welcome, Open all year.
Fourposter Lodge Hotel, 68-70 Heslington Road, Barbican Road, York YO1 5AU
Tel: 01904 651170 & 0802 383991   **Map Ref 120**

....

HEWORTH COURT HOTEL, a privately owned, family run hotel close to York Minster and surrounding countryside. Special short breaks. Bar, restaurant, car park and lounge.

B&B from £44, Dinner available, Rooms 5 single, 14 double, 4 triple, 2 family, all en-suite, No smoking, Children welcome, No pets, Open all year.
Heworth Court Hotel, 76-78 Heworth Green, York YO3 7TQ
Tel: 01904 425156 Fax: 01904 415290   **Map Ref 120**

JARVIS ABBEY PARK, explore York from its centrally located yet quiet hotel. Friendly service with a full bar and English restaurant. All rooms en-suite and most refurbished in 1997.

B&B from £44.50, Dinner available, Rooms 9 single, 28 double, 34 twin, 8 triple, 6 family, all en-suite, No smoking, Children welcome, Open all year.
Jarvis Abbey Park, 77 The Mount, York YO2 2BN
Tel: 01904 658301 Fax: 01904 621224 **Map Ref 120**

A warm welcome awaits you at **ASCOT HOUSE**, an attractive Victorian villa 15 minutes walk from York city centre. En-suite rooms, some with canopy/four-poster beds and a residents lounge for you to relax in. We are licensed and have an enclosed car park.

B&B from £19-£24pp, Rooms 1 single, 3 twin, 8 double, 3 family, most en-suite, Restricted smoking, Children & pets welcome, Open all year except Christmas.

Mr & Mrs Wood, **Ascot House,** 80 East Parade, York YO31 7YH
Tel: 01904 426826 Fax: 01904 431077 **Map Ref 120**

CAROUSEL GUEST HOUSE, a warm, friendly, licensed guest house in central location. All rooms en-suite with tea/coffee making facilities and colour TV. Parking.

B&B from £16.50, Dinner available, Rooms 2 single, 4 double, 1 twin, 1 triple, 1 family, all en-suite, Children welcome, No pets, Open all year.
Carousel Guest House, 83 Eldon Street, off Stanley Street, York YO3 7NH
Tel: 01904 646709 **Map Ref 120**

NUNMILL HOUSE, a splendid Victorian house lovingly restored to enhance all original features. Each bedroom, some with four poster beds, is individually furnished and ideal for those looking for comfortable yet affordable en-suite accommodation. Easy walk to all attractions. ETB 2 Crown Highly Commended. SAE for colour brochure.
B&B from £24-£28pp, Rooms 1 twin, 6 double, 1 family, all en-suite/private bathroom, No smoking, Children welcome, No pets, Open February - November.
Russell Whitbourn-Hammond, **Nunmill House,** 85 Bishopthorpe Road, York YO23 1NX
Tel: 01904 634047 Fax: 01904 655879 **Map Ref 120**

CHELMSFORD PLACE GUEST HOUSE, a small, friendly guest house offering comfortable en-suite accommodation, at a moderate price. Ten minutes walk from York centre.

B&B from £17, Rooms 3 double, 1 twin, 1 triple, 1 family, most en-suite, Children welcome, No pets, Open all year.

Chelmsford Place Guest House, 85 Fulford Road, York YO1 4BD
Tel: 01904 624491 Fax: 01904 674491 **Map Ref 120**

JUDGES LODGING, a Georgian town house of exceptional historic importance, set in the centre of this ancient city. Lavishly decorated and furnished. Private parking.

B&B from £50, Dinner available, Rooms 2 single, 6 double, 4 twin, 2 triple, all en-suite, No smoking, Children over 10, No pets, Open all year.

Judges Lodging, 9 Lendal, York YO1 2AQ
Tel: 01904 623587 & 638733 Fax: 01904 679947 **Map Ref 120**

David & Joyce offers a warm welcome to their delightful Victorian town house just ten minutes walk to city centre. At **BAY TREE GUEST HOUSE** all rooms are decorated to a high standard and include tea/coffee facilities. ETB Two Crown Commended. On street parking with free permit supplied.

B&B from £17pp, Rooms 2 single, 2 twin, 2 double, 1 family, some en-suite, No smoking, Children & pets welcome, Open all year except Christmas & New Year.
David & Joyce Ridley, **Bay Tree Guest House,** 92 Bishopthorne Road, York YO2 1JS
Tel: 01904 659462 Fax: 01904 659462   **Map Ref 120**

THE MOHAIR FARM, a secluded farmhouse set back from the main road, surrounded by conifers. Rooms have TV, radio alarms, private bathrooms and tea/coffee facilities. Easy access to York park and ride. Coast and Moors within easy reach. The farm produces mohair from a flock of Augoras.

B&B from £15pp, Rooms 1 twin, 1 double, 1 family, all en-suite, Smoking, children & pets welcome, Open all year.
Lesley Scott, **The Mohair Farm,** Barmby Moor, York YO4 5HU
Tel: 01759 38308 Fax: 01759 388119   **Map Ref 121**

INGLEWOOD GUEST HOUSE, relax and make yourself at home in this delightful Guest House, renowned for its warmth and friendly atmosphere. All the comfortable bedrooms have TV and some have en-suite facilities. Pleasant dining room. Parking. Open all year for Bed & Breakfast - details on request.

B&B from £17.50pp, Rooms 1 single, 2 twin, 6 double, 2 family, most en-suite, Children welcome, No pets, Open all year.
Mr & Mrs Tree, **Inglewood Guest House,** Clifton Green, York YO3 6LH
Tel: 01904 653523   **Map Ref 120**

GRANGE HOTEL, a classical Regency town house hotel with all bedrooms individually decorated with antiques and English chintz. Within easy walking distance of York Minister.

B&B from £78, Dinner available, Rooms 3 single, 9 double, 17 twin, 1 triple, all en-suite, Children welcome, Open all year.
Grange Hotel, Clifton, York YO3 6AA
Tel: 01904 644744 Fax: 01904 612453   **Map Ref 120**

DEAN COURT HOTEL, an elegant Victorian hotel, superbly situated next to York Minster in the centre of the city. Tearooms, restaurant, bar and conference facilities. Secure car park with free valet service.

B&B from £69.50, Dinner available, Rooms 10 single, 19 double, 8 twin, 1 triple, 2 family, all en-suite, No smoking, Children welcome, No pets, Open all year.
Dean Court Hotel, Duncombe Place, York YO1 2EF
Tel: 01904 625082 Fax: 01904 620305   **Map Ref 120**

BLUE BRIDGE HOTEL, a friendly, private hotel with a relaxed atmosphere and a warm welcome, Short riverside walk to city. Private car park.

B&B from £35, Rooms 2 single, 6 double, 3 twin, 5 triple, most en-suite, No smoking, Children welcome, Open all year.
Blue Bridge Hotel, Fishergate, York YO1 4AP
Tel: 01904 621193 Fax: 01904 671571   **Map Ref 120**

CLARENCE GARDENS HOTEL, comfortable accommodation with emphasis on service. 10 minutes walk to the city centre and York Minster. Large private car park.
B&B from £20, Dinner available, Rooms 1 single, 4 double, 8 twin, 1 triple, 4 family, all en-suite, Children welcome, No pets, Open all year.
Clarence Gardens Hotel, Haxby Road, York YO3 7JS
Tel: 01904 624252 Fax: 01904 671293 **Map Ref 120**

....

ROYAL YORK HOTEL, set in 3 acres of private grounds, this refurbished, magnificent Victorian hotel is in the centre of historic York. Major attractions within a short walking distance.

B&B from £49, Dinner available, Rooms 29 single, 59 double, 57 twin, 3 triple, 10 family, all en-suite, No smoking, Children welcome, Open all year.
Royal York Hotel, Station Road, York YO2 2AA
Tel: 01904 653681 Fax: 01904 653271 **Map Ref 120**

....

SWALLOW HOTEL, set on the edge of York racecourse on the Knavesmire. A traditional hotel with extensive leisure facilities, attractive bedrooms and a restaurant overlooking the hotel grounds. Short break packages available.
B&B from £70, Dinner available, Rooms 7 single, 42 double, 47 twin, 10 triple, 7 family, all en-suite, No smoking, Children welcome, Open all year.
Swallow Hotel, Tadcaster Road, York YO2 2QQ
Tel: 01904 701000 Fax: 01904 702308 **Map Ref 120**

....

ELMBANK, a city hotel with a country house atmosphere, close to York city centre, the Knavesmire and racecourse.

B&B from £40, Dinner available, Rooms 9 single, 14 double, 26 twin, 8 triple, 1 family, most en-suite, No smoking, Children welcome, Open all year.
Elmbank, The Mount, York YO2 2DD
Tel: 01904 610653 Fax: 01904 627139 **Map Ref 120**

....

THE MANOR COUNTRY HOUSE, an atmospheric manor in rural tranquillity, bordering river. Off the beaten track yet close for city, racecourse and A64. Private fishing in lake. En-suite rooms with full facilities. Wonderful conservatory dining room with a view of lake and gardens.
B&B from £38, Dinner available, Rooms 1 single, 4 double, 2 twin, 3 triple, all en-suite, No smoking, Children welcome, Open all year.
The Manor Country House, Acaster Malbis, York YO2 1UL
Tel: 01904 706723 Fax: 01904 706723 **Map Ref 122**

....

ALHAMBRA COURT HOTEL, an early Georgian town house in a quiet cul-de-sac near the city centre. Family run hotel with bar, restaurant, open to non residents. Lift and parking.

B&B from £32, Dinner available, Rooms 3 single, 9 double, 7 twin, 3 triple, 2 family, all en-suite, No smoking, Children welcome, Open all year.
Alhambra Court Hotel, 31 St Mary's, Bootham York YO3 7DD
Tel: 01904 628474 Fax: 01904 610690 **Map Ref 120**

....

23 ST. MARYS, Relax! Spend some time in our beautifully furnished elegant house. Antique furniture, fresh flowers and paintings throughout. En-suite rooms furnished individually to the highest standards, with all the little extras! Wonderful choices for breakfast served on linen tablecloths and napkins. A warm welcome awaits you.

B&B from £24pp, Rooms 2 single, 1 twin, 6 double, all en-suite, Restricted smoking, Children welcome, No pets, Open all year except Christmas & New Year.
Greta Hudson, **23 St. Marys,** Bootham, York, North Yorkshire YO3 7DD
Tel: 01904 622738 Fax: 01904 628802 **Map Ref 120**

ARNOT HOUSE, overlooks Bootham Park, five minutes walk from York Minster. All bedrooms are furnished with antiques and brass or wooded beds, colour TV, alarm clock, radio, hair dryers and hospitality tray. Breakfast includes fresh fruit salad, cereals, fruit juices, English and vegetarian options. Car parking.
B&B from £22.50pp, Rooms 1 twin, 3 double, all en-suite, no smoking or pets, Children over 10, Open all year.
Kim & Ann Sluter-Robbins, **Arnot House,** 17 Grosvenor Terrace, Bootham, York YO30 7AG
Tel: 01904 641966 Fax: 01904 641966 **Map Ref 120**

....

CROOK LODGE, an early Victorian residence 450 yards from city centre. Bedrooms all en-suite with colour TV and radio. Private car park. Special breaks, dinner, bed and breakfast. No smoking.

B&B from £25, Dinner available, Rooms 1 single, 4 double, 2 twin, all en-suite, No smoking, No pets, Open February - December.
Crook Lodge, 26 St Mary's, Bootham, York YO3 7DD
Tel: 01904 655614 **Map Ref 120**

....

CRAIG-Y-DON, under the Oliver ownership since 1979, where guests have become friends. Early booking is advisable to prevent disappointment.
B&B from £16, Rooms 3 single, 3 double, 2 twin, Children over 10, Open all year.
Craig-Y-Don, 3 Grosvenor Terrace, Bootham, York YO3 7AG
Tel: 01904 637186 & 0580 202795 Fax: 01904 637186 **Map Ref 120**

....

PARK VIEW GUEST HOUSE, a family run Victorian house with views of York Minster, close to city centre off the A19. Minimum 2 nights stay at weekends.

B&B from £25, Rooms 3 double, 2 triple, 1 family, some en-suite, No smoking, Children welcome, Open all year.
Park View Guest House, 34 Grosvenor Terrace, Bootham, York YO3 7AG
Tel: 01904 620437 Fax: 01904 620437 **Map Ref 120**

....

AARON GUEST HOUSE, an attractive and well decorated family guest house, a short walk from city centre. Most rooms en-suite. Ample parking.
B&B from £16, Rooms 1 single, 3 double, 1 twin, 1 triple, most en-suite, No smoking, Children welcome, No pets, Open all year.
Aaron Guest House, 42 Bootham Crescent, Bootham, York YO3 7AH
Tel: 01904 625927 **Map Ref 120**

....

JORVIK HOTEL, a well appointed central hotel overlooking the walls of St Mary's Abbey and Museum Gardens. Close to York Minster and shopping areas.

B&B from £28, Dinner available, Rooms 1 single, 12 double, 8 twin, 1 triple, all en-suite, No smoking, Children welcome, Open all year.
Jorvik Hotel, 50-52 Marygate, Bootham, York YO3 7BH
Tel: 01904 653511 Fax: 01904 627009 **Map Ref 120**

....

ABBOTS MEWS HOTEL, a converted Victorian coachmen's cottages, quietly located in a mews with easy access to the city centre.
B&B from £25, Dinner available, Rooms 7 single, 18 double, 15 twin, 9 triple, most en-suite, Children welcome, No pets, Open all year.
Abbots Mews Hotel, 6 Marygate Lane, Bootham, York YO3 7DE
Tel: 01904 6634866 & 622395 Fax: 01904 612848 **Map Ref 120**

....

ABBEY GUEST HOUSE, a small family run guest house on the banks of the River Ouse, 450 yards from the city centre.

B&B from £18, Rooms 2 single, 3 double, 1 twin, 1 family, some en-suite, No smoking, Children welcome, No pets, Open all year.

Abbey Guest House, 14 Earlsborough Terrace, Marygate, York YO3 7BQ
Tel: 01904 627782 Fax: 01904 671743 Email: rsummers@cix.co.uk **Map Ref 120**

AMBLESIDE GUEST HOUSE, a tastefully furnished Victorian town house, 5 minutes walk to city centre. Most rooms en-suite. Cleanliness and hospitality guaranteed at all times.

B&B from £36, Rooms 6 double, 1 twin, 1 triple, most en-suite, No smoking, Children over 10, No pets, Open February - December.
Ambleside Guest House, 62 Bootham Crescent, Bootham, York YO3 7AH
Tel: 01904 637165 Fax: 01904 637165   **Map Ref 120**

YORK LODGE GUEST HOUSE, we offer a warm friendly, relaxing stay with room facilities including full central heating, hand basin, clean towels daily, hot and cold air fans, clock radio alarms, colour television and welcome tray. We look forward to meeting you.
B&B from £17pp, Rooms 1 single, 2 twin, 3 double, 2 family, some en-suite, Children welcome, Pets by arrangement, Open all year.
Margaret Moore, **York Lodge Guest House,** 64 Bootham Crescent, Bootham, York YO3 7AH
Tel: 01904 654289 Fax: 01904 488803   **Map Ref 120**

FOUR SEASONS HOTEL, is a delightful Victorian residence situated in peaceful tree lined grove. 8 minutes stroll to city centre. Beautifully furnished en-suite rooms all fully equipped. Ample parking. Four course English breakfast. Cosy lounge and residential license. Awarded AA 4Q Selected and ETB Highly Commended.
B&B from £27pp, Rooms 1 twin, 2 double, 2 family, all en-suite, No smoking, Children welcome, Pets by arrangement, Open February - December.
Bernice & Steven Roe, **Four Seasons Hotel,** 7 St Peters Grove, Bootham, York YO30 6AQ
Tel: 01904 622621 Fax: 01904 620976   **Map Ref 120**

BRIAR LEA GUEST HOUSE, a Victorian house with all rooms en-suite, 5 minutes walk from the city centre and railway station.
B&B from £34, Rooms 1 double, 1 twin, 1 triple, 1 family, all en-suite, No smoking, Children welcome, No pets, Open all year.
Briar Lea Guest House, 8 Longfield Terrace, Bootham, York YO3 7DJ
Tel: 01904 635061 & 0589 178956   **Map Ref 120**

BOOTHAM PARK HOTEL, an elegant Victorian house 5 minutes walk from York Minster and tourist attractions. En-suite rooms with hair dryer, alarm clock, colour TV, drinks tray and telephone. Parking.
B&B from £28, Rooms 3 double, 1 twin, 1 triple, 1 family, all en-suite, No smoking, Children welcome, No pets, Open all year.
Bootham Park Hotel, 9 Grosvenor Terrace, Bootham, York YO3 7AG
Tel: 01904 644262 Fax: 01904 645647   **Map Ref 120**

SAVAGES HOTEL, a Victorian hotel in a quiet tree lined street close to city centre and all attractions. Comfortable, well equipped bedrooms and traditional restaurant serving fine food.
B&B from £25, Dinner available, Rooms 3 single, 9 double, 5 twin, 1 triple, 2 family, all en-suite, Children welcome, No pets, Open all year.
Savages Hotel, 15 St Peter's Grove, Clifton, York YO3 6AQ
Tel: 01904 610818 Fax: 01904 627729   **Map Ref 120**

CURZON LODGE & STABLE COTTAGES, a delightful 17th century former farmhouse and stables overlooking York Racecourse. 10 comfortable and well equipped en-suite rooms, some 4-posters. Country antiques, books, prints, fresh flowers and sherry in our cosy sitting room lend English house ambience. Parking in grounds. Restaurants close by. RAC, AA, ETB Highly Commended.
B&B from £27.50pp, Rooms 1 single, 3 twin, 4 double, 2 family, all en-suite, No smoking or pets, Children welcome, Open all year except Christmas.
Richard & Wendy Wood **Curzon Lodge & Stable Cottages,** 23 Tadcaster Road, Dringhouses, York YO24 1QG
Tel: 01904 703157   **Map Ref 120**

FIFTH MILESTONE COTTAGE, we stand in a rural setting close to York, views over open fields with car parking to rear of house. Central heating, colour television, hospitality tray, ground floor rooms with private bathroom with conservatory to relax in overlooking large gardens. Antique themed decor. Pubs in walking distance.
B&B from £15pp, Rooms 2 twin, 1 family, all private bathroom, No smoking, Children & Pets welcome, Open all year.
Karen & Alan Jackson, **Fifth Milestone Cottage,** Hull Road, Dunnington, York YO1 5LR
Tel: 01904 489361 **Map Ref 123**

MOORLAND HOUSE, purpose built guest house with car park, close to city centre, golf club & University. Pleasant en-suite ground floor rooms with colour TV, tea/coffee facilities and central heating. Comfortable guests lounge. Moorland House is an Ideal base for visiting York, the East coast, Yorkshire Dales and North Yorkshire Moors.
B&B from £16pp, Rooms 2 single, 5 twin, 3 double, 2 family, all en-suite, Restricted smoking, Children welcome, Pets by arrangement, Open all year.
Gordon Metcalfe, **Moorland House,** 1a Moorland Road, Fulford, York YO10 4HF
Tel: 01904 629354 **Map Ref 124**

YORK PAVILION HOTEL, a charming Georgian country house near city centre. Excellent restaurant, individually designed en-suite bedrooms, car parking, all within mature walled grounds.

B&B from £88, Dinner available, Rooms 22 double, 10 twin, 2 triple, all en-suite, No smoking, Children welcome, No pets, Open all year.
York Pavilion Hotel, 45 Main Street, Fulford, York YO1 4PJ
Tel: 01904 622099 Fax: 01904 626939 **Map Ref 124**

ALFREDA GUEST HOUSE, a double fronted, Edwardian residence in 1.5 acres, close to Fulford Golf Course and York University. Large parking area with security lighting.

B&B from £20, Rooms 3 double, 3 twin, 2 triple, 2 family, most en-suite, Children welcome, Open all year.

Alfreda Guest House, 61 Heslington Lane, Fulford, York YO1 4HN
Tel: 01904 631698 **Map Ref 124**

LAUREL MANOR FARM, a secluded Georgian house on the edge of Helperby which has four good pubs and lots of history. Two double and one twin room. All with private/en-suite, tea/coffee, TV etc. 30 minutes York, Harrogate and the Yorkshire Moors. Four and a half miles A1M.

B&B from £25pp, Dinner from £18, Rooms 1 twin, 2 double, all en-suite, Children & pets welcome, Open March - November.

Annie & Sam Atcherley Key, **Laurel Manor Farm,** Brafferton, Helperby, York YO61 2NZ
Tel: 01423 360 436 Fax: 01423 360436 **Map Ref 125**

JACOBEAN LODGE HOTEL, a converted 17th century farmhouse, 4 miles north of York. Set in picturesque gardens with ample parking. Warm, friendly atmosphere and traditional cuisine.

B&B from £30, Dinner available, Rooms 2 single, 9 double, 1 twin, 2 triple, all en-suite, No smoking, Children welcome, Open all year.

Jacobean Lodge Hotel, Plainville Lane, Wigginton, York YO3 8RG
Tel: 01904 762749 Fax: 01904 768403 **Map Ref 126**

553

Scotland

Scotland is without doubt a land steeped in history and romance. It is a land of noble castles and breathtaking scenery. With a turbulent history of tribal feuds, of dreadful battles and of lost causes. It was the Scandinavian invasion of Britain which forced the Picts of eastern Scotland and the Scots of Argyll to unite under Kenneth MacAlpin between 843 and 858 AD and establish the kingdom of Scotland. By the reign of Edward I most of Scotland was under English rule. However, Edward II, a weak king, allowed Robert Bruce to win back all that the Scots had lost and with Bruce's crushing defeat of the English army at Bannockburn, the Pope recognised Robert Bruce as King of the Scots and in 1328 the English made formal peace. The Scottish Highlands and Islands were divided into tribal districts each ruled by a clan chief and with the exception of the Lords of the Isles and the Princes of Galloway, the chiefs owed allegiance to the King of Scots. Every member of the same clan had a common surname and so, bonded together, the warlike clans attained a strong sense of patriotism. The weave of the cloth of their highland dress distinguished the clans. Following the slaughter of the clans by the English at Culloden and the fruitless attempt to restore Bonnie Prince Charlie to the Scottish throne, the clans were, in 1746, forbidden to wear the tartan. In 1782 the Duke of Montrose was able to force the repeal of this hated Act and many Scottish chiefs were restored to the peerage and the ancient titles were, by Act of Parliament, allowed to continue to be recorded by Lion King of Arms. The Disarming Act of 1746 and the years following that disastrous defeat at Culloden scattered the clans, many finding new homes in America and Canada.

left, Loch Eilein

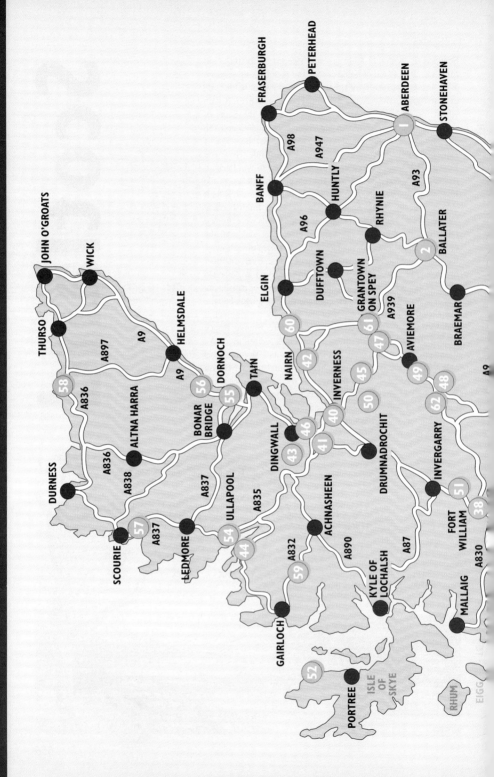

SCOTLAND

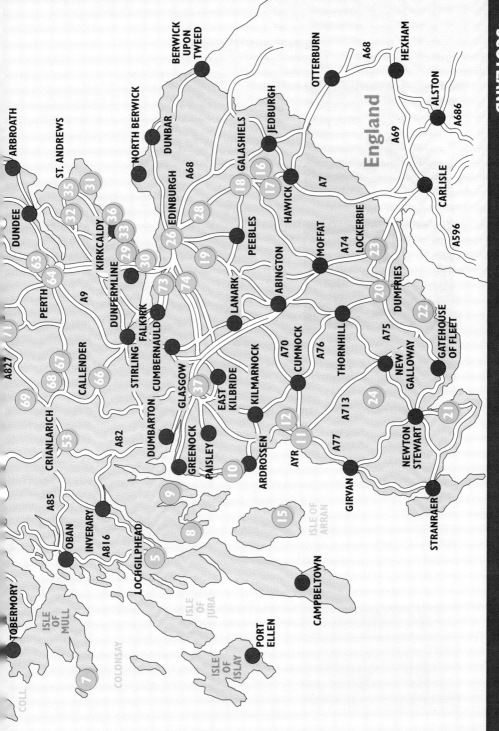

ABERDEENSHIRE

ABERDEEN NICOLL'S GUEST HOUSE, a very comfortable family run 'Listed' Victorian guest house. City centre location. An excellent standard of accommodation at affordable prices. En-suite and standard rooms available, each bedroom has remote control colour TV with cable, hospitality tray, radio alarm and hair dryer. Parking at rear.
B&B from £16-£20pp, Rooms 4 twin, 2 family, some en-suite, Restricted smoking, Children welcome, Open all year except Christmas & New Year.
Lillian Nicoll **Aberdeen Nicoll's Guest House,** 63 Springbank Terrace, Ferryhill, Aberdeen AB11 6JZ
Tel: 01224 572867 Fax: 01224 572867   **Map Ref 1**

DUNROVIN GUEST HOUSE, this family managed Victorian guest house is very central being only 10 minutes from bus, rail and ferry terminals, main shops, restaurants and parks. Well appointed bedrooms have colour TV, trouser press, iron, hair dryer and hospitality tray. Pay and display parking available on street.
B&B from £16pp, Rooms 3 single, 2 twin, 1 double, 2 family, Smoking, Children & pets welcome, Open all year.
Mr & Mrs Lee, **Dunrovin Guest House,** 168 Bon Accord Street, Aberdeen AB11 6TX
Tel: 01224 586081 Fax: 01224 586081   **Map Ref 1**

ROSELODGE GUEST HOUSE, a city centre, family run guest house. Within walking distance of most local amenities. Also train, bus and ferry terminals. All rooms have television, tea/coffee facilities, wash hand basin and central heating. Car park.

B&B from £15pp, Rooms 2 twin, 2 double, 1 family, Children welcome, No pets, Open all year except Christmas.

Mrs M. Wink, **Roselodge Guest House,** 3 Springbank Terrace, Aberdeen, AB11 6LS
Tel: 01224 586794 Fax: 01224 586794   **Map Ref 1**

GLENDALE GUEST HOUSE, a superior Victorian family run guest house, centrally located near Gateway to Royal Deeside. Full Scottish Breakfast. Cable TV all rooms some en-suite, all with tea/coffee facilities. Ideal touring base. Warm and friendly atmosphere. Restricted smoking. Fire certificate. Select accommodation at competitive rates.

B&B from £17-£20pp, Rooms 1 single, 2 twin, 1 double, 1 family, 2 en-suite, Restricted smoking, Children welcome, Pets by arrangement, Open all year.

Norma Smith, **Glendale Guest House,** 416 Great Western Road, Aberdeen, AB10 6NQ
Tel: 01224 315535   **Map Ref 1**

THE RUSSELL PRIVATE HOTEL, a family run guest house in west end of Aberdeen, just a few minutes walk from city centre. Residents lounge with cable television and complimentary light buffet. Tea/coffee facilities and colour TV in all rooms. Car parking for 8. Double glazed and centrally heated throughout. Email: 101335.2026@compuserve.com
B&B from £30pp, Rooms 9 single, 1 twin, 1 double, 1 family, most en-suite, Smoking, Children & pets welcome, Open all year except Christmas & New Year.
Anne Leith, **The Russell Private Hotel,** 50 St. Swithin Street, Aberdeen Aberdeenshire AB10 6XJ
Tel: 01224 323555 Fax: 01224 322805   **Map Ref 1**

RAVENSWOOD HOTEL, has a Victorian ambience, discreetly modernised. Personally run by Cathy and Scott, ensuring all guests a warm, friendly service and high standards. Ideal for relaxing in comfort with good whole some food. A homely base to explore Royal Deeside, walking, fishing or touring.

B&B from £20pp, Dinner from £13.95, Rooms 1 single, 3 twin, 4 double, 2 family, some en-suite, Restricted smoking, Children welcome, Pets by arrangement, Open December - October.
Cathy & Scott Fyfe, **Ravenswood Hotel,** Braemar Road, Ballater, Aberdeenshire AB35 5RQ
Tel: 013397 55539 Fax: 013397 55539   **Map Ref 2**

ABBOTSWELL GUEST HOUSE, a family run guest house. Town centre 10 minutes. Private off road parking. All rooms with tea/coffee, TV. Guest lounge with restricted license SKY TV. Easy access to Deeside and Dunochter Castle. Duthie Park with winter gardens close by.
B&B from £19pp, Dinner from £10, Rooms 1 single, 6 twin, 4 double, 1 family, some en-suite, No smoking or pets, Children over 5, Open all year except Christmas & New Year.
David & Grace Bremner, **Abbotswell Guest House,** 28 Abbotswell Crescent, Aberdeen, AB12 5AR
Tel: 01224 871788 Fax: 01224 891257   **Map Ref 1**

ANGUS

THE LIMES GUEST HOUSE, a family run Georgian style guest house, centrally situated. In a quiet residential part of town a few minutes walk from centre Railway station, beach and golf courses. Rooms have TV, hospitality tray, direct dial telephone, en-suite. Very clean, comfortable accommodation. Conservatory for visitors. Private parking.
B&B from £18pp, Rooms 2 single, 4 twin, 4 double, 2 family, some en-suite, Restricted smoking, Children welcome, Pets by arrangement, Open all year.
Mr & Mrs Dick, **The Limes Guest House,** 15 King Street, Montrose, Angus DD10 8NL
Tel/Fax: 01674 677236 Email: thelimes@easynet.co.uk   **Map Ref 3**

PARK HOTEL, is quietly yet conveniently situated near to all main road and rail routes. Family owned, Three Star Hotel with all in-room facilities. Easy car parking. Popular brasserie and Bar. Quality restaurant and full conference facilities. Sports and leisure centre, swimming pool, all within walking distance.

B&B from £29.50pp, Dinner from £12, Rooms 13 single, 31 twin, 11 double, 4 family, most en-suite, Restricted smoking, Children & Pets welcome, Open all year.
Mr Martin, **Park Hotel,** John Street, Montrose, Angus DD10 8RJ
Tel: 01674 673415 Fax: 01674 677091   **Map Ref 3**

ARGYLL & BUTE

TIGH AN LODAN, in a tranquil area at southern end of Loch Awe. Ideally situated for fishing, walking and other outdoor pursuits. We offer good food and comfort.

B&B from £22pp, Dinner from £14, Rooms 2 twin, 1 double, all en-suite, No smoking, Children over 13, Pets by arrangement, Open April - October.
Dr & Mrs Bannister, **Tigh an Lodan,** Ford by Lochgilphead, Argyll PA31 8RH
Tel: 01546 810287 Fax: 01546 810287   **Map Ref 5**

TIREE SCARINISH HOTEL, bedrooms have tea/coffee facilities, TV's. Guest lounge. Car park. Bar, dining room. Sea fishing, Loch fishing, golf, wind surfing, pony trekking, cycle/car hire can be arranged. Transport from ferry or airport can be arranged.

B&B from £23pp Dinner from £4.50, Rooms 2 single, 3 twin, 2 double, 2 family, some en-suite, Children welcome, Pets by arrangement, Open all year.
N & A Mac Arthur, **Tiree Scarinish Hotel**, Scarinish, Isle of Tiree, Argyll PA77 6UH
Tel: 018792 20308 Fax: 018792 20410

RED BAY COTTAGE, in an isolated shoreline position overlooking Iona. Good food available in adjoining licensed restaurant. Excellent centre for exploring Mull, Iona and the Treshnish Islands. Excellent walking and beautiful beaches.

B&B from £15.50pp, Dinner from £7.50, Rooms 2 twin, 1 double, Children & pets welcome, Open all year.
John & Eleanor Wagstaff, **Red Bay Cottage**, Deargphort, Fionnphort, Isle-of-Mull, Argyll PA66 6BP
Tel: 01681 700396   **Map Ref 7**

KAMES HOTEL, a warm welcome and magnificent views over the Kyles of Bute. Good food, fine wines, real ales. Frequent live music, close to golf, fishing and sailing school. Come for an activity week or just relax in peace on one of our off-season specials. Email: mark@waip.demon.co.uk

B&B from £25pp, Dinner from £8, Rooms 2 single, 1 twin, 4 double, 2 family, all en-suite, Children & pets welcome, Open all year except Christmas.

Mark Booth, **Kames Hotel**, Kames, Argyll PA21 2AF
Tel: 01700 811 489 Fax: 01700 811 283   **Map Ref 8**

ABBOT'S BRAE HOTEL, is a Victorian Country House Hotel in secluded two acre woodland glen with breath-taking views of the sea and hills. Seven tastefully furnished spacious bedrooms, all en-suite with all the extras. Quality dining and select wines. Easily accessible from major routes, including one hour from Glasgow Airport. Email: enquirykgp@abbotsbrae.ndirect.co.u
B&B from £25pp, Dinner from £15, Rooms 1 four poster, 4 double, 2 family, all en-suite, Restricted smoking, Children welcome, Pets by arrangement, Open all year.
Gavin & Helen Dick, **Abbot's Brae Hotel**, West Bay, Dunoon, Argyllshire PA23 7QJ
Tel: 01369 705021 Fax: 01369 701191 k   **Map Ref 9**

ALAMEIN HOUSE, superb location overlooking Rothesay Bay. Easy access for town centre. Colour TV's, tea/coffee facilities, smoking room, car park facilities. Near Mount Stuart House and Gardens. Easy access for ferry. Also fishing and golf course very popular. Relaxing holiday. All welcome.

B&B from £17pp, Rooms 3 twin, 3 double, 1 family, some en-suite, Restricted smoking, Children & pets welcome, Open all year.
Pat Scott, **Alamein House,** 28 Battery Place, Rothesay, Isle of Bute PA20 9DU
Tel: 01700 502395   **Map Ref 9**

AYRSHIRE

GLENFOOT HOUSE HOTEL, is a unique Country House in a unique location. Experience Scottish country living and superb cuisine at its very best. Spectacular views of the Firth of Clyde and Island of Arran. Within easy travelling distance of Glasgow, Prestwick, airports and Scotlands main championship Links Golf Courses. Email: glenfoothouse.co.uk
B&B from £55-£75pp, Dinner available, Rooms 4 single, 5 twin/double, 1 family, all en-suite, Restricted smoking, Children welcome, Pets by arrangement, Open all year.
Robert McAulay, **Glenfoot House Hotel,** North Shore Road, Ardrossan, Ayrshire KA22 8PQ
Tel: 01294 465143 Fax: 01294 462892   **Map Ref 10**

BELMONT GUEST HOUSE, is a Scottish town house built in 1877 in a quiet tree-lined conservation area. All bedrooms with TV, radio, tea/coffee making facilities. Guest lounge. Car parking. STB 2 Stars, Scotland's Best, Welcome Host and current fire certificate held. Member of Ayrshire and Arran Tourist Board.

B&B from £18.50pp, Rooms 2 double, 3 family, all en-suite, Children welcome, Pets by arrangement, Open all year except Christmas & New Year.
Andrew Hillhouse, **Belmont Guest House,** 15 Park Circus, Ayr KA7 2DJ
Tel: 01292 265588 Fax: 01292 290303   **Map Ref 11**

STAIR INN, here you will experience the peace and beauty of rural Ayrshire. Refurbished throughout the restaurant, bar and 6 en-suite rooms with TV and tea/coffee facilities have earned an enviable reputation. Award winning chefs provide outstanding and varied cuisine and friendly staff are always welcoming.
B&B from £27.50pp, Dinner available, Rooms 3 twin, 1 double, 2 family, all en-suite, Restricted smoking, Children welcome, No pets.
Mr & Mrs William Buchanan, **Stair Inn,** Stair, by Mauchline, Ayrshire KA5 5HW
Tel: 01292 591 650   **Map Ref 12**

GRANGE HOUSE HOTEL, come and discover Arran "Scotland in miniature" from our Victorian sea front hotel. All rooms have colour TV's and tea trays. One downstairs double bedroom, suitable for guests with wheelchairs. Delightful lounge and sauna. Parking. STB 3 Crowns Highly Commended, AA Selected QQQQ. Website:http://www.smoothhound.co.uk
B&B from £30pp, Rooms 1 single, 2 twin, 3 double, 1 family, all en-suite, No smoking, Children welcome, No pets, Open April - November.
Janet & Clive Hughes, **Grange House Hotel,** Whiting Bay, Isle of Arran KA27 8QH
Tel: 01770 700263 Fax: 01770 700263   **Map Ref 15**

BORDERS

KINGS ARMS HOTEL, a former 18th century Coaching Inn. Providing excellent accommodation combined with a superb selection of freshly prepared bar and restaurant menus. Our two bars provide a relaxed and friendly atmosphere to unwind after a busy day. Visiting the many local attractions. Car park available.

B&B from £27.50pp, Dinner from £12, Rooms 1 single, 3 twin, 1 double, 2 family, Children & pets welcome, Open all year except Christmas.
Mr Michael Dalgetty, **Kings Arms Hotel,** High Street, Melrose TD6 9PB
Tel: 01896 822143 Fax: 01896 823812 **Map Ref 16**

ETTRICKSHAWS COUNTRY HOUSE HOTEL, a delightful country house in 12 acres alongside Ettrick water in the beautiful Ettrick Valley. Refurbished to the highest standards, bedroom accommodation offers all modern conveniences - TV's, tea/coffee, telephones. Also Drawing Room, Dining Room and bar service. Car park. 2 miles single bank fishing. Many visitors attractions locally.
B&B from £27.50pp, Dinner from £17.50, Rooms 1 twin, 2 double, 2 family, all en-suite, Restricted smoking, Children over 12, Pets by arrangement, Open April - February.
Graham Hulme & Jenny Oldfield, **Ettrickshaws Country House Hotel,** Ettrickbridge, Selkirk, TD7 5HW
Tel: 01750 52229 **Map Ref 17**

MAPLEHURST GUEST HOUSE, an Edwardian family house on the southern outskirts of Galashiels. Private parking. TV and tea making facilities, guests lounge area. Spacious gardens with garden seating. Airport within one hour travel and most major border towns can be reached within half hours drive from Galashiels.
B&B from £22.50pp, Dinner from £15, Rooms 1 twin, 1 double, 1 family, all en-suite, No smoking, Children welcome, Open mid January - mid December.
Mrs Janice Richardson, **Maplehurst Guest House,** Abbotsford Road, Galashiels, Borders TD1 3HP
Tel: 01896 754700 Fax: 01896 754700 **Map Ref 18**

GREENMANTLE HOTEL, a family run hotel offering good food and hospitality. Beautiful area, near Peebles and Edinburgh.
B&B from £17.50-£20pp, Dinner from £8, Rooms 3 twin, 1 en-suite double, Children & pets welcome, Open all year.
David & Judy Bougourd, **Greenmantle Hotel,** Broughton, By Biggar, Peebleshire ML12 6HQ
Tel: 01899 830302 Email: greenmantle@vacations.scotland.co.uk **Map Ref 19**

DUMFRIES & GALLOWAY

ABERDOUR HOTEL, a family run hotel 2 minutes walk from town centre and railway station. All rooms have private facilities, tea/coffee making facilities and satellite TV. Bar meals available to non residents. Winner of 'Pub Grub' Award.
B&B from £25pp, Dinner from £9.75, Rooms 1 single, 6 twin,1 double, 4 family, all en-suite, Restricted smoking, Children welcome, No pets, Open all year except Christmas & New Year.
John McLatchie, **Aberdour Hotel,** 16-20 Newall Terrace, Dumfries, DG1 1LW
Tel: 01387 252060 Fax: 01387 262323 **Map Ref 20**

CRAIGMOUNT GUEST HOUSE, a former manse, listed building. Guests lounge with TV. Alcohol license. Tea/coffee making facilities. Ample car parking. Easy access to ferries for Northern Ireland from Stranraer, walking in the Galloway Hills, wild fowling, sea and river fishing, many golf course and beaches nearby.
B&B from £17pp, Dinner from £9, Rooms 1 single, 1 twin, 1 double, 2 family, most en-suite, Restricted smoking , Children & pets welcome, Open all year.
David & Pat Taylor, **Craigmount Guest House,** High Street, Wigtown, DG8 9EQ
Tel: 01988 402291   **Map Ref 21**

MAXWELL ARMS HOTEL, car park. Television, tea/coffee.Home cooked meals. Bar open all day. Golf course within 1 mile. Shooting, fishing and beaches all within a five mile radius. Threave Gardens, Hill walking and Castle's nearby.

B&B from £13.50pp, Dinner from £2.95, Rooms 2 single, 2 twin, 2 double, 2 family, 2 en-suite, Children & Pets welcome, Open all year.

Carolyn Maxwell, **Maxwell Arms Hotel,** Maxwell Street, Dalbeattie, Dumfries & Galloway DG5 4AH
Tel: 01566 610431 Fax: 01556 610431   **Map Ref 22**

KINGS ARMS HOTEL, is one of the oldest establishments in Lockerbie, dating from the 17th Century.The hotel is fully centrally heated, our 14 rooms are all en-suite with tea/coffee facilities, direct dial telephone and TV. Surrounded by Golf courses at Dumfries, Moffat, Powfoot, Lochmaben and of course Lockerbie.
B&B from £22.50pp, Dinner from £5, Rooms 3 single, 2 twin, 5 double, 3 family, most en-suite, Children & Pets welcome, Open all year.
Mrs A Carry, **Kings Arms Hotel,** High Street, Lockerbie, Dumfriesshire DG11 2JL
Tel: 01576 202410 Fax: 01576 202410   **Map Ref 23**

LEAMINGTON HOUSE HOTEL, enjoy the warmest welcome at this family run 9 bedroomed 18th Century hotel. Ideally situated for most sports including golf and walking. Evening meals available. TV, coffee/tea facilities. Car park. Weekly family and 3 day rates. Table licence. Guest lounge. Visit Kenmure Castle.
B&B from £18.50-£20pp, Dinner from £3.50, Rooms 2 single, 1 twin, 4 double, 1 family, most en-suite, Restricted smoking, Children welcome, Open all year.
Martha & Allan Young, **Leamington House Hotel,** High Street, New Galloway, Castle Douglas, Kirkcudbrightshire DG7 3RN
Tel: 01644 420327 http://www.galloway.co.uk   **Map Ref 24**

EDINBURGH

CLASSIC HOUSE, is a non-smoking elegant Victorian house, it has been beautifully restored. Near city centre, castle, Holywood Palace, University, Royal Colleges of Surgeons/Physicians. Warm welcome assured. Delicious breakfast and value for money. AA Selected. Quality house listed in Which? STB 3 Stars.

B&B from £19-£30pp, Rooms 2 single, 2 twin, 2 double, 1 family, all en-suite, No smoking or pets, Children welcome, Open all year.
Mr & Mrs Smail, **Classic House,** 50 Mayfield Rd, Edinburgh EH9 2NH
Tel: 0131 667 5847 Fax: 0131 662 1016   **Map Ref 26**

44 EAST CLAREMONT STREET, offers comfortable accommodation in Edinburgh's Victorian new town. McCrae's is only 15 minutes walk from the city centre giving easy access to all attractions. The bedrooms retain original features, have TV and tea/coffee facilities. Excellent breakfast using fresh local produce. Unrestricted on-street parking.

B&B from £24.50pp, Rooms 3 en-suite twin, Restricted smoking, Children welcome, Pets by arrangement, Open all year.
Ian McCrae, **44 East Claremont Street,** Edinburgh, EH7 4JR
Tel: 0131 556 2610   **Map Ref 26**

....

HAYMARKET HOTEL, family run hotel. Close to all amenities i.e. Princes Street, Airport, Railway all walking distance. TV, tea/coffee facilities. Lounge. Bar. Licensed. Horse riding on request. Parking outside hotel. All meals and packed lunches catered for. Very friendly atmosphere.

B&B from £??pp, Dinner from £5.75, Rooms 2 single, 1 twin, 2 double, 3 family, Children & Pets welcome, Open all year.
Pauline & Adam Brock, **Haymarket Hotel,** 1 Coates Gardens, Edinburgh, EH12 5LG
Tel: 0131 337 1775 Fax: 0131 313 0330   **Map Ref 26**

....

ELLESMERE HOUSE, in central Edinburgh, a Victorian town house facing south over a park. Castle, Royal Mile and Princes Street are all within walking distance. Also close to the International Conference Centre, theatres, restaurants and pubs. All rooms are en-suite and well equipped with everything for your comfort in mind.

B&B from £25pp, Rooms 1 single, 2 twin, 2 double, 1 family, all en-suite, Children over 10, No pets, Open all year except Christmas.

Mrs C Leishman, **Ellesmere House,** 11 Glengyle Terrace, Edinburgh, EH3 9LN
Tel: 0131 229 4823 Fax: 0131 229 5285   **Map Ref 26**

....

BEN DORAN GUEST HOUSE, is a beautifully refurbished Georgian house with city and hillside views. Near city centre on bus routes, close to Edinburgh attractions. Welcoming and charming, full Scottish breakfast on finest China, TV, central heating, tea/coffee and parking. Lace in the windows and cozy downies on the beds. Email: bendoran.guesthouse@virgin.net
B&B from £20pp, Rooms, 1 twin, 5 double, 4 family, some en-suite, No smoking, Children welcome, Pets by arrangement, Open all year.
Dr. Joseph Labaki, **Ben Doran Guest House,** 11 Mayfield Gardens, Edinburgh, EH9 2AX
Tel: 0131 667 8488 Fax: 0131 667 0076   **Map Ref 26**

....

HOPETOUN, is a small, friendly, family-run guest house close to Edinburgh University, offering very comfortable accommodation in a smoke-free environment. Bedrooms with private facilities, central heating, wash basins, colour TV, tea/coffee facilities. Parking. AA QQ. Which? Books - Good B&B Guide. STB 2 Crowns Commended. Email: hopetoun@aol.com
B&B from £20pp, Rooms 1 twin, 1 double, 1 family, 2 en-suite, No smoking or pets, Children welcome, Open all year except Christmas.
Rhoda Mitchell, **Hopetoun,** 15 Mayfield Road, Edinburgh, EH9 2NG
Tel: 0131 667 7691 Fax: 0131 466 1691   **Map Ref 26**

ROYAL CIRCUS HOTEL, quietly located overlooking gardens to both front and rear yet in the city centre. Within easy walking distance of all the main attractions. This 3 crown hotel offers a lounge, bar and restaurant along with a complimentary full cooked buffet breakfast. We are pleased to assist with booking tickets and tours.

B&B from £26pp, Dinner from £6, Rooms 4 single, 10 twin, 12 double, 4 family, all en-suite, Restricted smoking, Children welcome, No pets, Open all year.
Mr Wadia, **Royal Circus Hotel,** 19-21 Royal Circus, Edinburgh EH3 6TL
Tel: 0131 220 5000 Fax: 0131 220 2020 **Map Ref 26**

NUMBERTWO, comfortable accommodation in newly refurbished house in Georgian Edinburgh. 10 minutes walk from city centre. TV, fridge, tea/coffee facilities and central heating in rooms. Easy access to shops, theatres, pubs and restaurants and close to bus and railway stations.
Email: number2@criper.com

B&B from £22.50pp, Rooms 1 single, 4 double, 3 family, most en-suite, No smoking or pets, Children welcome, Open April - December.
Dr & Mrs Criper, **Numbertwo,** 2 East Claremont St Edinburgh, EH7 4JP
Tel: 0131 556 7000 Fax: 0131 556 4907 **Map Ref 26**

AIRLIE GUEST HOUSE, is a totally non smoking establishment centrally located. 1.25 miles from the city centre in an area well served by buses. All rooms comfortably furnished with colour TV's, tea/coffee facilities and central heating, most rooms en-suite. Private parking.
Email: flynstone@msn.com

B&B from £15-£30pp, Rooms 2 single, 3 twin, 5 double, 2 family, most en-suite, No smoking, Children welcome, No pets, Open all except Christmas Eve & Day.
Mr & Mrs Flynn, **Airlie Guest House,** 29 Minto Street, Edinburgh EH9 1SB
Tel: 0131 667 3562 Fax: 0131 662 1399 **Map Ref 26**

ABBOTSFORD GUEST HOUSE, in a central location near the waterfront. 15 minutes to Princes Street. All rooms with washbasins, tea/coffee making facilities and colour TV. Cooked breakfast served. Friendly atmosphere. Street parking.

B&B from £16pp, Rooms 2 single, 5 twin, 3 double, 1 family, Restricted smoking, Children & pets welcome, Open all year except Christmas.

Paola Crolla, **Abbotsford Guest House,** 36 Pilrig Street, Edinburgh, EH6 5AL
Tel: 0131 554 2706 **Map Ref 26**

INTERNATIONAL GUEST HOUSE, an attractive stone built Victorian house situated one and a half miles south of Princes Street on the main A701. Private parking. Luxury rooms with colour television and tea/coffee making facilities. Magnificent views across the extinct volcano of Arthur's Seat. Full Scottish breakfast. STB 4 Stars.

B&B from £19.40pp, Rooms 3 single, 1 twin, 2 double, 3 family, all en-suite, Restricted smoking, Children welcome, Pets by arrangement, Open all year.

Mrs Niven, **International Guest House,** 37 Mayfield Gardens, Edinburgh, EH9 2BX
Tel: 0131 667 2511 Fax: 0131 667 1112 Email: intergh@easynet.co.uk **Map Ref 26**

ELLWYN HOTEL, a small, friendly, owner managed hotel conveniently situated on the east side of Edinburgh in a residential area. No parking restrictions. On the main bus route. 10 minutes from all tourist attractions. Fully licensed. All rooms are central heated with tea/coffee facilities and television.

B&B from £16pp, Dinner from £9.95, Rooms 1 single, 3 twin,5 double, 2 family, some en-suite, Smoking & children welcome, Pets by arrangement, Open all year except Christmas & New Year.

Mrs Owens **Ellwyn Hotel,** 37-39 Moira Terrace, Edinburgh, EH7 6TD
Tel: 0131 669 1033 & 9992   **Map Ref 26**

FORRES STREET B&B, a 4 star luxury bed and breakfast in an elegant Georgian town house in the heart of Edinburgh's historic new town. All rooms are en-suite and tastefully furnished with all conveniences. Quiet, central location. 5 minutes walk from Princes Street and close to all attractions and amenities.Email: Forres.Street@btinternet.com

B&B from £32.50-£45pp, Rooms 1 single, 4 double, all en-suite, No smoking or pets, Children over 7, Open all year except Christmas.

Maria Lennon, **Forres Street B&B,** 4 Forres Street, Edinburgh, EH3 6BJ
Tel/Fax: 0131 220 5073   **Map Ref 26**

NOVA HOTEL, situated in a quiet secluded cul-de-sac in the city centre. Ideal for business and tourist. Major theatres, concert halls, museums, Edinburgh Castle, EICC, Royal Mile, Princes Street are all within easy walking distance. Fifteen minutes to Edinburgh Airport. Licensed lounge bar. Central heating. TV and direct dial telephone. Free parking. 3 Stars.

B&B from £30pp, Rooms 2 single, 4 twin, 2 double, 4 family, all en-suite, Children & pets welcome, Open all year.

Jamie McBride, **Nova Hotel,** 5 Bruntsfield Crescent, Edinburgh EH10 4EZ
Tel: 0131 4476437 Fax: 0131 4528126   **Map Ref 26**

BRUNTSFIELD GUEST HOUSE, is in a pleasant area with parkland, shops, restaurants and pubs, although only 15 minutes walk to Princes Street, the Castle and the Royal Mile. Our bedrooms all have central heating, wash hand basin, colour television and tea/coffee making facilities.

B&B from £20pp, Rooms 2 single, 2 twin, 2 double 1 family, some en-suite, Children & pets welcome, Open all year.

Bruce & Rona Adam, **Bruntsfield Guest House,** 55 Leamington Terrace, Edinburgh, EH10 4JS
Tel: 0131 2286458 Fax: 0131 2286458   **Map Ref 26**

LINDEN HOTEL, is Edinburgh's best small hotel, located in the centre of the historic Georgian 'New Town' built in 1810. Close to the castle, mediaeval Edinburgh and shopping in Prince's Street. Also close to clubs, bars, theatres and discos yet set in quiet street next to Queen's Gardens. The hotel has a Thai restaurant.

B&B from £20pp, Dinner from £15, Rooms 2 single, 7 twin, 8 double, 3 family, some en-suite, Restricted smoking, Children & pets welcome, Open all year.

Tony Carrigan, **Linden Hotel,** 9-13 Neslon Street, Edinburgh, EH3 6LF
Tel: 0131 5574344 Fax: 0131 5587170   **Map Ref 26**

APEX EUROPEAN HOTEL, is a brand new 3 Star Hotel at the west end of the city. Two minutes from Haymarket train station and on the airport road. On site car park. Superb cuisine served in a stunning terrace level restaurant. Quality accommodation at an affordable price.

B&B from £40pp, Dinner from £10, Rooms 21 twin, 49 double, all en-suite, Restricted smoking, Children welcome, No pets, Open all year.
Ms Karen Boe, **Apex European Hotel,** 90 Haymarket Terrace, Edinburgh, EH12 5LQ
Tel: 0131 474 3456 Fax: 0131 474 3400   **Map Ref 26**

TUDORBANK LODGE, an enchanting Tudor style house (historic Scotland listed building) set in private gardens. Ideal for business, touring, golf. Edinburgh Festival, Fringe and Tattoo. Easy access to city, Zoo, Murrayfield, Forth Bridge and motorways. Superb breakfasts with ample choice for vegetarians. Fax/photocopying. Fire Certificate. Private parking.
B&B from £25pp, Rooms 1 single, 3 twin, 2 double, 2 family, some en-suite, Restricted smoking, Children welcome, No pets, Open all year.
William & Eleanor Clark, **Tudorbank Lodge,** 18 St John's Road, Corstorphine, Edinburgh, EH12 6NY
Tel: 0131 334 7845 Fax: 0131 334 5386   **Map Ref 26**

ABBEY LODGE HOTEL, is a family run hotel, all rooms are en-suite with television and tea/coffee facilities. Car park. License. Sky TV.

B&B from £25pp, Dinner available, Rooms 1 single, 3 twin, 5 double, 4 family, all en-suite, Children welcome, Open all year.

Sally McNicoll **Abbey Lodge Hotel,** 137 Drum Street, Gilmerton, Edinburgh, EH17 8RJ
Tel: 0131 664 9548 & 664 3965   **Map Ref 26**

ST VALERY GUEST HOUSE, is a traditionally pleasant, family run business, newly refurbished and situated one mile from the famous Royal Mile and half a mile fro Princes Street (station 100 yards). A full cooked Scottish breakfast is served every morning. All rooms en-suite with heating, TV and tea/coffee facilities.
B&B from £22.50pp, Dinner from £5, Rooms 5 single, 2 twin, 7 double, 5 family, all en-suite, Smoking & Children welcome, Pets by arrangement, Open all year.
George or Charlie Gardner, **St Valery Guest House,** 36 Coates Gardens, Haymarket, Edinburgh, EH12 5LE
Tel: 0131 337 1893 Fax: 0131 346 8529   **Map Ref 26**

KELLY'S GUEST HOUSE, rooms are en-suite with TV, tea/coffee facilities. Conservatory, residents lounge. Private car park and fire certificate. Kelly's located in west Edinburgh on A90 with easy access to city centre, airport, Forth road bridge, city by-pass and motorway network. STB 2 Stars.
B&B from £25pp, Rooms 2 twin, 2 double, 1 family, most en-suite, Restricted smoking, Children welcome, Pets by arrangement, Open all year.
Tony & Liz Kelly, **Kelly's Guest House,** 3 Hillhouse Road, Queensferry Road, Edinburgh EH4 3QP
Tel: 0131 332 3894 Fax: 0131 332 3894   **Map Ref 26**

BRUNTSFIELD PARK HOTEL, a fully licensed hotel, realistically prices. Closed to city centre. All rooms have TV, tea/coffee. Hotel overlooks historic Bruntsfield Links. Car parking available outside hotel.

B&B from £20pp, Rooms 2 single, 1 twin, 2 double, 1 family, most en-suite, Children & pets welcome, Open all year except Christmas.

John Speet, **Bruntsfield Park Hotel,** 4 Alvanley Terrace, Whitehouse Loan, Edinburgh, EH9 1DU
Tel: 0131 229 3834 Fax: 0131 229 9094   **Map Ref 26**

CRAIG COTTAGE, a warm welcome from the hosts and assorted pets. We are 100 yards off A701 within half mile Edinburgh by-pass. Good bus service to city centre. Bedrooms have TV. Ample off street parking. Variety of breakfasts to suit all tastes. Excellent restaurant nearby.

B&B from £15pp, Rooms 1 twin, 1 double, No smoking, Children over 6, Pets by arrangement, Open February - October.
Pat & Angus Ciupik, **Craig Cottage,** 5 New Pentland, By Loanhead, Midlothian EH20 9NT
Tel: 0131 440 0405   **Map Ref 28**

FIFE

THE CROWN HOTEL, is a family run hotel offering bed and breakfast and full board. All rooms central heated, colour TV, radio alarm, hair dryer, trouser press, tea/coffee facilities. Restaurant offering good quality food, bar. Lounge and ample car park facilities. A warm welcome awaiting for children and pets. STB Approved.

B&B from £43pp, Dinner available, Rooms 4 single, 3 twin, 4 double, 1 family, Children & Pets welcome, Open all year.
Mr Pownil **The Crown Hotel,** 6 High St, Cowden Beath, Fife KY4 9NA
Tel: 01383 610540 Fax: 01383 610340   **Map Ref 29**

FORTH VIEW HOTEL, located on Hawkcraig Point, this small secluded hotel on the seashore with a high standard of comfortable accommodation commands impressive views across the Forth to Edinburgh. Numerous leisure facilities include award winning Silver Sands Beach and 18 Hole Golf Course; with Edinburgh and St. Andrews accessible from Aberdour Station.
B&B from £18.30pp, Rooms 1 single, 2 twin, 1 double, 1 family, most en-suite, Restricted smoking, Children & pets welcome, Open April - October.
Pauleen Norman, **Forth View Hotel,** Hawkcraig Point, Aberdour, Fife KY3 0TZ
Tel: 01383 860402 Fax: 01383 860262   **Map Ref 30**

THE ROYAL HOTEL, a warm welcome awaiting at small family run hotel situated fifty yards from sea front. Home cooked foods, licensed bar, pool table. En-suite available, tea/coffee in rooms. TV in residents lounge. Local harbour trips to Isle of May. Golf course and Historical Secret Bunker nearby.
B&B from £15-£18pp, Dinner from £5, Rooms 2 single, 4 twin, 3 double, 1 family, 2 en-suite, Children welcome, Pets by arrangement, Open all year.
Jessie & Trevor Cook, **The Royal Hotel,** 20 Roger Street, Anstruther, Fife KY10 3DU
Tel: 01333 310581   **Map Ref 31**

BEAUMONT LODGE GUEST HOUSE, offers luxury accommodation at competitive rates. Our spacious rooms have private facilities, hospitality trays, colour TV and many extras found only in first class hotels. Breakfasts are a speciality. Private parking. Non smoking, STB 4 Stars, AA 4Q's. STB Welcome Host. Email: reservations@beau-lodge.demon.co.uk

B&B from £22pp, Dinner from £12.50, Rooms 2 twin, 2 double, 1 family, all en-suite, No smoking, Children welcome, No pets, Open all year.

Julie Anderson, **Beaumont Lodge Guest House,** 43 Pittenweem Road, Anstruther, Fife KY10 3DT

Tel: 01333 310315 Fax: 01333 310315 **Map Ref 31**

THE HERMITAGE GUEST HOUSE, two luxury suites, each comprising private sitting room , bathroom, two double/family bedrooms. The house faces south with superb views across, the River Forth. Our 'Secret Garden' is a joy. The area is a golfers mecca with St. Andrews only ten miles away. Licensed. STB 4 Stars. AA 5Q's.

B&B from £20-£25pp, Rooms 2 suites each comprising 2 dble bedrooms, bathroom, lounge, No smoking or pets, Children welcome, Open all year except Christmas.

Margaret McDonald, **The Hermitage Guest House,** Ladywalk, Anstruther, Fife KY10 3EX

Tel: 01333 310909 Fax: 01333 311505 Email: hermitage@protostar.ltd.uk **Map Ref 31**

TODHALL HOUSE, a Georgian style country house, peacefully located in glorious countryside. 7 miles from St. Andrews. The Kingdom of Fife - rich in history offers a wide variety of pursuits including National Trust properties, fishing Villages of the East Neuk and many sports. Quality accommodation, good food and personal service. AA Premier selection QQQQQ. STB Highly Commended.

B&B from £24-£30pp, Dinner from £17, Rooms 1 twin, 2 double, all en-suite, No smoking or pets, Children over 12, Open mid March - October.

John & Gill Donald, **Todhall House,** Dairsie, Cupar, Fife KY15 4RQ

Tel: 01334 656344 Fax: 01334 656344 **Map Ref 32**

ROYAL HOTEL, a warm welcome awaits you at this 19th century former Coaching Inn, situated in the National Trust village of Dysart. Located halfway between Edinburgh and St. Andrews makes us an ideal base for touring central Scotland. Award winning restaurant and golf and fishing breaks arranged. Email: royalhotel@aol.com

B&B from £17pp, Dinner from £4.50, Rooms 6 twin, 3 double, 1 family, some en-suite, Children & pets welcome, Open all year.

Fiona & Simon Di Marco, **Royal Hotel,** Townhead, Dysart, Fife KY1 2XQ

Tel: 01592 654112 Fax: 01592 598555 **Map Ref 33**

St Andrews 5 miles. A warm welcome from Keith & Rosie at **FALSIDE SMIDDY**, converted stone smithy with beautiful walk to a deserted coast. Our bedrooms have tea/coffee and TV. The sitting room is for guests alone. Some French and German spoken. 1 hour from Highlands.

B&B from £19pp, Dinner by arrangement, Rooms 2 en-suite twin, No smoking, Children & pets welcome, Open all year except Christmas & New Year.

Mrs A R Birkinshaw, **Falside Smiddy,** Boarhills, St. Andrews, Fife KY16 8PT

Tel/Fax: 01334 880479 Email: falside@globalnet.co.uk **Map Ref 35**

BELVEDERE HOTEL

BELVEDERE HOTEL, twenty-one en-suite bedrooms with all modern facilities and panoramic views across the Firth of Forth and to Edinburgh beyond. Comfortable lounge bar and restaurant renowned for excellent cuisine using only the very best products from Scotlands wonderful natural larder.
B&B from £25pp, Dinner from £10, Rooms 1 single, 7 twin, 10 double, 5 family, all en-suite, Children welcome, Pets by arrangement, Open all year.
Gordon Mackintosh, **Belvedere Hotel,** Coxstool, West Wemyss, Fife KY1 4SL
Tel: 01592 654167 Fax: 01592 655279   **Map Ref 36**

HIGHLANDS

ASHBURN HOUSE

ASHBURN HOUSE, a completely refurbished Victorian house only 500 yards from town centre. Quietly located overlooking Loch Linnhe. Off-road parking. Central heating. Credit cards. AA 5Q Highly Acclaimed. Scottish breakfast. Tea making facilities, TV. Close to all Highland visitor attractions yet only two and a half hours from Glasgow. A truly restful holiday. Non-smoking.Email: ashburnhouse@ark.uk.co
B&B from £30-£40pp, Rooms 3 single, 1 twin, 3 double, all en-suite, No smoking or pets, Children welcome, Open February - December.
A Henderson, **Ashburn House,** Achintore Rd, Fort William PH33 6RD
Tel: 01397 706000 Fax: 01397 706000   **Map Ref 38**

Situated in own extensive grounds, midway between town centre and Ben Nevis. 10 of 12 rooms are en-suite, all rooms have colour TV and teas made. Special rates for 3 or more night bookings. Large private car park. **GLENLOCHY GUEST HOUSE** is recommended by Which and Best Bed & Breakfast Guide. Colour brochure available.
B&B from £15-£25pp, Rooms 4 twin, 6 double, 2 family, 10 en-suite, Restricted smoking, Children welcome, Open all year.
Margaret Macbeth, **Glenlochy Guest House,** Nevis Bridge, Fort William, DH33 6PF
Tel: 01397 702909   **Map Ref 39**

MACRAE HOUSE, a superior Victorian guest house overlooking River. AA QQQ. 5 minutes town centre. Private parking. Non-smoking. Ground floor bedroom. Near theatre. All rooms with big comfy armchairs. Owned by local lady for 10 years, lovely garden with seats overlooking River. Member of Tourist Board.

B&B from £18pp, Rooms 1 single, 2 twin, 2 double, 1 family, all with private bathrooms, No smoking or pets, Children welcome, Open all year.
Joyce Plent, **Macrae House,** 24 Ness Bank, Inverness, IV2 4SF
Tel: 01463 243658   **Map Ref 40**

ACORN HOUSE, all rooms en-suite, TV, tea/coffee etc. Ample car parking. Residents lounge, sauna, spa bath. Central to town and theatre, Aquadrome Sports centre. The premiere guest house in Inverness where you will find a truly Highland welcome. All food freshly prepared by the hostess.

B&B from £23.50pp, Dinner from £8.50-£15, Rooms 1 twin, 3 double, 3 family, most en-suite, Restricted smoking, Children & pets welcome, Open all year.
Dugie & Fiona Cameron, **Acorn House,** 2A Bruce Gardens, Inverness, IV3 5EN
Tel: 01463 717021 & 01463 240000 Fax: 01463 714236   **Map Ref 40**

ST. ANN'S HOUSE, a friendly family-run guest house. Ten minutes walk from town centre, rail and bus stations. TV, hostess tray, hair dryer all rooms. Guest lounge, restricted license. Parking. Brochure available. STB - 3 Star. AA - QQQ. RAC - Acclaimed. Day tours - Loch Ness, Skye, Orkney. Dolphin cruises. Email: stannshous@aol.com
B&B from £22pp, Rooms 1 single, 2 twin, 2 double, 1 family, all en-suite/private, Restricted smoking, Children welcome, No pets, Open February - October.
Brenda & Graham Wilson, **St. Ann's House,** 37 Harrowden Road, Inverness, IV3 5QN
Tel: 01463 236157 Fax: 01463 236157   **Map Ref 40**

ROSENEATH GUEST HOUSE, has tea/coffee facilities, hair dryers and TV's in all rooms. Credit cards accepted. Small fridge in the family rooms. Private parking. 5 minutes walk from centre. High chairs available. Pay phone. Close to Loch Ness. 3 Star Commended.

B&B from £19pp, Rooms 1 single, 1 twin, 2 double, 3 family, all en-suite, Children welcome, Pets by arrangement, Open all year.

Carol McIver, **Roseneath Guest House,** 39 Greig St, Inverness IV3 5PX
Tel: 01463 220201 Fax: 01463 220201   **Map Ref 41**

MELNESS GUEST HOUSE, is a small family run, no smoking B&B where our guests are made welcome in a true Highland fashion. We are close to all amenities and have private parking. To help you enjoy your stay our rooms are nicely decorated with central heating, tea/coffee, colour TV.

B&B from £18-£25pp, Rooms 1 twin, 1 double, 1 family en-suite, No smoking or pets, Children over 10, Open all year.
Mrs Joyce, **Melness Guest House,** 8 Old Edinburgh Road, Inverness, IV2 3HF
Tel: 01463 220963 Fax: 01463 220963   **Map Ref 40**

GROUSE & TROUT HOTEL, is a historic country house hotel linked to Bonny Prince Charlie. Cosy atmosphere, outstandingly beautiful surroundings, comfortable accommodation, renowned Scottish and International cuisine, Loch-View Restaurant and Bar. Popular fishing, deer stalking, shooting, Golf, Horse-riding and trekking, cycling and hill-walking. Own free Tennis Court.
B&B from £29pp, Dinner available???, Rooms ????single,????twin,?????double,????? family, all en-suite, Children & Pets welcome, Open all year.
Grouse & Trout Hotel, Farr, Loch Ness, Inverness, IV1 2XE
Tel: 01808 521314 Fax: 01808 521314   **Map Ref 40**

TOM AN T'SILIDH, a comfortable detached villa. Rooms have TV and tea/coffee making facilities. Guests lounge. Private parking. Personal service assured. Quiet location yet close to all amenities. Ideal hill walking centre amidst the Monadhliaths, Grampians, Cairngorms and the Lochaber peaks. 5 minutes from Golf course and River Spey.

B&B from £17pp, Dinner from £10, Rooms 1 twin, 1 double, 1 family, all en-suite, No smoking, Children & pets welcome, Open all year except Christmas & New Year.
Fiona Smith, **Tom an T'Silidh,** Station Road, Newtonmore, PH20 1AR
Tel: 01540 673554   **Map Ref 62**

DUNRAVEN LODGE HOTEL, a grade two listed building overlooking the spa village of Strathpeffer. All rooms have full en-suite facilities, TV and tea/coffee. A full menu is available to guests and visitors. Our comfortable bar lounge offers many fine wines and a full selection of malt whiskey. Children welcome. Spring and Autumn breaks at reduced prices.
B&B from £22.50pp, Dinner from £2.95, Rooms 5 twin, 2 double, 3 family, all en-suite, Restricted smoking, Children welcome, Pets by arrangement, Open March - December.
Andrew Harris, **Dunraven Lodge Hotel,** Golf Road, Strathpeffer IV14 9AG
Tel: 01997 421210   **Map Ref 43**

TAIGN NA MARA, offers a free Scottish Vegetarian information service, guide book £4.95 and cookbook 'Rainbows and Wellies' £14.95. Ideal for Highlands and Inverness. Idyllic loch side home. 1 hour from airport and station. Wildlife and walker paradise. Scottish vegetarian cooking, personal service and honeymoon suite. Email: mara@veganvillage.co.uk
B&B from £19.50pp, Dinner from £14.50, Rooms 1 twin, 2 double, one en-suite, No smoking, Pets by arrangement, Open all year.
Tony Weston, **Taign Na Mara,** The Shore, Ardindrean, Loch Broom, Ullapool, IV23 2SE
Tel: 01854 655282 Fax: 01854 655292   **Map Ref 44**

TORGUISH HOUSE, is set in beautiful countryside, once the home of famous author Alistair MacLean. It has now been converted into a very homely B&B, generous rooms, en-suite, TV, tea/coffee facilities, own sitting room with coal fire. Large garde with summerhouse and books just to relax. Email: torguish@torguish.com

B&B from £18pp, Rooms 2 twin, 2 double, 3 family, all en-suite, Children & Pets welcome, Open all year.
Mr & Mrs Allan, **Torguish House,** Daviot, Inverness IV1 2XQ
Tel: 01463 772208 Fax: 01463 772308   **Map Ref 45**

THE PRIORY HOTEL, is a privately owned hotel situated in village square. All facilities complimented with excellent service and good food. Ideal location for touring the North and West Highlands. "The only way to stay in the Beautiful Scottish Highlands".

B&B from £29.50pp, Dinner available, Rooms 3 single, 17 twin, 13 double, 2 family, all en-suite, Children & Pets welcome, Open all year.

The Priory Hotel, Beauly, Inverness-shire IV4 7BX
Tel: 01463 782309 Fax: 01463 782531   **Map Ref 46**

FEITH MHOR COUNTRY HOUSE, has all the charm and character of a Victorian country house, peacefully secluded, 1 mile from the village, so you can relax and enjoy the beauty of the Highlands. All bedrooms en-suite. Wonderful bird watching, walking and touring. STB 2 Stars. AA Recommended 3Q's.
B&B from £26pp, Rooms 3 twin, 2 double, 1 family, all en-suite, Restricted smoking, Children over 10, Pets by arrangement, Open January - November.
Peter & Penny Rawson, **Feith Mhor Country House,** Station Road, Carrbridge, Inverness-shire PH23 3AP
Tel: 01479 841621   **Map Ref 47**

OSPREY HOTEL, a small hotel in area of outstanding beauty offering warm welcome en-suite accommodation with colour TV, tea/coffee, hair dryers and Award winning food and extensive wine list. Ideal base for touring, walking, golf, fishing, etc. Members of "Taste of Scotland", AA Rosettes for food, brochure available.

B&B from £24pp, Dinner from £22, Rooms 2 single, 3 twin, 3 double, all en-suite, Restricted smoking, Children over 10, Pets by arrangement, Open all year.

Robert & Aileen Burrow, **Osprey Hotel,** Ruthven Road, Kingussie, Inverness-shire PH21 1EN
Tel: 01540 661510 Fax: 01540 661510   **Map Ref 48**

GRAMPIAN VIEW, an elegant Victorian house, six miles south Aviemore, with all amenities close by hill walking, bird watching, water sports etc. or just relaxing. All rooms tea/coffee facilities. Guest lounge with TV, central heating, newly refurbished. Home from home just ring and ask for Sandra. 3 Stars.

B&B from £18pp, Rooms 1 single, 2 twin, 3 double, all private/en-suite, Restricted smoking, Children & pets welcome, Open all year.

Sandra Neck, **Grampian View,** Kincraig, Kingussie, Inverness-shire PH21 1NA
Tel: 01540 651383   **Map Ref 49**

BALCRAGGAN HOUSE, for peace, quiet and a relaxing holiday. Double or twin bedroom en-suite, tea/coffee making facilities plus TV. Guests lounge. Ample parking. Walking and cycling from the house or visit the reindeer herd, castles, Culloden battlefield, wildlife park, distillery - the list is endless!

B&B from £25pp, Dinner from £15, Rooms 1 twin, 1 double, all en-suite, No smoking or pets, Children over 10, Open all year except Christmas.

Helen & Jim Gillies, **Balcraggan House,** Feshiebridge, Kincraig, Kingussie, Inverness-shire PH21 1NG
Tel: 01540 651488   **Map Ref 49**

FOYERS BAY HOUSE, a genuine Victorian villa in a spectacular position overlooking Loch Ness. Next to the Falls of Foyers. An ideal location for visiting the many attractions in the area. The guesthouse is not licensed but guests are welcome to bring their own wine for dinner, no corkage charge is made.

B&B from £19.50pp, Dinner from £10.50, Rooms 2 twin, 3 double, all en-suite, Restricted smoking, Children welcome, No pets, Open all year.

Otto & Carol Panciroli, **Foyers Bay House,** Lower Foyers, Loch Ness, Inverness-shire IV1 2YB
Tel: 01456 486624 Fax: 01456 486337   **Map Ref 50**

GREENLAWNS, is a comfortable, friendly, Victorian Guest House. Car park. Garden. Residents lounge. Open fire. Private Bar. Close to both Nairn's Championship Golf Courses, swimming pool, beaches and town. All rooms have colour TV's, tea/coffee facilities. AA 4Q Selected. STB 3 Star.

B&B from £16pp, Dinner from £8.50, Rooms 3 twin, 5 double, most en-suite, Restricted smoking, Children welcome, Pets by arrangement, Open all year except Christmas.

Sheelagh & David Southwell, **Greenlawns,** 13 Seafield Street, Nairn, Inverness-shire IV12 4HG
Tel: 01667 452738 Fax: 01667 452738   **Map Ref 42**

INVERGLOY HOUSE, a warm welcome to peaceful stables/coach house in beautiful Great Glen. Guests' sitting room overlooks Loch Lochy, superb views in 50-acre woodland. En-suite bedrooms, tastefully furnished with hospitality trays. Excellent meals nearby. Five and a half miles north of Spean Bridge. Non-smoking house.

B&B from £21pp, Rooms 3 twin, all en-suite, No smoking or pets, Children over 8, Open all year.

Mrs M.H. Cairns, **Invergloy House,** Spean Bridge, Inverness-shire PH34 4DY
Tel: 01397 712681   **Map Ref 51**

GLENVIEW INN & RESTAURANT, a charming inn nestling between mountains and sea and ideally situated for exploring the magnificent scenery of North Skye. We offer pretty bedrooms. A cosy lounge with open fire and seafood, ethnic and vegetarian delicacies in our high acclaimed restaurant.

B&B from £25pp, Dinner from £12.95, Rooms 1 twin, 3 double, 1 family, all en-suite, Restricted smoking, Children & pets welcome, Open mid March - November.

Cathie & Paul Booth, **Glenview Inn & Restaurant,** Culnacnoc, Staffin, Isle of Skye IV51 9JH
Tel: 01470 562248 Fax: 01470 562211   **Map Ref 52**

ALLT-CHAORAIN HOUSE, welcome to my home - come and relax admist some of the central Highlands most beautiful scenery. The log fire and the friendly atmosphere, complements our traditional Scottish meals made from local fresh produce, and allows the most reserved guests to exchange their day's experience with others from our trust bar.
B&B from £35pp, Dinner from £18, Rooms 1 single, 3 twin, 3 double, 1 family, No smoking, Children over 7, Pets welcome, Open April - October.
Roger McDonald, **Allt-Chaorain House,** Invierherive, Crianlarich, Perthshire FK20 8RU
Tel: 01838 300283 Fax: 01838 300238   **Map Ref 53**

LADYSMITH HOUSE

LADYSMITH HOUSE, a family run guesthouse serving a varied and substantial breakfast. Tea/coffee and TV all rooms, also a comfortable sitting-room is available. The informal licensed restaurant provides good home cooking using fresh, and as much, local produce as possible. We specialise in seafood and cater for vegetarian.
B&B from £15-£25pp, Dinner from £4.95-£10.50, Rooms 2 single, 1 twin, 2 double, 1 family, most en-suite, Children & pets welcome, Open all year.
Lauri Chilton, **Ladysmith House,** 24 Pulteney St, Ullapool, Ross-shire IV26 2UP
Tel: 01854 612185   **Map Ref 54**

POLOCHAR INN, a comfortable family run hotel by the seaside with outstanding views across the sound of Bara. Fully licensed. Tea/coffee making facilities in bedrooms. TV phone. Residents lounge and car park facilities. See the standing stone situated at Polochar and wild flowers and bird life. Ideal for hill walkers and sightseers.

B&B from £25pp, A la carte & bar meals available, Rooms 3 single, 4 twin, 2 double, 2 family, all en-suite, No smoking, Children welcome, Open all year.
Polochar Inn, Polochar South Uist HS8 5TT
Tel: 01878 700215 Fax: 01878 700768

BURNSIDE GUEST HOUSE, is a cozy guest house situated very close to town. Ideal base for golf, walking, cycling or simply relaxing. Tea/coffee making facilities. Private parking, Guests lounge. Continental breakfast available in your bedroom. Excellent home cooking and international cuisine. Email: burnsideguesthouse@msn.com
B&B from £19pp, Dinner from £12, Rooms 1 single, 2 twin, 1 double, 1 en-suite family, Restricted smoking, Children & pets welcome, Open all year.
Kerry & Dave, **Burnside Guest House,** Shore Road, Dornoch, Sutherland IV25 3LS
Tel: 01862 810919 Fax: 01862 810919   **Map Ref 55**

THE GOLF LINKS HOTEL, a family run hotel. Fully licensed, two bars, selection of wines. Centrally heated throughout, all rooms have colour television, electric blankets, tea/coffee facilities. Varied menu of homemade foods using local produce. Golf course and fabulous sandy beach literally on the doorstep.
B&B from £25pp, Dinner from £9, Rooms 5 twin, 3 double, 1 family, all en-suite, Children & pets welcome, Open all year.
Murray Galloway & Andrea Bates, **The Golf Links Hotel,** Church Street, Golspie, Sutherland KW10 6TT
Tel: 01408 633408 Fax: 01408 634184   **Map Ref 56**

EDDRACHILLES
HOTEL

EDDRACHILLES HOTEL, is set in an outstanding position at the head of the island studded. Eddrachilles Bay, a good area for bird watching and hill walking or touring amidst the magnificent scenery of the north-west. Modern bedrooms have TV, telephone, trouser press, hair dryer and tea/coffee facilities.
B&B from £34.50pp, Dinner from £11.60, Rooms 7 twin, 3 double, 1 family, all en-suite, Smoking allowed, Children over 3, No pets, Open 10th March - 25th October.
Mr & Mrs Wood, **Eddrachilles Hotel,** Badcall Bay, Scourie, Sutherland IV27 4TH
Tel: 01971 502080 Fax: 01971 502477   **Map Ref 57**

CATALINA GUEST HOUSE, located on the far north Atlantic coastline with fantastic scenery. We accept only two visitors who have their own private suite; twin bedroom, shower room, lounge and dining room. Delicious meal served at the time you want. High grades from the Automobile Association, Scottish Tourist Board, Rosette Award and Which? Guide.

B&B from £18pp, Dinner from £10, Rooms 1 twin with en-suite facilities, No smoking, children or pets, Open all year except Christmas.

Jane Salisbury, **Catalina Guest House,** Aultivullin, Strathy Point, Sutherland KW14 7RY
Tel: 01641 541279 Fax: 01641 541314   **Map Ref 58**

Set amidst the majestic splendour of the Torridon Mountains and adjacent to the acclaimed Beinn Eighe Nature Reserve. The **KINLOCHEWE HOTEL & BUNKHOUSE** offers relaxed and informal accommodation for lovers of the great outdoors. Excellent food and a well stocked bar complete a truly memorable holiday experience.
B&B from £22pp, Dinner from £4.95, Rooms 3 single, 5 twin, 2 double, some en-suite, Restricted smoking, Children & pets welcome, Open all year.
Gerry & Denise Thatcher, **Kinlochewe Hotel & Bunkhouse,** Kinlochewe, Wester Ross IV22 2PA
Tel: 01445 760253 Fax: 01445 760253   **Map Ref 59**

MORAY

MINTON HOUSE, a magnificent pink mansion with sanctuary and ballroom, stands on the shoreline of Findhorn Bay, well known for its wildlife. Set in 6 acres of grounds, the house has outstanding views of the sea and mountains. Email: minton@findhorn.org

B&B from £17 - £29pp, Dinner from £7, Rooms 2 twin en-suite, 2 double en-suite, 1 twin, 1 single, 1 family, Children welcome, No smoking. Vegetarian. Open all year.

Judith Meynell, **Minton House,** Findhorn Bay, Forres, Moray IV36 0YY
Tel: 01309 690819 Fax: 01309 691583   **Map Ref 60**

FEARNA HOUSE, an attractive period house one hundred yards from River Spey on outskirts of Grantown. All rooms prettily furnished with secondary glazing and tea/coffee facilities. Sitting room with TV and log fire. Wonderful local walks and easy access to Distilleries, Castles, Mountains, Moray Firth, beaches, fishing. Parking.
B&B from £20pp, Dinner by arrangement from £10, Rooms 2 twin, 1 double, all en-suite/private bathroom, No smoking, Children welcome, Dogs welcome, Open all year.
Miss Palmer, **Fearna House,** Old Spey Bridge, Grantown-on-Spey, Moray PH26 3NQ
Tel/Fax: 01479 872016   **Map Ref 61**

CULDEARN HOUSE, a country house on the edge of Grantown which has been sympathetically modernised. A friendly informal atmosphere where service is professional and attention to detail meticulous. Many castles and distilleries to be visited whilst golf, fishing, riding, bird watching and walking is available close by.
B&B from £60pp (includes Dinner), Rooms 1 single, 3 twin, 5 double, all en-suite, Restricted smoking, Children over 10, No pets, Open March - October.
Mr & Mrs Alasdair & Isobel Little, **Culdearn House,** Woodlands Terrace, Grantown on Spey, Morayshire PH26 3JU
Tel: 01479 872106 Fax: 01479 873641   **Map Ref 61**

KINROSS HOUSE, is a superb Guest House in the heart of the Scottish Highlands. Peacefully situated in small country town. Lovely en-suite rooms are warm and restful - all with TV and welcome trays. Excellent meals prepared and served by your Scottish hosts. Licensed. No-smoking house. Parking.
B&B from £24pp, Dinner from £14, Rooms 2 single, 2 twin, 1 double, 1 family, most en-suite, No smoking, Children or Pets, Open April - October.
David & Katherine Elder, **Kinross House,** Woodside Avenue, Grantown-on-Spey, Morayshire PH26 3JR
Tel: 01479 872042 Fax: 01479 873504   **Map Ref 61**

PERTHSHIRE & KINROSS

DUNALLAN GUEST HOUSE, a semi-detached Victorian villa on A94. Approx 5 minutes from city centre. All rooms have tea/coffee trays, colour TV's. Off-street parking, early breakfasts catered for if required. 10% discounts offered for stays of three nights or longer. Convenient for visits to Scone Palace or numerous golf course in area.
B&B from £20pp, Dinner from £10, Rooms 3 single, 2 twin, 1 double, 1 family, all en-site, Restricted smoking, Children welcome, Pets by arrangement, Open all year.
Cathy & Jim Brown, **Dunallan Guest House,** 10 Pitcullen Crescent, Perth, PH2 7HT
Tel: 01738 622551 Fax: 01738 622551   **Map Ref 63**

BEECHES GUEST HOUSE, a family run Victorian house. Strictly no smoking. Guest lounge. Off street car parking. Tea/coffee facilities in all rooms also television, video and satellite. Situated close to the centre of Perth (about 15 minutes walk). Ideal touring base.

B&B from £18pp, Dinner from £8, Rooms 2 single, 1 twin, 1 double, all en-suite, No smoking, Children welcome, Pets by arrangement, Open all year.

Pat & Brian Smith, **Beeches Guest House,** 2 Comely Bank, Perth, PH2 7HU
Tel: 01738 624486 Fax: 01738 624486 **Map Ref 64**

DALRULZION HOUSE HOTEL, is a quiet rural, family run hotel situated on A93 midway between Perth & Braemar. Coffee shop. Malt bar. Home cooking. Beer garden on riverside, salmon fishing available. Central for touring, hill walking, bird watching, deer, golfing & skiing. No TV or telephones in rooms. **B&B from £25pp,** Dinner from £12, Rooms 1 single, 1 twin, 2 double, 3 family, most en-suite, Restricted smoking, Children welcome, Open all year except Christmas & New Year.

Bill & Jean Alexander, **Dalrulzion House Hotel,** Glenshee, Blairgowrie, Perthshire PH10 7LJ
Tel: 01250 882222 **Map Ref 65**

ARDEN HOUSE, an elegant Victorian country house set above the town with own gardens and car park. Home of BBC TV's "Dr Finlay's Casebook". Comfortable en-suite rooms with TV and thoughtful extras. Excellent touring centre for Trossachs, Highlands, Edinburgh, Glasgow, East and West Coasts. **B&B from £25pp,** Rooms 1 single, 2 twin, 3 double, all en-suite, No smoking, Children over 14, No pets, Open March - November.

William R Jackson & Ian M Mitchell, **Arden House,** Bracklinn Road, Callander, Perthshire FK17 8EQ
Tel: 01877 330235 Fax: 01877 330235 **Map Ref 66**

POPPIES HOTEL, is a very comfortable fully licensed family run hotel. Rooms are en-suite with Direct Dial telephone, colour TV, radio and tea/coffee making facilities. The private car park is monitored by CCTV. A grand touring base.

B&B from £18pp, Rooms 1 twin, 5 double, 2 family, Restricted smoking, Children welcome, No pets, Open April - October.

Ian & Virginia Keppie, **Poppies Hotel,** Leny Road, Callander, Perthshire FK17 8AL
Tel: 01877 330329 Fax: 01877 330 329 **Map Ref 66**

THE ROYAL HOTEL, built in 1765 the hotel has 11 rooms, 2 four posters, one suite, among it's rooms. Also available is shooting, fishing, golf, walking and a wide selection of local attractions and also a beautifully appointed restaurant for the most desiring of dinners. Email: reception@royalhotel.co.uk
B&B from £65pp, Dinner from £12.95, Rooms 3 twin, 8 double, all en-suite, Children welcome, Pets by arrangement, Open all year.

Edward Gibbons, **The Royal Hotel,** Melville Square, Comrie, Perthshire PH6 2DN
Tel: 01764 679200 Fax: 01764 679219 **Map Ref 67**

THE COACH HOUSE HOTEL, family run hotel overlooking River Lochay. Good home cooked food, spacious comfortable rooms with mountain views, all have tea/coffee facilities, televisions, some en-suite. Private car parks. Live traditional Scottish music in our lounge bar most weekends throughout the summer. Friendly welcome awaits.
B&B from £25pp, Dinner available, Rooms 1 single, 2 twin, 2 double, 3 family, some en-suite, Restricted smoking, Children welcome, No pets, Open all year.
John, Ann, Peter & Mark Shuttleworth, **The Coach House Hotel,** Lochay Road, Killin, Perthshire FK21 8TN
Tel: 01567 820349 **Map Ref 68**

DALL LODGE COUNTRY HOUSE HOTEL, a century old mansion recently modernised. Commanding stunning views of mountains and river. Ideal for golfing, fishing and touring. Home cooking. En-suite rooms with colour TV, hair dryer, tea/coffee and 4 poster bed. Conservatory. Lounge. Ground floor rooms for wheelchairs guests. AA 3 Star. STB 4 Crown Highly Commended.
B&B from £29.50pp, Dinner from £21.50, Rooms 1 single, 2 twin, 5 double, 2 family, all en-suite, Open March - October.
David & Fatima Wilson, **Dall Lodge Country House Hotel,** Main Street, Killin, Perthshire FK21 8TN
Tel: 01567 820217 Fax: 01567 820726 **Map Ref 69**

BREADALBANE HOUSE , all rooms en-suite, TV, kettle, hair dryer. SKY TV residents lounge. Car park. Dinners served using best local produce Salmon, Venison. Ideal touring base. Hill walking, golfing haven. Wildlife and scenery a must. Close to famous falls of Dochart Loch Tay. Breadalbane Folklore centre.
B&B from £20pp, Dinner from £12, Rooms 2 twin, 2 double, 1 family, all en-suite, Restricted smoking, Children & pets welcome, Open February - November.
Dani Grant, **Breadalbane House ,** Main Street, Killin, Perthshire FK21 8UT
Tel: 01567 820386/798 Fax: 01567 820386 **Map Ref 69**

WESTLANDS OF PITOCHRY, a beautifully presented stone-built hotel of quality. All rooms en-suite with TV, radio and tea/coffee facilities. Cocktail bar and restaurant have appealing 'taste of Scotland' to a high standard. Great golf, theatre, walking and theatre. STB 4 Crown Commended Award.
B&B from £26pp, Dinner from £17.50, Rooms 1 single, 6 twin, 6 double, 2 family, all en-suite, Smoking, Children & pets welcome, Open all year.
Andrew Mathieson, **Westlands of Pitochry,** 160 Atholl Road Pitlochry Perthshire PH16 5AR
Tel: 01796 472266 Fax: 01796 473994 **Map Ref 70**

TIR ALUINN GUEST HOUSE, overlooking the Tummel Valley, we are a family run, friendly, licensed guest house catering for the discerning visitor. Our home cooking is renowned and includes traditional Scottish, Asian and Oriental cuisines. Quiet location. Ample parking. TV, courtesy tray in all rooms.
B&B from £17pp, Dinner from £8, Rooms 3 double, 2 family, 2 en-suite, Restricted smoking, Children welcome, Pets by arrangement, Open all year.
Pete & Dawn Burgoyne, **Tir Aluinn Guest House,** 10 Higher Oakfield, Pitlochry, Perthshire PH16 5HT
Tel: 01796 472231 **Map Ref 70**

BUTTONBOSS LODGE, coffee/tea facilities, TV in rooms. Sky TV in lounge. Private parking. Garage for motorbikes. Centrally positioned in Pitlochry. Easy walking distance from theatre, shops, Fish Ladder Restaurant. Guaranteed friendly welcome, relaxed atmosphere. Colin PGA Golf professional. Marleen former Stewardess with KLM airlines.
B&B from £15pp, Rooms 2 single, 3 twin, 4 double, some en-suite, Restricted smoking, Children welcome, Open all year except Christmas & New Year.
Colin & Marleen Mackay, **Buttonboss Lodge,** 25 Atholl Road, Pitlochry, Perthshire PH16 5BX
Tel: 01796 472065 Fax: 01796 472065 **Map Ref 65**

POPLARS HOTEL, a family run Victorian house hotel with large garden and panoramic views of Tummel Valley. Ample car parking. All rooms TVs, tea/coffee facilities. Licensed restaurant specialising in traditional Scottish Fayre. Close to local amenities. Ideal location for exploring Highland Scotland and for all outdoor activities. Email: hotelpops@aol.com
B&B from £19.50pp, Dinner from £12, Rooms 4 twin, 4 double, 3 family, all en-suite, Children welcome, Pets by arrangement, Open all year.
Kathleen Shepherd & Ian Goodlet, **Poplars Hotel,** 27 Lower Oakfield, Pitlochry, Perthshire PH16 5DS
Tel: 01796 472129 Fax: 01796 472554 **Map Ref 70**

BALROBIN HOTEL, traditional country house of quality with panoramic views, owned and run by the Hohman family offering the highest standards of comfort and services. 15 en-suite rooms with colour TV, refreshments tray, hair dryers etc. Resident's only bar. Ample car parking. Ideal base for golf and touring.
B&B from £25pp, Dinner from £15, Rooms 1 single, 3 twin, 10 double, 1 family, all en-suite, Restricted smoking, Children over 5, Pets welcome, Open March - October.
Mr & Mrs Hohman, **Balrobin Hotel,** Higher Oakfield, Pitlochry, Perthshire PH16 5HT
Tel: 01796 472901 Fax: 01796 474200 **Map Ref 70**

BENDARROCH HOUSE, a refurbished Victorian house set in landscaped grounds, panoramic views with the River Tay running past the estate. Situated between Aberfeldy/Pitlochry. Golf course, fishing, canoeing, 2 minutes, other sports nearby. B&B £25 per person per night. Spacious bedrooms, 3 separate lounges. Evening meals 2 courses £10. Restricted hotel licence.
B&B from £25pp, Dinner from £10, Rooms 1 twin, 3 double, 1 family, all en-suite, Restricted smoking, Children welcome, Pets by arrangement, Open April - October.
Mrs Jacqueline Warschau, **Bendarroch House,** Strathtay, Pitlochry, Perthshire PH9 0PG
Tel: 01887 840420 Fax: 01887 840438 **Map Ref 71**

RENFREWSHIRE

KIRKLEE HOTEL, recently awarded 4 Stars for quality by the Scottish Tourist Board, is set in the leafy "West-End" conservation area, but is only a short walk from many restaurants and bars. Stylish Edwardian elegance with antiques, paintings and award-winning garden.

B&B from £29.50pp, Rooms 2 twin, 4 double, 3 family, all en-suite, Smoking & Children welcome, No pets, Open all year except Christmas.

Douglas Rogen, **Kirklee Hotel,** 11 Kensington Gate, Glasgow, G12 9LG
Tel: 0141 334 5555 Fax: 0141 339 3828 **Map Ref 37**

SHETLAND

THE WESTING HOTEL, licensed country hotel situated eight miles west of Lerwick. In the centre of Shetland. Breathtaking views from rooms, restaurants and bars. All bedrooms have television, tea/coffee facilities. Awarded Three Star, Scottish Tourist Board rating. Ideal centre for exploring the Shetland Islands.

B&B from £35pp, Dinner from £10, Rooms 3 single, 2 twin, 1 double, all en-suite, Restricted smoking, Children welcome, No pets, Open all year.
Mr J.D. Macrae, **The Westing Hotel,** Whiteness, Shetland ZE2 9LJ
Tel: 01595 840242 Fax: 01595 840500

WEST LOTHIAN

RICHMOND PARK HOTEL, is a privately owned 4 Crown Commended Hotel over-looking River Forth. Centrally located between Stirling and Edinburgh. 46 luxury en-suite bedrooms, full facilities including SKY television. Several ground floor rooms, suitable for disabled guests. Restaurant, lounge-diner, bar, conservatory and fitness suite. Large private gardens and car park.
B&B from £30pp, Dinner from £9, Rooms 1 single, 20 twin, 21 double, 4 family, all en-suite, Children welcome, Pets by arrangement, Open all year.
Mr Miller, **Richmond Park Hotel,** 26 Linlithgow Road, Boness, West Lothian EH51 0DN
Tel: 01506 823213 Fax: 01506 822717   **Map Ref 73**

Douglas and Lorna extend a warm welcome with all rooms on ground level. All bedrooms are furnished to the highest standard. Each room has a remote control colour TV and tea/coffee facilities. **WHITECROFT** is surround by farmland yet only 10 miles from Edinburgh city centre. Private parking. A full hearty Scottish breakfast is served using local produce, even whisky marmalade. STB 3 Stars, AA QQQQ Selected.
B&B from £22pp, Rooms 1 twin, 2 double, all en-suite, No smoking, Children over 12, Guide dogs only, Open all year.
Lorna Scott, **Whitecroft,** East Calder, Livingston, West Lothian EH53 0ET
Tel: 01506 882494 Fax: 01506 882598   **Map Ref 74**

Please mention
THE BED & BREAKFAST
DIRECTORY
when booking your
accommodation

Wales, from its rugged coast to spectacular mountains, is steeped in history and legend. The country's backbone is the Cambrian Mountains, their highest point being the three thousand five hundred and sixty feet Snowdon, in North Wales, which is only ten miles from the sea. The popularity of North Wales stems from Snowdonia, which takes its name from Snowdon and its sea and great beaches. From the Snowdonia National Park to the east the landscape rises again to the Clwydian Range, an area of outstanding natural beauty.

A land of ancient rocks and ancient people, a wild people who kept the might of the Roman army at bay, who fought off the raiding Saxons, the Danish pirates and the fierce Irish and even when all England was subject to Norman rule, the Welsh continued to remain free for many years. They were superb guerrilla fighters, but were finally no match for the military genius of Edward I of England. Even so this turbulent principality managed to preserve its wild independence almost to the end of the 13th century, when Llywelyn at Gruffyd, ruler of Gwynedd and known to the Welsh as Ein Elyw Olaf, our last leader, was forced to make peace. Edward's ultimate weapon against the threat of Welsh uprising was a chain of eight magnificent and impregnable castles, each strategically placed so that it could be provisioned from the sea. In 1301, to cement the peace Edward made his young son Prince of Wales.

Rich in tradition, every region has its own legendary lore, and richest in such memories is the inland the Romans called Mona and the English know as Anglesey. Maybe because this fertile island fed the barren mountainous regions of the mainland, it was called the Motherland of Wales, but to the Welsh it was the Sacred Isle, and the centre of a strong Bardic tradition. Probably a quarter of the population of Wales now speak the Welsh language as well as English and there are still a considerable number who speak only Welsh, the language of many of the Eisteddfords, Contests in Music and Verse, held each year. The best known takes place at Llangollen.

Today this country is a wonderful holiday venue offering the ultimate in spectacular scenery and a beautiful coastline with its quaint fishing villages and popular seaside resorts with good beaches and safe bathing. There are castles, abbeys, towns and cities of historic significance aplenty, but it is the essentially Welsh villages that are, to many, the charm and delight of this fine country.

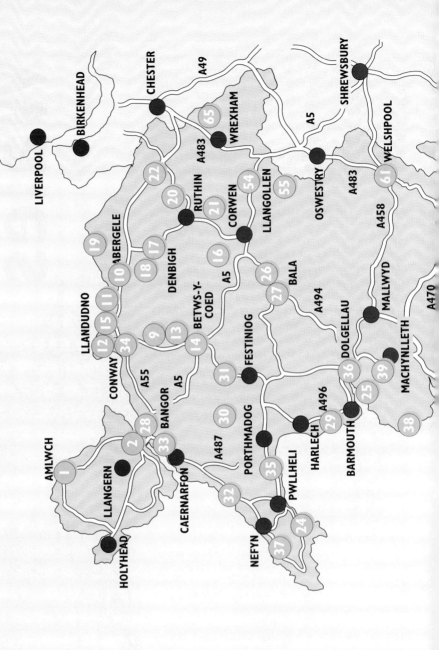

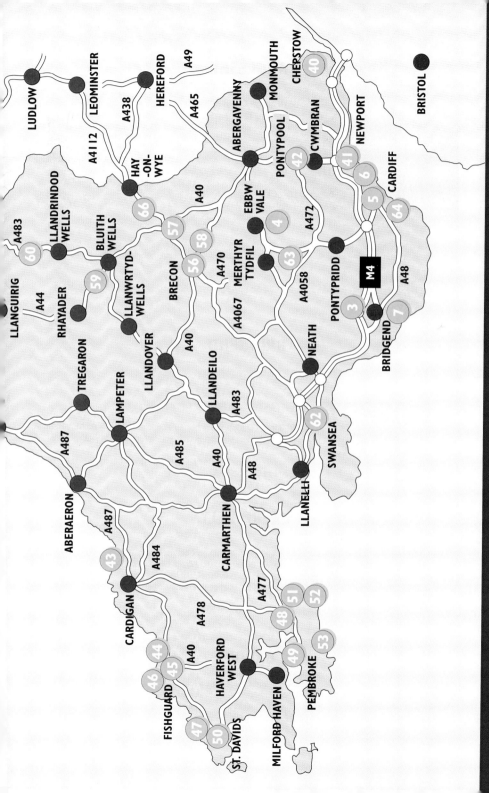

WALES

ANGLESEY

BRYN ARFOR GUEST HOUSE, is situated in a tremendous coastal location overlooking the picturesque Bull Bay. Lovely coastal walks, ideal for all watersports, close to 18 hole golf course and fabulous sandy beaches. Colour TV and hospitality trays. Licensed bar. Highly commended by WTB 2 Crowns. Welcome Host Award.
B&B from £16pp, Dinner from £3.95, Rooms 2 single, 4 twin, 4 double, 4 family, most en-suite, Restricted smoking, Open all year except Christmas & New Year.
Margaret & Ron Clays, **Bryn Arfor Guest House,** Pen-y-Bonc, Amlwch, Isle of Anglesey LL68 9DU
Tel: 01407 831 493   **Map Ref 1**

BWTHYN, a warm, welcoming, non-smoking B&B, former Victorian quarryman's terraced cottage. 1 minute from Menai Straits, with peaceful wooded shoreline walks to 8th century Church Island. Two very pretty en-suite doubles, power showers, colour TV's, tea makers, scrumptious food. , B&B Selected "Editor's" Top Twenty U.K, "Which" Recommended Guide 1999.
B&B from £15pp, Dinner £12.50, Rooms 2 en-suite double, No smoking or pets, Children over 12, Open all year.
Ms Rosemary Abas, **Bwthyn,** Brynafon, Menai Bridge, Isle of Anglesey LL59 5HA
Tel: 01248 713119 Fax: 01248 713119   **Map Ref 2**

BRIDGEND

MAERDY HOTEL, a small cozy, comfortable, family run hotel with all rooms en-suite, tea/coffee facilities, colour TV. Restaurant. Lounge Bar. Car park facilities. Recently refurbished.

B&B from £47.50pp, Dinner from £8.95, Rooms 4 single, 14 double, 6 family, all en-suite, Children welcome, Pets by arrangement, Open all year.

Firoz Nanji, **Maerdy Hotel,** Coychurch Road, Pencoed, Bridgend, Mid Glamorgan CF35 5NA
Tel: 01656 860654 Fax: 01656 864732   **Map Ref 3**

CAERPHILLY

WYRLOED LODGE, Victorian style house set in peaceful village with pub, church approx 20 houses. En-suites rooms, TV, tea/coffee, guests lounge and dining area, parking. Beautiful walks Moors Forestry. Excellent for touring Cardiff 45 minutes, Brecon 30 minutes, also converted barn, for self catering available.
B&B from £18pp, Dinner from £7, Rooms 1 twin, 1 double, 1 family, all en-suite, Restricted smoking, Children welcome, Pets by arrangement, Open January - November..
Mr & Mrs James, **Wyrloed Lodge,** Manmoel, Blackwood, Gwent NP2 0RW
Tel: 01495 371198 Fax: 01495 243322   **Map Ref 4**

CARDIFF

PRINCES GUEST HOUSE, small Victorian family run guest house situated close to town centre and tourist attraction like Cardiff Castle, Civic centre etc. Offering six bedrooms two with private showers. All rooms have washbasins colour TV and tea/coffee making facilities. Warm and friendly welcome to all guests.
B&B from £16pp, Rooms 2 single, 1 twin, 1 triple, 2 double, 1 family, 2 en-suite, Children over 3, No pets, Open all year.
Luz Burrows, **Princes Guest House,** 10 Princes Street, Roath, Cardiff, CF2 3PR
Tel: 01222 491732   **Map Ref 6**

THE GUEST HOUSE, small, friendly family run guest house with private car park. Conveniently situated, 15 minutes walk to the town centre or 3 minutes drive. Main bus route. Castle, shops, parks very close. All rooms central heated with washbasins, colour TV's and hospitality trays. M4 junction 29.
B&B from £15pp, Rooms 2 single, 3 twin, 3 double, 1 family, 2 en-suite, Children over 5, No pets, Open all year except Christmas.
Pete & Maggie Bird, **The Guest House,** 160 Richmond Road, Roath, Cardiff, South Glamorgan CF2 3BX
Tel: 01222 483619   **Map Ref 6**

CARMATHENSHIRE

THE HERONSTON HOTEL, ideally located seven minutes from the M4 whilst close to the Glamorgan heritage coast. Local places of interest include golf, castles and potteries. Hotel's leisure facilities: indoor and outdoor pools, sauna, jacuzzi, steam room and solarium. A'La Carte restaurant and Heron Bar with meals available.
B&B from £25pp, Dinner from £15.95, Rooms 11 twin, 61 double, 3 family, all en-suite, Children welcome, Pets by arrangement, Open all year except Christmas.
Tim Neill, **The Heronston Hotel,** Ewenny, Bridgend, Mid Glamorgan CF35 5AW
Tel: 01656 668811 Fax: 01656 767391   **Map Ref 7**

CEREDIGION

THE GEORGE BORROW HOTEL, famous hotel overlooking Rheidol Gorge. In foothills of Cambrian Mountains. Good food and beer. Log fires. All rooms have TV, coffee making facilities and are central heated. Lounge overlooking beautiful countryside. Ideal for walking, fishing, bird watching (Red Kite) or exploring Mid Wales. Email: 100672.3443@compuserve.com
B&B from £18pp, Dinner from £5.25, Rooms 2 single, 3 twin, 2 double, 2 family, most en-suite, Children welcome, Pets by arrangement, Open all year.
John & Jill Wall, **The George Borrow Hotel,** Ponterwyd, Aberystwyth SY23 3AD
Tel: 01970 890230 Fax: 01970 890 587   **Map Ref 8**

CONWY

HAFOD COUNTRY HOTEL, warm welcome, friendliness and a sense of quality and individuality, in furnishings and food, together with a general sense of peace and quiet, combine to make for a special experience. Car park. Licensed. Edge of Snowdonia National Park. Excellent base for exploring North Wales.
B&B from £27.50pp, Dinner from £15, Rooms 1 single, 2 twin, 6 double, all en-suite, Restricted smoking, Children over 11, Open February - December.
Chris & Rosina Nichols, **Hafod Country Hotel,** Trefriw, Aberconwy LL27 0RQ
Tel: 01492 640029 Fax: 01492 641351   **Map Ref 9**

LYNDALE HOTEL, AA, RAC 2 Star Hotel, offers all rooms with full en-suite facilities, bar/restaurant and car park. Situated in the village of old Colwyn. On the beautiful North Wales coast, central to Llandudno, Conway, Anglesey and Snowdonia.

B&B £45, Dinner from £15, Rooms 2 single, 3 twin, 7 double, 2 family, all en-suite, Restricted smoking, Children & pets welcome, Open all year.

Lyndale Hotel, 410 Abergate Road, Colwyn Bay, Conway, LL29 9AB
Tel: 01492 515429 Fax: 01492 518805   **Map Ref 11**

TUDNO LODGE, a warm and friendly guest house situated at the foot of the Great Orme, five minutes to beach and shops. Tea/coffee making facilities, TV lounge with views of the sea, south facing garden and patio area.

B&B from £14pp, Dinner from £6, Rooms 1 twin, 3 double, 3 family, 2 en-suite, Restricted smoking, Children welcome, Pets by arrangement, Open Easter - December.

Martin & Marcella Cooke, **Tudno Lodge,** 66 Church Walks, Llandudno, LL30 2HG
Tel: 01492 876174 **Map Ref 12**

....

THE STRATFORD HOTEL, an elegant sea front family run hotel with panoramic views of the bay. A wide choice of menu freshly cooked. All bedrooms en-suite with tea/coffee facilities, satellite TV and hair dryers. Luxury suite with spa bath. Licensed bar. Close to theatre, conference centre and shops.
B&B from £19, Dinner from £9, Rooms 2 twin, 4 double, 4 family, all en-suite, Smoking, Children & pets welcome, Open March - November.
Roy & Di Darlington, **The Stratford Hotel,** Promenade, Craig-y-don, Llandudno, LL30 1BG
Tel: 01492 877962 Fax: 01492 877962 **Map Ref 12**

....

FIRS COTTAGE,, our 17th century cottage and comfortable family home is near Bodnant Garden, Caernarfon and Snowdonia. Our Welsh breakfast includes homemade bread, jams and marmalade. From the garden patio we have lovely views of hills and the River Conwy.

B&B from £16pp, Rooms 2 twin, 1 double, Restricted smoking, Children welcome, Pets by arrangement, Open March - October.

Mary & Jack Marrow, **Firs Cottage,,** Maenan, Llanrwst, LL26 0YR
Tel: 01492 660 244 **Map Ref 13**

....

NANT-Y-GLYN HOTEL, a completely refurbished hotel. Has magnificent views, our perfect location beneath the great Orme offers the most discerning guests a holiday to remember. Our excellent food has been acclaimed in a Good Food Guide. En-suite rooms, colour TV, complimentary beverages. Licensed. Lounge bar. Non smoking hotel. WTB 3 Crowns Commended.
B&B from £17pp, Dinner from £9.50, Rooms 1 single, 1 twin, 6 double, some en-suite, No smoking or pets, Children over 10, Open all year.
Mavis & Eric Thomas, **Nant-y-Glyn Hotel,** 59 Church Walks, Llandudno Conwy LL30 2HL
Tel: 01492 875915 **Map Ref 12**

....

MAYVILLE HOTEL, is a small family-run licensed hotel. Close to sea, shops and rail station. All rooms are en-suite with colour TV's, radio, tea/coffee facilities. Car park. Easy access to Snowdonia, Great Orme, ski slope, toboggan run, pier, 2 beaches and copper mines.

B&B from £17pp, Dinner from £8, Rooms 3 twin, 1 double, 1 family, all en-suite, Children over 5, Pets by arrangement, Open all year.
Daivd Gilham, **Mayville Hotel,** 4 St. Davids Road, Llandudno, Conwy LL30 2UL
Tel: 01492 875406 Fax: 01492 875406 **Map Ref 12**

ST. HILARY HOTEL, is a well appointed Promenade Hotel providing superior accommodation. Positioned on the sea front affording magnificent views of Llandudno Bay and Great Orme. An ideal centre for touring North Wales and Snowdonia. Individually styled en-suite bedrooms, colour TV's, hospitality trays etc. "Bed & Breakfast at it's Best!" Email: sjprobert@compuserve.com
B&B from £15.75pp, Rooms 4 twin, 7 double, 4 family, most en-suite, Restricted smoking, Children welcome, No pets, Open mid February & mid November.
Mr & Mrs S.J. Probert, **St. Hilary Hotel,** Promenade, Llandudno, Conwy LL30 1BG
Tel: 01492 875551 Fax: 01492 875551   **Map Ref 12**

....

THE WHITE HORSE INN, is a 16th Century inn situated in the heart of Snowdonia National park. TV and tea/coffee facilities. Large car park. Notorious for real ales and fine wines, fresh produce used in our home made bar food. Cottage restaurant popular for fresh Salmon, Welsh Lamb. Log fires. Great welcome.
B&B from £24-£30pp, Restaurant 3 course from £15-£18, Rooms 1 twin, 5 double, all en-suite, Restricted smoking, Children over 12, Pets by arrangement, Open all year.
Roger & Megan Bower, **The White Horse Inn,** Capel Garmon, Betws y Coed, Llanrwst, Conwy LL26 0RW
Tel: 01690 710271 Fax: 01690 710271   **Map Ref 14**

....

SUNNY DOWNS HOTEL, 4 Crown family run hotel just 2 minutes walk to beach. All rooms en-suite with colour TV, video, satellite, clock radio, tea/coffee facilities, hair dryers, mini-bar/refrigerator, direct dial telephone and central heating. Hotel facilities bar, games room, restaurant, sauna and car park. Telephone for brochure.
B&B from £25pp, Dinner from £18, Rooms 2 single, 4 twin, 6 double, 3 family, all en-suite, Restricted smoking, Children & pets welcome, Open all year.
Mike Willington, **Sunny Downs Hotel,** 66 Abbey Road, Rhos-on-Sea, Conwy LL28 4NU
Tel: 01492 544256 Fax: 01492 543223   **Map Ref 15**

....

WHITE LODGE HOTEL, a sea front, family run, small hotel. All bedrooms have en-suite facilities, with colour television and tea/coffee making facilities. Licensed bar. Large car park. Well situated for touring Snowdonia and North Wales.

B&B from £26pp, Dinner from £9, Rooms 4 twin, 6 double, 2 family, all en-suite, Restricted smoking, Children over 5, No pets, Open March - November.
Eileen & Peter Rigby, **White Lodge Hotel,** Central Promenade, Llandudno, Gwynedd LL30 1AT
Tel: 01492 877713   **Map Ref 12**

....

DENBIGHSHIRE

....

GOLDEN PHEASANT HOTEL, an 18th century country hotel. In picturesque valley. All rooms centrally heated, colour TV's, tea/coffee facilities. 4 poster beds. Whirlpool baths. Restaurant bar. Gardens, patios. Ideal for visiting National Trust properties. Golf, fishing arranged. Car park. Special rates for groups. Children and pets welcome. Ideal for walkers.
B&B from £59pp, Dinner/Bar meals, Rooms 2 single, 6 twin, 6 double, 5 family, all en-suite, Children & pets welcome, Open all year.
John & Jannette Pugh, **Golden Pheasant Hotel,** Glyn Ceiriog, Llangollen, LL20 7BB
Tel: 01691 718281 Fax: 01691 718 479   **Map Ref 55**

THE OLD RECTORY, dating from 1714 in beautiful, quiet, hilly setting near Snowdonia National Park. Splendid views, large walled grounds and completely private. Beautiful home made/grown produce including biscuits, breads and marmalades. Lounge with inglenook. Conservatory. Secure parking. No TV and no smoking, Bring your own wine. Informal and charming.
B&B from £28pp, Meals from £9, Rooms 1 twin, 2 double, all en-suite, No smoking, Children welcome, No pets in house, Open all year.
Frank & Lesley Hart, **The Old Rectory,** Bettws Gwerfyl Goch, Corwen, Denbighshire LL21 9PU
Tel: 01490 460387   **Map Ref 16**

THE BULL HOTEL, 15th century grade II listed. Town centre. Car parking, Telephones, televisions, tea/coffee. Bar meals, restaurant. Golf and fishing in vicinity. Credit cards accepted. Owner run free house with real ale.

B&B from £16.50pp, Dinner from £2.50, Rooms 2 single, 3 twin, 5 double, 3 family, some en-suite, Children welcome, No pets, Open all year.

Alan Neaves, **The Bull Hotel,** Hall Square, Denbigh LL16 3NU
Tel: 01745 812582   **Map Ref 17**

HAWK & BUCKLE INN, is a 17th Century coaching inn in lovely countryside, very central for touring North Wales. Modern en-suite rooms, TV, telephone, tea/coffee facilities. Excellent meals available in both bar and dining room using local fresh produce where possible. W.T.B. four Crowns Highly Commended.
B&B from £25pp, Dinner from £10, Rooms 2 twin, 8 double, all en-suite, Restricted smoking, No pets, Open all year except Christmas.
Bob & Barbara Pearson, **Hawk & Buckle Inn,** Llannefydd, Denbighshire LL16 5ED
Tel: 01745 540249 Fax: 01745 540316   **Map Ref 18**

THE CLWYD GATE MOTEL, is situated on the A494 with easy access to places of interest. Most rooms overlook panoramic views overlook the Vale. Prices include continental breakfast use of swimming pool, sauna, jacuzzi, Satellite TV, tea/coffee facilities. Perfect venue for weddings, conferences. Situated on the offsdyke Path.
B&B from £24.75pp, Dinner from £4.50, Rooms 10 single, 4 twin, 10 double, 3 family, all en-suite, Restricted smoking, Children welcome, Pets by arrangement, Open all year.
Brian & Joyce O'Connor, **The Clwyd Gate Motel,** Mold Road, Llanbedr DC, Ruthin Denbighshire LL15 1YF
Tel: 01824 704444 Fax: 01824 703513   **Map Ref 20**

EYARTH STATION, a former railway station now converted country house with six en-suite bedrooms, TV lounge, swimming pool, car park and magnificent views. Located in beautiful countryside, 3 minutes drive to castle. Mediaeval banquets and town. Central for Chester, Snowdonia and Llangollen Bala and coast. Credit cards. BTA commended. AA. B&B Winner 96.
B&B from £22pp, Dinner from £7.50, rooms 2 twin, 2 double, 2 family, all en-suite, Smoking, Children & pets welcome, Open all year.
Jen & Bert Spencer, **Eyarth Station,** Llanfair DC, Ruthin, Denbighshire LL15 2EE
Tel: 01824 703643 Fax: 01824 707464   **Map Ref 21**

FLINTSHIRE

MAES GARMON FARM, a 17th century farmhouse with a wealth of beams and high standard of furnishing in oak and pine. Gardens, summer house, pond and stream. Secluded setting convenient for Chester and Snowdonia. Guest's own lounge with TV. Parking. WTB 2 Crowns Highly Commended. Welcome Host.

B&B from £18pp, Dinner from £10, Rooms 3 single, 1 twin, 2 double, all en-suite, No smoking or pets, Children over 7, Open all year.
Loraine Cook, **Maes Garmon Farm,** Gwernaffield Mold, Flintshire CH7 5DB
Tel: 01352 759887   **Map Ref 22**

GWYNEDD

The accommodation at **THE FERNS GUEST HOUSE** is under constant review, and the Guest House is renowned for the tasteful, high quality furnishing throughout. Hearty breakfast and packed lunches available. Betws is within easy reach of Llanwst, Conwy, Caernarfon, Blaenan Ffestiniog and Portmerrion. AA 3Q's. WTB Highly Commended. Which Recommended.
B&B from £20-£22pp, Rooms 1 single, 3 twin, 8 double, 2 family, all en-suite, No smoking, Children over 4, No pets, Open all year except Christmas Day & Boxing Day.
Teresa & Keith Roobottom, **The Ferns Guest House,** Holyhead Road, Betws-y-Coed, LL24 0AN
Tel: 01690 710587 Fax: 01690 710587   **Map Ref 14**

BRON CELYN GUEST HOUSE, a beautiful situation in Snowdonia National Park overlooking the village of Betws-y-Coed and Conwy/Llugwy valleys. Most rooms en-suite, all with colour TV and beverage trays. Car parking, hearty breakfasts, packed lunches and evening meals. We offer comfort and good home cooked food in a relaxed atmosphere.
B&B from £18pp, Dinner from £10, Rooms 1 twin, 2 double, 2 family, most en-suite, Restricted smoking, Children welcome, No pets, Open all year.
Jim & Lilian Boughton, **Bron Celyn Guest House,** Lon Muriau, Llanrwst Road, Betws-y-Coed, LL24 0HD
Tel: 01690 710333 Fax: 01690 710111   **Map Ref 14**

RIVERSIDE HOTEL, John & Wendy Bakewell's, delightful hotel situated on bank of River Soch and overlooking picturesque harbour, a warm welcoming atmosphere, canoe and dinghey available. Popular good food guide restaurant. Heated pool under conservatory. Large garden. Children welcome. Most sporting activities can be arranged from the hotel.

B&B from £36pp, Dinner from £23.50, Rooms 4 twin, 6 double, 2 family, all en-suite, Restricted smoking, Children welcome, Open March - November.
John & Wendy Bakewell, **Riverside Hotel,** Abersoch, Gwynedd LL53 7HW
Tel: 01758 712419 Fax: 01758 712671   **Map Ref 24**

MELIN MELOCH (WATER MILL), is a picturesque former watermill close to Bala stands in 2 acres of beautiful waterscaped gardens, a delight for garden lovers. En-suite rooms some with own front doors. TV and hot drinks tray. The spectacular galleried interior of the mill is furnished with antiques and paintings. Home cooked meals with fresh produce. 2 minutes drive to Bala lake and town, excellent for touring. Parking.
B&B from £22pp, Dinner by arrangement from £12.50, Rooms 2 single, 2 twin, 2 double, 1 family, most en-suite, No smoking, Children welcome, Open March - October.
Beryl Gunn & Richard Fullard, **Melin Meloch,** Llanfor Bala LL23 7DP
Tel: 01678 520101 **Map Ref 26**

FRONDDERW, a quietly situated period mansion overlooking Bala town/Lake. 50% en-suite accommodation. Home cooked meals with special diets catered for. Tea/coffee facilities. Licensed. TV room, separate lounge. Ideal centre for sightseeing in North/Mid Wales, walking, water sport, cycling etc. Concessional golf.
B&B from £16-£22pp, Dinner £10, Rooms 1 single, 2 twin, 2 double, 3 family, some en-suite, Restricted smoking, Children welcome, No pets, Open March - end November.
Glynn & Wenda Jones, **Frondderw,** Stryd-y-Fron, Bala, Gwynedd LL23 7YD
Tel: 01678 520301 **Map Ref 27**

Stunning views, comfortable rooms, relaxing bars and varied good food make the **ERYL MOR HOTEL** the ideal venue for your holiday or break. Please phone for our brochure or golf brochure. Bangor an ideal base for Snowdonia.
B&B from £18-£23pp, Dinner from £4.50-£9.95, Rooms 5 single, 7 twin, 8 double, 4 family, most en-suite, Children welcome, Pets by arrangement. Open all year.
Mr N Murray-Williams, **Eryl Mor Hotel,** 2 Upper Garth Road, Bangor, Gwynedd LL57 2SR
Tel: 01248 353789 Fax: 01248 354042 **Map Ref 28**

GARTH GUEST HOUSE, rooms are en-suite with colour TV, tea/coffee facilities. We are opposite Bangor swimming pool with all modern recreation facilities. Perfect central position for touring Snowdonia National Park - Castles of Bangor, Beaumaris, Conway, Caernarfon. Visit Bangor's Victorian pier. Also wonderful Slate Museum.
B&B from £17.50pp, Rooms 2 twin, 2 double, 1 family, all en-suite, Children welcome, No pets, Open all year except Christmas & New Year.
John & Sonia Thompson, **Garth Guest House,** Garth Road, Bangor, Gwynedd LL57 2RT
Tel: 01248 362277 Fax: 01248 362277 **Map Ref 28**

HARLEYS BAR & MOTEL

HARLEYS BAR & MOTEL, all rooms en-suite, television, tea/coffee facilities. Two bars. Snooker rooms. Pool entertainment. Home cooked meals, bar meals available. Two minutes from beach. Lots of rooms are sea view. Children welcome. Friendly atmosphere. Situated in main town. Car park facilities available.
B&B from £20pp, Dinner from £3.95, Rooms 10 double, 6 family, all en-suite, Restricted smoking, Children welcome, Pets by arrangement, Open all year.
Mrs Angelea Clarke, **Harleys Bar & Motel,** King Edward Street, Barmouth, Gwynedd LL42 1AB
Tel: 01341 280383 **Map Ref 29**

Nestling above Cardigan Bay, **LLWYNDU FARMHOUSE** offers relaxing, peaceful breaks. The house dates from around 1600 and is a wealth of original oak beams and inglenook with en-suite rooms, candlelight dinners and tranquillity brilliant.
B&B from £58pp, Dinner from £14.50, Rooms 1 twin, 4 double, 2 family, all en-suite, No smoking, Children welcome, Pets by arrangement, Open all year except Christmas & Boxing Day.
Peter & Paula Thompson, **Llwyndu Farmhouse,** Llanaber, Barmouth, Gwynedd LL42 1RR
Tel: 01341 280144 Fax: 01341 281236 **Map Ref 29**

SYGUN FAWR COUNTRY HOUSE HOTEL, this 17th century oaked beamed manor house with magnificent views of the Snowdon range is peacefully located on the edge of beautiful Beddgelert. Attractive en-suite accommodation offering quality and comfort with friendly attentive service. Imaginative menus using fresh local produce. WTB and AA Recommended.
B&B from £28pp, Dinner from £14.50, Rooms 1 single, 3 twin, 5 double, 1 family, all en-suite, Restricted smoking, Children & pets welcome, Open all year.
Ian Davies, **Sygun Fawr Country House Hotel,** Beddgelert, Gwynedd LL55 4NE
Tel: 01766 890258 **Map Ref 30**

BRYN EISTEDDFOD HOTEL, is set in own grounds overlooking the sea in a quiet location with plenty of parking. We offer good home cooked food including Vegetarian from £5, available in the bar or restaurant. All rooms have en-suite facilities with colour TV and coffee/tea facilities.

B&B from £20pp, Dinner from £5, Rooms 3 twin, 2 double, 3 family, all en-suite, Children welcome, No pets, Open all year except Christmas & New Year.
Jan & David Allen, **Bryn Eisteddfod Hotel,** Clynndg Fawr, Caernarfon, Gwynedd LL54 5DA
Tel/Fax: 01286 660431 **Map Ref 32**

GWERN, a warm Welsh welcome awaits you on our family run farm. Guests welcome to wander on farmland which runs to Menai Straits. Situated in open, peaceful countryside with beautiful sea and mountain views. Central heating, tea/coffee facilities and colour TV. Choice of breakfast using local produce.

B&B from £19pp, Rooms 1 double, 1 family, all en-suite, No smoking or pets, Children welcome, Open April - October.

Ellen Pierce Jones, **Gwern,** Saron, Caernarfon, Gwynedd LL54 5UH
Tel: 01286 831337 Fax: 01286 831337 **Map Ref 33**

CASTLE BANK HOTEL, an imposing Victorian house in own grounds, close to Conwy town walls. All rooms have colour TV, tea/coffee, hair dryer, telephone and many have good views of castle and town. AA Rosette for Food (6th year). RAC Restaurant Merit. Licensed. Ample private parking.
B&B from £27.50pp, Dinner from £13.50, Rooms 1 single, 3 twin, 2 double, 3 family, Children welcome, Well behaved dogs welcome, Open all year.
Mr M. J. Barber, **Castle Bank Hotel,** Mount Pleasant, Conwy, Gwynedd LL32 8NY
Tel: 01492 593888 Fax: 01492 596466 **Map Ref 34**

MOR-HELI, overlooking 100m of coast line from Aberdaron to Aberdyfei. All bedrooms sea front, en-suite, TV, hospitality trays etc. Noted for good food and atmosphere. Established over 20 years by Williams Family "Croeso Cynnes Gymreig". Close to Snowdonia, Portmeirion, Llyn Peninsula, Ffestiniog Railway etc.

B&B from £19pp, Dinner from £9, Rooms 1 single, 2 twin, 2 double, 2 family, all en-suite, Restricted smoking, Children & pets welcome, Open all year.

Eirwyn & Carolyn Williams, **Mor-Heli,** Min-y-Mor, Criccieth, Gwynedd LL52 0EF

Tel: 01766 522802 Fax: 01766 522878   **Map Ref 35**

Situated in the Snowdonia National Park **TREM HYFRYD GUEST HOUSE'S** high standard of accommodation comprises of five twin and three double en-suite with television, hot drinks facilities, hairdryers and shaver points. Two lounges one with bar and well appointed dining room. In beautiful grounds with adequate parking.

B&B from £21pp, Dinner from £14, Rooms 1 single, 5 twin, 3 double, all en-suite, No smoking, children or pets, Open March - November.

Stan & Sue Pepper, **Trem Hyfryd Guest House's,** Barmouth Road, Dolgellau, Gwynedd LL40 2SP

Tel/Fax: 01341 423192   **Map Ref 36**

LION HOTEL, a family run village pub on the beautiful Lleyn Peninsula. Extensive menu of wholesome pub meals in the bars, dining room, family dining room and courtyard or garden. A good selection of real ales and thirty malt whiskies. Nearby - beaches, walking golfing, riding etc.

B&B from £20pp, Dinner from £5, Rooms 1 twin, 2 double, 1 family, all en-suite, No smoking, Children welcome, Pets by arrangement, Open all year except Christmas & New Year.

Andrew, Carol & Martin Lee, **Lion Hotel,** Tudweiliog, Pwllheli LL53 8ND

Tel/Fax: 01758 770244   **Map Ref 37**

At **GREENFIELD HOTEL**, all rooms have colour TV's, tea/coffee trays and central heating throughout, residents bar good choice of menu. Convenient for BR and Talyllyon Narrow Grange Railways. Few minutes to beach. Directly opposite Tywyn's Leisure Centre with swimming pool. Large car park. Friendly atmosphere.

B&B from £16pp, Dinner from £6.75, Rooms 3 twin, 3 double, 2 family, some en-suite, Children welcome, No pets, Open January - November.

Cynthia Jenkins, **Greenfield Hotel,** High St, Tywyn, Gwynedd LL36 9AD

Tel: 01654 710354 Fax: 01654 710354   **Map Ref 38**

RHOSGADLAS, is a converted barn of character, situated near the beautiful Tal-y-llyn lake at the foot of Cader Idris in the Snowdonia National Park. All bedrooms have hospitality trays and TV. Breakfast is served in a conservatory overlooking a pretty cottage garden, and there is also a relaxing sitting room with beams and open fireplace. We offer a traditional 'Croeso' - a truly Welsh welcome - see and hear some authentic Welsh harps.

B&B from £20pp, Rooms 1 twin, 1 double, both en-suite, 1 double with private bathroom, No smoking or pets, Children over 14, Open March - October.

Mrs Rhian Bebb, **Rhosgadlas,** Tal-y-Llyn Tywyn, Gwynedd LL36 9AJ

Tel: 01654 761462 Fax: 01654 761462   **Map Ref 39**

MONMOUTHSHIRE

FIRST HURDLE GUEST HOUSE, a family owned bed and breakfast offering you the comforts of home. All bedroomsare en-suite with colour television and tea/coffee making facilities. Licensed. Borough parking available. Chepstow has an early Norman Castle, Museum, Stuart Crystal factory, delightful shops and the start of the Offa's Dyke and Wye Valley walks.

B&B from £20-£25pp, Rooms 1 single, 3 twin, 3 double, all en-suite, No smoking or pets, Children over 12, Open March - November.

Rob & Yvonne Westwood, **First Hurdle Guest House,** 9-10 Upper Church Street, Chepstow, Gwent NP6 5EX
Tel: 01291 622189 Fax: 01291 628421 **Map Ref 40**

NEWPORT

THE WEST USK LIGHTHOUSE, stay in a Grade II Listed Lighthouse with wedge-shaped rooms, water and 4-poster beds, flotation tank for deep relaxation. Champagne breakfast in Lantern room. Romantic and peaceful setting. Many amenities and attractions nearby. Long walks. Sea fishing, bird watching for enthusiasts unique experience. Distinctly different.
B&B from £37.50pp, Rooms 1 single, 2 double, 1 family, all en-suite, No smoking, Children welcome, Pets by arrangement, Open all year.
Frank & Danielle Sheahan, **The West Usk Lighthouse,** St. Brides, Wentloog, Newport, Gwent NP1 9SF
Tel: 01633 810126/815860 Fax: 01633 815582 **Map Ref 41**

TY'R YWEN FARM, is an isolated 16th century hill farm in the Brecon Beacons National Park. Spacious bedrooms with television, radio, tea/coffee making facilities and 4-poster beds. One room with jacuzzi. Magnificent views. Ideal for walking and bird watching. http://freespace.virgin.net/susan.armitage/webpage.htm Adventurous access.

B&B from £20pp, Rooms 1 twin, 3 double, all en-suite, No smoking, Children over 14, Pets welcome, Open all year except Christmas Eve/Day/Boxing Day & New Year.

Sue Armitage, **Ty'r Ywen Farm,** Lasgarn Lane, Mamhilad, via Trevethin, Pontypool, Gwent NP4 8TT
Tel: 01495 785200 Fax: 01495 785200 Email: susan.armitage@virgin.net **Map Ref 42**

PEMBROKESHIRE

BRYN BERWYN HOUSE, is an elegant Edwardian house set in 2 acres with beautiful views of the surrounding coast and valley. Close to several unspoilt National Trust beaches. Bryn Berwyn is an ideal location for exploring the beauty of West Wales.

B&B from £22.50pp, Room 7 double, 6 en-suite, 1 with private facilities, No smoking, Children over 14, Well behaved dogs accepted, Open all year.
Gillian & Gerry Lowe, **Bryn Berwyn House,** Tresaith, Cardigan, Ceredigion, SA43 2JG
Tel: 01239 811126 **Map Ref 43**

Antiques abound in the Georgian **MANOR HOUSE HOTEL** where 4 of the bedrooms overlook the picturesque harbour. Breakfast may be taken in the garden. Award winning restaurant. En-suite rooms with TV and tea/coffee facilities. WTB 3 Crowns Highly Commended, RAC Highly Acclaimed, "Which" Good Hotel Guide.

B&B from £22pp, Dinner from £16, Rooms 2 single, 2 twin, 3 double, all en-suite, Restricted smoking, Children welcome, Open all year except Christmas.

Beatrix & Ralph Davies, **Manor House Hotel,** Main Street, Fishguard, Pembrokeshire SA65 9HG

Tel: 01348 873260   **Map Ref 44**

ABERGWAUN HOTEL, a small family run hotel situated in the centre of the market town of Fishguard. Extensively refurbished in recent years and boasts en-suite bedrooms with colour TV, tea/coffee facilities a comfortable lounge bar with coffee and meals served all day. Children welcome. Garage parking available.

B&B from £26pp, Dinner from £5, Rooms 4 single, 2 twin, 3 double, 2 family, most en-suite, Children welcome, Pets by arrangement, Open all year except Christmas Day.

Richard Collier, **Abergwaun Hotel,** Market Square, Fishguard, Pembrokeshire SA65 9HA

Tel: 01348 872077 Fax: 01348 875412   **Map Ref 45**

BRYNAWEL COUNTRY HOUSE/ANNEXE, a Victorian guest house, annexe, self catering, sited on 4 acres, small holding. Tea/coffee facilities, TV in all rooms. Private, security car park. Half a mile from coastal path. Brochure, tariff on request. Welcome Host, Gold Award Finalists. Ferry to Ireland 5 minutes, Fishing, horse riding, golf within 5 miles.

B&B from £16pp, Dinner from £9, Rooms 3 triple, 1 twin, 2 double, 1 family, all en-suite, Restricted smoking, Children & pets welcome, Open all year.

Rhian C. Lloyd, **Brynawel Country House/Annexe,** Llanwnda, Goodwick, Fishguard, Pembrokeshire SA64 0HR

Tel/Fax: 01348 874155   **Map Ref 46**

YNYS BARRY COUNTRY HOTEL, a beautiful well appointed hotel. Adjacent to the famous coastal path of Pembrokeshire. With its rugged coastlines and sweeping beaches literally on your door step. Traditional and home cooking, tea room. Licensed bar and lounge. Set in the midst of superb countryside.

B&B from £16-£21pp, Dinner available, Rooms 4 twin, 10 double, 4 family, all en-suite, Children welcome, Pets by arrangement, Open all year.

Mr & Mrs P Bull, **Ynys Barry Country Hotel,** Porthgain, St David's, Haverfordwest, Pembrokeshire SA62 5BH

Tel: 01348 831180 Fax: 01348 831800   **Map Ref 47**

MANIAN LODGE HOTEL, is a country hotel, en-suite rooms, colour TV, tea/coffee facilities. Licensed bar. Pool table room. Sun terrace, children play lawn. Two bedrooms, four berth apartments, car parking. Evening meals optional. Families welcome. Near Folly Farm, Oakwood and Tenby Golden Beaches and golf course.

B&B from £15.50pp, Dinner from £8, Rooms 2 single, 1 twin, 3 double, 3 family, all en-suite, Restricted smoking, Children welcome, Open March - November.

Margaret West, **Manian Lodge Hotel,** Begelly, Kilgetty, Pembrokeshire SA68 0XE

Tel: 01834 813273 Fax: 01834 813273   **Map Ref 48**

RAMSEY HOUSE. Quiet relaxation exclusively for non-smoking adults. Traditional Welsh cuisine, fine wines, cosy bar. 7 superior en-suite rooms with colour TV and hospitality tray. Parking. Convenient location for Cathedral and Coast Path. Dogs welcome. WTB 3 Crowns Highly Commended. Dinner, B&B £41-£45pppn, £246-£270 weekly. Taste of Wales our speciality.
B&B from £27pp, Dinner from £14, Rooms 3 twin, 4 double, all en-suite, No smoking or children, Pets welcome, Open all year.
Mac & Sandra Thompson, **Ramsey House,** Lower Moor, St. David's Pembrokeshire SA62 6RP
Tel: 01437 720321 Fax: 01437 720025 **Map Ref 50**

TENBY HOUSE HOTEL, is a Grade 2 Listed town house and pub. Centrally situated. Lively bars. Serving traditional ales and good food. En-suite bedrooms. Colour TV's. Complimentary tray. Direct dial telephones. Family run hotel with friendly staff. Minutes away from the harbour and beaches. 3/4 mile Tenby station.
B&B From £30pp, Dinner from £7.50, Rooms 4 twin, 5 double, 2 family, all en-suite, Restricted smoking, Children welcome, No pets, Open all year.
Griff & Lesley Fisher, **Tenby House Hotel,** Tudor Square, Tenby, Pembrokeshire SA70 7AJ
Tel: 01834 842000 Fax: 01834 844647 **Map Ref 51**

WYCHWOOD HOUSE, an elegant country house with sea views and secure parking. Well appointed bedrooms with TV and tea/coffee making facilities. Situated in the National Park. Walking, fishing and two golf courses nearby. Penally is a quiet village only 20 minutes walk along path to Tenby. Beach is 10 minutes walk.

B&B from £21pp, Dinner from £15.50, Rooms 1 double, 2 en-suite family, Restricted smoking, Children welcome, Pets by arrangement, Open all year.

Lee & Mherly Ravenscroft, **Wychwood House,** Penally, Tenby, Pembrokeshire SA70 7PE
Tel: 01834 844387 **Map Ref 52**

THE OLD VICARAGE, is set in a peaceful coastal location and offers two spacious en-suite rooms with tea/coffee facilities. Manorbier is famous for its Norman Castle, sandy beach and stunning scenery. Irish ferries from Pembroke (20 minutes) or Fishguard (45 minutes).

B&B from £20pp, Rooms 1 twin, 1 double, both en-suite, No smoking or pets, Children welcome, Open all year.

Jill McHugh, **The Old Vicarage,** Manorbier, South Pembrokeshire SA70 7TN
Tel/Fax: 01834 871452 **Map Ref 53**

COACH HOUSE HOTEL, a warm welcome awaits at this traditional coaching inn situated in the mediaeval castle town of Pembroke. Tastefully refurbished. Dine beside an open log fire with fine cuisine freshly prepared. Outside patio area. Gallery displaying local artists paintings. 5 minutes to beaches and coastal paths.
B&B from £35pp sharing a double room, Dinner from £6.95, Rooms 10 twin, 3 double, 2 family, all en-suite, Children welcome, Open all year.
Mrs S. J Griffin, **Coach House Hotel,** 116 Main Street, Pembroke, South Pembrokeshire SA71 4HN
Tel: 01646 684602 Fax: 01646 687456 **Map Ref 49**

POWYS

MADRYN HOUSE, dated 1842, TV lounge with log fire we have two bathrooms, tea/coffee facilities in your room. We do a great breakfast. Vegetarians welcome and we make you tea/coffee on arrival. We treat all our customer's as VIP's. Children half price.
B&B from £15pp, Rooms 1 single, 1 twin, 1 double, 1 family, Children & pets welcome, Open all year except Christmas/Boxing & New Years Day.
Mrs E Kean **Madryn House,** 32 Regent Street, Llangollen, LL20 8HW
Tel: 01978 869052   **Map Ref 54**

THE HARP INN, a Welsh village pub, nearby River Wye, 4 miles Hay-on-Wye town of books. Ideal touring Black Mountains, Brecon Beacons. All rooms central heating, TV, tea/coffee facilities. Car parking. Canoeing, pony trekking, golf, walking available locally, also popular area artists, bird watchers. Home cooked food including Vegetarian. Children meals. Real Ale.
B&B from £17.50pp, Dinner from £8, Rooms 2 twin, 2 double, all en-suite, Restricted smoking, Children welcome, No pets, Open all year.
David & Lynda White, **The Harp Inn,** Hay Road, Glasbury-on-Wye, Hereford HR3 5NR
Tel: 01497 847 373   **Map Ref 66**

THE BEACONS, recently restored 17th/18th century house retaining many original features. Well-appointed standard, en-suite and luxury period rooms. Enjoy a drink in the original meat cellar before our award-winning chef spoils you with outstanding cuisine. Car park and cycle store. Ring Peter and Barbara Jackson for more information.
B&B from £18pp, Dinner from £9.95, Rooms 1 single, 3 twin, 4 double, 4 family, mostly en-suite, Restricted smoking, Children welcome, Pets by arrangement, Open all year except Christmas.
Peter & Barbara Jackson, **The Beacons,** 16 Bridge St, Brecon LD3 8AH
Tel: 01874 623339 Fax: 01874 623339   **Map Ref 56**

THE LAURELS, is an interesting, spacious, Victorian guest house offering good, non-smoking accommodation and ample parking. It is half-way between the book-town of Hay-on-Wye and Brecon, situated in the centre of a small village surrounded by the Black Mountains and Brecon Beacons.

B&B from £16-£22pp, Rooms 2 double, 1 family, all en-suite, No smoking, Children welcome, No pets, Open all year except Christmas & New Year.
Marie Gray, **The Laurels,** Church St, Bronllys, Brecon, Powys LD3 0HS
Tel: 01874 712188 Fax: 01874 712187   **Map Ref 57**

DOLYCOED, an attractive Edwardian house in mature garden offering home comforts in a beautiful part of Wales at the foot of the Brecon Beacons. 5 miles from Brecon. Directions to Dolycoed are: from Brecon A40/A470 take the A40 for Abergavenny, left onto the B4558 to Llangorse, turn right at the post office and next right, the house is on the right before the next "T" junction.
B&B from £18pp, Rooms 1 twin, 1 double, Restricted smoking, Children & pets welcome, Open all year
Mary Cole, **Dolycoed,** Talyllyn, Brecon, Powys LD3 7SY
Tel: 01874 658666   **Map Ref 58**

RHYDFELIN FARM GUEST HOUSE, an 18th century stone farmhouse on the A470 in Wye Valley. Easy access to "Heart of Wales" attractions, Builth Wells 3 miles. Licensed restaurant and cosy bar, TV lounge. Bedrooms with tea/coffee facilities and hot and cold. Cream teas served in summer. Adequate car parking.
B&B from £18pp, Dinner from £12, Rooms 1 twin, 2 double, 1 en-suite family, No smoking, Children welcome, Open all year except Christmas & Boxing Day.
Alan & Liz Moyes, **Rhydfelin Farm Guest House,** Cwmbach Llechrhyd, Builth Wells, Powys LD2 3RT
Tel: 01982 552493   **Map Ref 59**

GUIDFA HOUSE, this stylish Georgian house has earned an enviable reputation for it's comfort, good food and service. It offers superior accommodation including a ground floor rooms. Set in the very heart of Wales, 3 miles north of Llandrindod Wells. It's an excellent base for touring the wonderful local countryside. Email: guidfa@gobalnet.co.uk
B&B from £25pp, Dinner from £16.50, Rooms 2 single, 3 twin, 2 double, most en-suite, Restricted smoking, Children over 10, No pets, Open all year.
Tony & Anne Millan, **Guidfa House,** Crossgates, Llandrindod Wells, Powys LD1 6RF
Tel: 01597 851241 Fax: 01597 851875   **Map Ref 60**

BUTTINGTON HOUSE, a late Georgian Country House near Welshpool with lovely views of Severn Valley. En-suite luxury accommodation in the elegant period residence. Ideal centre for touring mid Wales borders, Powis Castle and walking Offa's Dyke.

B&B from £35pp, Dinner by arrangement, from £20 inc wine. No pets, Open all year.

Mrs J V Thomas, **Buttington House,** Welshpool, Powys SY21 8HD
Tel: 01938 553351   **Map Ref 61**

SWANSEA

TUDOR COURT HOTEL, situated close to Swansea city centre and the nearby Gower Coastline. Sea front location with excellent views of Swansea Bay. All rooms are comfortable and have colour television and tea/coffee facilities. Licensed bar and games rooms. Car parking on hotel forecourt.

B&B from £13pp, Rooms 6 single, 9 twin, 9 double, 2 family, some en-suite, Children welcome, No pets, Open all year except Christmas & New Year.
Nicola & Gary Quick, **Tudor Court Hotel,** 300 Oystermouth Road, Swansea, SA1 3UJ
Tel: 01792 650389   **Map Ref 62**

VALE OF GLAMORGAN

WESTBOURNE HOTEL, a family run, licensed guest house, clean comfortable rooms all have colour TV, hostess tray, some en-suite. Car park. Close to rail station, only 4 miles to Cardiff centre, short walk to Promenade, Pier, Cliffwalk. Ideal for holiday or business. Bristol Channel. Paddle Steamer trips in season. Short drive to mountains and valleys.
B&B from £20pp, Dinner from £3.50-£6.50 (Monday - Thursday), Rooms 6 single, 4 twin, 1 family, some en-suite, Restricted smoking, Children welcome, No pets, Open all year.
Brian & Mary Hardiman, **Westbourne Hotel,** 8 Victoria Road, Penarth, Cardiff, Vale of Glamorgan CF64 3EF
Tel: 01222 707268 Fax: 01222 708265 Mobile: 0410 315577   **Map Ref 64**

WREXHAM

BRACKENWOOD, quiet residential family guest house. Tea/coffee, TV in all rooms. Guest's lounge with Sky TV. Car parking. Home cooking, vegetarians welcome. Landscaped gardens. Near historic city of Chester. 40 minutes drive from Manchester, Liverpool and Airports. Within easy driving distance all North Wales tourist attractions and major motorways. Email: dglyon9@aol.com
B&B from £16pp, Dinner by arrangement £15, Rooms 3 single, 1 twin, 2 double, 1 family, some en-suite, Restricted smoking, Children welcome, Open all year.
Beryl & Derek Lyon, **Brackenwood,** 67 Wynnstay Lane, Marford, Wrexham LL12 8LH
Tel: 01978 852866 Fax: 01978 852065   **Map Ref 65**

Please mention

THE BED & BREAKFAST DIRECTORY

when booking your accommodation

A guide to many of the art galleries and museums in England, Scotland and Wales, available from all good bookshops from Spring 1999

NOTES

NOTES

NOTES

NOTES

NOTES

NOTES

NOTES